NEW ZEALAND SCHOOL

THE FUTURE OF NEW ZEALAND ENGLISH

OXFORD DICTIONARY

NEW ZEALAND SCHOOL

THE FUTURE OF NEW ZEALAND ENGLISH

OXFORD DICTIONARY

FIFTH EDITION

Edited by
Dianne Bardsley

OXFORD
UNIVERSITY PRESS

Oxford University Press is a department of the University of Oxford. It furthers the University's objective of excellence in research, scholarship, and education by publishing worldwide. Oxford is a registered trademark of Oxford University Press in the UK and in certain other countries.

Published in Australia by
Oxford University Press
253 Normanby Road, South Melbourne, Victoria 3205, Australia

First published 1991
Second edition 1995
Third edition 2001
Fourth edition 2006
Fifth edition 2013
Reprinted 2014 (three times), 2019, 2020, 2021

National Library of Australia Cataloguing-in-Publication data

New Zealand school Oxford dictionary / edited by Dianne Bardsley.
5th ed.

ISBN 978 0 19 558522 3 (pbk.)

For secondary school age.

English language—New Zealand—Dictionaries.
English language—New Zealand—Synonyms and antonyms—Dictionaries.

Bardsley, Dianne.

427.93

Typeset by diacriTech, Chennai, India
Proofread by Jamie Anderson
Printed in Hong Kong by Sheck Wah Tong Printing Press Ltd.

Contents

Preface

This dictionary is specially written for intermediate and secondary school students, and is a companion volume to the *New Zealand Oxford School Thesaurus*, first published in 2005. It is intended to provide an easy access to words, their spellings, and their meanings, while at the same time serving as an introduction to more complex styles of dictionaries. The dictionary contains few abbreviations, with the appropriate word class (e.g. noun) provided in full, following the headword. A simple method for indicating correct pronunciation is given for difficult or foreign words. Usage notes are also included, for example, where terms are commonly confused. (Refer to the example under **compliment**.) Occasionally, antonyms or direct opposites are given, e.g. under the headword **minimum**. Some etymologies or word histories are also provided, e.g. under the headword **turquoise**, the origin is provided. Words that are distinctive to various regions are labelled as such following the word class, e.g. **berm** *noun* (*NZ*). This helps to indicate which words are of the restricted variety and which are shared with other varieties, or with global English. Terms that are informal or slang are similarly noted.

Since the 2006 edition of this work, many new words have come into our New Zealand vocabulary, both from within New Zealand and from overseas. At the same time, many words previously in use have been given new or extended meanings. These new terms and meanings, all of which are recorded at the New Zealand Dictionary Centre, can be found in the main body of this dictionary. New terms relating to electronic communication and technology, such as **avatar**, **bitmap**, **emoticon**, and **wiki**, are amongst these.

One of the major areas of change in the lives of New Zealanders has been the introduction and use of foreign foods, with names that can both entrance and bewilder. Included in the middle section of this dictionary are the meanings of foreign food terms, along with their places of origin. Another feature of our lives is the increasing use of abbreviations, acronyms, and initialisms, which can similarly bewilder us. Those that are specific to New Zealand English can be found in a list in the middle pages of this work, while general and global usages such as **UFO** and **SGML** are found in the main body of the dictionary. The specific naming of various types of words is expanding, and the middle pages include definitions for terms of linguistic and literary significance, e.g. *acronym*, *eponym*, *toponym*, *simile*, etc.

The growing knowledge and use of te reo Māori is a specific aspect of New Zealand English vocabulary. In the middle pages are lists of Māori numerals, days of the week, and months of the year, and in the body of the dictionary, several new terms can be found. Further study notes and word lists are added and extended in the middle pages of this edition, including pictograms and text language.

While space does not permit all new New Zealand and borrowed English terms to be included in this dictionary, full lists of new usages are freely available. An extensive database of New Zealand words and usages is maintained at the New Zealand Dictionary Centre at Victoria University of Wellington, where inquiries and contributions are welcomed, and where assistance with research projects can be provided. Contact can be made by email to nzdc@vuw.ac.nz and by telephone 04 463 5644. Activities and projects based on New Zealand English can also be obtained from the New Zealand Dictionary Centre website: www.vuw.ac.nz/lals/research/nzdc.

September 2012 *Dianne Bardsley*

The English language

English is the chief language of Britain, the USA, Canada, New Zealand, Australia, and a number of other countries. More than 300 million people speak it as their first language, and millions more in all parts of the world learn it as a foreign language for use in communicating with people of other nations. It is the official language used between airline pilots and their air traffic controllers in all countries, and in shipping, and the main language of international business, science, medicine, and computing.

All languages have a history: they are constantly changing and evolving. It is probable that nearly all the languages of Europe came from one ancient community. As people moved away to the east and west they lost contact with each other and developed new and different life-styles. Naturally their language needs changed too. They invented new words and forgot old ones, and the grammar of the language also changed. Many varied languages grew from the original parent tongue, until the time came when people with the same ancestors would no longer have understood each other.

Invasions and conquests complicated the process. The English language shows this very well, for invaders brought their own languages to Britain, and the British took theirs to lands overseas. The earliest known inhabitants of Britain spoke a form of Celtic, related to modern Welsh and Gaelic. Very little of this Celtic survived the waves of invasion that drove its speakers into western and highland parts of the country, but the names of some cities, rivers, and hills date back to Celtic times (e.g. *Carlisle, Thames, Avon, Pendle*).

Old English

Old English, which is also called **Anglo-Saxon**, does not look very much like modern English (for example, *Fæder ure, þu þe eart on heofonum = Our Father, who are in heaven*), but many words, especially the most frequently used ones, can be traced back to it. *Eat, drink, sleep, speak, work, play,* and *sing* are all from Old English, so are *house, door, meat, bread, milk, fish*; and *head, nose, eye*; *man, woman, husband, wife*.

Old English did not originate in Britain. It was the language of the Angles, Saxons, and Jutes, Germanic tribes who went to Britain from the Continent in about AD 450. By about AD 700 the Anglo-Saxons had occupied most of the country and their language was the dominant one. Even the name of the country itself became 'England', which means 'land of the Angles', and from it came 'Englisc' or 'English'. The Anglo-Saxons were converted to Christianity in the 7th century, and many religious and educational terms came into English from the Latin language of the Church, such as *priest, pope, hymn,* and *school*.

The next great influence on Old English came from the Vikings, who arrived from Norway and Denmark in the 9th and 10th centuries and occupied much of eastern England. Their language was Old Norse, and from it we get many common words, such as *call, cast,* and *take,* and a number of words beginning with 'sc' or 'sk', including *scare, scrap, skirt,* and *sky*.

Middle English

In 1066 the Normans, led by William the Conqueror, invaded England. English life was greatly changed in the years that followed, and the language changed too, so much so that, with a little practice, we can now fairly easily read and understand the language of that time. These lines, for example, were written in about 1390: *This carpenter hadde wedded newe a wyf, Which that he lovede moore than his lyf.* We call this language 'Middle English' to distinguish it from Old English or Anglo-Saxon.

For much of this period the language used by the ruling classes was the French of the victorious Norman invaders, though most of the ordinary people still spoke English. Many words connected with government and law came into the language at this time through their French use, e.g. *advise, command, court, govern, people, reign, royalty, rule.*

Throughout all these centuries, although scholars in different countries spoke different languages, they all understood Latin, which had been the language of the ancient Roman Empire, and used it for writing about every subject that they studied. Some Latin words (e.g. *mint, pound, sack,* and *street*) had already been adopted by the Anglo-Saxons before they came to Britain, because they had lived on the fringe of the Roman Empire; others had arrived with the spread of Christianity. Then in the 14th to 16th centuries (the *Renaissance*) people throughout Europe became especially interested in Greek and Roman literature, philosophy, art, and buildings, and many more words from Greek and Latin were introduced into English (e.g. *architecture, column, comedy, educate, history, physics, tributary*). The Christian Church in all western countries had always used Latin, and continued to use this (not English or other local languages) in all its services.

Modern English

From about 1500 onwards the English language continued to change, and developed enormously. It adopted words from other languages with which people came into contact through trade or travel, and it was exported to other lands when English-speaking people travelled abroad. In the early 17th century colonies began to be established, first in North America and in India, then in the West Indies, and later in Australia, New Zealand, Hong Kong, and Africa. To each country the settlers took the English language of their own time, and in each country it changed, little by little, until it differed in various ways not only from the English of other settlements but from its parent form in Britain—where, of course, the language was changing too. Some words, such as names for birds and animals found in only one country, were adopted into the form of English used there and are not known elsewhere; others (e.g. *banana, potato,* and *tornado*) have made their way into international English and are known everywhere.

Nowadays travel is not the only way in which people acquire words from other countries. Films made in one country are shown in many others, and radio and television programmes from all over the world are received in people's homes. The result is that while American, Australian, and other vocabulary become familiar in Britain, English continues to be exported.

Dialects

There are different forms of English not only in different parts of the world but within the British Isles. These varieties of English are called dialects. Each is known, understood, and regarded as standard in its own area, but not outside it.

The way that the people of an area pronounce words is called an **accent**, and this too varies in different parts of a country.

Every language has a number of dialects, and most languages have one dialect and style of pronunciation that is regarded as standard for the whole country. In Britain, 'Standard English' is based on the form of English used in southern England. It is the basis of the written language, known (unlike other dialects) in all parts of the country, spoken by all well-educated people, used for national news bulletins on radio and television, and learnt by foreigners.

New Zealand English

Standard New Zealand English differs from Standard British English chiefly in its pronunciation and vocabulary; in grammar the two varieties are basically the same.

The distinctive vocabulary of New Zealand English clearly reflects the bicultural population of New Zealand, whose two cultures have travelled far from their origins. The earliest inhabitants of Aotearoa New Zealand came from Polynesia, and their language, te reo Māori, developed differently from other Polynesian languages. The first Pākehā settlers adopted Māori words for indigenous plants, birds and fish, such as *tōtara, tūi,* and *hāpuku,* and for other features of the environment, such as *pākihi* and *tomo.* They also borrowed words associated with Māori culture and society, such as *marae, mōkihi,* and *pā.* In the 21st century, New Zealand English includes a variety of terms from te reo Māori, all of which make our culture and language distinctive. Today, terms like *hapū, hui, mana, taonga,* and *tūrangawaewae* are used widely and meaningfully.

New Zealand English is also influenced by other Polynesian languages through Pacific Island immigration. Terms such as *afakasi, aiga, lava lava,* and *Palagi* are now in common usage, and new cultural terms, such as *White Sunday,* have also come into New Zealand English.

New words and usages have been generated by a variety of means within New Zealand English. Compounding is a common method, where words or word parts are combined to form a new one, e.g. *achievement standard, cyber-hui, sharemilking, woolshed,* and *All Black.* Prefixes and suffixes, new beginnings and endings, are added to existing terms, such as *Maoridom* and *Rogernomics.* Some words, known as acronyms, are formed from initials, such as *WINZ* and *DOC* while others are formed from abbreviations such as *Nat,* and initials such as *DPB.* New Zealanders have also taken words in use in British and other varieties of English and given them new senses or meanings. Examples are *berm, paddock,* and *unit.*

Much of our slang and informal vocabulary is shared with Australian English, such as *rattle your dags,* and *she'll be right,* while terms such as *a box of birds, howlybag, munted, poozle,* and *savs and pavs,* are limited to New Zealand use. Other terms, like *tiki tour,* are taken from proper nouns and used in a new colloquial sense. Toponyms include names that are from a place of invention, discovery or event, such as *Onehunga weed, Tukidale* sheep, and *Castlepoint daisy.* Words have also been generated from the names of people who have discovered, bred, invented, or had a special relationship with an article, product, or event, such as *Chewings fescue, Coopworth* and *Perendale* sheep, and *Hamilton jet.*

A characteristic that we share with Australian English is the generation of new words by using diminutive or shortened forms, and hypocoristics, or pet names. Well-known examples of these are *possie, Swannie,* and names of places, such as *Kune* for Ohakune, *Gissy* for Gisborne, and *Palmy* for Palmerston. Familiar landmarks have taken the definite article to become *the Mount, the Basin, the Brook,* and *the Park.* We have also given names to specific buildings and structures, such as the parliamentary *Beehive, Cake Tin* for the Wellington stadium, and *Nippon Clipon* for additional lanes on the Auckland Harbour Bridge.

The principal word-generating domains of recent times have included politics, sport, the rural world, and the environment. Words reflect our changing society, including our attitudes, and this is reflected particularly in terms relating to the environment. New terms like *open space covenants, insurance population, kawenta,* and *paunch dump* reflect an increasing concern for conservation of the natural world. Other words and phrases, such as *No 8,* and *on the sheep's back,* have taken on an 'iconic' identity. Since the 2006 edition of this dictionary, many New Zealanders have met a variety of experiences, including the major Canterbury earthquakes of 2010 and 2011. It has been interesting to note the terms that have been generated or used to describe the effects of the earthquakes, including *liquefaction* as a product rather than a process, *munted, muntage, mega-muntage,* historic buildings described as *old dungers,* and the largest quake described as the *grand mal.*

The New Zealand English lexicon continues to be influenced by terms from other languages, particularly in food (see the middle pages for a list of terms now used in New Zealand English) and sports, such as *pétanque, bocce,* and *boules.* Despite this, New Zealand English remains a distinctive variety of world English.

Formal and informal

We wear different clothes for different kinds of occasions, and often the words that we use when writing or speaking formally are different from those that we use informally to friends.

Very informal language (e.g. *nick* = to steal, *piffle* = nonsense) is called **slang**. It is used either for fun, or to express something in a more vivid or picturesque way than dignified words would do, or to shock people or attract their attention. Often, special slang words are used by members of a group, so that by using these they show that they belong to the group, and they recognise others who use them as belonging to it too. We use slang **euphemisms** to make things seem better (*fall off one's perch,* rather than die) and **dysphemisms** to make things seem bad or worse (*murder house* for dentist).

The dictionary

There are over 500 000 words in the English language, and the total is increasing all the time. Of these, about 3000 are known and used by almost everyone whose native language is English. Most people know the meaning of at least another 5000 words, though they may not use all of them in everyday speech or writing. In addition, those who specialise in a particular subject (e.g. music, chemistry, medicine, computers) have a wide vocabulary of words that are used by people working in that subject but are not generally known to others.

The biggest dictionary in the world is the *Oxford English Dictionary,* whose second edition (1989) fills twenty very large volumes, and it contains most of these words. Small dictionaries can find room for only a fraction of the whole language; they include most of the words that are in common use, but (in order to make the book a convenient size and not too expensive) they have to leave out a considerable number of words, and a larger dictionary must be consulted for information about these.

Notes on the use of the dictionary

Dictionary entries

Words defined are arranged in alphabetical order. Compounds of each word, and the words derived from it (*derivatives*), are often included in the same entry without definitions if their meaning can easily be worked out from that of the main word.

Words with the same spelling but with a different meaning or origin (*homographs*) are given separate entries, and numbered with a raised figure, e.g.

> **peer**[1] *verb* look at something closely or with difficulty. [from *appear*]
>
> **peer**[2] *noun* **1** a noble. **2** someone who is equal to another in rank or merit etc., *She had no peer.* **peeress** *noun* [from Latin *par* = equal]

Parts of speech

These are printed in italic or sloping print (e.g. *noun, adjective, verb*) after the word and before its definition. Some words can be used as more than one part of speech, e.g.

> **barricade** *noun* a barrier, especially one put up hastily across a street etc.
>
> **barricade** *verb* (**barricaded**, **barricading**) block or defend with a barricade.

Inflexions and plurals

Derived forms of verbs, plurals of nouns, and comparative and superlative forms of adjectives and adverbs are usually given if they are irregular or if there might be doubt about the spelling. When only two verb forms are given, e.g.

> **admit** *verb* (**admitted**, **admitting**)

the first form is both the past tense (as in 'he *admitted* it') and the past participle ('it was *admitted*'). When three forms are given, e.g.

> **come** *verb* (**came**, **come**, **coming**)
> **freeze** *verb* (**froze**, **frozen**, **freezing**)

the first is the past tense (as in 'he *came*'; 'it *froze*'), and the second is the past participle ('he had *come*'; 'it was *frozen*'). The last form given (ending in *-ing*) is the present participle.

In Māori the plural form of a noun is usually the same as its singular. Formerly, most Pākehā speakers of New Zealand English treated these words like native English words and added *s* to form their plurals, but many people now prefer to follow the Māori practice and say *many Māori, some Pākehā, all the marae,* etc.

Meanings

Many words have more than one meaning. Each meaning is numbered separately.

Labels

Words that are not standard English are labelled as *informal* or *slang* etc. (see p. ix).

Examples

Examples of words in use are given in italic or sloping print like *this* to help make a definition clearer, e.g.

> **beware** *verb* be careful, *Beware of pick-pockets.*

Phrases

These are listed and defined under the part of speech to which they belong, e.g.

> **jump** *verb* move up suddenly from the ground into the air.
> **jump at** (*informal*) accept something eagerly.
> **jump the queue** not wait your turn.
> **jump** *noun* a jumping movement.

Origins of words

The derivation (or **etymology**) of a word is given in square brackets at the end of the main part of an entry and before any phrases are listed, e.g.

> **alligator** *noun* a reptile, similar to a crocodile. [from Spanish *el lagarto* = the lizard]

These derivations often shed light on the word's meaning or on how its meaning has changed, or show the connection between words that have the same set of letters in them (e.g. at*tract*, con*tract*, ex*tract*, and *tract*or), and also help to indicate the number of languages from which words have been taken into English. For example, *exit* and *terminus* come from Latin, *kaleidoscope* from Greek, *fête* from French, *blitz* from German, *alert* from Italian, *alligator* from Spanish, *algebra* from Arabic, *mammoth* from Russian, *bungalow* from Hindi, *shawl* from Persian, and *skunk* from American Indian. There is not room to give the origin of every word (and some origins are very complicated; others are not known), and users who are interested in discovering these should look in a larger dictionary.

Spelling

Many verbs ending in **-ise** (such as *realise*) and their corresponding nouns ending in **-isation** (such as *realisation*) may also be spelt with *z* instead of *s*. However, only **-ise** should be used in *advertise, advise, arise, chastise, comprise, compromise, demise, despise, devise, disguise, enfranchise, enterprise, excise, exercise, franchise, improvise, incise, merchandise, practise, promise, revise, rise, supervise, surmise, surprise, televise,* and in verbs ending in *-aise, -oise* and *-uise.*

Pronunciation

Help is given with this when the word is difficult, or when two words with the same spelling are pronounced differently. The pronunciation is given in brackets with *say*, e.g.

chaos (*say* **kay**-oss) *noun*

Words are broken up into small units (usually of one syllable), and the syllable that is spoken with most stress is shown in thick black letters. In the pronunciation guide, note the following distinctions:

oo shows the sound as in *soon*
uu " " " " " *book*
th " " " " " *thin*
th " " " " " *this*
zh " " " " " *vision*

Māori loanwords

The pronunciation of loanwords from Māori is not given in the dictionary. Most New Zealanders will try to pronounce these words as closely as possible to the way they are said in te reo Māori. Unlike some letters in English words, each letter in Māori has just one pronunciation, as indicated below; note also that long vowels in Māori words are shown in this dictionary, and often elsewhere, with a macron (horizontal line) above the letter in question (as in *Māori, kōkopu, kūmara*). In some writings doubling of the vowel-letters is used instead (so *Maaori, kookopu, kuumara*).

There are no silent letters in Māori; each letter is sounded, including *h* in such words as *kahikatea* and *Pākehā*, and all final vowels.

The Māori short vowels *a, e, i, o, u* (as in *haka, mere, iwi, koro, umu*) are pronounced approximately as in English *putt, pet, pit, port* and *put* respectively.

The Māori long vowels *ā, ē, ī, ō, ū* (as in *hāngi, wētā, tītī, tōtara, pūkeko*) are pronounced approximately as in English *bard, bared, bead, board* and *booed* respectively.

Where two Māori vowels occur together, each one is given its own value, as in *kai, kauri, kea, poi, Aotearoa.*

The Māori consonants *h, k, m, n, p, r, t, w* are pronounced approximately as in English; *wh* is usually pronounced as *f*; *ng* is always pronounced as in *singer* (never as in *finger*).

All Māori syllables end in a vowel, and division into syllables is a recommended first step in determining the pronunciation of the word as a whole: e.g. *pō-hu-tu-ka-wa, me-re, kau-mā-tua, ta-ke, tū-ra-nga-wae-wae.*

Proprietary terms

This book includes some words that are or are asserted to be proprietary names. The presence or absence of such assertions should not be regarded as affecting the legal status of any proprietary name or trade mark.

Aa

a *adjective* (called the *indefinite article* and changing to **an** before most vowel sounds) **1** one (but not any special one), *Can you lend me a book?* **2** each; per. *We see it once a day* or *once an hour.*

a-[1] *prefix* **1** on; to; towards (as in *afoot, ashore, aside*). **2** in the process of (as in *a-hunting*). [from Old English *an, on* = on]

a-[2] *prefix* (**an-** is used before a vowel sound) not; without (as in *asymmetrical, anarchy*). [from Greek *a-* = not]

A[1] *adjective* excellent.

A & E *abbreviation* accident and emergency.

AA *abbreviation* **1** Automobile Association. **2** Alcoholics Anonymous.

A & P Show *noun* (*NZ*) an annual fair run by a local Agricultural and Pastoral Association.

aardvark *noun* an African mammal that feeds on ants and termites.

ab- *prefix* (changing to **abs-** before *c* and *t*) away; from (as in *abduct, abnormal, abstract*). [from Latin *ab* = away]

aback *adverb* **taken aback** surprised.

abacus (*say* **ab**-a-kus) *noun* (*plural* **abacuses**) a frame used for counting with beads sliding on wires.

abalone (*say* a-ba-**loh**-nee) *noun* an edible shellfish, called pāua in New Zealand.

abandon *verb* give up; leave something without intending to return, *Abandon ship!* **abandonment** *noun*

abandon *noun* a casual and careless manner, *dancing with great abandon.*

abase *verb* (**abased, abasing**) humiliate.

abashed *adjective* embarrassed.

abate *verb* (**abated, abating**) make or become less; die down, *The storm had abated.* **abatement** *noun*

abattoir (*say* **ab**-at-wahr) *noun* a slaughterhouse that produces meat for local shops. [French]

abbey *noun* (*plural* **abbeys**) **1** a monastery or convent. **2** a church that was once part of a monastery, *Westminster Abbey.*

abbot *noun* the head of an abbey.

abbreviate *verb* (**abbreviated, abbreviating**) shorten something.

abbreviation *noun* **1** a shortened form of a word or words, such as maths, St., USA. **2** abbreviating something.

ABC *noun* the alphabet.

abdicate *verb* (**abdicated, abdicating**) resign from a throne; give up an important responsibility. **abdication** *noun*

abdomen (*say* **ab**-dom-en) *noun* **1** the lower front part of a person's or animal's body, containing the stomach, intestines, and other digestive organs. **2** the rear section of an insect's body. **abdominal** (*say* ab-**dom**-in-al) *adjective*

abduct *verb* take a person away illegally; kidnap. **abduction** *noun*, **abductor** *noun* [from *ab-*, + Latin *ductum* = led]

abet *verb* (**abetted, abetting**) help or encourage someone to commit a crime.

abeyance (*say* ab-**ay**-ans) *noun* **in abeyance** suspended or postponed.

abhor *verb* (**abhorred, abhorring**) detest. **abhorrent** *adjective*, **abhorrence** *noun* [from Latin *abhorrere* shrink in fear]

abide *verb* (**abided, abiding**) **1** (*old use; past tense* **abode**) remain; dwell. **2** bear; tolerate, *I can't abide wasps.*
abide by keep a promise etc.

abiding *adjective* lasting; permanent.

ability *noun* (*plural* **abilities**) **1** being able to do something. **2** cleverness; talent.

abject (*say* **ab**-jekt) *adjective* **1** wretched; miserable, *living in abject poverty.* **2** humble, *an abject apology.* [from *ab-*, + Latin *-jectum* = thrown]

ablaze *adjective* blazing; on fire.

able *adjective* **1** having the power or skill or opportunity to do something. **2** skilful; clever. **ably** *adverb*

abnormal *adjective* not normal; unusual. **abnormally** *adverb*, **abnormality** *noun*

aboard *adverb & preposition* on or into a ship or aircraft or train.

abode *noun* (*old use*) the place where someone lives.

abolish *verb* put an end to a law or custom etc. **abolition** (*say* ab-ol-**ish**-on) *noun*

abominable *adjective* very bad; detestable. abominably *adverb*

abominate *verb* (**abominated**, **abominating**) detest. **abomination** *noun*

aborigine (*say* ab-er-**ij**-in-ee) *noun* one of the original inhabitants of a country. **Aborigine** one of the original inhabitants of Australia. **aboriginal** *adjective & noun* [from Latin *ab origine* = from the beginning]

abort *verb* put an end to something before it has been completed, *They aborted the space flight because of problems.*

abortion *noun* removal of a baby from the womb before it has developed enough to survive.

abortive *adjective* unsuccessful, *an abortive attempt.*

abound *verb* **1** be plentiful or abundant, *Fish abound in the river.* **2** have something in great quantities, *The river abounds in fish.*

about *preposition* **1** near in amount or size or time etc., *It costs about $5. Come about two o'clock.* **2** on the subject of; in connection with, *Tell me about your holiday.* **3** all round; in various parts of. *They ran about the playground.*

about *adverb* **1** in various directions, *They were running about.* **2** not far away, *He is somewhere about.*
be about to be going to do something.

above *preposition* **1** higher than. **2** more than.

above *adverb* at or to a higher place.

above-board *adjective & adverb* honest; without deception.

abrade *verb* (**abraded**, **abrading**) scrape or wear something away by rubbing it. **abrasion** *noun*

abrasive *adjective* **1** that abrades things. **2** harsh, *an abrasive manner.*

abrasive *noun* a rough substance used for rubbing or polishing things.

abreast *adverb* **1** side by side. **2** keeping up with something.

abridge *verb* (**abridged**, **abridging**) shorten a book etc. by using fewer words, *an abridged edition.* **abridgement** *noun* [from Old French *abregier* = shorten]

abroad *adverb* in or to another country.

abrupt *adjective* sudden; hasty. **abruptly** *adverb*, **abruptness** *noun* [from *ab-*, + Latin *ruptum* = broken]

abs- *prefix* see **ab-**.

abscess (*say* **ab**-sis) *noun* (*plural* **abscesses**) an inflamed place where pus has formed in the body.

abscond *verb* go away secretly, *The cashier had absconded with the money.*

abseil *verb* descend a rock-face by using a doubled rope that is fixed at a higher point.
abseil *noun* [from German *ab* = down, *seil* = rope]

absent *adjective* not here; not present, *absent from school.* **absence** *noun*

absent (*say* ab-**sent**) *verb* **absent yourself** stay away.

absentee *noun* a person who is absent. **absenteeism** *noun*

absent-minded *adjective* having your mind on other things; forgetful.

absolute *adjective* complete; not restricted. [same origin as *absolve*]

absolutely *adverb* **1** completely. **2** (*informal*) yes, I agree.

absolution *noun* a priest's formal declaration that people's sins are forgiven.

absolve *verb* (**absolved**, **absolving**) **1** clear a person of blame or guilt. **2** release from a promise or obligation. [from *ab-*, + Latin *solvere* = set free]

absorb *verb* **1** soak up; take in. **2** receive something and reduce its effects, *The buffers absorbed most of the shock.* **3** take up a person's attention or time. **absorbent** *adjective*, **absorption** *noun*

abstain *verb* keep yourself from doing something (e.g. from voting); refrain. **abstainer** *noun* **abstention** *noun*

abstemious (*say* ab-**steem**-ee-us) *adjective* eating or drinking only small amounts; not greedy. **abstemiously** *adverb*, **abstemiousness** *noun*

abstinence *noun* abstaining, especially from alcohol. **abstinent** *adjective*

abstract (*say* **ab**-strakt) *adjective* **1** concerned with ideas not with objects, *Truth is abstract.* **2** (of a painting or sculpture) showing the artist's ideas or feelings, not showing a recognisable person or thing.

abstract (*say* ab-**strakt**) *verb* take out; remove, *He abstracted some cards from the pack.* **abstraction** *noun*

abstract (*say* **ab**-strakt) *noun* a summary [from *abs-*, + Latin *tractum* = pulled]

abstracted *adjective* with your mind on other things; not paying attention.

abstruse (*say* ab-**stroos**) *adjective* hard to understand; obscure.

absurd *adjective* ridiculous; foolish. **absurdly** *adverb*, **absurdity** *noun* [from Latin *absurdus* = out of tune]

abundance *noun* plenty.

abundant *adjective* plentiful. **abundantly** *adverb*

abuse (*say* ab-**yooz**) *verb* (**abused**, **abusing**) **1** use badly or wrongly; misuse. **2** ill-treat. **3** say unpleasant things about a person or thing.

abuse (*say* ab-**yooss**) *noun* **1** a misuse. **2** ill-treatment. **3** words abusing a person or thing; insults, **abusive** *adjective* [from *ab-* + *use*]

abut *verb* (**abutted**, **abutting**) end against something, *Their shed abuts against ours.* **abutment** *noun*

abysmal (*say* ab-**iz**-mal) *adjective* extremely bad, *abysmal ignorance.*

abyss (*say* ab-**iss**) *noun* (*plural* **abysses**) an extremely deep pit.

ac- *prefix* see **ad-**.

a/c *abbreviation* account.

acacia *noun* a tree with yellow or white flowers.

academic *adjective* **1** of a school or college or university. **2** theoretical; having no practical application.

academy *noun* (*plural* **academies**) **1** a school or college, especially for specialised training. **2** a society of scholars or artists, *The Royal Academy.*

ACC *abbreviation* Accident Compensation Corporation.

accede (*say* ak-**seed**) *verb* (**acceded**, **acceding**) **1** agree to what is asked or suggested, *accede to a request.* **2** take office; become king or queen, *She acceded to the throne.* [from *ac-*, + Latin *cedere* = go]

accelerate *verb* (**accelerated**, **accelerating**) make or become quicker. **acceleration** *noun* [from *ac-*, + Latin *celer* = swift]

accelerator *noun* something that speeds things up; the pedal that a driver presses to make a motor vehicle go faster.

accent (*say* **ak**-sent) *noun* **1** the way a person pronounces words, *She has a French accent.* **2** emphasis; accenting of a word, *In 'action', the accent is on 'ac-'.* **3** a mark placed over a letter to show its pronunciation, e.g. on *café.*

accent (*say* ak-**sent**) *verb* pronounce part of a word more strongly than the other parts; emphasise.

accentuate (*say* ak-**sent**-yoo-ayt) *verb* (**accentuated**, **accentuating**) emphasise; accent. **accentuation** *noun*

accept *verb* take a thing that is offered or presented; say yes to an invitation etc. **acceptance** *noun*

acceptable *adjective* worth accepting; pleasing. **acceptably** *adverb*, **acceptability** *noun*

access (*say* **ak**-sess) *noun* a way in; a way to reach something.

access *verb* **1** find information that has been stored in a computer. **2** approach or enter (a place).

accessible *adjective* able to be reached. **accessibly** *adverb*, **accessibility** *noun*

accession *noun* **1** acceding; reaching a rank or position. **2** an addition, *recent accessions to our library.*

accessory (*say* ak-**sess**-er-ee) *noun* (*plural* **accessories**) **1** an extra thing that goes with something. **2** a person who helps another with a crime.

accident *noun* an unexpected happening, especially one causing injury or damage. **by accident** by chance; without its being arranged in advance. [from *ac-*, + Latin *cadens* = falling]

accidental *adjective* happening or done by accident. **accidentally** *adverb*

acclaim *verb* welcome or applaud. **acclaim** *noun*, **acclamation** *noun* [from *ac-*, + Latin *clamare* = to shout]

acclimatise *verb* (**acclimatised**, **acclimatising**) make or become used to a new climate or new conditions. **acclimatisation** *noun*

accolade (*say* ak-ol-**ayd**) *noun* **1** praise. **2** the ceremonial conferring of a knighthood by tapping a person on the shoulders with a sword.

accommodate *verb* (**accommodated**, **accommodating**) **1** provide room or lodging for somebody. **2** help by providing something, *We can accommodate you with skis.*

accommodation *noun* somewhere to live; lodgings.

accompanist *noun* a person who plays a musical accompaniment.

accompany *verb* (**accompanied**, **accompanying**) **1** go somewhere with somebody. **2** be present with something, *Thunder accompanied the storm.* **3** play music that supports a singer or another player etc. **accompaniment** *noun*

accomplice (*say* a-**kum**-pliss) *noun* a person who helps another in a crime etc.

accomplish *verb* do something successfully. **accomplishment** *noun*

accomplished *adjective* skilled.

accord *noun* agreement; consent. **of your own accord** voluntarily; without being asked or compelled.

accord *verb* **1** be consistent with something. **2** (*formal*) give, *He was accorded this privilege.*

accordance *noun* **in accordance with** in agreement with, *This is done in accordance with the rules.*

according *adverb* **according to** as stated by, *According to him, we are stupid*; in a way that suits, *Price the apples according to their size.* **accordingly** *adverb*

accordion *noun* a portable musical instrument like a large concertina.

accost *verb* approach and speak to a person.

account *noun* **1** a statement of money owed, spent, or received; a bill. **2** an arrangement to keep money in a bank etc. **3** a description; a report. **4** consideration, *Take it into account.*
on account of because of.
on no account certainly not.

account *verb* **account for** make it clear why something happens.

accountable *adjective* responsible; having to explain why you have done something. **accountability** *noun*

accountant *noun* a keeper or inspector of financial accounts. **accountancy** *noun*

accounting *noun* keeping financial accounts.

accoutrements (*say* a-**koo**-trim-ents) *plural noun* equipment. [French]

accredited *adjective* officially recognised, *our accredited agent.* **accreditation** *noun*

accretion (*say* a-**kree**-shon) *noun* a growth or increase in which things are added gradually.

accrue (*say* a-**kroo**) *verb* (**accrued**, **accruing**) accumulate. **accrual** *noun*

accumulate *verb* (**accumulated**, **accumulating**) collect; pile up. **accumulation** *noun* [from *ac-*, + Latin *cumulus* = heap]

accumulator *noun* a storage battery.

accurate *adjective* correct; exact. **accurately** *adverb*, **accuracy** *noun*

accusation *noun* accusing someone; a statement accusing a person of a fault or crime etc.

accuse *verb* (**accused**, **accusing**) say that a person (whom you name) has committed a crime etc.; blame. **accuser** *noun*

accustom *verb* make a person become used to something. [from *ac-*, + *custom*]

ace *noun* **1** a playing-card with one spot. **2** a very skilful person or thing.

acetylene (*say* a-**set**-il-een) *noun* a gas that burns with a bright flame, used in cutting and welding metal.

ache *noun* a dull continuous pain.

ache *verb* (**ached**, **aching**) have an ache.

achieve *verb* (**achieved**, **achieving**) succeed in doing or producing something; accomplish. **achievable** *adjective*, **achievement** *noun* [from Old French *a chief* = to a head]

achievement standard *noun* (*NZ*) a prescribed level of achievement required within a particular subject area or skill set, in order to gain a credit towards the National Certificate of Educational Achievement.

acid *noun* **1** a chemical substance that contains hydrogen and neutralises alkalis. **2** (*slang*) the drug LSD. **acidic** *adjective*, **acidity** *noun*

acid *adjective* **1** sharp-tasting; sour. **2** looking or sounding bitter, *an acid reply.* **acidly** *adverb*
acid rain rain made acid by mixing with waste gases from factories etc.

acidophilus (*say* ass-id-**off**-il-us) *noun* a *Lactobacillus* bacterium often added to yoghurt for easy digestion.

acknowledge *verb* (**acknowledged**, **acknowledging**) **1** admit that something is true. **2** state that you have received or noticed something, *Acknowledge this letter.* **3** express thanks or appreciation for something. **acknowledgement** *noun*

acme (*say* **ak**-mee) *noun* the highest degree of something, *the acme of perfection.* [from Greek *akme* = highest point]

acne (*say* **ak**-nee) *noun* inflamed red pimples on the face and neck.

acorn *noun* the seed of the oak-tree.

acoustic (*say* a-**koo**-stik) *adjective* **1** of sound or hearing. **2** (of a musical instrument) not electronic, *an acoustic guitar.* **acoustically** *adverb* [from Greek *akouein* = hear]

acoustics (*say* a-**koo**-stiks) *plural noun* **1** the qualities of a hall etc. that make it good or bad for carrying sound. **2** the properties of sound.

acquaint *verb* tell somebody about something, *Acquaint him with the facts.*
be acquainted with know slightly.

acquaintance *noun* **1** a person you know slightly. **2** being acquainted.

acquiesce (*say* ak-wee-**ess**) *verb* (**acquiesced**, **acquiescing**) agree to something. **acquiescent** *adjective*, **acquiescence** *noun*

acquire *verb* (**acquired**, **acquiring**) obtain. **acquirement** *noun*, **acquisition** *noun* [from *ac-*, + Latin *quaerere* = seek]

acquisitive (*say* a-**kwiz**-it-iv) *adjective* eager to acquire things.

acquit *verb* (**acquitted**, **acquitting**) decide that somebody is not guilty. **acquittal** *noun*

acre (*say* **ay**-ker) *noun* an imperial unit of area, equivalent to about 0.405 of a hectare. **acreage** *noun*

acrid *adjective* bitter, *an acrid smell.*

acrimonious (*say* ak-rim-**oh**-nee-us) *adjective* (of a person's manner or words) sharp and bad-tempered or bitter. **acrimony** (*say* **ak**-rim-on-ee) *noun*

acrobat *noun* a person who performs spectacular gymnastic stunts for entertainment. **acrobatic** *adjective*, **acrobatics** *plural noun* [from Greek *akrobatos* = walking on tiptoe]

acronym (*say* **ak**-ron-im) *noun* a word or name formed from the initial letters of other words, *Anzac is an acronym of Australian and New Zealand Army Corps*. [from Greek *akros* = top, + *onyma* = name]

across *preposition & adverb* **1** from one side to the other, *Swim across the river. Are you across yet?* **2** on the opposite side, *the house across the street.*

acrostic *noun* a word-puzzle or poem in which the first or last letters of each line form a word or words.

acrylic (*say* a-**kril**-ik) *noun* a kind of fibre, plastic, or resin made from an organic acid.

act *noun* **1** an action. **2** a law passed by a parliament. **3** one of the main divisions of a play or opera. **4** a short performance in a programme of entertainment, *a juggling act.* **5** (*informal*) a pretence, *She is only putting on an act.*

act *verb* **1** do something; perform actions. **2** perform a part in a play or film etc. **3** function; have an effect. [from Latin *actum* = done]

ACT *noun* a New Zealand political party. [acronym of *Association of Consumers and Taxpayers*]

action *noun* **1** doing something. **2** something done. **3** a battle; fighting, *He was killed in action.* **4** a lawsuit.
action song a traditional kind of Māori song accompanied by movements.
out of action not functioning.
take action do something.

activate *verb* (**activated**, **activating**) start something working. **activation** *noun*, **activator** *noun*

active *adjective* **1** doing things; moving about; taking part in activities. **2** functioning; in operation, *an active volcano.* **3** radioactive. **4** (of a form of a verb) used when the subject of the verb is performing the action. In 'The shop *sells* books' the verb is active; in 'Books *are sold* by the shop' the verb is passive. **actively** *adverb*, **activeness** *noun*

activist *noun* a person who believes in vigorous action, especially in politics.

activity *noun* (*plural* **activities**) **1** an action or occupation, *outdoor activities.* **2** being active or lively.

actor *noun* a performer in a play or film etc. **actress** *noun*

actual *adjective* real. **actually** *adverb*, **actuality** *noun*

actuate *verb* (**actuated**, **actuating**) activate, **actuation** *noun*

acumen (*say* **ak**-yoo-men) *noun* sharpness of mind. [Latin, = a point]

acupuncture (*say* **ak**-yoo-punk-cher) *noun* pricking parts of the body with needles to relieve pain or cure disease. **acupuncturist** *noun* [from Latin *acu* = with a needle, + *puncture*]

acute *adjective* **1** sharp; strong, *acute pain.* **2** having a sharp mind, **acutely** *adverb*, **acuteness** *noun*
acute accent a mark over a vowel, as over *e* in *café.*
acute angle an angle of less than 90°.

AD *abbreviation* Anno Domini (Latin = in the year of Our Lord), used in dates counted from the birth of Jesus Christ.

ad- *prefix* (changing to **ac-**, **af-**, **ag-**, **al-**, **an-**, **ap-**, **ar-**, **as-**, **at-** before certain consonants) to; towards (as in *adapt, admit*). [from Latin *ad* = to]

ad *noun* (*informal*) an advertisement.

adamant (*say* **ad**-am-ant) *adjective* firm and not giving way to requests.

Adam's apple the lump at the front of a person's neck.

adapt *verb* make or become suitable for a new purpose or situation. **adaptable** *adjective*, **adaptation** *noun* [from *ad-*, + Latin *aptus* = fitted]

adaptor *noun* a device to connect pieces of electrical or other equipment.

add *verb* **1** put one thing with another. **2** make another remark.
add up make or find a total; (*informal*) make sense; seem reasonable.

addenda *plural noun* things added at the end of a book. [Latin, = things to be added]

addict *noun* a person who does or uses something that he or she cannot give up. **addicted** *adjective*, **addiction** *noun* [from Latin *addictus* = person given as a servant to someone to whom he owes money]

addictive *adjective* causing people to become addicts.

addition *noun* **1** the process of adding. **2** something added. **additional** *adjective*, **additionally** *adverb*
in addition also; as an extra thing.

additive *noun* a substance added to another in small amounts for a special purpose, e.g. as a flavouring.

addled *adjective* (of eggs) rotted and producing no chick after being brooded.

address *noun* **1** the details of the place where someone lives or of where letters etc. should be delivered to a person or firm. **2** a speech to an audience.

address *verb* **1** write an address on a parcel etc. **2** make a speech or remark etc. to somebody.

addressee *noun* the person to whom a letter etc. is addressed.

addy *abbreviation* a shortened form of address, in electronic usage.

adenoids *plural noun* thick spongy flesh at the back of the nose and throat, which may hinder breathing.

adept (*say* **ad**-ept) *adjective* very skilful.

adequate *adjective* enough; good enough. **adequately** *adverb*, **adequacy** *noun*

adhere *verb* (**adhered**, **adhering**) stick to something. **adhesion** *noun* [from *ad-*, + Latin *haerere* = to stick]

adherent (*say* ad-**heer**-ent) *noun* a person who supports a certain group or theory etc. **adherence** *noun*

adhesive *adjective* causing things to stick together.

adhesive *noun* a substance used to stick things together; glue.

adieu (*say* a-**dew**) *interjection* goodbye. [from French *à* = to, + *Dieu* = God]

adjacent *adjective* near; next. [from *ad-*, + Latin *jacens* = lying]

adjective *noun* a word that describes a noun or adds to its meaning, e.g. *big, honest, strange, our*. **adjectival** *adjective*, **adjectivally** *adverb*

adjoin *verb* be next or nearest to something.

adjourn (*say* a-**jern**) *verb* **1** break off a meeting etc. until a later time. **2** break off and go somewhere else, *They adjourned to the library*. **adjournment** *noun* [from Latin, = to another day]

adjudge *verb* (**adjudged**, **adjudging**) judge; give a decision, *He was adjudged to be guilty*.

adjudicate (*say* a-**joo**-dik-ayt) *verb* (**adjudicated**, **adjudicating**) act as judge in a competition etc. **adjudication** *noun*, **adjudicator** *noun* [from *ad-*, + Latin *judicare* = to judge]

adjunct (*say* **aj**-unkt) *noun* something added that is useful but not essential. [from *ad-*, + Latin *junctum* = joined]

adjust *verb* **1** put a thing into its proper position or order. **2** alter so as to fit. **adjustable** *adjective*, **adjustment** *noun*

ad lib as you like; freely.

ad-lib *verb* (**ad-libbed**, **ad-libbing**) say or do something without any rehearsal or preparation. [from Latin *ad libitum* = according to pleasure]

administer *verb* **1** give; provide, *He administered a rebuke*. **2** manage business affairs; administrate.

administrate *verb* (**administrated**, **administrating**) manage public or business affairs. **administrator** *noun*, **administrative** *adjective*

administration *noun* **1** administering. **2** the management of public or business affairs. **3** the people who manage an organisation etc.; the government.

admirable *adjective* worth admiring; excellent. **admirably** *adverb*

admiral *noun* **1** a naval officer of high rank. **2** a kind of butterfly, *red admiral*. [from Arabic *amir* = commander]

admire *verb* (**admired**, **admiring**) **1** look at something and enjoy it. **2** think that someone or something is very good. **admiration** *noun*, **admirer** *noun* [from *ad-*, + Latin *mirari* = wonder at]

admissible *adjective* able to be admitted or allowed.

admission *noun* **1** admitting. **2** the charge for being allowed to go in. **3** a statement admitting something; a confession.

admit *verb* (**admitted**, **admitting**) **1** allow someone or something to come in. **2** state reluctantly that something is true; confess, *We admit that the task is difficult. He admitted his crime*. [from *ad-*, + Latin *mittere* = send]

admittance *noun* being allowed to go in, especially to a private place.

admittedly *adverb* as an agreed fact; without denying it.

admonish *verb* advise or warn firmly but mildly. **admonition** *noun*

ado *noun* fuss; excitement. [originally in *much ado* = much to do]

adolescence (*say* ad-ol-**ess**-ens) *noun* the time between being a child and being an adult. **adolescent** *adjective & noun*

adopt *verb* **1** take someone into your family as your own child. **2** accept something; take and use, *They adopted new methods of working*. **adoption** *noun* [from *ad-*, + Latin *optare* = choose]

adore *verb* (**adored**, **adoring**) love very much. **adorable** *adjective*, **adoration** *noun* [from *ad-*, + Latin *orare* = pray]

adorn *verb* decorate. **adornment** *noun*

adrenalin (*say* a-**dren**-al-in) *noun* a hormone that stimulates the nervous system.

adrift *adjective & adverb* drifting.

adroit (*say* a-**droit**) *adjective* skilful. [from French *à droit* = according to right]

adulation *noun* very great flattery.

adult (*say* **ad**-ult) *noun* a fully grown or mature person.

adulterate *verb* (**adulterated**, **adulterating**) make a thing impure or less good by adding something to it. **adulteration** *noun* [from Latin *adulterare* = corrupt]

adultery *noun* being unfaithful to your wife or husband by having sexual intercourse with someone else. **adulterer** *noun*, **adulterous** *adjective*

advance *noun* **1** a forward movement; progress. **2** an increase. **3** a loan; payment made before it is due.
in advance beforehand; ahead.

advance *verb* (**advanced**, **advancing**) **1** move forward; make progress. **2** lend or pay money ahead of the proper time, *Advance her a month's salary.* **advancement** *noun*

advantage *noun* **1** something useful or helpful. **2** the next point won after deuce in tennis.
take advantage of use profitably or unfairly.
to advantage making a good effect, *The painting shows to advantage here.*
to your advantage profitable or helpful to you.

advantageous (*say* ad-van-**tay**-jus) *adjective* giving an advantage; beneficial.

Advent *noun* the period before Christmas, when Christians commemorate the coming of Christ.

advent *noun* the arrival of a new person or thing, *the advent of computers.* [from *ad-*, + Latin *ventum-* = arrived]

adventure *noun* **1** an exciting or dangerous experience. **2** willingness to take risks. **adventurer** *noun*

adverb *noun* a word that adds to the meaning of a verb or adjective or another adverb and tells how, when, or where something happens, e.g. *gently*, *soon*, and *upstairs.* **adverbial** *adjective*, **adverbially** *adverb* [from *ad-*, + Latin *verbum* = word]

adversary (*say* **ad**-ver-ser-ee) *noun* (*plural* **adversaries**) an opponent; an enemy.

adverse *adjective* unfavourable; harmful, *adverse effects.* **adversely** *adverb*, **adversity** *noun* [from Latin *adversus* = opposite (*ad* = to, *versus* = turned)]

advert *noun* (*informal*) an advertisement.

advertise *verb* (**advertised**, **advertising**) **1** make something publicly known, *advertise a meeting.* **2** praise goods etc. in order to encourage people to buy or use them. **3** ask or offer by a public notice, *advertise for a secretary.* **advertisement** *noun*, **advertiser** *noun*

advice *noun* **1** a statement telling a person what you think he or she should do. **2** a piece of information, *We received advice that the goods had been dispatched.*

advisable *adjective* that is the wise thing to do. **advisability** *noun*

advise *verb* (**advised**, **advising**) **1** give somebody advice; recommend. **2** inform. **adviser** *noun*, **advisory** *adjective*

advocate (*say* **ad**-vok-ayt) *verb* (**advocated**, **advocating**) speak in favour of something; recommend, *We advocate reform.*

advocate (*say* **ad**-vok-at) *noun* **1** a person who advocates a policy etc., *She is an advocate of reform.* **2** a lawyer presenting someone's case in a lawcourt.

adze *noun* a tool rather like an axe for trimming wood.

aegis (*say* **ee**-jiss) *noun* protection; sponsorship, *The scheme is under the aegis of the Scout Association.* [from Greek *aigis* = magical shield of the god Zeus]

aerate (*say* **air**-ayt) *verb* (**aerated**, **aerating**) **1** add air to something. **2** add carbon dioxide to a liquid, *aerated water.*

aerial *adjective* **1** of or in or from the air. **2** of or by aircraft.
aerial topdressing the spreading of fertiliser from an aeroplane.

aerial *noun* a wire or rod etc. for receiving or transmitting radio or television signals.

aero- *prefix* of air or aircraft (as in *aeronautics*). [from Greek *aer* = air]

aerobatics *plural noun* spectacular performances by flying aircraft. **aerobatic** *adjective* [from *aero-* + *acrobatics*]

aerobics *plural noun* exercises to stimulate breathing and strengthen the heart and lungs. **aerobic** *adjective*

aerodrome *noun* an airfield. [from *aero-*, + Greek *dromos* running-track]

aeronautics *noun* the study of aircraft and flying. **aeronautic** *adjective*, **aeronautical** *adjective* [from *aero-* + *nautical*]

aeroplane *noun* a flying machine with wings. [from *aero-* + *plane*[1]]

aerosol *noun* a device for producing a fine spray of a substance. [from *aero-* + *solution*]

aerospace *noun* the earth's atmosphere and space beyond it.

aesthetic (*say* iss-**thet**-ik) *adjective* of or showing appreciation of beautiful things. [from Greek, = perceiving]

af- *prefix* see **ad-**.

afakasi (*say* **af**-a-kah-see) *noun* a person who is part-Pacific Islander, part-European. [from Samoan]

afar *adverb* far away, *The din was heard from afar.*

affable *adjective* polite and friendly. **affably** *adverb*, **affability** *noun*

affair *noun* **1** a thing; a matter; an event. **2** a temporary sexual relationship. [from French *à faire* = to do]

affect *verb* **1** have an effect on. **2** harm. **3** pretend, *She affected ignorance.*

USAGE Do not confuse with effect.

affectation *noun* a pretence; behaviour that is put on for show and not natural.

affected *adjective* pretended; unnatural.

affection *noun* love; a liking.

affectionate *adjective* showing affection; loving, **affectionately** *adverb*

affidavit (*say* af-id-**ay**-vit) *noun* a statement written down and sworn to be true, for use as legal evidence. [Latin, = he or she has stated on oath]

affiliated *adjective* officially connected with a larger organisation. [from Latin *affiliatum* = adopted (from *af-*, + *filius* = son)]

affinity *noun* (*plural* **affinities**) attraction, relationship, or similarity to each other, *There are many affinities between the two languages.*

affirm *verb* state definitely or firmly. **affirmation** *noun*

affirmative *adjective* that says 'yes', *an affirmative reply.* (Compare *negative.*) **affirmative action** acting in a way that benefits groups of people (e.g. women, Māori) that have been treated unfairly in the past.

affix (*say* a-**fiks**) *verb* attach; add in writing, *affix a stamp; affix your signature.*

affix (*say* **aff**-iks) *noun* a prefix or suffix.

afflict *verb* cause somebody distress. **affliction** *noun* [from *af-* + Latin *flictum* = struck]

affluent (*say* **af**-loo-ent) *adjective* rich. **affluence** *noun* [from Latin *affluens* = overflowing (see *fluent*)]

afford *verb* **1** have enough money to pay for something. **2** have enough time or resources etc. to do something.

afforestation *noun* the planting of trees to form a forest.

affray *noun* fighting or rioting in public.

affront *verb* insult; offend; embarrass.

affront *noun* an insult.

afghan (*say* **af**-gan) *noun* **1** a kind of woollen blanket or shawl. **2** a kind of chocolate biscuit.

afghan hound a large dog with long hair.

afield *adverb* at or to a distance; away from home, *travelling far afield.*

aflame *adjective & adverb* in flames; glowing.

afloat *adjective & adverb* floating; on the sea.

afoot *adjective* happening, *Great changes are afoot.*

aforesaid *adjective* mentioned previously.

afraid *adjective* frightened; alarmed. **I'm afraid** I regret, *I'm afraid I'm late.*

afresh *adverb* again; in a new way, *We must start afresh.*

African *adjective* of Africa or its people. **African American** (a) black American.

African *noun* an African person.

African Union *noun* an association of African states (formerly Organisation of African Unity).

Afrikaans (*say* af-rik-**ahns**) *noun* a language developed from Dutch, used in South Africa. [from Dutch, = African]

Afrikaner (*say* af-rik-**ah**-ner) *noun* a White person in South Africa whose language is Afrikaans.

Afro *noun* (*plural* **Afros**) a bushy frizzy hair-style. **Afro** *adjective*

Afro- *prefix* African.

aft *adverb* at or towards the back of a ship or aircraft.

after *preposition* **1** later than, *Come after tea.* **2** behind in place or order, *Which letter comes after H?* **3** trying to catch; pursuing, *Run after him.* **4** in spite of, *We can come after all.* **5** in imitation or honour of, *She is named after her aunt.* **6** about; concerning, *He asked after you.*

after *adverb* **1** behind, *Jill came tumbling after.* **2** later, *It came a week after.*

after *adjective* coming or done afterwards, *in after years; the after-effects.*

aftermath *noun* the conditions after something, *the aftermath of war.* [from *after* + *math* = mowing (i.e. new grass that grows after a mowing)]

afternoon *noun* the time from noon or lunch-time to evening. **afternoon tea** (*NZ*) a mid-afternoon break for tea or coffee and a snack.

afters *plural noun* (*informal*) dessert.

afterthought *noun* something thought of or added later.

afterwards *adverb* at a later time.

ag- *prefix* see **ad-**.

again *adverb* **1** another time; once more, *try again.* **2** as before, *You will soon be well again.* **3** besides; moreover.

against *preposition* **1** touching; hitting, *He leant against the wall.* **2** in opposition to; not in favour of, *They voted against the proposal.* **3** in preparation for, *Protect them against the cold.*

age *noun* **1** the length of time a person has lived or a thing has existed. **2** a special period of history or geology, *the Ice Age.*
ages *plural noun* (*informal*) a very long time, *We've been waiting for ages.*
come of age reach the age at which you have an adult's legal rights and obligations (now at 18 years; formerly 21).

age *verb* (**aged**, **ageing**) make or become old.

aged *adjective* **1** (*say* ayjd) having the age of, *a girl aged 9.* **2** (*say* **ay**-jid) very old, *an aged man.*

age-group *noun* people who are all of the same age.

agency *noun* (*plural* **agencies**) **1** the office or business of an agent, *a travel agency.* **2** the means by which something is done, *Flowers are pollinated by the agency of bees.*

agenda (*say* a-**jen**-da) *noun* (*plural* **agendas**) a list of things to be done or discussed, *The agenda is rather long.* [Latin, = things to be done]

agent *noun* **1** a person who organises things for other people. **2** a spy, *a secret agent.* [from Latin *agens* = doing things]

agglomeration *noun* a mass of things collected together. [from *ag-*, + Latin *glomus* = mass]

aggravate *verb* (**aggravated**, **aggravating**) **1** make a thing worse or more serious. **2** (*informal*) annoy. **aggravation** *noun* [from *ag-*, + Latin *gravare* = load heavily]

aggregate (*say* **ag**-rig-at) *adjective* combined; total, *the aggregate amount.* [from *ag-*, + Latin *gregatum* = herded together]

aggression *noun* starting an attack or war etc.; aggressive behaviour. [from *ag-* = against, + Latin *gressum* = gone]

aggressive *adjective* likely to attack people; forceful. **aggressively** *adverb*, **aggressiveness** *noun*

aggressor *noun* the person or nation that started an attack or war etc.

aggrieved (*say* a-**greevd**) *adjective* resentful because of being treated unfairly.

aggro *noun* (*slang*) **1** aggressive behaviour. **2** trouble, difficulties.

aghast *adjective* horrified.

agile *adjective* moving quickly or easily. **agilely** *adverb*, **agility** *noun*

agitate *verb* (**agitated**, **agitating**) **1** make someone feel upset or anxious. **2** stir up public interest or concern; campaign, *They agitated for a new bypass.* **3** shake something about. **agitation** *noun*, **agitator** *noun* [from Latin *agitare* = shake]

aglow *adjective* glowing.

AGM *abbreviation* Annual General Meeting.

agnostic (*say* ag-**nost**-ik) *noun* a person who believes that it is impossible to know whether God exists. **agnosticism** *noun* [from *a-* = not, + Greek *gnostikos* = knowing]

ago *adverb* in the past, *long ago.* [from an old word *agone* = gone by]

agog *adjective* eager and excited.

agony *noun* (*plural* **agonies**) extremely great pain or suffering. **agonising** *adjective* [from Greek *agon* = a struggle]

agoraphobia (*say* ag-er-a-**foh**-bee-a) *noun* abnormal fear of being in open spaces. [from Greek *agora* = market-place, + *phobia*]

agrarian (*say* a-**grair**-ee-an) *adjective* of farm land or its cultivation. [from Latin *ager* = field]

agree *verb* (**agreed**, **agreeing**) **1** think or say the same as another person etc. **2** consent, *She agreed to come.* **3** suit a person's health or digestion. *Curry doesn't agree with me.* **4** correspond in grammatical number, gender, or person. In 'They were good teachers', *they* agrees with *teachers* (both are plural forms) and *were* agrees with *they*; *was* would be incorrect because it is singular.

agreeable *adjective* **1** willing, *We shall go if you are agreeable.* **2** pleasant, *an agreeable place.* **agreeably** *adverb*

agreement *noun* **1** agreeing. **2** an arrangement that people have agreed on.

agriculture *noun* the process of cultivating land on a large scale and rearing livestock; farming. **agricultural** *adjective* [from Latin *agri* = of a field, + *culture*]

aground *adverb & adjective* stranded on the bottom in shallow water.

ah *interjection* an exclamation of surprise, pity, admiration, etc.

ahead *adverb* **1** further forward; in front. **2** forwards, *Full steam ahead!*

ahoy *interjection* an exclamation used by seamen to call attention.

AI *abbreviation* artificial insemination.

aid *noun* **1** help. **2** something that helps, *a hearing-aid.* **3** money, food, etc. sent to another country to help it, *overseas aid.*
in aid of for the purpose of; to help something.

aid *verb* help.

aide *noun* an assistant. [French]

Aids *noun* a disease that greatly weakens a person's ability to resist infections. [from the initial letters of 'acquired immune deficiency syndrome']

aiga (*say* ah-**eeng**-a) *noun* a Samoan extended family. [Samoan]

ail *verb* (*old use*) be ill; make a person ill.

ailing *adjective* ill; unwell.

ailment *noun* a slight illness.

aim *verb* **1** point a gun etc. **2** throw or kick in a particular direction. **3** try or intend to do something.

aim *noun* **1** aiming a gun etc. **2** purpose; intention.

aimless *adjective* without a purpose. **aimlessly** *adverb*

air *noun* **1** the mixture of gases that surrounds the earth and which everyone breathes. **2** the open space above the earth. **3** a tune; a melody. **4** an appearance or impression of something, *an air of mystery.* **5** an impressive or haughty manner, *He puts on airs.*
by air in or by aircraft.
on the air on radio or television.

air *verb* **1** put clothes etc. in a warm place to finish drying. **2** ventilate a room. **3** express, *He aired his opinions.*

airborne *adjective* **1** (of an aircraft) in flight. **2** carried by the air or by aircraft.

air-conditioning *noun* a system for controlling the temperature, purity, etc. of a room or building. **air-conditioned** *adjective*

aircraft *noun* (*plural* **aircraft**) an aeroplane, glider, or helicopter etc.

aircraft carrier *noun* a large ship with a long deck where aircraft can take off and land.

airfield *noun* an area equipped with runways etc. where aircraft can take off and land.

air force the part of a country's armed forces that is equipped with aircraft.

airgun *noun* a gun in which compressed air shoots a pellet or dart.

airlift *verb* transport supplies of food etc. by air, especially in an emergency. **airlift** *noun*

airline *noun* a company that provides a regular service of transport by aircraft.

airliner *noun* a large aircraft for carrying passengers.

airlock *noun* **1** a compartment with an airtight door at each end, through which people can go in and out of a pressurised chamber. **2** a bubble of air that stops liquid flowing through a pipe.

airmail *noun* mail carried by air.

airman *noun* (*plural* **airmen**) a member of an air force or of the crew of an aircraft. **airwoman** *noun* (*plural* **airwomen**)

airplane *noun* (especially in North American usage) an aeroplane.

airport *noun* an airfield for aircraft carrying passengers and goods.

air raid an attack by aircraft.

airship *noun* a large balloon with engines, designed to carry passengers or goods.

airstrip *noun* a strip of ground prepared for aircraft to land and take off.

airtight *adjective* not letting air in or out.

airworthy *adjective* (of an aircraft) fit to fly. **airworthiness** *noun*

airy *adjective* **1** with plenty of fresh air. **2** light as air. **3** light-hearted; insincere, *airy promises.* **airily** *adverb*

aisle (*say* I'll) *noun* **1** a passage between or beside rows of seats or pews. **2** a side part of a church.

ajar *adverb & adjective* slightly open, *Leave the door ajar.*

a.k.a. *abbreviation* also known as.

Ākarana *noun* Auckland, in Māori.

akeake *noun* an evergreen native tree with silver, green, or purple leaves. [Māori]

akimbo *adverb* **arms akimbo** with hands on hips and elbows out.

akin *adjective* related; similar.

al- *prefix* see **ad-**.

alabaster (*say* **al**-a-bast-er) *noun* a kind of hard stone, usually white.

alacrity *noun* speed and willingness, *She accepted with alacrity.*

alarm *noun* **1** a warning sound or signal; an apparatus for giving this. **2** being alarmed. **3** an alarm clock.
alarm clock a clock that can be set to make a sound at a fixed time to wake a sleeping person.

alarm *verb* make someone frightened or anxious. [from Italian *all' arme!* = to arms!]

alarmist *noun* a person who raises unnecessary alarm.

alas *interjection* an exclamation of sorrow.

albacore (*say* al-ber-**cor**-er) *noun* a kind of tuna fish. [Portuguese]

albatross *noun* (*plural* **albatrosses**) a large sea-bird with very long wings.

albino (*say* al-**been**-oh) *noun* (*plural* **albinos**) a person or animal with no colour in the skin and hair (which are white). [from Latin *albus* = white]

album *noun* **1** a book with blank pages in which to keep a collection of photographs, stamps, autographs, etc. **2** a collection of recordings on one disc. [Latin, = white piece of stone etc. on which to write things]

albumen (*say* **al**-bew-min) *noun* white of egg. [from Latin *albus* = white]

alchemy (*say* **al**-kim-ee) *noun* an early form of chemistry, the chief aim of which was to turn ordinary metals into gold. **alchemist** *noun* [from Arabic *al-kimiya* = the art of changing metals]

alcohol *noun* **1** a chemical compound C_2H_5OH, formed from the fermentation of sugars, which is the active ingredient of intoxicating drinks etc. **2** a drink containing this substance (wine, beer, whisky, etc.). [from Arabic *al-kuhl*]

alcoholic *adjective* of alcohol; containing alcohol.

alcoholic *noun* a person who is seriously addicted to alcohol. **alcoholism** *noun*

alcove *noun* a section of a room etc. that is set back from the main part; a recess. [from Arabic *al-kubba* = the arch]

alder *noun* a kind of tree, often growing in marshy places.

ale *noun* beer.

alert *adjective* watching for something; ready to act. **alertly** *adverb*, **alertness** *noun*

alert *noun* a warning or alarm.
on the alert on the look-out; watchful.

alert *verb* warn of danger etc.; make someone aware of something. [from Italian *all'erta!* = to the watch-tower!]

alga (*say* **al**-ga) *noun* (*plural* **algae**, *say* (**al**-jee) a kind of plant that grows in water, with no true stems or leaves.

algebra (*say* **al**-jib-ra) *noun* mathematics in which letters and symbols are used to represent quantities. **algebraic** (*say* al-jib-**ray**-ik) *adjective* [from Arabic *al-jabr* = putting together broken parts]

alias (*say* **ay**-lee-as) *noun* (*plural* **aliases**) a false or different name.

alias *adverb* also named, *Robert Zimmerman, alias Bob Dylan.* [Latin, = at another time]

alibi (*say* **al**-ib-I) *noun* (*plural* **alibis**) evidence that a person accused of a crime was somewhere else when it was committed. [Latin, = at another place]

USAGE It is incorrect to use this word as if it meant simply 'an excuse'.

alien (*say* **ay**-lee-en) *noun* a person who is not a citizen of the country where he or she is living; a foreigner.

alien *adjective* **1** foreign. **2** unnatural, *Cruelty is alien to her nature.* [from Latin *alius* = other]

alienate (*say* **ay**-lee-en-ayt) *verb* (**alienated**, **alienating**) make a person become unfriendly or hostile, alienation *noun*

alight[1] *adjective* **1** on fire. **2** lit up. [from *a-*[1]+ *light*[1]]

alight[2] *verb* **1** get out of a vehicle or down from a horse etc. **2** fly down and settle, *The bird alighted on a branch.* [from *a-*[1] + *light*[2]]

align (*say* al-**I'n**) *verb* **1** arrange in a line. **2** join as an ally, *They aligned themselves with the Germans.* **alignment** *noun* [from French *à ligne* = into line]

alike *adjective & adverb* like one another; in the same way, *The twins are very alike. Treat them alike.*

alimentary canal the tube along which food passes from the mouth to the anus in the process of being digested and absorbed by the body. [from Latin *alimentum* = food]

alive *adjective* **1** living. **2** alert, *Be alive to the possible dangers.*

alkali (*say* **alk**-al-I) *noun* (*plural* **alkalis**) a substance that neutralises acids. **alkaline** *adjective* [from Arabic *al-kily* = the ashes]

all *adjective* the whole number or amount of, *All my books are here; all day.*

all *noun* **1** everything, *That is all I know.* **2** everybody, *All are agreed.*

all *adverb* **1** completely, *She was dressed all in white.* **2** to each team or competitor, *The score is fifteen all.*
All Black a New Zealand national men's rugby union representative.
all-clear *noun* a signal that a danger has passed.
all in (*informal*) exhausted, *I'm all in.*
all-in *adjective* including or allowing everything, *an all-in price.*
all right satisfactory; in good condition; as desired; yes, I consent.
all-round *adjective* general; not specialist, *an all-round athlete,* **all-rounder** *noun*
all there (*informal*) having an alert mind.
all the same in spite of this; making no difference, *I like him, all the same.*
All White a New Zealand national men's soccer representative.

Allah the Muslim name of God.

allay (*say* a-**lay**) *verb* (**allayed**, **allaying**) calm, *to allay their fears.*

allegation (*say* al-ig-**ay**-shon) *noun* a statement made without proof.

allege (*say* a-**lej**) *verb* (**alleged**, **alleging**) say something without being able to prove it, *He alleged that I had cheated.* **allegedly** (*say* a-**lej**-id-lee) *adverb*

allegiance (*say* a-**lee**-jans) *noun* loyalty. [compare *liege*]

allegory (*say* **al**-ig-er-ee) *noun* (*plural* **allegories**) a story in which the characters and events represent or symbolise an underlying meaning. **allegorical** (*say* al-ig-**o**-rik-al) *adjective*

alleluia *interjection* praise to God. [from Hebrew]

allergic *adjective* very sensitive to something that may make you ill, *He is allergic to pollen, which gives him hay fever.* **allergy** (*say* **al**-er-jee) *noun*

alleviate (*say* a-**lee**-vee-ayt) *verb* (**alleviated**, **alleviating**) make a thing less severe, *to alleviate pain.* **alleviation** *noun* [from *al-*, + Latin *levis* = light]

alley *noun* (*plural* **alleys**) **1** a narrow street or passage. **2** a place where you can play bowls or skittles. [from French *aller* = go]

alliance *noun* an association formed by countries or groups who wish to support each other.
the Alliance a New Zealand political party.

allied *adjective* **1** joined as allies. **2** of the same kind.

alligator *noun* a reptile, similar to a crocodile. [from Spanish *el lagarto* = the lizard]

alliteration *noun* having the same letter or sound at the beginning of several words, e.g. in *Sit in solemn silence.* [from *al-*, + Latin *littera* = letter]

allocate *verb* (**allocated**, **allocating**) allot; set aside for a particular purpose. **allocation** *noun* [from *al-*, + Latin *locus* = a place]

allot *verb* (**allotted**, **allotting**) distribute portions, jobs, etc. to different people.

allotment *noun* the amount allotted.

allow *verb* **1** permit, *Smoking is not allowed.* **2** permit someone to have something; provide with, *She was allowed $100 for books.* **3** agree, *I allow that you have been patient.* **allowable** *adjective*

allowance *noun* **1** allowing something. **2** what is allowed, *an allowance of $100 for books.*
make allowances be considerate; excuse, *Make allowances for his age.*

alloy *noun* a metal formed by mixing two or more metals etc.

allude *verb* (**alluded**, **alluding**) mention something briefly or indirectly, *He alluded to his wealth.* **allusion** *noun*

allure *verb* (**allured**, **alluring**) entice; attract. **allurement** *noun* [from French *à* = to, + *lure*]

alluvium (*say* a-**loo**-vee-um) *noun* sand and soil etc. deposited by a river or flood. **alluvial** *adjective*

ally *noun* (*plural* **allies**) **1** a country in alliance with another. **2** a person who co-operates with another.

ally *verb* (**allied**, **allying**) form an alliance.

almanac *noun* an annual publication containing a calendar and other information.

almighty *adjective* **1** having complete power. **2** (*informal*) very great, *an almighty din.*

almond (*say* **ah**-mond) *noun* an oval edible nut.

almost *adverb* near to being something but not quite, *almost ready.*

alms (*say* ahmz) *noun* (*old use*) money and gifts given to the poor.

aloft *adverb* high up; up in the air.

alone *adjective* without any other people or things; without help. [from *all one*]

along *preposition* following the length of something, *Walk along the path.*

along *adverb* **1** on; onwards, *Push it along.* **2** accompanying somebody, *I've brought my brother along.*

alongside *preposition & adverb* next to something; beside.

aloof *adverb* apart; not taking part, *We stayed aloof from their quarrels.*

aloof *adjective* distant and not friendly in manner. *She seemed aloof.*

aloud *adverb* in a voice that can be heard.

alp *noun* a high mountain, *the Southern Alps.*

alpha *noun* the first letter of the Greek alphabet, = a.

alphabet *noun* the letters used in a language, usually arranged in a set order. **alphabetical** *adjective*, **alphabetically** *adverb* [from *alpha, beta*, the first two letters of the Greek alphabet]

alpine *adjective* of high mountains. [from the Alps, mountains in Switzerland]

already *adverb* by now; before now.

alright a form of *all right* considered by many people to be incorrect.

Alsatian (*say* al-**say**-shan) *noun* a large strong dog, often used by the police.

also *adverb* as an extra person or thing; besides; as well.

altar *noun* a table or similar structure used in religious ceremonies.

alter *verb* make or become different; change. **alteration** *noun* [from Latin *alter* = other]

altercation (*say* ol-ter-**kay**-shon) *noun* a noisy argument or quarrel.

alternate (*say* ol-**tern**-at) *adjective* happening or coming in turns; first the one and then the other. **alternately** *adverb.*

USAGE See the note on *alternative.*

alternate (*say* **ol**-tern-ayt) *verb* (**alternated**, **alternating**) use or come alternately. **alternation** *noun*

alternating current electric current that keeps reversing its direction at regular intervals. **alternator** *noun*

alternative *adjective* available instead of something else. **alternatively** *adverb*

USAGE Do not confuse *alternative* with *alternate*. If there are *alternative colours* it means that there is a choice of two or more colours, but *alternate colours* means that there is first one colour and then the other.

alternative *noun* one of two or more possibilities.
no alternative no choice.

although *conjunction* though.

altimeter *noun* an instrument used in aircraft etc. for showing the height above sea-level. [from Latin *altus* = high, + *meter*]

altitude *noun* the height of something, especially above sea-level. [from Latin *altus* = high]

alto *noun* (*plural* **altos**) **1** an adult male singer with a very high voice. **2** a contralto. [Italian, = high]

altogether *adverb* **1** with all included; in total, *The outfit costs $500 altogether.* **2** completely, *The stream dries up altogether in summer.* **3** on the whole, *Altogether, it was a good concert.*

USAGE Do not confuse *altogether* and *all together*.

altruistic (*say* al-troo-**ist**-ik) *adjective* unselfish; thinking of other people's welfare. **altruist** *noun*, **altruism** *noun* [from Italian *altrui* = somebody else]

aluminium *noun* a lightweight silver-coloured metal.

always *adverb* **1** at all times. **2** often, *You are always crying.* **3** whatever happens, *You can always sleep on the floor.*

AM *abbreviation* amplitude modulation.

a.m. *abbreviation* ante meridiem (Latin, = before noon).

amalgam *noun* **1** an alloy of mercury. **2** a soft mixture.

amalgamate *verb* (**amalgamated**, **amalgamating**) mix; combine. **amalgamation** *noun*

amass *verb* heap up; collect.

amateur (*say* **am**-at-er) *noun* a person who does something as a hobby, not as a professional. **amateurish** *adjective* [from Latin *amator* = lover]

amaze *verb* (**amazed**, **amazing**) surprise somebody greatly; fill with wonder. **amazement** *noun*

ambassador *noun* a person sent to a foreign country to represent his or her own government.

amber *noun* **1** a hard clear yellowish substance used for making ornaments. **2** a yellow traffic light shown between green and red as a signal to slow down and stop.

ambi- *prefix* both; on both sides (as in *ambidextrous*). [from Latin *ambo* = both]

ambidextrous *adjective* able to use either the left hand or the right hand equally well. [from *ambi-*, + Latin *dexter* = right-handed]

ambiguous *adjective* having more than one possible meaning; unclear. **ambiguously** *adverb*, **ambiguity** *noun*

ambition *noun* **1** a strong desire to achieve something. **2** the thing desired.

ambitious *adjective* full of ambition.

ambivalent (*say* am-**biv**-al-ent) *adjective* having mixed feelings about something (e.g. liking and disliking it). **ambivalence** *noun* [from *ambi-*, + Latin *valens* = strong]

amble *verb* (**ambled**, **ambling**) walk at a slow easy pace. [from Latin *ambulare* = walk]

ambrosia (*say* am-**broh**-zee-a) *noun* something delicious. [in Greek mythology, ambrosia was the food of the gods]

ambulance *noun* a vehicle equipped to carry sick or injured people.

ambush *noun* (*plural* **ambushes**) a surprise attack from troops etc. who have concealed themselves.

ambush *verb* lie in wait for someone; attack from an ambush.

ameliorate (*say* a-**mee**-lee-er-ayt) *verb* (**ameliorated**, **ameliorating**) make or become better; improve. **amelioration** *noun* [from *ad-*, + Latin *melior* = better]

amen *interjection* a word used at the end of a prayer or hymn, meaning 'may it be so'. [from Hebrew, = certainly]

amenable (*say* a-**meen**-a-bul) *adjective* willing to be guided or controlled by something, *He is not amenable to discipline.* [from French *amener* = to lead]

amend *verb* alter something so as to improve it. **amendment** *noun*
make amends make up for having done something wrong; atone.

amenity (*say* a-**men**-it-ee or a-**meen**-it-ee) *noun* (*plural* **amenities**) a pleasant or useful feature of a place etc., *The town has many amenities.*

American *adjective* **1** of the continent of America. **2** of the United States of America. **American** *noun*

American Indian (also **Native American**) a member or descendant of the original inhabitants of the continent of America (other than Inuit).

America's Cup an international yachting regatta; the winner's trophy (held by New Zealand from 1995 to 2003).

amethyst *noun* a purple precious stone.

amiable *adjective* friendly; good-tempered. **amiably** *adverb*

amicable *adjective* friendly. **amicably** *adverb* [from Latin *amicus* = friend]

amid or **amidst** *preposition* in the middle of; among.

amino acid (*say* a-**meen**-oh) an acid found in proteins.

amir (*say* a-**meer**) *noun* an emir. [Arabic, = ruler]

amiss *adjective* wrong; faulty, *There is nothing amiss with the engine.*

amiss *adverb* wrongly; faultily.
take amiss be offended by, *Don't take his criticism amiss.*

ammeter *noun* an instrument for measuring an electric current, usually in amperes.

ammo *noun* (slang) ammunition.

ammonia *noun* a colourless gas or liquid with a strong smell.

ammunition *noun* a supply of bullets, shells, grenades, etc. for use in fighting. [from French *la munition*, wrongly taken as *l'ammunition*]

amnesia (*say* am-**nee**-zee-a) *noun* loss of memory. [from Greek *a-* = without, + *-mnesis* = memory]

amnesty *noun* (*plural* **amnesties**) a general pardon for people who have committed a crime.

amoeba (*say* a-**mee**-ba) *noun* (*plural* **amoebas**) a microscopic creature consisting of a single cell which constantly changes shape.

amok *adverb* **run amok** rush about in a destructive or murderous frenzy. [from Malay, = fighting mad]

among or **amongst** *preposition* **1** surrounded by; in, *There were weeds among the flowers.* **2** between, *Divide the lollies among the children.* [from Old English *ongemang* = in a crowd]

amoral (*say* ay-**moral**) *adjective* not based on moral standards; neither moral nor immoral. [from *a-2* = not, + *moral*]

amorous *adjective* showing love, *amorous glances.* [from Latin *amor* = love]

amorphous (*say* a-**mor**-fus) *adjective* shapeless, *an amorphous mass.* [from *a-2* = not, + Greek *morphe* = form]

amount *noun* **1** a quantity. **2** a total.

amount *verb* **amount to** add up to; be equivalent to, *Their reply amounts to a refusal.* [from Latin *ad montem* = to the mountain, upwards]

amp *noun* **1** an ampere. **2** (*informal*) an amplifier.

ampere (*say* **am**-pair) *noun* a unit for measuring electric current. [named after the French scientist A. M. Ampère]

ampersand *noun* the symbol & (= and).

amphetamine (*say* am-**fet**-a-min) *noun* a drug often used as a stimulant.

amphi- *prefix* both; on both sides; in both places (as in *amphibian*). [from Greek *amphi* = around]

amphibian *noun* **1** an amphibious animal; an animal (e.g. a frog) that at first (as a tadpole) has gills and lives in water but later develops lungs and breathes air. **2** an amphibious aircraft or tank etc. [from *amphi-*, + Greek *bios* = life]

amphibious *adjective* able to live or move both on land and in water.

amphitheatre *noun* an oval or circular unroofed building with tiers of seats round a central arena. [from Greek *amphi* = all round, + *theatre*]

ample *adjective* **1** quite enough, *ample provisions.* **2** large. **amply** *adverb*

amplifier *noun* a device for making something louder.

amplify *verb* (**amplified**, **amplifying**) **1** make louder or stronger, *to amplify sound.* **2** give more details about something. [from Latin *amplificare* = make more ample]

amplitude *noun* **1** breadth. **2** largeness; abundance. **3** the largest amount by which an alternating current or electromagnetic wave can vary from its average.
amplitude modulation changing the amplitude of a radio wave. (Compare *frequency modulation.*)

amputate *verb* (**amputated**, **amputating**) cut off by a surgical operation. **amputation** *noun*

amuse *verb* (**amused**, **amusing**) **1** make a person laugh or smile. **2** make time pass pleasantly for someone. **amusement** *noun* [from French *amuser* = distract]

an *adjective* see **a**.

an-[1] *prefix* see **a-**[2].

an-[2] *prefix* see **ad-**.

ana- *prefix* up; back (as in *analysis*). [from Greek *ana* = up]

anachronism (*say* an-**ak**-ron-izm) *noun* something wrongly placed in a particular historical period, or regarded as out of date, *Bows and arrows would be an anachronism in modern warfare.* [from *ana-*, + Greek *chronos* = time]

anaemia (*say* a-**nee**-mee-a) *noun* a poor condition of the blood that makes a person pale. **anaemic** *adjective* [from *an-*[1] = without, + Greek *haima* = blood]

anaesthetic (*say* an-iss-**thet**-ik) *noun* a substance or gas that makes you unable to feel pain. **anaesthesia** *noun* [from *an-*[1] = without, + Greek *aisthesis* = sensation]

anaesthetist (*say* an-**ees**-thet-ist) *noun* a person trained to give anaesthetics. **anaesthetise** *verb*

anagram *noun* a word or phrase made by rearranging the letters of another, *'Trap' is an anagram of 'part'.* [from *ana-*, + Greek *gramma* = letter]

anal (*say* **ay**-nal) *adjective* of the anus.

analgesic (*say* an-al-**jee**-sik) *noun* a substance that relieves pain. [from *an-*[1] = without, + Greek *algesis* = pain]

analogue (*say* **an**-a-log) *adjective* of a watch or clock indicating time by the position of hour and minute hands.

analogy (*say* a-**nal**-oj-ee) *noun* (*plural* **analogies**) a partial likeness between two things that are compared, *the analogy between the human heart and a pump.* **analogous** *adjective*

analyse *verb* (**analysed**, **analysing**) **1** separate something into its parts. **2** examine and interpret something, *analyse the causes.* **analysis** *noun*, **analytic** *adjective*, **analytical** *adjective* [from *ana-*, + Greek *lysis* = loosening]

analyst *noun* a person who analyses things.

anarchist (*say* **an**-er-kist) *noun* a person who believes that all forms of government are bad and should be abolished.

anarchy (*say* **an**-er-kee) *noun* **1** lack of government or control, resulting in lawlessness. **2** disorder. [from *an-*[1] = without, + Greek *arche* = rule]

anatomy (*say* an-**at**-om-ee) *noun* the study of how the body is constituted. **anatomical** *adjective*, **anatomist** *noun* [from *ana-*, + Greek *tome* = cutting]

ANC *abbreviation* African National Congress.

ancestor *noun* anyone from whom a person is descended. **ancestral** *adjective*, **ancestry** *noun*

anchor *noun* **1** a heavy object joined to a ship by a chain or rope and dropped to the bottom of the sea to stop the ship from moving. **2** a presenter or coordinator of a media programme. **anchorage** *noun*

anchor *verb* **1** fix or be fixed by an anchor. **2** fix firmly.

anchovy *noun* (*plural* **anchovies**) a small fish with a strong flavour.

ancient *adjective* **1** very old. **2** of times long past, *ancient history.*

ancillary (*say* an-**sil**-er-ee) *adjective* helping people to do something, *ancillary services.* [from Latin *ancilla* = servant]

and *conjunction* **1** together with; in addition to, *We had cakes and buns.* **2** so that; with this result, *Work hard and you will pass.* **3** to, *Go and buy a pen.*

anecdote *noun* a short amusing or interesting story about a real person or thing.

anemone (*say* a-**nem**-on-ee) *noun* a plant with cup-shaped red, purple, or white flowers. [from Greek, = wind-flower]

anew *adverb* again; in a new or different way, *begin anew.*

angel *noun* **1** an attendant or messenger of God. **2** a very kind or beautiful person. **angelic** (*say* an-**jel**-ik) *adjective* [from Greek *angelos* = messenger]

angelica *noun* a fragrant plant whose crystallised stalks are used in cookery as a decoration.

anger *noun* a strong feeling that makes you want to quarrel or fight.

anger *verb* make a person angry.

angle *noun* **1** the space between two lines or surfaces that meet; the amount by which a line or surface must be turned to make it lie along another. **2** a point of view.

angle *verb* (**angled**, **angling**) **1** put something in a slanting position. **2** present news etc. from one point of view.

angler *noun* a person who fishes with a fishing-rod and line. **angling** *noun*

Anglican *adjective* of the Church of England or another church that is in communion with it, e.g. the Anglican Church of New Zealand. **Anglican** *noun*

Anglicise *verb* (**Anglicised**, **Anglicising**) give an English form or character to. **Anglicisation** *noun*

Anglo- *prefix* English or British, *an Anglo-French agreement.* [from the *Angles*, a Germanic tribe who came to England in the 5th century and eventually gave their name to it]

Anglo-Nubian *noun* a kind of goat kept for milking.

Anglo-Saxon *noun* **1** an English person, especially of the time before the Norman conquest in 1066. **2** the English language from about 450 to about 1100, also called *Old English.* **Anglo-Saxon** *adjective*

angora *noun* **1** a kind of long-haired goat, rabbit, or cat. **2** fabric made from the hair of angora goats or rabbits. **angora** *adjective*

angry *adjective* (**angrier, angriest**) feeling anger. **angrily** *adverb*

anguish *noun* severe suffering; great sorrow or pain. **anguished** *adjective*

angular *adjective* **1** having angles or sharp corners. **2** (of a person) bony, not plump.

Angus *noun* a kind of black cattle without horns.

animal *noun* **1** a living thing that can feel and usually move about, *Horses, birds, fish, bees, and people are all animals.* **2** a brutish person; someone not worthy of being called human. [from Latin *animalis* = having breath]

animate *verb* (**animated, animating**) **1** make a thing lively. **2** produce something as an animated cartoon. **animation** *noun*, **animator** *noun*
animated cartoon a film made by photographing a series of drawings.

animosity (*say* an-im-**oss**-it-ee) *noun* a feeling of hostility.

aniseed *noun* a sweet-smelling seed used for flavouring things.

ankle *noun* the part of the leg where it joins the foot.

annals *plural noun* a history of events, especially when written year by year. [from Latin *annales* = yearly books]

annex *verb* **1** take possession of something and add it to what you have already. **2** add or join a thing to something else. [from *an-*[2], + Latin *nexum* = tied]

annex or **annexe** *noun* a building added to a larger or more important building.

annihilate (*say* an-**I**-il-ayt) *verb* (**annihilated, annihilating**) destroy completely. **annihilation** *noun* [from *an-*[2], + Latin *nihil* = nothing]

anniversary *noun* (*plural* **anniversaries**) a day when you remember something special that happened on the same day in a previous year.
Anniversary Day a public holiday kept on different days in different New Zealand provinces. [from Latin *annus* = year, + *versum* = turned]

annotate (*say* **an**-oh-tayt) *verb* (**annotated, annotating**) add notes of explanation to something written or printed. **annotation** *noun*

announce *verb* (**announced, announcing**) make something known, especially by saying it publicly or to an audience. **announcement** *noun* [from *an-*[2], + Latin *nuntius* = messenger]

announcer *noun* a person who announces items in a broadcast.

annoy *verb* **1** make a person slightly angry. **2** be troublesome to someone. **annoyance** *noun* [from Latin *in odio* = hateful]

annual *adjective* **1** happening or done once a year, *her annual visit.* **2** of one year; reckoned by the year, *our annual income.* **3** living for one year or one season, *an annual plant.* **annually** *adverb*

annual *noun* **1** a book that comes out once a year. **2** an annual plant. [from Latin *annus* = year]

annuity (*say* a-**new**-it-ee) *noun* (*plural* **annuities**) a fixed annual allowance of money, especially from a kind of investment. [same origin as *annual*]

annul *verb* (**annulled, annulling**) cancel a law or contract; end something legally, *Their marriage was annulled.* **annulment** *noun* [from *an-*[2], + Latin *nullus* = none]

Annunciation *noun* the Christian festival (on 25 March) commemorating the announcement by the angel to the Virgin Mary that she was to be the mother of Jesus Christ.

anode *noun* the electrode by which electric current enters a device. (Compare *cathode.*) [from *ana-* = up, + Greek *hodos* = way]

anoint *verb* put oil or ointment on something, especially in a religious ceremony.

anomaly (*say* an-**om**-al-ee) *noun* (*plural* **anomalies**) something that does not follow the general rule or that is unlike the usual or normal kind. [from *an-*[1] = not, + Greek *homalos* = even]

anon *adverb* (*old use*) soon, *I will say more about this anon.*

anon. *abbreviation* anonymous.

anonymous (*say* an-**on**-im-us) *adjective* of or by a person whose name is not known or not made public, *an anonymous donor.* **anonymously** *adverb*, **anonymity** (*say* an-on-**im**-itee) *noun* [from *an-*[1] = not, + Greek *onyma* = name]

anorak *noun* a waterproof jacket with a hood. [from an Inuit word]

anorexia (*say* an-er-**eks**-ee-a) *noun* an illness that makes a person unwilling to eat. **anorexic** *adjective* [from *an-*[1] = not, + Greek *orexis* = appetite]

another *adjective & pronoun* a different or extra person or thing, *another day; choose another.*

answer *noun* **1** a reply. **2** the solution to a problem.

answer *verb* **1** give or find an answer to; reply. **2** respond to a signal, *Answer the telephone.* **answer back** reply cheekily.

answer for be responsible for.
answer to correspond to, *This answers to the description of the stolen bag.*

answerable *adjective* **1** able to be answered. **2** having to be responsible for something.

ant *noun* a very small insect that lives as one of an organised group.

ant- *prefix* see **anti-**.

antagonise *verb* (**antagonised, antagonising**) cause a person to feel antagonism.

antagonism (*say* an-**tag**-on-izm) *noun* an unfriendly feeling; hostility. **antagonist** *noun*, **antagonistic** *adjective* [from *ant-*, + Greek *agon* = struggle]

Antarctic *noun* the area round the South Pole. **Antarctic** *adjective*

Antarctica *noun* the ice-covered continent round the South Pole.

ante- *prefix* before (as in **ante-room**). [from Latin]

anteater *noun* an animal that feeds on ants and termites.

antediluvian (*say* an-tee-dil-**oo**-vee-an) *adjective* **1** of the time before Noah's Flood in the Old Testament. **2** (*informal*) very old or out of date. [from *ante-*, + Latin *diluvium* = deluge]

antelope *noun* (*plural* **antelope or antelopes**) an animal like a deer.

antenatal (*say* an-tee-**nay**-tal) *adjective* before birth; during pregnancy.

antenna *noun* **1** (*plural* **antennae**) a feeler on the head of an insect or crustacean. **2** (*plural* **antennas**) an aerial.

anterior *adjective* **1** situated at the front or the head. (The opposite is *posterior.*). **2** earlier. [Latin, = further forward]

ante-room *noun* a room leading to a more important room.

anthem *noun* a religious or patriotic song, usually sung by a choir or group of people.

anther *noun* the part of a flower's stamen that bears pollen.

anthill *noun* a mound over an ants' nest.

anthology *noun* a collection of poems, stories, songs, etc. in one book. [from Greek *anthos* = flower, + *-logia* = collection]

anthracite *noun* a kind of hard coal.

anthrax *noun* a disease of sheep and cattle that can also infect people.

anthropoid *adjective* resembling a human being, *Gorillas are anthropoid apes.* [from Greek *anthropos* = human being]

anthropology *noun* the study of human beings and their customs. **anthropological** *adjective*, **anthropologist** *noun* [from Greek *anthropos* = human being, + *-logy*]

anti- *prefix* (changing to **ant-** before a vowel) against; preventing (as in *anti-freeze*). [from Greek *anti* = against]

anti-aircraft *adjective* used against enemy aircraft.

antibiotic *noun* a substance (e.g. penicillin) that destroys bacteria or prevents them from growing. [from *anti-*, + Greek *bios* = life]

antibody *noun* (*plural* **antibodies**) a protein that forms in the blood as a defence against certain substances which it then attacks and destroys.

anticipate *verb* (**anticipated, anticipating**) **1** do something before the proper time or before someone else, *Others may have anticipated Columbus in discovering America.* **2** foresee, *They had anticipated our needs.* **3** expect, *We anticipate that it will rain.* **anticipation** *noun*, **anticipatory** *adjective* [from *ante-*, + Latin *capere* = take]

> USAGE Many people regard the use in sense 3 as incorrect; it is best to avoid it and use 'expect'.

anticlimax *noun* a disappointing ending or result where something exciting had been expected.

anticlockwise *adverb & adjective* moving in the direction opposite to clockwise.

antics *plural noun* comical or foolish actions.

anticyclone *noun* an area where air pressure is high, usually producing fine settled weather.

antidote *noun* something that acts against the effects of a poison or disease. [from *anti-*, + Greek *dotos* = given]

antifreeze *noun* a liquid added to water to make it less likely to freeze.

antihistamine *noun* a substance that protects people against unpleasant effects when they are allergic to something.

antimony *noun* a brittle silvery metal.

antioxidant *noun* a compound that protects the body from damage by free molecules, *Fresh fruit and vegetables are a good source of antioxidants.*

antipathy (*say* an-**tip**-ath-ee) *noun* a strong dislike. [from *anti-*, + Greek *pathos* = feeling]

antipodes (*say* an-**tip**-od-eez) *plural noun* places on opposite sides of the earth. **antipodean** *adjective*
the Antipodes Australia and New Zealand, and the areas near them, which are almost exactly opposite Europe. [from Greek, = having the feet opposite (*pod-* = foot)]

antiquarian (*say* anti-**kwair**-ee-an) *adjective* of the study of antiques.

antiquated *adjective* old-fashioned.

antique (*say* an-**teek**) *adjective* very old; belonging to the distant past.

antique *noun* something that is valuable because it is very old. [from Latin *antiquus* = ancient]

antiquity (*say* an-**tik**-wit-ee) *noun* ancient times.
antiquities *plural noun* objects that were made in ancient times.

anti-Semitic (*say* anti-sim-**it**-ik) *adjective* unfriendly or hostile towards Jews. **anti-Semitism** (*say* anti-**sem**-it-izm) *noun*

antiseptic *adjective* **1** able to destroy bacteria, especially those that cause things to become septic or to decay. **2** thoroughly clean and free from germs.

antiseptic *noun* a substance with an antiseptic effect.

antisocial *adjective* unfriendly or inconsiderate towards other people.

antistatic *adjective* counteracting the effects of static electricity.

antithesis (*say* an-**tith**-iss-iss) *noun* (*plural* **antitheses**) **1** the direct opposite of something, *Slavery is the antithesis of freedom.* **2** contrast of ideas. [from *anti-*, + Greek *thesis* = placing]

antitoxin *noun* a substance that neutralises a toxin and prevents it from having a harmful effect. **antitoxic** *adjective*

antivivisectionist *noun* a person who is opposed to making experiments on live animals.

antler *noun* the branching horn of a deer.

antonym (*say* **ant**-on-im) *noun* a word that is opposite in meaning to another. *'Soft' is an antonym of 'hard'.* [from *ant-*, + Greek *onyma* = name]

anus (*say* **ay**-nus) *noun* the opening at the lower end of the alimentary canal, through which solid waste matter is passed out of the body.

anvil *noun* a large block of iron on which a blacksmith hammers metal into shape. [from Old English *an* = on, + *filt-* = beat]

anxious *adjective* **1** worried. **2** eager, *She is anxious to please us.* **anxiously** *adverb*, **anxiety** *noun*

any *adjective & pronoun* **1** one or some, *Have you any wool? There isn't any.* **2** no matter which, *Come any day you like.* **3** every, *Any fool knows that!*

any *adverb* at all; in some degree, *Is that any better?*

anybody *noun & pronoun* any person.

anyhow *adverb* **1** anyway. **2** (*informal*) carelessly, *He does his work anyhow.*

anyone *noun & pronoun* anybody.

anything *noun & pronoun* any thing.

anyway *adverb* whatever happens; whatever the situation may be.

anywhere *adverb* in or to any place.

anywhere *pronoun* any place, *Anywhere will do.*

Anzac *noun* a soldier in the Australian and New Zealand Army Corps during the First World War (1914–1918).
Anzac biscuit a crunchy biscuit made from rolled oats, flour, sugar etc., given this name during the First World War.
Anzac Day 25 April, the anniversary of the Anzac landing at Gallipoli in 1915, a public holiday to honour all New Zealand's war dead.

aorta (*say* ay-**or**-ta) *noun* the great artery carrying blood away from the left side of the heart.

Aotearoa *noun* a Māori name for New Zealand. [from Māori, = (land of) long white cloud or long twilight]

ap-[1] *prefix* see **ad-**.

ap-[2] *prefix* see **apo-**.

apace *adverb* quickly.

apart *adverb* **1** away from each other; separately, *Keep your desks apart.* **2** into pieces, *It fell apart.* **3** excluded, *Joking apart, what do you think of it?* [from French *à* = to, + *part* = side]

apartheid (*say* a-**part**-hayt) *noun* the former policy in South Africa of keeping people of different races apart. [Afrikaans, = being apart]

apartment *noun* **1** a set of rooms. **2** a flat.

apathy (*say* **ap**-ath-ee) *noun* lack of interest or concern. **apathetic** (*say* ap-a-**thet**-ik) *adjective* [from *a-*[2] = without, + Greek *pathos* = feeling]

ape *noun* any of the four kinds of monkey (gorillas, chimpanzees, orang-utans, gibbons) that do not have a tail.

ape *verb* (**aped**, **aping**) imitate; mimic.

APEC *abbreviation* Asia-Pacific Economic Cooperation (an international forum established in 1989).

aperient (*say* a-**peer**-ee-ent) *noun* a laxative. [from Latin *aperiens* = opening]

aperitif (*say* a-**perri**-teef) *noun* an alcoholic drink taken before a meal to stimulate the appetite. [French]

aperture *noun* an opening. [from Latin *aperire* = to open]

apex (*say* **ay**-peks) *noun* (*plural* **apexes**) the tip or highest point.

aphid (*say* **ay**-fid) *noun* (*plural* **aphids**) a tiny insect (e.g. a greenfly) that sucks the juices from plants.

aphis (*say* **ay**-fiss) *noun* (*plural* **aphides**, *say* **ay**-fid-eez) an aphid.

aphorism (*say* **af**-er-izm) *noun* a short witty saying.

apiary (*say* **ay**-pee-er-ee) *noun* (*plural* **apiaries**) a place with a number of hives where bees are kept. **apiarist** *noun* [from Latin *apis* = bee]

apiece *adverb* to, for, or by each, *They cost fifty cents apiece.*

aplomb (*say* a-**plom**) *noun* dignity and confidence. [from French, = straight as a plumb-line]

apo- *prefix* (changing to **ap-** before a vowel or h) from; out or away (as in *Apostle*). [from Greek *apo* away from]

Apocalypse (*say* a-**pok**-a-lips) *noun* the Book of Revelation, the last book of the New Testament.

apocalypse *noun* a revelation of the end of the world. [from Greek *apokalypto* = reveal]

apocryphal (*say* a-**pok**-rif-al) *adjective* untrue; invented, *This account of his travels is apocryphal.* [from the *Apocrypha*, books of the Old Testament that were not accepted by the Jews as part of the Hebrew Scriptures]

apolitical (*say* ay-pol-**it**-ik-al) *adjective* **1** not political. **2** not concerned with politics. [from *a-*[2] = not, + *political*]

apologetic *adjective* making an apology. **apologetically** *adverb*

apologise *verb* (**apologised**, **apologising**) make an apology.

apology *noun* (*plural* **apologies**) **1** a statement saying that you are sorry for having done something wrong or badly. **2** a poor specimen, *this feeble apology for a meal.* [from Greek *apologia* = a speech in your own defence]

apoplexy (*say* **ap**-op-lek-see) *noun* sudden loss of the ability to feel and move, caused by the blocking or breaking of a blood-vessel in the brain. **apoplectic** *adjective* [from Greek, = a stroke]

Apostle *noun* any of the twelve men sent out by Christ to preach the Gospel. [from Greek *apostellein* = send out]

apostrophe (*say* a-**poss**-trof-ee) *noun* the punctuation mark ' used to show that letters have been missed out (as in *I can't* = I cannot) or to show possession (as in *the boy's book; the boys' books*). [from *apo-*, + Greek *strophe* = turning]

app *abbreviation* a shortened form of application (computer program).

appal *verb* (**appalled**, **appalling**) fill with horror; shock somebody very much. [from Old French *apalir* = become pale]

apparatus *noun* the equipment for a particular experiment or job etc.

apparel *noun* (*formal*) clothing.

apparent *adjective* **1** clear; obvious. **2** seeming; appearing to be true but not really so. **apparently** *adverb* [same origin as *appear*]

apparition *noun* **1** a ghost. **2** something strange or surprising that appears.

appeal *verb* **1** ask for something earnestly or formally, *They appealed for funds.* **2** ask for a decision to be changed, *He appealed against the prison sentence.* **3** seem attractive or interesting, *Cricket doesn't appeal to me.*

appeal *noun* **1** the action of appealing for something or about a decision; an earnest or formal request. **2** attraction; interest.

appear *verb* **1** come into sight. **2** seem. **3** take part in a play, film, or show etc.

appearance *noun* **1** appearing. **2** what somebody looks like; what something appears to be.

appease *verb* (**appeased**, **appeasing**) calm or pacify someone, especially by giving in to demands. **appeasement** *noun* [from French *à* = to, + *paix* = peace]

appellation *noun* a name or title.

append *verb* add at the end; attach. [from *ap-*, + Latin *pendere* = hang]

appendage *noun* something added or attached; a thing that forms a natural part of something larger.

appendicitis *noun* inflammation of the appendix.

appendix *noun* **1** (*plural* **appendixes**) a small tube leading off from the intestine. **2** (*plural* **appendices**) a section added at the end of a book. [same origin as *append*]

appetising *adjective* stimulating the appetite. **appetiser** *noun*

appetite *noun* a desire, especially for food. [from *ap-*, + Latin *petere* = seek]

applaud *verb* show that you like something, especially by clapping your hands. **applause** *noun* [from *ap-*, + Latin *plaudere* = clap hands]

apple *noun* a round fruit with a red, yellow, or green skin.
the apple of your eye a person or thing that you love and are proud of.

appliance *noun* a device, *electrical appliances.*

applicable (*say* **ap**-lik-a-bul) *adjective* able to be applied; suitable; relevant.

applicant *noun* a person who applies for something.

application *noun* **1** the action of applying. **2** a formal request. **3** the ability to apply yourself.

applied *adjective* put to practical use, *applied science.*

appliqué (*say* a-**plee**-kay) *noun* needlework in which cut-out pieces of material are sewn or fixed ornamentally on another piece. [French, = put on]

apply *verb* (**applied**, **applying**) **1** put one thing on another. **2** start using something. **3** concern; be relevant, *This rule does not apply to you.* **4** make a formal request, *apply for a job.*
apply yourself give all your attention to a job; work diligently.

appoint *verb* **1** choose a person for a job. **2** arrange officially, *They appointed a time for the meeting.*

appointment *noun* **1** an arrangement to meet or visit somebody at a particular time. **2** choosing somebody for a job. **3** a job or position.

apportion *verb* divide into shares; allot. **apportionment** *noun*

apposite (*say* **ap**-o-zit) *adjective* (of a remark) suitable; relevant.

apposition *noun* placing things together, especially nouns and phrases in a grammatical relationship. In *from Wellington, the capital of New Zealand,* 'the capital of New Zealand' is in apposition to 'Wellington'. [from *ap-* + *position*]

appraise *verb* (**appraised**, **appraising**) estimate the value or quality of a person or thing. **appraisal** *noun*

appreciable *adjective* enough to be noticed or felt; perceptible. **appreciably** *adverb*

appreciate *verb* (**appreciated**, **appreciating**) **1** enjoy; value. **2** understand. **3** increase in value. **appreciation** *noun*, **appreciative** *adjective* [from *ap-*, + Latin *pretium* = price]

apprehend *verb* **1** seize; arrest. **2** understand. **3** expect something with fear or worry. [from *ap-*, + Latin *prehendere* = to grasp]

apprehension *noun* **1** fear. **2** understanding. **3** arrest. **apprehensive** *adjective*

apprentice *noun* a person who is learning a trade or craft by a legal agreement with an employer. **apprenticeship** *noun*

apprentice *verb* (**apprenticed**, **apprenticing**) place a person as an apprentice. [from French *apprendre* = learn]

approach *verb* **1** come near. **2** go to someone with a request or offer, *They approached me for help.* **3** set about doing something or tackling a problem. **approachable** *adjective*

approach *noun* (*plural* **approaches**) **1** approaching. **2** a way or road.

approbation *noun* approval.

appropriate (*say* a-**proh**-pree-at) *adjective* suitable. **appropriately** *adverb*

appropriate (*say* a-**proh**-pree-ayt) *verb* (**appropriated**, **appropriating**) take something and use it as your own. **appropriation** *noun*

approval *noun* approving somebody or something.
on approval received by a customer to examine before deciding to buy.

approve *verb* (**approved**, **approving**) say or think that a person or thing is good or suitable.

approximate (*say* a-**proks**-im-at) *adjective* almost exact or correct but not completely so. **approximately** *adverb*

approximate (*say* a-**proks**-im-ayt) *verb* (**approximated**, **approximating**) make or be almost the same as something. [from *ap-*, + Latin *proximus* = very near]

après-ski *adjective* done or worn after skiing. [from French *après* = after, + *ski*]

apricot *noun* a juicy orange-coloured fruit with a stone in it.

April *noun* the fourth month of the year.

apron *noun* **1** a garment worn over the front of the body, especially to protect other clothes. **2** a hard-surfaced area on an airfield where aircraft are loaded and unloaded.
apron stage a part of a theatre stage in front of the curtain. [originally *a naperon*, from French *nappe* = tablecloth]

apropos (*say* ap-rop-**oh**) *adverb* concerning, *Apropos of tennis, who is the new champion?* [from French *à propos* = to the purpose]

apse *noun* a semicircular part projecting from a church or other building.

apt *adjective* **1** likely, *He is apt to be careless.* **2** suitable, *an apt quotation.* **3** quick at learning, *an apt pupil.* **aptly** *adverb*, **aptness** *noun* [from Latin *aptus* = fitted]

apteryx (*say* **ap**-ter-iks) *noun* the kiwi. [from *a-*[2] + Greek *pteryx* = wing]

aptitude *noun* a talent or skill.

aqualung *noun* a diver's portable breathing-apparatus, with cylinders of compressed air connected to a face-mask. [from Latin *aqua* = water, + *lung*]

aquamarine *noun* a bluish-green precious stone. [from Latin *aqua marina* = sea-water]

aquaplane *noun* a board on which a person stands to be towed by a speedboat. **aquaplane** *verb* [from Latin *aqua* = water, + *plane*[1]]

aquarium *noun* (*plural* **aquariums**) a tank or building in which live fish and other water animals are displayed. [from Latin *aquarius* = of water]

aquatic *adjective* of, on, or in water, *aquatic sports.* [from Latin *aqua* = water]

aquatint *noun* an etching made on copper by using nitric acid.

aqueduct *noun* a bridge carrying a water-channel across low ground or a valley. [from Latin *aqua* = water, + *ducere* = to lead]

aquiline (*say* **ak**-wil-I'n) *adjective* hooked like an eagle's beak, *an aquiline nose.* [from Latin *aquila* = eagle]

ar- *prefix* see **ad-**.

Arab *noun* a member of a people living in Arabia and other parts of the Middle East and North Africa. **Arabian** *adjective*

arabesque (*say* a-rab-**esk**) *noun* **1** (in dancing) a position with one leg stretched backwards in the air. **2** an ornamental design of leaves and branches.

Arabic *adjective* of the Arabs or their language.
Arabic numerals the symbols 1, 2, 3, 4, etc.

Arabic *noun* the language of the Arabs.

arable *adjective* suitable for ploughing or growing crops on, *arable land* [from Latin *arare* = to plough]

arachnid (*say* a-**rak**-nid) *noun* a member of the group of animals that includes spiders and scorpions. [from Greek *arachne* = spider]

arbiter *noun* a person who has the power to decide what shall be done or used etc.

arbitrary (*say* **ar**-bit-rer-ee) *adjective* chosen or done on an impulse, not according to a rule or law, *an arbitrary decision.* **arbitrarily** *adverb*

arbitration *noun* settling a dispute by calling in a person or persons from outside to make a decision. **arbitrate** *verb,* **arbitrator** *noun* [from Latin *arbitrari* = to judge]

Arbor Day a day (5 June) set aside every year for planting trees.

arboreal (*say* ar-**bor**-ee-al) *adjective* of trees; living in trees. [from Latin *arbor* = tree]

arboretum (*say* ar-ber-**ee**-tum) *noun* a place where trees are grown for study and display. [from Latin *arbor* = tree]

arbour (*say* **ar**-ber) *noun* a shady place among trees.

ARC *abbreviation* Auckland Regional Council.

arc *noun* **1** a curve; part of the circumference of a circle. **2** a luminous electric current passing between two electrodes. [same origin as *archer*]
arc lamp or **arc light** a light using an electric arc.

arcade *noun* a covered passage or area, especially for shopping.

arcane *adjective* secret; mysterious.

arch *noun* (*plural* **arches**) **1** a curved structure that helps to support a bridge or other building etc. **2** something shaped like this.

arch[1] *verb* form into an arch; curve. [same origin as *arc*]

arch[2] *adjective* pretending to be playful, *an arch smile.* **archly** *adverb*

arch- *prefix* chief; principal (as in *arch-enemy*).

archaeology (*say* ar-kee-**ol**-oj-ee) *noun* the study of the remains of ancient cultures. **archaeological** *adjective,* **archaeologist** *noun* [from Greek *archaios* = old, + *-logy*]

archaic (*say* ar-**kay**-ik) *adjective* belonging to former or ancient times. [from Greek *arche* = beginning]

archangel *noun* an angel of the highest rank.

archbishop *noun* the chief bishop of a province of the Church.

archdeacon *noun* a senior priest ranking next below a bishop.

arch-enemy *noun* the chief enemy.

archer *noun* a person who shoots with a bow and arrows. **archery** *noun* [from Latin *arcus* = a bow or curve]

archetype (*say* **ark**-i-typ) *noun* the original form or model from which others are copied. [from *arch-* + *type*]

archipelago (*say* ark-i-**pel**-ag-oh) *noun* (*plural* **archipelagos**) a large group of islands, or the sea containing these. [from *arch-*, + Greek *pelagos* = sea]

architect (*say* **ark**-i-tekt) *noun* a person who designs buildings. [from *arch-*, + Greek *tekton* = builder]

architecture *noun* **1** the process of designing buildings. **2** a particular style of building. **architectural** *adjective*

archives (*say* **ark**-I'vz) *plural noun* the historical documents etc. of an organisation or community. [from Greek *archeia* = public records]

archivist (*say* **ar**-kiv-ist) *noun* a person trained to deal with archives.

archway *noun* an arched passage or entrance.

Arctic *noun* the area round the North Pole. **Arctic** *adjective*

arctic *adjective* very cold, *The weather was arctic.*

ardent *adjective* full of ardour; enthusiastic. **ardently** *adverb* [from Latin *ardens* = burning]

ardour (*say* **ar**-der) *noun* great warmth of feeling.

arduous *adjective* needing much effort; laborious. **arduously** *adverb* [from Latin *arduus* = steep]

area *noun* **1** the extent or measurement of a surface. **2** a particular region.
area school (*NZ*) a school in a rural area for both primary and secondary pupils.

arena (*say* a-**reen**-a) *noun* the level area in the centre of an amphitheatre or sports stadium. [Latin, = sand]

aren't *(mainly spoken)* are not.
aren't I? (*informal*) am I not?

arête (*say* a-**ret**) *noun* a sharp ridge on a mountain. [French]

argosy *noun* (*plural* **argosies**) *(poetic)* a large merchant ship; a fleet of ships.

arguable *adjective* **1** able to be asserted; likely to be correct. **2** able to be doubted; not certain. **arguably** *adverb*

argue *verb* (**argued**, **arguing**) **1** say that you disagree; exchange angry comments. **2** state that something is true and give reasons.

argument *noun* **1** a disagreement; a quarrel. **2** a reason put forward; a series of reasons.

argumentative *adjective* fond of arguing.

aria (*say* **ar**-ee-a) *noun* a solo in an opera or oratorio. [Italian]

arid *adjective* dry and barren.

ariki *noun* **1** a chief. **2** the eldest member of a prominent Māori family. [Māori]

arise *verb* (**arose**, **arisen**, **arising**) **1** come into existence; come to people's notice, *Problems arose.* **2** (*old use*) rise; stand up, *Arise, Sir Francis.*

aristocracy (*say* a-ris-**tok**-ra-see) *noun* people of the highest social rank; members of the nobility. [from Greek *aristos* = best, + *-cracy*]

aristocrat (*say* **a**-ris-tok-rat) *noun* a member of the aristocracy. **aristocratic** *adjective*

arithmetic *noun* the science or study of numbers; calculating with numbers. **arithmetical** *adjective* [from Greek *arithmos* = number]

ark *noun* **1** the ship in which Noah and his family escaped the Flood. **2** a wooden box in which the writings of the Jewish Law were kept. [from Latin *arca* = box]

arm[1] *noun* **1** either of the two upper limbs of the body, between the shoulder and the hand. **2** a sleeve. **3** something shaped like an arm or jutting out from a main part; the raised side part of a chair. **armful** *noun* [Old English]

arm[2] *verb* **1** supply with weapons. **2** prepare for war.
armed forces or **armed services** a country's military forces; the army, navy, and air force. [from Latin *arma* = weapons]

armada (*say* ar-**mah**-da) *noun* a fleet of warships.
the Armada or **Spanish Armada** the warships sent by Spain to invade England in 1588. [Spanish, = navy]

armadillo *noun* (*plural* **armadillos**) a small burrowing South American animal whose body is covered with a shell of bony plates.

armaments *plural noun* the weapons of an army etc.

armature *noun* **1** the current-carrying part of a dynamo or electric motor. **2** the 'keeper' of a magnet.

armchair *noun* a chair with arms.

armistice *noun* an agreement to stop fighting in a war or battle. [from Latin *arma* = weapons, + *sistere* = stop]

armour *noun* **1** a protective covering for the body, formerly worn in fighting. **2** a metal covering on a warship, tank, or car to protect it from missiles. **armoured** *adjective* [same origin as *arm*[2]]

armoury *noun* a place where weapons and ammunition are stored.

armpit *noun* the hollow underneath the top of the arm, below the shoulder.

arms *plural noun* **1** weapons. **2** a coat of arms (see *coat*).
arms race competition between nations in building up supplies of weapons.
up in arms protesting vigorously. [same origin as *arm*[2]]

army *noun* (*plural* **armies**) **1** a large number of people trained to fight on land. **2** a large group.

aroha *noun* **1** love, affection. **2** sympathy. [Māori]

aroma (*say* a-**roh**-ma) *noun* a smell, especially a pleasant one. **aromatic** (*say* a-ro-**mat**-ik) *adjective*

around *adverb & preposition* all round; about.

arouse *verb* (**aroused**, **arousing**) rouse.

arpeggio (*say* ar-**pej**-ee-oh) *noun* (*plural* **arpeggios**) the notes of a musical chord played one after the other instead of together. [from Italian *arpa* = harp]

arrange *verb* (**arranged**, **arranging**) **1** put into a certain order; adjust. **2** form plans for something, *We arranged to be there.* **3** prepare music for a particular purpose. **arrangement** *noun*

arrant *adjective* thorough and obvious, *Arrant nonsense!*

array *noun* **1** a display. **2** an orderly arrangement.

array *verb* (**arrayed**, **arraying**) **1** arrange in order. **2** clothe; adorn. [from *ar*-, +old form of *ready*]

arrears *plural noun* **1** money that is owing and ought to have been paid earlier. **2** a backlog of work etc.
in arrears behind with payment.

arrest *verb* **1** seize a person by authority of the law. **2** stop a process or movement.

arrest *noun* **1** arresting somebody. **2** stopping something.

arrive *verb* (**arrived**, **arriving**) **1** reach the end of a journey or a point on it. **2** come, *The great day arrived.* **arrival** *noun*

arrogant *adjective* proud and dictatorial in manner. **arrogantly** *adverb*, **arrogance** *noun*

arrow *noun* **1** a pointed stick to be shot from a bow. **2** a sign with an outward-pointing V at the end, used to show direction or position. **arrowhead** *noun*

arrowroot *noun* an edible starch prepared from the root of an American plant.

arsenal *noun* a place where weapons and ammunition are stored or manufactured. [from Arabic, = workshop]

arsenic *noun* a very poisonous metallic substance. [from Persian *zar* = gold]

arson *noun* the crime of deliberately setting fire to a house or building etc. **arsonist** *noun*

art *noun* **1** producing something beautiful, especially by painting or drawing; things produced in this way. **2** a skill, *the art of sailing.*
arts *noun* subjects (e.g. languages, literature, history) in which opinion and understanding are very important, as opposed to sciences where measurements and calculations are used.
the arts painting, music, and writing etc. considered together.

artefact *noun* a manufactured object. [from Latin *arte* = by art, + *factum* = made]

artery *noun* (*plural* **arteries**) **1** any of the tubes that carry blood away from the heart to all parts of the body. (Compare *vein.*) **2** an important road or route. **arterial** (*say* ar-**teer**-ee-al) *adjective*

artesian well a well that is bored straight down into a place where water will rise easily to the surface.

artful *adjective* crafty. **artfully** *adverb*

arthritis (*say* arth-**ry**-tiss) *noun* a disease that makes joints in the body stiff and painful. **arthritic** (*say* arth-**rit**-ik) *adjective* [from Greek *arthron* = joint]

arthropod *noun* an animal of the group that includes insects, spiders, crabs, and centipedes. [from Greek *arthron* = joint, + *podos* = of a foot]

artichoke *noun* a kind of plant with a flower-head used as a vegetable.

article *noun* **1** a piece of writing published in a newspaper or magazine. **2** an object.
definite article the word 'the'.
indefinite article the word 'a' or 'an'.

articulate *adjective* able to express things clearly and fluently.

articulate *verb* (**articulated**, **articulating**) **1** say or speak clearly. **2** connect by a joint. **articulation** *noun*
articulated vehicle a vehicle that has sections connected by a flexible joint.

artifice *noun* a piece of trickery; a clever device. [same origin as *artificial*]

artificial *adjective* not natural; made by human beings in imitation of a natural thing. **artificially** *adverb*, **artificiality** *noun*
artificial insemination inserting semen into the womb artificially, so that an animal or baby can be conceived without sexual intercourse.
artificial respiration helping somebody to start breathing again after their breathing has stopped. [from Latin *ars* = art, + *facere* = make]

artillery *noun* **1** large guns. **2** the part of the army that uses large guns.

artisan (*say* art-iz-**an**) *noun* a skilled worker.

artist *noun* **1** a person who produces works of art, especially a painter. **2** an entertainer. **artistry** *noun*

artistic *adjective* **1** of art or artists. **2** showing skill and good taste. **artistically** *adverb*

artless *adjective* simple and natural; not artful. **artlessly** *adverb*

as *adverb* equally; similarly, *This is just as easy.*

as *preposition* in the character or function etc. of, *Use it as a handle.*

as *conjunction* **1** when; while, *She slipped as she got off the bus.* **2** because, *As he was late, we missed the train.* **3** in the way that, *Leave it as it is.*
as for with regard to, *As for you, I despise you.*
as it were in some way, *She became, as it were, her own enemy.*
as well also.

as- *prefix* see **ad-**.

a.s.a.p. *abbreviation* as soon as possible.

asbestos *noun* a soft fireproof material.

ascend *verb* go up.
ascend the throne become king or queen. [from Latin *ascendere* = climb up]

ascendancy *noun* being in control, *They gained ascendancy over others.*

ascendant *adjective* rising.
in the ascendant rising, especially in power or influence.

ascension *noun* ascending.
Ascension Day the 40th day after Easter, when Christians commemorate the ascension of Christ into heaven.

ascent *noun* **1** ascending. **2** a way up; an upward path or slope.

ascertain (*say* as-er-**tayn**) *verb* find out by asking. **ascertainable** *adjective*

ascetic (*say* a-**set**-ik) *adjective* not allowing yourself pleasure and luxuries. **asceticism** *noun*

ascetic *noun* a person who leads an ascetic life, often for religious reasons. [from Greek *asketes* = hermit]

ASCII *abbreviation* American Standard Code for Information Interchange.

ascorbic acid vitamin C.

ascribe *verb* (**ascribed**, **ascribing**) attribute.

ASEAN *abbreviation* Association of South-East Asian Nations.

aseptic (*say* ay-**sep**-tik) *adjective* clean and free from bacteria that cause things to become septic. [from *a*-[2] not, + *septic*]

asexual *adjective* (in biology, of reproduction) by other than sexual methods. [from *a*-[2] = not, + *sexual*]

ash[1] *noun* (*plural* **ashes**) the powder that is left after something has been burned. **ashen** *adjective*, **ashy** *adjective*
Ash Wednesday the first day of Lent.
the Ashes the trophy for which England and Australia play each other at cricket.

ash[2] *noun* (*plural* **ashes**) a tree with silver-grey bark.

ashamed *adjective* feeling shame.

ashore *adverb* to or on the shore.

ashtray *noun* a small bowl for tobacco ash.

Asian *adjective* of Asia or its people.

Asian *noun* an Asian person.

Asiatic *adjective* of Asia.

aside *adverb* **1** to or at one side, *pull it aside.* **2** away; in reserve.

aside *noun* words spoken so that only certain people will hear.

asinine (*say* **ass**-in-I'n) *adjective* silly; stupid. [same origin as *ass*]

ask *verb* **1** speak so as to find out or get something. **2** invite, *Ask her to the party.*

askance (*say* a-**skanss**) *adverb* **look askance at** regard with distrust or disapproval.

askew *adverb & adjective* crooked; not straight or level.

asleep *adverb & adjective* sleeping.

asp *noun* a small poisonous snake.

asparagus *noun* a plant whose young shoots are eaten as a vegetable.

aspect *noun* **1** one part of a problem or situation. *Violence was the worst aspect of the crime.* **2** a person's or thing's appearance, *The forest had a sinister aspect.* **3** the direction a house etc. faces, *This room has a southern aspect.* [from *as*-, + Latin *specere* = to look]

aspen *noun* a tree with leaves that move in the slightest wind.

asperity *noun* harshness; severity. [from Latin *asper* = rough]

aspersions *plural noun* an attack on someone's reputation, *He cast aspersions on his rivals.*

asphalt (*say* **ass**-falt) *noun* a sticky black substance like tar, often mixed with gravel to surface roads, etc.

asphyxia (*say* ass-**fiks**-ee-a) *noun* suffocation. [Greek, = stopping of the pulse]

asphyxiate (*say* ass-**fiks**-ee-ayt) *verb* (**asphyxiated**, **asphyxiating**) suffocate. **asphyxiation** *noun* [from *asphyxia*]

aspic *noun* a savoury jelly used for coating meats, eggs, etc.

aspidistra *noun* a house-plant with broad leaves. [from Greek *aspis* = a shield]

aspirant (*say* **asp**-er-ant) *noun* a person who aspires to something.

aspirate (*say* **asp**-er-at) *noun* the sound of 'h'. [same origin as *aspire*]

aspiration *noun* ambition; strong desire.

aspire *verb* (**aspired**, **aspiring**) have a high ambition, *He aspired to become a champion.* [from *ad*- = to, + Latin *spirare* breathe]

aspirin *noun* a medicinal drug used to relieve pain or reduce fever.

ass *noun* (*plural* **asses**) **1** a donkey. **2** (*informal*) a stupid person. [from Latin *asinus* = donkey]

assail *verb* attack. **assailant** *noun* [from Latin *assilire* = leap upon]

assassin *noun* a person who assassinates somebody. [from Arabic, = hashish-takers, Muslim fanatics who murdered people during the time of the Crusades]

assassinate *verb* (**assassinated**, **assassinating**) kill an important person deliberately and violently, especially for political reasons. **assassination** *noun*

assault *noun* a violent or illegal attack.

assault *verb* make an assault on someone. [same origin as *assail*]

assay (*say* a-**say**) *noun* a test made on metal or ore to discover its quality. [from French *essai* = trial]

assegai (*say* **ass**-ig-I) *noun* an iron-tipped spear used by South African peoples.

assemble *verb* (**assembled**, **assembling**) **1** bring or come together. **2** fit or put together. **assemblage** *noun*

assembly *noun* (*plural* **assemblies**) **1** assembling. **2** a regular meeting, such as when everybody in a school meets together. **3** people who regularly meet for a special purpose; a parliament.
assembly line a series of workers and machines along which a product passes to be assembled part by part.

assent *verb* consent; say you agree.

assent *noun* consent; approval.

assert *verb* state firmly. **assertion** *noun*
assert yourself use firmness or authority.

assertive *adjective* asserting yourself.
assertiveness *noun*

assess *verb* decide or estimate the value or quality of a person or thing. **assessment** *noun*, **assessor** *noun* [from Latin *assessor* = an assistant judge]

asset *noun* something useful.
assets *plural noun* a person's or firm's property, reckoned as having value.

assiduous (*say* a-**sid**-yoo-us) *adjective* working hard; persevering. **assiduously** *adverb*, **assiduity** *noun*

assign *verb* **1** allot; give. **2** appoint a person to perform a task. [from *as-*, + Latin *signare* = mark out]

assignation (*say* ass-ig-**nay**-shon) *noun* **1** assigning something. **2** an arrangement to meet someone.

assignment *noun* **1** assigning. **2** something assigned; a task given to someone.

assimilate *verb* (**assimilated**, **assimilating**) **1** take in and absorb something, e.g. nourishment into the body or knowledge into the mind or people into a group. **2** to become absorbed in this way.
assimilation *noun*

assist *verb* help. **assistance** *noun* [from Latin *assistere* = stand by]

assistant *noun* **1** a person who assists another; a helper. **2** a person who serves customers in a shop.

assistant *adjective* helping a person and ranking next below him or her, *the assistant manager.*

associate *verb* (**associated**, **associating**) **1** put or go naturally or regularly together. **2** work together.

associate *noun* a colleague or companion; a partner. **associate** *adjective* [from *as-*, + Latin *socius* = an ally]

association *noun* **1** an organisation of people; a society. **2** associating. **3** something associated.
association football soccer.

assonance (*say* **ass**-on-ans) *noun* similarity of vowel sounds, e.g. in vermin and furnish. [from *as-*, + Latin *sonus* = sound]

assorted *adjective* of various sorts put together; mixed. **assortment** *noun*

assuage (*say* a-**swayj**) *verb* (**assuaged**, **assuaging**) soothe; make less severe, *We drank to assuage our thirst.* [from *as-*, + Latin *suavis* = pleasant]

assume *verb* (**assumed**, **assuming**) **1** accept (without proof or question) that something is true or sure to happen. **2** take on; undertake, *She assumed the extra responsibility.* **3** put on, *He assumed an innocent expression.* **assumption** *noun*
assumed name a false name. [from *as-*, + Latin *sumere* = take]

assurance *noun* **1** a promise or guarantee that something is true or will happen. **2** life insurance. **3** self-confidence.

assure *verb* (**assured**, **assuring**) **1** tell somebody confidently; promise. **2** make certain.

aster *noun* a garden plant with daisy-like flowers in various colours. [from Greek *aster* = star]

asterisk *noun* a star-shaped sign * used to draw attention to something. [from Greek *asteriskos* = little star]

astern *adverb* **1** at the back of a ship or aircraft. **2** backwards, *Full speed astern!*

asteroid *noun* one of the small planets found mainly between the orbits of Mars and Jupiter. [same origin as *aster*]

asthma (*say* **ass**-ma) *noun* a disease that makes breathing difficult. **asthmatic** *adjective & noun*

astigmatism (*say* a-**stig**-mat-izm) *noun* a defect that prevents an eye or lens from focusing properly. **astigmatic** *adjective* [from *a-*[2] = not, + Greek *stigma* = a point]

astir *adverb & adjective* in motion; moving.

astonish *verb* surprise somebody greatly.
astonishment *noun*

astound *verb* astonish; shock greatly.

astral *adjective* of the stars. [same origin as *aster*]

astray *adverb & adjective* away from the right path or place or course of action.

astride *adverb & preposition* with one leg on each side of something.

astringent *adjective* **1** causing skin or body tissue to contract. **2** harsh; severe, *astringent criticism.* [from *as-*, + Latin *stringere* = bind tightly]

astrology *noun* the study of how the stars may affect people's lives. **astrologer** *noun*, **astrological** *adjective* [from Greek *astron* = star, + *-logy*]

astronaut *noun* a person who travels in a spacecraft. **astronautics** *noun* [from Greek *astron* = star, + *nautes* = sailor]

astronomy *noun* the study of the stars and planets and their movements. **astronomer** *noun*, **astronomical** *adjective* [from Greek *astron* = star, + *-nomia* = arrangement]

astute *adjective* clever; shrewd. **astutely** *adverb*, **astuteness** *noun*

asunder *adverb* apart; into pieces.

asylum *noun* **1** refuge and safety; a place of refuge, *The defeated rebels sought political asylum in another country.* **2** (*old use*) a mental hospital. [from Greek, = refuge]

asymmetrical (*say* ay-sim-**et**-rik-al) *adjective* not symmetrical. **asymmetrically** *adverb*

at *preposition* This word is used to show (**1**) position (*at the top*), (**2**) time (*at midnight*), (**3**) condition (*Stand at ease*), (**4**) direction towards something (*Aim at the target*), (**5**) level or price etc. (*Sell them at $5 each*), (**6**) cause (*We were annoyed at his failure*).
at all in any way; of any kind.
at it doing or working at something.
at once immediately; at the same time, *It all came out at once.*

at- *prefix* see **ad-**.

atheist (*say* **ay**th-ee-ist) *noun* a person who believes that there is no God. **atheism** *noun* [from *a-*[2] not, + Greek *theos* = god]

athlete *noun* a person who is good at athletics.

athletic *adjective* **1** physically strong and active. **2** of athletes. **athletically** *adverb*

athletics *plural noun* physical exercises and sports, e.g. running and jumping.

atlas *noun* (*plural* **atlases**) a book of maps. [named after Atlas, a giant in Greek mythology, who was made to support the universe]

ATM *abbreviation* automated teller machine.

atmosphere *noun* **1** the air round the earth. **2** a feeling given by surroundings, *the happy atmosphere of the fairground.* **atmospheric** *adjective* [from Greek *atmos* = vapour, + *sphere*]

atoll *noun* a ring-shaped coral reef.

atom *noun* the smallest particle of a substance.
atom bomb an atomic bomb. [from Greek *atomos* = indivisible]

atomic *adjective* of an atom or atoms.
atomic bomb a bomb using atomic energy.
atomic energy energy created by splitting the nuclei of certain atoms.

atomiser *noun* a device for making a liquid into a fine spray.

atone *verb* (**atoned**, **atoning**) make amends; make up for having done something wrong. **atonement** *noun* [from *at one*]

atrocious (*say* a-**troh**-shus) *adjective* extremely bad or wicked. **atrociously** *adverb* [from Latin *atrox* = cruel]

atrocity (*say* a-**tross**-it-ee) *noun* (*plural* **atrocities**) something extremely bad or wicked; wickedness.

attach *verb* **1** fix or join to something else. **2** regard as belonging to something, *We attach great importance to neatness.* **attachment** *noun*
attached to fond of.

attaché (*say* a-**tash**-ay) *noun* a special assistant to an ambassador, *our military attaché.*
attaché case a small case in which documents etc. may be carried. [French, = attached]

attachment *noun* a computer file added to an e-mail.

attack *noun* **1** a violent attempt to hurt or overcome somebody. **2** a piece of strong criticism. **3** sudden illness or pain.

attack *verb* make an attack. **attacker** *noun*

attain *verb* accomplish; succeed in doing or getting something. **attainable** *adjective*, **attainment** *noun*

attempt *verb* make an effort to do something; try.

attempt *noun* an effort to do something; a try. [from *at-*, + Latin *temptare* = try]

attend *verb* **1** give care and thought to something; look and listen, *Why don't you attend to your teacher?* **2** be present somewhere; go regularly to a meeting etc. **3** look after someone; be an attendant. **attendance** *noun*

attendant *noun* a person who helps or accompanies someone.

attention *noun* **1** attending to someone or something. **2** a position in which a soldier etc. stands with feet together and arms straight downwards.

attentive *adjective* giving attention. **attentively** *adverb*, **attentiveness** *noun*

attenuate *verb* (**attenuated**, **attenuating**) make a thing thinner or weaker. **attenuation** *noun*

attest *verb* declare or prove that something is true or genuine. **attestation** *noun* [from *at-*, + Latin *testari* be a witness]

attic *noun* a room in the roof of a house.

attire *noun* (*formal*) clothes.

attire *verb* (**attired**, **attiring**) (*formal*) clothe.

attitude *noun* **1** the position of the body or its parts; posture. **2** a way of thinking or behaving.

attorney *noun* (*plural* **attorneys**) **1** a person who is appointed to act on behalf of another in business matters. **2** (*American*) a lawyer.
Attorney-General *noun* the chief law minister in a New Zealand or Australian government.

attract *verb* **1** get someone's attention or interest; seem pleasant to someone. **2** pull something by an invisible force, *Magnets attract metal pins.* **attraction** *noun,* **attractive** *adjective,* **attractively** *adverb,* **attractiveness** *noun* [from *at-,* + Latin *tractum* = pulled]

attribute (*say* a-**trib**-yoot) *verb* (**attributed, attributing**) regard as belonging to or created by, *We attribute his success to hard work.* **attribution** *noun*

attribute (*say* **at**-rib-yoot) *noun* a quality or characteristic, *Kindness is one of his attributes.* [from *at-,* + Latin *tribuere* = allot]

attributive (*say* a-**trib**-yoo-tiv) *adjective* expressing an attribute and placed before the word it describes, e.g. *old* in *the old dog.* (Compare *predicative.*) **attributively** *adverb*

attrition (*say* a-**trish**-on) *noun* wearing something away gradually.

attune *verb* (**attuned, attuning**) bring into harmony.

atua *noun* a supernatural being; a god, demon or ghost. [Māori]

aubergine (*say* **oh**-ber-zheen) *noun* the deep-purple fruit of the egg-plant.

auburn *adjective* (of hair) reddish-brown.

auction *noun* a public sale where things are sold to the person who offers the most money for them.

auction *verb* sell by auction. **auctioneer** *noun* [from Latin *auctum* = increased]

audacious (*say* aw-**day**-shus) *adjective* bold; daring. **audaciously** *adverb,* **audacity** *noun* [from Latin *audax* = bold]

audible *adjective* loud enough to be heard. **audibly** *adverb,* **audibility** *noun* [from Latin *audire* = hear]

audience *noun* **1** people who have gathered to hear or watch something. **2** a formal interview with a king or queen etc. [from Latin *audire* = hear]

audio *noun* reproduced sounds.

audiotape *noun* magnetic tape for recording sound.

audio-visual *adjective* using both sound and pictures to give information.

audit *noun* an official examination of financial accounts to see that they are correct.

audit *verb* (**audited, auditing**) make an audit of accounts. **auditor** *noun*

audition *noun* a test to see if a performer is suitable for a job. **audition** *verb* [same origin as *audience*]

auditorium *noun* (*plural* **auditoriums**) the part of a building where the audience sits.

auē *interjection* an expression of astonishment or distress. [Māori]

auger *noun* a tool with a screw point for boring in wood or for boring holes in the ground for fence-posts etc.

augment *verb* increase or add to something. **augmentation** *noun* [from Latin *augere* = increase]

augur (*say* **awg**-er) *verb* be a sign of what is to come, *These exam results augur well.* [from Latin *augur* = prophet]

August *noun* the eighth month of the year. [named after the Roman emperor Augustus]

august (*say* aw-**gust**) *adjective* majestic; imposing. [from Latin *augustus* = majestic]

auk *noun* a kind of sea-bird.

aunt *noun* **1** the sister of your father or mother; your uncle's wife. **2** any female relative.

auntie or **aunty** *noun* (*informal*) aunt.

aura (*say* **or**-a) *noun* a general feeling surrounding a person or thing, *an aura of happiness.* [Greek, = breeze]

aural (*say* **or**-al) *adjective* of the ear; of hearing. **aurally** *adverb* [from Latin *auris* = ear]

USAGE Do not confuse *aural* with *oral.*

aurora (*say* aw-**raw**-ra) *noun* bands of coloured light appearing in the sky at night, the **aurora borealis** (*say* bor-ee-**ay**-liss) in the northern hemisphere and the **aurora australis** (*say* aw-**stray**-liss) in the southern hemisphere. [from Latin *aurora* = dawn]

auspices (*say* **aw**-spiss-eez) *plural noun* protection; sponsorship, *under the auspices of the Red Cross.*

auspicious (*say* aw-**spish**-us) *adjective* fortunate; favourable, *an auspicious start.*

Aussie *noun* (*informal*) **1** Australia. **2** an Australian. **Aussie** *adjective*

austere (*say* aw-**steer**) *adjective* very simple and plain; without luxuries. **austerely** *adverb,* **austerity** *noun* [from Greek, = severe]

Australasian *adjective* of Australasia, a region containing New Zealand and Australia and their outlying islands.

Australian *noun* a person born or living in Australia. **Australian** *adjective* **Australian Rules** an Australian form of football played with an oval ball by teams of eighteen.

aut- *prefix* see **auto-**.

authentic *adjective* genuine, *an authentic signature.* **authentically** *adverb,* **authenticity** *noun*

authenticate *verb* (**authenticated**, **authenticating**) confirm something as being authentic. **authentication** *noun*

author *noun* the writer of a book, play, poem, etc. **authorship** *noun* [from Latin *auctor* = originator]

authorise *verb* (**authorised**, **authorising**) give official permission for something. **authorisation** *noun*

authoritarian *adjective* believing that people should be completely obedient to those in authority.

authoritative *adjective* having proper authority or expert knowledge; official.

authority *noun* (*plural* **authorities**) **1** the right or power to give orders to other people. **2** a person or organisation with the right to give orders. **3** an expert; a book etc. that gives reliable information, *an authority on spiders.* [same origin as *author*]

autistic (*say* aw-**tist**-ik) *adjective* unable to communicate with people or respond to surroundings. [from *auto-*]

auto- *prefix* (changing to **aut-** before a vowel) self-; of or by yourself or itself (as in *autograph, automatic*). [from Greek *autos* = self]

autobiography *noun* (*plural* **autobiographies**) the story of a person's life written by himself or herself. **autobiographical** *adjective* [from *auto-* + *biography*]

autocracy (*say* aw-**tok**-ra-see) *noun* (*plural* autocracies) despotism; rule by a person with unlimited power. [from *auto-* + *-cracy*]

autocrat *noun* a person with unlimited power; a dictatorial person. **autocratic** *adjective*, **autocratically** *adverb*

autograph *noun* a person's signature.

autograph *verb* sign your name on or in a book etc. [from *auto-* + *-graph*]

automate *verb* (**automated**, **automating**) work something by automation.

automatic *adjective* **1** working on its own without continuous attention or control by people. **2** done without thinking. **automatically** *adverb* [from Greek *automatos* self-operating]

automation *noun* making processes automatic; using machines instead of people to do jobs.

automaton (*say* aw-**tom**-at-on) *noun* a robot; a person who seems to act mechanically without thinking.

automobile *noun* (*American*) a motor car. [from *auto-* + *mobile*]

autonomy (*say* aw-**ton**-om-ee) *noun* self-government. **autonomous** *adjective* [from *auto-*, + Greek *-nomia* = arrangement]

autopsy (*say* **aw**-top-see) *noun* (*plural* **autopsies**) a post-mortem. [from Greek *autopsia* = seeing with your own eyes]

autumn *noun* the season between summer and winter. **autumnal** *adjective*

auxiliary *adjective* giving help and support, *auxiliary services.*
auxiliary verb a verb used in forming tenses etc. of other verbs, e.g. *have* in *I have finished.*

auxiliary *noun* (*plural* **auxiliaries**) a helper. [from Latin *auxilium* = help]

avail *noun* usefulness; help, *Their pleas were of no avail.*

avail *verb* be useful or helpful, *Nothing availed against the storm.*
avail yourself of make use of something. [from Latin *valere* = be strong]

available *adjective* ready or able to be used; obtainable. **availability** *noun*

avalanche *noun* a mass of snow or rock falling down the side of a mountain. [French, from *avaler* = descend]

avarice (*say* **av**-er-iss) *noun* greed for gain. **avaricious** *adjective* [from Latin *avarus* = greedy]

avatar *noun* a digital image or symbol which represents a user on a computer program.

avenge *verb* (**avenged**, **avenging**) take vengeance for something done to harm you. **avenger** *noun*

avenue *noun* **1** a wide street. **2** a road with trees along both sides.

average *noun* **1** the value obtained by adding several quantities together and dividing by the number of quantities. **2** the usual or ordinary standard.

average *adjective* **1** worked out as an average, *Their average age is ten.* **2** of the usual or ordinary standard.

average *verb* (**averaged**, **averaging**) work out, produce, or amount to as an average.

averse *adjective* unwilling; feeling opposed to something. [same origin as *avert*]

aversion *noun* a strong dislike.

avert *verb* **1** turn something away, *People averted their eyes from the accident.* **2** prevent, *We averted a disaster.* [from *ab-* = away, + Latin *vertere* = turn]

aviary *noun* (*plural* **aviaries**) a large cage or building for keeping birds. [from Latin *avis* = bird]

aviation *noun* the flying of aircraft. **aviator** *noun* [from Latin *avis* = bird]

avid (*say* **av**-id) *adjective* eager, *an avid reader.* **avidly** *adverb*, **avidity** *noun*

avocado (*say* av-ok-**ah**-doh) *noun* (*plural* **avocados**) a pear-shaped tropical fruit.

avoid *verb* **1** keep yourself away from someone or something. **2** keep yourself from doing something; refrain from, *Avoid rash promises.* **avoidable** *adjective*, **avoidance** *noun*

avuncular *adjective* like a kindly uncle.

await *verb* wait for.

awake *verb* (**awoke**, **awoken**, **awaking**) wake up.

awake *adjective* not asleep.

awaken *verb* awake. **awakening** *noun*

award *verb* give something officially as a prize, payment, or penalty.

award *noun* **1** something awarded. **2** a legal agreement that fixes the minimum wages for a particular industry or job.

aware *adjective* knowing; realising, *Were you aware of the danger?* **awareness** *noun*

awash *adjective* with waves or water flooding over it.

away *adverb* **1** to or at a distance; not at the usual place. **2** out of existence. *The water had boiled away.* **3** continuously; persistently, *We worked away at it.*

away *adjective* played on an opponent's ground, *an away match.*

awe *noun* fearful or reverent wonder. **awed** *adjective*, **awestricken** *adjective*, **awestruck** *adjective*

aweigh *adverb* hanging just clear of the sea-bottom, *The anchor is aweigh.*

awesome *adjective* **1** causing awe. **2** (*informal*) excellent.

awful *adjective* **1** very bad, *an awful accident.* **2** (*informal*) very great, *That's an awful lot of money.* **3** causing awe or fear. **awfully** *adverb* [from *awe* + *-ful*]

āwhato *noun* (also **āwheto**) a large New Zealand caterpillar. [Māori]

awhile *adverb* for a short time.

awkward *adjective* **1** difficult to use or deal with; not convenient. **2** clumsy; not skilful. **awkwardly** *adverb*, **awkwardness** *noun* [from Old Norse *ofugr* = turned the wrong way]

awl *noun* a small pointed tool for making holes in leather, wood, etc.

awning *noun* a roof-like shelter made of canvas etc.

awry *adverb & adjective* twisted to one side; crooked; wrong, *plans went awry.*

axe *noun* **1** a tool for chopping things. **2** (*informal*) being axed.
have an axe to grind have a personal interest in something and want to take care of it.

axe *verb* (**axed**, **axing**) remove; reduce; abolish.

axiom *noun* an established general truth or principle, **axiomatic** *adjective*

axis *noun* (*plural* **axes**) **1** a line through the centre of a spinning object. **2** a line dividing a thing in half. [Latin, = axle]

axle *noun* the rod through the centre of a wheel, on which the wheel turns.

ayatollah (*say* I-a-**tol**-a) *noun* a Muslim religious leader in Iran. [Persian, = token of God]

aye (*say* as I) *adverb* yes.

azalea (*say* a-**zay**-lee-a) *noun* a kind of flowering shrub.

azure *adjective & noun* sky-blue.

Bb

BA *abbreviation* Bachelor of Arts.

baa *noun* the cry of a sheep or lamb.

babaco *noun* a yellow fruit.

babble *verb* (**babbled**, **babbling**) **1** talk in a meaningless way. **2** make a murmuring sound. **babble** *noun*, **babbler** *noun*

babe *noun* (*poetical*) a baby.

baboon *noun* a kind of large monkey.

baby *noun* (*plural* **babies**) a very young child or animal. **babyish** *adjective*

baby-sitter *noun* someone who looks after a child while its parents are out.

bach *noun* (*NZ*) a holiday cottage.

bachelor *noun* a man who has not married.
Bachelor of Arts or **Science** a person who has taken a first degree in arts or science at a university.

bacillus (*say* ba-**sil**-us) *noun* (*plural* **bacilli**) a rod-shaped bacterium.

back *noun* **1** the part furthest from the front. **2** the back part of the body from the shoulders to the buttocks. **3** the part of a chair etc. that your back rests against. **4** a player in a rugby team who is not part of the scrum. **5** a defensive player in soccer etc.

back *adjective* **1** placed at or near the back. **2** of the back.
back country the remote and thinly populated parts of a region.
back section a piece of land for building behind another that has a street boundary.

back *adverb* **1** to or towards the back. **2** to the place you have come from, *Go back home.* **3** to an earlier time or condition or position. *Put the clocks back one hour.*

back *verb* **1** move backwards. **2** give support or help to someone. **3** bet on something. **4** cover the back of something, *Back the rug with canvas.* **backer** *noun*
back out refuse to do what was agreed.
back up give support or help to a person or thing. **back-up** *noun*

backbiting *noun* spiteful talk.

backblocks *plural noun* (*NZ*) parts of the country a long way from cities or towns. **backblocker** *noun*

backbone *noun* the column of bones down the centre of the back.

backdrop *noun* a painted curtain at the back of a stage.

backfire *verb* (**backfired**, **backfiring**) **1** make an explosion when fuel burns too soon in an engine or ignites in the exhaust system. **2** produce an unwanted effect, *Their plans backfired.*

backgammon *noun* a game played on a board with draughts and dice. [from *back* (because sometimes pieces must go back to the start), + Old English *gamen* = game]

background *noun* **1** the back part of a scene or view etc. **2** the conditions influencing something. **3** a person's experience and education etc.

backhand *noun* a stroke made in tennis etc. with the back of the hand turned outwards. **backhanded** *adjective*

backing *noun* **1** support. **2** material that forms a support or lines the back of something. **3** musical accompaniment.
backing dog a kind of sheep-dog.

backlash *noun* (*plural* **backlashes**) a violent reaction to an event etc.

backline *noun* (in rugby) the players behind the scrum or line-out when they are lined out across the field.

backlog *noun* an amount of work that should have been finished but is still waiting to be done.

backpack *noun* a bag on straps for carrying on the back.

backpacker *noun* a traveller or tramper carrying belongings in a backpack.

backside *noun* (*informal*) the buttocks.
backspace *noun* a key on a keyboard used to move the cursor backwards.

backstroke *noun* a way of swimming on your back.

backward *adjective* **1** going backwards. **2** having made less than the normal progress. **backwardness** *noun*

backward *adverb* backwards.

backwards *adverb* **1** to or towards the back. **2** with the back end going first. **3** in reverse order, *Count backwards.*
backwards and forwards in each direction alternately; to and fro.

backwater *noun* **1** a branch of a river that comes to a dead end with stagnant water. **2** a place that is not affected by progress or new ideas.

bacon *noun* smoked or salted meat from the back or sides of a pig.

baconer *noun* a pig killed to make bacon and ham.

bacterium *noun* (*plural* **bacteria**) a microscopic organism. **bacterial** *adjective.*

bad *adjective* (**worse**, **worst**) **1** not having the right qualities; not good. **2** wicked; evil. **3** serious, *a bad accident.* **4** ill; unhealthy; diseased. **5** harmful, *Lollies are bad for your teeth.* **6** decayed, *This meat has gone bad.*
badness *noun*
not bad quite good.

bade *old past tense* of **bid**[2].

badge *noun* a thing that you wear on your clothes to show people who you are or what school or club etc. you belong to.

badger *noun* a grey burrowing animal with a white patch on its head.

badger *verb* pester. [named after the old sport of tormenting badgers]

badly *adverb* (**worse**, **worst**) **1** in a bad way; not well. **2** severely; so as to cause much injury, *He was badly wounded.* **3** very much, *She badly wanted to win.*

badminton *noun* a game in which a light object called a shuttlecock is hit to and fro with racquets across a high net. [named after Badminton in England, where it was invented in about 1870]

baffle *verb* (**baffled**, **baffling**) **1** puzzle or perplex somebody. **2** frustrate, *We baffled their attempts to capture us.*
bafflement *noun*

bag *noun* a flexible container for holding or carrying things.
bags (*informal*) plenty, *bags of room.*

bag *verb* (**bagged**, **bagging**) **1** (*informal*) seize; catch. **2** put into a bag or bags.

bagatelle *noun* **1** a game played on a board with small balls struck into holes. **2** a short piece of music, usually for the piano.

baggage *noun* luggage.

baggy *adjective* hanging loosely.

bagpipes *plural noun* a musical instrument in which air is squeezed out of a bag into pipes.

bail[1] *noun* money paid or promised as a guarantee that a person accused of a crime will return for trial if released temporarily.

bail[1] *verb* provide bail for a person.

bail[2] *noun* **1** one of the two small pieces of wood placed on top of the stumps in cricket. **2** a framework that holds a cow's head securely while it is being milked.

bail[2] *verb* secure a cow during milking.
bail up corner or detain a person (in conversation etc.).

bail[3] *verb* scoop out water that has entered a boat. [from French *baille* = bucket]

bailey *noun* the courtyard of a castle; the wall round this courtyard.

Bailey bridge a bridge that can be put up quickly because its sections have been made in advance.

bailiff *noun* a law officer who helps a sheriff by serving writs and performing arrests.

bairn *noun* (*Scottish*) a child.

bait *noun* food put on a hook or in a trap to catch fish or animals.

bait *verb* **1** put bait on a book or in a trap. **2** torment or tease by jeering.

baize *noun* thick green cloth used chiefly for covering snooker tables.

bake *verb* (**baked**, **baking**) **1** cook in an oven. **2** make or become very hot. **3** make a thing hard by heating it.
baked beans cooked white beans, usually tinned with tomato sauce.

baker *noun* a person who bakes and sells bread or cakes. **bakery** *noun*

baking powder *noun* a mixture including sodium bicarbonate, used to make cakes, pastry, etc. light.

balaclava *noun* a hood covering the head and neck and part of the face. [named after the battle of Balaclava (1854) in the Crimean War]

balance *noun* **1** a steady position; having the weight or amount evenly distributed. **2** an apparatus for weighing things, with two containers hanging from a bar. **3** the difference between money paid into an account and money taken out of it. **4** the money left after something has been paid for.

balance *verb* (**balanced**, **balancing**) make or be steady or equal. [from Latin *bilanx* = having two scale-pans]

balcony *noun* (*plural* **balconies**) **1** a platform projecting from an outside wall in a building. **2** the upstairs part of a theatre or cinema.

bald *adjective* **1** without hair on the top of the head. **2** with no details; blunt, *a bald statement.* **baldly** *adverb,* **baldness** *noun*

bale[1] *noun* a large compacted or tied bundle of wool, hay etc.

bale[1] *verb* make into bales.

bale[2] *verb* (**baled**, **baling**) **bale out** jump out of an aircraft with a parachute.

baleen *noun* whalebone, a horny stringy substance from the upper jaw of some kinds of whale.

baleful *adjective* bringing harm or evil; menacing, *a baleful frown.* **balefully** *adverb* [from Old English *balu* = evil]

baler *noun* a machine that compresses hay or straw into square or round bales.

ball[1] *noun* **1** a round object used in many games. **2** a solid or hollow sphere; a round mass, *a ball of string.*

ball[2] *noun* a grand gathering where people dance. [same origin as *ballet*]

ballad *noun* a simple song or poem telling a story.

ballast (*say* **bal**-ast) *noun* heavy material carried in a ship to keep it steady.

ball-bearings *plural noun* small steel balls rolling in a groove on which parts can move easily in machinery.

ballcock *noun* a floating device controlling the water-level in a cistern.

ballerina (*say* bal-er-**een**-a) *noun* a female ballet-dancer.

ballet (*say* **bal**-ay) *noun* a stage entertainment telling a story or expressing an idea in dancing and mime. [from Old French *baler* = to dance]

ballistic (*say* bal-**ist**-ik) *adjective* of projectiles such as bullets and missiles. [from Greek *ballein* = to throw]

balloon *noun* **1** an inflatable rubber pouch with a neck, used as a toy or decoration. **2** a large round bag inflated with hot air or light gases to make it rise in the air. **3** an outline round spoken words in a strip cartoon.

ballot *noun* **1** a secret method of voting by means of papers or tokens. **2** a piece of paper on which a vote is made.

ballot *verb* (**balloted**, **balloting**) vote or allow people to vote by a ballot. [from Italian *ballotta* = little ball (because originally this voting was by dropping balls into a box)]

ball-point pen *noun* a pen with a tiny ball round which the ink flows.

ballroom *noun* a large room where dances are held.

balm *noun* **1** a sweet-scented ointment. **2** a soothing influence.

balmy *adjective* **1** sweet-scented like balm. **2** soft and warm. **3** (*slang*) barmy.

balsa *noun* a kind of very lightweight wood.

balsam *noun* **1** a kind of gum produced by certain trees. **2** a tree producing balsam. **3** a kind of flowering plant.

balustrade *noun* a row of short posts or pillars supporting a rail or strip of stonework round a balcony or terrace.

bamboo *noun* **1** a tall plant with hard hollow stems. **2** a stem of the bamboo plant. [from a Malay word]

bamboozle *verb* (**bamboozled**, **bamboozling**) (*informal*) cheat or mystify someone.

ban *verb* (**banned**, **banning**) forbid something officially.

ban *noun* an order that bans something.

banal (*say* ban-**ahl**) *adjective* ordinary and uninteresting. **banality** *noun*

banana *noun* a finger-shaped yellow or green fruit.

band[1] *noun* **1** a strip or loop of something. **2** a range of values, wavelengths, etc.

band[2] *noun* **1** an organised group doing something together, *a band of robbers.* **2** a set of people playing music together.

band[2] *verb* form an organised group.

bandage *noun* a strip of material for binding up a wound. **bandage** *verb*

bandicoot *noun* (in Australia) a marsupial rather like a rat; (in India) a kind of very large rat.

bandit *noun* a member of a band of robbers. [from Italian *bandito* = out-lawed or banned]

bandstand *noun* a platform for a band playing music outdoors.

bandwagon *noun* a wagon for a band playing music in a parade.
jump or **climb on the bandwagon** join in something that is successful.

bandy[1] *adjective* having legs that curve outwards at the knees.

bandy[2] *verb* (**bandied**, **bandying**) pass to and fro, *The story was bandied about.*

bane *noun* a cause of trouble or worry etc., *Exams are the bane of our lives!* **baneful** *adjective*, **banefully** *adverb*

bang *noun* **1** a sudden loud noise like that of an explosion. **2** a sharp blow or knock.

bang *verb* **1** hit or shut noisily. **2** make a sudden loud noise.

bang *adverb* **1** with a bang; suddenly. **2** (*informal*) exactly, *bang in the middle.*

banger *noun* **1** a firework made to explode noisily. **2** (*slang*) a sausage. **3** (*slang*) a noisy old car.

bangle *noun* a stiff bracelet. [from Hindi *bangri*]

banish *verb* punish a person by sending him or her away. **banishment** *noun*

banisters *plural noun* a handrail with upright supports beside a staircase.

banjo *noun* (*plural* **banjos**) an instrument like a guitar with a round body.

bank[1] *noun* **1** a slope. **2** a long piled-up mass of sand, snow, cloud, etc. **3** a row of lights or switches etc.

bank[1] *verb* **1** build or form a bank. **2** tilt sideways while changing direction, *The plane banked as it prepared to land.*

bank[2] *noun* **1** a business that looks after people's money. **2** a reserve supply, *a blood bank.*

bank[2] *verb* put money in a bank.
bank on rely on.

banker *noun* a person who runs a bank.

banknote *noun* a piece of paper money issued by a bank.

bankrupt *adjective* unable to pay debts. **bankruptcy** *noun* [from *bank*[2], + Latin *ruptum* = broken]

banksia *noun* an Australia evergreen shrub with yellowish flowers.

banner *noun* **1** a flag. **2** a strip of cloth with a design or slogan, carried on a pole or two poles in a procession etc.

banns *plural noun* an announcement in a church that the two people named are going to marry each other. [from *ban* = proclamation]

banquet *noun* a formal public meal. **banqueting** *noun* [from Old French *banquet* = little bench]

bantam *noun* a kind of small fowl. [named after Bantan, in Java]

banter *noun* playful teasing or joking.

Bantu *noun* (*plural* **Bantu** or **Bantus**) a member of a group of Black African peoples. [Bantu word, = people]

bap *noun* a soft flat bread roll.

baptise *verb* (**baptised**, **baptising**) receive a person into the Christian Church in a ceremony in which he or she is sprinkled with or dipped in water, and usually given a name or names. [from Greek *baptizein* = to dip]

baptism *noun* baptising.

Baptist *noun* a member of a group of Christians who believe that a person should not be baptised until old enough to understand what baptism means.

bar *noun* **1** a long piece of hard substance. **2** a counter or room where refreshments, especially alcoholic drinks, are served. **3** a barrier; an obstruction. **4** one of the small equal sections into which music is divided, *three beats to the bar.* **the bar** barristers. **not to have a bar of** (*informal*) dislike, have nothing to do with.

bar *verb* (**barred**, **barring**) **1** fasten with a bar or bars. **2** block; obstruct, *A man with a dog barred the way.* **3** forbid; ban.

barb *noun* the backward-pointing part of a spear or fish-hook etc. [from Latin *barba* = beard]

barbarian *noun* an uncivilised or brutal person. **barbaric** *adjective*, **barbarous** *adjective*, **barbarity** *noun*, **barbarism** *noun* [from Greek *barbaros* = babbling, not speaking Greek]

barbecue *noun* **1** a metal frame for grilling food over an open fire outdoors. **2** a party where food is cooked in this way.

barbed *adjective* having a barb or barbs.
barbed wire wire with small spikes in it, used to make fences.

barber *noun* a men's hairdresser. [from Latin *barba* = beard]

barbie *noun* (*NZ, informal*) a barbecue.

barcode *noun* a set of striped identifying markings on products for sale, etc., for reading by a machine.

bard *noun* (*formal*) a poet or minstrel.

bare *adjective* **1** without clothing or covering. **2** empty of stores etc., *The cupboard was bare.* **3** plain; without details, *the bare facts.* **4** only just enough, *the bare necessities of life.* **barely** *adverb*, **bareness** *noun*

bare *verb* (**bared**, **baring**) uncover; reveal, *The dog bared its teeth in a snarl.*

bareback *adjective & adverb* riding on a horse without a saddle.

barefaced *adjective* shameless; bold and unconcealed, *It's barefaced robbery!*

bargain *noun* **1** an agreement about buying or selling or exchanging something. **2** something bought cheaply.

bargain *verb* argue over the price to be paid or what you will do in return for something.
bargain for be prepared for; expect, *He got more than he bargained for.*

barge *noun* a long flat-bottomed boat used especially on canals.

barge *verb* (**barged**, **barging**) move clumsily or heavily.

baritone *noun* a male singer with a voice between a tenor and a bass. [from Greek *barys* = heavy, + *tone*]

barium (*say* **bair**-ee-um) *noun* a soft silvery-white metal.

bark[1] *noun* the short harsh sound made by a dog. **bark** *verb*

bark[2] *noun* the outer covering of a tree's branches or trunk.

bark[3] *verb* scrape your skin accidentally.

barley *noun* a cereal plant from which malt is made.
barley sugar a sweet made from boiled sugar.

bar mitzvah a religious ceremony for Jewish boys aged 13. [Hebrew, = son of the commandment]

barmy *adjective* (*slang*) crazy.

barn *noun* a building for storing hay or grain etc. on a farm. **barnyard** *noun*
barn dance a kind of country dance; an informal gathering for dancing. [from Old English *bere ern* = barley-house]

barnacle *noun* a shellfish that attaches itself to rocks and the bottoms of ships.

barney *noun* (*slang*) a noisy quarrel. **barney** *verb*

barometer (*say* ba-**rom**-it-er) *noun* an instrument that measures air pressure, used in forecasting the weather. [from Greek *baros* = weight, + *meter*]

baron *noun* **1** a member of the lowest rank of noblemen. **2** an important owner of an industry or business, *a newspaper baron.* **baroness** *noun*, **barony** *noun*, **baronial** (*say* ba-**roh**-nee-al) *adjective*

baronet *noun* the holder of a hereditary British title ranking below a baron but above a knight. **baronetcy** *noun*

baroque (*say* ba-**rok**) *noun* **1** an elaborately decorated style of architecture used in the 17th and 18th centuries in Europe. **2** a style of music from the same period.

barrack *verb* **1** shout or jeer. **2** shout in support for a sports team etc.

barracks *noun* a large building or group of buildings for soldiers to live in. [from Spanish *barraca* = a soldier's tent]

barrage (*say* **ba**-rahzh) *noun* **1** an artificial barrier; a dam. **2** heavy gunfire. [from French *barre* = a bar]

barrel *noun* **1** a large rounded container with flat ends. **2** the metal tube of a gun, through which the shot is fired.

barrel-organ *noun* a musical instrument from which you produce tunes by turning a handle.

barren *adjective* not producing any fruit, seeds, children, etc.; not fertile, *barren land.* **barrenness** *noun*

barricade *noun* a barrier, especially one put up hastily across a street etc.

barricade *verb* (**barricaded**, **barricading**) block or defend with a barricade.

barrier *noun* something that prevents people or things from getting past; an obstacle.

barrister *noun* a lawyer who represents people in the higher lawcourts.

barrow[1] *noun* **1** a wheelbarrow. **2** a small cart pushed or pulled by hand. [from Old English *bearwe* = carrying]

barrow[2] *noun* a mound of earth over a prehistoric grave in Europe. [from Old English *beorg* = hill]

barrow[3] *noun* a castrated male pig.

barter *verb* trade by exchanging goods for other goods, not for money.

barter *noun* the system of bartering.

basalt (*say* **bas**-awlt) *noun* a kind of dark volcanic rock.

base[1] *noun* **1** the lowest part of something; the part on which a thing stands. **2** a basis. **3** a headquarters. **4** each of the four corners that must be reached by a runner in softball or baseball. **5** a substance that can combine with an acid to form a salt.

base[1] *verb* (**based**, **basing**) use something as a basis, *The story is based on facts.* [from Greek *basis* = stepping]

base[2] *adjective* **1** dishonourable, *base motives.* **2** not of great value, *base metals.* **basely** *adverb*, **baseness** *noun* [from French *bas* low]

baseball *noun* **1** a ball-game played mainly in North America on a field with four bases. **2** the ball used in this game.

basement *noun* a room or rooms below ground level.

bash *verb* hit hard; attack violently.

bash *noun* (*plural* **bashes**) **1** a hard hit. **2** (*informal*) a try, *Have a bash at it.*

bashful *adjective* shy and self-conscious. **bashfully** *adverb* [from *abash*]

BASIC *abbreviation* Beginner's All-purpose Symbolic Instruction Code.

basic *adjective* forming a basis or starting-point; very important, *Bread is a basic food.* **basically** *adverb* [from *base*[1]]

basilica (*say* ba-**zil**-ik-a) *noun* a large oblong hall or church with two rows of columns and an apse at one end.

basilisk (*say* **baz**-il-isk) *noun* a mythical reptile said to cause death by its glance or breath.

basin *noun* **1** a deep bowl. **2** a washbasin. **3** an enclosed area of water. **4** the area from which water drains into a river, *the Amazon basin.*

basis *noun* (*plural* **bases**) something to start from or add to; the main principle or ingredient. [same origin as *base*[1]]

bask *verb* sit or lie comfortably warming yourself.

basket *noun* a container for holding or carrying things, made of interwoven strips of flexible material or wire.

basketball *noun* **1** an indoor game in which goals are scored by throwing the ball through a raised hoop. **2** the ball used in this game.

basking shark a shark that lies near the surface of the water.

bass[1] (*say* bayss) *adjective* deep-sounding; of the lowest notes in music.

bass[1] *noun* (*plural* **basses**) **1** a male singer with a very deep voice. **2** a bass instrument or part. [from *base*[1]]

bass[2] (*say* bas) *noun* (*plural* **bass**) a kind of fish especially one with spiny fins.

basset *noun* a short-legged dog used for hunting hares. [from French *bas* = low]

bassoon *noun* a bass woodwind instrument.

bastard *noun* **1** (*old use*) an illegitimate child. **2** (*slang*) a person, *lucky bastard!* **3** (*slang*) an unpleasant or difficult person or thing. **bastardy** *noun*

baste *verb* (**basted**, **basting**) **1** moisten meat with fat while it is cooking. **2** tack material or a hem.

bastion *noun* **1** a projecting part of a fortified building. **2** a centre of support for a cause.

bat[1] *noun* **1** a wooden implement used to hit the bail in cricket, softball, etc. **2** a batsman or batswoman, *their opening bat.*
off your own bat without help from other people.

bat[1] *verb* (**batted**, **batting**) **1** use a bat in cricket etc. **2** hit.

bat[2] *noun* a flying animal that looks like a mouse with wings.

batch *noun* (*plural* **batches**) a set of things or people dealt with together.

bated *adjective* **with bated breath** anxiously; hardly daring to speak. [from *abate*]

bath *noun* **1** washing your whole body while sitting in water. **2** a large container for water in which to wash your whole body; this water, *Your bath is getting cold.* **3** a liquid in which something is placed, *an acid bath.*

bath *verb* wash in a bath.

bathe *verb* (**bathed**, **bathing**) **1** go swimming. **2** wash something gently. **bathe** *noun*, **bather** *noun*

bathroom *noun* **1** a room containing a bath. **2** a room with a toilet.

baths *plural noun* **1** a building with rooms where people can bathe. **2** a public swimming-bath.

batik *noun* **1** a method of printing coloured designs on cotton etc. by waxing the parts that are not to be dyed. **2** the fabric treated in this way.

baton *noun* a short stick, e.g. one used to conduct an orchestra.

batsman *noun* (*plural* **batsmen**) *noun* a player who uses a bat in cricket etc. **batswoman** *noun* (*plural* **batswomen**)

battalion *noun* an army unit containing two or more companies. [from Italian *battaglia* = battle]

batten[1] *noun* **1** a strip of wood or metal holding something in place. **2** the upright part of a fence that is not fixed in the ground but is used to keep the wires an equal distance apart.

batten[1] *verb* fasten with battens.

batten[2] *verb* feed or grow fat on something, *Pigeons battened on the crops.*

batter *verb* hit hard and often.

batter *noun* **1** a beaten mixture of flour, eggs, and milk, used for making pancakes etc. **2** a batsman or batswoman in cricket, softball, etc. [from Latin *battuere* = to beat]

battering-ram *noun* a heavy pole used to break down walls or gates.

battery *noun* (*plural* **batteries**) **1** a portable device for storing and supplying electricity. **2** a set of similar pieces of equipment; a group of large guns. **3** a series of cages in which poultry or animals are kept close together. [same origin as *batter*]

battle *noun* **1** a fight between large organised forces. **2** a struggle. **battlefield** *noun*, **battleground** *noun*

battle *verb* (**battled**, **battling**) fight; struggle. [same origin as *batter*]

battlements *plural noun* the top of a castle wall, often with gaps from which the defenders could fire at the enemy.

battler *noun* a person who struggles against great difficulties.

battleship *noun* a heavily armed warship.

batty *adjective* (*slang*) crazy. [from *bat*[2]]

bauble *noun* a showy but valueless thing.

baulk *verb* **1** shirk or jib at something; stop and refuse to go on, *The horse baulked at the fence.* **2** frustrate; prevent from doing or getting something.

bauxite *noun* the clay-like substance from which aluminium is obtained.

bawdy *adjective* (**bawdier**, **bawdiest**) funny but vulgar. **bawdiness** *noun*

bawl *verb* **1** shout. **2** cry noisily.

bay[1] *noun* **1** a place where the shore curves inwards. **2** an alcove.
bay window a window projecting from the main wall of a house.

bay[2] *noun* a kind of laurel-tree.
bay-leaf *noun* its leaf, used in cooking.

bay[3] *noun* the long deep cry of a hunting hound or other large dog.
at bay cornered but defiantly facing attackers, *a stag at bay*; prevented from coming near or causing harm, *We need laws to keep poverty at bay.*

bay[4] *adjective* reddish-brown.

bayonet *noun* a stabbing-blade attached to a rifle. [named after *Bayonne* in France, where it was first used]

bazaar *noun* **1** a set of shops or stalls in an oriental country. **2** a sale to raise money for a charity etc. [from Persian *bazar*]

bazooka *noun* a portable weapon for firing anti-tank rockets. [the word originally meant a musical instrument rather like a trombone]

BBC *abbreviation* British Broadcasting Corporation.

BC *abbreviation* before Christ (used of dates reckoned back from the birth of Jesus Christ).

be *verb* (**am**, **are**, **is**; **was**, **were**; **been**, **being**) **1** exist; occupy a position, *The shop is on the corner.* **2** happen; take place, *The wedding is tomorrow.* This verb is also used (**1**) to join subject and predicate (*He is my teacher*). (**2**) to form parts of other verbs (*It is raining. He was killed*).
have been have gone or come as a visitor etc., *We have been to Rome.*

be- *prefix* used to form verbs (as in befriend, belittle) or strengthen their meaning (as in begrudge).

beach *noun* (*plural* **beaches**) the part of the sea-shore nearest to the water.

beachcomber *noun* a person who searches beaches for objects of value.

beacon *noun* a light (or formerly a fire) used as a signal.

bead *noun* **1** a small piece of a hard substance with a hole in it for threading with others on a string or wire, e.g. to make a necklace. **2** a drop of liquid.

beady *adjective* like beads; small and bright, *beady eyes.*

beagle *noun* a small hound used for hunting hares.

beak *noun* the hard horny part of a bird's mouth.

beaker *noun* **1** a tall drinking-mug, often without a handle. **2** a glass container used for pouring liquids in a laboratory.

beam *noun* **1** a long thick bar of wood or metal. **2** a ray or stream of light or other radiation. **3** a bright look on someone's face; a happy smile.

beam *verb* **1** smile happily. **2** send out a beam of light or other radiation.

bean *noun* **1** a kind of plant with seeds growing in pods. **2** its seed or pod eaten as food. **3** the seed of coffee etc.

bear[1] *noun* a large heavy animal with thick fur.

bear[2] *verb* (**bore**, **borne**, **bearing**) **1** carry; support. **2** have a mark etc., *She still bears the scar.* **3** endure; tolerate, *I can't bear this pain.* **4** produce; give birth to, *She bore him two sons.* **bearer** *noun*

bearable *adjective* able to be borne; tolerable.

beard *noun* hair on a man's chin. **bearded** *adjective*

beard *verb* come face to face with a person and challenge him or her boldly.

beardie *noun* a kind of long-haired collie dog.

bearing *noun* **1** the way a person stands, walks, behaves, etc. **2** relevance, *It has no bearing on this problem.* **3** the direction or position of one thing in relation to another. **4** a device for preventing friction in a machine, *ball-bearings.*
get your bearings work out where you are in relation to things.

beast *noun* **1** any large four-footed animal. **2** (*informal*) a person you dislike. **beastly** *adjective*

beat *verb* (**beat**, **beaten**, **beating**) **1** hit often, especially with a stick. **2** shape or flatten something by beating it. **3** stir vigorously. **4** make repeated movements, *The heart beats.* **5** do better than somebody; overcome. **beater** *noun*

beat *noun* **1** a regular rhythm or stroke, *the beat of your heart.* **2** emphasis in rhythm; the strong rhythm of pop music. **3** a policeman's regular route. **4** (*NZ*) an area covered by a musterer of sheep, *a lambing beat.* **5** (*Yachting*) a course sailed to windward.

beatific (*say* bee-a-**tif**-ik) *adjective* showing great happiness, *a beatific smile.*

beatify (*say* bee-**at**-i-fy) *verb* (**beatified**, **beatifying**) (in the Roman Catholic Church) honour a person who has died by declaring that he or she is among the blessed, as a step towards declaring that person a saint. **beatification** *noun* [from Latin *beatus* = blessed]

Beaufort scale a scale that measures wind speeds.

beaut *noun* (*NZ, slang*) an excellent person or thing, *you beaut!*

beaut *adjective* (*NZ, slang*) excellent, *beaut day!*

beautiful *adjective* having beauty. **beautifully** *adverb*

beautify *verb* (**beautified**, **beautifying**) make beautiful. **beautification** *noun*

beauty *noun* (*plural* **beauties**) **1** a quality that gives pleasure to your senses or your mind. **2** a person or thing that has beauty.

beaver *noun* an amphibious animal with soft brown fur and strong teeth.

beaver *verb* work hard, *beavering away.*

becalmed *adjective* (in sailing) unable to move because there is no wind.

because *conjunction* for the reason that.
because of for the reason of, *He limped because of his bad leg.*

beck *noun* **at someone's beck and call** always ready and waiting to do what he or she asks. [from *beckon*]

beckon *verb* make a sign to a person asking him or her to come.

become *verb* (**became**, **become**, **becoming**) **1** come or grow to be; start being, *It became dark.* **2** be suitable for; make a person look attractive.
become of happen to, *What became of it?*

bed *noun* **1** a thing to sleep or rest on; a piece of furniture with a mattress and coverings. **2** a piece of a garden where plants are grown. **3** the bottom of the sea or of a river. **4** a flat base; a foundation. **5** a layer of rock or soil.

bedclothes *plural noun* sheets, blankets, etc.

bedding *noun* mattresses and bedclothes.

bedlam *noun* uproar. [from 'Bedlam', the popular name of the Hospital of St Mary of Bethlehem, a London mental hospital in the 14th century]

Bedouin (*say* **bed**-oo-in) *noun* (*plural* **Bedouin**) a member of an Arab people living in tents in the desert. [from Arabic *badawi* = desert-dweller]

bedpan *noun* a container for use as a toilet by a bedridden person.

bedraggled (*say* bid-**rag**-eld) *adjective* very untidy; wet and dirty.

bedridden *adjective* too weak to get out of bed.

bedrock *noun* solid rock beneath soil.

bedroom *noun* a room for sleeping in.

bedspread *noun* a covering spread over a bed during the day.

bedstead *noun* the framework of a bed.

bedtime *noun* the time for going to bed.

bee *noun* a stinging insect with four wings that makes honey.

beech *noun* (*plural* **beeches**) a tree with smooth bark and glossy leaves.

beef *noun* meat from an ox, bull, or cow.

beefy *adjective* having a solid muscular body.
beefiness *noun*

beehive *noun* a box or other container for bees to live in.
the Beehive a large dome-shaped annex to the New Zealand parliament building.

beeline *noun* **make a beeline for** go straight or quickly towards something.

beer *noun* an alcoholic drink made from malt and hops. **beery** *adjective*

beeswax *noun* a yellow substance produced by bees, used for polishing wood.

beet *noun* (*plural* **beet** or **beets**) a plant with a thick root used as a vegetable or for making sugar.

beetle *noun* an insect with hard shiny wing-covers.

beetling *adjective* prominent; overhanging, *beetling brows.*

beetroot *noun* (*plural* **beetroot**) the crimson root of beet used as a vegetable.

befall *verb* (**befell**, **befallen**, **befalling**) (*formal*) happen; happen to someone.

befitting *adjective* suitable.

before *adverb* at an earlier time, *Have you been here before?*

before *preposition & conjunction* **1** earlier than, *I was here before you!* **2** ahead of; in front of, *leg before wicket.*

beforehand *adverb* earlier; in readiness.

befriend *verb* act as a friend to someone.

beg *verb* (**begged**, **begging**) **1** ask to be given money, food, etc. **2** ask earnestly or humbly or formally.
go begging be available.
I beg your pardon I apologise; I did not hear what you said.

beget *verb* (**begot**, **begotten**, **begetting**) (*old use*) **1** be the father of someone. **2** produce, *War begets misery.*

beggar *noun* **1** a person who lives by begging. **2** (*informal*) a person, *You lucky beggar!*
beggary *noun*

begin *verb* (**began**, **begun**, **beginning**) **1** do the earliest or first part of something; start speaking. **2** come into existence, *The problem began last year.* **3** have something as its first element, *The word begins with B.*

beginner *noun* a person who is just beginning to learn a subject.

begone *verb* (*old use*) go away immediately, *Begone dull care!*

begonia (*say* big-**oh**-nee-a) *noun* a garden plant with brightly coloured flowers.

begot *past tense* of beget.

begrudge *verb* (**begrudged**, **begrudging**) grudge.

beguile (*say* big-**I'll**) *verb* (**beguiled**, **beguiling**) **1** amuse. **2** deceive.

behalf *noun* **on behalf of** for a person; done to help a person or charity etc.
on my behalf for me.

behave *verb* (**behaved**, **behaving**) **1** act in a particular way, *They behaved badly.* **2** show good manners, *Behave yourself!*
behaviour *noun*, **behavioural** *adjective*

behead *verb* cut the head from; execute a person in this way.

behest *noun* (*formal*) a command.

behind *adverb* **1** at or to the back; at a place people have left, *Don't leave it behind.* **2** not making good progress; late, *I'm behind with my rent.*
get in behind! (*NZ*) (to a dog) come to heel; (to a person) behave.

behind *preposition* **1** at or to the back of; on the further side of. **2** having made less progress than, *He is behind the others in French.* **3** supporting; causing, *What is behind all this trouble?*
behind a person's back kept secret from him or her deceitfully.
behind the times out of date.

behind *noun* (*informal*) a person's bottom.

behold *verb* (**beheld**, **beholding**) (*old use*) see. **beholder** *noun*

beholden *adjective* owing thanks; indebted, *We are greatly beholden to you.*

behove *verb* (**behoved**, **behaving**) (*formal*) be a person's duty, *It behoves you to be loyal.*

beige (*say* bay*zh*) *noun & adjective* light fawn colour.

being *noun* **1** existence. **2** a creature.

belated *adjective* coming very late or too late. **belatedly** *adverb*

belay *verb* (**belayed**, **belaying**) fasten a rope by winding it round a peg or spike.

belch *verb* **1** send out wind from your stomach through your mouth noisily. **2** send out fire or smoke etc. from an opening. **belch** *noun*

beleaguered (*say* bil-**eeg**-erd) *adjective* besieged; oppressed. [from Dutch *belegeren* = camp round]

belfry *noun* (*plural* **belfries**) a tower or part of a tower in which bells hang.

belief *noun* **1** believing. **2** something a person believes.

believe *verb* (**believed**, **believing**) think that something is true or that someone is telling the truth. **believable** *adjective*, **believer** *noun*
believe in think that something exists or is good or can be relied on.

belittle *verb* (**belittled**, **belittling**) make something seem of little value. *Do not belittle their success.* **belittlement** *noun*

bell *noun* **1** a cup-shaped metal instrument that makes a ringing sound when struck by the clapper hanging inside it; any device that makes a ringing or buzzing sound to attract attention. **2** a bell-shaped object.

belladonna *noun* deadly nightshade.
belladonna lily a kind of flower with white or pink flowers.

bellbird *noun* (*NZ*) a bird with a clear ringing note, the makomako.

belle *noun* a beautiful woman. [French]

bellicose (*say* **bel**-ik-ohs) *adjective* eager to fight. [from Latin *bellum* = war]

belligerent (*say* bil-**ij**-er-ent) *adjective* **1** aggressive; eager to fight. **2** fighting; engaged in a war. **belligerently** *adverb*, **belligerence** *noun* [from Latin *bellum* = war, *gerens* = waging]

bellow *noun* **1** the loud deep sound made by a bull or other large animal. **2** a deep shout.

bellow *verb* give a bellow; shout.

bellows *plural noun* a device for pumping air into a fire, organ-pipes. etc.

belly *noun* (*plural* **bellies**) the abdomen; the stomach.

belong *verb* have a proper place, *The pans belong in the kitchen.*
belong to be the property of; be a member of, *We belong to the same club.*

belongings *plural noun* a person's possessions.

beloved *adjective* dearly loved.

below *adverb* at or to a lower position; underneath, *There's fire down below.*

below *preposition* lower than; under, *The temperature was ten degrees below zero.*

belt *noun* **1** a strip of cloth or leather etc. worn round the waist. **2** a band of flexible material used in machinery. **3** a long narrow area, *a belt of rain.*

belt *verb* **1** put a belt round something. **2** (*slang*) hit. **3** (*slang*) rush along.

bemused *adjective* **1** bewildered. **2** lost in thought.

bench *noun* (*plural* **benches**) **1** a long seat. **2** a long table for working at. **3** the seat where judges sit; the judges hearing a lawsuit.

benchmark *noun* a required or standard measurement or level. *Full attendance is the benchmark that we aim for.*

bend[1] *verb* (**bent**, **bending**) **1** change from being straight. **2** turn downwards; stoop, *She bent to pick it up.*

bend[1] *noun* a place where something bends; a curve or turn.

bend[2] *noun* a kind of knot.

bene- (*say* **ben**-ee) *prefix* well (as in *benefit*, *benevolent*). [from Latin *bene* = well]

beneath *preposition* **1** under. **2** unworthy of. *Cheating is beneath you.*

beneath *adverb* underneath.

benediction *noun* a blessing. [from *bene-*, + Latin *dicere* = to say]

benefactor *noun* a person who gives money or other help. [from *bene-*, + Latin *factor* = doer]

beneficial *adjective* having a good or helpful effect; advantageous.

beneficiary (*say* ben-if-**ish**-er-ee) *noun* (*plural* **beneficiaries**) **1** a person who receives benefits from a will. **2** a person who receives payment from the government while sick, unemployed, etc.

benefit *noun* **1** something that is helpful or profitable. **2** a payment to which a person is entitled from government funds or from an insurance policy.

benefit *verb* (**benefited**, **benefiting**) **1** do good to a person or thing. **2** receive a benefit. [from *bene-*, + Latin *facere* = do]

benevolent *adjective* **1** kind and helpful. **2** formed for charitable purposes, *a benevolent fund.* **benevolently** *adverb*, **benevolence** *noun* [from *bene-*, + Latin *volens* = wishing]

benign (*say* bin-**I'n**) *adjective* **1** kindly. **2** favourable. **3** (of a disease) mild, not malignant. **benignly** *adverb* [from Latin *benignus* = kind-hearted]

benignant (*say* bin-**ig**-nant) *adjective* kindly.

benison *noun* (*old use*) a blessing.

bent *adjective* curved; crooked.
bent on intending to do something.

bent *noun* a talent for something.

benzene *noun* a substance obtained from coal tar and used as a solvent, motor fuel, and in the manufacture of plastics.

benzine *noun* a spirit obtained from petroleum and used in dry cleaning.

bequeath *verb* leave something to a person, especially in a will.

bequest *noun* something bequeathed.

bereaved *adjective* deprived of a relative or friend who has died. **bereavement** *noun* [from *reave* = take forcibly]

bereft *adjective* deprived of something.

beret (*say* **bair**-ay) *noun* a round flat cap.

beriberi (*say as* berry-berry) *noun* a disease caused by a vitamin deficiency. [from a Sinhalese word]

berm *noun* (*NZ*) a grass verge between street and footpath in a residential area.

berry *noun* (*plural* **berries**) any small round juicy fruit without a stone.

berserk (*say* ber-**serk**) *adjective* **go berserk** become uncontrollably violent. [from Icelandic *berserkr* = wild warrior (*ber-* = bear, *serkr* = coat)]

berth *noun* **1** a sleeping-place on a ship or train. **2** a place where a ship can moor.
give a wide berth keep at a safe distance from a person or thing.

berth *verb* moor in a berth.

beryl *noun* a pale-green precious stone.

beseech *verb* (**besought**, **beseeching**) ask earnestly; implore. [from *be-* + *seek*]

beset *verb* (**beset**, **besetting**) surround, *They are beset with problems.*

beside *preposition* **1** by the side of; near. **2** compared with.
be beside himself or **herself** etc. be very excited or upset.

besides *preposition & adverb* in addition to; also, *Who came besides you? And besides, it's the wrong colour.*

besiege *verb* (**besieged**, **besieging**) **1** surround a place with troops in order to capture it. **2** crowd round, *Fans besieged the pop star after the concert.*

besotted *adjective* infatuated.

besought *past tense of* **beseech**.

best *adjective* most excellent.
best man the bridegroom's chief attendant at a wedding.

best *adverb* **1** in the best way; most. **2** most usefully; most wisely, *We had best go.*

bestial (*say* **best**-ee-al) *adjective* of or like a beast; cruel. **bestiality** *noun* [from Latin *bestia* = beast]

bestow *verb* present. **bestowal** *noun*

bet *noun* **1** an agreement that you will pay money etc. if you are wrong in forecasting the result of a race etc. **2** the money that you agree to pay in this way.

bet *verb* (**bet** or **betted**, **betting**) **1** make a bet. **2** (*informal*) think most likely; predict, *I bet he will forget.*

beta (*say* **beet**-a) *noun* the second letter of the Greek alphabet, = b.

betide *verb* **woe betide you** trouble will come to you. [from *be-*, + an old word *tide* = befall]

betoken *verb* be a sign of.

betray *verb* **1** be disloyal to a person or country etc. **2** reveal something that should have been kept secret. **betrayal** *noun*, **betrayer** *noun* [from *be-*, + Latin *tradere* = hand over]

betrothed *adjective* (*formal*) engaged to be married. **betroth** *verb*, **betrothal** *noun*

better *adjective* **1** more excellent; more satisfactory. **2** recovered from illness.

better *adverb* **1** in a better way; more. **2** more usefully; more wisely, *We had better go.*

better *verb* **1** improve something. **2** do better than. **betterment** *noun*

between *preposition & adverb* **1** within two or more given limits, *between the walls.* **2** connecting two or more people, places, or things, *The train runs between Christchurch* *and Greymouth.* **3** shared by, *Divide this money between you.* **4** separating; comparing, *Can you tell the difference between them?*

> USAGE The preposition *between* needs the object form of a pronoun (*me, her, him, them,* or *us*) after it. The expression 'between you and I' is incorrect; say *between you and me.*

betwixt *preposition & adverb* (*old use*) between.

bevel *verb* (**bevelled**, **bevelling**) give a sloping edge to something.

beverage *noun* any kind of drink.

bevy *noun* (*plural* **bevies**) a large group.

bewail *verb* mourn for something.

beware *verb* be careful, *Beware of pick-pockets.* [from *be-*, + *ware* = wary]

bewilder *verb* puzzle someone hopelessly. **bewilderment** *noun* [from *be-*, + an old word *wilder* = lose your way]

bewitch *verb* **1** put a magic spell on someone. **2** delight someone very much.

beyond *preposition & adverb* **1** further than; further on, *Don't go beyond the boundary.* **2** outside the range of; too difficult for, *The problem is beyond me.*

bi- *prefix* two (as in *bicycle*); twice (as in *biannual*). [from Latin *bis* = twice]

biannual *adjective* happening twice a year. **biannually** *adverb.*

> USAGE Do not confuse this word with *biennial.*

bias *noun* (*plural* **biases**) **1** a feeling or influence for or against someone or something; a prejudice. **2** a tendency to swerve. **3** a slanting direction. **biased** *adjective*

bib *noun* **1** a cloth or covering put under a baby's chin during meals. **2** the part of an apron above the waist.

Bible *noun* the sacred book of the Jews (the Old Testament) and of the Christians (the Old and New Testament). [from Greek *biblia* = books (originally = rolls of papyrus from Byblos, a port now in Lebanon)]

biblical *adjective* of or in the Bible.

bibliography (*say* bib-lee-**og**-ra-fee) *noun* (*plural* **bibliographies**) **1** a list of books about a subject or by a particular author. **2** the study of books and their history. **bibliographical** *adjective* [from Greek *biblion* = book, + *-graphy*]

bicarbonate *noun* a kind of carbonate.

bicentenary (*say* by-sen-**teen**-er-ee) *noun* a 200th anniversary. **bicentennial** (*say* by-sen-**ten**-ee-al) *adjective*

biceps (*say* **by**-seps) *noun* the large muscle at the front of the arm above the elbow. [Latin, = two-headed (because its end is attached at two points)]

bicker *verb* quarrel over unimportant things; squabble.

bicultural *adjective* combining two distinct cultures. **biculturalism** *noun*

bicuspid *noun* a tooth with two points. [from *bi-*, + Latin *cuspis* = sharp point]

bicycle *noun* a two-wheeled vehicle driven by pedals. **bicyclist** *noun*

bid[1] *noun* **1** the offer of an amount you are willing to pay for something, especially at an auction. **2** an attempt.

bid[1] *verb* (**bid**, **bidding**) make a bid. **bidder** *noun*

bid[2] *verb* (**bid** (or *old use* **bade**), **bid** or **bidden**, **bidding**) **1** command, *Do as you are bid* or *bidden.* **2** say as a greeting or farewell, *bidding them good night.*

bidding *noun* a command.

biddy-bid *noun* (also **biddy-biddy** or **bidibidi**) a New Zealand plant with prickly brown burrs. [from Māori *piripiri*]

bide *verb* (**bided**, **biding**) wait.

biennial (*say* by-**en**-ee-al) *adjective* **1** lasting for two years. **2** happening every second year. **biennially** *adverb*

biennial *noun* a plant that lives for two years, flowering and dying in the second year. [from *bi-*, + Latin *annus* = year]

bier (*say as* beer) *noun* a movable stand on which a coffin or a dead body is placed before it is buried.

biff *verb* (*slang*) **1** strike. **2** throw. **biff** *noun*

biffo *noun* (*slang*) aggression or body contact.

bifocal (*say* by-**foh**-kal) *adjective* (of spectacle lenses) made in two sections, with the upper part for looking at distant objects and the lower part for reading.

bifocals *plural noun* bifocal spectacles.

big *adjective* (**bigger**, **biggest**) **1** large. **2** important, *the big match.* **3** more grown-up; elder, *my big sister.*
the Big Smoke (*NZ*) the city.

bigamy (*say* **big**-a-mee) *noun* the crime of marrying a person when you are already married to someone else. **bigamous** *adjective*, **bigamist** *noun* [from *bi-*, + Greek *gamos* = marriage]

bight *noun* **1** a long inward curve in a coast, *the Canterbury Bight.* **2** a loop of rope.

bigot *noun* a bigoted person.

bigoted *adjective* narrow-minded and intolerant. **bigotry** *noun*

bike *noun* (*informal*) a bicycle or motor cycle.
don't get off your bike calm down.
get on one's bike leave, move on.

biker *noun* a cyclist or motorcyclist.

bikie *noun* (*NZ, informal*) a member of a gang of motor-cyclists.

bikini *noun* (*plural* **bikinis**) a woman's very small two-piece swim-suit. [named after the island of Bikini in the Pacific Ocean, which was laid bare by an atomic bomb test in 1946]

bilateral *adjective* **1** of or on two sides. **2** of two people or groups, *a bilateral agreement.* [from *bi-* + *lateral*]

bile *noun* a bitter liquid produced by the liver, helping to digest fats.

bilge *noun* **1** the bottom of a ship; the water that collects there. **2** (*slang*) nonsense; worthless ideas.

bilingual (*say* by-**ling**-wal) *adjective* **1** written in two languages. **2** able to speak two languages. [from *bi-*, + Latin *lingua* = language]

bilious *adjective* feeling sick; sickly. **biliousness** *noun* [from *bile*]

bilk *verb* cheat someone by not paying them what you owe; defraud.

bill[1] *noun* **1** a written statement of charges for goods or services that have been supplied. **2** a poster. **3** a list; a programme of entertainment. **4** the draft of a proposed law to be discussed by Parliament. **5** (*American*) a banknote.
bill of fare a menu.

bill[2] *noun* a bird's beak.

billabong *noun* (in Australia) a backwater.

billet *noun* a lodging for troops, especially in a private house.

billet *verb* (**billeted**, **billeting**) house someone in a billet.

billhook *noun* a tool with a hooked blade, used for pruning trees etc.

billiards *noun* a game in which three balls are struck with cues on a cloth-covered table (**billiard-table**). [from French *billard* = cue]

billion *noun* **1** a thousand million (1,000,000,000). **2** (*old use*) a million million (1,000,000,000,000). **billionth** *adjective & noun.* [from *bi-* + *million*]

billow *noun* a huge wave.

billow *verb* rise or roll like waves.

billy *noun* (*plural* **billies**) a pot with a lid, used by campers etc. as a kettle or cooking-pot. **billycan** *noun*

billy-goat *noun* a male goat. (Compare *nanny-goat.*) [from the name *Billy*]

bin *noun* a large or deep container.

binary (*say* **by**-ner-ee) *adjective* involving sets of two; consisting of two parts.
binary digit either of the two digits (0 and 1) used in the system of numbers known as binary notation or the binary scale. [from Latin *binarius* = two together]

bind *verb* (**bound**, **binding**) **1** fasten material round something. **2** fasten the pages of a book into a cover. **3** tie up; tie together. **4** make somebody agree to do something; oblige. **binder** *noun*
bind a person over make him or her agree not to break the law.

bind *noun* (*slang*) a nuisance; a bore.

bine *noun* the flexible stem of the hop plant.

binge *noun* (*slang*) a bout of excessive eating, drinking, etc.

bingo *noun* housie.

binoculars *plural noun* a device with lenses for both eyes, making distant objects seem nearer. [from Latin *bini* = two together, + *oculus* = eye]

bio- *prefix* life (as in *biology*). [from Greek *bios* = life]

biochemistry *noun* the study of the chemical composition and processes of living things. **biochemical** *adjective*, **biochemist** *noun*

biodegradable *adjective* able to be broken down by bacteria in the environment.

biography (*say* by-**og**-ra-fee) *noun* the story of a person's life. **biographical** *adjective*, **biographer** *noun* [from *bio-* + *-graphy*]

biology *noun* the study of the life and structure of living things. **biological** *adjective*, **biologist** *noun* [from *bio-* + *-logy*]

bionic (*say* by-**on**-ik) *adjective* (of a person or parts of the body) operated by electronic devices. [from *bio-* + electro*nic*]

biopsy (*say* **by**-op-see) *noun* (*plural* **biopsies**) examination of tissue from a living body. [from *bio-* + auto*psy*]

bipartite *adjective* having two parts; involving two groups, *a bipartite agreement.*

biped (*say* **by**-ped) *noun* a two-footed animal. [from *bi-*, + Latin *pedis* = of a foot]

biplane *noun* an aeroplane with two sets of wings, one above the other.

birch *noun* (*plural* **birches**) **1** a deciduous tree with slender branches. **2** (*NZ*) a beech tree. **3** a bundle of birch branches for flogging people.

bird *noun* **1** an animal with feathers, two wings, and two legs. **2** (*slang*) a person. **3** (*slang*) a young woman.
bird's-eye view a view from above.

bird-cage *noun* **1** a cage for keeping birds. **2** (*NZ*) the enclosure where horses are paraded before a race.

birdie *noun* **1** (*informal*) a bird. **2** a score of one stroke under par for a hole at golf.

birl see **burl**.

biro *noun* (*plural* **biros**) (*trade mark*) a kind of ball-point pen. [named after its Hungarian inventor L. Biro]

birth *noun* **1** the process by which a baby or young animal comes out from its mother's body. **2** origin; parentage, *He is of noble birth.*
birth control ways of avoiding conceiving a baby.
birth rate the number of children born in one year for every 1,000 people.

birthday *noun* the anniversary of the day a person was born.

birthmark *noun* a coloured mark that has been on a person's skin since birth.

birthright *noun* a right or privilege to which a person is entitled through being born into a particular family (especially as the eldest son) or country.

biscuit *noun* a small flat piece of pastry baked crisp. [from Latin *bis* = twice, + *coctus* = cooked]

bisect (*say* by-**sekt**) *verb* divide into two equal parts. **bisection** *noun*, **bisector** *noun* [from *bi-*, + Latin *sectum* = cut]

bishop *noun* **1** an important member of the clergy in charge of all the churches in a city or district. **2** a chess piece shaped like a bishop's mitre.

bishopric *noun* the position or diocese of a bishop.

bismuth *noun* **1** a greyish-white metal. **2** a compound of this used in medicine.

bison (*say* **by**-son) *noun* (*plural* **bison**) a wild ox found in North America and Europe, with a large shaggy head.

bit[1] *noun* **1** a small piece or amount of something. **2** the metal part of a horse's bridle that is put into its mouth. **3** the part of a tool that cuts or grips things when twisted.
a bit a short distance or time, *Wait a bit*; slightly, *I'm a bit worried.*
bit by bit gradually.

bit[2] *past tense* of **bite**.

bit[3] *noun* (in computers) a unit of information expressed as a choice between two possibilities. [from *bi*nary digi*t*]

bitch *noun* (*plural* **bitches**) **1** a female dog, fox, or wolf. **2** (*informal*) a spiteful woman.
bitchy *adjective*

bite *verb* (**bit**, **bitten**, **biting**) **1** cut or take with your teeth. **2** penetrate; sting. **3** accept bait, *The fish are biting.*
bite the dust fall wounded and die.

bite *noun* **1** biting. **2** a mark or spot made by biting, *an insect bite.* **3** a snack.

bitmap *noun* any visible picture on a webpage, usually composed of dots or pixels.

bitter *adjective* **1** tasting sharp, not sweet. **2** feeling or causing mental pain or resentment, *a bitter disappointment.* **3** very cold. **bitterly** *adverb*, **bitterness** *noun*

bittern *noun* a marsh bird, the male of which makes a booming cry.

bitumen (*say* **bit**-yoo-min) *noun* a black substance used for covering roads etc.
bituminous (*say* bit-**yoo**-min-us) *adjective*

bivalve *noun* a shellfish (e.g. an oyster) that has a shell with two hinged parts.

bivouac (*say* **biv**-oo-ak) *noun* a temporary camp without tents; a temporary shelter.

bivouac *verb* (**bivouacked**, **bivouacking**) camp in a bivouac.

bivvy *noun* (*plural* **bivvies**) (*slang*) a bivouac.

bizarre (*say* biz-**ar**) *adjective* very odd in appearance or effect.

blab *verb* (**blabbed**, **blabbing**) tell tales; let out a secret.

Black *noun* a person with a very dark or black skin. **Black** *adjective*
Black Power a movement seeking rights and political power for Blacks; the name of a Māori gang.

black *noun* the very darkest colour, like coal or soot.

black *adjective* **1** of the colour black. **2** very dirty. **3** dismal; not hopeful, *The outlook is black.* **4** hostile; disapproving, *He gave me a black look.* **blackly** *adverb*, **blackness** *noun*
Black Cap a New Zealand national men's cricket representative.
black coffee coffee without milk.
black eye an eye with a bruise round it.
Black Fern a New Zealand national women's rugby union representative.
black hole a region in outer space with such a strong gravitational field that no matter or radiation can escape from it.
black magic evil magic.
black market illegal trading.
black pine a New Zealand tree, the mataī.
black robin a very rare New Zealand bird.
black sand black ironsands.
black sheep one bad character in a well-behaved group.
Black Sox a New Zealand national men's softball team.
black spot a dangerous place.
Black Stick a New Zealand national men's or women's hockey representative.

black *verb* make a thing black.
black out cover windows etc. so that no light can penetrate; faint, lose consciousness. **black-out** *noun*

blackball[1] *noun* (*NZ*) a round black and white striped boiled sweet.

blackball[2] *verb* exclude or reject a person or idea.

blackberry *noun* (*plural* **blackberries**) a sweet black berry.

blackbird *noun* a European songbird, the male of which is black.

blackboard *noun* a dark board for writing on with chalk.

blacken *verb* make or become black.

blackguard (*say* **blag**-ard) *noun* a scoundrel.

blackhead *noun* a small black spot in the skin.

blackleg *noun* a person who works while fellow workers are on strike.

blacklist *verb* put someone on a list of those who are disapproved of.

blackmail *verb* demand money etc. from someone by threats. **blackmail** *noun*, **blackmailer** *noun*

blacksmith *noun* a person who makes and repairs iron things, especially one who makes and fits horseshoes.

bladder *noun* **1** the bag-like part of the body in which urine collects. **2** the inflatable bag inside a football.

blade *noun* **1** the flat cutting-part of a knife, sword, axe, etc. **2** the flat wide part of an oar, spade, propeller, etc. **3** a flat narrow leaf, *blades of grass.* **4** a broad flat bone, *shoulder-blade.*

blame *verb* (**blamed**, **blaming**) **1** say that somebody or something has caused what is wrong, *They blamed me.* **2** find fault with someone, *We can't blame them for wanting a holiday.*

blame *noun* blaming; responsibility for what is wrong.

blameless *adjective* deserving no blame; innocent.

blanch *verb* make or become white or pale, *He blanched with fear.*

blancmange (*say* bla-**monj**) *noun* a jelly-like pudding made with milk. [from French *blanc* = white, + *mange* = eat]

bland *adjective* **1** having a mild flavour not a strong one. **2** gentle and casual; not irritating or stimulating, *a bland manner.* **blandly** *adverb*, **blandness** *noun* [from Latin *blandus* = soothing]

blandishments *plural noun* flattering or coaxing words. [same origin as *bland*]

blank *adjective* **1** not written or printed on; unmarked. **2** without interest or expression, *a blank look.* **3** without an opening, *a blank wall.* **blankly** *adverb*, **blankness** *noun*
blank cartridge a cartridge that makes a noise but does not fire a bullet.
blank cheque a cheque with the amount not yet filled in.
blank verse poetry without rhymes.

blank *noun* **1** an empty space. **2** a blank cartridge. [from French *blanc* = white]

blanket *noun* **1** a warm cloth covering used on a bed etc. **2** any thick soft covering, *a blanket of snow.*

blanket *adjective* covering a wide range of conditions etc., *a blanket agreement.*

blare *verb* (**blared**, **blaring**) make a loud harsh sound. **blare** *noun*

blasé (*say* **blah**-zay) *adjective* bored or unimpressed by things because you are used to them. [French]

blaspheme (*say* blas-**feem**) *verb* (**blasphemed**, **blaspheming**) utter blasphemies. [from Greek *blasphemos* = evil-speaking]

blasphemy (*say* **blas**-fim-ee) *noun* (*plural* **blasphemies**) irreverent talk about sacred things. **blasphemous** *adjective*

blast *noun* **1** a strong rush of wind or air. **2** a loud noise, *the blast of the trumpets.*

blast *verb* blow up with explosives.
blast off launch by the firing of rockets. **blast-off** *noun*

blast-furnace *noun* a furnace for smelting ore, with hot air driven in.

blatant (*say* **blay**-tant) *adjective* very obvious, *a blatant lie.* **blatantly** *adverb* [from an old word meaning 'noisy']

blaze[1] *noun* a very bright flame, fire, or light.

blaze[1] *verb* (**blazed**, **blazing**) **1** burn or shine brightly. **2** show great feeling, *He was blazing with anger.*

blaze[2] *noun* **1** a white mark on an animal's face. **2** a mark chipped in the bark of a tree to show a route.

blaze[2] *verb* (**blazed**, **blazing**) mark a tree or route by cutting blazes.
blaze a trail show the way for others to follow.

blazer *noun* a kind of jacket, often with a badge or in the colours of a school or team etc. [from *blaze*[1]]

bleach *verb* make or become white.

bleach *noun* (*plural* **bleaches**) a substance used to bleach things.

bleak *adjective* **1** bare and cold, *a bleak hillside.* **2** dreary; miserable, *a bleak future.* **bleakly** *adverb*, **bleakness** *noun*

bleary *adjective* watery and not seeing clearly, *bleary eyes.* **blearily** *adverb*

bleat *noun* the cry of a lamb, goat, or calf.

bleat *verb* make a bleat.

bleed *verb* (**bled**, **bleeding**) **1** lose blood. **2** draw blood or fluid from.

bleep *noun* a short high sound used as a signal. **bleep** *verb*

blemish *noun* (*plural* **blemishes**) a flaw; a mark that spoils a thing's appearance. **blemish** *verb*

blench *verb* flinch.

blend *verb* mix smoothly or easily. **blender** *noun*

blend *noun* a mixture.

bless *verb* **1** make sacred or holy. **2** bring God's favour on a person or thing.

blessing *noun* **1** a prayer that blesses a person or thing being blessed. **2** something that people are glad of.

blight *noun* **1** a disease that withers plants. **2** an insect that causes blight. **3** a bad or evil influence.

blight *verb* **1** affect with blight. **2** spoil something.

blind *adjective* **1** without the ability to see. **2** without any thought or understanding, *blind obedience.* **3** (of bulbs) not producing a flower. **4** (in cookery) without a filling, *bake the pastry cases blind.* **5** (of a tube, passage, or road) closed at one end. **blindly** *adverb*, **blindness** *noun*

blind *verb* make a person blind.

blind *noun* **1** a screen for a window. **2** a deception; something used to hide the truth, *His journey was a blind.*

blindfold *verb* cover someone's eyes with a cloth etc.

bling (also **bling bling**) *noun* **1** showy costume jewellery. **2** money.

blink *verb* shut and open your eyes rapidly. **blink** *noun*
on the blink (*slang*) not working properly.

blinkers *plural noun* leather pieces fixed on a bridle to prevent a horse from seeing sideways. **blinkered** *adjective*

blip *noun* **1** an error or problem. **2** a sudden fast pipping sound. **3** a small image of an object on a radar screen.

bliss *noun* perfect happiness. **blissful** *adjective*, **blissfully** *adverb*

blister *noun* a swelling like a bubble, especially on skin. **blister** *verb*

blithe *adjective* casual and carefree. **blithely** *adverb*

blitz *noun* (*plural* **blitzes**) a violent or intensive attack (originally referring to the bombing of London in 1940). **blitz** *verb* [short for German *blitzkrieg* (*blitz* = lightning, *krieg* = war)]

blizzard *noun* a severe snowstorm.

bloated *adjective* swollen by fat, gas, or liquid.

bloater *noun* a salted smoked herring.

blob *noun* a small round mass of something, *blobs of paint.*

bloc *noun* a group of parties or countries who unite to support a particular interest.

block *noun* **1** a solid piece of something. **2** an obstruction. **3** a large building divided into flats or offices. **4** a group of buildings. **5** a large plot of land that people can settle on or develop.
do one's block (*NZ, slang*) become angry.
block letters plain capital letters.

block *verb* obstruct; prevent from moving or being used. **blockage** *noun*

blockade *noun* the blocking of a city or port etc. in order to prevent people and goods from going in or out.

blockade *verb* (**blockaded**, **blockading**) set up a blockade of a place.

blockbuster *noun* something very powerful or successful.

blog *noun* a weblog or Internet-based diary. **blogger** *noun*, **blogging** *noun*, **frogblog** *noun* a New Zealand Green Party weblog.

bloke *noun* (*informal*) a fellow. **blokey** *adjective*, **blokish** *adjective.*

blond or **blonde** *adjective* fair-haired; fair. [from Latin *blondus* = yellow]

blonde *noun* a fair-haired girl or woman.

blood *noun* **1** the red liquid that flows through veins and arteries. **2** family relationship; ancestry, *He is of royal blood.*
blood and bone (*NZ*) a garden fertiliser.
in cold blood deliberately and cruelly.

blood-bath *noun* a massacre.

bloodhound *noun* a large dog formerly used to track people by their scent.

bloodshed *noun* the killing or wounding of people.

bloodshot *adjective* (of eyes) streaked with red.

bloodstock *noun* thoroughbred horses.

bloodthirsty *adjective* eager for bloodshed.

blood-vessel *noun* a tube carrying blood in the body; an artery, vein, or capillary.

bloody *adjective* (**bloodier**, **bloodiest**) **1** blood-stained; with much bloodshed. **2** (*slang*) very great, *a bloody nuisance.*
bloody-minded *adjective* deliberately awkward and not helpful.

bloom *noun* **1** a flower. **2** the fine powder on fresh ripe grapes etc.

bloom *verb* produce flowers.

blooper *noun* (*informal*) an embarrassing mistake.

blossom *noun* a flower or mass of flowers, especially on a fruit-tree.

blossom *verb* **1** produce flowers. **2** develop into something, *She blossomed into a fine singer.*

blot *noun* **1** a spot of ink. **2** a flaw or fault; something ugly, *a blot on the landscape.*

blot *verb* (**blotted**, **blotting**) **1** make a blot or blots on something. **2** dry with blotting-paper.
blot out cross out thickly; obscure, *Fog blotted out the view.*

blotch *noun* (*plural* **blotches**) an untidy patch of colour. **blotchy** *adjective*

blotter *noun* a pad of blotting-paper; a holder for blotting-paper.

blotting-paper *noun* absorbent paper for soaking up ink from writing.

blouse *noun* a garment like a shirt.

blow[1] (**blew**, **blown**, **blowing**) **1** send out a current of air. **2** move in or with a current of air, *His hat blew off.* **3** make or sound something by blowing, *blow bubbles; blow the whistle.* **4** melt with too strong an electric current, *A fuse has blown.* **5** (*slang*) damn, *Blow you!*
blow up inflate; explode; shatter by an explosion.

blow[1] *noun* the action of blowing.

blow[2] *noun* **1** a hard knock or hit. **2** a shock; a disaster.

blowfly *noun* **1** a fly that lays its eggs on meat or on the skin of a living sheep. **2** a bluebottle.

blowlamp *noun* a portable device for directing a very hot flame at something.

blowpipe *noun* a tube for sending out a dart or pellet by blowing.

blubber *noun* the fat of whales.

bludgeon (*say* **bluj**-on) *noun* a short stick with a thickened end, used as a weapon.

bludger *noun* (*NZ, slang*) a person who lives off other people or exploits them.
bludge *verb*

blue *noun* **1** the colour of a cloudless sky. **2** (*NZ, slang*) a mistake. **3** (*NZ, slang*) a fight.
out of the blue unexpectedly.

blue *adjective* **1** of the colour blue. **2** unhappy; depressed. **3** indecent; obscene, *blue films.*
blueness *noun*
blue blood aristocratic family.
blue duck (*NZ*) whio.
blue pointer a kind of shark.

bluebell *noun* a plant with blue bell-shaped flowers.

blueberry *noun* (*plural* **blueberries**) a small blue-black edible berry.

bluebottle *noun* **1** a large bluish fly. **2** a Portuguese man-of-war.

blueprint *noun* a detailed plan.

blues *noun* a slow sad jazz song or tune.
the blues a very sad feeling; depression.

bluestone *noun* (*NZ*) a kind of rock used for building, roads, etc.

bluff[1] *verb* deceive someone, especially by pretending to be able to do something.

bluff[1] *noun* bluffing; a threat that you make but do not intend to carry out. [from Dutch *bluffen* = boast]

bluff[2] *adjective* frank and hearty in manner.
bluffness *noun*

bluff[2] *noun* a cliff with a broad steep front.

bluish *adjective* rather blue.

blunder *noun* a stupid mistake.

blunder *verb* **1** make a blunder. **2** move clumsily and uncertainly.

blunderbuss *noun* an old type of gun that fired many balls in one shot. [from Dutch *donderbus* = thunder-gun]

blunt *adjective* **1** not sharp. **2** speaking in plain terms; straightforward, *a blunt refusal.*
bluntly *adverb*, **bluntness** *noun*

blunt *verb* make a thing blunt.

blur *verb* (**blurred**, **blurring**) make or become indistinct or smeared.

blur *noun* an indistinct appearance; a smear.

blurt *verb* say something suddenly or tactlessly, *He blurted it out.*

blush *verb* become red in the face because you are ashamed or embarrassed.

blush *noun* (*plural* **blushes**) reddening in the face.

bluster *verb* **1** blow in gusts; be windy. **2** talk threateningly. **blustery** *adjective*

BMX *abbreviation* a kind of bicycle for use in racing on a dirt track. [from *bicycle moto-cross*]

BNZ *abbreviation* Bank of New Zealand.

BO *abbreviation* body odour.

boa (*say* **boh**-a) *noun* (also **boa constrictor**) a large South American snake that squeezes its prey so as to suffocate it.

boar *noun* **1** a wild pig. **2** a male pig.

board *noun* **1** a flat piece of wood. **2** a flat piece of stiff material, e.g. a chessboard. **3** daily meals supplied in return for payment or work, *board and lodging.* **4** a committee. **5** (*NZ*) the part of the floor of a shearing shed where the shearers work. **6** (*NZ*) the part of a meat-processing plant where animals are killed.
on board on or in a ship, aircraft, etc.

board *verb* **1** go on board a ship, etc. **2** give or get meals and accommodation.
board up block with fixed boards.

boarder *noun* **1** a pupil who lives at a boarding-school during the term. **2** a lodger who receives meals.

boarding-house *noun* a house where people obtain board and lodging for payment.

boarding-school *noun* a school where pupils live during the term.

boardsailing *noun* windsurfing.
boardsailer *noun*

boast *verb* **1** speak with great pride and try to impress people. **2** have something to be proud of, *The town boasts a fine park.* **boaster** *noun*, **boastful** *adjective*, **boastfully** *adverb*

boast *noun* a boastful statement.

boat *noun* a hollow structure built to travel on water and carry people etc.
boat people refugees leaving a country by sea.
in the same boat in the same situation; suffering the same difficulties.

boatie *noun* (*NZ, informal*) a person who runs a small motor boat.

boatswain (*say* **boh**-sun) *noun* a ship's officer in charge of rigging, boats, anchors, etc.

bob *verb* (**bobbed**, **bobbing**) move quickly, especially up and down.

bobbin *noun* a small spool holding thread or wire in a machine.

bobble *noun* a small round ornament, often made of wool.

bobby *noun* (*informal*) a policeman.

bobby calf *noun* (also **bobby**, *plural* **bobbies**) (*NZ*) a calf that is killed for its meat before it has been weaned.

bob-sleigh or bob-sled *noun* a sledge with two sets of runners.

bobsy-die *noun* (*NZ, slang*) a fuss; an uproar.

bocce (*say* **bot**-chee) *noun* a form of bowls, usually played with wooden balls on a long gravel or dirt court. [Italian]

bode *verb* (**boded**, **boding**) be a sign or omen of what is to come, *It bodes well.*

bodice *noun* the upper part of a dress.

bodkin *noun* a thick blunt needle for drawing tape etc. through a hem.

body *noun* (*plural* **bodies**) **1** the structure consisting of bones and flesh etc. of a person or animal; the main part of this apart from the head and limbs. **2** a corpse. **3** the main part of something. **4** a group or quantity regarded as a unit, *the school's governing body.* **5** a distinct object or piece of matter, *Stars and planets are heavenly bodies.* **bodily** *adjective & adverb*

bodyguard *noun* a guard to protect a person's life.

Boer (*say* **boh**-er) *noun* **1** an Afrikaner. **2** (in history) an early Dutch inhabitant of South Africa. [from Dutch, = farmer]

bog *noun* an area of wet spongy ground.
boggy *adjective*
bogged down stuck and unable to make any progress.

boggle *verb* (**boggled**, **boggling**) hesitate in fear or doubt, *Our minds boggled at the idea.* [from dialect *bogle* = bogy]

bogus *adjective* not real; sham.

bogy *noun* (*plural* **bogies**) **1** an evil spirit. **2** something that frightens people. **bogyman** *noun* [originally *Old Bogey* = the Devil]

boil *verb* **1** make or become hot enough to bubble and give off steam. **2** cook or wash something in boiling water. **3** be very hot.
boil up make tea.

boil *noun* **1** an inflamed swelling under the skin. **2** boiling-point, *Bring the milk to the boil.* [from Latin *bulla* = a bubble]

boiler *noun* a container in which water is heated or clothes are boiled.

boisterous *adjective* noisy and lively.

bold *adjective* **1** brave; courageous. **2** impudent. **3** (of colours) strong and vivid. **boldly** *adverb*, **boldness** *noun*

bole *noun* the trunk of a tree.

bollard *noun* a short thick post to which a ship's mooring-rope may be tied.

bolster *noun* a long pillow for placing across a bed under other pillows.

bolster *verb* add extra support.

bolt *noun* **1** a sliding bar for fastening a door. **2** a thick metal pin for fastening things together. **3** a sliding bar that opens and closes the breech of a rifle. **4** a shaft of lightning. **5** an arrow shot from a crossbow. **6** the action of bolting.
a bolt from the blue a surprise, usually an unpleasant one.
bolt upright quite upright.

bolt *verb* **1** fasten with a bolt or bolts. **2** run away; (of a horse) run off out of control. **3** swallow food quickly.

bomb *noun* **1** an explosive device. **2** (*NZ, slang*) a dilapidated old car.
the bomb an atomic or hydrogen bomb.

bomb *verb* attack with bombs. **bomber** *noun* [from Greek *bombos* = loud humming]

bombard *verb* **1** attack with gunfire or many missiles. **2** direct a large number of questions or comments etc. at somebody. **bombardment** *noun*

bombastic (*say* bom-**bast**-ik) *adjective* using pompous words.

bombshell *noun* a great shock.

bonanza (*say* bon-**an**-za) *noun* sudden great wealth or luck.

bond *noun* **1** something that binds, restrains, or unites people or things. **2** a document stating an agreement.
in bond (of goods) stored by a customs department until duty has been paid.

bond *verb* connect or unite with a bond.

bondage *noun* slavery; captivity.

bone *noun* one of the hard parts of a person's or animal's body (excluding teeth, nails, horns, and cartilage).

bone *verb* (**boned**, **boning**) remove the bones from meat or fish.

bone-dry *adjective* quite dry.

boner *noun* (*NZ*) **1** a skilled workman in a freezing works who removes bones from carcasses. **2** a low-grade cattle beast whose meat is used for tinned meat, sausages, etc.

bonfire *noun* an outdoor fire to burn rubbish or celebrate something. [originally *bone fire*, = a fire to dispose of people's or animals' bones]

bonnet *noun* **1** a hat with strings that tie under the chin. **2** a Scottish beret. **3** the hinged cover over a car engine.

bonny *adjective* (**bonnier**, **bonniest**) **1** healthy-looking. **2** (Scottish) good-looking. [from French *bon* = good]

bonus (*say* **boh**-nus) *noun* (*plural* **bonuses**) an extra payment or benefit.
bonus bond (*NZ*) a government security that gives a chance of winning money. [from Latin *bonus* = good]

bony *adjective* **1** with large bones; having bones with little flesh on them. **2** full of bones. **3** like bones.

bonzer *adjective* (*NZ, old-fashioned slang*) excellent; very good.

boo *verb* shout 'boo' in disapproval.

booay *noun* (also **booai** and **boohai**) (*NZ, slang*) a remote rural area.
up the booay completely wrong.

booby *noun* (*plural* **boobies**) a babyish or stupid person.
booby prize a prize given as a joke to someone who comes last in a contest.
booby trap something designed to hit or injure someone unexpectedly.

book *noun* a set of sheets of paper, usually with printing or writing on them, fastened together inside a cover. **bookseller** *noun*, **bookshop** *noun*, **bookstall** *noun*

book *verb* **1** reserve a place in a theatre, hotel, train, etc. **2** write something down in a book or list; enter in a police record, *The police booked him for speeding.*

bookcase *noun* a piece of furniture with shelves for books.

bookkeeping *noun* recording details of buying, selling, etc. **bookkeeper** *noun*

booklet *noun* a small thin book.

bookmaker *noun* a person whose business is taking bets.

bookmark *noun* **1** something to mark a place in a book. **2** (*Computing*) the address to a web page that is saved by a browser for future use. **bookmark** *verb*

bookworm *noun* **1** a grub that eats holes in books. **2** a person who loves reading.

boom[1] *verb* **1** make a deep hollow sound. **2** be growing and prospering, *Business is booming.*

boom[1] *noun* **1** a booming sound. **2** prosperity; growth.

boom[2] *noun* **1** a long pole at the bottom of a sail to keep it stretched. **2** a long pole carrying a microphone etc. **3** a chain or floating barrier that can be placed across a river or a harbour entrance.

boomer *noun* (*informal*) something that is large or remarkable.

boomerang *noun* a curved piece of wood that can be thrown so that it returns to the thrower, originally used by Australian Aborigines.

boon *noun* a benefit. [from Old Norse *bon* = prayer]

boon companion a friendly companion. [from French *bon* = good]

boonga *noun* (*offensive*) a person from a Pacific Island nation.

boor *noun* an ill-mannered person. **boorish** *adjective*

boost *verb* **1** increase the strength, value, or reputation of a person or thing. **2** push something upwards. **booster** *noun*

boost *noun* **1** an increase. **2** an upward push.

boot *noun* **1** a shoe that covers the foot and ankle or leg. **2** the compartment for luggage in a car. **booted** *adjective*
boots and all (*NZ, slang*) without holding back.

boot *verb* **1** kick. **2** (usually **boot up**) start up (a computer).

bootee *noun* a baby's knitted boot.

booth *noun* a small enclosure.

booty *noun* loot.

booze *verb* (**boozed**, **boozing**) (*slang*) drink alcohol.

booze *noun* (*slang*) alcoholic drink.

borax *noun* a soluble white powder used in making glass, detergents, etc.

border *noun* **1** the boundary of a country; the part near this. **2** an edge. **3** something placed round an edge to strengthen or decorate it. **4** a strip of ground round a garden or part of it.

border *verb* put or be a border to something.

borderline *noun* a boundary.
borderline case something that is on the borderline between two different groups or kinds of things.

bore[1] *verb* (**bored**, **boring**) **1** drill a hole. **2** get through by pushing.

bore[1] *noun* **1** the internal width of a gun-barrel. **2** a hole made by boring (for water, oil, etc.)

bore[2] *verb* (**bored**, **boring**) make somebody feel uninterested by being dull.

bore[2] *noun* a boring person or thing.
boredom *noun*

bore[3] *noun* a tidal wave with a steep front that moves up some estuaries.

bore[4] *past tense* of **bear**[2].

borer *noun* insect-larvae which bore holes in timber.

born *adjective* **1** having come into existence by birth. (See the note on *borne.*). **2** having a certain natural quality or ability, *a born leader*.

borne *past participle* of **bear**[2].

> USAGE The word *borne* is used before *by* or after *have, has,* or *had,* e.g. *children borne by Eve; she had borne him a son.* The word *born* is used e.g. in *a son was born.*

boronia *noun* an aromatic Australian shrub.

borough (*say* **bu**-rra) *noun* (*British*) an important town or district. [from Old English *burg* = fortress or fortified town]

borrow *verb* **1** get something to use for a time, with a promise to give it back afterwards. **2** obtain money as a loan. **3** adopt words from another language.
borrower *noun*

bosom *noun* a person's breast.

boss[1] *noun* (*plural* **bosses**) (*informal*) a manager; a person whose job is to give orders to workers etc.

boss[1] *verb* (*slang*) order someone about. [from Dutch *baas* = master]

boss[2] *noun* a round raised knob or stud.
bossy *adjective* (*informal*) fond of ordering people about. **bossiness** *noun*

bot *noun* (*NZ, slang*) a minor illness.

botany *noun* the study of plants. **botanical** *adjective*, **botanist** *noun* [from Greek *botane* = a plant]

botch *verb* spoil something by poor or clumsy work.

both *adjective & pronoun* the two; not only one, *Are both films good? Both are old.*

both *adverb* **both ... and** not only ... but also, *The house is both small and ugly.*

bother *verb* **1** cause somebody trouble or worry; pester. **2** take trouble; feel concern, *Don't bother to reply.*

bother *noun* trouble; worry.

bottle *noun* a narrow-necked container for liquids.

bottle *verb* (**bottled**, **bottling**) put or store in bottles.

bottlebrush *noun* an Australian plant with large bristly flowers, usually red in colour.

bottleneck *noun* a narrow place where something (especially traffic) cannot flow freely.

bottler *noun* (*NZ, informal*) an excellent person or thing.

bottom *noun* **1** the lowest part; the base. **2** the part furthest away, *the bottom of the garden.* **3** a person's buttocks.

bottom *adjective* lowest, *the bottom shelf.*

bottomless *adjective* extremely deep.

boudoir (*say* **boo**-dwar) *noun* a woman's private room. [from French, = place to sulk in]

bougainvillaea (*say* boo-gan-**vil**-ee-a) *noun* a tropical shrub with large red or purple bracts.

bough *noun* a large branch coming from the trunk of a tree.

boulder *noun* a very large smooth stone.

boules (*say* bools) (*plural noun*) (*French*) a form of bowls played on rough ground, usually with metal balls.

bounce *verb* (**bounced**, **bouncing**) **1** spring back when thrown against something. **2** cause a ball etc. to bounce. **3** (*slang,* of a cheque) be sent back by the bank as worthless. **4** jump suddenly; move in a lively manner.

bounce *noun* **1** the action or power of bouncing. **2** a lively confident manner, *full of bounce.* **bouncy** *adjective*

bouncer *noun* **1** a ball in cricket that bounces high after pitching. **2** a person employed to remove troublesome people from a club or bar etc. or to prevent them from entering.

bound[1] *verb* jump or spring; run with jumping movements, *bounding along.*

bound[1] *noun* a bounding movement.

bound[2] *past tense* of **bind**.

bound[2] *adjective* obstructed or hindered by something, *We were fog-bound.*
bound to certain to, *He is bound to fail.*
bound up with closely connected with, *Happiness is bound up with success.*

bound[3] *adjective* going towards something, *We are bound for Fiji.*

bound[4] *verb* limit; be the boundary of, *Their land is bounded by the river.*

boundary *noun* (*plural* **boundaries**) **1** a line that marks a limit. **2** a hit to the boundary of a cricket field. [from *bound*[4]]

bounden *adjective* obligatory, *your bounden duty.* [from *bind*]

bounds *plural noun* limits.
out of bounds where you are not allowed to go. [from *bound*[4]]

bountiful *adjective* **1** plentiful; abundant, *bountiful harvest.* **2** giving generously.

bounty *noun* (*plural* **bounties**) **1** a generous gift. **2** generosity in giving things. **3** a reward for doing something. [from Latin *bonitas* = goodness]

bouquet (*say* boh-**kay**) *noun* a bunch of flowers. [French, = group of trees]

bout *noun* **1** a boxing or wrestling contest. **2** a period of exercise or work or illness, *a bout of flu.*

boutique (*say* boo-**teek**) *noun* a small shop selling fashionable clothes. [French]

bovine (*say* **boh**-vyn) *adjective* of or like oxen. [from Latin *bovis* = of an ox]

bow[1] (*rhymes with* go) *noun* **1** a strip of wood curved by a tight string joining its ends, used for shooting arrows. **2** a wooden rod with horsehair stretched between its ends, used for playing a violin etc. **3** a knot made with loops.
bow-legged *adjective* bandy.
bow-tie *noun* a man's necktie tied into a bow.
bow-window *noun* a curved window.

bow[2] (*rhymes with* cow) *verb* **1** bend your body forwards to show respect or as a greeting. **2** bend downwards, *bowed by the weight.*

bow[2] *noun* bowing your body.

bow[3] (*rhymes with* cow) *noun* the front part of a ship.

bowel *noun* the intestine. [from Latin *botellus* = little sausage]

bower *noun* a leafy shelter.

bower-bird *noun* an Australian bird that decorates its nest with feathers, shells, etc.

bowl[1] *noun* **1** a rounded usually deep container for food or liquid. **2** the rounded part of a spoon or tobacco-pipe etc.

bowl[2] *noun* a ball used in the game of **bowls** or in (**tenpin**) **bowling**, when heavy balls are rolled towards a target.

bowl[2] *verb* **1** send a ball to be played by a batsman; get a batsman out by bowling. **2** send a ball etc. rolling.

bowler[1] *noun* a person who bowls.

bowler[2] *noun* (also **bowler hat**) a man's stiff felt hat with a rounded top.

box[1] *noun* (*plural* **boxes**) **1** a container made of wood, cardboard, etc., usually with a top or lid. **2** a compartment in a theatre, lawcourt, etc., *witness-box.* **3** a hut or shelter, *sentry-box.* **4** a small evergreen shrub.
a box of birds (*NZ, slang*) very well.
box number the number of a pigeon-hole to which letters may be addressed in a newspaper office or postal centre.
the box (*informal*) television.

box[1] *verb* **1** put something into a box. **2** (*NZ*) mix mobs or drafts of sheep.

box[2] *verb* fight with the fists.

boxer *noun* **1** a person who boxes. **2** a dog that looks like a bulldog.

Boxing Day the day after Christmas Day. [from the old custom of giving presents (*Christmas boxes*) to tradesmen and servants on that day]

box-office *noun* an office for booking seats at a theatre or cinema etc.

boy *noun* **1** a male child. **2** a young man.
boyhood *noun*, **boyish** *adjective*

boycott *verb* refuse to use or have anything to do with, *They boycotted the buses when the fares went up.* **boycott** *noun* [from the name of Captain Boycott, a harsh landlord in Ireland whose tenants in 1880 refused to deal with him]

boyfriend *noun* a boy that a girl regularly goes out with.

boysenberry *noun* (*plural* **boysenberries**) a juicy purple edible berry.

bra *noun* a piece of underwear worn by women to support their breasts.

brace *noun* **1** a device for holding things in place. **2** a pair, *a brace of pheasants.*

brace *verb* (**braced**, **bracing**) support; make a thing firm against something. [from Latin *bracchia* = arms]

bracelet *noun* an ornament worn round the wrist. (same origin as *brace*]

braces *plural noun* straps to hold trousers up, passing over the shoulders.

bracing *adjective* invigorating.

bracken *noun* **1** a large fern. **2** a mass of ferns.

bracket *noun* **1** a mark used in pairs to enclose words or figures, *There are round brackets* (-) *and square brackets* [-]. **2** a support attached to a wall etc. **3** a group or range between certain limits, *a high income bracket.*

bracket *verb* (**bracketed**, **bracketing**) **1** enclose in brackets. **2** put things together because they are similar.

brackish *adjective* (of water) slightly salt.

bract *noun* a leaf-like part of a plant that is often coloured like a petal.

bradawl *noun* a small tool for boring holes.

brae (*say* bray) *noun* (*Scottish*) a hillside.

brag *verb* (**bragged**, **bragging**) boast.

braggart *noun* a person who brags.

brahmin *noun* a member of the highest Hindu class, originally priests. [from Sanskrit *brahman* = priest]

braid *noun* **1** a plait of hair. **2** a strip of cloth with a woven decorative pattern, used as trimming.

braid *verb* **1** plait. **2** trim with braid.

Braille *noun* a system of representing letters etc. by raised dots which blind people can read by feeling them. [named after Louis Braille, a blind French teacher who invented it in about 1830]

brain *noun* **1** the organ inside the top of the head that controls the body. **2** the mind; intelligence.

brainwash *verb* force a person to give up one set of ideas or beliefs and accept new ones; indoctrinate.

brainwave *noun* a sudden bright idea.

brainy *adjective* clever; intelligent.

braise *verb* (**braised**, **braising**) cook slowly in a little liquid in a closed container. [from French *braise* = burning coals]

brake *noun* a device for slowing or stopping something.

brake *verb* (**braked**, **braking**) use a brake.

bramble *noun* a blackberry bush or a prickly bush like it.

bran *noun* ground-up husks of grain.

branch *noun* (*plural* **branches**) **1** a woody arm-like part of a tree or shrub. **2** a part of a railway, road, or river etc. that leads off from the main part. **3** a shop or office etc. that belongs to a large organisation.

branch *verb* form a branch.
branch out start something new. [from Latin *branca* = a paw]

brand *noun* **1** a particular make of goods. **2** a mark made by branding. **3** a piece of burning wood.

brand *verb* **1** mark cattle or sheep etc. with a hot iron to identify them. **2** sell goods under a particular trade mark.

brandish *verb* wave something about.

brand-new *adjective* completely new.

brandy *noun* (*plural* **brandies**) a strong alcoholic drink. [from Dutch *brande-wijn* = burnt (distilled) wine]

brash *adjective* **1** impudent. **2** reckless.

brass *noun* (*plural* **brasses**) **1** a metal that is an alloy of copper and zinc. **2** wind instruments made of brass, e.g. trumpets and trombones. **brass** *adjective*, **brassy** *adjective*

brassière (*say* **bras**-ee-air) *noun* a bra. [French]

brat *noun* (*contemptuous*) a child.

bravado (*say* brav-**ah**-doh) *noun* a display of boldness. [from Spanish *bravata*]

brave *adjective* **1** having or showing courage. **2** spectacular, *a brave show of poppies.* **bravely** *adverb*, **bravery** *noun*

brave *noun* an American Indian warrior.

brave *verb* (**braved**, **braving**) face and endure something bravely.

bravo (*say* **brah**-voh) *interjection* well done!

brawl *noun* a noisy quarrel or fight.

brawl *verb* take part in a brawl.

brawn *noun* **1** muscular strength. **2** cold boiled pork or veal pressed in a mould.

brawny *adjective* strong and muscular.

bray *noun* the loud harsh cry of a donkey. **bray** *verb*

brazen *adjective* **1** made of brass. **2** shameless, *brazen impudence.*

brazen *verb* **brazen it out** behave as if there is nothing to be ashamed of when you know you have done wrong.

brazier (*say* **bray**-zee-er) *noun* a metal framework for holding burning coals.

breach *noun* (*plural* **breaches**) **1** the breaking of an agreement or rule etc. **2** a broken place; a gap.

breach *verb* break through; make a gap.

bread *noun* a food made by baking flour and water, usually with yeast. **breadcrumbs** *noun*

breadth *noun* width; broadness.

breadwinner *noun* the member of a family who earns money to support the others.

break *verb* (**broke**, **broken**, **breaking**) **1** divide or fall into pieces by hitting or pressing. **2** fail to keep a promise or law etc. **3** stop for a time; end, *She broke her silence.* **4** change, *the weather broke.* **5** damage; stop working properly. **6** (of waves) fall in foam. **7** go suddenly

or with force, *They broke through.* **8** appear suddenly, *Dawn had broken.*
breakage *noun*
break a record do better than anyone else has done before.
break down stop working properly; collapse.
break in clear new land for cultivation.
break out begin suddenly; escape.
break the news make something known.
break up break into small parts; separate at the end of a school term.

break *noun* **1** a broken place; a gap. **2** an escape; a sudden dash. **3** a short rest from work. **4** a number of points scored continuously in snooker etc. **5** (*informal*) a piece of luck; an opportunity.
break of day dawn.

breakable *adjective* able to be broken.

break-dancing *noun* energetic dancing performed in the street to loud music with a strong beat.

breakdown *noun* **1** breaking down; failure. **2** collapse of mental or physical health. **3** an analysis of accounts or statistics.

breaker *noun* a large wave breaking on the shore.

breakfast *noun* the first meal of the day. [from *break* + *fast*[2]]

breakneck *adjective* dangerously fast.

breakthrough *noun* an important advance or achievement.

breakwater *noun* a wall built out into the sea to protect a coast from heavy waves.

bream *noun* (*plural* **bream**) a kind of fish with an arched back.

breast *noun* **1** one of the two parts on the upper front of a woman's body that produce milk to feed a baby. **2** a person's or animal's chest.

breastbone *noun* the flat bone down the centre of the chest or breast.

breast-feed *verb* feed a baby from the breast.

breastplate *noun* a piece of armour covering the chest.

breath (*say* breth) *noun* **1** air drawn into the lungs and sent out again. **2** a gentle blowing, *a breath of wind.*
out of breath panting.
take your breath away surprise or delight you greatly.
under your breath in a whisper.

breathalyser *noun* a device for measuring the amount of alcohol in a person's breath. **breathalyse** *verb* [from *breath* + *analyse*]

breathe (*say* bree*th*) *verb* (**breathed**, **breathing**) **1** take air into the body and send it out again. **2** speak; utter, *Don't breathe a word of this.*

breather (*say* **bree**-*th*er) *noun* a pause for rest, *Let's take a breather.*

breathless *adjective* out of breath.

breathtaking *adjective* very surprising or delightful.

breech *noun* (*plural* **breeches**) the back part of a gun-barrel, where the bullets are put in.

breeches (*say* **brich**-iz) *plural noun* trousers reaching to just below the knees.

breed *verb* (**bred**, **breeding**) **1** produce young creatures. **2** keep animals so as to produce young ones from them. **3** bring up; train. **4** create; produce, *Poverty breeds illness.*
breeder *noun*

breed *noun* a variety of animals with qualities inherited from their parents.

breeze *noun* a wind. **breezy** *adjective*

breeze-block *noun* a lightweight building-block made of cinders and cement.

brethren *plural noun* (*old use*) brothers.

breve (*say* breev) *noun* a note in music, equal to two semibreves in length.

brevity *noun* shortness; briefness.

brew *verb* **1** make beer or tea. **2** develop, *Trouble is brewing.*

brew *noun* a brewed drink.

brewer *noun* a person who brews beer for sale.

brewery *noun* (*plural* **breweries**) a place where beer is brewed.

briar *noun* a brier.

bribe *noun* money or a gift offered to a person to influence him or her.

bribe *verb* (**bribed**, **bribing**) give someone a bribe. **bribery** *noun*

brick *noun* **1** a small hard block of baked clay etc. used to build walls. **2** a rectangular block of something.

brick *verb* close something with bricks, *We bricked up the gap in the wall.*

bricklayer *noun* a worker who builds with bricks.

bride *noun* a woman on her wedding-day. **bridal** *adjective* [from Old English *bryd*]

bridegroom *noun* a man on his wedding-day.

bridesmaid *noun* a girl or unmarried woman who attends the bride at a wedding.

bridge *noun* **1** a structure built over and across a river, railway, or road etc. to allow people to cross it. **2** a high platform above a ship's deck, for the officer in charge. **3** the bony upper part of the nose. **4** something that connects things. **5** a card-game usually for two pairs of players.

bridge *verb* (**bridged**, **bridging**) make or form a bridge over something.

bridle *noun* the part of a horse's harness that fits over its head.

bridle-path or **bridle-road** *noun* a road suitable for horses but not for vehicles.

brief *adjective* short. **briefly** *adverb*, **briefness** *noun*
in brief in a few words.

brief *noun* instructions and information given to someone, especially to a barrister.

brief *verb* **1** give a brief to a barrister. **2** instruct or inform someone concisely in advance. [from Latin *brevis* = short]

briefcase *noun* a flat case for carrying documents etc.

briefing *noun* a meeting to give someone concise instructions or information.

briefs *plural noun* very short underpants.

brier *noun* **1** a thorny bush, especially the wild rose. **2** a hard root used especially for making tobacco-pipes.

brigade *noun* **1** a large unit of an army. **2** a group of people organised for a special purpose, *the fire brigade.* [from Italian *brigata* = a troop]

brigadier *noun* a brigade-commander.

brigand *noun* a member of a band of robbers.

bright *adjective* **1** giving a strong light; shining. **2** clever. **3** cheerful. **brightly** *adverb*, **brightness** *noun*

brighten *verb* make or become brighter.

brill *noun* a large oval New Zealand flatfish.

brilliant *adjective* **1** very bright; sparkling. **2** very clever. **brilliantly** *adverb*, **brilliance** *noun* [from Italian *brillare* = shine]

brim *noun* **1** the edge of a cup etc. **2** the projecting edge of a hat.
brim-full *adjective* completely full.

brim *verb* (**brimmed**, **brimming**) be full to the brim.
brim over overflow.

brimstone *noun* (*old use*) sulphur.

brine *noun* salt water. **briny** *adjective*

bring *verb* (**brought**, **bringing**) cause a person or thing to come; lead; carry.
bring about cause to happen.
bring off achieve; do something successfully.
bring up look after and train growing children; mention a subject; vomit; cause to stop suddenly.

brink *noun* **1** the edge of a steep place or of a stretch of water. **2** the point beyond which something will happen, *We were on the brink of war.*

brisk *adjective* quick and lively. **briskly** *adverb*, **briskness** *noun*

bristle *noun* **1** a short stiff hair. **2** one of the stiff pieces of hair, wire, or plastic etc. in a brush. **bristly** *adjective*

bristle *verb* (**bristled**, **bristling**) **1** (of an animal) raise its bristles in anger or fear. **2** show indignation.
bristle with be full of, *The plan bristled with problems.*

Brit *noun* (*informal*) a Briton.

British *adjective* of or from Britain.

Briton *noun* a British person.

brittle *adjective* hard but easy to break or snap. **brittleness** *noun*

bro *noun* (*NZ, informal*) a brother, mate. [*abbreviation* of *brother*]

broach *verb* **1** make a hole in something and draw out liquid. **2** start a discussion of something, *They broached the subject.*

broad *adjective* **1** large across; wide. **2** full and complete, *broad daylight.* **3** in general terms; not detailed, *We are in broad agreement.* **4** strong and unmistakable, *a broad hint; a broad accent.* **broadly** *adverb*, **broadness** *noun*
broad bean a bean with large flat seeds.

broadband *noun* a method of accessing the Internet.

broadcast *noun* a programme sent out on the radio or on television.

broadcast *verb* (**broadcast**, **broadcasting**) send out or take part in a broadcast.
broadcaster *noun*

broaden *verb* make or become broader.

broadleaf *noun* a small tree or shrub with large glossy leaves.

broad-minded *adjective* tolerant; not easily shocked.

broadside *noun* **1** firing by all guns on one side of a ship. **2** a verbal attack.
broadside on sideways on.

brocade *noun* material woven with raised patterns.

broccoli *noun* (*plural* **broccoli**) a kind of cauliflower with greenish flower-heads. [Italian, = cabbage-heads]

brochure (*say* **broh**-shoor) *noun* a booklet or pamphlet containing information. [from French, = stitching]

brogue (*rhymes with* rogue) *noun* **1** a strong kind of shoe. **2** a strong accent, *He spoke with an Irish brogue.*

broil *verb* **1** cook on a fire or gridiron. **2** make or be very hot. [from French *brûler* = to burn]

broiler *noun* a young chicken reared for broiling or roasting.

broke *adjective* (*informal*) having spent all your money; bankrupt.

broken-hearted *adjective* overwhelmed with grief.

broken home a family lacking one parent through divorce or separation.

broker *noun* a person who buys and sells things for other people.

bromide *noun* a substance used in medicine to calm the nerves.

bronchial (*say* **bronk**-ee-al) *adjective* of the tubes that lead from the windpipe to the lungs. [from Greek *bronchos* = windpipe]

bronchitis (*say* bronk-**I**-tiss) *noun* a disease with bronchial inflammation.

brontosaurus *noun* (*plural* **brontosauruses**) a large dinosaur that fed on plants. [from Greek *bronte* = thunder, + *sauros* = lizard]

bronze *noun* **1** a metal that is an alloy of copper and tin. **2** something made of bronze; a bronze medal, usually given as third prize. **3** yellowish-brown. **bronze** *adjective*
Bronze Age the time when tools and weapons were made of bronze.

brooch *noun* (*plural* **brooches**) an ornament with a hinged pin for fastening it on to clothes.

brood *noun* young birds that were hatched together.
brood mare a mare kept for breeding.

brood *verb* **1** sit on eggs to hatch them. **2** keep thinking about something, especially with resentment.

broody *adjective* **1** (of a hen) wanting to sit on eggs. **2** thoughtful; brooding.

brook[1] *noun* a small stream.

brook[2] *verb* tolerate, *brook no delay*.

broom *noun* **1** a brush with a long handle, for sweeping. **2** a shrub with yellow, white, or pink flowers.

broomstick *noun* a broom-handle.

broth *noun* a kind of thin soup.

brothel *noun* a house in which women work as prostitutes.

brother *noun* **1** a son of the same parents as another person. **2** a man who is a fellow member of a Church, trade union, etc. **3** a member of a religious community, *a Marist brother*. **brotherhood** *noun*, **brotherly** *adjective* (from Old English *brothor*]

brother-in-law *noun* (*plural* **brothers-in-law**) the brother of a married person's husband or wife; the husband of a person's sister.

brow *noun* **1** an eyebrow. **2** the forehead. **3** the ridge at the top of a hill; the edge of a cliff.

brown *noun* a colour between orange and black.

brown *adjective* **1** of the colour brown. **2** having a brown skin; sun-tanned.

brown *verb* make or become brown.

Brownie *noun* a member of a junior branch of the Guides.

brownie *noun* **1** a rich chocolate square. **2** (*NZ*) a bread or pudding containing currants or raisins.

browse *verb* (**browsed**, **browsing**) **1** feed on grass or leaves. **2** read or look at something casually. **3** (*Computing*) read or look over (documents etc.) on a network.

browser *noun* **1** an animal or person that browses. **2** (*Computing*) a program that gives users access to the Internet.

brucellosis *noun* a disease in cattle etc., that can be caught by human beings.

bruise *noun* a dark mark made on the skin by hitting it.

bruise *verb* (**bruised**, **bruising**) give or get a bruise or bruises.

brunette *noun* a woman with dark-brown hair. [from French *brun* = brown]

brunt *noun* the chief impact or strain, *They bore the brunt of the attack.*

brush *noun* (*plural* **brushes**) **1** an implement used for cleaning or painting things or for smoothing the hair, usually with pieces of hair, wire, or plastic etc. set in a solid base. **2** a fox's bushy tail. **3** brushing, *Give it a good brush.* **4** a short fight, *They had a brush with the enemy.* **5** (*NZ*) thick undergrowth, small trees and shrubs.

brush *verb* **1** use a brush on something. **2** touch gently in passing.
brush up revise a subject.

brusque (*say* bruusk) *adjective* curt and offhand in manner. **brusquely** *adverb* [from Italian *brusco* = sour]

Brussels sprouts the edible buds of a kind of cabbage. [named after Brussels, the capital of Belgium]

brutal *adjective* very cruel. **brutally** *adverb*, **brutality** *noun*

brute *noun* **1** a brutal person. **2** an animal. **brutish** *adjective* [from Latin *brutus* = stupid]

BSc *abbreviation* Bachelor of Science.

bubble *noun* **1** a thin transparent ball of liquid filled with air or gas. **2** a small ball of air in something. **bubbly** *adjective*
bubble gum chewing-gum that can be blown into large bubbles.

bubble *verb* (**bubbled**, **bubbling**) **1** send up bubbles; rise in bubbles. **2** show great liveliness.

buccaneer *noun* a pirate.

buck[1] *noun* a male deer, rabbit, or hare.

buck[2] *verb* (of a horse) jump with its back arched.
buck up (*slang*) hurry; cheer up.

buck[3] *noun* an object used in the game of poker to show whose turn it is.
pass the buck (*slang*) pass the responsibility for something to another person. **buck-passing** *noun*

buck[4] *noun* (*slang*) a dollar.

bucket *noun* a container with a handle, for carrying liquids etc. **bucketful** *noun*

buckle *noun* a device through which a belt or strap is threaded to fasten it.

buckle *verb* (**buckled**, **buckling**) **1** fasten with a buckle. **2** bend or crumple.
buckle down to start working hard at.

buckler *noun* a small round shield.

bucolic (*say* bew-**kol**-ik) *adjective* of country life. [from Greek *boukolos* = herdsman]

bud *noun* a flower or leaf before it opens.

Buddhism (*say* **buud**-izm) *noun* a faith that started in Asia and follows the teaching of the Indian philosopher Gautama Buddha, who lived in the 5th century BC. **Buddhist** *noun* [from Sanskrit *Buddha* = enlightened one]

budding *adjective* beginning to develop.

buddy *noun* (*plural* **buddies**) (*informal*) a friend.

budge *verb* (**budged**, **budging**) move slightly.

budgerigar *noun* an Australian bird often kept as a pet in a cage. [from Australian Aboriginal *budgeri* = good, + *gar* = cockatoo]

budget *noun* **1** a plan for spending money wisely. **2** an amount of money set aside for a purpose. **budgetary** *adjective*
the Budget estimates of government income and expenditure presented to Parliament.

budget *verb* (**budgeted**, **budgeting**) plan a budget. [from French *bouge* = leather bag]

budgie *noun* (*informal*) a budgerigar.

buff *adjective* of a dull yellow colour.

buff *verb* polish with soft material. [from *buff leather* = leather of buffalo hide]

buffalo *noun* (*plural* **buffalo** or **buffaloes**) a large ox. Different kinds are found in Asia, Africa, and North America (where they are also called *bison*).

buffer *noun* something that softens a blow, especially a device on a railway engine or wagon or at the end of a track.

buffet[1] (*say* **buf**-ay) *noun* **1** a refreshment counter. **2** a meal where guests serve themselves. [from French = stool]

buffet[2] (*say* **buf**-it) *noun* a hit, especially with the hand.

buffet[2] *verb* (**buffeted**, **buffeting**) hit, knock, *Strong winds buffeted the aircraft.* [from Old French *buffe* a blow]

buffoon *noun* a clown; a person who plays the fool. **buffoonery** *noun* [from Latin *buffo* = clown]

bug *noun* **1** an insect. **2** (*informal*) a germ or microbe. **3** (*informal*) a secret hidden microphone.

bug *verb* (**bugged**, **bugging**) (*slang*) **1** fit with a 'bug'. **2** annoy.

bugbear *noun* something you fear or dislike. [from an old word *bug* = bogy]

buggy *noun* (*plural* **buggies**) **1** (*old use*) a light horse-drawn carriage. **2** a small strong vehicle.

bugle *noun* a brass instrument like a small trumpet, used for sounding military signals. **bugler** *noun*

build *verb* (**built**, **building**) make something by putting parts together.
build in include. **built-in** *adjective*
build up establish gradually; accumulate; cover an area with buildings; make stronger or more famous, *build up a reputation.*
built-up *adjective*

build *noun* the shape of someone's body, *of slender build.*

builder *noun* someone who puts up buildings.

building *noun* **1** the process of constructing houses etc. **2** a permanent built structure that people can go into.

bulb *noun* **1** a thick rounded part of a plant from which a stem grows up and roots grow down. **2** a rounded part of something, *the bulb of a thermometer.* **3** a glass globe that produces electric light. **bulbous** *adjective*

bulge *noun* a rounded swelling; an outward curve. **bulgy** *adjective*

bulge *verb* (**bulged**, **bulging**) form or cause to form a bulge.

bulk *noun* **1** the size of something, especially when it is large. **2** the greater portion; the majority, *The bulk of the population voted for it.*
in bulk in large amounts.

bulk *verb* increase the size or thickness of something, *bulk it out.*

bulky *adjective* (**bulkier**, **bulkiest**) taking up much space. **bulkiness** *noun*

bull[1] *noun* the fully-grown male of cattle or of certain other large animals (e.g. elephant, whale, seal).

bull[2] *noun* an edict issued by the pope.

bull-a-bull *noun* (*NZ*) poroporo.

bulldog *noun* a dog of a powerful courageous breed with a short thick neck.

bulldoze *verb* (**bulldozed**, **bulldozing**) clear with a bulldozer.

bulldozer *noun* a powerful tractor with a wide metal blade or scoop in front, used for shifting soil or clearing ground.

bullet *noun* a small lump of metal shot from a rifle or revolver.

bulletin *noun* a public statement giving news.

bullet-proof *adjective* able to keep out bullets.

bullfight *noun* a public entertainment in which bulls are tormented and killed in an arena. **bullfighter** *noun*

bullion *noun* bars of gold or silver.

bullock *noun* a young bull.

bullroarer *noun* a flat strip of wood on the end of a string that makes a roaring sound when it is whirled round. Australian Aborigines use it in religious ceremonies.

bull's-eye *noun* **1** the centre of a target. **2** a hard shiny peppermint sweet.

bully *verb* (**bullied**, **bullying**) **1** use strength or power to hurt or frighten a weaker person. **2** start play in hockey, when two opponents tap the ground and each other's stick, *bully off.*

bully *noun* (*plural* **bullies**) someone who bullies people.

bulrush *noun* (*plural* **bulrushes**) a tall rush with a thick velvety head.

bulwark *noun* a wall of earth built as a defence; a protection.
bulwarks *plural noun* a ship's side above the level of the deck.

bum *noun* (*slang*) **1** a person's bottom. **2** a lazy person.

bumble *verb* (**bumbled**, **bumbling**) move or behave or speak clumsily.

bumble-bee *noun* a large bee with a loud hum.

bump *verb* **1** knock against something. **2** move along with jolts.
bump into (*informal*) meet by chance.
bump off (*slang*) kill.

bump *noun* **1** the action or sound of bumping. **2** a swelling or lump. **bumpy** *adjective*

bumper *noun* a bar along the front or back of a motor vehicle to protect it in collisions.

bumper *adjective* unusually large or plentiful, *a bumper crop.*

bumpkin *noun* a country person with awkward manners.

bumptious (*say* **bump**-shus) *adjective* conceited. **bumptiousness** *noun*

bun *noun* **1** a small round sweet cake. **2** hair twisted into a round bunch at the back of the head.

bunch *noun* (*plural* **bunches**) a number of things joined or fastened together.

bundle *noun* a number of things tied or wrapped together.

bundle *verb* (**bundled**, **bundling**) **1** make into a bundle. **2** push hurriedly or carelessly, *They bundled him into a taxi.*

bung[1] *noun* a stopper for closing a hole in a barrel or jar.

bung[1] *verb* (*slang*) throw. *Bung it here.*
bunged up (*informal*) blocked.

bung[2] *adjective* **go bung** (*NZ, slang*) break down, fail. [Aboriginal]

bungalow *noun* a house without any upstairs rooms. [from Hindi *bangla* = of Bengal]

bungle *verb* (**bungled**, **bungling**) do something unsuccessfully; spoil by being clumsy. **bungler** *noun*

bungy jumping (*say* **bun**-jee) *noun* diving into a river or gorge or off a building while supported by a long rubber rope (a **bungy**) that is tied to your ankles. **bungy jump** *noun* and *verb*, **bungy jumper** *noun*

bunion *noun* a swelling at the side of the joint where the big toe joins the foot.

bunk[1] *noun* a bed built like a shelf.

bunk[2] *noun* **do a bunk** (*slang*) run away.
bunk *verb*

bunker *noun* **1** a container for storing fuel. **2** a sandy hollow built as an obstacle on a golf-course. **3** an underground shelter.

bunny *noun* (*plural* **bunnies**) (*informal*) a rabbit. [from dialect *bun* = rabbit]

bunt *verb* (in softball and baseball) let the ball gently rebound from the bat without swinging at it. **bunt** *noun*

bunting[1] *noun* a kind of small bird.

bunting[2] *noun* strips of cloth hung up to decorate streets and buildings.

buoy (*say* boi) *noun* (*plural* **buoys**) a floating object anchored to mark a channel or underwater rocks etc.

buoy *verb* **1** keep something afloat. **2** hearten; cheer, *They were buoyed up with new hope.*

buoyant (*say* **boi**-ant) *adjective* **1** able to float. **2** light-hearted; cheerful. **buoyantly** *adverb*, **buoyancy** *noun*

burb *noun* (*informal*) a suburb.

burble *verb* (**burbled**, **burbling**) make a gentle murmuring sound. **burble** *noun*

burden *noun* **1** something carried; a heavy load. **2** something troublesome that you have to bear, *Exams are a burden.* **burdensome** *adjective*

burden *verb* put a burden on a person etc.

bureau (*say* **bewr**-oh) *noun* (*plural* **bureaux** or **bureaus**) **1** a writing-desk. **2** a business office, *They will tell you at the Information Bureau.* [French, = desk]

bureaucracy (*say* bewr-**ok**-ra-see) *noun* (*plural* **bureaucracies**) **1** government by officials, not by elected representatives. **2** too much official routine. **bureaucratic** (*say* bewr-ok-**rat**-ik) *adjective* [from *bureau* + *-cracy*]

bureaucrat (*say* **bewr**-ok-rat) *noun* an official of a bureaucracy.

burgeon (*say* **ber**-jon) *verb* grow rapidly.

burger *noun* a hamburger.

burglar *noun* a person who enters a building illegally, especially in order to steal things. **burglary** *noun*

burgle *verb* (**burgled**, **burgling**) rob a place as a burglar.

burgundy *noun* a rich red or white wine. [originally made in Burgundy in France]

burial *noun* burying somebody.

burl *noun* (also **birl**) (*NZ, informal*) a try, a go, *give it a burl.*

burlesque (*say* ber-**lesk**) *noun* a comical imitation.

burly *adjective* (**burlier**, **burliest**) with a strong heavy body; sturdy.

burn[1] *verb* (**burned** or **burnt**, **burning**) **1** blaze or glow with fire; produce heat or light by combustion. **2** damage or destroy something by fire, heat, or chemicals. **3** be damaged or destroyed by fire etc. **4** feel very hot. **5** copy a CD or DVD. **burn off** *verb* (*NZ*) clear land of vegetation by fire. **burn-off** *noun*

USAGE The word *burnt* (not *burned*) is always used when an *adjective* is required. e.g. in *burnt wood.* As parts of the verb, either *burned* or *burnt* may be used, e.g. *the wood had burned or had burnt completely.*

burn[1] *noun* **1** a mark or injury made by burning. **2** the firing of a spacecraft's rockets.

burn[2] *noun* (*Otago-Southland*) a small stream.

burner *noun* the part of a lamp or cooker that gives out the flame.

burning *adjective* **1** intense, *a burning ambition.* **2** very important; hotly discussed, *a burning question.*

burnish *verb* polish by rubbing.

burr *noun* **1** a plant's seed-case or flower that clings to hair or clothes. **2** a whirring sound. **3** a soft country accent.

burrow *noun* a hole or tunnel dug by a rabbit or fox etc. as a dwelling.

burrow *verb* **1** dig a burrow. **2** push your way through or into something; search deeply, *She burrowed in her handbag.*

bursar *noun* a person who manages the finances and other business of a school or college. [from Latin *bursa* = a bag]

bursary *noun* (*plural* **bursaries**) a grant awarded to a student.
Bursary *noun* (*NZ*) an examination that used to be taken at the end of Year 13.

burst *verb* (**burst**, **bursting**) **1** break or force apart. **2** come or start suddenly, *It burst into flame. They burst out laughing.* **3** be very full, *bursting with energy.*

burst *noun* **1** bursting; a split. **2** something short and forceful, *a burst of gunfire.*

bury *verb* (**buried**, **burying**) **1** place a dead body in the earth, a tomb, or the sea. **2** put underground; cover up.
bury the hatchet agree to stop quarrelling or fighting.

bus *noun* (*plural* **buses**) a large vehicle for passengers to travel in. [short for *omnibus*]

bush *noun* (*plural* **bushes**) **1** a shrub. **2** (*NZ*) native forest. **3** (*NZ*) land in its natural, uncultivated state. **bushy** *adjective*
bush carpenter (*NZ*) an amateur carpenter with rough methods.
bush lawyer (*NZ*) **1** an unqualified person who claims knowledge of the law. **2** a kind of bramble.
bush telegraph a means by which information or rumour spreads quickly.
go bush (*NZ*) take up an outdoor or rural way of life.

bush-clad *adjective* (*NZ*) (of hills etc.) covered with bush.

bushcraft *noun* (*NZ*) knowledge of the bush and how to survive in it.

bushed *adjective* (*informal*) **1** exhausted. **2** (*NZ*) lost; baffled.

bushel *noun* an imperial unit of volume for grain and fruit, equivalent to about 36.4 litres.

bushfire *noun* a fire that burns through native forest.

bushline *noun* (*NZ*) the height on a mountain above which bush does not grow.

bushman *noun* (*NZ*) a person skilled in bushcraft; a person who clears bush or fells trees for timber.

bush-shirt *noun* (*NZ*) a long woollen shirt worn outside other clothing.

bushwhacker *noun* a person who fells bush or trees. **bushwhack** *verb*

busily *adverb* in a busy way.

business (*say* **biz**-niss) *noun* (*plural* **businesses**) **1** a person's concern or responsibilities, *Mind your own business.* **2** an affair or subject, *I'm tired of the whole business.* **3** a shop or firm. **4** buying and selling things; trade.

businesslike *adjective* practical; well-organised.

busker *noun* a person who entertains people in the street. **busking** *noun* [from an old word *busk* = be a pedlar]

bust[1] *noun* **1** a sculpture of a person's head, shoulders, and chest. **2** the upper front part of a woman's body.

bust[2] *verb* (**bust, busting**) (*informal*) burst.

buster *noun* a cool southerly gale.

bustle[1] *verb* (**bustled, bustling**) hurry in a busy or excited way.

bustle[1] *noun* hurried or excited activity.

bustle[2] *noun* padding used to puff out the top of a long skirt at the back.

busy *adjective* (**busier, busiest**) **1** having much to do; occupied. **2** full of activity. **busily** *adverb*, **busyness** *noun*

busy *verb* (**busied, busying**) **busy yourself** occupy yourself; keep busy.

busybody *noun* (*plural* **busybodies**) a person who interferes.

but *conjunction* however; nevertheless, *I wanted to go, but I couldn't.*

but *preposition* except, *There is no one here but me.*

but *adverb* only; no more than, *We can but try.*

butcher *noun* **1** a person who cuts up meat and sells it. **2** a person who kills cruelly or needlessly. **butchery** *noun*

butcher *verb* kill cruelly or needlessly. **go butcher's (hook)** (*NZ, slang*) become angry.

butler *noun* (*British*) the chief male servant of a household, in charge of the wine-cellar. [from Old French *bouteillier* = bottler]

butt[1] *noun* **1** the thicker end of a weapon or tool. **2** a stub, *cigarette butts.* [from Dutch *bot* = stumpy]

butt[2] *noun* a large cask or barrel. [from Latin *buttis* = cask]

butt[3] *noun* **1** a person or thing that is a target for ridicule or teasing, *He was the butt of their jokes.* **2** a mound of earth behind the targets on a shooting-range. **butts** *plural noun* a shooting-range. [from Old French *but* = goal]

butt[4] *verb* **1** push or hit with the head as a ram or goat does. **2** place the edges of things together. **butt in** interrupt; intrude; meddle. [from Old French *buter* = hit]

butter *noun* a soft fatty food made by churning cream. **buttery** *adjective*

buttercup *noun* a wild plant with bright yellow cup-shaped flowers.

butterfat *noun* the natural fat that is present in milk and is used to make butter.

butter-fingers *noun* (*informal*) a person who often drops things.

butterfish *noun* (*NZ*) an edible fish with mucus-coated skin.

butterfly *noun* (*plural* **butterflies**) **1** an insect with large white or coloured wings. **2** a swimming-stroke in which both arms are lifted at the same time.

buttermilk *noun* the liquid that is left after butter has been made.

butterscotch *noun* a kind of hard toffee.

buttock *noun* either of the two fleshy rounded parts at the lower or rear end of the back.

button *noun* **1** a knob or disc sewn on clothes as a fastening or ornament. **2** a small knob, *Press the button.*

button *verb* fasten with a button or buttons.

buttonhole *noun* **1** a slit through which a button passes to fasten clothes. **2** a flower worn on a lapel.

buttonhole *verb* (**buttonholed, buttonholing**) stop somebody so that you can talk to him or her.

buttress *noun* (*plural* **buttresses**) a support built against a wall. [same origin as *butt*[4]]

buy *verb* (**bought, buying**) get something by paying for it. **buyer** *noun*

buy *noun* something bought; a purchase.

buzz *noun* (*plural* **buzzes**) **1** a vibrating humming sound. **2** (*informal*) a feeling of excitement.

buzz *verb* **1** make a buzz. **2** threaten an aircraft by deliberately flying close to it.

buzzard *noun* a kind of hawk.

buzzer *noun* a device that makes a buzzing sound as a signal.

by *preposition* This word is used to show (**1**) closeness (*Sit by me*), (**2**) direction or route (*We got here by a short cut*), (**3**) time (*They came by night*), (**4**) manner or method (*cooking by gas*), (**5**) amount (*You missed it by inches*). **by the way** incidentally. **by yourself** alone; without help.

by *adverb* **1** past, *I can't get by.* **2** in reserve; for future use, *Put it by.*
by and by soon; later on.
by and large on the whole.

bye *noun* **1** a run scored in cricket when the ball goes past the batsman without being touched. **2** having no opponent for one round in a tournament and so going on to the next round as if you had won.

bye-bye *interjection* goodbye.

by-election *noun* an election to replace a Member of Parliament who has died or resigned.

bygone *adjective* belonging to the past.
let bygones be bygones forgive and forget.

by-law *noun* a law that applies only to a particular town or district.

BYO *abbreviation* (*NZ*) bring your own (liquor).

bypass *noun* (*plural* **bypasses**) **1** a road taking traffic past a city etc. **2** a channel that allows something to flow when the main route is blocked.

bypass *verb* avoid by means of a bypass.

by-product *noun* something produced while something else is being made.

byre *noun* (*Otago-Southland*) a cowshed.

bystander *noun* a person standing near but not taking part in something.

byte *noun* a fixed number of bits (= binary digits) in a computer, often representing a single character.

byway *noun* a minor road.

byword *noun* a person or thing spoken of as a famous example, *Their firm became a byword for quality.*

Cc

c. *abbreviation* about. [Latin *circa*]

cab *noun* **1** a taxi. **2** a compartment for the driver of a truck, train, bus, or crane.

cabaret (*say* **kab**-er-ay) *noun* an entertainment, especially one provided for the customers in a restaurant or nightclub. [French, = tavern]

cabbage *noun* a vegetable with green or purple leaves.
cabbage-tree a palm-like New Zealand tree with leaves whose shoots can be eaten.

cabin *noun* **1** a hut or shelter. **2** a compartment in a ship, aircraft, or spacecraft. **3** a driver's cab.

cabinet *noun* a cupboard or container with drawers or shelves.

Cabinet *noun* the group of chief ministers, including the Prime Minister, who meet to decide government policy.

cable *noun* **1** a thick rope of fibre or wire; a thick chain. **2** cable television.
cable television the transmission of television programmes by means of cable.

cable-car *noun* a car or carriage drawn up and down a steep slope by an endless cable by means of a stationary engine at one end.

cacao (*say* ka-**kay**-oh) *noun* (*plural* **cacaos**) a tropical tree with a seed from which cocoa and chocolate are made.

cache (*say* kash) *noun* hidden stores or treasure; a hiding-place for treasure or stores. [from French *cacher* = hide]

cackle *noun* **1** the loud clucking noise a hen makes. **2** a loud silly laugh. **3** noisy chatter. **cackle** *verb*

cacophony (*say* kak-**off**-on-ee) *noun* a loud harsh unpleasant sound. [from Greek *kakos* = bad, + *phone* = sound]

cactus *noun* (*plural* **cacti**) a fleshy plant, usually with prickles, from a hot dry climate.

cadaverous (*say* kad-**av**-er-us) *adjective* pale and gaunt. [from Latin *cadaver* = corpse]

caddie *noun* a person who carries a golfer's clubs during a game.

caddy *noun* (*plural* **caddies**) a small box for holding tea.

cadence (*say* **kay**-denss) *noun* **1** rhythm; the rise and fall of the voice in speaking. **2** the final notes of a musical phrase.

cadenza (*say* ka-**den**-za) *noun* an elaborate passage for a solo instrument or singer, to show the performer's skill.

cadet *noun* **1** a young person being trained for the armed forces or the police. **2** (in full **farm cadet**) (*NZ*) an apprentice farmer.

cadge *verb* (**cadged**, **cadging**) get something by begging for it. **cadger** *noun*

cadmium *noun* a metal that looks like tin.

Caesarean section (*say* siz-**air**-ee-an) a surgical operation for taking a baby out of the mother's womb when it is due to be born. [so called because Julius Caesar is said to have been born in this way]

café (*say* **kaf**-ay) *noun* a small restaurant. [French, = coffee]

cafeteria (*say* kaf-it-**eer**-ee-a) *noun* a self-service cafe.

caffeine (*say* **kaf**-een) *noun* a stimulant substance found in tea and coffee.

caftan *noun* alternative spelling of **kaftan**.

cage *noun* **1** a container with bars or wires, in which birds or animals are kept. **2** the enclosed platform of a lift.

cairn *noun* a pile of loose stones set up as a landmark or monument.

cajole *verb* (**cajoled**, **cajoling**) coax.

cake *noun* **1** a baked food made from a mixture of flour, fat, eggs, sugar, etc. **2** a shaped or hardened mass, *a cake of soap*; *fish cakes*.

caked *adjective* covered with dried mud etc.

calamari *noun* squid (as food). [Italian]

calamine *noun* a pink powder used to make a soothing lotion for the skin.

calamity *noun* (*plural* **calamities**) a disaster. **calamitous** *adjective*

calcium *noun* a chemical substance found in teeth, bones, and lime. [from Latin *calcis* = of lime]

calculate *verb* (**calculated**, **calculating**) **1** find out by using mathematics; count. **2** plan something deliberately; intend. **calculable** *adjective*, **calculation** *noun*

calculator *noun* a small electronic device for making calculations.

calculus *noun* mathematics for working out problems about rates of change. [from Latin *calculus* = small stone (used on an abacus)]

calendar *noun* something that shows the dates of the month or year.

calf[1] *noun* (*plural* **calves**) a young cow, whale, seal, etc.

calf[2] *noun* (*plural* **calves**) the fleshy back part of the leg below the knee.

calibre (*say* **kal**-ib-er) *noun* **1** the diameter of a tube or gun-barrel, or of a bullet etc. **2** ability; importance, *someone of your calibre.* (from Arabic *kalib* = mould]

calico *noun* a kind of cotton cloth. [from Calicut, a town in India]

caliph (*say* **kal**-if or **kay**-lif) *noun* the former title of the ruler in certain Muslim countries. [from Arabic *khalifa* = successor of Muhammad]

call *noun* **1** a shout or cry. **2** a visit. **3** a summons. **4** telephoning somebody.

call *verb* **1** shout or speak loudly, e.g. to attract someone's attention; utter a call. **2** tell somebody to come to you; summon. **3** wake a person up. **4** telephone somebody. **5** make a short visit. **6** name a person or thing. **caller** *noun*
call a person's bluff challenge a person to do what was threatened, and expose the fact that it was a bluff.
call for come and collect; require, *The scandal calls for investigation.*
call up summon to join the armed forces.

call-box *noun* a telephone-box.

calligraphy (*say* kal-**ig**-raf-ee) *noun* beautiful handwriting. [from Greek *kalos* = beautiful, + *-graphy*]

calling *noun* an occupation; a profession or trade.

calliper *noun* a support for a weak or injured leg.

callipers *plural noun* compasses for measuring the width of tubes or of round objects.

callous (*say* **kal**-us) *adjective* hardhearted; unsympathetic. **callously** *adverb,* **callousness** *noun*

callow *adjective* immature and inexperienced. **callowly** *adverb,* **callowness** *noun*

callus *noun* (*plural* **calluses**) a small patch of skin that has become thick and hard through being continually pressed or rubbed.

calm *adjective* **1** quiet and still; not windy. **2** not excited or agitated. **calmly** *adverb,* **calmness** *noun*

calm *verb* make or become calm.

calorie *noun* a unit for measuring an amount of heat or the energy produced by food. **calorific** *adjective* [from Latin *calor* = heat]

calumny (*say* **kal**-um-nee) *noun* (*plural* **calumnies**) slander.

calve *verb* (**calved**, **calving**) give birth to a calf.

calypso *noun* (*plural* **calypsos**) a West Indian song about current happenings.

calyx (*say* **kay**-liks) *noun* (*plural* **calyxes** or **calyces**) a ring of leaves (*sepals*) forming the outer case of a bud.

camaraderie (*say* kam-er-**ah**-der-ee) *noun* comradeship. [French]

camber *noun* a slight upward curve or arch, e.g. on a road to allow drainage.

cambric *noun* thin linen or cotton cloth.

camcorder *noun* a combination video camera and sound recorder.

camel *noun* a large animal with a long neck and either one or two humps on its back, used in desert countries for riding and for carrying goods.

camellia *noun* a kind of evergreen flowering shrub.

cameo (*say* **kam**-ee-oh) *noun* (*plural* **cameos**) **1** a small hard piece of stone carved with a raised design in its upper layer. **2** a short well-performed part in a play etc.

camera *noun* a device for taking photographs, films, or television pictures. **cameraman** *noun*
in camera in a judge's private room; in private.

camomile *noun* a plant with sweet-smelling daisy-like flowers.

camouflage (*say* **kam**-off-lah*zh*) *noun* a way of hiding things by making them look like part of their surroundings.

camouflage *verb* (**camouflaged**, **camouflaging**) hide by camouflage. [from French *camoufler* = disguise]

camp *noun* a place where people live in tents or huts etc. **campsite** *noun*

camp *verb* make a camp; live in a camp. [same origin as *campus*]

campaign *noun* **1** a series of battles in one area or with one purpose. **2** a planned series of actions, *an advertising campaign.*

campaign *verb* take part in a campaign. **campaigner** *noun*

camper *noun* a person who camps.

campervan *noun* a motor vehicle with a kitchen, bunks, etc., that you can live in while camping.

camphor *noun* a strong-smelling white substance used in medicine and mothballs and in making plastics. **camphorated** *adjective*

campus *noun* (*plural* **campuses**) the grounds of a university or college. [Latin, = field]

can[1] *noun* **1** a metal or plastic container for liquids. **2** a sealed tin in which food or drink is preserved.

can[1] *verb* (**canned**, **canning**) preserve in a sealed can. **canner** *noun*

can[2] *auxiliary verb* (*past tense* **could**) **1** be able to, *He can play the violin.* **2** have the right or permission to, *You can go.* [from an old word meaning 'know']

USAGE It is more formal to say *You may go.*

canal *noun* **1** an artificial river cut through land so that boats can sail along it or so that it can drain or irrigate an area. **2** a tube through which something passes in the body, *the alimentary canal.* [same origin as *channel*]

canary *noun* (*plural* **canaries**) a small yellow bird that sings.

cancan *noun* a lively dance in which the legs are kicked very high.

cancel *verb* (**cancelled**, **cancelling**) **1** say that something planned will not be done or will not take place. **2** stop an order or instruction for something. **3** mark a stamp or ticket etc. so that it cannot be used again. **cancellation** *noun*
cancel out stop each other's effect, *The good and harm cancel each other out.*

cancer *noun* **1** a disease in which harmful growths form in the body. **2** a tumour, especially a harmful one. **cancerous** *adjective* [from Latin *cancer* = crab]

candelabrum (*say* kan-dil-**ab**-rum) *noun* (*plural* **candelabra**) a candlestick with several branches for holding candles. [from Latin *candela* = candle]

candid *adjective* frank. **candidly** *adverb*, **candidness** *noun* [from Latin *candidus* = white]

candidate *noun* **1** a person who wants to be elected or chosen for a particular job or position etc. **2** a person taking an examination. **candidacy** *noun*, **candidature** *noun* [from Latin *candidus* = white (because Roman candidates for office had to wear a pure white toga)]

candied *adjective* coated or preserved in sugar.
candied peel bits of the peel of citrus fruits candied for use in cooking. [from *candy*]

candle *noun* a stick of wax with a wick through it, giving light when burning. **candlelight** *noun*

candlestick *noun* a holder for a candle or candles.

candour (*say* **kan**-der) *noun* being candid; frankness.

candy *noun* (*plural* **candies**) (*American*) sweets; a sweet. [from Arabic *kand* = sugar]

candyfloss *noun* a fluffy mass of very thin strands of spun sugar.

cane *noun* **1** the stem of a reed or tall grass etc. **2** a thin stick.

cane *verb* (**caned**, **caning**) beat with a cane.

canine (*say* **kayn**-I'n) *adjective* of dogs.
canine tooth a pointed tooth.

canine *noun* **1** a dog. **2** a canine tooth. [from Latin *canis* = dog]

canister *noun* a metal container.

canker *noun* a disease that rots the wood of trees and plants or causes ulcers and sores on animals.

cannabis *noun* hemp, especially when smoked as a drug. [from *Cannabis*, the Latin name of the hemp plant]

cannibal *noun* **1** a person who eats human flesh. **2** an animal that eats animals of its own kind. **cannibalism** *noun* [named after the Caribs, a former man-eating tribe in the West Indies]

cannibalise *verb* (**cannibalised**, **cannibalising**) take a machine etc. apart to provide spare parts for others. **cannibalisation** *noun*

cannon *noun* **1** (*plural* **cannon**) a large heavy gun. **2** the hitting of two balls in billiards by the third ball.

cannon *verb* (**cannoned**, **cannoning**) bump into something heavily.

cannon-ball *noun* a large solid ball fired from a cannon.

cannot can not.

canny *adjective* (**cannier**, **canniest**) shrewd. **cannily** *adverb*

canoe *noun* a narrow lightweight boat.

canoe *verb* (**canoed**, **canoeing**) travel in a canoe. **canoeist** *noun*

canon *noun* **1** a clergyman of a cathedral. **2** a general principle; a rule.

canonise *verb* (**canonised**, **canonising**) declare officially that someone is a saint. **canonisation** *noun*

canopy *noun* (*plural* **canopies**) **1** a hanging cover forming a shelter above a throne, bed, or person etc. **2** the part of a parachute that spreads in the air.

cant[1] *verb* slope; tilt. [from a Dutch word meaning 'edge']

cant² *noun* **1** insincere talk. **2** jargon. [from Latin *cantare* = sing]

can't (*mainly spoken*) cannot.

Cantabrian *noun* a person born or living in Canterbury, New Zealand. **Cantabrian** *adjective*

cantaloup (also **cantaloupe**) *noun* a round melon often known as rock melon or honey melon.

cantankerous *adjective* bad-tempered.

cantata (*say* kant-**ah**-ta) *noun* a musical composition for singers, like an oratorio but shorter. [from Italian *cantare* = sing]

canteen *noun* **1** a restaurant for workers in a factory, office, etc. **2** a case or box containing a set of cutlery. **3** a soldier's or camper's water-flask.

canter *noun* a gentle gallop.

canter *verb* go or ride at a canter. [short for 'Canterbury gallop', the gentle pace at which pilgrims were said to travel to Canterbury, England in the Middle Ages]

canticle *noun* a religious song with words taken from the Bible, e.g. the Magnificat. [from Latin, = little song]

cantilever *noun* a projecting beam or girder supporting a bridge etc.

canton *noun* each of the districts into which Switzerland is divided.

canvas *noun* (*plural* **canvases**) **1** a kind of strong coarse cloth. **2** a piece of canvas for painting on; a painting. [from Latin *Cannabis* = hemp, from whose fibres cloth was made]

canvass *verb* visit people to ask for votes, opinions, etc. **canvasser** *noun*

canyon *noun* a deep valley, usually with a river running through it. [from Spanish *cañon* = tube]

cap *noun* **1** a soft hat without a brim but often with a peak. **2** a special head-dress, e.g. that worn by a nurse; an academic mortar-board; a cap showing membership of a sports team. **4** a cap-like cover or top. **5** something that makes a bang when fired in a toy pistol.

cap *verb* (**capped**, **capping**) **1** put a cap or cover on something; cover. **2** award a sports cap to a person chosen as a member of a team. **3** do better than something, *Can you cap that joke?* **4** (*NZ*) confer a university degree.
capping ceremony (*NZ*) a degree ceremony at a university.

capable *adjective* able to do something. **capably** *adverb*, **capability** *noun*

capacious (*say* ka-**pay**-shus) *adjective* roomy; able to hold a large amount.

capacity *noun* (*plural* **capacities**) **1** the amount that something can hold. **2** ability; capability. **3** the position that someone occupies, *In my capacity as your guardian I am responsible for you.*

cape¹ *noun* a cloak.

cape² *noun* a promontory on the coast.
cape weed a weed with yellow flowers.

caper¹ *verb* jump or run about playfully.

caper¹ *noun* **1** capering. **2** (*slang*) an activity; an adventure.

caper² *noun* a bud of a prickly shrub, pickled for use in sauces etc.

capillary (*say* ka-**pil**-er-ee) *noun* (*plural* **capillaries**) any of the very fine blood-vessels that connect veins and arteries.

capillary *adjective* of or occurring in a very narrow tube; of a capillary. [from Latin *capillus* = hair]

capital *adjective* **1** important. **2** (*informal*) excellent.
capital city the city where the government of a country or state is located.
capital gain profit from the sale of property or other investments.
capital letter a large letter of the kind used at the start of a name or sentence.
capital punishment punishing criminals by putting them to death.

capital *noun* **1** a capital city. **2** a capital letter. **3** the top part of a pillar. **4** money or property that can be used to produce more wealth. [from Latin *caput* = head]

capitalise (*say* **kap**-it-al-I'z) *verb* (**capitalised**, **capitalising**) **1** write or print as a capital letter. **2** change something into capital; provide with capital (= money).
capitalisation *noun*
capitalise on profit by something; use it to your own advantage, *You could capitalise on your skill at drawing.*

capitalism (*say* **kap**-it-al-izm) *noun* a system in which trade and industry are controlled by private owners for profit. (Compare *Communism*.)

capitalist (*say* **kap**-it-al-ist) *noun* **1** a person who has much money or property being used to make more wealth; a very rich person. **2** a person who is in favour of capitalism.

capitulate *verb* (**capitulated**, **capitulating**) admit that you are defeated and surrender.
capitulation *noun*

cappuccino *noun* coffee made with frothy milk.

caprice (*say* ka-**preess**) *noun* a capricious action or impulse; a whim.

capricious (*say* ka-**prish**-us) *adjective* deciding or changing your mind in an impulsive way. **capriciously** *adverb*, **capriciousness** *noun*

capsize *verb* (**capsized**, **capsizing**) overturn, *the boat capsized.*

capstan *noun* a thick post that can be turned to pull in a rope or cable etc. that winds round it as it turns.

capsule *noun* **1** a hollow pill containing medicine. **2** a plant's seed-case that splits open when ripe. **3** a compartment that can be separated from the rest of a spacecraft.

captain *noun* **1** a person in command of a ship, aircraft, sports team, etc. **2** an army officer ranking next below a major; a naval officer ranking next below a commodore.
captaincy *noun*

captain *verb* be the captain of a sports team etc. [same origin as *capital*]

Captain Cooker (*NZ*) a wild boar. [brought into the country by Captain Cook]

caption *noun* **1** the words printed with a picture to describe it. **2** a short title or heading in a newspaper or magazine.

captious (*say* **kap**-shus) *adjective* pointing out small mistakes or faults.

captivate *verb* (**captivated**, **captivating**) charm or delight someone.
captivation *noun*

captive *noun* someone taken prisoner.

captive *adjective* taken prisoner; unable to escape. **captivity** *noun*

captor *noun* someone who has captured a person or animal.

capture *verb* (**captured**, **capturing**) **1** seize; make a prisoner of someone. **2** take or obtain by force, trickery, skill, or attraction, *He captured her heart.*

capture *noun* **1** capturing. **2** a person or thing captured. [from Latin *capere* = take]

car *noun* **1** a motor car. **2** a carriage, *dining-car.* [from Latin *carrus* = wagon]

carafe (*say* ka-**raf**) *noun* a glass bottle holding wine or water for pouring out at the table. [from Arabic *gharrafa*]

caramel *noun* **1** a kind of toffee tasting like burnt sugar. **2** burnt sugar used for colouring and flavouring food.

carapace (*say* **ka**-ra-payss) *noun* the shell on the back of a tortoise or crustacean.

carat *noun* **1** a measure of weight for precious stones. **2** a measure of the purity of gold, *Pure gold is 24 carats.*

caravan *noun* **1** an enclosed carriage equipped for living in, able to be towed by a motor vehicle or a horse. **2** a group of people travelling together across desert country.
caravanning *noun* [from Persian *karwan*]

caraway *noun* a plant with spicy seeds that are used for flavouring food.

carbohydrate *noun* a compound of carbon, oxygen, and hydrogen (e.g. sugar).

carbolic *noun* a kind of disinfectant.

carbon *noun* **1** a substance that is present in all living things and that occurs in its pure form as diamond and graphite. **2** carbon paper. **3** a carbon copy.
carbon copy a copy made with carbon paper; an exact copy.
carbon credit an ecological benefit earned by a person or corporation from forest planting or maintenance, which can be traded with another group.
carbon dioxide a gas formed when things burn, or breathed out by animals.
carbon paper thin paper with a coloured coating, placed between sheets of paper to make copies of what is written or typed on the top sheet.
carbon tax a tax on motor vehicle fuels and emissions which contribute to the greenhouse effect.

carbonate *noun* a compound that gives off carbon dioxide when mixed with acid.

carbonated *adjective* with carbon dioxide added, *Carbonated drinks are fizzy.*

carboniferous *adjective* producing coal. [from *carbon*, + Latin *ferre* = to bear]

carbuncle *noun* **1** a bad abscess in the skin. **2** a bright-red gem.

carburettor *noun* a device for mixing fuel and air in an engine.

carcass *noun* (*plural* **carcasses**) **1** the dead body of an animal. **2** the bony part of a bird's body before or after it is cooked. **3** a framework, e.g. of a tyre.

card[1] *noun* **1** a small usually oblong piece of stiff paper or of plastic. **2** a playing-card. **3** cardboard.
cards *plural noun* a game using playing-cards.
on the cards likely; possible.

card[2] *verb* clean and disentangle wool-fibres with a wire brush or toothed instrument called a *card.*

cardboard *noun* a kind of thin board made of layers of paper or wood-fibre.

cardiac (*say* **kard**-ee-ak) *adjective* of the heart. [from Greek *kardia* = heart]

cardie *noun* (*informal*) a cardigan.

cardigan *noun* a knitted jacket. [named after the Earl of Cardigan, who led the Charge of the Light Brigade in the Crimean War (1854)]

cardinal *noun* a senior priest in the Roman Catholic Church.

cardinal *adjective* **1** chief; most important, *the cardinal features of our plan.* **2** deep scarlet (like a cardinal's cassock).
cardinal numbers the whole numbers one, two, three, etc. (Compare *ordinal.*)
cardinal points the four main points of the compass (North, East, South, West).

cardiology *noun* the study of the structure and diseases of the heart. **cardiological** *adjective*, **cardiologist** *noun* [from Greek *kardia* = heart, + *-logy*]

care *noun* **1** serious attention and thought, *Plan your holiday with care.* **2** caution to avoid damage or loss, *Glass—handle with care.* **3** protection; supervision, *Leave the child in my care.* **4** worry; anxiety, *freedom from care.* [from Old English *caru* = sorrow]

care *verb* (**cared**, **caring**) **1** feel interested or concerned. **2** feel affection.
care for have in your care; be fond of.

career *noun* **1** progress through life, especially in work. **2** an occupation with opportunities for promotion.

career *verb* rush along wildly.

carefree *adjective* without worries or responsibilities.

careful *adjective* **1** giving serious thought and attention to something. **2** avoiding damage or danger etc.; cautious. **carefully** *adverb*, **carefulness** *noun*

caregiver *noun* someone who regularly cares for a child or sick person etc.

careless *adjective* not careful. **carelessly** *adverb*, **carelessness** *noun*

caress *noun* a gentle loving touch.

caress *verb* touch lovingly.

caret *noun* a mark (∧ or /) showing where something is to be inserted in writing or printing. [Latin, = it is lacking]

caretaker *noun* a person employed to look after a school, block of flats, etc.

cargo *noun* (*plural* **cargoes**) goods carried in a ship or aircraft.

Caribbean *adjective* of or from the Caribbean Sea, a part of the Atlantic Ocean east of Central America.

caribou (*say* **ka**-rib-oo) *noun* (*plural* **caribou**) a North American reindeer.

caricature *noun* an amusing or exaggerated picture of someone. [from Italian *caricare* = exaggerate]

caries (*say* **kair**-eez) *noun* (*plural* **caries**) decay in teeth or bones. [Latin]

carmine *adjective & noun* deep red.

carnage *noun* the killing of many people.

carnal *adjective* of the body as opposed to the spirit; not spiritual. [from Latin *carnis* = of flesh]

carnation *noun* a garden flower with a sweet smell.

carnival *noun* a festival, often with a procession in fancy dress. [originally this meant the festivities before Lent when meat (Latin *carnis* = of flesh) was given up until Easter]

carnivorous (*say* kar-**niv**-er-us) *adjective* meat-eating. (Compare *herbivorous.*)
carnivore *noun* [from Latin *carnis* = of flesh, + *vorare* = devour]

carol *noun* a joyful song; a Christmas hymn. **caroller** *noun*, **carolling** *noun*

carouse *verb* (**caroused**, **carousing**) drink and be merry.

carousel (*say* ka-roo-**sel**) *noun* **1** (*American*) a merry-go-round. **2** a rotating conveyor, e.g. for baggage at an airport.

carp[1] *noun* an edible freshwater fish.

carp[2] *verb* keep finding fault.

carpenter *noun* a person who makes things out of wood. **carpentry** *noun*

carpet *noun* a thick soft covering for a floor. **carpeted** *adjective*, **carpeting** *noun*

carport *noun* a shelter for a car.

carriage *noun* **1** one of the separate parts of a train, where passengers sit. **2** a passenger vehicle pulled by horses. **3** a moving part carrying or holding something in a machine.

carriageway *noun* the part of a road on which vehicles travel.

carrier *noun* a person or thing that carries something.

carrion *noun* dead and decaying flesh. [same origin as *carnal*]

carrot *noun* a plant with a thick orange-coloured root used as a vegetable.

carry *verb* (**carried**, **carrying**) **1** take something from one place to another. **2** support the weight of something. **3** travel clearly, *Sound carries in the mountains.* **4** win; approve, *The motion was carried by ten votes to six.*
be carried away be very excited.
carry on continue; manage; (*informal*) behave excitedly; (*informal*) complain. [same origin as *car*]

cart *noun* an open vehicle for carrying loads.

cart *verb* **1** carry in a cart. **2** (*informal*) carry something heavy or tiring, *I've carted these books all round the school.*

cartage *noun* the act or cost of transporting goods.

cart-horse *noun* a large strong horse used for pulling heavy loads.

cartilage *noun* tough white flexible tissue attached to a bone.

cartography *noun* drawing maps. **cartographer** *noun*, **cartographic** *adjective* [from French *carte* = map, + *-graphy*]

carton *noun* a cardboard or plastic container.

cartoon *noun* **1** an amusing drawing. **2** a comic strip (see *comic*). **3** an animated film. **cartoonist** *noun*

cartridge *noun* **1** a case containing the explosive for a bullet or shell. **2** a container holding film for a camera, ink for a pen or printer, etc.

cartwheel *noun* **1** the wheel of a cart. **2** a handstand balancing on each hand in turn with arms and legs spread like spokes of a wheel.

carve *verb* (**carved**, **carving**) **1** make by cutting wood or stone etc. **2** cut cooked meat into slices. **carver** *noun*

cascade *noun* a waterfall.

cascade *verb* (**cascaded**, **cascading**) fall like a cascade.

case[1] *noun* **1** a container. **2** a suitcase. [from Latin *capsa* = box]

case[2] *noun* **1** an example of something existing or occurring; a situation, *In every case we found that someone had cheated.* **2** something investigated by police etc. or by a lawcourt, *a murder case.* **3** a set of facts or arguments to support something, *She put forward a good case for equality.* **4** the form of a word that shows how it is related to other words. *Fred's* is the possessive case of *Fred*; *him* is the object case of *he*.
in any case anyway.
in case because something may happen; lest. [from Latin *casus* = occasion]

casein (*say* **kay**-seen) *noun* a protein found in milk. It is the basis of cheese. [from Latin *caseus* = cheese]

casement *noun* a window that opens on hinges at its side.

cash *noun* **1** money in coin or notes. **2** immediate payment for goods etc.
cash register a device that registers the amount of money put in, used in a shop.

cash *verb* change a cheque etc. for cash.

cashew *noun* a kind of small nut.

cashgora *noun* (*NZ*) **1** a crossbred variety of goat. **2** its fleece. [from *cash*mere + *angora*]

cashier *noun* a person who takes in and pays out money in a bank or takes payments in a shop.

cashmere *noun* very fine soft wool especially that of the Kashmir goat.

casing *noun* a protective covering.

casino *noun* (*plural* **casinos**) a public building or room for gambling.

cask *noun* **1** a barrel. **2** (*NZ*) a cardboard container lined with plastic or foil and filled with wine or juice.

casket *noun* a small box for jewellery etc.

cassava *noun* a tropical plant with starchy roots that are an important source of food in tropical countries.

casserole *noun* **1** a covered dish in which food is cooked and served. **2** food cooked in a casserole. [from Greek, = little cup]

cassette *noun* a small sealed case containing recording tape, film, etc. [French, = little case]

cassock *noun* a long garment worn by clergy and members of a church choir.

cassowary *noun* (*plural* **cassowaries**) a large flightless Australian bird related to the emu.

cast *verb* (**cast**, **casting**) **1** throw. **2** shed or throw off. **3** make a vote. **4** make something of metal or plaster in a mould. **5** choose performers for a play or film etc.
casting vote the vote that decides which group wins when the votes on each side are equal.
cast iron a hard alloy of iron made by casting it in a mould.

cast *noun* **1** a shape made by pouring liquid metal or plaster into a mould. **2** all the performers in a play or film.

castanets *plural noun* two pieces of wood, ivory, etc. held in one hand and clapped together to make a clicking sound, usually for dancing. [from Spanish *castañetas* = little chestnuts]

castaway *noun* a shipwrecked person.

caste *noun* (in India) one of the social classes into which Hindus are born. [from Spanish *casta* = descent from ancestors]

caster *noun* (also **castor**) **1** a small wheel on the leg of a table, chair, etc. **2** a container with holes for sprinkling sugar. [from *cast*]
caster sugar finely-ground white sugar.

castigate *verb* (**castigated**, **castigating**) punish or rebuke severely. **castigation** *noun* [from Latin *castigare* = punish]

castle *noun* **1** a large old fortified building. **2** a piece in chess, also called a *rook*.
castles in the air daydreams. [from Latin *castellum* = fort]

castor oil oil from the seeds of a tropical plant, used as a laxative.

castrate *verb* (**castrated**, **castrating**) remove the testicles of a male animal; geld. (Compare *spay*.) **castration** *noun*

casual *adjective* **1** happening by chance; not planned. **2** not careful; not methodical. **3** informal; suitable for informal occasions, *casual clothes.* **4** not permanent, *casual work.* **casually** *adverb*, **casualness** *noun*

casualty *noun* (*plural* **casualties**) a person who is killed or injured in war or in an accident.

cat *noun* **1** a small furry domestic animal. **2** an animal of the same family as the domestic cat, *Lions and tigers are cats.* **3** (*informal*) a spiteful girl or woman.
let the cat out of the bag reveal a secret.

cata- *prefix* (becoming **cat-** before a vowel; combining with an *h* to become **cath-**) **1** down (as in *catapult*). **2** thoroughly (as in *catalogue*). [from Greek *kata* = down]

cataclysm (*say* **kat**-a-klizm) *noun* a violent upheaval or disaster.

catacombs (*say* **kat**-a-koomz) *plural noun* underground passages with compartments for tombs.

catafalque (*say* **kat**-a-falk) *noun* a decorated platform for a person's coffin.

catalogue *noun* **1** a list of things (e.g. of books in a library), usually arranged in order. **2** a book containing a list of things available, *Christmas catalogue.*

catalogue *verb* (**catalogued**, **cataloguing**) enter something in a catalogue. [from Greek *katalogos* = list]

catalyst (*say* **kat**-a-list) *noun* something that starts or speeds up a change or reaction. [from *cata-*, + Greek *lysis* = loosening]

catamaran *noun* a boat with twin hulls. [from Tamil *kattumaram* = tied wood]

catapult *noun* **1** a device with elastic for shooting small stones. **2** an ancient military device for hurling stones etc.

catapult *verb* hurl or rush violently. [from *cata-*, + Greek *pellein* = throw]

cataract *noun* **1** a large waterfall or rush of water. **2** a cloudy area that forms in the eye and prevents a person from seeing clearly.

catarrh (*say* ka-**tar**) *noun* inflammation in your nose that makes it drip a watery fluid. [from Greek, = flow down]

catastrophe (*say* ka-**tass**-trof-ee) *noun* a sudden great disaster. **catastrophic** (*say* kat-a-**strof**-ik) *adjective*, **catastrophically** *adverb*

catch *verb* (**caught**, **catching**) **1** take and hold something. **2** capture. **3** overtake. **4** be in time to get on a bus or train etc. **5** be infected with an illness. **6** hear, *I didn't catch what he said.* **7** surprise or detect somebody, *caught in the act.* **8** trick somebody. **9** make or become fixed or unable to move; snag; entangle, *I caught my dress on a nail.* **10** hit; strike, *The blow caught him on the nose.*
catch fire start burning.
catch it (*informal*) be scolded or punished.
catch on (*informal*) become popular; understand.

catch *noun* (*plural* **catches**) **1** catching something. **2** something caught or worth catching. **3** a hidden difficulty. **4** a device for fastening something.

catcher *noun* **1** a person or thing that catches. **2** (in softball and baseball) the fielder positioned behind the batter.

catching *adjective* infectious.

catchment area **1** the whole area from which water drains into a river etc. **2** the area from which a school takes pupils or a hospital takes patients.

catchphrase *noun* a popular phrase.

catchy *adjective* easy to remember; soon becoming popular, *a catchy tune.*

catechism (*say* **kat**-ik-izm) *noun* a set of questions and answers that give the basic beliefs of a religion.

categorical (*say* kat-ig-**o**-rik-al) *adjective* definite and absolute, *a categorical refusal.* **categorically** *adverb*

category *noun* (*plural* **categories**) a set of people or things classified as being similar to each other.

cater *verb* **1** provide food etc. **2** satisfy or make allowances for. **caterer** *noun*

caterpillar *noun* the creeping worm-like creature that will turn into a butterfly or moth. [from Old French *chatepelose* = hairy cat]

cath- *prefix* see **cata-**.

cathedral *noun* the most important church of a district, usually containing the bishop's throne. [from Greek *kathedra* = seat]

Catherine wheel a firework that spins round. [named after St Catherine, who was martyred on a spiked wheel]

cathode *noun* the electrode by which electric current leaves a device. (Compare *anode.*) [from *cata-* = down, + Greek *hodos* = way]

Catholic *adjective* **1** of all Christians, *the Holy Catholic Church.* **2** Roman Catholic (see *Roman*). **Catholicism** *noun*

Catholic *noun* a Roman Catholic.

catholic *adjective* including most things, *Her taste in literature is catholic.* [from Greek *katholikos* = universal]

catkin *noun* a spike of small soft flowers on trees such as hazel and willow. [from Dutch *katteken* = kitten]

catnap *noun* a short sleep.

catseye *noun* **1** (*trade mark*) one of a line of reflecting studs marking the centre or edge of a road. **2** a New Zealand shellfish.

cattle *plural noun* animals with horns and hoofs, kept by farmers for their milk and beef.

cattle-dog *noun* a dog trained to herd cattle.

cattle-stop *noun* (*NZ*) a grid over a ditch, that vehicles and people can cross but not animals, used instead of a gate.

catty *adjective* (**cattier**, **cattiest**) speaking or spoken spitefully.

caucus *noun* (*plural* **caucuses**) (*NZ*) **1** all the Members of Parliament of a single political party, *the Labour Party caucus.* **2** a meeting of such a group.

cauldron *noun* a large deep pot for boiling things in. [from Latin *caldarium* = hot bath]

cauliflower *noun* a cabbage with a large head of white flowers. [from French *chou fleuri* flowered cabbage]

cause *noun* **1** a person or thing that makes something happen or produces an effect. **2** a reason, *There is no cause for worry.* **3** a purpose for which people work; an organisation or charity.

cause *verb* (**caused**, **causing**) be the cause of; make something happen.

causeway *noun* a raised road across low or marshy ground.

caustic *adjective* **1** able to burn or wear things away by chemical action. **2** sarcastic. **caustically** *adverb* [from Greek *kaustikos* = capable of burning]

cauterise *verb* (**cauterised**, **cauterising**) burn the surface of flesh to destroy infection or stop bleeding. **cauterisation** *noun* [from Greek *kauterion* = branding-iron]

caution *noun* **1** care taken so as to avoid danger etc. **2** a warning.

caution *verb* warn someone.

cautionary *adjective* giving a warning.

cautious *adjective* showing caution. **cautiously** *adverb*, **cautiousness** *noun*

cavalcade *noun* a procession. [from Italian *cavalcare* = ride]

cavalry *noun* soldiers who fight on horseback or in armoured vehicles. (Compare *infantry.*) [from Latin *caballus* = horse]

cave *noun* a large hollow place in the side of a hill or cliff, or underground.

cave *verb* (**caved**, **caving**) **cave in** fall inwards; give way in an argument. [from Latin *cavus* = hollow]

caveat (*say* **kav**-ee-at) *noun* a warning. [Latin, = let a person beware]

caveman *noun* (*plural* **cavemen**) a person living in a cave in ancient times.

cavern *noun* a large cave. **cavernous** *adjective*

caviare (*say* **kav**-ee-ar) *noun* the pickled roe of sturgeon or other large fish.

cavil *verb* (**cavilled**, **cavilling**) raise petty objections.

caving *noun* exploring caves.

cavity *noun* (*plural* **cavities**) a hollow or hole. [same origin as *cave*]

cavort (*say* ka-**vort**) *verb* caper about.

caw *noun* the harsh cry of a crow etc.

CBD *abbreviation* central business district.

cc *abbreviation* cubic centimetre(s).

CD *abbreviation* compact disc.
CD-ROM a compact disc with read-only memory, used for storing large databases for access via a computer.

cease *verb* (**ceased**, **ceasing**) stop; end.

cease *noun* **without cease** not ceasing.

cease-fire *noun* a period of truce.

ceaseless *adjective* not ceasing.

cedar *noun* an evergreen tree with hard fragrant wood. **cedarwood** *noun*

cede (*say* seed) *verb* (**ceded**, **ceding**) give up your rights to something; surrender. *They had to cede some of their territory.* [from Latin *cedere* = yield]

cedilla (*say* sid-**il**-a) *noun* a mark under c in certain languages to show that it is pronounced as *s*, e.g. in *façade.* [from Spanish, = a little *z*]

ceiling *noun* **1** the flat surface under the top of a room. **2** the highest limit that something can reach.

celandine *noun* a small wild plant with yellow flowers.

celebrate *verb* (**celebrated**, **celebrating**) **1** do something special or enjoyable to show that a day or event is important. **2** perform a religious ceremony. **celebrant** *noun*, **celebration** *noun*

celebrated *adjective* famous.

celebrity *noun* (*plural* **celebrities**) **1** a famous person. **2** fame; being famous.

celery *noun* a vegetable with crisp white or green stems.
celery pine (*NZ*) an evergreen tree with leaves that look like celery.

celestial (*say* sil-**est**-ee-al) *adjective* **1** of the sky. **2** of heaven; divine.
celestial bodies stars etc.

celibate (*say* **sel**-ib-it) *adjective* abstaining from sexual relations or from marrying. **celibacy** *noun*

cell *noun* **1** a very small room. e.g. in a monastery or a prison. **2** a microscopic unit of living matter. **3** a compartment of a honeycomb. **4** a device for producing electric current chemically. **5** a small group or unit in an organisation etc. [from Latin *cella* = store-room]

cellar *noun* an underground room. [same origin as *cell*]

cello (*say* **chel**-oh) *noun* a musical instrument like a large violin, placed between the knees of a player. **cellist** *noun* [short for *violoncello* (same origin as *violin*)]

cellphone short for **cellular telephone**

cellular *adjective* **1** of or containing cells. **2** with an open mesh, *cellular blankets.* **cellular telephone** a portable radiotelephone using a network of transmitters, each of which covers a particular area or 'cell'.

cellulite *noun* a lumpy form of fat producing puckering of the skin.

celluloid *noun* a kind of plastic.

cellulose *noun* **1** tissue that forms the main part of all plants and trees. **2** paint made from cellulose.

Celsius (*say* **sel**-see-us) *adjective* (of a temperature scale) centigrade. [named after A. Celsius, a Swedish astronomer]

Celtic *adjective* of the languages or inhabitants of ancient Britain and France before the Romans came, or of their descendants, e.g. Irish, Welsh, Gaelic. **Celt** *noun*

cement *noun* **1** a mixture of lime and clay used in building, to join bricks together, etc. **2** a strong glue.

cement *verb* **1** put cement on something. **2** join firmly; strengthen.

cemetery (*say* **sem**-et-ree) *noun* (*plural* **cemeteries**) a place where people are buried. [from Greek *koimeterion* = dormitory]

cenotaph (*say* **sen**-o-taf) *noun* a monument, especially as a war memorial, to people who are buried elsewhere. [from Greek *kenos* = empty, + *taphos* = tomb]

censer *noun* a container in which incense is burnt. [same origin as *incense*]

censor *noun* a person who examines films, books, letters, etc. and removes or bans anything that seems harmful. **censor** *verb,* **censorship** *noun* [Latin, = magistrate with power to ban unsuitable people from ceremonies]

censorious (*say* sen-**sor**-ee-us) *adjective* criticising something strongly.

censure (*say* **sen**-sher) *noun* strong criticism or disapproval of something.

census *noun* (*plural* **censuses**) an official count or survey of population, traffic, etc. [Latin, from *censere* = estimate]

cent *noun* one-hundredth of a dollar. [from Latin *centum* = 100]

centenarian (*say* sent-in-**air**-ee-an) *noun* a person who is 100 years old or more.

centenary *noun* (also **centennial**) a 100th anniversary.

centi- *prefix* **1** one hundred (as in *centipede*). **2** one-hundredth (as in *centimetre*). [from Latin *centum* = 100]

centigrade *adjective* measuring temperature on a scale using 100 degrees, where water freezes at 0°, and boils at 100°. [from *centi-*, + Latin *gradus* = step]

centimetre *noun* one-hundredth of a metre.

centipede *noun* a small crawling creature with a long body and many legs. [from *centi-*, + Latin *pedes* = feet]

central *adjective* **1** of or at the centre. **2** most important. **centrally** *adverb* **central heating** a system of heating a building from one source by circulating hot water or hot air or steam in pipes or by linked radiators.

centralise *verb* (**centralised**, **centralising**) bring under a central authority's control. **centralisation** *noun*

centre *noun* **1** the middle point or part. **2** an important place, e.g. from which things are organised; a place where certain things happen, *shopping centre.*

centre *verb* (**centred**, **centring**) place something in or at the centre. [from Greek *kentron* = sharp point]

centrifugal *adjective* moving away from the centre; using centrifugal force. **centrifugal force** a force that makes a thing that is travelling round a central point fly outwards off its circular path. [from Latin *centrum* = centre, + *fugere* = flee]

centurion (*say* sent-**yoor**-ee-on) *noun* an officer in the ancient Roman army. [originally he was in charge of 100 men (Latin *centum* = 100)]

century *noun* (*plural* **centuries**) **1** a period of one hundred years. **2** a hundred runs scored by a batsman in an innings at cricket. [from Latin *centum* = 100]

cephalopod (*say* **sef**-al-o-pod) *noun* a mollusc (such as an octopus) that has a head with a ring of tentacles round the mouth. [from Greek *kephale* = head, + podos = of a foot]

CER *abbreviation* Closer Economic Relations (a New Zealand-Australia trade agreement signed in 1983).

ceramic *adjective* of pottery.

ceramics *plural noun* pottery-making.

cereal *noun* **1** grass producing seeds which are used as food, e.g. wheat, barley, rice. **2** a breakfast food made from these seeds. [from the name of Ceres, Roman goddess of the corn]

cerebral (*say* **se**-rib-ral) *adjective* of the brain. **cerebral palsy** a condition involving muscle spasms and involuntary movements. [from Latin *cerebrum* = brain]

ceremonial *adjective* of or used in a ceremony; formal. **ceremonially** *adverb*

ceremonious *adjective* full of ceremony; elaborately performed.

ceremony *noun* (*plural* **ceremonies**) the formal actions carried out on an important occasion, e.g. at a wedding or a funeral.

cert[1] *noun* (*informal*) a certificate.

cert[2] *noun* (*informal*) a sure thing or certainty, *dead cert.*

certain *adjective* sure; without doubt.
a certain person or **thing** a person or thing that is known but not named.

certainly *adverb* **1** for certain. **2** yes.

certainty *noun* (*plural* **certainties**) **1** something that is sure to happen. **2** being sure.

certificate *noun* an official written or printed statement giving information about a person etc., *a birth certificate.*

certify *verb* (**certified**, **certifying**) declare something formally; show on a certificate. **certification** *noun*

certitude *noun* a feeling of certainty.

cervena *noun* (*NZ*) venison.

cervix *noun* **1** the neck. **2** the neck of the womb. **cervical** *adjective* [Latin, = neck]

cessation *noun* ceasing.

cession *noun* ceding something.

cesspit or **cesspool** *noun* a covered pit where liquid waste or sewage is stored temporarily.

cetacean (*say* sit-**ay**-shan) *noun* a member of a group of mammals that includes whales, porpoises, and dolphins. **cetacean** *adjective* [from Greek *ketos* = whale]

cf. *abbreviation* compare. [from Latin *confer*]

CFC *abbreviation* chlorofluorocarbon (a compound released into the atmosphere from aerosol sprays etc.)

ch. *abbreviation* chapter.

chafe *verb* (**chafed**, **chafing**) **1** rub a person's skin to make it warm again. **2** make or become sore by rubbing. **3** become irritated or impatient, *We chafed at the delay.* [from French *chauffer* = make warm]

chaff *noun* **1** husks of corn, separated from the seed. **2** hay or straw cut up for livestock food. **3** teasing; joking.

chaff *verb* tease; joke.

chaffinch *noun* (*plural* **chaffinches**) a kind of finch.

chagrin (*say* **shag**-rin) *noun* a feeling of being annoyed and embarrassed or disappointed. [French]

chain *noun* **1** a row of metal rings fastened together. **2** a connected series of things, *a chain of mountains; a chain of events.* **3** (*NZ*) the mechanism from which animals are suspended for slaughter and processing at a freezing works.
chain-letter a letter that you are asked to copy and send to several other people.
chain reaction a series of happenings in which each causes the next.
chain saw a power saw with teeth on an endless chain.
chain store one of a number of similar shops owned by the same firm.
drag the chain (*NZ, informal*) lag behind.

chain *verb* fasten with a chain or chains.

chair *noun* **1** a movable seat, with a back, for one person. **2** a position of authority at a meeting, *Mr Bloggs was in the chair.* **3** a chairperson.

chair *verb* be in charge of, *Who will chair this meeting?*

chairman *noun* (*plural* **chairmen**) the person who chairs a meeting. **chairwoman** *noun* (*plural* **chairwomen**), **chairperson** *noun*

chalet (*say* **shal**-ay) *noun* **1** a Swiss mountain hut or cottage. **2** a house or other accommodation in a style similar to this.

chalice *noun* a large goblet for holding wine, especially one used at Holy Communion. [from Latin *calix* = cup]

chalk *noun* **1** a soft white or coloured stick used for writing on blackboards or for drawing. **2** soft white limestone. **chalky** *adjective*

challenge *noun* a demand to have a contest, do something difficult, say who you are, etc.

challenge *verb* (**challenged**, **challenging**) **1** make a challenge to someone. **2** question whether something is true or correct. **challenger** *noun*

chamber *noun* **1** (*old use*) a room. **2** a hall used for meetings of a parliament etc.; the members of the group using it. **3** a compartment in machinery etc.
chamber music music for a small group of players.

chambermaid *noun* a woman employed to clean bedrooms at a hotel etc.

chameleon (*say* kam-**ee**-lee-on) *noun* a small lizard that can change its colour to that of its surroundings.

chamois *noun* (*plural* **chamois**) **1** (*say* **sham**-wa) a small wild antelope living in the mountains of Europe and Asia. **2** (*say* **sham**-ee) a piece of soft yellow leather used for washing and polishing things. [French]

champ *verb* munch or bite something noisily.

champagne (*say* sham-**payn**) *noun* a bubbly wine, especially from Champagne in France.

champion *noun* **1** a person or thing that has defeated all the others in a sport or competition etc. **2** someone who supports a cause by fighting, speaking, etc. **championship** *noun*

champion *verb* support a cause by fighting or speaking for it.

chance *noun* **1** a possibility; an opportunity, *Now is your chance to escape.* **2** the way things happen without being planned, *I met her by chance.*
take a chance take a risk.

chance *verb* (**chanced**, **chancing**) **1** happen by chance. *I chanced to meet her.* **2** (*informal*) risk, *Let's chance it.*

chancel *noun* the part of a church nearest to the altar.

chancellor *noun* an important official in a country, university, or diocese.

chancy *adjective* risky.

chandelier (*say* shand-il-**eer**) *noun* a hanging support for several lights. [from French *chandelle* = candle]

change *verb* (**changed**, **changing**) **1** make or become different. **2** exchange. **3** put fresh clothes or coverings etc. **4** go from one train or bus etc. to another.

change *noun* **1** changing; alteration. **2** coins or notes of small values. **3** money given back to the payer when the price is less than the amount handed over. **4** a fresh set of clothes. **5** a variation in routine, *Let's walk home for a change.*

changeable *adjective* likely to change; changing frequently.

changeling *noun* a child believed to have been substituted secretly for another, especially by fairies.

channel *noun* **1** a stretch of water connecting two seas. **2** a way for water to flow along. **3** the part of a river or sea etc. that is deep enough for ships. **4** a broadcasting wavelength.

channel *verb* (**channelled**, **channelling**) **1** make a channel in something. **2** direct something through a channel or other route. [from Latin *canalis* = canal]

chant *noun* **1** a tune to which words with no regular rhythm are fitted, e.g. one used in singing psalms. **2** a rhythmic call or shout.

chant *verb* **1** sing. **2** call out words in a rhythm. [from Latin *cantare* = sing]

chaos (*say* **kay**-oss) *noun* great disorder. **chaotic** *adjective*, **chaotically** *adverb* [Greek, = bottomless pit]

chap *noun* (*informal*) a man. [short for *chapman*, an old word for a pedlar]

chapel *noun* **1** a place used for Christian worship, other than a cathedral or parish church; a religious service in this. **2** a section of a large church, with its own altar.

chaperone (*say* **shap**-er-ohn) *noun* an older woman in charge of a young one on social occasions.

chaplain *noun* a member of the clergy who looks after a college or hospital or regiment etc.

chapped *adjective* with skin split or cracked from cold etc.

chapter *noun* **1** a division of a book. **2** the clergy of a cathedral or members of a monastery. The room where they meet is called a **chapter house**.

char *verb* (**charred**, **charring**) make or become black by burning. [from *charcoal*]

character *noun* **1** a person in a story or play etc. **2** all the qualities that make a person or thing what he, she, or it is. **3** a letter of the alphabet. **4** (*informal*) an eccentric or amusing person

characterise *verb* (**characterised**, **characterising**) **1** be a characteristic of. **2** describe the character of. **characterisation** *noun*

characteristic *noun* a quality that forms part of a person's or thing's character.

characteristic *adjective* typical of a person or thing. **characteristically** *adverb*

charade (*say* sha-**rahd**) *noun* **1** a scene in the game of *charades*, in which people try to guess a word from other people's acting. **2** a pretence.

charcoal *noun* a black substance made by burning wood slowly.

charge *noun* **1** the price asked for something. **2** a rushing attack. **3** the amount of explosive needed to fire a gun etc. **4** electricity in something. **5** an accusation of having committed a crime. **6** a person or thing in someone's care.
charge nurse a supervising or head nurse in a ward or department of a clinic or hospital.
in charge in control; deciding what shall happen to a person or thing.

charge *verb* (**charged**, **charging**) **1** ask a particular price. **2** rush forward in an attack. **3** give an electric charge to something. **4** accuse someone of committing a crime. **5** entrust someone with a responsibility or task.

charger *noun* (*old use*) a cavalry horse.

chariot *noun* a horse-drawn vehicle with two wheels, used in ancient times for fighting, racing, etc. **charioteer** *noun*

charisma (*say* ka-**riz**-ma) *noun* the special quality that makes a person popular, influential, etc. [Greek, = divine favour]

charismatic (*say* ka-riz-**mat**-ik) **1** *adjective* having charisma. **2** believing that God still gives people special qualities or gifts, *a charismatic Church.*

charity *noun* (*plural* **charities**) **1** an organisation set up to help people who are poor or have suffered a disaster. **2** giving money or help etc. to the needy. **3** loving kindness towards others; being unwilling to think badly of people. **charitable** *adjective*, **charitably** *adverb* [from Latin *caritas* = love]

charlatan (*say* **shar**-la-tan) *noun* a person who falsely claims to be an expert. [from Italian, = babbler]

charm *noun* **1** the power to please or delight people; attractiveness. **2** a magic spell; a small object believed to bring good luck. **3** an ornament worn on a bracelet etc.

charm *verb* **1** give pleasure or delight to people. **2** put a spell on; bewitch. **charmer** *noun* [from Latin *carmen* = song or spell]

Charolais (*say* **sha**-roh-lay) *noun* a kind of cattle farmed for milk and meat.

chart *noun* **1** a map for people sailing ships or flying aircraft. **2** an outline map showing special information, *a weather chart.* **3** a diagram or list etc. giving information in an orderly way.
the charts a list of the records that are most popular.

chart *verb* make a chart of something; map. [from Latin *charta* = card]

charter *noun* **1** an official document giving somebody certain rights etc. **2** chartering an aircraft, ship, or vehicle.

charter *verb* **1** hire an aircraft, ship, or vehicle. **2** give a charter to someone.
chartered accountant an accountant who is qualified according to the rules of an association that has a royal charter.

chary (*say* **chair**-ee) *adjective* cautious about doing or giving something.

chase *verb* (**chased**, **chasing**) go quickly after a person or thing in order to capture or catch them up or drive them away.
chase *noun*

chasm (*say* kazm) *noun* a deep opening in the ground. [Greek, = wide hollow]

chassis (*say* **shas**-ee) *noun* (*plural* **chassis**) the framework under a car etc., on which other parts are mounted.

chaste *adjective* not having sexual intercourse at all, or only with the person to whom you are married. **chastity** *noun* [from Latin *castus* = pure]

chasten (*say* **chay**-sen) *verb* discipline a person by punishing them; make someone feel subdued.

chastise *verb* (**chastised**, **chastising**) punish severely. **chastisement** *noun*

chat *noun* a friendly conversation. **chat room** *noun* an online messaging facility, often dedicated to a specific topic.

chat *verb* (**chatted**, **chatting**) have a chat. [from *chatter*]

chattel *noun* something you own that can be moved from place to place (distinguished from a house or land).

chatter *verb* **1** talk quickly about unimportant things; keep on talking. **2** make a rattling sound. **chatterer** *noun*

chatter *noun* chattering talk or sound.

chatterbox *noun* a talkative person.

chauffeur (*say* **shoh**-fer) *noun* a person employed to drive a car. [French, = stoker]

chauvinism (*say* **shoh**-vin-izm) *noun* prejudiced belief that your own group or country etc. is superior to others, *male chauvinism.* **chauvinist** *noun*, **chauvinistic** *adjective* [from the name of Nicolas Chauvin, a French soldier under Napoleon, noted for his extreme patriotism]

ChCh *abbreviation* (*NZ*) Christchurch.

cheap *adjective* **1** low in price; not expensive. **2** of poor quality; of low value. **cheaply** *adverb*, **cheapness** *noun* [from Old English *ceap* = a bargain]

cheapen *verb* make or become cheap.

cheat *verb* **1** trick or deceive somebody. **2** try to do well in an examination or game etc. by breaking the rules.

cheat *noun* a person who cheats.

check[1] *verb* **1** make sure that something is correct or in good condition. **2** make something stop or go slower.
check out 1 leave (a hotel etc.). **2** (*informal*) investigate, examine.

check[1] *noun* **1** checking something. **2** stopping or slowing; a pause. **3** a receipt; a bill in a restaurant. **4** the situation in chess when a king may be captured. [from Persian *shah* = king]

check[2] *noun* a pattern of squares. **checked** *adjective* [from *chequered*]

checker *noun* **1** a person working on a checkout counter. **2** a person who checks or tests. **3** a person or program that checks usage or spelling.

checkmate *noun* the winning situation in chess. **checkmate** *verb* [from Persian *shah mat* = the king is dead]

checkout *noun* a place where goods are paid for in a supermarket etc.

checkpoint *noun* a place where cars, documents, etc. are checked.

Cheddar *noun* a kind of cheese. [named after Cheddar in England]

cheek *noun* **1** the side of the face below the eye. **2** impudence.

cheek *verb* be cheeky to someone.

cheeky *adjective* impudent. **cheekily** *adverb*, **cheekiness** *noun*

cheer *noun* **1** a shout of praise or pleasure or encouragement, especially 'hurray'. **2** cheerfulness, *full of good cheer*.

cheer *verb* **1** give a cheer. **2** gladden or encourage somebody.
cheer up make or become cheerful.

cheerful *adjective* **1** looking or sounding happy. **2** pleasantly bright. **cheerfully** *adverb*, **cheerfulness** *noun*

cheerio[1] *noun* (*NZ*) a small saveloy.

cheerio[2] *interjection* (*informal*) goodbye.

cheerleader *noun* a supporter, especially in organised display at sports matches.

cheerless *adjective* gloomy; dreary.

cheery *adjective* bright and cheerful.

cheese *noun* a solid food made from milk.

cheetah *noun* a kind of leopard.

chef (*say* shef) *noun* the cook in a hotel or restaurant. [French, = chief]

chemical *adjective* of or produced by chemistry.

chemical *noun* a substance obtained by or used in chemistry.

chemist *noun* **1** a person who makes or sells medicines. **2** an expert in chemistry.

chemistry *noun* **1** the way that substances combine and react with one another. **2** study of substances and their reactions etc. [same origin as *alchemy*]

cheque *noun* a printed form on which you write instructions to a bank to pay out money from your account. [from *check*[1]]

chequered *adjective* marked with a pattern of squares.

cherish *verb* **1** look after a person or thing lovingly. **2** be fond of. [from French *cher* = dear]

cherry *noun* (*plural* **cherries**) a small soft round fruit with a stone.

cherub *noun* (*plural* **cherubim** or **cherubs**) **1** an angel, usually conveyed as a chubby child with wings. **2** an innocent child. **3** (*NZ*) a class of racing dinghy. **cherubic** (*say* che-**roo**-bik) *adjective* [from Hebrew]

chess *noun* a game for two players with sixteen pieces each (called **chessmen**) on a board of 64 squares (a **chessboard**). [same origin as *check*[1]]

chest *noun* **1** the front part of the body between the neck and the waist. **2** a large strong box for storing things in.
chest of drawers a piece of furniture with drawers for storing clothes etc.

chestnut *noun* **1** a tree that produces hard brown nuts. **2** the nut of this tree. **3** an old joke or story.

chevron (*say* **shev**-ron) *noun* a V-shaped stripe.

chew *verb* grind food between the teeth. **chewy** *adjective*

chewing-gum *noun* a sticky flavoured substance for chewing.

Chewings fescue *noun* (*NZ*) a kind of grass used for lawns and pasture.

chiack *verb* (*NZ, informal*) taunt, tease.

chic (*say* sheek) *adjective* stylish and elegant. [French]

chicanery (*say* shik-**ayn**-er-ee) *noun* trickery. [from French *chicaner* = quibble]

chick *noun* a very young bird.

chicken *noun* **1** a domesticated bird kept for its eggs and flesh. **2** the flesh of this bird as food.

chicken *adjective* (*slang*) afraid to do something; cowardly.

chicken *verb* **chicken out** (*slang*) withdraw because you are afraid.

chicken-pox *noun* a disease that produces red spots on the skin.

chicory *noun* a plant whose leaves are used as salad.

chide *verb* (**chided**, **chidden**, **chiding**) (*old use*) scold.

chief *noun* a person with the highest rank or authority.

chief *adjective* most important; main. **chiefly** *adverb*

Chiefs *noun* a New Zealand rugby union Super 14 franchise based in Hamilton.

chieftain *noun* the chief of a tribe, band of robbers, etc.

chiffon (*say* **shif**-on) *noun* a very thin almost transparent fabric. [French]

chilblain *noun* a sore swollen place, usually on a hand or foot, caused by cold weather. [from *chill* + *blain* = a sore]

child *noun* (*plural* **children**) **1** a young person; a boy or girl. **2** someone's son or daughter.

childhood *noun* the time when a person is a child.

childish *adjective* like a child; unsuitable for a grown person. **childishly** *adverb*

childless *adjective* having no children.

chill *noun* **1** unpleasant coldness. **2** an illness that makes you shiver.

chill *verb* make a person or thing cold.

chilli *noun* (*plural* **chillies**) the hot-tasting pod of a red pepper.

chilly *adjective* **1** rather cold. **2** unfriendly.
chilliness *noun*
chilly bin (*NZ*) an insulated container that keeps food or drink cool and can be carried around.

chime *noun* a series of notes sounded by a set of bells each making a different musical sound.

chime *verb* (**chimed**, **chiming**) make a chime.

chimney *noun* (*plural* **chimneys**) a tall pipe or structure that carries away smoke from a fire.

chimney-pot *noun* a pipe fitted to the top of a chimney.

chimney-sweep *noun* a person who cleans soot from inside chimneys.

chimpanzee *noun* an African ape, smaller than a gorilla.

chin *noun* the lower part of the face below the mouth.

china *noun* thin delicate pottery.

Chinese *adjective* of China.
Chinese gooseberry an older name for the kiwi-fruit.

chink *noun* **1** a narrow opening, *a chink in the curtains.* **2** a chinking sound.

chink *verb* make a sound like glasses or coins being struck together.

chintz *noun* a shiny cotton cloth used for making curtains etc. [from Hindi]

chip *noun* **1** a thin piece cut or broken off something hard. **2** an oblong strip of potato fried and eaten hot. **3** a thin slice of potato fried crisp and eaten cold. **4** a place where a small piece has been knocked off something. **5** a small counter used in games. **6** a microchip. **7** a punnet.
a chip off the old block a child who is very like his or her father.
have a chip on your shoulder have a grievance and feel bitter or resentful.

chip *verb* (**chipped**, **chipping**) **1** knock small pieces off something. **2** cut a potato into chips.

chipboard *noun* board made from chips of wood pressed and stuck together.

chip-heater *noun* (*NZ*) a domestic water-heater that burns wood chips.

chipolata *noun* a small thin sausage.

chippie *noun* (*slang*) **1** a carpenter. **2** a potato chip.

chiropody (*say* ki-**rop**-od-ee *or* shi-) *noun* treatment of ailments of the feet, e.g. corns.
chiropodist *noun* [from Greek *cheir* = hand, + *pod-* = foot]

chirp *verb* make short sharp sounds like a small bird. **chirp** *noun*

chirpy *adjective* lively and cheerful.

chisel *noun* a tool with a sharp end for shaping wood, stone, etc.

chisel *verb* (**chiselled**, **chiselling**) shape or cut with a chisel.

chivalrous (*say* **shiv**-al-rus) *adjective* being considerate and helpful towards people less strong than yourself. **chivalry** *noun*

chive *noun* a small herb with leaves that taste like onions.

chivvy *verb* (**chivvied**, **chivvying**) try to make someone hurry.

chlorinate *verb* (**chlorinated**, **chlorinating**) put chlorine into something.
chlorination *noun*

chlorine (*say* **klor**-een) *noun* a greenish-yellow gas used to disinfect water etc. [from Greek *chloros* = green]

chloroform (*say* **klo**-ro-form) *noun* a liquid that gives off a vapour that makes people unconscious.

chlorophyll (*say* **klo**-ro-fil) *noun* the substance that makes plants green. [from Greek *chloros* = green, + *phyllon* = leaf]

chock *noun* a block or wedge used to prevent something from moving.

chock-a-block *adjective* crammed or crowded together.

chock-full *adjective* crammed full.

chocolate *noun* **1** a solid brown food or powder made from roasted cacao seeds. **2** a drink made with this powder. **3** a sweet made of or covered with chocolate. [from Mexican *chocolatl*]

CHOGM *abbreviation* Commonwealth Heads of Government Meeting.

choice *noun* **1** choosing; the power to choose between things. **2** a variety from which someone can choose, *There is a wide choice of holidays.* **3** a person or thing chosen, *This is my choice.*

choice *adjective* **1** of the best quality, *choice bananas.* **2** (*slang*) excellent, enjoyable.

choir *noun* a group of people trained to sing together, especially in a church. **choirboy** *noun* [from Latin *chorus* = choir]

choke *verb* (**choked**, **choking**) **1** cause somebody to stop breathing properly. **2** be unable to breathe properly. **3** clog.

choke *noun* a device controlling the flow of air into the engine of a motor vehicle.

choko *noun* (*plural* **chokos**) a green vegetable shaped like a pear.

cholera (*say* **kol**-er-a) *noun* an infectious disease that is often fatal. [from Greek *chole* = bile]

cholesterol (*say* kol-**est**-er-ol) *noun* a fatty substance that can clog the arteries. [from Greek *chole* = bile, + *stereos* = stiff]

chook *noun* (*NZ, informal*) a chicken.

choose *verb* (**chose**, **chosen**, **choosing**) take one or more from among a number of people or things; select. **choosy** *adjective*

chop *verb* (**chopped**, **chopping**) cut or hit something with a heavy blow.

chop *noun* **1** a chopping blow. **2** a small thick slice of meat, usually on a rib.
not much chop (*informal*) not up to much.

chopper *noun* **1** a chopping tool; a small axe. **2** (*slang*) a helicopter.

choppy *adjective* (**choppier**, **choppiest**) not smooth; full of small waves, *a choppy sea*. **choppiness** *noun*

chopsticks *plural noun* a pair of thin sticks used for lifting Chinese and Japanese food to your mouth.

choral *adjective* of or for or sung by a choir or chorus.

chorale (*say* kor-**ahl**) *noun* a choral composition using the words of a hymn.

chord[1] (*say* kord) *noun* a number of musical notes sounded together. [from *accord*]

chord[2] (*say* kord) *noun* a straight line joining two points on a curve. [from *cord*]

chore (*say* chor) *noun* a regular or dull task.

choreography (*say* ko-ree-**og**-ra-fee) *noun* the composition of ballets or stage dances. **choreographer** *noun* [from Greek *choreia* = dance, + *-graphy*]

chorister (*say* **ko**-rist-er) *noun* a member of a choir.

chortle *noun* a loud chuckle. [a mixture of *chuckle* and *snort*]

chorus *noun* (*plural* **choruses**) **1** the words repeated after each verse of a song or poem. **2** music sung by a group of people. **3** a group singing together.

chorus *verb* (**chorused**, **chorusing**) sing or speak in chorus. [from Greek]

christen *verb* **1** baptise. **2** give a name or nickname to a person or thing. **christening** *noun*

Christian *noun* a person who believes in Jesus Christ and his teachings.

Christian *adjective* of Christians or their beliefs. **Christianity** *noun*
Christian name a name given to a person at his or her christening.

Christmas *noun* (*plural* **Christmases**) the day (25 December) when Christians commemorate the birth of Jesus Christ; the days round it.
Christmas pudding a dark pudding containing dried fruit etc., eaten at Christmas.
Christmas tree an evergreen or artificial tree decorated at Christmas; the pōhutukawa. [from *Christ* + *mass*[2]]

chromatic (*say* krom-**at**-ik) *adjective* of colours.
chromatic scale a musical scale going up or down in semitones. [from Greek *chroma* = colour]

chrome (*say* krohm) *noun* chromium. [from Greek *chroma* = colour (because its compounds have brilliant colours)]

chromium (*say* **kroh**-mee-um) *noun* a shiny silvery metal. [from *chrome*]

chromosome (*say* **kroh**-mos-ohm) *noun* a tiny thread-like part of an animal cell or plant cell, carrying genes. [from Greek *chroma* = colour, + *soma* = body]

chronic *adjective* lasting for a long time, *a chronic illness*. **chronically** *adverb* [from Greek *chronikos* = of time]

chronicle *noun* a record of events in the order of their happening. [same origin as *chronic*]

chronological *adjective* arranged in the order of happening. **chronologically** *adverb*

chronology (*say* kron-**ol**-oj-ee) *noun* the arrangement of events in the order in which they happened. e.g. in history or geology. [from Greek *chronos* = time, + *-logy*]

chronometer (*say* kron-**om**-it-er) *noun* a very exact device for measuring time. [from Greek *chronos* = time, = *meter*]

chrysalis *noun* (*plural* **chrysalises**) a caterpillar that is changing into a butterfly or moth. [from Greek *chrysos* = gold (the colour of its covering)]

chrysanthemum *noun* a garden flower that blooms in autumn. [from Greek *chrysos* = gold, + *anthemon* flower]

chubby *adjective* (**chubbier**, **chubbiest**) plump. **chubbiness** *noun*

chuck[1] *verb* (*informal*) throw.
chuck off at (*NZ*) sneer or scoff at, criticise.

chuck[2] *noun* **1** the gripping-part of a lathe. **2** the part of a drill that holds the bit.

chuckle *noun* a quiet laugh.

chuckle *verb* (**chuckled**, **chuckling**) give a chuckle.

chuddy *noun* (*NZ, informal*) chewing-gum.

chuffed *adjective* (*slang*) pleased.

chug *verb* (**chugged**, **chugging**) make the sound of an engine.

chum *noun* (*informal*) a friend. **chummy** *adjective*

chunk *noun* a thick piece of something. **chunky** *adjective*

church *noun* (*plural* **churches**) **1** a public building for Christian worship. **2** a religious service in a church, *I will see you after church.*
the Church all Christians; a group of these, *the Anglican Church.* [from Greek *kuriakon* = Lord's house]

churchyard *noun* the ground round a church, often used as a graveyard.

churlish *adjective* ill-mannered; surly.

churn *noun* **1** a large can in which milk is carried from a farm. **2** a machine in which milk is beaten to make butter.

churn *verb* **1** make butter in a churn. **2** stir or swirl vigorously.
churn out produce in large quantities.

chute (*say* shoot) *noun* a steep channel for people or things to slide down. [French, = a fall]

chutney *noun* a strong-tasting mixture of fruit, peppers, etc., eaten with meat. [from Hindi *catni*]

CIA *abbreviation* Central Intelligence Agency (in the US).

CIB *abbreviation* Criminal Investigation Branch (of the New Zealand Police).

cicada *noun* an insect rather like a grasshopper, that makes a shrill chirping sound.

cider *noun* an alcoholic drink made from apples.

cigar *noun* a roll of compressed tobacco-leaves for smoking. [from Spanish *cigarro*]

cigarette *noun* a small roll of shredded tobacco in thin paper for smoking. [French, = little cigar]

cinder *noun* a small piece of partly burnt coal or wood.

cine-camera (*say* **sin**-ee) *noun* a camera used for taking moving pictures.

cinema *noun* a place where movies are shown. [from Greek *kinema* = movement]

cinnamon (*say* **sin**-a-mon) *noun* a yellowish-brown spice.

cipher (*say* **sy**-fer) *noun* **1** the symbol 0, representing nought or zero. **2** a kind of code. [from Arabic *sifr* = nought]

circle *noun* **1** a perfectly round flat shape or thing. **2** a number of people with similar interests. **3** the balcony of a cinema or theatre.

circle *verb* (**circled**, **circling**) move in a circle; go round something.

circuit (*say* **ser**-kit) *noun* **1** a circular line or journey. **2** a motor-racing track. **3** the path of an electric current. [from Latin *circum* = round, + *itum* = gone]

circuitous (*say* ser-**kew**-it-us) *adjective* going a long way round, not direct.

circular *adjective* **1** shaped like a circle; round. **2** moving round a circle. **circularity** *noun*

circular *noun* a letter or advertisement etc. sent to a number of people.

circulate *verb* (**circulated**, **circulating**) **1** go round something continuously, *Blood circulates in the body.* **2** pass from place to place. **3** send round; send to a number of people. **circulation** *noun*

circum- *prefix* around (as in *circumference*). [from Latin *circum* = around]

circumcise *verb* (**circumcised**, **circumcising**) cut off the fold of skin at the tip of the penis. **circumcision** *noun* [from *circum-*, + Latin *caedere* = cut]

circumference *noun* the line or distance round something, especially round a circle. [from *circum-*, + Latin *ferens* = carrying]

circumflex accent a mark over a vowel, as over *e* in *fête.*

circumlocution *noun* a roundabout expression. using many words where a few would do, e.g. 'at this moment in time' for 'now'.

circumnavigate *verb* (**circumnavigated**, **circumnavigating**) sail completely round something. **circumnavigation** *noun* [from *circum- + navigate*]

circumscribe *verb* (**circumscribed**, **circumscribing**) **1** draw a line round something. **2** limit; restrict, *Her powers are circumscribed by many regulations.* [from *circum-*, + Latin *scribere* = write]

circumspect *adjective* cautious and watchful. **circumspection** *noun* [from *circum-*, + Latin *specere* = to look]

circumstance *noun* a fact or condition connected with an event or person or action. [from *circum-*, + Latin *stans* = standing]

circumstantial (*say* ser-kum-**stan**-shal) *adjective* **1** giving full details, *a circumstantial account of her journey.* **2** consisting of facts that strongly suggest something but do not actually prove it, *circumstantial evidence.*

circumvent *verb* find a way of avoiding, *We managed to circumvent the rules.* **circumvention** *noun* [from *circum-*, + Latin *ventum* = come]

circus *noun* (*plural* **circuses**) a travelling show with clowns, acrobats, animals, etc. [Latin, = ring]

cistern *noun* a tank for storing water.

citadel *noun* a fortress protecting a city.

cite (*say* sight) *verb* (**cited**, **citing**) **1** quote as an example. **2** report poor behaviour. **citation** *noun*

citizen *noun* a person belonging to a particular city or country and having certain rights and duties because of this. **citizenship** *noun* [same origin as *city*]

citizenry *noun* all the citizens.

citrus fruit a lemon, orange, etc.

city *noun* (*plural* **cities**) a large important town. [from Latin *civitas* = city]

civic *adjective* of a city or town; of citizens. [from Latin *civis* = citizen]

civics *noun* the study of the way citizens and towns are governed and of the rights and duties of citizens.

civil *adjective* **1** of citizens. **2** of civilians; not military, *civil aviation*. **3** polite. **civilly** *adverb*
civil defence the protection of civilians in a natural disaster; the organisation responsible for this.
civil rights the rights of citizens, especially to have freedom, equality, and the right to vote.
civil war war between groups of people of the same country.

civilian *noun* a person who is not serving in the armed forces.

civilisation *noun* **1** a civilised condition or society. **2** making or becoming civilised.

civilise *verb* (**civilised**, **civilising**) bring culture and education etc. to a primitive community.

civility *noun* (*plural* **civilities**) politeness; a polite act.

clack *noun* a short sharp sound like that of plates struck together. **clack** *verb*

clad *adjective* clothed.

claim *verb* **1** ask for something to which you believe you have a right. **2** declare; state something without being able to prove it. **claimant** *noun*

claim *noun* **1** claiming. **2** something claimed. **3** a piece of ground claimed or assigned to someone for mining etc. [same origin as *clamour*]

clairvoyant *noun* a person who is said to be able to perceive future events or things that are happening out of sight. **clairvoyance** *noun* [from French *clair* = clear, + *voyant* = seeing]

clam *noun* a large shellfish.

clamber *verb* climb with difficulty.

clammy *adjective* damp and slimy.

clamour *noun* **1** a loud confused noise. **2** an outcry; a loud protest or demand. **clamorous** *adjective*

clamour *verb* make a loud protest or demand. [from Latin *clamare* = call out]

clamp *noun* a device for holding things tightly.

clamp *verb* fix with a clamp; fix firmly.
clamp down on become stricter about something; put a stop to it.

clan *noun* a group sharing the same ancestor, especially in Scotland.

clandestine (*say* klan-**dest**-in) *adjective* done secretly; kept secret.

clang *noun* a loud ringing sound. **clang** *verb*

clangour *noun* a clanging noise.

clank *noun* a sound like heavy pieces of metal banging together. **clank** *verb*

clap *verb* (**clapped**, **clapping**) **1** strike the palms of the hands together loudly, especially as applause. **2** slap in a friendly way, *clapped him on the shoulder*. **3** put quickly, *They clapped him in jail.*

clap *noun* **1** a sudden sharp noise, *a clap of thunder*. **2** clapping; applause. **3** a friendly slap.

clapper *noun* the tongue or hanging piece inside a bell that strikes against the bell to make it sound.

claptrap *noun* insincere talk.

claret *noun* a kind of red wine.

clarify *verb* (**clarified**, **clarifying**) make or become clear or easier to understand. **clarification** *noun* [from Latin *clarus* = clear]

clarinet *noun* a woodwind instrument. **clarinettist** *noun*

clarion *noun* an old type of trumpet.

clarity *noun* clearness.

clash *verb* **1** make a loud sound like that of cymbals banging together. **2** conflict. **3** happen inconveniently at the same time. **4** (of colours) look unpleasant together. **clash** *noun*

clasp *noun* **1** a device for fastening things, with interlocking parts. **2** a grasp.

clasp *verb* **1** grasp or hold tightly. **2** fasten with a clasp.

class *noun* (*plural* **classes**) **1** a group of children, students, etc. who are taught together. **2** a group of similar people, animals, or things. **3** people of the same social or economic level. **4** level of quality, *first class*.

class *verb* classify. [from Latin *classis* = a social division of the Roman people]

classic *adjective* generally agreed to be excellent or important.

classic *noun* a classic book, film, writer, etc. [from Latin *classicus* = of the highest class]

classic car *noun* an early model of car, especially one made between 1925 and 1948.

classical *adjective* **1** of ancient Greek or Roman literature, art, etc. **2** serious or conventional in style, *classical music.*

classics *noun* the study of ancient Greek and Latin languages and literature etc.

classified *adjective* **1** put into classes or groups. **2** (of information) declared officially to be secret and available only to certain people.

classify *verb* (**classified**, **classifying**) arrange things in classes or groups. **classification** *noun*, **classificatory** *adjective*

classmate *noun* someone in the same class at school etc.

classroom *noun* a room where a class of children or students is taught.

clatter *verb & noun* rattle.

clause *noun* **1** a single part of a treaty, law, or contract. **2** part of a complex sentence, with its own verb, *There are two clauses in 'We choose what we want'.*

claustrophobia *noun* fear of being inside something. [from Latin *claustrum* = enclosed space, + *phobia*]

claw *noun* **1** a sharp nail on a bird's or animal's foot. **2** a claw-like part or device used for grasping things.

claw *verb* grasp, pull, or scratch with a claw or hand.

clay *noun* a kind of stiff sticky earth that becomes hard when baked, used for making bricks and pottery. **clayey** *adjective*

clean *adjective* **1** without any dirt or marks or stains. **2** fresh; not yet used. **3** honourable; not unfair, *a clean fight.* **4** not indecent. **cleanness** *noun*

clean *verb* make a thing clean.

clean *adverb* completely, *I clean forgot.*

cleaner *noun* **1** a person who cleans things, especially rooms etc. **2** something used for cleaning things.

cleanly (*say* **kleen**-lee) *adverb* in a clean way.

cleanly (*say* **klen**-lee) *adjective* taking care to be clean, *cleanly habits.* **cleanliness** *noun*

cleanse (*say* klenz) *verb* (**cleansed**, **cleansing**) **1** clean. **2** make pure. **cleanser** *noun*

clear *adjective* **1** transparent; not muddy or cloudy. **2** easy to see or hear or understand; distinct. **3** free from obstacles or unwanted things; free from guilt, *a clear conscience.* **4** complete, *Give three clear days' notice.* **clearly** *adverb*, **clearness** *noun*

clear *adverb* **1** distinctly; clearly, *We heard you loud and clear.* **2** completely, *He got clear away.* **3** apart; not in contact, *Stand clear of the doors.*

clear *verb* **1** make or become clear. **2** show that someone is innocent or reliable. **3** jump over something without touching it. **4** get approval or authorisation for something, *Clear this with the principal.*
clear away remove used plates etc. after a meal.
clear off or **out** (*informal*) go away.
clear up make things tidy; become better or brighter; solve, *clear up the mystery.* [from Latin *clarus* = clear]

clearance *noun* **1** clearing something. **2** getting rid of unwanted goods. **3** the space between two things.

clearing *noun* an open space in a forest.

cleave[1] *verb* (*past tense* **cleaved**, **clove**, or **cleft**; *past participle* **cleft** or **cloven**; *present participle* **cleaving**) **1** divide by chopping; split. **2** make a way through, *cleaving the waves.* **cleavage** *noun*

cleave[2] *verb* (**cleaved**, **cleaving**) (*old use*) cling to something.

cleaver *noun* a butcher's chopper.

clef *noun* a symbol on a stave in music, showing the pitch of the notes, *treble clef; bass clef.* [French, = key]

cleft *past tense* of **cleave**[1].

cleft *noun* a split; a separation.

clematis *noun* a climbing flowering plant.

clemency *noun* gentleness or mildness; mercy.

clench *verb* close teeth or fingers tightly.

clergy *noun* the people who have been ordained as priests or ministers of the Christian Church. **clergyman** *noun*

clerical *adjective* **1** of clerks or their work. **2** of the clergy.

clerk (*say* klark) *noun* a person employed to keep records or accounts, deal with papers in an office, etc.

clever *adjective* quick at learning and understanding things; skilful. **cleverly** *adverb*, **cleverness** *noun*

clianthus *noun* (*NZ*) kākā-beak.

cliché (*say* **klee**-shay) *noun* a phrase or idea that is used too often. [French, = stereotyped]

click *noun* a short sharp sound.

click *verb* **1** make a clicking sound. **2** press a computer mouse button. **3** connect a buckle etc. **4** become aware.

client *noun* a person who gets help from a lawyer, architect, or professional person other than a doctor; a customer.

clientele (*say* klee-on-**tel**) *noun* clients.

cliff *noun* a steep rock-face, especially on a coast.

climate *noun* the regular weather conditions of an area. **climatic** (*say* kly-**mat**-ik) *adjective*

climax *noun* (*plural* **climaxes**) the most interesting or important point of a story, series of events, etc. **climactic** *adjective* [from Greek *klimax* = ladder]

climb *verb* **1** go up or over or down something. **2** grow upwards. **3** go higher. **climb** *noun*, **climber** *noun*
climb down admit that you have been wrong.

clinch *verb* **1** fasten securely. **2** settle definitely, *clinch the deal.* **3** (in boxing) be clasping each other. **clinch** *noun* [from *clench*]

cline *noun* a grade within a sequence or continuum.

cling *verb* (**clung**, **clinging**) hold on tightly.

clinic *noun* a place where people see doctors etc. for treatment or advice. **clinical** *adjective* [from Greek *klinikos* = of a bed]

clink *noun* a thin sharp sound like glasses being struck together. **clink** *verb*

clinker *noun* a piece of rough stony material left after coal has burned.

clinker-built *adjective* (of a boat) made with the outside planks or plates overlapping downwards.

clip[1] *noun* a fastener for keeping things together, usually worked by a spring.

clip[1] *verb* (**clipped**, **clipping**) fasten with a clip.

clip[2] *verb* (**clipped**, **clipping**) **1** cut with shears or scissors etc. **2** (*informal*) hit.

clip[2] *noun* **1** clipping something. **2** a piece clipped off or out. **3** the amount of wool obtained from a flock.

clipper *noun* an old type of fast sailing-ship.

clippers *plural noun* an instrument for cutting hair.

clique (*say* kleek) *noun* a small group of people who stick together and keep others out.

cloak *noun* a sleeveless garment that hangs loosely from the shoulders.

cloak *verb* cover; conceal.

cloakroom *noun* **1** a place where people can leave outdoor clothes, luggage, etc. **2** a toilet.

clobber *verb* (*slang*) **1** hit hard again and again. **2** defeat completely.

cloche (*say* klosh) *noun* a glass or plastic cover to protect plants. [French, = bell]

clock *noun* **1** a device (other than a watch) that shows what the time is. **2** a measuring device with a dial or showing figures. [from Latin *clocca* = bell]

clock *verb* **clock in** or **out** register the time you arrive at work or leave work.
clock up achieve a certain speed.

clockwise *adverb & adjective* moving round a circle in the same direction as a clock's hands. [from *clock* + *-wise[2]*]

clockwork *noun* a mechanism with a spring that has to be wound up.
like clockwork very regularly.

clod *noun* a lump of earth or clay.

clog *noun* a shoe with a wooden sole.

clog *verb* (**clogged**, **clogging**) block up.

cloister *noun* a covered path along the side of a church or monastery etc., round a courtyard. [from Latin *claustrum* = enclosed place]

clone *noun* an animal or plant made from the cells of another animal or plant and therefore exactly like it.

close[1] (*say* klohss) *adjective* **1** near. **2** detailed; concentrated, *with close attention.* **3** tight; with little empty space, *a close fit.* **4** in which competitors are nearly equal, *a close contest.* **5** stuffy. **closely** *adverb*, **closeness** *noun*

close[1] *adverb* closely, *close behind.*

close[1] *noun* **1** a cul-de-sac. **2** an enclosed area, especially round a cathedral.

close[2] (*say* klohz) *verb* (**closed**, **closing**) **1** shut. **2** end.
close in get nearer; get shorter.

close[2] *noun* end, *at the close of play.* [from Latin *clausum* = shut]

closet *noun* (*American*) a cupboard; a storeroom.

closet *verb* (**closeted**, **closeting**) shut away in a private room.

close-up *noun* a photograph etc. showing a subject at close range.

closure *noun* a closing or resolution.

clot *noun* **1** a small mass of blood, cream, etc. that has become solid. **2** (*slang*) a stupid person.

clot *verb* (**clotted**, **clotting**) form clots.

cloth *noun* **1** woven material or felt. **2** a piece of this material. **3** a tablecloth.

clothe *verb* (**clothed**, **clothing**) put clothes on someone.

clothes *plural noun* things worn to cover the body. [originally the plural of *cloth*]

clothing *noun* clothes.

cloud *noun* **1** a mass of condensed water-vapour floating in the sky. **2** a mass of smoke, dust, etc., in the air. **3** *Computing* an electronic or Internet storage service.

cloud *verb* fill or obscure with clouds.

cloudburst *noun* a sudden violent rainstorm.

cloudless *adjective* without clouds.

cloudy *adjective* (**cloudier**, **cloudiest**) **1** full of clouds. **2** not transparent, *The liquid became cloudy.* **cloudiness** *noun*

clout *verb & noun* (*informal*) hit.

clove[1] *noun* the dried bud of a tropical tree, used as a spice.

clove[2] *noun* one of the small bulbs in a compound bulb, *a clove of garlic.*

clove[3] *past tense* of **cleave**[1].
clove hitch a kind of knot.

cloven *past participle* of **cleave**[1].
cloven hoof a hoof that is divided, like those of cows and sheep.

clover *noun* a small plant usually with three leaves on each stalk, used as fodder.
in clover in ease and luxury.

clown *noun* **1** a performer who does comical tricks and actions, especially in a circus. **2** a person who clowns.

clown *verb* behave comically.

cloying *adjective* sickeningly sweet.

club *noun* **1** a heavy stick used as a weapon. **2** a stick with a shaped head used to hit the ball in golf. **3** a group of people who meet because they are interested in the same thing; the premises where they meet. **4** a playing-card with black clover-leaves on it.

club *verb* (**clubbed**, **clubbing**) hit with a heavy stick.
club together join with other people in subscribing, *club together to buy a boat.*

cluck *verb* make a hen's throaty cry.
cluck *noun*

clue *noun* something that helps a person to solve a puzzle or a mystery.
not have a clue (*informal*) be stupid or helpless.

clump *noun* **1** a cluster or mass of things. **2** a clumping sound.

clump *verb* **1** form a cluster or mass. **2** walk with a heavy tread.

clumsy *adjective* (**clumsier**, **clumsiest**) **1** heavy and ungraceful; likely to knock things over or drop things. **2** not skilful; not tactful, *a clumsy apology.* **clumsily** *adverb*, **clumsiness** *noun*

cluster *noun* a small close group.

cluster *verb* form a cluster.

clutch[1] *verb* grasp tightly.

clutch[1] *noun* (*plural* **clutches**) **1** a tight grasp. **2** a device for connecting and disconnecting the engine of a motor vehicle from its gears.

clutch[2] *noun* (*plural* **clutches**) a set of eggs for hatching.

clutter *noun* things lying about untidily.

clutter *verb* fill with clutter.

CND *abbreviation* Campaign for Nuclear Disarmament.

CNG *abbreviation* compressed natural gas.

co. *abbreviation* company.

c/o *abbreviation* care of.

co- *prefix* together, jointly (as in *coexistence*); joint (as in *co-pilot*). [from *com-*]

coach *noun* (*plural* **coaches**) **1** a bus used for long journeys. **2** a carriage of a railway train. **3** a large horse-drawn carriage with four wheels. **4** an instructor in sports. **5** a teacher giving private specialised tuition.

coach *verb* instruct or train somebody, especially in sports.

coagulate *verb* (**coagulated**, **coagulating**) change from liquid to semi-solid; clot.
coagulant *noun*, **coagulation** *noun*

coal *noun* a hard black mineral substance used for burning to supply heat; a piece of this.
coalfield *noun*

coalesce (*say* koh-a-**less**) *verb* combine and form one whole thing. **coalescence** *noun*, **coalescent** *adjective*

coalition *noun* a union or alliance, especially of political parties in order to form a government.

coarse *adjective* **1** not smooth, not delicate; rough. **2** composed of large particles; not fine. **3** not refined; vulgar. **coarsely** *adverb*, **coarseness** *noun*

coarsen *verb* make or become coarse.

coast *noun* the sea-shore; the land close to it.
coastal *adjective*, **coastline** *noun*
the Coast (*NZ*) the West Coast (of the South Island).
the coast is clear there is no chance of being seen or hindered.

coast *verb* ride without using power.

Coaster *noun* (*NZ*) a person from the West Coast of the South Island.

coaster *noun* a small protective mat used under glasses and mugs.

coastguard *noun* a person whose job is to keep watch on the coast, detect or prevent smuggling, etc.

coat *noun* **1** an outdoor garment with sleeves. **2** the hair or fur on an animal's body. **3** a coating, *a coat of paint.*
coat of arms a design on a shield, used as an emblem by a family, city, etc.

coat *verb* cover with a coating.

coating *noun* a covering layer.

coax *verb* persuade gently or patiently.

cob *noun* **1** the central part of an ear of maize, on which the corn grows. **2** a sturdy horse for riding. **3** a male swan. (The female is a *pen.*)

cobalt *noun* a hard silvery-white metal.

cobber *noun* (*NZ, informal*) a friend; a companion.

cobble[1] *noun* a rounded stone used for paving streets etc. **cobbled** *adjective*

cobble[2] *verb* (**cobbled, cobbling**) make or mend roughly.

cobbler *noun* (*old use*) a shoe-repairer.

cobra (*say* **koh**-bra) *noun* a poisonous snake that can rear up.

cobweb *noun* the thin sticky net made by a spider to trap insects. [from an old word *coppe* = spider, + *web*]

cocaine *noun* a drug made from the leaves of a tropical plant called *coca*.

cock *noun* **1** a male bird; a male fowl. **2** a stopcock. **3** a lever in a gun.

cock *verb* **1** make a gun ready to fire by raising the cock. **2** turn something upwards or in a particular direction. *The dog cocked its ears.*

cockabully *noun* (*plural* **cockabullies**) (*NZ*) a small fish with a blunt nose. [from Māori *kōkopu*]

cockatoo *noun* a crested parrot.

cocked hat a triangular hat worn with some uniforms.

cockerel *noun* a young male fowl.

cocker spaniel a kind of small spaniel.

cock-eyed *adjective* (*slang*) **1** crooked; not straight. **2** absurd.

cockle *noun* an edible shellfish.

cockney *noun* (*plural* **cockneys**) **1** a person born in the East End of London. **2** the dialect or accent of cockneys.

cockpit *noun* the compartment where the pilot of an aircraft sits.

cockroach *noun* (*plural* **cockroaches**) a beetle-like insect.

cocksure *adjective* very sure; too confident.

cocktail *noun* **1** a mixed alcoholic drink. **2** a food containing shellfish or fruit.

cocky[1] *noun* (*plural* **cockies**) (*NZ, informal*) a farmer, *cow-cocky*.

cocky[2] *adjective* (**cockier, cockiest**) (*informal*) conceited. **cockiness** *noun*

cocoa *noun* **1** a hot drink made from a powder of crushed cacao seeds. **2** this powder. [an alteration of *cacao*]

coconut *noun* **1** a large round nut that grows on a kind of palm-tree. **2** its white lining, used in sweets and cookery. [from Spanish *coco* = grinning face (the base of the nut looks like a monkey's face)]

cocoon *noun* **1** the covering round a chrysalis. **2** a protective wrapping.

cocoon *verb* protect by wrapping.

cod *noun* (*plural* **cod**) a large edible sea-fish.

COD *abbreviation* cash on delivery.

coddle *verb* (**coddled, coddling**) cherish and protect carefully.

code *noun* **1** a word or phrase used to represent a message in order to keep its meaning secret. **2** a set of signs used in sending messages by machine etc., *the Morse code*. **3** a set of laws or rules, *the Road Code*.

code *verb* (**coded, coding**) put into code.

codicil *noun* an addition to a will.

codify *verb* (**codified, codifying**) arrange laws or rules into a code or system. **codification** *noun*

coeducation *noun* educating boys and girls together. **coeducational** *adjective*

coefficient *noun* a number by which another number is multiplied; a factor.

coerce (*say* koh-**erss**) *verb* (**coerced, coercing**) compel someone by using threats or force. **coercion** *noun*

coexist *verb* exist together. **coexistence** *noun*, **coexistent** *adjective*

C. of E. *abbreviation* Church of England.

coffee *noun* **1** a hot drink made from the roasted ground seeds (*coffee-beans*) of a tropical plant. **2** these seeds. [from Arabic *kahwa*]

coffer *noun* a large strong box for holding money and valuables.

coffin *noun* a long box in which a body is buried or cremated.

cog *noun* one of a number of projections round the edge of a wheel, fitting into and pushing those on another wheel. **cog-wheel** *noun* a wheel with cogs.

cogent (*say* **koh**-jent) *adjective* convincing, *a cogent argument*.

cogitate *verb* (**cogitated, cogitating**) think deeply. **cogitation** *noun*

cognac (*say* **kon**-yak) *noun* brandy, especially from Cognac in France.

cohere *verb* (**cohered, cohering**) stick to each other in a mass. **cohesion** *noun*, **cohesive** *adjective* [from *co-*, + Latin *haerere* = to stick]

coherent (*say* koh-**heer**-ent) *adjective* **1** cohering. **2** clear and reasonable; not incoherent. **coherently** *adverb*

coil *noun* something wound into a spiral.

coil *verb* wind into a coil.

coin *noun* a shaped piece of metal used to buy things.

coin *verb* **1** manufacture coins. **2** (*informal*) make a lot of money as profit. **3** invent a word or phrase.

coinage *noun* **1** coining. **2** coins; a system of money. **3** a new word or phrase.

coincide *verb* (**coincided, coinciding**) **1** happen at the same time as something else. **2** be in the same place. **3** be the same, *My opinion coincided with hers.* [from *co-*, + Latin *incidere* = fall on]

coincidence *noun* the happening of similar events at the same time by chance.

coke *noun* the solid fuel left when gas and tar have been extracted from coal.

col *noun* a dip in a range of mountains, *Erewhon Col.*

col- *prefix* see **com-**.

colander *noun* a bowl-shaped container with holes for straining water from vegetables etc. after cooking.

cold *adjective* **1** having or at a low temperature; not warm. **2** not friendly or loving; not enthusiastic. **coldly** *adverb*, **coldness** *noun*
cold shoulder deliberate unfriendliness.
cold-shoulder *verb*
cold war a situation where nations are enemies without actually fighting.
get cold feet feel afraid or reluctant to do something.

cold *noun* **1** lack of warmth; low temperature; cold weather. **2** an infectious illness that makes your nose run, your throat sore, etc.

cold-blooded *adjective* **1** having a body temperature that changes according to the surroundings. **2** callous; deliberately cruel.

coleslaw *noun* a salad made with raw sliced cabbage.

colic *noun* stomach-ache.

Coll. *abbreviation* College.

collaborate *verb* (**collaborated, collaborating**) work together on a job. **collaboration** *noun*, **collaborator** *noun* [from *col-*, + Latin *laborare* = to work]

collage (*say* kol-**ah***zh*) *noun* a picture made by fixing small objects to a surface. [French, gluing]

collapse *verb* (**collapsed, collapsing**) **1** fall down or inwards suddenly; break. **2** become very weak or ill. **3** fold up.

collapse *noun* collapsing; a breakdown. [from *col-*, + Latin *lapsum* = slipped]

collapsible *adjective* able to be folded up.

collar *noun* **1** an upright or turned-over band round the neck of a garment etc. **2** a band that goes round the neck of a dog, cat, horse, etc.

collar *verb* (*informal*) seize. [from Latin *collum* = neck]

collate *verb* (**collated, collating**) bring together and compare lists, books, etc. **collation** *noun*

collateral *adjective* **1** parallel to something. **2** additional but less important.

colleague *noun* a person you work with.

collect[1] (*say* kol-**ekt**) *verb* **1** bring people or things together from various places. **2** obtain examples of things as a hobby, *She collects stamps.* **3** come together. **4** ask for money or contributions etc. from people. **5** fetch, *Collect your coat from the cleaners.*
collector *noun*

collect[2] (*say* **kol**-ekt) *noun* a short prayer.

collection *noun* **1** collecting. **2** things collected. **3** money collected for a charity etc.

collective *adjective* of a group taken as a whole, *our collective opinion.*
collective noun a noun that is singular in form but refers to many individuals taken as a unit, e.g. *army, herd.*

college *noun* **1** a place where people can continue learning something after they have left school. **2** a secondary school, *Nelson College.*
College of Education a place where people are trained to become teachers.

collide *verb* (**collided, colliding**) crash into something. **collision** *noun*

collie *noun* a dog with a long pointed face.

colliery *noun* (*plural* **collieries**) a coal-mine and its buildings. [from *coal*]

colloquial (*say* col-**oh**-kwee-al) *adjective* suitable for conversation but not for formal speech or writing. **colloquially** *adverb*, **colloquialism** *noun* [from *col-*, + Latin *loqui* = speak]

collusion *noun* a secret agreement between two or more people who are trying to deceive or cheat someone. [from *col-*, + Latin *ludere* = to play]

cologne (*say* kol-**ohn**) *noun* eau-de-Cologne or a similar liquid.

colon[1] *noun* a punctuation mark (:), often used to introduce lists.

colon[2] *noun* the largest part of the intestine.

colonel (*say* **ker**-nel) *noun* an army officer in charge of a regiment. [from French]

colonial *adjective* of a colony.
colonial goose (*NZ*) a leg of mutton that has been boned and stuffed.

colonialism *noun* the policy of acquiring and keeping colonies.

colonise *verb* (**colonised, colonising**) establish a colony in a country. **colonist** *noun*, **colonisation** *noun*

colonnade *noun* a row of columns.

colony *noun* (*plural* **colonies**) **1** an area of land that the people of another country settle in and control. **2** the people of a colony. **3** a group of people or animals of the same kind living close together.

coloration *noun* colouring.

colossal *adjective* immense; enormous.

colossus *noun* (*plural* **colossi**) **1** a huge statue. **2** a person of immense importance. [from the bronze statue of Apollo at Rhodes, the *Colossus of Rhodes*]

colour *noun* **1** the effect produced by waves of light of a particular wavelength. **2** the use of various colours, not only black and white. **3** the colour of someone's skin. **4** a substance used to colour things. **5** the special flag of a ship or regiment.

colour *verb* **1** put colour on; paint or stain. **2** blush. **3** influence what someone says or believes. **colouring** *noun*

colour-blind *adjective* unable to see the difference between certain colours.

coloured *adjective* **1** having colour. **2** having a dark skin; Black.

colourful *adjective* **1** full of colour. **2** lively; with vivid details.

colourless *adjective* without colour.

colt *noun* **1** a young male horse. **2** a rugby player under a certain age, usually 21.

column *noun* **1** a pillar. **2** something long or tall and narrow, *a column of smoke.* **3** a vertical section of a page, *There are two columns on this page.* **4** a regular article in a newspaper. **columnist** *noun*

com- *prefix* (becoming **col-** before *l*, **cor-** before *r*, **con-** before many other consonants) with; together (as in *combine*, *connect*). [from Latin *cum* with]

coma (*say* **koh**-ma) *noun* a state of deep unconsciousness, especially in someone who is ill or injured. [from Greek, = deep sleep]

comb *noun* **1** a strip of wood or plastic etc. with teeth, used to tidy hair or hold it in place. **2** something used like this, e.g. to separate strands of wool. **3** the red crest on a fowl's head. **4** a honeycomb.

comb *verb* **1** tidy with a comb. **2** search thoroughly.

combat *noun & verb* (**combated**, **combating**) fight. **combatant** (*say* **kom**-batant) *noun*

combination *noun* **1** combining. **2** a number of people or things that are combined. **3** a series of numbers or letters used to open a combination lock.
combination lock a lock that can be opened only by setting a dial or dials to positions shown by numbers or letters.

combine (*say* komb-**I'n**) *verb* (**combined**, **combining**) join or mix together.

combine (*say* **komb**-I'n) *noun* a group of people or firms combining in business.
combine harvester a machine that both reaps and threshes grain.
[from *com-*, + Latin *bini* = pair]

combustible *adjective* able to be set on fire and burn.

combustion *noun* the process of burning, a chemical process (accompanied by heat) in which substances combine with oxygen in air.

come *verb* (**came**, **come**, **coming**) This word is used to show (**1**) movement towards somewhere (*Come here!*), (**2**) arrival, reaching a place or condition or result (*They came to a city. We came to a decision.*), (**3**) happening (*How did you come to lose it?*), (**4**) occurring (*It comes on the next page.*), (**5**) resulting (*That's what comes of being careless.*).
come by obtain.
come in for receive a share of.
come to amount to; become conscious again.
come to pass happen.

comedian *noun* someone who entertains people by making them laugh.

comedy *noun* (*plural* **comedies**) **1** a play or film etc. that makes people laugh. **2** humour. [from Greek *komos* = merrymaking, + *oide* = song]

comely *adjective* good-looking.

comet *noun* an object moving across the sky with a bright tail of light. [from Greek *kometes* = long-haired]

comfort *noun* **1** a comfortable feeling or condition. **2** soothing somebody who is unhappy or in pain. **3** a person or thing that gives comfort.

comfort *verb* make a person less unhappy; soothe.

comfortable *adjective* **1** free from worry or pain. **2** making someone feel comfortable; not tight or harsh. **comfortably** *adverb*

comfy *adjective* (*informal*) comfortable.

comic *adjective* making people laugh. **comical** *adjective*, **comically** *adverb*
comic strip a series of drawings telling a comic story or a serial.

comic *noun* **1** a paper full of comic strips. **2** a comedian.

comma *noun* a punctuation mark (,) used to mark a pause in a sentence or to separate items in a list. [from Greek *komma* = clause]

command *noun* **1** a statement telling somebody to do something; an order. **2** authority; control. **3** ability to use something; mastery, *She has a good command of Spanish.*

command *verb* **1** give a command to somebody; order. **2** have authority over. **3** deserve and get, *They command our respect.* **commander** *noun*

commandant (*say* **kom**-an-dant) *noun* a military officer in charge of a fortress etc.

commandeer *verb* take or seize something for military purposes or for your own use.

commandment *noun* a sacred command, especially one of the Ten Commandments given to Moses.

commando *noun* (*plural* **commandos**) a soldier trained for making dangerous raids.

commemorate *verb* (**commemorated**, **commemorating**) be a celebration or reminder of some past event or person etc. **commemoration** *noun*, **commemorative** *adjective* [compare *memory*]

commence *verb* (**commenced**, **commencing**) begin. **commencement** *noun*

commend *verb* **1** praise, *He was commended for bravery.* **2** entrust, *We commend him to your care.* **commendation** *noun*

commendable *adjective* deserving praise.

comment *noun* an opinion given about an event etc. or to explain something.

comment *verb* make a comment.

commentary *verb* (*plural* **commentaries**) a set of comments, especially describing an event while it is happening. **commentate** *verb*, **commentator** *noun*

commerce *noun* trade and the services that assist it, e.g. banking and insurance. [from *com-*, + Latin *merx* = merchandise]

commercial *adjective* **1** of commerce. **2** paid for by firms etc. whose advertisements are included, *commercial radio.* **3** profitable. **commercially** *adverb*

commercial *noun* a broadcast advertisement.

commercialised *adjective* altered in order to become profitable, *a commercialised resort.* **commercialisation** *noun*

commiserate *verb* (**commiserated**, **commiserating**) sympathise. **commiseration** *noun* [from *com-*, + Latin *miserari* = to pity]

commission *noun* **1** committing something. **2** authorisation to do something; the task etc. authorised, *a commission to paint a portrait.* **3** an appointment to be an officer in the armed forces. **4** a group of people given authority to do or investigate something. **5** payment to someone for selling your goods etc.

commission *verb* give a commission to a person or for a task etc.

commissionaire *noun* an attendant in uniform at the entrance to a theatre, large shop, offices, etc.

commissioner *noun* **1** an official appointed by commission. **2** a member of a commission (see *commission* **4**).

commit *verb* (**committed**, **committing**) **1** do; perform, *commit a crime.* **2** place in someone's care or custody; consign, *He was committed to prison.* **3** pledge; assign, *Don't commit all your spare time to helping him.*

committal *noun* **1** committing a person to prison etc. **2** giving a body ceremonially for burial or cremation.

committee *noun* a group of people appointed to deal with something.

commodious *adjective* roomy.

commodity *noun* (*plural* **commodities**) a useful thing; a product. [from Latin *commodus* = convenient]

commodore *noun* **1** a naval officer ranking next below a rear admiral. **2** the commander of part of a fleet.

common *adjective* **1** ordinary; usual; occurring frequently, *a common weed.* **2** of all or most people, *They worked for the common good.* **3** shared, *Music is their common interest.* **4** vulgar. **commonly** *adverb*, **commonness** *noun*
common noun see **noun**
common sense normal good sense in thinking or behaviour.
in common shared by two or more people or things.

common *noun* a piece of land that everyone can use. [from Latin *communis* = common]

commoner *noun* a member of the ordinary people, not of the nobility.

commonplace *adjective* ordinary; usual.

Commonwealth *noun* **1** an association of countries, *The Commonwealth consists of Britain and various other countries, including New Zealand, Australia, and Canada.* **2** a federal association of States, *the Commonwealth of Australia.* **3** the republic set up in Britain by Cromwell, lasting from 1649 to 1660.

commotion *noun* an uproar; a fuss.

communal (*say* **kom**-yoo-nal) *adjective* shared by several people. **communally** *adverb* [same origin as *common*]

commune[1] (*say* **kom**-yoon) *noun* **1** a group of people sharing a home, food, etc. **2** a district of local government in France and some other countries.

commune[2] *verb* (**communed**, **communing**) talk together.

communicant *noun* **1** a person who communicates with someone. **2** a person who receives Holy Communion.

communicate *verb* (**communicated**, **communicating**) **1** pass news, information, etc. to other people. **2** (of rooms etc.) open into each other; connect.

communication *noun* **1** communicating. **2** something communicated; a message. **communications** *plural noun* links between places (e.g. roads, railways, telephones, radio).

communicative *adjective* willing to talk.

communion *noun* religious fellowship. **Communion** or **Holy Communion** the Christian ceremony in which consecrated bread and wine are given to worshippers.

communiqué (*say* ko-**mew**-nik-ay) *noun* an official message giving a report. [French, = communicated]

communism *noun* a system where property is shared by the community.

Communism *noun* a political system where the State controls property, production, trade, etc. (Compare *capitalism*.) **Communist** *noun* [from French *commun* = common]

community *noun* (*plural* **communities**) **1** the people living in one area. **2** a group with similar interests or origins. **3** a collection.

commute *verb* (**commuted**, **commuting**) **1** travel a fairly long way by train, bus, or car to and from your daily work. **2** exchange; alter a punishment to something less severe. [from *com-*, + Latin *mutare* = change]

commuter *noun* a person who commutes to and from work.

compact[1] *noun* an agreement; a contract. [from *com-* + *pact*]

compact[2] *adjective* **1** closely or neatly packed together. **2** concise. **compactly** *adverb*, **compactness** *noun*
compact disc a small disc from which recorded sound etc. is reproduced by means of a laser beam.

compact[2] *noun* a small flat container for face-powder.

compact[2] *verb* join or press firmly together or into a small space. [from Latin *compactum* = put together]

companion *noun* **1** a person who accompanies another. **2** one of a matching pair of things. **3** (in book-titles) a guidebook or reference book, *The Oxford Companion to New Zealand Literature*. **4** a member of the three highest levels of the New Zealand Order of Merit. **companionship** *noun* [from *com-*, Latin *panis* = bread, = 'person who eats bread with another']

companionable *adjective* sociable.

company *noun* (*plural* **companies**) **1** a number of people together. **2** a business firm. **3** having people with you; companionship. **4** visitors, *We've got company*. **5** a section of a battalion.

comparable (*say* **kom**-per-a-bul) *adjective* similar. **comparably** *adverb*

comparative *adjective* of comparisons; comparing a thing with something else, *They live in comparative comfort*. **comparatively** *adverb*

comparative *noun* the form of an *adjective* or *adverb* that expresses 'more', *The comparative of 'big' is 'bigger'*.

compare *verb* (**compared**, **comparing**) **1** put things together so as to tell in what ways they are similar or different. **2** form the comparative and superlative of an *adjective* or *adverb*.
compare notes share information.
compare with be similar to; be as good as, *Our stadium cannot compare with Eden Park*. [from Latin *comparare* = match with each other]

comparison *noun* comparing.

compartment *noun* one of the spaces into which something is divided; a separate room or enclosed space. [from *com-*, + Latin *partiri* = to share]

compass *noun* (*plural* **compasses**) a device with a pointer that points north.
compasses or **pair of compasses** a device for drawing circles, usually with two rods hinged together at one end.

compassion *noun* pity; mercy. **compassionate** *adjective*, **compassionately** *adverb* [from *com-*, + Latin *passum* = suffered]

compatible *adjective* able to exist or be used together; not incompatible. **compatibly** *adverb*, **compatibility** *noun*

compel *verb* (**compelled**, **compelling**) force somebody to do something. [from *com-*, + Latin *pellere* = to drive]

compendious *adjective* giving much information concisely.

compendium *noun* a package of notepaper and envelopes, or of games. [Latin, = a saving]

compensate *verb* (**compensated**, **compensating**) **1** give a person money etc. to make up for a loss or injury. **2** have a balancing effect, *This victory compensates for our earlier defeats*. **compensation** *noun*, **compensatory** *adjective*

compère (*say* **kom**-pair) *noun* a person who introduces the performers in a show or broadcast. **compère** *verb* [French, = godfather]

compete *verb* (**competed**, **competing**) take part in a competition.

competent *adjective* able to do a particular thing. **competently** *adverb*, **competence** *noun*

competition *noun* **1** a game or race or other contest in which people try to win. **2** competing. **3** the people competing with yourself. **competitive** *adjective*

competitor *noun* someone who competes; a rival.

compile *verb* (**compiled**, **compiling**) put things together into a list or collection, e.g. to form a book. **compiler** *noun*, **compilation** *noun*

complacent *adjective* self-satisfied. **complacently** *adverb*, **complacency** *noun* [from *com-*, + Latin *placens* = pleasing]

complain *verb* say that you are annoyed or unhappy about something.

complaint *noun* **1** a statement complaining about something. **2** an illness.

complement *noun* **1** the quantity needed to fill or complete something, *The ship had its full complement of sailors.* **2** the word or words used after verbs such as *be* and *become* to complete the sense. In *She was brave* and *He became king of England*, the complements are *brave* and *king of England.*

complement *verb* make a thing complete, *The hat complements the outfit.* [same origin as *complete*]

USAGE Do not confuse with *compliment.*

complementary *adjective* completing, forming a complement.
complementary angles angles that add up to 90°.

USAGE Do not confuse with *complimentary.*

complete *adjective* **1** having all its parts. **2** finished. **3** thorough; in every way, *a complete stranger.* **completely** *adverb*, **completeness** *noun*

complete *verb* (**completed**, **completing**) make a thing complete; add what is needed. **completion** *noun* [from Latin *completum* = filled up]

complex *adjective* **1** made up of parts. **2** complicated. **complexity** *noun*

complex *noun* **1** a complex whole; a set of buildings. **2** a group of feelings or ideas that influence a person's behaviour etc., *a persecution complex.* [from Latin *complexum* = embraced, plaited]

complexion *noun* **1** the natural colour and appearance of the skin of the face. **2** the way things seem, *That puts a different complexion on the matter.*

compliant *adjective* complying; obedient. **compliance** *noun*

complicate *verb* (**complicated**, **complicating**) make a thing complex or complicated. [from *com-*, + Latin *plicare* = to fold]

complicated *adjective* **1** made up of many parts. **2** difficult through being complex.

complication *noun* **1** something that complicates things or adds difficulties. **2** a complicated condition.

complicity *noun* being involved in a crime etc.

compliment *noun* something said or done to show that you approve of a person or thing, *pay compliments.*
compliments *plural noun* formal greetings given in a message.

compliment *verb* pay someone a compliment; congratulate.

USAGE Do not confuse with *complement.*

complimentary *adjective* **1** expressing a compliment. **2** given free of charge.

USAGE Do not confuse with *complementary.*

comply *verb* (**complied**, **complying**) obey laws or rules.

compo *noun* (*informal*) compensation.

component *noun* each of the parts of which a thing is composed.

compose *verb* (**composed**, **composing**) **1** form; make up, *The class is composed of 20 students.* **2** write music or poetry etc. **3** arrange in good order. **4** make calm, *compose yourself.* [from Latin *compositum* = put together]

composed *adjective* calm, *a composed manner.* **composedly** *adverb*

composer *noun* a person who composes music etc.

composite (*say* **kom**-poz-it) *adjective* made up of a number of parts or different styles. [same origin as *compose*]

composition *noun* **1** composing. **2** something composed, especially a piece of music. **3** an essay or story written as a school exercise. **4** the parts that make something, *the composition of the soil.*

compost *noun* **1** decayed leaves and grass etc. used as a fertiliser. **2** a soil-like mixture for growing seedlings, cuttings, etc. [same origin as *compose*]

composure *noun* calmness of manner.

compound[1] *adjective* made of two or more parts or ingredients.

compound[1] *noun* a compound substance.

compound[1] *verb* put together; combine. [from Latin *componere* = put together]

compound[2] *noun* a fenced area containing buildings. [from Malay *kampong* = enclosure]

comprehend *verb* **1** understand. **2** include.

comprehensible *adjective* understandable.

comprehensive *adjective* including all or many kinds of people or things.

compress (*say* kom-**press**) *verb* press together or into a smaller space. **compression** *noun*, **compressor** *noun*

compress (*say* **kom**-press) *noun* a soft pad or cloth pressed on the body to stop bleeding or to cool inflammation etc.

comprise *verb* (**comprised**, **comprising**) include; consist of, *The decathlon comprises ten events.*

> USAGE Do not use *comprise* with *of*. It is incorrect to say 'The group was comprised of 20 men'; correct usage is 'was composed of'.

compromise (*say* **kom**-prom-I'z) *noun* settling a dispute by each side accepting less than it asked for.

compromise *verb* (**compromised**, **compromising**) **1** settle by a compromise. **2** expose to danger or suspicion etc., *His confession compromises his sister.*

compulsion *noun* compelling.

compulsive *adjective* having or resulting from an uncontrollable urge, *a compulsive gambler.*

compulsory *adjective* that must be done; not optional.

compunction *noun* a guilty feeling, *She felt no compunction about hitting the burglar.* [from *com-*, + Latin *punctum* = pricked (by conscience)]

compute *verb* (**computed**, **computing**) calculate. **computation** *noun*

computer *noun* an electronic machine for storing and analysing information put into it, or controlling machinery automatically.

computerise *verb* (**computerised**, **computerising**) equip with computers; perform or produce by computer. **computerisation** *noun*

computing *noun* the use of computers.

comrade *noun* a companion who shares in your activities. **comradeship** *noun* [from Spanish *camarada* = room-mate]

con[1] *noun & verb* (**conned**, **conning**) (*slang*) swindle. [short for *confidence trick*]

con[2] *noun* a reason against something, *There are pros and cons.* [from Latin *contra* = against]

con- *prefix* see **com-**.

concave *adjective* curved like the inside of a ball or circle. (The opposite is *convex*.) **concavity** *noun* [from *con-*, Latin *cavus* = hollow]

conceal *verb* hide; keep something secret. **concealment** *noun*

concede *verb* (**conceded**, **conceding**) **1** admit that something is true. **2** grant; allow, *They conceded us the right to cross their land.* **3** admit that you have been defeated.

conceit *noun* being too proud of yourself; vanity. **conceited** *adjective*

conceivable *adjective* able to be imagined or believed. **conceivably** *adverb*

conceive *verb* (**conceived**, **conceiving**) **1** become pregnant; form a baby in the womb. **2** form an idea or plan; imagine, *I can't conceive why you want to come.*

concentrate *verb* (**concentrated**, **concentrating**) **1** give your full attention or effort to something. **2** bring or come together in one place. **3** make a liquid etc. less dilute. [from *con-* + *centre*]

concentration *noun* concentrating. **concentration camp** a place where political prisoners etc. are brought together and confined.

concentric *adjective* having the same centre, *concentric circles.*

concept *noun* an idea.

conception *noun* **1** conceiving. **2** an idea.

concern *verb* **1** be important to or affect somebody. **2** worry somebody. **3** be about; have as its subject, *The story concerns a group of rabbits.*

concern *noun* **1** something that concerns you; a responsibility. **2** worry. **3** a business.

concerned *adjective* **1** worried. **2** involved in or affected by something.

concerning *preposition* on the subject of; about, *laws concerning seatbelts.*

concert *noun* a musical entertainment.

concerted *adjective* done in co-operation with others, *We made a concerted effort.*

concertina *noun* a portable musical instrument with bellows, played by squeezing.

concerto (*say* kon-**chert**-oh) *noun* (*plural* **concertos**) a piece of music for a solo instrument and an orchestra. [Italian]

concession *noun* **1** conceding. **2** something conceded. **concessionary** *adjective*

conch *noun* the spiral shell of a kind of shellfish. It can be used as a horn.

concierge (*say* **con**-see-er*zh*) *noun* a porter or hotel assistant.

conciliate *verb* (**conciliated**, **conciliating**) **1** win over an angry or hostile person by friendliness. **2** reconcile people who disagree. **conciliation** *noun*

concise *adjective* brief; giving much information in a few words. **concisely** *adverb*, **conciseness** *noun*

conclave *noun* a private meeting.

conclude *verb* (**concluded**, **concluding**) **1** bring or come to an end. **2** decide; form an opinion by reasoning, *The jury concluded that he was guilty.* [from *con-*, + Latin *claudere* = shut]

conclusion *noun* **1** an ending. **2** an opinion formed by reasoning.

conclusive *adjective* putting an end to all doubt. **conclusively** *adverb*

concoct *verb* **1** make something by putting ingredients together. **2** invent, *concoct an excuse.* **concoction** *noun* [from *con-*, + Latin *coctum* = cooked]

concord *noun* friendly agreement or harmony. [from *con-*, + Latin *cor* = heart]

concordance *noun* **1** agreement. **2** an index of the words used in a book or an author's works.

concourse *noun* **1** a crowd. **2** an open area through which people pass, e.g. at an airport. [same origin as *concur*]

concrete *noun* cement mixed with sand and gravel, used in building.

concrete *adjective* **1** able to be touched and felt; not abstract. **2** definite, *We need concrete evidence, not theories.*

concur *verb* (**concurred**, **concurring**) **1** agree. **2** happen together; coincide. **concurrence** *noun*, **concurrent** *adjective* [from *con-*, + Latin *currere* = run]

concussion *noun* a temporary injury to the brain caused by a hard knock. **concussed** *adjective* [from Latin *concussum* = shaken violently]

condemn *verb* **1** say that you strongly disapprove of something. **2** convict or sentence a criminal. **3** destine to something unhappy, *condemned to a lonely life.* **4** declare that houses etc. are not fit to be used. **condemnation** *noun* [from *con-*, + Latin *damnare* = damn]

condense *verb* (**condensed**, **condensing**) **1** make a liquid denser or more compact. **2** put something into fewer words. **3** change from gas or vapour to liquid, *Steam condenses on windows.* **condensation** *noun*, **condenser** *noun*

condescend *verb* **1** behave in a way which shows that you feel superior. **2** allow yourself to do something that seems unsuitable for a person of your high rank. **condescension** *noun*

condiment *noun* a seasoning (e.g. salt or pepper) for food.

condition *noun* **1** the state or fitness of a person or thing, *This bicycle is in good condition.* **2** the situation or surroundings etc. that affect something, *working conditions.* **3** something required as part of an agreement.
on condition that only if; on the understanding that something will be done.

condition *verb* **1** put something into a proper condition. **2** train; accustom.

conditional *adjective* containing a condition (see *condition* 3); depending. **conditionally** *adverb*

condole *verb* (**condoled**, **condoling**) express sympathy. **condolence** *noun* [from *con-*, + Latin *dolere* grieve]

condom *noun* a sheath for the penis.

condominium *noun* a complex of houses or apartments.

condone *verb* (**condoned**, **condoning**) forgive or ignore wrongdoing, *Do not condone violence.* **condonation** *noun*

condor *noun* a kind of large vulture.

conducive *adjective* helping to cause or produce something, *Noisy surroundings are not conducive to work.*

conduct (*say* kon-**dukt**) *verb* **1** lead or guide. **2** be the conductor of an orchestra or choir. **3** manage or direct something, *conduct an experiment.* **4** allow heat, light, sound, or electricity to pass along or through. **5** behave, *They conducted themselves with dignity.*

conduct (*say* **kon**-dukt) *noun* behaviour. [from *con-*, + Latin *ducere* = to lead]

conduction *noun* the conducting of heat or electricity etc. (see *conduct* 4).

conductor *noun* **1** a person who directs the performance of an orchestra or choir by movements of the arms. **2** something that conducts heat or electricity etc.

conduit (*say* **kon**-dit) *noun* **1** a pipe or channel for liquid. **2** a tube protecting electric wire.

cone *noun* **1** an object that is circular at one end and narrows to a point at the other end. **2** the dry cone-shaped fruit of a pine, fir, or cedar tree. **3** a cone-shaped wafer for ice cream.

confection *noun* something made of various things, especially sweet ones, put together.

confectioner *noun* someone who makes or sells sweets. **confectionery** *noun*

confederacy *noun* (*plural* **confederacies**) a union of States; a confederation.

confederate *adjective* allied; joined by an agreement or treaty.

confederate *noun* **1** a member of a confederacy. **2** an ally; an accomplice. [from *con-*, + Latin *foederatum* = allied]

confederation *noun* **1** the process of joining in an alliance. **2** a group of people, organisations, or States joined together by an agreement or treaty.

confer *verb* (**conferred**, **conferring**) **1** grant; bestow. **2** hold a discussion.

conference *noun* a meeting for holding a discussion.

confess *verb* state openly that you have done something wrong or have a weakness; admit. **confession** *noun*

confessional *noun* an enclosed stall where a priest hears confessions.

confessor *noun* a priest who hears confessions.

confetti *noun* tiny pieces of coloured paper thrown by wedding guests at the bride and bridegroom. [Italian]

confidant *noun* (**confidante** is used of a woman) a person in whom someone confides.

confide *verb* (**confided**, **confiding**) **1** tell confidentially, *confide a secret to someone* or *confide in someone*. **2** entrust. [from *con-*, + *Latin fidere* = to trust]

confidence *noun* **1** firm trust. **2** a feeling of certainty or boldness; being sure that you can do something. **3** something told confidentially.
confidence trick swindling a person after persuading him or her to trust you.
in confidence as a secret.
in a person's confidence trusted with his or her secrets.

confident *adjective* showing or feeling confidence; bold. **confidently** *adverb*

confidential *adjective* **1** that should be kept secret. **2** trusted to keep secrets, *a confidential secretary*. **confidentially** *adverb*, **confidentiality** *noun*

configuration *noun* **1** a method of arrangement of parts etc. **2** a shape.

confine *verb* (**confined**, **confining**) **1** keep within limits; restrict, *Please confine your remarks to the subject being discussed.* **2** keep somebody in a place. [from *con-*, + Latin, *finis* = limit, end]

confined *adjective* narrow; restricted, *a confined space.*

confinement *noun* **1** confining. **2** the time of giving birth to a baby.

confines (*say* **kon**-fynz) *plural noun* the limits or boundaries of an area.

confirm *verb* **1** prove that something is true or correct. **2** make a thing definite, *Please write to confirm your booking.* **3** make a person a full member of the Christian Church. **confirmation** *noun*, **confirmatory** *adjective*

confiscate *verb* (**confiscated**, **confiscating**) take something away as a punishment. **confiscation** *noun*

conflagration *noun* a great and destructive fire. [same origin *as flagrant*]

conflict (*say* **kon**-flikt) *noun* a fight, struggle, or disagreement.

conflict (*say* kon-**flikt**) *verb* have a conflict; differ or disagree. [from *con-* = together, + Latin *flictum* = struck]

confluence *noun* the place where two rivers unite. [from *con-*, + Latin *fluens* = flowing]

conform *verb* keep to accepted rules or customs etc. **conformist** *noun*, **conformity** *noun* [from Latin *conformare* = shape evenly]

confound *verb* **1** astonish or puzzle someone. **2** confuse.

confront *verb* **1** come or bring face to face, especially in a hostile way. **2** be present and have to be dealt with, *Problems confront us.* **confrontation** *noun*

confuse *verb* (**confused**, **confusing**) **1** make a person puzzled or muddled. **2** mistake one thing for another. **confusion** *noun*

confute *verb* (**confuted**, **confuting**) prove a person or statement to be wrong. **confutation** *noun*

congeal (*say* kon-**jeel**) *verb* become jelly-like instead of liquid, especially in cooling. [from Latin *congelare* = freeze]

congenial *adjective* pleasant through being similar to yourself or suiting your tastes; agreeable, *a congenial companion.* **congenially** *adverb*

congenital (*say* kon-**jen**-it-al) *adjective* existing in a person from birth. **congenitally** *adverb* [from *con-*, + Latin *genitus* = born]

congested *adjective* crowded; too full of something. **congestion** *noun*

conglomeration *noun* a mass of different things put together. [from *con-*, + Latin *glomus* = mass]

congratulate *verb* (**congratulated**, **congratulating**) tell a person that you are pleased about his or her success or good fortune. **congratulation** *noun*, **congratulatory** *adjective* [from *con-*, + Latin *gratulari* = show joy]

congregate *verb* (**congregated**, **congregating**) assemble; flock together. [from *con-*, + Latin *-gregatum* = herded]

congregation *noun* a group who have gathered to take part in worship.

congress *noun* a conference.

Congress *noun* the parliament of the USA. [from *con-*, + Latin *-gressus* = going]

congruent *adjective* **1** suitable; consistent. **2** (of geometrical figures) having exactly the same shape and size. **congruence** *noun*

conic *adjective* of a cone.

conical *adjective* cone-shaped. **conically** *adverb*

conifer (*say* **kon**-if-er) *noun* an evergreen tree with cones. **coniferous** *adjective* [from *cone* + Latin *ferens* = bearing]

conjecture *noun* a guess. **conjecture** *verb*, **conjectural** *adjective*

conjugal (*say* **kon**-jug-al) *adjective* of a husband and wife.

conjunction *noun* **1** a word that joins words or phrases or sentences, e.g. *and, but*. **2** combination, *The four armies acted in conjunction*. [from Latin *conjunctum* = yoked together]

conjure *verb* (**conjured**, **conjuring**) perform puzzling tricks. **conjuror** *noun*
conjure up produce, *Mention of the Antarctic conjures up visions of snow*.

conker *noun* the hard shiny brown nut of the horse-chestnut tree.
conkers a game between players who each have a conker threaded on a string. [from a dialect word, = snail-shell]

connect *verb* **1** join together; link. **2** think of as being associated with each other. **connection** *noun*, **connective** *adjective*, **connector** *noun* [from *con-*, + Latin *nectere* = bind]

conning-tower *noun* a projecting part on top of a submarine, containing the periscope.

connive (*say* kon-**I'v**) *verb* (**connived**, **conniving**) **connive at** take no notice of wrongdoing that ought to be reported or punished. **connivance** *noun* [from Latin *connivere* = shut the eyes]

connoisseur (*say* kon-a-**ser**) *noun* a person with great experience and appreciation of something, *a connoisseur of wine*. [French, = one who knows]

conquer *verb* defeat; overcome. **conqueror** *noun*

conquest *noun* **1** conquering. **2** conquered territory.

conscience (*say* **kon**-shens) *noun* knowing what is right and wrong, especially in your own actions. [from *con-*, + Latin *sciens* = knowing]

conscientious (*say* kon-shee-**en**-shus) *adjective* careful and honest, *conscientious workers*. **conscientiously** *adverb*
conscientious objector a person who refuses to serve in the armed forces because he or she believes it is wrong.

conscious (*say* **kon**-shus) *adjective* awake; aware of what is happening. **consciously** *adverb*, **consciousness** *noun*

conscript (*say* kon-**skript**) *verb* make a person join the armed forces. **conscription** *noun*

conscript (*say* **kon**-skript) *noun* a conscripted person. [from *con-*, + Latin *scriptus* = written in a list, enlisted]

consecrate *verb* (**consecrated**, **consecrating**) make a thing sacred; dedicate to God. **consecration** *noun*

consecutive *adjective* following one after another. **consecutively** *adverb* [from Latin *consecutum* = following]

consensus *noun* (*plural* **consensuses**) general agreement; the opinion of most people. [same origin as *consent*]

consent *noun* agreement to what someone wishes; permission.

consent *verb* say that you are willing to do or allow what someone wishes. [from *con-*, + Latin *sentire* = feel]

consequence *noun* **1** something that happens as the result of an event or action. **2** importance, *It is of no consequence*.

consequent *adjective* happening as a result. **consequently** *adverb* [same origin as *consecutive*]

consequential *adjective* consequent.

conservation *noun* conserving; preservation, especially of the natural environment. **conservationist** *noun*

conservation park *noun* (*NZ*) a protected natural area, formerly known as forest park.

conservative *adjective* **1** liking traditional ways and disliking changes. **2** (of an estimate) moderate; low. **conservatively** *adverb*, **conservatism** *noun*

conservatory *noun* **1** a room with glass roof and walls, attached to a house. **2** a school of music or other arts.

conserve *verb* (**conserved**, **conserving**) prevent something valuable from being changed, spoilt, or wasted. [from *con-*, + Latin *servare* = keep safe]

consider *verb* **1** think carefully about or give attention to something, especially in order to make a decision. **2** have an opinion; think to be, *Consider yourself lucky*.

considerable *adjective* fairly great, *a considerable amount*. **considerably** *adverb*

considerate *adjective* taking care not to inconvenience or hurt others. **considerately** *adverb*

consideration *noun* **1** being considerate. **2** careful thought or attention. **3** a fact that must be kept in mind. **4** payment given as a reward.
take into consideration allow for.

considering *preposition* taking something into consideration, *The car runs well, considering its age.*

consign *verb* hand something over formally; entrust.

consignment *noun* **1** consigning. **2** a batch of goods etc. sent to someone.

consist *verb* be made up or composed of, *The flat consists of three rooms.*

consistency *noun* (*plural* **consistencies**) **1** being consistent. **2** thickness or stiffness, especially of a liquid.

consistent *adjective* **1** keeping to a regular pattern or style; not changing. **2** not contradictory. **consistently** *adverb*

consolation *noun* **1** consoling. **2** something that consoles someone.
consolation prize a prize given to a competitor who has just missed winning one of the main prizes.

console[1] (*say* kon-**sohl**) *verb* (**consoled**, **consoling**) comfort someone who is unhappy or disappointed. [from *con-*, + Latin *solari* = to comfort]

console[2] (*say* **kon**-sohl) *noun* **1** a frame containing the keyboard and stops etc. of an organ. **2** a panel or unit holding the controls of equipment. [French]

consolidate *verb* (**consolidated**, **consolidating**) **1** make or become secure and strong. **2** combine two or more organisations, funds, etc. into one. **consolidation** *noun*
Consolidated Fund a central government fund made up of taxes and other forms of revenue.
[from *con-* + *solid*]

consonant *noun* **1** any of the sounds of speech in which the breath is obstructed in some way, e.g. the first and last sounds of *dog, cheese, thing*. **2** any letter of the alphabet that is not a vowel, e.g. *c, m, q, x*. [from *con-*, + Latin *sonans* = sounding]

consort (*say* **kon**-sort) *noun* a husband or wife, especially of a monarch.

consort (*say* kon-**sort**) *verb* be in someone's company, *consort with criminals*. [from Latin *consors* = sharer]

consortium *noun* (*plural* **consortia**) a combination of countries, companies, or other groups acting together.

conspicuous *adjective* easily seen; noticeable; remarkable. **conspicuously** *adverb*, **conspicuousness** *noun*

conspiracy *noun* (*plural* **conspiracies**) planning with others to do something illegal; a plot.

conspire *verb* (**conspired**, **conspiring**) take part in a conspiracy. **conspirator** *noun*, **conspiratorial** *adjective* [from *con-*, + Latin *spirare* = breathe]

constable *noun* a police officer of the lowest rank. [from Latin, originally = officer in charge of the stable]

constant *adjective* **1** not changing; happening all the time. **2** faithful; loyal. **constantly** *adverb*, **constancy** *noun* [from *con-*, + Latin *stans* = standing]

constellation *noun* a group of stars. [from *con-*, + Latin *stella* star]

constipated *adjective* unable to empty the bowels easily or regularly. **constipation** *noun*

constituency *noun* (*plural* **constituencies**) (*British*) an electorate (sense 2).

constituent *noun* **1** one of the parts that form a whole thing. **2** someone who lives in a particular electorate. **constituent** *adjective*

constitute *verb* (**constituted**, **constituting**) make up or form something, *Twelve months constitute a year*. [from *con-*, + Latin *statuere* = set up]

constitution *noun* **1** the group of laws or principles that state how a country is to be organised and governed. **2** the nature of the body in regard to healthiness. *She has a strong constitution.* **3** constituting. **4** the composition of something. **constitutional** *adjective*

constrain *verb* compel; oblige.

constraint *noun* **1** constraining; compulsion. **2** a restriction. **3** a strained manner caused by holding back feelings.

constrict *verb* squeeze or tighten something by making it narrower. **constriction** *noun* [from *con-*, + Latin *strictum* = bound]

construct *verb* make something by placing parts together; build. **constructor** *noun* [from *con-*, + Latin *structum* = built]

construction *noun* **1** constructing. **2** something constructed; a building. **3** two or more words put together to form a phrase or clause or sentence. **4** an explanation or interpretation, *They put a bad construction on our refusal.*

constructive *adjective* constructing; being helpful, *constructive suggestions.*

construe *verb* (**construed**, **construing**) interpret; explain.

consul *noun* **1** a government official appointed to live in a foreign city to help people from his or her own country who visit there. **2** either of the two chief officials in ancient Rome. **consular** *adjective* [Latin]

consulate *noun* the building where a consul works.

consult *verb* go to a person or book etc. for information or advice. **consultation** *noun*

consultant *noun* a person who is qualified to give expert advice.

consultative *adjective* for consultation, *a consultative committee.*

consume *verb* (**consumed**, **consuming**) **1** eat or drink something. **2** use up, *Much time was consumed in waiting.* **3** destroy, *Fire consumed the building.* [from *con-*, + Latin *sumere* = take up]

consumer *noun* a person who buys or uses goods or services.

consummate (*say* **kon**-sum-ayt) *verb* accomplish; make complete. **consummation** *noun*

consummate (*say* kon-**sum**-at) *adjective* perfect; highly skilled, *a consummate artist.* [from *con-*, + Latin *summus* = highest]

consumption *noun* **1** consuming. **2** (*old use*) tuberculosis of the lungs.

cont. *abbreviation* continued.

contact *noun* **1** touching. **2** being in touch; communication. **3** a person to communicate with when you need information or help. **contact lens** a tiny lens worn against the eyeball, instead of spectacles.

contact *verb* get in touch with a person. [from *con-*, + Latin *tactum* = touched]

contagion *noun* a contagious disease.

contagious *adjective* spreading by contact with an infected person, *a contagious disease.*

contain *verb* **1** have inside, *The box contains chocolates.* **2** restrain; hold back, *Try to contain your laughter.* [from *con-*, + Latin *tenere* = hold]

container *noun* **1** a box or bottle etc. designed to contain something. **2** a large box-like object of standard design in which goods are transported.

containerise *verb* (**containerised**, **containerising**) pack into containers; transport by containers. **containerisation** *noun*

contaminate *verb* (**contaminated**, **contaminating**) make a thing dirty or impure or diseased etc.; pollute. **contamination** *noun*

contemplate *verb* (**contemplated**, **contemplating**) **1** look at something thoughtfully. **2** consider or think about doing something, *We are contemplating a visit to Sydney.* **contemplation** *noun*, **contemplative** *adjective*

contemporary *adjective* **1** belonging to the same period, *Dickens was contemporary with Thackeray.* **2** modern; up-to-date, *contemporary furniture.*

contemporary *noun* (*plural* **contemporaries**) a person who is contemporary with another or who is about the same age, *She was my contemporary at college.* [from *con-*, + Latin *tempus* = time]

contempt *noun* a feeling of despising a person or thing.

contemptible *adjective* deserving contempt.

contemptuous *adjective* feeling or showing contempt. **contemptuously** *adverb*

contend *verb* **1** struggle in a battle etc. or against difficulties. **2** compete. **3** assert; declare in an argument etc., *We contend that he is innocent.* **contender** *noun* [from *con-*, + Latin *tendere* = strive]

content[1] (*say* kon-**tent**) *adjective* contented.

content[1] *noun* contentment.

content[1] *verb* make a person contented. [from Latin *contentum* = restrained]

content[2] (*say* **kon**-tent) *noun* (also **contents** *plural noun*) what something contains. [from Latin *contenta* = things contained]

contented *adjective* happy with what you have; satisfied. **contentedly** *adverb*

contention *noun* **1** contending; arguing. **2** an assertion put forward.

contentment *noun* a contented state.

contest (*say* **kon**-test) *noun* a competition; a struggle in which rivals try to obtain something or to do best.

contest (*say* kon-**test**) *verb* **1** compete for or in, *contest an election.* **2** dispute; argue that something is wrong or not legal.

contestant *noun* a person taking part in a contest; a competitor.

context *noun* **1** the circumstances or relevant facts concerning something. **2** the words that come before and after a particular word or phrase and help to fix its meaning. **3** position or surroundings. [from *con-*, + Latin *textum* = woven]

contiguous *adjective* adjoining.

continent *noun* one of the main masses of land in the world, *The continents are Europe, Asia, Africa, North America, South America, Australia, and Antarctica.* **continental** *adjective* [from Latin, = continuous land]

contingency *noun* (*plural* **contingencies**) something that may happen but is not intended.

contingent *adjective* **1** depending, *His future is contingent on success in this exam.* **2** possible but not certain, *other contingent events.*

contingent *noun* a group contributed to a larger group or gathering.

continual *adjective* continuing for a long time without stopping or with only short breaks, *Stop this continual quarrelling!* **continually** *adverb*

continuance *noun* continuing.

continue *verb* (**continued, continuing**) **1** do something without stopping. **2** begin again after stopping, *The game will continue after lunch.* **continuation** *noun* [same origin as *contain*]

continuous *adjective* continuing; without a break. **continuously** *adverb,* **continuity** *noun*

contort *verb* twist or force out of the usual shape. **contortion** *noun* [from *con-,* + Latin *tortum* twisted]

contortionist *noun* a person who can twist his or her body into unusual postures.

contour *noun* **1** a line (on a map) joining the points that are the same height above sea-level. **2** an outline.

contra- *prefix* against. [Latin]

contraband *noun* smuggled goods. [from *contra-,* + Italian *banda* = a ban]

contraception *noun* preventing conception; birth-control. [from *contra-* + *conception*]

contraceptive *noun* a substance or device that prevents conception.

contract (*say* **kon**-trakt) *noun* **1** a formal agreement to do something. **2** a document stating the terms of an agreement. **contract shearing** (*NZ*) shearing done on a farm by a gang of workers for an agreed price.

contract (*say* kon-**trakt**) *verb* **1** make or become smaller. **2** make a contract. **3** get an illness, *She contracted measles.* [from *con-,* + Latin *tractum* = pulled]

contraction *noun* **1** contracting. **2** a shortened form of a word or words. *Can't* is a contraction of *cannot.*

contractor *noun* a person who makes a contract, especially for building.

contradict *verb* **1** say that something said is not true or that someone is wrong. **2** say the opposite of, *These rumours contradict previous ones.* **contradiction** *noun,* **contradictory** *adjective* [from *contra-,* + Latin *dicere* say]

contralto *noun* (*plural* **contraltos**) a female singer with a low voice. [Italian, from *contra-* + *alto*]

contraption *noun* a strange-looking device or machine.

contrary *adjective* **1** (*say* **kon**-tra-ree) of the opposite kind or direction etc.; opposed; unfavourable. **2** (*say* kon-**trair**-ee) awkward and obstinate.

contrary (*say* **kon**-tra-ree) *noun* the opposite. **on the contrary** the opposite is true. [from Latin *contra* = against]

contrast *noun* **1** a difference clearly seen when things are compared. **2** something showing a clear difference.

contrast *verb* **1** compare or oppose two things so as to show that they are clearly different. **2** be clearly different when compared. [from *contra-,* + Latin *stare* = to stand]

contravene *verb* (**contravened, contravening**) act against a rule or law. **contravention** *noun* [from *contra-,* + Latin *venire* = come]

contretemps (*say* **kawn**-tre-tahn) *noun* an unfortunate happening. [French, = out of time (in music)]

contribute *verb* (**contributed, contributing**) **1** give money or help etc. when others are doing the same. **2** write something for a newspaper or magazine etc. **3** help to cause something. **contribution** *noun,* **contributor** *noun,* **contributory** *adjective* [from *con-,* + Latin *tribuere* = bestow]

contrite *adjective* penitent.

contrivance *noun* a device.

contrive *verb* (**contrived, contriving**) plan cleverly; find a way of doing or making something.

control *verb* (**controlled, controlling**) have the power to give orders or to restrain something. **controller** *noun*

control *noun* controlling a person or thing; authority.

controversial *adjective* causing controversy.

controversy (*say* **kon**-tro-ver-see or **kon-trov**-er-see) *noun* a long argument or disagreement. [from *contra-,* + Latin *versum* = turned]

contusion *noun* a bruise.

conundrum *noun* a riddle; a hard question.

conurbation *noun* a large urban area where towns have spread into each other. [from *con-,* + Latin *urbs* = city]

convalesce *verb* (**convalesced, convalescing**) be recovering from an illness. **convalescence** *noun,* **convalescent** *adjective & noun* [from *con-,* + Latin *valescere* = grow strong]

convection *noun* the passing on of heat within liquid, air, or gas by circulation of the warmed parts. [from *con-,* + Latin *vectum* = carried]

convector *noun* a device that circulates warmed air.

convene *verb* (**convened**, **convening**) summon or assemble for a meeting etc. **convener** *noun* [from *con-*, + Latin *venire* = come]

convenience *noun* **1** being convenient. **2** something that is convenient. **3** a public toilet.
at your convenience whenever you find convenient; as it suits you.

convenient *adjective* easy to use or deal with or reach. **conveniently** *adverb* [from Latin *convenire* = to suit]

convent *noun* a place where nuns live and work. [same origin as *convene*]

convention *noun* **1** an accepted way of doing things. **2** a formal assembly.

conventional *adjective* **1** done or doing things in the accepted way; traditional. **2** (of weapons) not nuclear. **conventionally** *adverb*, **conventionality** *noun*

converge *verb* (**converged**, **converging**) come to or towards the same point from different directions. **convergence** *noun*, **convergent** *adjective* [from *con*, + Latin *vergere* = turn]

conversant *adjective* familiar with something, *Are you conversant with the rules of this game?* [from *converse*[1]]

conversation *noun* talk between people. **conversational** *adjective*

converse[1] (*say* kon-**verss**) *verb* (**conversed**, **conversing**) hold a conversation. [from Latin, = keep company]

converse[2] (*say* **kon**-verss) *adjective* opposite; contrary. **conversely** *adverb*

converse[2] *noun* an opposite idea or statement etc. [same origin as *convert*]

conversion *noun* **1** (*NZ*) farmland area with a new use, *a dairy conversion*. **2** the act of changing to a new use. **3** a successful kick at goal following a rugby try. **4** (*NZ*) the theft of a car. **5** changing of mind, belief, or religion.

convert (*say* kon-**vert**) *verb* **1** change. **2** cause a person to change his or her beliefs. **3** kick a goal after scoring a try at rugby. **4** (*NZ*) steal a motor vehicle. **5** (*NZ*) change the use of land. **converter** *noun* [from *con-*, + Latin *vertere* = turn]

convertible *adjective* able to be converted. **convertibility** *noun*

convex *adjective* curved like the outside of a ball or circle. (The opposite is *concave*.) **convexity** *noun*

convey *verb* **1** transport. **2** communicate a message or idea etc. **conveyor** *noun*

conveyance *noun* **1** conveying. **2** a vehicle for transporting people.

conveyancing *noun* transferring the legal ownership of land etc. from one person to another.

conveyor belt a continuous moving belt for conveying objects.

convict (*say* kon-**vikt**) *verb* prove or declare that a certain person is guilty of a crime.

convict (*say* **kon**-vikt) *noun* (*old use*) a convicted person who is in prison. [from *con-*, + Latin *victum* = conquered]

conviction *noun* **1** convicting or being convicted of a crime. **2** being convinced. **3** a firm opinion or belief.
carry conviction be convincing.

convince *verb* (**convinced**, **convincing**) make a person feel certain that something is true. [from *con-*, + Latin *vincere* = conquer]

convivial *adjective* sociable and lively. [from Latin *convivium* = feast]

convoke *verb* (**convoked**, **convoking**) summon people to an assembly or meeting. [from *con-*, + Latin *vocare* = to call]

convoluted *adjective* **1** coiled; twisted. **2** complicated. **convolution** *noun* [from *con-*, + Latin *volutum* = rolled]

convoy *noun* a group of ships or trucks travelling together.

convulse *verb* (**convulse**, **convulsing**) cause violent movements or convulsions. **convulsive** *adjective* [from *con-*, + Latin *vulsum* = pulled]

convulsion *noun* **1** a violent movement of the body. **2** a violent upheaval.

coo *verb* (**cooed**, **cooing**) make a dove's soft murmuring sound. **coo** *noun*

cooee *noun* (*NZ*) a call used to attract someone's attention.
within cooee within hailing distance, i.e. close. [Aboriginal]

cook *verb* make food ready to eat by heating it.
cook up (*informal*) concoct; invent.

cook *noun* a person who cooks.

cooker *noun* a stove for cooking food.

cookery *noun* the action or skill of cooking food.

cookie *noun* **1** a biscuit. **2** (*informal*) a person, *a shrewd cookie*. **3** a means of identifying a computer user's access to a server.

Cook Islander a person born in, or living in, the Cook Islands.

cool *adjective* **1** fairly cold; not hot or warm. **2** calm; not enthusiastic. **3** (*slang*) excellent; fashionable. **coolly** *adverb*, **coolness** *noun*

cool *verb* make or become cool. **cooler** *noun*

coolie *noun* an unskilled labourer in countries of eastern Asia.

coop *noun* a cage for poultry.

co-op *noun* a cooperative factory etc. [*abbreviation*]

cooperate *verb* (**cooperated**, **cooperating**) work helpfully with other people. **cooperation** *noun*, **cooperative** *adjective*

co-opt *verb* invite someone to become a member of a committee etc. [from *co-*, + Latin *optare* choose]

Coopworth *noun* (*NZ*) a cross-bred sheep, farmed for its meat and wool. [named after I.E. Coop, an animal scientist]

coordinate *verb* (**coordinated**, **coordinating**) organise people or things to work properly together. **coordination** *noun*, **coordinator** *noun*

coordinate *noun* **1** a coordinated thing. **2** a quantity used to fix the position of something. [from *co-*, + Latin *ordinare* = arrange]

coot *noun* a water-bird with a horny white patch on its forehead.

cop *verb* (**copped**, **copping**) (*slang*) catch, *You'll cop it!*

cop *noun* (*slang*) **1** a police officer. **2** capture; arrest, *It's a fair cop!*

cope[1] *verb* (**coped**, **coping**) manage or deal with something successfully.

cope[2] *noun* a long loose cloak worn by clergy in ceremonies etc.

copier *noun* a device for copying things.

coping *noun* the top row of stones or bricks in a wall, usually slanted so that rainwater will run off. [from *cope*[2]]

copious *adjective* plentiful; in large amounts. **copiously** *adverb*

copper[1] *noun* **1** a reddish-brown metal used to make wire, coins, etc. **2** a reddish-brown colour. **3** a coin made of copper or metal of this colour. **copper** *adjective* [from Latin *cuprum* = Cyprus metal (because the Romans got most of their copper from Cyprus)]

copper[2] *noun* (*slang*) a policeman. [from *cop*]

copperplate *noun* neat handwriting.

copra *noun* dried coconut-kernels.

coprosma *noun* (*NZ*) a kind of small evergreen tree or shrub.

copse *noun* (*British*) a group of small trees.

copulate *verb* (**copulated**, **copulating**) have sexual intercourse with someone. **copulation** *noun*

copy *noun* (*plural* **copies**) **1** a thing made to look like another. **2** something written or typed out again from its original form. **3** one of a number of specimens of the same book or newspaper etc.

copy *verb* (**copied**, **copying**) **1** make a copy of something. **2** do the same as someone else; imitate. **copyist** *noun*

copyright *noun* the legal right to print a book, reproduce a picture, record a piece of music, etc.

coquette (*say* ko-**ket**) *noun* a woman who flirts. **coquettish** *adjective* [French]

cor- *prefix* see **com-**.

coral *noun* **1** a hard red, pink, or white substance formed by the skeletons of tiny sea-creatures massed together. **2** a pink colour.

cor anglais (*say* kor **ong**-lay) *noun* a woodwind instrument rather like an *oboe*.

corbel *noun* a piece of stone or wood projecting from a roof to support something.

cord *noun* **1** a long thin flexible strip of twisted threads or strands. **2** a piece of flex. **3** a cord-like structure in the body, *the spinal cord*. **4** corduroy.

cordial *noun* a fruit-flavoured drink.

cordial *adjective* warm and friendly. **cordially** *adverb*, **cordiality** *noun* [from Latin *cordis* = of the heart]

cordless *adjective* (of a telephone or other appliance) working without connection to a mains supply or central unit.

cordon *noun* a line of people, ships, fortifications, etc. placed round an area to guard or enclose it.

cordon *verb* surround with a cordon.

corduroy *noun* cotton cloth with velvety ridges.

core *noun* **1** the part in the middle of something. **2** the hard central part of an apple or pear etc., containing the seeds.

corgi *noun* (*plural* **corgis**) a small dog with short legs and upright ears.

cork *noun* **1** the lightweight bark of a kind of oak-tree. **2** a stopper for a bottle, made of cork or other material.

cork *verb* close with a cork.

corker *adjective* (*NZ & Australia, informal*) excellent.

corkscrew *noun* **1** a device for removing corks from bottles. **2** a spiral.

corm *noun* a part of a plant rather like a bulb.

cormorant *noun* a shag.

corn[1] *noun* **1** a cereal plant or crop, especially maize. **2** the seed of maize and other cereal plants.

corn[2] *noun* a small hard lump on the foot.

cornea *noun* the transparent covering over the pupil of the eye. **corneal** *adjective*

corned *adjective* preserved with salt, *corned beef.*

corner *noun* **1** the angle or area where two lines or sides or walls meet or where two streets join. **2** a free hit or kick from the corner of a hockey or soccer field. **3** a region, *a quiet corner of the world.*

corner *verb* **1** drive someone into a corner or other position from which it is difficult to escape. **2** travel round a corner. **3** obtain possession of all or most of something, *corner the market.*

cornerstone *noun* **1** a stone built into the corner at the base of a building. **2** something that is a vital foundation.

cornet *noun* a musical instrument rather like a trumpet. [from Latin *cornu* = horn, trumpet]

cornflakes *plural noun* toasted maize flakes eaten for breakfast.

cornflour *noun* flour made from maize or rice, used in sauces, milk puddings, etc.

cornflower *noun* a plant with blue flowers that grows wild in fields of corn.

cornice *noun* a band of ornamental moulding on walls just below a ceiling or at the top of a building.

cornucopia *noun* a horn-shaped container overflowing with fruit and flowers; a plentiful supply. [from Latin *cornu* = horn, + *copiae* = of plenty]

corny *adjective* (**cornier**, **corniest**) (*informal*) repeated so often that people are bored, *corny jokes.* [from *corn*[1]]

corollary (*say* ker-**ol**-er-ee) *noun* (*plural* **corollaries**) a fact etc. that logically accompanies another, *The work is difficult and, as a corollary, tiring.*

corona (*say* kor-**oh**-na) *noun* a circle of light round something. [Latin, = crown]

coronary *noun* short for **coronary thrombosis**, blockage of an artery carrying blood to the heart.

coronation *noun* the crowning of a king or queen. [same origin as *corona*]

coroner *noun* an official who holds an inquiry into the cause of a death thought to be from unnatural causes.

coronet *noun* a small crown.

Corp. *abbreviation* Corporation.

corporal[1] *noun* a soldier ranking next below a sergeant.

corporal[2] *adjective* of the body.
corporal punishment punishment by being whipped or beaten. [from Latin *corpus* = body]

corporate *adjective* shared by members of a group, *corporate responsibility.*

corporation *noun* a group of people legally authorised to act as an individual in business etc.

corporatise *verb* (**corporatised**, **corporatising**) change a government department into a corporation.
corporatisation *noun*

corps (*say* kor) *noun* (*plural* **corps**, *say* korz) **1** a special army unit, *the Medical Corps.* **2** a large group of soldiers. **3** a set of people engaged in the same activity, *the diplomatic corps.*

corpse *noun* a dead body. [from Latin *corpus* = body]

corpulent *adjective* having a bulky body; fat.
corpulence *noun*

corpuscle *noun* one of the red or white cells in blood. [from Latin, = little body]

corral (*say* kor-**ahl**) *noun* (*American*) an enclosure for horses, cattle, etc.

correct *adjective* **1** true; accurate; without any mistakes. **2** proper; done or said in an approved way. **correctly** *adverb*, **correctness** *noun*

correct *verb* **1** make a thing correct by altering or adjusting it. **2** mark the mistakes in something. **3** point out or punish a person's faults. **correction** *noun*, **corrective** *adjective*, **corrector** *noun* [from *cor-*, + Latin *rectus* = straight]

correlate *verb* (**correlated**, **correlating**) compare or connect things systematically.
correlation *noun* [from *cor-* + *relate*]

correspond *verb* **1** write letters to each other. **2** agree; match, *Your story corresponds with his.* **3** be similar or equivalent, *Their assembly corresponds to our parliament.* [from *cor-* + *respond*]

correspondence *noun* **1** letters; writing letters. **2** similarity; agreement.

correspondent *noun* **1** a person who writes letters to another. **2** a person employed to gather news and send reports to a newspaper or radio station etc.

corridor *noun* a passage in a building.

Corriedale *noun* (*NZ*) a cross-bred sheep farmed for its meat and wool. [named after the Corriedale Station in North Otago]

corroborate *verb* (**corroborated**, **corroborating**) help to confirm a statement etc. **corroboration** *noun*

corrode *verb* (**corroded**, **corroding**) destroy metal gradually by chemical action.
corrosion *noun*, **corrosive** *adjective* [from *cor-*, + Latin *rodere* = gnaw]

corrugated *adjective* shaped into alternate ridges and grooves, *corrugated iron.* [from *cor-*, + Latin *ruga* = wrinkle]

corrupt *adjective* **1** dishonest; accepting bribes. **2** wicked. **3** decaying.

corrupt *verb* **1** cause to become dishonest or wicked. **2** spoil; cause to decay. **corruption** *noun*, **corruptible** *adjective* [from *cor-*, + Latin *ruptum* = broken]

corsair *noun* a pirate ship; a pirate.

corset *noun* a piece of underwear worn to shape or support the body.

CORSO *abbreviation* (*NZ*) Council of Organisations for Relief Services Overseas.

cortège (*say* kort-**ay***zh*) *noun* a funeral procession. [French]

cosh *noun* a heavy weapon for hitting people.

cosine *noun* (in a right-angled triangle) the ratio of the length of a side adjacent to one of the acute angles to the length of the hypotenuse. (Compare *sine*.)

cosmetic *noun* a substance (e.g. face-powder, lipstick) put on the skin to make it look more attractive.

cosmic *adjective* **1** of the universe. **2** of outer space, *cosmic rays*. [from *cosmos*]

cosmonaut *noun* a Russian astronaut. [from *cosmos* + *astronaut*]

cosmopolitan *adjective* of or from many countries; containing people from many countries. [from *cosmos* + Greek *polites* = citizen]

cosmos (*say* **koz**-moss) *noun* the universe. [from Greek, = the world]

Cossack *noun* a member of a people of south Russia, famous as horsemen.

cosset *verb* (**cosseted**, **cosseting**) pamper; cherish lovingly.

cost *noun* the price of something.

cost *verb* (**cost**, **costing**) **1** have a certain price. **2** (*past tense* is **costed**) estimate the cost of something.

costly *adjective* (**costlier**, **costliest**) expensive. **costliness** *noun*

costume *noun* clothes, especially for a particular purpose or of a particular place or period.

cosy *adjective* (**cosier**, **cosiest**) warm and comfortable. **cosily** *adverb*, **cosiness** *noun*

cosy *noun* (*plural* **cosies**) a cover placed over a teapot or boiled egg to keep it hot.

cot *noun* a baby's bed with high sides. [from Hindi *khat* = bedstead]

cottage *noun* a small simple house, especially in the country.
cottage pie a dish of minced meat covered with mashed potato and baked.

cotton *noun* **1** a soft white substance covering the seeds of a tropical plant; the plant itself. **2** thread made from this substance. **3** cloth made from cotton thread.
cotton wool soft fluffy wadding originally made from cotton.

cottonwood *noun* (*NZ*) tauhinu.

couch *noun* (*plural* **couches**) **1** a long soft seat like a sofa but with only one end raised. **2** a sofa or settee.

couch *verb* **1** express in words of a certain kind. *The request was couched in polite terms.* **2** lie in a lair etc. or in ambush.

cougar (*say* **koo**-ger) *noun* (*American*) a puma.

cough (*say* kof) *verb* send out air from the lungs with a sudden sharp sound.

cough *noun* **1** the act or sound of coughing. **2** an illness that makes you cough.

could *past tense* of **can**².

couldn't (*mainly spoken*) could not.

council *noun* a group of people chosen or elected to organise or discuss something, especially those elected to organise the affairs of a district or city. [from Latin *concilium* = assembly]

councillor *noun* a member of a district or city council.

counsel *noun* **1** advice, *give counsel.* **2** a barrister or group of barristers representing someone in a lawsuit. [from Latin *consulere* = consult]

counsel *verb* (**counselled**, **counselling**) give advice to someone; recommend.

counsellor *noun* an adviser.

count¹ *verb* **1** say numbers in their proper order. **2** find the total of something by using numbers. **3** include in a total, *There are six of us, counting the dog.* **4** be important, *It's what you do that counts.* **5** regard; consider, *I should count it an honour to be invited.*
count on rely on.

count¹ *noun* **1** counting. **2** a number reached by counting; a total. **3** any of the points being considered, e.g. in accusing someone of crimes, *guilty on all counts.*

count² *noun* a European nobleman.

countdown *noun* counting numbers backwards to zero before an event.

countenance *noun* a person's face; the expression on the face.

countenance *verb* (**countenanced**, **countenancing**) give approval to; allow, *Will they countenance this plan?*

counter¹ *noun* **1** a flat-topped fitment over which customers are served in a shop, bank, etc. **2** a small round token used for keeping accounts or scores in certain games. **3** a device for counting things.
under the counter sold or obtained in an underhand way.

counter[2] *verb* **1** counteract. **2** counterattack; return an opponent's blow by hitting back.

counter[2] *adverb* contrary to something, *This is counter to what we really want.*

counter- *prefix* **1** against; opposing; done in return (as in *counter-attack*). **2** corresponding (as in *countersign*). [from Latin *contra* = against]

counteract *verb* act against something and reduce or prevent its effects. **counteraction** *noun*

counter-attack *verb* attack to oppose or return an enemy's attack. **counter-attack** *noun*

counterbalance *noun* a weight or influence that balances another. **counterbalance** *verb*

counterfeit (*say* **kownt**-er-feet) *adjective, noun, & verb* fake. [from Old French *countrefait* = made in opposition]

counterfoil *noun* a section of a cheque or receipt etc. that is detached and kept as a record.

countermand *verb* cancel a command or instruction that has been given.

counterpane *noun* a bedspread.

counterpart *noun* a person or thing that corresponds to another, *Their President is the counterpart of our Prime Minister.*

counterpoint *noun* a method of combining melodies in harmony.

counterpoise *noun & verb* counterbalance.

countersign *noun* a password or signal that has to be given in response to something.

countersign *verb* add another signature to a document to give it authority.

counterweight *noun & verb* counterbalance.

countless *adjective* too many to count.

countrified *adjective* like the country.

country *noun* (*plural* **countries**) **1** the land occupied by a nation. **2** all the people of a country. **3** less densely settled areas outside cities.

countryman *noun* (*plural* **countrymen**) **1** a man who lives in the countryside. **2** a man who belongs to the same country as yourself. **countrywoman** *noun* (*plural* **countrywomen**)

countryside *noun* country areas.

county *noun* (*plural* **counties**) a territorial division in some countries for local government purposes.

coup (*say* koo) *noun* a sudden action taken to win power; a clever victory. [French, = a blow]

couple *noun* two people or things considered together; a pair.

couple *verb* (**coupled**, **coupling**) fasten or link together.

couplet *noun* a pair of lines in rhyming verse.

coupling *noun* a link that connects two railway vehicles or two parts of machinery.

coupon *noun* a piece of paper that gives you the right to receive or do something. [French, = piece cut off]

courage *noun* the ability to face danger or difficulty or pain even when you are afraid; bravery. **courageous** *adjective* [from Latin *cor* = heart]

courgette (*say* koor-*zh***et**) *noun* a kind of small vegetable marrow.

courier (*say* **koor**-ee-er) *noun* **1** a messenger. **2** a person employed to guide and help a group of tourists. [from Latin *currere* = to run]

course *noun* **1** the direction in which something goes; a route, *the ship's course.* **2** a series of events or actions etc., *Your best course is to start again.* **3** a series of lessons, exercises, etc. **4** part of a meal, *the meat course.* **5** a racecourse. **6** a golf-course. **of course** without a doubt; as we expected.

course *verb* (**coursed**, **coursing**) move or flow freely, *Tears coursed down his cheeks.* [from Latin *cursus* = running]

court *noun* **1** the royal household. **2** a lawcourt; the judges etc. in a lawcourt. **3** an enclosed area for games such as tennis or netball. **4** a courtyard.

court *verb* try to win somebody's love or support. **courtship** *noun*

courteous (*say* **ker**-tee-us) *adjective* polite. **courteously** *adverb*, **courtesy** *noun*

courtier *noun* (*old use*) one of a king's or queen's companions at court.

courtly *adjective* dignified and polite.

court martial (*plural* **courts martial**) **1** a court for trying people who have broken military law. **2** a trial in this court.

court-martial *verb* (**court-martialled**, **court-martialling**) try a person by a court martial.

courtyard *noun* a space surrounded by walls or buildings.

cousin *noun* a child of your uncle or aunt.

cove *noun* a small bay.

coven (*say* **kuv**-en) *noun* a group of witches.

covenant (*say* **kuv**-en-ant) *noun* a formal agreement; a contract.

cover *verb* **1** place one thing over or round another; conceal. **2** travel a certain distance, *We covered ten miles a day.* **3** aim a gun at somebody, *I've got you covered.* **4** protect by insurance or a guarantee, *These goods are covered against fire or theft.* **5** be enough money to pay for something, *$20 will cover my fare.* **6** deal with or include, *The book covers all kinds of farming.* **coverage** *noun*

cover *noun* **1** a thing used for covering something else; a lid, wrapper, envelope, etc. **2** the binding of a book. **3** something that hides or shelters or protects you.

coverlet *noun* a bedspread.

covert (*say* **kuv**-ert) *noun* an area of thick bushes etc. in which birds and animals hide.

covert *adjective* stealthy; done secretly.

covet (*say* **kuv**-it) *verb* (**coveted**, **coveting**) wish to have something, especially a thing that belongs to someone else. **covetous** *adjective*

covey (*say* **kuv**-ee) *noun* (*plural* **coveys**) a group of partridges.

cow[1] *noun* **1** the fully-grown female of cattle or of certain other large animals (e.g. elephant, whale, seal). **2** (*NZ, slang*) an unpleasant or annoying person or happening etc.

cow[2] *verb* intimidate; subdue someone by bullying.

coward *noun* a person who shows fear in a shameful way, or who attacks people who cannot defend themselves. **cowardice** *noun*, **cowardly** *adjective*

cowboy *noun* a man in charge of grazing cattle on a ranch in the USA.

cow-cocky *noun* (*NZ, informal*) a dairy farmer.

cower *verb* crouch or shrink back in fear.

cowl *noun* **1** a monk's hood. **2** a hood-shaped covering, e.g. on a chimney.

cowshed *noun* a shed for cattle.

cowslip *noun* a wild plant with small yellow flowers in spring.

cox *noun* (*plural* **coxes**) a coxswain.

coxswain (*say* **kok**-swayn or **kok**-sun) *noun* **1** a person who steers a rowing-boat. **2** a sailor with special duties.

coy *adjective* pretending to be shy or modest; bashful. **coyly** *adverb*, **coyness** *noun*

CPI *abbreviation* (*NZ*) Consumers Price Index.

crab *noun* a shellfish with ten legs.

crab-apple *noun* a small sour apple.

crabby *adjective* (*informal*) grumbly or irritated.

crabstick *noun* a stick of crab-flavoured surimi.

crack *noun* **1** a line on the surface of something where it has broken but not come completely apart. **2** a narrow gap. **3** a sudden sharp noise. **4** a knock, *a crack on the head.* **5** (*informal*) a joke; a wisecrack. **6** a drug made from cocaine.

crack *adjective* (*informal*) first-class, *He is a crack shot.*

crack *verb* **1** make or get a crack; split. **2** make a sudden sharp noise. **3** break down, *He cracked under the strain.*
crack a joke tell a joke.
crack down on (*informal*) stop something that is illegal or against rules.
get cracking (*informal*) get busy.

cracker *noun* **1** a paper tube that bangs when pulled apart. **2** a firework that explodes with a crack. **3** a thin biscuit.

cracker *adjective* (*NZ, slang*) excellent, *it was a cracker game.*

crackle *verb* (**crackled**, **crackling**) make small crackling sounds. **crackle** *noun*

crackling *noun* crisp skin on roast pork.

-cracy *suffix* forming nouns meaning 'ruling' or 'government' (e.g. *democracy*). [from Greek *-kratia* = rule]

cradle *noun* **1** a small cot for a baby. **2** a supporting framework.

cradle *verb* (**cradled**, **cradling**) hold gently.

craft *noun* **1** a job that needs skill, especially with the hands. **2** skill. **3** cunning; trickery. **4** (*plural* is **craft**) a ship or boat; an aircraft or spacecraft.

craftsman *noun* (*plural* **craftsmen**) a person who is good at a craft. **craftsmanship** *noun*

crafty *adjective* (**craftier**, **craftiest**) cunning. **craftily** *adverb*, **craftiness** *noun*

crag *noun* a steep piece of rough rock. **craggy** *adjective*, **cragginess** *noun*

cram *verb* (**crammed**, **cramming**) **1** push many things into a space. **2** fill very full.

cramp *noun* pain caused by a muscle tightening suddenly.

cramp *verb* **1** keep in a very small space. **2** hinder someone's freedom or growth etc. **cramped** *adjective*

crampon *noun* an iron plate with spikes, fixed to boots for climbing on ice.

cranberry *noun* (*plural* **cranberries**) a small sour red berry used for making jelly and sauce.

crane *noun* **1** a machine for lifting and moving heavy objects. **2** a large wading bird with long legs and neck.

crane *verb* (**craned**, **craning**) stretch your neck to try and see something.

crane-fly *noun* a flying insect with very long thin legs.

cranium *noun* the skull.

crank *noun* **1** an L-shaped part used for changing the direction of movement in machinery. **2** a person with strange or fanatical ideas. **cranky** *adjective*

crank *verb* **1** move by means of a crank. **2** increase the intensity or performance of a process or object.

cranny *noun* (*plural* **crannies**) a crevice.

crape *noun* crêpe.
crape fern a New Zealand fern with tall green plumes.

crash *noun* **1** the loud noise of something breaking or colliding. **2** a violent collision or fall. **3** a sudden drop or failure.

crash *verb* **1** make or have a crash; cause to crash. **2** move with a crash.

crash *adjective* intensive, *a crash course.*

crash-helmet *noun* a padded helmet worn to protect the head in a crash.

crash-landing *noun* an emergency landing of an aircraft, which usually damages it.

crass *adjective* **1** very obvious or shocking; gross, *crass ignorance.* **2** very stupid. [from Latin *crassus* = thick]

crate *noun* **1** a packing-case made of strips of wood. **2** an open container with compartments for carrying bottles.

crater *noun* **1** a bowl-shaped cavity or hollow. **2** the mouth of a volcano.

cravat *noun* **1** a short scarf. **2** a wide necktie.

crave *verb* (**craved**, **craving**) **1** desire strongly. **2** (*formal*) beg for something.

craven *adjective* cowardly.

craving *noun* a strong desire; a longing.

crawl *verb* **1** move with the body close to the ground or other surface, or on hands and knees. **2** move slowly. **3** be covered with crawling things.

crawl *noun* **1** a crawling movement. **2** a very slow pace. **3** an overarm swimming stroke.

crawler *noun* **1** a person who seeks favour by behaving in a servile way. **2** (*NZ*) the kōura or freshwater crayfish.

cray *noun* (*informal*) a crayfish.

crayfish *noun* (*NZ*) **1** a kind of sea lobster. **2** a small freshwater lobster. **crayfishing** *noun*

crayon *noun* a stick or pencil of coloured wax etc. for drawing.

craze *noun* a temporary enthusiasm.

crazed *adjective* driven insane.

crazy *adjective* (**crazier**, **craziest**) **1** insane. **2** very foolish, *this crazy idea.* **crazily** *adverb*, **craziness** *noun*

crazy paving paving made of oddly-shaped pieces of stone etc.

creak *noun* a harsh squeak like that of a stiff door-hinge. **creaky** *adjective*

creak *verb* make a creak.

cream *noun* **1** the fatty part of milk. **2** a yellowish-white colour. **3** a food containing or looking like cream, *chocolate cream.* **4** a soft substance, *shoe-cream.* **5** the best part. **creamy** *adjective*

cream *verb* make creamy; beat butter etc. until it is soft like cream.
cream off remove the best part of something.

crease *noun* **1** a line made in something by folding, pressing, or crushing it. **2** a line on a cricket pitch marking a batter's or bowler's position.

crease *verb* (**creased**, **creasing**) make a crease or creases in something.

create *verb* (**created**, **creating**) **1** bring into existence; make or produce, especially something that no one has made before. **2** (*slang*) make a fuss; grumble. **creation** *noun*, **creative** *adjective*, **creativity** *noun*

creator *noun* a person who creates something.
the Creator God.

creature *noun* a person or animal.

crèche *noun* a place where babies and young children are looked after while their parents are at work. [French]

credence *noun* belief, *Don't give it any credence.* [from Latin *credere* = believe]

credentials *plural noun* documents showing a person's identity, qualifications, etc. [same origin as *credit*]

credible *adjective* able to be believed; convincing. **credibly** *adverb*, **credibility** *noun.* [same origin as *credit*]

credit *noun* **1** honour; acknowledgement. **2** an arrangement trusting a person to pay for something later on. **3** an amount of money in someone's account at a bank etc., or entered in an account-book as paid in. (Compare *debit.*) **4** belief; trust, *I put no credit in this rumour.*
credit card a card authorising a person to buy on credit.
credits or **credit titles** a list of people who have helped to produce a film or television programme.

credit *verb* (**credited**, **crediting**) **1** believe. **2** attribute; say that a person has done or achieved something, *Columbus is credited with the discovery of America.* **3** enter something as a credit in an account-book. (Compare *debit.*) [from Latin *credere* = believe, trust]

creditable *adjective* deserving praise. **creditably** *adverb.*

creditor *noun* a person to whom money is owed.

credulous *adjective* too ready to believe things; gullible.

creed *noun* a set or formal statement of beliefs. [from Latin *credo* = I believe]

creek *noun* **1** (*NZ*) a small stream. **2** (*British*) a narrow inlet.
up the creek (*slang*) in difficulties.

creep *verb* (**crept**, **creeping**) **1** move along close to the ground. **2** move quietly. **3** come gradually. **4** prickle with fear, *It makes my flesh creep.*

creep *noun* **1** a creeping movement. **2** (*slang*) an unpleasant person, especially one who seeks to win favour.
the creeps (*informal*) a nervous feeling caused by fear or dislike.

creeper *noun* a plant that grows along the ground or up a wall etc.

creepy *adjective* (**creepier**, **creepiest**) making people's flesh creep.

cremate *verb* (**cremated**, **cremating**) burn a dead body to ashes. **cremation** *noun*

crematorium *noun* (*plural* **crematoria**) a place where corpses are cremated.

creosote *noun* an oily brown liquid used to prevent wood from rotting. [from Greek, = flesh-preserver]

crêpe (*say* krayp) *noun* cloth, paper, or rubber with a wrinkled surface.

crescendo (*say* krish-**end**-oh) *noun* (*plural* **crescendos**) a gradual increase in loudness. [Italian]

crescent *noun* **1** a narrow curved shape (e.g. the new moon) coming to a point at each end. **2** a curved street. [from Latin *crescens* = growing]

cress *noun* a plant with hot-tasting leaves, used in salads and sandwiches.

crest *noun* **1** a tuft of hair, skin, or feathers on an animal's or bird's head. **2** the top of a hill or wave etc. **3** a design used on notepaper etc. **crested** *adjective*

crestfallen *adjective* disappointed; dejected.

cretin (*say* **kret**-in) *noun* a person who is mentally undeveloped through lack of certain hormones.

crevasse (*say* kri-**vass**) *noun* a deep open crack, especially in a glacier.

crevice *noun* a narrow opening, especially in a rock or wall.

crew[1] *noun* **1** the people working in a ship or aircraft. **2** a group working together, *the camera crew.*

crew[2] *past tense* of **crow**[2].

CRI *abbreviation* (*NZ*) Crown Research Institute.

crib *noun* **1** a baby's cot. **2** a framework holding fodder for animals. **3** a model representing the Nativity of Jesus Christ. **4** something cribbed. **5** a translation for use by students. **6** a light meal. **7** (*NZ, southern South Island*) a bach. **cribbie** (*NZ*) *noun* one who lives in a crib or small house. **8** cribbage.

crib *verb* (**cribbed**, **cribbing**) copy someone else's work.

cribbage *noun* a card-game.

crick *noun* painful stiffness in the neck or back.

cricket[1] *noun* a game played outdoors between teams with a ball, bats, and two wickets. **cricketer** *noun*

cricket[2] *noun* a brown insect like a grasshopper.

crime *noun* **1** an action that breaks the law. **2** law-breaking.

criminal *noun* a person who has committed a crime or crimes. **criminal** *adjective*, **criminally** *adverb*

criminology *noun* the study of crime. [from Latin *crimen* offence, + *-logy*]

crimp *verb* press into small ridges.

crimson *adjective & noun* deep-red.

cringe *verb* (**cringed**, **cringing**) shrink back in fear; cower.

cringe *noun* the act of cringing.
cultural cringe (*NZ*) feeling inferior to other cultures.

crinkle *verb* (**crinkled**, **crinkling**) make or become wrinkled. **crinkly** *adjective*

crinoline *noun* a long skirt worn over a framework that makes it stand out.

cripple *noun* a person who is permanently lame.

cripple *verb* (**crippled**, **crippling**) **1** make a person a cripple. **2** weaken or damage something seriously.

crisis *noun* (*plural* **crises**) an important and dangerous or difficult situation.

crisp *adjective* **1** very dry so that it breaks with a snap. **2** fresh and stiff, *a crisp $20 note.* **3** cold and dry, *a crisp morning.* **4** brisk and sharp, *a crisp manner.* **crisply** *adverb*, **crispness** *noun*

criss-cross *adjective & adverb* with crossing lines.

criterion (*say* kry-**teer**-ee-on) *noun* (*plural* **criteria**) a standard by which something is judged. [from Greek, = means of judging]

USAGE Note that *criteria* is a plural. It is incorrect to say 'a criteria' or 'this criteria'; correct usage is *this criterion, these criteria.*

critic *noun* **1** a person who gives opinions on books, plays, films, music, etc. **2** a person who criticises. [from Greek *krites* = judge]

critical *adjective* **1** criticising. **2** of critics or criticism. **3** of or at a crisis; very serious. **critically** *adverb*

criticise *verb* (**criticised**, **criticising**) say that a person or thing has faults.

criticism *noun* **1** criticising; pointing out faults. **2** the work of a critic.

croak *noun* a deep hoarse sound like that of a frog. **croak** *verb*

crochet (*say* **kroh**-shay) *noun* a kind of needlework done by using a hooked needle to loop a thread into patterns. **crochet** *verb* (**crocheted**, **crocheting**)

crock[1] *noun* a piece of crockery.

crock[2] *noun* (*informal*) a decrepit person *or* thing.

crockery *noun* household china.

crocodile *noun* **1** a large tropical reptile with a thick skin, long tail, and huge jaws. **2** a long line of schoolchildren walking in pairs.
crocodile tears sorrow that is not sincere (so called because the crocodile was said to weep while it ate its victim).

crocus *noun* (*plural* **crocuses**) a small plant with yellow, purple, or white flowers.

croft *noun* a small rented farm in Scotland. **crofter** *noun*

croissant (*say* **krwah**-sahn) *noun* a crescent-shaped roll made of sweet flaky pastry. [French, = crescent]

crone *noun* a very old woman.

crony *noun* (*plural* **cronies**) a close friend or companion.

crook *noun* **1** a shepherd's stick with a curved end. **2** something bent or curved. **3** (*informal*) a person who makes a living dishonestly.

crook *verb* bend, *She crooked her finger.*

crook *adjective* (*NZ, slang*) **1** sick. **2** unsatisfactory; out of order.
go crook get angry.

crooked *adjective* **1** bent; twisted; not straight. **2** dishonest.

croon *verb* sing softly and gently.

crop *noun* **1** something grown for food, *a good crop of wheat.* **2** a whip with a loop instead of a lash. **3** part of a bird's throat. **4** a very short haircut.

crop *verb* (**cropped**, **cropping**) **1** cut or bite off, *sheep were cropping the grass.* **2** produce a crop.
crop up happen unexpectedly.

cropper *noun* **come a cropper** (*slang*) fall heavily; fail badly.

croquet (*say* **kroh**-kay) *noun* a game played with wooden balls and mallets.

crosier (*say* **kroh**-zee-er) *noun* a bishop's staff shaped like a shepherd's crook.

cross *noun* **1** a mark or shape made like + or ×. **2** an upright post with another piece of wood across it, used in ancient times for crucifixion; **the Cross** the cross on which Christ was crucified, used as a symbol of Christianity. **3** a mixture of two different things.

cross *verb* **1** go across something. **2** draw a line or lines across something. **3** make the sign or shape of a cross, *Cross your fingers for luck.* **4** produce something from two different kinds.
cross out draw a line across something because it is unwanted, wrong, etc.

cross *adjective* **1** going from one side to another. **2** annoyed; bad-tempered. **crossly** *adverb*, **crossness** *noun*

cross- *prefix* **1** across; crossing something (as in *crossbar*). **2** from two different kinds (as in *cross-breed*).

crossbar *noun* a horizontal bar, especially between two uprights.

crossbow *noun* a powerful bow with mechanism for pulling and releasing the string.

cross-breed *verb* (**cross-bred**, **cross-breeding**) breed by mating an animal with one of a different kind. **cross-breed** *noun* (Compare *hybrid*.)

cross-examine *verb* cross-question someone, especially in a lawcourt. **cross-examination** *noun*

cross-eyed *adjective* with eyes that look or seem to look towards the nose.

crossfire *noun* lines of gunfire that cross each other.

crossing *noun* a place where people can cross a road, railway, etc.

cross-legged *adjective & adverb* with ankles crossed and knees spread apart.

crosspatch *noun* a bad-tempered person.

cross-question *verb* question someone carefully in order to test answers given to previous questions.

cross-reference *noun* a note telling people to look at another part of a book etc. for more information.

crossroads *noun* a place where two or more roads cross one another.

cross-section *noun* **1** a drawing of something as if it has been cut through. **2** a typical sample.

crosswise *adverb & adjective* with one thing crossing another.

crossword *noun* short for **crossword puzzle**, a puzzle in which words have to be guessed from clues and then written into the blank squares in a diagram.

crotch *noun* the part between the legs where they join the body; a similar angle in a forked part.

crotchet *noun* a note in music, lasting half as long as a minim (written ♩).

crotchety *adjective* peevish.

crouch *verb* lower your body, with your arms and legs bent.

croup (*say* kroop) *noun* a disease causing a hard cough and difficulty in breathing.

crow[1] *noun* a large black bird.
as the crow flies in a straight line.
crow's nest a look-out platform high up on a ship's mast.
stone the crows! (*NZ, slang*) an expression of surprise, amazement, etc.

crow[2] *verb* (**crowed** or **crew**, **crowing**) **1** make a shrill cry as a cock does. **2** boast; be triumphant. **crow** *noun*

crowbar *noun* an iron bar used as a lever.

crowd *noun* a large number of people in one place.

crowd *verb* **1** come together in a crowd. **2** cram; fill uncomfortably full.

crown *noun* **1** an ornamental head-dress worn by a king or queen. **2** (often **Crown**) the sovereign or his or her representatives, *This land belongs to the Crown.* **3** the highest part, *the crown of the road.*

crown *verb* **1** place a crown on as a symbol of royal power or victory. **2** form or cover or decorate the top of something. **3** reward; make a successful end to something, *Our efforts were crowned with victory.* **4** (*slang*) hit on the head. [from Latin *corona* = garland or crown]

crucial (*say* **kroo**-shal) *adjective* most important. **crucially** *adverb* [from Latin *crucis* = of a cross]

crucible *noun* a melting-pot for metals.

crucifix *noun* (*plural* **crucifixes**) a model of the Cross or of Jesus Christ on the Cross. [from Latin, = fixed to a cross]

crucify *verb* (**crucified**, **crucifying**) put a person to death by nailing or binding the hands and feet to a cross. **crucifixion** *noun*

crude *adjective* **1** in a natural state; not yet refined, *crude oil.* **2** not well finished; rough, *a crude carving.* **3** vulgar. **crudely** *adverb*, **crudity** *noun* [from Latin *crudus* = raw, rough]

cruel *adjective* (**crueller**, **cruellest**) causing pain or suffering. **cruelly** *adverb*, **cruelty** *noun*

cruet *noun* a set of small containers for salt, pepper, oil, etc. for use at the table.

cruise *noun* a pleasure-trip in a ship.

cruise *verb* (**cruised**, **cruising**) **1** sail or travel at a moderate speed. **2** have a cruise.

cruiser *noun* **1** a fast warship. **2** a large motor boat.

crumb *noun* a tiny piece of bread, etc.

crumble *verb* (**crumbled**, **crumbling**) break or fall into small fragments. **crumbly** *adjective*

crumpet *noun* a soft flat cake made with yeast, eaten toasted with butter.

crumple *verb* (**crumpled**, **crumpling**) **1** crush or become crushed into creases. **2** collapse loosely.

crunch *verb* **1** crush something noisily between the teeth. **2** make a sound like crunching.

crunch *noun* crunching; a crunching sound.
crunchy *adjective*
the crunch (*informal*) a crucial event.

Crusade *noun* a military expedition made by Christians in the Middle Ages to recover Palestine from the Muslims who had conquered it. **Crusader** *noun*

crusade *noun* a campaign against something bad.

crush *verb* **1** press something so that it gets broken or harmed. **2** squeeze tightly. **3** defeat.

crush *noun* (*plural* **crushes**) **1** a crowd of people pressed together. **2** a drink made with crushed fruit.

crust *noun* **1** the hard outer layer of something, especially bread. **2** the rocky outer layer of the earth. **3** (*NZ, slang*) a livelihood, a living, *What do you do for a crust?*

crustacean (*say* krust-**ay**-shon) *noun* an animal with a shell, e.g. a crab.

crusty *adjective* (**crustier**, **crustiest**) **1** having a crisp crust. **2** having a harsh or irritable manner. **crustiness** *noun*

crutch *noun* (*plural* **crutches**) a support like a long walking-stick for helping a lame person to walk.

crutch *verb* (*NZ*) clip away the wool from the hindquarters of a sheep.

cry *noun* (*plural* **cries**) **1** a loud wordless sound expressing pain, grief, joy, etc. **2** a shout. **3** crying, *Have a good cry.*

cry *verb* (**cried**, **crying**) **1** shed tears; weep. **2** call out loudly.

crypt *noun* a room under a church.

cryptic *adjective* hiding its meaning in a puzzling way. **cryptically** *adverb* [from Greek *kryptos* = hidden]

cryptogram *noun* something written in cipher. [from Greek *kryptos* = hidden, + *-gram*]

crystal *noun* **1** a transparent colourless mineral rather like glass. **2** very clear high-quality glass. **3** a small solid piece of certain substances, *crystals of snow and ice.* **crystalline** *adjective*

crystallise *verb* (**crystallised**, **crystallising**) **1** form into crystals. **2** become definite in form. **crystallisation** *noun*
crystallised fruit fruit preserved in sugar.

CTU *abbreviation* (*NZ*) Council of Trade Unions.

cub *noun* a young lion, tiger, fox, bear, etc.

Cub or **Cub Scout** a member of the junior branch of the Scout Association.

cubby-hole *noun* a small compartment.

cube *noun* **1** something that has six equal square sides. **2** the number produced by multiplying something by itself twice, *The cube of 3 is 3 × 3 × 3 = 27.*
cube root the number that gives a particular number if it is multiplied by itself twice, *The cube root of 27 is 3.*

cube *verb* (**cubed**, **cubing**) **1** multiply a number by itself twice, *4 cubed is 4 × 4 × 4 = 64.* **2** cut into small cubes.

cubic *adjective* three-dimensional.
cubic metre etc., the volume of a cube with sides that are one metre etc. long.

cubicle *noun* a compartment of a room.

cuckoo *noun* a bird that makes a sound like 'cuck-oo'.

cucumber *noun* a long green-skinned vegetable eaten raw or pickled.

cud *noun* half-digested food that a cow etc. brings back from its first stomach to chew again.

cuddle *verb* (**cuddled**, **cuddling**) put your arms closely round a person or animal that you love. **cuddly** *adjective*

cudgel *noun* a short thick stick used as a weapon.

cudgel *verb* (**cudgelled**, **cudgelling**) beat with a cudgel.
cudgel your brains think hard about a problem.

cue[1] *noun* something said or done that acts as a signal for an actor etc. to say or do something. [origin unknown]

cue[2] *noun* a long rod for striking the ball in billiards or snooker. [from *queue*]

cuff *noun* **1** the end of a sleeve that fits round the wrist. **2** hitting somebody with your hand; a slap.

cuff *verb* hit somebody with your hand.

cuisine (*say* kwiz-**een**) *noun* a style of cooking. [French, = kitchen]

cul-de-sac *noun* (*plural* **culs-de-sac**) a street with an opening at one end only; a dead end. [French, = bottom of a sack]

culinary *adjective* of cooking; for cooking.

cull *verb* **1** pick, *culling fruit.* **2** select and use, *culling lines from several poems.* **3** pick out and kill surplus animals from a flock. **cull** *noun*

culler *noun* (*NZ*) a person whose job is to kill pests such as deer, possums, etc.

culminate *verb* (**culminated**, **culminating**) reach its highest or last point. **culmination** *noun* [from Latin *culmen* = summit]

culpable *adjective* deserving blame. [from Latin *culpare* = to blame]

culprit *noun* the person who has done something wrong.

cult *noun* a religion; devotion to a person or thing.

cultivate *verb* (**cultivated**, **cultivating**) **1** use land to grow crops. **2** grow or develop things by looking after them. **cultivation** *noun*, **cultivator** *noun*

culture *noun* **1** appreciation and understanding of literature, art, music, etc. **2** customs and traditions, *Polynesian culture.* **3** improvement by care and training, *physical culture.* **4** cultivating things. **cultural** *adjective*
culture group (*NZ*) a group that performs haka, waiata, action songs, and poi dances.

cultured *adjective* educated to appreciate literature, art, music, etc.
cultured pearl a pearl formed by an oyster when a speck of grit etc. is put into its shell.

culvert *noun* a drain that passes under a road or railway etc.

cumbersome *adjective* clumsy to carry or manage. (Compare *encumber.*)

cummerbund *noun* a broad sash.

cumulative *adjective* accumulating; increasing by continuous additions. [from Latin *cumulus* = heap]

cunning *adjective* **1** clever at deceiving people. **2** cleverly designed or planned.

cunning *noun* being cunning.

cup *noun* **1** a small bowl-shaped container for drinking from. **2** anything shaped like a cup. **3** a goblet-shaped ornament given as a prize. **cupful** *noun*

cup *verb* (**cupped**, **cupping**) form into the shape of a cup, *cup your hands.*

cupboard *noun* a recess or piece of furniture with a door, for storing things.

cupidity (*say* kew-**pid**-it-ee) *noun* greed for gain. [from Latin *cupido* = desire]

cupola (*say* **kew**-pol-a) *noun* a small dome on a roof.

cur *noun* a scruffy or bad-tempered dog.

curable *adjective* able to be cured.

curate *noun* a member of the clergy who helps a vicar. [same origin as *cure*]

curative (*say* **kewr**-at-iv) *adjective* helping to cure illness.

curator (*say* kewr-**ay**-ter) *noun* a person in charge of a museum or other collection. [same origin as *cure*]

curb *verb* restrain, *curb your impatience.*

curb *noun* a restraint, *Put a curb on spending.* [from Latin *curvare* = to curve]

curd *noun* (also called **curds**) a thick substance formed when milk turns sour.

curdle *verb* (**curdled**, **curdling**) form into curds.
make someone's blood curdle horrify or terrify them.

cure *verb* (**cured**, **curing**) **1** get rid of someone's illness. **2** stop something bad. **3** treat something so as to preserve it, *Fish can be cured in smoke.*

cure *noun* **1** something that cures a person or thing; a remedy. **2** curing; being cured, *We cannot promise a cure.* [from Latin *curare* = take care of something]

curfew *noun* a time or signal after which people must remain indoors until the next day.

curio *noun* (*plural* **curios**) an object that is a curiosity.

curiosity *noun* (*plural* **curiosities**) **1** being curious. **2** something unusual and interesting.

curious *adjective* **1** wanting to find out about things; inquisitive. **2** strange; unusual. **curiously** *adverb* [from Latin, = careful (compare *cure*)]

curl *noun* a carve or coil, e.g. of hair.

curl *verb* form into curls.
curl up sit or lie with knees drawn up.

curler *noun* **1** a device for curling hair. **2** a player involved in a curling game. **3** a curving wave.

curlew *noun* a wading bird with a long curved bill.

curling *noun* a game played on ice with large flat stones.

curly *adjective* **1** full of curls. **2** (*NZ, informal*) difficult.

currant *noun* **1** a small black dried grape used in cookery. **2** a small round red, black, or white berry.

currency *noun* (*plural* **currencies**) **1** the money in use in a country. **2** the general use of something, *Some words have no currency now.* [from *current*]

current *adjective* happening now; used now. **currently** *adverb*

current *noun* **1** water or air etc. moving in one direction. **2** the flow of electricity along a wire etc. or through something. [from Latin *currens* = running]

curriculum *noun* (*plural* **curricula**) a course of study.

curriculum vitae *noun* a written summary of one's education, qualifications, etc. [Latin]

curry[1] *noun* (*plural* **curries**) food cooked with spices that taste hot. **curried** *adjective* [from Tamil *kari* = sauce]

curry[2] *verb* (**curried**, **currying**) groom a horse with a rubber or plastic pad (called a **curry-comb**).
curry favour seek to win favour by flattering someone.

curse *noun* **1** a call or prayer for a person or thing to be harmed; the evil produced by this. **2** something very unpleasant. **3** an angry word or words.

curse *verb* (**cursed**, **cursing**) **1** make a curse. **2** use a curse against a person or thing.
be cursed with something suffer from it.

cursor *noun* a movable indicator on a display screen, showing the point at which the next keystroke will be entered. [Latin, = runner (compare *current*)]

cursory *adjective* hasty and not thorough, *a cursory inspection.* **cursorily** *adverb* [from Latin, = of a runner]

curt *adjective* brief and hasty or rude, *a curt reply.* **curtly** *adverb*, **curtness** *noun*

curtail *verb* **1** cut short, *The lesson was curtailed.* **2** reduce, *We must curtail our spending.* **curtailment** *noun*

curtain *noun* **1** a piece of material hung at a window or door. **2** the large cloth screen hung at the front of a stage.

curtsy *noun* (*plural* **curtsies**) a movement of respect made by women and girls, putting one foot behind the other and bending the knees.

curtsy *verb* (**curtsied**, **curtsying**) make a curtsy. [= *courtesy*]

curvature *noun* curving; a curved shape.

curve *verb* (**curved**, **curving**) bend smoothly.

curve *noun* a curved line or shape. **curvy** *adjective*

cushion *noun* **1** a bag, usually of cloth, filled with soft material so that it is comfortable to sit on or lean against. **2** anything soft or springy that protects or supports something, *A hovercraft travels on a cushion of air.*

cushion *verb* **1** supply with cushions, *cushioned seats.* **2** protect from the effects of a knock or shock etc., *His fur hat cushioned the blow.*

cushy *adjective* (*informal*) pleasant and easy, *a cushy job.* [from Hindi *khus* = pleasant]

cusp *noun* a pointed end where two curves meet, e.g. the tips of the crescent moon. [from Latin *cuspis* = point]

custard *noun* **1** a sweet yellow sauce made with milk. **2** a pudding made with beaten eggs and milk.

custodian *noun* a person who has custody of something; a keeper.

custody *noun* **1** care and supervision; guardianship. **2** imprisonment. [from Latin *custos* = guardian]
take into custody arrest.

custom *noun* **1** the usual way of behaving or doing something. **2** regular business from customers.

customary *adjective* according to custom; usual. **customarily** *adverb*

custom-built *adjective* made according to a customer's order.

customer *noun* a person who uses a shop, bank, or other business.

customs *plural noun* taxes charged on goods brought into a country; the place at a port or airport where officials examine your luggage; these officials or their department.

cut *verb* (**cut**, **cutting**) **1** divide or wound or separate something by using a knife, axe, scissors, etc. **2** make a thing shorter or smaller; remove part of something, *They are cutting all their prices.* **3** divide a pack of playing-cards. **4** hit a ball with a chopping movement. **5** go through or across something. **6** stay away from something deliberately, *She cut her music lesson.* **7** make a sound-recording. **8** switch off electrical power or an engine etc.
cut a corner pass round it very closely.
cut and dried already decided.
cut in interrupt.

cut *noun* **1** cutting; the result of cutting. **2** a small wound. **3** (*slang*) a share.
be a cut above something be superior.

cute *adjective* (*informal*) **1** clever. **2** attractive. **cutely** *adverb*, **cuteness** *noun* [from *acute*]

cuticle (*say* **kew**-tik-ul) *noun* the skin round a nail.

cutlass *noun* (*plural* **cutlasses**) a short sword with a broad curved blade.

cutlery *noun* knives, forks, and spoons.

cutlet *noun* a thick slice of meat for cooking.

cut-out *noun* a shape cut out of paper, cardboard, etc.

cutter *noun* **1** a person or thing that cuts. **2** a small fast sailing-ship.

cutting *noun* **1** a steep-sided passage cut through high ground for a road or railway. **2** a clipping. **3** a piece cut from a plant to form a new plant.

cutting edge *noun* new form; the forefront of innovation, *Her work was at the cutting edge of research.*

cuttlefish *noun* (*plural* **cuttlefish**) a sea creature that sends out a black liquid when attacked.

cutty grass (*NZ*) a kind of sedge with leaves that have sharp edges.

CV *abbreviation* curriculum vitae.

cyanide *noun* a very poisonous chemical.

cyberbullying *noun* the use of electronic communication to bully a person, typically by sending messages of an intimidating or threatening nature.

cybercafe *noun* an Internet café.

cyberspace *noun* virtual reality or the imagined space between electronic communication systems.

cycle *noun* **1** a bicycle or motor cycle. **2** a series of events that are regularly repeated in the same order. **cyclic** *adjective*, **cyclical** *adjective*

cycle *verb* (**cycled**, **cycling**) ride a bicycle or tricycle. **cyclist** *noun* [from Greek *kyklos* = circle]

cyclone *noun* a wind that rotates round a calm central area. **cyclonic** *adjective*

CYFS *abbreviation* (*NZ*) Child, Youth and Family Services.

cygnet *noun* (*say* **sig**-nit) a young swan.

cylinder *noun* an object with straight sides and circular ends. **cylindrical** *adjective* [from Greek *kylindein* = to roll]

cymbal *noun* a percussion instrument consisting of a metal plate that is hit to make a ringing sound.

cynic (*say* **sin**-ik) *noun* a person who believes that people's reasons for doing things are selfish or bad, and shows this by sneering at them. **cynical** *adjective*, **cynically** *adverb*, **cynicism** *noun*

cypress *noun* (*plural* **cypresses**) an evergreen tree with dark leaves.

cyst (*say* sist) *noun* an abnormal swelling containing fluid or soft matter.

czar (*say* zar) *noun* a tsar.

Dd

dab *noun* **1** a quick gentle touch. **2** a small lump, *a dab of butter.*

dab *verb* (**dabbed, dabbing**) touch quickly and gently.

dabble *verb* (**dabbled, dabbling**) **1** splash something about in water. **2** do something as a hobby, *dabble in chemistry.*

dab hand *noun* (*informal*) a person with skill or expertise.

dachshund (*say* **daks**-huund or **dash**-und) *noun* a small dog with a long body and very short legs. [German, = badger-dog]

dad or daddy *noun* (*plural* **daddies**) (*informal*) father.

daddy-long-legs *noun* (*plural* **daddy-long-legs**) **1** a crane-fly. **2** a long-legged spider.

daffodil *noun* a yellow flower that grows from a bulb.

daft *adjective* (*informal*) silly; crazy.

dag *noun* (*NZ*) **1** a piece of wool clotted with dung on a sheep's hindquarters. **2** (*slang*) a funny person or thing. **daggy** *adjective*

dag *verb* (**dagged, dagging**) (*NZ*) remove dags from (a sheep).

dagger *noun* a pointed knife with two sharp edges, used as a weapon.

dahlia (*say* **day**-lee-a) *noun* a garden plant with brightly-coloured flowers. [named after a Swedish botanist, A. Dahl]

daily *adverb & adjective* every day.

dainty *adjective* (**daintier, daintiest**) small, delicate, and pretty. **daintily** *adverb*, **daintiness** *noun*

dairy *noun* (*plural* **dairies**) **1** a place where milk, butter, etc. are produced or sold. **2** (*NZ*) a local shop that sells groceries etc.
dairy cow a cow kept for milk production.
dairy farm a farm that produces dairy products.
dairy products milk, butter, cheese, etc.

dais (*say* **day**-iss) *noun* a low platform, especially at the end of a room.

daisy *noun* (*plural* **daisies**) a small flower with white petals and a yellow centre. [from *day's eye*]

daks *plural noun* (*informal*) underpants or trousers.

dale *noun* a valley, especially in the north of England.

dally *verb* (**dallied, dallying**) dawdle.

dam[1] *noun* a wall built to hold water back.

dam[1] *verb* (**dammed, damming**) hold water back with a dam.

dam[2] *noun* the mother of a horse or dog etc. (Compare *sire.*) [from *dame*]

damage *noun* something that reduces the value or usefulness of a thing or spoils its appearance.

damage *verb* (**damaged, damaging**) cause damage to something.

damages *plural noun* money paid as compensation for an injury or loss.

Dame *noun* the title of a woman who has been given the equivalent of a knighthood.

damn *verb* curse. [from Latin *damnare* = condemn]

damnation *noun* being damned or condemned to hell.

damned *adjective* hateful; annoying.

damp *adjective* slightly wet; not quite dry.
damply *adverb*, **dampness** *noun*

damp *noun* moisture in the air or on a surface or all through something.
damp course a layer of material built into a wall to prevent dampness in the ground from rising.

damp *verb* **1** make damp; moisten. **2** reduce the strength of something. *The defeat damped their enthusiasm.*

dampen *verb* damp.

damper *noun* **1** a metal plate that can be moved to increase or decrease the amount of air flowing into a fire or furnace etc. **2** something that reduces sound or enthusiasm etc. **3** a flat cake or kind of bread baked in hot ashes.

damsel *noun* (*old use*) a young woman.

damson *noun* a small dark-purple plum.

dance *verb* (**danced, dancing**) move about in time to music.

dance *noun* **1** a set of movements used in dancing. **2** a piece of music for dancing to. **3** a party or gathering where people dance.
dancer *noun*

dandelion *noun* a yellow wild flower with jagged leaves. [from French *dent-de-lion* = tooth of a lion]

dandruff *noun* tiny white flakes of dead skin in a person's hair.

dandy *noun* (*plural* **dandies**) a man who likes to look very smart.

danger *noun* something dangerous.

dangerous *adjective* likely to kill or do great harm. **dangerously** *adverb*

dangle *verb* (**dangled, dangling**) bang or swing loosely.

dank *adjective* damp and chilly.

danthonia *noun* (*NZ*) a kind of tufted grass.

dapper *adjective* dressed neatly and smartly.

dappled *adjective* marked with patches of a different colour.

dare *verb* (**dared, daring**) **1** be brave or bold enough to do something. **2** challenge a person to do something risky.

dare *noun* a challenge to do something risky.

daredevil *noun* a person who is very bold and reckless.

dark *adjective* **1** with little or no light. **2** not light in colour, *a dark suit.* **3** having dark hair. **4** secret, *Keep it dark!* **darkly** *adverb*, **darkness** *noun*

dark *noun* **1** absence of light, *Cats can see in the dark.* **2** the time when darkness has come, *She went out after dark.*

darken *verb* make or become dark.

darkroom *noun* a room kept dark for developing and printing photographs.

darling *noun* someone who is loved very much. [from Old English *deorling* = little dear]

darn *verb* mend a hole by weaving threads across it.

darn *noun* a place that has been darned.

dart *noun* **1** an object with a sharp point, thrown at a target. **2** a darting movement. **3** a tapering tuck stitched in something to make it fit.

dart *verb* run suddenly and quickly.

darts *noun* a game in which darts are thrown at a circular board (**dartboard**).

dash *verb* **1** run quickly; rush. **2** throw a thing violently against something, *The storm dashed the ship against the rocks.*

dash *noun* (*plural* **dashes**) **1** a short quick run; a rush. **2** energy; liveliness. **3** a small amount, *Add a dash of brandy.* **4** a short line (—) used in writing or printing.

dashboard *noun a* panel with dials and controls in front of the driver of a car etc.

dashing *adjective* lively and showy.

dastardly *adjective* contemptible and cowardly.

data (*say* **day**-ta) *plural noun* pieces of information, which in computing can be held in a database. **databank** *noun*, **database** *noun*

> USAGE It is best to use this word as a plural (e.g. *Here are the data*) because it is really a Latin plural meaning 'things given'. (The singular is *datum*.)

date[1] *noun* **1** the time when something happens or happened or was written, stated as the day, month, and year (or any of these). **2** an appointment to meet.

date[1] *verb* (**dated, dating**) **1** give a date to something. **2** have existed from a particular time, *The church dates from 1884.* **3** seem old-fashioned. [from Latin *data* = given (at a certain time)]

date[2] *noun* a small sweet brown fruit that grows on a kind of palm-tree.

daub *verb* paint or smear something clumsily. **daub** *noun*

daughter *noun* a girl or woman who is someone's child.

daughter-in-law *noun* (*plural* **daughters-in-law**) a son's wife.

daunt *verb* make somebody afraid or discouraged.

dauntless *adjective* brave; not to be daunted. **dauntlessly** *adverb*

dawdle *verb* (**dawdled, dawdling**) go slowly and lazily. **dawdler** *noun*

dawn *noun* the time when the sun rises. **dawn parade** *noun* (also **dawn service**) a memorial service held on Anzac Day.

dawn *verb* **1** begin to grow light in the morning. **2** begin to be realised, *The truth dawned on them.*

day *noun* **1** the 24 hours between midnight and the next midnight. **2** the light part of this time. **3** a particular day, *sports day.* **4** a period of time, *in Queen Victoria's day.*

daybreak *noun* dawn.

daydream *noun* pleasant thoughts of something you would like to happen.

daydream *verb* have daydreams.

daylight *noun* **1** the light of day. **2** dawn.

dazed *adjective* unable to think or see clearly. **daze** *noun*

dazzle *verb* (**dazzled, dazzling**) **1** make a person unable to see clearly because of too much bright light. **2** amaze or impress a person by a splendid display.

DB *abbreviation* (*NZ*) Dominion Breweries.

DDT *noun* an insecticide. [*abbreviation*]

de- *prefix* **1** removing (as in *defrost*). **2** down, away (as in *descend*). **3** completely (as in *denude*). [from Latin *de* = away from]

deacon *noun* **1** a member of the clergy ranking below bishops and priests. **2** (in some Churches) a church officer who is not a member of the clergy. **deaconess** *noun* [from Greek *diakonos* = servant]

dead *adjective* **1** no longer alive. **2** not lively. **3** not functioning; no longer in use. **4** exact; complete, *a dead loss.*
dead end a road or passage with one end closed; a situation where there is no chance of making progress.
dead heat a race in which two or more winners finish exactly together.
dead spit (*informal*) an identical person or object.

deaden *verb* make pain or noise etc. weaker.

deadline *noun* a time-limit. [originally this meant a line round an American military prison; if a prisoner went beyond it he could be shot]

deadlock *noun* a situation in which no progress can be made.

deadly *adjective* (**deadlier, deadliest**) likely to kill.

dead man *noun* **1** (*NZ*) anchor for a strainer or angle post. **2** (*informal*) an empty bottle.

deaf *adjective* **1** unable to hear. **2** unwilling to hear. **deafness** *noun*

deafen *verb* make somebody become deaf, especially by a very loud noise.

deal[1] *verb* (**dealt, dealing**) **1** hand something out; give. **2** give out cards for a card-game. **3** do business; trade, *He deals in scrap metal.* **dealer** *noun*
deal with be concerned with, *This book deals with words and meanings*; do what is needed, *deal with the problem.*

deal[1] *noun* **1** an agreement or bargain. **2** someone's turn to deal at cards.
a good deal or **a great deal** a large amount.

deal[2] *noun* sawn fir or pine wood.

dean *noun* **1** an important member of the clergy in a cathedral etc. **2** a college or university official; the head of a university faculty etc.

dear *adjective* **1** loved very much. **2** a polite greeting in letters, *Dear Sir.* **3** expensive. **dearly** *adverb*, **dearness** *noun*

dearth (*say* derth) *noun* a scarcity.

death *noun* dying; the end of life.

deathly *adjective & adverb* like death.

death-trap *noun* a very dangerous place.

debar *verb* (**debarred, debarring**) forbid; ban, *He was debarred from the contest.*

debase *verb* (**debased, debasing**) reduce the quality or value of something. **debasement** *noun*

debatable *adjective* questionable; that can be argued against.

debate *noun* a formal discussion.

debate *verb* (**debated, debating**) hold a debate. **debater** *noun*

debilitating *adjective* causing debility.

debility (*say* dib-**il**-it-ee) *noun* weakness.

debit *noun* an entry in an account-book showing how much money is owed. (Compare *credit.*)

debit *verb* (**debited, debiting**) enter something as a debit in an account-book. [from Latin *debitum* = what is owed]

debonair (*say* deb-on-**air**) *adjective* cheerful and confident. [from French *de bon air* = of good disposition]

debris (*say* **deb**-ree) *noun* scattered broken pieces of something; rubbish left behind. [from French *débris* = broken down]

debt (*say* det) *noun* something that you owe someone. [same origin as *debit*]
in debt owing money etc.

debtor (*say* **det**-or) *noun* a person who owes money to someone.

début (*say* **day**-bew) *noun* someone's first public appearance. [from French *débuter* = begin]

deca- *prefix* ten (as in *decathlon*). [from Greek *deka* = ten]

decade (*say* **dek**-ayd) *noun* a period of ten years.

decadent (*say* **dek**-a-dent) *adjective* becoming less good than it was. **decadence** *noun* [same origin as *decay*]

decamp *verb* **1** pack up and leave a camp. **2** go away suddenly or secretly.

decant (*say* dik-**ant**) *verb* pour wine etc. gently from one container into another.

decanter (*say* dik-**ant**-er) *noun* a decorative glass bottle into which wine etc. is poured for serving.

decapitate *verb* (**decapitated, decapitating**) behead. **decapitation** *noun* [from *de-*, + Latin *caput* = head]

decathlon *noun* an athletic contest in which each competitor takes part in ten events. [from *deca-*, + Greek *athlon* = contest]

decay *verb* **1** go bad; rot. **2** become less good or less strong. **decay** *noun*

decease (*say* dis-**eess**) *noun* death.

deceased *adjective* dead.

deceit (*say* dis-**eet**) *noun* a deception. **deceitful** *adjective*, **deceitfully** *adverb*

deceive *verb* (**deceived, deceiving**) cause a person to believe something that is not true. **deceiver** *noun*

December *noun* the twelfth month of the year. [from Latin *decem* = ten (in Roman times it was the tenth month)]

decent *adjective* **1** respectable; proper; suitable. **2** (*informal*) kind. **decently** *adverb*, **decency** *noun*

deception *noun* deceiving someone. **deceptive** *adjective*, **deceptively** *adverb*

deci- (*say* **dess**-ee) *prefix* one-tenth (as in *decimetre*). [same origin as *decimal*]

decibel (*say* **dess**-ib-el) *noun* a unit for measuring the loudness of sound. [originally one-tenth of the unit called a *bel*]

decide *verb* (**decided, deciding**) **1** make up your mind; make a choice. **2** settle a contest or argument. **decider** *noun*

decided *adjective* **1** having clear and definite opinions. **2** noticeable, *a decided difference.* **decidedly** *adverb*

deciduous (*say* dis-**id**-yoo-us) *adjective* losing its leaves in autumn, *a deciduous tree, not an evergreen tree.* [from Latin *decidere* = fall off]

decimal *adjective* using tens or tenths.
decimal fraction a fraction with tenths shown as numbers after a dot ($^3/_{10}$ is 0.3; $1^1/_2$ is 1.5).
decimal point the dot in a decimal fraction.

decimal *noun* a decimal fraction. [from Latin *decimus* = tenth]

decimalise *verb* (**decimalised, decimalising**) express something as a decimal. **decimalisation** *noun*

decimate *verb* **1** to destroy one-tenth of something. **2** to destroy a large amount or number. [from Latin *decimare* = kill every tenth man (this was the ancient Roman punishment for an army guilty of mutiny or other serious crime)]

decipher (*say* dis-**I**-fer) *verb* **1** decode. **2** work out the meaning of something written badly. **decipherment** *noun*

decision *noun* **1** deciding; what you have decided. **2** determination.

decisive (*say* dis-**I**-siv) *adjective* **1** that settles or ends something, *a decisive battle.* **2** full of determination; resolute. **decisively** *adverb*, **decisiveness** *noun*

deck *noun* **1** a floor on a ship or bus. **2** a level surface in various devices.

deck *verb* decorate with something.

deckchair *noun* a folding chair with a canvas or plastic seat.

declaim *verb* make a speech etc. loudly and dramatically. **declamation** *noun* [from *de-*, + Latin *clamare* = to shout]

declare *verb* (**declared, declaring**) **1** say something clearly or firmly. **2** tell customs officials that you have goods on which you ought to pay duty. **3** end a cricket innings before all the batters are out. **declaration** *noun*
declare war announce that you are starting a war against someone. [from *de-*, + Latin *clarare* = make clear]

decline *verb* (**declined, declining**) **1** refuse. **2** become weaker or smaller. **3** slope downwards.

decline *noun* a gradual decrease or loss of strength. [from *de-*, + Latin *clinare* = bend]

decode *verb* (**decoded, decoding**) **1** find the meaning of something in code. **2** convert signals into a different form. **decoder** *noun*

decompose *verb* (**decomposed, decomposing**) decay. **decomposition** *noun*

decompression *noun* reducing air-pressure.

decontamination *noun* getting rid of the harmful effects caused by poisonous chemicals or radioactive material.

decor (*say* **day**-kor) *noun* the style of furnishings and decorations used in a room etc. [French (compare *decorate*)]

decorate *verb* (**decorated, decorating**) **1** make something look more beautiful or colourful. **2** put fresh paint or paper on walls. **3** give somebody a medal. **decoration** *noun*, **decorator** *noun*, **decorative** *adjective* [from Latin *decor* = beauty]

decorous (*say* **dek**-er-us) *adjective* polite and dignified. **decorously** *adverb*

decorum (*say* dik-**or**-um) *noun* decorous behaviour.

decoy (*say* **dee**-koi) *noun* something used to tempt a person or animal into a trap or into danger.

decoy (*say* dik-**oi**) *verb* tempt into a trap etc.

decrease *verb* (**decreased, decreasing**) make or become smaller or fewer.

decrease *noun* decreasing; the amount by which something decreases. [from *de-*, + Latin *crescere* = grow]

decree *noun* an official order or decision.

decree *verb* (**decreed, decreeing**) make a decree.

decrepit (*say* dik-**rep**-it) *adjective* old and weak; dilapidated. **decrepitude** *noun* [from Latin, = creaking]

dedicate *verb* (**dedicated, dedicating**) **1** devote to a special use, *She dedicated herself to her work.* **2** name a person as a mark of respect, e.g. at the beginning of a book. **dedication** *noun*

deduce *verb* (**deduced, deducing**) work something out by reasoning. **deducible** *adjective* [from *de-*, + Latin *ducere* = to lead]

deduct *verb* subtract part of something.

deductible *adjective* able to be deducted.

deduction *noun* **1** deducting; something deducted. **2** deducing; something deduced.

deed *noun* **1** something that someone has done; an act. **2** a legal document.

deem *verb* (*formal*) consider, *I should deem it an honour to be invited.*

deep *adjective* **1** going a long way down or back or in, *a deep well; deep cupboards.* **2** measured from top to bottom or front to back, *a hole a metre deep.* **3** intense; strong, *deep colours; deep feelings.* **4** low-pitched, not shrill, *a deep voice.* **deeply** *adverb,* **deepness** *noun*
the deep south (*NZ*) Otago and Southland.

deepen *verb* make or become deeper.

deep-freeze *noun* a freezer.

deer *noun* (*plural* **deer**) a fast-running graceful animal, the male of which usually has antlers.

deer-culler *noun* (*NZ*) a professional killer of wild deer.

deface *verb* (**defaced, defacing**) spoil the surface of something, e.g. by scribbling on it. **defacement** *noun*

de facto (*say* dee **fak**-toh) *adjective* existing in fact even if not officially.

de facto *noun* (*NZ*) a person living with a partner as if they were married to each other.

defame *verb* (**defamed, defaming**) attack a person's good reputation; slander, libel. **defamation** (*say* def-a-**may**-shon) *noun,* **defamatory** (*say* dif-**am**-a-ter-ee) *adjective*

default *verb* fail to do what you have agreed to do. **defaulter** *noun*

default *noun* failure to do something.

defeat *verb* **1** win a victory over someone. **2** baffle; be too difficult for someone.

defeat *noun* **1** defeating someone. **2** being defeated; a lost game or battle.

defeatist *noun* a person who expects to be defeated. **defeatism** *noun*

defecate (*say* **dee**-fik-ayt) *verb* (**defecated, defecating**) get rid of faeces from your body. **defecation** *noun*

defect (*say* dif-**ekt** or **dee**-fekt) *noun* a flaw.

defect (*say* dif-**ekt**) *verb* desert your own country etc. and join the enemy. **defection** *noun,* **defector** *noun*

defective *adjective* having defects; incomplete. **defectiveness** *noun*

defence *noun* **1** defending something. **2** something that defends or protects. **3** a reply put forward by a defendant.

defenceless *adjective* having no defences.

defend *verb* **1** protect, especially against an attack. **2** try to prove that a statement is true or that an accused person is not guilty. **defender** *noun*

defendant *noun* a person accused of something in a lawcourt.

defensible *adjective* able to be defended. **defensibility** *noun*

defensive *adjective* used or done for defence; protective. **defensively** *adverb*
on the defensive ready to defend yourself.

defer[1] *verb* (**deferred, deferring**) postpone. **deferment** *noun,* **deferral** *noun* [same origin as *differ*]

defer[2] *verb* (**deferred, deferring**) give way to a person's wishes or authority; yield. [from Latin *deferre* = to grant]

deference (*say* **def**-er-ens) *noun* polite respect. **deferential** (*say* def-er-**en**-shal) *adjective,* **deferentially** *adverb*

defiant *adjective* defying; openly disobedient. **defiantly** *adverb,* **defiance** *noun*

deficiency *noun* (*plural* **deficiencies**) **1** a lack; a shortage. **2** a defect. **deficient** *adjective*

deficit (*say* **def**-iss-it) *noun* **1** the amount by which a total is smaller than what is required. **2** the amount by which spending is greater than income.

defile *verb* (**defiled, defiling**) make a thing dirty or impure. **defilement** *noun* [from an old word *defoul*]

define *verb* (**defined, defining**) **1** explain what a word or phrase means. **2** show clearly what something is; specify. **3** show a thing's outline. **definable** *adjective* [from *de-,* + Latin *finis* = limit]

definite *adjective* **1** clearly stated; exact, *Fix a definite time.* **2** certain; settled, *Is it definite that we are to move?* **definitely** *adverb*
definite article the word 'the'.

definition *noun* **1** a statement of what a word or phrase means or of what a thing is. **2** being distinct; clearness of outline (e.g. in a photograph).

definitive (*say* dif-**in**-it-iv) *adjective* finally settling something; conclusive, *a definitive victory.*

deflate *verb* (**deflated, deflating**) **1** let out air from a tyre or balloon etc. **2** make someone feel less proud or less confident. **3** reduce or reverse inflation. **deflation** *noun,* **deflationary** *adjective* [from *de-* + *inflate*]

deflect *verb* make something turn aside. **deflection** *noun,* **deflector** *noun* [from *de-,* + Latin *flectere* = to bend]

defoliant *noun* a chemical substance or process that destroys leaves.

deforest *verb* clear away the trees from an area. **deforestation** *noun*

deform *verb* spoil a thing's shape or appearance. **deformation** *noun*

deformed *adjective* badly or abnormally shaped. **deformity** *noun*

defraud *verb* take something from a person by fraud; cheat, swindle.

defray *verb* (**defrayed, defraying**) provide money to pay costs or expenses. **defrayal** *noun*

defrost *verb* thaw out something frozen.

deft *adjective* skilful and quick. **deftly** *adverb*, **deftness** *noun*

defunct *adjective* dead.

defuse *verb* (**defused, defusing**) **1** remove the fuse from a bomb etc. **2** make a situation less dangerous.

defy *verb* (**defied, defying**) **1** resist something openly; refuse to obey, *They defied the law.* **2** challenge a person to do something you believe cannot be done, *I defy you to prove this.* **3** prevent something being done, *The door defied all efforts to open it.*

degenerate *verb* (**degenerated, degenerating**) become worse; lose good qualities. **degeneration** *noun*

degenerate *adjective* having degenerated. **degeneracy** *noun*

degrade *verb* (**degraded, degrading**) **1** humiliate; disgrace. **2** decompose. **degradation** (*say* deg-ra-**day**-shon) *noun*

degree *noun* **1** a unit for measuring temperature. **2** a unit for measuring angles. **3** extent, *to some degree.* **4** an award to someone at a university or college who has successfully finished a course.

dehydrated *adjective* dried up, with its moisture removed. **dehydration** *noun* [from *de-*, + Greek *hydor* = water]

de-ice *verb* (**de-iced, de-icing**) remove ice from a windscreen etc. **de-icer** *noun*

deign (*say* dayn) *verb* condescend, be gracious enough to do something.

deity (*say* **dee**-it-ee) *noun* (*plural* **deities**) a god or goddess. [from Latin *deus* = god]

déjà vu *noun* (*say* day-zhah **voo**) a feeling that you have experienced something before, in French.

dejected *adjective* sad; gloomy; downcast. **dejectedly** *adverb*, **dejection** *noun* [from *de-*, + Latin *-jectum* = cast]

delay *verb* (**delayed, delaying**) **1** make someone or something late; hinder. **2** postpone. **3** wait; linger.

delay *noun* delaying; the time for which something is delayed, *a two-hour delay.*

delectable *adjective* delightful. **delectably** *adverb*

delegate (*say* **del**-ig-at) *noun* a person who represents others and acts on their instructions.

delegate (*say* **del**-ig-ayt) *verb* (**delegated, delegating**) **1** appoint as a delegate. *We delegated Jones to represent us.* **2** entrust, *We delegated the work to Jones.* [from Latin *delegare* = entrust]

delegation (*say* del-ig-**ay**-shon) *noun* **1** delegating. **2** a group of delegates.

delete (*say* dil-**eet**) *verb* (**deleted, deleting**) strike out something written or printed. **deletion** *noun*

deliberate (*say* dil-**ib**-er-at) *adjective* **1** done on purpose, intentional. **2** slow and careful. **deliberately** *adverb*

deliberate (*say* dil-**ib**-er-ayt) *verb* (**deliberated, deliberating**) discuss or think carefully. **deliberation** *noun*

deliberative *adjective* for deliberating or discussing things.

delicacy *noun* (*plural* **delicacies**) **1** being delicate. **2** a delicious food.

delicate *adjective* **1** fine; soft; fragile. **2** pleasant and not strong or intense. **3** becoming ill easily. **4** using or needing great care, *a delicate situation.* **delicately** *adverb*, **delicateness** *noun*

delicatessen *noun* a shop that sells cooked meats, cheeses, salads, etc. [from German, = delicacies to eat]

delicious *adjective* tasting or smelling very pleasant. **deliciously** *adverb*

delight *verb* **1** please someone greatly. **2** feel great pleasure.

delight *noun* great pleasure. **delightful** *adjective*, **delightfully** *adverb*

delinquent (*say* dil-**ing**-kwent) *noun* someone who breaks the law or commits an offence. **delinquent** *adjective*, **delinquency** *noun*

delirium (*say* dil-**irri**-um) *noun* **1** a state of mental confusion and agitation during a feverish illness. **2** wild excitement. **delirious** *adjective*, **deliriously** *adverb*

deliver *verb* **1** take letters or goods etc. to someone's house or place of work. **2** give a speech or lecture etc. **3** help with the birth of a baby. **4** aim or strike a blow or an attack. **5** rescue; set free. **deliverer** *noun*, **deliverance** *noun*, **delivery** *noun* [from *de-*, + Latin *liberare* = set free]

dell *noun* (*poetic*) a small valley with trees.

delphinium *noun* a garden plant with tall spikes of flowers, usually blue.

delta *noun* a triangular area at the mouth of a river where it spreads into branches. [shaped like the Greek letter delta (= D), written Δ]

delude *verb* (**deluded, deluding**) deceive.

deluge *noun* **1** a large flood. **2** a heavy fall of rain. **3** something coming in great numbers, *a deluge of questions.*

deluge *verb* (**deluged, deluging**) overwhelm by a deluge.

delusion *noun* a false belief.

de luxe of very high quality. [French, = of luxury]

delve *verb* (**delved, delving**) search deeply, e.g. for information, *delving into history.* [the original meaning was *dig*]

demagogue (*say* **dem**-a-gog) *noun* a leader who wins support by making emotional speeches rather than by careful reasoning. [from Greek *demos* = people, + *agogos* = leading]

demand *verb* **1** ask for something firmly or forcefully. **2** need, *It demands skill.*

demand *noun* **1** a firm or forceful request. **2** a desire to have something, *There is a great demand for computers.*
in demand wanted; desired. [from *de-*, + Latin *mandare* = to order]

demarcation (*say* dee-mar-**kay**-shon) *noun* marking the boundary of something.

demean *verb* lower a person's dignity, *I wouldn't demean myself to ask for it!*

demeanour (*say* dim-**een**-er) *noun* a person's behaviour or manner.

demented *adjective* driven mad; crazy. [from *de-*, + Latin *mentis* = of the mind]

demerara (*say* dem-er-**air**-a) *noun* light-brown cane sugar. [named after Demarara in South America]

demerit *noun* a fault; a defect.

demi- *prefix* half (as in *demisemiquaver*).

demigod *noun* a partly divine being.

demise (*say* dim-**I'z**) *noun* (*formal*) death.

demisemiquaver *noun* a note in music, equal to half a semiquaver.

demist *verb* remove misty condensation from a windscreen etc. **demister** *noun*

demo *noun* (*plural* **demos**) (*informal*) a demonstration.

democracy *noun* (*plural* **democracies**) **1** government of a country by representatives elected by the whole people. **2** a country governed in this way. **democrat** *noun*, **democratic** *adjective*, **democratically** *adverb* [from Greek *demos* = people, + *-cracy*]

demographic *noun* a specific feature or defined part of a population, as in *Old age is a demographic.*

demographic *adjective* relating to the structure or features of a population.

demography *noun* the study of a population, such as births, deaths, or ethnicity.

demolish *verb* knock something down and break it up. **demolition** *noun* [from *de-*, + Latin *moliri* = build]

demon *noun* **1** a devil an evil spirit. **2** a fierce or forceful person. **demonic** (*say* dim-**on**-ik) *adjective* [from Greek *daimon* = a spirit]

demonstrable (*say* **dem**-on-strab-ul) *adjective* able to be shown or proved. **demonstrably** *adverb*

demonstrate *verb* (**demonstrated, demonstrating**) **1** show; prove. **2** take part in a demonstration. **demonstrator** *noun*

demonstration *noun* **1** demonstrating; showing how to do or work something. **2** a meeting or procession etc. held to show everyone what you think about something.

demonstrative (*say* dim-**on**-strat-iv) *adjective* **1** showing or proving something. **2** showing feelings or affections openly. **3** (in grammar) pointing out the person or thing referred to. *This, that, these,* and *those* are demonstrative adjectives and pronouns. **demonstratively** *adverb*, **demonstrativeness** *noun*

demoralise *verb* (**demoralised, demoralising**) dishearten someone; weaken someone's confidence or morale. **demoralisation** *noun*

demote *verb* (**demoted, demoting**) reduce to a lower position or rank. **demotion** *noun* [from *de-* + *promote*]

demur (*say* dim-**er**) *verb* (**demurred, demurring**) raise objections.

demur *noun* an objection raised.

demure *adjective* quiet and serious. **demurely** *adverb*, **demureness** *noun*

den *noun* **1** a lair. **2** a person's private room. **3** a place where something illegal happens, *a gambling den.*

deniable *adjective* able to be denied.

denial *noun* denying or refusing something.

denier (*say* **den**-yer) *noun* a unit for measuring the fineness of silk, rayon, or nylon thread.

denim *noun* a kind of strong cotton cloth. [from *serge de Nim* = fabric of Nîmes (a town in southern France)]

denizen (*say* **den**-iz-en) *noun* an inhabitant, *Lions are denizens of the jungle.*

denomination *noun* **1** a name or title. **2** a religious group with a special name. *Baptists, Methodists, and other denominations.* **3** a unit of weight or of money, *coins of small denomination.*

denominator *noun* the number below the line in a fraction, showing how many parts the whole is divided into, e.g. 4 in $^1/_4$. (Compare *numerator.*)

denote *verb* (**denoted, denoting**) mean; indicate, *In road signs, P denotes a car park.* **denotation** *noun*

dénouement (*say* day-**noo**-mahn) *noun* the final outcome of a plot or story, revealed at the end. [French, = unravelling]

denounce *verb* (**denounced, denouncing**) speak strongly against something; accuse, *They denounced him as a spy.* **denunciation** *noun* [from *de-*, + Latin *nuntiare* = announce]

dense *adjective* **1** thick; packed close together. **2** stupid. **densely** *adverb*

density *noun* (*plural* **densities**) **1** thickness. **2** (in physics) the proportion of weight to volume.

dent *noun* a hollow left in a surface where something has pressed or hit it.

dent *verb* make a dent in something.

dental *adjective* of or for the teeth; of dentistry.
dental floss a thread used to clean between the teeth. [from Latin *dentis* = of a tooth]

dentist *noun* a person who is trained to treat teeth, fill or extract them, fit false ones, etc. **dentistry** *noun*

denture *noun* a set of false teeth.

denude *verb* (**denuded, denuding**) make bare or naked; strip something away. **denudation** *noun*

denunciation *noun* denouncing.

deny *verb* (**denied, denying**) **1** say that something is not true. **2** refuse to give or allow something, *deny a request.*

deodorant (*say* dee-**oh**-der-ant) *noun* a substance that removes smells.

deodorise *verb* (**deodorised, deodorising**) remove smells. **deodorisation** *noun* [from *de-*, + Latin *odor* = a smell]

depart *verb* go away; leave.

department *noun* one part of a large organisation. **departmental** *adjective*

departure *noun* departing.

depend *verb* **depend on** rely on, *We depend on your help*; be controlled by something else, *Whether we can picnic depends on the weather.* [from *de-*, + Latin *pendere* = hang]

dependable *adjective* reliable.

dependant *noun* a person who depends on another, *She has two dependants.*

> USAGE Note that the spelling ends in *-ant* for this noun but *-ent* for the adjective *dependent.*

dependency *noun* (*plural* **dependencies**) **1** dependence. **2** a country that is controlled by another.

dependent *adjective* depending, *She has two dependent children; they are dependent on her.*

dependence *noun* **1** having support from a person, process, organisation, or nation. **2** addiction to a food, drink or substance.

depict *verb* **1** show in a painting or drawing etc. **2** describe. **depiction** *noun* [from *de-*, + Latin *pictum* = painted]

deplete (*say* dip-**leet**) *verb* (**depleted, depleting**) reduce the amount of something by using up large amounts. **depletion** *noun* [from *de-*, + Latin *pletum* = filled]

deplore *verb* (**deplored, deploring**) be very upset or annoyed by something. **deplorable** *adjective*, **deplorably** *adverb* [from *de-*, + Latin *plorare* = weep]

deploy *verb* spread out; place troops etc. in good positions. **deployment** *noun*

deport *verb* send an unwanted foreign person out of a country. **deportation** *noun* [from *de-*, + Latin *portare* = carry]

deportment *noun* a person's manner of standing, walking, and behaving.

depose *verb* (**deposed, deposing**) **1** remove a person from power. **2** make a sworn statement. **deposition** *noun*

deposit *noun* **1** an amount of money paid into a bank etc. **2** money paid as a first instalment. **3** a layer of solid matter in or on the earth.

deposit *verb* (**deposited, depositing**) **1** put down. **2** pay money as a deposit. **depositor** *noun* [from *de-*, + Latin *positum* = placed]

depot (*say* **dep**-oh) *noun* **1** a place where things are stored. **2** a headquarters. [same origin as *deposit*]

depraved *adjective* behaving wickedly; of bad character. **depravity** *noun*

deprecate (*say* **dep**-rik-ayt) *verb* (**deprecated, deprecating**) say that you disapprove of something. **deprecation** *noun* [from Latin *deprecari* = keep away misfortune by prayer]

depreciate (*say* dip-**ree**-shee-ayt) *verb* (**depreciated, depreciating**) make or become lower in value. **depreciation** *noun* [from *de-*, + Latin *pretium* = price]

depredation (*say* dep-rid-**ay**-shon) *noun* the act of plundering or damaging something. (Compare *predator*.)

depress *verb* **1** make somebody sad. **2** lower the value of something, *Threat of war depressed prices.* **3** press down, *Depress the lever.* **depressive** *adjective*

depression *noun* **1** a great sadness or feeling of hopelessness. **2** a long period when trade is very slack because no one can afford to buy things. **3** a shallow hollow in the ground or on a surface. **4** an area of low air-pressure which may bring rain. **5** pressing something down.

deprive *verb* (**deprived, depriving**) take or keep something away from somebody. **deprival** *noun*, **deprivation** *noun* [from *de-*, + Latin *privare* = rob]

dept. *abbreviation* department.

depth *noun* **1** being deep; how deep something is. **2** the deepest or lowest part.
in depth thoroughly.
out of your depth in water that is too deep to stand in; trying to do something that is too difficult for you.

deputation *noun* a group of people sent as representatives of others.

depute (*say* dip-**yoot**) *verb* (**deputed, deputing**) **1** appoint a person to do something, *We deputed Hone to take the message.* **2** assign or delegate a task to someone, *We deputed the task to him.*

deputise *verb* (**deputised, deputising**) act as someone's deputy.

deputy *noun* (*plural* **deputies**) a person appointed to act as a substitute for another.

derail *verb* cause a train to leave the rails. **derailment** *noun*

derange *verb* (**deranged, deranging**) **1** throw into confusion; disturb. **2** make a person insane. **derangement** *noun*

derelict (*say* **derri**-likt) *adjective* abandoned and left to fall into ruin. **dereliction** *noun* [from *de-* = completely, + Latin *relictum* = left behind]

deride *verb* (**derided, deriding**) laugh at with contempt or scorn; ridicule. [from *de-*, + Latin *ridere* = to laugh]

derision *noun* scorn; ridicule. **derisive** (*say* dir-**I**-siv) *adjective*, **derisively** *adverb*, **derisory** *adjective*

derivation *noun* **1** deriving. **2** the origin of a word from another language or from a simple word to which a prefix or suffix is added; etymology.

derivative *adjective* derived from something. **derivative** *noun*

derive *verb* (**derived, deriving**) **1** obtain from a source, *She derived great enjoyment from music.* **2** form or originate from something, *Many English words are derived from Latin words.* [from *de-*, + Latin *rivus* = a stream]

dermatology *noun* the study of the skin and its diseases. **dermatologist** *noun* [from Greek *derma* = skin, + *-logy*]

dermis *noun* the layer of skin below the epidermis.

derogatory (*say* dir-**og**-at-er-ee) *adjective* contemptuous; disparaging, *He made a derogatory remark about his friend's new haircut.*

derrick *noun* **1** a kind of crane for lifting things. **2** a tall framework holding the machinery used in drilling an oil-well etc. [this word originally meant 'a gallows', named after Derrick, a London hangman in about 1600]

dervish *noun* (*plural* **dervishes**) a member of a Muslim religious group who vowed to live a life of poverty. [from Persian *darvish* = poor]

descant *noun* a tune sung or played above the main tune. [from *dis-*, + Latin *cantus* = song]

descend *verb* go down.
be descended from have as an ancestor; come by birth from a certain person or family. **descendant** *noun* [from Latin *descendere* = climb down]

descent *noun* descending.

describe *verb* (**described, describing**) **1** say what someone or something is like. **2** draw in outline; move in a pattern. **description** *noun*, **descriptive** *adjective* [from *de-*, + Latin *scribere* = write]

desecrate (*say* **dess**-ik-rayt) *verb* (**desecrated, desecrating**) treat a sacred thing irreverently. **desecration** *noun* [from *de-* + *consecrate*]

desert (*say* **dez**-ert) *noun* a large area of dry often sandy land.
desert island an uninhabited island.

desert (*say* diz-**ert**) *verb* abandon; leave without intending to return. **deserter** *noun*, **desertion** *noun*

deserts (*say* diz-**erts**) *plural noun* what a person deserves, *He got his deserts.* [from *deserve*]

deserve *verb* (**deserved, deserving**) have a right to something; be worthy of something. **deservedly** *adverb*

desiccated *adjective* dried.

design *noun* **1** a drawing that shows how something is to be made. **2** the way something is made or arranged. **3** lines and shapes that form a decoration; a pattern. **4** a mental plan or scheme.
have designs on plan to get hold of.

design *verb* **1** draw a design for something. **2** plan or intend something for a special purpose. **designer** *noun* [from *de-*, + Latin *signare* = mark out]

designate *verb* (**designated, designating**) mark or describe as something particular, *They designated the river as the boundary.* **designation** *noun*

designate *adjective* appointed to a job but not yet doing it, *the bishop designate.* [same origin as *design*]

desirable *adjective* **1** causing people to desire it; worth having. **2** worth doing; advisable. **desirability** *noun*

desire *noun* a feeling of wanting something very much. **desirous** *adjective*

desire *verb* (**desired, desiring**) have a desire for something.

desist (*say* diz-**ist**) *verb* cease.

desk *noun* **1** a piece of furniture with a flat top and often drawers, used when writing or reading etc. **2** a counter at which a cashier or receptionist sits.

desktop *noun* **1** the working surface of a desk. **2** a personal computer that is suitable for use at a desk. (Compare *laptop.*) **3** the representation of a desktop on a VDU screen.

desolate *adjective* **1** lonely; sad. **2** uninhabited. **desolation** *noun*

despair *noun* a feeling of hopelessness.

despair *verb* feel despair. [from *de-*, + Latin *sperare* = to hope]

despatch *noun & verb* dispatch.

desperado (*say* dess-per-**ah**-doh) *noun* (*plural* **desperadoes**) a reckless criminal.

desperate *adjective* **1** extremely serious; hopeless, *a desperate situation.* **2** reckless and ready to do anything. **desperately** *adverb*, **desperation** *noun* [same origin as *despair*]

despicable *adjective* deserving to be despised; contemptible.

despise *verb* (**despised, despising**) think someone or something is inferior or worthless. [from *de-*, + Latin *-spicere* = to look]

despite *preposition* in spite of.

despondent *adjective* sad; gloomy. **despondently** *adverb*, **despondency** *noun*

despot (*say* **dess**-pot) *noun* a tyrant. **despotism** *noun*, **despotic** (*say* dis-**pot**-ik) *adjective*

dessert (*say* diz-**ert**) *noun* fruit or a sweet food as the last course of a meal. [from French *desservir* = clear the table]

dessertspoon *noun* a medium-sized spoon used for eating puddings etc.

destination *noun* the place to which a person or thing is travelling.

destined *adjective* having as a destiny; intended.

destiny *noun* (*plural* **destinies**) fate.

destitute *adjective* left without anything; living in extreme poverty. **destitution** *noun*

destroy *verb* ruin or put an end to something. **destruction** *noun*, **destructive** *adjective* [from *de-*, + Latin *struere* = build]

destroyer *noun* a fast warship.

desultory (*say* **dess**-ul-ter-ee) *adjective* casual and disconnected, *desultory talk.*

detach *verb* unfasten; separate. **detachable** *adjective*, **detachment** *noun*

detached *adjective* **1** separated. **2** not prejudiced; not involved in something.

detail *noun* **1** a very small part of a design or plan or decoration etc. **2** a small piece of information. **detailed** *adjective*

detain *verb* **1** keep someone waiting. **2** keep someone at a place. **detention** *noun* [from *de-*, + Latin *tenere* = hold]

detainee *noun* a person who is officially detained or kept in custody.

detect *verb* discover. **detection** *noun*, detector *noun* [from *de-*, + Latin *tectum* = covered]

detective *noun* a person who investigates crimes.

detention *noun* detaining; being detained; being made to stay late in school as a punishment.

deter *verb* (**deterred, deterring**) discourage or prevent a person from doing something. **determent** *noun* [from *de-*, + Latin *terrere* = frighten]

detergent *noun* a substance used for cleaning or washing things.

deteriorate (*say* dit-**eer**-ee-er-ayt) *verb* (**deteriorated, deteriorating**) become worse. **deterioration** *noun* [from Latin *deterior* = worse]

determination *noun* **1** strong intention; having decided firmly. **2** determining or deciding something.

determine *verb* (**determined, determining**) **1** decide, *determine what is to be done.* **2** find out; calculate, *determine the height of the mountain.* [from *de-*, Latin *terminare* = set a limit]

determined *adjective* full of determination; with your mind firmly made up.

determiner *noun* a word (such as *a, the, many*) that modifies a noun.

deterrent *noun* something that may deter people; a nuclear weapon that deters countries from making war on the one that has it. **deterrence** *noun*

detest *verb* dislike very much; loathe. **detestable** *adjective*, **detestation** *noun*

detonate (*say* **det**-on-ayt) *verb* (**detonated, detonating**) explode; cause something to explode. **detonation** *noun*, **detonator** *noun* [from *de-* = thoroughly, + Latin *tonare* = to thunder]

detour (*say* **dee**-toor) *noun* a roundabout route instead of the normal one. [from French *détourner* = turn away]

detract *verb* lessen the amount or value, *It will not detract from our pleasure.* **detraction** *noun* [from *de-*, + Latin *tractum* = pulled]

detriment (*say* **det**-rim-ent) *noun* harm; damage, *She worked long hours, to the detriment of her health.*

detrimental (*say* det-rim-**en**-tal) *adjective* harmful. **detrimentally** *adverb*

deuce *noun* a score in tennis where both sides have 40 points and must gain two consecutive points to win.

devalue *verb* (**devalued, devaluing**) reduce a thing's value. **devaluation** *noun*

devastate *verb* (**devastated, devastating**) ruin or cause great destruction to something. **devastation** *noun*

develop *verb* (**developed, developing**) **1** make or become bigger or better. **2** come gradually into existence, *Storms developed.* **3** begin to have or use, *They developed bad habits.* **4** use an area of land for building houses, shops, factories, etc. **5** treat photographic film with chemicals so that pictures appear. **developer** *noun*, **development** *noun*

deviate (*say* **dee**-vee-ayt) *verb* (**deviated, deviating**) turn aside from a course or from what is usual or true. [from *de-*, + Latin *via* = way]

deviation *noun* **1** a realignment of a river, road, passageway, or railway. **2** moving away from a conventional way of doing things. **3** changing the subject in a conversation.

device *noun* **1** something made for a particular purpose, *a device for opening tins.* **2** a design used as a decoration or emblem. **leave him to his own devices** leave him to do as he wishes.

devil *noun* **1** an evil spirit. **2** a wicked, cruel, or annoying person. **devilish** *adjective*, **devilry** *noun*

devilment *noun* mischief.

devious (*say* **dee**-vee-us) *adjective* **1** roundabout; not direct, *a devious route.* **2** not straightforward; underhand. **deviously** *adverb*, **deviousness** *noun*

devise *verb* (**devised, devising**) invent; plan.

devoid *adjective* lacking or without something, *His work is devoid of merit.*

devolution *noun* devolving; giving authority to another person etc.; handing over responsibility for government.

devolve *verb* (**devolved, devolving**) pass or be passed to a deputy or successor.

devote *verb* (**devoted, devoting**) give completely, *He devoted his time to sport.*

devoted *adjective* very loving or loyal.

devotee (*say* dev-o-**tee**) *noun* a person who is devoted to something; an enthusiast.

devotion *noun* great love or loyalty; being devoted.

devotions *plural noun* prayers.

devour *verb* eat or swallow something hungrily or greedily. [from *de-* = completely, + Latin *vorare* = to swallow]

devout *adjective* earnestly religious or sincere. **devoutly** *adverb*, **devoutness** *noun*

dew *noun* tiny drops of water that form during the night on surfaces of things in the open air. **dewdrop** *noun*, **dewy** *adjective*

dexterity (*say* deks-**te**rri-tee) *noun* skill in handling things. dexterous adjective [from Latin *dexter* = on the right-hand side]

di-[1] *prefix* two; double (as in *dioxide*). [from Greek *dis* = twice]

di-[2] *prefix* see **dis-**.

dia- *prefix* through (as in *diarrhoea*); across (as in *diagonal*). [from Greek *dia* = through]

diabetes (*say* dy-a-**bee**-teez) *noun* a disease in which there is too much sugar in a person's blood. **diabetic** (*say* dy-a-**bet**-ik) *adjective & noun*

diabolical *adjective* **1** like a devil; very wicked. **2** very clever or annoying.

diacritic *noun* a symbol or sign above or below a letter (e.g. accent, macron, or cedilla) to indicate a particular sound or value.

diadem (*say* **dy**-a-dem) *noun* a crown or headband worn by a royal person.

diagnose *verb* (**diagnosed, diagnosing**) find out what disease a person has or what is wrong. **diagnosis** *noun*, **diagnostic** *adjective*

diagonal (*say* dy-**ag**-on-al) *noun* a straight line joining opposite corners. **diagonal** *adjective*, **diagonally** *adverb* [from *dia-*, + Greek *gonia* = angle]

diagram *noun* a kind of drawing or picture that shows the parts of something or how it works. [from *dia-* + *-gram*]

dial *noun* a circular object with numbers or letters round it.

dial *verb* (**dialled, dialling**) telephone a number by turning a telephone dial or pressing numbered buttons.

dialect *noun* the pronunciation and usage of people in a particular region or social class.

dialogue *noun a* conversation.

dial-up *noun* a method of accessing Internet service.

dialysis (*say* dy-**al**-iss-iss) *noun* a way of removing harmful substances from the blood by letting it flow through a machine. [from *dia-*, + Greek *lysis* = loosening]

diameter (*say* dy-**am**-it-er) *noun* **1** a line drawn straight across a circle or sphere and passing through its centre. **2** the length of this line. [from Greek, = measuring across]

diametrically *adverb* completely, *diametrically opposite.*

diamond *noun* **1** a very hard precious stone that looks like clear glass. **2** a shape with four equal sides and four angles that are not right angles. **3** a playing-card with red diamond shapes on it. [from Greek *adamas* = adamant (= a very hard stone)]

diaper *noun* a nappy.

diaphanous (*say* dy-**af**-an-us) *adjective* (of fabric) almost transparent.

diaphragm (*say* **dy**-a-fram) *noun* **1** the muscular partition inside the body that separates the chest from the abdomen and is used in breathing. **2** a hole that can be altered in size to control the amount of light that passes through a camera lens.

diarist *noun* a person who keeps a diary.

diarrhoea (*say* dy-a-**ree**-a) *noun* too frequent and too watery emptying of the bowels. [from *dia-*, + Greek *rhoia* = a flow]

diary *noun* (*plural* **diaries**) a book in which someone writes down what happens each day. [from Latin *dies* = day]

diatribe *noun* a strong verbal attack.

dice *noun* (strictly this is the plural of **die**[2], but it is often used as a singular, *plural* **dice**) a small cube marked with dots (1 to 6) on its sides, used in games.

dice *verb* (**diced, dicing**) **1** play gambling games using dice. **2** cut into small cubes.

dictate *verb* (**dictated, dictating**) **1** speak or read something aloud for someone else to write down. **2** give orders in an officious way. **dictation** *noun* [from Latin *dictare* = keep saying]

dictates (*say* **dik**-tayts) *plural noun* orders, commands.

dictator *noun* a ruler who has unlimited power. **dictatorial** (*say* dik-ta-**tor**-ee-al) *adjective*, **dictatorship** *noun*

diction *noun* a person's way of speaking words, *clear diction.*

dictionary *noun* (*plural* **dictionaries**) a book that contains words in alphabetical order so that you can find out how to spell them and what they mean. [from Latin *dictio* = word]

didactic (*say* dy-**dak**-tik) *adjective* having the manner of someone who is lecturing people. **didactically** *adverb* [from Greek *didaktikos* = teaching]

diddle *verb* (**diddled, diddling**) (*slang*) cheat; swindle.

didgeridoo *noun* an Aboriginal wind instrument shaped like a long tube. [Aboriginal]

didn't (*mainly spoken*) did not.

die[1] *verb* (**died**, **dying**) **1** stop living or existing. **2** stop burning or functioning, *The fire had died down.*

die[2] *noun* singular of **dice**.

die[3] *noun* a device that stamps a design on coins etc. or that cuts or moulds metal.

diehard *noun* a person who obstinately refuses to give up old ideas or policies.

diesel (*say* **dee**-zel) *noun* **1** an engine that works by burning oil in compressed air. **2** fuel for this kind of engine. [named after a German engineer, R. Diesel]

diet[1] *noun* **1** special meals that someone eats in order to be healthy or to become less fat. **2** the sort of foods usually eaten by a person or animal.

diet[1] *verb* (**dieted**, **dieting**) keep to a diet. [from Greek *diaita* = way of life]

diet[2] *noun* the parliament of certain countries (e.g. Japan). [from Latin *dieta* = day's business]

dietitian (*say* dy-it-**ish**-an) *noun* an expert in diet and nutrition.

dif- *prefix* see **dis-**.

differ *verb* **1** be different. **2** disagree. [from *dif-* = apart, + Latin *ferre* = carry]

difference *noun* **1** being different; the way in whi ch things differ. **2** the remainder left after one number is subtracted from another, *The difference between 8 and 3 is 5.* **3** a disagreement.

different *adjective* unlike; not the same. **differently** *adverb.*

USAGE It is acceptable to use either *from* or *to* after *different* or *differently*, *Yours is different from* or *to mine. Different(ly) than* is more acceptable in North American English than in New Zealand English.

differential *noun* **1** a difference in wages between one group of workers and another. **2** a differential gear.
differential gear a system of gears that makes a vehicle's driving wheels revolve at different speeds when going round corners.

differentiate *verb* (**differentiated, differentiating**) **1** make different, *These things differentiate one breed from another.* **2** distinguish; recognise differences, *We do not differentiate between them.* **differentiation** *noun*

difficult *adjective* needing much effort or skill; not easy. **difficulty** *noun*

diffident (*say* **dif**-id-ent) *adjective* shy and not self-confident; hesitating to put yourself or your ideas forward. **diffidently** *adverb*, **diffidence** *noun* [from *dif-* = not, + Latin *fidere* = to trust]

diffract *verb* break up a beam of light etc. **diffraction** *noun* [from *dif-* = apart, + Latin *fractum* = broken]

diffuse *verb* (**diffused, diffusing**) **1** spread something widely or thinly, *diffused lighting.* **2** mix slowly, *diffusing gases.* **diffusion** *noun*

diffuse *adjective* **1** diffused; spread widely; not concentrated. **2** using many words; not concise. **diffusely** *adverb*, **diffuseness** *noun* [from *dif-* = apart, + Latin *fusum* = poured]

dig *verb* (**dug, digging**) **1** break up soil and move it; make a hole or tunnel by moving soil. **2** poke; push, *Dig a knife into it.* **3** seek or discover by investigating, *We dug up some facts.*

dig *noun* **1** a piece of digging. **2** a poke.

digest (*say* dy-**jest**) *verb* **1** soften and change food in the stomach etc. so that the body can absorb it. **2** take information into your mind and think it over. **digestible** *adjective*, **digestion** *noun*

digest (*say* **dy**-jest) *noun* a summary of news, information, etc.

digestive *adjective* of digestion; digesting, *the digestive system.*
digestive biscuit a wholemeal biscuit.

digger *noun* **1** a person or thing that digs. **2** a New Zealand or Australian soldier.

digit (*say* **dij**-it) *noun* **1** any of the numbers from 0 to 9. **2** a finger or toe. [from Latin *digitus* = finger or toe]

digital *adjective* **1** of or using digits. **2** (of a computer) operating on data represented by (usually binary) digits. **3** (of a recording) with the sound information represented by digits for more reliable transmission. **digitally** *adverb*
digital camera a camera that produces digital images that can be stored in a computer and displayed on a screen.
digital clock or **watch** one that shows the time with a row of figures.
digital television television where the picture is transmitted in digital form.

dignified *adjective* having dignity.

dignitary *noun* (*plural* **dignitaries**) an important official.

dignity *noun* **1** a calm and serious manner. **2** a high rank. [from Latin *dignus* = worthy]

digress *verb* stray from the main subject or focus. **digression** *noun* [from *di-*[2] = away, + Latin *gressum* = gone]

dike *noun* **1** a long wall or embankment to hold back water and prevent flooding. **2** a ditch for draining water from land.

dilapidated *adjective* falling to pieces. **dilapidation** *noun*

dilate *verb* (**dilated, dilating**) make or become wider or larger. [from *di-*[2] = apart, + Latin *latus* = wide]

dilatory (*say* **dil**-at-er-ee) *adjective* slow in doing something; not prompt.

dilemma (*say* dil-**em**-a) *noun* a situation where someone has to choose between two possible actions, each of which will bring difficulties. [from Greek, = double proposal]

diligent (*say* **dil**-ij-ent) *adjective* working hard. **diligently** *adverb*, **diligence** *noun* [from Latin *diligens* = conscientious]

dill *noun* (*NZ, slang*) a silly or stupid person.

dilute *verb* (**diluted, diluting**) make a liquid weaker by adding water or other liquid. **dilution** *noun*

dilute *adjective* diluted, *a dilute acid.*

dim *adjective* (**dimmer, dimmest**) **1** not bright or clear; only faintly lit. **2** (*informal*) stupid. **dimly** *adverb*, **dimness** *noun*

dim *verb* (**dimmed, dimming**) make or become dim. **dimmer** *noun*

dimension *noun* **1** a measurement such as length, width, area, or volume. **2** size; extent. **dimensional** *adjective*

diminish *verb* make or become smaller. **diminution** *noun*

diminutive (*say* dim-**in**-yoo-tiv) *adjective* very small.

dimple *noun* a small hollow or dent, especially in the skin. **dimpled** *adjective*

din *noun* a loud annoying noise.

din *verb* (**dinned, dinning**) **1** make a din. **2** force a person to learn something by continually repeating it, *Din it into him.*

dine *verb* (**dined, dining**) have dinner. **diner** *noun*

dinette *noun* a small room or part of a room where people eat.

ding *noun* (*informal*) **1** a minor accident. **2** the damaged part of a car etc.

ding *verb* (*informal*) dent or damage a car etc.

dingbat *noun* (*NZ, slang*) a crazy or stupid person.

ding-dong *noun* the sound of a bell or alternate strokes of two bells.

dinghy (*say* **ding**-ee) *noun* (*plural* **dinghies**) a kind of small boat. [from Hindi, = Indian river-boat]

dingle *noun* a small valley with trees.

dingo *noun* (*plural* **dingoes**) an Australian wild dog.

dingy (*say* **din**-jee) *adjective* dirty-looking. **dingily** *adverb*, **dinginess** *noun*

dinkum *adjective* (*NZ, informal*) genuine, real.

dinner *noun* the main meal of the day, either at midday or in the evening.

dinosaur (*say* **dy**-noss-or) *noun* a prehistoric lizard-like animal, often of enormous size. [from Greek *demos* = terrible, + *sauros* = lizard]

dint *noun* a dent.
by dint of by means of.

diocese (*say* **dy**-oss-iss) *noun* a district under the care of a bishop. **diocesan** (*say* dy-**oss**-iss-an) *adjective*

dioxide *noun* an oxide with two atoms of oxygen to one of another element. *carbon dioxide.* [from *di-*[1] + *oxide*]

dip *verb* (**dipped, dipping**) put down or go down, especially into a liquid.
dip out (**on**) (*NZ, slang*) fail, miss out (on).

dip *noun* **1** dipping. **2** a downward slope. **3** a quick swim. **4** a substance into which things are dipped.

diphtheria (*say* dif-**theer**-ee-a) *noun* a serious disease that causes inflammation in the throat. [from Greek, = leather (because a tough skin forms)]

diphthong (*say* **dif**-thong) *noun* a compound vowel-sound made up of two sounds, e.g. *oi* in *point* (made up of 'aw' + 'ee') or *ou* in *loud* ('ah' + 'oo'). [from *di-*[1], + Greek *phthongos* = sound]

diploma *noun* a certificate awarded by a college etc. for skill in a particular subject. [from Greek, = folded paper]

diplomacy *noun* keeping friendly with other nations or other people.

diplomat *noun* **1** a person employed in diplomacy on behalf of his or her country. **2** a tactful person.

diplomatic *adjective* **1** of diplomats or diplomacy. **2** tactful. **diplomatically** *adverb*

dipper *noun* **1** a kind of bird that dives for its food. **2** a ladle.

dire *adjective* dreadful; serious, *dire need.*

direct *adjective* **1** as straight as possible. **2** going straight to the point; frank. **3** exact, *the direct opposite.* **directly** *adverb & conjunction*, **directness** *noun*
direct current electric current flowing only in one direction.
direct object the word that receives the action of the verb. In *she hit him* 'him' is the direct object.

direct *verb* **1** tell someone the way. **2** guide or aim in a certain direction. **3** control; manage. **4** order, *He directed his troops to advance.* **director** *noun* [from Latin *directum* = kept straight]

direction *noun* **1** directing. **2** the line along which something moves or faces. **directional** *adjective*

directions *plural noun* information on how to use or do something.

directive *noun* a command.

directory *noun* (*plural* **directories**) a book containing a list of people with their telephone numbers, addresses, etc.

dirge *noun* a slow sad song.

dirk *noun* a kind of dagger.

dirt *noun* earth, soil; anything that is not clean.

dirty *adjective* (**dirtier, dirtiest**) **1** not clean; soiled. **2** unfair; dishonourable, *a dirty trick.* **3** indecent; obscene. **dirtily** *adverb*, **dirtiness** *noun*

dis- *prefix* (changing to **dif-** before words beginning with *f*, and to **di-** before some consonants) **1** not; the reverse of (as in *dishonest*). **2** apart; separated (as in *disarm, disperse*). [from Latin, = not; away]

disabled *adjective* made unable to do something because of illness or injury. **disability** *noun*, **disablement** *noun*

disadvantage *noun* something that hinders or is unhelpful. **disadvantaged** *adjective*, **disadvantageous** *adjective*

disagree *verb* (**disagreed, disagreeing**) **1** have or express a different opinion from someone. **2** have a bad effect, *Rich food disagrees with me.* **disagreement** *noun*

disagreeable *adjective* unpleasant; bad-tempered.

disappear *verb* stop being visible; vanish. **disappearance** *noun*

disappoint *verb* fail to do what someone hopes for. **disappointment** *noun*

disapprobation *noun* disapproval.

disapprove *verb* (**disapproved, disapproving**) have or show an unfavourable opinion; not approve. **disapproval** *noun*

disarm *verb* **1** reduce the size of armed forces. **2** take away someone's weapons. **3** overcome a person's anger or doubt, *Her friendliness disarmed their suspicions.* **disarmament** *noun*

disarray *noun* disorder.

disaster *noun* **1** a very bad accident or misfortune. **2** a complete failure. **disastrous** *adjective*, **disastrously** *adverb* [literally 'an unlucky star', from *dis-*, + Latin *astrum* = star]

disband *verb* break up a group.

disbelief *noun* refusal or unwillingness to believe something.

disburse *verb* (**disbursed, disbursing**) pay out money. **disbursement** *noun*

disc *noun* **1** any round flat object. **2** a compact disc.
disc jockey a person who introduces and plays records. [from Latin *discus* = disc]

discard *verb* throw away; put something aside as being useless or unwanted.

discern (*say* dis-**sern**) *verb* perceive; see or recognise clearly. **discernible** *adjective*, **discernment** *noun*

discerning *adjective* perceptive; showing good judgement.

discharge *verb* (**discharged, discharging**) **1** release a person. **2** send something out, *discharge smoke*. **3** pay or do what was agreed, *discharge the debt*.

discharge *noun* **1** discharging. **2** something that is discharged.

disciple *noun* a person who accepts the teachings of another whom he or she regards as a leader; any of the original followers of Jesus Christ. [from Latin *discipulus* = learner]

disciplinarian *noun* a person who believes in strict discipline.

discipline *noun* orderly and obedient behaviour. **disciplinary** (*say* **dis**-ip-lin-er-ee) *adjective*

discipline *verb* (**disciplined, disciplining**) **1** train to be orderly and obedient. **2** punish. [from Latin *disciplina* = training]

disclaim *verb* disown; say that you are not responsible for something.

disclose *verb* (**disclosed, disclosing**) reveal. **disclosure** *noun*

disco *noun* (*plural* **discos**) (*informal*) a discothèque.

discolour *verb* spoil a thing's colour; stain. **discolouration** *noun*

discomfit *verb* (**discomfited, discomfiting**) disconcert; dismay. **discomfiture** *noun*

discomfort *noun* being uncomfortable.

disconcert (*say* dis-kon-**sert**) *verb* make a person feel uneasy.

disconnect *verb* break a connection; detach. **disconnection** *noun*

disconnected *adjective* not having a connection between its parts.

disconsolate (*say* dis-**kon**-sol-at) *adjective* disappointed.

discontent *noun* lack of contentment; dissatisfaction. **discontented** *adjective*; **discontentment** *noun*

discontinue *verb* (**discontinued, discontinuing**) put an end to something.

discord *noun* **1** disagreement; quarrelling. **2** musical notes sounded together and producing a harsh or unpleasant sound. **discordant** *adjective* [from *dis-* = not, + Latin *cordis* = of the heart]

discothèque (*say* **dis**-ko-tek) *noun* a place where people dance to recorded pop music. [French, = record-library]

discount *noun* an amount by which a price is reduced.

discount *verb* ignore; disregard. *We cannot discount the possibility.*

discourage *verb* (**discouraged, discouraging**) **1** take away someone's enthusiasm or confidence. **2** try to persuade someone not to do something; dissuade; deter. **discouragement** *noun*

discourse *noun* **1** a conversation. **2** a formal speech or piece of writing.

discourse *verb* (**discoursed, discoursing**) speak or write at length about something.

discourteous *adjective* not courteous; rude. **discourteously** *adverb*, **discourtesy** *noun*

discover *verb* **1** find. **2** be the first person to find something. **discoverer** *noun*, **discovery** *noun* [from *dis-* = apart, + *cover*]

discredit *verb* (**discredited, discrediting**) **1** destroy people's confidence in a person or thing; disgrace. **2** distrust.

discredit *noun* **1** disgrace. **2** distrust. **discreditable** *adjective*

discreet *adjective* **1** not giving away secrets. **2** not showy. **discreetly** *adverb*

> USAGE Do not confuse with *discrete*.

discrepancy (*say* dis-**krep**-an-see) *noun* (*plural* **discrepancies**) difference; lack of agreement, *There are several discrepancies in the two accounts.* **discrepant** *adjective* [from Latin, = discord]

discrete *adjective* separate; distinct from each other.

> USAGE Do not confuse with *discreet*.

discretion (*say* dis-**kresh**-on) *noun* **1** being discreet; keeping secrets. **2** power to take action according to your own judgement, *The treasurer has full discretion.*

discriminate *verb* (**discriminated, discriminating**) **1** notice the differences between things; distinguish; prefer one thing to another. **2** treat people differently or unfairly, e.g. because of their race, sex, or religion. **discrimination** *noun*. [from Latin *discrimen* = separator]

USAGE Note that these words have both a 'good' sense and a 'bad' sense. A *discriminating* person can mean someone who judges carefully and well, but it can also mean someone who judges unfairly.

discus *noun* (*plural* **discuses**) a thick heavy disc thrown in athletic contests.

discuss *verb* talk with other people about a subject. **discussion** *noun*

disdain *noun* scorn; contempt. **disdainful** *adjective*, **disdainfully** *adverb*

disdain *verb* **1** regard or treat with disdain. **2** not do something because of disdain, *She disdained to reply*. [from *dis-* = not, + Latin *dignus* = worthy]

disease *noun* an unhealthy condition; an illness. **diseased** *adjective* [from *dis-* = not, + *ease*]

disembark *verb* put or go ashore. **disembarkation** *noun*

disembodied *adjective* freed from the body, *a disembodied spirit.*

disembowel *verb* (**disembowelled, disembowelling**) take out the bowels or inside parts of something.

disengage *verb* (**disengaged, disengaging**) disconnect; detach.

disentangle *verb* (**disentangled, disentangling**) free from tangles or confusion.

disfavour *noun* disapproval; dislike.

disfigure *verb* (**disfigured, disfiguring**) spoil a person's or thing's appearance. **disfigurement** *noun*

disgorge *verb* (**disgorged, disgorging**) pour or send out, *The pipe disgorged its contents.* [from *dis-* + *gorge* = throat]

disgrace *noun* **1** shame; loss of approval or respect. **2** something that causes shame. **disgraceful** *adjective*, **disgracefully** *adverb*

disgrace *verb* (**disgraced, disgracing**) bring disgrace upon someone.

disgruntled *adjective* discontented; resentful.

disguise *verb* (**disguised, disguising**) make a person or thing look different so as to deceive people.

disguise *noun* something used for disguising.

disgust *noun* a feeling that something is very unpleasant or disgraceful.

disgust *verb* cause disgust. **disgusted** *adjective*, **disgusting** *adjective* [from *dis-* = not, + Latin *gustare* = to taste]

dish *noun* (*plural* **dishes**) **1** a plate or bowl for food. **2** food served on a dish. **3** a receptacle or other object in the shape of a dish.

dish *verb* (*informal*) ruin; spoil people's hopes, *It had dished our chances.*

dishcloth *noun* a cloth for washing dishes.

dishearten *verb* cause a person to lose hope or confidence.

dishevelled (*say* dish-**ev**-eld) *adjective* ruffled and untidy. **dishevelment** *noun* [from *dis-* = apart, + Old French *chevel* = hair]

dishonest *adjective* not honest. **dishonestly** *adverb*, **dishonesty** *noun*

dishonour *noun & verb* disgrace. **dishonourable** *adjective*

dishwasher *noun* a machine for washing dishes etc. automatically.

disillusion *verb* get rid of someone's pleasant but wrong beliefs. **disillusionment** *noun*

disincentive *noun* something that discourages an action or effort.

disinclination *noun* unwillingness.

disinclined *adjective* unwilling to do something.

disinfect *verb* destroy the germs in something. **disinfection** *noun*

disinfectant *noun* a substance used for disinfecting things.

disinherit *verb* deprive a person of the right to inherit something.

disintegrate *verb* (**disintegrated, disintegrating**) break up into small parts or pieces. **disintegration** *noun*

disinter *verb* (**disinterred, disinterring**) dig up something buried; unearth.

disinterested *adjective* impartial; not biased; not influenced by hope of gaining something yourself, *She gave us some disinterested advice.*

USAGE Do not use this word as if it meant 'not interested' or 'bored' (the word for this is *uninterested*).

disjointed *adjective* disconnected.

disk *noun* a round flat plate coated with magnetic material on which computer data can be stored. (See also *floppy disk, hard disk.*)

diskette *noun* (*Computing*) a floppy disk.

dislike *noun* a feeling of not liking somebody or something.

dislike *verb* (**disliked, disliking**) not to like somebody or something.

dislocate *verb* (**dislocated, dislocating**) **1** dislodge a bone from its proper position in one of the joints. **2** disrupt, *Fog dislocated the traffic.* **dislocation** *noun*

dislodge *verb* (**dislodged, dislodging**) move or force something from its place.

disloyal *adjective* not loyal. **disloyally** *adverb*, **disloyalty** *noun*

dismal *adjective* gloomy. **dismally** *adverb* [from Latin *dies mali* = unlucky days]

dismantle *verb* (**dismantled, dismantling**) take something to pieces.

dismay *noun* a feeling of surprise and discouragement. **dismayed** *adjective*

dismiss *verb* **1** send someone away. **2** tell a person that you will no longer employ him or her. **3** stop considering an idea etc. **4** (in cricket) get a batter or side out. **dismissal** *noun*, **dismissive** *adjective* [from *dis-*, + Latin *missum* = sent]

dismount *verb* get off a horse or bicycle.

disobedient *adjective* not obedient. **disobediently** *adverb*, **disobedience** *noun*

disobey *verb* (**disobeyed, disobeying**) not to obey; disregard orders.

disorder *noun* **1** untidiness. **2** a disturbance. **3** an illness. **disorderly** *adjective*

disorganise *verb* (**disorganised, disorganising**) throw into confusion. **disorganisation** *noun*

disown *verb* refuse to acknowledge that a person or thing has any connection with you.

disparage (*say* dis-**pa**-rij) *verb* (**disparaged, disparaging**) belittle; declare that something is small or unimportant. **disparagement** *noun*

disparity *noun* (*plural* **disparities**) difference; inequality.

dispassionate *adjective* calm and impartial. **dispassionately** *adverb*

dispatch *verb* **1** send off to a destination. **2** kill.

dispatch *noun* **1** dispatching. **2** a report or message sent. **3** promptness; speed.

dispatch-box *noun* a container for carrying official documents.

dispatch-rider *noun* a messenger who travels by motor cycle.

dispel *verb* (**dispelled, dispelling**) drive away; scatter, *Wind dispels fog.* [from *dis-* = apart, + Latin *pellere* = to drive]

dispensary *noun* (*plural* **dispensaries**) a place where medicines are dispensed.

dispense *verb* (**dispensed, dispensing**) **1** distribute; deal out. **2** prepare medicine according to prescriptions. **dispensation** *noun*, **dispenser** *noun*
dispense with do without something. [from *dis-* = separately, + Latin *pensum* = weighed]

disperse *verb* (**dispersed, dispersing**) scatter. **dispersal** *noun*, **dispersion** *noun* [from Latin *dispersum* = scattered]

displace *verb* (**displaced, displacing**) **1** shift from its place. **2** take a person's or thing's place. **displacement** *noun*

display *verb* show; arrange something so that it can be clearly seen.

display *noun* **1** the displaying of something; an exhibition. **2** something displayed. [from *dis-* = separately, + Latin *plicare* = to fold]

displease *verb* (**displeased, displeasing**) annoy or not please someone. **displeasure** *noun*

disposable *adjective* made to be thrown away after it has been used.

disposal *noun* getting rid of something.
at your disposal for you to use; ready for you.

dispose *verb* (**disposed, disposing**) **1** place in position; arrange, *Dispose your troops in two lines.* **2** make a person ready or willing to do something, *I feel disposed to help him.*
be well disposed be friendly.
dispose of get rid of. [from *dis-* = away, + French *poser* = to place]

disposition *noun* **1** a person's nature or qualities. **2** arrangement.

disproportionate *adjective* out of proportion; too large or too small.

disprove *verb* (**disproved, disproving**) show that something is not true.

disputation *noun* a debate; an argument.

dispute *verb* (**disputed, disputing**) **1** argue; debate. **2** quarrel. **3** raise an objection to, *We dispute their claim.*

dispute *noun* **1** an argument; a debate. **2** a quarrel.
in dispute being argued about. [from *dis-* = apart, + Latin *putare* = consider]

disqualify *verb* (**disqualified, disqualifying**) bar someone from a competition etc. because he or she has broken the rules or is not properly qualified to take part. **disqualification** *noun*

disquiet *noun* anxiety; worry. **disquieting** *adjective*

disregard *verb* ignore.

disregard *noun* the act of ignoring something.

disrepair *noun* bad condition caused by not doing repairs.

disreputable *adjective* not respectable.

disrepute *noun* discredit; bad reputation.

disrespect *noun* lack of respect; rudeness. **disrespectful** *adjective*, **disrespectfully** *adverb*

disrupt *verb* put into disorder; interrupt a continuous flow, *Fog disrupted traffic.* **disruption** *noun*, **disruptive** *adjective* [from *dis-* = apart, + Latin *ruptum* = broken]

dissatisfied *adjective* not satisfied. **dissatisfaction** *noun*

dissect (*say* dis-**sekt**) *verb* cut something up so as to examine it. **dissection** *noun* [from *dis-* = apart, + Latin *sectum* = cut]

disseminate *verb* (**disseminated, disseminating**) spread ideas etc. widely. **dissemination** *noun* [from *dis-* = apart, + Latin *seminare* = sow (scatter seeds)]

dissent *noun* disagreement.

dissent *verb* disagree. [from *dis-* = apart, + Latin *sentire* = feel]

dissertation *noun* a discourse.

disservice *noun* a harmful action done by someone who was intending to help.

dissident *noun* a person who disagrees; someone who opposes the authorities. **dissident** *adjective*, **dissidence** *noun*

dissipate *verb* (**dissipated, dissipating**) **1** dispel; disperse. **2** squander; waste; fritter away. **dissipation** *noun* [from Latin *dissipare* scatter]

dissociate *verb* (**dissociated, dissociating**) separate something in your thoughts. **dissociation** *noun*

dissolute *adjective* living a frivolous and selfish life.

dissolution *noun* dissolving.

dissolve *verb* (**dissolved, dissolving**) **1** mix something with a liquid so that it becomes part of the liquid. **2** make or become liquid; melt. **3** put an end to a marriage or partnership etc. **4** dismiss an assembly, *Parliament was dissolved and a general election was held.* [from *dis-* = separate, + Latin *solvere* = loosen]

dissuade *verb* (**dissuaded, dissuading**) persuade somebody not to do something. **dissuasion** *noun* [from *dis-* = apart, + Latin *suadere* = advise]

distaff *noun* a stick holding raw wool etc. for spinning into yarn.

distance *noun* the amount of space between two places.
in the distance far away.

distant *adjective* **1** far away. **2** not friendly; not sociable. **distantly** *adverb* [from *dis-* = apart, + Latin *stans* = standing]

distaste *noun* dislike.

distasteful *adjective* unpleasant.

distemper *noun* **1** a disease of dogs and certain other animals. **2** a kind of paint.

distend *verb* make or become swollen because of pressure from inside. **distension** *noun* [from *dis-* = apart, + Latin *tendere* = stretch]

distil *verb* (**distilled, distilling**) purify a liquid by boiling it and condensing the vapour. **distillation** *noun* [from *dis-* = apart, + Latin *stillare* drip down]

distiller *noun* a person who makes alcoholic liquors by distillation. **distillery** *noun*

distinct *adjective* **1** easily heard or seen; noticeable. **2** clearly separate or different. **distinctly** *adverb*, **distinctness** *noun*

> USAGE See *distinctive.*

distinction *noun* **1** a difference. **2** distinguishing; making a difference. **3** excellence; honour. **4** an award for excellence; a high mark in an examination.

distinctive *adjective* that distinguishes one thing from another or others, *The school has a distinctive uniform.* **distinctively** *adverb*

> USAGE Do not confuse this word with *distinct.* A *distinct* mark is a clear mark; a *distinctive* mark is one that is not found anywhere else.

distinguish *verb* **1** make or notice differences between things. **2** see or hear something clearly. **3** bring honour to, *He distinguished himself by his bravery.* **distinguishable** *adjective* [from Latin *distinguere* = to separate]

distinguished *adjective* excellent; famous.

distort *verb* **1** pull or twist out of its normal shape. **2** misrepresent; give a false account of something, *distort the truth.* **distortion** *noun* [from *dis-* = apart, + Latin *tortum* = twisted]

distract *verb* take a person's attention away from something. [from *dis-* = apart, + Latin *tractum* = pulled]

distracted *adjective* distraught.

distraction *noun* **1** something that distracts a person's attention. **2** an amusement. **3** great worry or distress.

distraught (*say* dis-**trawt**) *adjective* greatly upset by worry or distress.

distress *noun* great sorrow, pain, or trouble.

distress *verb* cause distress to a person.

distribute *verb* (**distributed, distributing**) **1** deal or share out. **2** spread or scatter. **distribution** *noun*, **distributor** *noun* [from *dis-* = separate, + Latin *tributum* = given]

district *noun* an area or region of a country. **District Court** (*NZ*) a lawcourt where all cases except the most serious are heard.

distrust *noun* lack of trust; suspicion. **distrustful** *adjective*

distrust *verb* not to trust.

disturb *verb* **1** spoil someone's peace or rest. **2** cause someone to worry. **3** move a thing from its position. **disturbance** *noun* [from *dis-* = thoroughly, + Latin *turbare* = confuse, upset]

disuse *noun* the state of not being used.

disused *adjective* no longer used.

ditch *noun* (*plural* **ditches**) a trench dug to hold water or carry it away, or to serve as a boundary.
the ditch (*NZ, slang*) the Tasman Sea.

ditch *verb* **1** (*informal*) bring an aircraft down in a forced landing on the sea. **2** (*slang*) abandon; discard.

dither *verb* **1** tremble. **2** hesitate nervously.

ditto *noun* (used in lists) the same again.

ditty *noun* (*plural* **ditties**) a short song.

divan *noun* a bed or couch without a raised back or sides. [Persian, = cushioned bench]

dive *verb* (**dived, diving**) **1** go under water, especially head first. **2** move down quickly. **dive** *noun*

diver *noun* **1** someone who dives. **2** a person who works under water in a special suit with an air supply. **3** a bird that dives for its food.

diverge *verb* (**diverged, diverging**) go aside or in different directions. **divergent** *adjective*, **divergence** *noun* [from *di-*[2] = apart, + Latin *vergere* = to slope]

divers (*say* **dy**-verz) *adjective* (*old use*) various.

diverse (*say* dy-**verss**) *adjective* varied; of several different kinds. **diversity** *noun*

diversify *verb* (**diversified, diversifying**) make or become varied; involve yourself in different kinds of things. **diversification** *noun*

diversion *noun* **1** diverting something from its course; an alternative route for traffic when a road is closed. **2** a recreation; an entertainment. **diversionary** *adjective*

divert *verb* **1** turn something aside from its course. **2** entertain; amuse. [from *di-*[2] = apart, + Latin *vertere* = to turn]

divest *verb* **1** strip of clothes, *He divested himself of his robes.* **2** take away; deprive, *They divested him of power.*

divide *verb* (**divided, dividing**) **1** separate from something or into smaller parts; split up. **2** find how many times one number is contained in another, *Divide six by three* (6 ÷ 3 = 2). **divider** *noun*

dividend *noun* **1** a share of a business's profit. **2** a number that is to be divided by another. (Compare *divisor*.)

dividers *plural noun* a pair of compasses for measuring distances.

divine *adjective* **1** of God; coming from God. **2** like a god. **3** (*informal*) excellent; extremely beautiful. **divinely** *adverb*

divine *verb* (**divined, divining**) prophesy or guess what is about to happen. [from Latin *divus* = god]

division *noun* **1** dividing. **2** a dividing line; a partition. **3** one of the parts into which something is divided. **4** (in Parliament) separation of members into two sections for counting votes. **divisional** *adjective*

divisive (*say* div-**I**-siv) *adjective* causing disagreement within a group.

divisor *noun* a number by which another is to be divided. (Compare *dividend*[2].)

divorce *noun* the legal ending of a marriage; dissolution.

divorce *verb* (**divorced, divorcing**) **1** end a marriage by divorce. **2** separate; think of things separately.

divulge *verb* (**divulged, divulging**) reveal information. **divulgence** *noun*

DIY *abbreviation* do-it-yourself.

dizzy *adjective* (**dizzier, dizziest**) giddy. **dizzily** *adverb*, **dizziness** *noun*

DJ *abbreviation* disc jockey.

DLitt. *abbreviation* Doctor of Letters.

DNA *abbreviation* deoxyribonucleic acid, a substance in chromosomes that stores genetic information.

do *verb* (**did, done, doing**) This word has many different uses, most of which mean performing or dealing with something (*Do your best. I can't do this. She is doing well at school*) or being suitable or enough (*This will do*).
The verb is also used with other verbs (**1**) in questions (*Do you want this?*), (**2**) in statements with 'not' (*He does not want it*), (**3**) for emphasis (*I do like nuts*), (**4**) to avoid repeating a verb that has just been used (*We work as hard as they do*).
do away with get rid of.
do up fasten, *Do your coat up*; repair or redecorate, *Do up the spare room.*

do *noun* (*plural* **dos**) (*informal*) **1** a party; an entertainment. **2** a success.

DOC *abbreviation* (*NZ*) Department of Conservation.

docile (*say* **doh**-syl) *adjective* willing to obey. **docilely** *adverb*, **docility** *noun* [from Latin *docilis* = easily taught]

dock[1] *noun* a place where ships are loaded, unloaded, or repaired.

dock[1] *verb* **1** bring or come into a dock. **2** (of spacecraft) join together in space.

dock[2] *noun* an enclosure for the prisoner on trial in a lawcourt. [from Flemish *dok* = cage]

dock[3] *noun* a weed with broad leaves.

dock[4] *verb* **1** cut short an animal's tail. **2** castrate a lamb. **3** reduce or take away part of someone's wages or supplies etc.

docket *noun* **1** a document or label listing the contents of a package. **2** (*NZ & Australia*) an itemised receipt provided by a shop, service, or supermarket.

dockyard *noun* an open area with docks and equipment for building or repairing ships.

doco *noun* (*informal*) a documentary.

doctor *noun* **1** a person who is trained to treat sick or injured people. **2** a person who holds an advanced degree (a **doctorate**) at a university, *Doctor of Music*. [from Latin *doctor* = teacher]

doctrine *noun* a belief held by a religious, political, or other group. **doctrinal** *adjective* [same origin as *doctor*]

document *noun* a piece of written, printed, or electronic matter giving information or evidence about something. **documentation** *noun*

documentary *adjective* **1** consisting of documents, *documentary evidence*. **2** showing real events or situations.

documentary *noun* (*plural* **documentaries**) a film giving an account of something, often showing real events etc.

dodder *verb* totter. **doddery** *adjective*

dodge *verb* (**dodged, dodging**) move quickly to avoid someone or something.

dodge *noun* **1** a dodging movement. **2** (*informal*) a trick; a clever way of doing something.

dodgem *noun* a small electrically-driven car at a fair, in which each driver tries to bump some cars and dodge others.

dodgy *adjective* (*informal*) tricky; awkward.

dodo *noun* (*plural* **dodos**) a large heavy bird that used to live on an island in the Indian Ocean but has been extinct for over 200 years. [from Portuguese *doudo* = fool]

doe *noun* a female deer, rabbit, or hare.

doer *noun* a person who does things.

doesn't (*mainly spoken*) does not.

doff *verb* take off, *He doffed his hat*. [from *do off*; compare *don*]

dog *noun* a four-legged animal that barks, often kept as a pet.

dog *verb* (**dogged, dogging**) follow closely or persistently, *Reporters dogged his footsteps*.

doge (*say* dohj) *noun* the elected ruler of the former republics of Venice and Genoa. [from Latin *dux* = leader]

dog-eared *adjective* (of a book) having the corners of the pages bent from constant use.

dogfish *noun* (*plural* **dogfish**) a kind of small shark.

dogged (*say* **dog**-id) *adjective* persistent; obstinate. **doggedly** *adverb*

doggerel *noun* bad verse.

doggo *adverb* **lie doggo** (*informal*) lie motionless or hidden.

dog-leg fence (*NZ*) a rough fence made of logs that rest on crossed poles.

dogma *noun* a belief or principle that a Church or other authority declares is true and must be accepted.

dogmatic *adjective* expressing ideas in a very firm authoritative way. **dogmatically** *adverb* [from *dogma*]

doh *noun* a name for the keynote of a scale in music, or the note C.

doily *noun* (*plural* **doilies**) a small ornamental table-mat.

do-it-yourself *adjective* suitable for an amateur handyman to make or use.

doldrums *plural noun* **1** the ocean regions near the equator where there is little or no wind. **2** a time of depression or inactivity.

dole *verb* (**doled, doling**) distribute.

dole *noun* (*informal*) money paid by the State to unemployed people.

doleful *adjective* mournful. **dolefully** *adverb* [from an old word *dole* = grief]

doll *noun* a toy model of a person.

dollar *noun* a unit of money in New Zealand, Australia, the USA, and some other countries. [from German *thaler* = a silver coin]

dolly *noun* (*plural* **dollies**) (*informal*) a doll.

dolphin *noun* a sea mammal like a small whale with a beak-like snout.

domain (*say* dom-**ayn**) *noun* **1** realm. **2** (*NZ*) a public park, *Auckland Domain*. **3** an Internet server subset with addresses that share a common suffix.

dome *noun* a roof shaped like the top half of a ball. **domed** *adjective*

domestic *adjective* **1** of the home or household. **2** (of animals) kept by people, not wild. **domestically** *adverb*, **domesticated** *adjective*
domestic purposes benefit (*NZ*) a government payment to a person without other income who is raising a child or children. [from Latin *domus* = home]

domicile (*say* **dom**-iss-syl) *noun* a residence; home. **domiciled** *adjective*

dominate *verb* (**dominated, dominating**) **1** control by being stronger or more powerful. **2** be conspicuous or prominent, *The mountain dominated the whole landscape*. **dominant** *adjective*, **dominance** *noun*, **domination** *noun* [from Latin *dominus* = master]

domineer *verb* behave in a dominating way. **domineering** *adjective*

dominion *noun* **1** authority to rule others; control. **2** an area over which someone rules; a domain.
the Dominion (*older usage*) New Zealand. [the country's official title after 1907]

domino *noun* (*plural* **dominoes**) a small flat oblong piece of wood or plastic with dots (1 to 6) or a blank space at each end, used in the game of dominoes.

don *verb* (**donned, donning**) put on, *don a cloak.* [from *do on*; compare *doff*]

donate *verb* (**donated, donating**) present money or a gift to a fund or institution etc. **donation** *noun*

donkey *noun* (*plural* **donkeys**) an animal that looks like a small horse with long ears.

donor *noun* someone who gives something, *a blood donor.*

don't (*mainly spoken*) do not.

doodle *verb* (**doodled, doodling**) scribble or draw absent-mindedly. **doodle** *noun*

doom *noun* a grim fate; death; ruin.

doom *verb* destine to a grim fate.

doomsday *noun* the day of the Last Judgement; the end of the world.

door *noun* a movable barrier on hinges (or one that slides or revolves), used to open or close an entrance. **doorknob** *noun*, **doormat** *noun*

doorstep *noun* the step or piece of ground just outside a door.

doorway *noun* the opening into which a door fits.

dope *noun* **1** (*informal*) a drug, especially one taken or given illegally. **2** (*slang*) a stupid person. **dopey** *adjective*

dope *verb* (**doped, doping**) (*informal*) give a drug to a person or animal. [from Dutch *doop* = sauce]

dormant *adjective* **1** sleeping. **2** living or existing but not active; not extinct, *a dormant volcano.* [from French, = sleeping]

dormitory *noun* (*plural* **dormitories**) a room for several people to sleep in, especially in a school or institution. [from Latin *dormire* = to sleep]

dormouse *noun* (*plural* **dormice**) an animal like a large mouse that hibernates in winter.

dorsal *adjective* of or on the back, *Some fish have a dorsal fin.* [from Latin *dorsum* = the back]

DOS *abbreviation* (*computing*) disk operating system.

dosage *noun* **1** the giving of medicine in doses. **2** the size of a dose.

dose *noun* an amount of medicine etc. taken at one time.

dose *verb* (**dosed, dosing**) give a dose of medicine to a person or animal.

dossier (*say* **doss**-ee-er or **doss**-ee-ay) *noun* a set of documents containing information about a person or event.

dot *noun* a tiny spot.

dot *verb* (**dotted, dotting**) mark with dots.

dotage (*say* **doh**-tij) *noun* a condition of weakness of mind caused by old age, *He is in his dotage.*

dote *verb* (**doted, doting**) **dote on** be very fond of.

dotty *adjective* (**dottier, dottiest**) (*informal*) crazy; silly. **dottiness** *noun*

double *adjective* **1** twice as much; twice as many. **2** having two things or parts that form a pair, *a double-barrelled gun.* **3** suitable for two people, *a double bed.* **doubly** *adverb*

double *noun* **1** a double quantity or thing. **2** a person or thing that looks exactly like another. **3** a bet picking the winners of two selected races.

double *verb* (**doubled, doubling**) **1** make or become twice as much or as many. **2** bend or fold in two. **3** turn back sharply, *The deer doubled back on its tracks.* **4** (also **double-bank**) (*NZ*) let someone ride with you on your horse or bicycle.
double-bass *noun* a musical instrument with strings, like a large cello.
double-cross *verb* deceive or cheat someone who thinks you are working with them.
double-decker *noun* (*British*) a bus with two decks.

doublet *noun* a man's close-fitting jacket worn in the 15th–17th centuries.

doubt *noun* a feeling of not being sure about something.

doubt *verb* feel doubt. **doubter** *noun* [from Latin *dubitare* = hesitate]

doubtful *adjective* **1** feeling doubt. **2** casting doubt. **doubtfully** *adverb*

doubtless *adverb* certainly.

dough *noun* **1** a thick mixture of flour and water used for making bread, pastry, etc. **2** (*slang*) money. **doughy** *adjective*

doughnut *noun* a round bun that has been fried and covered in sugar.

doughty (*say* **dow**-tee) *adjective* valiant.

dour (*say* doo-er) *adjective* stern and gloomy-looking. **dourly** *adverb* [from Gaelic *dur* = dull, obstinate]

douse *verb* (**doused, dousing**) **1** put into water; pour water over something. **2** put out, *douse the light.*

dove *noun* a kind of pigeon.

dovetail *noun* a wedge-shaped joint used to join two pieces of wood.

dovetail *verb* **1** join pieces of wood with a dovetail. **2** fit neatly together, *My plans dovetailed with hers.*

dowager *noun* a woman who holds a title or property after her husband has died, *the dowager duchess.*

dowdy *adjective* (**dowdier, dowdiest**) shabby; unfashionable. **dowdily** *adverb*

dowel *noun* a headless wooden or metal pin for holding together two pieces of wood, stone, etc. **dowelling** *noun*

down[1] *adverb* **1** to or in a lower place or position or level, *It fell down.* **2** to a source or place etc., *Track them down.* **3** in writing, *Take down these instructions.* **4** as a payment, *We will pay $50 down and the rest later.* **5** out of action, *the computer is down.*
be down on disapprove of, *She is down on smoking.*
down under (*informal*) in or to New Zealand and/or Australia.

down[1] *preposition* downwards through or along or into, *Pour it down the drain.*

down[2] *noun* very fine soft feathers or hair. **downy** *adjective*

down[3] *noun* (*in plural*) undulating grassland, *the South Canterbury Downs.*

downcast *adjective* **1** looking downwards, *downcast eyes.* **2** dejected.

downfall *noun* **1** a fall from power or prosperity. **2** a heavy fall of rain or snow.

downhill *adverb & adjective* down a slope.

download *verb* (*Computing*) transfer data to one's computer from another system.

downpipe *noun* a pipe that carries rainwater from the roof to a drain.

downpour *noun* a great fall of rain.

downright *adjective* **1** frank; straightforward. **2** thorough; complete, *a downright lie.*

downside *noun* the undesirable aspect of something.

downsize *verb* (**downsized, downsizing**) make smaller.

downstairs *adverb & adjective* to or on a lower floor.

downstream *adjective & adverb* in the direction in which a stream flows.

downward *adjective & adverb* going towards what is lower. **downwards** *adverb*

dowry *noun* (*plural* **dowries**) property or money brought by a bride to her husband when she marries him.

doze *verb* (**dozed, dozing**) sleep lightly.

doze *noun* a light sleep. **dozy** *adjective*

dozen *noun* a set of twelve.

> USAGE Correct use is *ten dozen* (not *ten dozens*).

DPB *abbreviation* (*NZ*) domestic purposes benefit.

Dr *abbreviation* Doctor; Drive; debtor.

drab *adjective* (**drabber, drabbest**) **1** not colourful. **2** dull; uninteresting, *a drab life.* **drably** *adverb*, **drabness** *noun*

Draconian (*say* drak-**oh**-nee-an) *adjective* very harsh, *Draconian laws.* [named after Draco, who established very severe laws in ancient Athens]

draft *noun* **1** a rough sketch or plan. **2** a written order for a bank to pay out money. **3** (*NZ*) a group of livestock selected from a larger mob.

draft *verb* **1** prepare a draft. **2** select for a special duty, *She was drafted to our office in Paris.* **3** (*NZ*) separate livestock from a larger mob.

drafting *noun* **1** (*NZ*) selecting livestock. **2** an alternative spelling of **draughting**.
drafting race (*NZ*) a narrow alley down which animals are driven for drafting.

drag *verb* (**dragged, dragging**) **1** pull something heavy along. **2** search a river or lake etc. with nets and hooks. **3** continue slowly and dully. **4** move an image or part of a text on a computer screen.

drag *noun* **1** a hindrance; something boring. **2** (*slang*) women's clothes worn by men.

dragon *noun* **1** a mythological monster, usually with wings and able to breathe out fire. **2** a fierce person. [from Greek *drakon* = serpent]

dragonfly *noun* (*plural* **dragonflies**) an insect with a long thin body and two pairs of transparent wings.

dragoon *noun* a member of certain cavalry regiments in Europe.

dragoon *verb* force someone into doing something.

drain *noun* **1** a pipe or ditch etc. for taking away water or other liquid. **2** something that takes away strength or resources. **drainpipe** *noun*

drain *verb* **1** take away water etc. through a drain. **2** flow or trickle away. **3** empty liquid out of a container. **4** take away strength etc.; exhaust. **drainage** *noun*

drainlayer *noun* a person who lays or repairs drains.

drake *noun* a male duck.

drama *noun* **1** a play. **2** writing or performing plays. **3** a series of exciting events.

dramatic *adjective* **1** of drama. **2** exciting; impressive, *a dramatic change.* **dramatics** *plural noun,* **dramatically** *adverb*

dramatise *verb* (**dramatised, dramatising**) **1** make a story etc. into a play. **2** make something seem exciting. **dramatisation** *noun*

dramatis personae *plural noun* (*say* **dram**-uh-tuhs per-**soh**-nuy) the characters in a play.

dramatist *noun* a person who writes plays.

drape *verb* (**draped, draping**) hang cloth etc. loosely over something.

draper *noun* a shopkeeper who sells cloth or clothes.

drapery *noun* (*plural* **draperies**) **1** a draper's stock. **2** cloth arranged in loose folds.

drastic *adjective* having a strong or violent effect. **drastically** *adverb*

draught (*say* drahft) *noun* **1** a current of usually cold air indoors. **2** a haul of fish in a net. **3** the depth of water needed to float a ship. **4** a swallow of liquid. **5** one of the pieces in the game of draughts. **draughty** *adjective*

draughting *noun* the drawing of sketches and plans for new buildings etc. **draughter** *noun*

draughts *noun* a game played with 24 round pieces on a chess-board.

draw *verb* (**drew, drawn, drawing**) **1** produce a picture or outline by making marks on a surface. **2** pull. **3** take out, *draw water.* **4** attract, *The fair drew large crowds.* **5** end a game or contest with the same score on both sides. **6** move; come, *The ship drew nearer.* **7** make out by thinking, *draw conclusions.* **8** write out a cheque to be cashed.

draw *noun* **1** the drawing of lots (see *lot*). **2** the drawing out of a gun etc., *He was quick on the draw.* **3** an attraction. **4** a drawn game.

drawback *noun* a disadvantage.

drawbridge *noun* a bridge over a moat, hinged at one end so that it can be raised or lowered.

drawer *noun* **1** a sliding box-like compartment in a piece of furniture. **2** a person who draws something. **3** someone who draws (= writes out) a cheque.

drawing *noun* a picture or outline drawn.

drawing-pin *noun* a short pin with a flat top to be pressed with your thumb, used for fastening paper etc. to a surface.

drawing-room *noun* a sitting-room.

drawl *verb* speak very slowly or lazily.

drawl *noun* a drawling way of speaking.

dray *noun* a strong low flat cart for carrying heavy loads.

dread *noun* great fear.

dread *verb* fear greatly.

dreadful *adjective* (*informal*) very bad, *dreadful weather.* **dreadfully** *adverb*

dreadlocks *plural noun* hair worn in many ringlets or plaits, especially by Rastafarians.

dream *noun* **1** things a person seems to see while sleeping. **2** something imagined; an ambition or ideal. **dreamy** *adjective,* **dreamily** *adverb*

dream *verb* (**dreamt** or **dreamed, dreaming**) **1** have a dream or dreams. **2** have an ambition. **3** think something might happen, *I never dreamt she would leave.* **dreamer** *noun*

dreary *adjective* (**drearier, dreariest**) **1** dull; boring. **2** gloomy. **drearily** *adverb,* **dreariness** *noun*

dredge *verb* (**dredged, dredging**) drag something up, especially by scooping at the bottom of a river or the sea. **dredger** *noun*

dregs *plural noun* worthless bits that sink to the bottom of a liquid.

drench *verb* **1** make wet all through. **2** give drench to.

drench *noun* a dose of medicine for an animal.

dress *noun* (*plural* **dresses**) **1** a woman's or girl's garment with a bodice and skirt. **2** clothes; costume, *fancy dress.*
dress rehearsal a rehearsal at which the cast wear their costumes.

dress *verb* **1** put clothes on. **2** arrange a display in a window etc.; decorate, *dress the shop windows.* **3** prepare food for cooking or eating. **4** put a dressing on a wound. **dresser** *noun*

dressage (*say* **dress**-ah*zh*) *noun* management of a horse to show its obedience and style. [French, = training]

dresser *noun* a sideboard with shelves at the top for dishes etc.

dressing *noun* **1** a bandage, plaster, or ointment etc. for a wound. **2** a sauce of oil, vinegar, etc. for a salad. **3** manure or other fertiliser for spreading on the soil.

dressing-gown *noun* a loose garment for wearing when you are not fully dressed.

dressmaker *noun* a woman who makes women's clothes. **dressmaking** *noun*

dribble *verb* (**dribbled, dribbling**) **1** let saliva trickle out of your mouth. **2** move the ball forward in soccer or hockey with slight touches of your feet or stick.

drier *noun* a device for drying hair, laundry, etc.

drift *verb* **1** be carried gently along by water or air. **2** move slowly and casually; live casually with no definite objective. **drifter** *noun*

drift *noun* **1** a drifting movement. **2** a mass of snow or sand piled up by the wind. **3** the general meaning of a speech etc.

drift-net *noun* a fishing net several kilometres long that is allowed to drift. **drift-net** *verb*, **drift-netting** *noun*, **drift-netter** *noun*

driftwood *noun* wood floating on the sea or washed ashore by it.

drill *noun* **1** a tool for making holes; a machine for boring holes or wells. **2** repeated exercises in gymnastics, military training, etc.

drill *verb* **1** make a hole etc. with a drill. **2** do repeated exercises; make people do exercises.

drily *adverb* in a dry way.

drink *verb* (**drank, drunk, drinking**) **1** swallow liquid. **2** drink a lot of alcoholic drinks. **drinker** *noun*

drink *noun* **1** a liquid for drinking; an amount of liquid swallowed. **2** an alcoholic drink.

drip *verb* (**dripped, dripping**) fall or let something fall in drops.

drip *noun* **1** liquid falling in drops; the sound it makes. **2** apparatus for dripping liquid into the veins of a sick person.

drip-dry *adjective* made of material that dries easily and does not need ironing.

dripping *noun* fat melted from roasted meat and allowed to set.

drive *verb* (**drove, driven, driving**) **1** make something or someone move. **2** operate a motor vehicle or a train etc. **3** cause; compel, *Hunger drove them to steal.* **4** force someone into a state, *She is driving me crazy.* **5** rush; move rapidly, *Rain drove against the window.* **driver** *noun*

drive *noun* **1** a journey in a vehicle. **2** a hard stroke in cricket or golf etc. **3** the transmitting of power to machinery, *four-wheel drive.* **4** energy; enthusiasm. **5** an organised effort, *a sales drive.* **6** a track for vehicles through the grounds of a house.

drive-in *adjective* (also **drive-through**) that you can use without getting out of your car.

drivel *noun* silly talk; nonsense.

drizzle *noun* very fine rain.

droll *adjective* amusing in an odd way.

dromedary *noun* (*plural* **dromedaries**) a camel with one hump, bred for riding on. [from Greek *dromas* = runner]

drone *verb* (**droned, droning**) **1** make a deep humming sound. **2** talk in a boring voice.

drone *noun* **1** a droning sound. **2** a male bee.

drongo *noun* (*plural* **drongos** or **drongoes**) (*NZ, informal*) a stupid person. [from the name of a tropical bird]

drool *verb* dribble. **drool over** be very emotional about liking something.

droop *verb* hang down weakly.

drop *noun* **1** a tiny amount of liquid. **2** a small round sweet. **3** a hanging ornament. **4** a fall; a decrease. **5** a descent.

drop *verb* (**dropped, dropping**) **1** fall. **2** let something fall. **3** put down a passenger etc., *Drop me at the station.*
drop in visit someone casually.
drop-kick (in rugby) a kick made by dropping the ball and kicking it as it touches the ground. **drop-kick** *verb*
drop out stop taking part in something.
drop-out *noun* **1** a person who drops out. **2** (in rugby union) a drop-kick to restart play.
dropped goal (in rugby) a field goal.

droplet *noun* a small drop.

drought (*say* drout) *noun* a long period of dry weather.

drove *noun* a moving herd, flock, or crowd, *droves of people.*

drown *verb* **1** die or kill by suffocation under water. **2** flood; drench. **3** make so much noise that another sound cannot be heard.

drowsy *adjective* sleepy. **drowsily** *adverb*, **drowsiness** *noun*

drubbing *noun* a beating; a severe defeat.

drudge *noun* a person who does dull work. **drudgery** *noun*

drug *noun* **1** a substance used in medicine. **2** a substance that affects your senses or your mind, *a drug addict.*

drug *verb* (**drugged, drugging**) give a drug to someone, especially to make them unconscious.

Druid (*say* **droo**-id) *noun* a priest of an ancient Celtic religion in Britain and France.

drum *noun* **1** a musical instrument made of a cylinder with a skin or parchment stretched over one or both ends. **2** a cylindrical object or container, *an oil drum.*

drum *verb* (**drummed, drumming**) **1** play a drum or drums. **2** tap or thrum on something.

drummer *noun* **1** a drum-player. **2** (*NZ*) a greyish-green fish.

drumstick *noun* **1** a stick for beating a drum. **2** the lower part of a cooked bird's leg.

drunk *adjective* excited or helpless through drinking too much alcohol.

drunk *noun* a person who is drunk.

drunkard *noun* a person who is often drunk.

drunken *adjective* **1** drunk, *a drunken man.* **2** caused by drinking alcohol.

dry *adjective* (**drier, driest**) **1** without water or moisture. **2** thirsty. **3** boring; dull. **4** (of remarks or humour) said in a matter-of-fact or ironical way, *dry wit.* **drily** *adverb,* **dryness** *noun*
dry cleaning a method of cleaning clothes etc. by a liquid that evaporates quickly.
dry dock a dock that can be emptied of water so that ships can float in and then be repaired.

dry *verb* (**dried, drying**) make or become dry.

dryad *noun* a wood-nymph.

Drysdale *noun* (*NZ*) a kind of cross-bred sheep farmed for its wool. [named after F. W. Dry, an animal scientist]

dual *adjective* composed of two parts; double.
dual carriageway a road with a dividing strip between lanes of traffic in opposite directions. [from Latin *duo* = two]

dub[1] *verb* (**dubbed, dubbing**) **1** make someone a knight by touching him on the shoulder with a sword. **2** give a person or thing a nickname. [from an old French word, = knight a person]

dub[2] *verb* (**dubbed, dubbing**) **1** change or add new sound to the sound-track of a film or magnetic tape. **2** copy a recording. **3** (*NZ, informal*) double (sense 4). [short for *double*]

dub-dub-dub *abbreviation* shortened form of www or World Wide Web.

dubbin *noun* thick grease used to soften leather and make it waterproof.

dubious (*say* **dew**-bee-us) *adjective* doubtful. **dubiously** *adverb* [from Latin *dubium* = doubt]

ducal *adjective* of a duke.

duchess *noun* (*plural* **duchesses**) a duke's wife or widow.

duck *noun* **1** a swimming bird with a flat beak; the female of this. **2** a batter's score of nought at cricket. **3** a ducking movement.

duck *verb* **1** bend down quickly to avoid something. **2** go or push quickly under water. **3** dodge; avoid doing something.

duckling *noun* a young duck.

duckweed *noun* a plant that covers the surface of ponds etc.

duct *noun* a tube or channel through which liquid, gas, air, or cables can pass. [from Latin *ductum* = conveyed]

ductile *adjective* (of metal) able to be drawn out into fine strands.

dud *noun* (*slang*) something that is useless or a fake or fails to work.

dudgeon (*say* **duj**-on) *noun* indignation.

due *adjective* **1** expected; scheduled to do something or to arrive, *The train is due in ten minutes.* **2** owing; needing to be paid. **3** that ought to be given; rightful, *Treat her with due respect.*
due to caused by.

> USAGE Correct use is as in *His lateness was due to an accident.* Many people dislike the use of 'due to' without a preceding noun (e.g. 'lateness') to which it refers. It is best to avoid uses such as 'He was late, due to an accident' where there is no such noun. (Use *because of* or *owing to* instead.)

due *adverb* exactly, *We sailed due east.*

due *noun* **1** a person's right; something deserved; proper respect, *Give him his due.* **2** a fee, *harbour dues.*

duel *noun* a fight between two people, especially with pistols or swords. **duelling** *noun,* **duellist** *noun*

> USAGE Do not confuse this word with *dual.*

duet *noun* a piece of music for two players or singers. [from Latin *duo* = two]

duff *adjective* (*slang*) worthless.

duffel coat *noun* a thick overcoat with a hood, fastened with toggles. [named after Duffel, a town in Belgium]

duffer *noun* (*informal*) a person who is stupid or not good at doing something.

dugout *noun* **1** an underground shelter. **2** a canoe made by hollowing out a tree-trunk.

duke *noun* a member of the highest rank of noblemen. **dukedom** *noun* [from Latin *dux* = leader]

dulcet (*say* **dul**-sit) *adjective* sweet-sounding. [from Latin *dulcis* = sweet]

dulcimer *noun* a musical instrument with strings that are struck by two small hammers.

dull *adjective* **1** not bright or clear, *dull weather.* **2** stupid. **3** boring, *a dull concert.* **4** not sharp, *a dull pain; a dull thud.* **dully** *adverb,* **dullness** *noun*

dullard *noun* a stupid person.

duly *adverb* in the due or proper way.

dumb *adjective* **1** unable to speak; silent. **2** (*informal*) stupid. **dumbly** *adverb,* **dumbness** *noun*

dumbfound *verb* astonish; strike a person dumb with surprise. [from *dumb* + *confound*]

dummy *noun* (*plural* **dummies**) **1** something made to look like a person or thing. **2** an imitation teat given to a baby to suck.

3 (in rugby and soccer) a pretended pass or move, to trick an opponent. [from *dumb*]
dummy half (in rugby league) the player picking up the ball when it is passed back with the foot by a tackled team-mate.

dump *noun* **1** a place where something (especially rubbish) is left or stored. **2** (*informal*) a dull or unattractive place.

dump *verb* **1** get rid of something that is not wanted. **2** put down carelessly. **3** (*NZ*) compress bales of wool together.

dumpling *noun* a lump of dough cooked in a stew etc. or baked with fruit inside.

dumps *plural noun* (*informal*) low spirits, *in the dumps.*

dumpy *adjective* short and fat.

dunce *noun* a person who is slow at learning. [from Duns Scotus, a Scottish philosopher in the Middle Ages, whose followers were said by their opponents to be unable to understand new ideas]

dune *noun* a mound of loose sand shaped by the wind.

Dunedinite *noun* (*NZ*) a person born or living in Dunedin.

dung *noun* solid waste matter excreted by an animal.

dungarees *plural noun* overalls made of thick strong cloth. [from Hindi *dungri*]

dungeon (*say* **dun**-jon) *noun* an underground cell for prisoners.

dunger *noun* (*informal*) an old or decrepit object, especially a vehicle.

dunk *verb* dip something into liquid.

dunny *noun* (*plural* **dunnies**) (*NZ, informal*) an outside toilet.

duodenum (*say* dew-o-**deen**-um) *noun* the part of the small intestine that is just below the stomach. **duodenal** *adjective*

dupe *verb* (**duped, duping**) deceive.

duplicate *noun* **1** something that is exactly the same as something else. **2** an exact copy.

duplicate *verb* (**duplicated, duplicating**) make or be a duplicate. **duplication** *noun*, **duplicator** *noun* [from Latin *duplex* = double]

duplicity (*say* dew-**plis**-it-ee) *noun* deceitfulness. [from Latin *duplex* = double]

duplicitous (*say* due-**pliss**-it-is) *adjective* two-faced or deceitful.

durable *adjective* strong and likely to last.
durably *adverb*, **durability** *noun* [from Latin *durare* = endure]

duration *noun* the time something lasts.

duress (*say* dewr-**ess**) *noun* the use of force or threats to get what you want.

during *preposition* while something else is going on.

dusk *noun* twilight in the evening.

dusky *adjective* dark; shadowy.

dust *noun* tiny particles of earth or other solid material.

dust *verb* **1** wipe away dust. **2** sprinkle with dust or something powdery.

duster *noun* a cloth for dusting things.

dustpan *noun* a pan into which dust is brushed from a floor.

dusty *adjective* (**dustier, dustiest**) **1** covered with dust. **2** like dust.

dutiful *adjective* doing your duty; obedient.
dutifully *adverb* [from *duty* + *-ful*]

duty *noun* (*plural* **duties**) **1** what you ought to do or must do. **2** a task that must be done. **3** a tax charged on imports and on certain other things.
on duty actually doing what is your regular work.

duvet (*say* **doo**-vay) *noun* a kind of quilt used instead of other bedclothes.

DVD *abbreviation* digital video disc.

DVD-R *abbreviation* a DVD that can be recorded only once.

DVD-ROM *abbreviation* a DVD used in a computer for displaying data.

DVD-RW *abbreviation* a DVD on which many recordings can be made and erased a number of times.

dwang *noun* (*NZ*) a short piece of timber placed between joists or studs.

dwarf *noun* (*plural* **dwarves**) a very small person or thing.

dwarf *verb* make something seem small by contrast, *The cruise ship dwarfed the tugs that were towing it.*

dwell *verb* (**dwelt, dwelling**) live somewhere.
dweller *noun*
dwell on think or talk about something for a long time.

dwelling *noun* a house etc. to live in.

dwindle *verb* (**dwindled, dwindling**) get smaller gradually.

dye *verb* (**dyed, dyeing**) colour something by putting it into a liquid. **dyer** *noun*

dye *noun* a substance used to dye things.

dyke *noun* a dike.

dynamic *adjective* **1** energetic; active. **2** changing.
dynamically *adverb* [from Greek dynamis = power]

dynamite *noun* **1** a powerful explosive. **2** something likely to make people very excited or angry. [same origin as *dynamic*]

dynamo *noun* (*plural* **dynamos**) a machine that makes electricity.

dynasty (*say* **din**-a-stee) *noun* (*plural* **dynasties**) a succession of rulers all from the same family. **dynastic** *adjective* [same origin as *dynamic*]

dys- *prefix* bad; difficult. [from Greek]

dysentery (*say* **dis**-en-tree) *noun* a disease causing severe diarrhoea. [from *dys-*, + Greek *entera* = bowels]

dysfunctional *adjective* not functioning normally.

dyslexia (*say* dis-**leks**-ee-a) *noun* unusually great difficulty in being able to read and spell. **dyslexic** *adjective* [from *dys-*, + Greek *lexis* = speech]

dyspepsia (*say* dis-**pep**-see-a) *noun* indigestion. **dyspeptic** *adjective* [from *dys-*, + Greek *peptikos* = able to digest]

dysphemism *noun* a harsh or offensive word or expression, the opposite of euphemism. *Murder house is a dysphemism for dentist.*

dystrophy (*say* **dis**-trof-ee) *noun* a disease that weakens the muscles. [from *dys-*, + Greek *-trophia* = nourishment]

Ee

E. *abbreviation* east; eastern.

e-[1] *prefix* see **ex-**.

e-[2] *prefix* short for *electronic*, as in *e-mail, e-banking.*

each *adjective & pronoun* every; every one, *each child; each of you.*

eager *adjective* strongly wanting to do something; enthusiastic. **eagerly** *adverb*, **eagerness** *noun*

eagle *noun* a large bird of prey with very strong sight.

E & OE *abbreviation* errors and omissions excepted.

ear[1] *noun* **1** the organ of the body that is used for hearing. **2** hearing ability, *She has a good ear for music.*

ear[2] *noun* the spike of seeds at the top of a stalk of corn.

earache *noun* pain in the ear.

earbash *verb* (*NZ*) to talk at length to a person. **earbashing** *noun*

eardrum *noun* a membrane in the ear that vibrates when sounds reach it.

earl *noun* a British nobleman. **earldom** *noun*

early *adjective & adverb* (**earlier**, **earliest**) **1** before the usual or expected time. **2** near the beginning, *early in the book.* **earliness** *noun*

earmark *verb* put aside for a particular purpose. [from the custom of marking an animal's ear to identify it]

earn *verb* get something by working or in return for what you have done.

earnest *adjective* showing serious feelings or intentions. **earnestly** *adverb*, **earnestness** *noun*

earnings *plural noun* money earned.

earphone *noun* a listening device that fits over the ear.

earring *noun* an ornament worn on the ear.

earshot *noun* the distance within which a sound can be heard.

eartag *noun* (*NZ*) an identity tag attached to the ear of a farm animal.

earth *noun* **1** the planet (*Earth*) that we live on. **2** its surface; the ground; soil. **3** connection to the ground to complete an electrical circuit.

earth *verb* connect an electrical circuit to the ground.

earthenware *noun* pottery made of coarse baked clay.

earthly *adjective* of this earth or our life on it.

earthquake *noun* a violent movement of part of the earth's surface.

earthworm *noun* a worm that lives in the soil.

earthy *adjective* like earth or soil.

earwig *noun* a crawling insect with pincers at the end of its body.

ease *noun* freedom from trouble or effort or pain.

ease *verb* (**eased**, **easing**) **1** make less painful or less tight or troublesome. **2** move gently or gradually, *ease it in.* **3** become less severe, *The pressure eased.*

easel *noun* a stand for supporting a blackboard or a painting. [from Dutch *ezel* = donkey (which carries a load)]

easily *adverb* **1** without difficulty; with ease. **2** by far, *easily the best.* **3** very likely, *He could easily be lying.*

east *noun* **1** the direction where the sun rises. **2** the eastern part of a country, city, etc. **the East** regions and countries to the east of Europe, Asian countries.

east *adjective & adverb* towards or in the east; coming from the east. **easterly** *adjective*, **eastern** *adjective*, **easterner** *noun*, **easternmost** *adjective*

Easter *noun* the Sunday (in March or April) when Christians commemorate the resurrection of Christ; the days around it.

eastward *adjective & adverb* towards the east. **eastwards** *adverb*

easy *adjective* (**easier**, **easiest**) able to be done or used or understood without trouble. **easiness** *noun*
easy chair a comfortable armchair.

easy *adverb* in an easy way; with ease; comfortably, *Take it easy!*

eat *verb* (**ate**, **eaten**, **eating**) **1** chew and swallow as food. **2** have a meal, *When do we eat?* **3** use up; destroy gradually, *Extra expenses ate up our savings.*

eatable *adjective* fit to be eaten.

eau-de-Cologne (*say* oh-de-kol-**ohn**) *noun* a perfume first made at Cologne.

eaves *plural noun* the overhanging edges of a roof.

eavesdrop *verb* (**eavesdropped, eavesdropping**) listen secretly to a private conversation. **eavesdropper** *noun* (as if outside a wall, where water drops from the eaves]

ebb *noun* **1** the movement of the tide when it is going out, away from the land. **2** a low point, *Our courage was at a low ebb.*

ebb *verb* **1** flow away from the land. **2** weaken; become less, *strength ebbed.*

ebony *noun* a hard black wood.

eccentric (*say* ik-**sen**-trik) *adjective* behaving strangely. **eccentrically** *adverb*, **eccentricity** (*say* ek-sen-**triss**-it-ee) *noun* [from Greek *ekkentros* = away from the centre]

ecclesiastical (*say* ik-lee-zee-**ast**-ik-al) *adjective* of the Church or the clergy. [from Greek *ekklesia* church]

echidna (*say* ik-**id**-na) the Australian spiny ant-eater.

echo *noun* (*plural* **echoes**) a sound that is heard again as it is reflected off something.

echo *verb* (**echoed, echoing**) **1** make an echo. **2** repeat a sound or saying.

éclair (*say* ay-**klair**) *noun* a finger-shaped cake of pastry with a creamy filling.

eclipse *noun* the blocking of the sun's or moon's light when the moon or the earth is in the way.

eclipse *verb* (**eclipsed, eclipsing**) **1** block the light and cause an eclipse. **2** outshine, seem better or more important, *Her performance eclipsed all the others.*

ecobach *noun* a cottage or holiday house built with sustainable materials and on sustainable principles using, for example, solar or wind power.

ecology (*say* ee-**kol**-o-jee) *noun* the study of living things in relation to each other and to where they live. **ecological** *adjective*, **ecologically** *adverb*, **ecologist** *noun* [from Greek *oikos* = house, + *-logy*]

economic (*say* ee-kon-**om**-ik) *adjective* of economy or economics.

economical *adjective* using as little as possible. **economically** *adverb*

economics *noun* the study of how money is used and how goods and services are provided and used. **economist** *noun*

economise *verb* (**economised, economising**) be economical; use or spend less.

economy *noun* (*plural* **economies**) **1** a country's or household's income (e.g. from what it sells or earns) and the way this is spent (e.g. on goods and services). **2** being economical. **3** a saving, *We made economies.* [from Greek *oikos* = house, + *-nomia* = management]

ecotourism (*say* **ee**-koh-) *noun* **1** tourism carried out in a way that no environmental damage occurs. **2** tourism designed to feature places of great ecological interest, such as unusual ecosystems, the habitats of rare species, etc. **ecotourist** *noun*

ecowhare *noun* a house or lodge built on sustainable principles and using sustainable materials and processes, for example, solar or wind power.

ecstasy (*say* **ek**-sta-see) *noun* a feeling of great delight. **ecstatic** (*say* ik-**stat**-ik) *adjective*, **ecstatically** *adverb* [from Greek, = standing outside yourself]

eczema (*say* **eks**-im-a) *noun* a skin disease causing rough itching patches.

ed. *abbreviation* edition; editor; edited by.

eddy *noun* (*plural* **eddies**) a swirling patch of water or air or smoke etc.

eddy *verb* (**eddied, eddying**) swirl.

edge *noun* **1** the part along the side or end of something. **2** the sharp part of a knife or axe or other cutting-instrument.
be on edge be tense and irritable.

edge *verb* (**edged, edging**) **1** be the edge or border of something. **2** put a border on. **3** move gradually, *He edged away.*

edger *noun* a tool for trimming the edges of lawns etc.

edgeways *adverb* with the edge forwards or outwards.

edgy *adjective* tense and irritable. **edginess** *noun*

edible *adjective* suitable for eating, not poisonous, edible fruits.

edict (*say* **ee**-dikt) *noun* an official command. [from e-, Latin *dictum* = said]

edifice (*say* **ed**-if-iss) *noun* a large building.

edify *verb* (**edified, edifying**) be an improving influence on a person's mind. **edification** *noun*

edit *verb* (**edited, editing**) **1** be the editor of a newspaper or other publication. **2** make written material ready for printing or publishing. **3** choose and put the parts of a film or tape-recording etc. into order.

edition *noun* **1** the form in which something is published, *a paperback edition.* **2** all the copies of a book etc. issued at the same time, *the first edition.*

editor *noun* **1** the person in charge of a newspaper or a section of it. **2** a person who edits something.

editorial *adjective* of editing or editors.

editorial *noun* a newspaper article giving the editor's comments on something.

educate *verb* (**educated**, **educating**) provide with education. **educative** *adjective*, **educator** *noun* [from Latin *educare* = bring up, train]

education *noun* the process of training people's minds and abilities so that they acquire knowledge and develop skills. **educational** *adjective*, **educationally** *adverb*, **educationist** *noun*

eel *noun* a long fish that looks like a snake.

EEO *abbreviation* Equal Employment Opportunities.

eerie *adjective* (**eerier**, **eeriest**) strange in a frightening or mysterious way. **eerily** *adverb*, **eeriness** *noun*

EEZ *abbreviation* (*NZ*) exclusive economic zone.

ef- *prefix* see **ex-**.

efface *verb* (**effaced**, **effacing**) wipe or rub out. **effacement** *noun*

effect *noun* **1** a change produced by an action or cause; a result. **2** an impression produced, *a cheerful effect.*

effect *verb* cause; produce, *We want to effect a change.* [from *ef-*, + Latin *-fectum* = done]

USAGE Do not confuse with *affect*.

effective *adjective* producing an effect; impressive. **effectively** *adverb*, **effectiveness** *noun*

effectual *adjective* producing the result desired. **effectually** *adverb*

effeminate *adjective* (of a man) having qualities that are thought to be feminine. **effeminacy** *noun*

effervesce (*say* ef-er-**vess**) *verb* (**effervesced**, **effervescing**) give off bubbles of gas; fizz. **effervescent** *adjective*, **effervescence** *noun* [from Latin, = bubble over (compare *fervent*)]

efficacious (*say* ef-ik-**ay**-shus) *adjective* able to produce the result desired. **efficacy** (*say* **ef**-ik-a-see) *noun*

efficient *adjective* doing work well; effective. **efficiently** *adverb*, **efficiency** *noun* [same origin as *effect*]

effigy *noun* (*plural* **effigies**) a model or sculptured figure.

effort *noun* **1** the use of energy; the energy used. **2** something difficult or tiring. **3** an attempt, *This painting is a good effort.*

effortless *adjective* done with little or no effort. **effortlessly** *adverb*

effusive *adjective* making a great show of affection or enthusiasm. **effusively** *adverb*, **effusiveness** *noun*

EFL *abbreviation* English as a Foreign Language.

EFTPOS *abbreviation* electronic funds transfer at point of sale.

e.g. *abbreviation* for example. [short for Latin *exempli gratia* = for the sake of an example]

egalitarian (*say* ig-al-it-**air**-ee-an) *adjective* believing that everybody is equal and that nobody should be given special privileges. [from French *égal* = equal]

egg[1] *noun* **1** a more or less round object produced by the female of birds, fishes, reptiles, and insects, which may develop into a new individual if fertilised. **2** a hen's or duck's egg used as food.

egg[2] *verb* encourage with taunts or dares etc., *We egged him on.*

eggplant *noun* a plant with dark-purple fruit (*aubergine*) used as a vegetable.

ego (*say* **eeg**-oh) *noun* (*plural* **egos**) a person's self or self-respect. [Latin, = I]

egotist (*say* **eg**-oh-tist) *noun* a conceited person who is always talking about himself or herself. **egotism** *noun*, **egotistic** *adjective*

egress *noun* **1** an action of leaving. **2** an exit way.

eh *interjection* (*informal*) **1** asking for something to be said again. **2** inviting agreement, *quick thinking, eh?*

e hoa *interjection* a form of address similar to 'mate', *bad luck, e hoa!* [Māori]

eiderdown *noun* a quilt stuffed with soft material. [originally the soft down of the *eider*, a kind of Arctic duck]

eight *noun & adjective* the number 8; one more than seven. **eighth** *adjective & noun*

eighteen *noun & adjective* the number 18; one more than seventeen. **eighteenth** *adjective & noun*

eighty *noun & adjective* (*plural* **eighties**) the number 80; eight times ten. **eightieth** *adjective & noun*

either *adjective & pronoun* **1** one or the other of two, *Either team can win; either of them.* **2** both of two, *There are fields on either side of the river.*

either *adverb* also; similarly, *If you won't go, I won't either.*

either *conjunction* (used with *or*) the first of two possibilities, *He is either ill or drunk. Either come right in or go away.*

eject *verb* **1** send out forcefully. **2** expel; compel to leave. **ejection** *noun*, **ejector** *noun* [from *e-*, + Latin *-jectum* = thrown]

eke (*say* eek) *verb* (**eked**, **eking**) **eke out** manage to make something enough.

elaborate (*say* il-**ab**-er-at) *adjective* having many parts or details; complicated. **elaborately** *adverb*, **elaborateness** *noun*

elaborate (*say* il-**ab**-er-ayt) *verb* (**elaborated**, **elaborating**) describe or work out in detail. **elaboration** *noun* [from e-, + Latin *laborare* = to work]

elan *noun* style or dash.

elapse *verb* (**elapsed**, **elapsing**) (of time) pass. [from *e*-, + Latin *lapsum* slipped]

elastic *noun* cord or material woven with strands of rubber etc. so that it can stretch.

elastic *adjective* able to be stretched or squeezed and then go back to its original length or shape. **elasticity** *noun*

elated *adjective* with raised spirits, feeling very pleased. **elation** *noun* [from *e*-, + Latin *latum* = carried]

elbow *noun* the joint in the middle of the arm.

elbow *verb* push with the elbow.

elder[1] *adjective* older, *my elder brother.*

elder[1] *noun* **1** an older person, *Respect your elders!* **2** an official in certain Churches. **3** an older influential member of a tribe; a kaumātua. [an old form of *older*]

elder[2] *noun* a tree with white flowers and black berries. **elderberry** *noun*

elderly *adjective* rather old.

eldest *adjective* oldest. [an old form of *oldest*]

elect *verb* **1** choose by voting. **2** choose to do something; decide. [from *e*-, + Latin *lectum* = chosen]

election *noun* electing; the process of electing Members of Parliament.

elector *noun* a person who has the right to vote in an election. **electoral** *adjective*

electorate *noun* **1** all the electors. **2** (*NZ*) the area represented by a Member of Parliament.
electorate vote (*NZ*) one of the two votes a person casts in a general election, for an MP to represent the voter's electorate. (Compare *list vote.*)

electric *adjective* **1** of or worked by electricity. **2** causing sudden excitement, *The news had an electric effect.* **electrical** *adjective*, **electrically** *adverb* [from Greek *elektron* = amber (which is easily given a charge of static electricity)]

electrician *noun* a person whose job is to deal with electrical equipment.

electricity *noun* a form of energy carried by certain particles of matter (electrons and protons), used for lighting and heating and for making machines work.

electrify *verb* (**electrified**, **electrifying**) **1** give an electric charge to something. **2** supply with electric power; cause to work with electricity. **3** thrill with sudden excitement. **electrification** *noun*

electro- *prefix* of or using electricity.

electrocute *verb* (**electrocuted**, **electrocuting**) kill by electricity. **electrocution** *noun*

electrode *noun* a solid conductor through which electricity enters or leaves a vacuum tube. [from *electro*-, + Greek *hodos* = way]

electromagnet *noun* a magnet worked by electricity. **electromagnetic** *adjective*

electron *noun* a particle of matter with a negative electric charge. [see *electric*]

electronic *adjective* **1** (of a device) having components such as microchips and transistors that control electric currents. **2** (of music) produced by electronic instruments. **3** of or concerning electrons or electronics, *electronic engineering.* **4** carried out using a computer, especially over a network, *electronic banking.* **electronically** *adverb*
electronic mail 1 the sending of messages and documents from one computer to another. **2** the messages sent in this way.

electronics *noun* the use or study of electronic devices.

elegant *adjective* graceful and dignified. **elegantly** *adverb*, **elegance** *noun*

elegy (*say* **el**-ij-ee) *noun* (*plural* **elegies**) a sorrowful or serious poem.

element *noun* **1** each of the parts that make up a whole thing. **2** each of about 100 substances composed of atoms that have the same number of protons. **3** a basic or elementary principle, *the elements of algebra.* **4** a wire or coil that gives out heat in an electric heater or stove etc. **5** a suitable or satisfying environment, *Water is a fish's element.*
the elements the forces of weather, such as rain, wind, and cold.

elementary *adjective* dealing with the simplest stages of something; easy.

elephant *noun* a very large animal with a trunk and tusks.
elephant fish a large silvery fish with a bulge on its snout. [from Greek *elephas* = ivory (the material of its tusks)]

elephantine (*say* el-if-**ant**-I'n) *adjective* very large; clumsy.

elevate *verb* (**elevated**, **elevating**) lift up; put high up. **elevation** *noun* [from *e*-, + Latin *levare* = to lift]

elevator *noun* **1** something that raises things. **2** a lift.

eleven *adjective & noun* the number 11; one more than ten. **eleventh** *adjective & noun*

elf *noun* (*plural* **elves**) (in fairy-tales) a small being with magic powers. **elfin** *adjective*

elicit (*say* ill-**iss**-it) *verb* draw out information by reasoning or questioning.

eligible (*say* **el**-ij-ib-ul) *adjective* qualified or suitable for something. **eligibility** *noun*

eliminate *verb* (**eliminated**, **eliminating**) get rid of; remove. **elimination** *noun* [from Latin *e-* = out, + *limen* = entrance]

elision (*say* il-**lizh**-on) *noun* omitting part of a word in pronouncing it, e.g. in saying *I'm* for *I am*.

élite (*say* ay-**leet**) *noun* a group of people given privileges which are not given to others. [from Old French *élit* = chosen]

elixir (*say* il-**iks**-er) *noun* a sweetened and flavoured liquid medicine. [from Arabic *al-iksir* = substance that would cure illness and change metals into gold]

Elizabethan (*say* il-iz-a-**beeth**-an) *adjective* of the time of Queen Elizabeth I (1558–1603). **Elizabethan** *noun*

elk *noun* a large kind of deer.

ellipse (*say* il-**ips**) *noun* an oval shape.

elliptical (*say* il-**ip**-tik-al) *adjective* **1** shaped like an ellipse. **2** with some words omitted, *an elliptical phrase*. **elliptically** *adverb*

elm *noun* a tall tree with rough leaves.

El Niño (*say* el-**nee**-nyoh) a warming of Pacific Ocean currents causing unusual weather patterns, including drier and windier conditions than normal in New Zealand. [from Spanish *El Niño de Navidad* = the child of Christmas (roughly the time when this phenomenon occurs)]

elocution (*say* el-o-**kew**-shon) *noun* speaking clearly. [same origin as *eloquent*]

elongated *adjective* made longer; lengthened. **elongation** *noun*

elope *verb* (**eloped**, **eloping**) run away secretly with a lover to get married. **elopement** *noun*

eloquent *adjective* speaking fluently and expressing ideas vividly. **eloquently** *adverb*, **eloquence** *noun* [from *e-*, + Latin *loqui* = speak]

else *adverb* **1** besides; other, *Nobody else knows*. **2** otherwise; if not, *Run or else you'll be late*.

elsewhere *adverb* somewhere else.

elucidate (*say* il-**oo**-sid-ayt) *verb* (**elucidated**, **elucidating**) make something clear by explaining it. **elucidation** *noun* [compare *lucid*]

elude (*say* il-**ood**) *verb* (**eluded**, **eluding**) avoid being caught by someone, *The deer eluded the hunter*. **elusive** *adjective*

elver *noun* a young eel.

em- *prefix* see **en-**.

emaciated (*say* im-**ay**-see-ay-tid) *adjective* very thin from illness or starvation. **emaciation** *noun*

e-mail *noun* (also **email**) short for **electronic mail**.

e-mail *verb* (also **email**) send e-mail to (someone); send (a message) by e-mail.

emanate (*say* **em**-an-ayt) *verb* (**emanated**, **emanating**) come from a source.

emancipate (*say* im-**an**-sip-ayt) *verb* (**emancipated**, **emancipating**) set free from slavery or other restraints. **emancipation** *noun*

embalm *verb* preserve a corpse from decay by using spices or chemicals.

embankment *noun* a bank of earth or stone built to retain water, to support a road or railway, or to provide seating or shelter.

embargo *noun* (*plural* **embargoes**) a ban. [from Spanish *embargar* = restrain]

embark *verb* put or go on board a ship or aircraft. **embarkation** *noun*
embark on begin, *They embarked on a dangerous exercise*.

embarrass *verb* make someone feel awkward or ashamed. **embarrassment** *noun*

embassy *noun* (*plural* **embassies**) **1** an ambassador and his or her staff. **2** the building where they work.

embed *verb* (**embedded**, **embedding**) fix firmly in something solid.

embellish *verb* ornament something; add details to it. **embellishment** *noun*

embers *plural noun* small pieces of glowing coal or wood in a dying fire.

embezzle *verb* (**embezzled**, **embezzling**) take dishonestly money that was left in your care. **embezzlement** *noun*

emblazon *verb* ornament with heraldic or other emblems.

emblem *noun* a symbol; a device representing something, *The silver fern is a New Zealand emblem*. **emblematic** *adjective*

embody *verb* (**embodied**, **embodying**) **1** express principles or ideas in a visible form, *The house embodies our idea of a modern home*. **2** incorporate; include, *Parts of the old treaty are embodied in the new one*. **embodiment** *noun*

emboss *verb* decorate with a raised design.

embrace *verb* (**embraced**, **embracing**) hold closely in your arms.

embrace *noun* embracing; a hug. [from *em-*, + Latin *bracchium* = an arm]

embrocation *noun* a lotion for rubbing on parts of the body that ache.

embroider *verb* **1** ornament cloth with needlework. **2** add made-up details to a story to make it more interesting. **embroidery** *noun*

embroil *verb* involve in an argument or quarrel.

embryo (*say* **em**-bree-oh) *noun* (*plural* **embryos**) **1** an animal in the early stage of its development, before it hatches or is born (in human beings, in the first eight weeks after fertilisation). **2** anything in its earliest stages of development. **embryonic** (*say* em-bree-**on**-ik) *adjective* [from *em-*, + Greek *bryein* = grow]

emerald *noun* **1** a bright-green precious stone. **2** its colour.

emerge *verb* (**emerged**, **emerging**) come out; appear. **emergence** *noun*, **emergent** *adjective*

emergency *noun* (*plural* **emergencies**) a sudden serious happening needing prompt action.

emery-paper *noun* paper with a gritty coating like sandpaper.

emetic (*say* im-**et**-ik) *noun* a medicine used to make a person vomit.

emigrate *verb* (**emigrated**, **emigrating**) leave your own country and go and live in another. **emigration** *noun*, **emigrant** *noun* [from *e-* + migrate]

USAGE People are *emigrants* from the country they leave and *immigrants* in the country where they settle.

eminence *noun* **1** being eminent; distinction. **2** a piece of ground; a hill.
His Eminence a cardinal's title.

eminent *adjective* famous; distinguished; outstanding. **eminently** *adverb*

emir (*say* em-**eer**) *noun* a Muslim ruler. [from Arabic *amir* = ruler]

emit *verb* (**emitted**, **emitting**) send out (light, heat, fumes, etc.). **emission** *noun*, **emitter** *noun* [from *e-*, + Latin *mittere* = send]

emolument (*say* im-**ol**-yoo-ment) *noun* payment for work; a salary.

emoticon *noun* a symbol showing a smile, a frown or another facial expression that is made from keyboard letters. *☺ and (^-^) are emoticons.*

emotion *noun* a strong feeling in the mind, such as love or hate. **emotional** *adjective*, **emotionally** *adverb*

emotive *adjective* causing emotion.

empathy *noun* identifying yourself mentally with another person and understanding him or her. [from *em-*, + Greek *pathos* = feeling]

emperor *noun* a man who rules an empire. **emperor penguin** the largest kind of penguin.

emphasis (*say* **em**-fa-sis) *noun* special importance given to something.

emphasise *verb* (**emphasised**, **emphasising**) put emphasis on something.

emphatic (*say* im-**fat**-ik) *adjective* using emphasis. **emphatically** *adverb*

emphysema (*say* em-fi-**seem**-a) *noun* a condition that makes it hard to breathe.

empire *noun* **1** a group of countries controlled by one person or government. **2** a set of shops or firms under one control.

employ *verb* **1** pay a person to work for you. **2** make use of, *Our doctor employs the most modern methods.* **employer** *noun*, **employment** *noun*

employee *noun* a person employed by someone (who is the *employer*).

emporium (*say* em-**por**-ee-um) *noun* a large shop.

empower *verb* give someone the power to do something; authorise.

empress *noun* (*plural* **empresses**) **1** a woman who rules an empire. **2** an emperor's wife.

empty *adjective* **1** with nothing in it. **2** with nobody in it. **3** with no meaning or no effect, *empty promises.* **emptily** *adverb*, **emptiness** *noun*

empty *verb* (**emptied**, **emptying**) make or become empty.

emu *noun* (*plural* **emus**) a large Australian bird rather like an ostrich.

emulate *verb* (**emulated**, **emulating**) try to do as well as someone or something, especially by imitating them, *He is emulating his father.* **emulation** *noun*

emulsion *noun* **1** a creamy or slightly oily liquid. **2** the coating on photographic film which is sensitive to light.

en- *prefix* (changing to **em-** before words beginning with *b*, *m*, or *p*) in; into; on. [from Latin or Greek, = in]

enable *verb* (**enabled**, **enabling**) give the means or ability to do something.

enact *verb* **1** make into a law by a formal process, *Parliament enacted new laws* *against drugs.* **2** perform, *enact a play.* **enactment** *noun*

enamel *noun* **1** a shiny substance for coating metal. **2** paint that dries hard and shiny. **3** the shiny surface of teeth.

enamel *verb* (**enamelled**, **enamelling**) coat or decorate with enamel.

enamoured (*say* in-**am**-erd) *adjective* in love with someone. [from *en-*, + French *amour* = love]

encamp *verb* settle in a camp.

encampment *noun* a camp.

encase *verb* (**encased**, **encasing**) enclose in a case.

enchant *verb* **1** put under a magic spell. **2** fill with intense delight. **enchanter** *noun*, **enchantment** *noun*, **enchantress** *noun*

encircle *verb* (**encircled**, **encircling**) surround. **encirclement** *noun*

enclose *verb* (**enclosed**, **enclosing**) **1** put a wall or fence round; shut in on all sides. **2** put into a box or envelope etc.

enclosure *noun* **1** enclosing. **2** an enclosed area. **3** something enclosed with a letter or parcel.

encompass *verb* **1** surround. **2** contain.

encore (*say* **on**-kor) *noun* an extra item performed at a concert etc. after previous items have been applauded. [French, = again]

encounter *verb* **1** meet someone unexpectedly. **2** experience, *We encountered some difficulties.*

encounter *noun* **1** an unexpected meeting. **2** a baffle.

encourage *verb* (**encouraged**, **encouraging**) **1** give confidence or hope; hearten. **2** try to persuade; urge. **3** stimulate; help to develop, *Encourage healthy eating.* **encouragement** *noun*

encroach *verb* intrude upon someone's rights; go further than the proper limits, *The extra work would encroach on their free time.* **encroachment** *noun*

encrust *verb* cover with a crust or layer. **encrustation** *noun*

encrypt *verb* convert (data) into code, to stop those not authorised having access to it. **encryption** *noun*

encumber *verb* be a burden to; hamper. **encumbrance** *noun*

encyclopedia *noun* a book or set of books containing all kinds of information. **encyclopedic** *adjective* [from Greek, = general education]

end *noun* **1** the last part of something. **2** the half of a sports pitch or court defended or occupied by one team or player. **3** destruction; death. **4** purpose, *She did it to gain her own ends.*

end *verb* bring or come to an end.

endanger *verb* cause danger to.

endear *verb* cause to be loved, *She endeared herself to us all.* **endearing** *adjective*

endeavour (*say* in-**dev**-er) *verb* attempt.

endeavour *noun* an attempt.

endemic (*say* en-**dem**-ik) *adjective* (of a disease) often found in a certain area or group of people. [from *en-*, + Greek *demos* = people]

ending *noun* the last part.

endless *adjective* **1** never stopping. **2** with the ends joined to make a continuous strip for use in machinery etc., *an endless belt.* **endlessly** *adverb*

endorse *verb* (**endorsed**, **endorsing**) **1** sign your name on the back of a cheque or document. **2** make an official entry on a licence about an offence committed by its holder. **3** confirm or give your approval to something. **endorsement** *noun* [from Latin *in dorsum* = on the back]

endow *verb* **1** provide a source of income to establish something, *She endowed a scholarship.* **2** provide with an ability or quality, *He was endowed with great talent.* **endowment** *noun*

endure *verb* (**endured**, **enduring**) **1** suffer or put up with pain or hardship etc. **2** continue to exist; last. **endurable** *adjective*, **endurance** *noun*

enemy *noun* (*plural* **enemies**) **1** one who hates and opposes or seeks to harm another. **2** a nation or army etc. at war with another.

energetic *adjective* full of energy. **energetically** *adverb*

energy *noun* **1** strength to do things, liveliness. **2** the ability of matter or radiation to do work, *electrical energy.* [from *en-*, + Greek *ergon* = work]

enfold *verb* **1** wrap up. **2** clasp.

enforce *verb* (**enforced**, **enforcing**) compel people to obey a law or rule. **enforcement** *noun*, **enforceable** *adjective*

enfranchise *verb* (**enfranchised**, **enfranchising**) give the right to vote in elections. **enfranchisement** *noun*

engage *verb* (**engaged**, **engaging**) **1** arrange to employ or use, *Engage a typist.* **2** occupy the attention of, *They engaged her in conversation.* **3** promise. **4** begin a battle with, *We engaged the enemy.*

engaged *adjective* **1** having promised to marry somebody. **2** in use; occupied.

engagement *noun* **1** engaging something. **2** a promise to marry somebody. **3** an arrangement to meet somebody or do something. **4** a battle.

engaging *adjective* attractive; charming.

engine *noun* **1** a machine that provides power. **2** a vehicle that pulls a railway train, a locomotive. [from Latin *ingenium* = clever invention (compare ingenious)]

engineer *noun* an expert in engineering. **engineer** *verb* plan and construct or cause to happen, *He engineered a meeting between them.*

engineering *noun* the design and building or control of machinery or of structures such as roads and bridges.

English *adjective* **1** of England. **2** of English.

English *noun* the principal language of Britain, New Zealand, and other countries.

engrave *verb* (**engraved**, **engraving**) carve words or lines etc. on a surface. **engraver** *noun*, **engraving** *noun*

engross *verb* occupy a person's whole attention, *He was engrossed in his book.*

engulf *verb* flow over and cover; swamp.

enhance *verb* (**enhanced**, **enhancing**) make a thing more attractive; increase its value. **enhancement** *noun*

enigma (*say* in-**ig**-ma) *noun* something very difficult to understand; a puzzle.

enigmatic (*say* en-ig-**mat**-ik) *adjective* mysterious and puzzling. **enigmatically** *adverb*

enjoy *verb* get pleasure from something. **enjoyable** *adjective*, **enjoyment** *noun*

enlarge *verb* (**enlarged**, **enlarging**) make or become bigger. **enlargement** *noun*

enlighten *verb* give knowledge to a person, inform. **enlightenment** *noun*

enlist *verb* **1** join the armed forces. **2** obtain someone's support or services etc., *enlist their help.* **enlistment** *noun*

enliven *verb* make more lively. **enlivenment** *noun*

enmity *noun* being somebody's enemy; hostility.

enormity *noun* (*plural* **enormities**) **1** great wickedness, *the enormity of this crime.* **2** great size; hugeness, *the enormity of their task.*

> USAGE Many people regard the use of sense 2 as incorrect. It is best to avoid it and use *magnitude.*

enormous *adjective* very large; huge. **enormously** *adverb*, **enormousness** *noun* [from *e*-, + Latin *norma* = standard]

enough *adjective* (e.g. 'enough food'), *noun* (e.g. 'I have had enough'), & *adverb* (e.g. 'Are you warm enough?') as much or as many as necessary.

enquire *verb* (**enquired**, **enquiring**) ask, *He enquired if I was well.* **enquiry** *noun.*

> USAGE See the note under *inquire.*

enrage *verb* (**enraged**, **enraging**) make someone very angry.

enrapture *verb* (**enraptured**, **enrapturing**) fill someone with intense delight.

enrich *verb* make richer. **enrichment** *noun*

enrol *verb* (**enrolled**, **enrolling**) **1** become a member of a society etc. **2** make into a member. **enrolment** *noun*

ensconce *verb* (**ensconced**, **ensconcing**) settle comfortably, *ensconced in a chair.*

ensemble (*say* on-**sombl**) *noun* **1** a group of things that go together. **2** a group of musicians. [French]

enshrine *verb* (**enshrined**, **enshrining**) keep as if in a shrine, *His memory is enshrined in our hearts.*

ensign *noun* **1** a military or naval flag. **2** the lowest-ranking officer in the New Zealand navy. [the word is related to *insignia*]

enslave *verb* (**enslaved**, **enslaving**) make a slave of; force into slavery. **enslavement** *noun*

ensue *verb* (**ensued**, **ensuing**) happen afterwards or as a result.

ensuite (*say* on-**sweet**) *noun* a bathroom directly connected to a bedroom. [from French, = in sequence]

ensure *verb* (**ensured**, **ensuring**) make certain of; guarantee, *Good food will ensure good health.*

> USAGE Do not confuse with *insure.*

entail *verb* make necessary, involve, *This plan entails danger.* **entailment** *noun*

entangle *verb* (**entangled**, **entangling**) tangle. **entanglement** *noun*

entente (*say* on-**tont**) *noun* a friendly understanding between countries. [French]

enter *verb* **1** come in; go in. **2** put into a list or book. **3** register as a competitor.

enterprise *noun* **1** being enterprising; adventurous spirit. **2** an undertaking or project. **3** business activity, *private enterprise.*

enterprising *adjective* willing to undertake new or adventurous projects.

entertain *verb* **1** amuse. **2** have people as guests and give them food and drink. **3** consider, *He refused to entertain the idea.* **entertainer** *noun*

entertainment *noun* **1** entertaining; being entertained. **2** something performed before an audience to amuse or interest them.

enthral (*say* in-**thrawl**) *verb* (**enthralled, enthralling**) hold spellbound; fascinate.

enthusiasm *noun* a strong liking, interest, or excitement. **enthusiast** *noun*

enthusiastic *adjective* full of enthusiasm. **enthusiastically** *adverb*

entice *verb* (**enticed, enticing**) attract or persuade by offering something pleasant. **enticement** *noun*

entire *adjective* whole, complete. **entirely** *adverb*

entirety (*say* int-**I**-rit-ee) *noun* completeness; the total.
in its entirety in its complete form.

entitle *verb* (**entitled, entitling**) give the right to have something, *This coupon entitles you to a ticket.* **entitlement** *noun*

entitled *adjective* having as a title.

entomb (*say* in-**toom**) *verb* place in a tomb. **entombment** *noun*

entomology (*say* en-tom-**ol**-ojee) *noun* the study of insects. **entomologist** *noun* [from Greek *entomon* = insect, + *-logy*]

entrails *plural noun* the intestines.

entrance[1] (*say* **en**-trans) *noun* **1** the way into a place. **2** entering, *Her entrance is the signal for applause.* [from *enter*]

entrance[2] (*say* in-**trahns**) *verb* (**entranced, entrancing**) fill with intense delight; enchant. [from *en-* + *trance*]

entrant *noun* someone who enters for an examination or contest etc.

entreat *verb* request earnestly; beg.

entreaty *noun* an earnest request.

entrench *verb* **1** fix or establish firmly, *These ideas are entrenched in his mind.* **2** settle in a well-defended position. **entrenchment** *noun*

entrust *verb* place a person or thing in someone's care.

entry *noun* (*plural* **entries**) **1** an entrance. **2** something entered in a list or in a diary etc.

entwine *verb* (**entwined, entwining**) twine round.

enumerate *verb* (**enumerated, enumerating**) count; list one by one. [from *e-*, + Latin *numerare* = to number]

envelop (*say* en-**vel**-op) *verb* (**enveloped, enveloping**) wrap thoroughly.

envelope (*say* **en**-vel-ohp) *noun* a wrapper or covering, especially a folded cover for a letter.

enviable *adjective* likely to be envied.

envious *adjective* feeling envy. **enviously** *adverb*

environment *noun* **1** surroundings, especially as they affect people's lives. **2** (**the environment**) the natural world, as a whole or in a particular region, especially as affected by human activity, *We are polluting the environment.* **environmental** *adjective*

environmentalist *noun* a person who wishes to protect or improve the environment.

environs (*say* in-**vy**-ronz) *plural noun* the surrounding districts, *They all lived in the environs of Christchurch.*

envisage (*say* in-**viz**-ij) *verb* (**envisaged, envisaging**) picture in the mind; imagine as being possible, *It is difficult to envisage such a change.*

envoy *noun* an official representative, especially one sent by one government to another. [from French *envoyé* = sent]

envy *noun* **1** a feeling of discontent aroused when someone possesses things that others would like to have for themselves. **2** something causing this, *Their car is the envy of all their friends.*

envy *verb* (**envied, envying**) feel envy towards someone.

Enzed *noun* (*informal*) New Zealand.

enzyme *noun* a kind of substance that assists chemical processes.

epaulette (*say* **ep**-al-et) *noun* an ornamental flap on the shoulder of a coat.

ephemeral (*say* if-**em**-er-al) *adjective* lasting only a very short time.

epi- *prefix* on; above; in addition. [from Greek *epi* = on]

epic *noun* **1** a long poem or story about heroic deeds or history. **2** a spectacular film.

epicentre *noun* the point where an earthquake reaches the earth's surface.

epidemic *noun* an outbreak of a disease that spreads quickly among the people of an area. [from *epi-*, + Greek *demos* = people]

epidermis *noun* the outer layer of the skin. [from *epi-*, + Greek *derma* = skin]

epigram *noun* a short witty saying. [from *epi-* + *-gram*]

epilepsy *noun* a disease of the nervous system, causing convulsions. **epileptic** *adjective & noun*

epilogue (*say* **ep**-il-og) *noun* a short section at the end of a book or play etc. [from *epi-*, + Greek *logos* = speech]

epiphany *noun* discovery, enlightenment, or realisation.

Epiphany (*say* ip-**if**-an-ee) *noun* a Christian festival on 6 January, commemorating the showing of the infant Christ to the 'wise men' from the East.

episcopal (*say* ip-**iss**-kop-al) *adjective* **1** of a bishop or bishops. **2** (of a Church) governed by bishops.

episode *noun* **1** one event in a series of happenings. **2** one programme in a radio or television serial.

epistle *noun* a letter, especially one forming part of the New Testament.

epitaph *noun* words written on a tomb or describing a person who has died. [from *epi-*, + Greek *taphos* = tomb]

epithet *noun* an adjective; words expressing something special about a person or thing, e.g. 'the Great' in *Alfred the Great.*

epoch (*say* **ee**-pok) *noun* an era. **epoch-making** *adjective* very important.

equable (*say* **ek**-wa-bul) *adjective* steady; calm, *She has an equable manner.*

equal *adjective* **1** the same in amount, size, or value etc. **2** having the necessary strength, courage, or ability etc., *She was equal to the task.* **equally** *adverb*

equal *noun* a person or thing that is equal to another, *She has no equal.*

equal *verb* (**equalled**, **equalling**) be the same in amount, size, or value etc.

equalise *verb* (**equalised**, **equalising**) make things equal. **equalisation** *noun*

equality *noun* being equal.

equanimity (*say* ekwa-**nim**-it-ee) *noun* calmness of mind or temper. [from *equi-*, + Latin *animus* = mind]

equate *verb* (**equated**, **equating**) say things are equal or equivalent.

equation *noun* a statement that two amounts etc. are equal, e.g. $3 + 4 = 2 + 5$.

equator *noun* an imaginary line round the earth at an equal distance from the North and South Poles.

equatorial (*say* ek-wa-**tor**-ee-al) *adjective* of or near the equator.

equestrian (*say* ik-**wes**-tree-an) *adjective* of horse-riding. [from Latin *equus* = horse]

equi- *prefix* equal; equally. [from Latin *aequus* = equal]

equilateral (*say* ee-kwi-**lat**-er-al) *adjective* (of a triangle) having all sides equal. [from *equi-* + *lateral*]

equilibrium (*say* ee-kwi-**lib**-ree-um) *noun* balance, being balanced. [from *equi-*, + Latin *libra* = balance]

equine (*say* **ek**-wyn) *noun* of or like a horse. [from Latin *equus* = horse]

equinox (*say* **ek**-win-oks) *noun* (*plural* **equinoxes**) the time of year when day and night are equal in length (about 20 March in autumn, about 22 September in spring). **equinoctial** *adjective* [from *equi-*, + Latin *nox* = night]

equip *verb* (**equipped**, **equipping**) supply with what is needed.

equipment *noun* the things needed for a particular purpose.

equity (*say* **ek**-wit-ee) *noun* fairness, justice. **equitable** *adjective*

equivalent *adjective* equal in importance, meaning, value, etc. **equivalence** *noun* [from *equi-*, + Latin *valens* = worth]

equivocal (*say* ik-**wiv**-ok-al) *adjective* **1** able to be interpreted in two ways, ambiguous. **2** questionable, suspicious, *an equivocal character.* **equivocally** *adverb* [from *equi-*, + Latin *vocare* = to call]

era (*say* **eer**-a) *noun* a period of history.

eradicate *verb* (**eradicated**, **eradicating**) get rid of something; remove all traces of it. **eradication** *noun* [from Latin, = root out (*e-* = out, *radix* = a root)]

erase *verb* (**erased**, **erasing**) **1** rub out. **2** wipe out a recorded signal from a magnetic tape or disk. **eraser** *noun* [from *e-*, + Latin *rasum* = scraped]

erasure *noun* **1** erasing. **2** the place where something has been erased.

ere (*say as* air) *preposition & conjunction* (*old use*) before.

erect *adjective* standing on end; upright.

erect *verb* set up; build. **erection** *noun*, **erector** *noun*

ermine *noun* **1** a kind of weasel with brown fur that turns white in winter. **2** this valuable white fur.

erode *verb* (**eroded**, **eroding**) wear away, *Water eroded the rocks.* **erosion** *noun* [from *e-*, + Latin *rodere* = gnaw]

erotic *adjective* arousing sexual feelings. **erotically** *adverb*

err (*say* er) *verb* **1** make a mistake. (Compare *error.*) **2** do wrong. [from Latin *errare* = wander]

errand *noun* a short journey to take a message or fetch goods etc.

errant (*say* **e**-rant) *adjective* **1** misbehaving. **2** wandering; travelling in search of adventure, *a knight errant.* [same origin as *err*]

erratic (*say* ir-**at**-ik) *adjective* not reliable; not regular. **erratically** *adverb*

erroneous (*say* ir-**oh**-nee-us) *adjective* incorrect. **erroneously** *adverb*

error *noun* a mistake. [same origin as *err*]

erudite (*say* **e**-rew-dyt) *adjective* having great knowledge or learning. **eruditely** *adverb*, **erudition** *noun*

erupt *verb* **1** burst out. **2** (of a volcano) shoot out lava, eruption *noun* [from *e*-, + Latin *ruptum* = burst]

escalate *verb* (**escalated**, **escalating**) make or become greater or more serious, *The riots escalated into a war*. **escalation** *noun*

escalator *noun* a staircase with an endless line of steps moving up or down.

escapade (*say* eska-**payd**) *noun* a reckless adventure; a piece of mischief.

escape *verb* (**escaped**, **escaping**) **1** get yourself free; get out or away. **2** avoid something, *He escaped punishment*.

escape *noun* **1** escaping. **2** a way to escape.

escapist *noun* a person who likes to avoid thinking about serious matters by occupying his or her mind in entertainments, day-dreams, etc. **escapism** *noun*

escarpment *noun* a steep slope at the edge of some high level ground.

escort (*say* **ess**-kort) *noun* a person or group accompanying a person or thing, especially as a protection.

escort (*say* iss-**kort**) *verb* act as an escort to somebody or something.

Eskimo *noun* (*plural* **Eskimo** or **Eskimos**) a member of a people living near the Arctic coast of North America, Greenland, and Siberia.

> **Usage** In Canada the term *Inuit* is now preferred to *Eskimo*.

esp. *abbreviation* especially.

ESP *abbreviation* extra-sensory perception.

especial *adjective* special.

especially *adverb* specially; more than anything else.

espionage (*say* **ess**-pee-on-ahzh) *noun* spying. [from French *espion* = spy]

esplanade *noun* a flat open area used as a promenade, especially by the sea.

espresso *noun* (*plural* **espressos**) coffee made by forcing steam through ground coffee-beans. [Italian, = pressed out]

espy *verb* (**espied**, **espying**) catch sight of.

essay (*say* **ess**-ay) *noun* **1** a short piece of writing in prose. **2** an attempt.

essay (*say* ess-**ay**) *verb* attempt.

essence *noun* **1** the most important quality or element of something. **2** a concentrated liquid. [from Latin *esse* = to be]

essential *adjective* not able to be done without. **essentially** *adverb*

essential *noun* an essential thing.

est. *abbreviation* estimated.

establish *verb* **1** set up a business, government, or relationship etc. on a firm basis. **2** show to be true; prove, *He established his innocence*.

establishment *noun* **1** establishing something. **2** a business firm or other institution.
the Establishment people who are established in positions of power and influence.

estate *noun* **1** an area of land with a set of houses or factories on it. **2** a large area of land owned by one person. **3** all that a person owns when he or she dies. **4** (*old use*) a condition or status, *the holy estate of matrimony*.
estate agent a land agent, a person whose business is selling or letting houses and land.

esteem *verb* think that a person or thing is excellent.

esteem *noun* respect and admiration. [the word is related to *estimate*]

ester *noun* a kind of chemical compound.

estimable *adjective* worthy of esteem.

estimate (*say* **ess**-tim-at) *noun* a calculation or guess about amount or value.

estimate (*say* **ess**-tim-ayt) *verb* (**estimated**, **estimating**) make an estimate.
estimation *noun*

estranged *adjective* unfriendly after having been friendly or loving. **estrangement** *noun*

estuary (*say* **ess**-tew-er-ee) *noun* (*plural* **estuaries**) the mouth of a river where it reaches the sea and the tide flows in and out. [from Latin *aestus* = tide]

ETA *abbreviation* estimated time of arrival.

et al. *abbreviation* and others. [from Latin *et alia*]

etc. *abbreviation* (short for **et cetera**) and other similar things; and so on. [from Latin *et* = and, + *cetera* = the other things]

etch *verb* **1** engrave a picture with acid on a metal plate, especially for printing. **2** cut or impress deeply, *The scene is etched on my memory*. **etcher** *noun*

etching *noun* a picture printed from an etched metal plate.

eternal *adjective* lasting for ever; not ending or changing. **eternally** *adverb*, **eternity** *noun*

ether (*say* **ee**-ther) *noun* **1** a colourless liquid that evaporates easily into fumes that are used as an anaesthetic. **2** the upper air.

ethereal (*say* ith-**eer**-ee-al) *adjective* light and delicate. **ethereally** *adverb*

ethical (*say* **eth**-ik-al) *adjective* **1** of ethics. **2** morally right; honourable. **ethically** *adverb*

ethics (*say* **eth**-iks) *plural noun* standards of right behaviour; moral principles. [from Greek *ethos* = character]

ethnic *adjective* belonging to a particular racial group within a larger set of people. [from Greek *ethnos* = nation]

etiquette (*say* **et**-ik-et) *noun* the rules of correct behaviour.

etymology (*say* et-im-**ol**-oj-ee) *noun* (*plural* **etymologies**) **1** an account of the origin of a word and its meaning. **2** the study of the origins of words. **etymological** *adjective* [from Greek *etymon* = original word, + *-logy*]

eu- (*say* yoo) *prefix* well. [from Greek]

EU *abbreviation* European Union.

eucalyptus (*say* yoo-kal-**ip**-tus) *noun* (*plural* **eucalyptuses**) **1** a kind of evergreen tree. **2** a strong-smelling oil obtained from its leaves.

Eucharist (*say* **yoo**-ker-ist) *noun* the Christian sacrament in which bread and wine are consecrated and swallowed, commemorating the Last Supper of Christ and his disciples. [from Greek, = thanksgiving]

eulogy (*say* **yoo**-loj-ee) *noun* a piece of praise for a person or thing. [from *eu-*, + Greek *-logia* = speaking]

euphemism (*say* **yoo**-fim-izm) *noun* a mild word or phrase used instead of an offensive or frank one, *'To pass away' is a euphemism for 'to die'.* **euphemistic** *adjective*, **euphemistically** *adverb* [from *eu-*, + Greek *pheme* = speech]

euphonium (*say* yoof-**oh**-nee-um) *noun* a large brass musical instrument. [from *eu-*, + Greek *phone* = sound]

euphoria (*say* yoo-**for**-ee-a) *noun* a feeling of general happiness. [from *eu-*, + Greek *phoros* = bearing]

Eurasian *adjective* having European and Asian parents or ancestors. **Eurasian** *noun* [from *European* + *Asian*]

euro *noun* a unit of money in Europe.

European *adjective* of Europe or its people. **European** *noun*

euthanasia (*say* yooth-an-**ay**-zee-a) *noun* the act of causing somebody to die gently and without pain, especially when they are suffering from a painful incurable disease. [from *eu-*, + Greek *thanatos* = death]

evacuate *verb* (**evacuated**, **evacuating**) **1** move people away from a dangerous place. **2** make a thing empty of air or other contents. **evacuation** *noun* [from *e-*, + Latin *vacuus* = empty]

evacuee *noun* a person who has been evacuated.

evade *verb* (**evaded**, **evading**) avoid a person or thing by cleverness or trickery. [from *e-*, + Latin *vadere* = go]

evaluate *verb* (**evaluated**, **evaluating**) estimate the value of something; assess. **evaluation** *noun*

Evangelist *noun* any of the writers (Matthew, Mark, Luke, John) of the four Gospels.

evangelist *noun* a person who preaches the Christian faith enthusiastically. **evangelism** *noun*, **evangelical** *adjective* [from Greek, = announce good news (*eu* = well, *angelos* = messenger)]

evaporate *verb* (**evaporated**, **evaporating**) **1** change from liquid into steam or vapour. **2** cease to exist, *Their enthusiasm had evaporated.* **evaporation** *noun* [from *e-* = out, + Latin *vapor* = steam]

evasion *noun* **1** evading. **2** an evasive answer or excuse.

evasive *adjective* evading something; not frank or straightforward. **evasively** *adverb*, **evasiveness** *noun*

eve *noun* **1** the day or evening before an important day or event, *Christmas Eve.* **2** (*old use*) evening.

even[1] *adjective* **1** level; smooth; not varying. **2** calm; not easily upset, *an even temper.* **3** equal, *Our scores were even.* **4** able to be divided exactly by two, *Six and fourteen are even numbers.* (Compare *odd*.) **evenly** *adverb*, **evenness** *noun*

even[1] *verb* make or become even.

even[1] *adverb* (used to emphasise a word or statement) *She ran even faster.*
even so although that is correct.

even[2] *noun* (*old use*) evening.

evening *noun* the time at the end of the day before most people go to bed.

evensong *noun* the service of evening prayer in the Anglican Church.

event *noun* **1** something that happens, especially something important. **2** an item in a sports contest. [from *e-*, + Latin *ventum* = come]

eventful *adjective* full of happenings.

eventual *adjective* happening at last, *his eventual success.* **eventually** *adverb*

eventuality (*say* iv-en-tew-**al**-it-ee) *noun* (*plural* **eventualities**) something that may happen.

ever *adverb* **1** at any time, *the best thing I ever did.* **2** always, *ever hopeful.* **3** (*informal*, used for emphasis), *Why ever didn't you tell me?*

evergreen *adjective* having green leaves all the year. **evergreen** *noun*

everlasting *adjective* lasting for ever or for a very long time.

every *adjective* each without any exceptions, *We enjoyed every minute.*
every one each one, *Every one of them is growing.*
every other day or **week** etc., each alternate one; every second one.

everybody *pronoun* every person.

everyday *adjective* ordinary; usual, *everyday clothes.*

everyone *pronoun* everybody.

everything *pronoun* **1** all things; all. **2** the only or most important thing, *Beauty is not everything.*

everywhere *adverb* in every place.

evict *verb* make people move out from where they are living. **eviction** *noun* [from Latin *evictum* = expelled]

evidence *noun* **1** anything that gives people reason to believe something. **2** statements made or objects produced in a lawcourt to prove something.

evident *adjective* obvious; clearly seen. **evidently** *adverb*

evil *adjective* wicked; harmful. **evilly** *adverb*

evil *noun* something evil; a sin.

evoke *verb* (**evoked**, **evoking**) produce or inspire a memory or feelings etc., *The photographs evoked happy memories.* **evocation** *noun*, **evocative** *adjective* [from *e-* = out, + Latin *vocare* = call]

evolution (*say* ee-vol-**oo**-shon) *noun* **1** evolving; gradual change into something different. **2** the development of animals and plants from earlier or simpler forms. **evolutionary** *adjective*

evolve *verb* (**evolved**, **evolving**) develop gradually or naturally. [from *e-*,+ Latin *volvere* = to roll]

ewe (*say* yoo) *noun* a female sheep.

ewer (*say* **yoo**-er) *noun* a large water-jug.

ex- *prefix* (changing to **ef-** before words beginning with *f*; shortened to **e-** before many consonants) **1** out; away (as in *extract*). **2** up, upwards; thoroughly (as in *extol*). **3** formerly (as in *ex-president*). [from Latin *ex* = out of]

exacerbate (*say* eks-**ass**-er-bayt) *verb* (**exacerbated**, **exacerbating**) make a pain or disease or other problem worse.

exact *adjective* **1** correct. **2** clearly stated; giving all details, *exact instructions.* **exactly** *adverb*, **exactness** *noun*

exact *verb* insist on something and obtain it, *He exacted obedience from the recruits.* **exaction** *noun* [from *ex-* = out, + Latin *actum* = performed]

exacting *adjective* making great demands, *an exacting task.*

exactitude *noun* exactness.

exaggerate *verb* (**exaggerated**, **exaggerating**) make something seem bigger, better, or worse etc. than it really is. **exaggeration** *noun* [from *ex-* = upwards, + Latin *agger* = heap]

exalt (*say* ig-**zawlt**) *verb* **1** raise in rank or status etc. **2** praise highly. **3** delight; elate. **exaltation** *noun* [from *ex-* = up, + Latin *altus* = high]

exam *noun* (*informal*) an examination.

examination *noun* **1** a test of a person's knowledge or skill. **2** examining something; an inspection.

examine *verb* (**examined**, **examining**) **1** test a person's knowledge or skill. **2** inspect; look at something closely. **examiner** *noun*

examinee *noun* a person being tested in an examination.

example *noun* **1** anything that shows what others of the same kind are like or how they work. **2** a person or thing good enough to be worth imitating.

exasperate *verb* (**exasperated**, **exasperating**) annoy someone greatly. **exasperation** *noun* [from *ex-* = thoroughly, + Latin *asper* = rough]

excavate *verb* (**excavated**, **excavating**) dig out; uncover by digging. **excavation** *noun*, **excavator** *noun* [from *ex-* = out, + Latin *cavus* = hollow]

exceed *verb* **1** be greater than, surpass. **2** do more than you need or ought to do; go beyond a thing's limits. *He has exceeded his authority.* [from *ex-* = out, beyond, + Latin *cedere* = go]

exceedingly *adverb* very; extremely.

excel *verb* (**excelled**, **excelling**) be better than others at doing something. [from *ex-*, + Latin *celsus* = lofty]

Excellency *noun* the title of high officials such as ambassadors and Governors-General.

excellent *adjective* extremely good. **excellently** *adverb*, **excellence** *noun*

except *preposition* excluding; not including, *They all left except me.*

except *verb* exclude; leave out, *I blame you all, no one is excepted.* [from *ex-* = out, + Latin *-ceptum* = taken]

excepting *preposition* except.

exception *noun* **1** a person or thing that is left out or does not follow the general rule. **2** exclusion; excepting, *All were pardoned with the exception of traitors.*

take exception raise objections to something.

exceptional *adjective* **1** forming an excepton; very unusual. **2** outstandingly good. **exceptionally** *adverb*

excerpt (*say* **ek**-serpt) *noun* a passage taken from a book or speech or film etc.

excess *noun* (*plural* **excesses**) too much of something. [from *exceed*]

excessive *adjective* too much; too great. **excessively** *adverb*

exchange *verb* (**exchanged**, **exchanging**) give something and receive something else for it. **exchangeable** *adjective*

exchange *noun* **1** exchanging. **2** a place where things (especially stocks and shares) are bought and sold, *a stock exchange*. **3** a place where telephone lines are connected to each other when a call is made.
exchange rate the value of one currency in relation to that of another.

exchequer *noun* a national treasury into which public funds (such as taxes) are paid. [the word refers to the table, covered with a cloth divided into squares (a *chequered* pattern), on which the accounts of the Norman kings of England were kept by means of counters]

excise[1] (*say* **eks**-I'z) *noun* a tax charged on certain goods and licences etc. [from a Dutch word meaning 'tax']

excise[2] (*say* iks-**I'z**) *verb* (**excised**, **excising**) remove something by cutting it away, *The surgeon excised the tumour*. [from *ex-* = out, + Latin *caesum* = cut]

excitable *adjective* easily excited.

excite *verb* (**excited**, **exciting**) **1** rouse a person's feelings; make eager, *The thought of finding gold excited them*. **2** cause a feeling; arouse, *The invention excited great interest*. **excitedly** *adverb* [from *ex-* = out, + Latin *citare* = wake]

excitement *noun* a strong feeling of eagerness or pleasure.

exclaim *verb* shout or cry out in eagerness or surprise. [from *ex-* = out, + Latin *clamare* = cry]
exclamation *noun* **1** exclaiming. **2** a word or words exclaimed expressing joy or pain or surprise etc.
exclamation mark the punctuation mark placed after an exclamation.

exclude *verb* (**excluded**, **excluding**) **1** keep somebody or something out. **2** leave out, *Do not exclude the possibility of rain*. **exclusion** *noun* [from *ex-* = out, + Latin *claudere* = shut]

exclusive *adjective* **1** allowing only certain people to be members etc., *an exclusive club*. **2** not shared with others, *This newspaper has an exclusive report*. **exclusively** *adverb*, **exclusiveness** *noun*
exclusive economic zone (*NZ*) the area of sea extending 200 miles out from the coastline, in which fishing is controlled by a quota system and other regulations.
exclusive of excluding, not including, *This is the price exclusive of meals*. [same origin as *exclude*]

excommunicate *verb* (**excommunicated**, **excommunicating**) cut off a person from membership of a Church. **excommunication** *noun* [from Latin, = put out of the community]

excrement (*say* **eks**-krim-ent) *noun* waste matter excreted from the bowels, dung.

excrescence (*say* iks-**kress**-ens) *noun* **1** an outgrowth on a plant or animal's body. **2** an ugly addition or part. [from *ex-* = out, + Latin *crescens* = growing]

excrete *verb* (**excreted**, **excreting**) expel waste matter from the body. **excretion** *noun*, **excretory** *adjective* [from *ex-* = out, + Latin *cretum* = separated]

excruciating (*say* iks-**kroo**-shee-ayt-ing) *adjective* extremely painful; agonising. **excruciatingly** *adverb* [from *ex-* = thoroughly, + Latin *cruciatum* = tortured]

exculpate (*say* **eks**-kul-payt) *verb* (**exculpated**, **exculpating**) clear a person from blame. **exculpation** *noun* [from *ex-* = away, + Latin *culpa* = blame]

excursion *noun* a short journey made for pleasure. [from *ex-* = out, + Latin *cursus* = course]

excusable *adjective* able to be excused. **excusably** *adverb*

excuse (*say* iks-**kewz**) *verb* (**excused**, **excusing**) **1** forgive. **2** allow someone not to do something or to leave a room etc., *Please may I be excused swimming?*

excuse (*say* iks-**kewss**) *noun* a reason given to explain why something wrong has been done. [from *ex-* = away, + Latin *causa* = accusation]

execrable (*say* **eks**-ik-rab-ul) *adjective* very bad; abominable.

execute *verb* (**executed**, **executing**) **1** put someone to death as a punishment. **2** perform or produce something, *She executed the somersault perfectly*. **execution** *noun* [from *ex-* = out, + Latin *sequi* = follow]

executioner *noun* an official who executes a condemned person.

executive (*say* ig-**zek**-yoo-tiv) *noun* a senior person with authority in a business or government organisation.

executive *adjective* having the authority to carry out plans or laws.

executor (*say* ig-**zek**-yoo-ter) *noun* a person appointed to carry out the instructions in someone's will.

exemplary (*say* ig-**zem**-pler-ee) *adjective* very good; being an example to others, *His conduct was exemplary.*

exemplify *verb* (**exemplified**, **exemplifying**) be an example of something.

exempt *adjective* not having to do something that others have to do, *Charities are exempt from paying tax.*

exempt *verb* make someone or something exempt. **exemption** *noun* [from *ex-* = out, + Latin *emptum* = taken]

exercise *noun* **1** using your body to make it strong and healthy. **2** a piece of work done for practice.

exercise *verb* (**exercised**, **exercising**) **1** do exercises. **2** give exercise to an animal etc. **3** use, *exercise patience.* [from Latin *exercere* = keep someone working]

exert *verb* use power or influence etc., *He exerted all his strength.* **exertion** *noun*
exert yourself make an effort.

exhale *verb* (**exhaled**, **exhaling**) breathe out. **exhalation** *noun* [from *ex-*, + Latin *halare* = breathe]

exhaust *verb* **1** make somebody very tired. **2** use up something completely. **exhaustion** *noun*

exhaust *noun* **1** the waste gases or steam from an engine. **2** the pipe etc. through which they are sent out. [from *ex-* = out, + Latin *haustum* = drained]

exhaustive *adjective* thorough; trying everything possible. *We made an exhaustive search.* **exhaustively** *adverb*

exhibit *verb* (**exhibited**, **exhibiting**) show in public. **exhibitor** *noun*

exhibit *noun* something exhibited.

exhibition *noun* a collection of things arranged for people to look at.

exhibitionist *noun* a person who behaves in a way that is meant to attract attention. **exhibitionism** *noun*

exhilarate (*say* ig-**zil**-er-ayt) *verb* (**exhilarated**, **exhilarating**) make someone very happy; elate. **exhilaration** *noun* [from *ex-* = thoroughly, + Latin *hilaris* = cheerful (compare *hilarious*)]

exhort (*say* ig-**zort**) *verb* urge someone earnestly. **exhortation** *noun* [from *ex-*, + Latin *hortari* = encourage]

exhume (*say* ig-**zewm**) *verb* (**exhumed**, **exhuming**) dig up something that has been buried. **exhumation** *noun* [from *ex-* = out, + Latin *humare* = bury]

exile *verb* (**exiled**, **exiling**) banish.

exile *noun* **1** a banished person. **2** having to live away from your own country, *He was in exile for ten years.*

exist *verb* **1** have a place as part of what is real, *Do ghosts exist?* **2** stay alive, *We cannot exist without food.* **existence** *noun*, **existent** *adjective* [from *ex-*, + Latin *sistere* = stand]

exit *verb* he or she leaves the stage.

exit *noun* **1** the way out of a building. **2** going off the stage, *The actress made her exit.* [Latin, = he or she goes out]

ex-nuptial *adjective* that takes place or is born outside marriage.

exodus *noun* (*plural* **exoduses**) the departure of many people. [from Greek, = a way out (*ex* = out, *hodos* = way)]

exonerate *verb* (**exonerated**, **exonerating**) declare or prove that a person is not to blame for something. **exoneration** *noun* [from *ex-* = out, + Latin *oneris* = of a burden]

exorbitant *adjective* much too great; excessive, *exorbitant prices.* [from *ex-* = out, + Latin *orbita* = orbit]

exorcise *verb* (**exorcised**, **exorcising**) get rid of an evil spirit. **exorcism** *noun*, **exorcist** *noun*

exotic *adjective* **1** very unusual, *exotic clothes.* **2** from another part of the world, *exotic plants.* **exotically** *adverb* [from Greek *exo* = outside]

expand *verb* make or become larger or fuller. **expansion** *noun*, **expansive** *adjective* [from *ex-* = out, + Latin *pandere* = spread]

expanse *noun* a wide area.

expatriate (*say* eks-**pat**-ree-at) *noun* a person living away from his or her own country. [from *ex-* = away, + Latin *patria* = native land]

expect *verb* **1** think or believe that something will happen or that someone will come. **2** think that something ought to happen, *She expects obedience.* [from *ex-* = out, + Latin *spectare* = to look]

expectant *adjective* expecting something to happen; hopeful. **expectantly** *adverb*, **expectancy** *noun*
expectant mother a woman who is pregnant.

expectation *noun* **1** expecting something; being hopeful. **2** something you expect to happen or get.

expedient (*say* iks-**pee**-dee-ent) *adjective* **1** suitable, convenient. **2** useful and practical though perhaps unfair. **expediently** *adverb*, **expediency** *noun*

expedient *noun* a means of doing something, especially when in difficulty.

expedite (*say* **eks**-pid-dyt) *verb* (**expedited**, **expediting**) make something happen more quickly.

expedition *noun* **1** a journey made in order to do something. **2** speed; promptness. **expeditionary** *adjective*

expeditious (*say* eks-pid-**ish**-us) *adjective* quick and efficient. **expeditiously** *adverb*

expel *verb* (**expelled**, **expelling**) **1** send or force something out, *This fan expels stale air.* **2** make a person leave a school or country etc. **expulsion** *noun* [from *ex-* = out, + Latin *pellere* = drive]

expend *verb* spend; use up.

expendable *adjective* **1** able to be expended. **2** able to be sacrificed in order to gain something.

expenditure *noun* expending; the spending of money or effort etc.

expense *noun* the cost of doing something.

expensive *adjective* costing a lot. **expensively** *adverb*, **expensiveness** *noun*

experience *noun* **1** what you learn from doing or seeing things. **2** something that has happened to you.

experience *verb* (**experienced**, **experiencing**) have something happen to you. [same origin as *experiment*]

experienced *adjective* having great skill or knowledge from much experience.

experiment *noun* a test made in order to find out what happens or to prove something. **experimental** *adjective*, **experimentally** *adverb*

experiment *verb* carry out an experiment. **experimentation** *noun* [from Latin *experiri* = to test]

expert *noun* a person with great knowledge or skill in something.

expert *adjective* having great knowledge or skill. **expertly** *adverb*, **expertness** *noun*

expertise (*say* eks-per-**teez**) *noun* expert ability.

expiate (*say* **eks**-pee-ayt) *verb* (**expiated**, **expiating**) atone for; make amends for wrongdoing. **expiation** *noun*

expire *verb* (**expired**, **expiring**) **1** come to an end; stop being usable. *Your season ticket has expired.* **2** die. **3** breathe out air. **expiration** *noun*, **expiry** *noun* [from *ex-*, + Latin *spirare* = breathe]

explain *verb* **1** make something clear to somebody else; show its meaning. **2** account for something, *That explains his absence.* **explanation** *noun* [from *ex-*, + Latin *planare* = make level or plain]

explanatory (*say* iks-**plan**-at-er-ee) *adjective* giving an explanation.

explicit (*say* iks-**pliss**-it) *adjective* stated or stating something openly and exactly. (Compare *implicit.*) **explicitly** *adverb* [from Latin, = unfolded]

explode *verb* (**exploded**, **exploding**) **1** burst or suddenly release energy with a loud noise. **2** cause a bomb to go off. **3** increase suddenly or quickly. [from *ex-* = out, + Latin *plaudere* = clap the hands (originally said of the audience clapping or hissing to drive a player off the stage)]

exploit (*say* **eks**-ploit) *noun* a brave or exciting deed.

exploit (*say* iks-**ploit**) *verb* **1** use or develop resources. **2** use selfishly. **exploitation** *noun*

exploratory (*say* iks-**plorra**-ter-ee) *adjective* for the purpose of exploring.

explore *verb* (**explored**, **exploring**) **1** travel through a country etc. in order to learn about it. **2** examine something, investigate, *We explored the possibilities.* **exploration** *noun*, **explorer** *noun* [from Latin, = search out]

explosion *noun* **1** the exploding of a bomb etc.; the noise made by exploding. **2** a sudden great increase.

explosive *adjective* able to explode.

explosive *noun* an explosive substance.

exponent *noun* **1** a person who expounds something. **2** someone who uses a certain technique. **3** the raised number etc. written to the right of another (e.g. 3 in 2^3) showing how many times the first one is to be multiplied by itself.

exponential (*say* eks-po-**nen**-shal) *adjective* (of an increase) more and more rapid.

export *verb* send goods abroad to be sold. **exportation** *noun*, **exporter** *noun*

export *noun* **1** exporting things. **2** something exported. [from *ex-* = away, + Latin *portare* = carry]

expose *verb* (**exposed**, **exposing**) **1** reveal, uncover. **2** allow light to reach a photographic film so as to take a picture. **exposure** *noun* [from *ex-* = out, + Latin *positum* = put]

expostulate *verb* (**expostulated**, **expostulating**) make a protest. **expostulation** *noun*

expound *verb* explain in detail.

express *adjective* **1** going or sent quickly. **2** expressed; clearly stated, *This was done against my express orders.*

express *noun* (*plural* **expresses**) a fast train or bus that makes very few stops.

express *verb* **1** put ideas etc. into words; make your feelings known. **2** press or squeeze out, *Express the juice.*

expression *noun* **1** the look on a person's face that shows his or her feelings. **2** a word or phrase etc. **3** a way of speaking or of playing music etc. so as to show feeling for its meaning. **4** expressing, *this expression of opinion.*

expressive *adjective* full of expression.

expressly *adverb* **1** clearly; plainly, *This was expressly forbidden.* **2** specially, *designed expressly for children.*

expulsion *noun* expelling; being expelled. **expulsive** *adjective*

expunge *verb* (**expunged**, **expunging**) erase; wipe out.

exquisite (*say* **eks**-kwiz-it) *adjective* very beautiful. **exquisitely** *adverb* [from *ex-* = out, + Latin *quaesitum* = sought]

extemporise *verb* (**extemporised**, **extemporising**) speak or produce or do something without advance preparation. **extemporisation** *noun* [from Latin *ex tempore* = impromptu (literally 'out of the time')]

extend *verb* **1** stretch out. **2** make something become longer or larger. **3** offer; give, *Extend a warm welcome to our friends.* **extendible** *adjective.* **extensible** *adjective* **extended family** a family including relatives in addition to parents and children. [from *ex-* = out, + Latin *tendere* = stretch]

extension *noun* **1** extending; being extended. **2** something added on; an addition to a building. **3** one of a set of telephones in an office or house etc.

extensive *adjective* covering a large area or range, *extensive gardens.* **extensively** *adverb,* **extensiveness** *noun*

extent *noun* **1** the area or length over which something extends. **2** the amount, level, or scope of something, *the full extent of his power.*

extenuating *adjective* making a crime seem less great by providing a partial excuse, *There were extenuating circumstances.* **extenuation** *noun*

exterior *adjective* outer.

exterior *noun* the outside of something. [Latin, = further out]

exterminate *verb* (**exterminated**, **exterminating**) destroy or kill all the members or examples. **extermination** *noun,* **exterminator** *noun* [from *ex-* = out, +Latin *terminus* = boundary]

external *adjective* outside. **externally** *adverb*

extinct *adjective* **1** not existing any more, *The moa is an extinct bird,* **2** not burning; not active, *an extinct volcano.* [same origin as *extinguish*]

extinction *noun* **1** making or becoming extinct. **2** extinguishing; being extinguished.

extinguish *verb* **1** put out a fire or light. **2** put an end to; destroy, *Our hopes of victory were extinguished.* [from Latin *extinguere* = quench]

extinguisher *noun* a portable device for sending out water, chemicals, or gases to extinguish a fire.

extol *verb* (**extolled**, **extolling**) praise.

extort *verb* obtain something by force or threats. **extortion** *noun* [from *ex-* = out, + Latin *tortum* = twisted]

extortionate *adjective* charging or demanding far too much.

extra *adjective* additional; more than is usual, *extra strength.*

extra *adverb* more than usually, *extra strong.*

extra *noun* **1** an extra person or thing. **2** a person acting as part of a crowd in a movie. [Latin, = outside]

extra- *prefix* outside; beyond (as in *extraterrestrial*). [from Latin, = outside]

extract (*say* iks-**trakt**) *verb* take out; remove. **extractor** *noun*

extract (*say* **eks**-trakt) *noun* **1** a passage taken from a book, speech, movie, etc.; an excerpt. **2** a substance separated or obtained from another. [from *ex-* = out, + Latin *tractum* = pulled]

extraction *noun* **1** extracting. **2** descent; ancestry, *He is of Chinese extraction.*

extradite *verb* (**extradited**, **extraditing**) **1** hand over an accused person to the country where the crime was committed. **2** obtain such a person for trial or punishment. **extradition** (*say* eks-tra-**dish**-on) *noun* [from *ex-*, + Latin *tradere* = hand over]

extraneous (*say* iks-**tray**-nee-us) *adjective* **1** added from outside. **2** not belonging to the matter in hand; irrelevant.

extraordinary *adjective* very unusual or strange. **extraordinarily** *adverb*

extra-sensory *adjective* outside the range of the known human senses.

extravagant *adjective* spending or using too much. **extravagantly** *adverb,* **extravagance** *noun* [from *extra-*, + Latin *vagans* = wandering]

extravaganza *noun* a very spectacular show.

extreme *adjective* **1** very great or intense. *extreme cold.* **2** furthest away, *the extreme north.* **3** going to great lengths in actions or opinions; not moderate. **extremely** *adverb*

extreme *noun* **1** something extreme. **2** either end of something. [from Latin, = furthest outside]

extremist *noun* a person who holds extreme (not moderate) opinions in political or other matters.

extremity (*say* iks-**trem**-it-ee) *noun* (*plural* **extremities**) **1** an extreme point; the very end. **2** an extreme need or feeling of danger etc.

extricate (*say* **eks**-trik-ayt) *verb* (**extricated**, **extricating**) release from a difficult position. **extrication** *noun* [from *ex-*, + Latin *tricae* = entanglements]

extrovert *noun* a person who is generally friendly and likes company. (The opposite is *introvert*.) [from *extro-* = outside, + Latin *vertere* = to turn]

extrude *verb* (**extruded**, **extruding**) push or squeeze out. **extrusion** *noun* [from *ex-*, + Latin *trudere* = to push]

exuberant (*say* ig-**zew**-ber-ant) *adjective* very lively. **exuberantly** *adverb*, **exuberance** *noun*

exude *verb* (**exuded**, **exuding**) **1** give off like sweat or a smell etc. **2** ooze out.

exult *verb* rejoice greatly. **exultant** *adjective*, **exultation** *noun*

eye *noun* **1** the organ of the body that is used for seeing, **2** the power of seeing, *She has sharp eyes*. **3** the small hole in a needle. **4** a spot or leaf-bud that seems like an eye. **5** the centre of a storm. **6** the best part.

eye *verb* (**eyed**, **eyeing**) look at; watch.

eyeball *noun* the ball-shaped part of the eye inside the eyelids.

eyebrow *noun* the fringe of hair growing on the face above the eye.

eye-dog *noun* (*NZ*) a dog that controls sheep by staring at them.

eyelash *noun* (*plural* **eyelashes**) one of the short hairs that grow on an eyelid.

eyelid *noun* either of the two folds of skin that can close over the eyeball.

eye-opener *noun* something that is unexpectedly enlightening.

eyepiece *noun* the lens of a telescope or microscope etc. that you put to your eye.

eyesight *noun* the ability to see.

eyesore *noun* something that is ugly to look at.

eyewitness *noun* (*plural* **eyewitnesses**) a person who actually saw an accident or crime etc.

eyrie (*say* **ee**-ree) *noun* the nest of an eagle or other bird of prey.

e-zine *noun* a magazine published regularly in electronic form.

Ff

fa'afafine *noun* a Samoan person who is born biologically male, but embodies both male and female gender traits.

fa'a-Samoa (*say* **fah**-ah-sah-moh-a) *noun* the Samoan way of life; the language, customs, etc. of Samoa. [Samoan]

fable *noun* a short story that teaches about behaviour, often with animals as characters. [from Latin *fabula* = story]

fabric *noun* **1** cloth. **2** the framework of a building (walls, floors, and roof).

fabricate *verb* (**fabricated**, **fabricating**) **1** construct; manufacture. **2** invent, *fabricate an excuse*. **fabrication** *noun*

fabulous *adjective* **1** (*informal*) wonderful. **2** incredibly *great, fabulous wealth*. **3** told of in fables. **fabulously** *adverb*

façade (*say* fas-**ahd**) *noun* **1** the front of a building. **2** an outward appearance, especially a deceptive one. [French (same origin as *face*)]

face *noun* **1** the front part of the head. **2** the expression on a person's face. **3** the front or upper side of something. **4** a surface, *A cube has six faces*.

face *verb* (**faced**, **facing**) **1** look or have the front towards something, *Our room faced the sea*. **2** meet and have to deal with something; encounter, *Explorers face many dangers*. **3** cover a surface with a layer of different material. [from Latin *facies* = appearance]

facet (*say* **fas**-it) *noun* **1** one of the many sides of a cut stone or jewel. **2** one aspect of a situation or problem.

facetious (*say* fas-**ee**-shus) *adjective* trying to be funny at an unsuitable time, *facetious remarks*. **facetiously** *adverb*

facial (*say* **fay**-shal) *adjective* of the face.

facial eczema a skin disease of livestock.

facile (*say* **fas**-I'll) *adjective* done or produced easily or with little thought or care. [from Latin *facilis* = easy]

facilitate (*say* fas-**il**-it-ayt) *verb* (**facilitated**, **facilitating**) make easy or easier. **facilitation** *noun*

facility (*say* fas-**il**-it-ve) *noun* (*plural* **facilities**) **1** something that provides you with the means to do things, *There are sports facilities*. **2** easiness.

facsimile (*say* fak-**sim**-il-ee) *noun* an exact reproduction of a document etc. [from Latin *fac* = make, + *simile* = a likeness]

fact *noun* something that is certainly true. [from Latin *factum* = thing done]

faction *noun* a small united group within a larger one, especially in politics.

factor *noun* **1** something that helps to bring about a result, *Hard work was a factor in her success*. **2** a number by which a larger number can be divided exactly, *2 and 3 are factors of 6*.

factory *noun* (*plural* **factories**) a large building where machines are used to make things. [from Latin *facere* = make or do]

factotum (*say* fakt-**oh**-tum) *noun* a servant or assistant who does all kinds of work. [from Latin *fac* = do, + *totum* = everything)

factual *adjective* based on facts; containing facts. **factually** *adverb*

faculty *noun* (*plural* **faculties**) **1** any of the powers of the body or mind (e.g. sight, speech, understanding). **2** one section of a university, usually made up of several departments, *History is part of the Faculty of Arts*.

fad *noun* a person's particular like or dislike; a craze. **faddy** *adjective*

fade *verb* (**faded**, **fading**) **1** lose or cause to lose colour or freshness or strength. **2** disappear gradually. **3** make a sound etc. become gradually weaker (*fade it out*) or stronger (*fade it in* or *up*).

faeces (*say* **fee**-seez) *plural noun* solid waste matter expelled from the body.

fag *noun* (*informal*) **1** tiring work; drudgery. **2** a cigarette.

fagged out tired out; exhausted.

faggot *noun* **1** a meat ball made with chopped liver and baked. **2** a bundle of sticks bound together, especially as firewood.

Fahrenheit *adjective* measuring temperature on a scale where water freezes at 32° and boils at 212°. [named after a German scientist, G. D. Fahrenheit]

fail *verb* **1** try to do something but be unable to do it. **2** become weak or useless; break down, *The brakes failed.* **3** not to do something, *He failed to warn me.* **4** grade a candidate or be graded as not having passed an examination.

fail *noun* **without fail** for certain; whatever happens.

failing *noun* a weakness; a fault.

failure *noun* **1** not being able to do something. **2** a person or thing that has failed.

faint *adjective* **1** weak; not clear, not distinct. **2** exhausted; nearly unconscious. **faintly** *adverb*, **faintness** *noun*

faint *verb* become unconscious.

fair[1] *adjective* **1** right or just; according to the rules, *a fair fight.* **2** (of hair or skin) light in colour; (of a person) having fair hair. **3** (*old use*) beautiful. **4** fine; favourable, *fair weather.* **5** moderate; quite good, *a fair number of people.* **fairness** *noun*
fair go (*NZ, informal*) just treatment, *they didn't get a fair go*; (as exclamation) really? be reasonable!
[from Old English *faeger*]

fair[1] *adverb* fairly, *Play fair!*

fair[2] *noun* **1** a group of entertainments such as roundabouts and sideshows. **2** an exhibition; a market. [from Latin *feriae* = holiday]

fairly *adverb* **1** justly; according to the rules. **2** moderately, *It is fairly hard.*

fairy *noun* (*plural* **fairies**) an imaginary very small creature with magic powers. **fairyland** *noun*, **fairytale** *noun* [from an old word *fay*, from *Latin fata* = the Fates, three goddesses who were believed to control people's lives]

faith *noun* strong belief; trust.
in good faith with honest intentions.

faithful *adjective* **1** loyal and trustworthy. **2** sexually loyal to one partner. **faithfully** *adverb*, **faithfulness** *noun*
Yours faithfully see *yours.*

fakaalofa *noun* love. [Niuean]

fakaalofa lahi atu *exclamation* love to you. [Niuean]

fake *noun* something that looks genuine but is not; a forgery.

fake *verb* (**faked**, **faking**) **1** make something that looks genuine, so as to deceive people. **2** pretend. *They faked illness.* **faker** *noun*

fakir (*say* **fay**-keer) *noun* a Muslim or Hindu religious beggar regarded as a holy man. [Arabic, = a poor man]

falcon *noun* a kind of hawk often used in the sport of hunting other birds or game. **falconry** *noun*

fale (*say* **fah**-lay) a Samoan house. [Samoan]

fall *verb* (**fell**, **fallen**, **falling**) **1** come or go down without being pushed or thrown etc. **2** decrease; become lower, *Prices fell.* **3** be captured or overthrown, *The city fell.* **4** die in battle. **5** happen, *Silence fell.* **6** become, *She fell asleep.* **7** cut down (trees).
fall back retreat.
fall back on use for support or in an emergency.
fall for (*informal*) be attracted by a person; be taken in by a deception.
fall out quarrel.
fall through fail, *plans fell through.*

fall *noun* **1** the action of falling. **2** (*American*) autumn, when leaves fall.

fallacy (*say* **fal**-a-see) *noun* (*plural* **fallacies**) a false idea or belief. **fallacious** (*say* fal-**ay**-shus) *adjective* [from Latin *fallere* = deceive]

fallible (*say* **fal**-ib-ul) *adjective* liable to make mistakes; not infallible, *All people are fallible.* **fallibility** *noun*

fall-out *noun* particles of radioactive material carried in the air after a nuclear explosion.

fallow *adjective* (of land) ploughed but left without crops in order to restore its fertility.

fallow deer a kind of light-brown deer.

falls *plural noun* a waterfall.

false *adjective* **1** untrue; incorrect. **2** not genuine; sham; faked. **3** treacherous; deceitful. **falsely** *adverb*, **falseness** *noun*, **falsity** *noun* [from Latin *falsum* = deceived]

falsehood *noun* **1** a lie. **2** telling lies.

falsetto *noun* (*plural* **falsettos**) a man's voice forced into speaking or singing higher than is natural.

falsify *verb* (**falsified**, **falsifying**) alter a thing dishonestly. **falsification** *noun*

falsity *noun* falseness.

falter *verb* **1** hesitate when you move or speak. **2** become weaker; begin to give way, *His courage faltered.*

fame *noun* being famous. **famed** *adjective*

familiar *adjective* **1** well-known; often seen or experienced. **2** knowing something well, *Are you familiar with this book?* **3** very friendly. **familiarly** *adverb*, **familiarity** *noun* [same origin as *family*]

familiarise *verb* (**familiarised**, **familiarising**) make familiar; accustom. **familiarisation** *noun*

family *noun* (*plural* **families**) **1** parents and their children, sometimes including grandchildren and other relations. **2** a group of things that are alike in some way.
Family Court (*NZ*) a court that administers family law (cases of dissolution of marriage, the custody of children, etc.).
family planning birth control.
family tree a diagram showing how people in a family are related. [from Latin *familia* = household]

famine *noun* a very bad shortage of food in an area. [from Latin *fames* = hunger]

famished *adjective* very hungry. **famishing** *adjective* [same origin as *famine*]

famous *adjective* known to very many people.

famously *adverb* (*informal*) very well, *They get on famously.*

fan[1] *noun* a device for making air move about so as to cool people or things.

fan[1] *verb* (**fanned**, **fanning**) send a current of air on something.

fan[2] *noun* an enthusiast; a great admirer or supporter. [short *for fanatic*]

fanatic *noun* a person who is very enthusiastic or too enthusiastic about something. **fanatical** *adjective*, **fanatically** *adverb*, **fanaticism** *noun*

fanciful *adjective* **1** imagining things. **2** quaint; unusual, *fanciful designs.*

fancy *noun* (*plural* **fancies**) **1** a liking or desire for something. **2** imagination.

fancy *adjective* decorated; elaborate.

fancy *verb* (**fancied**, **fancying**) **1** believe, *I fancy it's raining.* **2** imagine. **3** have a liking or desire for something. [originally a shortened spelling of *fantasy*]

fanfare *noun* a short piece of loud music played on trumpets.

fang *noun* a long sharp tooth.

fanlight *noun* a window above a door.

fantail *noun* a small New Zealand bird with fan-like tail.

fantasia (*say* fan-**tay**-zee-a) *noun* an imaginative piece of music or writing.

fantasise *verb* (**fantasised**, **fantasising**) imagine in fantasy; daydream.

fantastic *adjective* **1** (*informal*) excellent. **2** designed in a very fanciful way. **fantastically** *adverb*

fantasy *noun* (*plural* **fantasies**) something imaginary or fantastic.

far *adverb* **1** at or to a great distance, *We didn't go far.* **2** much; by a great amount, *This is far better.*

far *adjective* distant; remote, *On the far side of the river.*

farce *noun* **1** an exaggerated comedy. **2** events that are ridiculous or a pretence. **farcical** *adjective*

fare *noun* **1** the price charged for a passenger to travel. **2** food and drink, *There was only very plain fare.*

fare *verb* (**fared**, **faring**) get along; progress, *How did they fare?*

farewell *interjection & noun* goodbye.

farewell *verb* **1** *say* goodbye to. **2** (*NZ*) honour someone who is leaving or retiring.

farm *noun* **1** an area of land where someone grows crops or keeps animals for food or other use. **2** the farmer's house. **farmhouse** *noun*, **farmyard** *noun*

farm *verb* **1** grow crops or keep animals for food etc. **2** use land for growing crops; cultivate.

farmer *noun* a person who owns or manages a farm.

farrier (*say* **fa**-ree-er) *noun* a smith who shoes horses. **farriery** *noun* [from Latin *ferrum* = iron, an iron horseshoe]

farrow *noun* a litter of young pigs.

farther *adverb & adjective* at or to a greater distance; more distant.

> USAGE *Farther* and *farthest* are used only in connection with distance (e.g. *She lives farther from the school than I do*), but even in such cases many people prefer to use *further*. Only *further* can be used to mean 'additional', e.g. in *We must make further inquiries.* If you are not sure which is right, use *further.*

farthest *adverb & adjective* at or to the greatest distance; most distant.

fascinate *verb* (**fascinated**, **fascinating**) be very attractive or interesting to somebody. **fascination** *noun*, **fascinator** *noun* [from Latin, = cast a spell]

Fascist (*say* **fash**-ist) *noun* a person who supports an extreme right-wing dictatorial type of government. **Fascism** *noun* [from Latin *fasces*, the bundle of rods with an axe through it, carried before a judge in ancient Rome as a symbol of his power to punish people]

fashion *noun* **1** the style of clothes or other things that most people like at a particular time. **2** a way of doing something, *Continue in the same fashion.* **fashionable** *adjective*, **fashionably** *adverb*

fashion *verb* make in a particular shape or style.

fast[1] *adjective* **1** moving or done quickly; rapid. **2** allowing fast movement, *a fast road.* **3** showing a time later than the correct time, *Your watch is fast.* **4** firmly fixed or attached. **5** not likely to fade, *fast colours.* **fastness** *noun*

fast[1] *adverb* **1** quickly, *Run fast!* **2** firmly; securely, *They are fast asleep.*

fast[2] *verb* go without food. **fast** *noun*

fasten *verb* fix one thing firmly to another. **fastener** *noun*, **fastening** *noun*

fast forward *noun* a mechanism for running a videotape or audiotape forward quickly. **fast forward** *verb*

fastidious *adjective* choosing carefully and liking only what is very good. **fastidiously** *adverb*, **fastidiousness** *noun*

fat *noun* **1** the white greasy part of meat. **2** oil or grease used in cooking.

fats *plural noun* (*NZ*) cattle or sheep that are ready to be killed for their meat.
the fat of the land the best food.

fat *adjective* (**fatter**, **fattest**) **1** having a very thick round body. **2** thick, *a fat book*. **3** full of fat. **fatness** *noun*

fatal *adjective* causing death or disaster, *a fatal accident*. **fatally** *adverb*

fatalist *noun* a person who accepts whatever happens and thinks it could not have been avoided. **fatalism** *noun*, **fatalistic** *adjective*

fatality (*say* fa-**tal**-it-ee) *noun* (*plural* **fatalities**) a death caused by an accident, war, or other disaster.

fate *noun* **1** a power that is thought to make things happen. **2** what will happen or has happened to somebody or something; destiny.

fated *adjective* destined by fate; doomed, *the fated lovers, Romeo and Juliet*.

fateful *adjective* bringing events that are important and usually unpleasant. **fatefully** *adverb*

father *noun* **1** a male parent. **2** the title of certain priests. **fatherly** *adjective*

father *verb* be the father of, *He fathered six children*. [from Old English *faeder*]

father-in-law *noun* (*plural* **fathers-in-law**) the father of a married person's husband or wife.

fathom *noun* a unit used in measuring the depth of water, equivalent to about 1.83 metres.

fathom *verb* **1** measure the depth of something. **2** get to the bottom of something; work it out. **fathomless** *adjective*

fatigue *noun* **1** tiredness. **2** weakness in metals, caused by stress. **fatigued** *adjective* [from Latin *fatigare* = tire]

fatten *verb* make or become fat.

fatty *adjective* like fat; containing fat.

fatuous *adjective* silly. **fatuously** *adverb*, **fatuousness** *noun*, **fatuity** *noun*

fault *noun* **1** anything that makes a person or thing imperfect; a flaw or mistake. **2** the responsibility for something wrong, *It wasn't your fault*. **3** a break in a layer of rock.

fault *verb* **1** find faults in something. **2** form a fault. [from Latin *fallere* = deceive]

faultless *adjective* without a fault. **faultlessly** *adverb*, **faultlessness** *noun*

faulty *adjective* having a fault or faults. **faultily** *adverb*, **faultiness** *noun*

faun *noun* an ancient country-god with a goat's legs, horns, and tail. [from the name of Faunus, an ancient Roman country-god (see *fauna*)]

fauna *noun* the animals of a certain area or period of time. (Compare *flora*.) [from the name of Fauna, an ancient Roman country-goddess, sister of Faunus (see *faun*)]

favour *noun* **1** a kind or helpful act. **2** approval; goodwill. **3** friendly support shown to one person or group but not to another, *without fear or favour*.

favour *verb* be in favour of something; show favour to a person.

favourable *adjective* helpful; approving; pleasing. **favourably** *adverb*

favourite *adjective* liked more than others. **favourite** *noun*

favouritism *noun* unfairly being kinder to one person than to others.

fawn[1] *noun* **1** a young deer. **2** a light-brown colour.

fawn[2] *verb* try to win a person's favour or affection by flattery and humility.

fax *noun* **1** the transmission by electronic means of an exact copy of a document etc., *send it by fax*. **2** a copy produced in this way. [from *facsimile*]

fax *verb* send a fax to; send (a letter etc.) by fax.

FBI *abbreviation* Federal Bureau of Investigation (in the US).

fear *noun* a feeling that something unpleasant may happen.

fear *verb* feel fear; be afraid of somebody or something.

fearful *adjective* **1** feeling fear; afraid. **2** causing fear or horror, *a fearful monster*. **3** (*informal*) very great or bad. **fearfully** *adverb*

fearless *adjective* without fear. **fearlessly** *adverb*, **fearlessness** *noun*

fearsome *adjective* frightening.

feasible *adjective* **1** able to be done; possible. **2** likely, *a feasible explanation*. **feasibly** *adverb*, **feasibility** *noun*

feast *noun* **1** a large splendid meal. **2** a religious festival. **feast** *verb* [from Latin *festus* = joyful]

feat *noun* a brave or clever deed.

feather *noun* one of the very light coverings that grow from a bird's skin. **feathery** *adjective*

feather *verb* cover or line with feathers.

featherweight *noun* **1** a person who weighs very little. **2** a boxer weighing less than 57 kg.

feature *noun* **1** any part of the face (e.g. mouth, nose, eyes). **2** an important or noticeable part; a characteristic. **3** a long or important film, broadcast programme, or newspaper article.

feature *verb* (**featured**, **featuring**) make or be a noticeable part of something.

February *noun* the second month of the year.

feckless *adjective* feeble and incompetent, irresponsible. [from Scottish *feck* = effect, + *-less* without]

fed *past tense* of **feed**.

fed up (*informal*) discontented.

federal *adjective* of a system in which several States are ruled by a central government but are responsible for their own internal affairs. **federation** *noun* [from Latin *foederis* of a treaty]

fee *noun* a charge for something.

feeble *adjective* weak; without strength. **feebly** *adverb*, **feebleness** *noun* [from Latin *flebilis* = wept over]

feed *verb* (**fed**, **feeding**) **1** give food to a person or animal. **2** take food. **3** supply something to a machine etc. **feeder** *noun*

feed *noun* **1** a meal. **2** food for animals.

feedback *noun* the return of information about an event or thing; a response.

feel *verb* (**felt**, **feeling**) **1** touch something to find out what it is like. **2** be aware of something; have an opinion. **3** give a certain sensation, *It feels warm.*
feel like (*informal*) want.

feel *noun* the sensation caused by feeling something, *I like the feel of silk.*

feeler *noun* **1** a long thin projection on an insect's or crustacean's body, used for feeling; an antenna. **2** a cautious question or suggestion etc. to test people's reactions.

feeling *noun* **1** the ability to feel things; the sense of touch. **2** what a person feels.

feign (*say* fayn) *verb* pretend.

feijoa (*say* fee-**joh**-a) *noun* a fruit with bright-green skin. [named after a naturalist, Feijo]

feint (*say* faynt) *noun* a sham attack or blow etc. meant to deceive an opponent.

feint *verb* make a feint.

felicity *noun* **1** great happiness. **2** a pleasing manner or style. *He expressed himself with great felicity.* **felicitous** *adjective*, **felicitously** *adverb*

feline (*say* **feel**-I'n) *adjective* of cats; catlike. [from Latin *feles* cat]

fell[1] *past tense* of **fall**.

fell[2] *verb* cause to fall; cut or knock down. *They were felling the trees.*

fell[3] *noun* a piece of wild hilly country, especially in the north of England.

fellow *noun* **1** a friend or companion; one who belongs to the same group. **2** (*informal*) a man or boy. **3** a member of a learned society.

fellow *adjective* of the same group or kind, *Her fellow teachers supported her.*

fellowship *noun* **1** friendship. **2** a group of friends; a society.

felon (*say* **fel**-on) *noun* a criminal. [from Latin *fellonis* = of an evil person]

felony (*say* **fel**-on-ee) *noun* (*plural* **felonies**) a serious crime.

felt[1] *past tense* of **feel**.

felt[2] *noun* a thick fabric made of fibres of wool or fur etc. pressed together.

female *adjective* of the sex that can bear offspring or produce eggs or fruit.

female *noun* a female person, animal, or plant.

feminine *adjective* of or like women; suitable for women. **femininity** *noun* [from Latin *femina* = woman]

feminist *noun* a person who believes that women should be given the same rights and status as men. **feminism** *noun*

femur (*say* **fee**-mer) *noun* the thigh-bone.

fen *noun* an area of low-lying marshy or flooded ground.

fence *noun* **1** a barrier made of wood or wire etc. round an area. **2** a structure for a horse to jump over. **3** (*informal*) a person who buys stolen goods and sells them again.

fence *verb* (**fenced**, **fencing**) **1** put a fence round or along something. **2** fight with long narrow swords (called *foils*) as a sport. **fencer** *noun* [from *defence*]

fend *verb* **fend for** provide things for someone.

fend off keep a person or thing away from yourself. [from *defend*]

fender *noun* **1** something placed round a fireplace to stop coals from falling into the room. **2** something hung over the side of a boat to protect it from knocks.

fennel *noun* a herb with yellow flowers.

feral *adjective* **1** wild. **2** (*NZ*) (of goats) formerly wild but now farmed.

ferment (*say* fer-**ment**) *verb* bubble and change chemically by the action of a substance such as yeast. **fermentation** *noun*

ferment (*say* **fer**-ment) *noun* **1** fermenting. **2** an excited or agitated condition.

fern *noun* a plant with feathery leaves and no flowers.

fernbird *noun* a small New Zealand bird with spiny tail-feathers.

fern-leaf *noun* the leaf of a fern; this used as the emblem of New Zealand.

ferocious *adjective* fierce; savage. **ferociously** *adverb*, **ferocity** *noun* [from Latin *ferox* = bold, fierce]

ferret *noun* a small animal used for catching rabbits and rats. **ferrety** *adjective*

ferret *verb* (**ferreted, ferreting**) **1** hunt with a ferret. **2** search; rummage. [from Latin *fur* = thief]

ferric or **ferrous** *adjectives* containing iron. [from Latin *ferrum* = iron]

ferry *verb* (**ferried, ferrying**) transport people or things, especially across water.

ferry *noun* (*plural* **ferries**) a boat or aircraft used in ferrying.

fertile *adjective* **1** producing good crops, *fertile soil.* **2** able to produce offspring. **3** able to produce ideas, *a fertile imagination.* **fertility** *noun*

fertilise *verb* (**fertilised, fertilising**) **1** add substances to the soil to make it more fertile. **2** put pollen into a plant or sperm into an egg or female animal so that it develops seed or young. **fertilisation** *noun*, **fertiliser** *noun*

fervent or **fervid** *adjectives* showing warm or strong feeling. **fervently** *adverb*, **fervency** *noun*, **fervour** *noun* [from Latin *fervens* = boiling]

fester *verb* **1** become septic and filled with pus. **2** cause resentment for a long time.

festival *noun* a time when people arrange special celebrations, performances, etc. [same origin as *feast*]

festive *adjective* of a festival; suitable for a festival, joyful. **festively** *adverb*

festivity *noun* (*plural* **festivities**) a festive occasion or celebration.

festoon *noun* a chain of flowers or ribbons etc. hung as a decoration.

festoon *verb* decorate with ornaments.

fetch *verb* **1** go for and bring back, *fetch some milk; fetch a doctor.* **2** be sold for a particular price, *The chairs fetched $50.*

fête (*say* fayt) *noun* an outdoor entertainment with stalls and sideshows.

fête *verb* (**fêted, fêting**) honour a person with celebrations. [same origin as *feast*]

fetish *noun* an object supposed to have magical powers. [from Portuguese *feitiço* = a charm]

fetlock *noun* the part of a horse's leg above and behind the hoof.

fetter *noun* a chain or shackle put round a prisoner's ankle.

fetter *verb* put fetters on a prisoner.

fettle *noun* condition, *in fine fettle.*

fettuccine (also **fettucine**) *noun* pasta in the form of ribbons.

feud (*say* fewd) *noun* a long-lasting quarrel or enmity.

feudal (*say* **few**-dal) *adjective* of the system used in the Middle Ages in which people could farm land in exchange for work done for the owner. **feudalism** *noun*

fever *noun* **1** an abnormally high body-temperature, usually with an illness. **2** excitement; agitation. **fevered** *adjective*, **feverish** *adjective*, **feverishly** *adverb*

few *adjective* not many. **fewness** *noun*

few *noun* a small number of people or things.

fez *noun* (*plural* **fezzes**) a high flat-topped red hat with a tassel, worn by Muslim men in some countries. [named after Fez, a town in Morocco]

ff. *abbreviation* and the following (pages etc.).

fiancé (*say* fee-**ahn**-*say*) *noun* a man who is engaged to be married. [French, = betrothed]

fiancée (*say* fee-**ahn**-*say*) *noun* a woman who is engaged to be married.

fiasco (*say* fee-**as**-koh) *noun* (*plural* **fiascos**) a complete failure.

fib *noun* a lie about something unimportant. **fibber** *noun*, **fibbing** *noun*

fibre *noun* **1** a very thin thread. **2** a substance made of thin threads. **3** indigestible material in certain foods that stimulates the action of the intestines. **fibrous** *adjective*
fibre optics thin glass fibres used for the transmission of telephone and television signals etc.

fibreglass *noun* **1** fabric made from glass fibres. **2** plastic containing glass fibres.

fickle *adjective* constantly changing, not loyal to one person or group etc. **fickleness** *noun*

fiction *noun* **1** writings about events that have not really happened; stories and novels. **2** something imagined or untrue. **fictional** *adjective* [from Latin *fictio* = pretending]

fictitious *adjective* imagined; untrue.

fiddle *noun* **1** (*informal*) a violin. **2** (*slang*) a swindle.

fiddle *verb* (**fiddled, fiddling**) **1** (*informal*) play the violin. **2** fidget or tinker with something, using your fingers. **3** (*slang*) swindle; get or change something dishonestly. **fiddler** *noun*

fiddly *adjective* small and awkward to use or do.

fidelity *noun* **1** faithfulness; loyalty. **2** accuracy; the exactness with which sound is reproduced. [from Latin *fidelitas* = faithfulness]

fidget *verb* (**fidgeted, fidgeting**) **1** make small restless movements. **2** worry. **fidgety** *adjective*

fidget *noun* a person who fidgets. [from a dialect word *fidge* = twitch]

field *noun* **1** a piece of land with grass or crops growing on it. **2** an area or section, *recent advances in the field of science.* **3** a battlefield. **4** those who are taking part in a race or outdoor game etc.
field goal a drop-kick between the goal posts in rugby.

field *verb* **1** stop or catch the ball in cricket etc. **2** be on the side not batting in cricket etc. **3** put a team into a match etc., *They fielded their best players.* **fielder** *noun*, **fieldsman** *noun*

fieldwork *noun* practical work or research done in various places, not in a library or museum or laboratory etc.

fiend (*say* feend) *noun* **1** an evil spirit; a devil. **2** a very wicked or cruel person. **3** an enthusiast, *a fresh-air fiend.* **fiendish** *adjective*

fierce *adjective* **1** angry and violent or cruel. **2** intense, *fierce heat.* **fiercely** *adverb*, **fierceness** *noun*

fiery *adjective* **1** full of flames or heat. **2** full of emotion. **3** easily made angry.

FIFA *noun* the governing body of international soccer. [abbreviation, from French]

fife *noun* a small shrill flute.

fifteen *noun & adjective* **1** the number 15; one more than fourteen. **2** a team in rugby union. **fifteenth** *adjective & noun*

fifth *adjective & noun* next after the fourth. **fifthly** *adverb*

fifty *noun & adjective* (*plural* **fifties**) the number 50; five times ten. **fiftieth** *adjective & noun*

fifty-fifty *adjective & adverb* **1** shared equally between two people or groups. **2** evenly balanced, *a fifty-fifty chance.*

fig *noun* a soft fruit full of small seeds.

fight *noun* **1** a struggle against somebody using hands, weapons, etc. **2** an attempt to achieve or overcome something, *the fight against poverty.*

fight *verb* (**fought, fighting**) **1** have a fight. **2** attempt to achieve or overcome something. **fighter** *noun*

figment *noun* something imagined, a figment of the imagination.

figurative *adjective* using a figure of speech (see *figure*); metaphorical, not literal. **figuratively** *adverb*

figure *noun* **1** the symbol of a number. **2** a diagram or illustration. **3** a pattern or shape; the shape of someone's body. **4** a representation of a person or animal in painting, sculpture, etc.
figure of speech a word or phrase used for dramatic effect and not intended literally, e.g. 'a *flood* of letters'.

figure *verb* (**figured, figuring**) **1** imagine. **2** work out. **3** appear or take part in something. [from Latin *figura* = shape]

figure-head *noun* **1** a carved figure decorating the prow of a sailing-ship. **2** a person who is head of a country or organisation but has no real power.

Fijian *noun* **1** a person born in or living in Fiji. **2** the language of Fiji. **Fijian** *adjective*

filament *noun* a thread or thin wire. [same origin as *file*[2]]

filch *verb* steal something slyly; pilfer.

file[1] *noun* a metal tool with a rough surface that is rubbed on things to shape them or make them smooth.

file[1] *verb* (**filed, filing**) shape or smooth with a file.

file[2] *noun* **1** a folder or box etc. for keeping papers in order. **2** a set of data stored under one reference in a computer. **3** a line of people one behind the other.

file[2] *verb* (**filed, filing**) **1** put into a file. **2** walk in a file. *They filed out.* [from Latin *filum* = thread (because a string or wire was put through papers to hold them in order)]

filial (*say* **fil**-ee-al) *adjective* of a son or daughter. [from Latin *filius* = son, *filla* = daughter]

filibuster *verb* try to delay or prevent the passing of a law by making long speeches. **filibuster** *noun*

filigree *noun* ornamental lace-like work of twisted metal wire.

fill *verb* **1** make or become full. **2** block up a hole or cavity. **filler** *noun*

fill *noun* enough to fill a person or thing.

fillet *noun* a piece of fish or meat without bones.

fillet *verb* (**filleted, filleting**) remove the bones from fish or meat.

filling *noun* **1** something used to fill a hole or gap, e.g. in a tooth. **2** something put in pastry to make a pie, or between layers of bread to make a sandwich.

filly *noun* (*plural* **fillies**) a young female horse.

film *noun* **1** a rolled strip or sheet of thin plastic coated with material that is sensitive to light, used for taking photographs or making a motion picture. **2** a story or event recorded by a camera as a set of moving images and shown in a cinema or on television. **3** a very thin layer, *a film of grease.*

film *verb* make a film of a story etc.

filmy *adjective* (**filmier**, **filmiest**) thin and almost transparent. **filminess** *noun*

filo pastry pastry made in very thin leaves. [from Greek *phullon* = leaf]

filter *noun* **1** a device for holding back dirt or other unwanted material from a liquid or gas etc. that passes through it. **2** a screen for preventing light of certain wavelengths from passing through.

filter *verb* **1** pass through a filter. **2** move gradually, *They filtered into the hall.* [from *felt*[2], originally used for making filters]

filth *noun* disgusting dirt.

filthy *adjective* (**filthier**, **filthiest**) disgustingiy dirty. **filthiness** *noun*

fin *noun* **1** a thin flat part projecting from a fish's body, that helps it to swim. **2** a small projection on an aircraft or rocket etc., that helps its balance.

final *adjective* **1** coming at the end, last. **2** that puts an end to an argument etc., *You must go, and that's final!* **finally** *adverb*, **finality** *noun*

final *noun* the last in a series of contests. [same origin as *finish*]

finale (*say* fin-**ah**-lee) *noun* the final section of a piece of music or a play etc.

finalise *verb* (**finalised**, **finalising**) put into its final form. **finalisation** *noun*

finalist *noun* competitor in the final.

finance *noun* the use or management of money.

finance *verb* (**financed**, **financing**) provide the money for something. **financier** *noun* [from Old French *finer* = settle a debt]

finances *plural noun* money resources; funds.

financial *adjective* **1** of finance. **2** (*NZ, informal*) having some money. **financially** *adverb*
financial member a person who has paid the subscription to belong to a club or society, etc.

finch *noun* (*plural* **finches**) a small bird with a short stubby bill.

find *verb* (**found**, **finding**) **1** get or see something by looking for it or by chance. **2** learn by experience, *He found that digging was hard work.*

find *noun* something found.

fine[1] *adjective* **1** of high quality; excellent. **2** dry and clear; sunny, *fine weather*. **3** very thin; consisting of small particles. **4** in good health; comfortable, *I'm fine*. **finely** *adverb*, **fineness** *noun*

fine[1] *adverb* **1** finely, chop it fine. **2** (*informal*) very well, *That will suit me fine.* [same origin as finish]

fine[2] *noun* money which has to be paid as a punishment.

fine[2] *verb* (**fined**, **fining**) make somebody pay a fine. [from Latin *finis* = end (in the Middle Ages it referred to the sum paid to settle a lawsuit)]

finery *noun* fine clothes or decorations.

finesse (*say* fin-**ess**) *noun* clever management; artfulness. [French, = fineness]

finger *noun* **1** one of the separate parts of the hand. **2** a narrow piece of something, *fish fingers*.

finger *verb* touch or feel with your fingers.

fingerprint *noun* a mark made by the tiny ridges on the fingertip, used as a way of identifying someone.

fingertip *noun* the tip of a finger.
have something at your fingertips be very familiar with a subject etc.

finicky *adjective* fussy about details; hard to please.

finish *verb* bring or come to an end. **finisher** *noun*

finish *noun* (*plural* **finishes**) **1** the last stage of something; the end. **2** the surface or coating on woodwork etc. [from Latin *finis* = end]

finite (*say* **fy**-nyt) adjective limited; not infinite, We have only a finite supply of coal.
finite verb a verb that agrees with its subject in person and number, *'was', 'went', and 'says' are finite verbs; 'going' and 'to say' are not.* [from Latin *finitum* = ended]

fiord (*say* **fee**-ord) *noun* an inlet of the sea between high cliffs, as in Norway, Fiordland (New Zealand), etc. [a Norwegian word]

fir *noun* an evergreen tree with needle-like leaves, that produces cones.

fire *noun* **1** the process of burning that produces light and heat. **2** coal and wood etc. burning in a grate or furnace to give heat. **3** a device using electricity or gas to heat a room. **4** the shooting of guns, *Hold your fire!*
fire brigade a team of people organised to fight fires.
on fire burning.
set fire to start something burning.

fire *verb* (**fired**, **firing**) **1** set fire to. **2** bake pottery or bricks etc. in a kiln. **3** shoot a gun; send out a bullet or missile. **4** dismiss someone from a job. **5** excite, *fire them with enthusiasm*. **firer** *noun*

firearm *noun* a small gun; a rifle, pistol, or revolver.

firebrand *noun* a person who stirs up trouble.

fire-engine *noun* a large vehicle that carries firemen and equipment to put out large fires.

fire-escape *noun* a special staircase or apparatus by which people may escape from a burning building etc.

firefighter *noun* a member of a fire brigade.

firefly *noun* (*plural* **fireflies**) a kind of beetle that gives off a glowing light.

fireplace *noun* an open structure for holding a fire in a room.

fireside *noun* the part of the room near a fireplace.

firewood *noun* wood for use as fuel.

firework *noun* a device containing chemicals that burn attractively or noisily.

firing-squad *noun* a group ordered to fire a salute during a military funeral, or to shoot a condemned person.

firm[1] *noun* a business organisation.

firm[2] *adjective* **1** not giving way when pressed; hard, solid. **2** steady; not shaking or moving. **3** definite and not likely to change, *a firm belief.* **firmly** *adverb*, **firmness** *noun*

firm[2] *adverb* firmly, *Stand firm!*

firm[2] *verb* make something become firm.

firmament *noun* the sky with its clouds and stars.

first *adjective* coming before all others in time or order or importance. **firstly** *adverb*
first aid treatment given to an injured person before a doctor comes.

first *adverb* before everything else, *Finish this work first.*

first *noun* a person or thing that is first.

firth *noun* an estuary or inlet of the sea.

fiscal *adjective* of public finances. [from Latin *fiscus* = treasury]

fish *noun* (*plural* **fish** or **fishes**) an animal that always lives and breathes in water.

fish *verb* **1** try to catch fish. **2** search for something; try to get something, *He is only fishing for praise.*

fisherman *noun* (*plural* **fishermen**) a person who tries to catch fish.

fishery *noun* (*plural* **fisheries**) **1** the part of the sea where fishing is carried on. **2** the business of fishing.

fish-hook *noun* **1** a barbed hook for catching fish. **2** (*NZ, informal*) a drawback or difficulty.

fishmonger *noun* a shopkeeper who sells fish.

fishy *adjective* (**fishier, fishiest**) **1** smelling or tasting of fish. **2** (*informal*) causing doubt or suspicion, a *fishy excuse.* **fishily** *adverb*, **fishiness** *noun*

fissile *adjective* **1** likely to split. **2** capable of undergoing nuclear fission.

fission *noun* splitting something; splitting the nucleus of an atom so as to release energy. **fissionable** *adjective* [from Latin *fissum* = split]

fissure (*say* **fish**-er) *noun* a narrow opening made where something splits.

fist *noun* a tightly closed hand with the fingers bent into the palm.

fisticuffs *noun* fighting with the fists.

fit[1] *adjective* (**fitter, fittest**) **1** suitable; good enough, a meal fit for a king. **2** healthy, *Keep fit!* **3** ready; likely, *They worked till they were fit to collapse.* **fitly** *adverb*, **fitness** *noun*

fit[1] *verb* (**fitted, fitting**) **1** be the right size and shape for something; be suitable. **2** put into place, *Fit a lock on the door.* **3** alter something to make it the right size and shape. **4** make suitable, *His training fits him for the job.* **fitter** *noun*

fit[1] *noun* the way something fits, *a good fit.*

fit[2] *noun* **1** a sudden illness, especially one that makes you move violently or become unconscious. **2** an outburst, *a fit of rage.*

fitful *adjective* happening in short periods, not steadily. **fitfully** *adverb*

fitment *noun* a piece of fixed furniture etc.

fitting *adjective* proper; suitable.

fittings *plural noun* the fixtures and fitments of a building.

five *noun & adjective* the number 5; one more than four.

five-eighth *noun* (*NZ*) (rugby union) one of two players (*first five-eighth, second five-eighth*) positioned between the half back and the centre three-quarter.

fix *verb* **1** fasten or place firmly. **2** make permanent and unable to change. **3** decide; arrange, *We fixed a date for the party.* **4** repair; put into working condition, *He is fixing my bike.* **fixer** *noun*
fix up arrange, organise.

fix *noun* (*plural* **fixes**) **1** (*informal*) an awkward situation, *I'm in a fix.* **2** finding the position of something. **3** (*slang*) an addict's dose of a drug.

fixation *noun* **1** fixing something. **2** a strong interest or a concentration on one idea etc.; an obsession.

fixative *noun* a substance used to keep something in position or make it permanent.

fixedly *adverb* in a fixed way.

fixity *noun* a fixed condition; permanence.

fixture *noun* **1** something fixed in its place. **2** a sports event planned for a particular day.

fizz *verb* make a hissing or spluttering sound; produce a lot of small bubbles. **fizzy** *adjective*, **fizziness** *noun*

fizzle *verb* (**fizzled, fizzling**) make a slight fizzing sound.
fizzle out end feebly or unsuccessfully.

fjord *noun* a fiord.

flabbergast *verb* astonish greatly.

flabby *adjective* fat and soft, not firm. **flabbily** *adverb*, **flabbiness** *noun*

flaccid (*say* **flak**-sid) *adjective* soft and limp. **flaccidly** *adverb*, **flaccidity** *noun*

flag[1] **1** a piece of cloth with a coloured pattern or shape on it, used as a sign or signal. **2** a small piece of paper or plastic that looks like a flag. **flag-pole** *noun*, **flagstaff** *noun*

flag[1] *verb* (**flagged**, **flagging**) **1** become weak; droop. **2** signal with a flag or by waving. **flag away** (*NZ, informal*) give (a thing) up. [from an old word *flag* = drooping]

flag[2] *noun* a flagstone. [from Old Norse *flaga* = slab of stone]

flagon *noun* a large bottle or container for wine or cider etc.

flagrant (*say* **flay**-grant) *adjective* very bad and noticeable, *flagrant disobedience.* **flagrantly** *adverb*, **flagrancy** *noun* [from Latin *flagrans* = blazing]

flagship *noun* a ship that carries an admiral and flies his flag.

flagstone *noun* a flat slab of stone used for paving. [from *flag*[2] + stone]

flail *noun* an old-fashioned tool for threshing grain.

flail *verb* beat as if with a flail; wave about wildly. [from Latin *flagellum* = a whip]

flair *noun* a natural ability, talent. [French, = power to smell things]

flak *noun* **1** shells fired by anti-aircraft guns. **2** (*informal*) criticism or abuse. [short for German *fliegerabwehrkanone* = aircraft-defence-cannon]

flake *noun* **1** a very light thin piece of something. **2** a small flat piece of falling snow. **flaky** *adjective*

flake *verb* (**flaked**, **flaking**) come off in flakes.

flamboyant *adjective* very showy in appearance or manner. [French, = blazing]

flame *noun* a tongue-shaped portion of fire or burning gas.

flame *verb* (**flamed**, **flaming**) **1** produce flames. **2** become bright red.

flame-tree *noun* a tree with bright scarlet flowers.

flamingo *noun* (*plural* **flamingoes**) a wading bird with long legs, a long neck, and pinkish feathers.

flammable *adjective* able to be set on fire. **flammability** *noun*

flan *noun* a pastry or sponge shell with no cover over the filling.

flank *noun* the side of something.

flank *verb* place or be placed at the side of something or somebody. **flanker** *noun*

flannel *noun* **1** a soft cloth for washing yourself. **2** a soft woollen material.

flap *verb* (**flapped**, **flapping**) **1** wave about. **2** (*slang*) panic; fuss.

flap *noun* **1** a part that is fixed at one edge on to something else, often to cover an opening. **2** the action or sound of flapping. **3** (*slang*) a panic or fuss, *in a flap.*

flapjack *noun* (*US*) a pancake.

flare *verb* (**flared**, **flaring**) **1** blaze with a sudden bright flame. **2** become angry suddenly. **3** become gradually wider.

flare *noun* **1** a sudden bright flame or light. **2** a gradual widening.

flash *noun* (*plural* **flashes**) **1** a sudden bright flame or light. **2** a device for making a sudden bright light for taking photographs. **3** a sudden display of anger, wit, etc. **4** a short item of news. **5** a computer application used to produce animated items.

flash *verb* **1** make a flash. **2** appear suddenly; move quickly, *The train flashed past us.*

flashback *noun* going back in a film or story to something that happened earlier.

flashy *adjective* gaudy; showy.

flask *noun* **1** a bottle with a narrow neck. **2** a vacuum flask.

flat *adjective* (**flatter**, **flattest**) **1** with no curves or bumps; smooth and level. **2** spread out; lying at full length, *Lie flat on the ground.* **3** (of a tyre) with no air inside. **4** (of feet) without the normal arch underneath. **5** absolute, *a flat refusal.* **6** dull; not changing. **7** (of a drink) having lost its fizziness. **8** (of a battery) unable to produce any more electric current. **9** (in music) one semitone lower than the natural note, *E flat.* **flatly** *adverb*, **flatness** *noun*

flat *adverb* **1** so as to be flat, *Press it flat.* **2** (*informal*) exactly, *in ten seconds flat.* **3** (in music) below the correct pitch. **flat out** as fast as possible.

flat *noun* **1** a flat thing or area. **2** a set of rooms for living in, usually on one floor of a building. **3** (*in music*) a note one semitone lower than the natural note; the sign (♭) that indicates this.

flatfish *noun* a kind of fish with a flattened body that swims on its side.

flathead *noun* any of several fish with a flattened head.

flatten *verb* make or become flat.

flatter *verb* **1** praise somebody more than he or she deserves. **2** make a person or thing seem better or more attractive than they really are. **flatterer** *noun*, **flattery** *noun* [from Old French *flater* = smooth down]

flattie *noun* (*NZ, informal*) a flat tyre.

flaunt *verb* display something proudly, show it off, *They flaunted the trophy.*

USAGE Do not confuse this word with *flout*, which has a different meaning.

flavour *noun* the taste of something.

flavour *verb* give something a flavour, season it. **flavouring** *noun*

flaw *noun* something that makes a person or thing imperfect. **flawed** *adjective*

flawless *adjective* without a flaw; perfect. **flawlessly** *adverb*, **flawlessness** *noun*

flax *noun* **1** a plant that produces fibres from which linen is made and seeds from which linseed oil is obtained. **2** a plant that produces fibres used for weaving baskets etc.

flaxen *adjective* pale-yellow like flax fibres, *flaxen hair.*

flay *verb* strip the skin from an animal.

flea *noun* a small jumping insect that sucks blood.

fleck *noun* **1** a very small patch of colour. **2** a particle; a speck, *flecks of dirt.* **flecked** *adjective*

fledged *adjective* (of young birds) having grown feathers and able to fly. **fully-fledged** *adjective* fully trained, a fully-fledged engineer.

fledgeling *noun* a young bird that is just fledged.

flee *verb* (**fled**, **fleeing**) run or hurry away from something.

fleece *noun* the woolly hair of a sheep or similar animal. **fleecy** *adjective*

fleece *verb* (**fleeced**, **fleecing**) **1** shear the fleece from a sheep. **2** swindle a person out of some money.

fleece-picker *noun* (*NZ*) a person whose job it is to pick up fleeces in the shearing shed.

fleet[1] *noun* a number of ships, aircraft, or vehicles owned by one country or company. [from Old English *fleot* = ships]

fleet[2] *adjective* moving swiftly; nimble. **fleeting** *adjective* passing quickly; brief.

flesh *noun* **1** the soft substance of the bodies of people and animals, consisting of muscle and fat. **2** the pulpy part of fruits and vegetables. **fleshy** *adjective*

flex *verb* bend or stretch something that is flexible, *flex your muscles.*

flex *noun* (*plural* **flexes**) flexible insulated wire for carrying electric current. [from Latin *flexum* = bent]

flexible *adjective* **1** easy to bend or stretch. **2** able to be changed or adapted, *Our plans are flexible.* **flexibility** *noun*

flexitime *noun* a system of flexible working hours.

flick *noun* a quick light hit or movement.

flick *verb* hit or move with a flick.

flicker *verb* **1** burn or shine unsteadily. **2** move quickly to and fro.

flicker *noun* a flickering light or movement.

flier *noun* a flyer.

flight[1] *noun* **1** flying. **2** a journey in an aircraft etc. **3** a series of stairs. **4** the feathers or fins on a dart or arrow.

flight[2] *noun* fleeing; an escape.

flightless *adjective* (of birds) unable to fly.

flighty *adjective* (**flightier**, **flightiest**) silly and frivolous. **flightiness** *noun*

flimsy *adjective* (**flimsier**, **flimsiest**) light and thin; fragile; not strong. **flimsily** *adverb*, **flimsiness** *noun*

flinch *verb* move or shrink back because you are afraid; wince. **flinch** *noun*

fling *verb* (**flung**, **flinging**) throw something violently or carelessly.

fling *noun* **1** the movement of flinging. **2** a vigorous dance, *the Highland fling.* **3** a short time of enjoyment, *have a fling.*

flint *noun* **1** a very hard kind of stone. **2** a piece of flint or hard metal used to produce sparks. **flinty** *adjective*

flip *verb* (**flipped**, **flipping**) **1** flick. **2** (*slang*) become crazy or very angry.

flip *noun* a flipping movement.

flippant *adjective* not showing proper seriousness. **flippantly** *adverb*, **flippancy** *noun*

flipper *noun* **1** a limb that water-animals use for swimming. **2** a device that you wear on your feet to help you to swim.

flirt *verb* behave lovingly towards somebody to amuse yourself. **flirtation** *noun*

flirt *noun* a person who flirts. **flirtatious** *adjective*, **flirtatiously** *adverb*

flit *verb* (**flitted**, **flitting**) fly or move lightly and quickly. **flit** *noun*

flitter *verb* flit about. **flitter** *noun*

float *verb* **1** stay or move on the surface of a liquid or in air. **2** make something float. **floater** *noun*

float *noun* **1** a device designed to float. **2** a vehicle with a platform used for carrying a display in a parade etc. **3** a small amount of money kept for paying small bills or giving change etc.

floating voter *noun* a person who does not support any political party permanently.

flock[1] *noun* a group of sheep, goats, or birds.

flock[1] *verb* gather or move in a crowd.

flock[2] *noun* a tuft of wool or cotton etc.

floe *noun* a sheet of floating ice. [from Norwegian *flo* = layer]

flog *verb* (**flogged, flogging**) **1** beat hard with a whip or stick as a punishment. **2** (*slang*) sell. **3** (*slang*) steal. **flogging** *noun*

flood *noun* **1** a large amount of water spreading over a place that is usually dry. **2** a great amount, *a flood of requests.* **3** the movement of the tide when it is coming in towards the land.

flood *verb* **1** cover with a flood. **2** come in great amounts, *Letters flooded in.*

floodlight *noun* a lamp that makes a broad bright beam to light up a stage or building etc. **floodlit** *adjective*

floor *noun* **1** the part of a room that people walk on. **2** a storey of a building; all the rooms at the same level.

floor *verb* **1** put a floor into a building. **2** knock a person down. **3** baffle somebody.

floorboard *noun* one of the boards forming the floor of a room.

flop *verb* (**flopped, flopping**) **1** fall or sit down clumsily. **2** hang or sway heavily and loosely. **3** (*slang*) be a failure.

flop *noun* **1** a flopping movement or sound. **2** (*slang*) a failure.

floppy *adjective* hanging loosely; not firm or rigid. **floppiness** *noun*
floppy disk a flexible, removable disk holding data for use in a computer.

flora *noun* the plants of a particular area or period. (Compare *fauna.*) [from the name of Flora, the ancient Roman goddess of flowers (Latin *flores* = flowers)]

floral *adjective* of flowers.

florist *noun* a shopkeeper who sells flowers.

floss *noun* **1** silky thread or fibres. **2** dental floss. **flossy** *adjective*

floss *verb* clean (teeth) with dental floss.

flotation *noun* floating something.

flotilla (*say* flot-**il**-a) *noun* a fleet of boats or small ships. [Spanish, = little fleet]

flotsam *noun* wreckage or cargo found floating after a shipwreck.
flotsam and jetsam odds and ends.

flounce[1] *verb* (**flounced, flouncing**) go in an impatient or annoyed manner, *She flounced out of the room.* **flounce** *noun*

flounce[2] *noun* a wide frill.

flounder *verb* **1** move clumsily and with difficulty. **2** make mistakes or become confused when trying to do something.

flounder *noun* a small edible flatfish.

flour *noun* a fine powder of wheat or other grain, used in cooking. **floury** *adjective* [old spelling of *flower*]

flourish *verb* **1** grow or develop strongly. **2** be successful; prosper. **3** wave something about dramatically.

flourish *noun* (*plural* **flourishes**) a dramatic sweeping movement, curve, or passage of music. [from *Latin florere* = to flower]

flout *verb* disobey openly and scornfully, *They flouted the rules.*

> USAGE Do not confuse this word with *flaunt*, which has a different meaning.

flow *verb* **1** move along smoothly or continuously. **2** gush out, *Water flowed from the tap.* **3** hang loosely, *flowing hair.* **4** (of the tide) come in towards the land.

flow *noun* **1** a flowing movement or mass. **2** the movement of the tide when it is coming in towards the land, *the ebb and flow of the tide.*

flower *noun* **1** the part of a plant from which seed and fruit develops. **2** a blossom and its stem used for decoration, usually in groups. [compare *flora*]

flower *verb* produce flowers.

flowerpot *noun* a pot in which a plant may be grown.

flowery *adjective* **1** full of flowers. **2** full of ornamental phrases.

flu *noun* influenza.

fluctuate *verb* (**fluctuated, fluctuating**) rise and fall; vary, *Prices fluctuated.* **fluctuation** *noun* [from Latin *fluctus* = a wave]

flue *noun* a pipe or tube through which smoke or hot gases are drawn off.

fluent (*say* **floo**-ent) *adjective* skilful at speaking; using a language easily and well. **fluently** *adverb*, **fluency** *noun* [from Latin *fluens* = flowing]

fluff *noun* a fluffy substance.

fluffy *adjective* having a mass of soft fur or fibres. **fluffiness** *noun*

fluid *noun* a substance that is able to flow freely as liquids and gases do.

fluid *adjective* able to flow freely, not solid or stiff. **fluidity** *noun* [from Latin *fluere* = to flow]

fluke[1] *noun* a piece of good luck that makes you able to do something you thought you could not do.

fluke[2] *noun* a parasitic worm that lives in a sheep's liver.

flummox *verb* (*informal*) baffle.

fluorescent (*say* floo-er-**ess**-ent) *adjective* creating light from radiations. **fluorescence** *noun*

fluoridation *noun* adding fluoride to drinking-water.

fluoride *noun* a chemical substance that is thought to prevent tooth-decay.

flurry *noun* (*plural* **flurries**) **1** a sudden whirling gust of wind, rain, or snow **2** an excited or flustered disturbance.

flush *verb* **1** blush. **2** clean or remove something with a fast flow of water.

flush *noun* **1** a blush. **2** a fast flow of water.

flush *adjective* **1** level; without projections, *The doors are flush with the walls.* **2** having plenty of money.

fluster *verb* make somebody nervous and confused. **fluster** *noun*

flute *noun* a musical instrument consisting of a long pipe with holes that are stopped by fingers or keys.

flutter *verb* **1** flap wings quickly. **2** move or flap quickly and irregularly.

flutter *noun* **1** a fluttering movement. **2** a nervously excited condition. **3** (*informal*) a small bet, *Have a flutter!*

flux *noun* continual change or flow.

fly[1] *noun* (*plural* **flies**) **1** a small flying insect with two wings. **2** a real or artificial fly used as bait in fishing.

fly[2] *verb* (**flew**, **flown**, **flying**) **1** move through the air by means of wings or in an aircraft. **2** travel through the air or through space. **3** wave in the air, *Flags were flying.* **4** make something fly, *They flew model aircraft.* **5** move or pass quickly, *Time flies.* **6** flee from, *You must fly the country!* **flyer** *noun*

fly[2] *noun* (*plural* **flies**) **1** flying. **2** the front opening of a pair of trousers.

fly[3] *noun* **1** a waterproof sheet spread over a tent for shelter. **2** a shelter or windbreak made from a fly.

fly-blown *adjective* tainted by flies' eggs.

flying fox *noun* **1** a kind of bat. **2** a device to carry people etc. across a gorge, operated by cables.

flying saucer a mysterious saucer-shaped object reported to have been seen in the sky.

flying squad a team of police or doctors etc. organised so that they can move rapidly.

flyleaf *noun* (*plural* **flyleaves**) a blank page at the beginning or end of a book.

flyover *noun* a bridge that carries one road or railway over another.

flywheel *noun* a heavy wheel used to regulate machinery.

FM *abbreviation* frequency modulation.

foal *noun* a young horse.

foal *verb* give birth to a foal.

foam *noun* **1** froth. **2** a spongy kind of rubber or plastic. **foamy** *adjective*

foam *verb* form foam; send out foam.

fob[1] *noun* an ornament hanging from a watch-chain; a tab on a key-ring.

fob[2] *verb* (**fobbed**, **fobbing**) **fob off** get rid of someone by an excuse or a trick.

focal *adjective* of or at a focus.

focus *noun* (*plural* **focuses** or **foci**) **1** the distance from an eye or lens at which an object appears clearest. **2** the point at which rays etc. seem to meet. **3** something that is a centre of interest or attention etc.
in focus appearing clearly.
out of focus not appearing clearly.

focus *verb* (**focused**, **focusing**) **1** use or adjust a lens so that objects appear clearly. **2** concentrate, *She focused her attention on it.* [Latin, = hearth (the central point of a household)]

fodder *noun* food for horses and farm animals.

foe *noun* (*old use*) an enemy.

foetus (*say* **fee**-tus) *noun* (*plural* **foetuses**) **1** a developing embryo. **2** a human embryo more than eight weeks after conception. **foetal** *adjective*

fog *noun* thick mist. **foggy** *adjective*

foghorn *noun* a loud horn for warning ships in fog.

fogy *noun* (*plural* **fogies**) **old fogy** a person with old-fashioned ideas.

foible *noun* a slight peculiarity in someone's character or tastes.

foil[1] *noun* **1** a very thin sheet of metal. **2** a person or thing that makes another look better in contrast.

foil[2] *noun* a long narrow sword used in the sport of fencing.

foil[3] *verb* frustrate, prevent from being successful, *We foiled his evil plan.*

foist *verb* make a person accept something inferior or unwelcome, *They foisted the job on me.* [originally = dishonestly substitute a loaded dice]

fold[1] *verb* bend or move so that one part lies on another part.

fold[1] *noun* a line where something is folded.

fold[2] *noun* an enclosure for sheep.

folder *noun* a folding cover for loose papers.

foliage *noun* the leaves of a tree or plant. [from Latin *folium* = leaf]

folk *noun* people.

folk-dance, folk-song *nouns* a dance or song in the traditional style of a country.

folklore *noun* old beliefs and legends.

follow *verb* **1** go or come after. **2** do a thing after something else. **3** take a person or thing as a guide or example. **4** take an interest in the progress of events or a sport or team etc. **5** understand, *Did you follow what he said?* **6** result from something.
follower *noun*

following *preposition* after, as a result of, *Following the burglary, we had new locks fitted.*

folly *noun* (*plural* **follies**) foolishness; a foolish action etc. [from French *folie* = madness]

foment (*say* fo-**ment**) *verb* arouse or stimulate deliberately, *foment trouble.* [from Latin *fomentum* = poultice]

fomentation *noun* **1** fomenting. **2** hot liquid used to bathe an inflamed or aching part of the body.

fond *adjective* **1** loving. **2** foolishly hopeful, *fond hopes.* **fondly** *adverb*, **fondness** *noun* [from *fon* = a fool]

fondle *verb* (**fondled**, **fondling**) touch or stroke lovingly.

font[1] *noun* a basin (often of carved stone) in a church, to hold water for baptism. [from Latin *fontis* = of a fountain]

font[2] *noun* (*printing*) a set of type characters of the same style and size, e.g. Times, Helvetica.

food *noun* any substance that a plant or animal can take into its body to help it to grow and be healthy.
food chain a series of plants and animals each of which serves as food for the one above it in the series.

fool *noun* **1** a stupid person; someone who acts unwisely. **2** a jester or clown, *Stop playing the fool.* **3** a creamy pudding with crushed fruit in it, *gooseberry fool.*
fool's errand a useless errand.
fool's gold pyrites.
fool's paradise happiness that comes only from being mistaken about something.

fool *verb* **1** behave in a joking way; play about. **2** trick or deceive someone.

foolery *noun* foolish acts or behaviour.

foolhardy *adjective* bold but foolish; reckless.
foolhardiness *noun*

foolish *adjective* without good sense or judgement; unwise. **foolishly** *adverb*, **foolishness** *noun*

foolproof *adjective* easy to use or do correctly.

foot *noun* (*plural* **feet**) **1** the lower part of the leg below the ankle. **2** any similar part, e.g. one used by certain animals to move or attach themselves to things. **3** the lowest part, *the foot of the hill.* **4** an imperial unit of length, equivalent to about 0.305 of a metre. **5** a unit of rhythm in a line of poetry, e.g. each of the four divisions in *Jack / and Jill / went up / the hill.*
on foot walking.

football *noun* **1** an inflated leather ball. **2** any of the team games played with a football; in New Zealand *football* refers mainly to rugby union, in Britain mainly to soccer.
footballer *noun*

footer *noun* (in word processing) words etc. programmed to appear at the foot of every page. (Compare *header.*)

foothill *noun* a low hill near the bottom of a mountain or range of mountains.

foothold *noun* **1** a place to put your foot when climbing. **2** a small but firm position from which you can advance in business etc.

footie *noun* (*informal*) football.

footing *noun* **1** having your feet placed on something; a foothold, *He lost his footing and slipped.* **2** a status, *We are on a friendly footing with that country.*

footlights *plural noun* a row of lights along the front of the floor of a stage.

footnote *noun* a note printed at the bottom of the page.

footpath *noun* a path for pedestrians.

footprint *noun* a mark made by a foot or shoe.

footrot *noun* a disease in sheep or cattle.

footsore *adjective* having feet that are painful or sore from walking.

footstep *noun* **1** a step taken in walking or running. **2** the sound of this.

footstool *noun* a stool for resting your feet on when you are sitting.

for *preposition* This word is used to show (**1**) purpose or direction (*This letter is for you. We set out for home*), (**2**) distance or time (*Walk for ten kilometres or two hours*), (**3**) price or exchange (*We bought it for $2. New lamps for old*), (**4**) cause (*She was fined for speeding*), (**5**) defence or support (*He fought for his country. Are you for us or against us?*), (**6**) reference (*For all her wealth, she is bored*), (**7**) similarity or correspondence (*We took him for a fool*).
for ever for all time; always.

for *conjunction* because, *They hesitated, for they were afraid.*

for- *prefix* **1** away, off (as in *forgive*). **2** prohibiting (as in *forbid*). **3** abstaining or neglecting (as in *forgo, forsake*).

forage *noun* **1** food for horses and cattle. **2** the action of foraging.

forage *verb* (**foraged**, **foraging**) go searching for something; rummage.

foray *noun* a raid.

forbear *verb* (**forbore**, **forborne**, **forbearing**) **1** refrain from something, *We forbore to mention it.* **2** be patient or tolerant. **forbearance** *noun*

forbid *verb* (**forbade**, **forbidden**, **forbidding**) **1** order someone not to do something. **2** refuse to allow, *We shall forbid the marriage.*

forbidding *adjective* looking stern or unfriendly.

force *noun* **1** strength; power; intense effort. **2** (in science) an influence, which can be measured, that causes something to move. **3** an organised group of police, soldiers, etc. **in** or **into force** in or into effectiveness, *The new law comes into force next week.*

force *verb* (**forced**, **forcing**) **1** use force in order to get or do something, or to make somebody obey. **2** break something open by force. **3** cause plants to grow or bloom earlier than is normal, *You can force them in a greenhouse.*

forceful *adjective* strong and vigorous. **forcefully** *adverb*

forceps *noun* (*plural* **forceps**) pincers or tongs used by dentists, surgeons, etc.

forcible *adjective* done by force; forceful. **forcibly** *adverb*

ford *noun* a shallow place where you can walk, cycle, or drive across a river.

ford *verb* cross a river at a ford.

fore *adjective & adverb* at or towards the front, *fore and aft.*

fore *noun* the front part. **to the fore** to or at the front; in or to a prominent position.

fore- *prefix* before (as in *forecast*); in front (as in *foreleg*).

forearm[1] *noun* the arm from the elbow to the wrist or fingertips.

forearm[2] *verb* arm or prepare in advance against possible danger.

forebears *plural noun* ancestors.

foreboding *noun* a feeling that trouble is coming.

forecast *noun* a statement that tells in advance what is likely to happen.

forecast *verb* (**forecast**, **forecasting**) make a forecast. **forecaster** *noun*

forecastle (*say* **foh**-ksul) *noun* the forward part of certain ships.

forecourt *noun* an enclosed area in front of a building etc.

forefathers *plural noun* ancestors.

forefinger *noun* the finger next to the thumb.

forefoot *noun* (*plural* **forefeet**) an animal's front foot.

forefront *noun* the very front.

foregoing *adjective* preceding; previous.

foregone conclusion a result that can be foreseen easily and with certainty.

foreground *noun* the front part of a scene or view etc.

forehand *noun* a stroke made in tennis etc. with the palm of the hand turned forwards.

forehead (*say* **fo**rrid or **for**-hed) *noun* the part of the face above the eyes.

foreign *adjective* **1** of or in another country; of other countries. **2** not belonging, unnatural, *Lying is foreign to her nature.* [from Latin *foris* = outside, abroad]

foreigner *noun* a person from another country.

foreleg *noun* an animal's front leg.

foreman *noun* (*plural* **foremen**) **1** a workman in charge of a group of other workers. **2** a man acting as president and spokesman of a jury.

foremost *adjective & adverb* first in position or rank; most important.

forensic (*say* fer-**en**-sik) *adjective* of or used in lawcourts.

forensic medicine medical knowledge needed in legal matters.

forerunner *noun* a person or thing that comes before another; a sign of what is to come.

foresee *verb* (**foresaw**, **foreseen**, **foreseeing**) realise what is going to happen.

foreseeable *adjective* able to be foreseen.

foreshadow *verb* be a sign of something that is to come.

foreshorten *verb* show an object in a drawing etc. with some lines shortened to give an effect of distance or depth.

foresight *noun* the ability to foresee and prepare for future needs.

forest *noun* trees and undergrowth covering a large area. **forested** *adjective*

forestall *verb* prevent somebody or something by taking action first. [from Old English *foresteall* = ambush]

forestry *noun* planting forests and looking after them. **forester** *noun*

foretaste *noun* an experience of something that is to come in the future.

foretell *verb* (**foretold**, **foretelling**) forecast; prophesy.

forethought *noun* careful thought and planning for the future.

forewarn *verb* warn someone beforehand.

forewoman *noun* (*plural* **forewomen**) **1** a woman worker in charge of other workers. **2** a woman acting as president and spokesman of a jury.

foreword *noun* a preface.

forfeit (*say* **for**-fit) *verb* pay or give up something as a penalty. **forfeiture** *noun*

forfeit *noun* something forfeited.

forge[1] *noun* a place where metal is heated and shaped; a blacksmith's workshop.

forge[1] *verb* (**forged**, **forging**) **1** shape metal by heating and hammering. **2** copy something so as to deceive people. **forger** *noun*, **forgery** *noun*

forge[2] *verb* (**forged**, **forging**) **forge ahead** move forward by a strong effort.

forget *verb* (**forgot**, **forgotten**, **forgetting**) **1** fail to remember. **2** stop thinking about, *Forget your troubles.*
forget yourself behave rudely or thoughtlessly.

forgetful *adjective* tending to forget. **forgetfully** *adverb*, **forgetfulness** *noun*

forget-me-not *noun* a plant with small blue flowers.

forgive *verb* (**forgave**, **forgiven**, **forgiving**) stop feeling angry with somebody about something. **forgiveness** *noun*

forgo *verb* (**forwent**, **forgone**, **forgoing**) give something up; go without.

fork *noun* **1** a small device with prongs for lifting food to your mouth. **2** a large device with prongs used for digging or lifting things. **3** a place where something separates into two or more parts.

fork *verb* **1** lift or dig with a fork. **2** form a fork by separating into two branches. **3** follow one of these branches, *Fork left.*
fork out (*slang*) pay out money.

fork-lift truck a truck with two metal bars at the front for lifting and moving heavy loads.

forlorn *adjective* left alone and unhappy.
forlorn hope the only faint hope left.

form *noun* **1** the shape, appearance, or condition of something. **2** the way something exists, *Ice is a form of water.* **3** a bench. **4** a piece of paper with spaces to be filled in.

form *verb* **1** shape or construct something; create. **2** come into existence; develop, *Icicles formed.*

formal *adjective* strictly following the accepted rules or customs; ceremonious. **formally** *adverb*

formality *noun* (*plural* **formalities**) **1** formal behaviour. **2** something done to obey a rule or custom.

format *noun* the shape and size of something; the way it is arranged.

format *verb* (**formatted**, **formatting**) (especially *Computing*) put (text etc.) into a particular format.

formation *noun* **1** the act of forming something. **2** a thing formed. **3** a special arrangement or pattern, *flying in formation.* [from Latin *formare* = to mould]

formative *adjective* forming or developing something.

former *adjective* of an earlier period; of past times. **formerly** *adverb*
the former the first of two people or things just mentioned.

formidable (*say* **for**-mid-a-bul) *adjective* frightening; difficult to deal with or do, *a formidable task.* **formidably** *adverb* [from Latin *formido* = fear]

formula *noun* (*plural* **formulae**) **1** a set of chemical symbols showing what a substance consists of. **2** a rule or statement expressed in symbols or numbers. **3** a list of substances needed for making something. **4** a fixed wording for a ceremony etc. **5** one of the groups into which racing-cars are placed according to the size of their engines. [Latin, = little form]

formulate *verb* (**formulated**, **formulating**) express clearly and exactly. **formulation** *noun* [from *formula*]

forsake *verb* (**forsook**, **forsaken**, **forsaking**) abandon.

fort *noun* a fortified building. [from Latin *fortis* = strong]

forth *adverb* **1** out; into view. **2** onwards; forwards, *from this day forth.*
and so forth and so on.

forthcoming *adjective* **1** about to come forth or happen, *forthcoming events.* **2** made available when needed, *Money for the trip was not forthcoming.* **3** (*informal*) willing to give information.

forthright *adjective* frank; outspoken.

forthwith *adverb* immediately.

fortification *noun* **1** fortifying something. **2** a wall or building constructed to make a place strong against attack.

fortify *verb* (**fortified**, **fortifying**) **1** make a place strong against attack, especially by building fortifications. **2** strengthen. [same origin as *fort*]

fortissimo *adverb* very loudly. [Italian]

fortitude *noun* courage in bearing pain or trouble. [from Latin *fortis* = strong]

fortnight *noun* a period of two weeks. **fortnightly** *adverb & adjective* [from an old word meaning 'fourteen nights']

fortress *noun* (*plural* **fortresses**) a fortified building or town. [same origin as *fort*]

fortuitous (*say* for-**tew**-it-us) *adjective* happening by chance. **fortuitously** *adverb* [from Latin, = accidental]

USAGE Note that *fortuitous* does not mean the same as *fortunate.*

fortunate *adjective* lucky. **fortunately** *adverb*

fortune *noun* **1** luck; chance; fate. **2** a great amount of money. [from Latin *fortuna* = luck]

forty *noun & adjective* (*plural* **forties**) the number 40; four times ten. **fortieth** *adjective & noun*
forty winks a short sleep; a nap.

forum *noun* **1** the public square in an ancient Roman city. **2** a meeting where a public discussion is held. [Latin]

forward *adjective* **1** going forwards. **2** placed in the front. **3** having made more than the normal progress. **4** too eager or bold. **forwardness** *noun*

forward *adverb* forwards.

forward *noun* **1** a player in the front line of a team in soccer, hockey, etc. **2** any of the players who form the scrum in rugby.

forward *verb* **1** send on a letter etc. to a new address. **2** help something to improve or make progress.

forwards *adverb* **1** to or towards the front. **2** in the direction you are facing.

fossick *verb* (*NZ*) rummage, search, *fossick around.*

fossil *noun* the remains or traces of a prehistoric animal or plant that has been buried in the ground for a very long time and become hardened in rock.
fossil fuel coal, oil, and natural gas.

fossilise *verb* (**fossilised**, **fossilising**) turn into a fossil. **fossilisation** *noun*

foster *verb* **1** bring up someone else's child as if he or she was your own. **2** help to grow or develop. **foster-child** *noun*, **foster-father** *noun*, **foster-mother** *noun* [from Old English *foster* = food]

foul *adjective* **1** disgusting; filthy; tasting or smelling unpleasant. **2** (of weather) rough; stormy. **3** unfair; breaking the rules of a game. **4** colliding or entangled with something. **foully** *adverb*, **foulness** *noun*
foul play unfair play; a violent crime, especially murder.

foul *noun* an action that breaks the rules of a game.

foul *verb* **1** make or become foul, *Smoke had fouled the air.* **2** commit a foul against a player in a game.

found[1] *past tense* of **find**.

found[2] *verb* **1** establish; provide money for starting, *They founded a hospital.* **2** base, *This novel is founded on fact.* [from Latin *fundus* = bottom]

foundation *noun* **1** the founding of something. **2** a base or basis. **3** the solid base on which a building is built up. **foundation-stone** *noun*

founder[1] *noun* a person who founds something, *the founder of the hospital.*

founder[2] *verb* **1** fill with water and sink, *The ship foundered.* **2** stumble; fall. **3** fail completely, *Their plans foundered.* [same origin as *found*[2]]

foundling *noun* a child found abandoned, whose parents are not known.

foundry *noun* (*plural* **foundries**) a factory or workshop where metal or glass is made.

fount *noun* (in poetry) a fountain.

fountain *noun* a device that makes a jet of water shoot up into the air.

fountain-pen *noun* a pen that can be filled with a supply of ink.

four *noun & adjective* the number 4; one more than three.
on all fours on hands and knees.

fourteen *noun & adjective* the number 14; one more than thirteen. **fourteenth** *adjective & noun*

fourth *adjective* next after the third. **fourthly** *adverb*

fourth *noun* **1** the fourth person or thing. **2** one of four equal parts; a quarter.

fowl *noun* a chicken, especially a hen kept or farmed for its eggs and meat.

fox *noun* (*plural* **foxes**) a wild animal that looks like a dog with a long furry tail. **foxy** *adjective*

fox *verb* deceive; puzzle.

foxglove *noun* a tall plant with flowers like the fingers of gloves.

foyer (*say* **foi**-ay) *noun* the entrance hall of a theatre, cinema, or hotel. [French, = hearth]

fracking *noun* a method of extracting oil and natural gas from beneath the earth's crust through fractures caused by the application of a pressurised fluid (also called hydrofracking).

fraction *noun* **1** a number that is not a whole number, e.g. ½, 0.5. **2** a tiny part. **fractional** *adjective*, **fractionally** *adverb* [same origin as *fracture*]

fractious (*say* **frak**-shus) *adjective* irritable. **fractiously** *adverb*, **fractiousness** *noun*

fracture *noun* the breaking of something, especially of a bone.

fracture *verb* (**fractured**, **fracturing**) break. [from Latin *fractum* = broken]

fragile *adjective* easy to break or damage. **fragilely** *adverb*, **fragility** *noun*

fragment *noun* **1** a small piece broken off. **2** a small part. **fragmentary** *adjective*, **fragmentation** *noun*, **fragmented** *adjective*

fragrant *adjective* having a pleasant smell. **fragrance** *noun*

frail *adjective* **1** (of things) fragile. **2** (of people) not strong; not robust, *a frail old man.* **frailty** *noun*

frame *noun* **1** a holder that fits round the outside of a picture. **2** a rigid structure that supports something. **3** a human or animal body, *He has a small frame.* **4** a single exposure on a cinema film.
frame of mind the way you think or feel for a while.

frame *verb* (**framed**, **framing**) **1** put a frame on or round. **2** construct, *They framed the question badly.* **3** make an innocent person seem guilty by arranging false evidence. **frame-up** *noun*

framework *noun* **1** a frame supporting something. **2** a basic plan or system.

franc *noun* a unit of money in France, Switzerland, and other countries, prior to the use of the euro.

franchise *noun* **1** the right to vote in elections. **2** a licence to sell a firm's goods or services in a certain area.

frank *adjective* making your thoughts and feelings clear to people; candid. **frankly** *adverb*, **frankness** *noun*

frank *verb* mark a letter etc. automatically in a machine to show that postage has been paid.

frankincense *noun* a sweet-smelling gum burnt as incense.

frantic *adjective* wildly agitated or excited. **frantically** *adverb* [from Greek *phrenetikos* = mad]

fraternal (*say* fra-**tern**-al) *adjective* of a brother or brothers. **fraternally** *adverb* [from Latin *frater* = brother]

fraternise *verb* (**fraternised**, **fraternising**) associate with other people in a friendly way. **fraternisation** *noun*

fraternity *noun* (*plural* **fraternities**) **1** a brotherly feeling. **2** a group of people who have the same interests or occupation, *the medical fraternity.*

fraud *noun* **1** a dishonest trick; a swindle. **2** an impostor; a person or thing that is not what it pretends to be. **fraudulent** *adjective*, **fraudulently** *adverb*, **fraudulence** *noun*

fraught *adjective* filled; involving, *The situation is fraught with danger.* [from an old use, = loaded with freight]

fray[1] *noun* a fight; a conflict, *ready for the fray.* [same origin as *affray*]

fray[2] *verb* **1** make or become ragged so that loose threads show. **2** (of tempers or nerves) become strained or upset.

freak *noun* a very strange or abnormal person, animal, or thing. **freakish** *adjective*

freckle *noun* a small brown spot on the skin. **freckled** *adjective*

free *adjective* (**freer**, **freest**) **1** able to do what you want to do or go where you want to go. **2** not costing anything. **3** not fixed, *Leave one end free.* **4** not having or affected by something, *The harbour is free of ice.* **5** available; not being used or occupied. **6** generous, *She is very free with her money.* **freely** *adverb*

free *verb* (**freed**, **freeing**) set free.

freebie *noun* (*informal*) something given away free.

freedom *noun* being free; independence.

freehand *adjective* (of a drawing) done without a ruler or compasses etc.

freehold *noun* possessing land or a house as its absolute owner, not as a tenant renting from a landlord.

Freemason *noun* a member of a certain secret society. **Freemasonry** *noun*

freewheel *verb* ride a bicycle without needing to pedal.

freeze *verb* (**froze**, **frozen**, **freezing**) **1** turn into ice; become covered with ice. **2** make or be very cold. **3** keep wages or prices etc. at a fixed level. **4** suddenly stand completely still. **5** the sudden locking of a computer screen.

freeze *noun* **1** a period of freezing weather. **2** the freezing of prices etc.

freezer *noun* a refrigerator in which food can be frozen quickly and stored.

freezing works (*NZ*) a place where animals are killed and their carcasses prepared and frozen for export. **freezing worker** *noun*

freight (*say* frayt) *noun* **1** the transport of goods from one place to another. **2** the goods transported. **3** the charge for this, *Freight is extra.*

freighter (*say* **fray**-ter) *noun* a ship or aircraft carrying mainly cargo.

French fries *plural noun* = **chips** (sense 2).

French window a long window that serves as a door on an outside wall.

frenzy *noun* wild excitement or agitation. **frenzied** *adjective*, **frenziedly** *adverb* [same origin as *frantic*]

frequency *noun* (*plural* **frequencies**) **1** being frequent. **2** how often something happens. **3** the number of oscillations per second of a wave of sound or light etc.
frequency modulation changing the frequency of a radio wave.

frequent (*say* **freek**-went) *adjective* happening often. **frequently** *adverb*

frequent (*say* frik-**went**) *verb* be in or go to a place often, *They frequented the club.* [from Latin *frequens* = crowded]

fresco *noun* (*plural* **frescoes**) a picture painted on a wall or ceiling before the plaster is dry. [Italian, = fresh]

fresh *adjective* **1** newly made or produced or arrived; not stale, *fresh bread.* **2** not tinned, not preserved, *fresh fruit.* **3** cool and clean, *fresh air.* **4** not salty, *fresh water.* **freshly** *adverb*, **freshness** *noun*

freshen *verb* make or become fresh.

freshwater *adjective* of fresh water not sea water; living in rivers or lakes.

fret[1] *verb* (**fretted**, **fretting**) worry or be upset about something. **fretful** *adjective*, **fretfully** *adverb*

fret[2] *noun* a bar or ridge on the finger-board of a guitar etc.

fretsaw *noun* a very narrow saw used for making fretwork.

fretwork *noun* cutting decorative patterns in wood; wood cut in this way.

friable *adjective* easily crumbled.

friar *noun* a man who is a member of certain Roman Catholic religious orders, who has vowed to live a life of poverty. **friary** *noun* [from Latin *frater* = brother]

friction *noun* **1** rubbing. **2** disagreement, quarrelling. **frictional** *adjective* [from Latin *frictum* = rubbed]

Friday *noun* the day after Thursday.

fridge *noun* (*informal*) a refrigerator.

friend *noun* **1** a person you like who likes you. **2** a helpful or kind person.

friendless *adjective* without a friend.

friendly *adjective* behaving like a friend. **friendliness** *noun*

friendship *noun* being friends.

Friesian *noun* one of a breed of large black-and-white dairy cattle.

frieze (*say* freez) *noun* a strip of designs or pictures round the top of a wall.

frigate *noun* a small warship.

fright *noun* **1** sudden great fear. **2** a person or thing that looks ridiculous.

frighten *verb* make or become afraid. be frightened of be afraid of.

frightful *adjective* awful; very great or bad. **frightfully** *adverb*

frigid *adjective* **1** extremely cold. **2** unfriendly; not affectionate. **frigidly** *adverb*, **frigidity** *noun* [from Latin *frigidus* = cold]

frill *noun* **1** a decorative gathered or pleated trimming on a dress, curtain, etc. **2** something extra that is pleasant but unnecessary, *a simple life with no frills.* **frilled** *adjective*, **frilly** *adjective*

fringe *noun* **1** a decorative edging with many threads hanging down loosely. **2** a straight line of short hair hanging down over the forehead. **3** the edge of something. **fringed** *adjective*

frisk *verb* **1** jump or run about playfully. **2** search somebody by running your hands over his or her clothes. **frisky** *adjective*, **friskily** *adverb*, **friskiness** *noun*

fritter[1] *noun* a slice of meat or fruit or potato etc. coated in batter and fried. [from Latin *frictum* = fried]

fritter[2] *verb* waste something gradually; spend money or time on trivial things. [from an old word *fritters* = fragments]

frivolous *adjective* seeking pleasure in a light-hearted way; not serious, not sensible. **frivolously** *adverb*, **frivolity** *noun*

frizz *noun* hair curled into a wiry mass. **frizzy** *adjective*, **frizziness** *noun*

frizzle *verb* (**frizzled**, **frizzling**) **1** fry with a spluttering noise. **2** shrivel something by burning it.

fro *adverb* **to and fro** backwards and forwards.

frock *noun* a girl's or woman's dress.

frog *noun* a small jumping animal that can live both in water and on land.
a frog in your throat hoarseness.

frogman *noun* (*plural* **frogmen**) a swimmer equipped with a rubber suit, flippers, and breathing-apparatus for swimming and working underwater.

frolic *noun* a lively cheerful game or entertainment. **frolicsome** *adjective*

frolic *verb* (**frolicked**, **frolicking**) play about in a lively cheerful way.

from *preposition* This word is used to show (**1**) starting-point in space or time or order (*We flew from London to Paris. We work from 9 to 5 o'clock. Count from one to ten*), (**2**) source or origin (*Get water from the tap*), (**3**) separation or release (*Take the gun from him. She was freed from prison*), (**4**) difference (*Can you tell margarine from butter?*), (**5**) cause (*I suffer from headaches*).

frond *noun* a leaf-like part of a fern, palm-tree, etc. [from Latin *frondis* = of a leaf]

front *noun* **1** the part or side that comes first or is the most important or furthest forward. **2** the place where fighting is happening in a war. **3** an outward appearance or show; a cover for illegal activities. **4** the forward edge of an advancing mass of cold or warm air. **frontal** *adjective*

front *adjective* of the front; in front. [from Latin *frontis* = of the forehead]

frontage *noun* the front of a building; the land beside this.

frontier *noun* the boundary between two countries or regions.

frontispiece *noun* an illustration opposite the title-page of a book.

front-person *noun* a presenter or host of a radio or television programme.

front-runner *noun* a favourite or expected winner.

frost *noun* **1** powdery ice that forms on things in freezing weather. **2** weather with a temperature below freezing-point. **frosty** *adjective*

frost *verb* cover with frost or frosting.

frostbite *noun* harm done to the body by very cold weather. **frostbitten** *adjective*

frosted glass glass made cloudy so that you cannot see through it.

frosting *noun* sugar icing for cakes.

froth *noun* a white mass of tiny bubbles on a liquid. **frothy** *adjective*

frown *verb* wrinkle your forehead because you are angry or worried.

frown *noun* a frowning movement or look.

frugal (*say* **froo**-gal) *adjective* **1** very economical and careful. **2** costing very little money; not plentiful, *a frugal meal*. **frugally** *adverb*, **frugality** *noun*

fruit *noun* (*plural* **fruits** or **fruit**) **1** the seed-container that grows on a tree or plant and is often used as food. **2** the result of doing something, *the fruits of his efforts*. **fruity** *adjective*

fruit *verb* produce fruit.

fruitful *adjective* producing good results, *fruitful discussions*. **fruitfully** *adverb*

fruition (*say* froo-**ish**-on) *noun* the achievement of what was hoped or worked for, *Our plans never came to fruition*. [from Latin *frui* = enjoy]

fruitless *adjective* producing no results. **fruitlessly** *adverb*

frustrate *verb* (**frustrated**, **frustrating**) prevent somebody from doing something; prevent from being successful, *frustrate their wicked plans*. **frustration** *noun* [from Latin *frustra* = in vain]

fry[1] *verb* (**fried**, **frying**) cook something in very hot fat. **fryer** *noun*

fry[2] *plural noun* very young fishes. **small fry** **1** young children. **2** people or things of no importance.

frying-pan *noun* a shallow pan for frying things.

ftp *abbreviation* an abbreviated form of file transfer protocol, a method for copying files on a computer network.

fuchsia (*say* **few**-sha) *noun* an ornamental plant with flowers that hang down.

fudge *noun* **1** a soft sugary sweet. **2** an attempt to hide or confuse an issue.

fudge *verb* deliberately confuse or manipulate.

fuel *noun* something that is burnt to produce heat or power.

fuel *verb* (**fuelled**, **fuelling**) supply something with fuel.

fug *noun* (*informal*) a stuffy atmosphere. **fuggy** *adjective*, **fugginess** *noun*

fugitive (*say* **few**-jit-iv) *noun* a person who is running away from something. [from Latin *fugere* = flee]

fugue (*say* fewg) *noun* a piece of music in which tunes are repeated in a pattern.

fulcrum *noun* the point on which a lever rests.

fulfil *verb* (**fulfilled**, **fulfilling**) **1** do what is required; satisfy; carry out, *You must fulfil your promises*. **2** make something come true, *It fulfilled an ancient prophecy*. **fulfilment** *noun*

full *adjective* **1** containing as much or as many as possible. **2** having many people or things, *full of ideas*. **3** complete, *the full story*. **4** the greatest possible, *at full speed*. **5** fitting loosely; with many folds, *a full skirt*. **fully** *adverb*, **fullness** *noun*
full back (*rugby*) the player positioned closest to a team's own goal-line.
full moon the moon when you can see its whole disc.
full stop the dot used as a punctuation mark at the end of a sentence or an abbreviation.

full *adverb* completely; exactly, *It hit him full in the face*.

full-blown *adjective* fully developed.

fully *adverb* completely.

fulsome *adjective* praising something too much or too emotionally.

fumble *verb* (**fumbled**, **fumbling**) hold or handle something clumsily.

fume *noun* (also **fumes**) strong-smelling smoke or gas.

fume *verb* (**fumed**, **fuming**) **1** give off fumes. **2** be very angry. [from Latin *fumus* = smoke]

fumigate (*say* **few**-mig-ayt) *verb* (**fumigated**, **fumigating**) disinfect something by fumes. **fumigation** *noun*

fun *noun* amusement; enjoyment. **make fun of** make people laugh at a person or thing.

function *noun* **1** what somebody or something is there to do, *The function of a knife is to cut things.* **2** an important event or party. **3** a basic operation in a computer.

function *verb* perform a function; work properly. [from Latin *functum* = performed]

functional *adjective* **1** working properly. **2** practical without being decorative or luxurious. **functionally** *adverb*

fund *noun* **1** money collected or kept for a special purpose. **2** a stock or supply.

fund *verb* supply with money.

fundamental *adjective* basic. **fundamentally** *adverb* [from Latin *fundamentum* = foundation]

fundamentalism *noun* a form of religion that keeps strictly to traditional beliefs. **fundamentalist** *noun*

funeral *noun* the ceremony when a dead person is buried or cremated. [from *Latin funeris* = of a burial]

funereal (*say* few-**neer**-ee-al) *adjective* dark; dismal.

fungus *noun* (*plural* **fungi**, *say* **fung**-I) a plant without leaves or flowers that grows on other plants or on decayed material, *Mushrooms are fungi.*

funk *noun* (*slang*) **1** fear. **2** a coward.

funk *verb* (*slang*) be afraid of doing something and avoid it.

funky *adjective* (*slang*) **1** (of jazz etc.) soulful, with a strong rhythm. **2** fashionable; excellent, exciting.

funnel *noun* **1** a metal chimney on a ship or steam-engine. **2** a tube that is wide at the top and narrow at the bottom to help you pour things into a narrow opening. [from Latin *fundere* = pour]

funnel-web spider a large black poisonous Australian spider.

funny *adjective* (**funnier**, **funniest**) **1** that makes you laugh or smile. **2** strange; odd, *a funny smell.* **funnily** *adverb*

fur *noun* **1** the soft hair that covers some animals. **2** animal skin with the fur on it, used for clothing; fabric that looks like animal fur.

furbelows *plural noun* showy trimmings, frills and furbelows.

furbish *verb* polish or clean; renovate.

furious *adjective* **1** very angry. **2** violent; intense, *furious heat.* **furiously** *adverb*

furl *verb* roll up a sail, flag, or umbrella.

furlong *noun* (in the imperial system) one-eighth of a mile, or about 200 metres.

furlough (*say* **ferl**-oh) *noun* leave of absence from duty; a holiday.

furnace *noun* a device in which great heat can be produced, e.g. for melting metals or making glass.

furnish *verb* **1** provide a place with furniture. **2** provide; supply.

furnishings *plural noun* furniture and fitments, curtains, etc.

furniture *noun* tables, chairs, and other movable things that you need in a house or school or office etc.

furore (*say* few-**ror**-ee) *noun* an excited or angry uproar. [from Latin *furor* = madness]

furrow *noun* **1** a long cut in the ground made by a plough or other implement. **2** a groove. **3** a deep wrinkle in the skin.

furrow *verb* make furrows in something.

furry *adjective* like fur; covered with fur.

further *adverb & adjective* **1** at or to a greater distance; more distant. **2** more; additional, *We made further inquiries.*

USAGE See the note under *farther.*

further *verb* help something to progress, *This success will further your career.* **furtherance** *noun*

furthermore *adverb* also; moreover.

furthest *adverb & adjective* at or to the greatest distance; most distant.

USAGE See the note under *farther.*

furtive *adjective* stealthy; trying not to be seen. **furtively** *adverb*, **furtiveness** *noun* [from Latin *furtivus* = stolen]

fury *noun* wild anger; rage. [from Latin *furia* = rage; an avenging spirit]

fuse[1] *noun* a safety device containing a short piece of wire that melts if too much electricity is passed through it.

fuse[1] *verb* (**fused**, **fusing**) **1** stop working because a fuse has melted. **2** blend together, especially through melting. [from Latin *fusum* = melted]

fuse[2] *noun* a length of material that burns easily, used for setting off an explosive. [from Latin *fusus* = a spindle]

fuselage (*say* **few**-zel-ah*zh*) *noun* the body of an aircraft.

fusillade (*say* few-zil-**ayd**) *noun* a great outburst of firing guns or questions etc. [from French *fusil* = gun]

fusion *noun* **1** the action of blending or uniting things. **2** the uniting of atomic nuclei, usually releasing energy.

fuss *noun* (*plural* **fusses**) **1** unnecessary excitement or bustle. **2** an agitated protest.

fuss *verb* make a fuss about something.

fussy *adjective* (**fussier**, **fussiest**) **1** fussing; inclined to make a fuss. **2** choosing very carefully; hard to please. **3** full of unnecessary details or decorations. **fussily** *adverb*, **fussiness** *noun*

fusty *adjective* (**fustier**, **fustiest**) smelling stale or stuffy. **fustiness** *noun*

futile (*say* **few**-tyl) *noun* useless; having no result. **futility** *noun* [from Latin *futilis* = leaking]

futon *noun* a kind of low bed with a wooden frame. [Japanese]

future *noun* the time that will come; what is going to happen then.

future *adjective* belonging or referring to the future.

fuzz *noun* something fluffy or frizzy.

fuzzy *adjective* **1** like fuzz; covered with fuzz. **2** blurred; not clear. **fuzzily** *adverb*, **fuzziness** *noun*

Gg

gabardine *noun* a strong fabric woven in a slanting pattern.

gabble *verb* (**gabbled**, **gabbling**) talk so quickly that it is difficult to know what is being said.

gable *noun* the pointed part at the top of an outside wall, between two sloping roofs. **gabled** *adjective*

gad *verb* (**gadded**, **gadding**) **gad about** gallivant. **gadabout** *noun*

gadget *noun* any small useful tool. **gadgetry** *noun*

gaff *noun* a stick with a metal hook for landing large fish.

gaffe *noun* a blunder or lapse in manners.

gag *noun* **1** something put into a person's mouth or tied over it to prevent speaking. **2** a joke.

gag *verb* (**gagged**, **gagging**) **1** put a gag on a person. **2** prevent from making comments, *We cannot gag the press.* **3** retch.

gaiety *noun* cheerfulness.

gaily *adverb* in a cheerful way.

gain *verb* **1** get something that you did not have before; obtain. **2** (of a clock or watch) become ahead of the correct time. **3** reach; arrive at, *At last we gained the shore.* **gainer** *noun*
gain on come closer to a person or thing in chasing them or in a race.

gain *noun* something gained; a profit or improvement. **gainful** *adjective*

gait *noun* a way of walking or running, *He walked with a shuffling gait.* [from a dialect word *gate* = going]

gaiter *noun* a leather or cloth covering for the lower part of the leg.

gala (*say* **gah**-la) *noun* **1** a celebration with cheerful festivities. **2** a set of sports contests.

galah *noun* a grey Australian cockatoo with a pink breast.

galaxy *noun* (*plural* **galaxies**) a very large group of stars. **galactic** *adjective*

gale *noun* a very strong wind.

gall[1] (*say* gawl) *noun* **1** bile. **2** bitterness of feeling. **3** (*slang*) impudence.

gall[2] (*say* gawl) *noun* a sore spot on an animal's skin.

gall[2] *verb* **1** rub sore. **2** vex or humiliate someone.

gallant (*say* **gal**-lant) *adjective* **1** brave; chivalrous. **2** fine; stately, *our gallant ship.* **gallantly** *adverb*, **gallantry** *noun*

galleon *noun* a large Spanish sailing-ship used in the 16th–17th centuries.

gallery *noun* (*plural* **galleries**) **1** a platform jutting out from the wall in a church or hall. **2** the highest balcony in a cinema or theatre. **3** a long room or passage. **4** a room or building for showing works of art.

galley *noun* (*plural* **galleys**) **1** an ancient type of ship driven by oars. **2** the kitchen in a ship or aircraft.

galling (*say* **gawl**-ing) *adjective* vexing; humiliating.

gallivant *verb* go about in search of pleasure.

gallon *noun* an imperial unit of volume for liquids, equivalent to about 4.55 litres (British gallon) or about 3.79 litres (US gallon).

gallop *noun* **1** the fastest pace a horse can go. **2** a fast ride on a horse.
gallops (*NZ*) races for thoroughbred horses. (Compare *trots*.)

gallop *verb* (**galloped**, **galloping**) go or ride at a gallop.

gallows *noun* a framework with a noose for hanging criminals.

galore *adverb* in plenty; in great numbers, *bargains galore.*

galoshes *plural noun* a pair of waterproof shoes worn over ordinary shoes.

galvanise *verb* (**galvanised**, **galvanising**) **1** stimulate into sudden activity. **2** coat iron with zinc to protect it from rust. **galvanisation** *noun* [named after an Italian scientist, Luigi Galvani]

gambit *noun* **1** a kind of opening move in chess. **2** an action or remark intended to gain an advantage.

gamble *verb* (**gambled**, **gambling**) **1** bet on the result of a game, race, or other event. **2** take great risks in the hope of gaining something. **gambler** *noun*

gamble *noun* **1** gambling. **2** a risky attempt.

gambol *verb* (**gambolled**, **gambolling**) jump or skip about in play.

game *noun* **1** a form of play or sport, especially one with rules. **2** a section of a long game such as tennis or bridge. **3** a scheme or plan; a trick. **4** wild animals or birds hunted for sport or food.

game *adjective* **1** able and willing to do something, *She is game for all kinds of tricks.* **2** brave. **gamely** *adverb*

gamekeeper *noun* a person employed to protect game-birds and animals, especially from poachers.

gamelan (*say* **gam**-i-lan) *noun* an Indonesian orchestra that consists of sets of gongs, xylophones, and drums etc. as well as string and woodwind instruments.

gaming *noun* gambling.

gamma *noun* the third letter of the Greek alphabet, = g.
gamma rays very short X-rays.

gammon *noun* a kind of ham.

gander *noun* a male goose.

gang *noun* a number of people who do things together, especially with some antisocial or criminal purpose. **gang-member** noun

gang *verb* join in a gang, *gang up.*

gangling *adjective* tall, thin, and awkward-looking.

gangplank *noun* a plank placed so that people can walk into or out of a boat.

gangrene (*say* **gang**-green) *noun* decay of body tissue in a living person.

gangster *noun* a member of a gang of violent criminals.

gangway *noun* **1** a gap left for people to pass between rows of seats or through a crowd. **2** a movable bridge placed so that people can walk into or out of a ship or building.

gannet *noun* a large sea-bird.

gaol (*say* jayl) *noun* & *verb* = *jail.*

gap *noun* **1** a break or opening in something continuous such as a hedge or fence. **2** an interval. **3** a wide difference in ideas.

gape *verb* (**gaped**, **gaping**) **1** have your mouth open. **2** stare with your mouth open. **3** be open wide.

garage (*say* **ga**-rahzh or **ga**-rij) **1** a building in which a motor vehicle or vehicles may be kept. **2** an establishment where motor vehicles are repaired or serviced.
garage sale a sale of second-hand articles held in a private house.

garb *noun* special clothing. **garb** *verb*

garbage *noun* rubbish.

garble *verb* (**garbled**, **garbling**) give a confused account of a story or message so that it is misunderstood.

garden *noun* a piece of ground where flowers, fruit, or vegetables are grown. **gardener** *noun*, **gardening** *noun*

garfish *noun* (*NZ*) a sea-fish with slender body and elongated lower jaw.

gargantuan (*say* gar-**gan**-tew-an) *adjective* gigantic. [from the name of Gargantua, a giant in a story]

gargle *verb* (**gargled**, **gargling**) hold a liquid at the back of the mouth and breathe air through it to wash the inside of the throat. **gargle** *noun*

gargoyle *noun* an ugly or comical face or figure carved on a building, especially on a water-spout.

garish (*say* **gair**-ish) *adjective* too bright or highly coloured; gaudy. **garishly** *adverb*

garland *noun* a wreath of flowers worn or hung as a decoration. **garland** *verb*

garlic *noun* a plant rather like an onion, used for flavouring food.

garment *noun* a piece of clothing.

garner *verb* store up; gather; collect.

garnet *noun* a dark-red stone used as a gem.

garnish *verb* decorate.

garnish *noun* something used to decorate food or give it extra flavour.

garret *noun* an attic.

garrison *noun* **1** troops stationed in a town or fort to defend it. **2** the building they occupy. **garrison** *verb*

garrotte (*say* ga-**rot**) *noun* a cord or wire used for strangling a victim.

garrotte *verb* (**garrotted**, **garrotting**) strangle with a garrotte.

garrulous (*say* **ga**-rool-us) *adjective* talkative. **garrulousness** *noun*

garter *noun* a band of elastic to hold up a sock or stocking.

gas[1] *noun* (*plural* **gases**) **1** a substance that (like air) can move freely and is not liquid or solid at ordinary temperatures. **2** a flammable gas used for lighting, heating, or cooking.

gas[1] *verb* (**gassed**, **gassing**) **1** kill or injure with gas. **2** (*informal*) talk idly for a long time.

gas[2] *noun* (*informal*) petrol.

gash *noun* a long deep cut or wound.

gash *verb* make a gash in something.

gasket *noun* a flat ring or strip of soft material for sealing a joint between metal surfaces.

gasoline *noun* (*American*) petrol.

gasometer (*say* gas-**om**-it-er) *noun* a large round tank in which gas is stored.

gasp *verb* **1** breathe in suddenly when you are shocked or surprised. **2** struggle to breathe with your mouth open when you are tired or ill. **3** speak in a breathless way. **gasp** *noun*

gassy *adjective* of or like gas.

gastric *adjective* of the stomach. [from Greek *gaster* = stomach]

gastronomy (*say* gas-**tron**-om-ee) *noun* the science of good eating. **gastronomic** *adjective* [from Greek *gaster* = stomach, + *-nomia* = management]

gastropod *noun* an animal (e.g. a snail) that moves by means of a fleshy 'foot' on its stomach. [from Greek *gaster* = stomach, + *podos* = of the foot]

gate *noun* **1** a movable barrier, usually on hinges, serving as a door in a wall or fence. **2** the opening it covers. **3** a barrier for controlling the flow of water in a dam or lock. **4** the number of people attending a match etc.

gateau (*say* **gat**-oh) *noun* a large rich cream cake. [from French *gâteau* = cake]

gatecrash *verb* go to a private party without being invited. **gatecrasher** *noun*

gateway *noun* **1** an opening containing a gate. **2** a way to reach something, *The gateway to success.*

gather *verb* **1** come or bring together. **2** collect; obtain gradually, *gather information.* **3** collect as harvest; pluck, *Gather the corn when it is ripe; gather flowers.* **4** understand; learn, *We gather you have been on holiday.* **5** pull cloth into folds by running a thread through it. **6** (of a sore) swell up and form pus.

gathering *noun* **1** an assembly of people. **2** a swelling that forms pus.

gaudy *adjective* too showy and bright. **gaudily** *adverb*, **gaudiness** *noun* [from Latin *gaudere* = rejoice]

gauge (*say* gayj) *noun* **1** a standard measurement. **2** the distance between a pair of rails on a railway. **3** a measuring-instrument.

gauge *verb* (**gauged**, **gauging**) **1** measure. **2** estimate; form a judgement.

gaunt *adjective* **1** (of a person) lean and haggard. **2** (of a place) grim or desolate-looking. **gauntness** *noun*

gauntlet[1] *noun* a glove with a wide cuff covering the wrist. [from French *gant* = glove]

gauntlet[2] *noun* **run the gauntlet** have to suffer continuous severe criticism or risk. [from a former military and naval punishment in which the victim was made to pass between two rows of men who struck him as he passed; the word is from Swedish *gatlopp* = passage]

gauze *noun* **1** thin transparent woven material. **2** fine wire mesh. **gauzy** *adjective* [from Gaza, a town in the Palestinian territories]

gay *adjective* **1** homosexual. **2** (*old use*) cheerful; brightly coloured. **gayness** *noun*

gay *noun* a homosexual person.

gaze *verb* (**gazed**, **gazing**) look at something steadily for a long time.

gaze *noun* a long steady look.

gazelle *noun* a small antelope.

gazette *noun* **1** a newspaper. **2** an official journal.

gazetteer (*say* gaz-it-**eer**) *noun* a list of place-names.

GDP *abbreviation* gross domestic product (the total value of goods produced and services provided in a country in one year).

GE *abbreviation* genetic engineering.

gear *noun* **1** a cog-wheel, especially one of a set in a motor vehicle that transmit movement from the engine to the wheels when they are connected. **2** equipment; apparatus, *camping gear.*

gear *verb* **1** provide with a gear or gears. **2** provide with equipment etc.

gearbox *noun* a case enclosing gears.

gecko *noun* (*plural* **geckos**) a small lizard found in houses.

geek[1] *noun* (*slang*) **1** a foolish or despised person. **2** an obsessive enthusiast or expert, *He is a real computer geek.*

geek[2] *noun* (*slang*) a look.

Geiger counter (*say* **gy**-ger) *noun* an instrument that detects and measures radioactivity. [named after the German scientist H. W. Geiger]

gelatine *noun* a clear jelly-like substance made by boiling animal tissue and used to make jellies and other foods and in photographic film. **gelatinous** (*say* jil-**at**-in-us) *adjective* [same origin as *jelly*]

geld *verb* castrate, spay.

gelding *noun* a castrated horse or other male animal.

gelignite (*say* **jel**-ig-nyt) *noun* a kind of explosive. [from *gelatine*, + Latin *ignis* = fire]

gem *noun* **1** a precious stone. **2** an excellent person or thing.

gender *noun* **1** the group in which a noun is classed in the grammar of some languages (e.g. *masculine*, *feminine*, *neuter*). **2** a person's sex. [from Latin *genus* = a kind]

gene (*say* jeen) *noun* one of the factors controlling which characteristics (such as the colour of hair or eyes) are inherited from parents. [from Greek, = born]

genealogy (*say* jeen-ee-**al**-o-jee) *noun* **1** a statement or diagram showing how people are descended from an ancestor; a pedigree. **2** the study of family history and ancestors. **genealogical** (*say* jeen-ee-a-**loj**-ik-al) *adjective* [from Greek *genea* = race of people, + *-logy*]

general *adjective* **1** of all or most people or things, *general approval.* **2** not detailed; not exact, *a general account.* **3** chief; head, *the general secretary.*
general election an election of Members of Parliament for the whole country.
general practitioner a doctor who treats cases of all kinds (as opposed to a *specialist*).

general *noun* a senior army officer.

generalise *verb* (**generalised**, **generalising**) **1** make a statement that is true of most cases. **2** bring into general use. **generalisation** *noun*

generality *noun* (*plural* **generalities**) **1** being general. **2** a general statement without exact details.

generally *adverb* **1** usually. **2** in a general sense; without regard to details, *I was speaking generally.*

generate *verb* (**generated**, **generating**) produce; create.

generation *noun* **1** generating. **2** a single stage in a family. *Three generations were included: children, parents, and grandparents.* **3** all the people born at about the same time.

generator *noun* **1** an apparatus for producing gases or steam. **2** a machine for converting mechanical energy into electricity.

generic (*say* jin-**e**-rik) *adjective* of a whole genus or kind. **generically** *adverb*

generous *adjective* **1** willing to give things or share them. **2** given freely; plentiful, *a generous helping.* **3** kindly and not petty in making judgements. **generously** *adverb*, **generosity** *noun*

genesis *noun* beginning; origin. [Greek, = creation or origin]

genetic (*say* jin-**et**-ik) *adjective* of genes; of characteristics inherited from parents or ancestors. **genetically** *adverb* [from *genesis*]

genetic engineering *noun* altering the features of an animal or plant by experimenting with its genetic material.

genetic fingerprinting *noun* analysis of DNA from body samples for identification purposes.

genetics (*say* jin-**et**-iks) *noun* the study of heredity.

genial (*say* **jee**-nee-al) *adjective* kindly and cheerful. **genially** *adverb*, **geniality** (*say* jee-nee-**al**-it-ee) *noun*

genie (*say* **jee**-nee) *noun* (in Arabian tales) a spirit with strange powers. [from Arabic *jinni*]

genital (*say* **jen**-it-al) *adjective* of animal reproduction or reproductive organs.

genitals (*say* **jen**-it-alz) *plural noun* external sexual organs.

genius *noun* (*plural* **geniuses**) **1** an unusually clever person. **2** a very great natural ability. [Latin, = a spirit]

genocide (*say* **jen**-o-syd) *noun* deliberate extermination of a race of people. [from Greek *genos* = a race, + Latin *caedere* = kill]

gent *noun* (*slang*) a gentleman; a man.

genteel (*say* jen-**teel**) *adjective* trying to seem polite and refined. **genteelly** *adverb*, **gentility** (*say* jen-**til**-it-ee) *noun*

gentile *noun* a person who is not Jewish.

gentle *adjective* kind and quiet; not rough or severe. **gently** *adverb*, **gentleness** *noun*

gentleman (*plural* **gentlemen**) **1** a well-mannered or honourable man. **2** a man of good social position. **3** (in polite use) a man.

genuine *adjective* really what it is said to be; not faked or pretending. **genuinely** *adverb*, **genuineness** *noun*

genus (*say* **jee**-nus) *noun* (*plural* **genera**, *say* **jen**-er-a) a group of similar animals or plants, *Lions and tigers belong to the same genus.* [Latin, = family or race]

geo- *prefix* earth. [from Greek *ge* = earth]

geography (*say* jee-**og**-ra-fee) *noun* the study of the earth's surface and of its climate, peoples, and products. **geographer** *noun*, **geographical** *adjective*, **geographically** *adverb* [from *geo-* + *-graphy*]

geology (*say* jee-**ol**-o-jee) *noun* the study of the structure of the earth's crust and its layers. **geological** *adjective*, **geologically** *adverb*, **geologist** *noun* [from *geo-* + *-logy*]

geometry (*say* jee-**om**-it-ree) *noun* the study of lines, angles, surfaces and solids in mathematics. **geometric** *adjective*, **geometrical** *adjective*, **geometrically** *adverb* [from *geo-*, + Greek *-metria* = measurement]

geothermal *adjective* of the earth's internal heat, especially in the form of steam and hot water rising to the surface, *Rotorua is situated in a geothermal region.*

geranium *noun* a garden plant with red, pink, or white flowers.

geriatric (*say* je-ree-**at**-rik) *adjective* concerned with the care of old people and their health. [from Greek *geras* = old age, + *iatros* = doctor]

germ *noun* **1** a micro-organism, especially one that can cause disease. **2** a tiny living structure from which a plant or animal may develop. **3** part of the seed of a cereal plant.

germane *adjective* relevant.

germicide *noun* a substance that kills germs. [from *germ*, + Latin *caedere* = kill]

germinate *verb* (**germinated**, **germinating**) begin to grow and develop; put forth shoots. **germination** *noun*

gestation (*say* jes-**tay**-shun) *noun* **1** the process of carrying or being carried in the womb. **2** the time from conception until birth. **3** the private development of a plan etc. **gestate** *verb*

gesticulate (*say* jes-**tik**-yoo-layt) *verb* (**gesticulated**, **gesticulating**) make expressive movements with hands and arms. **gesticulation** *noun*

gesture (*say* **jes**-cher) *noun* a movement or action that expresses what a person feels. **gesture** *verb*

get *verb* (**got**, **getting**) This word has many different uses, including (**1**) obtain or receive, *She got first prize.* (**2**) become, *Don't get angry!* (**3**) reach a place, *We got there by midnight.* (**4**) put or move, *I can't get my shoe on.* (**5**) prepare, *Will you get the tea?* (**6**) persuade or order, *Get him to wash up.* (**7**) catch or suffer from an illness. (**8**) (*informal*) understand, *Do you get what I mean?*
get away with escape with something; avoid being punished for what you have done.
get by (*informal*) manage.
get on make progress; be friendly with somebody.
get over recover from an illness etc.
get up stand up; get out of your bed in the morning; prepare or organise, *We got up a concert.*
get your own back (*informal*) have your revenge.

getaway *noun* an escape after committing a crime.

get-together *noun* a gathering.

geyser (*say* **gy**-zer) *noun* a natural spring that shoots up columns of hot water. [from the name of a hot spring in Iceland (*geysa* = gush)]

ghastly *adjective* **1** very unpleasant or bad. **2** looking pale and ill. **ghastliness** *noun* [related to *aghast* = horrified]

gherkin (*say* **ger**-kin) *noun* a small cucumber used for pickling.

ghetto (*say* **get**-oh) *noun* (*plural* **ghettos**) a slum area inhabited by a group of people who are treated unfairly in comparison with others. [from Italian *getto* = foundry (the first ghetto was in Venice, on the site of a foundry)]

ghost *noun* the spirit of a dead person. **ghostly** *adjective*

ghoulish (*say* **gool**-ish) *adjective* enjoying things that are grisly or unpleasant. **ghoulishly** *adverb*, **ghoulishness** *noun* [from *ghoul* = a demon in Muslim stories]

giant *noun* **1** (in fairy-tales) a man-like creature of very great height and size. **2** a man, animal, or plant that is much larger than the usual size.

giantess *noun* (*plural* **giantesses**) a female giant.

gibber (*say* **jib**-er) *verb* make quick meaningless sounds, especially when shocked or terrified.

gibberish (*say* **jib**-er-ish) *noun* meaningless speech; nonsense.

gibbet (*say* **jib**-it) *noun* **1** a gallows. **2** an upright post with an arm from which a criminal's body was hung after execution.

gib board *noun* (*NZ*) short for **gibraltar board** (*trade mark*), a form of plaster board used to line the interior walls of houses.

gibbon *noun* an ape with very long arms.

gibe (*say* jyb) *noun & verb* jeer.

giblets (*say* **jib**-lits) *plural noun* the edible parts of the inside of a bird, taken out before it is cooked.

gidday *interjection* (*NZ, informal*) good day.

giddy *adjective* having or causing the feeling that everything is spinning round. **giddily** *adverb*, **giddiness** *noun*

gift *noun* **1** a present. **2** a talent, *She has a gift for music.*

gifted *adjective* talented.

gig *noun* (*informal*) a show when a musician or band plays pop music in public.

gigantic *adjective* very large.

giggle *verb* (**giggled**, **giggling**) laugh in a silly way.

giggle *noun* **1** a silly laugh. **2** (*informal*) something amusing, a joke.

gild *verb* cover with a thin layer of gold or gold paint.

gills *plural noun* **1** the part of the body through which fishes and certain other water animals breathe while in water. **2** the thin upright parts under the cap of a mushroom.

gilt *noun* a thin gold covering.

gilt *adjective* gilded; gold-coloured.

gimlet *noun* a small tool with a screw-like tip for boring holes.

gimmick *noun* something unusual done or used to attract people's attention.

gin[1] *noun* a colourless alcoholic spirit flavoured with juniper berries. [from the name of Geneva, a city in Switzerland]

gin² *noun* **1** a kind of trap for catching animals. **2** a machine for separating the fibres of the cotton-plant from its seeds.

gin² *verb* (**ginned**, **ginning**) treat cotton in a gin. [from Old French *engin* = engine]

ginger *noun* **1** a flavouring made from the hot-tasting root of a tropical plant. **2** this root. **3** liveliness; energy. **4** reddish yellow.
ginger *adjective*

ginger *verb* make more lively, *This will ginger things up!*

gingerbread *noun* a ginger-flavoured cake or biscuit.

gingerly *adverb* cautiously.

ginkgo *noun* (*plural* **ginkgos**) a tree with fan-shaped leaves and yellow flowers.

giraffe *noun* an African animal rather like a horse but with a very long neck.

gird *verb* **1** fasten with a belt or band. *He girded on his sword.* **2** prepare for an effort, *gird yourself for action.*

girder *noun* a metal beam supporting part of a building or a bridge.

girdle *noun* a belt or cord worn round the waist.

girl *noun* **1** a female child. **2** a young woman.
girlhood *noun*, **girlish** *adjective*

girlfriend *noun* a girl that a boy regularly goes out with.

girt *adjective* girded.

girth *noun* **1** the distance round a thing. **2** a band passing under a horse's body to hold the saddle in place.

gist (*say* jist) *noun* the essential points or general sense of a speech etc.

give *verb* (**gave**, **given**, **giving**) **1** cause another person to receive something that you have or can provide. **2** make or perform an action or effort, *He gave a laugh.* **3** be flexible or springy; bend or collapse when pressed. **giver** *noun*
give away make a gift of; reveal (a secret etc.); stop doing, *she gave gymnastics away.*
give in acknowledge that you are defeated; yield.
give up stop doing or trying something; surrender, *the burglar gave himself up.*
give way collapse, *the scaffolding gave way*; let (a car etc.) go before you.

given *adjective* named or stated in advance, *All the people in a given area.*

gizzard *noun* a bird's second stomach, in which food is ground up.

glacé (*say* **glas**-ay) *adjective* iced with sugar; crystallised. [French, = iced]

glacial (*say* **glay**-shal) *adjective* icy; of or from ice. **glacially** *adverb* [from Latin *glacies* = ice]

glacier (*say* **glas**-ee-er) *noun* a river of ice that moves very slowly.

glad *adjective* **1** pleased; expressing joy. **2** giving pleasure, *We brought the glad news.*
gladly *adverb*, **gladness** *noun*
glad of grateful for; pleased with.

gladden *verb* make a person glad.

glade *noun* an open space in a forest.

gladiator (*say* **glad**-ee-ay-ter) *noun* a man trained to fight in public shows in ancient Rome. **gladiatorial** (*say* glad-ee-at-**or**-ee-al) *adjective* [from Latin *gladius* = sword]

glamorise *verb* (**glamorised**, **glamorising**) make glamorous or romantic.

glamour *noun* attractiveness, romantic charm. **glamorous** *adjective* [from an old use of *grammar* = magic]

glance *verb* (**glanced**, **glancing**) **1** look at something briefly. **2** strike something at an angle and slide off it, *The ball glanced off his bat.* **glance** *noun*

gland *noun* an organ of the body that separates substances from the blood so that they can be used or expelled. **glandular** *adjective*

glare *verb* (**glared**, **glaring**) **1** shine with an unpleasant dazzling light. **2** stare angrily or fiercely. **glare** *noun*

glasnost *noun* open reporting of news etc. in the former Soviet Union. [Russian, = publicity]

glass *noun* (*plural* **glasses**) **1** a hard brittle substance that is usually transparent. **2** a container made of glass for drinking from. **3** a mirror. **4** a lens or telescope.
glassy *adjective*

glasses *plural noun* **1** spectacles. **2** binoculars.

glaze *verb* (**glazed**, **glazing**) **1** fit or cover with glass. **2** give a shiny surface to something. **3** become glassy.

glaze *noun* a shiny surface or coating, especially on pottery. [from *glass*]

glazier (*say* **glay**-zee-er) *noun* a person whose job is to fit glass in windows.

gleam *noun* **1** a beam of soft light, especially one that comes and goes. **2** a small amount of hope, humour, etc.

gleam *verb* send out gleams.

glean *verb* **1** pick up grain left by harvesters. **2** gather bit by bit, *glean some information.*
gleaner *noun*

glee *noun* lively or triumphant delight.
gleeful *adjective*, **gleefully** *adverb*

glen *noun* a narrow valley.

glib *adjective* speaking or writing readily but not sincerely or thoughtfully. **glibly** *adverb*, **glibness** *noun* [from an old word *glibbery* = slippery]

glide *verb* (**glided**, **gliding**) **1** fly or move along smoothly. **2** fly without using an engine. **glide** *noun*
glide time (*NZ*) flexitime.

glider *noun* an aeroplane that does not use an engine.

glimmer *noun* a faint gleam.

glimmer *verb* gleam faintly.

glimpse *noun* a brief view.

glimpse *verb* (**glimpsed**, **glimpsing**) catch a glimpse of.

glint *noun* very brief flash of light.

glint *verb* send out a glint.

glissade (*say* gliss-**ayd**) *verb* (**glissaded**, **glissading**) glide or slide skilfully; especially down a steep slope.

glisten (*say* **glis**-en) *verb* shine like something wet or polished.

glitter *verb & noun* sparkle.

gloaming *noun* the evening twilight.

gloat *verb* be full of greedy or unkind pleasure.

global *adjective* **1** of the whole world; world-wide. **2** of or in the whole system. **globally** *adverb*

globe *noun* **1** something shaped like a ball, especially one with a map of the whole world on it. **2** the world. *She has travelled all over the globe.* **3** a hollow round glass object.

globular (*say* **glob**-yoo-ler) *adjective* shaped like a globe.

globule (*say* **glob**-yool) *noun* a small rounded drop.

gloom *noun* a gloomy condition or feeling;

gloomy *adjective* (**gloomier**, **gloomiest**) **1** almost dark. **2** depressed; depressing; sad. **gloomily** *adverb*, **gloominess** *noun*

glorify *verb* (**glorified**, **glorifying**) **1** give glory or honour. **2** make a thing seem more splendid than it really is. **glorification** *noun*

glorious *adjective* having glory; splendid. **gloriously** *adverb*

glory *noun* **1** fame and honour. **2** praise. **3** beauty; magnificence.

glory *verb* (**gloried**, **glorying**) rejoice; pride yourself, *They gloried in victory.*

glory-box *noun* (*plural* **glory-boxes**) (*NZ*) clothes, linen, etc. stored by a girl or woman in preparation for marriage.

gloss *noun* (*plural* **glosses**) the shine on a smooth surface.

gloss *verb* make a thing glossy.
gloss over make a fault or mistake etc. seem less serious than it really is.

glossary *noun* (*plural* **glossaries**) a list of specific or technical terms with their meanings. [from Greek *glossa* = tongue, language.]

glossy *adjective* (**glossier**, **glossiest**) shiny. **glossily** *adverb*, **glossiness** *noun*

glove *noun* a covering for the hand, usually with separate divisions for each finger and thumb. **gloved** *adjective*

glow *noun* **1** brightness and warmth without flames. **2** a warm or cheerful feeling, *We felt a glow of pride.*

glow *verb* produce a glow.

glower (*rhymes with* flower) *verb* stare angrily; scowl.

glow-worm *noun* **1** a kind of beetle whose tail gives out a green light. **2** (*NZ*) a luminous gnat larva.

glucose *noun* a form of sugar found in fruit-juice. [same origin as *glycerine*]

glue *noun* a sticky substance used for joining things. **gluey** *adjective*

glue *verb* (**glued**, **gluing**) **1** stick with glue. **2** attach or hold closely, *His ear was glued to the keyhole.*

glue ear *noun* a blocking of the middle ear with fluid.

glue-sniffing *noun* breathing in the fumes of plastic glue that act as a drug. **glue-sniffer** *noun*

glum *adjective* sad and gloomy. **glumly** *adverb*, **glumness** *noun* [from dialect *glum* = to frown]

glut *verb* (**glutted**, **glutting**) **1** supply with much more than is needed. **2** satisfy fully with food.

glut *noun* an excessive supply. [same origin as *glutton*]

gluten (*say* **gloo**-ten) *noun* a sticky protein substance in flour. [from Latin, = glue]

glutinous (*say* **gloo**-tin-us) *adjective* glue-like, sticky. [same origin as *gluten*]

glutton *noun* a person who eats too much. **gluttonous** *adjective*, **gluttony** *noun* [from Latin *gluttire* = to swallow]

glycerine (*say* **glis**-er-een) *noun* a thick sweet colourless liquid used in ointments and medicines and in explosives. [from Greek *glykys* = sweet]

GM *abbreviation* genetically modified, *GM foods.*

GMT *abbreviation* Greenwich Mean Time.

gnarled (*say* narld) *adjective* twisted and knobbly, like an old tree.

gnash (*say* nash) *verb* grind teeth together.

gnat (*say* nat) *noun* a tiny fly that bites.

gnaw (*say* naw) *verb* keep on biting something hard.

gnome (*say* nohm) *noun* a kind of dwarf in fairy-tales, usually living underground.

gnu (*say* noo) *noun* a large ox-like antelope.

go *verb* (**went**, **gone**, **going**) This word is used to show (**1**) movement, especially away from somewhere (*Where are you going?*), (**2**) direction (*The road goes to Taupo*), (**3**) change (*Milk went sour*), (**4**) progress or result (*The gun went bang*), (**5**) place (*Plates go on that shelf*), (**6**) sale (*The house went very cheaply*), (**7**) (*informal*) speech (*She goes, 'I thought you were lost.'*).

go *noun* (*plural* **goes**) **1** a turn or try, *May I have a go?* **2** (*informal*) a success, *They made a go of it.* **3** (*informal*) energy; liveliness, *She is full of go.*
on the go active; always working or moving.

goad *noun* a stick with a pointed end for prodding cattle to move onwards.

goad *verb* stir into action by being annoying, *He goaded me into fighting.*

go-ahead *noun* a signal to proceed.

go-ahead *adjective* energetic; willing to try new methods.

goal *noun* **1** the place where a ball must go to score a point in soccer, hockey, etc. **2** a point scored in this way. **3** an objective. [from an old word *gol* = boundary]

goalkeeper *noun* the player who stands in the goal to try and keep the ball from entering.

goalpost *noun* either of the two upright posts of a goal.

goanna *noun* a large Australian lizard.

goat *noun* a small animal with horns, kept for its milk.

gobble *verb* (**gobbled**, **gobbling**) eat quickly and greedily.

gobbledegook *noun* (*slang*) pompous language used by officials. [imitation of the sound a turkey-cock makes]

go-between *noun* a person who acts as a messenger or negotiator between others.

goblet *noun* a drinking-glass with a stem and a foot.

goblin *noun* a mischievous ugly elf.

gobsmacked *adjective* (*informal*) shocked.

God *noun* the creator of the universe in Christian, Jewish, and Muslim belief.

god *noun* a person or thing that is worshipped, *Mars was a Roman god.*

goddess *noun* (*plural* **goddesses**) a female god.

godhead *noun* the divine nature of God.

godly *adjective* (**godlier**, **godliest**) sincerely religious. **godliness** *noun*

godparent *noun* a person at a child's christening who promises to see that he or she is brought up as a Christian. **godchild** *noun*, **god-daughter** *noun*, **godfather** *noun*, **godmother** *noun*, **godson** *noun*

godsend *noun* a piece of unexpected good luck.

godwit *noun* a wading bird with a straight bill or one curved upwards, that migrates to New Zealand from Siberia in summer.

Godzone *noun* (*informal*) New Zealand. [from *God's own country*]

goggle *verb* (**goggled**, **goggling**) stare with wide-open eyes.

goggles *plural noun* large spectacles for protecting the eyes from wind, water, dust, etc.

going *present participle of* **go**.
be going to do something be ready or likely to do it.

gold *noun* **1** a precious yellow metal. **2** a deep yellow colour. **3** a gold medal, usually given as first prize. **gold** *adjective*

gold-digger *noun* a person who mines for gold.

gold-dredge *noun* a boat equipped with machinery to dredge for gold.

golden *adjective* **1** made of gold. **2** coloured like gold. **3** precious; excellent, *a golden opportunity*.
golden wedding the 50th anniversary of a wedding.

goldfield *noun* an area where gold is found.

goldfinch *noun* (*plural* **goldfinches**) a bird with yellow feathers in its wings.

goldfish *noun* (*plural* **goldfish**) a small red or orange fish, often kept as a pet.

goldrush *noun* the movement of many people to a goldfield.

goldsmith *noun* a person who makes things in gold.

golf *noun* an outdoor game played by hitting a small white ball with a club into a series of holes on a specially prepared ground (a **golf-course** or **golf-links**). **golfer** *noun*, **golfing** *noun*

golliwog *noun* a black (male) doll with woolly hair.

gong *noun a* large metal disc that makes an echoing sound when it is hit.

good *adjective* (**better**, **best**) **1** having the right qualities; of the kind that people like, *a good book.* **2** kind, *It was good of you to help us.* **3** well-behaved, *Be a good boy.* **4** healthy; giving benefit, *Exercise is good for you.* **5** thorough, *Give it a good clean.* **6** large; considerable, *It's a good distance from the shops.*
good as gold (*NZ, informal*) satisfactory, excellent.
good day a form of greeting or farewell.

Good Friday the Friday before Easter, when Christians commemorate the Crucifixion of Christ.

good *noun* **1** something good, *Do good to others.* **2** benefit, *It's for your own good.*
good on you (*informal*) well done.
for good for ever.
no good useless.

goodbye *interjection* a word used when you leave somebody or at the end of a phone call. [short for *God be with you*]

goodness *noun* **1** being good. **2** the good part of something.

goods *plural noun* **1** things that are bought and sold. **2** things that are carried on trains, trucks, etc.

goodwill *noun* a kindly feeling.

goody *noun* (*plural* **goodies**) (*informal*) **1** something good or attractive, especially to eat. **2** a person of good character.

google *verb* use an Internet search engine, *I googled for pāua.* [from proprietary name *Google*]

goose *noun* (*plural* **geese**) a kind of bird with webbed feet, larger than a duck.

gooseberry *noun* (*plural* **gooseberries**) a small green fruit that grows on a prickly bush.

goose-flesh *noun* (also called **goose-pimples**) skin that has turned rough with small bumps on it because a person is cold or afraid.

gore[1] *verb* (**gored**, **goring**) wound by piercing with a horn or tusk.

gore[2] *noun* thickened blood from a cut or wound. [from Old English *gor* = dirt]

gorge *noun* **1** a narrow valley with steep sides. **2** the throat or gullet.

gorge *verb* (**gorged**, **gorging**) eat greedily; stuff with food. [French, = throat]

gorgeous *adjective* magnificent; beautiful.
gorgeously *adverb*

gorilla *noun* a large strong African ape.

gorse *noun* a prickly bush with small yellow flowers.

gory *adjective* **1** covered with blood. **2** with much bloodshed, *a gory battle.*

gosh *interjection* (*slang*) an exclamation of surprise.

gosling *noun* a young goose.

gospel *noun* **1** the teachings of Jesus Christ. **2** something you can safely believe.
the Gospels the first four books of the New Testament, telling of the life and teachings of Jesus Christ. [from Old English *god* = good, + *spel* = news]

gossamer *noun* **1** fine cobwebs made by small spiders. **2** any fine delicate material.

gossip *verb* (**gossiped**, **gossiping**) talk a lot about other people.

gossip *noun* **1** gossiping talk. **2** a person who enjoys gossiping. **gossipy** *adjective*

got *past tense* of **get**.
have got possess, *Have you got a car?*
have got to must.

Gothic *adjective* of the style of building common in the 12th–16th centuries, with pointed arches and much carving.

gouge (*say* gowj) *verb* (**gouged**, **gouging**) scoop or force out by pressing.

goulash (*say* **goo**-lash) *noun* a meat stew seasoned with red pepper. [from Hungarian *gulyashus* = herdsman's meat]

gourd (*say* goord) *noun* the rounded hard-skinned fruit of a climbing plant.

gourmet (*say* **goor**-may) *noun* a person who understands and appreciates good food and drink. [French, = wine-taster]

gout *noun* a disease that causes painful inflammation of the toes, knees, and fingers.
gouty *adjective*

govern *verb* be in charge of the public affairs of a country or an organisation.

governess *noun* a woman employed to teach children in a private household.

government *noun* **1** the group of people who govern a country. **2** the process of governing.
governmental *adjective*

governor *noun* **1** a person who governs a State or a colony etc. **2** the representative of the Queen in an Australian state. **3** a member of the governing body of a school or other institution.

Governor-General *noun* (*plural* **Governors-General**) (in New Zealand and some other Commonwealth countries) the representative of the Queen.

gown *noun* a loose flowing garment.

GP *abbreviation* general practitioner.

grab *verb* (**grabbed**, **grabbing**) take hold of suddenly or greedily.

grace *noun* **1** beauty of movement or manner or design. **2** goodwill; favour. **3** a short prayer of thanks before or after a meal. **4** the title of a duke, duchess, or archbishop.

grace *verb* (**graced**, **gracing**) bring honour or dignity to something.

graceful *adjective* full of grace. **gracefully** *adverb*, **gracefulness** *noun*

gracious *adjective* kind and pleasant.
graciously *adverb*, **graciousness** *noun*

grade *noun* a step in a scale of quality or value or rank; a standard.

grade *verb* (**graded**, **grading**) arrange in grades. [from Latin *gradus* = a step]

gradient (*say* **gray**-dee-ent) *noun* a slope.

gradual *adjective* happening slowly but steadily. **gradually** *adverb*

graduate (*say* **grad**-yoo-ayt) *verb* (**graduated**, **graduating**) **1** get a university degree. **2** divide into graded sections; mark with units of measurement.

graduate (*say* **grad**-yoo-at) *noun* a person who has a university degree.

graffiti *plural noun* words or drawings sprayed, scratched, or scribbled on a wall or other surface, *These graffiti are a problem.* [Italian, = scratchings]

> USAGE Note that this word is a plural (the singular is *graffito*). It is incorrect to say 'a graffiti' or 'this graffiti'.

graft[1] *noun* **1** a shoot from one plant or tree fixed into another to form a new growth. **2** a piece of living tissue transplanted by a surgeon to replace what is diseased or damaged, *a skin graft.*

graft[1] *verb* insert or transplant as a graft.

graft[2] *noun* (*NZ, informal*) hard work.

graft[2] *verb* (*NZ, informal*) work hard.

grain *noun* **1** a small hard seed or similar particle. **2** cereal plants when they are growing or after being harvested. **3** the pattern of lines made by the fibres in a piece of wood. **grainy** *adjective*

gram *noun* one-thousandth of a kilogram.

-gram *suffix* forming nouns meaning something written or drawn etc. (e.g. *diagram*). [from Greek *gramma* = thing written]

grammar *noun* **1** a set of rules for the form and use of words in a language. **2** a book about these rules. [from Greek, = the art of letters]

grammatical *adjective* of grammar; according to its rules. **grammatically** *adverb*

gramophone *noun* (*old use*) a record-player. [altered from 'phonogram', from Greek *phone* = a sound, + *-gram*]

grampus *noun* (*plural* **grampuses**) a large dolphin-like sea animal.

granary *noun* (*plural* **granaries**) a storehouse for grain.

grand *adjective* **1** splendid, magnificent. **2** including everything; complete, *The grand total.*
grandly *adverb*, **grandness** *noun*
grand mal *noun* a major seizure.
grand piano a large piano with the strings fixed horizontally.

grandad (*informal*) grandfather.

grandchild *noun* (*plural* **grandchildren**) the child of a person's son or daughter.
granddaughter *noun*, **grandson** *noun*

grandeur (*say* **grand**-yer) *noun* grandness; splendour.

grandfather *noun* the father of a person's father or mother.
grandfather clock a clock in a tall wooden case.

grandiose (*say* **grand**-ee-ohss) *adjective* imposing; trying to seem grand.

grandma *noun* (*informal*) grandmother.

grandmother *noun* the mother of a person's father or mother.

grandpa *noun* (*informal*) grandfather.

grandparent *noun* a grandfather or grandmother.

grandstand *noun* a building with a roof and rows of seats for spectators at a racecourse or sports ground.

granite *noun* a very hard kind of rock.

granny *noun* (*plural* **grannies**) (*informal*) grandmother.
granny flat a self-contained part of a house, for an older relative.
granny knot a reef-knot with the strings crossed the wrong way.

grant *verb* **1** give or allow what is asked for, *grant a request.* **2** admit; agree that something is true.
take for granted assume that something is true or will always be available.

grant *noun* something granted, especially a sum of money.

granular *adjective* like grains.

granule *noun* a small grain.

grape *noun* a small green or purple berry that grows in bunches on a vine.

grapefruit *noun* (*plural* **grapefruit**) a large round yellow citrus fruit.

grapevine *noun* **1** a vine on which grapes grow. **2** a way by which news is passed on unofficially.

graph *noun* a diagram showing how two qualities are related. [from Greek *-graphia* = writing]
graph paper paper printed with small squares. used for drawing graphs.

-graph *suffix* forming nouns and verbs meaning something written or drawn etc. (e.g. *photograph*). [same origin as *graph*]

graphic *noun* an example of graphics, especially one created by a computer program.

graphic *adjective* **1** of drawing or painting, *a graphic artist.* **2** giving a lively description.
graphically *adverb*

graphics *plural noun* diagrams, lettering, and drawings.

graphite *noun* a soft black form of carbon used for the lead in pencils, as a lubricant, and in nuclear reactors.

-graphy *suffix* forming names of descriptive sciences (e.g. *geography*) or methods of writing or drawing etc. (e.g. *photography*). [same origin as *graph*]

grapnel *noun* a heavy metal device with claws for hooking things.

grapple *verb* (**grappled**, **grappling**) **1** struggle; wrestle. **2** seize or hold firmly.

grasp *verb* **1** seize and hold firmly. **2** understand. **grasp** *noun*

grasping *adjective* greedy for money or possessions.

grass *noun* (*plural* **grasses**) **1** a plant with green blades and stalks that are eaten by animals. **2** ground covered with grass. **3** (*slang*) cannabis (marijuana). **grassy** *adjective*

grass roots the ordinary people in a political party or other group.

grass-grub *noun* any of various insect-larvae that feed on grass roots.

grasshopper *noun* a jumping insect that makes a shrill noise.

grassland *noun* a wide area covered in grass with few trees.

grass-tree *noun* any of various small New Zealand and Australian trees with long grass-like leaves, e.g. the horoeka or lancewood.

grate[1] *noun* **1** a metal framework that keeps fuel in a fireplace. **2** a fireplace.

grate[2] *verb* (**grated**, **grating**) **1** shred into small pieces by rubbing on a rough surface. **2** make an unpleasant noise by rubbing. **3** sound harshly.

grateful *adjective* feeling or showing that you value what was done for you. **gratefully** *adverb* [from Latin *gratus* = thankful, pleasing]

grater *noun* a device with a jagged surface for grating food.

gratify *verb* (**gratified**, **gratifying**) **1** give pleasure. **2** satisfy a wish etc., *Please gratify our curiosity*. **gratification** *noun* [from Latin *gratus* = pleasing]

grating *noun* a framework of metal or wooden bars placed across an opening.

gratis (*say* **grar**-tiss) *adverb & adjective* free of charge, *You can have the leaflet gratis.* [Latin, = out of kindness]

gratitude *noun* being grateful.

gratuitous (*say* gra-**tew**-it-us) *adjective* given or done without payment or without good reason. **gratuitously** *adverb*

gratuity (*say* gra-**tew**-it-ee) *noun* (*plural* **gratuities**) money given in gratitude; a tip.

graunch *verb* (*NZ*) **1** make a crunching noise. **2** damage or break something.

grave[1] *noun* the place where a corpse is buried, [from Old English *graef* = hole dug out]

grave[2] *adjective* serious, solemn. **gravely** *adverb* [from Latin *gravis* = heavy]

gravel *noun* small stones often mixed with coarse sand. **gravelled** *adjective*, **gravelly** *adjective*

graven (*say* **gray**-ven) *adjective* carved.

gravestone *noun* a stone monument over a grave.

graveyard *noun* a burial ground.

gravitate *verb* (**gravitated**, **gravitating**) move or be attracted towards something.

gravitation *noun* **1** gravitating. **2** the force of gravity. **gravitational** *adjective*

gravity *noun* **1** the force that pulls everything towards the earth. **2** seriousness. [same origin as *grave*[2]]

gravy *noun* a hot brown liquid served with meat.

gravy-beef *noun* a cheap cut of meat used to make stews etc.

graze *verb* (**grazed**, **grazing**) **1** feed on growing grass. **2** scrape slightly in passing, *I grazed my elbow on the wall.*

graze *noun* a raw place where skin has been scraped.

grease *noun* melted fat; any thick oily substance.

grease *verb* (**greased**, **greasing**) put grease on something.

great *adjective* **1** very large; much above average. **2** very important or talented, *a great composer.* **3** (*informal*) very good or enjoyable, *It's great to see you again.* **4** older or younger by one generation, *great-grandfather*. **greatly** *adverb*, **greatness** *noun*

grebe (*say* greeb) *noun* a kind of diving bird.

greed *noun* being greedy.

greedy *adjective* wanting more food, money, or other things than you need. **greedily** *adverb*, **greediness** *noun*

Green *noun* (also **Greenie** *informal*) a member or supporter of a political party or group concerned with protecting the natural environment.

green *noun* **1** the colour of growing grass. **2** an area of grass, *the putting green.*

green *adjective* **1** of the colour green. **2** inexperienced and likely to make mistakes. **3** concerned with the natural environment. **greenness** *noun*
green belt an area kept as open land round a town or city.

greenery *noun* green leaves or plants.

greenfeed *noun* forage grown to be fed fresh (not dried) to cattle etc.

greenfly *noun* (*plural* **greenfly**) a small green insect that sucks the juices from plants.

greengrocer *noun* a person who keeps a shop that sells fruit and vegetables. **greengrocery** *noun*

greenhouse *noun* a glass building where plants are protected from cold.
greenhouse effect the warming up of the earth's surface when radiation from the sun is trapped by the atmosphere.

greenie *noun* (*informal*) an environmental conservationist.

greenstone *noun* a New Zealand variety of jade used for tools, ornaments, etc.; pounamu.

Greenwich Mean Time (*say* **gren**-ich) the time on the line of longitude which passes through Greenwich in London, used as a basis for calculating time throughout the world.

greet *verb* **1** speak to a person who arrives. **2** receive, *They greeted the song with applause.* **3** present itself to, *A strange sight greeted our eyes.*

greeting *noun* **1** words or actions used to greet somebody. **2** good wishes.

gregarious (*say* grig-**air**-ee-us) *adjective* **1** fond of company. **2** living in flocks or communities. **gregariously** *adverb*, **gregariousness** *noun* [from Latin *gregis* = of a flock]

grenade (*say* grin-**ayd**) *noun* a small bomb, usually thrown by hand.

grey *noun* the colour between black and white, like ashes. **grey** *adjective*, **greyness** *noun*
grey nurse a large shark.
grey warbler a small New Zealand bird, the riroriro.

greyhound *noun* a slender dog with smooth hair, used in racing.

grid *noun* **1** a framework or pattern of bars or lines crossing each other. **2** a computer Internet grouping. **3** (*NZ & Australia, slang*) a bicycle. **4** a pattern of lines at the start of a racing track. **5** a rectangular arrangement of town or city streets.
national grid the network of transmission lines that carry electric power around the country.

griddle *noun* a round iron plate for cooking things on.

gridiron *noun* **1** a framework of bars for cooking on. **2** American football.

gridlock *noun* a traffic jam affecting an entire network of intersecting streets.

grief *noun* deep sorrow.
come to grief suffer a disaster.

grievance *noun* something that people are discontented about.

grieve *verb* (**grieved**, **grieving**) **1** cause a person grief. **2** feel grief.

grievous (*say* **gree**-vus) *adjective* **1** causing grief. **2** serious. **grievously** *adverb*

griffin *noun* a creature in fables, with an eagle's head and wings on a lion's body.

grill *noun* **1** a heated element on a cooker, for sending heat downwards. **2** food cooked under this. **3** a grille.

grill *verb* **1** cook under a grill. **2** question closely and severely, *The police grilled him for an hour.*

grille *noun* a metal grating covering a window or similar opening.

grim *adjective* (**grimmer**, **grimmest**) **1** stern; severe. **2** without cheerfulness; unattractive, *a grim prospect.* **grimly** *adverb*, **grimness** *noun*

grimace (*say* grim-**ayss**) *noun* a twisted expression on the face made in pain or disgust.

grimace *verb* (**grimaced**, **grimacing**) make a grimace.

grime *noun* dirt clinging to a surface or to the skin. **grimy** *adjective*

grin *noun* a broad smile.

grin *verb* (**grinned**, **grinning**) smile broadly.

grind *verb* (**ground**, **grinding**) *verb* **1** crush into grains or powder. **2** sharpen or smooth by rubbing on a rough surface. **3** rub harshly together, *He ground his teeth in fury.* **4** move with a harsh grating noise, *The bus ground to a halt.* **grinder** *noun*

grindstone *noun* a thick round rough revolving stone for sharpening or grinding things.

grip *verb* (**gripped**, **gripping**) **1** hold firmly. **2** hold a person's attention.

grip *noun* **1** a firm hold. **2** understanding. **3** a handle. **4** a suitcase or travel-bag.

gripe *verb* (**griped**, **griping**) (*slang*) grumble. **gripe** *noun*

grisly *adjective* (**grislier**, **grisliest**) causing horror or disgust; gruesome.

grist *noun* grain for grinding.

gristle *noun* tough rubbery tissue in meat. **gristly** *adjective*

grit *noun* **1** tiny pieces of stone or sand. **2** courage and endurance. **gritty** *adjective*, **grittiness** *noun*

grit *verb* (**gritted**, **gritting**) **1** spread with grit, *grit the roads*. **2** clench the teeth when in pain or trouble.

grizzle *verb* (**grizzled**, **grizzling**) whimper; whine.

grizzled *adjective* streaked with grey hairs.

grizzly *adjective* grey-haired.
grizzly bear a large fierce bear.

groan *verb* **1** make a long deep sound in pain or distress or disapproval. **2** creak loudly under a heavy load. **groan** *noun*, **groaner** *noun*

grocer *noun* a person who keeps a shop that sells food and household supplies. **grocery** *noun* (*plural* **groceries**)

grog *noun* (*NZ, slang*) alcoholic drink, especially beer.

groggy *adjective* (**groggier**, **groggiest**) weak and unsteady, especially after illness. **groggily** *adverb*, **grogginess** *noun*

groin *noun* the groove where the thigh joins the trunk of the body.

grommet[1] *noun* a tube inserted in the eardrum to drain fluid and prevent glue ear.

grommet[2] *noun* (*NZ & Australia, slang*) an inexperienced participant or candidate.

groom *noun* **1** a person whose job is to look after horses. **2** a bridegroom.

groom *verb* **1** clean and brush (an animal). **2** make neat and trim. **3** train a person for a certain job or position.

groove *noun* a long narrow furrow or channel cut in the surface of something. **grooved** *adjective*

grope *verb* (**groped**, **groping**) feel about for something you cannot see.

groper *noun* a large New Zealand food fish, the hāpuku.

gross (*say* grohss) *adjective* **1** fat and ugly. **2** having bad manners; vulgar. **3** very obvious or shocking, *gross stupidity*. **4** total; without anything being deducted, *our gross income*. (Compare *net*[2].) **grossly** *adverb*, **grossness** *noun*

gross *noun* (*plural* **gross**) twelve dozen (144) of something.

grotesque (*say* groh-**tesk**) *adjective* very strange; fantastically ugly. **grotesquely** *adverb*, **grotesqueness** *noun*

grotto *noun* (*plural* **grottoes**) a picturesque cave.

grouchy *adjective* (*informal*) grumpy.

ground[1] *past tense* of **grind**.

ground[2] *noun* **1** the solid surface of the earth. **2** a sports field.
ground parrot the kākāpō.
ground zero site of New York's World Trade Center building, destroyed on 11 September 2001.

ground[2] *verb* **1** run aground. **2** prevent from flying, *All aircraft are grounded because of the fog*. **3** give a good basic training, *Ground them in the rules of spelling*. **4** base, *This theory is grounded on known facts*.

grounding *noun* basic training.

groundless *adjective* without foundation or reasons, *Your fears are groundless*.

grounds *plural noun* **1** the gardens of a large house. **2** solid particles that sink to the bottom, *coffee grounds*. **3** reasons, *There are grounds for suspicion*.

groundsheet *noun* a piece of waterproof material for spreading on the ground.

groundsman *noun* (*plural* **groundsmen**) a person whose job is to look after a sports ground.

groundwork *noun* work that lays the basis for something.

group *noun* a number of people, animals, or things that come together or belong together in some way.

group *verb* put together or come together in a group or groups.

groupie *noun* (*informal*) a young person (usually female) who follows pop groups or other celebrities around.

grouse[1] *noun* (*plural* **grouse**) a bird with feathered feet, hunted as game.

grouse[2] *verb* (**groused**, **grousing**) (*informal*) grumble. **grouse** *noun*, **grouser** *noun*

grouse[3] *adjective* (*NZ, old-fashioned slang*) excellent, attractive.

grove *noun* a group of trees, a small wood.

grovel *verb* (**grovelled**, **grovelling**) **1** crawl on the ground, especially in a show of fear or humility. **2** act in an excessively humble way. **groveller** *noun*

grow *verb* (**grew**, **grown**, **growing**) **1** become bigger or greater. **2** develop; put out shoots. **3** cultivate; plant and look after, *She grows roses*. **4** become, *He grew rich*. **grower** *noun*

growl *verb* **1** make a deep angry sound. **2** speak angrily. **growl** *noun*, **growling** *noun*

grown-up *noun* an adult person.

growth *noun* **1** the process of growing; development. **2** something that has grown.

grub *noun* **1** a tiny worm-like creature that will become an insect; a larva. **2** (*slang*) food.

grub *verb* (**grubbed**, **grubbing**) **1** dig up by the roots. **2** rummage.

grubber *noun* a tool for digging plants.

grubby *adjective* (**grubbier**, **grubbiest**) rather dirty. **grubbiness** *noun*

grudge *noun* a feeling of resentment or ill will.

grudge *verb* (**grudged**, **grudging**) resent having to give or allow something.

gruelling *adjective* exhausting.

gruesome *adjective* causing people to feel horror or disgust.

gruff *adjective* having a rough unfriendly voice or manner. **gruffly** *adverb*, **gruffness** *noun*

grumble *verb* (**grumbled**, **grumbling**) complain in a bad-tempered way. **grumble** *noun*, **grumbler** *noun*

grumpy *adjective* bad-tempered. **grumpily** *adverb*, **grumpiness** *noun*

grunge *noun* (*slang*) dirt, grime; anything repulsive or unpleasant.

grunt *verb* **1** make a pig's gruff snort. **2** speak or say gruffly. **grunt** *noun*

GST *abbreviation* (*NZ*) Goods and Services Tax.

guarantee *noun* a formal promise to do something or to repair an object if it breaks or goes wrong.

guarantee *verb* (**guaranteed**, **guaranteeing**) give a guarantee; promise. **guarantor** *noun*

guard *verb* **1** protect; keep safe. **2** watch over and prevent from escaping.

guard *noun* **1** guarding; protection, *Keep the prisoners under close guard.* **2** someone who guards a person or place. **3** a group of soldiers or police officers etc. acting as a guard. **4** a railway official in charge of a train. **5** a protecting device, *a fire-guard.*

guardian *noun* **1** someone who guards. **2** a person who is legally in charge of a child whose parents cannot look after him or her. **guardianship** *noun*

guava a tropical fruit.

guerrilla (*say* ger-**il**-a) *noun* a person who fights by making surprise attacks as one of a small group. [Spanish, = little war]

guess *noun* (*plural* **guesses**) an opinion given without making careful calculations or without certain knowledge.

guess *verb* make a guess. **guesser** *noun*

guest *noun* **1** a person who is invited to visit or stay at another's house. **2** a person staying at a hotel. **3** a person who takes part in another's show as a visiting performer.

guffaw *verb* give a noisy laugh. **guffaw** *noun*

guidance *noun* **1** guiding. **2** advising or advice on problems.

Guide *noun* a member of the Girl Guides Association, an organisation for girls.

guide *noun* **1** a person who shows others the way or points out interesting sights. **2** a book giving information about a place or subject.

guide *verb* (**guided**, **guiding**) act as guide to.

guidebook *noun* a book of information about a place, for travellers or visitors.

guidelines *plural noun* statements that give general advice about something.

guild (*say* gild) *noun* a society of people with similar skills or interests.

guile (*rhymes with* mile) *noun* craftiness.

guillotine (*say* **gil**-ot-een) *noun* **1** a machine with a heavy blade for beheading criminals. **2** a machine with a long blade for cutting paper or metal. **3** fixing a time for a vote to be taken in Parliament in order to cut short a debate.

guillotine *verb* (**guillotined**, **guillotining**) cut with a guillotine. [named after Dr Guillotin, who suggested its use in France in 1789]

guilt *noun* **1** the fact of having committed an offence. **2** a feeling of being to blame for something that has happened.

guilty *adjective* **1** having done wrong. **2** feeling or showing guilt. **guiltily** *adverb*

guinea-pig *noun* **1** a small furry animal without a tail. **2** a person who is used as the subject of an experiment.

guise (*say as* guys) *noun* a manner or appearance put on to conceal the truth; a pretence, *under the guise of friendship.*

guitar *noun* a musical instrument played by plucking its strings. **guitarist** *noun*

gulf *noun* **1** a large area of the sea that is partly surrounded by land. **2** a wide gap; a great difference.

gull *noun* a seagull.

gullet *noun* the tube from the throat to the stomach.

gullible *adjective* easily deceived. [from an old word *gull* = a fool]

gully *noun* (*plural* **gullies**) a narrow channel that carries water.

gulp *verb* **1** swallow hastily or greedily. **2** make a loud swallowing noise.

gulp *noun* **1** the act of gulping. **2** a large mouthful of liquid.

gum[1] *noun* the firm flesh in which teeth are rooted. [from Old English *goma*]

gum[2] *noun* **1** a sticky substance produced by some trees and shrubs, used as glue. **2** a sweet made with gum or gelatine. **3** chewing-gum. **4** a gum-tree. **gummy** *adjective*

gum[2] *verb* (**gummed**, **gumming**) cover or stick with gum. [from Latin *gummi*]

gumboot *noun* a waterproof rubber boot.

gum-digger *noun* (*NZ*) a person who digs for kauri gum.

gumption *noun* (*informal*) common sense.

gum-tree *noun* a eucalyptus.

gun *adjective* (*NZ, informal*) expert, top, *a gun footballer.*

gun *noun* **1** a weapon that fires shells or bullets from a metal tube. **2** a starting-pistol. **3** a device that forces a substance out of a tube, *a grease-gun.* **4** (*NZ, informal*) a fast shearer, hence any highly skilled person. **gunfire** *noun*, **gunshot** *noun*

gun *verb* (**gunned**, **gunning**) shoot with a gun, *They gunned him down.*

gunboat *noun* a small warship.

gunk *noun* any sticky or unpleasant substance.

gunman *noun* (*plural* **gunmen**) a criminal with a gun.

gunner *noun* a person who operates a gun.

gunnery *noun* the making or use of guns.

gunpowder *noun* a kind of explosive.

gunwale (*say* **gun**-al) *noun* the upper edge of a small ship's or boat's side. [from *gun* + *wale* = a ridge (because it was formerly used to support guns)]

gurgle *verb* (**gurgled**, **gurgling**) make a low bubbling sound. **gurgle** *noun*

gurnard *noun* a food fish of coastal waters.

gush *verb* **1** flow suddenly or quickly. **2** talk effusively. **gush** *noun*

gust *noun* **1** a sudden rush of wind. **2** a burst of rain, smoke, or sound. **gusty** *adjective*, **gustily** *adverb*

gust *verb* blow in gusts.

gusto *noun* great enjoyment; zest.

gut *noun* the lower part of the digestive system; the intestine.

gut *verb* (**gutted**, **gutting**) **1** remove the guts from a dead fish or other animal. **2** remove or destroy the inside of something, *The fire gutted the factory.*

guts *plural noun* **1** the digestive system; the inside parts of a person or thing. **2** (*informal*) courage.

gutter *noun* a long narrow channel at the side of a street, or along the edge of a roof, for carrying away rainwater.

gutter *verb* (of a candle) burn unsteadily so that melted wax runs down. [from Latin *gutta* = a drop]

guttural (*say* **gut**-er-al) *adjective* throaty, harsh-sounding, *a guttural voice.* [*from* Latin *guttur* = throat]

guy[1] (*informal*) a man; (especially in *plural*) any person, female or male, *Are you guys ready?*

guy[2] or **guy-rope** *noun* a rope used to hold something in place.

guzzle *verb* (**guzzled**, **guzzling**) eat or drink greedily. **guzzler** *noun*

gybe *verb* **1** (of a sail or boom) swing across. **2** (of a boat) change course so that this happens.

gym (*say* jim) *noun* (*informal*) **1** a gymnasium. **2** gymnastics.

gymkhana (*say* jim-**kah**-na) *noun* a series of horse-riding contests and other sports events.

gymnasium *noun* a place fitted up for gymnastics. [from Greek *gymnos* = naked (because Greek men exercised naked)]

gymnast *noun* an expert in gymnastics.

gymnastics *plural noun* exercises performed to develop the muscles or to show the performer's agility. **gymnastic** *adjective*

gypsy *noun* (*plural* **gypsies**) a member of a people who live in caravans and wander from place to place in Europe.

gyrate (*say* jy-**rayt**) *verb* (**gyrated**, **gyrating**) revolve; move in circles or spirals. **gyration** *noun* [from Greek *gyros* = a ring or circle]

gyroscope (*say* **jy**-ro-skohp) *noun* a device that keeps steady because of a heavy wheel spinning inside it. [same origin as *gyrate*]

Hh

ha *interjection* an exclamation of triumph or surprise.

haberdashery *noun* dress accessories and small articles used in sewing, e.g. ribbons, buttons, thread.

habit *noun* **1** something that you do without thinking because you have done it so often; a settled way of behaving. **2** the long dress worn by a monk or nun. **habitual** *adjective*, **habitually** *adverb*

habitat *noun* where an animal or plant lives naturally.

habitation *noun* **1** a dwelling. **2** inhabiting a place.

hack[1] *verb* **1** chop or cut roughly. **2** (*informal*) access a computer file or phone without authorisation. **3** (*slang*) accept; cope with. **hacker** *noun*

hack[2] *noun* a horse for ordinary riding.

hackles *plural noun* **with his** or **her hackles up** angry and ready to fight. [*hackles* are the long feathers on some birds' necks]

hackneyed *adjective* used so often that it is no longer interesting.

hacksaw *noun* a saw for cutting metal.

haddock *noun* (*plural* **haddock**) a North Atlantic sea-fish like cod but smaller, used as food.

hadn't (*mainly spoken*) had not.

haemoglobin (*say* heem-a-**gloh**-bin) *noun* the red substance that carries oxygen in the blood. [from Greek *haima* = blood]

haemophilia (*say* heem-o-**fil**-ee-a) *noun* a disease that causes people to bleed dangerously from even a slight cut. [from Greek *haima* = blood, + *philia* = loving]

haemorrhage (*say* **hem**-er-ij) *noun* bleeding. [from Greek *haima* = blood, + *rhegnunai* = burst]

haere mai *interjection* welcome! [Māori, = come here]

haere rā *interjection* farewell! [Māori = go away]

hag *noun* an ugly old woman.

haggard *adjective* looking ill or very tired.

haggis *noun* (*plural* **haggises**) a Scottish food made from sheep's offal.

haggle *verb* (**haggled, haggling**) argue about a price or agreement.

ha ha *interjection* laughter.

haiku (*say* **hy**-koo) *noun* (*plural* **haiku**) a kind of short poem of 17 syllables, usually with three lines. [Japanese]

hail[1] *noun* frozen drops of rain. **hail** *verb*, **hailstone** *noun*, **hailstorm** *noun*

hail[2] *interjection* an exclamation of greeting.

hail[2] *verb* call out to somebody.
hail from come from, *He hails from Timaru.*

hair *noun* **1** a soft covering that grows on the heads and bodies of people and animals. **2** one of the threads that make up this covering. **hairbrush** *noun*, **haircut** *noun*
keep your hair on (*informal*) do not lose your temper.
split hairs make petty or unimportant distinctions of meaning. **hair-splitting** *noun*

hairdresser *noun* a person whose job is to cut and arrange people's hair.

hairpin *noun* a U-shaped pin for keeping hair in place.
hairpin bend a sharp bend in a road.

hair-raising *adjective* terrifying.

hairy *adjective* **1** with a lot of hair. **2** (*slang*) hair-raising; difficult.

haka *noun* **1** a Māori war-dance with chanting. **2** a similar dance performed by a sports team etc. [Māori]

hākari *noun* a feast after a ceremonial occasion. [Māori]

hake *noun* (*plural* **hake**) a sea-fish used as food.

hakea *noun* an ornamental Australian shrub.

halal *noun* meat prepared according to Muslim law.

halcyon (*say* **hal**-see-on) *noun* happy and peaceful, *halcyon days.*

hale *adjective* strong and healthy, *hale and hearty.*

half *noun* (*plural* **halves**) *one* of the two equal parts or amounts into which something is or can be divided.

half *adverb* partly; not completely, *This meat is only half cooked.*
not half (*slang*) extremely, *Was she cross? Not half!*

half-back *noun* (in rugby) the player whose position is close to the scrum.

half-baked *adjective* (*informal*) not well planned; foolish.

half-brother *noun* a brother to whom you are related by one parent but not by both parents.

half-hearted adjective not very enthusiastic. **half-heartedly** *adverb*

half-pie *adjective & adverb* (*NZ*) not complete(ly), *it was only half-pie finished.* [Māori *pai* good]

half-sister *noun* a sister to whom you are related by one parent but not by both parents.

half-time *noun* the point or interval halfway through a game.

halfway *adjective & adverb* between two others and equally distant from each.

halfwitted *adjective* mentally deficient; stupid. **halfwit** *noun*

halibut *noun* (*plural* **halibut**) a large flat fish used as food.

hall *noun* **1** a space or passage into which the front entrance of a house etc. opens. **2** a very large room or building used for meetings, concerts, etc.

hallelujah *interjection & noun* alleluia.

hallmark *noun* an official mark made on gold, silver, and platinum to show its quality.

hallo *interjection* a word used to greet somebody or to attract their attention.

hallow *verb* make a thing holy; honour something as being holy.

Halloween *noun* 31 October, when some people think magical things happen.

hallucination *noun* something you think you can see or hear that is not really there.

halo *noun* (*plural* **haloes**) a circle of light round something, especially round the head of a saint etc. in paintings.

halt *verb* stop.

halt *noun* a stop, *Work came to a halt.*

halter *noun* a rope or strap put round a horse's head so that it can be led or fastened by this.

halve *verb* (**halved**, **halving**) **1** divide into halves. **2** reduce to half its size.

ham *noun* **1** meat from a pig's leg. **2** (*slang*) an actor or performer who is not very good. **3** (*informal*) someone who operates a radio to send and receive messages as a hobby.

hamburger *noun* a flat round cake of minced beef served fried, often in a bread roll. [named after Hamburg in Germany (not after *ham*)]

hamlet *noun* a small village.

hammer *noun* a tool with a heavy metal head used for driving nails in, breaking things, etc.

hammer *verb* **1** hit with a hammer. **2** strike loudly. **3** (*informal*) defeat.

hammock *noun* a bed made of a strong net or piece of cloth hung by cords.

hamper[1] *noun* a large box-shaped basket with a lid.

hamper[2] *verb* hinder; prevent from moving or working freely.

hamster *noun* a small furry animal with cheek-pouches for carrying grain.

Hamutana *noun* Hamilton, in Māori.

hand *noun* **1** the end part of the arm below the wrist. **2** a pointer on a clock or dial. **3** a worker; a member of a ship's crew, *All hands on deck!* **4** the cards held by one player in a card-game. **5** side or direction, *on the other hand.* **6** control; care, *You are in good hands.* **7** influence; help, *Give me a hand with these boxes.*
at hand near.
by hand using your hand or hands.
hands down winning easily.
hands off not involving active participation.
hands on involving active participation.
in hand in your possession; being dealt with.
on hand available.
out of hand out of control.

hand *verb* give or pass something to somebody, *Hand it over.*

handbag *noun* a small bag for holding a purse and personal articles.

handball *noun* **1** a team game similar to soccer but using hands instead of feet. **2** a game in which a ball is hit with the hand against a wall.

handbook *noun* a small book that gives useful facts about something.

handcuff *noun* one of a pair of metal rings linked by a chain, for fastening wrists together.

handcuff *verb* fasten with handcuffs.

handful *noun* (*plural* **handfuls**) **1** as much as can be carried in one hand. **2** a few people or things. **3** (*informal*) a troublesome person or task.

handicap *noun* **1** a disadvantage. **2** a physical or mental disability. **handicapped** *adjective*

handicraft *noun* artistic work done with the hands, e.g. woodwork, needlework.

handily *adverb* in a handy way.

handiwork *noun* **1** something made by hand. **2** something done, *Is this mess your handiwork?*

handkerchief *noun* a small square of cloth for wiping the nose or face. [from *hand* + *kerchief*]

handle *noun* **1** the part of a thing by which it is carried or controlled. **2** (*NZ*) a glass mug for beer. **3** (*informal*) a person's name or title.

handle *verb* (**handled, handling**) **1** touch or feel something with your hands. **2** deal with; manage, *Will you handle the catering?* **handler** *noun*

handlebar *noun* (also **handlebars**) the bar, with a handle at each end, that steers a bicycle or motor cycle etc.

handrail *noun* a narrow rail for people to hold as a support.

handshake *noun* shaking hands with someone as a greeting etc.

handsome *adjective* **1** good-looking. **2** generous. **handsomely** *adverb*

handstand *noun* balancing on your hands with your feet in the air.

handwriting *noun* writing done by hand. **handwritten** *adjective*

handy *adjective* (**handier, handiest**) **1** convenient; useful. **2** good at using the hands. **handily** *adverb*, **handiness** *noun*

handyman *noun* (*plural* **handymen**) a person who does household repairs or odd jobs.

hang *verb* (**hung, hanging**) **1** fix the top or side of something to a hook or nail etc.; be supported in this way. **2** stick wallpaper to a wall. **3** decorate with drapery or hanging ornaments etc., *The tree was hung with lights.* **4** droop; lean, *People hung over the gate.* **5** (with *past tense* & *past participle* **hanged**) execute someone by hanging them from a rope that tightens round the neck.
hang about loiter; not go away.
hang back hesitate to go forward or to do something.
hang on hold tightly; (*informal*) wait.
hang up end a telephone conversation by putting back the receiver.

hang *noun* the way something hangs.
get the hang of (*informal*) learn how to do or use something.

hangar *noun* a large shed where aircraft are kept.

hanger *noun* a device on which to hang things, *a coat-hanger.*

hang-glider *noun* a framework in which a person can glide through the air. **hang-gliding** *noun*

hāngi *noun* a feast of food that has been cooked by steam in an underground pit. [Māori]

hangman *noun* (*plural* **hangmen**) a man whose job it is to hang people condemned to death.

hangover *noun* an unpleasant feeling after drinking too much alcohol.

hank *noun* a coil or piece of wool, thread, etc.

hanker *verb* feel a longing for something.

hanky *noun* (*plural* **hankies**) (*informal*) a handkerchief.

haphazard *adjective* done or chosen at random, not by planning. [same origin as *happen*, + *hazard*]

hapless *adjective* having no luck. [same origin as *happen*, + *-less*]

happen *verb* **1** take place; occur. **2** do something by chance, *I happened to see him.* [from Old Norse *happ* = luck]

happening *noun* something that happens; an event.

happy *adjective* (**happier, happiest**) pleased; contented; fortunate. **happily** *adverb*, **happiness** *noun* [same origin as *happen*]

hapū *noun* **1** a division of a Māori tribe; sub-tribe. **2** a family group within an iwi. [Māori]

hapū *adjective* pregnant. [Māori]

hāpuku *noun* a New Zealand fish, the groper. [Māori]

harangue (*say* ha-**rang**) *verb* (**harangued, haranguing**) make a long speech to somebody. **harangue** *noun*

harass *verb* trouble or annoy somebody often. **harassment** *noun* [from Old French *harer* = set the dog on someone]

harbour *noun* a place where ships can shelter or unload.

harbour *verb* **1** give shelter to somebody, *harbouring a criminal.* **2** keep in your mind, *harbouring a grudge.*

hard *adjective* **1** firm; solid; not soft. **2** difficult, *hard sums.* **3** severe; stern. **4** causing suffering, *hard luck.* **5** using great effort, *a hard worker.* **hardness** *noun*
hard cheese (*informal*) misfortune.
hard disk a rigid, non-removable disk for storing large amounts of data in a computer.
hard drive a computer part that reads and processes data stored on computer disks.
hard of hearing slightly deaf.
hard up (*informal*) short of money.
hard water water containing minerals that prevent soap from making much lather.

hard *adverb* **1** so as to be hard, *The ground froze hard.* **2** with great effort; intensively, *We worked hard. It is raining hard.* **3** with difficulty, *hard-earned.*

hardboard *noun* stiff board made of compressed wood-pulp.

harden *verb* make or become hard or hardy. **hardener** *noun*

hard-hearted *adjective* unsympathetic.

hardly *adverb* only just; only with difficulty, *She can hardly walk.*

hardship *noun* difficult conditions that cause discomfort or suffering.

hardware *noun* **1** metal implements and tools etc.; machinery. **2** the machinery of a computer. (Compare *software*.)

hardwood *noun* hard heavy wood from trees such as beech and rātā. (Compare *softwood*.)

hardy *adjective* (**hardier, hardiest**) able to endure cold or difficult conditions. **hardiness** *noun*

hare *noun* an animal like a rabbit but larger.

harem (*say* **har**-eem) *noun* the part of a Muslim palace or house where the women live; the women living there. [from Arabic *harim* forbidden]

haricot (*say* **ha**-rik-co) *noun* a kind of bean.

hark *verb* listen.
hark back return to an earlier subject.

harlequin *adjective* in mixed colours.

harm *verb* damage; injure.

harm *noun* damage; injury, **harmful** *adjective*, **harmless** *adjective*

harmonic *adjective* of harmony in music.

harmonica *noun* a mouth-organ.

harmonious *adjective* full of harmony.

harmonise *verb* (**harmonised, harmonising**) make harmonious; produce harmony. **harmonisation** *noun*

harmony *noun* (*plural* **harmonies**) **1** a pleasant combination, especially of musical notes. **2** being friendly to each other and not quarrelling.

harness *noun* (*plural* **harnesses**) the straps and fittings by which a horse is controlled and fastened to the cart etc. that it pulls.
harness racing the racing of pacers and trotters.

harness *verb* **1** put a harness on a horse. **2** control and use something, *Could we harness the power of the wind?*

harp *noun* a musical instrument made of strings stretched across a frame and plucked by the fingers. **harpist** *noun*

harp *verb* keep on talking about something in a tiresome way, *He is always harping on his misfortunes.*

harpoon *noun* a spear attached to a rope, used for catching whales etc. **harpoon** *verb*

harpsichord *noun* an instrument like a piano but with strings that are plucked (not struck) by a mechanism. [from *harp*, + Latin *chorda* = string]

harrow *noun* a heavy device pulled over the ground to break up the soil.

harrowing *adjective* causing horror and distress.

harry *verb* (**harried, harrying**) harass.

harsh *adjective* **1** rough and unpleasant. **2** severe; cruel. **harshly** *adverb*, **harshness** *noun*

hart *noun* a male deer. (Compare *hind*[2].)

harvest *noun* **1** the time when farmers gather in the grain, fruit, or vegetables that they have grown. **2** the crop that is gathered in.

harvest *verb* gather in a crop; reap. **harvester** *noun*

hash *noun* a mixture of small pieces of meat and vegetables, usually fried.
make a hash of (*informal*) make a mess of something; bungle.

hashish *noun* a drug made from hemp.

hasn't (*mainly spoken*) has not.

hassle *noun* (*informal*) trouble, annoyance.

hassle *verb* (*informal*) harass, pester.

hassock *noun* a small thick cushion for kneeling on in church.

haste *noun* a hurry.
make haste act quickly.

hasten *verb* hurry.

hasty *adjective* hurried; done too quickly. **hastily** *adverb*, **hastiness** *noun*

hat *noun* a shaped covering for the head.
hat trick getting three goals, wickets, victories, etc. one after the other.
keep it under your hat keep it secret.

hatch[1] *noun* (*plural* **hatches**) an opening in a floor, wall, or door, usually with a covering.

hatch[2] *verb* **1** break out of an egg. **2** keep an egg warm until a baby bird comes out. **3** plan, *They hatched a plot.*

hatchback *noun* a car with a sloping back hinged at the top.

hatchet *noun* a small axe.

hate *verb* (**hated, hating**) dislike very strongly.

hate *noun* hatred.

hateful *adjective* arousing hatred.

hate speech *noun* verbally abusive or antagonistic behaviour.

hatred *noun* strong dislike.

hatter *noun* a person who makes hats.

haughty *adjective* proud of yourself and looking down on other people. **haughtily** *adverb*, **haughtiness** *noun*

Hau-Hauism *noun* a 19th-century Māori religion.

haul *verb* pull or drag with great effort. **haulage** *noun*

haul *noun* **1** hauling. **2** the amount obtained by an effort; booty, *The robbers made a good haul.* **3** a distance to be covered, *a long haul.*

haunch *noun* (*plural* **haunches**) the buttock and top part of the thigh.

haunt *verb* **1** (of ghosts) appear often in a place or to a person. **2** visit a place often. **3** stay in your mind, *Memories haunt me.*

haurangi *adjective* drunk. [Māori]

have *verb* (**had, having**) This word has many uses, including (**1**) possess; own (*We have two dogs*), (**2**) contain (*This tin has sweets in it*), (**3**) experience (*He had a shock*), (**4**) be obliged to do something (*We have to go now*), (**5**) allow (*I won't have him bullied*), (**6**) receive; accept (*Will you have a biscuit?*), (**7**) get something done (*I'm having my watch mended*), (**8**) (*slang*) cheat; deceive (*We've been had!*).
have somebody on (*informal*) fool him or her.

have *auxiliary verb* used to form the past tense of verbs, e.g. *He has gone.*

haven *noun* a refuge.

haven't (*mainly spoken*) have not.

haversack *noun* a strong bag carried on your back or over your shoulder.

havoc *noun* great destruction or disorder.

Hawaiian *noun* a person from Hawaii.
Hawaiian *adjective*

Hawaiki *noun* (in legend) the place where the Māori came from. [Māori]

hawk[1] *noun* a bird of prey with very strong eyesight.

hawk[2] *verb* carry goods about and try to sell them. **hawker** *noun*

hawthorn *noun* a thorny tree with small red berries (called *haws*).

hay *noun* dried grass for feeding to animals.
hay baler a machine for packing hay or straw into bales.
hay fever irritation of the nose, throat, and eyes, caused by pollen or dust.

haystack or **hayrick** *noun* a large neat pile of hay packed for storing.

haywire *adjective* (*informal*) badly disorganised; out of control.

hazard *noun* **1** a danger; a risk. **2** an obstacle, hazardous *adjective*

haze *noun* thin mist.

hazel *noun* **1** a bush with small nuts. **2** a light-brown colour. **hazelnut** *noun*

hazy *adjective* **1** misty. **2** vague; uncertain.
hazily *adverb*, **haziness** *noun*

H-bomb *noun* a hydrogen bomb.

he *pronoun* **1** the male person or animal being talked about. **2** a person (male or female), *He who hesitates is lost.*

head *noun* **1** the part of the body containing the brains, eyes, and mouth. **2** brains; the mind; intelligence, *Use your head!* **3** a talent or ability, *She has a good head for figures.* **4** the side of a coin on which someone's head is shown. **5** a person, *It costs $5 per head.* **6** the top, *a pin-head*; the leading part of something, *at the head of the procession.* **7** the chief; the person in charge; a headteacher. **8** a crisis, *Matters came to a head.*
keep your head stay calm.

head *verb* **1** be at the top or front of something. **2** (in soccer) hit a ball with your head. **3** move in a particular direction, *We headed for the coast.* **4** force someone to turn by getting in front, *head him off.*

headache *noun* **1** a pain in the head. **2** (*informal*) a worrying problem.

head-dress *noun* a covering or decoration for the head.

header *noun* **1** heading the ball in soccer. **2** a dive or fall with the head first. **3** a reaping machine that cuts only the heads of the grain. **4** (in word processing) words etc. programmed to appear at the top of every page. (Compare *footer.*)

heading *noun* **1** a word or words put at the top of a piece of printing or writing. **2** compass direction; bearing.
heading dog (*NZ*) a dog trained to drive the sheep towards their owner.

headland *noun* a promontory.

headlight *noun* a powerful light at the front of a car, locomotive, etc.

headline *noun* a heading in a newspaper.
the headlines the main items of news.

headlong *adverb & adjective* **1** head first. **2** in a hasty or thoughtless way.

headmaster *noun* the man in charge of a school.

headmistress *noun* (*plural* **headmistresses**) the woman in charge of a school.

head-on *adverb & adjective* with the front parts colliding, *a head-on collision.*

headphone *noun* a radio or telephone receiver that fits over the head.

headquarters *noun* or *plural noun* the place from which an organisation is controlled.

headstrong *adjective* determined to do as you want.

heads-up *noun* advanced information or a warning.

headteacher *noun* a headmaster or headmistress.

headway *noun* progress, *make headway.*

heal *verb* **1** make or become healthy flesh again, *The wound healed.* **2** (*old use*) cure, *healing the sick.*

health *noun* **1** the condition of a person's body or mind, *His health is bad.* **2** being healthy, *in sickness and in health.*
health camp (*NZ*) an outdoor camp for delicate children.
health stamp (*NZ*) a postage stamp that is sold to help support health camps.

healthy *adjective* (**healthier**, **healthiest**) **1** being well; free from illness. **2** producing good health, *Fresh air is healthy.* **healthily** *adverb*, **healthiness** *noun*

heap *noun* a pile, especially if untidy.
heaps *plural noun* (*informal*) a great amount; plenty, *There's heaps of time.*

heap *verb* **1** make into a heap. **2** put on large amounts, *She heaped the plate with food.*

hear *verb* (**heard**, **hearing**) **1** take in sounds through the ears. **2** receive news or information etc. **hearer** *noun*
hear! hear! (in a debate) I agree.

hearing *noun* **1** the ability to hear. **2** a chance to be heard; a trial in a lawcourt.

hearing-aid *noun* a device to help a deaf person to hear.

hearsay *noun* something heard, e.g. in a rumour or gossip.

hearse (*say* herss) *noun* a vehicle for taking the coffin to a funeral.

heart *noun* **1** the organ of the body that makes the blood circulate. **2** a person's feelings or emotions; sympathy. **3** enthusiasm; courage, *Take heart.* **4** the middle or most important part. **5** a curved shape representing a heart; a playing-card with red heart shapes on it.
break a person's heart make him or her very unhappy. **heartbroken** *adjective*
by heart memorised.
heart attack or **heart failure** a sudden failure of the heart to work properly.

hearten *verb* make a person feel encouraged.

heartfelt *adjective* felt deeply.

hearth *noun* the floor of or near a fireplace.

heartland *noun* an important, typical, or traditional region in a nation.

heartless *adjective* without pity or sympathy.

hearty *adjective* **1** strong; vigorous. **2** enthusiastic; sincere, *hearty congratulations.* **3** (of a meal) large. **heartily** *adverb*, **heartiness** *noun*

heat *noun* **1** hotness or (in scientific use) the form of energy causing this. **2** hot weather. **3** a race or contest to decide who will take part in the final.
heat wave a long period of hot weather.

heat *verb* make or become hot.

heater *noun* a device for warming the air in a room, car, etc.

heath *noun* flat land with low shrubs.

heathen *noun* a person who does not believe in one of the chief religions.

heather *noun* an evergreen plant with small purple, pink, or white flowers.

heave *verb* (**heaved** (in sense 4 **hove**), **heaving**) **1** lift or move something heavy. **2** (*informal*) throw. **3** rise and fall like sea-waves; pant; retch. **4** (of ships) **heave in sight** appear; **heave to** stop without mooring or anchoring, *The ships hove to.*
heave a sigh utter a deep sigh.

heaven *noun* **1** the place where God and angels are thought to live. **2** a very pleasant place or condition.
the heavens the sky.

heavenly *adjective* **1** of heaven. **2** in the sky, *Stars are heavenly bodies.* **3** (*informal*) very pleasing.

heavy *adjective* (**heavier**, **heaviest**) **1** having great weight; difficult to lift or carry. **2** great in amount or force etc., *heavy rain*; *a heavy penalty.* **3** needing much effort, *heavy work.* **4** full of sadness or worry, *with a heavy heart.* **heavily** *adverb*, **heaviness** *noun*
heavy industry industry producing metal, machines, etc.
heavy metal a kind of loud, pounding rock music.

heavyweight *noun* **1** a heavy person. **2** a boxer of the heaviest weight.
heavyweight *adjective*

hebe (*say* **hee**-bee) *noun* any of various kinds of evergreen New Zealand shrubs.

Hebrew *noun* the language of the Jews in ancient Palestine and modern Israel.

heckle *verb* (**heckled**, **heckling**) harass a speaker with interruptions and questions.
heckler *noun*

hectare (*say* **hek**-tar) *noun* a unit of area equal to 10,000 square metres.

hectic *adjective* full of activity.

hecto- *prefix* one hundred (as in *hectogram* = 100 grams). [from Greek *hekaton* = a hundred]

hector *verb* frighten by bullying talk.

hedge *noun* a row of bushes forming a barrier or boundary.

hedge *verb* (**hedged**, **hedging**) **1** surround with a hedge or other barrier. **2** make or trim a hedge. **3** avoid giving a definite answer.
hedger *noun*

hedgehog *noun* a small animal covered with long prickles.

hedgerow *noun* a hedge round a field etc.

heed *verb* pay attention to.

heed *noun* attention given to something, *take heed.* **heedful** *adjective*, **heedless** *adjective*

hee-haw *noun* a donkey's bray.

heel[1] *noun* **1** the back part of the foot. **2** the part round or under the heel of a sock or shoe etc.
take to your heels run away.

heel[1] *verb* (in rugby) move (the ball) through the scrum with the heel.

heel[2] *verb* lean over to one side; tilt.

hefty *adjective* (**heftier**, **heftiest**) large and strong. **heftily** *adverb*

heifer (*say* **hef**-er) *noun* a young cow.

height *noun* **1** how high something is; the distance from the base to the top or from head to foot. **2** a high place. **3** the highest or most intense part, *at the height of the holiday season*.

heighten *verb* make or become higher or more intense.

heir (*say as* air) *noun* a person who inherits something.
heir apparent an heir whose right to inherit cannot be cancelled.
heir presumptive an heir whose right to inherit will be cancelled if someone with a stronger right is born.

heiress (*say* **air**-ess) *noun* (*plural* **heiresses**) a female heir, especially to great wealth.

heirloom (*say* **air**-loom) *noun* a valued possession that has been handed down in a family for several generations.

heitiki *noun* a neck-ornament made of greenstone. (Compare *tiki*.) [Māori]

helicopter *noun* a kind of aircraft with a large horizontal propeller or rotor. [from *helix* + Greek *pteron* = wing]

heliotrope *noun* a plant with small fragrant purple flowers. [from Greek *helios* = sun, + *trope* = turning (the plant turns its flowers to the sun)]

helium (*say* **hee**-lee-um) *noun* a light colourless gas that does not burn. [from Greek *helios* = sun]

helix (*say* **hee**-liks) *noun* (*plural* **helices**, *say* **hee**-liss-eez) a spiral. [Greek, = coil]

hell *noun* **1** a place where wicked people are thought to be punished after they die. **2** a very unpleasant place. **3** (*informal*) an exclamation of anger.
hell for leather (*informal*) at high speed.

hello *interjection* hallo.

helm *noun* the handle or wheel used to steer a ship. **helmsman** *noun*

helmet *noun* a strong covering worn to protect the head.

help *verb* **1** do part of another person's work for him or her. **2** benefit; make something better or easier, *This will help you to sleep.* **3** avoid, *I can't help coughing.* **4** serve food etc. to somebody. **helper** *noun*, **helpful** *adjective*, **helpfully** *adverb*

help *noun* **1** helping somebody. **2** a person or thing that helps.

helping *noun* a portion of food.

helpless *adjective* not able to do things. **helplessly** *adverb*, **helplessness** *noun*

helpmate *noun* a helper.

helter-skelter *adverb* in great haste.

hem *noun* the edge of a piece of cloth that is folded over and sewn down.

hem *verb* (**hemmed**, **hemming**) put a hem on something.
hem in surround and restrict.

hemisphere *noun* **1** half a sphere. **2** half the earth. **hemispherical** *adjective* [from Greek *hemi-* = half, + *sphere*]

hemlock *noun* a poisonous plant; poison made from it.

hemp *noun* **1** a plant that produces coarse fibres from which cloth and ropes are made. **2** a drug made from this plant. **hempen** *adjective*

hen *noun* **1** a female bird. **2** a female fowl.

hence *adverb* **1** henceforth. **2** therefore. **3** (*old use*) from here.

henceforth *adverb* from now on.

henchman *noun* (*plural* **henchmen**) a trusty supporter.

henna *noun* a reddish-brown dye.

hepatitis *noun* inflammation of the liver.

hepta- *prefix* seven. [from Greek *hepta* = seven]

heptagon *noun* a flat shape with seven sides and seven angles. **heptagonal** *adjective* [from *hepta-*, + Greek *gonia* = angle]

heptathlon *noun* an athletic contest in which each competitor takes part in seven events. [from *hepta-*, + Greek *athlon* = contest]

her *pronoun* the form of *she* used as the object of a verb or after a preposition.

her *adjective* belonging to her, *her book.*

herald *noun* **1** an official in former times who made announcements and carried messages for a king or queen. **2** a person or thing that heralds something.

herald *verb* show that something is coming.

heraldry *noun* the study of coats of arms. **heraldic** (*say* hir-**al**-dik) *adjective*

herb *noun* a plant used for flavouring or for making medicine. **herbal** *adjective* [from Latin *herba* = grass]

herbaceous (*say* her-**bay**-shus) *adjective* **1** of or like herbs. **2** containing many flowering plants, *a herbaceous border.*

herbicide *noun* a chemical that kills weeds. [from Latin *herba* = grass, + *caedere* = kill]

herbivorous (*say* her-**biv**-er-us) *adjective* plant-eating. (Compare *carnivorous.*) **herbivore** *noun* [from Latin *herba* = grass, + *vorare* = devour]

herculean (*say* her-kew-**lee**-an) *adjective* **1** needing great strength or effort, *a herculean task.* **2** as strong as Hercules (a hero in ancient Greek legend).

herd *noun* **1** a group of cattle or other animals that feed together. **2** a mass of people; a mob. **herdsman** *noun*

herd *verb* **1** gather or move or send in a herd, *We all herded into the dining-room.* **2** look after a herd of animals.

herd-testing *noun* (*NZ*) testing how much butterfat a dairy herd is producing. **herd-tester** *noun*

here *adverb* in or to this place etc. **here and there** in various places or directions.

hereafter *adverb* from now on; in future.

hereby *adverb* by this act or decree etc.

hereditary *adjective* **1** inherited, *a hereditary disease.* **2** inheriting a position, *Our Queen is a hereditary monarch.*

heredity (*say* hir-**ed**-it-ee) *noun* inheriting characteristics from parents or ancestors. [from Latin *heredis* = of an heir]

Hereford *noun* a kind of red and white beef cattle. [from *Herefordshire*, the name of a city and county in England]

heresy (*say* **he**rri-see) *noun* (*plural* **heresies**) an opinion that disagrees with the beliefs accepted by the Christian Church or other authority.

heretic (*say* **he**rri-tik) *noun* a person who supports a heresy. **heretical** (*say* hi-**ret**-ik-al) *adjective*

heritage *noun* the things that someone has inherited.

hermetically *adverb* so as to be airtight, *The tin is hermetically sealed.*

hermit *noun* a person who lives alone and keeps away from people. [from Greek *eremites* = of the desert]

hermitage *noun* a hermit's home.

hernia *noun* a condition in which an internal part of the body pushes through another part; a rupture.

hero *noun* (*plural* **heroes**) **1** a man or boy who is admired for doing something very brave or great. **2** the chief male character in a story etc. **heroic** *adjective*, **heroically** *adverb*, **heroism** *noun*

heroin *noun* an addictive drug.

heroine *noun* **1** a woman or girl who is admired for doing something very brave or great. **2** the chief female character in a story, play, or poem.

heron *noun* a wading bird with long legs and a long neck.

herring *noun* (*plural* **herring** or **herrings**) a sea-fish used as food.

herring-bone *noun* a zigzag pattern.

hers *possessive pronoun* belonging to her, *Those books are hers.*

> **USAGE** It is incorrect to write *her's.*

herself *pronoun* she or her and nobody else. The word is used to refer back to the subject of a sentence (e.g. *She cut herself*) or for emphasis (e.g. *She herself has said it*). **by herself** alone; on her own.

hertz *noun* (*plural* **hertz**) a unit of frequency of electromagnetic waves, = one cycle per second. [named after the German scientist H. R. Hertz]

hesitant *adjective* hesitating. **hesitantly** *adverb*, **hesitancy** *noun*

hesitate *verb* (**hesitated**, **hesitating**) be slow or uncertain in speaking, moving, etc. **hesitation** *noun* [from Latin *haesitare* = get stuck]

hessian *noun* sackcloth.

hetero- *prefix* other; different. [from Greek *heteros* = other]

heterogeneous (*say* het-er-o-**jeen**-ee-us) *adjective* composed of people or things of different kinds. [from *hetero-*, + Greek *genos* = a kind]

heterosexual *adjective* attracted to people of the opposite sex; not homosexual.

hew *verb* (**hewed**, **hewn**, **hewing**) chop or cut with an axe or sword etc.

hex *verb* bewitch; put a spell on someone. **hex** *noun*

hexa- *prefix* six. [from Greek *hex* = six]

hexagon *noun* a flat shape with six sides and six angles. **hexagonal** *adjective* [from *hexa-*, + Greek *gonia* = angle]

hey *interjection* an exclamation calling attention or expressing surprise or inquiry.

heyday *noun* the time of a thing's greatest success or prosperity.

hi *interjection* an exclamation calling attention or expressing a greeting.

hiatus (*say* hy-**ay**-tus) *noun* (*plural* **hiatuses**) a gap in something that is otherwise continuous. [Latin, = gaping]

hibernate *verb* (**hibernated**, **hibernating**) spend the winter in a state like deep sleep. **hibernation** *noun* [from Latin *hibernus* = of winter]

hibiscus *noun* a shrub with large brightly coloured flowers.

hiccup *noun* **1** a high gulping sound made when your breath is briefly interrupted. **2** a brief hitch. **hiccup** *verb* (**hiccuped**, **hiccuping**)

hickory *noun* (*plural* **hickories**) a North American tree rather like the walnut tree.

hide[1] *verb* (**hid**, **hidden**, **hiding**) **1** keep a person or thing from being seen; conceal. **2** get into a place where you cannot be seen. **3** keep a thing secret.

hide[2] *noun* an animal's skin.

hide-and-seek *noun* a game in which one person looks for others who are hiding.

hidebound *adjective* narrow-minded.

hideous *adjective* very ugly or unpleasant. **hideously** *adverb*

hide-out *noun* a place where somebody hides.

hiding[1] *noun* being hidden, *She went into hiding.* **hiding-place** *noun*

hiding[2] *noun* a thrashing; a beating.

hierarchy (*say* **hyr**-ark-ee) *noun* an organisation that ranks people one above another according to the power or authority that they hold. [from Greek *hieros* = sacred, + *archein* = to rule]

hieroglyphics (*say* hyr-o-**glif**-iks) *plural noun* pictures or symbols used in ancient Egypt to represent words. [from Greek *hieros* = sacred, + *glyphe* = carving]

hiff *verb* (*NZ, informal*) throw.

hi-fi *noun* (*informal*) **1** high fidelity. **2** equipment that gives high fidelity.

higgledy-piggledy *adverb & adjective* completely mixed up; in great disorder.

high *adjective* **1** reaching a long way upwards, *high hills.* **2** far above the ground or above sea-level, *high clouds.* **3** measuring from top to bottom, *two metres high.* **4** above average level in importance, quality, amount, etc., *high rank*; *high prices.* **5** (of meat) beginning to go bad. **6** (*slang*) affected by a drug.
high country (*NZ*) mountain foothills used for sheep farming (especially in the South Island).
high explosive a powerful explosive.
high fidelity reproducing sound with very little distortion.
high school a secondary school.
high time fully time, *It's high time we left.*

high *adverb* at or to a high level or position etc., *They flew high above us.*

highbrow *adjective* intellectual.

higher *adjective & adverb* more high.
higher education education at a university, polytechnic, or college.

high five *noun* a salutation in which two people slap the palms of their hands together above their heads, often to express solidarity or victory.

highlands *plural noun* mountainous country, especially in Scotland. **highland** *adjective*, **highlander** *noun*

high-level *adjective* of a computer programming language with instructions that resemble an existing language.

highlight *noun* **1** a light area in a painting etc. **2** the most interesting part.

highlight *verb* **1** draw special attention to something. **2** mark with a highlighter. **3** select text on a computer screen.

highlighter *noun* a pen with a broad felt tip for emphasising printed words etc. with a transparent colour.

highly *adverb* **1** extremely, *highly amusing.* **2** very favourably, *We think highly of her.*

Highness *noun* (*plural* **Highnesses**) the title of a prince or princess.

high-octane *adjective* powerful or fast-moving.

high-rise *adjective* with many storeys.

highway *noun* a main road or route.

highwayman *noun* (*plural* **highwaymen**) a man who robbed travellers on highways in former times.

hijack *verb* seize control of an aircraft or vehicle during a journey. **hijack** *noun*, **hijacker** *noun*

hike *noun* a long walk. **hike** *verb* (**hiked**, **hiking**), **hiker** *noun*

hīkoi *noun* a protest march. [Māori]

hīkoi *verb* march in protest.

hilarious *adjective* very funny or merry. **hilariously** *adverb*, **hilarity** *noun* [from Greek *hilaros* = cheerful]

hill *noun* a piece of land that is higher than the ground around it. **hillside** *noun*, **hilly** *adjective*
hill country (*NZ*) hillside land used for grazing (especially in the North Island).
over the hill (*informal*) past the prime of life; in decline.

hillock *noun* a small hill; a mound.

hilt *noun* the handle of a sword or dagger etc.
to the hilt completely.

him *pronoun* the form of *he* used as the object of a verb or after a preposition.

himself *pronoun* he or him and nobody else. (Compare *herself.*)

hīnau *noun* a tree that gives a black dye. [Māori]

hind[1] *adjective* at the back, *the hind legs.*

hind[2] *noun* a female deer. (Compare *hart.*)

hinder *verb* get in someone's way; make it difficult for a person to do something quickly or for something to happen. **hindrance** *noun*

Hindi *noun* one of the languages of India.

hindmost *adjective* furthest behind.

hindquarters *plural noun* an animal's hind legs and rear parts.

hindsight *noun* looking back on an event with knowledge or understanding that you did not have at the time.

Hindu *noun* (*plural* **Hindus**) a person who believes in Hinduism, which is one of the religions of India.

Hindustani *noun* a group of languages and dialects of NW India.

hine *noun* girl. [Māori]

hinge *noun* a joining device on which a lid or door etc. turns when it opens.

hinge *verb* (**hinged**, **hinging**) **1** fix with a hinge. **2** depend, *Everything hinges on this meeting.*

hint *noun* **1** a slight indication or suggestion, *Give me a hint of what you want.* **2** a useful suggestion, *household hints.*

hint *verb* make a hint.

hinterland *noun* the district behind a coast or port etc.

hip[1] *noun* the bony part at the side of the body between the waist and the thigh.

hip[2] *noun* the fruit of the wild rose.

hip[3] *interjection* part of a cheer, *Hip, hip, hooray!*

hip hop *noun* a style of music and dance featuring rap, originating in the US.

hippie *noun* (*slang*) a young person who joins with others to live in an unconventional way.

hippo *noun* (*plural* **hippos**) (*informal*) a hippopotamus.

hippopotamus *noun* (*plural* **hippopotamuses**) a very large African animal that lives near water. [from Greek *hippos* = horse, + *potamos* = river]

hire *verb* (**hired**, **hiring**) **1** pay to borrow something. **2** lend for payment, *He hires out bicycles.* **hirer** *noun*

hire *noun* hiring, *for hire.*

hire-purchase *noun* buying something by paying in instalments.

hirsute (*say* **herss**-yoot) *adjective* hairy.

his *adjective & possessive pronoun* belonging to him, *That is his book. That book is his.*

hiss *verb* make a sound like an *s*, *The snakes were hissing.* **hiss** *noun*

historian *noun* a person who writes or studies history.

historic *adjective* famous or important in history, *a historic town.*

history *noun* (*plural* **histories**) **1** what happened in the past. **2** study of past events. **3** a description of important events. **historical** *adjective*, **historically** *adverb* [from Greek *historia* = finding out, narrative]

hit *verb* (**hit**, **hitting**) **1** come forcefully against a person or thing; knock or strike. **2** have a bad effect on, *Famine has hit the poor countries.* **3** reach, *I can't hit that high note.*
hit on discover something by chance.

hit *noun* **1** hitting; a knock or stroke. **2** a shot that hits the target. **3** a success; a successful song, show, etc. **4** a murder. **5** a website response to a search with a search engine, *I had 665 hits when I entered pāua.*

hitch *verb* **1** raise or pull with a slight jerk. **2** fasten with a loop or hook etc. **3** hitch-hike.

hitch *noun* **1** a hitching movement. **2** a knot. **3** a difficulty causing delay.

hitchhike *verb* travel by begging rides in passing vehicles. **hitchhiker** *noun*

hither *adverb* to or towards this place.

hitherto *adverb* until this time.

hive *noun* **1** a beehive. **2** the bees living in a beehive.
hive of industry a place full of people working busily.

HMNZS *abbreviation* Her Majesty's New Zealand Ship.

ho *interjection* an exclamation of triumph, surprise, etc.

hoard *noun* a carefully saved store of money, treasure, food, etc.

hoard *verb* store away. **hoarder** *noun*

hoarding *noun* a tall fence covered with advertisements.

hoar-frost *noun* a white frost.

hoarse *adjective* with a rough voice. **hoarsely** *adverb*, **hoarseness** *noun*

hoary *adjective* **1** white or grey from age, *hoary hair.* **2** old, *hoary jokes.*

hoax *verb* deceive somebody as a joke. **hoax** *noun*, **hoaxer** *noun*

hob *noun* a flat surface on a stove or beside a fireplace, where food etc. can be cooked or kept warm.

hobble *verb* (**hobbled**, **hobbling**) limp.

hobby *noun* (*plural* **hobbies**) something you do for pleasure in your spare time.

hobby-horse *noun* **1** a stick with a horse's head, used as a toy. **2** a subject that a person likes to talk about.

hobgoblin *noun* a mischievous or evil spirit; a bogy.

hobnob *verb* (**hobnobbed**, **hobnobbing**) spend time together in a friendly way, *hobnobbing with pop stars.*

hock *noun* the middle joint of an animal's hind leg.

hockey *noun* a game played by two teams with curved sticks and a hard ball.

hoe *noun* a tool for scraping up weeds.

hoe *verb* (**hoed**, **hoeing**) scrape or dig with a hoe.

hog *noun* **1** a male pig. **2** (*informal*) a greedy person.
go the whole hog (*slang*) do something completely or thoroughly.

hog *verb* (**hogged**, **hogging**) (*slang*) take more than your fair share of something; hoard selfishly.

hogget *noun* (*NZ*) a lamb of either sex between the age of ten months and when it cuts its first two adult teeth; its meat.

Hogmanay *noun* New Year's Eve in Scotland.

hōhā *adjective* bored; annoying. [Māori]

hōiho *noun* the yellow-eyed penguin. [Māori]

hoi polloi *noun* the common mass of people. [Greek]

hoist *verb* lift; raise something by using ropes and pulleys etc.

hokey-pokey *noun* (*NZ*) a kind of toffee, often added to ice-cream.

hoki *noun* an edible fish. [Māori]

hold *verb* (**held**, **holding**) This word has many uses, including (**1**) have and keep, especially in your hands, (**2**) have room for (*The jug holds a litre*), (**3**) support (*This plank won't hold my weight*), (**4**) stay unbroken; continue (*Will the fine weather hold?*), (**5**) believe; consider (*We shall hold you responsible*), (**6**) cause to take place (*hold a meeting*), (**7**) restrain; stop (*Hold everything!*).
hold forth make a long speech.
hold out last; continue.
hold up hinder; stop and rob somebody by threats or force.
hold with approve of, *We don't hold with bullying.*
hold your tongue (*informal*) stop talking.

hold *noun* **1** holding something; a grasp. **2** something to hold on to for support. **3** the part of a ship where cargo is stored, below the deck.
get hold of grasp; obtain; make contact with a person.

holdall *noun* a large portable bag or case.

holder *noun* a person or thing that holds something.

hold-up *noun* **1** a delay. **2** a robbery with threats or force.

hole *noun* **1** a hollow place; a gap or opening. **2** a burrow. **3** (*informal*) an unpleasant place. **4** (*slang*) an awkward situation.
holey *adjective*

hole *verb* (**holed**, **holing**) **1** make a hole or holes in something. **2** put into a hole.

holiday *noun* **1** a day or week etc. when people do not go to work or to school. **2** a time when you go away to enjoy yourself. [from *holy* + *day* (because holidays were originally religious festivals)]

holiness *noun* being holy or sacred.
His Holiness the title of the pope.

holistic *adjective* treating something as a whole unit rather than as a collection of parts.

hollow *adjective* with an empty space inside; not solid. **hollowly** *adverb*

hollow *adverb* completely, *We beat them hollow.*

hollow *noun* a hollow or sunken place.

hollow *verb* make a thing hollow.

holly *noun* (*plural* **hollies**) an evergreen bush with shiny prickly leaves and red berries.

hollyhock *noun* a plant with large flowers on a very tall stem.

holocaust *noun* an immense destruction, especially by fire, *the nuclear holocaust.* [from Greek *holos* = whole, + *kaustos* = burnt]

holster *noun* a leather case in which a pistol or revolver is carried.

holy *adjective* (**holier**, **holiest**) **1** belonging or devoted to God. **2** consecrated, *holy water.*
holiness *noun*

homage *noun* an act or expression of respect or honour, *We paid homage to his achievements.*

home *noun* **1** the place where you live. **2** the place where you were born or where you feel you belong. **3** a place where those who need help are looked after, *an old people's home.* **4** the place to be reached in a race or in certain games. **5** (often **Home**) (*NZ*) formerly, a name for Britain.
home economics the study of household management.
home page (*Computing*) a document providing an introduction or index to a website.
home run (in softball and baseball) a hit allowing the batter to make a complete circuit of the bases.
home unit a flat.

home *adjective* **1** of a person's own home or country, *home industries.* **2** played on a team's own ground, *a home match.*

home *adverb* **1** to or at home, *Is she home yet?* **2** to the point aimed at, *Push the bolt home.*
home and dry, (*NZ*) **home and hosed** (*informal*) close to success.
bring something home to somebody make him or her realise it.

home *verb* (**homed**, **homing**) make for a target, *The missile homed in.*

homeless *adjective* having no home.

homely *adverb* simple and ordinary, *a homely meal.* **homeliness** *noun*

home-made *adjective* made at home, not bought from a shop.

homesick *adjective* sad because you are away from home. **homesickness** *noun*

homestead *noun* **1** a farmhouse, usually with the land and buildings round it. **2** (*NZ*) the owner's house on a sheep or cattle station.

homeward *adjective & adverb* going towards home. **homewards** *adverb*

homework *noun* school work that a pupil has to do at home.

homicide *noun* the killing of one person by another. **homicidal** *adjective* [from Latin *homo* = person, + *caedere* = kill]

homily *noun* (*plural* **homilies**) a lecture about behaviour.

homing *adjective* trained to fly home, *a homing pigeon.*

homo- *prefix* same. [from Greek *0* = same]

homogeneous (*say* hom-o-**jeen**-ee-us) *adjective* composed of people or things of the same kind. [from *homo-*, + Greek *genos* = a kind]

homograph *noun* a word that is spelt like another but has a different meaning or origin, e.g. *bat* (a flying animal) and *bat* (for hitting a ball). [from *homo-* + *-graph*]

homonym (*say* **hom**-o-nim) *noun* a homograph or homophone. [from *homo-*, + Greek *onyma* = name]

homophone *noun* a word with the same sound as another, e.g. *son, sun.* [from *homo-*, + Greek *phone* = sound]

homosexual *adjective* attracted to people of the same sex. **homosexual** *noun,* **homosexuality** *noun*

Hon. *abbreviation* Honourable; honorary.

honest *adjective* not stealing or cheating or telling lies; truthful. **honestly** *adverb,* **honesty** *noun* [from Latin *honestus* = honourable]

honey *noun* a sweet sticky food made by bees.

honeycomb *noun* a wax structure of small six-sided sections made by bees to hold their honey and eggs.

honeycombed *adjective* with many holes or tunnels.

honeymoon *noun* a holiday spent together by a newly-married couple.

honeysuckle *noun* a climbing plant with fragrant yellow or pink flowers.

hongi *noun* the pressing of noses together as a greeting. **hongi** *verb* [Māori]

honk *noun* a loud sound like that made by an old-fashioned car-horn. **honk** *verb*

honorary *adjective* **1** given or received as an honour, *an honorary degree.* **2** unpaid, *the honorary treasurer.*

honour *noun* **1** great respect. **2** a person or thing that brings honour. **3** honesty and loyalty, *a man of honour.* **4** an award for distinction.

honour *verb* **1** feel or show honour for a person. **2** acknowledge and pay a cheque etc. **3** keep to the terms of an agreement or promise.

honourable *adjective* deserving honour; honest and loyal. **honourably** *adverb.*

hood *noun* **1** a covering of soft material for the head and neck. **2** a folding roof or cover. **hooded** *adjective*

hoodwink *verb* deceive.

hoof *noun* (*plural* **hooves**) the horny part of the foot of a horse etc.

hook *noun* a bent or curved piece of metal etc. for hanging things on or for catching hold of something.

hook *verb* **1** catch with a hook. **2** fasten with or on a hook. **3** send a ball in a curving direction.
be hooked on something (*slang*) be addicted to it.

hookah *noun* an oriental tobacco-pipe with a long tube passing through a jar of water.

hooked *adjective* hook-shaped.

hooker *noun* the player in the middle of the front row of the scrum in rugby.

hooley *noun* (*NZ, slang*) a wild party.

hooligan *noun* a rough lawless young person. **hooliganism** *noun*

hoon *noun* (*NZ, informal*) a hooligan.

hoon *verb* (*NZ, informal*) behave like a hooligan.

hoop *noun* a ring made of metal or wood.

hoop-la *noun* a game in which people try to throw hoops round objects.

hooray *interjection* **1** hurray. **2** (*NZ*) goodbye.

hoot[1] *noun* **1** the sound made by an owl or a vehicle's horn or a steam whistle. **2** a cry of scorn or disapproval. **3** laughter; a cause of this. **hoot** *verb,* **hooter** *noun*

hoot[2] *noun* (*informal*) money. [from Māori *utu*]

hop[1] *verb* (**hopped, hopping**) **1** jump on one foot. **2** (of an animal) spring from all feet at once. **3** (*informal*) move quickly, *Here's the car—hop in!*
hop it (*slang*) go away.

hop[1] *noun* a hopping movement.

hop[2] *noun* a climbing plant used to give beer its flavour.

hope *noun* **1** a wish for something to happen. **2** a person or thing that gives hope, *You are our only hope.*

hope *verb* (**hoped, hoping**) feel hope; want and expect something.

hopeful *adjective* **1** feeling hope. **2** likely to be good or successful.

hopefully *adverb* **1** in a hopeful manner. **2** (*informal*) it is to be hoped, *Hopefully, our team will win.*

hopeless *adjective* **1** without hope. **2** very bad at something. **hopelessly** *adverb*, **hopelessness** *noun*

hopper *noun* **1** one who hops. **2** a V-shaped container with an opening at the bottom.

hopscotch *noun* a game of hopping into squares drawn on the ground.

horde *noun* a large group or crowd.

horizon *noun* the line where the earth and the sky seem to meet. [from Greek *horizein* = form a boundary]

horizontal *adjective* level, so as to be parallel to the horizon; going across from left to right. (The opposite is *vertical*.) **horizontally** *adverb*

hormone *noun* a substance that stimulates an organ of the body or of a plant.

horn *noun* **1** a hard substance that grows into a point on the head of a bull, cow, ram, etc. **2** a pointed part. **3** a brass instrument played by blowing. **4** a device for making a warning sound. **horned** *adjective*, **horny** *adjective*

hornet *noun* a large kind of wasp.

hornpipe *noun* a sailors' dance.

horoeka *noun* a small tree. [Māori]

horopito *noun* the pepper-tree. [Māori]

horoscope *noun* an astrologer's forecast of future events. [from Greek *hora* = hour (of birth), + *skopos* = observer]

horrendous *adjective* horrifying.

horrible *adjective* horrifying; unpleasant. **horribly** *adverb*

horrid *adjective* horrible. **horridly** *adverb*

horrific *adjective* horrifying. **horrifically** *adverb*

horrify *verb* (**horrified, horrifying**) arouse horror in somebody; shock.

horror *noun* **1** great fear and dislike or dismay. **2** a person or thing causing horror.

horse *noun* **1** a large four-legged animal used for riding on and for pulling carts etc. **2** a framework for hanging clothes on to dry. **3** a vaulting-horse.
on horseback mounted on a horse.

horse-chestnut *noun* a large tree that produces dark-brown nuts (conkers).

horseman *noun* (*plural* **horsemen**) a man who rides a horse, especially a skilled rider. **horsemanship** *noun*

horseplay *noun* rough play.

horsepower *noun* a unit for measuring the power of an engine.

horseshoe *noun* a U-shaped piece of metal nailed to a horse's hoof.

horsewoman *noun* (*plural* **horsewomen**) a woman who rides a horse, especially a skilled rider.

horticulture *noun* the art of cultivating gardens. **horticultural** *adjective* (from Latin *hortus* = garden, + *culture*]

hose *noun* **1** (also **hose-pipe**) a flexible tube for taking water to something. **2** (*old use*) breeches, *doublet and hose.*

hose *verb* (**hosed, hosing**) water or spray with a hose.
hose down (*NZ, slang*) rain hard.

hosiery *noun* (in shops) socks and stockings.

hospice (*say* **hosp**-iss) *noun* **1** a nursing home for people who are very ill. **2** a lodging-house for travellers, especially one kept by a religious institution.

hospitable *adjective* welcoming; liking to give hospitality. **hospitably** *adverb*

hospital *noun* a place providing medical and surgical treatment for people who are ill or injured. [from Latin *hospitium* = hospitality]

hospitality *noun* welcoming people and giving them food and entertainment.

host[1] *noun* a person who has guests and looks after them. [same origin as *hospital*]

host[2] *noun* a large number of people or things. [same origin as *hostile*]

host[3] *noun* the bread consecrated at Holy Communion. [from Latin *hostia* = sacrifice]

hostage *noun* a person who is held prisoner until the holder gets what he or she wants.

hostel *noun* a lodging-house for travellers, students, or other groups.

hostess *noun* a woman who has guests and looks after them.

hostile *adjective* **1** of an enemy. **2** unfriendly, *a hostile glance.* **hostility** *noun* [from Latin *hostis* = an enemy]

hot *adjective* (**hotter, hottest**) **1** having great heat or a high temperature. **2** giving a burning sensation when tasted. **3** enthusiastic; excitable, *a hot temper*. **hotly** *adverb*, **hotness** *noun*
hot cross bun a fresh spicy bun marked with a cross, to be eaten on Good Friday.
hot dog a hot sausage in a bread roll.
in hot water (*informal*) in trouble or disgrace.

hot *verb* (**hotted, hotting**) **hot up** (*informal*) make or become hot or hotter or more exciting.

hotel *noun* **1** a building where people pay to have meals and stay for the night. **2** (*NZ*) a public house.

hotfoot *adverb* in eager haste.

hothead *noun* an impetuous person.

hothouse *noun* a heated greenhouse.

hotplate *noun* a heated surface for cooking food etc. or keeping it hot.

hotpot *noun* a stew.

hottie *noun* (*informal*) **1** a hot-water bottle. **2** a physically attractive person.

houhere *noun* a small tree. [Māori]

hound *noun* a dog used in hunting or racing.

hound *verb* chase; harass.

hour *noun* **1** one twenty-fourth part of a day and night; sixty minutes. **2** a time, *Why are you up at this hour?*
hours *plural noun* a fixed period for work, *Office hours are 9 a.m. to 5 p.m.*

hourglass *noun* a glass container with a very narrow part in the middle through which sand runs from the top half to the bottom half, taking one hour.

hourly *adverb & adjective* every hour.

house (*say* howss) *noun* **1** a building made for people to live in, usually designed for one family. **2** a building or establishment for a special purpose, *the opera house.* **3** a building for a government assembly; the assembly itself, *the House of Representatives.* **4** each of the divisions of a school for sports competitions etc. **5** a family or dynasty, *the royal house of Tudor.*

house (*say* howz) *verb* (**housed, housing**) provide accommodation or room for someone or something.

houseboat *noun* a barge-like boat for living in.

household *noun* all the people who live together in the same house.

householder *noun* a person who owns or rents a house.

housekeeper *noun* a person employed to look after a household.

housekeeping *noun* **1** looking after a household. **2** (*informal*) the money for a household's food and other necessities.

housemaid *noun* a woman servant in a house, especially one who cleans rooms.

house-proud *adjective* very careful to keep a house clean and tidy.

house-trained *adjective* (of an animal) trained to be clean in the house.

house-warming *noun* a party to celebrate moving into a new home.

housewife *noun* (*plural* **housewives**) a woman who does the housekeeping for her family.

housework *noun* the cleaning and cooking etc. done in housekeeping.

housie *noun* a game in which the players have pieces of card marked with numbers which they cover up as the numbers are drawn at random and called out.

housing *noun* **1** accommodation; houses. **2** a stiff cover or guard for a piece of machinery.

hove *past tense* of **heave** (when used of ships).

hovel *noun* a small shabby house.

hover *verb* **1** stay in one place in the air. **2** wait about near someone or something; linger.

hovercraft *noun* (*plural* **hovercraft**) a vehicle that travels just above the surface of land or water, supported by a strong current of air sent downwards from its engines.

how *adverb* **1** in what way; by what means, *How did you do it?* **2** to what extent or amount etc., *How high can you jump?* **3** in what condition, *How are you?*
how about would you like, *How about a game of cards?*
how do you do? a formal greeting.

however *adverb* **1** in whatever way; to whatever extent, *You will never catch him, however hard you try.* **2** all the same; nevertheless, *Later, however, he decided to go.*

howl *noun* a long loud sad-sounding cry or sound, such as that made by a dog or wolf.

howl *verb* **1** make a howl. **2** weep loudly.

howler *noun* **1** an animal that howls. **2** (*informal*) a foolish mistake.

howly-bag *noun* (*NZ, informal*) a crybaby or sissy.

HP *abbreviation* hire purchase.

HQ *abbreviation* headquarters.

HRH *abbreviation* Her/His Royal Highness.

HTML *abbreviation* Hypertext Markup Language, a system for tagging text files to achieve links between pages of a website or home page.

http *abbreviation* an abbreviated form of hypertext transfer protocol, a means of connecting to a website.

hub *noun* the central part of a wheel.

hubbub *noun* a loud confused noise of voices.

huddle *verb* (**huddled, huddling**) **1** crowd together into a small space. **2** curl your body closely. **huddle** *noun*

hue[1] *noun* a colour or tint.

hue[2] *noun* **hue and cry** a general outcry of demand, alarm, or protest.

huff *noun* an annoyed or offended mood. *She went away in a huff.* **huffy** *adjective*

huff *verb* blow, *huffing and puffing.*

hug *verb* (**hugged**, **hugging**) **1** clasp tightly in your arms; embrace. **2** keep close to. *The ship hugged the shore.*

hug *noun* hugging; an embrace.

huge *adjective* extremely large; enormous. **hugely** *adverb*, **hugeness** *noun*

huhu *noun* an edible grub. [Māori]

hui *noun* **1** a meeting or conference. **2** a social gathering. [Māori]

hūia *noun* a bird which is now extinct, with white tail-feathers. [Māori]

hula *noun* a Hawaiian women's dance. [Hawaiian]

hulk *noun* **1** the body or wreck of an old ship. **2** a large clumsy person or thing. **hulking** *adjective*

hull *noun* the framework of a ship.

hullabaloo *noun* an uproar.

hullo *interjection* hallo.

hum *verb* (**hummed**, **humming**) **1** sing a tune with your lips closed. **2** make a low continuous sound as some flying insects do.

hum *noun* a humming sound.

human *adjective* of human beings.
human being a creature distinguished from other animals by its better mental development, power of speech, and upright posture.
human rights the rights that any living person can claim.

human *noun* a human being.

humane (*say* hew-**mayn**) *adjective* kind-hearted; merciful. **humanely** *adverb*

humanise *verb* (**humanised**, **humanising**) make human or humane. **humanisation** *noun*

humanism *noun* a way of thinking that concerns itself with human, not religious, matters.

humanist *noun* a humanitarian person.

humanitarian *adjective* concerned with people's welfare and the reduction of suffering. **humanitarian** *noun*

humanity *noun* **1** human beings; people. **2** being human. **3** being humane. **humanities** *plural noun* arts subjects.

humble *adjective* **1** modest; not proud or showy. **2** of low rank or importance. **humbly** *adverb*, **humbleness** *noun*

humble *verb* (**humbled**, **humbling**) make humble. [from Latin *humilis* = lowly]

humbug *noun* **1** deceitful talk or behaviour. **2** a person who tries to win sympathy by deceit. **3** a hard peppermint sweet.

humdrum *adjective* dull and not exciting; commonplace; without variety.

humid (*say* **hew**-mid) *adjective* (of air) moist. **humidity** *noun*

humiliate *verb* (**humiliated**, **humiliating**) make a person feel disgraced. **humiliation** *noun*

humility *noun* being humble.

humming-bird *noun* a small tropical bird that makes a humming sound by moving its wings rapidly.

hummock *noun* a hump in the ground.

humorist *noun* a humorous person.

humorous *adjective* full of humour.

humour *noun* **1** being amusing; what makes people laugh. **2** the ability to enjoy comical things, *a sense of humour.* **3** a mood, *in a good humour.*

humour *verb* keep a person contented by doing what he or she wants.

hump *noun* **1** a rounded projecting part. **2** an abnormal outward curve at the top of a person's back. **humpback** *noun*, **humpbacked** *adjective*

hump *verb* **1** form a hump. **2** carry something on your back.

humus (*say* **hew**-mus) *noun* rich earth made by decayed plants.

hunch *noun* (*plural* **hunches**) **1** a hump. **2** a feeling that you can guess what will happen.

hunch *verb* bend into a hump, *He hunched his shoulders.*

hunchback *noun* a person with a hump on his or her back; this hump.

hundred *noun & adjective* the number 100; ten times ten. **hundredth** *adjective & noun*

hundredfold *adjective & adverb* one hundred times as much or as many.

hunger *noun* the feeling that you have when you have not eaten for some time; need for food.
hunger strike refusing to eat, as a way of making a protest.

hungry *adjective* (**hungrier**, **hungriest**) feeling hunger. **hungrily** *adverb*

hunk *noun* a large or clumsy piece.

hunt *verb* **1** chase and kill animals for food or as a sport. **2** search for something. **hunter** *noun*, **huntsman** *noun*

hunt *noun* **1** hunting. **2** a group of hunters.

huntaway *noun* (*NZ*) a farm dog trained to drive sheep forward when mustering.

hurdle *noun* **1** an upright frame to be jumped over in hurdling. **2** an obstacle.

hurdling *noun* racing in which the runners jump over hurdles. **hurdler** *noun*

hurl *verb* throw something violently.

hurly-burly *noun* a rough bustle of activity.

hurrah or **hurray** *interjection* a shout of joy or approval; a cheer.

hurricane *noun* a storm with violent wind, especially a cyclone.

Hurricanes *noun* a New Zealand rugby union Super 14 franchise based in Wellington.

hurry *verb* (**hurried**, **hurrying**) **1** move quickly; do something quickly. **2** try to make somebody or something be quick. **hurried** *adjective*, **hurriedly** *adverb*

hurry *noun* hurrying; a need to hurry.

hurt *verb* (**hurt**, **hurting**) cause or feel pain or damage or injury.

hurt *noun* an injury; harm. **hurtful** *adjective*

hurtle *verb* (**hurtled**, **hurtling**) move rapidly, *The train hurtled along.*

husband *noun* the man to whom a woman is married.

husband *verb* manage economically and try to save, *husband your strength.* [from Old English *husbonda* = master of a house (*hus*)]

husbandry *noun* **1** farming. **2** management of resources. [from an old use of *husband* = person who manages things]

hush *verb* make or become silent or quiet.

hush *noun* silence.

husk *noun* the dry outer covering of some seeds and fruits.

husky[1] *adjective* (**huskier**, **huskiest**) **1** hoarse. **2** big and strong; burly. **huskily** *adverb*, **huskiness** *noun*

husky[2] *noun* (*plural* **huskies**) a large dog used in the Arctic for pulling sledges.

hustle *verb* (**hustled**, **hustling**) hurry; bustle. **hustle** *noun*, **hustler** *noun*

hut *noun* a small roughly-made house or shelter.

hut-bagging *noun* a tallying of the number of tramping huts that a tramper has visited.

hutch *noun* (*plural* **hutches**) a box-like cage for a pet rabbit etc.

hyacinth *noun* a fragrant flower that grows from a bulb.

hybrid *noun* **1** a plant or animal produced by combining two different species or varieties. **2** something that combines parts or characteristics of two different things.

hydatids *plural noun* a condition in dogs caused by a kind of tapeworm.

hydra *noun* a microscopic freshwater animal with a tubular body.

hydrangea (*say* hy-**drayn**-ja) *noun* a shrub with pink, blue, or white flowers growing in large clusters.

hydrant *noun* a special water-tap to which a large hose can be attached for fire-fighting or street-cleaning etc.

hydraulic *adjective* worked by the force of water or other fluid, *hydraulic brakes.* [from *hydro-*, + *aulos* = pipe]

hydro- *prefix* **1** water (as in *hydroelectric*). **2** (in chemical names) containing hydrogen (as in *hydrochloric*). [from Greek *hydor* = water]

hydrochloric acid a colourless acid containing hydrogen and chlorine.

hydroelectric *adjective* using water-power to produce electricity. **hydroelectricity** *noun*

hydrofoil *noun* a boat designed to skim over the surface of water.

hydrogen *noun* a lightweight gas that combines with oxygen to form water. **hydrogen bomb** a very powerful bomb using energy created by the fusion of hydrogen nuclei. [from *hydro-*, + *-gen* = producing]

hydrophobia *noun* abnormal fear of water, as in someone suffering from rabies. [from *hydro-* + *phobia*]

hyena *noun* a wild animal that looks like a wolf and makes a shrieking howl.

hygiene (*say* **hy**-jeen) *noun* keeping things clean in order to remain healthy and prevent disease. **hygienic** *adjective*, **hygienically** *adverb* [from Greek *hygieine* = of health]

hymn *noun* a religious song, usually of praise to God. **hymn-book** *noun*

hymnal *noun* a hymn-book.

hyper- *prefix* over or above; excessive. [from Greek *hyper* = over]

hyperbola (*say* hy-**per**-bol-a) *noun* a kind of curve. [same origin as *hyperbole*]

hyperbole (*say* hy-**per**-bol-ee) *noun* a dramatic exaggeration that is not meant to be taken literally, e.g. 'I've got a stack of work a mile high.' [from *hyper-*, + Greek *bole* = a throw]

hypermedia *noun* a computer hypertext extension handling sound and video.

hypertext *noun* (*Computing*) the provision of many linked texts on one system, as on the World Wide Web.

hyphen *noun* a short dash used to join words or parts of words together (e.g. in *hymn-book.* [from Greek, = together]

hyphenate *verb* (**hyphenated**, **hyphenating**) join with a hyphen. **hyphenation** *noun*

hypnosis (*say* hip-**noh**-sis) *noun* a condition like a deep sleep in which a person's actions may be controlled by someone else. [from Greek *hypnos* = sleep]

hypnotise *verb* (**hypnotised**, **hypnotising**) produce hypnosis in somebody. **hypnotism** *noun*, **hypnotic** *adjective*, **hypnotist** *noun*

hypo- *prefix* below; under. [from Greek *hypo* = under]

hypochondriac (*say* hy-po-**kon**-dree-ak) *noun* a person who constantly imagines that he or she is ill. **hypochondria** *noun*

hypocrite (*say* **hip**-o-krit) *noun* a person who pretends to be more virtuous than he or she really is. **hypocrisy** (*say* hip-**ok**-riss-ee) *noun*, **hypocritical** *adjective* [from Greek, = acting a part]

hypodermic *adjective* injecting something under the skin, *a hypodermic syringe.* [from *hypo-*, + Greek *derma* = skin]

hypotenuse (*say* hy-**pot**-i-newz) *noun* the side opposite the right angle in a right-angled triangle.

hypothermia *noun* being too cold; the condition in which someone's temperature is below normal. [from *hypo-*, + Greek *therme* = heat]

hypothesis (*say* hy-**poth**-i-sis) *noun* (*plural* **hypotheses**) a suggestion or guess that tries to explain something. **hypothetical** *adjective*

hysterectomy (*say* hist-er-**ek**-tom-ee) *noun* surgical removal of the womb. [from Greek *hystera* = womb, + *-ectomy* = cutting out]

hysteria *noun* wild uncontrollable excitement or emotion. **hysterical** *adjective*, **hysterically** *adverb*, **hysterics** *noun* [from Greek *hystera* = womb (once thought to be the cause of hysterics)]

Ii

I *pronoun* a word used by a person to refer to himself or herself.

I. *abbreviation* Island.

IAAF *abbreviation* International Amateur Athletic Federation.

ice *noun* **1** frozen water, a brittle transparent solid substance. **2** an ice-cream.
ice block frozen juice on a stick.
ice-cap *noun* the permanent covering of ice at the North and South Poles.
ice rink a place made for skating.
the Ice (*NZ, informal*) Antarctica.

ice *verb* (**iced**, **icing**) **1** make or become icy. **2** put icing on a cake.

iceberg *noun* a large mass of ice floating in the sea with most of it under water.

ice-cream *noun* a sweet creamy frozen food.

ice-plant *noun* a low, spreading plant with fleshy leaves.

icicle *noun* a pointed hanging piece of ice formed when dripping water freezes.

icing *noun* a sugary substance for decorating cakes.
icing sugar finely powdered sugar used to make icing.

icon (*say* **I**-kon) *noun* **1** a sacred painting or mosaic etc. **2** a person or thing seen as a prominent and respected representative of something, *James K. Baxter is one of New Zealand's literary icons.* **3** a graphic symbol for a program etc. on a computer screen. **iconic** *adjective* [from Greek *eikon* = image]

icy *adjective* (**icier**, **iciest**) like ice; very cold.
icily *adverb*, **iciness** *noun*

ID *abbreviation* identity; identification, *Do you have ID?*

idea *noun* a plan etc. formed in the mind; an opinion.

ideal *adjective* perfect; completely suitable.
ideally *adverb*

ideal *noun* a person or thing regarded as perfect or worth trying to achieve.

idealist *noun* a person who has high ideals and wishes to achieve them. **idealism** *noun*, **idealistic** *adjective*

identical *adjective* exactly the same.
identically *adverb* [same origin as *identity*]

identify *verb* (**identified**, **identifying**) **1** recognise as being a certain person or thing. **2** treat as being identical, *Don't identify wealth with happiness.* **3** think of yourself as sharing someone's feelings etc., *We can identify with the hero of this play.*
identification *noun*

identity *noun* (*plural* **identities**) **1** who or what a person or thing is. **2** being identical; sameness. **3** distinctive character.
old identity (*NZ*) a person who is well-known in a particular place. [from Latin *idem* = same]

ideology (*say* I-dee-**ol**-o-jee) *noun* (*plural* **ideologies**) a set of beliefs and aims, especially in politics, *a socialist ideology*, **ideological** *adjective* [from *idea* + *-logy*]

ides (*say* **I**'dz) *plural noun* the ancient Roman name for the 15th day of March, May, July, and October, and the 13th day of other months.

idiocy *noun* **1** being an idiot. **2** stupid behaviour.

idiom *noun* **1** a phrase that means something different from the meanings of the words in it, e.g. *in hot water* (= in disgrace), *hell for leather* (= at high speed). **2** a special way of using words, e.g. *wash up the dishes but not wash up the baby.* **idiomatic** *adjective*, **idiomatically** *adverb* [from Greek *idios* = your own]

idiosyncrasy (*say* id-ee-o-**sink**-ra-see) *noun* (*plural* **idiosyncrasies**) one person's own way of behaving or doing something. [from Greek *idios* = your own, + *syn* = with, + *krasis* = mixture]

idiot *noun* **1** a person who is mentally deficient. **2** (*informal*) a very stupid person.
idiocy *noun*, **idiotic** *adjective*, **idiotically** *adverb* [from Greek *idiotes* = private citizen, uneducated person]

idle *adjective* **1** doing no work; lazy. **2** not in use, *The machines were idle.* **3** useless; with no special purpose, *idle gossip.* **idly** *adverb*, **idleness** *noun*

idle *verb* (**idled**, **idling**) **1** be idle. **2** (of an engine) work slowly. **idler** *noun*

idol *noun* **1** a statue or image that is worshipped as a god. **2** a person who is idolised. [from Greek *eidolon* = image]

idolatry *noun* **1** worship of idols. **2** idolising someone. **idolatrous** *adjective* [from *idol*, + Greek *latreia* = worship]

idolise *verb* (**idolised, idolising**) admire someone intensely. **idolisation** *noun*

idyll (*say* **id**-il) *noun* a poem describing a peaceful or romantic scene. **idyllic** (*say* id-**il**-ik) *adjective*

i.e. *abbreviation* id est (Latin, = that is), *The world's highest mountain (i.e. Mount Everest) is in the Himalayas.*

USAGE Do not confuse with *e.g.*

if *conjunction* **1** on condition that; supposing that, *He will do it if you pay him.* **2** even though, *I'll finish this job if it kills me.* **3** whether, *Do you know if dinner is ready?* **if only** I wish, *If only I were rich!*

iffy *adjective* (*informal*) doubtful; unreliable.

igloo *noun* an Eskimo's round house built of blocks of hard snow. [from Eskimo, = house]

igneous *adjective* formed by the action of a volcano, *igneous rocks*. [from Latin *igneus* = fiery]

ignite *verb* (**ignited, igniting**) **1** set fire to something. **2** catch fire. [from Latin *ignis* = fire]

ignition *noun* **1** igniting. **2** starting the fuel burning in an engine.

ignoble *adjective* not noble; shameful.

ignominious *adjective* humiliating; with disgrace. **ignominy** *noun*

ignoramus *noun* (*plural* **ignoramuses**) an ignorant person. [Latin, = we do not know]

ignorant *adjective* not knowing about something or about many things. **ignorantly** *adverb*, **ignorance** *noun*

ignore *verb* (**ignored, ignoring**) take no notice of a person or thing. [from Latin *ignorare* = not know]

iguana (*say* ig-**wah**-na) *noun* a large tree-climbing tropical lizard.

IHC *abbreviation* New Zealand Society for the Intellectually Handicapped (formerly Intellectually Handicapped Children's Society).

il- *prefix* see **in-**.

ilk *noun* **of that ilk** (*informal*)of that kind.

ill *adjective* **1** unwell; in bad health. **2** bad; harmful, *There were no ill effects.* **ill will** unkind feeling.

ill *adverb* badly, *She was ill-treated.* **ill at ease** uncomfortable; embarrassed.

illegal *adjective* not legal; against the law. **illegally** *adverb*, **illegality** *noun*

illegible *adjective* not legible. **illegibly** *adverb*, **illegibility** *noun*

illegitimate *adjective* not lawful or acceptable. **illegitimately** *adverb*, **illegitimacy** *noun*

illicit *adjective* unlawful; not allowed. **illicitly** *adverb* [from *il-* = not, + Latin *licitus* = allowed]

illiterate *adjective* unable to read or write; uneducated. **illiterately** *adverb*, **illiteracy** *noun*

illness *noun* (*plural* **illnesses**) being ill; a particular form of bad health.

illogical *adjective* not logical; not reasoning correctly. **illogically** *adverb*, **illogicality** *noun*

illuminate *verb* (**illuminated, illuminating**) **1** light something up. **2** decorate streets etc. with lights. **3** decorate a manuscript with coloured designs. **4** clarify or help to explain something. **illumination** *noun* [from *il-* = in, + Latin *lumen* = light]

illusion *noun* something unreal or imaginary; a false impression, *The train went so fast that we had the illusion that it was flying.* (Compare *delusion*.) **illusive** *adjective*, **illusory** *adjective* [from Latin *illudere* = mock]

illusionist *noun* a conjuror.

illustrate *verb* (**illustrated, illustrating**) **1** show something by pictures, examples, etc. **2** put illustrations in a book. **illustrator** *noun*

illustration *noun* **1** a picture in a book etc. **2** illustrating something. **3** an example.

illustrious *adjective* famous; distinguished.

im- *prefix* see **in-**.

image *noun* **1** a picture or statue of a person or thing. **2** the appearance of something as seen in a mirror or through a lens etc. **3** a person or thing that is very much like another, *He is the image of his father.* **4** reputation.

imagery *noun* **1** a writer's or speaker's use of words to produce effects. **2** images; statues.

imaginable *adjective* able to be imagined.

imaginary *adjective* existing only in the imagination; not real.

imagination *noun* the ability to imagine things, especially in a creative or inventive way. **imaginative** *adjective*

imagine *verb* (**imagined, imagining**) form pictures or ideas in your mind.

imam *noun* a Muslim religious leader. [Arabic, = leader]

imbalance *noun* lack of balance; disproportion.

imbecile (*say* **imb**-i-seel) *noun* an idiot. **imbecile** *adjective*, **imbecility** *noun*

imbibe *verb* (**imbibed**, **imbibing**) **1** drink. **2** take ideas etc. into the mind.

IMF *abbreviation* International Monetary Fund.

imitate *verb* (**imitated**, **imitating**) copy; mimic. **imitation** *noun*, **imitator** *noun*, **imitative** *adjective*

immaculate *adjective* **1** perfectly clean; spotless. **2** without any fault or blemish. **immaculately** *adverb*

immaterial *adjective* **1** having no material body, *as immaterial as a ghost.* **2** unimportant; not mattering, *it is immaterial whether he goes or stays.*

immature *adjective* not mature. **immaturity** *noun*

immediate *adjective* **1** happening or done without any delay. **2** nearest; with nothing or no one between, *our immediate neighbours.* **immediately** *adverb*, **immediacy** *noun*

immemorial *adjective* existing from before what can be remembered or found in histories, *from time immemorial.*

immense *adjective* exceedingly great; huge. **immensely** *adverb*, **immensity** *noun* [from *im-* = not, + Latin *mensum* = measured]

immerse *verb* (**immersed**, **immersing**) **1** put something completely into a liquid. **2** absorb or involve deeply, *She was immersed in her work.*

immersion *noun* a method of teaching a language by excluding the use of all others. **immersion heater** a device that heats water by means of an electric element immersed in the water in a tank etc.
[from *im-* = in, + Latin *mersum* = dipped]

immigrate *verb* (**immigrated**, **immigrating**) come into another country to live there. **immigration** *noun*, **immigrant** *noun* [from *im-* = in, + *migrate*]

USAGE See the note on *emigrate*.

imminent *adjective* likely to happen at any moment, *an imminent storm.* **imminence** *noun*

immobile *adjective* not moving; immovable. **immobility** *noun*

immobilise *verb* (**immobilised**, **immobilising**) stop a thing from moving or working. **immobilisation** *noun*

immodest *adjective* **1** without modesty; indecent. **2** conceited.

immoral *adjective* morally wrong; wicked. **immorally** *adverb*, **immorality** *noun*

immortal *adjective* **1** living for ever; not mortal. **2** famous for all time. **immortal** *noun*, **immortality** *noun*, **immortalise** *verb*

immovable *adjective* unable to be moved. **immovably** *adverb*

immune *adjective* safe from or protected against something, *immune from* (or *against* or *to*) *infection* etc. **immunity** *noun* [from Latin *immunis* = exempt]

immunise *verb* (**immunised**, **immunising**) make a person immune from a disease etc., e.g. by vaccination. **immunisation** *noun*

immutable (*say* i-**mewt**-a-bul) *adjective* unchangeable. **immutably** *adverb*

imp *noun* **1** a small devil. **2** a mischievous child. **impish** *adjective*

impact *noun* **1** a collision; the force of a collision. **2** an influence or effect, *the impact of computers on our lives.* [from *im-* = in, + Latin *pactum* = driven]

impair *verb* damage; weaken, *Smoking impairs health.* **impairment** *noun* [from *im-* = in, + Latin *peior* = worse]

impala (*say* im-**pah**-la) *noun* (*plural* **impala**) a small African antelope. [Zulu]

impale *verb* (**impaled**, **impaling**) pierce or fix something on a sharp pointed object. **impalement** *noun* [from *im-* = in, + Latin *palus* = a stake]

impart *verb* **1** tell, *She imparted the news to her brother.* **2** give, *Lemon imparts a sharp flavour to drinks.*

impartial *adjective* not favouring one side more than the other; not biased; fair. **impartially** *adverb*, **impartiality** *noun*

impassable *adjective* not able to be travelled along or over, *The roads are impassable because of floods.*

impasse (*say* **am**-pahss) *noun* a deadlock. [French, = impassable place]

impassive *adjective* not feeling or not showing emotion. **impassively** *adverb*

impatient *adjective* not patient. **impatiently** *adverb*, **impatience** *noun*

impeach *verb* bring a person to trial for a serious crime against his or her country. **impeachment** *noun*

impeccable *adjective* faultless. **impeccably** *adverb*, **impeccability** *noun* [from *im-* = not, + Latin *peccare* = to sin]

impecunious *adjective* having little or no money.

impede *verb* (**impeded**, **impeding**) hinder. [from Latin *impedire* = to shackle the feet (*im-* = in, + *pedis* = of a foot)]

impediment *noun* **1** a hindrance. **2** a defect, *He has an impediment in his speech* (= a lisp or stammer). [same origin as *impede*]

impel *verb* (**impelled**, **impelling**) **1** urge or drive someone to do something; *Curiosity impelled her to investigate.* **2** drive forward; propel. [from *im-* = towards, + Latin *pellere* = drive]

impending *adjective* imminent. [from *im-* = in, + Latin *pendere* = hang]

impenetrable *adjective* not able to be penetrated.

impenitent *adjective* not penitent; unrepentant.

imperative *adjective* **1** expressing a command. **2** essential. *Speed is imperative.*

imperative *noun* a command; the form of a verb used in making commands (e.g. 'come' in *Come here!*). [from Latin *imperare* = to command]

imperceptible *adjective* not perceptible; difficult or impossible to see.

imperfect *adjective* not perfect. **imperfectly** *adverb*, **imperfection** *noun*
imperfect tense a tense of a verb showing a continuous action, e.g. *She was singing.*

imperial *adjective* **1** of an empire or its rulers. **2** (of weights and measures) fixed by British law, *an imperial gallon.* **imperially** *adverb* [from Latin *imperium* = supreme power]

imperialism *noun* the policy of extending a country's empire or its influence; colonialism. **imperialist** *noun*

imperious *adjective* commanding; bossy.

impersonal *adjective* **1** not affected by personal feelings; showing no emotion. **2** not referring to a particular person. **impersonally** *adverb*
impersonal verb a verb used only with 'it', e.g. in *It is raining.*

impersonate *verb* (**impersonated**, **impersonating**) pretend to be another person. **impersonation** *noun*, **impersonator** *noun*

impertinent *adjective* **1** insolent; not showing proper respect. **2** not pertinent; irrelevant. **impertinently** *adverb*, **impertinence** *noun*

imperturbable *adjective* not excitable; calm. **imperturbably** *adverb*

impervious *adjective* **1** impenetrable, *impervious to water.* **2** not influenced by something, *impervious to criticism.* [from *im-* = not, + Latin *per* through, *via* = way]

impetuous *adjective* **1** hasty; rash. **2** eager impulsive.

impetus *noun* force or energy of movement. [Latin, = an attack]

impiety *noun* lack of reverence. **impious** (*say* **imp**-ee-us) *adjective*

impinge *verb* (**impinged**, **impinging**) make an impact; encroach.

implacable *adjective* not able to be placated; relentless. **implacably** *adverb*

implant *verb* insert; fix something in. **implant** *noun*, **implantation** *noun*

implement *noun* a tool.

implement *verb* put into action, *We shall implement these plans next month.* **implementation** *noun*

implicate *verb* (**implicated**, **implicating**) involve a person in a crime etc.; show that a person is involved, *His evidence implicates his sister.*

implication *noun* **1** implicating. **2** implying; something that is implied.

implicit (*say* im-**pliss**-it) *adjective* **1** implied but not stated openly. (Compare *explicit.*) **2** absolute; unquestioning, *She expects implicit obedience.* **implicitly** *adverb* [from Latin, = folded in]

implore *verb* (**implored**, **imploring**) beg somebody to do something; entreat. [from *im-* = in, + Latin *plorare* = weep]

imply *verb* (**implied**, **implying**) suggest something without actually saying it. **implication** *noun* [same origin as *implicate*]

impolite *adjective* not polite.

imponderable *adjective* not able to be estimated.

import *verb* bring in goods etc. from another country.

import *noun* **1** importing; something imported. **2** meaning; importance, *The message was of great import.* [from *im-* = in, + Latin *portare* = carry]

important *adjective* **1** having or able to have a great effect. **2** having great authority or influence. **importantly** *adverb*, **importance** *noun*

impose *verb* (**imposed**, **imposing**) put; inflict, *It imposes a strain upon us.*
impose on somebody put an unfair burden on him or her.
[from *im-* = on, + Latin *positum* = placed]

imposing *adjective* impressive.

imposition *noun* **1** something imposed; a burden imposed unfairly. **2** imposing something.

impossible *adjective* **1** not possible. **2** (*informal*) very annoying; unbearable, *He really is impossible!* **impossibly** *adverb*, **impossibility** *noun*

impostor *noun* a person who dishonestly pretends to be someone else.

imposture *noun* a dishonest pretence.

impotent *adjective* **1** powerless; unable to take action. **2** (of a man) unable to have sexual intercourse. **impotently** *adverb*, **impotence** *noun*

impound *verb* confiscate.

impoverish *verb* **1** make a person poor. **2** make a thing poor in quality, *impoverished soil.* **impoverishment** *noun*

impracticable *adjective* not practicable.

impractical *adjective* not practical; unwise.

imprecise *adjective* not precise.

impregnable *adjective* strong enough to be safe against attack.

impregnate *verb* (**impregnated**, **impregnating**) **1** fertilise; make pregnant. **2** saturate; fill throughout, *The air was impregnated with the scent.* **impregnation** *noun*

impresario *noun* (*plural* **impresarios**) a person who organises concerts, shows, etc. [Italian]

impress *verb* **1** cause a person to admire or think something is very good. **2** fix firmly in the mind, *He impressed on them the need for secrecy.* **3** press a mark into something.

impression *noun* **1** an effect produced on the mind. **2** a vague idea. **3** an imitation of a person or a sound etc. **4** a reprint of a book.

impressionism *noun* a style of painting that gives the general effect of a scene etc. but without details. **impressionist** *noun*

impressive *adjective* making a strong impression; seeming very good.

imprint *noun* a mark pressed into or on something.

imprison *verb* put into prison; keep in confinement. **imprisonment** *noun*

improbable *adjective* unlikely. **improbably** *adverb*, **improbability** *noun*

impromptu *adjective & adverb* done without any rehearsal or preparation. [from Latin *in promptu* = in readiness]

improper *adjective* **1** incorrect; wrong. **2** indecent. **improperly** *adverb*, **impropriety** (*say* im-pro-**pry**-it-ee) *noun*
improper fraction a fraction that is greater than unity, with the numerator greater than the denominator, e.g. 5/3.

improve *verb* (**improved**, **improving**) **1** make or become better. **2** (*NZ*) increase the value of a property by renewal or addition. **improvement** *noun*

improvident *adjective* not providing or planning for the future; not thrifty.

improvise *verb* (**improvised**, **improvising**) **1** compose something impromptu. **2** make something quickly with whatever is available. **improvisation** *noun*

imprudent *adjective* unwise.

impudent *adjective* impertinent; cheeky. **impudently** *adverb*, **impudence** *noun*

impulse *noun* **1** a sudden desire to do something. **2** a push; impetus. **3** (in physics) a force acting for a very short time, *electrical impulses.* [same origin as *impel*]

impulsive *adjecttve* done or doing things on impulse, not after careful thought. **impulsively** *adverb*, **impulsiveness** *noun*

impunity (*say* im-**pewn**-it-ee) *noun* freedom from punishment or injury. [from *im-* = without, + Latin *poena* = penalty]

impure *adjective* not pure. **impurity** *noun*

impute *verb* (**imputed**, **imputing**) attribute; ascribe. **imputation** *noun*

in *preposition* This word is used to show position or condition, e.g. (**1**) at or inside; within the limits of something (*in a box; in two hours*), (**2**) into (*He fell in a puddle*), (**3**) arranged as; consisting of (*a serial in four parts*), (**4**) occupied with; a member of (*He is in the army*), (**5**) by means of (*We paid in cash*).
in all in total number; altogether.

in *adverb* (**1**) so as to be in something or inside (*Get in*), (**2**) inwards (*The top caved in*), (**3**) at home; indoors (*Is anybody in?*), (**4**) in action; (in cricket) batting; (of a fire) burning. (**5**) having arrived (*The train is in*).
in for likely to get, *You're in for a shock.*
in on (*informal*) aware of or sharing in, *I want to be in on this project.*

in- *prefix* (changing to **il-** before *l*, **im-** before *b, m, p*, **ir-** before *r*) **1** in; into; on; towards (as in *include, invade*). [from Latin *in.*] **2** not (as in *incorrect, indirect*). [Compare the prefixes *an-*[1] and *un-*.]

inability *noun* being unable.

inaccessible *adjective* not accessible.

inaccurate *adjective* not accurate.

inactive *adjective* not active. **inaction** *noun*, **inactivity** *noun*

inadequate *adjective* **1** not enough. **2** not capable enough. **inadequately** *adverb*, **inadequacy** *noun*

inadvertent *adjective* unintentional.

inadvisable *adjective* not advisable.

inalienable *adjective* that cannot be taken away, *an inalienable right.*

inane *adjective* silly; without sense. **inanely** *adverb*, **inanity** *noun* [from Latin *inanis* = empty]

īnanga *noun* (also **īnaka**) a small fish eaten young as whitebait. [Māori]

inanimate *adjective* **1** not living. **2** not moving.

inappropriate *adjective* not appropriate.

inarticulate *adjective* **1** not able to speak or express yourself clearly, *inarticulate with rage.* **2** not expressed in words, *an inarticulate cry.*

inattention *noun* not being attentive; not listening, **inattentive** *adjective*

inaudible *adjective* not audible. **inaudibly** *adverb*, **inaudibility** *noun*

inaugurate *verb* (**inaugurated**, **inaugurating**) **1** start or introduce something new and important. **2** install a person in office, *inaugurate a new President.* **inaugural** *adjective*, **inauguration** *noun*, **inaugurator** *noun*

inauspicious *adjective* not auspicious.

inborn *adjective* present in a person or animal from birth, *an inborn ability.*

inbred *adjective* **1** inborn. **2** produced by inbreeding.

inbreeding *noun* breeding from closely related individuals.

incalculable *adjective* not able to be calculated or predicted.

incandescent *adjective* giving out light when heated; shining. **incandescence** *noun* [from Latin, = becoming white]

incantation *noun* a spoken spell or charm; the chanting of this. [from *in-* = in, + Latin *cantare* = sing]

incapable *adjective* not able to do something, *incapable of working alone.*

incapacitate *verb* (**incapacitated**, **incapacitating**) make unable to do something; disable.

incapacity *noun* inability; lack of sufficient strength or power.

incarcerate *verb* (**incarcerated**, **incarcerating**) shut in; imprison. **incarceration** *noun* [from *in-* = in, + Latin *carcer* = prison]

incarnate *adjective* having a body or human form, *a devil incarnate.* **incarnation** *noun* **the Incarnation** the embodiment of God in human form as Jesus Christ.
[from *in-* = in, + Latin *carnis* = of flesh]

incautious *adjective* rash.

incendiary *adjective* starting or designed to start a fire, *an incendiary bomb.*

incense (*say* **in**-sens) *noun* a substance making a spicy smell when burnt.

incense (*say* in-**sens**) *verb* (**incensed**, **incensing**) make a person angry.

incentive *noun* something that encourages a person to do something or to work harder.

inception *noun* a beginning.

incessant *adjective* unceasing.

incest *noun* sexual intercourse between two people who are so closely related that they cannot marry each other. **incestuous** *adjective*

inch *noun* (*plural* **inches**) an imperial unit of length, equivalent to about 2.54 centimetres.

incidence *noun* the extent or frequency of something, *Study the incidence of the disease.* [from Latin *incidens* = happening]

incident *noun* an event.

incidental *adjective* happening with something else, *incidental expenses.*

incidentally *adverb* by the way.

incinerate *verb* (**incinerated**, **incinerating**) destroy something by burning. **incineration** *noun* [from *in-* = in, + Latin *cineris* = of ashes]

incinerator *noun* a device for burning rubbish.

incipient (*say* in-**sip**-ee-ent) *adjective* just beginning, *incipient decay.*

incise *verb* (**incised**, **incising**) cut or engrave something into a surface. [from *in-* = into, + Latin *caesum* = cut]

incision *noun* a cut, especially one made in a surgical operation.

incisive *adjective* clear and sharp, *incisive comments.*

incisor (*say* in-**sy**-zer) *noun* each of the sharp-edged front teeth in the upper and lower jaws.

incite *verb* (**incited**, **inciting**) urge a person to do something; stir up, *They incited a riot.* **incitement** *noun* [from *in-* = towards, + Latin *citare* = rouse]

incivility *noun* being uncivil; rudeness.

inclement *adjective* (*formal*) cold, wet, or stormy, *inclement weather.*

inclination *noun* **1** a tendency. **2** a liking or preference. **3** a slope or slant.

incline *verb* (**inclined**, **inclining**) **1** lean; slope. **2** bend the head or body forward, as in a nod or bow. **3** cause or influence, *Her frank manner inclines me to believe her.*
be inclined have a tendency, *The door is inclined to bang.*
[from Latin *inclinare* = to bend]

include *verb* (**included**, **including**) make or consider something as part of a group of things. [from Latin, = enclose]

inclusive *adjective* including everything.

incognito (*say* in-kog-**neet**-oh or in-**kog**-nit-oh) *adjective & adverb* with your name or identity concealed, *The film star was travelling incognito.* [Italian, = unknown]

incoherent *adjective* not speaking or reasoning in an orderly way.

incombustible *adjective* unable to be set on fire.

income *noun* money received regularly from wages, investments, etc.
income tax tax charged on income.

incomparable *adjective* without an equal; unsurpassed, *incomparable beauty.*

incompatible *adjective* not compatible.

incompetent *adjective* not competent.

incomplete *adjective* not complete.

incomprehensible *adjective* not able to be understood. **incomprehension** *noun*

inconceivable *adjective* not able to be imagined; most unlikely.

inconclusive *adjective* not conclusive.

incongruous *adjective* unsuitable; not harmonious; out of place. **incongruously** *adverb*, **incongruity** *noun*

inconsiderable *adjective* of small value.

inconsiderate *adjective* not considerate.

inconsistent *adjective* not consistent. **inconsistently** *adverb*, **inconsistency** *noun*

inconsolable *adjective* not able to be consoled; very sad.

inconspicuous *adjective* not conspicuous. **inconspicuously** *adverb*

incontinent *adjective* not able to control excretion. **incontinence** *noun*

incontrovertible *adjective* indisputable.

inconvenience *noun* being inconvenient.

inconvenience *verb* (**inconvenienced**, **inconveniencing**) cause inconvenience or slight difficulty to someone.

inconvenient *adjective* not convenient.

incorporate *verb* (**incorporated**, **incorporating**) include something as a part. **incorporation** *noun*

incorporated *adjective* (of a business firm) formed into a legal corporation.

incorrect *adjective* not correct. **incorrectly** *adverb*

incorrigible *adjective* not able to be reformed, *an incorrigible liar.*

incorruptible *adjective* **1** not liable to decay. **2** not able to be bribed.

increase *verb* (**increased**, **increasing**) make or become larger or more.

increase *noun* increasing; the amount by which a thing increases.
on the increase increasing.
[from *in-* = in, + Latin *crescere* = grow]

incredible *adjective* unbelievable. **incredibly** *adverb*, **incredibility** *noun.*

incredulous *adjective* not believing somebody; showing disbelief. **incredulously** *adverb*, **incredulity** *noun.*

increment (*say* **in**-krim-ent) *noun* an increase; an added amount.

incriminate *verb* (**incriminated**, **incriminating**) show a person to have been involved in a crime etc. **incrimination** *noun*

incrustation *noun* encrusting; a crust or deposit formed on a surface.

incubate *verb* (**incubated**, **incubating**) **1** hatch eggs by keeping them warm. **2** cause bacteria or a disease etc. to develop. **incubation** *noun*

incubator *noun* **1** a device for incubating eggs etc. **2** a device in which a baby born prematurely can be kept warm and supplied with oxygen.

incumbent *adjective* forming an obligation, *It is incumbent on you to warn people of the danger.*

incumbent *noun* a person who holds a particular office or position. [from *in-* = on, + Latin *-cumbens* = lying]

incur *verb* (**incurred**, **incurring**) bring something on yourself, *incur expense.* [from *in-* = on, + Latin *currere* = to run]

incurable *adjective* not able to be cured. **incurably** *adverb*

incurious *adjective* feeling or showing no curiosity about something.

incursion *noun* a raid or brief invasion. [same origin as *incur*]

indebted *adjective* owing money or gratitude to someone.

indecent *adjective* not decent; improper. **indecently** *adverb*, **indecency** *noun*

indecipherable *adjective* not able to be deciphered.

indecision *noun* being unable to make up your mind; hesitation.

indecisive *adjective* not decisive.

indeed *adverb* **1** really; truly, *I am indeed surprised*; (used to strengthen a meaning), *very nice indeed.* **2** admittedly, *It is, indeed, his first attempt.*

indefensible *adjective* unable to be defended; unable to be justified.

indefinable *adjective* unable to be defined or described clearly.

indefinite *adjective* not definite; vague. **indefinite article** the word 'a' or 'an'.

indefinitely *adverb* for an indefinite or unlimited time.

indelible *adjective* impossible to rub out or remove. **indelibly** *adverb* [from *in-* = not, + Latin *delere* = destroy]

indelicate *adjective* **1** slightly indecent. **2** tactless. **indelicacy** *noun*

indemnify *verb* (**indemnified**, **indemnifying**) **1** protect or insure someone against possible penalties. **2** compensate.

indent *verb* **1** make notches or recesses in something. **2** start a line of writing or printing further in from the margin than other lines, *Always indent the first line of a new paragraph.* **3** place an official order for goods or stores, *Indent for a new office desk.* **indentation** *noun*

indenture *noun* (also **indentures**) an agreement binding an apprentice to work for a certain employer. **indentured** *adjective*

independent *adjective* **1** not dependent; not controlled by any other person or thing. **2** (of a country) governing itself. **3** (of broadcasting) not financed by money from licences. **independently** *adverb*, **independence** *noun*

indescribable *adjective* unable to be described. **indescribably** *adverb*

indestructible *adjective* unable to be destroyed. **indestructibility** *noun*

indeterminate *adjective* not fixed or decided exactly; left vague.

index *noun* **1** (*plural* **indexes**) an alphabetical list of things, especially at the end of a book. **2** a number showing how prices or wages have changed from a previous level. **3** (*plural* **indices**) the exponent of a number.
index finger the forefinger.

index *verb* make an index to a book etc.; put into an index. [Latin, = pointer]

Indian *adjective* **1** of India or its people. **2** of American Indians. **Indian** *noun*
Indian summer a warm period in late autumn (orginally in North America).

indicate *verb* (**indicated**, **indicating**) **1** point out; make known. **2** be a sign of. **indication** *noun* [from *in-* = towards, + Latin *dicatum* = proclaimed]

indicative *adjective* giving an indication.

indicative *noun* the form of a verb used in making a statement (e.g. 'he said' or 'he is coming') not in a command or question etc.

indicator *noun* **1** a thing that indicates or points to something. **2** a flashing light used to signal that a motor vehicle is turning.

indict (*say* ind-**I**t) *verb* charge a person with having committed a crime. **indictment** *noun*

indifferent *adjective* **1** not caring about something, not interested. **2** not very good, *an indifferent cricketer.* **indifferently** *adverb*, **indifference** *noun*

indigenous (*say* in-**dij**-in-us) *adjective* growing or originating in a particular country; native, *The koala is indigenous to Australia.* [from Latin *indigena* = born in a country]

indigent (*say* **in**-dij-ent) *adjective* needy.

indigestible *adjective* difficult or impossible to digest.

indigestion *noun* pain caused by difficulty in digesting food.

indignant *adjective* angry at something that seems unfair or wicked. **indignantly** *adverb*, **indignation** *noun* [from Latin *indignari* = regard as unworthy]

indignity *noun* (*plural* **indignities**) treatment that makes a person feel undignified or humiliated; an insult.

indigo *noun a* deep-blue colour.

indirect *adjective* not direct. **indirectly** *adverb*

indiscreet *adjective* **1** not discreet; revealing secrets. **2** incautious; unwise. **indiscreetly** *adverb*, **indiscretion** *noun*

indiscriminate *adjective* showing no discrimination; not making a careful choice. **indiscriminately** *adverb*

indispensable *adjective* not able to be dispensed with; essential. **indispensability** *noun*

indisposed *adjective* **1** slightly unwell. **2** unwilling. *They seem indisposed to help us.* **indisposition** *noun*

indisputable *adjective* undeniable.

indissoluble *adjective* that cannot be dissolved; lasting. **indissolubility** *noun*

indistinct *adjective* not distinct. **indistinctly** *adverb*, **indistinctness** *noun*

indistinguishable *adjective* not distinguishable.

individual *adjective* **1** of or for one person. **2** single; separate, *Count each individual word.* **individually** *adverb*

individual *noun* one person, animal, or plant.

individuality *noun* the things that make one person or thing different from another; distinctive identity.

indivisible *adjective* not able to be divided or separated. **indivisibly** *adverb*

indoctrinate *verb* (**indoctrinated**, **indoctrinating**) fill a person's mind with particular ideas or beliefs, especially so as to make him or her accept them uncritically. **indoctrination** *noun* [from *in-* = in, + *doctrine*]

indolent *adjective* lazy. **indolently** *adverb*, **indolence** *noun*

indomitable *adjective* not able to be overcome or conquered. [from *in-* = not, + Latin *domitare* = to tame]

indoor *adjective* used or placed or done etc. inside a building, *indoor games.*

indoors *adverb* inside a building.

indubitable (*say* in-**dew**-bit-a-bul) *adjective* not able to be doubted; certain. **indubitably** *adverb* [from *in-* = not, + Latin *dubium* = doubt]

induce *verb* (**induced**, **inducing**) **1** persuade. **2** produce; cause, *Some substances induce sleep.* **induction** *noun* [from *in-* = in, + Latin *ducere* = to lead]

inducement *noun* an incentive.

indulge *verb* (**indulged, indulging**) allow a person to have or do what he or she wishes. **indulgence** *noun*, **indulgent** *adjective* **indulge in** allow yourself to have or do something that you like.

industrial *adjective* of industry; working or used in industry. **industrially** *adverb* **industrial action** striking or working slowly. **industrial relations** relations between workers and their employers in industry. **Industrial Revolution** the expansion of British industry by the use of machines in the late 18th and early 19th century.

industrialised *adjective* (of a country or district) having many industries. **industrialisation** *noun*

industrialist *noun* a person who owns or manages an industrial business.

industrious *adjective* working hard. **industriously** *adverb*

industry *noun* (*plural* **industries**) **1** making or producing goods etc., especially in factories. **2** a branch of this; any business activity, *the tourist industry.* **3** being industrious. [from Latin *industria* = hard work]

inebriated *adjective* drunk; drunken.

inedible *adjective* not edible.

ineffective *adjective* not effective; inefficient. **ineffectively** *adverb*

ineffectual *adjective* not effectual; not confident, not convincing.

inefficient *adjective* not efficient. **inefficiently** *adverb*, **inefficiency** *noun*

inelegant *adjective* not elegant.

ineligible *adjective* not eligible.

inept *adjective* unsuitable; bungling. **ineptly** *adverb*, **ineptitude** *noun* [from *in-* = not, + Latin *aptus* = suitable]

inequality *noun* (*plural* **inequalities**) not being equal.

inequity *noun* (*plural* **inequities**) unfairness. **inequitable** *adjective*

inert *adjective* not moving; not reacting. **inertly** *adverb* [from Latin *iners* = idle]

inertia (*say* in-**er**-sha) *noun* **1** inactivity; being inert or slow to take action. **2** the tendency for a moving thing to keep moving in a straight line.

inescapable *adjective* unavoidable.

inessential *adjective* not essential.

inestimable *adjective* too great or precious to be able to be estimated.

inevitable *adjective* unavoidable; sure to happen. **inevitably** *adverb*, **inevitability** *noun* [from *in-* = not, + Latin *evitare* = avoid]

inexact *adjective* not exact.

inexcusable *adjective* not excusable.

inexhaustible *adjective* so great that it cannot be used up completely.

inexorable (*say* in-**eks**-er-a-bul) *adjective* relentless; not yielding to requests or entreaties. **inexorably** *adverb*

inexpensive *adjective* not expensive; cheap. **inexpensively** *adverb*

inexperience *noun* lack of experience. **inexperienced** *adjective*

inexpert *adjective* unskilful.

inexplicable *adjective* impossible to explain. **inexplicably** *adverb*

infallible *adjective* never wrong; never failing, *an infallible remedy.* **infallibly** *adverb*, **infallibility** *noun*

infamous (*say* **in**-fam-us) *adjective* having a bad reputation; wicked. **infamously** *adverb*, **infamy** *noun*

infancy *noun* **1** early childhood; babyhood. **2** an early stage of development.

infant *noun* a baby or young child. [from Latin, = person unable to speak]

infantile *adjective* **1** of an infant. **2** very childish.

infantry *noun* soldiers who fight on foot. (Compare *cavalry.*) [from Italian *infante* = a youth]

infatuated *adjective* filled with foolish or unreasoning love. **infatuation** *noun* [from *in-* = in, + Latin *fatuus* = foolish]

infect *verb* pass on a disease or bacteria etc. to a person, animal, or plant. [from Latin *infectum* = tainted]

infection *noun* **1** infecting. **2** an infectious disease or condition.

infectious *adjective* **1** (of a disease) able to be spread by air or water etc. (Compare *contagious.*) **2** quickly spreading to others, *His fear was infectious.*

infer *verb* (**inferred, inferring**) form an opinion by reasoning; conclude, *I infer from your luggage that you are going on holiday.* **inference** *noun* [from *in-*, + Latin *ferre* = bring]

USAGE Do not confuse with *imply.*

inferior *adjective* less good or less important; low or lower in position, quality, etc. **inferiority** *noun* [Latin, = lower]

infernal *adjective* **1** of or like hell, *the infernal regions.* **2** (*informal*) detestable; tiresome. **infernally** *adverb*

inferno *noun* (*plural* **infernos**) a terrifying fire.

infertile *adjective* not fertile. **infertility** *noun*

infest *verb* (of pests) be numerous and troublesome in a place. **infestation** *noun* [from Latin, = hostile]

infidel (*say* **in**-fid-el) *noun* a person who does not believe in a religion. [from *in-* = not, + Latin *fidelis* = faithful]

infidelity *noun* unfaithfulness.

infiltrate *verb* (**infiltrated**, **infiltrating**) get into a place or organisation gradually and without being noticed. **infiltration** *noun*, **infiltrator** *noun*

infinite *adjective* **1** endless; without a limit. **2** too great to be measured. **infinitely** *adverb*

infinitesimal *adjective* extremely small. **infinitesimally** *adverb*

infinitive *noun* a form of a verb that does not indicate a particular tense or number or person, in English used with or without *to*, e.g. *go* in 'Let him go' or 'Allow him to go'. [from *in-* = not, + Latin *finitivus* definite]

infinitude *noun* infinity.

infinity *noun* an infinite number or distance or time.

infirm *adjective* weak, especially from old age or illness. **infirmity** *noun*

infirmary *noun* (*plural* **infirmaries**) **1** a hospital. **2** a place where sick people are cared for in a school or monastery etc.

inflame *verb* (**inflamed**, **inflaming**) **1** arouse strong feelings or anger in people. **2** cause redness, heat, and swelling in a part of the body. **inflammation** *noun*, **inflammatory** *adjective*

inflammable *adjective* able to be set on fire.

> USAGE This word means the same as *flammable*; its opposite is *non-inflammable*.

inflatable *adjective* able to be inflated.

inflate *verb* (**inflated**, **inflating**) **1** fill with air or gas and expand. **2** increase too much; raise prices or wages etc. more than is justifiable. [from *in-* = in, + Latin *flatum* = blown]

inflation *noun* **1** inflating. **2** a general rise in prices and fall in the purchasing power of money. **inflationary** *adjective*

inflect *verb* **1** change the ending or form of a word to show its tense or its grammatical relation to other words, e.g. *sing* changes to *sang* or *sung*, *child* changes to *children*. **2** alter the voice in speaking. [from *in-* = in, + Latin *flectere* = to bend]

inflection *noun* (also **inflexion**) **1** a suffix used in inflecting, e.g. *-ren* on *children*, *-s* on *prays* or *prayers*. **2** a change in the pitch of the voice when speaking.

inflexible *adjective* not able to be bent or changed or persuaded. **inflexibly** *adverb*, **inflexibility** *noun*

inflict *verb* make a person suffer something, *She inflicted a severe blow on him.* **infliction** *noun* [from *in-* = on, + Latin *flictum* = struck]

inflow *noun* flowing in; what flows in.

influence *noun* the power to produce an effect; a person or thing with this power.

influence *verb* (**influenced**, **influencing**) have influence on a person or thing; affect.

influential *adjective* having influence.

influenza *noun* an infectious disease that causes fever, catarrh, and pain.

influx *noun* a flowing in, especially of people or things coming in.

info *noun* (*informal*) information.

inform *verb* give information to somebody. **informant** *noun*

informal *adjective* not formal. **informally** *adverb*, **informality** *noun*
informal vote (*NZ*) a voting paper that has been incorrectly filled in; a vote that does not count.

> USAGE In this dictionary, words marked *informal* are used in talking but not when you are writing or speaking formally.

information *noun* facts told or heard or discovered, or put into a computer etc.
information superhighway *noun* a means of rapid informatiom transfer in different digital forms via the Internet or other electronic networks.
information technology the study or use of computers and telecommunications for storing and sending information.

informative *adjective* giving a lot of useful information.

informed *adjective* knowing about something.

informer *noun* a person who gives information against someone.

infotainment *noun* factual material presented in an entertaining way [*inf*ormation + enter*tainment*]

infra- *prefix* below. [Latin]

infra-red *adjective* below or beyond red in the spectrum.

infrequent *adjective* not frequent.

infringe *verb* (**infringed**, **infringing**) break a rule or an agreement etc.; violate. **infringement** *noun*

infuriate *verb* (**infuriated, infuriating**) make a person very angry; enrage. **infuriation** *noun*

infuse *verb* (**infused, infusing**) **1** add or inspire with a feeling etc., *infuse them with courage; infuse courage into them.* **2** soak or steep tea or herbs etc. in a liquid to extract the flavour. **infusion** *noun* [from Latin *infusum* = poured in]

ingenious *adjective* clever at inventing things; cleverly made. **ingeniously** *adverb,* **ingenuity** *noun* [from Latin *ingenium* = genius]

ingenuous *adjective* naive. **ingenuously** *adverb,* **ingenuousness** *noun*

ingot *noun* a lump of gold or silver etc. cast in a brick shape.

ingrained *adjective* **1** (of dirt) marking a surface deeply. **2** (of feelings or habits etc.) firmly fixed.

ingratiate *verb* (**ingratiated, ingratiating**) **ingratiate yourself** get yourself into favour. **ingratiation** *noun* [from Latin *in gratiam* = into favour]

ingratitude *noun* lack of gratitude.

ingredient *noun* one of the parts of a mixture; one of the things used in a recipe. [from Latin *ingrediens* = going in]

inhabit *verb* (**inhabited, inhabiting**) live in a place. **inhabitant** *noun*

inhale *verb* (**inhaled, inhaling**) breathe in. **inhalation** *noun* [from *in-* = in, Latin *halare* = breathe]

inhaler *noun* a device that produces or sends out a medicinal vapour for inhaling.

inharmonious *adjective* not harmonious.

inherent (*say* in-**heer**-ent) *adjective* existing in something as one of its natural or permanent qualities. **inherently** *adverb,* **inherence** *noun* [from *in-* = in, + Latin *haerere* = to stick]

inherit *verb* (**inherited, inheriting**) **1** receive money, property, or a title etc. when its previous owner dies. **2** get certain qualities etc. from parents or predecessors. **inheritance** *noun,* **inheritor** *noun* [from *in-* = in, + Latin *heres* = heir]

inhibit *verb* (**inhibited, inhibiting**) restrain; hinder; repress. **inhibition** *noun*

inhospitable *adjective* not hospitable.

inhuman *adjective* cruel; without pity or kindness. **inhumanity** *noun*

inhumane *adjective* not humane.

inimitable *adjective* impossible to imitate.

iniquitous *adjective* very unjust. **iniquity** *noun* [from *in-* = not, + *equity*]

initial *noun* the first letter of a word or name.

initial *verb* (**initialled, initialling**) mark or sign something with the initials of your names.

initial *adjective* of the beginning, *the initial stages.* **initially** *adverb* [from Latin *initium* = the beginning]

initiate *verb* (**initiated, initiating**) **1** start something. **2** admit a person as a member of a society or group, often with special ceremonies. **initiation** *noun,* **initiator** *noun*

initiative (*say* in-**ish**-a-tiv) *noun* the power or courage to start a new process; enterprising ability.
take the initiative take action to start something happening.

inject *verb* **1** put a medicine or drug into the body by means of a hollow needle. **2** put liquid into something by means of a syringe etc. **3** add a new quality, *Inject some humour into it.* **injection** *noun* [from *in-* = in, + Latin *-jectum* = thrown]

injudicious *adjective* unwise.

injunction *noun* a command given with authority, e.g. by a lawcourt.

injure *verb* (**injured, injuring**) harm; damage; hurt. **injury** *noun,* **injurious** (*say* in-**joor**-ee-us) *adjective*

injustice *noun* lack of justice; an unjust action or treatment.

ink *noun* a black or coloured liquid used in writing and printing.

inkling *noun* a hint; a slight knowledge or suspicion.

inky *adjective* **1** stained with ink. **2** black like ink, *inky darkness.*

inland *adjective & adverb* in or towards the interior of a country; away from the coast.
Inland Revenue the government department responsible for collecting taxes and similar charges.

in-laws *plural noun* (*informal*) relatives by marriage.

inlay *verb* (**inlaid, inlaying**) set pieces of wood or metal etc. into a surface to form a design. **inlay** *noun*

inlet *noun* **1** a strip of water reaching into the land from a sea or lake. **2** a passage that lets something in (e.g. to a tank).

in-line skate *noun* a skate with four narrow wheels in a single line along the sole.

inmate *noun* one of the occupants of a prison, hospital, or other institution.

inmost *adjective* most inward.

inn *noun* a hotel or public house, especially for travellers. **innkeeper** *noun*

innate *adjective* inborn. [from *in-* = in, + Latin *natus* = born]

inner *adjective* inside; internal; nearer to the centre. **innermost** *adjective*

inning *noun* one section of a softball or baseball game, during which both sides have a turn at batting.

innings *noun* (*plural* **innings**) the time when a cricket team or player is batting.

innocent *adjective* **1** not guilty. **2** not wicked. **3** harmless. **innocently** *adverb*, innocence *noun* [from *in-* = not, + Latin *nocens* = doing harm]

innocuous *adjective* harmless.

innovation *noun* **1** introducing new things or new methods. **2** something newly introduced. **innovative** *adjective*, **innovator** *noun* [from *in-* = in, + Latin *novus* = new]

innuendo *noun* (*plural* **innuendoes**) an unpleasant insinuation or hint.

innumerable *adjective* countless.

innumerate *adjective* not knowing basic mathematics. (Compare *illiterate.*)

inoculate *verb* (**inoculated, inoculating**) inject or treat with a vaccine or serum as a protection against a disease. **inoculation** *noun*

inoffensive *adjective* harmless.

inordinate *adjective* excessive. **inordinately** *adverb*

inorganic *adjective* not of living organisms; of mineral origin.

input *noun* what is put into something (e.g. data into a computer). **input** *verb*

inquest *noun* an official inquiry to find out how a person died.

inquire *verb* (**inquired, inquiring**) make an investigation. **inquiry** *noun*. [from *in-* = into, + Latin *quaerere* = seek]

> USAGE It is best to use *enquire* and *enquiry* of asking something, and *inquire* and *inquiry* of investigating.

inquisition *noun* a detailed questioning or investigation. **inquisitor** *noun*
the Inquisition a council of the Roman Catholic Church in the Middle Ages set up to discover and punish heretics.

inquisitive *adjective* always asking questions or trying to look at things; prying. **inquisitively** *adverb*

inroad *noun* an invasion; a raid.
make inroads on or **into** use up large quantities of stores etc.

inrush *noun* (*plural* **inrushes**) a sudden rush in; an influx.

insane *adjective* **1** not sane; mad. **2** foolish or irrational. **insanely** *adverb*, **insanity** *noun*

insanitary *adjective* unclean and likely to be harmful to health.

insatiable (*say* in-**say**-sha-bul) *adjective* impossible to satisfy, *an insatiable appetite.*

inscribe *verb* (**inscribed, inscribing**) write or carve words etc. on something. [from *in-* = on, + Latin *scribere* = write]

inscription *noun* **1** words or names inscribed on a monument, coin, stone, etc. **2** inscribing.

inscrutable *adjective* enigmatic; impossible to interpret, *an inscrutable smile.*

insect *noun* a small animal with six legs, no backbone, and a body divided into three parts (head, thorax, abdomen).

insecticide *noun* a substance for killing insects. [from *insect*, + Latin *caedere* = kill]

insectivorous *adjective* feeding on insects and other small invertebrate creatures. **insectivore** *noun* [from *insect*, + Latin *vorare* = devour]

insecure *adjective* not secure; unsafe. **insecurely** *adverb*, **insecurity** *noun*

inseminate *verb* (**inseminated, inseminating**) insert semen into the womb. **insemination** *noun*

insensible *adjective* **1** unconscious. **2** unaware. **3** imperceptible.

insensitive *adjective* not sensitive. **insensitively** *adverb*, **insensitivity** *noun*

inseparable *adjective* **1** not able to be separated. **2** liking to be constantly together, *inseparable friends.* **inseparably** *adverb*

insert *verb* put a thing into something else. **insertion** *noun*

inshore *adverb & adjective* near or nearer to the shore.

inside *noun* **1** the inner side, surface, or part. **2** (usually as **insides** *informal*) the organs in the abdomen; the stomach and bowels.
inside out with the inside turned to face outwards.

inside *adjective* on or coming from the inside; in or nearest to the middle.

inside *adverb & preposition* on or to the inside of something; in, *Come inside. It's inside that box.*

insider *noun a* member of a certain group, especially someone with access to private information.

insidious *adjective* inconspicuous but harmful. **insidiously** *adverb*

insight *noun* being able to perceive the truth about things; understanding.

insignia *plural noun* emblems; a badge.

insignificant *adjective* not important; not influential. **insignificance** *noun*

insincere *adjective* not sincere. **insincerely** *adverb*, **insincerity** *noun*

insinuate *verb* (**insinuated**, **insinuating**) **1** hint artfully or unpleasantly. **2** insert gradually or craftily. **insinuation** *noun*

insipid *adjective* **1** lacking flavour. **2** not lively or interesting. **insipidity** *noun*

insist *verb* be very firm in saying or asking for something. **insistent** *adjective*, **insistence** *noun* [from Latin *insistere* = stand firm]

insole *noun* the inner sole of a boot or a shoe.

insolent *adjective* very impudent; insulting. **insolently** *adverb*, **insolence** *noun*

insoluble *adjective* **1** impossible to solve, *an insoluble problem.* **2** impossible to dissolve. **insolubility** *noun*

insolvent *adjective* unable to pay money that is owed. **insolvency** *noun*

insomnia *noun* being unable to sleep. **insomniac** *noun* [from *in-* = without, + Latin *somnus* = sleep]

inspect *verb* examine carefully and critically. **inspection** *noun* [from *in-* = in, + Latin *specere* = to look]

inspector *noun* **1** a person whose job is to inspect or supervise things. **2** a police officer ranking next above a sergeant.

inspiration *noun* **1** a sudden brilliant idea. **2** inspiring; an inspiring influence.

inspire *verb* (**inspired**, **inspiring**) fill a person with good or useful feelings or ideas, *The applause inspired us with confidence.* [from *in-* = into, + Latin *spirare* = breathe]

instability *noun* lack of stability.

install *verb* **1** put something in position and ready to use, *They installed central heating.* **2** put a person into an important position with a ceremony, *He was installed as pope.* **installation** *noun*

instalment *noun* each of the parts in which something is given or paid for gradually, *an instalment of a serial.*

instance *noun* an example, *for instance.*

instant *adjective* **1** happening immediately, *instant success.* **2** (of food) designed to be prepared quickly and easily, *instant coffee.* **instantly** *adverb*

instant *noun* a moment, *not an instant too soon.* [from Latin *instans* = urgent]

instantaneous *adjective* happening immediately. **instantaneously** *adverb*

instead *adverb* in place of something else; as a substitute.

instep *noun* the top of the foot between the toes and the ankle.

instigate *verb* (**instigated**, **instigating**) urge; incite; cause something to be done, *instigate a rebellion.* **instigation** *noun*, **instigator** *noun*

instil *verb* (**instilled**, **instilling**) put ideas into a person's mind gradually. [from *in-* = in, + Latin *stilla* = a drop]

instinct *noun* a natural tendency or ability, *Birds fly by instinct.* **instinctive** *adjective*, **instinctively** *adverb*

institute *noun* a society or organisation; the building used by this.

institute *verb* (**instituted**, **instituting**) establish; found; start an inquiry or custom etc. [from *in-* = in, + Latin *statuere* = set up]

institution *noun* **1** an institute; a public organisation, e.g. a hospital or university. **2** a habit or custom. **3** instituting something. **4** a significant organisation within a country, e.g. the Reserve Bank. **5** a familiar custom, person, or object, *The All Blacks are a Kiwi institution.* **institutional** *adjective*

instruct *verb* **1** teach a person a subject or skill. **2** inform. **3** tell a person what he or she must do. **instruction** *noun*, **instructional** *adjective*, **instructor** *noun* [same origin as *structure*]

instructive *adjective* giving knowledge.

instrument *noun* **1** a device for producing musical sounds. **2** a tool used for delicate or scientific work. **3** a measuring device.

instrumental *adjective* **1** of or using musical instruments. **2** being the means of doing something, *She was instrumental in getting me a job.*

instrumentalist *noun* a person who plays a musical instrument.

insubordinate *adjective* disobedient; rebellious. **insubordination** *noun*

insufferable *adjective* unbearable.

insufficient *adjective* not sufficient.

insular *adjective* **1** of or like an island. **2** narrow-minded. **insularity** *noun*

insulate *verb* (**insulated**, **insulating**) cover or protect something to prevent heat, cold, or electricity etc. from passing in or out. **insulation** *noun*, **insulator** *noun* [from Latin *insula* = island]

insulin *noun* a substance that controls the amount of sugar in the blood.

insult (*say* in-**sult**) *verb* hurt a person's feelings or pride.

insult (*say* **in**-sult) *noun* an insulting remark or action.

insuperable *adjective* unable to be overcome, *an insuperable difficulty.*

insurance *noun* an agreement to compensate someone for a loss, damage, or injury etc., in return for a payment (called a *premium*) made in advance.

insure *verb* (**insured**, **insuring**) protect with insurance.

USAGE Do not confuse with *ensure*.

insurgent *noun* a rebel. **insurgent** *adjective* [from *in-* = against, + Latin *surgere* = to rise]

insurmountable *adjective* insuperable.

insurrection *noun* a rebellion.

intact *adjective* not damaged; complete. [from *in-* = not, + Latin *tactum* = touched]

intake *noun* **1** taking something in. **2** the number of people or things taken in.

intangible *adjective* not tangible.

integer *noun* a whole number (e.g. 0, 3, 19), not a fraction. [Latin, = whole]

integral (*say* **in**-tig-ral) *adjective* **1** an essential part of a whole thing, *An engine is an integral part of a car.* **2** whole; complete.

integrate *verb* (**integrated**, **integrating**) **1** make parts into a whole; combine. **2** join together harmoniously into a single community. **integration** *noun* [from Latin *integrare* = make whole]

integrity (*say* in-**teg**-rit-ee) *noun* honesty.

intellect *noun* the ability to think (contrasted with *feeling* and *instinct*).

intellectual *adjective* **1** of or using the intellect. **2** having a good intellect and a liking for knowledge. **intellectually** *adverb*

intellectual *noun* an intellectual person.

intelligence *noun* **1** being intelligent. **2** information, especially of military value; the people who collect and study this information.

intelligent *adjective* able to learn and understand things; having great mental ability. **intelligently** *adverb*

intelligentsia *noun* intellectual people regarded as a group.

intelligible *adjective* able to be understood. **intelligibly** *adverb*, **intelligibility** *noun*

intend *verb* have something in mind as what you want to do; plan. [from Latin *intendere* = stretch, aim]

intense *adjective* very strong or great. **intensely** *adverb*, **intensity** *noun*

intensify *verb* (**intensified**, **intensifying**) make or become more intense. **intensification** *noun*

intensive *adjective* concentrated; thorough; using a lot of effort. **intensively** *adverb* **intensive care** special medical services for very seriously ill patients in a hospital.

intent *noun* intention.

intent *adjective* with concentrated attention; very interested. **intently** *adverb* [same origin as *intend*]

intention *noun* what a person intends; a purpose or plan.

intentional *adjective* intended; deliberate, not accidental. **intentionally** *adverb*

inter *verb* (**interred**, **interring**) bury. [from *in-* = in, + Latin *terra* = earth]

inter- *prefix* between; among. [from Latin]

interact *verb* have an effect upon one another. **interaction** *noun*, **interactive** *adjective*

interbreed *verb* (**interbred**, **interbreeding**) breed with each other; cross-breed.

intercede *verb* (**interceded**, **interceding**) intervene on behalf of another person or as a peacemaker. **intercession** *noun* [from *inter-*, + Latin *cedere* = go]

intercept *verb* stop or catch a person or thing that is going from one place to another. **interception** *noun* [from *inter-*, + Latin *captum* = seized]

interchange *verb* (**interchanged**, **interchanging**) **1** put each of two things into the other's place. **2** exchange. **3** alternate. **interchangeable** *adjective*

interchange *noun* **1** interchanging. **2** a road junction where vehicles can move from one motorway etc. to another. **3** a station where passengers can change from one bus or train service to another.

intercom *noun* (*informal*) a system of communication between rooms or compartments, operating rather like a telephone. [short for *intercommunication*]

intercourse *noun* **1** communication or dealings between people. **2** sexual intercourse (see *sexual*).

interdependent *adjective* dependent upon each other.

interdict *noun* a prohibition. [from *inter-*, + Latin *dictum* = said]

interest *noun* **1** a feeling of wanting to know about or help with something. **2** a thing that interests somebody, *Science fiction is one of my interests.* **3** advantage, *She looks after her own interests.* **4** money paid regularly in return for money lent or deposited.

interest *verb* arouse a person's interest. **interested** *adjective*, **interesting** *adjective* [Latin, = it matters]

interface *noun* a point where two systems, subjects, etc. meet and interact.

interfere *verb* (**interfered**, **interfering**) **1** take part in something that has nothing to do with you. **2** get in the way; obstruct. **interference** *noun*

interim *noun* an interval of time between two events.

interim *adjective* of or in the interim; temporary, *an interim arrangement.* [Latin, = meanwhile]

interior *adjective* inner.

interior *noun* the inside of something; the central or inland part of a country. [Latin, = further in]

interisland *adjective* (*NZ*) between the North and South Islands.

Interislander *noun* (*NZ*) **1** the ferry service between Wellington and Picton. **2** a ferry boat on the service between Wellington and Picton.

interject *verb* break in with a remark while someone is speaking. [from *inter-*, + Latin *jactum* = thrown]

interjection *noun* **1** an exclamation such as *oh!* or *good heavens!* **2** interjecting; a remark interjected.

interlock *verb* fit into each other.

interloper *noun* an intruder.

interlude *noun* **1** an interval. **2** something happening in an interval or between other events. [from *inter-*, + Latin *ludus* = game]

intermarry *verb* (**intermarried**, **intermarrying**) become connected by marriage. **intermarriage** *noun*

intermediary *noun* (*plural* **intermediaries**) a mediator; a go-between.

intermediate *adjective* coming between two things in time, place, or order. **intermediate school** (*NZ*) a school for pupils in years 7 and 8.

intermediate *noun* an intermediate school.

interment *noun* interring; burial.

interminable *adjective* endless; long and boring. **interminably** *adverb* [from *in-* = not, + *terminable*]

intermission *noun* an interval or pause.

intermittent *adjective* happening at intervals; not continuous. **intermittently** *adverb* [from *inter-*, + Latin *mittere* = let go]

intern *verb* imprison in a special camp or area, usually in wartime.

internal *adjective* inside. **internally** *adverb* **internal-combustion engine** an engine that produces power by burning fuel inside the engine itself.

international *noun* **1** a sporting contest between teams representing different countries. **2** a person who has taken part in such a contest.

international *adjective* of or belonging to more than one country; agreed between nations. **internationally** *adverb*

Internet *noun* (as **the Internet**) an international computer network allowing users to exchange e-mail and obtain information from websites.

internment *noun* being interned.

interplanetary *adjective* between planets.

interplay *noun* interaction.

interpolate *verb* (**interpolated**, **interpolating**) **1** interject. **2** insert words; put terms into a mathematical series. **interpolation** *noun*

interpose *verb* (**interposed**, **interposing**) **1** insert; interject. **2** intervene. [from *inter-*, + Latin *positum* = put]

interpret *verb* **1** explain what something means. **2** translate what someone says into another language orally. **interpretation** *noun*, **interpreter** *noun*

interprovincial *adjective* between two or more New Zealand provinces, *interprovincial rugby matches.*

interregnum *noun* an interval between the reign of one ruler and that of his or her successor. [from *inter-*, + Latin *regnum* = reign]

interrelated *adjective* related to each other.

interrogate *verb* (**interrogated**, **interrogating**) question closely or formally. **interrogation** *noun*, **interrogator** *noun* [from *inter-*, + Latin *rogare* = ask]

interrogative *adjective* questioning; expressing a question. **interrogatory** *adjective*

interrupt *verb* prevent from continuing; break in on a person's speech etc. by inserting a remark. **interruption** *noun* [from *inter-*, + Latin *ruptum* = broken]

intersect *verb* divide a thing by passing or lying across it; (of lines or roads etc.) cross each other. **intersection** *noun* [from *inter-*, + Latin *sectum* = cut]

intersperse *verb* (**interspersed**, **interspersing**) insert things here and there in something. [from *inter-*, + Latin *sparsum* = scattered]

interval *noun* **1** a time between two events or parts of a play etc. **2** a space between two things. **3** a half-time break in a sports match. **4** the morning break between school classes.
at intervals with some time or distance between each one.
[from Latin *intervallum* = space between ramparts]

intervene *verb* (**intervened, intervening**) **1** come between two events, *in the intervening years.* **2** interrupt a discussion or fight etc. to try and stop it or change its result. **intervention** *noun* [from *inter-*, + Latin *venire* = come]

interview *noun* a formal meeting with someone to ask him or her questions or to obtain information.

interview *verb* hold an interview with someone. **interviewer** *noun*

intestine *noun* the long tube along which food passes while being absorbed by the body, between the stomach and the anus. **intestinal** *adjective*

intimate (*say* **in**-tim-at) *adjective* **1** very friendly with someone. **2** private and personal, *intimate thoughts.* **3** detailed, *an intimate knowledge of the country.* **intimately** *adverb*, **intimacy** *noun*

intimate (*say* **in**-tim-ayt) *verb* (**intimated, intimating**) tell or hint. **intimation** *noun*

intimidate *verb* (**intimidated, intimidating**) frighten a person by threats into doing something. **intimidation** *noun* [from *in-* = in, + Latin *timidus* = timid]

into *preposition* used to express (**1**) movement to the inside (*Go into the house*), (**2**) change of condition or occupation etc. (*It broke into pieces. She went into politics*), (**3**) (in division) *4 into 20* = 20 divided by 4.

intolerable *adjective* unbearable. **intolerably** *adverb*

intolerant *adjective* not tolerant. **intolerantly** *adverb*, **intolerance** *noun*

intonation *noun* **1** the tone or pitch of the voice in speaking. **2** intoning.

intone *verb* (**intoned, intoning**) recite in a chanting voice.

intoxicate *verb* (**intoxicated, intoxicating**) make a person drunk or very excited. **intoxication** *noun* [from *in-* = in, + Latin *toxicum* = poison]

intra- *prefix* within. [from Latin]

intractable *adjective* unmanageable; difficult to deal with or control. **intractability** *noun*

intransigent *adjective* stubborn. **intransigence** *noun*

intransitive *adjective* (of a verb) used without a direct object after it, e.g. *hear* in *we can hear* (but not in *we can hear you*). Compare *transitive.* **intransitively** *adverb*

intravenous (*say* in-tra-**veen**-us) *adjective* into a vein.

intrepid *adjective* fearless; brave. **intrepidly** *adverb*, **intrepidity** *noun* (from *in-* = not, + Latin *trepidus* = alarmed]

intricate *adjective* very complicated. **intricately** *adverb*, **intricacy** *noun* [from Latin *intricatum* = entangled]

intrigue (*say* in-**treeg**) *verb* (**intrigued, intriguing**) **1** plot with someone in an underhand way. **2** interest very much, *The subject intrigues me.*

intrigue *noun* **1** plotting; an underhand plot. **2** (*old use*) a secret love affair. [from Latin *intricare* = to tangle]

intrinsic *adjective* belonging naturally in something; inherent. **intrinsically** *adverb*

intro- *prefix* into; inwards. [from Latin]

introduce *verb* (**introduced, introducing**) **1** make a person known to other people. **2** announce a broadcast, speaker, etc. **3** bring something into use or for consideration. [from *intro-*, + Latin *ducere* = to lead]

introduction *noun* **1** introducing somebody or something. **2** an explanation put at the beginning of a book or speech etc. **introductory** *adjective*

introspective *adjective* examining your own thoughts and feelings. **introspection** *noun* [from *intro-*, + Latin *specere* = to look]

introvert *noun* an introspective person. (The opposite is *extrovert.*) [from *intro-*, + Latin *vertere* = to turn]

intrude *terb* (**intruded, intruding**) come in or join in without being wanted; interfere. **intrusion** *noun*, **intrusive** *adjective* [from *in-* = in, + Latin *trudere* = to push]

intruder *noun* **1** someone who intrudes. **2** a burglar.

intuition *noun* the power to know or understand things without having to think hard or without being taught. **intuitive** *adjective*, **intuitively** *adverb*

Inuit (*say* **in**-yoo-it) *noun* **1** an indigenous person of Canada, Greenland, and Alaska who speaks an Inupiaq language. **2** one of the Inupiaq languages.

inundate *verb* (**inundated, inundating**) flood. **inundation** *noun* [from *in-* = in, + Latin *unda* = a wave]

inure (*say* in-**yoor**) *verb* (**inured, inuring**) accustom, especially to something unpleasant.

invade *verb* (**invaded, invading**) **1** attack and enter a country etc. **2** crowd into a place, *Tourists invade Whangamatā in summer.* **invader** *noun* [from *in-* = into, + Latin *vadere* = go]

invalid (*say* **in**-va-lid) *noun* a person who is ill or who is weakened by illness.

invalid (*say* in-**val**-id) *adjective* not valid, *This passport is invalid.* **invalidity** *noun*

invalidate *verb* (**invalidated, invalidating**) make a thing invalid. **invalidation** *noun*

invaluable *adjective* having a value that is too great to be measured; extremely valuable. [from *in-* = not, + *valuable*]

invariable *adjective* not variable; never changing. **invariably** *adverb*

invasion *noun* invading; being invaded.

invective *noun* abusive words.

inveigle (*say* in-**vay**-gul) *verb* (**inveigled, inveigling**) entice. **inveiglement** *noun*

invent *verb* **1** be the first person to make or think of a particular thing. **2** make up a false story etc., *invent an excuse.* **invention** *noun,* **inventor** *noun,* **inventive** *adjective*

inventory (*say* **in**-ven-ter-ee) *noun* (*plural* **inventories**) a detailed list of goods or furniture.

inverse *adjective* reversed; opposite. **inversely** *adverb* [same origin as *invert*]

invert *verb* turn something upside down. **inversion** *noun*
inverted commas punctuation marks " " or ' ' put round quoted words. [from *in-* = in, + Latin *vertere* = to turn]

invertebrate *noun* an animal without a backbone. **invertebrate** *adjective*

invest *verb* **1** use money to make a profit, e.g. by lending it in return for interest to be paid, or by buying stocks and shares or property. **2** give somebody a rank, medal, etc. in a formal ceremony. **investment** *noun,* **investor** *noun*

investigate *verb* (**investigated, investigating**) find out as much as you can about something; make a systematic inquiry. **investigation** *noun,* **investigator** *noun,* **investigative** *adjective*

investiture *noun* the process of investing someone with an honour etc.

inveterate *adjective* firmly established; habitual, *an inveterate reader.*

invidious *adjective* causing resentment because of unfairness.

invigilate *verb* (**invigilated, invigilating**) supervise candidates at an examination. **invigilation** *noun,* **invigilator** *noun* [from *in-* = on, + Latin *vigilare* = keep watch]

invigorate *verb* (**invigorated, invigorating**) give a person strength or courage. [compare *vigour*]

invincible *adjective* not able to be defeated; unconquerable. **invincibly** *adverb,* **invincibility** *noun* [from *in-* = not, + Latin *vincere* = conquer]

invisible *adjective* not visible; not able to be seen. **invisibly** *adverb,* **invisibility** *noun*

invite *verb* (**invited, inviting**) **1** ask a person to come or do something. **2** be likely to cause something to happen, *You are inviting disaster.* **invitation** *noun*

inviting *adjective* attractive; tempting. **invitingly** *adverb*

invoice *noun* a list of goods sent or work done, with the prices charged. [from French *envoyer* = send]

invoke *verb* (**invoked, invoking**) **1** call upon a god in prayer asking for help etc. **2** appeal to for help or protection, *invoke the law.* **invocation** *noun* [from *in-* = in, + Latin *vocare* = to call]

involuntary *adjective* not deliberate; unintentional. **involuntarily** *adverb*

involve *verb* (**involved, involving**) **1** have as a part; make a thing necessary, *The job involves hard work.* **2** make someone share in something, *They involved us in their charity work.* **involvement** *noun* [from *in-* = in, + Latin *volvere* = to roll]

involved *adjective* **1** complicated. **2** concerned; sharing in something.

invulnerable *adjective* not vulnerable.

inward *adjective* **1** on the inside. **2** going or facing inwards.

inward *adverb* inwards.

inwards *adverb* towards the inside.

iodine *noun* a chemical substance used as an antiseptic.

ion *noun* an electrically charged particle.

ionosphere (*say* I-**on**-os-feer) *noun* a region of the upper atmosphere, containing ions.

IOU *noun* a written declaration of a debt. [= *I owe you*]

iPad (*trade mark*) *noun* a mobile tablet computer launched by Apple Inc in 2010.

iPhone (*trade mark*) *noun* an Internet-enabled smartphone first released by Apple Inc in 2007.

IQ *abbreviation* intelligence quotient, a number showing how a person's intelligence compares with that of an average person.

ir- *prefix* see **in-**.

IRA *abbreviation* Irish Republican Army.

irascible (*say* ir-**as**-ib-ul) *adjective* easily becoming angry; irritable.

irate (*say* I-**rayt**) *adjective* angry.

IRB *abbreviation* International Rugby Board.

IRD *abbreviation* Inland Revenue Department.

iridescent *adjective* showing rainbow-like colours. **iridescence** *noun*

iris *noun* (*plural* **irises**) **1** a plant with long pointed leaves and large flowers. **2** the coloured part of the eyeball. [Greek, = rainbow]

irk *verb* annoy.

irksome *adjective* annoying; tiresome.

iron *noun* **1** a hard grey metal. **2** a device with a flat base that is heated for smoothing clothes or cloth. **3** a tool etc. made of iron.
iron *adjective*
Iron Age the time when tools and weapons were made of iron.
irons *plural noun* fetters.

iron *verb* smooth clothes or cloth with an iron.

ironic (*say* I-**ron**-ik) *adjective* using irony; full of irony. **ironical** *adjective*, **ironically** *adverb*

Ironman *noun* a demanding triathlon contest of swimming, cycling, and running.

ironmonger *noun* a shopkeeper who sells tools and other metal objects. **ironmongery** *noun*

ironsands *noun* (*NZ*) sands containing iron ore.

ironstone *noun* **1** hard iron ore. **2** a kind of hard white pottery.

irony (*say* **I**-ron-ee) *noun* (*plural* **ironies**) **1** saying the opposite of what you mean in order to emphasise it, e.g. saying 'What a lovely day' when it is pouring with rain. **2** an oddly contradictory situation, *The irony of it is that I tripped while telling someone else to be careful.*

irrational *adjective* not rational; illogical. **irrationally** *adverb*

irreducible *adjective* unable to be reduced, *an irreducible minimum.*

irrefutable (*say* ir-**ef**-yoo-ta-bul) *adjective* unable to be refuted.

irregular *adjective* **1** not regular; uneven. **2** against the rules or usual custom. **3** (of troops) not in the regular armed forces. **irregularly** *adverb*, **irregularity** *noun*

irrelevant (*say* ir-**el**-iv-ant) *adjective* not relevant. **irrelevantly** *adverb*, **irrelevance** *noun*

irreparable (*say* ir-**ep**-er-a-bul) *adjective* unable to be repaired or replaced. **irreparably** *adverb*

irreplaceable *adjective* unable to be replaced.

irrepressible *adjective* unable to be repressed. **irrepressibly** *adverb*

irreproachable *adjective* blameless; faultless. **irreproachably** *adverb*

irresistible *adjective* unable to be resisted; very attractive. **irresistibly** *adverb*

irresolute *adjective* feeling uncertain; hesitant. **irresolutely** *adverb*

irrespective *adjective* not taking something into account, *Prizes are awarded to winners, irrespective of age.*

irresponsible *adjective* not showing a proper sense of responsibility. **irresponsibly** *adverb*, **irresponsibility** *noun*

irretrievable *adjective* not able to be retrieved. **irretrievably** *adverb*

irreverent *adjective* not reverent; not respectful. **irreverently** *adverb*, **irreverence** *noun*

irreversible *adjective* not able to be reversed or changed. **irreversibly** *adverb*

irrevocable (*say* ir-**ev**-ok-a-bul) *adjective* unable to be revoked or altered. **irrevocably** *adverb*

irrigate *verb* (**irrigated**, **irrigating**) supply land with water so that crops etc. can grow. **irrigation** *noun*

irritable *adjective* easily annoyed; bad-tempered. **irritably** *adverb*, **irritability** *noun*

irritate *verb* (**irritated**, **irritating**) **1** annoy. **2** cause itching. **irritation** *noun*, **irritant** *adjective & noun*

irrupt *verb* enter forcibly or violently. **irruption** *noun*. [from *ir-* = into, + Latin *ruptum* = burst]

ISBN *abbreviation* international standard book number.

Islam *noun* the religion of Muslims. **Islamic** *adjective* [Arabic, = submission to God]

island *noun* **1** a piece of land surrounded by water. **2** something resembling an island because it is isolated.
the Islands (*NZ*) the South Pacific Islands, especially those from which many people have emigrated to New Zealand.

islander *noun* an inhabitant of an island.

Islander *noun* (*NZ*) a Pacific Islander.

isle (*say* as I'll) *noun* (*poetic & in names*) an island. [from Latin *insula* = island]

isn't (*mainly spoken*) is not.

iso- *prefix* equal (as in *isobar*). [from Greek *isos* = equal]

isobar (*say* **I**-so-bar) *noun* a line (on a map) connecting places that have the same atmospheric pressure.

isolate *verb* (**isolated**, **isolating**) place a person or thing apart or alone; separate. **isolation** *noun* [from Latin *insula* = island]

isosceles (*say* I-**soss**-il-eez) *adjective* having two sides equal, *an isosceles triangle.* [from *iso-*, + Greek *skelos* = leg]

isotope *noun* a form of an element that differs from other forms in its nuclear properties but not in its chemical properties.

ISP *abbreviation* Internet Service Provider.

ISSN *abbreviation* international standard serial number; a number given to journal publications.

issue *verb* (**issued**, **issuing**) **1** come out; go out; flow out. **2** supply; give out, *We issued one blanket to each refugee.* **3** put out for sale; publish. **4** send out, *They issued a gale warning.* **5** result.

issue *noun* **1** a subject for discussion or concern, *What are the real issues?* **2** a result, *Await the issue of the trial.* **3** something issued, *The Christmas issue of our magazine.* **4** issuing something, *The issue of passports is held up.*

isthmus (*say* **iss**-mus) *noun* (*plural* **isthmuses**) a narrow strip of land connecting two larger pieces of land.

it *pronoun* **1** the thing being talked about. **2** the player who has to catch others in a game. The word is also used (**3**) in statements about the weather (*It is raining*) or about circumstances etc. (*It is six miles to Levin*), (**4**) as an indefinite object (*Run for it!*), (**5**) to refer to a phrase (*It is unlikely that she will fail*).

IT *abbreviation* information technology.

italic (*say* it-**al**-ik) *adjective* printed with sloping letters (called **italics**) *like this.*

itch *verb* **1** have or feel a tickling sensation in the skin that makes you want to scratch it. **2** long to do something.

itch *noun* (*plural* **itches**) **1** an itching feeling. **2** a longing. **itchy** *adjective*, **itchiness** *noun*

item *noun* **1** one thing in a list or group of things. **2** one piece of news in a newspaper or bulletin.

itinerant (*say* it-**in**-er-ant) *adjective* travelling from place to place, *an itinerant preacher.*

itinerary (*say* I-**tin**-er-er-ee) *noun* (*plural* **itineraries**) a list of places to be visited on a journey; a route. [from Latin *itineris* = of a journey]

its *possessive pronoun* belonging to it, *The cat hurt its paw.*

> USAGE Do not put an apostrophe into *its* unless you mean 'it is' or 'it has' (see the next entry).

it's (*mainly spoken*) **1** it is, *It's very hot.* **2** it has, *It's broken all records.*

> USAGE Do not confuse with *its.*

itself *pronoun* it and nothing else. (Compare *herself.*)
by itself on its own; alone.

ivory *noun* **1** the hard creamy-white substance that forms elephants' tusks. **2** a creamy-white colour.

ivy *noun* (*plural* **ivies**) a climbing evergreen plant with shiny leaves.

iwi *noun* a tribe or nation. [Māori]

Jj

jab *verb* (**jabbed**, **jabbing**) poke roughly; push a thing into something.

jab *noun* **1** a jabbing movement. **2** (*informal*) an injection.

jabber *verb* speak quickly and not clearly; chatter. **jabber** *noun*

jack *noun* **1** a device for lifting something heavy off the ground. **2** a playing-card with a picture of a young man. **3** a small white ball aimed at in bowls.
jack of all trades someone who can do many different kinds of work.

jack *verb* lift with a jack.
jack it in (*slang*) give up or abandon an attempt etc.
jack up (*NZ, slang*) fix, arrange.

jackal *noun* a wild animal rather like a dog.

jackass *noun* (*plural* **jackasses**) **1** a male donkey. **2** a stupid person.

jackdaw *noun* a kind of small crow.

jackeroo *noun* (also **jackaroo**) (*NZ*) **1** a learner or novice. **2** (*old use*) a trainee farmer.

jacket *noun* **1** a short coat, usually reaching to the hips. **2** a cover to keep the heat in a water-tank etc. **3** a paper wrapper for a book. **4** the skin of a potato that is baked without being peeled.

jack-in-the-box *noun* a toy figure that springs out of a box when the lid is lifted.

jackknife *verb* (**jackknifed**, **jackknifing**) fold one part against another, like a folding knife.

jackpot *noun* an amount of prize-money that increases until someone wins it.

jack-up *noun* (*NZ, slang*) a wangle or shady deal.

jacuzzi *noun* (*British*) a spa-bath.

jade *noun* a green stone that is carved to make ornaments.

jaded *adjective* tired and bored.

JAFA *abbreviation* (*NZ, slang*) just another f-ing Aucklander.

jagged (*say* **jag**-id) *adjective* having an uneven edge with sharp points.

jaguar *noun* a large fierce South American animal rather like a leopard.

jail *noun* a prison.

jail *verb* to put into prison. **jailer** *noun* [from Latin *cavea* = a cage]

jake *adjective* (*NZ, slang*) all right.
she's jake it's OK.

jam *noun* **1** a sweet food made of fruit boiled with sugar until it is thick. **2** a lot of people, cars, or logs etc. crowded together so that movement is difficult. **3** (*informal*) a difficult situation, *in a jam.*

jam *verb* (**jammed**, **jamming**) **1** crowd or squeeze into a space. **2** make or become fixed and difficult to move. **3** push something forcibly, *jam the brakes on.* **4** block a broadcast by causing interference with the transmission.

jamb (*say* jam) *noun* a side-post of a doorway or window-frame. [from French *jambe* = leg]

jamboree *noun* **1** a large party or celebration. **2** a large gathering of Scouts.

jandals *plural noun* (*NZ, trade mark*) plastic or rubber sandals with two straps that meet between the big toe and the toe next to it.

jangle *verb* (**jangled**, **jangling**) make a loud harsh ringing sound. **jangle** *noun*

janitor *noun* a caretaker. [from Latin *janua* = door]

January *noun* the first month of the year. [named after the Roman god Janus, guardian of gates and beginnings]

jar[1] *noun* a container made of glass or pottery. [from Arabic *jarra* = pot]

jar[2] *verb* (**jarred**, **jarring**) **1** cause an unpleasant jolt or shock. **2** sound harshly.

jar[2] *noun* a jarring effect.

jargon *noun* special words used by a group of people, *scientists' jargon.*

jarrah *noun* a kind of eucalyptus tree.

jasmine *noun* a shrub with yellow or white flowers.

jaundice *noun* a disease in which the skin becomes yellow. [from French *jaune* = yellow]

jaunt *noun* a short trip. **jaunting** *noun*

jaunty *adjective* (**jauntier**, **jauntiest**) lively and cheerful. **jauntily** *adverb*, **jauntiness** *noun*

javelin *noun* a lightweight spear.

jaw *noun* **1** either of the two bones that form the framework of the mouth. **2** the lower part of the face. **3** something shaped like the jaws or used for gripping things. **4** (*slang*) talking.

jay *noun* a noisy brightly-coloured bird.

jazz *noun* a kind of music with strong rhythm. **jazzy** *adjective*

jealous *adjective* **1** unhappy or resentful because you feel that someone is your rival or is better or luckier than yourself. **2** careful in keeping something, *He is very jealous of his own rights.* **jealously** *adverb,* **jealousy** *noun*

jeans *plural noun* trousers made of strong cotton fabric.

jeer *verb* laugh or shout at somebody rudely or scornfully. **jeer** *noun*

jelly *noun* (*plural* **jellies**) **1** a soft transparent food. **2** any soft slippery substance. **jellied** *adjective* [from Latin *gelare* = freeze]

jellyfish *noun* (*plural* **jellyfish**) a sea animal with a body like jelly.

jemmy *noun* (*plural* **jemmies**) a burglar's crowbar.

jeopardise (*say* **jep**-er-dyz) *verb* (**jeopardised**, **jeopardising**) endanger.

jeopardy (*say* **jep**-er-dee) *noun* danger.

jerk *verb* make a sudden sharp movement; pull suddenly; move unevenly.

jerk *noun* **1** a jerking movement. **2** (*slang*) an objectionable or stupid person. **jerky** *adjective,* **jerkily** *adverb*

jerkin *noun* a sleeveless jacket.

jerry-built *adjective* built badly and with poor materials.

jersey *noun* (*plural* **jerseys**) **1** a pullover with sleeves. **2** a plain machine-knitted material used for making clothes.

jest *noun* a joke.

jest *verb* make jokes.

jester *noun* a professional entertainer at a royal court in the Middle Ages.

Jesuit *noun* a member of the Society of Jesus (a Roman Catholic religious order).

jet[1] *noun* **1** a stream of water, gas, flame, etc. shot out from a narrow opening. **2** a narrow opening from which a jet comes. **3** an aircraft driven by engines that send out a high-speed jet of hot gases at the back. **jet-boat** *noun* (*NZ*) a river-boat driven by engines that send out a high-speed jet of water at the back.

jet[1] *verb* (**jetted**, **jetting**) **1** come or send out in a strong stream. **2** (*informal*) travel in a jet aircraft. [from French *jeter* = to throw]

jet[2] *noun* **1** a hard black mineral substance. **2** a deep glossy black colour.

jetsam *noun* goods thrown overboard and washed ashore from a ship in distress. [from *jettison*]

jettison *verb* throw overboard or away; release or drop something from an aircraft or spacecraft in flight. [same origin as *jet*[1]]

jetty *noun* (*plural* **jetties**) a small landing-stage. [same origin as *jet*[1]]

Jew *noun* a member of a people descended from the ancient tribes of Israel, or who believes in the religion of this people. **Jewess** *noun,* **Jewish** *adjective* [from Hebrew, = of the tribe of Judah]

jewel *noun* a precious stone; an ornament containing precious stones. **jewelled** *adjective*

jeweller *noun* a person who sells or makes jewellery.

jewellery *noun* jewels and similar ornaments for wearing.

jib[1] *noun* **1** a triangular sail stretching forward from a ship's front mast. **2** the projecting arm of a crane.

jib[2] *verb* (**jibbed**, **jibbing**) be reluctant or unwilling to do something.

jibe *noun* an insulting or mocking remark.

jiffy *noun* (*informal*) a moment.

jig *noun* **1** a lively jumping dance. **2** a device that holds something in place while you work on it with tools.

jig *verb* (**jigged**, **jigging**) move up and down quickly and jerkily.

jiggle *verb* (**jiggled**, **jiggling**) rock or jerk something lightly.

jigsaw *noun* **1** a saw that can cut curved shapes. **2** a jigsaw puzzle. **jigsaw puzzle** a picture cut into irregular pieces which are then shuffled and fitted together again for amusement.

jihad *noun* (in Islam) a holy war. [Arabic]

jilt *verb* abandon a boyfriend or girlfriend, especially after promising to marry him or her.

jingle *verb* (**jingled**, **jingling**) make or cause to make a tinkling sound.

jingle *noun* **1** a jingling sound. **2** a very simple verse or tune.

jitters *plural noun* (*informal*) nervousness. **jittery** *adjective*

job *noun* **1** work that someone does regularly to earn a living. **2** a piece of work to be done. **3** (*informal*) a difficult task, *You'll have a job to lift that box.* **4** (*informal*) a thing; a state of affairs, *It's a good job you're here.*

jockey *noun* (*plural* **jockeys**) a person who rides horses in races.

jocular *adjective* joking. **jocularly** *adverb,* **jocularity** *noun*

jodhpurs (*say* **jod**-perz) *plural noun* trousers for horse-riding, fitting closely from the knee to the ankle. [named after Jodhpur in India]

joey *noun* a young kangaroo, possum, etc.

jog *verb* (**jogged, jogging**) **1** run or trot slowly, especially for exercise. **2** give something a slight push. **jogger** *noun*
jog someone's memory help him or her to remember something.

jog *noun* **1** a slow run or trot. **2** a slight knock or push.

joggle *verb* (**joggled, joggling**) shake slightly; move jerkily. **joggle** *noun*

jogtrot *noun* a slow steady trot.

join *verb* **1** put or come together; fasten; unite; connect. **2** do something together with others, *We all joined in the chorus.* **3** become a member of a group or organisation etc., *Join the Navy.*
join up enlist in the armed forces.

join *noun* a place where things join.

joiner *noun* a person whose job is to make furniture and fitments out of wood. **joinery** *noun*

joint *noun* **1** a join. **2** the place where two bones fit together. **3** a large piece of meat cut ready for cooking.

joint *adjective* shared or done by two or more people, nations, etc., *a joint project*; combined. **jointly** *adverb*

joist *noun* any of the long beams supporting a floor or ceiling.

joke *noun* something said or done to make people laugh.

joke *verb* (**joked, joking**) make jokes.

joker *noun* **1** someone who jokes. **2** an extra playing-card with a jester on it. **3** (*NZ, informal*) a man.

jolly *adjective* (**jollier, jolliest**) cheerful; merry. **jollity** *noun*

jolly *adverb* (*informal*) very, *jolly good.*

jolly *verb* (**jollied, jollying**) (*informal*) keep someone in a good humour.

jolt *verb* **1** shake or dislodge with a sudden sharp movement. **2** move along jerkily, e.g. on a rough road. **3** give someone a shock.

jolt *noun* **1** a jolting movement. **2** a shock.

jostle *verb* (**jostled, jostling**) push roughly, especially in a crowd.

jot *verb* (**jotted, jotting**) write something quickly, *jot it down.*

jotter *noun* a note-pad or notebook.

joule (*say* jool) *noun* a unit of work or energy. [named after the English scientist J. P. Joule]

journal *noun* **1** a newspaper or magazine. **2** a diary. [from Latin, = by day]

journalist *noun* a person who writes for a newspaper or magazine. **journalism** *noun*, **journalistic** *adjective*

journey *noun* (*plural* **journeys**) **1** going from one place to another. **2** the distance or time taken to travel somewhere, *two days' journey.*

journey *verb* make a journey. [from French, = a day's travel (*jour* = day)]

journo *noun* (*informal*) a journalist.

joust (*say* jowst) *verb* fight on horseback with lances.

jovial *adjective* cheerful and goodhumoured. **joviality** *noun*, **jovially** *adverb*

jowl *noun* **1** the jaw or cheek. **2** loose skin on the neck.

joy *noun* **1** a feeling of great pleasure; gladness. **2** a thing that causes joy. **joyful** *adjective*, **joyfully** *adverb*, **joyfulness** *noun*, **joyous** *adjective*, **joyously** *adverb*

joyride *noun* a car ride taken for pleasure, usually without the owner's permission. **joyriding** *noun*

joystick *noun* **1** the control lever of an aircraft. **2** a device for moving a cursor etc. on a VDU screen.

JP *abbreviation* Justice of the Peace.

jubilant *adjective* rejoicing; triumphant. **jubilantly** *adverb*, **jubilation** *noun* [from Latin *jubilans* = shouting for joy]

jubilee (*say* **joo**-bil-ee) *noun* a special anniversary, *silver* (25th), *golden* (50th), and *diamond* (60th) *jubilee.*

Judaism (*say* **joo**-day-izm) *noun* the religion of the Jewish people. [same origin as *Jew*]

judder *verb* shake noisily or violently.
judder bar (*NZ*) a hump in the road to slow down cars etc.

judge *noun* **1** a person appointed to hear cases in a lawcourt and decide what should be done. **2** a person deciding who has won a contest or competition, or the value or quality of something.

judge *verb* (**judged, judging**) **1** act as a judge. **2** form and give an opinion. **3** estimate, *He judged the distance carefully.* [from Latin *judex* = judge]

judgment (also **judgement**) *noun* **1** judging. **2** the decision made by a lawcourt. **3** someone's opinion. **4** the ability to judge wisely. **5** something considered as a punishment from God, *It's a judgement on you!*

judicial *adjective* of lawcourts, judges, or judgments. **judicially** *adverb*

judiciary (*say* joo-**dish**-er-ee) *noun* all the judges in a country.

judicious (*say* joo-**dish**-us) *adjective* having or showing good sense. **judiciously** *adverb*

judo *noun* a Japanese method of self-defence without using weapons. [from Japanese *ju* = gentle, + *do* = way]

jug *noun* a container for holding and pouring liquids, with a handle and a lip.

juggernaut *noun* a huge truck. [named after a Hindu god whose image was dragged in procession on a huge wheeled vehicle]

juggle *verb* (**juggled**, **juggling**) **1** toss and keep a number of objects in the air, for entertainment. **2** rearrange or alter things skilfully or in order to deceive people.
juggler *noun*

jugular *adjective* of or in the throat or neck, *the jugular veins.*

juice *noun* **1** the liquid from fruit, vegetables, or other food. **2** a liquid produced by the body, *the digestive juices.* **juicy** *adjective*

juke-box *noun* a machine that plays a record when you put a coin in.

July *noun* the seventh month of the year. [named after Julius Caesar]

jumble *verb* (**jumbled**, **jumbling**) mix things up into a confused mass.

jumble *noun* a confused mixture of things; a muddle.
jumble sale a sale of second-hand goods.

jumbo *noun* (*plural* **jumbos**) **1** something very large; a jumbo jet. **2** an elephant.
jumbo jet a very large jet aircraft.

jump *verb* **1** move up suddenly from the ground into the air. **2** go over something by jumping, *jump the fence.* **3** pass over something; miss out part of a book etc. **4** move suddenly in surprise. **5** pass quickly to a different place or level.
jump at (*informal*) accept something eagerly.
jump the gun start before you should.
jump the queue not wait your turn.

jump *noun* **1** a jumping movement. **2** an obstacle to jump over. **3** a sudden rise or change.

jumper *noun* **1** a person or animal that jumps. **2** a jersey.

jumpy *adjective* nervous.

junction *noun* **1** a join. **2** a place where roads or railway lines meet. [from Latin *junctum* = joined]

juncture *noun* **1** a point of time, especially in a crisis. **2** a join.

June *noun* the sixth month of the year. [named after the Roman goddess Juno]

jungle *noun* a thick tangled forest, especially in the tropics. **jungly** *adjective* [from Hindu *jangal* = forest]

junior *adjective* **1** younger. **2** for young children, *a junior school.* **3** lower in rank or importance, *junior officers.*

junior *noun* a junior person. [Latin, = younger]

juniper *noun* an evergreen shrub.

junk[1] *noun* rubbish; things of no value.
junk food food that is not nourishing.

junk[2] *noun* a Chinese sailing-boat.

jurisdiction *noun* authority; official power, especially to interpret and apply the law. [from Latin *juris* = of the law, + *dictum* = said]

juror *noun* a member of a jury.

jury *noun* (*plural* **juries**) a group of people (usually twelve) appointed to give a verdict about a case in a lawcourt. **juryman** *noun*, **jurywoman** *noun* [from Latin *jurare* = take an oath]

jury-mast *noun* a temporary mast.

just *adjective* **1** giving proper consideration to everyone's claims. **2** deserved; right in amount etc., *a just reward.* **justly** *adverb*, **justness** *noun*

just *adverb* **1** exactly, *It's just what I wanted.* **2** only; simply, *I just wanted to see him.* **3** barely; by only a small amount, *just below the knee.* **4** at this moment or only a little while ago, *She has just gone.* [from Latin *justus* = rightful]

justice *noun* **1** being just; fair treatment. **2** legal proceedings, *a court of justice.* **3** a judge.
Justice of the Peace a person with the legal authority to judge minor criminal cases, witness documents, etc.

justify *verb* (**justified**, **justifying**) show that something is fair, just, or reasonable.
justification *noun*

jut *verb* (**jutted**, **jutting**) stick out. [same origin *as jet*[1]]

jute *noun* fibre from tropical plants, used for making sacks etc.

juvenile *adjective* of or for young people.
juvenile delinquent a young person who has broken the law. [from Latin *juvenis* = young person]

juxtapose *verb* (**juxtaposed**, **juxtaposing**) put things side by side. **juxtaposition** *noun* [from Latin *juxta* = next, *positum* = put]

kaftan *noun* a long belted tunic or loosely-fitting dress.

kahawai *noun* a fish rather like a salmon. [Māori]

kahikatea *noun* the white pine. [Māori]

kai *noun* (also **kaikai**) (*informal*) food. [Māori]

kaiako *noun* a teacher. [Māori]

kāika *noun* = **kāinga**.

kaikōmako *noun* a small tree with white flowers and black fruit. [Māori]

kaimoana *noun* seafood. [Māori]

kāinga *noun* a settlement or village. [Māori]

kaitiakitanga *noun* guardianship, especially of land. [Māori]

kākā *noun* a large olive-brown parrot. **kākā-beak** or **kākā-bill** a New Zealand climbing plant with bright-red flowers. [Māori]

kākāpō *noun* a large dark-green flightless parrot. [Māori]

kākāriki *noun* a green parakeet with a red forehead. [Māori]

kale *noun* a kind of cabbage.

kaleidoscope (*say* kal-**I**-dos-kohp) *noun* a tube that you look through to see brightly coloured patterns which change as you turn the end of the tube. **kaleidoscopic** *adjective* [from Greek *halos* = beautiful, + *eidos* = form, + *skopein* = look at]

kāmahi *noun* a hardwood tree. [Māori]

kamikaze *noun* **1** a Japanese aircraft in the Second World War laden with explosives and deliberately crashed on a target. **2** the pilot of this.

kamikaze *adjective* suicidal. [Japanese, = *divine wind*]

kangaroo *noun* an Australian animal that jumps along on its strong hind legs. (See *marsupial*.)

kānuka *noun* a small tree with white flowers. [Māori]

kaolin *noun* fine white clay used in making porcelain and in medicine.

ka pai *interjection* very good. [Māori]

karaka *noun* a tree with orange berries which contain poisonous seeds. [Māori]

karakia *noun* a prayer. [Māori]

karamū *noun* any of several kinds of small tree. [Māori]

karanga *noun* a call of welcome as visitors go on to a marae. [Māori]

karanga *verb* chant a karanga.

karaoke *noun* a form of entertainment in which a person sings along to a recorded track from which the vocal part has been removed. [from Japanese = empty orchestra]

karate (*say* ka-**rah**-tee) *noun* a Japanese method of self-defence in which the hands and feet are used as weapons. [from Japanese *kara* = empty, *te* = hand]

kārearea *noun* the New Zealand falcon. [Māori]

karengo *noun* (also **parengo**) an edible seaweed. [Māori]

Karitane hospital (*NZ*) a children's hospital set up by the Plunket Society.

Karitane nurse (*NZ*) a children's nurse trained by the Plunket Society. [from Karitane, a township near Dunedin]

karo *noun* a small tree with brown flowers. [Māori]

katipō *noun* a small poisonous spider with a red stripe along its back. [Māori]

kaumātua *noun* a Māori elder. [Māori]

kaupapa *noun* a principle or policy. **kura kaupapa Māori** a primary school where teachers and children use the Māori language. [Māori]

kauri *noun* **1** a tall tree. **2** its wood. **kauri gum** resin from kauri that has become fossilised. [Māori]

kava *noun* **1** a Pacific Island shrub. **2** an intoxicating drink made from its roots. [Tongan]

kawa *noun* proper behaviour. [Māori]

kawakawa *noun* a shrub with scented leaves. [Māori]

kāwanatanga *noun* governing. [from Māori *kāwana*, from English *governor*]

kayak *noun* a small canoe with a covering that fits round the canoeist's waist. [Inuit word]

kea *noun* a green parrot of the South Island high country. [Māori]

Kea *noun* (*NZ*) a member of a Scouting organisation for boys aged 6–7 years.

Kea crossing *noun* a school pedestrian crossing.

kebabs *plural noun* small pieces of meat etc. cooked on a skewer.

keel *noun* the long piece of wood or metal along the bottom of a boat.
on an even keel steady.

keel *verb* tilt; overturn, *The ship keeled over.*

keen[1] *adjective* **1** enthusiastic; very interested in or eager to do something, *a keen swimmer.* **2** sharp, *a keen edge.* **3** piercingly cold, *a keen wind.* **keenly** *adverb,* **keenness** *noun*

keen[2] *verb* wail, especially in mourning.

keep *verb* (**kept**, **keeping**) This word has many uses, including, (**1**) have something and look after it or not get rid of it, (**2**) stay or cause to stay in the same condition etc. (*keep still; keep it hot*), (**3**) do something continually (*She keeps laughing*), (**4**) respect and not break (*keep a promise*), (**5**) make entries in (*keep a diary*).
keep up make the same progress as others; continue something.

keep *noun* **1** maintenance; the food etc. that you need to live, *She earns her keep.* **2** a strong tower in a castle.
for keeps (*informal*) permanently; to keep. *Is this football mine for keeps?*

keeper *noun* **1** a person who looks after an animal, building, etc., *the zoo keeper.* **2** (*informal*) a goalkeeper or wicketkeeper.

keeping *noun* care; looking after something, *in safe keeping.*
in keeping with conforming to; suiting, *Modern furniture is not in keeping with an old house.*

keepsake *noun* a gift to be kept in memory of the person who gave it.

keg *noun* a small barrel.

kēhua *noun* a ghost. [Māori]

kelp *noun* a large seaweed.

kennel *noun* a shelter for a dog.

keno *noun* a gambling game similar to housie.

kerb *noun* the edge of a pavement.

kerchief *noun* (*old use*) **1** a square scarf worn on the head. **2** a handkerchief.

kererū *noun* a large green, bronze, and white bird of the bush, the New Zealand pigeon. [Māori]

kernel *noun* the part inside the shell of a nut etc.

kero *noun* (*NZ, informal*) kerosene.

kerosene *noun* an oil used for heating and lighting, paraffin oil. [from Greek *keros* = wax]

kestrel *noun* a small falcon.

ketchup *noun* a thick sauce made from tomatoes and vinegar etc.

kete *noun* a woven basket. [Māori]

kettle *noun* a container with a spout and handle, for boiling water in.

kettledrum *noun* a drum consisting of a large metal bowl with skin or plastic over the top.

key *noun* **1** a piece of metal shaped so that it will open a lock. **2** a device for winding up a clock or clockwork toy etc. **3** a small lever to be pressed by a finger, e.g. on a piano or a typewriter. **4** a system of notes in music, *the key of C major.* **5** a fact or clue that explains or solves something, *the key to the mystery.*

keyboard *noun* the set of keys on a piano, typewriter, computer, etc.

keycard *noun* a magnetically encoded plastic security card for entering rooms or buildings.

keyhole *noun* the hole through which a key is put into a lock.

keynote *noun* **1** the note on which a key in music is based, *The keynote of C major is C.* **2** the main idea in something said, written, or done; a theme.

keystone *noun* the central wedge-shaped stone in an arch, locking the others together.

khaki *noun* a dull yellowish-brown colour, used for military uniforms. [from Urdu, = dust-coloured]

kia ora *interjection* hello; good health! [Māori]

kibbutz *noun* (*plural* **kibbutzim**) a commune in Israel, especially for farming. [from Hebrew, = gathering]

kick *verb* **1** hit or move a person or thing with your foot. **2** move your legs about vigorously. **3** (of a gun) recoil when fired.
kick in begin.
kick out get rid of; dismiss.
kick up (*informal*) make a noise or fuss.

kick *noun* **1** a kicking movement. **2** the recoiling movement of a gun. **3** (*informal*) a thrill. **4** (*informal*) an interest or activity, *He's on a health kick.*

kid *noun* **1** a young goat. **2** fine leather made from goat's skin. **3** (*informal*) a child.

kid *verb* (**kidded**, **kidding**) (*informal*) deceive in fun; tease.

kiddie *noun* (*informal*) a child.

kidnap *verb* (**kidnapped**, **kidnapping**) abduct, especially in order to obtain a ransom. **kidnapper** *noun*

kidney *noun* (*plural* **kidneys**) either of the two organs in the body that remove waste products from the blood and excrete urine into the bladder.

kiekie *noun* a climbing plant whose leaves are used to weave baskets. [Māori]

kilikiti *noun* a Samoan version of cricket. [Samoan]

kill *verb* **1** make a person or thing die. **2** destroy or put an end to something.
killer *noun*
killing shed *noun* (*NZ*) a farm building where animals are killed.
kill time occupy time idly while waiting.

kill *noun* **1** killing. **2** the animal or animals killed by a hunter. **3** (*NZ*) livestock killed for processing into meat, *this year's lamb kill.*

killing *adjective* (*informal*) very amusing.

kiln *noun* an oven for hardening pottery or bricks, for drying hops, or for burning lime. [from Latin *culina* = kitchen]

kilo *noun* (*plural* **kilos**) (*informal*) a kilogram.

kilo- *prefix* one thousand (as in *kilolitre* = 1,000 litres, *kilohertz* = 1,000 hertz). [from Greek *khilioi* = thousand]

kilogram *noun* a unit of mass or weight equal to 1,000 grams.

kilometre (*say* **kil**-o-meet-er or kil-**om**-it-er) *noun* a unit of length equal to 1,000 metres.

kilowatt *noun* a unit of electrical power equal to 1,000 watts.

kilt *noun* a kind of pleated skirt worn especially by Scotsmen. **kilted** *adjective*

kimono *noun* (*plural* **kimonos**) a long loose Japanese robe.

kin *noun* a person's relatives. **kinsman** *noun*, **kinswoman** *noun*
next of kin a person's closest relative.

kina *noun* an edible sea-urchin. [Māori]

kind[1] *noun* a class of similar things or animals; a sort or type.
payment in kind payment in goods not in money.

> USAGE Correct use is *this kind of thing* or *these kinds of things* (not 'these kind of things').

kind[2] *adjective* friendly and helpful; considerate. **kind-hearted** *adjective*, **kindness** *noun*

kindergarten *noun* a school or class for very young children. [from German *kinder* = children, + *garten* = garden]

kindle *verb* (**kindled**, **kindling**) **1** start a flame; set light to something. **2** begin burning.

kindling *noun* small pieces of wood for use in lighting fires.

kindly *adjective* (**kindlier**, **kindliest**) kind, *a kindly smile.* **kindliness** *noun*

kindly *adverb* **1** in a kind manner. **2** please, *Kindly leave the room.*

kindred *noun* kin.

kindred *adjective* related; similar, *chemistry and kindred subjects.*

kindy *noun* (*plural* **kindies**) (*NZ, informal*) a kindergarten.

kinetic *adjective* of or produced by movement, *kinetic energy.* [from Greek *kinetikos* = moving]

king *noun* **1** a man who is the ruler of a country through inheriting the position. **2** a person or thing regarded as supreme, *the lion is the king of beasts.* **3** the most important piece in chess. **4** a playing-card with a picture of a king. **kingly** *adjective*, **kingship** *noun*
king fern any of several large New Zealand ferns.

kingdom *noun* a country ruled by a king or queen.

kingfish *noun* (*NZ*) a large fish rather like a trevally.

kingfisher *noun* a small bird with blue feathers that dives to catch fish.

kink *noun* **1** a short twist in a rope, wire, piece of hair, etc. **2** a peculiarity. **kinky** *adjective*

kiore *noun* the Polynesian rat. [Māori]

kiosk *noun* a small hut or stall where newspapers, refreshments, etc. are sold. [from Persian, = pavilion]

kipper *noun* a smoked herring.

Kirikiriroa *noun* a Māori name for Hamilton.

kirk *noun* (*Scottish*) a church.

kiss *noun* (*plural* **kisses**) touching somebody with your lips as a sign of affection.

kiss *verb* give somebody a kiss.

kit[1] *noun* **1** equipment or clothes for a particular occupation. **2** a set of parts sold ready to be fitted together.

kit[2] *noun* a basket woven from flax. [from Māori *kete*]

kitchen *noun* a room in which meals are prepared and cooked.
kitchen shower, kitchen tea (*NZ*) a party given for a bride-to-be.

kitchenette *noun* a small kitchen.

kite *noun* **1** a light framework covered with cloth, paper, etc. and flown in the wind on the end of a long piece of string. **2** a large hawk.

kith and kin friends and relatives.

kitset *noun* (*NZ*) = *kit*[1] (sense 2).

kitten *noun* a very young cat.

kitty *noun* (*plural* **kitties**) **1** an amount of money that you can win in a card-game. **2** a fund for use by several people.

Kiwanis *noun* an international organisation of clubs giving service to the community.

kiwano *noun* (*plural* **kiwanos**) a tropical fruit with a spiky orange skin.

kiwi *noun* **1** a flightless New Zealand bird with a long bill and no tail. **2** (**Kiwi**) a New Zealander; a New Zealand national rugby league representative. **3** the New Zealand dollar. **4** (**Kiwi**) New Zealand English, *He speaks broad Kiwi.* **5** a kiwifruit. **Kiwi** *adjective, Kiwi ingenuity, a Kiwi accent.* [Māori]

Kiwiana *noun* things associated uniquely with New Zealand history and society.

kiwifruit *noun* a fruit with a brown hairy skin and bright green flesh.

Kiwiland *noun* (*informal*) New Zealand.

kleptomania *noun* an uncontrollable tendency to steal things. **kleptomaniac** *noun* [from Greek *kleptes* = thief, + *mania*]

km/h *abbreviation* kilometres per hour.

knack *noun* a special skill.

knacker *noun* a person who buys and slaughters horses and sells the meat and hides.

knapsack *noun* a bag carried on the back by soldiers, trampers, etc.

knave *noun* **1** (*old use*) a dishonest man; a rogue. **2** a jack in playing-cards.

knead *verb* press and stretch something soft (especially dough) with your hands.

knee *noun* the joint in the middle of the leg.

kneecap *noun* the small bone covering the front of the knee-joint.

kneel *verb* (**knelt, kneeling**) be or get yourself in a position on your knees.

knell *noun* the sound of a bell rung solemnly after a death or at a funeral.

knickerbockers *plural noun* loose-fitting short trousers gathered in at the knees.

knickers *plural noun* a woman's or girl's underpants.

knick-knack *noun* a small ornament.

knife *noun* (*plural* **knives**) a cutting instrument consisting of a sharp blade set in a handle.

knife *verb* (**knifed, knifing**) stab with a knife.

knight *noun* **1** a man who has been given the rank that allows him to put 'Sir' before his name. **2** a piece in chess, with a horse's head. **knighthood** *noun*

knight *verb* make someone a knight.

knit *verb* (**knitted** or **knit, knitting**) make something by looping together wool or other yarn, using long needles or a machine. **knitter** *noun*, **knitting-needle** *noun*
knit your brow frown.

knob *noun* **1** the round handle of a door, drawer, etc. **2** a round projecting part. **3** a small lump. **knobbly** *adjective*, **knobby** *adjective*

knock *verb* **1** hit a thing hard or so as to make a noise. **2** produce by hitting, *knock a hole in it.* **3** (*slang*) criticise unfavourably, *Stop knocking the All Blacks!*
knock back (*informal*) **1** eat or drink quickly. **2** reject or refuse, *They knocked back our request for more staff.*
knock off (*informal*) stop working; deduct something from a price; (*slang*) steal.
knock on (in rugby) knock the ball forward with your lower arms.
knock out make a person unconscious, especially by a blow to the head.

knock *noun* the act or sound of knocking.

knock-back *noun* a rejection or refusal.

knocker *noun* a hinged metal device for knocking on a door.

knockout *noun* **1** knocking somebody out. **2** a contest in which the loser in each round has to drop out. **3** (*slang*) an amazing person or thing.

knoll *noun* a small round hill; a mound.

knot *noun* **1** a place where a piece of string, rope, or ribbon etc. is twisted round itself or another piece. **2** a tangle; a lump. **3** a round spot on a piece of wood where a branch joined it. **4** a cluster of people or things. **5** a unit for measuring the speed of ships and aircraft, equal to 1,852 metres per hour.

knot *verb* (**knotted, knotting**) **1** tie or fasten with a knot. **2** entangle.

knotty *adjective* (**knottier, knottiest**) **1** full of knots. **2** difficult; puzzling.

know *verb* (**knew, known, knowing**) **1** have something in your mind that you have learnt or discovered. **2** recognise or be familiar with a person or place, *I've known him for years.* **3** understand, *She knows how to please us.*

know-all *noun* a person who behaves as if he or she knows everything.

know-how *noun* skill; ability for a particular job.

knowing *adjective* showing that you know something, *a knowing look.*

knowingly *adverb* **1** in a knowing way. **2** deliberately.

knowledge *noun* **1** knowing. **2** all that a person knows. **3** all that is known.
to my knowledge as far as I know.

knowledgeable *adjective* well-informed. **knowledgeably** *adverb*

knuckle *noun* a joint in the finger.

knuckle *verb* (**knuckled, knuckling**)
knuckle down to buckle down to.
knuckle under be submissive.

KO *abbreviation* knockout.

koala (*say* koh-**ah**-la) *noun* an Australian animal that looks like a small bear.

koha *noun* a present or donation. [Māori]

kōhanga *noun* a kōhanga reo. [Māori]

kōhanga reo *noun* a pre-school where the teachers and children use the Māori language. [from Māori *kōhanga* = nest, + *reo* = language]

kohekohe *noun* a tree used for timber. [Māori]

kōkako *noun* a large bluish-grey forest bird. [Māori]

kōkiri *noun* a Māori group working together. [Māori *kōkiri* = go forward]

kōkopu *noun* the cockabully. [Māori]

kōkōwai *noun* a burnt red clay used in decoration. [Māori]

konaki *noun* a wooden sledge pulled by horses. [from Māori *kōneke* = sledge]

kōnini *noun* the New Zealand fuchsia or its berries. [Māori]

kookaburra *noun* a large Australian kingfisher.

Koori *noun* (*plural* **Kooris**) (*Australian*) an Aborigine.

Koran (*say* kor-**ahn**) *noun* the sacred book of Islam, written in Arabic.

kōrari *noun* the New Zealand flax. [Māori]

kōrero *noun* **1** talk or conversation. **2** a conference. [Māori]

korimako *noun* the bellbird. [Māori]

koro *noun* an elderly man, (grand)father; (used as a form of address) *kia ora, e koro.* [Māori]

koromiko *noun* a kind of shrub, hebe. [Māori]

korowai *noun* a chief's woven cloak. [Māori]

koru *noun* **1** a plant. **2** a coil shaped motif used in Māori carving and 'scroll' left out painting. [Māori]

kotahitanga *noun* **1** unity of purpose. **2** the name of a Māori political movement. [Māori]

kōtare *noun* the New Zealand kingfisher. [Māori]

kōtuku *noun* a large white heron. [Māori]

kōura *noun* a small freshwater crayfish. [Māori]

kōwhai *noun* a tree with yellow flowers. [Māori]

kremlin *noun* a citadel in a Russian city.
the Kremlin the government of Russia, in Moscow. [from Russian *kreml'*]

krill *noun* a mass of tiny shrimp-like creatures, the chief food of certain whales. [from Norwegian, = tiny fish]

kudos (*say* **kew**-doss) *noun* honour and glory. [from Greek]

kuia *noun* an elderly woman. [Māori]

kūkū *noun* the kererū. [Māori]

kūmara *noun* a sweet potato. [Māori]

kūmera a variant of **kūmara**.

kumquat *noun* a kind of fruit. [from Chinese *kam kwat* = gold orange]

kunekune *noun* **1** a popular squat and rounded breed of pig. **2** a wild pig. [Māori]

kung fu *noun* a Chinese method of self-defence, rather like karate.

kura *noun* a school.
kura kaupapa Māori a primary school where teachers and pupils speak Māori. [Māori]

kurī *noun* **1** a dog. **2** (*slang*) an unpleasant person. [Māori]

kutu *noun* a louse. [Māori]

Ll

lab *noun* (*informal*) a laboratory.

label *noun* a small piece of paper, cloth, or metal etc. fixed on or beside something to show what it is or what it costs, or its owner or destination etc.

label *verb* (**labelled**, **labelling**) put a label on something.

labial (*say* **lay**-bee-al) *adjective* of the lips. [from Latin *labia* = lips]

laboratory *noun* (*plural* **laboratories**) a room or building equipped for scientific experiments. [same origin as *labour*]

laborious *adjective* **1** needing or using much hard work. **2** explaining something at great length and with obvious effort. **laboriously** *adverb*

labour *noun* **1** hard work. **2** a task. **3** the contractions of the womb when a baby is being born.

Labour *noun* (in New Zealand and elsewhere) the Labour Party, a socialist political party.

labour *verb* **1** work hard. **2** explain something laboriously, *Don't labour the point.*
Labour Weekend (*NZ*) the weekend including Labour Day, a public holiday on the fourth Monday of October.
[from Latin *labor* = toil]

labourer *noun* a person who does hard manual work, especially outdoors.

labrador *noun* a large black or light-brown dog. [named after Labrador, a district of Canada]

laburnum *noun* a tree with hanging yellow flowers.

labyrinth *noun* a complicated arrangement of paths etc.

lace *noun* **1** net-like material with decorative patterns of holes in it. **2** a piece of thin cord or leather for fastening a shoe etc. **lacy** *adjective*

lace *verb* (**laced**, **lacing**) **1** fasten with a lace. **2** thread a cord etc. through something. **3** add spirits to a drink.

lacebark *noun* (*NZ*) a small tree with white flowers, the houhere.

lacerate *verb* (**lacerated**, **lacerating**) injure flesh by cutting or tearing it; wound. **laceration** *noun*

lachrymal (*say* **lak**-rim-al) *adjective* of tears; producing tears, *lachrymal ducts.* [from Latin *lacrima* = a tear]

lack *noun* being without something.

lack *verb* be without, *He lacks courage.*

lackadaisical *adjective* lacking vigour or determination; careless.

lackey *noun* (*plural* **lackeys**) a footman.

laconic *adjective* terse, a laconic reply. **laconically** *adverb*

lacquer *noun* a hard glossy varnish. **lacquered** *adjective*

lacrosse *noun* a game using a stick with a net on it (a *crosse*) to catch and throw a ball. [from French *la crosse* = the crosse]

lacy *adjective* of or like lace.

lad *noun* a boy; a youth.

ladder *noun* **1** a device with two upright pieces of wood or metal etc. and cross-pieces (*rungs*), for use in climbing. **2** a vertical ladder-like flaw in a stocking etc. where a stitch has become undone.

ladder *verb* cause or have a ladder in a stocking etc.

laden *adjective* carrying a heavy load.

ladle *noun* a large deep spoon with a long handle, used for lifting and pouring liquids.

ladle *verb* (**ladled**, **ladling**) lift and pour with a ladle.

lady *noun* (*plural* **ladies**) **1** a well-mannered woman. **2** a woman of good social position. **3** (in polite use) a woman. **ladylike** *adjective*, **ladyship** *noun* [from Old English *hlaefdige* = person who makes the bread (compare *lord*)]

Lady *noun* the title of a knight's wife or (in Britain) of a noblewoman.
Lady Chapel a chapel in a large church, dedicated to the Virgin Mary (**Our Lady**).

ladybird *noun* a small flying beetle, usually red with black spots.

lag[1] *verb* (**lagged**, **lagging**) go too slowly and fail to keep up with others.

lag[1] *noun* lagging; a delay.

lag[2] *verb* (**lagged**, **lagging**) wrap pipes or boilers etc. in insulating material to keep them warm.

lager (*say* **lah**-ger) *noun* a light beer.

laggard *noun* a person who lags behind.

lagoon *noun* **1** a saltwater lake separated from the sea by sandbanks or reefs. **2** a freshwater pond, especially a stagnant one. [from Latin *lacuna* a pool]

laid *past tense* of **lay**.

lain *past participle* of **lie**[2].

lair *noun* a sheltered place where a wild animal lives.

laity (*say* **lay**-it-ee) *noun* laymen.

lake *noun* a large area of water entirely surrounded by land.

lama *noun* a Buddhist priest or monk in Tibet and Mongolia. [from Tibetan *blama* = superior]

lamb *noun* **1** a young sheep. **2** meat from a lamb. **lambswool** *noun*

lamb *verb* give birth to lambs. **lambing** *noun*

lamb's fry *noun* sheep's liver as food.

lame *adjective* **1** unable to walk normally. **2** weak; not convincing, a *lame excuse*. **lamely** *adverb*, **lameness** *noun*

lament *noun* a statement, song, or poem expressing grief or regret.

lament *verb* express grief or regret about something. **lamentation** *noun* [from Latin *lamentari* = weep]

lamentable (*say* **lam**-in-ta-bul) *adjective* regrettable; deplorable.

laminated *adjective* made of layers joined together. [from Latin *lamina* = layer]

lamington *noun* a small square sponge-cake coated with chocolate and coconut. [named after Baron Lamington, Governor of Queensland 1895–1901]

lamp *noun* a device for producing light from electricity, gas, or oil. **lamplight** *noun*, **lampshade** *noun*

lamppost *noun* a tall post in a street etc., with a lamp at the top.

lamprey *noun* (*plural* **lampreys**) a small eel-like water animal.

lance *noun* a long spear.

lance *verb* (**lanced**, **lancing**) cut open with a surgeon's lancet.

lance-corporal *noun* a soldier ranking between a private and a corporal.

lancet *noun* **1** a pointed two-edged knife used by surgeons. **2** a tall narrow pointed window or arch.

lancewood *noun* a small New Zealand tree, the horoeka.

land *noun* **1** the part of the earth's surface not covered by sea. **2** the ground or soil; an area of country, *forest land*. **3** the area occupied by a nation; a country.
Land of the Long White Cloud New Zealand. [a translation of Māori *Aotearoa*]
Land Wars see **New Zealand Wars**

land *verb* **1** arrive or put on land from a ship or aircraft etc. **2** reach the ground after jumping or falling. **3** bring a fish out of the water. **4** obtain, *She landed an excellent job.* **5** arrive or cause to arrive at a certain place or position etc., *They landed up in jail.* **6** present with a problem, *He landed me with this task.*

land-agent *noun* a person whose job it is to sell land, houses, etc.

landed *adjective* **1** owning land. **2** consisting of land, *landed estates*.

landing *noun* **1** bringing or coming to land. **2** a place where people can land. **3** the level area at the top of stairs.

landing-stage *noun* a platform on which people and goods are landed from a boat.

landlord (also **landlady**) *noun* **1** a person who lets a house, room, or land to a tenant. **2** a person who looks after a public house.

landlubber *noun* (*informal*) a person who is not used to the sea.

landmark *noun* **1** an object that is easily seen in a landscape. **2** an important event in the history of something.

landowner *noun* a person who owns a large amount of land.

landscape *noun* the scenery or a picture of the countryside.
landscape gardening laying out a garden to imitate natural scenery.

landslide *noun* **1** a landslip. **2** an overwhelming victory in an election.

landslip *noun* a huge mass of soil and rocks sliding down a slope.

landward *adjective & adverb* towards the land. **landwards** *adverb*

lane *noun* **1** a narrow road. **2** a strip of road for a single line of traffic. **3** a strip of track or water for one runner, swimmer, etc. in a race.

language *noun* **1** the spoken and written means by which human beings communicate. **2** the spoken and written communication system of a particular country or people, *the Russian language, the Māori language*. **3** specialised usage, *the language of economics*. **4** any means of communication, *sign language, the language of dolphins*. **5** a system of symbols and rules for writing computer programs. [from Latin *lingua* = tongue]

languid *adjective* slow because of tiredness, weakness, or laziness. **languidly** *adverb*, **languor** *noun*

languish *verb* **1** become weak or listless and depressed; pine. **2** live in miserable conditions; be neglected.

La Niña (*say* la-**nee**-nyah) a climate change in the Pacific Ocean that brings unusually wet weather to New Zealand (the opposite of **El Niño**). [Spanish, = the (female) child]

lank *adjective* lanky; long and limp.

lanky *adjective* (**lankier**, **lankiest**) awkwardly thin and tall. **lankiness** *noun*

lanolin *noun* a kind of ointment, made of fat from sheep's wool.

lantern *noun* a transparent case for holding a light and shielding it from the wind.

lanyard *noun* a short cord for fastening or holding something.

lap[1] *noun* **1** the level place formed by the front of the legs above the knees when a person is sitting down. **2** going once round a racecourse. **3** one section of a journey, *the last lap.*

lap[1] *verb* (**lapped**, **lapping**) **1** fold or wrap round. **2** be a lap ahead of someone in a race.

lap[2] *verb* (**lapped**, **lapping**) **1** take up liquid by moving the tongue, as a cat does. **2** make a gentle splash against something, *Waves lapped the shore.*

lapel (*say* la-**pel**) *noun* a flap folded back at the front edge of a coat etc. [from *lap*[1]]

lapse *noun* **1** a slight mistake or failure, *a lapse of memory.* **2** a relapse, *a lapse into bad habits.* **3** an amount of time elapsed, *after a lapse of six months.*

lapse *verb* (**lapsed**, **lapsing**) **1** pass or slip gradually, *He lapsed into unconsciousness.* **2** be no longer valid, through not being renewed, *My insurance policy has lapsed.* [from Latin *lapsum* = slipped]

laptop *noun* a lightweight portable computer.

larceny *noun* stealing possessions.

larch *noun* (*plural* **larches**) a tall deciduous tree that bears small cones.

lard *noun* a white greasy substance prepared from pig-fat and used in cooking. **lardy** *adjective*

larder *noun* a cupboard or small room for storing food.

large *adjective* of more than the ordinary or average size; big. **largeness** *noun*
at large free to roam about, not captured, *The escaped prisoners are still at large*; in general, as a whole, *She is respected by the country at large.*

largely *adverb* to a great extent, *You are largely responsible for the accident.*

largesse (*say* lar-**jess**) *noun* money or gifts generously given.

lark[1] *noun* a small sandy-brown bird; the skylark.

lark[2] *noun* (*informal*) something amusing; a bit of fun, *We did it for a lark.*

lark[2] *verb* (*informal*) have fun; play.

larrikin *noun* (*NZ*) a hooligan.

larva *noun* (*plural* **larvae**) an insect in the first stage of its life, after it comes out of the egg. **larval** *adjective* [from Latin, = ghost, mask]

laryngitis *noun* inflammation of the larynx, causing hoarseness.

larynx (*say* **la**-rinks) *noun* (*plural* **larynxes**) the part of the throat that contains the vocal cords.

lasagne *noun* a form of pasta in wide strips or pieces; a dish with layers of this, together with mince, cheese, etc.

Laser *noun* a class of racing yacht.

laser *noun* a device that makes a very strong narrow beam of light or other electromagnetic radiation.
laser printer a machine using laser technology to print documents etc.
[from the initials of 'light amplification (by) stimulated emission (of) radiation']

lash *noun* (*plural* **lashes**) **1** a stroke with a whip etc. **2** the cord or cord-like part of a whip. **3** an eyelash. **4** (*informal*) an attempt, *Let's have a lash at that.*

lash *verb* **1** strike with a whip; beat violently. **2** move like a whip. **3** tie with cord etc., *Lash the sticks together.*

lass *noun* (*plural* **lasses**) a girl; a young woman.

lassitude *noun* tiredness; listlessness.

lasso *noun* (*plural* **lassoes**) a rope with a sliding noose at the end, used for catching cattle etc.

lasso *verb* (**lassoed**, **lassoing**) catch with a lasso. [from Spanish *lazo* = lace]

last[1] *adjective & adverb* **1** coming after all others; final. **2** latest; most recent, *last night.* **3** least likely, *She is the last person I'd have chosen.*
the last straw a final thing that makes problems unbearable.

last[1] *noun* **1** a person or thing that is last. **2** the end, *He was brave to the last.*
at last or **at long last** finally; after much delay. [originally short for *latest*]

last[2] *verb* **1** continue; go on existing or living or being usable. **2** be enough for, *The food will last us for three days.*

last[3] *noun* a block of wood or metal shaped like a foot, used in making and repairing shoes.

lasting *adjective* able to last for a long time.

lastly *adverb* in the last place; finally.

latch *noun* (*plural* **latches**) a small bar fastening a door or gate, lifted by a lever or spring. **latchkey** *noun*

latch *verb* fasten with a latch.

late *adjective & adverb* **1** after the usual or expected time. **2** near the end, *late in the afternoon.* **3** recent, *the latest news.* **4** who has died recently, *the late king.*
of late recently.
late night (*NZ*) a day when shops stay open in the evening, *late-night shopping.*

lately *adverb* recently.

latent (*say* **lay**-tent) *adjective* existing but not yet developed or active or visible, *latent heat.*

lateral *adjective* of, at, or towards the side or sides. **laterally** *adverb* [from Latin *lateris* = of a side]

lath *noun* a narrow thin strip of wood.

lathe (*say* layth) *noun* a machine for holding and turning pieces of wood while they are being shaped.

lather *noun* a mass of froth.

lather *verb* **1** cover with lather. **2** form a lather.

Latin *noun* the language of the ancient Romans.
Latin America the parts of Central and South America where the main language is Spanish or Portuguese. (These languages were developed from Latin.)
[from Latium, an ancient district of Italy including Rome]

latitude *noun* **1** the distance of a place from the equator, measured in degrees. **2** freedom from restrictions on what people can do or believe. [from Latin, = breadth]

latrine (*say* la-**treen**) *noun* a toilet in a camp or barracks etc.

latte *noun* espresso coffee with steamed milk.

latter *adjective* later, *the latter part of the year.*
the latter the second of two people or things just mentioned. (Compare *former.*)

latterly *adverb* lately; recently.

lattice *noun* a framework of crossed laths or bars with spaces between.

laud *verb* (*formal*) praise. **laudatory** (*say* **law**-dat-er-ee) *adjective* [from Latin *laudare* = to praise]

laudable *adjective* praiseworthy. **laudably** *adverb*

laugh *verb* make the sounds that show you think something is funny.

laugh *noun* an act or sound of laughing.

laughable *adjective* deserving to be laughed at.

laughter *noun* the act, sound, or manner of laughing.

launch[1] *verb* **1** send a ship from the land into the water. **2** set a thing moving by throwing or pushing it; send a rocket etc. into space. **3** start into action, *launch an attack.*

launch[1] *noun* (*plural* **launches**) the launching of a ship or spacecraft.

launch[2] *noun* (*plural* **launches**) a large motor boat.

launder *verb* wash and iron clothes etc.

laundrette *noun* a place fitted with washing-machines that people pay to use.

laundry *noun* (*plural* **laundries**) **1** a place where clothes etc. are laundered for customers. **2** clothes etc. sent to or from a laundry.

laurel *noun* an evergreen shrub with smooth shiny leaves.

lava *noun* molten rock that flows from a volcano; the solid rock formed when it cools.

lava-lava *noun* a kind of skirt worn by Pacific Islanders. [Samoan]

lavatory *noun* (*plural* **lavatories**) a toilet. [from Latin *lavare* = to wash]

lavender *noun* **1** a shrub with sweet-smelling purple flowers. **2** light-purple colour.

lavish *adjective* **1** generous. **2** plentiful. **lavishly** *adverb*, **lavishness** *noun*

lavish *verb* give generously, *They lavished praise upon him.* [from Old French *lavasse* = downpour of rain]

law *noun* **1** a rule or set of rules that everyone must obey. **2** (*informal*) the police. **3** a scientific statement of something that always happens, *the law of gravity.*

law-abiding *adjective* obeying the law.

lawcourt *noun* a room or building in which a judge hears evidence and decides whether someone has broken the law.

lawful *adjective* allowed or accepted by the law. **lawfully** *adverb*

lawless *adjective* **1** not obeying the law. **2** without proper laws, *a lawless country.* **lawlessly** *adverb*, **lawlessness** *noun*

lawn[1] *noun* an area of closely-cut grass in a garden or park.

lawn[2] *noun* very fine cotton material.

lawnmower *noun* a machine for cutting the grass of lawns.

lawsuit *noun* a dispute or claim etc. brought to a lawcourt for judgment.

lawyer *noun* an expert on law.

lax *adjective* slack; not strict, *discipline was lax.* **laxly** *adverb*, **laxity** *noun* [from Latin *laxus* = loose]

laxative *noun* a medicine that stimulates the bowels to empty.

lay[1] *verb* (**laid, laying**) **1** put something down in a particular place or way. **2** arrange things, especially for a meal, *lay the table.* **3** place, *He laid the blame on his sister.* **4** prepare; arrange, *We laid our plans.* **5** produce an egg.
lay off stop employing somebody for a while; (*informal*) stop doing something.
lay on supply; provide.
lay out arrange or prepare; knock a person unconscious; prepare a corpse for burial. [from Old English *lecgan*]

> USAGE Do not confuse *lay/laid/laying* = 'put down', with *lie/lay/lain/lying* = 'be in a flat position'. Correct uses are as follows: *Go and lie down; she went and lay down; please lay it on the floor.* 'Go and lay down' is incorrect.

lay[2] *past tense* of **lie**[2].

lay[3] *noun* (*old use*) a poem meant to be sung; a ballad. [from Old French *lai*]

lay[4] *adjective* of laymen; not belonging to the clergy or other profession, *a lay preacher; lay opinion.* [from Greek *laos* = people]

layabout *noun* a loafer; a person who lazily avoids working for a living.

lay-by *noun* (*plural* **lay-bys**) **1** (*NZ*) reserving something you want to buy, by paying a deposit and then making regular payments. **2** (in Britain) a place where vehicles can stop beside a main road.

layer *noun* a single thickness or coating.

layman *noun* (*plural* **laymen**) a person who does not have specialised knowledge or training (e.g. as a doctor or lawyer), or who is not ordained as a member of the clergy. [from *lay*[4] + *man*]

layout *noun* an arrangement of parts of something according to a plan.

laze *verb* (**lazed, lazing**) spend time in a lazy way.

lazy *adjective* (**lazier, laziest**) not wanting to work; doing little work. **lazily** *adverb*, **laziness** *noun*

LCD *abbreviation* liquid crystal display (as on a digital watch etc.).

lea *noun* (*poetic*) a meadow.

lead[1] (*say* leed) *verb* (**led, leading**) **1** take or guide, especially by going in front. **2** be winning in a race or contest etc.; be ahead. **3** be a way or route, *This path leads to the beach.* **4** play the first card in a card-game. **5** live or experience, *He leads a dull life.*

lead[1] (*say* leed) *noun* **1** the action of leading; guidance, *Give us a lead.* **2** a leading place or part or position, *She took the lead.* **3** (*NZ*) the front of a mob of sheep. **4** a strap or cord for leading a dog or other animal. **5** an electrical wire attached to something.

lead[2] (*say* led) *noun* **1** a soft heavy grey metal. **2** the writing substance (graphite) in a pencil. **lead** *adjective*

leaden (*say* **led**-en) *adjective* **1** made of lead. **2** heavy and slow. **3** lead-coloured; dark-grey, *leaden skies.*

leader *noun* a person or thing that leads; a chief. **leadership** *noun*

leaf *noun* (*plural* **leaves**) **1** a flat usually green part of a plant, growing out from its stem, branch, or root. **2** the paper forming one page of a book. **3** a very thin sheet of metal, *gold leaf.* **4** a flap that makes a table larger. **leafy** *adjective*, **leafless** *adjective*
turn over a new leaf make a fresh start and improve your behaviour.

leaflet *noun* **1** a piece of paper printed with information. **2** a small leaf.

league[1] *noun* **1** a group of people or nations who agree to work together. **2** a group of teams who compete against each other for a championship. **3** short for *rugby league.*
in league with working or plotting together.

league[2] *noun* an old measure of distance, about 5 kilometres.

leak *noun* **1** a hole or crack etc. through which liquid or gas wrongly escapes. **2** the revealing of secret information. **leaky** *adjective*

leak *verb* **1** get out or let out through a leak. **2** reveal secret information. **leakage** *noun*

lean[1] *adjective* **1** with little or no fat, *lean meat.* **2** thin, *a lean body.*

lean[2] *verb* (**leaned** or **leant, leaning**) **1** bend your body towards or over something. **2** put or be in a sloping position. **3** rest against something.

leaning *noun* a tendency or preference.

leap *verb* (**leaped** or **leapt, leaping**) jump vigorously. **leap** *noun*
leap year a year with an extra day in it (29 February).

leap-frog *noun* a game in which each player jumps with legs apart over another who is bending down.

learn *verb* (**learned** or **learnt, learning**) get knowledge or skill; find out about something.

learned (*say* **ler**-nid) *adjective* having much knowledge obtained by study.

learner *noun* a person who is learning something, especially to drive a car.

learning *noun* knowledge obtained by study.

lease *noun* **1** an agreement to allow a person to use land or a building for a fixed period of time in return for payment. **2** a leased area of land or building. **leaseholder** *noun*

lease *verb* (**leased**, **leasing**) allow or obtain the use of something by lease.

leash *noun* (*plural* **leashes**) a dog's lead.

least *adjective & adverb* very small in amount etc., *the least bit; the least expensive bike.*

least *noun* the smallest amount etc.

leather *noun* material made from animal skins. **leathery** *adjective*

leatherjacket *noun* any of several New Zealand and Australian fish with tough skins.

leave *verb* (**left**, **leaving**) **1** go away from a person or place. **2** stop belonging to a group. **3** cause or allow something to stay where it is or as it is, *You left the door open.* **4** go away without taking something, *I left my book at home.* **5** put something to be collected or passed on, *leave a message.*
leave off cease.
leave out omit; not include.

leave *noun* **1** permission. **2** official permission to be away from work; the time for which this permission lasts.

leaven (*say* **lev**-en) *noun* a substance (e.g. yeast) used to make dough rise.

lechery *noun* excessive sexual desire. **lecherous** *adjective*

lectern *noun* a stand to hold a Bible or other large book or notes for reading. [same origin as lecture]

lecture *noun* **1** a talk about a subject to an audience or a class. **2** a long serious warning or rebuke.

lecture *verb* (**lectured**, **lecturing**) give a lecture. **lecturer** *noun* [from Latin *lectum* = read]

led *past tense* of **lead**[1].

ledge *noun* a narrow shelf or similar projecting part.

ledger *noun* an account-book.

lee *noun* the sheltered side or part of something, away from the wind.

leech *noun* (*plural* **leeches**) a small blood-sucking worm that lives in water.

leek *noun* a white vegetable rather like an onion, with broad leaves.

leer *verb* look at someone in an insulting, sly, or unpleasant way. **leer** *noun*

leeward *adjective* on the lee side.

leeway *noun* **1** drift to leeward or off course. **2** extra space or time available.
make up leeway make up lost time; regain a lost position.

left[1] *adjective & adverb* of or on or towards the left-hand side.
left hand the hand that most people use less than the other, on the same side of the body as the heart. **left-hand** *adjective*
left-handed *adjective* using the left hand in preference to the right hand.

left[1] *noun* **1** the left-hand side or part etc. **2** (**Left**) the left wing of a political party or other group. [the word originally meant 'weak']

left[2] *past tense* of **leave**.

leftovers *plural noun* food not eaten.

left wing *noun* **1** the more socialist side of a political party or system. **2** (rugby etc.) the left-hand side of the field; a player positioned there. **left-wing** *adjective*, **left-winger** *noun*

leg *noun* **1** each of the projecting parts of a person's or animal's body, on which it stands or moves. **2** the part of a garment covering a leg. **3** each of the projecting supports of a chair or other piece of furniture. **4** one part of a journey. **5** one of a pair of matches between the same teams. **6** (*NZ*) one of the horse-races making up a double or treble etc.

legacy *noun* (*plural* **legacies**) something left to a person in a will.

legal *adjective* **1** lawful. **2** of the law or lawyers. **legally** *adverb*, **legality** *noun* [from Latin *legis* = of a law]

legalise *verb* (**legalised**, **legalising**) make a thing legal. **legalisation** *noun*

legate *noun* an official representative, especially of the pope.

legend *noun* an old story handed down from the past. **legendary** *adjective* (Compare *myth.*) [from Latin *legenda* = things to be read]

leggings *plural noun* an outer covering for each leg.

legible *adjective* clear enough to read. **legibly** *adverb*, **legibility** *noun* [from Latin *legere* = to read]

legion *noun* **1** a division of the ancient Roman army. **2** a group of soldiers or former soldiers.

legislate *verb* (**legislated**, **legislating**) make laws. **legislation** *noun*, **legislator** *noun* [from Latin *legis* = of a law, + *latio* = proposing]

legislative *adjective* making laws, *a legislative assembly.*

legislature *noun* a country's legislative assembly (parliament).

legitimate *adjective* **1** lawful. **2** born when parents are married to each other. **legitimately** *adverb*, **legitimacy** *noun*

leisure *noun* time that is free from work, when you can do what you like. **leisured** *adjective*, **leisurely** *adjective*
at leisure having leisure; not hurried.
at your leisure when you have time.

lemming *noun* a small mouse-like animal of Arctic regions that migrates in large numbers and is said to run headlong into the sea and drown.

lemon *noun* **1** an oval yellow citrus fruit with a sour taste. **2** pale-yellow colour.

lemonade *noun* a lemon-flavoured drink.

lemonwood *noun* (*NZ*) a small tree with scented leaves, the tarata.

lemur (*say* **lee**-mer) *noun* a monkey-like animal.

lend *verb* (**lent, lending**) **1** allow a person to use something of yours for a short time. **2** provide someone with money that they must repay, usually in return for payments (called *interest*). **lender** *noun*
lend a hand help somebody.

length *noun* **1** how long something is. **2** a piece of cloth, rope, wire, etc. cut from a larger piece. **3** the amount of thoroughness in an action, *They went to great lengths to make us comfortable.*
at length after a long time; taking a long time; in detail.

lengthen *verb* make or become longer.

lengthways or **lengthwise** *adverb* from end to end; along the longest part.

lengthy *adjective* very long; long and boring. **lengthily** *adverb*

lenient (*say* **lee**-nee-ent) *adjective* merciful; not severe. **leniently** *adverb*, **lenience** *noun* [from Latin *lenis* = gentle]

lens *noun* (*plural* **lenses**) **1** a curved piece of glass or plastic used to focus things. **2** the transparent part of the eye, immediately behind the pupil.

Lent *noun* a time of fasting and penitence observed by Christians for about six weeks before Easter. **Lenten** *adjective*

lent *past tense* of **lend**.

lentil *noun* a kind of small bean.

leopard (*say* **lep**-erd) *noun* a large lion-like spotted wild animal, also called a panther. **leopardess** *noun*

leotard (*say* **lee**-o-tard) *noun* a close-fitting garment worn by acrobats and dancers.

leper *noun* a person who has leprosy.

lepidopterous *adjective* of the group of insects that includes butterflies and moths.

leprechaun (*say* **lep**-rek-awn) *noun* (in Irish folklore) an elf who looks like a little old man. [from Irish, = a small body]

leprosy *noun* an infectious disease that makes parts of the body waste away. **leprous** *adjective*

lesbian *noun* a homosexual woman.

less *adjective & adverb* smaller in amount; not so much, *Make less noise. It is less important.*

less *noun* a smaller amount.

less *preposition* minus; deducting, *She earned $500, less tax.*

lessen *verb* make or become less.

lesser *adjective* not so great as the other, *the lesser evil.*

lesson *noun* **1** an amount of teaching given at one time. **2** something to be learnt by a pupil. **3** an example or experience from which you should learn, *Let this be a lesson to you!* **4** a passage from the Bible read aloud as part of a church service.

lest *conjunction* so that something should not happen, *Remind us, lest we forget.*

let *noun* an obstruction of the ball or player in tennis, squash, etc., requiring play to be restarted.

let *verb* (**let, letting**) **1** allow to do something; not prevent; not forbid, *Let me see it.* **2** cause to, *Let us know what happens.* **3** allow or cause to come or go or pass, *Let me out!* **4** allow someone to use a house or building etc. in return for payment (*rent*). **5** leave, *Let it alone.*
let down deflate; disappoint somebody.
let off cause to explode; excuse somebody from a duty or punishment etc.
let up (*informal*) relax. **let-up** *noun*

lethal (*say* **lee**-thal) *adjective* deadly; causing death. **lethally** *adverb*

lethargy (*say* **leth**-er-jee) *noun* extreme lack of energy or vitality; sluggishness. **lethargic** (*say* lith-**ar**-jik) *adjective*

letter *noun* **1** a symbol representing a sound used in speech. **2** a written message, usually sent by post. [from Latin *littera* = letter of the alphabet]

lettering *noun* letters drawn or painted.

lettuce *noun* a garden plant with broad crisp leaves eaten as salad.

leukaemia (*say* lew-**kee**-mee-a) *noun* a disease in which there are too many white corpuscles in the blood. [from Greek *leukos* white, + *haima* = blood]

level *adjective* **1** flat; horizontal. **2** at the same height or position etc. as others.
level crossing a place where a road crosses a railway at the same level.

level *noun* **1** height, depth, position, or value etc., *Fix the shelves at eye level.* **2** a level surface. **3** a device that shows whether something is level.
on the level (*informal*) honest.

level *verb* (**levelled, levelling**) **1** make or become level. **2** aim a gun or missile. **3** direct an accusation at a person. [from Latin *libra* = balance]

lever *noun* **1** a bar that turns on a fixed point (the *fulcrum*) in order to lift something or force something open. **2** a bar used as a handle to operate machinery etc., *a gear-lever.*

lever *verb* lift or move by means of a lever. [from Latin *levare* = raise]

leverage *noun* **1** the action or power of a lever. **2** influence.

leveret *noun* a young hare.

levitation *noun* rising into the air and floating there.

levity *noun* being humorous, especially at an unsuitable time; frivolity. [from Latin *levis* = lightweight]

levy *verb* (**levied**, **levying**) **1** impose or collect a tax or other payment by the use of authority or force. **2** enrol, *levy an army.* **levy** *noun*

lewd *adjective* indecent; obscene. **lewdly** *adverb*, **lewdness** *noun*

lexical *adjective* of or relating to words.

lexicography *noun* the process of writing dictionaries. **lexicographer** *noun* [from Greek *lexis* = word, + *-graphy*]

liability *noun* (*plural* **liabilities**) **1** being liable. **2** a debt or obligation. **3** (*informal*) a disadvantage; a handicap.

liable *adjective* **1** likely to do or get something, *She is liable to colds. The cliff is liable to crumble.* **2** legally responsible for something.

liaise (*say* lee-**ayz**) *verb* (**liaised**, **liaising**) (*informal*) act as a liaison or go-between.

liaison (*say* lee-**ay**-zon) *noun* **1** communication and co-operation between people or groups. **2** a person who is a link or go-between. [from French *lier* = bind]

liar *noun* a person who tells lies.

libel (*say* **ly**-bel) *noun* an untrue written, printed, or broadcast statement that damages a person's reputation. (Compare *slander.*) **libellous** *adjective*

libel *verb* (**libelled**, **libelling**) make a libel against someone. [from Latin *libellus* = little book]

liberal *adjective* **1** giving generously. **2** given in large amounts. **3** not strict; tolerant. **liberally** *adverb*, **liberality** *noun* [from Latin *liber* = free]

liberalise *verb* (**liberalised**, **liberalising**) make less strict. **liberalisation** *noun*

liberate *verb* (**liberated**, **liberating**) set free. **liberation** *noun*, **liberator** *noun* [same origin as *liberty*]

liberty *noun* freedom.
take liberties behave too casually; be presumptuous.
[from Latin *liber* = free]

librarian *noun* a person in charge of or assisting in a library. **librarianship** *noun*

library (*say* **ly**-bra-ree) *noun* (*plural* **libraries**) **1** a place where books are kept for people to use or borrow. **2** a collection of books, records, films, etc. [from Latin *libri* = books]

libretto *noun* (*plural* **librettos**) the words of an opera or other long musical work. [Italian, = little book]

lice *plural* of **louse**.

licence *noun* **1** an official permit to do or use or own something, *a driver's licence.* **2** special freedom to avoid the usual rules or customs. [from Latin *licere* = be allowed]

license *verb* (**licensed**, **licensing**) give a licence to a person; authorise. *We are licensed to sell tobacco.*

licensee *noun* a person who holds a licence, especially to sell alcohol.

licentious (*say* ly-**sen**-shus) *adjective* breaking the rules of conduct; immoral. **licentiousness** *noun*

lichee (*say* **ly**-chee) *noun* (*plural* **lichees**) a small fleshy fruit with a brown skin.

lichen (*say* **ly**-ken or **lich**-en) *noun* a dry-looking plant that grows on rocks, walls, trees, etc.

lick *verb* **1** pass the tongue over something. **2** (of a wave or flame) move like a tongue; touch lightly. **3** (*slang*) defeat.

lick *noun* **1** the act of licking. **2** a slight application of paint etc. **3** (*NZ*) a block of salt etc. for animals to lick. **4** (*slang*) a fast pace.

lid *noun* **1** a cover for a box or pot etc. **2** an eyelid.

lie[1] *noun* a statement that the person who makes it knows to be untrue.

lie[1] *verb* (**lied**, **lying**) tell a lie or lies; be deceptive.

lie[2] *verb* (**lay**, **lain**, **lying**) **1** be or get in a flat or resting position, *He lay on the grass. The cat has lain here all night.* **2** be or remain, *The island lies near the coast. The machinery lay idle.*
lie low keep yourself hidden.

USAGE See the note on **lay**[1].

lie[2] *noun* the way something lies, *the lie of the land.*

liege (*say* leej) *noun* (*old use*) a person entitled to receive feudal service or allegiance (*a liege lord*) or bound to give it (*a liege man*).

lieu (*say* lew) *noun* **in lieu** instead, *He accepted a cheque in lieu of cash.* [French, = place]

lieutenant (*say* lef-**ten**-ant or loo-**ten**-ant) *noun* **1** an officer in the army or navy. **2** a deputy or chief assistant. [from French *lieu* = place, + *tenant* = holding]

life *noun* (*plural* **lives**) **1** the ability to function and grow; the period between birth and death. **2** living things, *Is there life on Mars?* **3** liveliness, *full of life.* **4** a biography.

lifebelt *noun* a circle of material that will float, used to support someone's body in water.

lifeboat *noun* a boat for rescuing people at sea.

lifebuoy *noun* a device to support someone's body in water.

lifeguard *noun* someone whose job is to rescue swimmers in difficulty.

life-jacket *noun* a jacket of material that will float, used to support someone's body in water.

lifeless *adjective* **1** without life. **2** unconscious. **lifelessly** *adverb*

lifelike *adjective* looking exactly like a real person or thing.

lifelong *adjective* continuing for the whole of someone's life.

lifesaver *noun* **1** (*NZ*) a lifeguard working at a beach; a surf-lifesaver. **2** (*informal*) something that keeps you from having problems, *a fridge is a real lifesaver in hot weather.*

lifetime *noun* the time for which someone is alive.

lift *verb* **1** raise; pick up. **2** rise; go upwards. **3** (*informal*) steal. **4** remove; abolish, *The ban has been lifted.*

lift *noun* **1** the act of lifting. **2** a device for taking people or goods from one floor or level to another in a building. **3** a free ride in somebody else's vehicle.

lift-off *noun* the vertical take-off of a rocket or spacecraft.

ligament *noun* a piece of the tough flexible tissue that holds bones etc. together. [from Latin *ligare* = bind]

ligature *noun* a thing used in tying something, especially in surgical operations. [from Latin *ligare* = bind]

light[1] *noun* **1** radiation that stimulates the sense of sight and makes things visible. **2** something that provides light, especially an electric lamp. **3** a flame.
bring or **come to light** make or become known.
come to light with (*NZ*) produce.

light[1] *adjective* **1** full of light; not dark. **2** pale, *light blue.*

light[1] *verb* (**lit** or **lighted**, **lighting**) **1** start a thing burning; kindle. **2** provide the light.
light up put lights on, especially at dusk; make or become light or bright.

USAGE Say *He lit the lamps; the lamps were lit* (not 'lighted'), but *She carried a lighted torch* (not 'a lit torch').

light[2] *adjective* **1** having little weight; not heavy. **2** small in amount or force etc., *light rain; a light punishment.* **3** needing little effort, *light work.* **4** cheerful, not sad, *with a light heart.* **5** not serious or profound, *light music.* **6** small in quantity and easy to digest, *a light meal.* **7** low in fat, cholesterol, sugar, or alcohol. **8** in short supply. **lightly** *adverb*, **lightness** *noun*
light industry industry producing small or light articles.

light[2] *adverb* lightly; with only a small load, *We were travelling light.*

lighten[1] *verb* **1** make or become lighter or brighter. **2** produce lightning.

lighten[2] *verb* make or become lighter or less heavy.

lighter *noun* **1** a device for lighting cigarettes etc. **2** a flat-bottomed boat that carries goods between a ship and a wharf.

light-hearted *adjective* cheerful; free from worry; not serious.

lighthouse *noun* a tower with a bright light at the top to guide or warn ships.

lighting *noun* lamps, or the light they provide.

lightning *noun* a flash of bright light produced by natural electricity during a thunderstorm.
lightning conductor a metal rod or wire fixed on a building to divert lightning into the earth.
like lightning with very great speed.

lightweight *noun* **1** a person who is not heavy. **2** a boxer weighing less than 60 kilograms. **lightweight** *adjective*

light-year *noun* the distance that light travels in one year (about 9.5 million million kilometres).

like[1] *verb* (**liked**, **liking**) **1** think a person or thing is pleasant or satisfactory. **2** wish, *I should like to come.*

like[2] *adjective* similar; having some or all of the qualities of another person or thing, *They are as like as two peas.*

like[2] *noun* a similar person or thing, *We shall not see his like again.*

like[2] *preposition* **1** similar to; in the manner of, *He swims like a fish.* **2** in a suitable state for, *It looks like rain.*

likeable *adjective* easy to like; pleasant.

likelihood *noun* being likely; probability.

likely *adjective* (**likelier**, **likeliest**) **1** probable; expected to happen or be true etc., *Rain is likely*. **2** expected to be successful, *a likely lad*.

liken *verb* compare, *He likened the human heart to a pump*.

likeness *noun* (*plural* **likenesses**) **1** being like; a resemblance. **2** a portrait.

likewise *adverb* similarly.

liking *noun* a feeling that you like something, *She has a liking for ice-cream*.

lilac *noun* **1** a bush with fragrant purple or white flowers. **2** pale purple.

lilt *noun* a light pleasant rhythm. **lilting** *adjective*

lily *noun* (*plural* **lilies**) a garden plant with trumpet-shaped flowers, growing from a bulb.

limb *noun* **1** a leg, arm, or wing. **2** a projecting part, e.g. a bough of a tree.
out on a limb isolated; stranded.

limber *verb* **limber up** exercise in preparation for an athletic activity.

limbo *noun* an intermediate state where nothing is happening, *Lack of money has left our plans in limbo*. [from the name of a region formerly thought to exist on the border of hell]

lime[1] *noun* a white substance (calcium oxide) used in making cement and as a fertiliser.

lime[2] *noun* a green fruit like a small round lemon. **lime-juice** *noun*

lime[3] *noun* a tree with yellow flowers.

limelight *noun* great publicity. [from *lime*[1] which gives a bright light when heated, formerly used to light up the stage of a theatre]

limerick *noun* a type of comical poem with five lines. [named after Limerick, a town in Ireland]

limestone *noun* a kind of rock from which lime (calcium oxide) is obtained.

limit *noun* **1** a line, point, or level where something ends. **2** the greatest amount allowed, *the speed limit*.

limit *verb* **1** keep within certain limits. **2** be a limit to something. **limitation** *noun* [from Latin *limes* = boundary]

limited *adjective* **1** kept within limits; restricted; small. **2** that is a **limited company** or **limited liability company**, a business company whose members would have to pay only some of its debts, *'Ltd' after the name of a business shows that it is a limited company*.

limo *noun* (*informal*) a limousine.

limousine (*say* lim-oo-**zeen**) *noun* a luxurious car.

limp[1] *verb* walk lamely.

limp[1] *noun* a limping walk.

limp[2] *adjective* **1** not stiff or firm. **2** without strength or energy. **limply** *adverb*, **limpness** *noun*

limpet *noun* a small shellfish that attaches itself firmly to rocks.

limpid *adjective* (of liquids) clear; transparent. **limpidity** *noun*

linchpin *noun* a pin passed through the end of an axle to keep a wheel in position.

line[1] *noun* **1** a long thin mark. **2** a row or series of people or things; a row of words. **3** a length of rope, string, wire, etc. used for a special purpose, *a fishing-line*. **4** a telephone connection, *Please hold the line*. **5** a railway; a line of railway track. **6** a system of ships, aircraft, buses, etc. **7** a way of doing things or behaving; a type of business. **8** (*NZ*) a group of farm stock for exhibition or sale. **9** a group of products of the same type for sale.
in line forming a straight line; conforming.
on line (of a computer) connected to a database; (of a database) able to be accessed.

line[1] *verb* (**lined**, **lining**) **1** mark with lines, *Use lined paper*. **2** form into a line or lines, *Line them up*. [from Latin *linea* = linen thread]

line[2] *verb* (**lined**, **lining**) cover the inside of something. [from *linen* (used for linings)]

lineage (*say* **lin**-ee-ij) *noun* ancestry; a line of descendants from an ancestor.

lineal (*say* **lin**-ee-al) *adjective* of or in a line, especially as a descendant.

linear (*say* **lin**-ee-er) *adjective* **1** of a line; of length. **2** arranged in a line.

linen *noun* **1** cloth made from flax. **2** shirts, sheets, and tablecloths etc. (which were formerly made of linen). [from Latin *linum* = flax]

line-out *noun* (in rugby union) parallel lines of the forwards of each team, formed at right-angles to the touch-line.

liner *noun* a large ship on a regular route, usually carrying passengers.

ling *noun* an edible fish like an eel.

linger *verb* stay for a long time, as if unwilling to leave; be slow to leave.

lingerie (*say* **lon**-zher-ray) *noun* women's underwear. [from French *linge* = linen]

linguist *noun* **1** a specialist in linguistics. **2** a person able to speak foreign languages. [from Latin *lingua* = language]

linguistics *noun* the study of languages. **linguistic** *adjective*

liniment *noun* embrocation.

lining *noun* a layer that covers the inside of something. (Compare *line*[2].)

link *noun* **1** one ring or loop of a chain. **2** a connection. **3** contact between two places, *rail link, satellite link.* **4** a connection between one Internet website and another.

link *verb* join things together; connect. **linkage** *noun*

links *noun* or *plural noun* a golf-course, especially one by the sea.

linnet *noun* a kind of finch.

lino *noun* linoleum.

linocut *noun* a print made from a design cut into a block of thick linoleum.

linoleum *noun* a stiff shiny floor-covering. [from Latin *linum* = flax, + *oleum* = oil]

linseed *noun* the seed of flax, from which oil is obtained. [from Latin *linum* = flax, + *seed*]

lint *noun* a soft material for covering wounds.

lintel *noun* a horizontal piece of wood or stone etc. above a door or other opening.

lion *noun* a large strong flesh-eating animal found in Africa and India. **lioness** *noun*

lip *noun* **1** either of the two fleshy edges of the mouth. **2** the edge of something hollow, such as a cup or crater. **3** a projecting part at the top of a jug etc., shaped for pouring things.

lip-reading *noun* understanding what a person says by watching the movements of his or her lips, not by hearing.

lip-service *noun* **pay lip-service to something** say that you approve of it but do nothing to support it.

lipstick *noun* a stick of a waxy substance for colouring the lips.

liquefy *verb* (**liquefied, liquefying**) make or become liquid. **liquefaction** *noun*

liqueur (*say* lik-**yoor**) *noun* a strong sweet alcoholic drink. [French, = liquor]

liquid *noun* a substance (such as water or oil) that flows freely but is not a gas.

liquid *adjective* **1** in the form of a liquid; flowing freely. **2** easily converted into cash, *the firm's liquid assets.* **liquidity** *noun* [from Latin *liquidus* = flowing]

liquidate *verb* (**liquidated, liquidating**) **1** pay off or settle a debt. **2** close down a business and divide its value between its creditors. **3** get rid of, especially by killing. **liquidation** *noun*, **liquidator** *noun*

liquidise *verb* (**liquidised, liquidising**) cause to become liquid; crush into a liquid pulp. **liquidiser** *noun*

liquor *noun* **1** alcoholic drink. **2** juice produced in cooking; liquid in which food has been cooked.

liquorice *noun* **1** a black substance used in medicine and as a sweet. **2** the plant from whose root this substance is obtained. [from Greek *glykys* = sweet, + *rhiza* = root]

lisp *noun* a fault in speech in which *s* and *z* are pronounced like *th*. **lisp** *verb*

list¹ *noun* a number of names, items, or figures etc. written or printed one after another.
list vote (also **party vote**) (*NZ*) one of the two votes a person casts in a general election, for a political party not an individual candidate. Parties have ranked lists from which some MPs are drawn in proportion to each party's share of the list vote. (Compare *electorate vote.*)

list¹ *verb* make a list of people or things. [from Old English *liste* = border]

list² *verb* (of a ship) lean over to one side; tilt. **list** *noun* [origin unknown]

listen *verb* pay attention in order to hear something. **listener** *noun*

listless *adjective* too tired to be active or enthusiastic. **listlessly** *adverb*, **listlessness** *noun* [from an old word *list* = desire, + *-less*]

lit *past tense* of **light**¹.

litany *noun* (*plural* **litanies**) a formal prayer with fixed responses.

literacy *noun* being literate; the ability to read and write.

literal *adjective* meaning exactly what is said, not metaphorical or exaggerated; precise. **literally** *adverb* [same origin as *letter*]

literary (*say* **lit**-er-er-i) *adjective* of literature; interested in literature.

literate *adjective* able to read and write. [same origin as *letter*]

literature *noun* books and other writings, especially those considered to have been written well. [same origin as *letter*]

lithe *adjective* flexible; supple; agile.

litigant *noun* a person who is involved in a lawsuit. [from Latin *litigare* = start a lawsuit]

litigation *noun* a lawsuit; the process of carrying on a lawsuit.

litmus *noun* a blue substance that is turned red by acids and can be turned back to blue by alkalis.
litmus-paper *noun* paper stained with litmus.

litre *noun* a unit of volume for liquids, equal to one cubic decimetre.

litter *noun* **1** rubbish or untidy things left lying about. **2** straw etc. put down as bedding for animals. **3** the young animals born to one mother at one time. **4** a kind of stretcher. **5** granular material for use by cats etc. as an indoor toilet.

litter *verb* **1** make a place untidy with litter. **2** spread straw etc. for animals.

little *adjective* (**less, least**) small in amount or size or intensity etc.; not great or big or much.
little by little gradually; by a small amount at a time.

little *adverb* not much, *I eat very little.*

little theatre *noun* a non-professional, community, or repertory theatre association.

littlie *noun* (*NZ, slang*) a child.

liturgy *noun* (*plural* **liturgies**) a fixed form of public worship used in churches. **liturgical** *adjective*

live (rhymes with *give*) *verb* (**lived, living**) **1** have life; be alive; stay alive. **2** have your home, *She lives in Mangere.* **3** pass your life in a certain way, *He lived as a hermit.*
live on use something as food; depend on for your living.

live (rhymes with *hive*) *adjective* **1** alive. **2** burning, *live coals.* **3** carrying electricity. **4** broadcast while it is actually happening, not from a recording.
live wire a wire carrying electricity; a forceful energetic person.

livelihood *noun* a living (= *living*[3]).

lively *adjective* (**livelier, liveliest**) full of life or action vigorous and cheerful. **liveliness** *noun*

liven *verb* make or become lively, *liven things up.*

liver *noun* **1** a large organ of the body, found in the abdomen, that processes digested food and produces bile. **2** an animal's liver used as food.

livery stables a place where horses are kept for their owner or where horses may be hired.

livestock *noun* farm animals.

livid *adjective* **1** bluish-grey, *a livid bruise.* **2** (*informal*) furiously angry.

living *noun* **1** being alive. **2** the way that a person lives, *a good standard of living.* **3** a way of earning money or providing enough food to support yourself.

living room *noun* a sitting room for general or everyday use.

lizard *noun* a reptile with a rough or scaly skin, four legs, and a long tail.

llama (*say* **lah**-ma) *noun* a South American animal with woolly fur, like a camel but with no hump.

LMVD *abbreviation* (*NZ*) Licensed Motor Vehicle Dealer.

lo *interjection* (*old use*) see, behold.

load *noun* **1** something carried; a burden. **2** the quantity that can be carried. **3** the total amount of electric current supplied. **4** (*informal*) a large amount, *It's a load of nonsense.*

load *verb* **1** put a load in or on something. **2** fill heavily. **3** weight with something heavy, *loaded dice.* **4** put a bullet or shell into a gun; put a film into a camera. **5** enter data etc. into a computer.

loader *noun* a vehicle with a scoop for moving earth.

loading *noun* the electric current delivered to, or taken up by, an appliance.

loaf[1] *noun* (*plural* **loaves**) **1** a shaped mass of bread baked in one piece. **2** minced or chopped meat etc. moulded into an oblong shape. **3** (*slang*) the head, *Use your loaf.* [from Old English *hlaf*]

loaf[2] *verb* spend time idly; loiter or stand about. **loafer** *noun*

loam *noun* rich soil containing clay, sand, and decayed leaves etc. **loamy** *adjective*

loan *noun* **1** something lent, especially money. **2** lending; being lent, *These books are on loan from the library.*

loan *verb* lend.

USAGE Many people dislike the use of this verb except when it means to lend money. (It is really better to use *lend* in all cases.)

loanword *noun* a word adopted by one language from another, *'Pākehā' is a loanword from Māori.*

loath (rhymes with *both*) *adjective* unwilling, *I was loath to go.*

loathe (rhymes with *clothe*) *verb* (**loathed, loathing**) feel great hatred and disgust for something; detest. **loathing** *noun*

loathsome *adjective* arousing a feeling of loathing; detestable.

lob *verb* (**lobbed, lobbing**) send a ball in a high curve into the air.

lob *noun* a lobbed ball.

lobby *noun* (*plural* **lobbies**) **1** an entrance-hall. **2** a group who lobby Members of Parliament etc.

lobby *verb* (**lobbied, lobbying**) try to influence a Member of Parliament etc. in favour of a special interest.

lobe *noun* a rounded fairly flat part of a leaf or an organ of the body; the rounded soft part at the bottom of an ear. **lobar** *adjective*, **lobed** *adjective*

lobster *noun* **1** a large shellfish with eight legs and two long claws. **2** (*NZ*) a crayfish.

local *adjective* belonging to a particular place or a small area. **locally** *adverb*
local anaesthetic an anaesthetic affecting only the part of the body where it is applied.

local government the organisation of the affairs of a city or district by people elected by those who live there.

local *noun* **1** someone who lives in a particular district. **2** (*informal*) a pub close to one's home. **3** short for *local anaesthetic.* [from Latin *locus* = place]

localise *verb* (**localised, localising**) keep something within a particular area. **localisation** *noun*

locality *noun* (*plural* **localities**) a district; a location.

locate *verb* (**located, locating**) **1** discover where something is, *locate the electrical fault.* **2** situate something in a particular place, *The cinema is located in Queen Street.*

location *noun* **1** the place where something is situated. **2** discovering where something is; locating.
on location filmed in natural surroundings, not in a studio.

loch *noun* a lake in Scotland.

lock[1] *noun* **1** a fastening that is opened with a key or other device. **2** a section of a canal or river fitted with gates and sluices so that boats can be raised or lowered to the level beyond each gate. **3** a wrestling-hold that keeps an opponent's arm or leg from moving. **4** the distance that a vehicle's front wheels can be turned by the steering-wheel. **5** (in rugby) a player in the second row of the scrum.
lock, stock, and barrel completely.

lock[1] *verb* **1** fasten or secure by means of a lock. **2** store away securely. **3** become fixed in one place; jam.

lock[2] *noun* a clump of hair.
locks *plural noun* the hair of the head.

locker *noun* a small cupboard or compartment where things can be stowed safely.

locket *noun* a small ornamental case for holding a portrait or lock of hair etc., worn on a chain round the neck.

locksmith *noun* a person whose job is to make and mend locks.

locomotive *noun* a railway engine.

locomotive *adjective* of movement or the ability to move, *locomotive power.* **locomotion** *noun* [from Latin *locus* = place, + *motivus* = moving]

locum *noun* a doctor or member of the clergy who takes the place of another who is temporarily away. [short for Latin *locum tenens* = person holding the place]

locus (*say* **loh**-kus) *noun* (*plural* **loci**, *say* **loh**-sy) **1** the exact place of something. **2** (in geometry) the path traced by a moving point, or made by points placed in a certain way. [Latin, = place]

locust *noun* a kind of grasshopper that travels in large swarms which eat all the plants in an area.

locution *noun* a word or phrase. [from Latin *locutum* = spoken]

lodestone *noun* a kind of stone that can be used as a magnet.

lodge *noun* **1** a small house at a gate. **2** a ski hut or fishing lodge. **3** a large, exclusive hotel.

lodge *verb* (**lodged, lodging**) **1** stay somewhere as a lodger. **2** provide a person with somewhere to live temporarily. **3** deposit; be or become fixed, *The ball lodged in the tree.* **lodging-house** *noun*
lodge a complaint complain formally.

lodger *noun* a person who pays to live in another person's house.

lodgings *plural noun* a room or rooms (not in a hotel) rented for living in.

loft *noun* a room or storage-space under the roof of a house or barn etc.

lofty *adjective* **1** tall. **2** noble. **3** haughty. **loftily** *adverb*, **loftiness** *noun*

log[1] *noun* **1** a large piece of a tree that has fallen or been cut down; a piece cut off this. **2** a detailed record of a ship's voyage, aircraft's flight, etc. kept in a **logbook.**
log cabin a hut built of logs.
log of wood (*NZ, informal*) the Ranfurly Shield.

log[1] *verb* (**logged, logging**) **1** fell trees for timber. **2** enter facts in a logbook.
log in (or **on**), **log out** (or **off**) connect and disconnect a terminal correctly to or from a computer system.

log[2] *noun* a logarithm, *log tables.*

loganberry *noun* (*plural* **loganberries**) a dark-red fruit like a blackberry.

logarithm *noun* one of a series of numbers set out in tables which make it possible to do sums by adding and subtracting instead of multiplying and dividing. [from Greek *logos* = reckoning, + *arithmos* = number]

loggerheads *plural noun* **at loggerheads** arguing; quarrelling.

logic *noun* **1** reasoning; a system of reasoning. **2** the principles used in designing a computer; the circuits involved in this. [from Greek *logos* = word, reason]

logical *adjective* using logic; reasoning or reasoned correctly. **logically** *adverb*, **logicality** *noun*

logo (*say* **loh**-goh) *noun* (*plural* **logos**) a printed symbol used by a business company etc. as its emblem.

-logy *suffix* forming nouns meaning a subject of study (e.g. *biology*). [from Greek *-logia* = study]

loin *noun* the side and back of the body between the ribs and the hip-bone.

loincloth *noun* a piece of cloth worn round the hips as a garment.

loiter *verb* linger or stand about idly. **loiterer** *noun*

loll *verb* lean lazily against something.

lolly *noun* (*plural* **lollies**) (*informal*) **1** (*NZ*) a sweet. **2** (*slang*) money.
lolly scramble (*NZ*) throwing lollies into a group of children for them to catch.

lone *adjective* solitary. [from *alone*]

lonely *adjective* (**lonelier**, **loneliest**) **1** sad because you are on your own. **2** solitary. **3** far from inhabited places; not often visited or used, *a lonely road.*
loneliness *noun* [from *lone*]

lonesome *adjective* lonely.

long[1] *adjective* **1** measuring a lot or a certain amount from one end to the other. **2** taking a lot of time, *a long holiday.* **3** having a certain length, *The river is 50 kilometres long.*
long acre (*NZ*) (in the country) the grass verge between the roadway and a fence.
long division dividing one number by another and writing down all the calculations.

long[1] *adverb* **1** for a long time, *Have you been waiting long?* **2** at a long time before or after, *They left long ago.* **3** throughout a time, *all night long.*
as long as or **so long as** provided that; on condition that.

long[2] *verb* feel a strong desire.

longevity (*say* lon-**jev**-it-ee) *noun* long life. [from Latin *longus* = long, + *aevum* = age]

longhand *noun* ordinary writing, contrasted with shorthand or typing.

longing *noun* a strong desire.

longitude *noun* the distance east or west, measured in degrees, from the Greenwich meridian.

longitudinal *adjective* **1** of longitude. **2** of length; measured lengthwise.

long-life *adjective* that lasts or remains usable for a long time.

long-line *noun* (*NZ*) a long fishing line with many hooks. **long-lining** *noun*

long-suffering *adjective* putting up with things patiently.

long-winded *adjective* talking or writing at great length.

loo *noun* (*informal*) a toilet.

loofah *noun* a rough sponge made from a dried gourd. [from Arabic *lufa*]

look *verb* **1** use your eyes; turn your eyes in a particular direction. **2** face in a particular direction. **3** have a certain appearance; seem, *You look sad.*
look after protect; attend to somebody's needs; be in charge of something.
look down on despise.
look forward to be waiting eagerly for something you expect.
look into investigate.
look out be careful.
look up search for information about something; improve in prospects, *Things are looking up.*
look up to admire or respect.

look *noun* **1** the act of looking; a gaze or glance. **2** appearance, *I don't like the look of this place.*

looker-on *noun* (*plural* **lookers-on**) a spectator; someone who sees what happens but takes no part in it.

looking-glass *noun* a glass mirror.

lookout *noun* **1** looking out or watching for something. **2** a place from which you can keep watch. **3** a person whose job is to keep watch. **4** a future prospect, *It's a poor lookout for us.* **5** (*informal*) a person's own concern, *If he wastes his money, that's his lookout.*

loom[1] *noun* an apparatus for weaving cloth.

loom[2] *verb* appear suddenly; seem large or close and threatening, *An iceberg loomed up through the fog.*

loony *adjective* (**loonier**, **looniest**) (*slang*) crazy. [short for *lunatic*]

loop *noun* the shape made by a curve crossing itself; a piece of string, ribbon, wire, etc. made into this shape.
in the loop (*informal*) having access to information.

loop *verb* **1** make into a loop. **2** enclose in a loop.

loophole *noun* **1** a way of avoiding a law or rule or promise etc. without actually breaking it. **2** a narrow opening in the wall of a fort etc.

loose *adjective* **1** not tight; slack; not firmly fixed, *a loose tooth.* **2** not tied up or shut in, *There's a lion loose!* **3** not packed in a box or packet etc. **4** not exact, *a loose translation.*
loosely *adverb*, **looseness** *noun*
loose forward (rugby union) a player on the side of the scrum.
at a loose end with nothing to do.

loose *verb* (**loosed**, **loosing**) **1** loosen. **2** untie; release.

loose-leaf *adjective* with each leaf or page removable, *a loose-leaf notebook.*

loosen *verb* make or become loose or looser.

loosie *noun* (*NZ, informal*) a loose forward.

loot *noun* stolen things; goods taken from an enemy.

loot *verb* **1** rob a place or an enemy, especially in a time of war or disorder. **2** take as loot.
looter *noun*

lop *verb* (**lopped**, **lopping**) cut away branches or twigs; cut off.

lope *verb* (**loped**, **loping**) run with a long jumping stride. **lope** *noun*

lop-eared *adjective* with drooping ears.

lopsided *adjective* with one side lower than the other; uneven.

loquacious (*say* lok-**way**-shus) *adjective* talkative. **loquacity** (*say* lok-**wass**-it-ee) *noun* [from Latin *loqui* = speak]

loquat (*say* **loh**-kwot) *noun* a kind of reddish-yellow fruit.

lord *noun* **1** a nobleman, especially one who is allowed to use the title 'Lord' in front of his name. **2** a master or ruler. **lordly** *adjective*, **lordship** *noun*
Our Lord Jesus Christ.
the Lord God.

lord *verb* domineer; behave in a masterful way, *lording it over the whole club.* [from Old English *hlaford* = person who keeps the bread (compare *lady*)]

lore *noun* a set of traditional facts or beliefs, *ghost lore.* [from *learn*]

lorgnette (*say* lorn-**yet**) *noun* a pair of spectacles held on a long handle.

lorikeet *noun* any of various kinds of small brightly coloured Australian parrots.

lorry *noun* (*plural* **lorries**) (*chiefly British*) a truck (sense 1).

lose *verb* (**lost**, **losing**) **1** be without something that you once had, especially because you cannot find it. **2** be deprived of something; fail to keep or obtain, *We lost control.* **3** be defeated in a contest or argument etc. **4** cause the loss of, *That fall lost us the game.* **5** (of a clock or watch) become behind the correct time. **loser** *noun*
be lost or **lose your way** not know where you are or which is the right path.
lose it (*informal*) lose control.
lose your life be killed.
lost cause an idea or policy etc. that is failing.

loss *noun* (*plural* **losses**) **1** losing something. **2** something lost.
be at a loss be puzzled; not know what to do or say.

lot *noun* **1** a number of people or things. **2** one of a set of objects used in choosing or deciding something by chance, *We drew lots to see who should go first.* **3** a person's share or fate. **4** something for sale at an auction. **5** a piece of land.
the lot or **the whole lot** everything; all. [from Old English *hlot* = share]

loth *adjective* loath.

lotion *noun* a liquid for putting on the skin.

lottery *noun* (*plural* **lotteries**) a way of raising money by selling numbered tickets and giving prizes to people who hold winning numbers, which are chosen by a method depending on chance (compare *lot* 2).

Lotto *noun* (*NZ*) a national lottery in which monetary prizes are given to those who select on a card some or all of the same numbers as those drawn from the set of 1 to 40.

lotus *noun* (*plural* **lotuses**) a kind of tropical water-lily.

loud *adjective* **1** easily heard; producing much noise. **2** unpleasantly bright; gaudy, *loud colours.* **loudly** *adverb*, **loudness** *noun*

loudspeaker *noun* a device that changes electrical impulses into sound.

lounge *noun* a sitting-room.

lounge *verb* (**lounged**, **lounging**) sit or stand lazily; loll.

louring (rhymes with *flowering*) *adjective* looking dark and threatening, *a louring sky.*

louse *noun* (*plural* **lice**) a small insect that lives as a parasite on animals or plants.

lousy *adjective* (**lousier**, **lousiest**) **1** full of lice. **2** (*slang*) very bad.

lout *noun* a bad-mannered man.

lovable *adjective* easy to love.

love *noun* **1** great liking or affection. **2** sexual affection or passion. **3** a loved person; a sweetheart. **4** (in games) no score; nil.
in love feeling strong love.

love *verb* (**loved**, **loving**) feel love for a person or thing. **lover** *noun*, **lovingly** *adverb*

loveless *adjective* without love.

lovelorn *adjective* pining with love, especially when abandoned by a lover.

lovely *adjective* (**lovelier**, **loveliest**) **1** beautiful. **2** (*informal*) very pleasant or enjoyable. **loveliness** *noun*

lovesick *adjective* languishing with love.

low[1] *adjective* not high. **lowness** *noun*

low[1] *adverb* at or to a low level or position etc., *The plane was flying low.*

low[2] *verb* moo like a cow.

lower *adjective & adverb* less high.
lower case letters in printing or typing that are not capitals.

lower *verb* make or become lower.

lowest common denominator *noun* a group of people with the least understanding or sense of aesthetics.

lowlands *plural noun* low-lying country.
lowland *adjective*, **lowlander** *noun*

lowly *adjective* (**lowlier**, **lowliest**) humble. **lowliness** *noun*

loyal *adjective* always firmly supporting your friends or group or country etc. **loyally** *adverb*, **loyalty** *noun*

loyalist *noun* a person who is loyal to the government during a revolt.

lozenge *noun* **1** a small flavoured tablet, especially as medicine. **2** a diamond shape.

LPG *abbreviation* liquefied petroleum gas.

LSD *abbreviation* lysergic acid diethylamide, an illegal drug.

Ltd. *abbreviation* limited.

LTSA *abbreviation* (*NZ*) Land Transport Safety Authority.

lubricant *noun* a lubricating substance.

lubricate *verb* (**lubricated**, **lubricating**) oil or grease something so that it moves smoothly. **lubrication** *noun* [from Latin *lubricus* = slippery]

lucerne *noun* a plant rather like clover, used for fodder.

lucid *adjective* **1** clear and easy to understand. **2** sane. **lucidly** *adverb*, **lucidity** *noun* [from Latin *lucidus* = bright]

luck *noun* **1** the way things happen without being planned; chance. **2** good fortune, *It will bring you luck.*

luckless *adjective* unlucky.

lucky *adjective* (**luckier**, **luckiest**) having or bringing or resulting from good luck. **luckily** *adverb*

lucrative (*say* **loo**-kra-tiv) *adjective* profitable; producing much money.

lucre (*say* **loo**-ker) *noun* (*contemptuous*) money. [from Latin *lucrum* = profit]

ludicrous *adjective* ridiculous. **ludicrously** *adverb*

ludo *noun* a game played with dice and counters on a board. [Latin, = I play]

lug[1] *verb* (**lugged**, **lugging**) drag or carry something heavy.

lug[2] *noun* an ear-like part on an object, by which it may be carried or fixed.

luge *noun* (*say* loo*zh*) a light toboggan, ridden while sitting or lying on one's back.

luggage *noun* suitcases and bags etc. holding things for taking on a journey.

lugger *noun* a small sailing-ship.

lugubrious (*say* lug-**oo**-bree-us) *adjective* dismal. **lugubriously** *adverb* [from Latin *lugubris* = mourning]

lukewarm *adjective* **1** only slightly warm; tepid. **2** not very enthusiastic. [from *luke* = tepid, + *warm*]

lull *verb* soothe or calm; send to sleep.

lull *noun* a short period of quiet or inactivity.

lullaby *noun* (*plural* **lullabies**) a song that is sung to send a baby to sleep.

lumbago *noun* pain in the muscles of the loins. [from Latin *lumbus* = loin]

lumbar *adjective* of the loins.

lumber *noun* **1** unwanted furniture etc.; junk. **2** (*American*) timber.

lumber *verb* **1** encumber. **2** fill up space with junk. **3** move in a heavy clumsy way.

lumberjack *noun* (*American*) a person whose job is to cut or carry timber.

luminescent *adjective* giving out light. **luminescence** *noun* [from Latin *lumen* = light]

luminous *adjective* glowing in the dark. **luminosity** *noun* [from Latin *lumen* = light]

lump[1] *noun* **1** a solid piece of something. **2** a swelling. **lumpy** *adjective*
lump sum a single payment, especially one paid all at once rather than by instalments.

lump[1] *verb* put things together as being similar; deal with things together.

lump[2] *verb* **lump it** (*informal*) put up with something you dislike.

lunacy *noun* (*plural* **lunacies**) insanity; madness. [from *lunatic*]

lunar *adjective* of the moon.
lunar month the period between new moons; four weeks. [from Latin *luna* = moon]

lunatic *noun* an insane person. **lunatic** *adjective* [from Latin *luna* = moon (because formerly people were thought to be affected by changes of the moon)]

lunch *noun* (*plural* **lunches**) a meal eaten in the middle of the day. **lunch** *verb*

luncheon *noun* (*formal*) lunch.

lung *noun* either of the two parts of the body, in the chest, used in breathing.

lunge *verb* (**lunged**, **lunging**) thrust the body forward suddenly. **lunge** *noun*

lupin *noun* a garden plant with tall spikes of flowers.

lurch[1] *verb* stagger; lean suddenly to one side. **lurch** *noun*

lurch[2] *noun* **leave somebody in the lurch** leave somebody in difficulties.

lure *verb* (**lured**, **luring**) tempt a person or animal into a trap; entice. **lure** *noun*

lurid (*say* **lewr**-id) *adjective* **1** in very bright colours; gaudy. **2** sensational and shocking, *the lurid details of the murder.* **luridly** *adverb*, **luridness** *noun*

lurk *verb* wait where you cannot be seen.

luscious (*say* **lush**-us) *adjective* delicious. **lusciously** *adverb*, **lusciousness** *noun*

lush *adjective* **1** growing thickly and strongly, *lush grass.* **2** luxurious. **lushly** *adverb,* **lushness** *noun*

lush *noun* (*informal*) a habitual drinker.

lust *noun* powerful desire. **lustful** *adjective*

lustre *noun* brightness; brilliance. **lustrous** *adjective* [from Latin *lustrare* = illuminate]

lusty *adjective* (**lustier, lustiest**) strong and vigorous. **lustily** *adverb,* **lustiness** *noun*

lute *noun* a musical instrument rather like a guitar.

lux *verb* (*NZ*) use a vacuum cleaner. [abbreviation of *Electrolux,* a brand of vacuum cleaner]

luxuriant *adjective* growing abundantly.

luxuriate *verb* (**luxuriated, luxuriating**) enjoy something as a luxury, *luxuriating in the warm sunshine.*

luxury *noun* (*plural* **luxuries**) **1** something expensive that you enjoy but do not really need. **2** expensive and comfortable surroundings. **luxurious** *adjective,* **luxuriously** *adverb* [from Latin *luxus* = plenty]

lying *present participle* of **lie**[1] and **lie**[2].

lymph (*say* limf) *noun* a colourless fluid from the flesh or organs of the body, containing white blood-cells. **lymphatic** *adjective* [from Latin *lympha* = water]

lynch *verb* join together to execute or punish someone violently without a proper trial. [named after William Lynch, an American judge who allowed this kind of punishment in about 1780]

lynx *noun* (*plural* **lynxes**) a wild animal like a very large cat with thick fur and very sharp sight.

lyre *noun* an ancient musical instrument like a small harp, popular in Europe in the 14th–17th centuries.

lyric (*say* **li**rrik) *noun* **1** a short poem that expresses thoughts and feelings. **2** the words of a song. **lyrical** *adjective,* **lyrically** *adverb* [from *lyre*]

Mm

MA *abbreviation* Master of Arts.

ma *noun* (*slang*) mother. [short for *mama*]

macabre (*say* mak-**ahbr**) *adjective* gruesome.

macadam *noun* layers of broken stone rolled flat to make a firm road-surface. **macadamised** *adjective* [named after a Scottish engineer, J. McAdam]

macadamia *noun* an Australian rainforest tree bearing an edible nut; this nut.

macaroni *noun* pasta formed into tubes.

macaroon *noun* a small sweet cake or biscuit made with ground almonds.

macaw *noun* a brightly coloured parrot.

mace *noun* an ornamental staff carried or placed in front of an official.

mach (*say* mahk) *noun* **mach number** the ratio of the speed of a moving object to the speed of sound, *mach one is the speed of sound.* [named after the Austrian scientist Ernst Mach]

machete (*say* ma-**shet**-ee) *noun* a broad heavy knife used as a tool or weapon.

machiavellian (*say* mak-ee-a-**vel**-ee-an) *adjective* very cunning or deceitful. [named after an Italian statesman, Niccolo dei Machiavelli (1469–1527)]

machinations (*say* mash-in-**ay**-shonz) *plural noun* clever schemes or plots.

machine *noun* something with parts that work together to do a job.

machine *verb* (**machined**, **machining**) make something with a machine. [from Greek *mechane* = device]

machine-gun *noun* a gun that can keep firing bullets quickly one after another.

machinery *noun* **1** machines. **2** mechanism. **3** an organised system for doing something.

macho (*say* **mach**-oh) *adjective* showing off masculine strength. [Spanish, = male]

mackerel *noun* (*plural* **mackerel**) a sea-fish used as food.

mackintosh *noun* (*plural* **mackintoshes**) (*British*) a raincoat.

macrocarpa *noun* an evergreen Californian tree used in New Zealand to form a hedge or wind-break.

macron *noun* a mark over a long vowel (as in *Māori*). [from Greek *makros* = long]

mad *adjective* (**madder**, **maddest**) **1** having something wrong with the mind; insane. **2** extremely foolish. **3** very keen, *He is mad about football.* **4** (*informal*) very excited or annoyed. **madly** *adverb*, **madness** *noun*, **madman** *noun*
like mad (*informal*) with great speed, energy, or enthusiasm.

madam *noun* a word used when speaking politely to a woman, *Can I help you, madam?* [from French *ma dame* = my lady]

madcap *noun* a wildly impulsive person.

madden *verb* make a person mad or angry.

madonna *noun* a picture or statue of the Virgin Mary. [from Old Italian *ma donna* = my lady]

madrigal *noun* a song for several voices singing different parts together.

maelstrom (*say* **mayl**-strom) *noun* a great whirlpool. [from Dutch *malen* = whirl, + *stroom* stream]

maestro (*say* **my**-stroh) *noun* (*plural* **maestros**) a master, especially a musician. [Italian, = master]

MAF *abbreviation* (*NZ*) Ministry of Agriculture and Forestry.

Mafia *noun* an organised criminal group, originating in Sicily.

magazine *noun* **1** a paper-covered publication that comes out regularly, with articles or stories etc. by a number of writers. **2** the part of a gun that holds the cartridges. **3** a store for weapons and ammunition or for explosives. **4** a device that holds film for a camera or slides for a projector. [from Arabic *makhazin* = storehouses]

magenta (*say* ma-**jen**-ta) *noun* a colour between bright red and purple. [named after Magenta, a town in north Italy, where Napoleon III won a battle in the year when the dye was discovered (1859)]

maggot *noun* the larva of some kinds of fly. **maggoty** *adjective*

Magi (*say* **mayj**-I) *plural noun* the 'wise men' from the East who brought offerings to the infant Jesus at Bethlehem.

magic *noun* the art or pretended art of making things happen by secret or unusual powers. **magic** *adjective*, **magical** *adjective*, **magically** *adverb*

magician *noun* a person who is skilled in magic; a wizard.

magisterial *adjective* **1** of a magistrate. **2** masterful; full of authority; imperious. [same origin as *magistrate*]

magistrate *noun* (British, and formerly in New Zealand) an official who hears and judges minor cases in a local court. [from Latin *magister* = master]

magma *noun* a molten substance beneath the earth's crust.

magnanimous (*say* mag-**nan**-im-us) *adjective* generous and forgiving; not petty-minded. **magnanimously** *adverb*, **magnanimity** *noun* [from Latin *magnus* = great, + *animus* mind]

magnate *noun* a wealthy influential person, especially in business. [from Latin *magnus* = great]

magnesia *noun* a white powder that is a compound of magnesium, used in medicine.

magnesium *noun* a silvery-white metal that burns with a very bright flame.

magnet *noun* a piece of iron or steel etc. that can attract iron and that points north and south when it is hung up. **magnetism** *noun*

magnetic *adjective* having the powers of a magnet. **magnetically** *adverb*
magnetic tape a plastic strip coated with a magnetic substance for recording sound.

magnetise *verb* (**magnetised**, **magnetising**) **1** make into a magnet. **2** attract like a magnet. **magnetisation** *noun*

magneto (*say* mag-**neet**-oh) *noun* (*plural* **magnetos**) a small electric generator using magnets. [from *magnet*]

magnificent *adjective* **1** grand or splendid in appearance etc. **2** excellent. **magnificently** *adverb*, **magnificence** *noun* [same origin as *magnify*]

magnify *verb* (**magnified**, **magnifying**) **1** make something look or seem bigger than it really is. **2** (*old use*) praise, *My soul doth magnify the Lord*. **magnification** *noun*, **magnifier** *noun*
magnifying glass a lens that magnifies things.
[from Latin *magnus* = great, *facere* = make]

magnitude *noun* **1** largeness; size. **2** importance. [from Latin *magnus* = great]

magnolia *noun* a tree with large white or pale-pink flowers.

magnum *noun* a large bottle containing about 1.5 litres of wine or spirits. [Latin, = large thing]

magpie *noun* a noisy bird with black and white feathers.

maharajah *noun* the title of certain Indian princes. [Hindi, = great rajah]

mah-jong *noun* a Chinese game for four people, played with pieces called tiles.

māhoe *noun* a small bushy tree with whitish bark. [Māori]

mahogany *noun* a hard brown wood.

maid *noun* **1** a female servant. **2** (*old use*) a girl. **maidservant** *noun*

maiden *noun* (*old use*) a girl. **maidenhood** *noun*

maiden *adjective* **1** not married, *a maiden aunt*. **2** first, *a maiden voyage*.
maiden name a woman's family name before she married.
maiden over a cricket over in which no runs are scored.

mail[1] *noun* **1** letters or parcels etc. sent by post. **2** e-mail.
mail order ordering goods by post.

mail[1] *verb* send by post or by e-mail.

mail[2] *noun* armour made of metal rings joined together, *a suit of chain-mail*.

mailbox *noun* a box into which mail is delivered at your home, or one you put letters into for collection by the postal service.

mailman *noun* (*plural* **mailmen**) a postman.

maim *verb* injure a person so that part of his or her body is useless.

maimai *noun* (*NZ*) a hide for duck-shooters. [from Aboriginal *mia-mia* = hut]

main *adjective* principal; most important; largest.
main trunk (*NZ*) the railway line between Auckland and Wellington.

main *noun* **1** the main pipe or cable in a public system carrying water, gas, or (usually called **mains**) electricity to a building. **2** (*old use*) the seas, *Drake sailed the Spanish main*.

mainframe *noun* a large computer.

mainland *noun* the main part of a country or continent, not the islands round it.
the Mainland (*NZ, informal*) the South Island. **Mainlander** *noun*

mainly *adverb* chiefly; almost completely.

mainmast *noun* the principal mast of a sailing ship.

mainstay *noun* the chief support.

mainstream *verb* include all students in a single general education system, or all patients in a single general hospital.

maintain *verb* **1** cause something to continue; keep in existence. **2** keep a thing in good condition. **3** provide money for a person to live on. **4** state that something is true. **maintenance** *noun*

maire *noun* a New Zealand tree with dark brown wood. [Māori]

maize *noun* a tall cereal plant with large seeds on cobs.

majestic *adjective* stately and dignified; imposing. **majestically** *adverb*

majesty *noun* (*plural* **majesties**) **1** the title of a king or queen, *Her Majesty the Queen.* **2** being majestic.

major *adjective* **1** greater; very important, *major roads.* **2** of the musical scale that has a semitone after the 3rd and 7th notes. (Compare *minor.*) [Latin, = larger, greater]

major *noun* **1** an army officer ranking next above a captain. **2** a student's special course or subject, *Engineering is her major.*

major *verb* to specialise in a particular subject at university.

majority *noun* (*plural* **majorities**) **1** the greatest part of a group of people or things. (Compare *minority.*) **2** the difference between numbers of votes, *She had a majority of 25 over her opponent.* **3** the age at which a person becomes an adult according to the law (now 18, formerly 21 years of age), *He attained his majority.*

make *verb* (**made, making**) **1** bring something into existence, especially by putting things together. **2** gain or earn, *She makes $50,000 a year.* **3** cause or compel, *Make him repeat it.* **4** achieve, *The swimmer just made the shore.* **5** reckon, *What do you make the time?* **6** perform an action etc., *make an effort.* **7** arrange for use, *make the beds.* **8** cause to be successful or happy, *Her visit made my day.*
make do manage with something that is not what you really want.
make for go towards.
make love have sexual intercourse.
make off go away quickly.
make out manage to see, hear, or understand something; pretend.
make up build or put together; invent a story etc.; compensate for something; put on make-up.
make up your mind decide.

make *noun* **1** making; how something is made. **2** a brand of goods; something made by a particular firm.

make-believe *noun* pretending; imagining things.

makeover *noun* a complete transformation, especially of a person's appearance and clothing.

maker *noun* the person or firm that has made something.

makeshift *adjective* improvised or used because you have nothing better, *We used a box as a makeshift table.*

make-up *noun* **1** cosmetics. **2** the way something is made up. **3** a person's character.

mako *noun* the blue pointer shark. [Māori]

makomako[1] *noun* the bellbird. [Māori]

makomako[2] *noun* a small tree with reddish flowers. [Māori]

mākutu *noun* **1** magic. **2** a magic spell. [Māori]

mal- *prefix* bad; badly (as in *malnourished*). [from Latin *male* = badly]

maladjusted *adjective* not fitting well with his or her own circumstances.

maladministration *noun* bad administration, especially of business affairs.

malady *noun* (*plural* **maladies**) an illness or disease. [from French *malade* = ill]

malapropism *noun* a comical confusion of words, e.g. using *hooligan* instead of *hurricane.* [named after Mrs Malaprop in Sheridan's play *The Rivals,* who made mistakes of this kind]

malaria *noun* a feverish disease spread by mosquitoes. **malarial** *adjective* [from Italian *mala aria* = bad air, which was once thought to cause the disease]

malcontent *noun* a discontented person.

male *adjective* **1** of the sex that reproduces by fertilising egg-cells produced by the female. **2** of men, *a male voice choir.*

male *noun* a male person, animal, or plant.

malediction (*say* mal-id-**ik**-shon) *noun* a curse. [from Latin *male* = evilly, + *diction*]

malefactor (*say* **mal**-if-ak-ter) *noun* a wrongdoer. [from Latin *male* = evilly, + *factor* = doer]

malevolent (*say* ma-**lev**-ol-ent) *adjective* wishing to harm people. **malevolently** *adverb,* **malevolence** *noun* [from Latin *male* = evilly, + *volens* = wishing]

malformed *adjective* faultily formed.

malfunction *noun* faulty functioning.

malice *noun* a desire to harm others or to tease. **malicious** *adjective,* **maliciously** *adverb* [from Latin *malus* = evil]

malign (*say* mal-**I'**n) *adjective* **1** harmful, *a malign influence.* **2** showing malice. **malignity** (*say* mal-**ig**-nit-ee) *noun*

malign *verb* say unpleasant and untrue things about somebody. [same origin as *malice*]

malignant *adjective* **1** (of a tumour) growing uncontrollably. **2** full of ill will. **malignantly** *adverb,* **malignancy** *noun*

malinger *verb* pretend to be ill in order to avoid work. **malingerer** *noun*

mall *noun* a traffic-free street, or a large covered area (especially in the suburbs), for shopping.

malleable *adjective* **1** able to be pressed or hammered into shape. **2** easy to influence; adaptable. **malleability** *noun* [from Latin *malleare* = to hammer]

mallet *noun* **1** a large hammer, usually made of wood. **2** an implement with a long handle, used in croquet or polo for striking the ball. [from Latin *malleus* = a hammer]

malnutrition *noun* not having enough food to eat. **malnourished** *adjective*

malpractice *noun* wrongdoing.

malt *noun* dried barley used in brewing, making vinegar, etc. **malted** *adjective*

maltreat *verb* ill-treat. **maltreatment** *noun*

mama *noun* (*old use*) mother.

mammal *noun* any animal of which the female can feed her babies with her own milk. **mammalian** (*say* mam-**ay**-lee-an) *adjective* [from Latin *mamma* = breast]

mammoth *noun* an extinct elephant with a hairy skin and curved tusks.

mammoth *adjective* huge. [from Russian]

man *noun* (*plural* **men**) **1** a grown-up male human being. **2** an individual person. **3** mankind. **4** a piece used in chess etc. [from Old English *mann*]

man *verb* (**manned**, **manning**) supply with people to work something, *Man the pumps!*

mana *noun* power; prestige. [Māori]

manacle *noun* a fetter or handcuff.

manacle *verb* (**manacled**, **manacling**) fasten with manacles. [from Latin *manus* = hand]

manage *verb* (**managed**, **managing**) **1** be able to do something difficult. **2** control; be in charge of a shop, factory, etc. **manageable** *adjective* [from Latin *manus* = hand]

management *noun* **1** managing. **2** managers; the people in charge.

manager *noun* a person who manages something. **manageress** *noun*, **managerial** (*say* man-a-**jeer**-ee-al) *adjective*

manaia *noun* a carved figure with a bird's head and a human body. [Māori]

Mana Party *noun* a political party established in 2011 by Hone Harawira, former member of the Maori Party.

manchester *noun* (*NZ*) cotton or linen goods. [from Manchester, an industrial city in England]

mandarin *noun* **1** an important official. **2** a kind of small orange.

mandate *noun* authority given to someone to carry out a certain task or policy, *An elected government has a mandate to govern the country.* [from Latin *mandatum* = commanded]

mandatory *adjective* obligatory; compulsory.

mandible *noun* **1** a jaw, especially the lower one. **2** either part of a bird's beak or the similar part in insects etc. (Compare *maxilla*.)

mandolin *noun* a musical instrument rather like a guitar.

mane *noun* the long hair on a horse's or lion's neck.

manful *adjective* brave. **manfully** *adverb*

manganese *noun* a hard brittle metal.

mange *noun* a skin disease of dogs etc. **mangy** *adjective*

manger *noun* a trough in a stable etc., for horses or cattle to feed from.

mangle *verb* (**mangled**, **mangling**) damage something by crushing or cutting it roughly.

mango *noun* (*plural* **mangoes**) a tropical fruit with yellow pulp.

mangrove *noun* a tropical tree growing in mud and swamps, with many tangled roots above the ground.

manhandle *verb* (**manhandled**, **manhandling**) treat or push roughly.

manhole *noun* a space or opening, usually with a cover, by which a person can get into a sewer or boiler etc. to inspect or repair it.

manhood *noun* **1** the condition of being a man. **2** manly qualities.

mania *noun* **1** violent madness. **2** great enthusiasm, *a mania for sport.* **manic** *adjective* [Greek, = madness]

maniac *noun* a person with mania.

manicure *noun* care and treatment of the hands and nails. **manicure** *verb*, **manicurist** *noun* [from Latin *manus* = hand, + *cura* = care]

manifest *adjective* clear and obvious. **manifestly** *adverb*

manifest *verb* show a thing clearly. **manifestation** *noun*

manifesto *noun* (*plural* **manifestos**) a public statement of a group's or person's policy or principles.

manifold *adjective* of many kinds; very varied. [from *many* + *-fold*]

manipulate *verb* (**manipulated**, **manipulating**) handle or arrange something cleverly or cunningly. **manipulation** *noun*, **manipulator** *noun* [from Latin *manus* = hand]

mankind *noun* human beings in general.

manky *adjective* (*slang*) dirty or smelly.

manly *adjective* suitable for a man; strong, brave. **manliness** *noun*

manner *noun* **1** the way something happens or is done. **2** a person's way of behaving. **3** sort, *all manner of timings.*
manners *plural noun* how a person behaves with other people; politeness.

mannerism *noun* a person's habit or way of doing something.

mannish *adjective* like a man.

manoeuvre (*say* man-**oo**-ver) *noun* a difficult or skilful or cunning action.

manoeuvre *verb* (**manoeuvred**, **manoeuvring**) make a manoeuvre.
manoeuvrable *adjective* [from Latin, = work by hand (*manus* = hand, *operari* = to work)]

man-of-war *noun* (*plural* **men-of-war**) a warship.

manor *noun* (*British*) a large important house (*manor house*) in the country; the land belonging to it. **manorial** *adjective*

manpower *noun* the number of people who are working or needed or available for work on something.

manse *noun* a church minister's house, especially that of a Presbyterian minister.

mansion *noun* a large stately house.

manslaughter *noun* killing a person unlawfully but without meaning to.

mantelpiece *noun* a shelf above a fireplace.

mantilla *noun* a lace veil worn by Spanish women over the hair and shoulders.

mantle *noun* a cloak.

manual *adjective* of or done with the hands, *manual work.* **manually** *adverb*

manual *noun* **1** a handbook. **2** an organ keyboard played with the hands. [from Latin *manus* = hand]

manufacture *verb* (**manufactured**, **manufacturing**) make things. **manufacture** *noun*, **manufacturer** *noun* [from Latin *manu* = by hand, + *facere* = make]

manuhiri *noun* a visitor or guest. [Māori].

mānuka *noun* a shrub with pleasant-smelling leaves. [Māori]

manure *noun* fertiliser, especially dung.

manuscript *noun* something written or typed but not printed. [from Latin *manu* = by hand, + *scriptum* = written]

many *adjective* (**more**, **most**) great in number; numerous, *many people.*

many *noun* many people or things, *Many were found.*

maomao *noun* an edible fish with blue or pink skin. [Māori]

Māori *noun* (*plural* **Māori**) **1** a member of the indigenous people of New Zealand. **2** their language. [Māori]

Māori *adjective* of or relating to Māori people, culture, or language, *Māori English, Māori land.*

Māoridom *noun* **1** the Māori world. **2** Māori culture.

Māori Party *noun* a political party established in 2004, the ideology of which is indigenous rights.

Māoritanga *noun* Māori traditions, culture, and identity.

map *noun* a diagram of part or all of the earth's surface or of the sky.

map *verb* (**mapped**, **mapping**) make a map of an area.
map out plan the details of something.

māpau *noun* a small tree with dark berries. [Māori]

maple *noun* a tree with broad leaves.

māpou *noun* = **māpau**.

mar *verb* (**marred**, **marring**) spoil.

marae *noun* **1** the courtyard in front of a Māori meeting-house. **2** the meeting-house, courtyard, and other buildings together, forming a centre for Māori gatherings.

mararī *noun* the butterfish. [Māori]

marathon *noun* a long-distance race (about 42.2 km) for runners. [named after Marathon in Greece, from which a messenger ran to Athens in 490 BC to announce that Greeks had defeated the Persian army]

marauding *adjective* going about in search of plunder or prey. **marauder** *noun* [from French *maraud* = rogue]

marble *noun* **1** a small glass ball used in games. **2** a kind of limestone polished and used in sculpture or building.

march *verb* **1** walk with regular steps. **2** make somebody walk somewhere, *He marched them up the hill.* **marcher** *noun*

march *noun* (*plural* **marches**) **1** marching. **2** music suitable for marching to. [from Latin *marcus* = hammer]

March *noun* the third month of the year.

marching girl *noun* (*NZ*) a member of a team trained to march in formation, a participant in the female sport of **marching**.

mare *noun* a female horse or donkey.
mare's nest a discovery that seems interesting but turns out to be false or worthless.

margarine (*say* mar-ja-**reen**) *noun* a substance used like butter, made from animal or vegetable fats.

marge *noun* (*informal*) margarine.

margin *noun* **1** an edge or border. **2** the blank space between the edge of a page and the writing or pictures etc. on it. **3** the difference between two scores or prices etc., *She won by a narrow margin.*

marginal *adjective* **1** of or in a margin, *marginal notes.* **2** very slight, *a marginal difference.* **marginally** *adverb*
marginal seat a seat where a Member of Parliament was elected with only a small majority and may be defeated in the next election.

marigold *noun* a yellow or orange garden flower.

marijuana (*say* ma-ri-**wah**-na) *noun* a drug made from hemp.

marina *noun* a harbour for yachts, motor boats, etc. [same origin as *marine*]

marinade *noun* a flavoured liquid in which meat or fish is soaked before being cooked.
marinade (or **marinate**) *verb*

marine (*say* ma-**reen**) *adjective* of or concerned with the sea.

marine *noun* a member of a body of troops who are trained to serve at sea as well as on land. [from Latin *mare* = sea]

mariner (*say* **ma**-rin-er) *noun* a sailor.

marionette *noun* a puppet worked by strings or wires.

Marist *noun* a member of the Society of Mary (a Roman Catholic religious order).

marital *adjective* of marriage. [from Latin *maritus* = husband]

maritime *adjective* **1** of the sea or ships. **2** found near the sea. [same origin as *marine*]

mark[1] *noun* **1** a spot, dot, line, or stain etc. on something. **2** a number or letter etc. put on a piece of work to show its quality. **3** a distinguishing feature. **4** a symbol. **5** a target; the normal standard. **6** the position from which you start a race, *On your marks!*

mark[1] *verb* **1** put a mark on something. **2** give a mark to a piece of work; correct. **3** pay attention to something, *Mark my words!* **4** keep close to an opposing player in soccer etc. **marker** *noun*
mark time march on one spot without moving forward; occupy your time without making progress.
mark up prepare a text for formatting or printing.

mark[2] *noun* a German unit of money.

marked *adjective* noticeable, *a marked improvement.* **markedly** *adverb*

market *noun* **1** a place where things are bought and sold, usually from stalls in the open air. **2** demand for things; trade.
market-place *noun*

market *verb* (**marketed**, **marketing**) offer things for sale. **marketable** *adjective* [from Latin *merx* = merchandise]

marksman *noun* (*plural* **marksmen**) an expert in shooting at a target.
marksmanship *noun*

marlin *noun* a large deep-sea fish with a long pointed snout.

marmalade *noun* jam made from oranges, lemons, or other citrus fruit.

marmoset *noun* a kind of small monkey.

maroon[1] *verb* abandon or isolate somebody in a deserted place; strand.

maroon[2] *noun* dark brownish red.

marquee (*say* mar-**kee**) *noun* a large tent used for a party or exhibition etc.

marriage *noun* **1** the state of being married. **2** a wedding.

marrow *noun* **1** a large gourd eaten as a vegetable. **2** the soft substance inside bones.

marry *verb* (**married**, **marrying**) **1** become a person's husband or wife. **2** unite a man and woman legally for the purpose of living together. [from Latin *maritus* = husband]

marsh *noun* (*plural* **marshes**) an area of very wet ground. **marshy** *adjective*

marshal *noun* **1** an official who supervises a contest or ceremony etc. **2** an officer of very high rank, *a Field Marshal.*

marshal *verb* (**marshalled**, **marshalling**) **1** arrange neatly. **2** usher; escort.
marshalling yard a railway yard where wagons are put together to form goods trains.

marshmallow *noun* a soft spongy sweet.

marsupial (*say* mar-**soo**-pee-al) *noun* an animal such as a kangaroo or wallaby. The female has a pouch on the front of its body in which its babies are carried. [from Greek *marsypion* = pouch]

martial *adjective* of war; warlike.
martial arts fighting sports, such as judo and karate.
martial law government of a country by the armed forces during a crisis.
[from Latin, = of Mars, the Roman god of war]

martin *noun* a bird rather like a swallow.

martinet *noun* a very strict person.

martyr *noun* a person who is killed or suffers because of his or her beliefs.
martyrdom *noun*

martyr *verb* kill or torment someone as a martyr. [from Greek, = witness]

marvel *noun* a wonderful thing.

marvel *verb* (**marvelled**, **marvelling**) be filled with wonder.

marvellous *adjective* wonderful.

Marxism *noun* the Communist theories of the German writer Karl Marx (1818–83). **Marxist** *noun*

marzipan *noun* a soft sweet food made of ground almonds and sugar.

mascara *noun* a cosmetic for darkening the eyelashes. [from Italian, = mask]

mascot *noun* a person, animal, or thing that is believed to bring good luck.

masculine *adjective* of or like men; suitable for men. **masculinity** *noun*

mash *verb* crush into a soft mass.

mash *noun* **1** a soft mixture of cooked grain or bran etc. **2** (*informal*) mashed potatoes.

mask *noun* a covering worn over the face to disguise or protect it.

mask *verb* **1** cover with a mask. **2** disguise; screen; conceal.

masochist (*say* **mas**-ok-ist) *noun* a person who enjoys things that seem painful or tiresome. **masochism** *noun*

Mason *noun* a Freemason.

mason *noun* a person who builds or works with stone.

masonry *noun* **1** the stone parts of a building; stonework. **2** a mason's work.

masquerade *noun* a pretence.

masquerade *verb* (**masqueraded**, **masquerading**) pretend to be something, *He masqueraded as a policeman.* [from Spanish *mascara* = mask]

mass[1] *noun* (*plural* **masses**) **1** a large amount. **2** a heap or other collection of matter. **3** (in scientific use) the quantity of matter that a thing contains. In non-scientific use this is called *weight*.
mass production manufacturing goods in large quantities. **mass-produced** *adjective*

mass[1] *verb* collect into a mass.

mass[2] *noun* (*plural* **masses**) the Communion service in a Roman Catholic church.

massacre *noun* the killing of a large number of people. **massacre** *verb*

massage (*say* **mas**-ahzh) *verb* (**massaged**, **massaging**) rub and press the body to make it less stiff or less painful. **massage** *noun*, **masseur** *noun*, **masseuse** *noun*

massive *adjective* large and heavy; huge.

mast *noun* a tall pole that holds up a ship's sails or a flag or an aerial.

master *noun* **1** a man who is in charge of something. **2** a male teacher. **3** a great artist, composer, sportsman, etc. **4** something from which copies are made. **5** (**Master**) a title put before a boy's name.
Master of Arts or **Science** a person who has taken the next degree after Bachelor of Arts or Science.

master *verb* **1** learn a subject or a skill thoroughly. **2** overcome; bring under control. [from Latin *magister* = master]

masterful *adjective* **1** domineering. **2** very skilful. **masterfully** *adverb*

masterly *adjective* very skilful.

mastermind *noun* **1** a very clever person. **2** the person who is planning and organising a scheme etc.

mastermind *verb* plan and organise a scheme etc.

masterpiece *noun* **1** an excellent piece of work. **2** a person's best piece of work.

mastery *noun* complete control or thorough knowledge or skill in something.

masticate *verb* (**masticated**, **masticating**) chew food. **mastication** *noun* [from Greek *mastichan* = gnash the teeth]

mastiff *noun* a large kind of dog.

masturbate *verb* (**masturbated**, **masturbating**) excite yourself by fingering your genitals. **masturbation** *noun*

mat *noun* **1** a small carpet; a doormat. **2** a small piece of material put on a table to protect the surface.

matador *noun* a bullfighter who fights on foot. [from Spanish *matar* = kill]

matagouri *noun* (*NZ*) a prickly shrub found in the South Island. [from Māori *tūmatakuru*]

mataī *noun* the black pine. [Māori]

matai (*say* **mah**-tie) *noun* the head of a Samoan family. [Samoan]

match[1] *noun* (*plural* **matches**) a small thin stick with a head made of a substance that gives a flame when rubbed on something rough. **matchbox** *noun*, **matchstick** *noun*

match[2] *noun* (*plural* **matches**) **1** a game or contest between two teams or players. **2** one person or thing that matches another. **3** a marriage.

match[2] *verb* **1** be equal or similar to another person or thing. **2** put teams or players to compete against each other. **3** find something that is similar or corresponding.

matchboard *noun* a piece of board that fits into a groove in a similar piece.

mate[1] *noun* **1** a companion or friend. **2** one of a mated pair. **3** an officer on a merchant ship.

mate[1] *verb* (**mated**, **mating**) **1** come or put together so as to have offspring. **2** put together as a pair or as corresponding.

mate[2] *noun & verb* (*in chess*) checkmate.

material *noun* **1** anything used for making something else. **2** cloth; fabric. [from Latin *materia* = matter]

materialise *verb* (**materialised**, **materialising**) **1** become visible; appear, *The ghost didn't materialise.* **2** become a fact; happen, *The trip did not materialise.* **materialisation** *noun*

materialism *noun* regarding possessions as very important. **materialist** *noun*, **materialistic** *adjective*

maternal *adjective* **1** of a mother. **2** motherly. **maternally** *adverb* [from Latin *mater* = mother]

maternity *noun* **1** motherhood. **2** having a baby. [same origin as *maternal*]

matey *adjective* friendly; sociable.

mathematics *noun* the study of numbers, measurements, and shapes. **mathematical** *adjective*, **mathematically** *adverb*, **mathematician** *noun*

maths *noun* (*informal*) mathematics.

matinée *noun* an afternoon performance at a theatre or cinema.

matins *noun* the church service of morning prayer. [from Latin *matutinus* = of morning]

matipo *noun* = **māpau**.

matriarch (*say* **may**-tree-ark) *noun* a woman who is head of a family or tribe. (Compare *patriarch*.) **matriarchal** *adjective*, **matriarchy** *noun* [from Latin *mater* = mother, + Greek *archein* = to rule]

matrimony *noun* marriage. **matrimonial** *adjective*

matrix (*say* **may**-triks) *noun* (*plural* **matrices**) **1** an array of mathematical quantities etc. in rows and columns. **2** a mould or other place in which a thing is shaped or enclosed. [Latin *matrix* = womb]

matron *noun* **1** a mature married woman. **2** a woman in charge of nursing in a school etc. or (formerly) of the nursing staff in a hospital. **matronly** *adjective*

matt *adjective* not shiny, *matt paint.*

matted *adjective* tangled into a mass.

matter *noun* **1** something you can touch or see, not spirit or mind or qualities etc. **2** things of a certain kind, *printed matter.* **3** something to be thought about or done, *It's a serious matter.* **4** a quantity, *in a matter of minutes.*
no matter it does not matter.
what is the matter? what is wrong?
[same origin as *material*]

matter *verb* be important.

matter-of-fact *adjective* keeping to facts; not imaginative or emotional.

matting *noun* rough material for covering floors.

mattress *noun* (*plural* **mattresses**) soft or springy material in a fabric covering, used on or as a bed.

mature *adjective* fully grown or developed; grown-up. **maturely** *adverb*, **maturity** *noun*

mature *verb* (**matured**, **maturing**) make or become mature. [from Latin *maturus* = ripe]

maudlin *adjective* sentimental in a silly or tearful way.

maul *noun* a loose scrum in rugby union, with the ball in hand and not on the ground.

maul *verb* injure by handling or clawing, *He was mauled by a lion.*

Maundy Thursday the day before Good Friday, celebrated by Christians in commemoration of the Last Supper.

mauri *noun* the life principle; the source of the emotions. [Māori]

mausoleum (*say* maw-sol-**ee**-um) *noun* a magnificent tomb. [named after the tomb of Mausolus, a king in the 4th century BC in what is now Turkey]

Maussie *noun* a Maori living in Australia. [A blend of *Māori* and *Aussie*].

mauve *noun* pale purple.

maverick *noun* a person who belongs to a group but often disagrees with its beliefs.

maw *noun* the jaws, mouth, or stomach of a hungry or fierce animal.

maxi- *prefix* very large or long, *maxiyacht.* [abbreviation of *maximum*]

maxilla *noun* (*plural* **maxillae**) the upper jaw; a similar part in a bird or insect etc. (Compare *mandible*.)

maxim *noun* a short saying giving a general truth or rule of behaviour, e.g. 'Waste not, want not.'

maximise *verb* (**maximised**, **maximising**) increase something to a maximum.

maximum *noun* (*plural* **maxima**) the greatest possible number or amount. (The opposite is *minimum*.) [Latin, = greatest thing]

May *noun* the fifth month of the year.

may[1] *auxiliary verb* (*past tense* **might**) used to express (**1**) permission (*You may go now*), (**2**) possibility (*It may be true*), (**3**) wish (*Long may she reign*), (**4**) uncertainty (*whoever it may be*).

may[2] *noun* hawthorn blossom.

maybe *adverb* perhaps; possibly.

mayday *noun* an international radio signal calling for help. [from French *venez m'aider* = come and help me]

mayfly *noun* an insect that lives for only a short time, in spring.

mayhem *noun* violent confusion or damage, *The mob caused mayhem.*

mayonnaise *noun* a creamy sauce made from eggs, oil, vinegar, etc.

mayor *noun* the person in charge of the council in a city or district. **mayoral** *adjective*, **mayoress** *noun*

maypole *noun* a decorated pole round which people dance on 1 May.

maze *noun* a network of paths, especially one designed as a puzzle in which to try and find your way.

MB or Mb *abbreviation* megabyte.

me *pronoun* the form of *I* used as the object of a verb or after a preposition.

ME *abbreviation* myalgic encephalomyelitis, an illness with symptoms resembling those of influenza and depression.

mead *noun* an alcoholic drink made from honey and water.

meadow *noun* (*chiefly British*) a field of grass.

meagre *adjective* scanty in amount.

meal[1] *noun* food served and eaten at one sitting. **mealtime** *noun*

meal[2] *noun* coarsely-ground grain. **mealy** *adjective*

meal-ticket *noun* a source of food or money.

mealy-mouthed *adjective* too polite.

mean[1] *verb* (**meant**, **meaning**) **1** have as an equivalent, *'Maybe' means 'perhaps'.* **2** have as a purpose; intend, *I mean to win.* **3** indicate, *Dark clouds mean rain.*

mean[2] *adjective* **1** not generous; miserly. **2** unkind; spiteful, *a mean trick.* **3** poor in quality or appearance, *a mean little house.* **meanly** *adverb*, **meanness** *noun*

mean[3] *noun* a middle point or condition.

mean[3] *adjective* average.

meander (*say* mee-**an**-der) *verb* take a winding course; wander. **meander** *noun* [named after the Meander, a river in Turkey]

meaning *noun* what something means. **meaningful** *adjective*, **meaningless** *adjective*

means *noun* a way of achieving something or producing a result, *We transport our goods by means of trucks.*
by all means certainly.
by no means not at all.

means *plural noun* money or other wealth.
means test an inquiry into how much money etc. a person has, in order to decide whether he or she is entitled to get help from public funds.
[from *mean*[3]]

meantime *noun* the time between two events or while something else is happening, *in the meantime.* [from *mean*[3] + *time*]

meanwhile *adverb* in the time between two events or while something else is happening. [from *mean*[3] + *while*]

measles *noun* an infectious disease that causes small red spots on the skin.

measly *adjective* (*informal*) very small.

measure *verb* (**measured**, **measuring**) **1** find how big or heavy something is by comparing it with a unit of standard size or weight. **2** be a certain size. **measurable** *adjective*, **measurement** *noun*

measure *noun* **1** a unit used for measuring, *A kilometre is a measure of length.* **2** a device used in measuring. **3** the size or quantity of something. **4** the rhythm of poetry; time in music. **5** something done for a particular purpose; a law, *We took measures to stop vandalism.*

meat *noun* animal flesh used as food. **meaty** *adjective*
meat works (*NZ*) a freezing works.

mechanic *noun* a person who uses or repairs machinery.

mechanical *adjective* **1** of machines; produced or worked by machines. **2** automatic; done or doing things without thought. **mechanically** *adverb* [from Greek *mechane* = machine]

mechanics *noun* **1** the study of movement and force. **2** the study or use of machines.

mechanised *adjective* equipped with machines. **mechanisation** *noun*

mechanism *noun* **1** the moving parts of a machine. **2** the way a machine works.

medal *noun* a piece of metal shaped like a coin, star, or cross, given to a person for bravery or for achieving something.

medallion *noun* a large medal.

medallist *noun* a winner of a medal.

meddle *verb* (**meddled**, **meddling**) **1** interfere. **2** tinker, *Don't meddle with it.* **meddler** *noun*, **meddlesome** *adjective*

media *plural* of **medium** *noun*
the media newspapers, radio, and television, which convey information and ideas to the public. (See *medium* 2.)

> USAGE This word is a plural. Say *The media are* (not 'is') *very influential.* It is incorrect to speak of one of them (e.g. television) as 'this media'.

medial *adjective* in the middle; average [*from* Latin *medius* = middle]

median *adjective* in the middle.

median *noun* **1** a median point or line. **2** a median number or position.

median-strip *noun* a narrow raised strip of ground that separates the streams of traffic going in opposite directions.

mediate *verb* (**mediated**, **mediating**) negotiate between the opposing sides in a dispute. **mediation** *noun*, **mediator** *noun* [from Latin *medius* = middle]

medic *noun* (*informal*) a doctor or medical student.

medical *adjective* connected with the treatment of disease. **medically** *adverb* [from Latin *medicus* = doctor]

medicament *noun* a medicine or ointment etc.

medicated *adjective* treated with a medicinal substance. **medication** *noun*

medicine *noun* **1** a substance, usually swallowed, used to try to cure a disease. **2** the study and treatment of diseases. **medicinal** (*say* med-**iss**-in-al) *adjective*, **medicinally** *adverb*

medieval (*say* meddy-**ee**-v'l) *adjective* of the Middle Ages. [from Latin *medius* = middle, + *aevum* = age]

mediocre (*say* mee-dee-**oh**-ker) *adjective* not very good; of only medium quality; middling. **mediocrity** *noun*

meditate *verb* (**meditated**, **meditating**) think deeply and quietly. **meditation** *noun*, **meditative** *adjective*

Mediterranean *adjective* of the Mediterranean Sea (which lies between Europe and Africa) or the countries round it. [from Latin, = sea in the middle of the earth (*media* = middle, + *terra* = land)]

medium *adjective* of middle size or degree or quality etc.; moderate.

medium *noun* (*plural* **media**) **1** a middle size or degree or quality etc. **2** a thing in which something exists, moves, or is expressed, *Air is the medium in which sound travels. Television is used as a medium for advertising.* (See *media.*) **3** (with plural **mediums**) a person who claims to be able to communicate with the dead. [Latin, = middle thing]

medley *noun* (*plural* **medleys**) an assortment or mixture of things.

meek *adjective* quiet and obedient. **meekly** *adverb*, **meekness** *noun*

meerkat *noun* a South African mongoose.

meet[1] *verb* (**met**, **meeting**) **1** come together from different places; come face to face. **2** come into contact; touch. **3** go to receive an arrival, *We will meet your train.* **4** pay a bill or the cost of something. **5** deal with a problem.

meet[1] *noun* a gathering of sportspeople, including riders and hounds for a hunt.

meet[2] *adjective* (*old use*) suitable; proper.

meeting *noun* coming together; a number of people who have come together for a discussion, contest, etc.
meeting house (*NZ*) the principal building on a marae.

meg *noun* (*informal*) a megabyte, *128 megs of RAM.*

mega- *prefix* **1** large; great (as in *megaphone*). **2** one million (as in *megahertz* = one million hertz). [from Greek *megas* = great]

megabyte *noun* (*computing*) a measure of data capacity or memory size (a million bytes).

megalomania *noun* an exaggerated idea of your own importance. **megalomaniac** *noun* [from *mega-* + *mania*]

megaphone *noun* a funnel-shaped device for amplifying a person's voice. [from *mega-*, + Greek *phone* = voice]

melamine *noun* a strong kind of plastic.

melancholy *adjective* sad; gloomy.

melancholy *noun* sadness; gloom. [from Greek *melas* = black, + *chole* = bile]

Melanesian *noun* **1** a member of the people of Melanesia (which includes Fiji). **2** their language. **Melanesian** *adjective* [from Greek *melas* = black, + *nesos* = island]

mêlée (*say* **mel**-ay) *noun* **1** a confused fight. **2** a muddle. [French, = medley]

mellow *adjective* **1** not harsh; soft and rich in flavour, colour, or sound. **2** kindly and genial. **mellowness** *noun*

mellow *verb* make or become mellow.

melodious *adjective* full of melody.

melodrama *noun* a play full of dramatic excitement and emotion. **melodramatic** *adjective* [from Greek *melos* = music, + *drama*]

melody *noun* (*plural* **melodies**) a tune, especially a pleasing tune. [from Greek *melos* = music, + *oide* song]

melon *noun* a large sweet fruit with a yellow or green skin.

melt *verb* **1** make or become liquld by heating. **2** disappear slowly. **3** soften.

member *noun* **1** a person or thing that belongs to a particular society or group. **2** a part of something. **membership** *noun* [from Latin *membrum* = limb]

membrane *noun* a thin skin or similar covering. **membranous** *adjective*

meme *noun* a cultural element or behavioural trait that mimics a gene, that passes through a population. *A hairstyle is a meme.*

memento *noun* (*plural* **mementoes**) a souvenir. [Latin, = remember]

memo (*say* **mem**-oh) *noun* (*plural* **memos**) (*informal*) a memorandum.

memoir (*say* **mem**-wahr) *noun* a biography.

memoirs *plural noun* an autobiography.

memorable *adjective* worth remembering; easy to remember. **memorably** *adverb*

memorandum *noun* (*plural* **memoranda**) a written note, especially to remind yourself of something. [from Latin, = thing to be remembered]

memorial *noun* something to remind people of a person or event, *a war memorial.* **memorial** *adjective*

memorise *verb* (**memorised**, **memorising**) get something into your memory.

memory *noun* (*plural* **memories**) **1** the ability to remember things. **2** something that you remember. **3** the part of a computer where information is stored. [from Latin *memor* = remembering]

menace *noun* **1** a threat or danger. **2** a troublesome person or thing.

menace *verb* (**menaced**, **menacing**) threaten with harm or danger.

menagerie *noun* a small zoo.

mend *verb* **1** repair. **2** make or become better, improve. **mender** *noun*

mend *noun* a repair.

mendacious (*say* men-**day**-shus) *adjective* untruthful; telling lies. **mendaciously** *adverb*, **mendacity** *noun* [from Latin *mendax* = lying]

mendicant *noun* a beggar. [from Latin *mendicans* = begging]

menial (*say* **meen**-ee-al) *adjective* lowly; needing little or no skill, *menial tasks.* **menially** *adverb*

menial *noun* a person who does menial work; a servant.

meningitis *noun* a disease causing inflammation of the membranes (*meninges*) round the brain and spinal cord.

menopause *noun* the time of life when a woman finally ceases to menstruate. [from Greek *menos* = of a month, + *pause*]

menstruate *verb* (**menstruated**, **menstruating**) bleed from the womb about once a month, as normally happens to girls and women from their teens until middle age. **menstruation** *noun*, **menstrual** *adjective* [from Latin *menstruus* = monthly]

mental *adjective* **1** of or in the mind. **2** (*informal*) mad. **mentally** *adverb* [from Latin *mentis* = of the mind]

mentality *noun* (*plural* **mentalities**) a person's mental ability or attitude.

menthol *noun* a solid white peppermint-flavoured substance. [from Latin *mentha* = mint]

mention *verb* speak or write about a person or thing briefly; refer to.

mention *noun* mentioning something.

mentor *noun* a trusted adviser; a counsellor. [from Mentor in Greek legend, who advised Odysseus' son]

menu (*say* **men**-yoo) *noun* **1** a list of the food available in a restaurant or served at a meal. **2** a list of things, shown on a screen, from which you decide what you want a computer to do.

mercantile *adjective* trading; of trade.

mercenary *adjective* working only for money or some other reward.

mercenary *noun* (*plural* **mercenaries**) a soldier hired to serve in a foreign army.

merchandise *noun* goods for sale.

merchant *noun* a person involved in trade. **merchant navy** a country's ships that are involved in commercial activity, rather than in defence or warfare.

merciful *adjective* showing mercy. **mercifully** *adverb*

merciless *adjective* showing no mercy; cruel. **mercilessly** *adverb*

mercurial *adjective* **1** of mercury. **2** having sudden changes of mood.

mercury *noun* a heavy silvery metal (also called *quicksilver*) that is usually liquid, used in thermometers. **mercuric** *adjective* [from the name of the planet Mercury]

mercy *noun* (*plural* **mercies**) **1** kindness or pity shown in not punishing or harming a wrongdoer or enemy etc. **2** something to be thankful for.

mere[1] *adjective* not more than, *He's a mere child.*

mere[2] *noun* (*poetic*) a lake.

mere[3] *noun* a war-club, usually made of greenstone. [Māori]

merely *adverb* only; simply.

merest *adjective* very small, *the merest trace of colour.*

merge *verb* (**merged**, **merging**) combine; blend. [from Latin *mergere* = dip]

merger *noun* the combining of two business companies etc. into one.

meridian *noun* a line on a map or globe from the North Pole to the South Pole. The meridian that passes through Greenwich, England, is shown on maps as 0° longitude.

meringue (*say* mer-**ang**) *noun* a crisp cake made from egg-white and sugar.

merino *noun* (*plural* **merinos**) a kind of sheep with fine soft wool.

merit *noun* a quality that deserves praise; excellence. **meritorious** *adjective*

merit *verb* (**merited**, **meriting**) deserve. [from Latin *meritum* = deserved]

mermaid *noun* a mythical sea-creature with a woman's body but with a fish's tail instead of legs. **merman** *noun* [from *mere*[2] (old word, = sea), + *maid*]

merry *adjective* (**merrier**, **merriest**) cheerful and lively. **merrily** *adverb*, **merriment** *noun*

merry-go-round *noun* a circular revolving ride at fun-fairs.

mesh *noun* **1** the open spaces in a net, sieve, or other criss-cross structure. **2** material made like a net; network.

mesh *verb* (of gears) engage.

mesmerise *verb* (**mesmerised**, **mesmerising**) hypnotise; fascinate or hold a person's attention completely. **mesmerism** *noun*

mess *noun* (*plural* **messes**) **1** a dirty or untidy condition or thing. **2** a difficult or confused situation; trouble. **3** (in the armed forces) a dining-room.
make a mess of bungle.

mess *verb* **1** make a thing dirty or untidy. **2** bungle; spoil by muddling, *They messed up our plans.*
mess about behave stupidly; potter.
mess with interfere or tinker with.

message *noun* a piece of information etc. sent from one person to another.

messenger *noun* a person who carries a message.

Messiah (*say* mis-**I**-a) *noun* **1** the saviour expected by the Jews. **2** Jesus Christ, who Christians believe was this saviour. **Messianic** *adjective* [from Hebrew, = the anointed one]

Messrs *plural* of **Mr**.

messy *adjective* dirty; untidy. **messily** *adverb*, **messiness** *noun*

metabolism (*say* mit-**ab**-ol-izm) *noun* the process by which food is built up into living material in a plant or animal, or used to supply it with energy. **metabolic** *adjective*, **metabolise** *verb* [from Greek *metabole* = change]

metal *noun* **1** a hard mineral substance (e.g. gold, silver, copper, iron) that melts when it is heated. **2** broken stones forming the bed of a railway or the surface of a road. **metallic** *adjective*

metalled *adjective* made of or mended with road-metal.

metallurgy (*say* mit-**al**-er-jee) *noun* the study of metals; the craft of making and using metals. **metallurgical** *adjective*, **metallurgist** *noun* [from *metal*, + Greek *-ourgia* = working]

metamorphic *adjective* formed or changed by heat or pressure, *Marble is a metamorphic rock.* [from Greek *meta-* = change, + *morphe* = form]

metamorphosis (*say* met-a-**mor**-fo-sis) *noun* (*plural* **metamorphoses**) a change of form or character. **metamorphose** *verb* [same origin as *metamorphic*]

metaphor *noun* using a word or phrase in a way that is not literal, e.g. 'The pictures of starving people *touched our hearts*.' **metaphorical** *adjective*, **metaphorically** *adverb* [from Greek *metapherein* = transfer]

mete *verb* (**meted**, **meting**) **mete out** deal out; allot, *mete out punishment.*

meteor (*say* **meet**-ee-er) *noun* a piece of rock or metal that moves through space and burns up when it enters the earth's atmosphere. [from Greek *meteoros* = high in the air]

meteoric (*say* meet-ee-**o**-rik) *adjective* **1** of meteors. **2** like a meteor in brilliance or sudden appearance, *a meteoric career.*

meteorite *noun* a meteor that has landed on the earth.

meteorology *noun* the study of the conditions of the atmosphere, especially in order to forecast the weather. **meteorological** *adjective*, **meteorologist** *noun* [from Greek *meteoros* = high in the air, + *-logy*]

meter *noun* a device for measuring something, e.g. the amount supplied, *a parking meter*. **meter** *verb* [from *mete*]

methamphetamine (*say* meth-am-**fet**-a-mean) *noun* a habit-forming drug that leads to violent behaviour.

methane (*say* **mee**-thayn) *noun* an inflammable gas found in marshy areas and in coal-mines.

method *noun* **1** a procedure or way of doing something. **2** methodical behaviour; orderliness. [from Greek *methodos* pursuit of knowledge]

methodical *adjective* doing things in an orderly or systematic way. **methodically** *adverb*

Methodist *noun* a member of a Christian religious group started by John and Charles Wesley in the 18th century. **Methodism** *noun*

meths *noun* (*informal*) methylated spirit.

methylated spirit or spirits *noun* a liquid fuel made from alcohol.

meticulous *adjective* very careful and exact. **meticulously** *adverb*

metre *noun* **1** the basic unit of length in the metric system. **2** rhythm in poetry. [from Greek *metron* = measure]

metric *adjective* **1** of the metric system. **2** of metre in poetry. **metrically** *adverb*
metric system a measuring system based on decimal units (the metre, litre, and gram).

metrical *adjective* of or in rhythmic metre, not prose, *metrical psalms.*

metrication *noun* changing to the metric system.

metronome *noun* a device that makes a regular clicking noise to help a person keep in time when practising music. [from Greek *metron* = measure, + *nomos* = law]

metropolis *noun* the chief city of a country or region. **metropolitan** *adjective* [from Greek *meter* = mother, + *polis* = city]

metrosexual *noun* a male who takes care with his grooming and dresses fashionably.

mettle *noun* courage; strength of character. **mettlesome** *adjective*
be on your mettle be determined to show your courage or ability.

mew *verb* make a cat's cry. **mew** *noun*

miaow *verb & noun* mew.

miasma (*say* mee-**az**-ma) *noun* unpleasant or unhealthy air. [Greek, = pollution]

mica *noun* a mineral substance used to make electrical insulators.

mickey *noun* **take the mickey** (**out of**) tease, ridicule.

mickey mouse *adjective* (*informal*) shoddy, not to be taken seriously, *that firm is a real mickey mouse outfit.* [Walt Disney cartoon character]

micro- *prefix* very small (as in *microfilm*). [from Greek *mikros* = small]

microbe *noun* a microorganism. [from *micro-*, + Greek *bios* = life]

microchip *noun* a very small piece of silicon etc. made to work like a complex wired electric circuit.

microcomputer *noun* a very small computer.

microcosm *noun* a world in miniature; something regarded as resembling something else on a very small scale. [from Greek *mikros kosmos* = little world]

microfilm *noun* a length of film on which written or printed material is photographed in greatly reduced size.

microlight *noun* a very small, light aircraft.

micro-organism *noun* a microscopic creature, e.g. a bacterium or virus.

microphone *noun* an electrical device that picks up sound waves for recording, amplifying, or broadcasting. [from *micro-*, + Greek *phone* = sound]

microprocessor *noun* a miniature computer (or a unit of this) consisting of one or more microchips.

microscope *noun* an instrument with lenses that magnify tiny objects or details. [from *micro-*, + Greek *skopein* = look at]

microscopic *adjective* **1** extremely small; too small to be seen without the aid of a microscope. **2** of a microscope.

microwave *noun* **1** a very short electromagnetic wave. **2** a microwave oven.
microwave oven an oven that uses microwaves to heat food very quickly.

mid *adjective* in the middle of; middle.

midday *noun* the middle of the day; noon.

middle *noun* **1** the place or part of something that is at the same distance from all its sides or edges or from both its ends. **2** someone's waist.

middle *adjective* **1** placed or happening in the middle. **2** moderate in size or rank etc.
Middle Ages the period in history from about the 5th to the 15th centuries.
middle class the class of people between the upper class and the working class, including business and professional people.
Middle East the countries from Egypt to Iran inclusive.
Middle English the English language from about 1100 to 1500 AD.

middleman *noun* (*plural* **middlemen**) **1** a trader who buys from a producer and sells to a consumer. **2** an intermediary.

middling *adjective & adverb* moderately good; moderately.

midge *noun* a small insect like a gnat.

midget *noun* an extremely small person or thing. **midget** *adjective*

midnight *noun* twelve o'clock at night.

midriff *noun* the front part of the body just above the waist.

midshipman *noun* (*plural* **midshipmen**) a sailor ranking next above a cadet.

midst *noun* the middle of something.

midsummer *noun* the middle of summer.

midway *adverb* half-way.

midwife *noun* (*plural* midwives) a person trained to look after a woman who is giving birth to a baby. **midwifery** *noun*

mien (*say* meen) *noun* a person's manner.

might[1] *noun* great strength or power.

might[2] *auxiliary verb* used (**1**) as the past tense of *may*[1] (*We told her she might go*), (**2**) to express possibility (*It might be true*).

mighty *adjective* very impressive or powerful. **mightily** *adverb*, **mightiness** *noun.*

mignonette (*say* min-yon-**et**) *noun* a plant with fragrant leaves.

migraine (*say* **my**-grayn or **mee**-grayn) *noun* a severe kind of headache.

migrant *noun* a person or animal that migrates or has migrated.

migrate *verb* (**migrated, migrating**) **1** leave one place or country and settle in another. **2** (of birds or animals) move periodically from one area to another. **migration** *noun*, **migratory** *adjective* [from Latin *migrare* = migrate]

mihi *verb* to greet.

mihi *noun* a greeting. [Māori]

mike *noun* (*informal*) a microphone.

mild *adjective* **1** gentle; not harsh or severe. **2** not strongly flavoured. **mildly** *adverb*, **mildness** *noun*

mildew *noun* a tiny fungus that forms a white coating on things kept in damp conditions. **mildewed** *adjective*

mile *noun* a British and American unit of distance, equivalent to about 1.61 kilometres. [from Latin *mille* = thousand (paces)]

mileage *noun* the number of miles travelled.

milestone *noun* **1** a stone of a kind that used to be fixed beside a road to mark the distance between towns. **2** an important event in life or history.

militant *adjective* eager to fight or be aggressive. **militant** *noun*, **militancy** *noun*

militarism *noun* belief in the use of military strength and methods. **militarist** *noun*, **militaristic** *adjective*

military *adjective* of soldiers or the armed forces. [from Latin *miles* = soldier]

militate *verb* (**militated, militating**) have a strong effect or influence, *The weather militated against the success of our plans.*

USAGE Do not confuse with *mitigate.*

militia (*say* mil-**ish**-a) *noun* a military force, especially one raised from civilians. [same origin as *military*]

milk *noun* **1** a white liquid that female mammals produce in their bodies to feed their babies. **2** the milk of cows, used as food by human beings. **3** a milky liquid, e.g. that in a coconut.
milk vendor (*NZ*) a milkman.

milk *verb* get the milk from a cow or other animal.

milkman *noun* (*plural* **milkmen**) a man who delivers milk to customers' houses.

milky *adjective* like milk; white.
Milky Way the broad bright band of stars formed by our galaxy.

mill *noun* **1** machinery for grinding wheat to make flour; a building containing this machinery. **2** a grinding machine, *a coffee-mill.* **4** a factory for processing certain materials, *a paper-mill.*

mill *verb* **1** grind or crush in a mill. **2** cut markings round the edge of a coin. **3** move in a confused crowd, *The animals were milling around.* **miller** *noun*

millennium *noun* (*plural* **millenniums**) a period of 1,000 years. [from Latin *mille* = thousand, + *annus* = year]

millet *noun* a kind of cereal with tiny seeds.

milli- *prefix* **1** one thousand (as in *millipede*). **2** one-thousandth (as in *milligram, millilitre, millimetre*). [from Latin *mille* thousand]

milliner *noun* a person who makes or sells women's hats. **millinery** *noun*

million *noun & adjective* one thousand thousand (1,000,000). **millionth** *adjective & noun*

millionaire *noun* a person who has a million dollars or more.

millipede *noun* a small crawling creature like a centipede, with many legs. [from Latin *mille* = thousand, + *pedes* = feet]

millstone *noun* **1** either of a pair of large circular stones between which cereal grains are ground. **2** a heavy responsibility.

milt *noun* a male fish's sperm.

mime *noun* acting with movements of the body, not using words. **mime** *verb*

mimic *verb* (**mimicked, mimicking**) imitate. **mimicry** *noun*

mimic *noun* a person who mimics others, especially to amuse people.

mimosa *noun* a tropical tree or shrub with small ball-shaped flowers.

mina *noun* = **mynah**.

minaret *noun* the tall tower of a mosque. [from Arabic *manara* = lighthouse]

mince *verb* (**minced, mincing**) **1** cut into very small pieces in a machine. **2** walk in an affected way. **mincer** *noun*
not to mince matters speak bluntly.

mince *noun* minced meat.

mincemeat *noun* a sweet mixture of currants, raisins, apple, etc. used in pies.

mince pie a pie containing mincemeat or minced meat.

mind *noun* **1** the ability to think, feel, understand, and remember, originating in the brain. **2** a person's thoughts and feelings or opinion, *I changed my mind.*

mind *verb* **1** look after, *He was minding the baby.* **2** be careful about, *Mind the step.* **3** be sad or upset about something; object to, *We don't mind waiting.* **minder** *noun*

mindful *adjective* taking thought or care, *He was mindful of his reputation.*

mindless *adjective* without intelligence.

mine[1] *possessive pronoun* belonging to me.

mine[2] *noun* **1** a place where coal, metal, precious stones, etc. are dug out of the ground. **2** an explosive placed in or on the ground or in the sea etc. to destroy people or things that come close to it.

mine[2] *verb* (**mined**, **mining**) **1** dig from a mine. **2** lay explosive mines in a place.

minefield *noun* an area where explosive mines have been laid.

miner *noun* a person who works in a mine.

mineral *noun* a hard inorganic substance found in the ground. [from Latin *minera* = ore]

mineralogy (*say* min-er-**al**-o-jee) *noun* the study of minerals. **mineralogist** *noun* [from *mineral* + *-logy*]

minestrone (*say* mini-**stroh**-nee) *noun* an Italian soup containing vegetables and pasta.

mingimingi *noun* a shrub with small green flowers and red or white berries. [Māori]

mingle *verb* (**mingled**, **mingling**) mix.

mingy *adjective* (*informal*) mean; stingy.

mini- *prefix* miniature; very small. [short for *miniature*]

miniature *adjective* very small; copying something on a very small scale.

miniature *noun* **1** a very small portrait. **2** a small-scale model.

minibus *noun* (*plural* **minibuses**) a very small bus.

minicomputer *noun* a small computer.

minim *noun* a note in music, lasting half as long as a semibreve (written h.)

minimise *verb* (**minimised**, **minimising**) reduce something to a minimum.

minimum *noun* (*plural* **minima**) the lowest possible number or amount. (The opposite is *maximum*.) **minimal** *adjective* [Latin, = least thing]

minion *noun* (*contemptuous*) a very obedient assistant or servant.

minister *noun* **1** a person in charge of a government department. **2** a member of the clergy. **ministerial** *adjective*

minister *verb* attend to people's needs. [Latin, = servant]

ministry *noun* (*plural* **ministries**) **1** a government department, *the Ministry of Education*. **2** the work of the clergy.

mink *noun* **1** an animal rather like a stoat. **2** this animal's valuable brown fur.

minnow *noun* a tiny freshwater fish.

minor *adjective* **1** less important; not very important. **2** of the musical scale that has a semitone after the second note. (Compare *major*.) [Latin, = smaller, lesser]

minor *noun* a person below the age at which she or he legally becomes an adult.

minority *noun* (*plural* **minorities**) **1** the smallest part of a group of people or things. **2** a small group that is different from others. (Compare *majority*.)

minstrel *noun* a travelling singer and musician in the Middle Ages.

mint[1] *noun* **1** a plant with fragrant leaves that are used for flavouring things. **2** peppermint; a sweet flavoured with this. [from Latin *mentha* = mint]

mint[2] *noun* the place where a country's coins are made.

mint[2] *adjective* clean and new or unused.

mint[2] *verb* make coins. [from Latin *moneta* = coins; a mint]

minuet *noun* a slow stately dance.

minus *preposition* with the next number or thing subtracted, *Ten minus four equals six* (10 – 4 = 6).

minus *adjective* less than zero, *temperatures of minus ten degrees* (–10°). [Latin, = less]

minute[1] (*say* **min**-it) *noun* **1** one-sixtieth of an hour. **2** a very short time; a moment. **3** a particular time, *Come here this minute!* **4** one-sixtieth of a degree (used in measuring angles).
minutes *plural noun* a written summary of what was said at a meeting.

minute[2] (*say* my-**newt**) *adjective* **1** very small, *a minute insect*. **2** very detailed, *a minute examination*. **minutely** *adverb* [from Latin *minutus* = little]

minx *noun* (*plural* **minxes**) a cheeky or mischievous girl.

miracle *noun* something wonderful and good that happens, especially something believed to have a supernatural or divine cause.
miraculous *adjective*, **miraculously** *adverb* [from Latin *mirari* = to wonder]

mirage (*say* **mi**-rahzh) *noun* an illusion; something that seems to be there but is not, especially when a lake seems to appear in a desert. [from French *se mirer* = be reflected]

mire *noun* swampy ground; mud.

miro[1] *noun* a timber-tree. [Māori]

miro[2] *noun* (also **miromiro**) the New Zealand tomtit. [Māori]

mirror *noun* a device or surface of reflecting material, usually glass.
mirror boy (*informal*) a male concerned with his appearance.

mirror *verb* reflect in or like a mirror. [from Latin *mirare* = look at]

mirth *noun* merriment; laughter. **mirthful** *adjective*, **mirthless** *adjective*

mis- *prefix* badly; wrongly. (Compare *amiss*.)

misadventure *noun* a piece of bad luck.

misanthropy *noun* dislike of people. **misanthropist** *noun*, **misanthropic** *adjective* [from Greek *misos* = hatred, *anthropos* = human being]

misapprehend *verb* misunderstand. **misapprehension** *noun*

misappropriate *verb* take something dishonestly. **misappropriation** *noun*

misbehave *verb* behave badly. **misbehaviour** *noun*

miscalculate *verb* calculate incorrectly. **miscalculation** *noun*

miscarriage *noun* **1** the expulsion of a foetus before it has developed enough to live. **2** failure to achieve the right result, *a miscarriage of justice.*

miscellaneous (*say* mis-el-**ay**-nee-us) *adjective* of various kinds; mixed. **miscellany** (*say* mis-**el**-an-ee) *noun* [from Latin *miscellus* = mixed]

mischance *noun* misfortune.

mischief *noun* naughty or troublesome behaviour; trouble caused by this. **mischievous** *adjective*, **mischievously** *adverb*

misconception *noun* a mistaken idea.

misconduct *noun* bad behaviour.

misconstrue *verb* (**misconstrued**, **misconstruing**) misinterpret. **misconstruction** *noun*

miscreant (*say* **mis**-kree-ant) *noun* a wrongdoer; a villain.

misdeed *noun* a wrong or improper action.

misdemeanour *noun* a misdeed; an unlawful act.

miser *noun* a person who hoards money and spends as little as possible. **miserly** *adjective*, **miserliness** *noun* [same origin as *misery*]

miserable *adjective* **1** full of misery; very unhappy, poor, or uncomfortable. **2** disagreeable; unpleasant, *miserable weather*. **miserably** *adverb*

misericord (*say* **mis**-ere-re-cord) *noun* **1** a supporting ledge beneath a choir stall. **2** an area in a monastery that allows freedom. **3** a small dagger used to kill a dying enemy. [from Latin *miserēri* = pity + *cor cordis* = heart]

misery *noun* (*plural* **miseries**) **1** great unhappiness or discomfort or suffering. **2** (*informal*) a discontented or disagree-able person. [from Latin *miser* = wretched]

misfire *verb* (**misfired**, **misfiring**) fail to fire; fail to function correctly or to have the required effect, *The joke misfired.*

misfit *noun* **1** a person who does not fit in well with other people or who is not well suited to his or her work. **2** a garment that does not fit.

misfortune *noun* bad luck; an unlucky event or accident.

misgiving *noun* a feeling of doubt or slight fear or mistrust.

misguided *adjective* mistaken.

mishap (*say* **mis**-hap) *noun* an unlucky accident.

misinterpret *verb* interpret incorrectly. **misinterpretation** *noun*

misjudge *verb* (**misjudged**, **misjudging**) judge wrongly; form a wrong opinion or estimate. **misjudgement** *noun*

mislay *verb* (**mislaid**, **mislaying**) lose something for a short time.

mislead *verb* (**misled**, **misleading**) give somebody a wrong idea; deceive.

mismanagement *noun* bad management.

misnomer *noun* an unsuitable name for something. [from *mis-*, + Latin *nomen* = name]

misogynist (*say* mis-**oj**-in-ist) *noun* a person who hates women. **misogyny** *noun* [from Greek *misos* = hatred, + *gyne* = woman]

misplace *verb* (**misplaced**, **misplacing**) place wrongly. **misplacement** *noun*

misprint *noun* a mistake in printing.

mispronounce *verb* pronounce incorrectly. **mispronunciation** *noun*

misquote *verb* (**misquoted**, **misquoting**) quote incorrectly. **misquotation** *noun*

misread *verb* read or interpret incorrectly.

misrepresent *verb* represent in a false or misleading way. **misrepresentation** *noun*

misrule *noun* bad government.

Miss *noun* (*plural* **Misses**) a title put before a girl's or unmarried woman's name. [short for *mistress*]

miss *verb* **1** fail to hit, reach, catch, see, hear, or find something. **2** be sad because someone or something is not with you. **3** notice that something has gone. [from Old English *missan*]

miss *noun* (*plural* **misses**) missing something, *Was that shot a hit or a miss?*

missal *noun* a Roman Catholic prayer-book. [from Latin *missa* = mass (*mass*²)]

misshapen *adjective* badly shaped.

missile *noun* a weapon or other object for firing or throwing at a target. [from Latin *missum* = sent]

missing *adjective* **1** lost; not in the proper place. **2** absent.

mission *noun* **1** an important job that somebody is sent to do or feels he or she must do. **2** a place or building where missionaries work. [from Latin *missio* = a sending]

missionary *noun* (*plural* **missionaries**) a person who is sent to another country to spread the Christian faith.

mist *noun* **1** damp cloudy air near the ground. **2** condensed water-vapour on a window, mirror, etc.

mistake *noun* something done wrongly; an incorrect opinion.

mistake *verb* (**mistook**, **mistaken**, **mistaking**) **1** misunderstand, *Don't mistake my meaning.* **2** choose or identify wrongly, *We mistook her for her sister.*

mistaken *adjective* incorrect; unwise.

mistime *verb* (**mistimed**, **mistiming**) do or say something at a wrong time.

mistletoe *noun* a plant with white berries that grows as a parasite on trees.

mistreat *verb* treat badly.

mistress *noun* (*plural* **mistresses**) **1** a woman who is in charge of something. **2** a woman teacher. **3** a woman who is a man's lover but not his wife.

mistrust *verb* feel no trust in somebody or something. **mistrust** *noun*

misty *adjective* full of mist; not clear. **mistily** *adverb*, **mistiness** *noun*

misunderstand *verb* (**misunderstood**, **misunderstanding**) get a wrong idea or impression of something.

misuse *verb* (**misused**, **misusing**) **1** use incorrectly. **2** treat badly. **misuse** *noun*

mite *noun* **1** a tiny spider-like creature found in food, *cheese-mites.* **2** a very small amount. **3** a small child.

mitigate *verb* (**mitigated**, **mitigating**) make a thing less intense or less severe. **mitigation** *noun*
mitigating circumstances facts that may partially excuse wrongdoing.
[from Latin *mitigare* = make mild]

USAGE Do not confuse with *militate.*

mitre *noun* **1** the tall tapering hat worn by a bishop. **2** a mitred join.

mitre *verb* (**mitred**, **mitring**) join two tapered pieces of wood or cloth etc. so that they form a right angle.

mitten *noun* a kind of glove without separate parts for the fingers.

mix *verb* **1** put different things together so that the substances etc. are no longer distinct; blend; combine. **2** (of a person) get together with others. **mixer** *noun*
mix up mix thoroughly; confuse.

mix *noun* (*plural* **mixes**) a mixture.

mixed *adjective* containing two or more kinds of things or people.
mixed blessing something that has disadvantages as well as advantages.

mixture *noun* **1** something made of different things mixed together. **2** the process of mixing.

mizzen *noun* **1** (also **mizzen-mast**) a mast that is astern of a mainmast. **2** (also **mizzen-sail**) a sail on this mast.

MMP *abbreviation* mixed member proportional (the version of proportional representation used in New Zealand general elections).

mnemonic (*say* nim-**on**-ik) *noun* a verse or saying that helps you to remember something. [from Greek *mnemonikos* = for the memory]

moa *noun* a large flightless bird which is now extinct. [Māori]

moan *verb* **1** make a long low sound of pain or suffering. **2** grumble. **moan** *noun*

moat *noun* a deep wide ditch round a castle, usually filled with water. **moated** *adjective*

mob *noun* **1** a large disorderly crowd; a rabble. **2** a gang. **3** (*NZ*) a flock of animals.

mob *verb* (**mobbed**, **mobbing**) **1** crowd together. **2** gather farm stock together. [from Latin *mobile vulgus* = excitable crowd]

mobile *adjective* moving easily. **mobility** *noun*
mobile home a large caravan permanently parked and used for living in.
mobile phone a cellular telephone for use in a car etc.

mobile *noun* **1** a decoration for hanging up so that its parts move in currents of air. **2** a mobile phone. [from Latin *movere* = move]
mobile phone a portable cellphone.

mobilise *verb* (**mobilised**, **mobilising**) assemble people or things for a particular purpose, especially for war. **mobilisation** *noun*

moccasin *noun* a soft leather shoe.

mock *verb* **1** make fun of a person or thing. **2** imitate; mimic. **mockery** *noun*

mock *adjective* sham; imitation, not real, *a mock battle.*

mock-up *noun* a model of something, made in order to test or study it.

mode *noun* **1** the way a thing is done. **2** what is fashionable.

model *noun* **1** a copy of an object, usually on a smaller scale. **2** a particular design. **3** a person who poses for an artist or displays clothes by wearing them. **4** a person or thing that is worth copying.

model *verb* (**modelled**, **modelling**) **1** make a model of something. **2** make according to a model. **3** work as an artist's model or a fashion model.

modem *noun* a device which allows one to send data from one computer to another via a telephone line.

moderate *adjective* medium; not extremely small or great or hot etc., *a moderate climate.* **moderately** *adverb*

moderate (*say* **mod**-er-ayt) *verb* (**moderated**, **moderating**) make or become moderate. **moderation** *noun*
in moderation in moderate amounts.

modern *adjective* of the present or recent times; in fashion now. **modernity** *noun*

modernise *verb* (**modernised**, **modernising**) make a thing more modern. **modernisation** *noun*

modest *adjective* **1** not vain; not boasting. **2** moderate; not showy or splendid. **3** rather shy; decorous. **modestly** *adverb*, **modesty** *noun* [from Latin, = keeping the proper measure]

modicum *noun* a small amount.

modify *verb* (**modified**, **modifying**) **1** change something slightly. **2** qualify a word by describing it, *Adjectives modify nouns.* **modification** *noun*

modulate *verb* (**modulated**, **modulating**) **1** adjust; regulate. **2** vary in pitch or tone etc. **modulation** *noun*

module *noun* **1** an independent part of a spacecraft, building, etc. **2** a unit; a section of a course of study. **modular** *adjective*

mogul (*say* **moh**-gul) *noun* (*informal*) an important or influential person. [the Moguls were the ruling family in India in the 16th–19th centuries]

mohair *noun* fine silky wool from an angora goat. [from Arabic, = special]

moist *adjective* slightly wet; damp. **moistly** *adverb*, **moistness** *noun*

moisten *verb* make or become moist.

moisture *noun* water in the air or making a thing moist.

moki *noun* an edible fish. [Māori]

mōkī or mōkihi *noun* a kind of raft. [Māori]

moko[1] *noun* a tattoo, often on the face. [Māori]

moko[2] *noun* a mokopuna.

mokomoko *noun* a kind of lizard. [Māori]

mokopuna *noun* **1** a grandchild or descendant. **2** a toddler. [Māori]

molar *noun* any of the wide teeth at the back of the jaw, used in chewing. [from Latin *mola* = millstone]

molasses *noun* syrup from raw sugar.

mole[1] *noun* **1** a small furry animal in the Northern hemisphere that burrows under the ground. **2** a person who secretly gives confidential information to an enemy or rival.

mole[2] *noun* a small dark spot on skin.

mole[3] *noun* a stone wall built out into the sea as a breakwater or causeway.

molecule *noun* the smallest part into which a substance can be divided without changing its chemical nature; a group of atoms. **molecular** *adjective* [from Latin, = little mass]

molehill *noun* a small pile of earth thrown up by a burrowing mole.

molest *verb* pester. **molestation** *noun* [from Latin *molestus* = troublesome]

mollify *verb* (**mollified**, **mollifying**) make a person less angry. **mollification** *noun* [from Latin, = soften]

mollusc *noun* any of a group of animals with soft bodies and hard shells (e.g. snails, mussels) or no shell (e.g. octopuses). [from Latin *molluscus* = soft]

mollymawk *noun* (*NZ*) any of several kinds of small albatross.

molten *adjective* melted; made liquid by great heat.

moment *noun* **1** a very short time. **2** a particular time, *Call me the moment she arrives.* **3** importance, *These are matters of great moment.*

momentary *adjective* lasting for only a moment. **momentarily** *adverb*

momentous (*say* mo-**ment**-us) *adjective* very important.

momentum *noun* amount or force of movement. *The stone gathered momentum as it rolled downhill.* [Latin, = movement]

monarch *noun* a king, queen, emperor, or empress ruling a country. **monarch butterfly** a large orange and black butterfly. **monarchic** *adjective* [from Greek *monos* = alone, + *archein* = to rule]

monarchy *noun* (*plural* **monarchies**) a country ruled by a monarch. **monarchist** *noun*

monastery *noun* (*plural* **monasteries**) a building where monks or nuns live and work. **monastic** *adjective* [from Greek *monazein* = live alone]

Monday *noun* the day after Sunday.

monetary *adjective* of money.

money *noun* **1** coins and banknotes. **2** wealth. [same origin as *mint*[2]]

mongol *noun* a person suffering from Down's syndrome. **mongolism** *noun*

mongoose *noun* (*plural* **mongooses**) a small tropical animal rather like a stoat, that can kill snakes.

mongrel (*say* **mung**-rel) *noun* a dog of mixed breeds. [from *mingle*]

monitor *noun* **1** a device for watching or testing how something is working. **2** a pupil who is given a special responsibility in a school. **3** a visual display unit, a computer screen.

monitor *verb* watch or test how something is working. [from Latin *monere* = warn]

monk *noun* a member of a community of men who live according to the rules of a religious organisation. (Compare *nun*.) [same origin as *mono*]

monkey *noun* (*plural* **monkeys**) **1** an animal with long arms, hands with thumbs, and often a tail. **2** a mischievous person. [origin unknown]

monkfish *noun* a kind of flathead fish.

mono- *prefix* one; single. [from Greek *monos* = alone]

monochrome *adjective* done in one colour or in black and white. [from *mono-*, + Greek *chroma* = colour]

monocle *noun* an eyeglass for one eye. [from *mono-*, + Latin *oculus* = eye]

monocultural *adjective* having only one culture. **monoculturalism** *noun*

monogamy *noun* the custom of being married to only one person at a time. (Compare *polygamy*.) **monogamous** *adjective* [from *mono-*, + Greek *gamos* = marriage]

monogram *noun* a design made up of a letter or letters, especially a person's initials. **monogrammed** *adjective* [from *mono-* + *-gram*]

monograph *noun* a scholarly book on one particular subject. [from *mono-* + *-graph*]

monolith *noun* a large single upright block of stone. [from *mono-*, + Greek *lithos* = stone]

monolithic *adjective* **1** consisting of monoliths. **2** single and huge.

monologue *noun* a speech by one person. [from *mono-*, + Greek *logos* = word]

monoplane *noun* a type of aeroplane with only one set of wings.

monopolise *verb* (**monopolised**, **monopolising**) take the whole of something for yourself, *One girl monopolised my attention.* **monopolisation** *noun*

monopoly *noun* (*plural* **monopolies**) complete possession or control of something by one group, *The company had a monopoly in supplying electricity.* [from *mono-*, + Greek *polein* = sell]

monorail *noun* a railway that uses a single rail, not a pair of rails.

monosyllable *noun* a word with only one syllable. **monosyllabic** *adjective*

monotheism (*say* **mon**-oth-ee-izm) *noun* belief that there is only one god. **monotheist** *noun* [from *mono-*, + Greek *theos* = god]

monotone *noun* a level unchanging tone of voice in speaking or singing.

monotonous *adjective* boring because it does not change. **monotonously** *adverb*, **monotony** *noun*

monoxide *noun* an oxide with one atom of oxygen.

monsoon *noun* **1** a strong wind in and near the Indian Ocean, bringing heavy rain in summer. **2** the rainy season brought by this wind. [from Arabic *mausim* = fixed season]
monsoon bucket (*NZ*) a large bucket, carried by a helicopter, used to dump water on bushfires.

monster *noun* **1** a large frightening creature. **2** a huge thing.

monster *adjective* huge. [from Latin *monstrum* = marvel]

monstrosity *noun* (*plural* **monstrosities**) a monstrous thing.

monstrous *adjective* **1** like a monster; huge. **2** very shocking; outrageous.

month *noun* each of the twelve parts into which a year is divided. [related to *moon* (because time was measured by the changes in the moon's appearance)]

monthly *adjective & adverb* happening or done once a month.

monument *noun* a statue, building, or column etc. put up as a memorial of some person or event.

monumental *adjective* **1** of or as a monument. **2** extremely great; huge.

moo *verb* make the low deep sound of a cow. **moo** *noun*

mood *noun* the way someone feels, *She is in a cheerful mood.*

moody *adjective* gloomy or sullen; likely to become bad-tempered suddenly. **moodily** *adverb*, **moodiness** *noun*

moon *noun* **1** the natural satellite of the earth that can be seen in the sky at night. **2** a satellite of any planet. **moonbeam** *noun*, **moonlight** *noun*, **moonlit** *adjective*
over the moon (*informal*) very pleased or excited.

moon *verb* go about in a dreamy or listless way.

Moor *noun* a member of a Muslim people of north-west Africa. **Moorish** *adjective*

moor[1] *noun* (*British*) an area of rough land with bushes but no trees. **moorland** *noun*

moor[2] *verb* fasten a boat etc. to a fixed object by means of a cable.

moorhen *noun* a small water-bird.

moose *noun* (*plural* **moose**) a North American elk.

moot *adjective* debatable; undecided, *That's a moot point.*

moot *verb* put forward an idea for discussion.

mop *noun* **1** a bunch or pad of soft material fastened on the end of a stick, used for cleaning floors etc. **2** a thick mass of hair.

mop *verb* (**mopped**, **mopping**) clean or wipe with a mop etc.; wipe away.

mope *verb* (**moped**, **moping**) be sad.

moraine *noun* a mass of stones and earth etc. carried down by a glacier.

moral *adjective* **1** connected with what is right and wrong in behaviour. **2** virtuous. **morally** *adverb*, **morality** *noun*
moral support encouragement.

moral *noun* a lesson in right behaviour taught by a story or event.
morals *plural noun* standards of behaviour; virtuousness. [from Latin *mores* = customs]

morale (*say* mor-**ahl**) *noun* confidence; the state of someone's spirits, *Morale was high after the victory.*

moralise *verb* (**moralised**, **moralising**) talk or write about right and wrong behaviour. **moralist** *noun*

morass *noun* (*plural* **morasses**) **1** a marsh or bog. **2** a confused mass.

moratorium *noun* a temporary ban. [from Latin *morari* = to delay]

morbid *adjective* **1** thinking about gloomy or unpleasant things. **2** unhealthy.
morbidly *adverb*, **morbidity** *noun* [from Latin *morbus* = disease]

more *adjective* (comparative of **much** and **many**) greater in amount etc.

more *noun* a greater amount.

more *adverb* **1** to a greater extent, *more beautiful.* **2** again, *once more.*
more or less about; approximately.

moreover *adverb* besides; in addition to what has been said.

morepork *noun* a small brown New Zealand owl.

Moriori *noun* (*plural* **Moriori**) a member of the original Polynesian people of the Chatham Islands; their language.

Mormon *noun* a member of a religious group founded in the USA.

morn *noun* (*poetic*) morning.

morning *noun* the early part of the day, before noon or before lunchtime.
morning tea (*NZ*) a mid-morning break for tea or coffee and a snack.

morocco *noun* a kind of leather originally made in Morocco from goatskins.

moron *noun* (*informal*) a very stupid person. [from Greek *moros* = foolish]

morose *adjective* sullen and gloomy.
morosely *adverb*, **moroseness** *noun*

morphia or morphine (*say* **mor**-feen) *noun* a drug made from opium, used to lessen pain. [named after Morpheus. the Roman god of dreams]

morris dance a traditional English dance performed in costume by men with ribbons and bells. [originally 'Moorish dance']

morrow *noun* (*poetic*) the following day.

Morse code a signalling code using short and long sounds or flashes of light (dots and dashes) to represent letters. [named after its American inventor, S. F. B. Morse]

morsel *noun* a small piece of food; a small amount. [from Latin *morsus* = bite]

mortal *adjective* **1** that can die, *All of us are mortal.* **2** causing death; fatal, *a mortal wound.* **3** deadly, *mortal enemies.* **mortally** *adverb*, **mortality** *noun*

mortal *noun* a person who is not immortal. [from Latin *mortis* = of death]

mortar *noun* **1** a mixture of sand, cement, and water used in building to stick bricks together. **2** a hard bowl in which substances are pounded with a pestle. **3** a short cannon.

mortarboard *noun* an academic cap with a stiff square top.

mortgage (*say* **mor**-gij) *noun* an arrangement to borrow money to buy a house, with the house as security for the loan.

mortgage *verb* (**mortgaged**, **mortgaging**) offer a house etc. as security in return for a loan.

mortify *verb* (**mortified**, **mortifying**) humiliate a person greatly. **mortification** *noun* [same origin as *mortal*]

mortise *noun* a hole made in a piece of wood for another piece to be joined to it. (Compare *tenon.*)
mortise lock a lock set into a door.

mortuary *noun* a place where dead bodies are kept before being buried. [from Latin *mortuus* = dead]

mosaic (*say* mo-**zay**-ik) *noun* a picture or design made from small coloured pieces of stone or glass.

mosque (*say* mosk) *noun* a building where Muslims worship.

mosquito *noun* (*plural* **mosquitoes**) a kind of gnat that sucks blood. [Spanish, = little fly]

moss *noun* (*plural* **mosses**) a plant that grows in damp places and has no flowers. **mossy** *adjective*

most *adjective* (superlative of **much** and **many**) greatest in amount etc., *Most people came by bus.*

most *noun* the greatest amount, *Most of the food was eaten.*

most *adverb* **1** to the greatest extent; more than any other, *most beautiful.* **2** very; extremely, *most impressive.*

mostly *adverb* mainly.

MOTAT *abbreviation* (*NZ*) Museum of Transport and Technology (in Auckland).

motel *noun* a form of accommodation for those travelling in cars, with furnished units and space for parking. [from *mo*tor + ho*tel*]

moth *noun* an insect rather like a butterfly, that usually flies at night.

mother *noun* a female parent.
motherhood *noun*
Mother's Day the second Sunday in May, when people often give presents to their mothers.
[from Old English *modor*]

mother *verb* look after someone in a motherly way.

mother-in-law *noun* (*plural* **mothers-in-law**) the mother of a married person's husband or wife.

motherly *adjective* kind and gentle like a mother. **motherliness** *noun*

mother-of-pearl *noun* a pearly substance lining the shells of mussels etc.

motif *noun* a repeated design or theme.

motion *noun* **1** moving; movement. **2** a formal statement to be discussed and voted on at a meeting.
motion picture a cinema or television film, a movie.

motion *verb* signal by a gesture. *She motioned him to sit beside her.* [from Latin *motio* = movement]

motionless *adjective* not moving.

motivate *verb* (**motivated, motivating**) give a person a motive or incentive to do something. **motivation** *noun*

motive *noun* what makes a person do something, *a motive for murder.*

motive *adjective* producing movement, *The engine provides motive power.* [from Latin *motivus* = moving]

motley *adjective* **1** multicoloured. **2** made up of various sorts of things.

motocross *noun* cross-country racing on motor cycles.

motor *noun* a machine providing power to drive machinery etc.; an engine.

motor *verb* go or take someone in a car. [from Latin *motor* = mover]

motorcade *noun* a procession of cars. [from *motor* + *cavalcade*]

motorcycle a two-wheeled vehicle driven by a motor and that cannot be driven by pedals.
motorcyclist *noun*

motorised *adjective* equipped with a motor or with motor vehicles.

motorist *noun* a person who drives a car.

motor-racing *noun* the racing of motor vehicles, especially cars.

motorway *noun* a wide road for fast long-distance traffic.

mottled *adjective* marked with spots or patches of colour. [from *motley*]

motto *noun* (*plural* **mottoes**) **1** a short saying used as a guide for behaviour, *Their motto is 'Who dares, wins'.* **2** a short verse or riddle etc. found inside a cracker. [Italian, = word]

mould[1] *noun* a hollow container of a particular shape, in which a liquid or soft substance is put to set into this shape.

mould[1] *verb* make something have a particular shape or character.

mould[2] *noun* a fine furry growth of very small fungi. **mouldy** *adjective*

moulder *verb* rot away; decay into dust.

moult *verb* shed feathers, hair, or skin etc. while a new growth forms.

mound *noun* a pile of earth or stones etc.; a small hill.

mount *verb* **1** climb or go up; ascend. **2** get on a horse or bicycle etc. **3** increase in amount, *Our costs mounted.* **4** place or fix in position for use or display, *Mount your photos in an album.*

mount *noun* **1** a mountain, *Mount Taranaki.* **2** something on which an object is mounted. **3** a horse etc. for riding. [from Latin *mons* = mountain]

mountain *noun* **1** an area of natural high ground rising steeply to a peak. **2** a large heap or pile or quantity. **mountainous** *adjective*

mountaineer *noun* a person who climbs mountains. **mountaineering** *noun*

mounted *adjective* serving on horseback, *mounted police.*

mourn *verb* be sad, especially because someone has died. **mourner** *noun*

mournful *adjective* sad; sorrowful. **mournfully** *adverb*

mouse *noun* **1** (*plural* **mice**) a small animal with a long thin tail and a pointed nose. **2** (*plural* **mouses**) a device connected to a computer and handled on a flat surface to control the movement of the cursor on the computer screen. **mousetrap** *noun*, **mousy** *adjective.*

mousse (*say* mooss) *noun* **1** a creamy pudding flavoured with fruit or chocolate. **2** a frothy creamy substance. [French, = froth]

moustache (*say* mus-**tahsh**) *noun* hair allowed to grow on a man's upper lip.

mouth *noun* **1** the opening through which food is taken into the body. **2** the place where a river enters the sea. **3** an opening or outlet. **mouthful** *noun*

mouth *verb* form words carefully with your lips, especially without saying them aloud.

mouth-organ *noun* a small musical instrument that you play by blowing and sucking while passing it along your lips.

mouthpiece *noun* the part of a musical or other instrument that you put to your mouth.

movable *adjective* able to be moved.

move *verb* (**moved**, **moving**) **1** take or go from one place to another; change a person's or thing's position. **2** affect a person's feelings, *Their sad story moved us deeply.* **3** put forward a formal statement (a *motion*) to be discussed and voted on at a meeting. **mover** *noun*

move *noun* **1** moving; a movement. **2** a player's turn to move a piece in chess etc.
get a move on (*informal*) hurry up.
on the move moving; making progress.
[from Latin *movere* = to move]

movement *noun* **1** the action of moving or being moved. **2** a group of people working together to achieve something. **3** one of the main divisions of a symphony or other long musical work.

movie *noun* a cinema film.
the movies films generally; the film industry.

mow *verb* (**mowed**, **mown**, **mowing**) cut down grass etc. **mower** *noun*
mow down knock down and kill.

MP *abbreviation* Member of Parliament.

Mr (*say* **mist**-er) *noun* (*plural* **Messrs**) a title put before a man's name. [short for *mister*]

Mrs (*say* **mis**-iz) *noun* (*plural* **Mrs**) a title put before a married woman's name. [short for *mistress*]

Ms (*say* miz) *noun* a title put before a woman's name. [from *Mrs* and *Miss*]

MS *abbreviation* **1** (*plural* **MSS**) manuscript. **2** multiple sclerosis.

MSc *abbreviation* Master of Science.

Mt *abbreviation* mount or mountain.

much *adjective* (**more**, **most**) existing in a large amount, *much noise.*

much *noun* a large amount of something.

much *adverb* **1** greatly; considerably, *much to my surprise.* **2** approximately, *It is much the same.*

muck *noun* **1** farmyard manure. **2** (*informal*) dirt; filth. **3** (*informal*) a mess. **mucky** *adjective*

muck *verb* make dirty; mess.
muck about (*slang*) mess about.
muck up (*slang*) mess up; spoil.

mucous (*say* **mew**-kus) *adjective* like mucus; covered with mucus, *a mucous membrane.*

mucus (*say* **mew**-kus) *noun* the moist sticky substance on the inner surface of the throat etc.

mud *noun* wet soft earth. **muddy** *adjective*, **muddiness** *noun*

muddle *verb* (**muddled**, **muddling**) mix things up; confuse. **muddler** *noun*

muddle *noun* a muddled condition or thing; confusion; disorder.

mudfish *noun* a New Zealand freshwater fish that burrows in the mud.

mudflat *noun* a stretch of muddy land which is uncovered at low tide.

mudguard *noun* a curved cover over the top part of the wheel of a bicycle etc. to protect the rider from the mud and water thrown up by the wheel.

muesli (*say* **mews**-lee) *noun* a food made of mixed cereals, dried fruit, nuts, etc.

muff[1] *noun* a short tube-shaped piece of warm material into which the hands are pushed from opposite ends.

muff[2] *verb* (*informal*) bungle.

muffin *noun* a cup-shaped cake.

muffle *verb* (**muffled**, **muffling**) **1** cover or wrap something to protect it or keep it warm. **2** deaden the sound of something, *a muffled scream.* [from *muff*[1]]

muffler *noun* **1** a warm scarf. **2** (*NZ*) a silencer on a motor vehicle.

mufti *noun* ordinary clothes worn by someone who usually wears a uniform.

mug *noun* **1** a kind of large cup, usually used without a saucer. **2** (*slang*) a fool; a person who is easily deceived. **3** (*slang*) a person's face.

mug *verb* (**mugged**, **mugging**) attack and rob somebody in the street. **mugger** *noun*

muggy *adjective* unpleasantly warm and damp, *muggy weather*. **mugginess** *noun*

mulberry *noun* (*plural* **mulberries**) a purple or white fruit rather like a blackberry.

mule *noun* an animal that is the offspring of a donkey and a mare, known for being stubborn. **mulish** *adjective*

mull[1] *verb* heat wine or beer with sugar and spices, as a drink, *mulled ale*.

mull[2] *verb* think about something carefully; ponder, *mull it over*.

mullah *noun* a Muslim who has studied Islamic theology and law.

mullet *noun* **1** an edible sea fish. **2** a hairstyle in which hair is cut short at the front and sides and left long at the back.

multi- *prefix* many (as in *multicoloured* = with many colours). [from Latin *multus* = many]

multifarious (*say* multi-**fair**-ee-us) *adjective* of many kinds; very varied.

multilateral *adjective* (of an agreement or treaty) made between three or more people or countries etc.

multimedia *adjective* using more than one medium of communication or expression (text, video, sound, etc.).

multimillionaire *noun* a person with a fortune of several million dollars.

multinational *adjective* (of a business company) working in several countries.

multiple *adjective* having many parts. **multiple sclerosis** *noun* a disease causing gradual impairment of the central nervous system.

multiple *noun* a number that contains another number (a *factor*) an exact amount of times without remainder, *8 and 12 are multiples of 4*.

multiplex *noun* a number of cinemas on one site.

multiplicity *noun* a great variety.

multiply *verb* (**multiplied**, **multiplying**) **1** take a number a given quantity of times, *Five multiplied by four equals twenty* (5 × 4 = 20). **2** make or become many; increase. **multiplication** *noun*, **multiplier** *noun*

multiracial *adjective* consisting of people of many different races.

multitude *noun* a great number of people or things. **multitudinous** *adjective*

mum[1] *noun* (*informal*) mother.

mum[2] *adjective* (*informal*) silent, *keep mum*.

mum[3] *verb* (**mummed**, **mumming**) act in a mime. **mummer** *noun*

mumble *verb* (**mumbled**, **mumbling**) speak indistinctly and not be easy to hear. **mumble** *noun*, **mumbler** *noun*

mumbo-jumbo *noun* talk or ceremony that has no real meaning.

mummy[1] *noun* (*plural* **mummies**) (*informal*) mother.

mummy[2] *noun* (*plural* **mummies**) a corpse treated with preservatives before being buried, as was the custom in ancient Egypt. **mummify** *verb*

mumps *noun* an infectious disease that causes the neck to swell painfully.

munch *verb* chew vigorously.

mundane *adjective* **1** ordinary, not exciting. **2** concerned with practical matters, not ideals. [from Latin *mundus* = world]

municipal (*say* mew-**nis**-ip-al) *adjective* of a town or city.

municipality *noun* (*plural* **municipalities**) a town or city that has its own local government (see *local*).

munificent *adjective* extremely generous. **munificently** *adverb*, **munificence** *noun* [from Latin *munus* = gift]

munitions *plural noun* military weapons and ammunition etc. [from Latin *munitum* = fortified]

munted *adjective* (*NZ, slang*) broken or ruined.

muntage *noun* (*NZ, slang*) damage.

mural *adjective* of or on a wall.

mural *noun* a wall-painting. [from Latin *murus* = wall]

murder *verb* kill a person unlawfully and deliberately. **murderer** *noun*, **murderess** *noun*

murder *noun* the murdering of somebody. **murderous** *adjective*

murky *adjective* dark and gloomy. **murk** *noun*, **murkiness** *noun*

murmur *verb* **1** make a low continuous sound. **2** speak in a soft voice. **murmur** *noun*

muscle *noun* **1** a band or bundle of fibrous tissue that can contract and relax and so produce movement in parts of the body. **2** the power of muscles; strength. **muscular** *adjective*, **muscularity** *noun*

muse *verb* (**mused**, **musing**) think deeply about something; ponder; meditate.

museum *noun* a place where interesting objects, especially antiquities, are displayed for people to see. [from Greek, = place of the Muses (goddesses of the arts and sciences)]

mush *noun* soft pulp. **mushy** *adjective*

mushroom *noun* an edible fungus with a stem and a dome-shaped top.

mushroom *verb* grow or appear suddenly in large numbers, *Office blocks mushroomed in the city.*

music *noun* **1** pleasant or interesting sounds made by instruments or by the voice. **2** printed or written instructions for making music. [from Greek, = of the Muses (see *museum*)]

musical *adjective* **1** of or with music; producing music. **2** good at music; interested in music. **musically** *adverb*

musical *noun* a play or film containing a lot of songs.

musician *noun* someone who plays a musical instrument.

musk *noun* a strong-smelling substance used in perfumes. **musky** *adjective*

musket *noun* a kind of gun with a long barrel, formerly used by soldiers.

musketeer *noun* a soldier armed with a musket.

Muslim *noun* a person who follows the religious teachings of Muhammad (who lived in about 570–632), set out in the Koran.

muslin *noun* very thin cotton cloth.

mussel *noun* a black shellfish.

must *auxiliary verb* used to express (**1**) necessity or obligation (*You must go*), (**2**) certainty (*You must be joking!*).

mustang *noun* a wild horse of Mexico and California.

mustard *noun* a yellow paste or powder used to give food a hot taste.
mustard and cress small green plants eaten in salads.

muster *verb* **1** assemble; gather together. **2** (*NZ*) round up livestock, for shearing etc.

muster *noun* **1** an assembly of people or things. **2** (*NZ*) a round-up of animals.
pass muster be up to the required standard.

mustn't (*mainly spoken*) must not.

musty *adjective* smelling or tasting mouldy or stale. **mustiness** *noun*

mutable (*say* **mew**-ta-bul) *adjective* able or likely to change. **mutability** *noun* [from *Latin mutare* = to change]

mutation *noun* a change or alteration in the form of something.

mute *adjective* **1** silent; not speaking; not able to speak. **2** not pronounced, *The g in 'gnat' is mute.* **mutely** *adverb*, **muteness** *noun*

mute *noun* a person who cannot speak.

mute *verb* (**muted**, **muting**) make a thing quieter or less intense.

mutilate *verb* (**mutilated**, **mutilating**) damage something by breaking or cutting off part of it. **mutilation** *noun*

mutineer *noun* a person who mutinies.

mutiny *noun* (*plural* **mutinies**) rebellion against authority; refusal by members of the armed forces to obey orders. **mutinous** *adjective*, **mutinously** *adverb*

mutiny *verb* (**mutinied**, **mutinying**) take part in a mutiny.

mutter *verb* **1** speak in a low voice. **2** grumble. **mutter** *noun*

mutton *noun* meat from a sheep.

mutton-bird *noun* (*NZ*) a sea-bird related to the petrel and eaten as food.

mutual (*say* **mew**-tew-al) *adjective* given to each other; felt by each for the other, *mutual affection.* **mutually** *adverb*

muzzle *noun* **1** an animal's nose and mouth. **2** a cover put over an animal's nose and mouth so that it cannot bite. **3** the open end of a gun.

muzzle *verb* (**muzzled**, **muzzling**) **1** put a muzzle on an animal. **2** silence; prevent a person from expressing opmions.

MVP *abbreviation* most valuable player.

my *adjective* belonging to me.

mynah or myna *noun* a bird of the starling family that can mimic speech.

myriad (*say* **mi**rri-ad) *adjective* innumerable.

myriads *plural noun* a very great number, *myriads of gnats.* [from Greek *myrioi* = 10,000]

myrrh (*say* mer) *noun* a substance used in perfumes and incense and medicine.

myrtle *noun* an evergreen shrub with dark leaves and white flowers.

myself *pronoun* I or me and nobody else. (Compare *herself.*)

mysterious *adjective* full of mystery; puzzling. **mysteriously** *adverb*

mystery *noun* (*plural* **mysteries**) something that cannot be explained or understood; something puzzling.

mystic *adjective* **1** having a spiritual meaning. **2** mysterious and filling people with wonder. **mystical** *adjective*, **mystically** *adverb*, **mysticism** *noun*

mystic *noun* a person who seeks to obtain spiritual contact with God by deep religious meditation.

mystify *verb* (**mystified**, **mystifying**) puzzle; bewilder. **mystification** *noun*

mystique (*say* mis-**teek**) *noun* an air of mystery or mystical power.

myth (*say* mith) *noun* **1** an old story containing ideas about ancient times or about supernatural beings. (Compare *legend*.) **2** an untrue story or belief. [from Greek *mythos* = story]

mythical *adjective* imaginary; found in myths, *a mythical animal.*

mythology *noun* myths; the study of myths. **mythological** *adjective* [from *myth* + *-logy*]

myxomatosis (*say* miks-om-at-**oh**-sis) *noun* a disease that kills rabbits.

Study Pages

Punctuation

▪ A **full stop (.)** is used at the end of a sentence, unless the sentence is a question or an exclamation:
We're leaving now. That's all. Thank you.
It is also often used after an abbreviation:
Acacia Ave. a.m. Queen St.

? A **question mark (?)** is written at the end of a direct question:
'Who's that man?' Jenny asked.
but not after an indirect question:
Jenny asked who the man was.

! An **exclamation mark (!)** is used at the end of a sentence that expresses surprise, enthusiasm, shock or horror:
What an amazing story! How well you look! Oh no! The cat's been run over!
or after an interjection or a word describing a loud sound:
Bye! Ow! Crash!

, A **comma (,)** shows a slight pause in a sentence:
I ran all the way to the station, but I still missed the train. Although it was cold, the sun was shining. He did, nevertheless, leave his phone number. However, we may be wrong.
It is also used before a quotation or direct speech:
Fiona said, 'I'll help you.' 'I'll help you,' said Fiona, 'but you'll have to wait till Monday.'
Commas are also used between the items in a list, although they may be omitted before 'and':
It was a cold, rainy day. This shop sells videos, compact discs, DVDs, and iPods.
In relative clauses, commas are used around a phrase that adds some new, but not essential, information. Compare the two sentences:
The boy who had lots of sweets gave some to the boy who had none. The boy, who had lots of sweets, was already eating.
We cannot understand the first sentence without the information introduced by 'who'. However, in the second sentence, the phrase 'who had lots of sweets' only adds extra information and is kept separate from the main part of the sentence by commas.

: A **colon (:)** is used to introduce something, such as a long quotation or a list:
There is a choice of main course: fish, pasta or roast beef.

; A **semicolon (;)** is used to separate two contrasting parts of a sentence:
John wanted to go; I did not.
or to separate items in a list where commas have already been used:
The school uniform consists of navy skirt or trousers; grey, white or pale blue shirt; navy jumper or blazer; grey, blue or white socks.

' An **apostrophe (')** shows that a letter is missing in short forms:
hasn't, don't, I'm, he's
or that a person or thing belongs to somebody:
Peter's scarf, Jane's mother, my friend's car

With some names that end in ‘s’, another ‘s’ is not always added:
Jesus’ name
Notice the position of the apostrophe with singular and plural nouns:
the girl’s keys (= the keys belonging to the girl)
the girls’ keys (= the keys belonging to the girls).

“” **Quotation marks** or **inverted commas (‘’ or “”)** are used to show the words that somebody said:
‘Come and see,’ said Martin. ‘Oh, no!’ said Martin. ‘Come and see what’s happened.’
Angela shouted, ‘Over here!’
or what somebody thought, when the thoughts are presented like speech:
‘Will they get here on time?’ she wondered.
They are also used around a title, for example of a poem, song, etc:
The choir sang ‘God Defend New Zealand’.

- A **hyphen (-)** is used to join two words that together form one idea:
the deep-freeze, a ten-tonne truck
or sometimes to link a prefix to a word:
non-violent, anti-American
and in compound numbers:
thirty-four, seventy-nine.
You also write a hyphen at the end of a line if you have to divide a word and write part of it on the next line.

— A **dash (—)** can be used to separate a phrase from the rest of a sentence. It can be used near the end of the sentence before a phrase that sums up the rest of the sentence:
The burglars had taken the furniture, the TV and stereo, the paintings — absolutely everything.
or you can put a dash at the beginning and the end of a phrase that adds extra information:
A few people — not more than ten — had already arrived.
A dash can also show that the speaker has been interrupted in the middle of a sentence:
‘Have you seen —’ ‘Look out!’ she screamed as the ball flew towards them.

() **Brackets** or **parentheses ()** are also used to keep extra information separate from the rest of the sentence:
Two of the runners (Jones and Smith) finished the race in under an hour.
Numbers or letters used in sentences may also have a bracket after them or brackets around them:
The camera has three main advantages: 1) its compact size 2) its low price and 3) the quality of the photographs.
What would you do if you won a lot of money? (a) save it (b) travel round the world (c) buy a new house (d) buy presents for your friends.

Grammar

Words can be put into sets called word classes, or parts of speech. The main ones are: **noun pronoun verb adjective adverb preposition conjunction interjection**

Nouns

Nouns are words that are the names of things or persons, such as *child*, *danger*, *tree*.
Nouns divide up into names (or **proper nouns**) and descriptions (or **common nouns**).

proper nouns:	Tom, Hokitika, Moro bar, Labour Party, TV2
common nouns:	dog, creek, mystery, fire, tiki

Common nouns divide into those that stand for objects (**concrete nouns**), and those that stand for ideas (**abstract nouns**).

concrete nouns:	dog, creek, fire, tiki, waka
abstract nouns:	mystery, danger, happiness, mana

Nouns also divide into those that can be made plural (**countables**), and those that cannot (**uncountables**).

countables:	dog, creek, car, iPod
uncountables:	steel, air, clothing, china

Pronouns

Pronouns are words used instead of a noun, such as *it*, *me*, *they*.

Verbs and their tenses

Some verbs express actions or feeling:

*I **came**. She **ate**. They **know**.*

Other verbs connect words or phrases in a sentence:

*It **is** late. I **am** coming. You **have** eaten. They **must** not know.*

Verbs have several different forms, depending on their *tense*:

Present tense: *I speak, she speaks, they are speaking.*
Past tenses: *I spoke, she has spoken, you had spoken, they have been speaking.*
Future tense: *I will be speaking, they will be speaking.*

Regular verbs form their past tense and past participle by adding ***-ed*** to the verb stem:

*I **kicked**. He has **kicked**. I **washed**. She had **washed**.*

They form their present participle by adding ***-ing*** to the verb stem:

*I am **washing**. She was **playing**. They are **learning**.*

But many verbs are **irregular** and have rules of their own! The forms of these verbs are given in the dictionary in the same order every time:

speak *verb* (spoke, spoken, speaking)
speak: present tense after *I*, *you*, and *they*.
spoke: simple past tense.
spoken: past participle (used after *has*, *had*, etc.).
speaking: present participle (used after *is*, *are*, *was*, *has been*, etc.)

The connecting verb, **be**, is the most irregular of all:

be *verb* (present tense: *I* ***am***, *you* ***are***, *he or she* ***is***, *we* ***are***, *you* ***are***, *they* ***are***; present participle ***being***; past tense: *I* ***was***, *you* ***were***, *he or she* ***was***, *we* ***were***, *you* ***were***, *they* ***were***; past participle ***been***).

Adjectives

Adjectives are words that describe a noun and add to its meaning:

happy, important, old.

Adverbs

Adverbs are words that tell you how, when, where, or why something happens:

quickly, again, here, together.

Comparison of adjectives and adverbs

Adjectives and adverbs can be made **comparative** or **superlative** in the following ways:

positive	**comparative**	**superlative**
stiff	*stiffer*	*stiffest*
quick	*quicker*	*quickest*
funny	*funnier*	*funniest*
late	*later*	*latest*

(For general rules about adding **-er** and **-est**, see **Spelling**, pA7)

For longer adjectives, and for most adverbs, the comparative and superlative are formed by putting **more** or **most** in front of them:

positive	**comparative**	**superlative**
terrible	*more terrible*	*most terrible*
quickly	*more quickly*	*most quickly*

But watch out for exceptions:

bad	*worse*	*worst*
badly	*worse*	*worst*

If in doubt, look them up in the dictionary.

Prepositions

Prepositions are words put in front of nouns or pronouns to show how the nouns and pronouns are connected with other words:

against, in, on.

Conjunctions

Conjunctions are joining words:

and, but, whether.

Interjections

Interjections are words that express surprise, pain, delight, etc:

oh, ouch, hooray.

Spelling

Some useful rules

To make a noun plural:

Normally, just add **-s**: *skirts, socks, ties, pianos, pieces, stars.*

- ▶ But watch out for some words ending in **-o**, that need **-es**:
  echoes, heroes, potatoes, tomatoes, volcanoes, etc.

To words ending in **-ch, -s, -sh, -x**, or **-z**, add **-es**:
dress — dresses, box — boxes, stitch — stitches.

To some words ending in **-f** and **-fe**, change to **-ves**:
scarf — scarves, life — lives, half — halves.

- ▶ But watch out for the exceptions: *beliefs, proofs, roofs*, etc.

To words ending in a consonant followed by **-y**, change the **y** to **i** and add **-es**:
copy — copies, cry — cries, party — parties.

Adding -ing and -ed to verbs

Normally just add **-ing** or **ed**:
load — loading — loaded; open — opening — opened; stay — staying — stayed.

For short words ending in **-e**, usually leave off the **e**:
race — raced — racing; blame — blamed — blaming.

For many short words that end with one consonant, double the last consonant:
slam — slamming — slammed; tip — tipping — tipped.

For longer words ending with one consonant and having the stress on the last syllable, double the last consonant:
compel — compelling — compelled; prefer — preferring — preferred.

For words ending in **-y** after a consonant, change the **y** to an **i** before **-ed**:
try — trying — tried.

For words ending in **-ie**, change the **ie** to **y** before adding **-ing**:
lie — lying — lied; tie — tying — tied.

- ▶ Watch out for these exceptions: *lay — laid; pay — paid; say — said.*

Adding -er and -est to adjectives

Normally just add **-er** and **-est**, unless the word already ends in **-e**:
cold — colder — coldest; wide — wider — widest.

For many short words that end with one consonant, change to a double consonant:
wet — wetter — wettest; dim — dimmer — dimmest.

If the word has two syllables and ends in **-y**, change the **y** to an **i**;
dirty — dirtier — dirtiest; happy — happier — happiest.

(See also **Grammar**, pA5, on adjective and adverb forms.)

Adding -ly

Adding **-ly** to an adjective makes it into an adverb:
slowly, badly, awkwardly.

If the word ends in **-ll**, just add **-y**:
full — fully.

For words ending in **-y** and with more than one syllable, leave off the **-y** and add **-ily**:
happy — happily; hungry — hungrily.

For words ending in **-le**, leave off the **e**:
idle — idly; simple — simply.

For adjectives ending in **ic**, you usually add **-ally**:
basic — basically; drastic — drastically.

▶ But watch out for these special ones: *public — publicly*.

Confusing words

These pairs of words are often confused. Check that you know the differences in spelling and meaning.

accept/except
affect/effect
affection/affectation
affluent/effluent
allowed/aloud
atheist/agnostic
berth/birth
bought/brought
brake/break
cell/sell
cereal/serial
check/cheque
coarse/course
complement/compliment
confirm/conform
contemptible/contemptuous
continual/continuous
councillor/counsellor
creak/creek
currant/current
desert/dessert
diseased/deceased
dyeing/dying
emaciated/emancipated
eminent/imminent
except/accept
formally/formerly
gamble/gambol
honourable/honorary
horde/hoard
inedible/indelible
its/it's
know/no
know/now
lead/led
lightning/lightening
metre/meter
momentary/momentous
moral/morale
officious/official
perpetuate/perpetrate
persecute/prosecute
personal/personnel
piece/peace
plain/plane
political/politic
prey/pray
principal/principle
queue/cue
quite/quiet
recent/resent
respective/respectful
sceptic/septic
seam/seem
sealing/ceiling
site/sight
sole/soul
spacious/specious
stationary/stationery
straight/strait
successful/successive
superficial/superfluous
there/they're/their
threw/through
vocation/vacation
waist/waste
wet/whet
where/we're/wear
wrap/rap

When words sound alike, learn to use them in their correct context as their meaning will make their spelling clear.

Examples

The car stopped when I applied the brake. If I drop this glass it will break.
The food was inedible. She labelled her clothes with an indelible pen.

Some commonly misspelt words

acceptable
accessible
accidentally
accommodation
acquire
adjournment
admissible
affectation
aghast
alcoholism
align
allotted
amateur
ambiguous
analogue
annihilate
assign
asthma
autumn
ballet
believe
benign
bibliography
bureaucracy
calendar
campaign
capricious
carnivorous
catalogue
category
cemetery
certificate
chandelier
changeable
chasm
cheque
collectible
colloquial
column
committed
communication
condemn
conscience
conscious
consign
continuum

dachshund
debt
definitely
desiccated
deteriorate
dialogue
diesel
discernible
discipline
effervescence
embarrassment
enthusiasm
entrepreneurial
environmentalist
equipment
euthanasia
exception
exhilarate
exceed
familiar
fluorescent
foreign
fraudulent
freight
gaiety
gauge
genealogy
gnarled
gnawed
government
gracious
guarantee
guardian
haemorrhage
hearth
height
heterogeneous
hierarchy
hieroglyphic
idiosyncrasy
inadequacy
incoherent
independent
indict
innovative
inoculate

judgement
language
lascivious
leisure
liaison
library
ludicrous
luscious
malign
manoeuvre
medieval
miniature
miscellaneous
mischievous
moratorium
muscle
noticeable
noxious
numerous
oblique
occasion
occurrence
omitted
onomatopoeia
paradigm
paralleled
parliament
perceive
perseverance
persuade
pharmaceutical
phlegm
piece
piteous
playwright
pneumonia
privilege
pronunciation
psychiatrist
qualm
quarantine
queue
raucous
receipt
receive
recommend

reconnaissance
referred
relevant
rescuing
resign
rheumatism
rhyme
rhythm
ricochet
salmon
satisfactorily
scene
sceptic
schedule
scheme
schism
scintillate
scissors
seize
separate
simile
soldier
straight
succumb
supersede
synonymous
thoroughfare
tongue
traumatic
tsunami
twelfth
tyranny
ubiquitous
unequalled
vaccination
vacuum
ventriloquist
vicissitude
vogue
weight
weird
wrangle
wrath
wrench
yacht

List of prefixes and suffixes

Prefixes

a- not: *atypical.*

Anglo- English: *Anglo-Celtic background.*

ante- before: *antenatal* (= before birth).

anti- against: *antisocial.*

auto- self: *autobiography* (= the story of the writer's own life).

bi- two: *bicycle*, *bilingual* (= using two languages), *bimonthly* (= twice a month or every two months).

cent-, **centi-** hundred: *centenary* (= the hundredth anniversary), *centimetre* (= one hundredth of a metre).

circum- around: *circumnavigate* (= sail around).

co- with; together; *copilot*, *coexist*, *cooperation.*

con- (**col-**, **com-**) with; together: *context* (= the words or sentences that come before and after a particular word or sentence), *collide*, *combine.*

contra- against; opposite: *contradict* (= say the opposite).

counter- against; opposite: *counter-revolution*, *counter-productive* (= producing the opposite of the desired effect).

de- taking something away; the opposite: *defrost*, *decentralise.*

deci- one tenth: *decilitre.*

dis- reverse or opposite: *displease*, *disembark*, *discomfort.*

Euro- European: *Eurocentric.*

ex- former: *ex-wife*, *ex-president.*

extra- **1** very; more than usual: *extra-thin*, *extra-special.* **2** outside; beyond: *extraordinary*, *extra-terrestrial* (= coming from somewhere beyond the earth).

fore- **1** before; in advance: *foretell* (= say what is going to happen), *foreword* (= at the beginning of a book). **2** front: *foreground* (= the front part of a picture), *forehead.*

in- (**il-**, **im-**, **ir-**) not: *incorrect*, *invalid*, *illegal*, *illegible*, *immoral*, *impatient*, *impossible*, *irregular*, *irrelevant.*

Indo- Indian: *Indo-China.*

inter- between; from one to another: *international*, *interracial.*

kilo- thousand: *kilogram*, *kilowatt.*

maxi- most; very large: *maximum.*

mega- million; very large: *megabyte*, *megastar* (= a very famous person).

micro- one millionth; very small; *microgram*, *micro-organism.*

mid- in the middle of: *mid-afternoon*, *mid-air.*

milli- thousandth: *milligram*, *millilitre.*

mini- small: *miniskirt*, *minibus*, *miniseries.*

mis- bad or wrong; not: *misunderstand*, *misbehave*, *miscalculate.*

mono- one; single: *monolingual* (= using one language), *monorail.*

multi- many: *multinational* (= involving many countries).

non- not: *nonsense*, *non-resident*, *non-smoker.*

out- more; to a greater degree: *outdo*, *outrun* (= run faster or better than somebody).

over- more than normal; too much: *overeat*, *oversleep* (= sleep too long), *overestimate* (= guess too high).

post- after; *postwar.*

pre- before: *prepaid*, *preview.*

pro- for; in favour of: *pro-democracy.*

quad- four: *quadruple* (= multiply by four), *quadruplet* (= one of four babies born at the same time).

re- again: *rewrite*, *rebuild.*

semi- half: *semicircle*, *semitrailer.*

Sino- Chinese: *Sino-Japanese.*

sub- **1** below; less than: *subzero*, *subsonic* (= less than the speed of sound). **2** under: *subway*, *subtitles* (= translation under the pictures of a film).

super- extremely; more than: *superhuman* (= having greater power than humans normally have), *supersonic* (= faster than the speed of sound).

tele- far; over a long distance: *telecommunications*, *television*, *telephoto lens.*

trans- across; through: *transatlantic*, *transcontinental.*

tri- three: *triangle*, *tricolour* (= a flag with three colours).

ultra- extremely; beyond a certain limit: *ultramodern*, *ultraviolet* (= light that is beyond what we can normally see).

un- not; opposite; taking something away: *uncertain*, *uncomfortable*, *unsure*, *undo*, *undress.*

uni- one; single: *uniform* (= having the same form).

Suffixes

-able, -ible, -ble to make adjectives; possible to ~: *acceptable, noticeable, convertible, divisible* (= possible to divide), *irresistible* (= that you cannot resist).

-age to make nouns; a process or state: *shortage, storage.*

-al to make adjectives; connected with: *experimental, accidental, environmental.*

-ance, -ence (**-ancy, -ency**) to make nouns; an action, process or state: *appearance, performance, elegance, importance, existence, intelligence, patience.*

-ant, -ent to make nouns; a person who does something: *assistant, immigrant, student.*

-ation to make nouns; a state or action: *examination, imagination, organisation.*

-ble look at **-able**.

-ee to make nouns; a person to whom something is done: *employee* (= one who is employed), *trainee* (= one who is being trained).

-en to make verbs; to give something a particular quality; to make something more ~: *shorten, widen, blacken, sharpen, loosen*, (but note: *lengthen*).

-ence (**-ency**) look at **-ance**.

-ent look at **-ant**.

-er to make nouns; a person who does something: *rider, painter, baker, builder, driver, teacher.*

-ese to make adjectives; from a place: *Japanese, Chinese, Viennese.*

-ess to make nouns; a woman who does something as a job: *waitress, actress.*

-ful to make adjectives; having a particular quality: *helpful, useful, thankful, beautiful.*

-hood to make nouns; a state, often during a particular period of time: *childhood, motherhood.*

-ian to make nouns; a person who does something as a job or hobby: *historian, comedian, politician.*

-ible look at **-able**.

-ical to make adjectives from nouns ending in -y or -ics; connected with: *economical, mathematical, physical.*

-ify to make verbs; to produce a state or quality: *beautify, simplify, purify.*

-ise, -ize to make verbs; actions producing a particular state: *magnetise, standardise, modernise, generalise.*

-ish to make adjectives; **1** describing nationality or language: *English, Swedish, Polish.* **2** like something: *babyish, foolish.* **3** rather, quite: *longish* (= fairly long, but not very long), *youngish, brownish.*

-ist to make nouns; **1** a person who has studied something or does something as a job: *artist, scientist, typist.* **2** a person who believes in something or belongs to a particular group: *capitalist, pacifist, feminist.*

-ion to make nouns; a state or process: *action, connection, exhibition.*

-ive to make adjectives; able to ~, having a particular quality: *attractive, effective.*

-less to make adjectives; not having something: *hopeless, friendless.*

-like to make adjectives; similar to: *childlike.*

-ly to make adverbs; in a particular way: *badly, beautifully, completely.*

-ment to make nouns; a state, action or quality: *development, arrangement, excitement, achievement.*

-ness to make nouns; a state or quality: *kindness, sadness, happiness, weakness.*

-ology to make nouns; the study of a subject: *biology, psychology, zoology.*

-or to make nouns; a person who does something, often as a job: *actor, conductor, sailor.*

-ous to make adjectives; having a particular quality: *dangerous, religious, ambitious.*

-ship to make nouns; showing status: *friendship, membership, citizenship.*

-wards to make adverbs; in a particular direction: *backwards, upwards.*

-wise to make adverbs; in a particular way: *clockwise.*

-y to make adjectives; having the quality of the thing mentioned: *cloudy, rainy, fatty, thirsty, greeny* (= similar to green).

Some common linguistic and literary terms

acronym a word formed from the initial letters of words, e.g., *WINZ*/Work and Income New Zealand; *DOC*/Department of Conservation.

alliteration the repetition of consonant sounds at the beginning of words in close succession for effect, e.g., *the crafty kea kept its cool*; *where wild winds and wekas wither.*

antonym a word of opposite meaning to another, e.g., *generous* is an antonym of *miserly.*

assonance the repetition of vowel sounds in close succession for effect, e.g., *the rank brambles hid tan sandals and the cat by the sandy bank.*

dead metaphor a metaphor that has been accepted into common usage, and used without special attention or consideration, e.g., *the social thread was weakened*; *they passed the hat around*; *he pushed his luck*; *the funds dried up.*

dysphemism a harsh or offensive word or expression, the opposite of euphemism. *Murder house is a dysphemism for dentist.*

eponym a word that is formed from the name of an inventor, breeder or a person connected with it, e.g., *Perendale* (a New Zealand sheep breed, after Sir Geoffrey Peren, a New Zealand scientist and breeder); *Hamilton jet* after Sir Charles Hamilton, a New Zealand engineer.

euphemism a mild or polite word or phrase used instead of an offensive or frank one, *'To pass away' is a euphemism for 'to die'.*

heterocosm a believable imagined other world, created in fiction.

homonym a word having the same sound and spelling as another, but with a different origin and meaning, eg., *dog/a canine animal*; *dog/a gudgeon.*

homophone a word that is pronounced the same as another but has a different spelling and meaning, e.g., *wood/would*

initialism an abbreviation composed of a series of initials, e.g., *NZCER*, New Zealand Council for Educational Research.

metaphor a comparison of two ideas, objects or processes not normally thought of as being alike; rather like a direct simile and not containing 'like' or 'as'. e.g., *the giant cauliflower of sheep moved across the hill*; *the cunning kurī appointed somebody new*; *the moon's a balloon.*

metonymy when a characteristic or aspect of some object or process becomes the substitute term for it, e.g., *the bench* is used for the judge/judges as in *'You must address the Bench'*; *the high country* is used for high-country farmers, as in '*the high country is proceeding spasmodically with its shearing'*.

onomatopoeia a word that sounds like the meaning or sound that it conveys, e.g., *boom, buzz, swish, whisper.*

personification a figure of speech where inanimate objects or processes are given the characteristics of living beings (animate objects), e.g., *the wind whispered*; *the moon lifted its face to the stars*; *the city slept.*

sibilance the repetition of an s or z sound in close succession for effect, e.g., *she whispered sweet soft decibels of sound.*

simile a comparison between two ideas, objects or processes not normally thought of as being alike; containing either 'like' or 'as'. e.g., *the mob of sheep moved like a giant cauliflower across the hill*; *as cunning as a kurī*; *the moon's like a balloon.*

synonym a word of the same or similar meaning as another, e.g., *taonga* is a synonym for treasure.

toponym a place-name or a word that is formed from the name of a place or after an event at a place, e.g., *Corriedale*, *Mystery Creek*, *Washpool.*

verisimilitude the construction of credible reality in literature, as in '*the frailty of the characters adds to the verisimilitude*'.

Some common New Zealand abbreviations, acronyms and initialisms

ACC	Accident Compensation Corporation
Ak	Auckland
ALAC	Alcoholic Liquor Advisory Council
Anzac	Australian and New Zealand Army Corps
ARA	Auckland Regional Authority
BIA	Building Industry Authority
BSA	Broadcasting Standards Authority
BYO	Bring Your Own
CAB	Citizen's Advice Bureau
CCMAU	Crown Company Monitoring Advisory Unit
CD	Civil Defence
ChCh	Christchurch
COGS	Community Organisations Grant Scheme
CPI	Consumer Price Index
CRI	Crown Research Institute
CYF	Child Youth and Family
DIY	Do It Yourself
Dn	Dunedin
DOC	Department of Conservation
DPB	Domestic Purposes Benefit
EEO	Equal Employment Opportunity
EEZ	Exclusive Economic Zone
ERMA	Environmental Risk Management Authority
ERO	Education Review Office
EQC	Earthquake Commission
FRSNZ	Fellow, Royal Society of New Zealand
GRI	Guaranteed Retirement Income
GSF	Government Superannuation Fund
GST	Goods and Services Tax
Hn	Hamilton
IRD	Inland Revenue Department
JAFA	Just another f-ing Aucklander
LINZ	Land Information New Zealand
LMVD	Licensed Motor Vehicle Dealer
LSZ	Limited Speed Zone
LTNZ	Land Transport New Zealand
MAF	Ministry of Agriculture and Forestry
MONZ	Museum of New Zealand
MORST	Ministry of Research, Science and Technology
MOT	Ministry of Transport
MOTAT	Museum of Transport and Technology
MP	Minister of Parliament
NCEA	National Certificate of Educational Achievement

NIWA	National Institute of Water and Atmospheric Research
NZD	New Zealand Dollar
NZDF	New Zealand Defence Force
NZFSA	New Zealand Food Safety Authority
NZPA	New Zealand Press Association
NZPD	New Zealand Parliamentary Debates
NZQA	New Zealand Qualifications Authority
NZRU	New Zealand Rugby Union
NZSF	New Zealand Superannuation Fund
NZSO	New Zealand Symphony Orchestra
NZX	New Zealand Stock Exchange
OSH	Occupational Safety and Health
PHARMAC	Pharmaceutical Management Agency
PHO	Primary Health Organisation
PN	Palmerston North
RD	Rural Delivery
RNZ	Radio New Zealand
RNZAF	Royal New Zealand Air Force
RNZN	Royal New Zealand Navy
RONZ	Rest of New Zealand
SAR	Search and Rescue
SIS	Security Intelligence Service
SOE	State Owned Enterprise
SPARC	Sport and Recreation New Zealand
TAB	Totalisator Agency Board
TEC	Tertiary Education Commission
TPK	Te Puni Kōkiri (Ministry of Māori Affairs)
WEA	Workers' Education Association
WINZ	Work and Income New Zealand
Wn	Wellington
WOF	Warrant of Fitness

Universal Internet domain addresses

.com	top level domain for commerce
.edu	top level domain for education
.gov/.govt	top level domain for government
.mil	top level domain for military
.net	top level domain for network providers
.org	top level domain for non-profit organisations

Pictograms and text language

:-)	= smile
;-)	= wink
:-@	= screaming
(*o*)	= surprised
(^_^)	= cute
@	at
@oms	atoms
@wrk	at work
abt2	about to
addy	address
adn	any day now
afaict	as far as I can tell
afrd	afraid
aisb	as I said before
aisi	as I see it
aka	also known as
ambw	all my best wishes
asaik	as soon as I know
asap	as soon as possible
atb	all the best
atm	at the moment
ayt	are you there?
b	be
b4	before
bc / b/c	because
bbs	be back soon
bhl8	be home late
brb	be right back
btwn	between
btw	by the way
cya	see you later
2day	today
def	definitely
dno	don’t know
dw	don’t worry
ez / ezy	easy
f9	fine
fyi	for your information
gr8	great
gtg / g2g	got to go
hand	have a nice day
hru	how are you?
idc	I don't care
idk	I don't know
404	I don't know
jj / jk	just joking/just kidding
j2luk	just to let you know
lol	laugh out loud/lots of love
msg	message
mtf	more to follow
n1	nice one
ne1	anyone
nm	never mind
no1	no one
nty	no thank you
nm	not much
np	no problem
ofc	of course
omw	on my way
pcm	please call me
pls	please
?4u	I have a question for you

ruf2t	are you free to talk
ruok	are you OK?
som1	someone
sotmg	short of time must go
sry	sorry
2mi	too much information
2nte	tonight
thx	thanks
tom	tomorrow
ttyl	talk to you later
txt / tb	text/text back
ty / tyvm	thank you/ thank you very much
wb	welcome back
wknd	weekend
wu	what's up?
xlnt	excellent
yr	your
zzz	sleeping

A quick guide

Single letters:

- be = **b**
- see = **c**
- are = **r**
- you = **u**
- why = **y**

Single numbers:

- ate = **8**
- for = **4**
- to or too = **2**

Single letters or numbers can replace syllables and words:

- great = **gr8**
- mate = **m8**
- later becomes **l8r** or **l8a**
- tomorrow = **2mro**
- before = **b4**
- therefore = **thr4**

Some common descriptive terms of music

adagio	slow, leisurely
adagietto	slightly faster than adagio
adagissimo	very slowly
allegretto	moderately fast, but slower than allegro
allegro	lively, brisk
andante	moderately slow
ardente	fiery
baroque	of the 1600–1750 period, usually grand and elaborate in style
classical	of the 1750–1800 period, usually simple in style
crescendo	gradually becoming louder
diminuendo	gradually becoming softer
dolce	sweet
forte	loud, strong
fortissimo	very loud
istesso tempo	the same tempo
largo	broad, slow
legato	smooth and connected
lento	slow
mezzo forte	moderately loud
mezzo piano	moderately soft
pianissimo	very soft
piano	soft
presto	fast
romantic	of the 1800s period, usually rich, emotional, and harmonious in style
scherzando	playful, light, humorous
staccato	in a short, sharp separated manner
tempo	the speed at which a musical composition is performed
tutto, tutti	complete, all
vivace	bright, lively

Some foreign food terms

à la carte the separate pricing of each item on a menu. (French)
aioli a garlic mayonnaise. (French)
akra (also **acra**) a battered and fried savoury fritter. (Caribbean)
al dente of food that is cooked until tender but firm. (Italian)
al fresco eating out of doors. (Italian)
ambrosia a dessert, usually composed of fruit and cream. (Greek)
antipasto hot or cold appetiser served at the beginning of a meal. (Italian)
aperitif an alcoholic drink taken before a meal to stimulate the appetite. (French)
Arborio a type of short-grained rice used to make risotto. (Italian)
au choix of your choice. (French)
au gratin food browned under a grill, often with cheese topping. (French)
au naturel food served in its natural or raw state. (French)
baba ganoush a creamy dip with an eggplant base. (Middle East)
bagel a doughnut-shaped yeast roll with a varnished crust. (Jewish)
baguette a classic long thin loaf of bread with a crisp crust. (French)
balsamic vinegar a dark vintage vinegar used in salads, marinades, and sauces.
basmati a type of white long-grained rice. (Indian)
béarnaise a classic sauce made with egg yolks and butter. (French)
béchamel a basic white sauce of flour, milk, and butter. (French)
biltong dried strips of lean meat (also known as *jerky*). (South African)
biscotti crisp twice-cooked biscuits. (Italian)
blini a small yeast pancake. (Russian)
blintz a thin pancake cooked on one side only and filled. (Jewish)
bocconcini small balls of mozzarella cheese. (Italian)
bok choy a long-stemmed leafy green vegetable. (Chinese)
Bombay duck dried salted fish used to flavour curry dishes. (Indian)
borsch (also **borscht**) a hot or cold soup made with beetroot. (Russian)
bouquet garni a small bunch of herbs used to flavour meat dishes and sauces. (French)
Brie a soft cheese made from cows' milk. (French)
bruschetta slices of crusty bread lightly toasted and rubbed with garlic, oil, etc. (Italian)
cacciatore traditional stew of chicken or rabbit, tomatoes, and mushrooms. (Italian)
Caesar salad salad of lettuce, croutons, parmesan cheese, and anchovies. (American)
café au lait espresso coffee with warmed or steamed milk. (French)
café noir plain black espresso coffee. (French)
caffe espresso strong black coffee made by forcing steam through ground coffee. (Italian)
caffe latte espresso coffee combined with an equal amount of steamed milk. (Italian)
Cajun a spicy type of cooking developed by French settlers in Louisiana. (American)
calzone a small flat loaf made with pizza dough and stuffed with cheese, ham, etc. (Italian)
Camembert a soft cheese made from cows' milk. (French)
canapé bite-sized pieces of food served with cocktails or as antipasto. (French)
cannelloni pasta tubes stuffed with savoury filling. (Italian)
cappuccino espresso coffee with hot steamed and frothy milk. (Italian)
cassata a traditional ice-cream made with candied fruit, nuts, etc. (Italian)
caviar the pressed salted eggs of a sturgeon fish.
chasseur a sauce made with wine, mushrooms, tomatoes, and herbs. (French)

chilli con carne a Mexican-style dish made of minced meat, tomatoes, garlic, chillies, red beans, and herbs and spices. (American)

chorizo a spicy pork sausage. (Spanish)

choux a light pastry used for chocolate éclairs and cream puffs. (French)

chow mein a stir-fried dish of meat and vegetables. (Chinese)

ciabatta a flat bread made with olive oil. (Italian)

clotted cream lightly cooked cream that develops a thick layer used when cool. (English)

compote fruit poached in a sugar syrup. (French)

consommé meat, fish, or vegetable stock. (French)

coq au vin chicken cooked in wine with mushrooms and garlic. (French)

coulis a purée of fruit or vegetables or a thick seafood soup. (French)

couscous a savoury dish made from semolina grain. (North African)

crème anglais a light custard sauce. (French)

crème brulée a rich egg custard with a caramelised topping. (French)

crème fraîche a thick, velvety, naturally soured cream. (French)

Creole cooking a style of cooking originating in Louisiana from French, Spanish, African, and American Indian influences. (American)

crostini small pieces of toast like croutons, usually topped with savoury items. (Italian)

croustade a hollowed bread or pastry shell filled with savoury fillings. (French)

crouton a small cube of toasted or fried bread. (French)

crudités assorted raw vegetables served with a cold sauce as an appetiser. (French)

Danbo a semi-soft cheese made from cows' milk. (Danish)

Danish pastry a flaky yeast-dough pastry, filled with fruit or custard. (Danish)

daube a casserole made with meat, wine, herbs, and spices. (French)

dhal a name for lentils, beans, peas and chickpeas or a spicy dish made from these. (Indian)

dim sum a range of steamed or fried appetisers and dishes, usually served as a snack. (Chinese)

dolmas (also **dolmades**) vine leaves traditionally stuffed with rice, lamb, and mixed flavourings. (Greek)

Edam a semi-hard pressed cows' milk cheese with a bright red waxy coating. (Dutch)

Emmental a semi-hard, nutty-flavoured cows' milk cheese with large holes. (Swiss)

entrée in France, this is a dish between the fish and the roast course in a menu, in America it is the main course, and in New Zealand, it is usually the dish served before the main course.

escargot an edible snail. (French)

falafel a small patty made from spicy-flavoured beans or chickpeas and onions. (Mid Eastern)

feta a salty white cheese traditionally made from sheeps' milk. (Greek)

fettuccine/fettucine a long flat ribbon-like pasta. (Italian)

ficelle a small thin baguette. (French)

focaccia a flat bread made from leavened dough, traditionally brushed with olive oil, herbs, and salt. (Italian)

fondue a dish cooked in a burner at the table. (French)

fricassee a stew of white meat, white wine, cream, and eggs. (French)

frittata a savoury omelette. (Italian)

gado-gado a cooked vegetable salad with a peanut sauce. (Indonesian)

gazpacho a chilled uncooked soup of cucumber, tomato, onion, peppers, and garlic. (Spanish)
gelato a smooth creamy flavoured ice-cream made with egg yolks. (Italian)
gnocchi small dumplings often made with potatoes or flour. (Italian)
gorgonzola a strong blue-vein cheese. (Italian)
gouda a firm, nutty-flavoured cheese with small holes, made from cows' milk. (Dutch)
goulash a traditional beef stew flavoured with paprika, onions, and tomatoes. (Hungarian)
gremolata a blend of parsley, garlic and lemon zest, used as a garnish. (Italian)
gruyère a smooth cheese made from cows' milk, with small holes. (Swiss)
guacamole a dip made from avocado, onions, garlic, and lemon juice. (Mexican)
gumbo a thick soup or stew (also a name for okra). (American Creole)
haggis a traditional dish of sheep's stomach filled with oatmeal, herbs, and offal. (Scottish)
haloumi a firm mint-flavoured sheeps' milk cheese. (Middle Eastern)
harissa a hot spicy paste of chillies and olive oil. (North African)
havarti a mild-flavoured, semi-firm cows' milk cheese, with small holes. (Danish)
hummus a creamy dip made from chickpeas, lemon juice, olive oil, garlic, and tahini. (Middle Eastern)
jambalaya a highly spiced Creole rice dish. (American)
kofta small balls of spiced minced meat, fish, or vegetables. (Middle Eastern)
kosher food produced and served according to religious custom. (Jewish)
laksa a traditional soup made from coconut milk, noodles, lemongrass, and other herbs and spices. (Malaysian)
lasagne pasta cut into wide sheets (also a dish with layers of pasta, meat, tomatoes, and cheese sauce). (Italian)
mascarpone a rich, thick and sweet dairy product made from cream and used in desserts. (Italian)
mesclun a mix of salad greens such as rocket, radicchio, and mizuna. (French)
minestrone a traditional thick vegetable soup containing pasta. (Italian)
moussaka a traditional dish made with potato or eggplant, onions, tomato, and minced meat. (Greek)
mousse a light, cold dessert or moulded savoury dish. (French)
mozzarella a stretchy cows' milk cheese, often used in pizza and pasta dishes. (Italian)
naan a flat leavened bread, made of white flour, often baked on the side of a tandoori oven. (Indian)
nachos corn tortillas or chips topped with beans, tomatoes, chillies, and cheese. (Mexican)
nasi goreng a rice dish made with pork, chicken, prawns, and garlic, sometimes with strips of omelette. (Indonesian)
pad thai a traditional stir-fried dish of noodles, eggs, chilli, peanuts, and coriander. (Thai)
paella a traditional rice dish containing seafood, chicken, vegetables, and garlic. (Spanish)
panini a flat, filled bread roll, usually served toasted. (Italian)
pappadum (also **pappadam** and **poppadam**) a very thin crisp biscuit made from lentil flour and traditionally served with curry dishes. (Indian)
Parmesan a hard, low-fat cows' milk cheese, usually grated or shaved for garnishes or toppings. (Italian)
pastrami cuts of lean beef rubbed with salt and spices and cured and smoked. (Italian)
pâté de foie gras a richly flavoured pâté made from goose or duck liver. (French)

pecorino a variety of cheeses made from sheeps' milk. (Italian)

pesto a paste traditionally made of fresh basil or other fresh herbs, nuts, parmesan cheese, olive oil, and garlic. (Italian)

pita a round or oval bread pocket which can be filled or served in wedges with soups or dips. (Middle Eastern)

polenta a yellow cornmeal. (Italian)

pommes frites fine chips or French fries. (French)

Port-Salut a semi-soft cheese, made from cows' milk, with an orange rind. (French)

prix fixe a fixed price menu. (French)

prosciutto a lightly salted ham. (Italian)

quark an unripened low-fat white cheese. (German)

quiche a traditional tart, made with eggs, cheese, cream, and vegetables. (French)

raclette a pale, semi-firm cows' milk cheese, often melted for use with potato dishes. (Swiss)

ragout a rich stew made with meat, wine, herbs, and vegetables. (French)

raita a yoghurt and vegetable dish used as an accompaniment to curries. (Indian)

ratatouille a vegetable stew traditionally made from lightly cooked eggplant, tomatoes, peppers, and garlic. (French)

ravioli small pieces of pasta stuffed with meat or vegetables, usually served with a tomato-based sauce. (Italian)

rendang a hot beef curry. (Indonesian)

ricotta a white cheese-like product, made from the whey of sheeps' milk and used mainly in cooking. (Italian)

risotto a flavoured rice dish made from arborio rice. (Italian)

Roquefort a rich blue-vein cheese made from sheeps' milk. (French)

roti breads such as chapati, naan, and paratha. (Indian)

satay skewered meat or vegetables served with a spicy sauce. (Indonesian, Malaysian)

Stilton a rich, moist blue-vein cheese made from cows' milk. (English)

sushi (also **zushi**) a vinegared rice dish, often held together with nori, an edible seaweed. (Japanese)

tabbouleh/tabbouli a salad made with cracked wheat, onions, parsley, tomatoes, and lemon juice. (Middle Eastern)

taco a folded tortilla, often filled with minced meat, guacamole, and tomatoes. (Mexican)

tapas a selection of small snacks and appetisers served in bars and cafes. (Spanish)

tapenade a thick paste of black olives, capers, etc served with toast etc. (French)

taramasalata a thick paste made from fish roe, lemon juice, etc. and used as a dip or topping. (Greek)

tofu a bean curd, used in a variety of dishes. (Japanese)

tortilla a thin cornmeal bread, usually eaten with fillings (Mexican), a savoury omelette. (Spanish)

vinaigrette a dressing made from oil and vinegar, and flavoured with herbs, garlic, etc. (French)

won ton a small deep-fried dough pocket with a savoury filling. (Chinese)

yum cha a traditional weekend brunch composed of a variety of dishes. (Chinese)

Some foreign words and phrases used in English

ad hoc done or arranged only when necessary and not planned in advance. [Latin, = for this]

ad infinitum (*say* in-fin-**I**-tum) without limit; for ever. [Latin, = to infinity]

ad nauseam (*say* **naw**-see-am) until people are sick of it. [Latin, = to sickness]

aide-de-camp (*say* ayd-der-**kahm**) a military officer who is the assistant to a senior officer. [French, = camp helper]

à la carte ordered and paid for as separate items from a menu. (Compare *table d'hôte*.) [French, = from the menu]

alfresco *adjective & adverb* in the open air, *an alfresco meal*. [from Italian *al fresco* = in the fresh air]

alter ego another, very different, side of someone's personality. [Latin, = other self]

au fait (*say* oh **fay**) knowing a subject or procedure etc. well. [French, = to the point]

au gratin (*say* oh gra-**tan**) cooked with a crisp topping of breadcrumbs or grated cheese. [French]

au revoir (*say* oh rev-**wahr**) goodbye for the moment. [French, = to be seeing again]

avant-garde (*say* av-ahn-**gard**) *noun & adjective* people who use a very modern style in art or literature etc. [French, = vanguard]

bête noire (*say* bayt **nwahr**) a person or thing you greatly dislike. [French, = black beast]

bona fide (*say* **boh**-na-**fy**-dee) *adjective* genuine; without fraud, *Are they bona fide tourists or spies?* [Latin, = in good faith]

bona fides (*say* **boh**-na-**fy**-deez) *noun* honest intention; sincerity, *We do not doubt his bona fides*. [Latin, = good faith]

bon voyage (*say* bawn vwah-**yah***zh*) pleasant journey! [French]

carte blanche (*say* kart **blahnsh**) freedom to act as you think best. [French, = blank paper]

c'est la vie (*say* say la **vee**) life is like that. [French, = that is life]

chef-d'oeuvre (*say* shay **dervr**) a masterpiece. [French, = chief work]

compos mentis in your right mind; sane. (The opposite is **non compos mentis**.) [Latin, = having control of the mind]

cordon bleu (*say* kor-dawn **bler**) (of cooks and cookery) first-class. [French, = blue ribbon]

corps de ballet (*say* kor der **bal**-ay) the whole group of dancers (not the soloists) in a ballet. [French]

corps diplomatique (*say* kor dip-lom-at-**eek**) the diplomatic service. [French]

coup de grâce (*say* koo der **grahs**) a stroke or blow that puts an end to something. [French, = mercy-blow]

coup d'état (*say* koo day-**tah**) the sudden overthrow of a government. [French, = blow of state]

crème de la crème (*say* krem der la krem) the very best of something. [French, = cream of the cream]

curriculum vitae (*say* **veet**-I) a brief account of a person's education, career, etc. [Latin, = course of life]

déjà vu (*say* day-*zh*a **vew**) a feeling that you have already experienced what is happening now. [French, = already seen]

de rigueur (*say* der rig-**er**) proper; required by custom or etiquette. [French, = of strictness]

de trop (*say* der **troh**) not wanted; unwelcome. [French, = too much]

doppelgänger (*say* **dop**-el-geng-er) *noun* the ghost of a living person. [German, = double-goer]

dramatis personae (*say* **dram**-a-tis per-**sohn**-I) the characters in a play. [Latin, = persons of the drama]

en bloc (*say* ahn **blok**) all at the same time; in a block. [French]

en masse (*say* ahn **mass**) all together. [French, = in a mass]

en passant (*say* ahn **pas**-ahn) by the way. [French, = in passing]

en route (*say* ahn **root**) on the way. [French]

entente (*say* ahn-**tahnt** *or* on-**tont**) *noun* a friendly understanding between nations. [French]

esprit de corps (*say* es-pree der **kor**) loyalty to your group. [French, = spirit of the body]

eureka (*say* yoor-**eek**-a) *interjection* I have found it! [Greek]

exeunt (*say* **eks**-ee-unt) *verb* they leave the stage. [Latin, = they go out]

ex gratia (*say* eks **gray**-sha) given without being legally obliged to be given, *an ex gratia payment*. [Latin, = from favour]

faux pas (*say* foh **pah**) an embarrassing blunder. [French, = false step]

gratis free; for nothing. [Latin]

hara-kiri *noun* a form of suicide formerly used by Japanese officers when in disgrace. [from Japanese *hara* = belly, *kiri* = cutting]

hoi polloi the ordinary people; the masses. [Greek, = the many]

Homo sapiens human beings regarded as a species of animal. [Latin, = wise man]

hors-d'oeuvre (*say* or-**dervr**) *noun* food served as an appetiser at the start of a meal. [French, = outside the work]

in camera in a judge's private room, not in public. [Latin, = in the room]

in extremis (*say* eks-**treem**-iss) at the point of death; in very great difficulties. [Latin, = in the greatest danger]

in memoriam in memory (of). [Latin]

in situ (*say* **sit**-yoo) in its original place. [Latin]

joie de vivre (*say zh*wah der **veevr**) a feeling of great enjoyment of life. [French, = joy of life]

laissez-faire (*say* lay-say-**fair**) *noun* a government's policy of not interfering. [French, = let (them) act]

magnum opus a great achievement. [Latin]

maître d'hôtel (*say* metr doh-**tel**) a head waiter. [French, = master of house]

milieu (*say* **meel**-yer) *noun* environment; surroundings. [French, from *mi* = mid + *lieu* = place]

modus operandi (*say* moh-dus op-er-**and**-ee) **1** a person's way of working. **2** the way a thing works. [Latin, = way of working]

nem.con. *abbreviation* unanimously. [short for Latin *nemine contradicente* = with nobody disagreeing]

nom de plume a writer's pseudonym. [French, = pen-name (this phrase is not used in France)]

non sequitur (*say* non **sek**-wit-er) a conclusion that does not follow from the evidence given. [Latin, = it does not follow]

nota bene (*say* noh-ta-**ben**-ee) (usually shortened to NB) note carefully. [Latin, = note well]

nouveau riche (*say* noo-voh **reesh**) a person who has only recently become rich. [French, = new rich]

objet d'art (*say* ob-*zh*ay **dar**) a small artistic object. [French, = object of art]

par excellence (*say* par eks-el-**ahns**) more than all the others; to the greatest degree. [French, = because of special excellence]

pas de deux (*say* pah der **der**) a dance (e.g. in a ballet) for two persons. [French, = step of two]

pâté de foie gras (*say* pat-ay der fwah **grah**) a paste or pie of goose liver. [French, = paste of fat liver]

per annum for each year; yearly. [Latin]

per capita (*say* **kap**-it-a) for each person. [Latin, = for heads]

per diem by the day. [Latin]

persona grata (*say* per-soh-na **grah**-ta) a person who is acceptable to someone, especially a diplomat acceptable to a foreign government. (The opposite is **persona non grata**.) [Latin, = pleasing person]

pièce de résistance (*say* pee-ess der ray-zees-**tahns**) the most important item. [French]

placebo (*say* plas-**ee**-boh) *noun* (*plural* **placebos**) a harmless substance given as if it were medicine, usually to reassure a patient. [Latin, = I shall be pleasing]

poste restante (*say* rest-**ahnt**) a part of a post office where letters etc. are kept until called for. [French, = letters remaining]

prima facie (*say* pry-ma **fay**-see) at first sight; judging by the first impression. [Latin, = on first appearance]

quid pro quo (*say* kwoh) something given or done in return for something. [Latin, = something for something]

raison d'être (*say* ray-zawn **detr**) the purpose of a thing's existence. [French, = reason for being]

rigor mortis (*say* rig-er **mor**-tis) stiffening of the body after death. [Latin, = stiffness of death]

RIP *abbreviation* may he or she (or they) rest in peace. [short for Latin *requiescat* (or *requiescant*) *in pace*]

sang-froid (*say* sahn-**frawh**) *noun* calmness in danger or difficulty. [French, = cold blood]

savoir faire (*say* sav-wahr **fair**) *noun* knowledge of how to behave socially. [French, = knowing how to do]

sotto voce (*say* sot-oh **voh**-chee) in a very quiet voice. [Italian, = under the voice]

status quo (*say* stay-tus **kwoh**) the state of affairs as it was before a change. [Latin, = the state in which]

sub judice (*say* **joo**-dis-ee) being decided by a judge or lawcourt. [Latin, = under a judge]

table d'hôte (*say* tahbl **doht**) a restaurant meal served at a fixed inclusive price. (Compare **à la carte**.) [French, = host's table]

terra firma dry land; the ground. [Latin, = firm land]

tête-à-tête (*say* tayt-ah-**tayt**) *noun* a private conversation, especially between two people. [French, = head to head]

vis-à-vis (*say* veez-ah-**vee**) *adverb & preposition* **1** in a position facing one another, opposite to. **2** as compared with. [French, = face to face]

viva voce (*say* vy-va **voh**-chee) in a spoken test or examination. [Latin, = with the living voice]

volte-face (*say* volt-**fahs**) *noun* a complete change in your attitude towards something. [French]

Countries of the world (including some dependent territories)

Country	People	Adjective
Afghanistan	Afghans	Afghan
Albania	Albanians	Albanian
Algeria	Algerians	Algerian
America (*see* United States of America)		
Andorra	Andorrans	Andorran
Angola	Angolans	Angolan
Anguilla	Anguillans	Anguillan
Antigua and Barbuda	Antiguans, Barbudans	Antiguan, Barbudan
Argentina	Argentinians	Argentinian *or* Argentine
Armenia	Armenians	Armenian
Australia	Australians	Australian
Austria	Austrians	Austrian
Azerbaijan	Azerbaijanis *or* Azeris	Azerbaijani
Bahamas	Bahamians	Bahamian
Bahrain	Bahrainis	Bahraini
Bangladesh	Bangladeshis	Bangladeshi
Barbados	Barbadians	Barbadian
Belarus	Belorussians	Belorussian
Belgium	Belgians	Belgian
Belize	Belizians	Belizian
Benin	Beninese	Beninese
Bermuda	Bermudans	Bermudan
Bhutan	Bhutanese	Bhutanese
Bolivia	Bolivians	Bolivian
Bosnia and Herzegovina	Bosnians *or* Herzegovinians	Bosnian Herzegovinian
Botswana	Motswana, *plural* Batswana	Motswana, *plural* Batswana
Brazil	Brazilians	Brazilian
Britain (part of the United Kingdom)	British or Britons	British
Brunei	Bruneians	Bruneian
Bulgaria	Bulgarians	Bulgarian
Burkina Faso	Burkinese	Burkinese
Burma (*see* Myanmar)		
Burundi	Burundians	Burundi
Cambodia	Cambodians	Cambodian
Cameroon	Cameroonians	Cameroonian
Canada	Canadians	Canadian
Cape Verde Islands	Cape Verdeans	Cape Verdean
Cayman Islands	Cayman Islanders	Cayman Islands
Central African Republic	Central African	Central African Republic
Chad	Chadians	Chadian
Chile	Chileans	Chilean
China	Chinese	Chinese

Colombia	Colombians	Colombian
Comoros	Comorans	Comoran
Congo, Republic of	Congolese	Congolese
Congo, Democratic Republic of	Congolese	Congolese
Costa Rica	Costa Ricans	Costa Rican
Croatia	Croats *or* Croatians	Croatian
Cuba	Cubans	Cuban
Cyprus	Cypriots	Cypriot
Czech Republic	Czechs	Czech
Denmark	Danes	Danish
Djibouti	Djiboutians	Djiboutian
Dominica	Dominicans	Dominican
Dominican Republic	Dominicans	Dominican
East Timor	East Timorese	East Timorese
Ecuador	Ecuadoreans	Ecuadorean
Egypt	Egyptians	Egyptian
El Salvador	Salvadoreans	Salvadorean
England (part of the United Kingdom)	English	English
Equatorial Guinea	Equatorial Guineans	Equatorial Guinean
Eritrea	Eritreans	Eritrean
Estonia	Estonians	Estonian
Ethiopia	Ethiopians	Ethiopian
Falkland Islands	Falkland Islanders	Falkland Islands
Fiji	Fijians	Fijian *or* Fiji
Finland	Finns	Finnish
France	French	French
Gabon	Gabonese	Gabonese
Gambia	Gambians	Gambian
Georgia	Georgians	Georgian
Germany	Germans	German
Ghana	Ghanaians	Ghanaian
Gibraltar	Gibraltarians	Gibraltarian
Great Britain (*see* United Kingdom)		
Greece	Greeks	Greek
Grenada	Grenadians	Grenadian
Guatemala	Guatemalans	Guatemalan
Guinea	Guineans	Guinean
Guinea-Bissau	Guinean	Guinean
Guyana	Guyanese	Guyanese
Haiti	Haitians	Haitian
Honduras	Hondurans	Honduran
Hong Kong	People of Hong Kong	Hong Kong
Hungary	Hungarians	Hungarian
Iceland	Icelanders	Icelandic
India	Indians	Indian

Indonesia	Indonesians	Indonesian
Iran	Iranians	Iranian
Iraq	Iraqis	Iraqi
Ireland, Republic of	Irish	Irish
Israel	Israelis	Israeli *or* Israel
Italy	Italians	Italian
Ivory Coast	Ivorians	Ivorian
Jamaica	Jamaicans	Jamaican
Japan	Japanese	Japanese
Jordan	Jordanians	Jordanian
Kazakhstan	Kazakhs	Kazakh
Kenya	Kenyans	Kenyan
Kiribati	I-Kiribati	I-Kiribati
Korea (*see* North, South Korea)		
Kuwait	Kuwaitis	Kuwaiti
Kyrgyzstan	Kyrgyz	Kyrgyz
Laos	Laotians	Laotian
Latvia	Latvians	Latvian
Lebanon	Lebanese	Lebanese
Lesotho	Mosotho, *plural* Basotho	Basotho
Liberia	Liberians	Liberian
Libya	Libyans	Libyan
Liechtenstein	Liechtensteiners	Liechtenstein
Lithuania	Lithuanians	Lithuanian
Luxembourg	Luxembourgers	Luxembourgian
Madagascar	Madagascan	Malagasy *or* Madagascan
Malawi	Malawians	Malawian
Malaysia	Malaysians	Malaysian
Maldives	Maldivians	Maldivian
Mali	Malians	Malian
Malta	Maltese	Maltese
Marshall Islands	Marshall Islanders	Marshallese
Mauritania	Mauritanians	Mauritanian
Mauritius	Mauritians	Mauritian
Mexico	Mexicans	Mexican
Micronesia	Micronesians	Micronesian
Monaco	Monégasques	Monégasque
Mongolia	Mongolians	Mongolian
Montenegro	Montenegrins	Montenegrin
Montserrat	Montserratians	Montserrat
Morocco	Moroccans	Moroccan
Mozambique	Mozambicans	Mozambican
Myanmar (until 1989 called *Burma*)	People of Myanmar	Myanmar
Namibia	Namibians	Namibian
Nauru	Nauruans	Nauruan

Nepal	Nepalese	Nepalese
Netherlands	Dutch *or* Netherlanders	Dutch *or* Netherlands
New Zealand	New Zealanders	New Zealand
Nicaragua	Nicaraguans	Nicaraguan
Niger	Nigeriens	Nigerien
Nigeria	Nigerians	Nigerian
Northern Ireland (part of the United Kingdom)	Northern Irish	Northern Irish *or* Northern Ireland
North Korea	North Koreans	North Korean
Norway	Norwegians	Norwegian
Oman	Omanis	Omani *or* Oman
Pakistan	Pakistanis	Pakistani
Palau	Palauans	Palauan
Panama	Panamanians	Panamanian
Papua New Guinea	Papua New Guineans	Papua New Guinean
Paraguay	Paraguayans	Paraguayan
Peru	Peruvians	Peruvian
Philippines	Filipinos *or* Filipina	Filipino or Philippine
Pitcairn Islands	Pitcairn Islanders	Pitcairn
Poland	Poles	Polish
Portugal	Portuguese	Portuguese
Puerto Rico	Puerto Ricans	Puerto Rican
Qatar	Qataris	Qatari *or* Qatar
Romania	Romanians	Romanian
Russia	Russians	Russian
Rwanda	Rwandans	Rwandan
St Helena	St Helenians	St Helenian *or* St Helena
St Kitts-Nevis	People of St Kitts-Nevis	Nevisian Kittitian
St Lucia	St Lucians	St Lucian *or* St Lucia
St Vincent and the Grenadines	Vincentians	Vincentian *or* St Vincent
Samoa	Samoans	Samoan
San Marino	Sammarinese	Sammarinese
São Tomé and Principe	São Toméan	São Toméan
Saudi Arabia	Saudi Arabians *or* Saudis	Saudi Arabian *or* Saudi
Scotland (part of the United Kingdom)	Scots	Scottish, Scots, *or* Scotch
Senegal	Senegalese	Senegalese
Serbia	Serbians	Serbian
Seychelles	Seychellois	Seychelles *or* Seychellois
Sierra Leone	Sierra Leoneans	Sierra Leonean *or* Sierra Leone
Singapore	Singaporeans	Singaporean
Slovakia	Slovaks	Slovak
Slovenia	Slovenes *or* Slovenians	Slovenian
Solomon Islands	Solomon Islanders	Solomon Islander

Somalia	Somalis	Somali
South Africa	South Africans	South African
South Korea	South Koreans	South Korean
Spain	Spaniards	Spanish
Sri Lanka	Sri Lankans	Sri Lankan
Sudan	Sudanese	Sudanese
Suriname	Surinamers	Surinamese
Swaziland	Swazis	Swazi
Sweden	Swedes	Swedish
Switzerland	Swiss	Swiss
Syria	Syrians	Syrian
Taiwan	Taiwanese	Taiwanese
Tajikistan	Tajiks	Tajik
Tanzania	Tanzanians	Tanzanian
Thailand	Thais	Thai
Togo	Togolese	Togolese
Tonga	Tongans	Tongan
Trinidad and Tobago	Trinidadians *or* Tobagans *or* Tobagonians	Trinidadian *or* Tobagan *or* Tobagonian
Tunisia	Tunisians	Tunisian
Turkey	Turks	Turkish
Turkmenistan	Turkmens	Turkmen
Tuvalu	Tuvaluans	Tuvaluan
Uganda	Ugandans	Ugandan
Ukraine	Ukrainians	Ukrainian
United Arab Emirates	Emirians	Emirian
United Kingdom	British or Britons	British
United States of America	United States citizen *or* Americans	United States *or* American
Uruguay	Uruguayans	Uruguayan
Uzbekistan	Uzbeks	Uzbek
Vanuatu	Vanuatuans *or* Ni-vanuatu	Vanuatuan *or* Ni-vanuatu
Venezuela	Venezuelans	Venezuelan
Vietnam	Vietnamese	Vietnamese
Wales (part of the United Kingdom)	Welsh	Welsh
Yemen	Yemeni	Yemeni
Zaïre (see Congo, Democratic Republic of)		
Zambia	Zambians	Zambian
Zimbabwe	Zimbabweans	Zimbabwean *or* Zimbabwe

Shapes

circle

diamond

heptagon

hexagon

oblong

octagon

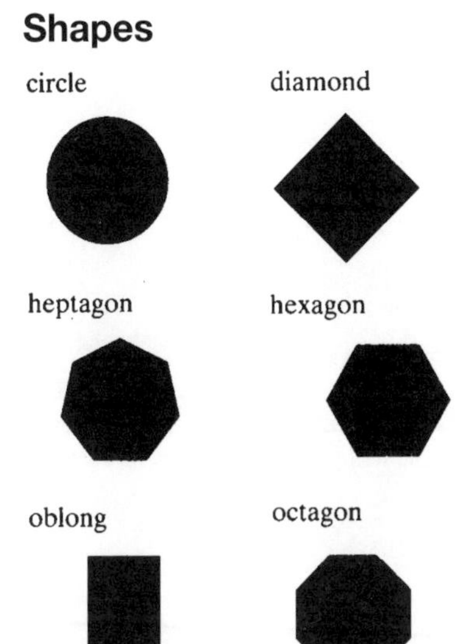

oval

pentagon

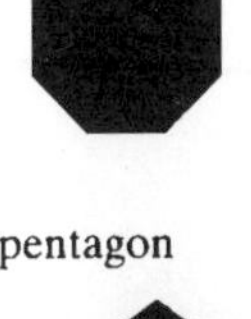

parallelogram

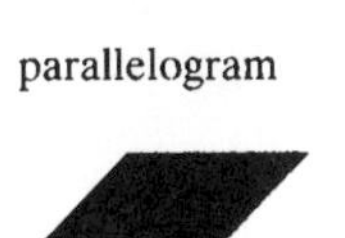

square

rectangle

triangle

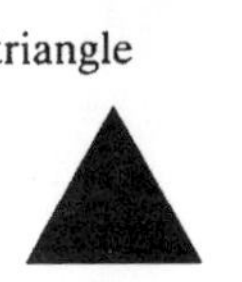

semi-circle

spiral

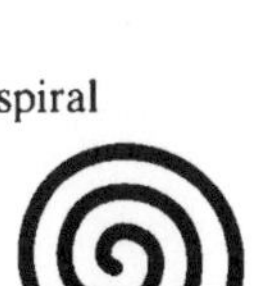

cone

cube

cuboid

cylinder

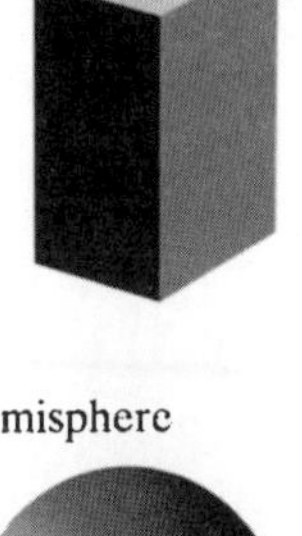

hemisphere

prism (triangular)

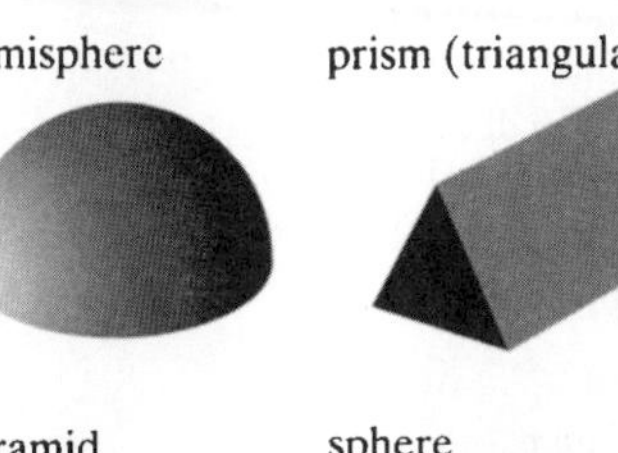

pyramid

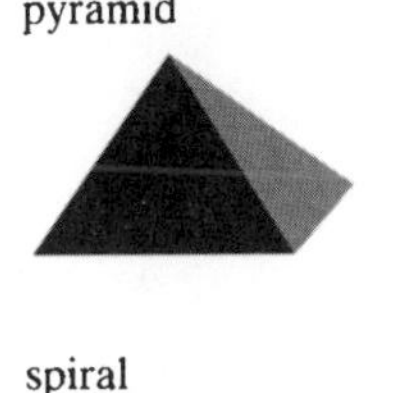

sphere

spiral

prism (rectangular)

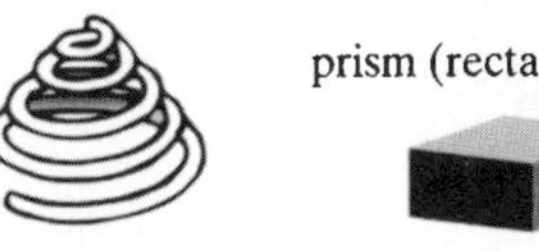

trapezium

rhombus

Measurements

Linear measure

1 millimetre
1 centimetre = 10 mm
1 decimetre = 10 cm
1 metre = 10 dm
1 decametre = 10 m
1 hectometre = 100 m
1 kilometre = 1000 m

Square measure

1 are = 100 square metres
1 hectare = 100 ares
1 square kilometre = 100 hectares

Capacity measure

1 millilitre
1 centilitre = 10 ml
1 decilitre = 10 cl
1 litre = 10 dl
1 decalitre = 10 l
1 hectolitre = 100 l
1 kilolitre = 1000 l

Weight

1 milligram
1 centigram = 10 mg
1 gram = 10 dg
1 decigram = 10 cg
1 decagram = 10 g
1 kilogram = 1000 g
1 tonne (metric ton) = 1000 kg

Time

60 seconds = 1 minute
60 minutes = 1 hour
24 hours = 1 day
365 days = 1 year
366 days = 1 leap year
10 years = 1 decade
10 decades = 1 century

Conversion from imperial measurements

Note The conversion factors are not exact unless so marked. They are given only to the accuracy likely to be needed in everyday calculations.

Linear measure

1 millimetre = 0.039 inch
1 centimetre = 10 mm = 0.394 inch
1 metre = 10 dm = 1.094 yards
1 kilometre = 1000 m = 0.6214 mile

Square measure

1 square centimetre = 0.155 sq. inch
1 square metre = 10,000 sq. cm = 1.196 sq. yards
1 are = 100 sq. metres = 119.6 sq. yards
1 hectare = 100 ares = 2.471 acres
1 square kilometre = 100 hectares = 0.386 sq. mile

Cubic measure

1 cubic centimetre = 0.061 cu. inch
1 cubic metre = 1,000,000 cu. cm = 1.308 cu. yards

Capacity measure

1 litre = 1.76 pints
1 decalitre = 10 l = 2.20 gallons

Weight

1 kilogram = 1000 g = 2.205 pounds
1 tonne (metric ton) = 1000 kg = 0.984 (long) ton

Temperature

Fahrenheit: Water boils (under standard conditions) at 212° and freezes at 32°.
Celsius or Centigrade: Water boils at 100° and freezes at 0°.
Kelvin: Water boils at 373.15 K and freezes at 273.15 K.

Celsius	Fahrenheit	Celsius	Fahrenheit
−17.8°	0°	50°	122°
−10°	14°	60°	140°
0°	32°	70°	158°
10°	50°	80°	176°
20°	68°	90°	194°
30°	86°	100°	212°
40°	104°		

To convert Celsius into Fahrenheit: multiply by 9, divide by 5, and add 32.
To convert Fahrenheit into Celsius: subtract 32, multiply by 5, and divide by 9.

Metric prefixes

	Abbreviation or symbol	Factor		Abbreviation or symbol	Factor
deca-	da	10	deci-	d	10^{-1}
hecto-	h	10^2	centi-	c	10^{-2}
kilo-	k	10^3	milli-	m	10^{-3}
mega-	M	10^6	micro-	µ	10^{-6}
giga-	G	10^9	nano-	n	10^{-9}
tera-	T	10^{12}	pico-	p	10^{-12}
peta-	P	10^{15}	femto-	f	10^{-15}
exa-	E	10^{18}	atto-	a	10^{-18}

These prefixes may be applied to any units of the metric system: hectogram (abbreviated hg) = 100 grams; kilowatt (abbreviated kW) = 1000 watts.

Mathematical signs

+	plus	=	equal to
−	minus	≠	not equal to
÷	divide	<	less than
×	multiply	>	more than

Māori and Roman numerals

Māori numerals

Numbers	Nga nama
0	kāhore, kore
1	kotahi, tahi
2	rua, tokorua
3	toru, tokotoru
4	whā, tokowhā
5	rima, tokorima
6	ono, tokoono
7	whitu, tokowhitu
8	waru, tokowaru
9	iwa, tokoiwa
10	tekau, ngahuru
11	tekau mā tahi, ngahuru mā tahi
12	tekau mā rua, ngahuru mā rua
13	tekau mā toru, ngahuru mā toru
14	tekau mā whā, ngahuru mā whā
15	tekau mā rima, ngahuru mā rima
16	tekau mā ono, ngahuru mā ono
17	tekau mā whitu, ngahuru mā whitu
18	tekau mā waru, ngahuru mā waru
19	tekau mā iwa, ngahuru mā iwa
20	rua tekau, hokotahi
21	rua tekau mā tahi
30	toru tekau
40	whā tekau, hokorua
50	rima tekau
60	ono tekau, hokotoru
70	whitu tekau
80	waru tekau, hokowhā
90	iwa tekau
100	rau, kotahi rau mā tahi
101	kotahi rau mā tahi
121	kotahi rau rua tekau mā tahi
1000	mano
1,000,000	miriona
1st	tuatahi, ātua, mua
2nd	tuarua
3rd	tuatoru
4th	tuawhā
5th	tuarima
6th	tuaono
7th	tuawhitu

8th	tuawaru
9th	tuaiwa
10th	te takau, te ngahuru
11th	te tekau mā tahi
12th	te tekau mā rua
13th	te rua tekau
100th	te kotahi rau

Roman numerals

Number	Roman numeral
1	I
2	II
3	III
4	IV
5	V
6	VI
7	VII
8	VIII
9	IX
10	X
11	XI
12	XII
13	XIII
14	XIV
15	XV
16	XVI
17	XVII
18	XVIII
19	XIX
20	XX
21	XXI
30	XXX
32	XXXII
40	XL
43	XLIII
50	L
54	LIV
60	LX
65	LXV
70	LXX
76	LXXVI
80	LXXX
87	LXXXVII
90	XC
98	XCVIII

100	C
101	CI
115	CXV
150	CL
200	CC
300	CCC
400	CD
500	D
600	DC
700	DCC
800	DCCC
900	CM
1000	M

Days of the week (English)

The days of the week were named more than a thousand years ago, in Anglo-Saxon times, and the English names are based on those given by the ancient Romans. They are named after the planets, taking the order of these from ancient astronomy.

Sunday	from Old English *sunnandæg* = day of the sun; the Latin name was *solis dies*.
Monday	from Old English *monandæg* = day of the moon; the Latin name was *lunae dies*. Compare French *lundi*.
Tuesday	from Old English *Tiwesdæg* = day of Tiw, the Old English name of the Norse god of War, whose name was substituted for that of Mars, the Roman god of war; the Latin name was *Martis dies* = day of Mars. Compare French *mardi*.
Wednesday	from Old English *Wodnesdæg* = day of Woden or Odin, the chief Norse god, whose name was substituted for that of Mercury, the Roman messenger-god; the Latin name was *Mercurii dies*. Compare French *mercredi*.
Thursday	from Old English *Thuresdæg* = day of thunder, named after Thor, the Norse god of thunder, whose name was substituted for that of Jove or Jupiter, the Roman god who controlled thunder and lightning; the Latin name was *Jovis dies* = day of Jupiter. Compare French *jeudi*.
Friday	from Old English *Frigedæg* = day of Frigg, wife of the god Odin (see *Wednesday*); the Latin name was *Veneris dies* = day of Venus. Compare French *vendredi*.
Saturday	from the Old English *Sæternesdæg* = day of Saturn, a Roman god; the Latin name was *Saturni dies*. Compare French *samedi*.

Days of the week (Māori)

Sunday	Rātapu
Monday	Mane
Tuesday	Tūrei
Wednesday	Wenerei
Thursday	Tāite
Friday	Paraire
Saturday	Rāhoroi or Hatarei

Months of the year (English)

The names of the months go back to ancient Roman times, and some are named after Roman gods and goddesses.

January is named after Janus, god of gates and beginnings, who faced two ways (past and future), and whose festival was held on 9 January.

February is named after *februa*, an ancient Roman feast of purification held in this month.

March is named after Mars, god of war, several of whose festivals were held in this month. It was originally the first month of the year and the months September–December were counted from here.

April is from its Latin name *Aprilis*. The Romans considered this month to be sacred to Venus, goddess of love, and its name may be taken from that of her Greek equivalent Aphrodite.

May is named after the goddess Maia, who was worshipped in this month.

June is named after Juno, queen of the gods.

July is named after Julius Caesar, who was born in this month.

August is named after Augustus Caesar, the first Roman emperor, who was given the name Augustus (Latin, = majestic) in 27 BC.

September is from Latin *septem* = seven, because it was the seventh month in the ancient Roman calendar (see the note on *March*).

October is from Latin *octo* = eight (eighth month).

November is from Latin *novem* = nine (ninth month).

December is from Latin *decem* = ten (tenth month).

Months of the year (Māori)

January	Kohi-tātea
February	Hui-tanguru
March	Poutū-te-rangi
April	Paenga-whāwhā
May	Haratua
June	Pipiri
July	Hōngongoi
August	Here-turi-kōkā
September	Mahuru
October	Whiringa-ā-nuku
November	Whiringa-ā-rangi
December	Hakihea

Some common New Zealand birds

* The most common name is in **bold** print.

Common name in English	Common name in Māori
albatross	toroa
banded rail	moho-pererū
bellbird	korimako, makomako
brown bittern	matuku-hūrepo
brown creeper	toitoi
bush wren	matuhi, piwauwau
crested grebe	pāteketeke
dabchick	totokipio, weweia
dotterel	pukunui, tūturiwhatu
duck	
blue	whio
brown	pāteke
paradise	pūtangitangi
falcon	kārearea
fantail	pīwakawaka
fernbird	mātātā
fluttering shearwater	pakahā
gannet	tākapu
godwit	kūaka
grey warbler	riroriro
gull	
black-backed	karoro
red-billed	tarāpunga
harrier hawk	kāhu
heron	
white	kōtuku
white-faced	matuku-moana
kingfisher	kōtare
kiwi	**kiwi**
little spotted kiwi	kiwi pukupuku
laughing owl	whēkau
long-tailed cuckoo	koekoeā
morepork	ruru
muttonbird	hakoakoa, tītī
New Zealand scaup	pāpango
oyster catcher	tōrea
parrot	
bush	**kākā**
mountain	**kea**
ground	**kākāpō**
parson bird	**tūī**

penguin	
blue	kororā
crested	tawaki
yellow-eyed	**hoiho**
pipit	pīhoihoi
plover	
shore	kukuruatu
wry-billed	ngutu-parore
red-crowned parakeet	powhaitere
red-tailed tropic bird	amokura
rifleman	piripiri, titipounamu
robin	pitoitoi, toutouwai
royal spoonbill	kotuku-ngutupapa
saddleback	tīeke
shag	kawau
little pied	kawaupaka
pied	kāruhiruhi
spotted	pārekareka
shining cuckoo	pīpīwharauroa
shoveller	kuruwhengi, pateke
silvereye	tauhou
skua	hākoakoa
spotless crake	pūtoto, pūweto
stilt	
black	kakī
pied	poaka
stitchbird	**hihi**
swamp hen	**pūkeko**
takahe	**takahe**
teal	
black	pāpango
brown	pateke
tern	tara
tomtit	miromiro, ngirungiru, toitoi
whitehead	mohua, pōpokatea/pōpokotea
wood pigeon	**kererū**
woodhen	**weka**
yellowhead	mohua

Some common New Zealand fish

* The most common name is in **bold** print.

Common name in English	Common name in Māori
bass	moeone
black bream, blackfish, shitfish	**parore**
blue mackerel	tawatawa
blue moki	**moki**
blue-nose, bluenose warehou	matiri
blue warehou, common warehou	**warehou**
bluefish	korokoro-pounamu
butterfish, greenbone	mararī, rarī
butterfly (red) perch	**oia**
cod	
blue cod	pākirikiri, rāwaru
red cod	hoka
dogfish, rig, **lemonfish**	koinga, okeoke, pīoke
eel	tuna
elephant fish	reperepe
flounder	mahue, pātiki
frostfish	hiku, pāra
giant stargazer, monkfish	kourepoua
groper	**hāpuku**
hake	tīkati
hoki	**hoki**
John Dory	kuparu
kingfish, yellowtail kingfish	haku
leatherjacket, creamfish	kōkiri
ling	hokarari
maomao	**maomao**
mullet	
grey	kanae
yellow-eyed	aua
orange roughy	
ray, skate	whai
red gurnard	kumukumu
sand flounder	pātiki
sea perch	pohui akaroa
shark	mangō
snapper	tamure
golden	koarea
tarakihi, terakihi	**tarakihi**
trevally	araara
whitebait	hiwi, inanga

Some common New Zealand shellfish and crustacea

abalone	**pāua**
cockle	tuangi
crab	pāpaka
crayfish	kōura
mussel (freshwater)	kākahi
mussel	kuku, kūtai
octopus	wheke
oyster	tio
pipi	**pipi**
sea egg	**kina**
scallop	tipa, tupa
toheroa	**toheroa**
tuatua	**tuatua**

Some common New Zealand trees

* The most common name is in **bold** print.

Common name in English	Common name in Māori
akeake	**akeake**
beech	tawhai
black	tawhairauriki
hard beech	tawhairanui
mountain beech	tawhairauriki
red beech	tawhairaunui
broadleaf	kāpuka
shining broadleaf	**puka**
bushman's friend	**rangiora**
cabbage tree	tī
cork tree	**whau**
cyathea tree fern	kōrau, mamaku, **ponga**
five finger	houhou, houpara
hinau	**hīnau**
horopito, pepper tree	**horopito**
ironwood	**rātā**
karamu	**karamū**
kowhai	**kōwhai**
kakabeak	kōwhai ngutu-kaka
karaka	**karaka**
lacebark	houhere
lancewood	horoeka
lemonwood	tarata
maire	**maire**
black maire	maire rau nui
manuka	
red manuka	**mānuka**
white manuka	**kānuka**
milktree	ewekuri, tōwai; tūrepo
New Zealand cedar	kaikawaka, kawaka
New Zealand Christmas tree	**pōhutukawa**
New Zealand honeysuckle	rewarewa
New Zealand mahogany	kohe, **kohekohe**
New Zealand palm	**nīkau**
ngaio	**ngaio**
pepper tree	**kawakawa**
pigeonwood	**kaiwhiria**
pine	paina
black pine	**matai**
brown pine	**miro**, toromiro
celery pine	**tānekaha**; toatoa

red pine	**rimu**; puaka
kauri pine	**kauri**
white pine	**kahikatea**
pukatea	**pukatea**
pururi	**pururi**
ribbonwood	mānatu
rata	**rātā**
titoki	**tītoki**
toro	**toro, toru**
totara	**tōtara**; amoka (South Island)
turpentine tree	**karo**
veronica shrub	**koromiko**
wharangi	koheriki, **wharangi**, tātaka
whiteywood	**māhoe**

Nn

N. *abbreviation* north; northern.

n/a *abbreviation* not applicable.

nab *verb* (**nabbed**, **nabbing**) (*slang*) catch or arrest (a wrongdoer); seize.

nacho *noun* (*plural* **nachos**) a corn chip. [Mexican Spanish]

nag[1] *verb* (**nagged**, **nagging**) **1** pester a person by keeping on criticising, complaining, or asking for things. **2** keep on hurting, *a nagging pain.*

nag[2] *noun* (*informal*) a horse.

nail *noun* **1** the hard covering over the end of a finger or toe. **2** a small sharp piece of metal hammered in to fasten pieces of wood etc. together.

nail *verb* **1** fasten with a nail or nails. **2** catch; arrest.

naive (*say* ny-**eev**) *adjective* showing a lack of experience or good judgement; innocent and unsophisticated. **naively** *adverb*, **naivety** *noun*

naked *adjective* without any clothes or coverings on. **nakedly** *adverb*, **nakedness** *noun*
the naked eye the eye when it is not helped by a telescope or microscope etc.

name *noun* **1** the word or words by which a person, animal, place, or thing is known. **2** a reputation.

name *verb* (**named**, **naming**) **1** give a name to. **2** state the name or names of.

nameless *adjective* without a name.

namely *adverb* that is to say, *My two favourite subjects are sciences, namely chemistry and biology.*

namesake *noun* a person or thing with the same name as another.

nanna *noun* (*informal*) a grandmother.

nanny *noun* (*plural* **nannies**) a nurse who looks after young children.

nanny-goat *noun* a female goat. (Compare *billy-goat.*)

nap[1] *noun* a short sleep.
catch a person napping catch a person unprepared for something or not alert.

nap[2] *noun* short raised fibres on the surface of cloth or leather.

napalm (*say* **nay**-pahm) *noun* a substance made of petrol, used in some incendiary bombs.

napkin *noun* **1** a piece of cloth or paper used to keep your clothes clean or to wipe your lips or fingers; a serviette, *a table-napkin.* **2** a piece of cloth or other fabric put round a baby's bottom.

nappy *noun* (*plural* **nappies**) a baby's napkin.

narcissus *noun* (*plural* **narcissi**) a garden flower like a daffodil.

narcotic *noun* a drug that makes a person sleepy or unconscious. **narcotic** *adjective*, **narcosis** *noun*

nark *verb* (*slang*) annoy; infuriate.

nark *noun* (*slang*) **1** (*NZ*) an annoying person or thing. **2** an informer.

narrate *verb* (**narrated**, **narrating**) tell a story; give an account of something. **narration** *noun*, **narrator** *noun*

narrative *noun* a spoken or written account of something.

narrow *adjective* **1** not wide; not broad. **2** uncomfortably close; with only a small margin of safety, *a narrow escape.* **narrowly** *adverb*

narrow *verb* make or become narrower.

narrow-minded *adjective* not tolerant of other people's beliefs and ways.

NASA *abbreviation* National Aeronautics and Space Administration (in the USA).

nasal *adjective* **1** of the nose. **2** sounding as if the breath comes out through the nose, *a nasal voice.* **nasally** *adverb* [from Latin *nasus* = nose]

nashi *noun* a kind of Japanese pear.

nasturtium (*say* na-**ster**-shum) *noun* a garden plant with round leaves and red, yellow, or orange flowers.

nasty *adjective* **1** unpleasant. **2** unkind. **nastily** *adverb*, **nastiness** *noun*

Nat *noun* (especially as plural **Nats**) (*informal*) a member of the New Zealand National Party.

natal (*say* **nay**-tal) *adjective* of birth; from birth. [from Latin *natus* = born]

nation *noun* a large community of people most of whom have the same ancestors, language, history, and customs, and who usually live in the same part of the world under one government. **national** *adjective & noun*, **nationally** *adverb* [from Latin *natio* = birth; race]

National *noun* (*NZ*) the National Party, a conservative political party.

nationalise *verb* (**nationalised**, **nationalising**) put an industry etc. under public ownership. **nationalisation** *noun*

nationalist *noun* **1** a person who is very patriotic. **2** a person who wants his or her country to remain independent. **nationalistic** *adjective*

nationality *noun* (*plural* **nationalities**) the condition of belonging to a particular nation, *What is his nationality?*

National Park *noun* an extensive protected outdoor region for public use, which is owned by the State.

nationals *plural noun* national championship event for sports, debating, etc., *Are you going to the nationals this year?*

native *noun* **1** a person born in a particular place, *He is a native of Southland.* **2** a plant or animal indigenous to a country.

native *adjective* **1** belonging to a person because of the place of his or her birth, *my native country.* **2** natural; belonging to a person by nature, *native ability.* **3** indigenous; indigenous to New Zealand, *native beech.*
Native American see **American**.
native bush (*NZ*) bush or forests made up of indigenous trees and shrubs. [from Latin *nativus* = born]

nativity *noun* a person's birth.
the Nativity the birth of Jesus Christ.

NATO *abbreviation* North Atlantic Treaty Organisation.

natty *adjective* (**nattier**, **nattiest**) neat and trim; dapper. **nattily** *adverb*

natural *adjective* **1** produced or done by nature, not by people or machines. **2** normal; not surprising. **3** (of a note in music) neither sharp nor flat. **naturally** *adverb*, **naturalness** *noun*
natural gas gas found in the earth's crust, not manufactured.
natural history the study of plants and animals.

natural *noun* **1** a person who is naturally good at something. **2** a natural note in music; a sign (♮) that shows this.

naturalise *verb* (**naturalised**, **naturalising**) **1** give a person full rights as a citizen of a country although they were not born there. **2** cause a plant or animal to grow or live naturally in a country that is not its own. **naturalisation** *noun*

naturalist *noun* an expert in natural history.

nature *noun* **1** everything in the world that was not made by people. **2** the qualities and characteristics of a person or thing, *She has a loving nature.* **3** a kind or sort of thing, *He likes things of that nature.* [from Latin *natus* = born]

naught *noun* (*old use*) nothing.

naughty *adjective* behaving badly; disobedient. **naughtily** *adverb*, **naughtiness** *noun* [from *naught*]

nausea (*say* **naw**-zee-a) *noun* a feeling of sickness or disgust. **nauseous** *adjective*, **nauseating** *adjective* [originally 'sea-sickness', from Greek *naus* = ship]

nautical *adjective* of ships or sailors.
nautical mile a measure of distance used in navigating, 1.852 kilometres.
[from Greek *nautes* = sailor]

nautilus *noun* a mollusc with a spiral shell that is divided into compartments.

naval *adjective* of a navy.

nave *noun* the main central part of a church (the other parts are the chancel, aisles, and transepts).

navel *noun* the small hollow in the centre of the abdomen, where the umbilical cord was attached.

navigable *adjective* **1** suitable for ships to sail in, *a navigable river.* **2** able to be steered. **navigability** *noun*

navigate *verb* (**navigated**, **navigating**) **1** sail in or through a river or sea etc., *The ship navigated the Suez Canal.* **2** make sure that a ship, aircraft, or vehicle is going in the right direction. **3** move around a website or the Internet. **navigation** *noun*, **navigator** *noun* [from Latin *navis* = ship, + *agere* = to drive]

navy *noun* (*plural* **navies**) **1** a country's warships; the people trained to use them. **2** (also **navy blue**) very dark blue, the colour of naval uniform. [from Latin *navis* = ship]

nay *adverb* (*old use*) no.

Nazi (*say* **nah**-tsee) *noun* (*plural* **Nazis**) a member of the National Socialist Party in Germany in Hitler's time, with Fascist beliefs. **Nazism** *noun*

NB *abbreviation* take note that (Latin *nota bene* = note well).

NCEA *abbreviation* (*NZ*) National Certificate of Educational Achievement.

NCO *abbreviation* non-commissioned officer.

NE *abbreviation* north-east; northeastern.

Neanderthal (say nee-**an**-da-tharl) *noun* **1** a primitive Ice Age human with a receding forehead. **2** (*slang*) an uncouth person. **3** (*slang*) a person with out-of-date ideas.

near *adverb & adjective* not far away. **near by** not far away, *They live near by.*

> USAGE This is written as two words except when it is an adjective (see *nearby*).

near *preposition* not far away from, *near the shops.*

near *verb* come near to, *The ship neared the harbour.*

nearby *adjective* near, *a nearby house.*

nearly *adverb* **1** almost, *We have nearly finished.* **2** closely, *They are nearly related.*

neat *adjective* **1** simple and clean and tidy. **2** skilful. **3** undiluted, *neat whisky.* **4** (*informal*) excellent. **neatly** *adverb*, **neatness** *noun*

neaten *verb* make or become neat.

nebula *noun* (*plural* **nebulae**) a bright or dark patch in the sky, caused by a distant galaxy or a cloud of dust or gas. [Latin, = mist]

nebulous *adjective* indistinct; vague, *nebulous ideas.* [from *nebula*]

necessary *adjective* not able to be done without; essential. **necessarily** *adverb*

necessitate *verb* (**necessitated**, **necessitating**) make a thing necessary.

necessitous *adjective* needy.

necessity *noun* (*plural* **necessities**) need; something necessary.

neck *noun* **1** the part of the body that joins the head to the shoulders. **2** the part of a garment round the neck. **3** a narrow part of something, especially of a bottle.

necklace *noun* an ornament worn round the neck.

necklet *noun* a necklace.

necktie *noun* a strip of material worn passing under the collar of a shirt and knotted in front.

nectar *noun* **1** a sweet liquid collected by bees from flowers. **2** a delicious drink.

nectarine *noun* a kind of peach with a smooth skin.

nectary *noun* (*plural* **nectaries**) the nectar-producing part of a plant.

née (*say* nay) *adjective* born (used in giving a married woman's maiden name), *Mrs Smith, née Jones.* [French]

need *verb* **1** be without something you should have; require, *We need two more chairs.* **2** (as an *auxiliary verb*) have to do something, *You need not answer.*

need *noun* **1** something needed; a necessary thing. **2** a situation where something is necessary, *There is no need to cry.* **3** great poverty or hardship. **needful** *adjective*, **needless** *adjective*

needle *noun* **1** a very thin pointed piece of steel used in sewing. **2** something long and thin and sharp, *a knitting-needle.* **3** the pointer of a meter or compass.

needlework *noun* sewing or embroidery.

needy *adjective* very poor; lacking things necessary for life. **neediness** *noun*

ne'er *adverb* (*poetic*) never.

nefarious (*say* nif-**air**-ee-us) *adjective* wicked. [from Latin *nefas* = wrong]

negate *verb* (**negated**, **negating**) **1** make a thing ineffective. **2** disprove. **negation** *noun* [from Latin *negare* = deny]

negative *adjective* **1** that says 'no', *a negative answer.* **2** not definite; not positive. **3** less than nought; minus. **4** of the kind of electric charge carried by electrons. **negatively** *adverb.*

> USAGE The opposite of sense **1** is *affirmative*, and of senses **2**, **3**, **4** *positive.*

negative *noun* **1** something negative. **2** a photograph on film with the dark parts light and the light parts dark, from which a positive print (with the dark and light or colours correct) can be made. [from Latin *negare* = deny]

neglect *verb* **1** not look after or attend to a person or thing. **2** not do something; forget, *He neglected to shut the door.*

neglect *noun* neglecting; being negiected. **neglectful** *adjective*

negligence *noun* lack of proper care or attention; carelessness. **negligent** *adjective*, **negligently** *adverb*

negligible *adjective* not big enough or important enough to be worth bothering about.

negotiable *adjective* **1** able to be changed after being discussed, *The salary is negotiable.* **2** (of a cheque) able to be changed for cash or transferred to another person.

negotiate *verb* (**negotiated**, **negotiating**) **1** bargain or discuss with others in order to reach an agreement. **2** arrange after discussion, *They negotiated a treaty.* **3** get over an obstacle or difficulty. **negotiation** *noun*, **negotiator** *noun* [from Latin *negotium* = business]

Negro *noun* (*plural* **Negroes**) a member of the black-skinned race of people originally from Africa. **Negress** *noun* [from Latin *niger* = black]

USAGE Offensive; the term *Black* is preferred.

neigh *verb* make the high-pitched cry of a horse. **neigh** *noun*

neighbour *noun* a person who lives next door or near to another. **neighbouring** *adjective*, **neighbourly** *adjective* [from Old English *neahgebur* = near dweller]

neighbourhood *noun* the surrounding district or area.

neinei *noun* a shrub with long narrow leaves. [Māori]

neither (*say* **ny**-ther or **nee**-ther) *adjective & pronoun* not either.

USAGE Correct use is *Neither of them likes it. Neither he nor his children like it.* Use a singular verb (e.g. *likes*) unless one of its subjects is plural (e.g. *children*).

neither *adverb & conjunction*
neither ... nor not one thing and not the other, *She neither knew nor cared.*

nemesis (*say* **nem**-i-sis) *noun* retribution; justifiable punishment that comes upon somebody who hoped to escape it. [named after Nemesis, goddess of retribution in Greek mythology]

neo- *prefix* new. [from Greek *neos* = new]

neolithic (*say* nee-o-**lith**-ik) *adjective* of the later part of the Stone Age. [from *neo-*, + Greek *lithos* = stone]

neon *noun* a gas that glows when electricity passes through it, used in glass tubes to make illuminated signs.

nephew *noun* the son of a person's brother or sister. [from Latin *nepos*]

nepotism (*say* **nep**-ot-izm) *noun* showing favouritism to relatives in appointing them to jobs. [from Latin *nepos* = nephew]

nerd *noun* (*slang*) a socially awkward person, often with an absorbing, singular interest. **nerdy** *adjective*

nerve *noun* **1** any of the fibres in the body that carry messages to and from the brain, so that parts of the body can feel and move. **2** courage; calmness in a dangerous situation, *Don't lose your nerve.* **3** (*informal*) impudence, *Oliver Twist had the nerve to ask for more.*
nerves *plural noun* nervousness.

nerve *verb* (**nerved**, **nerving**) give strength or courage to someone. [from Latin *nervus* = sinew]

nervous *adjective* **1** easily upset or agitated; excitable. **2** slightly afraid; timid. **3** of the nerves, *a nervous illness.* **nervously** *adverb*, **nervousness** *noun*

nervy *adjective* nervous.

nest *noun* **1** a structure or place in which a bird lays its eggs and feeds its young. **2** a place where some small creatures (e.g. mice, wasps) live. **3** a set of similar things that fit inside each other, *a nest of tables.*

nest *verb* **1** have or make a nest. **2** fit inside something.

nest-egg *noun* a sum of money saved up for future use.

nestle *verb* (**nestled**, **nestling**) curl up comfortably.

nestling *noun* a bird that is too young to leave the nest.

net[1] *noun* **1** material made of pieces of thread, cord, or wire etc. joined together in a criss-cross pattern with holes between. **2** something made of this. **3** (**the Net**) (*informal*) the Internet, *surfing the Net.*

net[1] *verb* (**netted**, **netting**) cover or catch with a net.

net[2] *adjective* remaining when nothing more is to be deducted, *The net weight, without the box, is 100 grams.* (Compare *gross.*)

net[2] *verb* (**netted**, **netting**) obtain or produce as net profit.

netball *noun* **1** a game similar to basketball, but played on a larger court with a lighter ball, and mostly by women. **2** the ball used in this game.

nether *adjective* lower, *the nether regions.*

netting *noun* a piece of net.

nettle *noun* a wild plant with leaves that sting when they are touched.

nettle *verb* (**nettled**, **nettling**) annoy or provoke someone.

network *noun* **1** any net-like arrangement of connected lines. **2** a group of linked television or radio stations. **3** a group of linked computers. **4** a group of people exchanging information etc. for professional or social reasons.

network *verb* **1** link (a set of computers) so that data can be transferred from one to the others. **2** establish contacts with other people for professional or social reasons. **networking** *noun*

neuralgia (*say* newr-**al**-ja) *noun* pain along a nerve. [from Greek *neuron* = nerve, + *algos* = pain]

neurology *noun* the study of nerves and their diseases. **neurological** *adjective*, **neurologist** *noun* [from Greek *neuron* = nerve, + *-logy*]

neurotic (*say* newr-**ot**-ik) *adjective* always abnormally worried about something.

neuter *adjective* neither masculine nor feminine. [Latin, = neither]

neuter *verb* castrate or spay.

neutral *adjective* **1** not supporting either side in a war or quarrel. **2** not very distinctive, *a neutral colour such as grey.* **neutrally** *adverb*, **neutrality** *noun*
neutral gear a gear that is not connected to the driving parts of an engine.
[from Latin *neuter* = neither]

neutralise *verb* (**neutralised, neutralising**) make a thing neutral or ineffective. **neutralisation** *noun*

neutron *noun* a particle with no electric charge. [from *neutral*]

never *adverb* at no time; not ever; not at all. [from *ne* = not, + *ever*]

never-never *noun* (*NZ & Australia, informal*) **1** hire purchase. **2** an isolated place.

nevertheless *adverb & conjunction* in spite of this; although this is a fact.

new *adjective* not existing before; just made, invented, discovered, or received etc. **newly** *adverb*, **newness** *noun*
New Year's Day 1 January.

new *adverb* newly, *new-born; new-laid.*

newcomer *noun* a person who has arrived recently.

newel *noun* the upright post to which the handrail of a stair is fixed, or that forms the centre pillar of a winding stair.

newfangled *adjective* disliked because it is new in method or style. [from *new*, + *fang* = seize]

newly *adverb* **1** recently. **2** in a new way.

news *noun* **1** information about recent events; a broadcast report of this. **2** a piece of new information.

newsagent *noun* a shopkeeper who sells newspapers.

newscast *noun* a radio or television broadcast of news. **newscaster** *noun*

newsgroup *noun* a group for sharing information on the Internet where we can post messages and reply to other users.

newspaper *noun* **1** a daily or weekly publication on large sheets of paper, containing news reports, articles, etc. **2** the sheets of paper forming a newspaper, *Wrap it in newspaper.*

newsy *adjective* (*informal*) full of news.

newt *noun* a small animal rather like a lizard, that lives near or in water.

New Zealand *adjective* of New Zealand, *New Zealand English, New Zealand butter.*
New Zealand Wars the fighting between Māori and Pākehā in the 19th century (also called **Land Wars**).

New Zealander *noun* a person born or living in New Zealand.

New Zealandism *noun* a word or usage distinctive to New Zealand English.

New Zild *noun* (*slang*) **1** New Zealand. **2** New Zealand English.

next *adjective* nearest; coming immediately after, *on the next day.*
next door in the next house or room.

next *adverb* in the next place; on the next occasion. *What happens next?*

nexus *noun* a central point or network link.

Ngāi, Ngāti *prefixes* denoting a Māori tribe or sub-tribe, *Ngāi Tahu, Ngāti Porou.*

ngaio *noun* a small evergreen tree. [Māori]

ngārara 1 a native lizard. **2** a monster in reptile form. [Māori]

NI *abbreviation* (*NZ*) North Island.

nib *noun* the pointed metal part of a pen.

nibble *verb* (**nibbled, nibbling**) take small quick or gentle bites.

nice *adjective* **1** pleasant; kind; satisfactory. **2** precise; careful, *Dictionaries make nice distinctions between meanings of words.* **nicely** *adverb*, **niceness** *noun* [the word originally meant 'stupid', from Latin *nescius* = ignorant]

nicety (*say* **ny**-sit-ee) *noun* (*plural* **niceties**) **1** precision. **2** a small detail or difference pointed out.

niche (*say* nich or neesh) *noun* **1** a small recess, especially in a wall, *The vase stood in a niche.* **2** a suitable place or position, *She found her niche in the drama club.* [from Latin *nidus* = nest]

nick *noun* **1** a small cut or notch. **2** (*slang*) a police station or prison. **3** (*slang*) condition, *in good nick.*
in the nick of time only just in time.

nick *verb* **1** make a nick in something. **2** (*slang*) steal. **3** (*slang*) catch; arrest.

nickel *noun* **1** a silvery-white metal. **2** (*American*) a 5-cent coin.

nickname *noun* a name given to a person instead of his or her real name. [originally *a nekename*, from *an eke-name* (*eke* = addition, + *name*)]

nicotine *noun* a poisonous substance found in tobacco. [from the name of J. Nicot, who introduced tobacco into France in 1560]

niece *noun* the daughter of a person's brother or sister. [from Latin *neptis*]

niggardly *adjective* mean; stingy. **niggardliness** *noun*

niggle *verb* (**niggled**, **niggling**) fuss over details or very small faults.

nigh *adverb & preposition* (*old use*) near.

night *noun* **1** the dark hours between sunset and sunrise. **2** a particular night or evening, *the first night of the play.* **nightdress** *noun*

nightcap *noun* **1** (*old use*) a cap worn in bed. **2** an alcoholic or hot drink taken at bedtime.

nightfall *noun* the coming of darkness at the end of the day.

nightingale *noun* a small brown bird that sings sweetly.

nightly *adjective & adverb* happening every night.

nightmare *noun* a frightening dream. **nightmarish** *adjective*

nightshade *noun* any of several kinds of wild plants, some with poisonous berries.

nīkau *noun* a palm. [Māori]

nil *noun* nothing; nought. [from Latin *nihil* = nothing]

nimble *adjective* able to move quickly; agile. **nimbly** *adverb*

nine *noun & adjective* the number 9; one more than eight. **ninth** *adjective & noun*
nine-eleven 11 September 2001, the date of the destruction of New York's World Trade Center.

ninepins *noun* the game of skittles played with nine objects.

nineteen *noun & adjective* the number 19; one more than eighteen. **nineteenth** *adjective & noun*

ninety *noun & adjective* (*plural* **nineties**) the number 90; nine times ten. **ninetieth** *adjective & noun*

nip *verb* (**nipped**, **nipping**) **1** pinch or bite quickly. **2** (*slang*) go quickly.

nip 1 *noun* a quick pinch or bite. **2** sharp coldness, *There's a nip in the air.*

nipple *noun* a small projecting part, especially at the front of a person's breast.

nippy *adjective* (**nippier**, **nippiest**) (*informal*) **1** quick; nimble. **2** cold.

nit *noun* a parasitic insect or louse; its egg.

nit-picking *noun* pointing out very small faults.

nitrate *noun* potassium or sodium nitrate used as a fertiliser.

nitric acid (*say* **ny**-trik) a very strong colourless acid containing nitrogen.

nitrogen (*say* **ny**-tro-jen) *noun* a gas that makes up about four-fifths of the air.

nitwit *noun* (*informal*) a stupid person. **nitwitted** *adjective*

Niuean *noun* **1** an inhabitant of the island of Niue, or someone with ancestors from there. **2** the language of Niue. **Niuean** *adjective*

Niu Tīrani, Niu Tīreni Māori forms of the name New Zealand.

no *adjective* not any, *We have no money.*
no man's land an area that does not belong to anybody.
no one no person; nobody.

no *adverb* **1** used to deny or refuse something, *Will you come? No.* **2** not at all. *She is no better.*

No. or **no.** *abbreviation* (*plural* **Nos.** or **nos.**) number. [from Latin *numero* = by number]

noa *adjective* free from tapu. [Māori]

noble *adjective* **1** of high social rank; aristocratic. **2** having a very good character or qualities, *a noble king.* **3** stately; impressive, *a noble building.* **nobly** *adverb*, **nobility** *noun*

noble *noun* a person of high social rank. **nobleman** *noun*, **noblewoman** *noun*

nobody *pronoun* no person; no one.

nocturnal *adjective* of or in the night; active at night, *nocturnal animals.* [from Latin *noctis* = of night]

nocturne *noun* a piece of music with the quiet dreamy feeling of night.

nod *verb* (**nodded**, **nodding**) **1** move the head up and down, especially as a way of agreeing with somebody or as a greeting. **2** be drowsy. **nod** *noun*

node *noun* a swelling like a small knob.

nodule *noun* a small node.

nogging *noun* (*NZ*) a short wooden strut placed at right angles to joists, studs, etc.; a dwang.

Noh *noun* a kind of traditional Japanese drama.

no-hoper (*informal*) a useless person, a failure.

noise *noun* a sound, especially one that is loud or unpleasant. **noisy** *adjective*, **noisily** *adverb*, **noiseless** *adjective*

noisome (*say* **noi**-sum) *adjective* smelling unpleasant; harmful. [from *annoy*]

nomad *noun* a member of a tribe that moves from place to place looking for pasture for their animals. **nomadic** *adjective*

nominal *adjective* **1** in name, *He is the nominal ruler, but the real power is held by the generals.* **2** small, *We charged them only a nominal fee.* **nominally** *adverb* [from Latin *nomen* = name]

nominate *verb* (**nominated**, **nominating**) name a person or thing to be appointed or chosen. **nomination** *noun*, **nominator** *noun* [from Latin *nominare* = to name]

nominee *noun* a person who is nominated.

non- *prefix* not. [from Latin *non* = not]

nonagenarian *noun* a person aged between 90 and 99. [from Latin *nonageni* = ninety each]

non-aligned *adjective* not allied with any major group of countries.

nonchalant (*say* **non**-shal-ant) *adjective* calm and casual; showing no anxiety or excitement. **nonchalantly** *adverb*, **nonchalance** *noun* [from French *non* = not, + *chaloir* = be concerned]

non-commissioned *adjective* not holding a commission, *Non-commissioned officers include corporals and sergeants.*

non-committal *adjective* not committing yourself; not showing what you think.

nonconformist *noun* a person who does not conform to generally accepted beliefs or practices.

non-custodial *adjective* **1** (non-custodial sentence) not involving imprisonment. **2** (non-custodial parent) not having custody or care of a child/children.

nondescript *adjective* having no special or distinctive qualities and therefore difficult to describe.

none *pronoun* **1** not any. **2** no one, *None can tell.*

USAGE In sense **1** it is better to use a singular verb (e.g. *None of them is here*), but the plural is not incorrect (e.g. *None of them are here*).

none *adverb* not at all, *He is none too bright.* [from *not one*]

nonentity (*say* non-**en**-tit-ee) *noun* (*plural* **nonentities**) an unimportant person. [from *non-* + *entity*]

non-existent *adjective* not existing; unreal.

non-fiction *noun* writings that are not fiction; books about real people and things and true events.

nong *noun* (*NZ, slang*) a fool.

no-no *noun* (*informal*) something unacceptable.

nonplus *verb* (**nonplussed**, **nonplussing**) puzzle someone completely. [from Latin *non plus* = not further]

non-profit organisation *noun* an institution or organisation that provides a service but does not benefit financially.

non-proliferation *noun* limiting the number of something, especially nuclear weapons.

nonsense *noun* **1** words put together in a way that does not mean anything. **2** stupid ideas or behaviour. **nonsensical** (*say* non-**sens**-ik-al) *adjective* [from *non-* + *sense*]

non-stop *adjective* **1** not stopping, *non-stop chatter.* **2** not stopping between two main stations, *a non-stop train.*

non-U *adjective* (of usage or habit) not upper class.

noodles *plural noun* pasta made in narrow strips, used in soups etc.

nook *noun* a sheltered corner; a recess.

noon *noun* twelve o'clock midday.

noose *noun* a loop in a rope that gets smaller when the rope is pulled.

nor *conjunction* and not, *She cannot do it; nor can I.*

Nordic (*say* **nor**-dik) *adjective* **1** of Scandinavia, Finland, and Iceland. **2** of a tall blond person, typical of Northern Europe. [from French *nordique* from *nord* = north]

Norfolk Island pine an evergreen pine tree.

norm *noun* a standard or average type, amount, level, etc.

normal *adjective* **1** usual or ordinary. **2** natural and healthy; without a physical or mental illness. **normally** *adverb*, **normality** *noun*

Norman *noun* a member of the people of Normandy in northern France, who conquered England in 1066. **Norman** *adjective*

Norse *noun* the Norwegian language or the Scandinavian group of languages. **Norse** *adjective* [from Dutch *noord* = north]

north *noun* **1** the direction to the left of a person who faces east. **2** the northern part of a country, city, etc.

north *adjective & adverb* towards or in the north. **northerly** *adjective*, **northern** *adjective*, **northernmost** *adjective*

north-east *noun, adjective, & adverb* midway between north and east. **north-easterly** *adjective*, **north-eastern** *adjective*

northerner *noun* a person who lives in the north.

Northerner *noun* (*NZ*) the overnight express train between Wellington and Auckland.

North Islander *noun* (*NZ*) a person born in or who lives in the North Island.

northward *adjective & adverb* towards the north. **northwards** *adverb*

north-west *noun, adjective, & adverb* midway between north and west. **north-westerly** *adjective*, **north-western** *adjective*

nor'wester *noun* (*NZ*) a warm wind from the north-west, especially in Canterbury.

Nos. or **nos.** *plural* of **No.** or **no.**

nose *noun* **1** the part of the face that is used for breathing and for smelling things. **2** the front end or part.

nose *verb* (**nosed**, **nosing**) **1** push the nose into or near something. **2** go forward cautiously, *Ships nosed through the ice.*

nosebag *noun* a bag containing fodder, for hanging on a horse's head.

nosebleed *noun* bleeding from the nose.

nosedive *noun* a steep downward dive, especially of an aircraft. **nosedive** *verb*

nosegay *noun* a small bunch of flowers. [from *nose* + *gay* = ornament]

nostalgia (*say* nos-**tal**-ja) *noun* sentimental remembering or longing for the past. **nostalgic** *adjective*, **nostalgically** *adverb* [from Greek *nostos* = return home, + *algos* = pain (= homesickness)]

nostril *noun* either of the two openings in the nose.

nosy *adjective* (**nosier**, **nosiest**) inquisitive. **nosily** *adverb*, **nosiness** *noun*

not *adverb* used to change the meaning of something to its opposite or absence.

notable *adjective* worth noticing; remarkable; famous. **notably** *adverb*, **notability** *noun*

notation *noun* a system of symbols representing numbers, quantities, musical notes, etc.

notch *noun* (*plural* **notches**) a small V-shape cut into a surface.

notch *verb* cut a notch or notches in. **notch up** score.

note *noun* **1** something written down as a reminder or as a comment or explanation. **2** a short letter. **3** a banknote, *a $5 note.* **4** a single sound in music. **5** any of the black or white keys on a piano etc. (see *key* 3). **6** a sound or quality that indicates something, *a note of warning.* **7** notice; attention, *Take note.*

note *verb* (**noted**, **noting**) **1** make a note about something; write down. **2** notice; pay attention to, *Note what we say.* [from Latin *nota* = a mark]

notebook *noun* a book with blank pages on which to write notes.

noted *adjective* famous; well-known.

notepaper *noun* paper for writing letters.

nothing *noun* **1** no thing; not anything. **2** no amount; nought.
for nothing without payment, free; without a result.

nothing *adverb* not at all; in no way, *It's nothing like as good.*

nothofagus *noun* the Southern hemisphere beech tree.

notice *noun* **1** something written or printed and displayed for people to see. **2** attention, *It escaped my notice.* **3** information that something is going to happen; warning that you are about to end an agreement or a person's employment etc., *We gave him a month's notice.*

notice *verb* (**noticed**, **noticing**) see; become aware of something. [from Latin *notus* = known]

noticeable *adjective* easily seen or noticed. **noticeably** *adverb*

noticeboard *noun* a board on which notices may be displayed.

notifiable *adjective* that must be reported.

notify *verb* (**notified**, **notifying**) inform, *Notify the police.* **notification** *noun*

notion *noun* an idea, especially one that is vague or incorrect.

notional *adjective* assumed or not definite. **notionally** *adverb*

notorious *adjective* well-known for something bad. **notoriously** *adverb*, **notoriety** (*say* noh-ter-**I**-it-ee) *noun* [from Latin *notus* = known]

notornis *noun* the takahē. [from Greek *notos* = south, + *ornis* = bird]

notwithstanding *preposition* in spite of.

nougat (*say* **noo**-gah) *noun* a chewy sweet made from nuts, sugar or honey, and egg-white. [French]

nought (*say* nawt) *noun* **1** the figure 0. **2** nothing.

noun *noun* a word that stands for a person, place, or thing. *Common nouns* are words such as *boy*, *dog*, *river*, *sport*, *table*, which are used of a whole kind of people or things; *proper nouns* are words such as *Charles*, *Waikato*, and *London*, which name a particular person or thing. [from Latin *nomen* = name]

nourish *verb* keep a person, animal, or plant alive and well by means of food. **nourishment** *noun*

novel *noun* a story that fills a whole book.

novel *adjective* of a new and unusual kind, *a novel experience.* **novelty** *noun* [from Latin *novus* = new]

novelist *noun* a person who writes novels.

November *noun* the eleventh month of the year. [from Latin *novem* = nine (in Roman times it was the ninth month)]

novice *noun* a beginner.

now *adverb* **1** at this time. **2** by this time. **3** immediately, *You must go now.* **4** I wonder or am telling you, *Now why didn't I think of that?*
now and again or **now and then** sometimes; occasionally.

now *conjunction* as a result of or at the same time as something, *Now that you have come, we'll start.*

now *noun* this moment, *They will be at home by now.*

nowadays *adverb* at the present time, as contrasted with years ago.

nowhere *adverb* not anywhere.

nowhere *noun* no place, *Nowhere is as beautiful as Fiordland.*

no-win *adjective* describing a situation where a successful outcome is impossible.

noxious *adjective* unpleasant and harmful.
noxious weeds (*NZ*) plants considered harmful to the environment. [from Latin *noxius* = harmful]

nozzle *noun* the spout of a hose or pipe etc. [= little nose]

NPC *abbreviation* (*NZ*) National Provincial Championship (rugby union).

NRL *abbreviation* (*Australian & NZ*) National Rugby League.

nuance (*say* **new**-ahns) *noun* a slight difference or shade of meaning.

nub *noun* **1** a small knob or lump. **2** the central point of a problem.

nuclear *adjective* **1** of a nucleus. **2** using the energy that is created by reactions in the nuclei of atoms.
nuclear family a mother, father, and their children.
nuclear-free zone an area that has no nuclear weapons or power plants.
nuclear power power derived from nuclear energy.

nucleus *noun* (*plural* **nuclei**) **1** the part in the centre of something, round which other things are grouped. **2** the central part of an atom or of a seed or a biological cell. [Latin, = kernel]

nud or **nuddy** *noun* (*NZ, slang*) **in the nud** naked.

nude *adjective* not wearing any clothes; naked. **nudity** *noun*

nudge *verb* (**nudged**, **nudging**) **1** poke a person gently with your elbow. **2** push slightly or gradually. **nudge** *noun*

nudist *noun* a person who believes that going naked is enjoyable and good for the health. **nudism** *noun*

nugget *noun* a rough lump of gold or platinum found in the earth.

nuggety *adjective* (also **nuggetty**) (*NZ*) **1** (of gold) in the form of nuggets. **2** (of a person or animal) stocky, thickset.

nuisance *noun* an annoying person or thing.

nuke *noun* (*informal*) a nuclear weapon.

nuke *verb* (**nuked**, **nuking**) (*informal*) **1** attack with nuclear weapons. **2** destroy, get rid of; cook or heat (food) in a microwave oven.

null *adjective* not valid, *null and void.* [from Latin *nullus* = none]

nullify *verb* (**nullified**, **nullifying**) make a thing null. **nullification** *noun*

numb *adjective* unable to feel or move. **numbly** *adverb*, **numbness** *noun*

numb *verb* make numb.

number *noun* **1** a symbol or word indicating how many; a numeral or figure. **2** a numeral given to a thing to identify it, *a telephone number.* **3** a quantity of people or things, *the number of people present.* **4** one issue of a magazine or newspaper. **5** a song or piece of music.
number eight *noun* **1** (*NZ*) the 4-millimetre wire used for fencing etc. **2** (rugby union) the player at the back of the scrum. **3** the New Zealand symbol for Kiwi ingenuity.

number *verb* **1** mark with numbers. **2** count. **3** amount to, *The crowd numbered 10,000.*

numberless *adjective* too many to count.

numeral *noun* a symbol that represents a certain number; a figure. [from Latin *numerus* = number]

numerate *adjective* having a good basic knowledge of mathematics. **numeracy** *noun* [same origin as *numeral*]

numeration *noun* numbering.

numerator *noun* the number above the line in a fraction, showing how many parts are to be taken, e.g. 2 in ⅔. (Compare *denominator.*)

numerical (*say* new-**merri**-kal) *adjective* of a number or series of numbers, *in numerical order.* **numerically** *adverb*

numerous *adjective* many. [from Latin *numerus* = number]

numismatics (*say* new-miz-**mat**-iks) *noun* the study of coins. **numismatist** *noun* [from Greek *nomisma* = coin]

nun *noun* a member of a community of women who live according to the rules of a religious organisation. (Compare *monk.*) [from Latin *nonna* = nun]

nunnery *noun* (*plural* **nunneries**) a convent for nuns.

nuptial *adjective* of marriage; of a wedding. **nuptials** *plural noun* a wedding.

nurse *noun* **1** a person trained to look after people who are ill or injured. **2** a woman employed to look after young children.

nurse *verb* (**nursed**, **nursing**) **1** look after someone who is ill or injured. **2** hold carefully. **3** feed a baby.
nursing home a small hospital or home for invalids or elderly people. [same origin as *nourish*]

nursery *noun* (*plural* **nurseries**) **1** a place where young children are looked after or play. **2** a place where young plants are grown and usually for sale.
nursery rhyme a simple rhyme or song of the kind that young children like.
nursery school a school for children below primary school age.

nurture *verb* (**nurtured**, **nurturing**) **1** nourish. **2** train and educate; bring up.

nurture *noun* nurturing; nourishment.

nut *noun* **1** a fruit with a hard shell. **2** a kernel. **3** a small piece of metal with a hole in the middle, for screwing on to a bolt. **4** (*slang*) the head. **5** (*slang*) a mad or eccentric person. **nutty** *adjective*

nutcrackers *plural noun* pincers for cracking nuts.

nutmeg *noun* the hard seed of a tropical tree, grated and used in cooking.

nutrient (*say* **new**-tree-ent) *noun* a nourishing substance. **nutrient** *adjective* [from Latin *nutrire* = nourish]

nutriment (*say* **new**-trim-ent) *noun* nourishing food.

nutrition (*say* new-**trish**-on) *noun* nourishment; the study of what nourishes people. **nutritional** *adjective*, **nutritionally** *adverb*

nutritious (*say* new-**trish**-us) *adjective* nourishing; giving good nourishment. **nutritiousness** *noun*

nutritive (*say* **new**-trit-iv) *adjective* nourishing.

nutshell *noun* the shell of a nut.
in a nutshell stated very briefly.

nuzzle *verb* (**nuzzled**, **nuzzling**) rub gently with the nose.

NW *abbreviation* north-west; north-western.

nylon *noun* a synthetic lightweight very strong cloth or fibre.

nymph (*say* nimf) *noun* (in myths) a young goddess living in the sea or woods etc.

NZ *abbreviation* New Zealand.

NZD *abbreviation* New Zealand dollar(s), *NZD 200.*

NZE *abbreviation* New Zealand English.

NZ First *noun* (*NZ*) a political party formed in 1993.

NZQA *abbreviation* New Zealand Qualifications Authority.

NZRU *abbreviation* New Zealand Rugby Union.

NZX *abbreviation* New Zealand Stock Exchange.

NZSO *abbreviation* New Zealand Symphony Orchestra.

Oo

O *interjection* oh.

oaf *noun* (*plural* **oafs**) a stupid lout.

oak *noun* a large deciduous tree with seeds called acorns. **oaken** *adjective*

Ōamaru stone (*NZ*) a white stone used for building. [from the name of a South Island town]

oar *noun* a pole with a flat blade at one end, used for rowing a boat. **oarsman** *noun*, **oarsmanship** *noun*

oasis (*say* oh-**ay**-sis) *noun* (*plural* **oases**) a fertile place in a desert, with a spring or well of water.

oath *noun* **1** a solemn promise to do something or that something is true, appealing to God or a holy person as witness. **2** use of the name of God in anger or to emphasise something.

oatmeal *noun* ground oats.

oats *plural noun* a cereal used to make food.

ob- *prefix* (changing to **oc-** before *c*, **of-** before *f*, **op-** before *p*) **1** to; towards (as in *observe*). **2** against (as in *opponent*). **3** in the way; blocking (as in *obstruct*). [from Latin *ob* = towards, against]

obedient *adjective* doing what you are told; willing to obey. **obediently** *adverb*, **obedience** *noun*

obeisance (*say* o-**bay**-sans) *noun* a deep bow or curtsy.

obelisk *noun* a tall pillar set up as a monument. [from Greek, = little rod]

obese (*say* o-**beess**) *adjective* very fat. **obesity** (*say* o-**beess**-it-ee) *noun* [from Latin *obesus* = having overeaten]

obey *verb* do what you are told to do by a person, law, etc.

obituary *noun* (*plural* **obituaries**) a printed notice of a person's death, often with a short account of his or her life.

object (*say* **ob**-jikt) *noun* **1** something that can be seen or touched. **2** a purpose or intention. **3** (in grammar) the word or words naming who or what is acted upon by a verb or by a preposition, e.g. *him* in *the dog bit him* and *against him.*

object (*say* ob-**jekt**) *verb* say that you are not in favour of something or do not agree; protest. **objector** *noun* [from *ob* = in the way, + Latin *-jectum* = thrown]

objection *noun* **1** objecting to something. **2** a reason for objecting.

objectionable *adjective* unpleasant; not liked. **objectionably** *adverb*

objective *noun* what you are trying to reach or do; an aim.

objective *adjective* **1** real; actual, *Dreams have no objective existence.* **2** not influenced by personal feelings or opinions, *an objective account of the quarrel.* (Compare *subjective.*) **objectively** *adverb*, **objectivity** *noun*

obligation *noun* **1** being obliged to do something. **2** what you are obliged to do; a duty.
under an obligation owing gratitude to someone who has helped you.

obligatory (*say* ob-**lig**-a-ter-ee) *adjective* compulsory, not optional.

oblige *verb* (**obliged**, **obliging**) **1** compel. **2** help and please someone, *Can you oblige me with a loan?*
be obliged to someone feel gratitude to a person who has helped you. [from *ob-* = to, + Latin *ligare* = bind]

obliging *adjective* polite and helpful.

oblique (*say* ob-**leek**) *adjective* **1** slanting. **2** not saying something straightforwardly, *an oblique reply.* **obliquely** *adverb*

obliterate *verb* (**obliterated**, **obliterating**) blot out; destroy and remove all traces of something. **obliteration** *noun* [from Latin, = erase (*ob* = over, *littera* = letter)]

oblivion *noun* **1** being forgotten. **2** being oblivious.

oblivious *adjective* unaware of something, *oblivious to the danger.*

oblong *adjective* rectangular in shape and longer than it is wide (like a page of this book). **oblong** *noun*

obnoxious *adjective* very unpleasant; objectionable.

oboe *noun* a high-pitched woodwind instrument. **oboist** *noun* [from French *haut* = high, + *bois* = wood]

obscene (*say* ob-**seen**) *adjective* indecent in a repulsive or very offensive way. **obscenely** *adverb*, **obscenity** *noun*

obscure *adjective* **1** difficult to see or to understand; not clear. **2** not famous. **obscurely** *adverb*, **obscurity** *noun*

obscure *verb* (**obscured**, **obscuring**) make a thing obscure; darken or conceal, *Clouds obscured the sun.*

obsequious (*say* ob-**seek**-wee-us) *adjective* respectful in an excessive or sickening way. **obsequiously** *adverb*, **obsequiousness** *noun*

observance *noun* obeying or keeping a law, custom, religious festival, etc.

observant *adjective* quick at observing or noticing things. **observantly** *adverb*

observation *noun* **1** observing; watching. **2** a comment or remark.

observatory *noun* (*plural* **observatories**) a building with telescopes etc. for observation of the stars or weather.

observe *verb* (**observed**, **observing**) **1** see and notice; watch carefully. **2** obey a law. **3** keep or celebrate a custom or religious festival etc. **4** make a remark. **observer** *noun* [from *ob-* = towards, + Latin *servare* = to watch]

obsess *verb* **1** occupy a person's thoughts continually. **2** worry constantly. **obsession** *noun*, **obsessive** *adjective.*

obsidian *noun* a dark glassy volcanic rock, formerly used by Māori to make tools.

obsolescent *adjective* becoming obsolete; going out of use or fashion. **obsolescence** *noun*

obsolete *adjective* not used any more; out of date. [from Latin *obsoletus* = worn out]

obstacle *noun* something that stands in the way or obstructs progress. [from *ob-* = in the way, + Latin *stare* to stand]

obstetrics *noun* the branch of medicine and surgery that deals with the birth of babies. [from Latin, = of a midwife]

obstinate *adjective* keeping firmly to your own ideas or ways, even though they may be wrong. **obstinately** *adverb*, **obstinacy** *noun*

obstreperous (*say* ob-**strep**-er-us) *adjective* noisy and unruly.

obstruct *verb* stop a person or thing from getting past; hinder. **obstruction** *noun*, **obstructive** *adjective*

obtain *verb* get; come into possession of something by buying, taking, or being given it. **obtainable** *adjective* [from *ob-* to, + Latin *tenere* = hold]

obtrude *verb* (**obtruded**, **obtruding**) force yourself or your ideas on someone; be obtrusive. **obtrusion** *noun* [from *ob-*, + Latin *trudere* = push]

obtrusive *adjective* obtruding; unpleasantly noticeable. **obtrusiveness** *noun*

obtuse *adjective* stupid. **obtusely** *adverb*, **obtuseness** *noun*
obtuse angle an angle of more than 90° but less than 180°. (Compare *acute.*) [from *ob-* = towards, + Latin *tusum* = blunted]

obverse *noun* the side of a coin or medal showing the head or chief design (the other side is the *reverse*). [from *ob-* = towards, + Latin *versum* = turned]

obvious *adjective* easy to see or understand. **obviously** *adverb* [from Latin *ob viam* = in the way]

oc- *prefix* see **ob-**.

occasion *noun* **1** the time when something happens. **2** a special event. **3** a suitable time; an opportunity.

occasion *verb* cause.

occasional *adjective* **1** happening at intervals. **2** for special occasions, *occasional music.* **occasionally** *adverb*

Occident *noun* countries of the West (compare *Orient*). [from Latin, = sunset]

occult *adjective* **1** mysterious; supernatural, *occult powers.* **2** secret except when people have special knowledge. [from Latin *occultum* = hidden]

occupant *noun* someone who occupies a place. **occupancy** *noun*

occupation *noun* **1** an activity that keeps a person busy; a job. **2** occupying.

occupational *adjective* of or caused by an occupation, *an occupational disease.*
occupational therapy creative work designed to help people to recover from certain illnesses.

occupy *verb* (**occupied**, **occupying**) **1** live in a place; inhabit. **2** fill a space or position. **3** capture enemy territory and place troops there. **4** keep somebody busy; fill with activity. **occupier** *noun*

occur *verb* (**occurred**, **occurring**) **1** happen; come into existence as an event or process. **2** be found to exist, *These plants occur in ponds.* **3** come into a person's mind, *An idea occurred to me.*

occurrence *noun* **1** occurring. **2** an incident or event; a happening.

ocean *noun* the seas that surround the continents of the earth, especially one of the large named areas of this, *the Pacific Ocean.* **oceanic** *adjective* [from Oceanus, the river that the ancient Greeks thought surrounded the world]

ocelot (*say* **oss**-il-ot) *noun* a leopard-like animal of Central and South America.

ochre (*say* **oh**-ker) *noun* **1** a mineral used as a pigment. **2** pale brownish-yellow.

Ocker *noun* (*NZ, slang*) an Australian.

ocker *adjective* (*NZ, slang*) Australian, *He's an ocker cricketer.*

o'clock *adverb* by the clock, *Lunch is at one o'clock.* [short for *of the clock*]

octa- or **octo-** *prefix* eight. [from Greek *okto* = eight]

octagon *noun* a flat shape with eight sides and eight angles. **octagonal** *adjective* [from *octa-*, + Greek *gonia* = angle]

octane *noun* a substance occurring in petrol.

octave *noun* the interval of eight steps between one musical note and the next note of the same name above or below it. [from Latin *octavus* = eighth]

octet *noun* a group of eight instruments or singers. [from *octo-*]

octo- *prefix* see **octa-**.

October *noun* the tenth month of the year. [from Latin *octo* = eight (in Roman times it was the eighth month)]

octogenarian *noun* a person aged between 80 and 89. [from Latin *octogeni* = 80 each]

octopus *noun* (*plural* **octopuses**) a sea animal with eight long tentacles. [from *octo-*, + Greek *pous* = foot]

ocular *adjective* of or for the eyes; visual. [from Latin *oculus* = eye]

oculist *noun* a doctor who treats diseases of the eye. [from Latin *oculus* = eye]

OD *abbreviation* overdose.

odd *adjective* **1** strange; unusual. **2** not an even number; not able to be divided exactly by 2. **3** left over from a pair or set, *I've got one odd sock.* **4** of various kinds; not regular, *odd jobs.* **oddly** *adverb*, **oddness** *noun*, **oddity** *noun*

oddments *plural noun* small things of various kinds.

odds *plural noun* the chances that a certain thing will happen; a measure of this, *When the odds are 10 to 1, you will win $10 if you bet $1.*
odds and ends oddments.
odds-on the situation when success is more likely than failure.
over the odds above the usual price etc.

ode *noun* a poem addressed to a person or thing. [from Greek *oide* = song]

ODI *abbreviation* one-day international (cricket match).

odious (*say* **oh**-dee-us) *adjective* hateful. **odiously** *adverb*, **odiousness** *noun*

odium (*say* **oh**-dee-um) *noun* general hatred or disgust felt towards a person or actions. [Latin, = hatred]

odometer *noun* an instrument for measuring the distance travelled by a car etc.

odour *noun* **1** a smell. **2** a quality or impression, *The odour of his argument was evident.* **odorous** *adjective*, **odourless** *adjective* [Latin *odor* = smell]

odyssey (*say* **od**-iss-ee) *noun* (*plural* **odysseys**) a long adventurous journey. [named after the *Odyssey*, a Greek poem telling of the wanderings of Odysseus]

OE *abbreviation* (*NZ*) overseas experience.

OECD *abbreviation* Organisation for Economic Cooperation and Development.

o'er *preposition & adverb* (*poetic*) over.

oesophagus (*say* ee-**sof**-a-gus) *noun* (*plural* **oesophagi**) the gullet.

of *preposition* (used to indicate relationships) **1** belonging to, *the mother of the child.* **2** concerning; about, *news of the disaster.* **3** made from, *built of stone.* **4** from, *north of the town.*

of- *prefix* see **ob-**.

off *preposition* **1** not on; away or down from, *He fell off the ladder.* **2** not taking or wanting, *She is off her food.* **3** deducted from, *$5 off the price.*

off *adverb* **1** away or down from something, *His hat blew off.* **2** not working; not happening, *The heating is off.* **3** to the end; completely, *Finish it off.* **4** as regards money or supplies, *How are you off for cash?* **5** behind or at the side of a stage, *There were noises off.* **6** (of food) beginning to go bad.

offal *noun* the organs of an animal (e.g. liver, kidneys) sold as food.

offcut *noun* a piece of wood etc. left over after cutting.

offence *noun* **1** an illegal action. **2** a feeling of annoyance or resentment. **3** in sport, attacking play or players.

offend *verb* **1** cause offence to someone; hurt a person's pride. **2** do wrong, *offend against the law.* **offender** *noun*

offensive *adjective* **1** causing offence; insulting. **2** disgusting, *an offensive smell.* **3** used in attacking, *offensive weapons.* **offensively** *adverb*, **offensiveness** *noun*

offensive *noun* an attack.
take the offensive be the first to attack.

offer *verb* (**offered**, **offering**) **1** present something so that people can accept it if they want to. **2** say that you are willing to do or give something or to pay a certain amount.

offer *noun* **1** offering something. **2** an amount offered. [from *of-* = to, + Latin *ferre* = bring]

offering *noun* what is offered.

offhand *adjective* **1** without preparation. **2** casual; curt. **offhanded** *adjective*

office *noun* **1** a room or building used for business, especially for clerical work or for a special department; the people who work there. **2** an important job or position.
be in office hold an official position.

officer *noun* **1** a person who is in charge of others, especially in the armed forces. **2** an official. **3** a member of the police.

official *adjective* **1** done or said by someone with authority. **2** of officials. **officially** *adverb*

official *noun* a person who holds a position of authority.

officiate *verb* (**officiated**, **officiating**) be in charge of a meeting, event, etc.

officious *adjective* too ready to give orders; bossy. **officiously** *adverb*

offing *noun* **in the offing** not far away; likely to happen.

offset *verb* (**offset**, **offsetting**) counter-balance or make up for something, *Defeats are offset by successes.*

offshoot *noun* **1** a side-shoot on a plant. **2** a by-product.

offshore *adjective & adverb* **1** from the land towards the sea, *an offshore breeze.* **2** in the sea some distance from the shore. **3** overseas, foreign, *offshore investments.*

offside *adjective & adverb* (of a player in rugby etc.) in a position where the rules do not allow him or her to play the ball.

offsider *noun* (*NZ*) an assistant.

offspring *noun* (*plural* **offspring**) a person's child or children; the young of an animal.

oft *adverb* (*old use*) often.

often *adverb* many times; in many cases.

ogle *verb* (**ogled**, **ogling**) stare at someone whom you find attractive.

ogre *noun* **1** a cruel giant in fairytales. **2** a terrifying person.

oh *interjection* an exclamation of pain, surprise, delight, etc., or used for emphasis (*Oh yes I will!*).

ohm *noun* a unit of electrical resistance. [named after a German scientist, G. S. Ohm]

OHP *abbreviation* overhead projector.

oil *noun* **1** a thick slippery liquid that will not dissolve in water. **2** a kind of petroleum used as fuel. **oil-well** *noun*
oil rig machinery etc. for drilling an oil-well.
oil-slick *noun* a patch of oil on water, the sea etc.

oil *verb* put oil on something, especially to make it work smoothly. [from Latin *oleum* = olive oil]

oilcake *noun* cattle feed made from linseed after the oil has been pressed out.

oil-colour *noun* paint made with oil.

oilfield *noun* an area where oil is found.

oil-painting *noun* a painting done with oil-colours.

oilskin *noun* cloth made waterproof by treatment with oil.

oily *adjective* of or like oil; covered or soaked with oil. **oiliness** *noun*

ointment *noun* a cream or slippery paste for putting on sore skin and cuts.

OK *adverb & adjective* (*informal*) all right. [perhaps from the initials of *oll* (or *orl*) *korrect*, a humorous spelling of *all correct*, first used in the USA in 1839]

old *adjective* **1** not new; born or made or existing from a long time ago. **2** of a particular age, *I'm ten years old.* **3** former; original, *in its old place.* **4** (*informal*, used casually or for emphasis), *good old mum!*
oldness *noun*
Old English the English language up to about 1100 AD.
old identity (*NZ*) a well-known person in a town or district who has lived there a long time.

olden *adjective* (*old use*) of former times.

old-fashioned *adjective* of the kind that was usual a long time ago.

olfactory *adjective* of the sense of smell.

oligarchy *noun* (*plural* **oligarchies**) a country ruled by a small group of people. **oligarch** *noun*, **oligarchic** *adjective* [from Greek *oligoi* = few, + *archein* = to rule]

olive *noun* **1** an evergreen tree with a small bitter fruit. **2** this fruit, from which an oil (*olive oil*) is made. **3** a shade of green like an unripe olive.

olive-branch *noun* something done or offered that shows you want to make peace.

Olympic Games or **Olympics** *plural noun* a series of international sports contests held every four years in a different part of the world. [from the name Olympia in Greece, the ancient venue for the games.]

ombudsman *noun* (*plural* **ombudsmen**) an official whose job is to investigate complaints against government organisations etc. [from Swedish, = legal representative]

omega (*say* **oh**-meg-a) *noun* the last letter of the Greek alphabet, a long *o*. [from Greek *o mega* = big O]

omelette *noun* eggs beaten together and cooked in a pan, often with a filling.

omen *noun* an event regarded as a sign of what is going to happen.

ominous *adjective* seeming as if trouble is coming. **ominously** *adverb* [from *omen*]

omission *noun* **1** omitting. **2** something that has been omitted or not done.

omit *verb* (**omitted**, **omitting**) **1** miss something out. **2** fail to do something.

omni- *prefix* all. [from Latin *omnis* = all]

omnibus *noun* (*plural* **omnibuses**) **1** (*old use*) a bus. **2** a book containing several stories or books that were previously published separately. [Latin, = for everybody]

omnipotent *adjective* having unlimited power or very great power. [from *omni-* + *potent*]

omniscient (*say* om-**nish**-ent) *adjective* knowing everything. **omniscience** *noun* [from *omni-*, + Latin *sciens* = knowing]

omnivorous (*say* om-**niv**-er-us) *adjective* feeding on all kinds of food. (Compare *carnivorous, herbivorous.*) [from *omni-*, + Latin *vorare* = devour]

on *preposition* **1** supported by; covering; added or attached to, *the sign on the door.* **2** close to; towards, *The army advanced on Paris.* **3** during; at the time of, *on my birthday.* **4** by reason of, *Arrest him on suspicion.* **5** concerning, *a book on butterflies.* **6** in a state of; using or showing, *The house was on fire.*

on *adverb* **1** so as to be on something, *Put it on.* **2** further forward, *Move on.* **3** working; in action, *Is the heater on?*
on and off not continually.

once *adverb* **1** for one time or on one occasion only, *They came only once.* **2** formerly, *They once lived here.*

once *noun* one time, *Once is enough.*

once *conjunction* as soon as, *You can go once I have taken your names.*

oncoming *adjective* approaching; coming towards you, *oncoming traffic.*

one *adjective* single; individual; united.

one *noun* **1** the smallest whole number, 1. **2** a person or thing alone.
one another each other.

one *pronoun* a person; any person, *One likes to help.* **oneself** *pronoun*

one-off *adjective* not repeated. **one-off** *noun*

onerous (*say* **oh**-ner-us) *adjective* burdensome. [from Latin *onus* = burden]

one-way *adjective* where traffic is allowed to travel in one direction only.

ongoing *adjective* continuing.

onion *noun* a round vegetable with a strong flavour. **oniony** *adjective*

online *adjective* **1** joined to the Internet. **2** having an Internet site. **3** directly joined to a computer.

onlooker *noun* a spectator.

only *adjective* being the one person or thing of a kind; sole, *my only wish.*
only child a child who has no brothers or sisters.

only *adverb* no more than; and that is all, *There are only three cakes left.*

only *conjunction* but then; however, *He makes promises, only he never keeps them.*

o.n.o. *abbreviation* or near offer.

onomatopoeia (*say* on-om-at-o-**pee**-a) *noun* the formation of words that imitate what they stand for, e.g. *cuckoo, sizzle.* **onomatopoeic** *adjective* [from Greek *onoma* = name, + *poiein* = make]

onrush *noun* an onward rush.

onset *noun* **1** a beginning, *the onset of winter.* **2** an attack.

onshore *adjective & adverb* **1** from the sea towards the land, *an onshore breeze.* **2** on land. **3** not overseas, *investing onshore.*

onslaught *noun* a fierce attack.

onto *preposition* to a position on.

onus (*say* **oh**-nus) *noun* the duty or responsibility of doing something. [Latin, = burden]

onward *adverb & adjective* going forward; further on. **onwards** *adverb*

onyx *noun* a stone rather like marble, with different colours in layers.

ONZ *abbreviation* Order of New Zealand.

OOS *abbreviation* occupational overuse syndrome, a condition in which pain in muscles and tendons is caused by continually repeating the same movements, or by remaining for long periods in the same posture, at one's work (compare *RSI*).

ooze *verb* (**oozed**, **oozing**) **1** flow out slowly; trickle. **2** allow something to flow out slowly, *The wound oozed blood.*

ooze *noun* mud at the bottom of a river or sea.

op- *prefix* see **ob-**.

opal *noun* a kind of stone with a rainbow sheen. **opalescent** *adjective*

opaque (*say* o-**payk**) *adjective* not transparent; not translucent.

ope *noun* a company or group of people. [Māori]

OPEC *abbreviation* Organisation of Petroleum Exporting Countries.

open *adjective* **1** allowing people or things to go in and out; not closed or covered; not blocked up. **2** spread out; unfolded. **3** not limited; not restricted, *an open championship.* **4** letting in visitors or customers. **5** with wide spaces between solid parts. **6** honest; frank; not secret or secretive, *Be open about the danger.* **7** not decided, *an open mind.* **openness** *noun*
in the open air not inside a house or building. **open-air** *adjective*
open day the opening of a building or institution to the general public.
open slather see **slather**.

open *verb* **1** make or become open or more open. **2** begin. **opener** *noun*

opencast *adjective* (of a mine) worked by removing layers of earth from the surface, not underground.

opening *noun* **1** a space or gap; a place where something opens. **2** the beginning of something. **3** an opportunity.

openly *adverb* without secrecy.

opera *noun* a play in which all or most of the words are sung. **operatic** *adjective*

opera *plural* of **opus**.

operate *verb* (**operated**, **operating**) **1** make something work. **2** be in action; work. **3** perform a surgical operation on somebody. **operable** *adjective* [from Latin *operari* = to work]
operating theatre *noun* a room where surgical operations are performed in a hospital.

operation *noun* **1** operating; working. **2** a piece of work. **3** something done to the body to take away or repair a part of it. **4** a planned military activity. **operational** *adjective*

operative *adjective* **1** working; functioning. **2** of surgical operations.

operator *noun* a person who works something, especially a telephone switchboard or exchange.

operetta *noun* a short light opera.

ophthalmic (*say* off-**thal**-mik) *adjective* of or for the eyes. [from Greek *ophthalmos* = eye]

opinion *noun* what you think of something; a belief or judgement.
opinion poll an estimate of what people think, made by questioning a sample of them. [from Latin *opinari* = believe]

opinionated *adjective* having strong opinions and holding them obstinately.

opium *noun* a drug made from the juice of certain poppies, used in medicine.

opossum *noun* **1** a North American marsupial that lives in trees. **2** (*Australia & NZ, old use*) a possum.

opponent *noun* a person or group opposing another in a contest or war. [from Latin *opponere* = set against]

opportune *adjective* **1** (of time) suitable for a purpose. **2** done or happening at a suitable time. **opportunely** *adverb* [from *op-*, + Latin *portus* = harbour (originally used of wind blowing a ship towards a harbour)]

opportunist *noun* a person who is quick to seize opportunities, often in an unprincipled way. **opportunism** *noun*

opportunity *noun* (*plural* **opportunities**) a time or set of circumstances that are suitable for doing a particular thing. [same origin as *opportune*]

oppose *verb* (**opposed**, **opposing**) **1** argue or fight against; resist. **2** contrast, *'Soft' is opposed to 'hard'.*

opposite *adjective* **1** placed on the other or further side; facing, *on the opposite side of the road.* **2** moving away from or towards each other, *The cars were travelling in opposite directions.* **3** completely different, *opposite characters.*

opposite *noun* an opposite person or thing.

opposite *adverb* in an opposite position or direction, *I'll sit opposite.*

opposite *preposition* opposite to, *They live opposite the school.* [from Latin *oppositum* = placed against]

opposition *noun* **1** opposing something; resistance. **2** the people who oppose something; **the Opposition** the political party or parties opposing the Government.

oppress *verb* **1** govern or treat somebody cruelly or unjustly. **2** weigh down with worry or sadness. **oppression** *noun*, **oppressive** *adjective*, **oppressor** *noun* [from *op-* = against, + *press*]

opt *verb* choose.
opt out decide not to join in. [from Latin *optare* = wish for]

optic *adjective* of the eye or sight.
optics *noun* the study of sight and of light as connected with this. [from Greek *optos* = seen]

optical *adjective* of sight; aiding sight, *optical instruments.* **optically** *adverb*
optical illusion a deceptive appearance that makes you see something wrongly. [from *optic*]

optician *noun* a person who makes or sells spectacles etc.

optimise *verb* (**optimised**, **optimising**) make the most of something.

optimist *noun* a person who expects that things will turn out well. (Compare *pessimist.*) **optimism** *noun*, **optimistic** *adjective*, **optimistically** *adverb* [from Latin *optimus* = best]

optimum *adjective* best; most favourable.
optimum *noun*, **optimal** *adjective* [Latin, = best thing]

option *noun* **1** the right or power to choose something. **2** something chosen or that may be chosen. **3** the right to buy or sell something at a certain price within a limited time. [same origin as *opt*]

optional *adjective* that you can choose, not compulsory. **optionally** *adverb*

optometrist *noun* a person who is qualified to test people's eyesight and prescribe spectacles etc. **optometry** *noun*

opulent *adjective* **1** wealthy; rich. **2** plentiful. **opulently** *adverb*, **opulence** *noun* [from Latin *opes* = wealth]

opus (*say* **oh**-pus) *noun* (*plural* **opera**) a numbered musical composition, *Beethoven, opus 15.* [Latin, = work]

or *conjunction* used to show that there is a choice or an alternative, *Do you want a bun or a biscuit?*

oracle *noun* **1** a shrine where the ancient Greeks consulted one of their gods for advice or a prophecy. **2** a wise adviser. **oracular** (*say* or-**ak**-yoo-ler) *adjective* [from Latin *orare* = speak]

oracy (*say* **or**-a-see) *noun* the ability to express yourself well in speaking.

oral *adjective* **1** spoken, not written. **2** of or using the mouth. **orally** *adverb* [from Latin *oris* = of the mouth]

orange *noun* **1** a round juicy citrus fruit with reddish-yellow peel. **2** a reddish-yellow colour. [from Persian *narang*]
orange roughy (*NZ*) an edible sea-fish.

orangeade *noun* an orange-flavoured drink.

orang-utan *noun* a large ape of Borneo and Sumatra. [from Malay, = wild man]

oration *noun* a long formal speech. [from Latin *orare* = speak]

orator *noun* a person who makes speeches. **oratory** *noun*, **oratorical** *adjective*

oratorio *noun* (*plural* **oratorios**) a piece of music for voices and an orchestra, usually on a religious subject.

orb *noun* a sphere or globe.

orbit *noun* **1** the curved path taken by something moving round a planet etc. in space. **2** the range of someone's influence or control. **orbital** *adjective*

orbit *verb* (**orbited**, **orbiting**) move in an orbit round something, *The spacecraft orbited the earth.* [from Latin *orbis* = circle]

orchard *noun* a piece of ground planted with fruit trees. [from Latin *hortus* = garden, + *yard*]

orchestra *noun* a large group of people playing various musical instruments together. **orchestral** *adjective* [Greek, = space where the chorus danced during a play]

orchestrate *verb* (**orchestrated**, **orchestrating**) **1** compose or arrange music for an orchestra. **2** coordinate things deliberately, *They orchestrated their campaigns.* **orchestration** *noun*

orchid *noun* a kind of flower, often with unevenly shaped petals.

ordain *verb* **1** appoint a person ceremonially to perform spiritual duties in the Christian Church. **2** destine. **3** declare authoritatively; decree.

ordeal *noun* something very hard to endure.

order *noun* **1** a command. **2** a request for something to be supplied. **3** the way things are arranged, *in alphabetical order.* **4** a neat arrangement; a proper arrangement or condition, *in working order.* **5** obedience to rules or laws, *law and order.* **6** a kind or sort, *She showed courage of the highest order.* **7** a special group; a religious organisation, *an order of monks.*
in order that or **in order to** for the purpose of.

order *verb* **1** command. **2** ask for something to be supplied. **3** put into order; arrange neatly.

orderly *adjective* **1** arranged neatly or well; methodical. **2** well-behaved; obedient. **orderliness** *noun*

orderly *noun* (*plural* **orderlies**) **1** a soldier whose job is to assist an officer. **2** an assistant in a hospital.

ordinal numbers numbers showing a thing's position in a series, e.g. *first, fifth, twentieth.* (Compare *cardinal.*) [same origin as *ordinary*]

ordinance *noun* a command; a decree.

ordinary *adjective* normal; usual; not special. **ordinarily** *adverb* [from Latin *ordinis* = of a row or an order]

ordination *noun* ordaining or being ordained as a member of the clergy.

ordnance *noun* military equipment.

ore *noun* rock with metal or other useful substances in it, *iron ore.*

oregano *noun* a herb used in cooking.

organ *noun* **1** a musical instrument from which sounds are produced by air forced through pipes, played by keys and pedals. **2** a part of the body with a particular function, *the digestive organs.* [from Greek *organon* = tool]

organdie *noun* a kind of thin fabric, usually stiffened.

organic *adjective* **1** of organs of the body, *organic diseases.* **2** of or formed from living things, *organic matter.* **3** grown or produced without using artificial fertilisers etc. **4** organised as a system of related parts, *an organic whole.* **organically** *adverb*

organisation *noun* **1** an organised group of people. **2** the organising of something. **organisational** *adjective*

organise *verb* (**organised**, **organising**) **1** plan and prepare something, *We organised a picnic.* **2** form people into a group to work together. **3** put things in order. **organiser** *noun* [same origin as *organ*]

organism *noun* a living thing; an individual animal or plant.

organist *noun* a person who plays the organ.

orgasm *noun* the climax of sexual excitement.

orgy *noun* (*plural* **orgies**) **1** a wild party. **2** an extravagant activity, *an orgy of spending.*

Orient *noun* the East; oriental countries (compare *Occident*). [from Latin, = sunrise]

orient *verb* orientate.

oriental *adjective* of the countries east of the Mediterranean Sea, especially China and Japan.

orientate *verb* (**orientated**, **orientating**) place something or face in a certain direction. **orientation** *noun*

orienteering *noun* the sport of finding your way across rough country with a map and compass.

orifice (*say* **o**-rif-iss) *noun* an opening. [from Latin *oris* = of the mouth]

origami (*say* o-rig-**ah**-mee) *noun* folding paper into decorative shapes. [from Japanese *ori* = fold, + *kami* = paper]

origin *noun* the start of something; the point or cause from which something began. [from Latin *origo* = source]

original *adjective* **1** existing from the start; earliest, *the original inhabitants.* **2** new in its design etc., not a copy. **3** producing new ideas; inventive. **originally** *adverb*, **originality** *noun*

originate *verb* (**originated**, **originating**) **1** cause to begin; create. **2** have its origin, *The quarrel originated in rivalry.* **origination** *noun*, **originator** *noun*

ornament *noun* a decoration. **ornamental** *adjective*

ornament *verb* decorate with things. **ornamentation** *noun* [from Latin *ornare* = adorn]

ornate *adjective* elaborately ornamented. **ornately** *adverb* [from Latin *ornatum* = adorned]

ornithology *noun* the study of birds. **ornithologist** *noun*, **ornithological** *adjective* [from Greek *ornithos* = of a bird, + *-logy*]

orphan *noun* a child whose parents are dead. **orphaned** *adjective*

orphanage *noun* a home for orphans.

ortho- *prefix* right; straight; correct. [from Greek *orthos* = straight]

orthodox *adjective* holding beliefs that are correct or generally accepted. **orthodoxy** *noun*
Orthodox Church the Christian Churches of eastern Europe. [from *ortho-*, + Greek *doxa* = opinion]

orthopaedics (*say* orth-o-**pee**-diks) *noun* the treatment of deformities and injuries to bones and muscles. **orthopaedic** *adjective* [from *ortho-*, + Greek *paideia* = rearing of children (because the treatment was originally of children)]

oryx *noun* a large African antelope.

oscillate *verb* (**oscillated**, **oscillating**) **1** move to and fro like a pendulum; vibrate. **2** waver; vary. **oscillation** *noun*, **oscillator** *noun*

osier (*say* **oh**-zee-er) *noun* a willow with flexible twigs used in making baskets.

osmosis *noun* the passing of fluid through a porous partition into another more concentrated fluid. [from Greek *osmos* = push]

ossify *verb* (**ossified**, **ossifying**) turn to bone, harden. **ossification** *noun*

ostensible *adjective* pretended; used to conceal the true reason, *Their ostensible reason for travelling was to visit friends.* **ostensibly** *adverb* [from Latin *ostendere* = to show]

ostentatious *adjective* making a showy display of something to impress people. **ostentatiously** *adverb*, **ostentation** *noun*

osteopath *noun* a person who treats certain diseases etc. by manipulating a patient's bones and muscles. **osteopathy** *noun*, **osteopathic** *adjective* [from Greek *osteon* = bone, + *-patheia* = suffering]

ostracise *verb* (**ostracised**, **ostracising**) exclude; ignore someone completely. **ostracism** *noun* [from Greek *ostrakon* = piece of pottery (because people voted that a person should be banished by writing his name on this)]

ostrich *noun* (*plural* **ostriches**) a large long-legged African bird that can run very fast but cannot fly. It is said to bury its head in the sand when pursued, believing that it cannot then be seen.

Ōtautahi *noun* a Māori name for Christchurch.

Ōtepoti *noun* a Māori name for Dunedin.

other *adjective* **1** different, *some other tune.* **2** remaining, *Try the other shoe.* **3** additional, *my other friends.* **4** just recent or past, *I saw him the other day.*

other *noun & pronoun* the other person or thing, *Where are the others?*

otherwise *adverb* **1** if things happen differently; if you do not, *Write it down, otherwise you'll forget.* **2** in other ways, *It rained, but otherwise the holiday was good.* **3** differently, *We could not do otherwise.*

otter *noun* a fish-eating animal of the Northern hemisphere with webbed feet, a flat tail, and thick brown fur, living near water.

ottoman *noun* **1** a long padded seat. **2** a storage box with a padded top.

ought *auxiliary verb* expressing duty (*We ought to feed them*), rightness or advisability (*You ought to take more exercise*), or probability (*At this speed, we ought to be there by noon*).

oughtn't (*mainly spoken*) ought not.

ounce *noun* an imperial unit of weight, equivalent to about 28.3 grams.

our *adjective* belonging to us.

ours *possessive pronoun* belonging to us, *These seats are ours.*

USAGE It is incorrect to write *our's.*

ourselves *pronoun* we or us and nobody else. (Compare *herself.*)

oust *verb* drive out; expel; eject from a position or employment etc.

out *adverb* **1** away from or not in a particular place or position or state etc.; not at home. **2** into the open; into existence or sight etc., *The sun came out.* **3** not in action or use etc.; (in cricket) having had an innings ended; (of a fire) not burning. **4** to or at an end; completely, *sold out; tired out.* **5** without restraint; boldly; loudly, *Speak out!*
be out for or **out to** be seeking or wanting, *They are out to make trouble.*
out of date old-fashioned; not valid any more.
out of doors in the open air.
out of the way remote; unusual.

out- *prefix* **1** out of; away from (as in *outcast*). **2** external; separate (as in *out-house*). **3** more than; so as to defeat or exceed (as in *outdo*).

out-and-out *adjective* thorough; complete, *an out-and-out villain.*

outback *noun* the remote inland districts of Australia, the back country.

outboard motor a motor fitted to the outside of a boat's stern.

outbreak *noun* the start of a disease or war or anger etc.

outburst *noun* the bursting out of anger or laughter etc.

outcast *noun* a person who has been rejected by family, friends, or society.

outcome *noun* the result of what happens or has happened.

outcrop *noun* a piece of rock from a lower level that sticks out on the surface of the ground.

outcry *noun* (*plural* **outcries**) **1** a loud cry. **2** a strong protest.

outdated *adjective* out of date.

outdistance *verb* (**outdistanced, outdistancing**) get far ahead of someone in a race etc.

outdo *verb* (**outdid, outdone, outdoing**) do better than another person etc.

outdoor *adjective* done or used outdoors.

outdoors *noun* the open air, *the great outdoors.*

outdoors *adverb* in the open air.

outer *adjective* outside; external; nearer to the outside. **outermost** *adjective*
on the outer (*NZ*) neglected; unpopular.

outfall *noun* the outlet of a river, drain, etc.

outfit *noun* **1** a set of clothes worn together. **2** a set of equipment.

outflow *noun* **1** flowing out; what flows out. **2** a pipe for liquid flowing out.

outgoing *adjective* **1** going out. **2** sociable and friendly.
outgoings *plural noun* expenditure.

outgrow *verb* (**outgrew, outgrown, outgrowing**) **1** grow out of clothes or habits etc. **2** grow faster or larger than another person or thing.

outgrowth *noun* something that grows out of another thing, *Feathers are outgrowths on a bird's skin.*

outhouse *noun* a small building (e.g. a shed or barn) that belongs to a house but is separate from it.

outing *noun* **1** a journey for pleasure. **2** an appearance in a race or contest.

outlandish *adjective* looking or sounding strange or foreign.

outlast *verb* last longer than something else.

outlaw *noun* a person who is punished by being excluded from legal rights and the protection of the law.

outlaw *verb* **1** make a person an outlaw. **2** declare something to be illegal; forbid.

outlay *noun* what is spent on something.

outlet *noun* **1** a way for something to get out. **2** a market for goods.

outline *noun* **1** a line round the outside of something, showing its boundary or shape. **2** a summary.

outline *verb* (**outlined, outlining**) **1** make an outline of something. **2** summarise.

outlive *verb* (**outlived, outliving**) live or last longer than another person etc.

outlook *noun* **1** a view on which people look out. **2** a person's mental attitude to something. **3** future prospects.

outlying *adjective* far from a centre; remote, *the outlying districts.*

outmoded *adjective* out of date.

outnumber *verb* be more numerous than another group.

out-patient *noun* a person who visits a hospital for treatment but does not stay there.

outpost *noun* a distant settlement.

output *noun* the amount produced.

outrage *noun* **1** something that shocks people by being very wicked or cruel. **2** great anger. **outrageous** *adjective*, **outrageously** *adverb*

outrage *verb* (**outraged**, **outraging**) shock and anger people greatly.

outrider *noun* a person riding on horseback or on a motor cycle as an escort.

outrigger *noun* a projecting framework attached to a boat, e.g. to prevent a canoe from capsizing.
outrigger canoe a canoe with an outrigger.

outright *adverb* **1** completely; entirely, not gradually. **2** frankly, *We told him this outright.*

outright *adjective* thorough; complete, *an outright fraud.*

outrun *verb* (**outran**, **outrun**, **outrunning**) **1** run faster or further than another. **2** go on for longer than it should.

outset *noun* the beginning, *from the outset of his career.*

outside *noun* the outer side, surface, or part.

outside *adjective* **1** on or coming from the outside, *the outside edge.* **2** greatest possible, *the outside price.* **3** remote; unlikely, *an outside chance.*
outside the square unconventional or unexpected.

outside *adverb* on or to the outside; outdoors, *Leave it outside. It's cold outside.*

outside *preposition* on or to the outside of, *Leave it outside the door.*

outsider *noun* **1** a person who does not belong to a certain group. **2** a horse or person thought to have no chance of winning a race or competition.

outsize *adjective* much larger than average.

outskirts *plural noun* the outer parts or districts, especially of a town.

outspoken *adjective* speaking or spoken very frankly.

outspread *adjective* spread out.

outstanding *adjective* **1** extremely good or distinguished. **2** conspicuous. **3** not yet paid or dealt with.

outstretched *adjective* stretched out.

outstrip *verb* (**outstripped**, **outstripping**) **1** outrun. **2** surpass.

outvote *verb* (**outvoted**, **outvoting**) defeat by a majority of votes.

outward *adjective* **1** going outwards. **2** on the outside. **outwardly** *adverb*, **outwards** *adverb*

outweigh *verb* be greater in weight or importance than something else.

outwit *verb* (**outwitted**, **outwitting**) deceive somebody by being crafty.

outworn *adjective* **1** worn out, exhausted. **2** no longer used, obsolete.

ova *plural* of **ovum**.

oval *adjective* shaped like a 0, rounded and longer than it is broad. **oval** *noun* [from Latin *ovum* = egg]

ovary *noun* (*plural* **ovaries**) **1** either of the two organs in which ova or eggcells are produced in a woman's or female animal's body. **2** part of the pistil in a plant, from which fruit is formed. [from Latin *ovum* = egg]

ovation *noun* enthusiastic applause. [from Latin *ovare* = rejoice]

oven *noun* a closed space in which things are cooked or heated.

over *preposition* **1** above. **2** more than, *It's over a mile away.* **3** concerning, *They quarrelled over money.* **4** across the top of; on or to the other side of, *They rowed the boat over the lake.* **5** during, *We can talk over dinner.* **6** in superiority or preference to, *their victory over Otago.*

over *adverb* **1** out and down from the top or edge; from an upright position, *He fell over.* **2** so that a different side shows, *Turn it over.* **3** at or to a place; across, *Walk over to our house.* **4** remaining, *There is nothing left over.* **5** all through; thoroughly, *Think it over.* **6** at an end, *The lesson is over.*
over and over many times; repeatedly.

over *noun* a series of six balls bowled in cricket.

over- *prefix* **1** over (as in *overturn*). **2** too much; too (as in *over-anxious*).

overall *adjective* including everything; total, *the overall cost.*

overalls *plural noun* a garment worn over other clothes to protect them.

overarm *adjective & adverb* with the arm lifted above shoulder level and coming down in front of the body.

overawe *verb* (**overawed**, **overawing**) overcome a person with awe.

overbalance *verb* (**overbalanced**, **overbalancing**) lose balance and fall over; cause to lose balance.

overbearing *adjective* domineering.

overblown *adjective* **1** (of a flower) too fully open; past its best. **2** exaggerated, pretentious, *overblown rhetoric.*

overboard *adverb* from in or on a ship into the water, *She jumped overboard.*

overcast *adjective* covered with cloud.

overcoat *noun* a warm outdoor coat.

overcome *verb* (**overcame**, **overcome**, **overcoming**) **1** win a victory over somebody; defeat. **2** make a person helpless, *He was overcome by the fumes.* **3** find a way of dealing with a problem etc.

overcrowd *verb* crowd too many people into a place or vehicle etc.

overdo *verb* (**overdid**, **overdone**, **overdoing**) **1** do something too much. **2** cook food for too long.

overdose *noun* too large a dose of a drug.

overdraft *noun* the amount by which a bank account is overdrawn.

overdraw *verb* (**overdrew**, **overdrawn**, **overdrawing**) draw more money from a bank account than the amount you have in it.

overdrive *noun* a mechanism that provides an extra high gear in a car etc.

overdue *adjective* late; not paid or arrived etc. by the proper time.

overestimate *verb* (**overestimated**, **overestimating**) estimate too highly.

overfish *verb* take too many fish from a river etc.

overflow *verb* flow over the edge or limits of something. **overflow** *noun*

overgrown *adjective* covered with weeds or unwanted plants.

overhang *verb* (**overhung**, **overhanging**) jut out over something. **overhang** *noun*

overhaul *verb* **1** examine something thoroughly and repair it if necessary. **2** overtake. **overhaul** *noun*

overhead *adjective & adverb* **1** above the level of your head. **2** in the sky.
overheads *plural noun* the expenses of running a business. **overhead projector** a machine for projecting writing etc. from a flat surface onto a screen behind the user.

overhear *verb* (**overheard**, **overhearing**) hear something accidentally or without the speaker intending you to hear it.

overjoyed *adjective* filled with great joy.

overland *adjective & adverb* travelling over the land, not by sea or air.

overlap *verb* (**overlapped**, **overlapping**) **1** lie across part of something. **2** happen partly at the same time. **overlap** *noun*

overlay *verb* (**overlaid**, **overlaying**) cover with a layer; lie on top of something.

overlay *noun* a thing laid over another.

overlie *verb* (**overlay**, **overlain**, **overlying**) be or lie over something.

overlook *verb* **1** not notice or consider something. **2** not punish an offence. **3** have a view over something.

overlord *noun* a supreme lord.

overnight *adjective & adverb* of or during a night, *an overnight stop in Rotorua.*

overpower *verb* overcome.

overpowering *adjective* very strong.

overrate *verb* (**overrated**, **overrating**) have too high an opinion of something.

overreach *verb* **overreach yourself** fail through being too ambitious.

override *verb* (**overrode**, **overridden**, **overriding**) **1** overrule. **2** be more important than. *Safety overrides all other considerations.*

overripe *adjective* too ripe.

overrule *verb* (**overruled**, **overruling**) reject a suggestion etc. by using your authority, *We voted for having a picnic but the principal overruled the idea.*

overrun *verb* (**overran**, **overrun**, **overrunning**) **1** spread over and occupy or harm something, *Mice overran the place.* **2** go on for longer than it should, *The broadcast overran its time.*

overseas *adverb* across or beyond the sea; abroad.
overseas experience living and working for a while outside New Zealand.

oversee *verb* (**oversaw**, **overseen**, **overseeing**) superintend. **overseer** *noun*

overshadow *verb* **1** cast a shadow over something. **2** make a person or thing seem unimportant in comparison.

overshoot *verb* (**overshot**, **overshooting**) go beyond a target or limit, *The plane overshot the runway.*

oversight *noun* a mistake made by not noticing something.

oversleep *verb* (**overslept**, **oversleeping**) sleep for longer than you intended.

overstay *verb* stay in a country for longer than your work permit allows. **overstayer** *noun*

overstep *verb* (**overstepped**, **overstepping**) go beyond a limit.

overt *adjective* done or shown openly, *overt hostility.* **overtly** *adverb*

overtake *verb* (**overtook**, **overtaken**, **overtaking**) **1** pass a moving vehicle or person etc. **2** catch up with someone.

overtax *verb* **1** tax too heavily. **2** put too heavy a burden or strain on someone.

overthrow *verb* (**overthrew**, **overthrown**, **overthrowing**) cause the downfall of, *They overthrew the king.*

overthrow *noun* **1** overthrowing; downfall. **2** throwing a ball too far.

overtime *noun* time spent working outside the normal hours; payment for this.

overtone *noun* an extra quality, *There were overtones of envy in his speech.*

overture *noun* **1** a piece of music written as an introduction to an opera, ballet, etc. **2** a friendly attempt to start a discussion, *They made overtures of peace.*

overturn *verb* **1** turn over or upside-down. **2** upset; overthrow.

overweight *adjective* too heavy.

overwhelm *verb* **1** bury or drown beneath a huge mass. **2** overcome completely.

overwork *verb* **1** work or cause to work too hard. **2** use too often, *'Nice' is an overworked word.* **overwork** *noun*

overwrought *adjective* very upset and nervous or worried.

ovoid *adjective* egg-shaped. [from *ovum*]

ovulate *verb* (**ovulated**, **ovulating**) produce an ovum from an ovary. [from Latin *ovum* = egg]

ovum (*say* **oh**-vum) *noun* (*plural* **ova**) a female cell that can develop into a new individual when fertilised. [Latin, = egg]

owe *verb* (**owed**, **owing**) **1** have a duty to pay or give something to someone, especially money. **2** have something because of the action of another person or thing, *They owed their lives to the pilot's skill.*
owing to because of; caused by.

owl *noun* a bird of prey with large eyes, usually flying at night.

own *adjective* belonging to yourself or itself.
get your own back get revenge.
on your own alone.

own *verb* **1** possess; have something as your property. **2** acknowledge; admit, *I own that I made a mistake.*
own up (*informal*) confess; admit guilt.

owner *noun* the person who owns something.
ownership *noun*

ox *noun* (*plural* **oxen**) a large animal kept for its meat and for pulling carts.

oxide *noun* a compound of oxygen and one other element.

oxidise *verb* (**oxidised**, **oxidising**) **1** combine or cause to combine with oxygen. **2** coat with an oxide. **oxidation** *noun*

oxtail *noun* the tail of an ox, used to make soup or stew.

oxygen *noun* a colourless, odourless, tasteless gas that exists in the air and is essential for living things.

oyster *noun* a kind of shellfish whose shell sometimes contains a pearl.

oystercatcher *noun* a wading bird that feeds on shellfish.

Oz *noun* (*slang*) Australia.

ozone *noun* a form of oxygen with a sharp smell.
ozone layer a layer of ozone high in the atmosphere, protecting the world from harmful amounts of the sun's rays. [from Greek *ozein* = to smell]

Pp

P *abbreviation* (*NZ, informal*) methamphetamine.

p. *abbreviation* (*plural* **pp.**) page.

pa *noun* (*slang*) father. [short for *papa*]

pā *noun* **1** (*old use*) a fortified Māori settlement. **2** a Māori village or marae. [Māori]

PA *abbreviation* public address (system).

pace *noun* **1** one step in walking, marching, or running. **2** speed.

pace *verb* (**paced, pacing**) **1** walk with slow or regular steps. **2** measure a distance in paces, *pace it out.* **3** (of a horse) to run with the two legs on one side moving forward together.

pacemaker *noun* **1** a person who sets the pace for another in a race. **2** an electrical device to keep the heart beating.

pacer *noun* **1** a pacemaker. **2** a racehorse trained to pace.

pacific (*say* pa-**sif**-ik) *adjective* peaceful; making or loving peace. **pacifically** *adverb* [from Latin *pacis* = of peace]

Pacific *noun* **the Pacific** the Pacific Ocean.

Pacific Islander a person from or with ancestors from Niue, Samoa, Tonga, or other islands in the South Pacific.

Pacific Islands Forum (also **Pacific Forum**) *noun* an organisation of independent Pacific countries whose leaders meet annually.

Pacific Rim the countries and regions bordering the Pacific Ocean.

pacifist (*say* **pas**-if-ist) *noun* a person who believes that war is always wrong. **pacifism** *noun*

pacify *verb* (**pacified, pacifying**) make peaceful or calm. **pacification** *noun* [from Latin *pacis* = of peace]

pack *noun* **1** a bundle; a collection of things wrapped or tied together. **2** a set of playing-cards (usually 52). **3** a group of hounds or wolves etc. **4** a group of people; a group of Brownies or Cub Scouts. **5** a large amount, *a pack of lies.* **6** a mass of pieces of ice floating in the sea, *packice.* **7** a backpack.
go to the pack (*NZ, informal*) go into decline, collapse.

pack *verb* **1** put things into a suitcase, bag, or box etc. in order to move or store them. **2** crowd together; fill tightly.
pack a sad (*NZ, slang*) become angry or break down, *My iPod's packed a sad.*
pack off send a person away.
send a person packing dismiss him or her.

package *noun* **1** a parcel or packet. **2** a package deal. **packaging** *noun*
package deal a number of things offered or accepted together.
package tour a holiday with everything arranged and included in the price.

packet *noun* a small parcel.

pact *noun* an agreement; a treaty.

pad[1] *noun* **1** a soft thick mass of material, used e.g. to protect or stuff something. **2** a device worn to protect the leg in cricket and other games. **3** a set of sheets of paper fastened together at one edge. **4** the soft fleshy part under an animal's foot or the end of a finger or toe. **5** a flat surface from which spacecraft are launched or where helicopters take off and land.

pad[1] *verb* (**padded, padding**) put a pad on or in something.

pad[2] *noun* (*NZ*) a path or track, *cattle-pad.*

pad[3] *verb* (**padded, padding**) walk softly.

padding *noun* material used to pad things.

paddle[1] *verb* (**paddled, paddling**) walk about in shallow water. **paddle** *noun*

paddle[2] *noun* a short oar with a broad blade; something shaped like this.

paddle[2] *verb* (**paddled, paddling**) move a boat along with a paddle or paddles; row gently.

paddock *noun* **1** (*NZ*) a field. **2** (*British*) a small field where horses are kept.

paddy[1] *noun* (*plural* **paddies**) a field where rice is grown. **paddy-field** *noun*

paddy[2] *noun* (*informal*) a rage.

padlock *noun* a detachable lock with a metal loop that passes through a ring or chain etc.

padre (*say* **pah**-dray) *noun* (*informal*) a chaplain in the armed forces. [Italian, = father]

paean (*say* **pee**-an) *noun* a song of praise or triumph. [from Greek, = hymn]

paediatrics (*say* peed-ee-**at**-riks) *noun* the study of children's diseases. **paediatric** *adjective*, **paediatrician** *noun* [from Greek *paidos* = of a child, + *iatros* = doctor]

pagan (*say* **pay**-gan) *adjective & noun* heathen. [same origin as *peasant*]

page[1] *noun* **1** a piece of paper that is part of a book or newspaper etc.; one side of this. **2** a section of data on a computer screen. [from Latin *pagina* = page]

page[2] *noun* a boy or man employed to go on errands or be an attendant. [from Greek *paidion* = small boy]

pageant *noun* **1** a play or entertainment about historical events and people. **2** a procession of people in costume as an entertainment. **pageantry** *noun*

pagoda (*say* pag-**oh**-da) *noun* a Buddhist tower, or a Hindu temple shaped like a pyramid, in India and the Far East.

paid *past tense* of **pay**.
put paid to (*informal*) put an end to someone's activity or hope etc.

pail *noun* a bucket.

pain *noun* **1** an unpleasant feeling caused by injury or disease. **2** suffering in the mind. **painful** *adjective*, **painfully** *adverb*, **painless** *adjective*
take pains make a careful effort with work etc. **painstaking** *adjective*

pain *verb* cause pain to someone. [from Latin *poena* = punishment]

paint *noun* a liquid substance put on something to colour it. **paintbox** *noun*, **paintbrush** *noun*

paint *verb* **1** put paint on something. **2** make a picture with paints.

painter[1] *noun* a person who paints.

painter[2] *noun* a rope used to tie up a boat. [from Old French *penteur* = rope]

painting *noun* a painted picture.

pair *noun* a set of two things or people; a couple. **2** something made of two joined parts, *a pair of scissors*.

pair *verb* put together as a pair. [from Latin *paria* = equal things]

Pākehā *noun* (*plural* **Pākehā**) a New Zealander whose ancestors came from Europe. **Pākehā** *adjective*. [Māori]

pākihi *noun* **1** an area of open swampy land. **2** a bush clearing. [Māori]

pal *noun* (*informal*) a friend. [from a gypsy word *pal* = brother]

palace *noun* a mansion where a king, queen, or other important person lives. [from Palatium, the name of a hill on which the house of the emperor Augustus stood in ancient Rome]

palaeolithic (*say* pal-ee-o-**lith**-ik) *adjective* of the early part of the Stone Age. [from Greek *palaios* = old, + *lithos* = stone]

Palagi a person whose ancestors came from Europe. [Samoan]

palatable *adjective* tasting pleasant.

palate *noun* **1** the roof of the mouth. **2** a person's sense of taste.

palatial (*say* pa-**lay**-shal) *adjective* like a palace; large and splendid.

pale[1] *adjective* **1** almost white, *a pale face*. **2** not bright in colour or light, *pale green; the pale moonlight*. **palely** *adverb*, **paleness** *noun* [from Latin *pallidus* = pallid]

pale[2] *noun* a boundary.
beyond the pale beyond the limits of good taste or behaviour etc.
[from Latin *palus* = pointed stick set in the ground]

palette *noun* a board on which an artist mixes colours ready for use.

paling *noun* a fence made of wooden posts or railings; one of its posts.

palisade *noun* a fence of pointed sticks or boards. [same origin as *pale*[2]]

pall[1] (*say* pawl) **1** a cloth spread over a coffin. **2** a dark covering, *A pall of smoke lay over the town*. [from Latin *pallium* = cloak]

pall[2] (*say* pawl) *verb* become uninteresting or boring to someone. [from *appal*]

pallbearer *noun* a person helping to carry the coffin at a funeral.

pallet *noun* **1** a mattress stuffed with straw. **2** a hard narrow bed.

palliate *verb* (**palliated**, **palliating**) make a thing less serious or less severe. **palliation** *noun*, **palliative** *adjective & noun* [same origin as *pall*[1]]

pallid *adjective* pale, especially because of illness. **pallor** *noun*

palm *noun* **1** the inner part of the hand, between the fingers and the wrist. **2** a palmtree.
Palm Sunday the Sunday before Easter, commemorating Jesus Christ's entry into Jerusalem when people spread palm leaves in his path.

palm *verb* conceal something in the palm of your hand.
palm off deceive a person into accepting something.

palmistry *noun* fortune-telling by looking at the creases in the palm of a person's hand. **palmist** *noun*

palm-tree *noun* a tropical tree with large leaves at the top and no branches.

palpable *adjective* **1** able to be touched or felt. **2** obvious, *a palpable lie.* **palpably** *adverb* [from Latin *palpare* = touch]

palpitate *verb* (**palpitated**, **palpitating**) **1** (of the heart) beat hard and quickly. **2** (of a person) quiver with fear or excitement. **palpitation** *noun*

palsy (*say* **pawl**-zee) *noun* **1** paralysis. **2** uncontrollable trembling.

paltry (*say* **pol**-tree) *adjective* very small and almost worthless, *a paltry amount.*

pampas *noun* wide grassy plains in South America.

pampas-grass *noun* a tall ornamental grass with feathery flowers.

pamper *verb* treat very kindly and indulgently; coddle.

pamphlet *noun* a leaflet or booklet giving information on a subject.

pan *noun* **1** a wide container with a flat base, used for cooking etc. **2** something shaped like this. **3** the bowl of a toilet.

pan- *prefix* **1** all (as in *panorama*). **2** of the whole of a continent or group etc. (as in *pan-African*). [from Greek *pan* = all]

panacea (*say* pan-a-**see**-a) *noun* a cure for all kinds of diseases or troubles. [from *pan-*, + Greek *akos* = remedy]

panama *noun* a hat made of a fine straw-like material. [from Panama in Central America]

pancake *noun* a thin round cake of batter fried on both sides. [from *pan* + *cake*]

pancreas (*say* **pan**-kree-as) *noun* a gland near the stomach, producing insulin and digestive juices. [from *pan-*, + Greek *kreas* = flesh]

panda *noun* a large bear-like black-and-white animal found in China.

pandemonium *noun* uproar. [from *pan-* + *demon*]

pander *verb* **pander to** indulge someone by providing things, *Don't pander to his taste for sweet things!*

pane *noun* a sheet of glass in a window.

panegyric (*say* pan-i-**jirrik**) *noun* a piece of praise; a eulogy.

panel *noun* **1** a long flat piece of wood, metal, etc. that is part of a door, wall, piece of furniture, etc. **2** a group of people appointed to discuss or decide something. **panelled** *adjective*, **panelling** *noun*

pang *noun* a sudden sharp pain.

panic *noun* sudden uncontrollable fear. **panic-stricken** *adjective*, **panicky** *adjective*

panic *verb* (**panicked**, **panicking**) fill or be filled with panic. [from the name of Pan, an ancient Greek god thought to be able to cause sudden fear]

pannier *noun* a large bag or basket hung on one side of a bicycle or horse etc. [from Latin *panarium* = bread-basket]

panoply *noun* (*plural* **panoplies**) a splendid array. [from *pan-*, + Greek *hopla* = weapons]

panorama *noun* a view or picture of a wide area. **panoramic** *adjective* [from *pan-*, + Greek *horama-* = view]

pansy *noun* (*plural* **pansies**) a small brightly coloured garden flower with velvety petals. [from French *pensée* = thought]

pant *verb* take short quick breaths, usually after running or working hard.

pantaloons *plural noun* wide trousers.

panther *noun* a leopard.

panties *plural noun* (*informal*) underpants for women and girls.

pantihose *noun* (also **pantyhose**) women's tights.

pantile *noun* a curved tile for a roof. [from *pan* + *tile*]

pantomime *noun* **1** a Christmas entertainment based on a fairytale. **2** mime. [from *pan-* + *mime* (because in its most ancient form an actor mimed the different parts)]

pantry *noun* (*plural* **pantries**) **1** a room where china, glasses, cutlery, etc. are kept. **2** a larder. [from Latin *panis* = bread]

pants *plural noun* (*informal*) **1** trousers. **2** underpants. [short for *pantaloons*]

pap *noun* soft food suitable for babies.

papa[1] *noun* (*old use*) father.

papa[2] *noun* a soft bluish clay. [Māori]

papacy (*say* **pay**-pa-see) *noun* the position of pope. [from Latin *papa* = pope]

papal (*say* **pay**-pal) *adjective* of the pope.

Papalagi *noun* a Palagi or European. [Samoan]

paparazzi *plural noun* photographers who take pictures of celebrities. [Italian]

papaw *noun* = **pawpaw**.

paper *noun* **1** a substance made in thin sheets from wood, rags, etc. and used for writing or printing or drawing on or for wrapping things. **2** a newspaper. **3** wallpaper. **4** a document. **5** an examination paper; a course at university, etc., *She's doing six papers.*

paper *verb* cover with wallpaper. [from *papyrus*]

paperback *noun* a book with a thin flexible cover.

papier mâché (*say* pap-yay **mash**-ay) paper made into pulp and moulded to make models, ornaments, etc. [French, = chewed paper]

paprika (*say* **pap**-rik-a) *noun* red pepper. [Hungarian]

papyrus (*say* pap-**I**-rus) *noun* (*plural* **papyri**) **1** a kind of paper made from the stems of a plant like a reed, used in ancient Egypt. **2** a document written on this paper.

par *noun* an average or normal amount or condition. [from Latin *par* = equal]

para[1] *noun* (*informal*) a paratrooper.

para[2] *noun* a large New Zealand fern. [Māori]

para-[1] *prefix* **1** beside (as in *parallel*). **2** beyond (as in *paradox*). [from Greek *para* = beside or past]

para-[2] *prefix* projecting (as in *parasol*). [from Italian *para* = defend]

parable *noun* a story told to teach people something, especially one of those told by Jesus Christ. [from Greek *parabole* = comparison (same origin as *parabola*)]

parabola (*say* pa-**rab**-ol-a) *noun* a curve like the path of an object thrown into the air and falling down again. **parabolic** *adjective* [from *para-*[1] = beside, + Greek *bole* = a throw]

parachute *noun* an expanding device on which people or things can float slowly to the ground from an aircraft. **parachuting** *noun*, **parachutist** *noun* [from *para-*[2] + *chute*]

parade *noun* **1** a procession that displays people or things. **2** an assembly of troops for inspection, drill, etc.; a ground for this. **3** a public square or promenade.

parade *verb* (**paraded**, **parading**) **1** move in a parade. **2** assemble for a parade.

paradigm (*say* **pa**-ruh-dime) *noun* a pattern or model.

paradise *noun* **1** heaven; a heavenly place. **2** the Garden of Eden.
paradise duck a brightly coloured New Zealand duck.
[from ancient Persian, = a park or garden]

paradox *noun* (*plural* **paradoxes**) a statement that seems to contradict itself but which contains a truth, e.g. 'More haste, less speed.' **paradoxical** *adjective*, **paradoxically** *adverb* [from *para-*[1], + *doxa* = opinion]

paraffin *noun* (*British*) kerosene.

paragliding *noun* a sport like hang-gliding, using a wide parachute-like canopy attached to the body by a harness.

paragon *noun* a person or thing that seems to be perfect.

paragraph *noun* one or more sentences on a single subject, forming a section of a piece of writing and beginning on a new line, usually away from the margin of the page. [from *para-*[1] + *-graph*]

parakeet *noun* a kind of small parrot.

parallax *noun* what seems to be a change in the position of something when you look at it from a different place.

parallel *adjective* **1** (of lines etc.) always at the same distance from each other, like the rails on which a train runs. **2** similar; corresponding, *When petrol prices rise there is a parallel rise in bus fares.* **parallelism** *noun*

parallel *noun* **1** a line etc. that is parallel to another. **2** a line of latitude. **3** something similar or corresponding. **4** a comparison.

parallel *verb* (**paralleled**, **paralleling**) find or be a parallel to something. [from *para-*[1], + Greek *allelos* = each other]

parallelogram *noun* a quadrilateral with its opposite sides equal and parallel. [from *parallel* + *-gram*]

paralyse *verb* (**paralysed**, **paralysing**) **1** cause paralysis in a person etc. **2** make something be unable to move.

paralysis *noun* being unable to move, especially because of a disease or an injury to the nerves. **paralytic** (*say* pa-ra-**lit**-ik) *adjective* [from Greek *para* = on one side, + *lysis* = loosening]

parameter (*say* pa-**ram**-it-er) *noun* a quantity or quality etc. that is variable and affects other things (which depend on it) by its changes. [from *para-*[1] = beside, + Greek *metron* = measure]

paramilitary *adjective* organised like a military force but not part of the armed services. [from *para-*[1] = beside, + *military*]

paramount *adjective* more important than anything else, *Secrecy is paramount.*

paranoia *noun* an abnormal mental condition in which a person has delusions or suspects and distrusts people. **paranoid** *adjective* [Greek, = distraction]

parapet *noun* a low wall along the edge of a balcony, bridge, roof, etc.

paraphernalia *noun* numerous pieces of equipment, possessions, etc. [from Greek, = personal articles that a woman could keep after her marriage, as opposed to her dowry which went to her husband (Greek *para* = beside, *pherne* = dowry)]

paraphrase *verb* (**paraphrased**, **paraphrasing**) give the meaning of something by using different words. **paraphrase** *noun* [from *para-*[1] + *phrase*]

paraplegic *adjective* paralysed from the waist down. **paraplegic** *noun*

parasite *noun* an animal or plant that lives in or on another, from which it gets its food. **parasitic** *adjective* [from Greek *parasitos* = guest at a meal]

parasol *noun* a lightweight umbrella used to shade yourself from the sun. [from *para-*[2], + Italian *sole* = sun]

paratroops *plural noun* troops trained to come down from aircraft by parachute. **paratrooper** *noun* [from *parachute* + *troops*]

parboil *verb* boil food until it is partly cooked.

parcel *noun* something wrapped up to be sent by post or carried.

parcel *verb* (**parcelled**, **parcelling**) **1** wrap up as a parcel. **2** divide into portions, *parcel out the work* [same origin as *particle*]

parched *adjective* very dry or thirsty.

parchment *noun* a kind of heavy paper, originally made from animal skins. [from the city of Pergamum, now in Turkey, where parchment was made in ancient times]

pardon *noun* forgiveness.

pardon *verb* **1** forgive. **2** excuse somebody kindly. **pardonable** *adjective*, **pardonably** *adverb*

pare (*say as* pair) (**pared**, **paring**) **1** trim by cutting away the edges; peel. **2** reduce gradually, *We had to pare down our expenses.* [from Latin *parare* = prepare]

parengo *noun* (also **karengo**) an edible seaweed. [Māori]

parent *noun* **1** a father or mother; a living thing that has produced others of its kind. **2** a source from which others are derived, *the parent company*. **parenthood** *noun*, **parenting** *noun*, **parental** (*say* pa-**rent**-al) *adjective* [from Latin *parens* = producing offspring]

parentage *noun* descent from parents; lineage; ancestry.

parenthesis (*say* pa-**ren**-thi-sis) (*plural* **parentheses**) **1** something extra that is inserted in a sentence, usually between brackets or dashes. **2** either of the pair of brackets (like these) used to mark off words from the rest of a sentence. **parenthetical** *adjective* [Greek, = putting in besides]

pārera *noun* the New Zealand grey duck. [Māori]

pariah (*say* pa-**ry**-a) *noun* an outcast.

parish *noun* (*plural* **parishes**) a district with its own church. **parishioner** *noun* [from Greek, = neighbourhood (Greek *para* = beside, *oikein* = dwell)]

parity *noun* equality. [from *par*]

park *noun* **1** a large garden or recreation ground for public use. **2** an area of grassland belonging to a mansion.
car park an area where cars may be parked.

park *verb* leave a vehicle somewhere for a time.

parka *noun* a warm jacket with a hood attached.

parley *verb* (**parleyed**, **parleying**) hold a discussion with someone. **parley** *noun* [from French *parler* = speak]

parliament *noun* the assembly that makes a country's laws. **parliamentary** *adjective* [same origin as *parley*]

parliamentarian *noun* a member of parliament.

parlour *noun* **1** a shop or business providing specific goods or services, *ice-cream parlour, beauty parlour.* **2** (*old use*) a sitting-room. [from French *parler* = speak]

parochial (*say* per-**oh**-kee-al) *adjective* **1** of a parish. **2** local; interested only in your own area, *a narrow parochial attitude.*

parody *noun* (*plural* **parodies**) an imitation that makes fun of a person or thing.

parody *verb* (**parodied**, **parodying**) make or be a parody of a person or thing. [from *para-*[1] = beside, + Greek *oide* = song]

parole *noun* the release of a prisoner before the end of his or her sentence on condition of good behaviour, *He was on parole.* [French, = word of honour]

parore *noun* the blackfish, a dark-brown striped fish. [Māori]

paroxysm (*say* **pa**-roks-izm) *noun* a spasm; a sudden outburst of rage, laughter, etc.

parquet (*say* **par**-kay) *noun* wooden blocks arranged in a pattern to make a floor.

parrot *noun* a brightly-coloured tropical bird that can learn to repeat words etc.

parrotfish *noun* a brightly coloured fish with teeth like a parrot's beak.

parry *verb* (**parried**, **parrying**) **1** turn aside an opponent's weapon or blow by using your own to block it. **2** avoid an awkward question skilfully.

parse *verb* (**parsed**, **parsing**) state what is the grammatical form and function of a word or words in a sentence. [from Latin *pars* = part (of speech)]

parsimonious *adjective* stingy; very sparing in the use of something. **parsimony** *noun*

parsley *noun* a plant with crinkled green leaves used to flavour and decorate food.

parsnip *noun* a plant with a pointed pale-yellow root used as a vegetable.

parson *noun* a clergyman.

parsonage *noun* a parson's house.

parson-bird *noun* (*old use*) the tūī.

part *noun* **1** some but not all of a thing or number of things; anything that belongs to something bigger. **2** the character played by an actor or actress. **3** the words spoken by a character in a play. **4** one side in an agreement or in a dispute or quarrel.
part of speech any of the groups into which words are divided in grammar (noun, pronoun, adjective, verb, adverb, preposition, conjunction, interjection)
take in good part not be offended at something.
take part join in an activity.

part *verb* separate; divide.
part with give away or get rid of something.

partake *verb* (**partook**, **partaken**, **partaking**) **1** participate. **2** eat or drink something, *We all partook of the food.*

part-exchange *noun* giving something that you own, as part of the price of what you are buying.

Parthian shot a sharp remark made by a person who is just leaving. [named after the horsemen of Parthia (an ancient kingdom in what is now Iran), who were famous for shooting arrows at the enemy while retreating]

partial *adjective* **1** of a part; not complete, not total, *a partial eclipse.* **2** biased; unfair. **partially** *adverb*, **partiality** *noun*
be partial to be fond of something.

participate *verb* (**participated**, **participating**) take part or have a share in something. **participant** *noun*, **participation** *noun*, **participator** *noun* [from Latin *pars* = part, + *capere* = take]

participle *noun* a word formed from a verb (e.g. *gone, going; guided, guiding*) and used with an auxiliary verb to form certain tenses (e.g. *It has gone. It is going*) or the passive (e.g. *We were guided to our seats*), or as an adjective (e.g. *a guided missile; a guiding light*).
The **past participle** (e.g. *gone, guided*) describes a completed action or past condition. The **present participle** (which ends in *-ing*) describes a continuing action or condition.

particle *noun* a very small portion or amount. [from Latin, = little part]

particoloured *adjective* partly of one colour and partly of another; variegated.

particular *adjective* **1** of this one and no other; individual, *This particular stamp is very rare.* **2** special, *Take particular care of it.* **3** giving something close attention; choosing carefully, *He is very particular about his clothes.* **particularly** *adverb*, **particularly** *noun*

particular *noun* a single fact; a detail.
in particular especially, *We liked this one in particular*; special, *We did nothing in particular.*
[same origin as *particle*]

parting *noun* **1** leaving; separation. **2** a line where hair is combed away in different directions.

partisan *noun* **1** a strong supporter of a party or group etc. **2** a member of an organisation resisting the authorities in a conquered country.

partition *noun* **1** a thin wall that divides a room or space. **2** dividing something into parts.

partition *verb* **1** divide into parts. **2** divide a room or space by means of a partition.

partly *adverb* to some extent but not completely.

partner *noun* one of a pair of people who do something together, e.g. in business or dancing or playing a game. **partnership** *noun*

partner *verb* be a person's partner; put together as partners.

partook *past tense* of **partake**.

partridge *noun* a game-bird with brown feathers.

part-time *adjective & adverb* working for only some of the normal hours. **part-timer** *noun*

party *noun* (*plural* **parties**) **1** a gathering of people to enjoy themselves, *a birthday party.* **2** a group working or travelling together. **3** an organised group of people with similar political beliefs, *the Labour Party.* **4** a person who is involved in an action or lawsuit etc., *the guilty party.* [from *part*]
party vote (*NZ*) see **list vote**.

party *verb* (**partied**, **partying**) enjoy oneself (at a party etc.), *let's party!*

paspalum *noun* coarse pasture grass, originally from South America.

pass *verb* (**passed**, **passing**) **1** go past something; go onwards. **2** cause to move, *Pass the cord through the ring.* **3** give or transfer to another person, *Pass the butter to your father.* **4** be successful in a test or examination. **5** approve or accept, *They passed a law.* **6** occupy time. **7** happen, *We heard what passed when they met.* **8** disappear. **9** utter, *Pass a remark.* **10** let your turn go by at cards or in a competition etc., *Pass!*
pass out complete military training; (*informal*) faint.

pass *noun* (*plural* **passes**) **1** passing something. **2** a permit to go in or out of a place. **3** a route through a gap in a range of mountains, *Arthur's Pass.* **4** a critical state of affairs, *Things have come to a pretty pass!* [from Latin *passus* = pace]

passable *adjective* **1** able to be passed. **2** satisfactory but not especially good.
passably *adverb*

passage *noun* **1** a way through something; a corridor. **2** a journey by sea. **3** a section of a piece of writing or music. **4** passing, *the passage of time.* **passageway** *noun*

passbook *noun* a special notebook in which a bank writes down how much a customer has paid in or drawn out.

passenger *noun* a person who is driven or carried in a car, train, ship, or aircraft etc.

passer-by *noun* (*plural* **passers-by**) a person who happens to be going past something.

passion *noun* **1** strong emotion. **2** great enthusiasm.
the Passion the sufferings of Jesus Christ at the Crucifixion.
[from Latin *passio* = suffering]

passionate *adjective* full of passion.
passionately *adverb*

passionfruit *noun* a small round fruit with a black or purple wrinkled skin.

passive *adjective* **1** acted upon and not active; not resisting or fighting against something. **2** (of a form of a verb) used when the subject of the sentence receives the action, e.g. *was hit* in 'She was hit on the head'. (Compare *active.*) **passively** *adverb*, **passiveness** *noun*, **passivity** *noun*
passive smoking the involuntary inhaling of other people's tobacco smoke.

Passover *noun* a Jewish religious festival commemorating the freeing of the Jews from slavery in Egypt. [from *pass over*, because God spared the Jews from the fate which affected the Egyptians]

passport *noun* an official document that entitles the person holding it to travel abroad. [from *pass* + *port*[1]]

password *noun* **1** a secret word or phrase used to distinguish friends from enemies. **2** a word or phrase you enter into a computer to gain access to its data.

past *adjective* of the time before now, *during the past week.*

past *noun* past times or events.

past *preposition* **1** beyond, *Walk past the school.* **2** after, *It is past midnight.*
past it (*slang*) too old to be able to do something.

pasta *noun* an Italian food consisting of a dried paste made from flour and shaped into macaroni, spaghetti, etc. [Italian, = paste]

paste *noun* **1** a soft and moist or gluey substance. **2** a hard glassy substance used to make imitation gems.

paste *verb* (**pasted**, **pasting**) **1** stick by using paste. **2** coat something with paste. **3** (*slang*) beat or thrash. **4** to insert text into a computer document.

pastel *noun* **1** a crayon that is like chalk. **2** a light delicate colour.

pastern *noun* the part of a horse's foot between the fetlock and the hoof.

pasteurise *verb* (**pasteurised**, **pasteurising**) purify milk by heating and then cooling it. [named after a French scientist, Louis Pasteur]

pastille *noun* a small flavoured sweet for sucking.

pastime *noun* something done to make time pass pleasantly; a recreation.

pastor *noun* a member of the clergy who is in charge of a church or congregation. [Latin, = shepherd]

pastoral *adjective* **1** of sheep or cattle farming. **2** (of farmland) used for grazing, raising livestock. **3** of country life, *a pastoral scene.* **4** of a pastor or a pastor's duties.

pastoralist *noun* a sheep-farmer or cattle-farmer.

pastry *noun* (*plural* **pastries**) **1** dough made with flour, fat, and water, rolled flat and baked. **2** something made of pastry. [from *paste*]

pasture *noun* land covered with grass etc. that cattle, sheep, or horses can eat.

pasture *verb* (**pastured**, **pasturing**) put animals to graze in a pasture. [same origin as *pastor*]

pasty[1] (*say* **pas**-tee) *noun* (*plural* **pasties**) pastry with a filling of meat, fruit, or jam etc., baked without a dish to shape it.

pasty[2] (*say* **pay**-stee) *adjective* **1** like paste. **2** looking pale and unhealthy.

pat *verb* (**patted**, **patting**) tap gently with the open hand or with something flat.

pat *noun* **1** a patting movement or sound. **2** a small piece of butter or other soft substance.
a pat on the back praise.

pātaka *noun* a storehouse built on posts. [Māori]

patch *noun* (*plural* **patches**) **1** a piece of material or metal etc. put over a hole or damaged place. **2** an area that is different from its surroundings. **3** a piece of ground, *the kūmara patch.* **4** a small area or piece of something, *There are patches of fog.* **5** an area for which one is responsible or frequents, *That's not that cop's patch.* **6** a small insertion to correct or enhance a computer program.
not a patch on (*informal*) not nearly as good as.

patch *verb* **1** put a patch on something. **2** piece things together.
patch up repair something roughly; settle a quarrel.

patchwork *noun* needlework in which small pieces of different cloth are sewn edge to edge.

patchy *adjective* occurring in patches; uneven. **patchily** *adverb*, **patchiness** *noun*

pate *noun* (*old use*) the head.

pâté (*say* **pat**-ay) *noun* paste made of meat or fish. [French]

patent (*say* **pat**-ent or **pay**-tent) *noun* the official right given to an inventor to make or sell his or her invention and to prevent other people from copying it.

patent (*say* **pay**-tent) *adjective* **1** protected by a patent, *patent medicines*. **2** obvious. **patently** *adverb*
patent leather glossy leather.

patent *verb* get a patent for something.

patentee (*say* pay-ten-**tee** or pat-en-**tee**) *noun* a person who holds a patent.

paternal *adjective* **1** of a father. **2** fatherly. **paternally** *adverb* [from Latin *pater* = father]

paternalistic *adjective* treating people in a paternal way, providing for their needs but giving them no responsibility. **paternalism** *noun*

paternity *noun* **1** fatherhood. **2** being the father of a particular baby. [from Latin *pater* = father]

path *noun* **1** a narrow way along which people or animals can walk. **2** a line along which a person or thing moves.

pathetic *adjective* **1** arousing pity or sadness. **2** miserably inadequate or useless, *a pathetic attempt*. **pathetically** *adverb* [same origin as *pathos*]

pathfinder *noun* an explorer.

pathology *noun* the study of diseases of the body. **pathological** *adjective*, **pathologist** *noun* [from Greek *pathos* = suffering, + *-logy*]

pathos (*say* **pay**-thoss) *noun* a quality that arouses pity or sadness. [Greek, = feeling or suffering]

patience *noun* **1** being patient. **2** a card-game for one person.

patient *adjective* **1** able to wait or put up with annoyances without becoming angry. **2** able to persevere. **patiently** *adverb*

patient *noun* a person who has treatment from a doctor or dentist etc. [from Latin *patiens* = suffering]

patio *noun* (*plural* **patios**) a paved area beside a house. [Spanish]

patriarch (*say* **pay**-tree-ark) *noun* **1** a man who is head of a family or tribe. **2** a bishop of high rank in certain Churches. **patriarchal** *adjective* [from Greek *patria* = family, + *archein* = to rule]

patrician *noun* an ancient Roman noble. (Compare *plebeian*.) **patrician** *adjective* [from Latin, = having a noble father]

patriot (*say* **pay**-tree-ot or **pat**-ree-ot) *noun* a person who loves his or her country and supports it loyally. **patriotic** *adjective*, **patriotically** *adverb*, **patriotism** *noun* [from Greek *patris* = fatherland]

patrol *verb* (**patrolled**, **patrolling**) walk or travel regularly over an area so as to guard it and see that all is well.

patrol *noun* **1** a patrolling group of people, ships, aircraft, etc. **2** a group of Scouts or Guides.
on patrol patrolling.
[from French *patouiller* = paddle in mud]

patron (*say* **pay**-tron) *noun* **1** someone who supports a person or cause with money or encouragement. **2** a regular customer. **patronage** (*say* **pat**-ron-ij) *noun*
patron saint a saint who is thought to protect a particular place or activity.
[from Latin *patronus* = protector]

patronise (*say* **pat**-ron-I'z) *verb* (**patronised**, **patronising**) **1** be a patron or supporter of something. **2** treat someone in a condescending way.

patter *noun* **1** a series of light tapping sounds. **2** the quick talk of a comedian, conjuror, salesman, etc.

patter *verb* make light tapping sounds.

pattern *noun* **1** an arrangement of lines, shapes, or colours etc. **2** a thing to be copied in order to make something, *a dress pattern*. **3** an excellent example; a model.

patty *noun* (*plural* **patties**) a small pie or pasty.

patu *noun* a short weapon similar to a club. [Māori]

pāua *noun* a large edible shellfish with a shell that can be used to make ornaments etc. [Māori]

paucity *noun* scarcity; fewness. [from Latin *pauci* = few]

paunch *noun* a large belly.

pauper *noun* a person who is very poor. [Latin, = poor]

pause *noun* a temporary stop in speaking or doing something.

pause *verb* (**paused**, **pausing**) make a pause. [from Greek *pauein* = to stop]

pav *noun* (*NZ, informal*) a pavlova.

pave *verb* (**paved**, **paving**) lay a hard surface on a road or path etc. **paving-stone** *noun*
pave the way prepare for something. [from Latin *pavire* = ram down]

pavement *noun* a paved path along the side of a street.

pavilion *noun* **1** a building for use by players and spectators etc. **2** an ornamental building or shelter used for dances, concerts, exhibitions, etc.

pavlova *noun* (*NZ*) a dessert with a meringue base covered with whipped cream and fruit. [from the name of the Russian ballerina Anna Pavlova]

paw *noun* the foot of an animal that has claws.

paw *verb* touch with a hand or foot.

pawl *noun* a bar with a catch that fits into the notches of a ratchet.

pawn[1] *noun* **1** any of the least valuable pieces in chess. **2** a person whose actions are controlled by somebody else. [from Latin *pedo* = foot-soldier]

pawn[2] *verb* leave something with a pawnbroker as security for a loan. [from Old French *pan* = pledge]

pawnbroker *noun* a shopkeeper who lends money to people in return for objects that they leave as security. **pawnshop** *noun*

pawpaw *noun* an orange-coloured tropical fruit used as food.

pay *verb* (**paid**, **paying**) **1** give money in return for goods or services. **2** give what is owed, *pay your debts; pay the rent.* **3** be profitable or worth while, *It pays to advertise.* **4** give or express, *pay attention; pay them a visit; pay compliments.* **5** suffer a penalty. **6** let out a rope by loosening it gradually. **payer** *noun*
pay up pay fully; pay what is asked.

pay *noun* payment; wages. [from Latin *pacare* = appease]

payable *adjective* that must be paid.

PAYE *abbreviation* pay-as-you-earn, a method of collecting income tax by deducting it from wages before these are paid to people who earn them.

payee *noun* a person to whom money is paid or is to be paid.

paymaster *noun* an official who pays troops or workmen etc.

payment *noun* **1** paying. **2** money paid.

payroll *noun* a list of a company's employees.

PC *abbreviation* police constable; political correctness, politically correct; personal computer.

pdf *abbreviation* a system for storing and moving documents between computers that allows you to read or print but not change the documents. *Pdf is short for portable document format.*

PE *abbreviation* physical education.

pea *noun* the small round green seed of a climbing plant, growing inside a pod and used as a vegetable.

peace *noun* **1** a condition in which there is no war, violence, or disorder. **2** quietness; calm. **peaceful** *adjective*, **peacefully** *adverb*, **peacefulness** *noun* [from Latin *pax* = peace]

peaceable *adjective* peaceful; not quarrelsome. **peaceably** *adverb*

peach *noun* (*plural* **peaches**) **1** a round soft juicy fruit with a pinkish or yellowish skin and a large stone. **2** (*slang*) a beauty.

peacock *noun* a male bird with a long brightly-coloured tail that it can spread out like a fan. **peahen** *noun*

peak *noun* **1** a pointed top, especially of a mountain. **2** the highest or most intense part of something, *Traffic reaches its peak at 5 p.m.* **3** the part of a cap that sticks out in front. **peaked** *adjective*

peak *verb* reach its highest point.

peaky *adjective* looking pale and ill.

peal *noun* **1** the loud ringing of a bell or set of bells. **2** a loud burst of thunder or laughter.

peal *verb* sound in a peal.

peanut *noun* a small round nut that grows in a pod in the ground.
peanut butter roasted peanuts crushed into a paste.

pear *noun* a juicy fruit that gets narrower near the stalk.

pearl *noun* **1** a small shiny white ball found in the shells of some oysters and used as a jewel. **2** something shaped like this. **pearly** *adjective*
pearl barley grains of barley made small by grinding.

peasant *noun* (in some countries) a person who works on a farm. **peasantry** *noun* [from Latin *paganus* = villager]

peat *noun* rotted plant material that can be dug out of the ground and used as fuel or in gardening. **peaty** *adjective*

pebble *noun* a small round stone. **pebbly** *adjective*

pecan (*say* pe-**kan** or **pee**-kan) *noun* a kind of edible nut.

peccadillo *noun* (*plural* **peccadilloes**) an unimportant offence. [Spanish, = little sin]

peck *verb* **1** bite or eat something with the beak. **2** kiss lightly.

peck *noun* a pecking movement.

peckish *adjective* (*informal*) hungry.

pectin *noun* a substance found in ripe fruits, causing jam to set firmly.

pectoral *adjective* of the chest or breast, *pectoral muscles.* [from Latin *pectoris* = of the breast]

peculiar *adjective* **1** strange; unusual. **2** special, *This point is of peculiar interest.* **3** restricted, *This custom is peculiar to this tribe.* **peculiarly** *adverb,* **peculiarity** *noun* [from Latin *peculium* = private property]

pecuniary *adjective* of money, *pecuniary aid.* [from Latin *pecunia* = money (from *pecu* = cattle, because in early times wealth consisted of cattle and sheep)]

pedagogue (*say* **ped**-a-gog) *noun* a teacher who teaches in a pedantic way. [from Greek, = slave who led a boy to school]

pedal *noun* a lever pressed by the foot to operate a bicycle, car, machine, etc. or in certain musical instruments.

pedal *verb* (**pedalled**, **pedalling**) use a pedal; move or work something by means of pedals. [from Latin *pedis* = of a foot]

pedant *noun* a pedantic person.

pedantic *adjective* being very careful and strict about exact meanings and facts etc. in learning. **pedantically** *adverb* [same origin as *pedagogue*]

peddle *verb* (**peddled**, **peddling**) sell goods as a pedlar. [from *pedlar*]

pedestal *noun* the raised base on which a statue or pillar etc. stands.
put someone on a pedestal admire him or her greatly.
[from Italian *piede* = foot, + *stall*]

pedestrian *noun* a person who is walking. [from Latin *pedis* = of a foot]

pedestrian *adjective* **1** on foot; for walkers. **2** dull.

pedigree *noun* a list of a person's or animal's ancestors, especially to show how well an animal has been bred.

pediment *noun* a wide triangular part decorating the top of a building.

pedlar *noun* **1** a person who goes from house to house selling small things. **2** a person who sells illegal drugs. **3** a person who promotes an idea or view.

peek *verb & noun* peep.

peel *noun* the skin of certain fruits and vegetables.

peel *verb* **1** remove the peel or covering from something. **2** come off in strips or layers. **3** lose a covering or skin.

peelings *plural noun* strips of skin peeled from potatoes etc.

peep *verb* **1** look quickly or secretly. **2** look through a narrow opening. **3** show slightly or briefly, *The moon peeped out from behind the clouds.* **peep** *noun,* **peep-hole** *noun*

peer[1] *verb* look at something closely or with difficulty. [from *appear*]

peer[2] *noun* **1** a noble. **2** someone who is equal to another in rank or merit etc., *She had no peer.* **peeress** *noun* [from Latin *par* = equal]

peerless *adjective* without an equal; superb.

peeved *adjective* (*slang*) annoyed.

peevish *adjective* irritable.

peewit *noun* a kind of plover, named after its cry.

peg *noun* a piece of wood or metal or plastic for fastening things together or for hanging things on.

peg *verb* (**pegged**, **pegging**) **1** fix with pegs. **2** keep wages or prices at a fixed level.
peg away work diligently; persevere.
peg out 1 mark out the boundaries of a mining claim. **2** (*slang*) die.

pejorative (*say* pij-**o**rra-tiv) *adjective* derogatory; insulting. [from Latin *pejor* = worse]

peke *noun* (*informal*) a Pekingese.

Pekingese *noun* (*plural* **Pekingese**) a small kind of dog with short legs, a flat face, and long silky hair. [from Peking, now Beijing, the capital of China]

pelican *noun* a large bird with a pouch in its long beak for storing fish.

pellet *noun* a tiny ball of metal, food, paper, etc.

pell-mell *adverb & adjective* in a hasty untidy way.

pelmet *noun* an ornamental strip of wood or material etc. above a window, especially to conceal a curtain rail.

pelt[1] *verb* **1** throw a lot of things at someone. **2** run fast. **3** rain very hard.

pelt[2] *noun* an animal skin, especially with the fur still on it.

pelvis *noun* (*plural* **pelvises**) the round framework of bones at the lower end of the spine. **pelvic** *adjective*

pen[1] *noun* a device with a point for writing with ink. [from Latin *penna* = feather (because a pen was originally a sharpened quill)]

pen[2] *noun* an enclosure for cattle, sheep, hens, or other animals.

pen[2] *verb* (**penned**, **penning**) shut into a pen or other enclosed space.

pen[3] *noun* a female swan. (Compare *cob*.)

penal (*say* **peen**-al) *adjective* of punishment; used for punishment. [from Latin *poena* = punishment]

penalise *verb* (**penalised**, **penalising**) punish; put a penalty on someone. **penalisation** *noun*

penalty *noun* (*plural* **penalties**) **1** a punishment. **2** a point or advantage given to one side in a game when a member of the other side has broken a rule.

penance *noun* something done to show penitence.

pence *plural noun* see **penny**.

pencil *noun* a device for drawing or writing, made of a thin stick of graphite or coloured chalk etc. enclosed in a cylinder of wood or metal.

pencil *verb* (**pencilled**, **pencilling**) write, draw, or mark with a pencil.

pendant *noun* an ornament worn hanging on a cord or chain round the neck. [from Latin *pendens* = hanging]

pendent *adjective* hanging.

pending *preposition* **1** until, *Please take charge, pending his return.* **2** during, *pending these discussions.*

pending *adjective* waiting to be decided or settled. [same origin as *pendant*]

pendulous *adjective* hanging down.

pendulum *noun* a weight hung so that it can swing to and fro, especially in the works of a clock.

penetrable *adjective* able to be penetrated.

penetrate *verb* (**penetrated**, **penetrating**) make or find a way through or into something; pierce. **penetration** *noun*, **penetrative** *adjective* [from Latin *penitus* = inside]

pen-friend *noun* a friend to whom you write without meeting.

penguin *noun* an Antarctic sea-bird that cannot fly but uses its wings as flippers for swimming.

penicillin *noun* an antibiotic obtained from mould. [from the Latin name of the mould used]

peninsula *noun* a piece of land that is almost surrounded by water. **peninsular** *adjective* [from Latin *paene* = almost, + *insula* = island]

penis (*say* **peen**-iss) *noun* (*plural* **penises**) the part of the body with which a male urinates and has sexual intercourse. [Latin, = tail]

penitence *noun* regret for having done wrong. **penitent** *adjective*, **penitently** *adverb*

penknife *noun* (*plural* **penknives**) a small folding knife. [originally used for sharpening quill pens]

pennant *noun* a long pointed flag.

penniless *adjective* having no money; very poor.

penny *noun* (*plural* **pennies** for separate coins, **pence** for a sum of money) **1** a British coin worth one hundredth of a pound; a former British and New Zealand coin worth one twelfth of a shilling. **2** (in the US) a one-cent coin.

pension *noun* an income consisting of regular payments made by a government or firm to someone who is retired, widowed, or disabled.

pension *verb* pay a pension to someone. [from Latin *pensio* = payment]

pensioner *noun* a person who receives a pension.

pensive *adjective* thinking deeply; thoughtful. **pensively** *adverb* [from Latin *pensare* = consider]

pent *adjective* shut in, *pent in* or *up*. [from *pen*[2]]

penta- *prefix* five. [from Greek *pente* = five]

pentagon *noun* a flat shape with five sides and five angles. **pentagonal** (*say* pent-**ag**-on-al) *adjective*
the Pentagon a five-sided building in Washington, headquarters of the American armed forces.
[from *penta-*, + Greek *gonia* = angle]

pentameter *noun* a line of verse with five rhythmic beats. [from *penta-*, + Greek *metron* = measure]

Pentecost (*say* **pent**-ee-kost) *noun* **1** the Jewish harvest festival, fifty days after Passover. **2** Whit Sunday. [from Greek, = fiftieth day]

Pentecostal *adjective* believing that God still bestows special abilities on people, as he did on the disciples of Jesus at Pentecost, *a Pentecostal Church.*

penthouse *noun* a flat at the top of a tall building.

penultimate *adjective* last but one. [from Latin *paene* = almost, + *ultimate*]

penumbra *noun* an area that is partly but not fully shaded, e.g. during an eclipse. [from Latin *paene* = almost, + *umbra* = shade]

penurious (*say* pin-**yoor**-ee-us) *adjective* **1** in great poverty. **2** mean; stingy. **penury** (*say* **pen**-yoor-ee) *noun* [from Latin *penuria* = poverty]

peony *noun* (*plural* **peonies**) a plant with large round red, pink, or white flowers.

people *plural noun* human beings; persons, especially those belonging to a particular country, area, or group etc.

people *noun* a community or nation, *a warlike people; the English-speaking peoples.*

people *verb* fill a place with people; populate. [from Latin *populus* = people]

pep *noun* (*slang*) vigour; energy. [from *pepper*]

pepper *noun* **1** a hot-tasting powder used to flavour food. **2** a bright green, red, or yellow vegetable. **peppery** *adjective*

pepper *verb* **1** sprinkle with pepper. **2** pelt with small objects.

peppercorn *noun* the dried black berry from which pepper is made.

peppermint *noun* **1** a kind of mint used for flavouring. **2** a sweet flavoured with this mint.

pepper-tree *noun* a New Zealand shrub with strong-smelling leaves, the horopito.

per *preposition* for each, *The charge is $2 per person.* [from Latin, = through]
per annum for each year; yearly.
per cent for or in every hundred, *three per cent* (3%). [from *per*, + Latin *centum* = hundred]

per- *prefix* **1** through (as in *perforate*). **2** thoroughly (as in *perturb*). **3** away entirely; towards badness (as in *pervert*). [from Latin *per* = through]

perambulate *verb* (**perambulated**, **perambulating**) walk through or round an area. **perambulation** *noun* [from *per-*, + Latin *ambulare-* = to walk]

perambulator *noun* (*old use*) a baby's pram.

perceive *verb* (**perceived**, **perceiving**) see; notice. [from Latin *percipere* = seize, understand]

percentage *noun* the amount per cent (see *per*); a proportion or part.

perceptible *adjective* able to be perceived. **perceptibly** *adverb*, **perceptibility** *noun*

perception *noun* perceiving.

perceptive *adjective* quick to notice things.

perch[1] *noun* (*plural* **perches**) **1** a place where a bird sits or rests. **2** a seat high up.

perch[1] *verb* rest or place on a perch. [from Latin *pertica* = pole]

perch[2] *noun* (*plural* **perch**) an edible freshwater fish.

percipient *adjective* perceptive. **percipience** *noun*

percolate *verb* (**percolated**, **percolating**) flow through small holes or spaces. **percolation** *noun* [from *per-*, + Latin *colum* = strainer]

percolator *noun* a pot for making coffee, in which boiling water percolates through coffee grounds.

percussion *noun* the striking of one thing against another. **percussive** *adjective*
percussion instruments musical instruments (e.g. drum, cymbals) played by being struck or shaken.
[from Latin *percussum* = hit]

perdition *noun* eternal damnation. [from Latin *perditum* = destroyed]

peregrination *noun* travelling about; a journey. [from Latin *per* = through, + *ager* = field]

peregrine *noun* a kind of falcon.

peremptory *adjective* giving commands; imperious.

Perendale *noun* (*NZ*) a kind of cross-bred sheep farmed for its wool and its meat. [named after G. S. Peren, an animal scientist]

perennial *adjective* lasting for many years; keeping on recurring. **perennially** *adverb*

perennial *noun* a plant that lives for many years. [from *per-*, + Latin *annus* = year]

perestroika (*say* peri-**stroik**-a) *noun* restructuring, especially of the former Soviet economy. [Russian]

perfect (*say* **per**-fikt) *adjective* **1** so good that it cannot be made any better. **2** complete, *a perfect stranger.* **perfectly** *adverb*
perfect tense a tense of a verb showing a completed action, e.g. He *has arrived.*

perfect (*say* per-**fekt**) *verb* make a thing perfect. **perfection** *noun*
to perfection perfectly.
[from Latin *perfectum* = completed]

perfectionist *noun* a person who likes everything to be done perfectly.

perfidious *adjective* treacherous; disloyal. **perfidiously** *adverb*, **perfidy** *noun* [from *per-* = becoming bad, + Latin *fides* = faith]

perforate *verb* (**perforated**, **perforating**) **1** make tiny holes in something, especially so that it can be torn off easily. **2** pierce. **perforation** *noun* [from *per-*, + Latin *forare* = bore through]

perforce *adverb* by necessity; unavoidably.

perform *verb* **1** do something in front of an audience, *perform a play.* **2** do something, *perform an operation.* **performance** *noun*, **performer** *noun*

perfume *noun* **1** a pleasant smell. **2** a liquid for giving something a pleasant smell; scent. **perfume** *verb*, **perfumery** *noun* [from *per-* + *fume* (originally used of smoke from a burning substance)]

perfunctory *adjective* done without much care or interest, *a perfunctory glance.* **perfunctorily** *adverb*

pergola *noun* an arched structure, often for the support of climbing plants.

perhaps *adverb* it may be; possibly.

peri- *prefix* around (as in *perimeter*). [from Greek *peri* = around]

peril *noun* danger. **perilous** *adjective*, **perilously** *adverb* [from Latin *periculum* = danger]

perimeter *noun* **1** the outer edge or boundary of something. **2** the distance round the edge. [from *peri-*, + Greek *metron* measure]

period *noun* **1** a length of time. **2** the time when a woman menstruates. **3** (in punctuation) a full stop. **periodic** *adjective*

periodical *adjective* periodic; at set times. **periodically** *adverb*

periodical *noun* a magazine published at regular intervals (e.g. monthly).

peripatetic *adjective* going from place to place. [from *peri-*, + Greek *patein* = to walk]

periphery (*say* per-**if**-er-ee) *noun* the part at the edge or boundary. **peripheral** *adjective* [from Greek, = circumference]

periphrasis (*say* per-**if**-ra-sis) *noun* (*plural* **periphrases**) a roundabout way of saying something; a circumlocution. [from *peri-*, + Greek *phrasis* = speech]

periscope *noun* a device with a tube and mirrors by which a person in a trench or submarine etc. can see things that are otherwise out of sight. [from *peri-*, + Greek *skopein* = look at]

perish *verb* **1** die; be destroyed. **2** rot, *The rubber ring has perished.* **3** (*informal*) make a person etc. feel very cold. **perishable** *adjective*

periwinkle *noun* a trailing plant with blue or white flowers.

perjure *verb* (**perjured**, **perjuring**) **perjure yourself** commit perjury.

perjury *noun* telling a lie while you are on oath to speak the truth. [from Latin *perjurare* = break an oath]

perk[1] *verb* raise the head quickly or cheerfully. **perk up** make or become more cheerful. [from *perch*[1]]

perk[2] *noun* (*informal*) a perquisite or benefit, *One of the perks of this job is a free lunch.*

perky *adjective* lively and cheerful. **perkily** *adverb*

perm *noun* a permanent wave. **perm** *verb*

permanent *adjective* lasting for always or for a very long time. **permanently** *adverb*, **permanence** *noun*
permanent wave treatment of the hair to give it long-lasting waves.
[from *per-*, + Latin *manens* = remaining]

permeable *adjective* able to be permeated by fluids etc. **permeability** *noun*

permeate *verb* (**permeated**, **permeating**) spread into every part of something; pervade, *Smoke had permeated the hall.* **permeation** *noun* [from *per-*, + Latin *meare* = to pass]

permissible *adjective* allowable.

permission *noun* the right to do something, given by someone in authority; authorisation.

permissive *adjective* permitting things; allowing much freedom to do things.

permit (*say* per-**mit**) *verb* (**permitted**, **permitting**) give permission or consent or a chance to do something; allow.

permit (*say* **per**-mit) *noun* written or printed permission to do something or go somewhere. [from *per-*, + Latin *mittere* = send]

permutation *noun* **1** changing the order of a set of things. **2** a changed order, *3, 1, 2 is a permutation of 1, 2, 3.* [from *per-*, + Latin *mutare* to change]

pernicious *adjective* very harmful.

peroration *noun* an elaborate ending to a speech. [from *per-* + *oration*]

perpendicular *adjective* upright; at a right angle (90°) to a line or surface. [from Latin, = plumb-line]

perpetrate *verb* (**perpetrated**, **perpetrating**) commit or be guilty of, *perpetrate a crime or an error.* **perpetration** *noun*, **perpetrator** *noun*

perpetual *adjective* lasting for ever; continuous. **perpetually** *adverb* [from Latin, = uninterrupted]

perpetuate *verb* (**perpetuated**, **perpetuating**) make a thing perpetual; cause to be remembered for a long time, *The statue will perpetuate his memory.* **perpetuation** *noun*

perpetuity *noun* being perpetual. **in perpetuity** for ever.

perplex *verb* bewilder or puzzle somebody. **perplexity** *noun* [from *per-*, + Latin *plexus* = twisted together]

perquisite (*say* **per**-kwiz-it) *noun* something extra given to a worker, *Use of the firm's car is a perquisite of this job.*

persecute *verb* (**persecuted**, **persecuting**) be continually cruel to somebody, especially because you disagree with his or her beliefs; harass. **persecution** *noun*, **persecutor** *noun* [from Latin *persecutum* = pursued]

persevere *verb* (**persevered**, **persevering**) go on doing something even though it is difficult. **perseverance** *noun* [from *per-*, + Latin *severus* = strict]

persimmon *noun* a sweet edible fruit.

persist *verb* **1** continue firmly or obstinately, *She persists in breaking the rules.* **2** continue to exist, *The custom persists in some countries.* **persistent** *adjective*, **persistently** *adverb*, **persistence** *noun*, **persistency** *noun* [from *per-*, + Latin *sistere* = to stand]

person *noun* **1** a human being; a man, woman, or child. **2** (in grammar) any of the three groups of personal pronouns and forms taken by verbs. The **first person** (= *I, me, we, us*) refers to the person(s) speaking; the **second person** (= *thou, thee, you*) refers to the person(s) spoken to; the **third person** (= *he, him, she, her, it, they, them*) refers to the person(s) spoken about.
in person being actually present oneself, *She was there in person.*
[from Latin *persona* = mask used by an actor]

personable *adjective* good-looking.

personage *noun* a person; someone important.

personal *adjective* **1** belonging to, done by, or concerning a particular person. **2** criticising a person, *making personal remarks.* **personally** *adverb*

personalise *verb* (**personalised, personalising**) make for, or mark as belonging to, a particular person, *personalised number plates.*

personality *noun* (*plural* **personalities**) **1** a person's character, *She has a cheerful personality.* **2** a well-known person.

personify *verb* (**personified, personifying**) represent a quality or idea etc. as a person. **personification** *noun*

personnel (*say* per-sa-**nel**) *noun* the people employed by a firm etc. [French, = personal]

perspective *noun* the impression of depth and space in a picture or scene.
in perspective giving a well-balanced view of things.
[from Latin *perspectum* = looked through]

perspicacious *adjective* perceptive. **perspicacity** *noun*

perspire *verb* (**perspired, perspiring**) sweat. **perspiration** *noun* [from *per-*, + Latin *spirare* breathe]

persuade *verb* (**persuaded, persuading**) cause a person to believe or agree to do something. **persuasion** *noun*, **persuasive** *adjective* [from *per-*, + Latin *suadere* = induce]

pert *adjective* cheeky. **pertly** *adverb*, **pertness** *noun*

pertain *verb* be relevant to something, *evidence pertaining to the crime.* [from Latin *pertinere* = belong]

pertinacious *adjective* persistent and determined. **pertinaciously** *adverb*, **pertinacity** *noun* [from *per-* + *tenacious*]

pertinent *adjective* pertaining; relevant. **pertinently** *adverb*, **pertinence** *noun*

perturb *verb* worry someone. **perturbation** *noun* [from *per-*, + Latin *turbare* = disturb]

peruse (*say* per-**ooz**) *verb* (**perused, perusing**) read something carefully. **perusal** *noun* [from *per-* + *use*]

pervade *verb* (**pervaded, pervading**) spread all through something; permeate. **pervasion** *noun*, **pervasive** *adjective* [from *per-*, + Latin *vadere* = go]

perverse *adjective* obstinately doing something different from what is reasonable or required. **perversely** *adverb*, **perversity** *noun* [same origin as *pervert*]

pervert (*say* per-**vert**) *verb* **1** turn something from the right course of action, *By false evidence they perverted the course of justice.* **2** cause a person to behave wickedly or abnormally.

pervert (*say* **per**-vert) *noun* a person who behaves wickedly or abnormally. [from *per-*, + Latin *vertere* to turn]

pessimist *noun* a person who expects that things will turn out badly. (Compare *optimist.*) **pessimism** *noun*, **pessimistic** *adjective*, **pessimistically** *adverb* [from Latin *pessimus* = worst]

pest *noun* **1** a destructive insect or animal, such as a locust or a mouse. **2** a nuisance. [from Latin *pestis* = plague]

pester *verb* keep annoying someone by frequent questions or requests.

pesticide *noun* a substance for killing harmful insects etc. [from *pest*, + Latin *caedere* = kill]

pestiferous *adjective* troublesome. [from *pest*, + Latin *ferre* = carry]

pestilence *noun* a deadly epidemic. [same origin as *pest*]

pestilential *adjective* troublesome.

pestle *noun* a tool with a heavy rounded end for pounding substances in a mortar.

pet *noun* **1** a tame animal kept for companionship and amusement. **2** a person treated as a favourite, *teacher's pet.*

pet *verb* (**petted, petting**) treat or fondle affectionately.

petal *noun* any of the separate coloured outer parts of a flower.

pétanque *noun* a game of outdoor bowls usually played with metal balls and wooden jack on gravel or sand. [French]

peter *verb* **peter out** become gradually less and cease to exist.

petition *noun* a formal request for something, especially a written one signed by many people.

petition *verb* request by a petition. **petitioner** *noun* [from Latin *petere* = seek]

petrel *noun* a kind of sea-bird.

petrify *verb* (**petrified, petrifying**) **1** paralyse someone with terror, surprise, etc. **2** change into a stony mass. **petrifaction** *noun* [from *Greek petra* = rock]

petrol *noun* a liquid made from petroleum, used as fuel for engines.

petroleum *noun* an oil found underground that is refined to make fuel (e.g. petrol, kerosene) or for use in dry-cleaning etc. [from Greek *petra* = rock, + *oleum* = oil]

petticoat *noun* a woman's or girl's dress-length undergarment. [from *petty* = little, + *coat*]

pettifogging *adjective & noun* paying too much attention to unimportant details.

petting *noun* affectionate treatment or fondling.

pettish *adjective* peevish.

petty *adjective* (**pettier, pettiest**) unimportant; trivial, *petty regulations.* **pettily** *adverb*, **pettiness** *noun*
petty cash cash kept by an office for small payments.
petty officer an NCO in the navy.
[from French *petit* = small]

petulant *adjective* peevish. **petulantly** *adverb*, **petulance** *noun*

petunia *noun* a garden plant with funnel-shaped flowers.

pew *noun* a long wooden seat, usually fixed in rows, in a church.

pewter *noun* a grey alloy of tin and lead.

PGD *abbreviation* postgraduate diploma.

phalanger *noun* a marsupial, such as the possum, that lives in trees. [from Greek *phalangion* = spider's web]

phalanx *noun* (*plural* **phalanxes**) a number of people or soldiers in a close formation. [Greek]

phantasm *noun* a phantom.

phantom *noun* a ghost; something that is not real. [from Greek, = made visible]

Pharaoh (*say* **fair**-oh) *noun* the title of the king of ancient Egypt.

pharmaceutical (*say* farm-as-**yoot**-ik-al) *adjective* of pharmacy; of medicines.

pharmacist *noun* a person who is trained in pharmacy; a pharmaceutical chemist.

pharmacology *noun* the study of medicinal drugs. **pharmacological** *adjective*, **pharmacologist** *noun* [from Greek *pharmakon* = drug, + *-logy*]

pharmacy *noun* (*plural* **pharmacies**) **1** a shop selling medicines; a dispensary. **2** the process of preparing medicines. [from Greek *pharmakon* = drug]

pharynx (*say* **fa**-rinks) *noun* the cavity at the back of the mouth and nose.

phase *noun* a stage in the progress or development of something.

phase *verb* (**phased, phasing**) do something in stages, *a phased withdrawal.*

PhD *abbreviation* Doctor of Philosophy.

pheasant (*say* **fez**-ant) *noun* a game-bird with a long tail.

phenomenal *adjective* amazing; remarkable. **phenomenally** *adverb*

phenomenon *noun* (*plural* **phenomena**) an event or fact, especially one that is remarkable. [from Greek, = thing appearing]

USAGE Note that *phenomena* is a plural; it is incorrect to say 'this phenomena' or 'these phenomenas'.

phial *noun* a small glass bottle.

phil- *prefix* see **philo-**.

philander *verb* flirt. **philanderer** *noun*

philanthropy *noun* love of mankind, especially as shown by kind and generous acts that benefit large numbers of people. **philanthropist** *noun*, **philanthropic** *adjective* [from *phil-*, + Greek *anthropos* = human being]

philately (*say* fil-**at**-il-ee) *noun* stamp-collecting. **philatelist** *noun* [from *phil-*, + Greek *ateleia* = not needing to pay (because postage has been paid for by buying a stamp)]

philharmonic *adjective* (in names of orchestras etc.) devoted to music.

philistine (*say* **fil**-ist-I'n) *noun* a person who dislikes art, poetry, etc. [named after the Philistines, who were enemies of the Israelites in the Old Testament]

philo- *prefix* (becoming **phil**- before vowels and *h*) fond of; lover of (as in *philosophy*). [from Greek *philein* = to love]

philology *noun* the study of languages, especially the history of languages preserved in ancient texts. **philological** *adjective*, **philologist** *noun* [from *philo-*, + Greek *logos* = word]

philosopher *noun* an expert in philosophy.

philosophical *adjective* **1** of philosophy. **2** calm and not upset, *Be philosophical about losing.* **philosophically** *adverb*

philosophy *noun* (*plural* **philosophies**) **1** the study of truths about life, morals, etc. **2** a set of ideas or principles or beliefs. [from *philo-*, + Greek *sophia* = wisdom]

philtre (*say* **fil**-ter) *noun* a magic drink; a love potion.

phlegm (*say* flem) *noun* thick mucus that forms in the throat and lungs when someone has a bad cold.

phlegmatic (*say* fleg-**mat**-ik) *adjective* not easily excited or worried; sluggish. **phlegmatically** *adverb*

phobia (*say* **foh**-bee-a) *noun* great or abnormal fear of something. [from Greek *phobos* = fear]

phoenix (*say* **feen**-iks) *noun* (*plural* **phoenixes**) a mythical bird that was said to burn itself to death in a fire and be born again from the ashes.

phone *noun* a telephone.

phone *verb* (**phoned**, **phoning**) telephone. [short for *telephone*]

phonetic (*say* fon-**et**-ik) *adjective* of speech-sounds. **phonetically** *adverb* [from Greek *phonein* = speak]

phonetics *noun* the study of speech-sounds.

phoney *adjective* (*slang*) sham; not genuine. [origin unknown]

phonology *noun* the speech-sounds of a particular language; a description of these.

phosphate *noun* a substance containing phosphorus.

phosphorescent (*say* fos-fer-**ess**-ent) *adjective* luminous. **phosphorescence** *noun*

phosphorus *noun* a chemical substance that glows in the dark. [from Greek *phos* = light, + *-phoros* bringing]

photo *noun* (*plural* **photos**) a photograph.

photo- *prefix* light (as in *photograph*). [from Greek *photos* = of light]

photocopy *noun* (*plural* **photocopies**) a copy of a document or page etc. made by photographing it. **photocopy** *verb*, **photocopier** *noun*

photoelectric *adjective* using the electrical effects of light.

photogenic *adjective* looking attractive in photographs.

photograph *noun* a picture made by the effect of light or other radiation on film or special paper.

photograph *verb* take a photograph of a person or thing. **photographer** *noun* [from *photo-* + *-graph*]

photography *noun* taking photographs. **photographic** *adjective*

photosynthesis *noun* the process by which green plants use sunlight to turn carbon dioxide and water into complex substances, giving off oxygen. [from *photo-* + *synthesis*]

phrase *noun* **1** a group of words that form a unit in a sentence or clause, e.g. *in the garden* in 'The Queen was in the garden'. **2** a short section of a tune.

phrase *verb* (**phrased**, **phrasing**) **1** put something into words. **2** divide music into phrases. [from Greek *phrazein* = declare]

phraseology (*say* fray-zee-**ol**-o-jee) *noun* wording; the way something is worded. [from *phrase* + *-logy*]

physical *adjective* **1** of the body. **2** of things that you can touch or see. **3** of physics.
physically *adverb*
physical education or **physical training** gymnastics or other exercises done to keep the body healthy.
[same origin as *physics*]

physician *noun* a doctor, especially one who is not a surgeon.

physicist (*say* **fiz**-i-sist) *noun* an expert in physics.

physics (*say* **fiz**-iks) *noun* the study of the properties of matter and energy (e.g. heat, light, sound, movement). [from Greek *physikos* = natural]

physiognomy (*say* fiz-ee-**on**-o-mee) *noun* the features of a person's face. [from Greek *physis* = nature, + *gnomon* = indicator]

physiology (*say* fiz-ee-**ol**-o-jee) *noun* the study of the body and its parts and how they function. **physiological** *adjective*, **physiologist** *noun* [from Greek *physis* = nature, + *-logy*]

physiotherapy (*say* fiz-ee-o-th'**e**-ra-pee) *noun* the treatment of a disease or weakness by massage, exercises, etc. **physiotherapist** *noun* [from Greek *physis* = nature, + *therapy*]

physique (*say* fiz-**eek**) *noun* a person's build. [French]

pianist *noun* a person who plays the piano.

piano *noun* (*plural* **pianos**) a large musical instrument with a keyboard. [short for *pianoforte*, from Italian *piano* = soft, + *forte* = loud (because it can produce soft notes and loud notes)]

PIC *abbreviation* (*NZ*) Pacific Island Church.

piccolo *noun* (*plural* **piccolos**) a small high-pitched flute. [Italian, = small]

pick[1] *verb* **1** separate a flower or fruit from its plant, *We picked apples.* **2** choose; select carefully. **3** pull bits off or out of something. **4** open a lock by using something pointed, not with a key. **5** (*NZ, informal*) predict, reckon, *I'm picking the Silver Ferns will win.*
pick a quarrel deliberately provoke a quarrel with somebody.
pick holes in find fault with.
pick on keep criticising or harassing a particular person.
pick someone's pocket steal from it.
pick up lift, take up; collect; take someone into a vehicle; manage to hear something; get better, recover.

pick[1] *noun* **1** choice. **2** the best of a group.

pick[2] *noun* **1** a pickaxe. **2** a plectrum.

pickaxe *noun* a heavy pointed tool with a long handle, used for breaking up hard ground etc.

picker-up *noun* (*NZ*) a person who gathers fleeces which have been shorn from sheep.

picket *noun* **1** a striker or group of strikers who try to persuade other people not to go into a place during a strike. **2** a group of sentries. **3** a pointed post as part of a fence.

picket *verb* (**picketed**, **picketing**) act as a picket; place people as pickets. [from French *piquet* = pointed post]

pickle *noun* **1** a strong-tasting food made of pickled vegetables. **2** (*informal*) a mess.

pickle *verb* (**pickled**, **pickling**) preserve in vinegar or salt water.

pickpocket *noun* a thief who picks people's pockets (see *pick*).

picnic *noun* a meal eaten in the open air away from home.

picnic *verb* (**picnicked**, **picnicking**) have a picnic. **picnicker** *noun*

pictogram *noun* a visual shape, symbol, or picture that represents an object or idea. *Emoticons and smileys are pictograms.*

pictorial *adjective* with or using pictures. **pictorially** *adverb*

picture *noun* **1** a representation of a person or thing made by painting, drawing, or photography. **2** a film at the cinema. **3** how something seems; an impression.

picture *verb* (**pictured**, **picturing**) **1** show in a picture. **2** imagine. [from Latin *pictum* = painted]

picturesque *adjective* **1** forming an attractive scene, *a picturesque village.* **2** vividly described; expressive, *picturesque language.* **picturesquely** *adverb*

pidgin *noun* a simplified form of English or another language used between people who speak different languages, especially in the Far East [from the Chinese pronunciation of *business* (because it was used by traders)]

pie *noun* a baked dish of meat, fish, or fruit covered with pastry.
pie chart a diagram showing quantities as sectors of a circle.

piebald *adjective* with patches of black and white, *a piebald donkey.* [from *pie* = magpie, + *bald*]

piece *noun* **1** a part or portion of something; a fragment. **2** a separate thing or example, *a fine piece of work.* **3** something written, composed, or painted etc., *a piece of music.* **4** any of the objects used to play a game on a board, *a chess-piece.*

piece *verb* (**pieced**, **piecing**) put pieces together to make something.

piecemeal *adjective & adverb* done or made one piece at a time.

pier *noun* **1** a long structure built out into the sea for people to walk on. **2** a pillar supporting a bridge or arch.

pierce *verb* (**pierced**, **piercing**) make a hole through something; penetrate.

piercing *adjective* **1** very loud. **2** penetrating; very strong, *a piercing wind.*

piety *noun* piousness. [from Latin *pietas* = dutiful behaviour]

piffle *noun* (*slang*) nonsense.

pig *noun* **1** a fat animal with short legs and a blunt snout, kept for its meat. **2** (*informal*) someone greedy, dirty, or unpleasant. **piggy** *adjective & noun*
on the pig's back (*slang*) prosperous.
Pig Island(s) (*informal*) New Zealand.
Pig Islander *noun*

pig-dog *noun* (*NZ*) a dog used in hunting wild pigs.

pigeon[1] *noun* a bird with a fat body and a small head. [from Old French *pijon* = young bird]

pigeon[2] *noun* (*informal*) a person's business or responsibility, *That's your pigeon.* [same origin as *pidgin*]

pigeon-hole *noun* a small compartment above a desk etc., used for holding letters or papers.

piggery *noun* (*plural* **piggeries**) a place where pigs are bred or kept.

piggyback *adverb* carried on somebody else's back or shoulders. **piggyback** *noun* [from *pick-a-back*]

piggy bank a money-box made in the shape of a hollow pig.

pig-headed *adjective* obstinate.

pig-iron iron that has been processed in a smelting-furnace.

piglet *noun* a young pig.

pigment *noun* a substance that colours something. **pigmented** *adjective*, **pigmentation** *noun* [from Latin *pingere* = to paint]

pigsty *noun* (*plural* **pigsties**) a partly-covered pen for pigs.

pigtail *noun* a plait of hair worn hanging at the back of the head.

pīkau *noun* bundle, swag. [Māori]

pike[1] *noun* **1** a heavy spear. **2** (*plural* **pike**) a large freshwater fish.

pike[2] *verb* **pike out** (*NZ*, *informal*) back out of or fail to do something (in a cowardly way). **piker** *noun*

pikelet *noun* a small pancake. [from Welsh *bara pyglyd* = pitchy bread]

pilchard *noun* a small sea-fish.

pile[1] *noun* **1** a number of things on top of one another. **2** (*informal*) a large quantity; a lot of money. **3** a tall building.

pile[1] *verb* (**piled**, **piling**) put things into a pile; make a pile. [from Latin *pila* = pillar]

pile[2] *noun* a heavy beam made of metal, concrete, or timber driven into the ground to support something.
pile-driver a machine for driving piles.
[from Latin *pilum* = spear]

pile[3] *noun* a raised surface on fabric, made of upright threads, *a carpet with a thick pile.* [from Latin *pilus* = hair]

pilfer *verb* steal small things. **pilferer** *noun*, **pilferage** *noun*

pilgrim *noun* a person who travels to a holy place for religious reasons. **pilgrimage** *noun*

pill *noun* a small solid piece of medicinal substance for swallowing.
the pill a contraceptive pill.
[from Latin *pila* = ball]

pillage *verb* (**pillaged**, **pillaging**) plunder. **pillage** *noun*

pillar *noun* a tall stone or wooden post. [from Latin *pila* = pillar]

pillion *noun* a seat behind the driver on a motor cycle.

pillory *noun* (*plural* **pillories**) a wooden framework with holes for a person's head and hands, in which offenders were formerly made to stand and be ridiculed and scorned by the public as a punishment.

pillory *verb* (**pilloried**, **pillorying**) **1** put into a pillory. **2** expose a person to public ridicule and scorn, *He was pilloried in the newspapers for what he had done.*

pillow *noun* a cushion for a person's head to rest on, especially in bed.

pillow *verb* rest the head on a pillow etc.

pillowcase or **pillowslip** *noun* a cloth cover for a pillow.

pilot *noun* **1** a person who works the controls for flying an aircraft. **2** a person qualified to steer a ship in and out of a port or through a difficult stretch of water. **3** a guide.

pilot *verb* (**piloted**, **piloting**) **1** be pilot of an aircraft or ship. **2** guide; steer.

pilot *adjective* testing on a small scale how something will work, *a pilot scheme.*

pilot-light *noun* **1** a small flame that lights a larger burner on a gas cooker etc. **2** an electric indicator light.

pimpernel (*say* **pimp**-er-nel) *noun* a plant with small red, blue, or white flowers that close in cloudy weather.

pimple *noun* a small round raised spot on the skin. **pimply** *adjective*

pin *noun* **1** a short thin piece of metal with a sharp point and a rounded head, used to fasten pieces of cloth or paper etc. together. **2** a pointed device for fixing or marking something.
pins and needles a prickling feeling.

pin *verb* (**pinned**, **pinning**) **1** fasten with a pin or pins. **2** make a person or thing unable to move, *He was pinned under the wreckage.* **3** fix, *They pinned the blame on her.*

PIN *abbreviation* Personal Identification Number.

pinafore *noun* an apron. [from *pin* + *afore* = before]

pincer *noun* the claw of a shellfish such as a crayfish.
pincers a tool with two parts that are pressed together for gripping and holding things.

pinch *verb* **1** squeeze tightly or painfully between two things, especially between the finger and thumb. **2** (*informal*) steal. **3** (*informal*) arrest.

pinch *noun* (*plural* **pinches**) **1** a pinching movement. **2** difficulty; stress or pressure of circumstances, *They began to feel the pinch.* **3** the amount that can be held between the tips of the thumb and forefinger, *a pinch of salt.*
at a pinch if necessary.

pincushion *noun* a small pad into which pins are stuck to keep them ready for use.

pine[1] *noun* an evergreen tree with needle-shaped leaves.

pine[2] *verb* (**pined**, **pining**) feel an intense longing; become weak through longing for somebody or something.

pineapple *noun* a large tropical fruit with a tough prickly skin and yellow flesh.

ping *noun* a short sharp ringing sound.

pīngao *noun* a sand-plant with bronze-coloured leaves. [Māori]

ping-pong *noun* table tennis.

pinion[1] *noun* a bird's wing, especially the outer end.

pinion[1] *verb* **1** clip a bird's wings to prevent it from flying. **2** hold or fasten a person's arms or legs so as to prevent movement.

pinion[2] *noun* a small cog-wheel that engages with another or with a rod (called a *rack*).

pink[1] *adjective* pale red. **pinkness** *noun*

pink[1] *noun* **1** pink colour. **2** a garden plant with fragrant flowers, often pink or white.
in the pink (*informal*) in good health.

pink[2] *verb* **1** pierce slightly. **2** cut a zigzag edge on cloth.

pinko *noun* (*informal*) a person with left-wing views.

pinnacle *noun* **1** a pointed ornament on a roof. **2** a peak.

pinny *noun* (*informal*) a pinafore.

pinpoint *adjective* exact; precise, *with pinpoint accuracy.*

pinpoint *verb* find or identify something precisely.

pinprick *noun* a small annoyance.

pin-stripe *noun* a very narrow stripe.
pin-striped *adjective*

pint *noun* a unit of volume for liquids, equivalent to about 0.57 of a litre (British pint) or about 0.47 of a litre (US pint).

pin-up *noun* (*informal*) a picture of an attractive or famous person for pinning on a wall.

pinus radiata the radiata pine tree, and its timber. [Latin]

pioneer *noun* one of the first people to go to a place or do or investigate something. **pioneer** *verb* [from French *pionnier* = foot-soldier]

piopio *noun* a kind of thrush, now extinct. [Māori]

pious *adjective* very religious; devout. **piously** *adverb*, **piousness** *noun* [from Latin *pius* = dutiful]

pip *noun* **1** a small hard seed of an apple, pear, orange, etc. **2** one of the spots on playing-cards, dice, or dominoes. **3** a short high-pitched sound. *She heard the pips of the time-signal on the radio.*

pip *verb* (**pipped**, **pipping**) (*informal*) defeat.

pipe *noun* **1** a tube through which water or gas etc. can flow from one place to another. **2** a short narrow tube with a bowl at one end in which tobacco can burn for smoking. **3** a tube forming a musical instrument or part of one.
the pipes bagpipes.

pipe *verb* (**piped**, **piping**) **1** send something along pipes. **2** transmit music or other sound by wire or cable. **3** play music on a pipe or the bagpipes. **4** trim or ornament with piping.
pipe down (*informal*) be quiet.

pipedream *noun* an impossible wish.

pipeline *noun* a pipe for carrying oil or water etc. a long distance.
in the pipeline in the process of being made or organised.

piper *noun* **1** a person who plays a pipe or bagpipes. **2** (*NZ*) garfish.

pipette *noun* a small glass tube used in a laboratory, usually filled by suction.

pipi *noun* an edible shellfish. [Māori]

piping *noun* **1** pipes; a length of pipe. **2** a long narrow pipe-like fold or line decorating something.

piping *adjective* shrill, *a piping voice.*
piping hot very hot.

pipit *noun* a small songbird.

pippin *noun* a kind of apple.

piquant (*say* **pee**-kant) *adjective* pleasantly sharp and appetising or stimulating, *a piquant smell.* **piquancy** *noun* [same origin as *pique*]

pique (*say* peek) *noun* a feeling of hurt pride. **pique** *verb* [from French *piquer* = to prick]

piranha *noun* a fierce freshwater fish.

pirate *noun* **1** a person on a ship who robs other ships at sea or makes a plundering raid on the shore. **2** someone who produces or publishes or broadcasts without authorisation. **piratical** *adjective*, **piracy** *noun* [from Greek *peiraein* = to attack]

pirouette (*say* pir-oo-**et**) *noun* a spinning movement of the body made while balanced on the point of the toe or on one foot. **pirouette** *verb* [French, = spinning-top]

pistachio *noun* (*plural* **pistachios**) a nut with an edible green kernel.

pistil *noun* the part of a flower that produces the seed, consisting of the ovary, style, and stigma.

pistol *noun* a small hand-gun.

piston *noun* a disc or cylinder that fits inside a tube in which it moves up and down as part of an engine or pump etc.

pit *noun* **1** a deep hole or depression. **2** a coalmine. **3** the part of a racetrack where racing-cars are refuelled and repaired during a race.

pit *verb* (**pitted**, **pitting**) **1** make pits or depressions in something, *The ground was pitted with holes.* **2** put somebody in competition with somebody else, *He was pitted against the champion.* [from Latin *puteus* = a well]

pitch[1] *noun* (*plural* **pitches**) **1** a piece of ground marked out for cricket, football, or another game. **2** the highness or lowness of a voice or a musical note. **3** intensity; strength, *Excitement was at fever pitch.* **4** the steepness of a slope, *the pitch of the roof.*

pitch[1] *verb* **1** throw; fling. **2** fix a tent etc. **3** fall heavily. **4** move up and down on a rough sea. **5** set something at a particular level, *They pitched their hopes high.* **6** (of a bowled ball in cricket) strike the ground.
pitched battle a battle between troops in prepared positions.
pitch in (*informal*) start working or eating vigorously.

pitch² *noun* a black sticky substance rather like tar. **pitchy** *adjective*
pitch-black or **pitch-dark** *adjectives* very black or very dark.

pitchblende *noun* a mineral ore (uranium oxide) from which radium is obtained.

pitcher *noun* a large jug.

pitchfork *noun* a large fork with two prongs, used for lifting hay.

pitchfork *verb* **1** lift with a pitchfork. **2** put a person somewhere suddenly.

piteous *adjective* causing pity. **piteously** *adverb*

pitfall *noun* an unsuspected danger or difficulty.

pith *noun* the spongy substance in the stems of certain plants or lining the rind of oranges etc.

pithy *adjective* **1** like pith; containing much pith. **2** short and full of meaning, *pithy comments.*

pitiable *adjective* pitiful.

pitiful *adjective* arousing pity; pathetic. **pitifully** *adverb*

pitiless *adjective* showing no pity. **pitilessly** *adverb*

pit-saw *noun* (*formerly*) a cross-cut saw for cutting timber, operated by two people, one of whom worked in a pit. **pit-sawyer** *noun*

pitta (also **pita**) (*say* **pee**-ta) a kind of flat bread, hollow inside, that can be filled with meat, salad, etc.

pittance *noun* a very small allowance of money. [same origin as *pity* and *piety* (the word *pittance* originally meant 'pious gift')]

pittosporum *noun* any of various kinds of New Zealand and Australian shrubs that have white or yellowish flowers with sticky seeds.

pity *noun* **1** the feeling of being sorry because someone is in pain or trouble. **2** a cause for regret, *It's a pity that you can't come.*
take pity on feel sorry for someone and help them.

pity *verb* (**pitied**, **pitying**) feel pity for someone. [same origin as *piety*]

piupiu *noun* a skirt made of grass or flax. [Māori]

pivot *noun* a point or part on which something turns or swings. **pivotal** *adjective*

pivot *verb* (**pivoted**, **pivoting**) turn or place something to turn on a pivot.

pīwakawaka *noun* the fantail. [Māori]

pixel *noun* a tiny component of an image on an electronic display screen.

pixie *noun* a small fairy; an elf.

pizza (*say* **peets**-a) *noun* an Italian food consisting of a layer of dough baked with a savoury topping. [Italian, = pie]

pizzicato (*say* pits-i-**kah**-toh) *adjective & adverb* plucking the strings of a musical instrument. [Italian]

placard *noun* a poster; a notice.

placate *verb* (**placated**, **placating**) pacify; conciliate. **placatory** *adjective*

place *noun* **1** a particular part of space, especially where something belongs; an area; a position. **2** a seat, *Save me a place.* **3** a job; employment. **4** a building; a home, *Come round to our place.* **5** a duty or function, *It's not my place to interfere.* **6** a point in a series of things, *In the first place, the date is wrong.*
in place in the right position; suitable.
out of place in the wrong position; unsuitable.

place *verb* (**placed**, **placing**) put something in a particular place. **placement** *noun* [from Greek *plateia* = broad way]

placenta *noun* a piece of body tissue that forms in the womb during pregnancy and supplies the foetus with nourishment.

placid *adjective* calm and peaceful; not easily made anxious or upset. **placidly** *adverb*, **placidity** *noun* [from Latin *placidus* = gentle]

placket *noun* an opening in a skirt to make it easy to put on and take off.

plagiarise (*say* **play**-jee-er-I'z) *verb* (**plagiarised**, **plagiarising**) copy and use someone else's writings or ideas etc. as if they were your own. **plagiarism** *noun*, **plagiarist** *noun* [from Latin *plagiarius* = kidnapper]

plague *noun* **1** a dangerous illness that spreads very quickly. **2** a large number of pests, *a plague of locusts.*

plague *verb* (**plagued**, **plaguing**) pester; annoy.

plaid (*say* plad) *noun* cloth with a tartan or similar pattern.

plain *adjective* **1** not decorated; not elaborate; not flavoured. **2** not beautiful. **3** easy to see or hear or understand. **4** frank; straightforward. **plainly** *adverb*, **plainness** *noun*
plain clothes civilian clothes worn instead of a uniform, e.g. by police.

plain *noun* a large area of flat country. [from Latin *planus* = flat]

plaintiff *noun* the person who brings a complaint against somebody else to a lawcourt. (Compare *defendant.*) [same origin as *complain*]

plaintive *adjective* sounding sad. [same origin as *complain*]

plait (*say* plat) *verb* weave three or more strands to form one length.

plait *noun* something plaited. [from Latin *plicatum* = folded]

plan *noun* **1** a way of doing something thought out in advance. **2** a drawing showing the arrangement of parts of something. **3** a map of a town or district.

plan *verb* (**planned**, **planning**) make a plan for something. **planner** *noun*

plane[1] *noun* **1** an aeroplane. **2** a tool for making wood smooth by scraping its surface. **3** a flat or level surface.

plane[1] *verb* (**planed**, **planing**) smooth wood with a plane.

plane[1] *adjective* flat; level, *a plane surface.* [same origin as *plain*]

plane[2] *noun* a tall tree with broad leaves.

planet *noun* any of the heavenly bodies that move in an orbit round the sun, *The main planets are Mercury, Venus, Earth, Mars, Jupiter, Saturn, Uranus, and Neptune.* **planetary** *adjective* [from Greek *planetes* = wanderer (because it was not a 'fixed star')]

plank *noun* **1** a long flat piece of wood. **2** an item in a political or other programme.

plankton *noun* microscopic plants and animals that float in the sea, lakes, etc. [from Greek, = wandering]

plant *noun* **1** a living thing that cannot move and that makes its food from chemical substances, *Flowers, trees, and shrubs are plants.* **2** a small plant, not a tree or shrub. **3** a factory or its equipment. **4** (*slang*) something planted to deceive people (see *plant* verb 3).

plant *verb* **1** put something in soil for growing. **2** fix firmly in place. **3** place something where it will be found, usually to mislead people or cause trouble. **planter** *noun* [from Latin *planta* = a shoot]

plantation *noun* **1** a large area of land where cotton, tobacco, or tea etc. is planted. **2** a group of planted trees.

plaque (*say* plak) *noun* **1** a flat piece of metal or porcelain fixed on a wall as an ornament or memorial. **2** a filmy substance that forms on teeth and gums, where bacteria can live.

plasma *noun* the colourless liquid part of blood, carrying the corpuscles.

plaster *noun* **1** a mixture of lime, sand, and water etc. for covering walls and ceilings. **2** plaster of Paris. **3** a piece of sticking-plaster.
plaster of Paris a white paste used for making moulds or for casts round a broken limb etc.

plaster *verb* **1** cover with plaster. **2** cover thickly; daub.

plastic *noun* **1** a strong light synthetic substance that can be moulded into a permanent shape. **2** (*informal*) a credit card, *I can pay for it with my plastic.*

plastic *adjective* **1** made of plastic. **2** soft and easy to mould, *Clay is a plastic substance.* **3** artificial or unnatural, *a plastic smile.*
plasticity *noun*
plastic surgery surgery to repair deformed or injured parts of the body.

plate *noun* **1** an almost flat usually circular object from which food is eaten or served. **2** (*NZ*) a plate of cakes, sandwiches, etc., brought as a contribution to a social event. **3** a thin flat sheet of metal, glass, or other hard material. **4** an illustration on special paper in a book. **plateful** *noun*

plate *verb* (**plated**, **plating**) **1** coat metal with a thin layer of gold, silver, tin etc. **2** cover with sheets of metal.

plateau (*say* **plat**-oh) *noun* (*plural* **plateaux** or **plateaus**, *say* **plat**-ohz) a flat area of high land. [from French *plat* = flat]

platelayer *noun* a person whose job is to fix and repair railway rails.

platform *noun* **1** a flat surface that is above the level of the ground or the rest of the floor, e.g. in a hall or beside a railway line at a station. **2** the policy that a political party puts forward when there is an election.

platinum *noun* a valuable silver-coloured metal that does not tarnish. [from Spanish *plata* = silver]

platitude *noun* a very ordinary remark. **platitudinous** *adjective*

platoon *noun* a small group of soldiers.

platter *noun* a flat dish or plate.

platypus *noun* (*plural* **platypuses**) an Australian animal with a bill like that of a duck, that lays eggs like a bird but is a mammal and suckles its young. [from Greek *platys* = broad, + *pous* = foot]

plaudits *plural noun* applause; expressions of approval. [same origin as *applaud*]

plausible *adjective* seeming to be honest or worth believing but perhaps deceptive, *a plausible excuse.* **plausibly** *adverb*, **plausibility** *noun*

play *verb* **1** take part in a game or other amusement. **2** make music or sound with a musical instrument, stereo, etc. **3** perform a part in a play or film.
play down give people the impression that something is not important.
play up (*informal*) be mischievous or annoying.

play *noun* **1** a story acted on a stage or on radio or television. **2** playing.

playback *noun* playing back something that has been recorded.

playcentre *noun* (*NZ*) a place for preschool children to meet and play, with parents supervising them.

player *noun* **1** a participant in a game. **2** a person playing a musical instrument. **3** an actor in a play. **4** a person or body involved in a particular process or area, *He is one of the central players in the design team.* **5** a device for playing CDs, DVDs, etc.

playful *adjective* wanting to play; full of fun; not serious. **playfully** *adverb*, **playfulness** *noun*

playground *noun* a piece of ground for children to play on.

playing-card *noun* each of a set of cards (usually 52) used for playing games.

playing-field *noun* a field used for outdoor games.

play-lunch *noun* (*NZ*) a mid-morning snack for schoolchildren.

playmate *noun* a person you play games with.

playstation *noun* a video game console introduced in 1995.

plaything *noun* a toy.

playtime *noun* the time when young schoolchildren may go out to play.

playwright *noun* a dramatist. [from *play*, + *wright* = maker]

PLC or **p.l.c.** *abbreviation* public limited company (see *limited*).

plea *noun* **1** a request; an appeal, *a plea for mercy.* **2** an excuse, *He stayed at home on the plea of a headache.* **3** a formal statement of 'guilty' or 'not guilty' made in a lawcourt by someone accused of a crime. [same origin as *please*]

plead *verb* make a plea.

pleasant *adjective* pleasing; giving pleasure. **pleasantly** *adverb*, **pleasantness** *noun*

pleasantry *noun* (*plural* **pleasantries**) being humorous; a humorous remark.

please *verb* (**pleased**, **pleasing**) **1** make a person feel satisfied or glad. **2** (used to make a request or an order polite), *Please ring the bell.* **3** like; think suitable, *Do as you please.* [from Latin *placere* = satisfy]

pleasurable *adjective* causing pleasure.

pleasure *noun* **1** a feeling of satisfaction or gladness; enjoyment. **2** something that pleases you.

pleat *noun* a flat fold made by doubling cloth upon itself. **pleated** *adjective* [from *plait*]

plebeian (*say* plib-**ee**-an) *noun* a member of the common people in ancient Rome. (Compare *patrician*.) **plebeian** *adjective* [from Latin *plebs* = the common people]

plebiscite (*say* **pleb**-iss-it) *noun* a referendum. [from Latin *plebs* the common people, + *scitum* = decree]

plectrum *noun* (*plural* **plectra**) a small piece of metal or bone etc. for plucking the strings of a musical instrument.

pledge *noun* **1** a solemn promise. **2** a thing handed over as security for a loan or contract.

pledge *verb* (**pledged**, **pledging**) **1** promise solemnly. **2** hand something over as security.

plenary (*say* **pleen**-er-ee) *adjective* attended by all members, *a plenary session of the council.* [from Latin *plenus* = full]

plenipotentiary (*say* plen-i-pot-**en**-sher-ee) *adjective* having full authority to make decisions on behalf of a government, *Our ambassador has plenipotentiary power.* **plenipotentiary** *noun* [from Latin *plenus* = full, + *potentia* = power]

plentiful *adjective* quite enough in amount; abundant. **plentifully** *adverb*

plenty *noun* quite enough; as much as is needed or wanted.

plenty *adverb* (*informal*) quite; fully, *It's plenty big enough.* [from Latin *plenus* = full]

pleurisy (*say* **ploor**-i-see) *noun* inflammation of the membrane round the lungs. [from Greek *pleura* = ribs]

pliable *adjective* easy to bend or influence; flexible. **pliability** *noun* [from French *plier* = to bend]

pliant *adjective* pliable.

pliers *plural noun* pincers that have jaws with flat surfaces for gripping things.

plight[1] *noun* a difficult situation.

plight[2] *verb* (*old use*) pledge.

Plimsoll line a mark on a ship's side showing how deeply it may legally go down in the water when loaded. [named after an English politician, S. Plimsoll, who in the 1870s protested about ships being overloaded]

plinth *noun* a block or slab forming the base of a column or a support for a statue or vase etc.

PLO *abbreviation* Palestine Liberation Organisation.

plod *verb* (**plodded**, **plodding**) **1** walk slowly and heavily. **2** work slowly but steadily. **plodder** *noun*

plop *noun* the sound of something dropping into water. **plop** *verb*

plot *noun* **1** a secret plan. **2** the story in a play, novel, or film. **3** a small piece of land. **lose the plot** (*informal*) become confused or exasperated.

plot *verb* (**plotted**, **plotting**) **1** make a secret plan. **2** make a chart or graph of something, *We plotted the ship's route on our map.*

plough *noun* a farming implement for turning the soil over.

plough *verb* **1** turn over soil with a plough. **2** go through something with great effort or difficulty, *He ploughed through the book.*
ploughman *noun*
plough back reinvest profits in the business that produced them.

ploughshare *noun* the cutting-blade of a plough.

plover (*say* **pluv**-er) *noun* a kind of wading bird. [from Latin *pluvia* rain]

ploy *noun* a cunning manoeuvre to gain an advantage; a ruse.

pluck *verb* **1** pick a flower or fruit. **2** pull the feathers off a bird. **3** pull something up or out. **4** pull a string (e.g. on a guitar) and let it go again.
pluck up courage summon up courage and overcome fear.

pluck *noun* **1** courage; bravery. **2** plucking; a pull.

plucky *adjective* (**pluckier**, **pluckiest**) showing pluck; brave. **pluckily** *adverb*

plug *noun* **1** something used to stop up a hole. **2** a device that fits into a socket to connect wires to a supply of electricity. **3** (*informal*) a piece of publicity for something.

plug *verb* (**plugged**, **plugging**) **1** stop up a hole. **2** (*informal*) publicise something.
plug in put a plug into an electrical socket.

plum *noun* **1** a soft juicy fruit with a pointed stone in the middle. **2** (*old use*) a dried grape or raisin used in cooking, *plum pudding.* **3** reddish-purple colour. **4** (*informal*) something good, *a plum job.*

plumage (*say* **ploom**-ij) *noun* a bird's feathers. [same origin as *plume*]

plumb *verb* **1** measure how deep something is. **2** get to the bottom of a matter, *We could not plumb the mystery.* **3** fit with a plumbing system.

plumb *adjective* exactly upright; vertical, *The wall was plumb.*

plumb *adverb* (*informal*) exactly, *It fell plumb in the middle.* [from Latin *plumbum* = lead[2] (the metal)]

plumber *noun* a person who fits and mends plumbing.

plumbing *noun* **1** the water-pipes, water-tanks, and drainage-pipes in a building. **2** the work of a plumber.

plumb-line *noun* a cord with a weight on the end, used to find how deep something is or whether a wall etc. is vertical.

plume *noun* **1** a large feather. **2** something shaped like a feather, *a plume of smoke.*

plume *verb* (**plumed**, **pluming**) preen. [from Latin *pluma* = feather]

plumed *adjective* ornamented with plumes, *a plumed helmet.*

plummet *noun* a plumb-line or the weight on its end.

plummet *verb* (**plummeted**, **plummeting**) drop downwards quickly.

plump[1] *adjective* slightly fat; rounded.
plumpness *noun*

plump[2] *verb* drop or fall quickly.
plump for (*informal*) choose.

plunder *verb* rob a person or place forcibly or systematically; loot. **plunderer** *noun*

plunder *noun* **1** plundering. **2** goods etc. that have been plundered; loot.

plunge *verb* (**plunged**, **plunging**) **1** go or push forcefully into something; dive. **2** fall or go downwards suddenly. **3** go or force into action etc., *They plunged the world into war.*
plunger *noun*

plunge *noun* plunging; a dive.
take the plunge start a bold course of action.

Plunket *noun* (*NZ*) the Plunket Society.
Plunket baby a baby raised on the lines advocated by the Plunket Society.
Plunket nurse a Karitane nurse.
Plunket Society the Royal New Zealand Plunket Society, formerly the Royal New Zealand Society for the Health of Women and Children (founded 1907). [named after Lady Plunket, its first President]

pluperfect tense a tense of the verb showing that an action was completed before a point of time in the past, e.g. He *had arrived.* (Compare *perfect tense.*) [from Latin *plus quam perfectum* = more than perfect]

plural *noun* the form of a noun or verb used when it stands for more than one person or thing, *The plural of 'child' is 'children'.* (Compare *singular.*) **plural** *adjective*, **plurality** *noun* [from Latin *pluris* = of more]

plus *preposition* with the next number or thing added, *2 plus 2 equals four* (2 + 2 = 4). [Latin, = more]

plush *noun* a thick velvety cloth used in furnishings. **plushy** *adjective* [from Latin *pilus* = hair]

plutocrat *noun* a person who is powerful because of his or her wealth. [from Greek *ploutos* = wealth, + *-kratia* = power]

plutonium *noun* a radioactive substance used in nuclear weapons and reactors. [named after the planet Pluto]

pluty *adjective* (*NZ, informal*) wealthy. [from *plutocrat*]

ply[1] *noun* **1** a thickness or layer of wood or cloth etc. **2** a strand in yarn, *4-ply wool.* [same origin as *pliable*]

ply[2] *verb* (**plied**, **plying**) **1** use or wield a tool or weapon. **2** work at, *Tailors plied their trade.* **3** keep offering, *They plied her with food* or *with questions.* **4** go regularly, *The boat plies between the two harbours.* **5** drive or wait about looking for custom, *Taxis are allowed to ply for hire.* [from *apply*]

plywood *noun* strong thin board made of layers of wood glued together.

PM *abbreviation* Prime Minister.

p.m. *abbreviation* post meridiem (Latin, = after noon).

PMS *abbreviation* pre-menstrual syndrome.

PMT *abbreviation* pre-menstrual tension.

pneumatic (*say* new-**mat**-ik) *adjective* filled with or worked by compressed air, *a pneumatic drill.* **pneumatically** *adverb* [from Greek *pneuma* = wind]

pneumonia (*say* new-**moh**-nee-a) *noun* inflammation of one or both lungs. [from Greek *pneumon* = lung]

PNG *abbreviation* Papua New Guinea.

poach *verb* **1** cook an egg (removed from its shell) in or over boiling water. **2** cook fish or fruit etc. in a small amount of liquid. **3** steal game or fish from someone else's land or water. **4** take unfairly, *One club was poaching members from another.* **poacher** *noun* [same origin as *pouch*]

poaka *noun* **1** a long-legged black and white bird, a kind of stilt. **2** a pig. [Māori]

pocket *noun* **1** a small bag-shaped part, especially in a garment. **2** a person's supply of money, *The expense is beyond my pocket.* **3** an isolated part or area, *small pockets of rain.* **pocketful** *noun*
be out of pocket have spent more money than you have gained.

pocket *adjective* small enough to carry in a pocket, *a pocket calculator.*

pocket *verb* (**pocketed**, **pocketing**) put something into a pocket. [from Old French *pochet* = little pouch]

pocket-knife *noun* a knife for carrying in the pocket, with a folding blade or blades.

pocket-money *noun* money given to a child to spend as he or she likes.

pod *noun* a long seed-container of the kind found on a pea or bean plant.

podcast *noun* a digital recording of a broadcast, made available on the Internet for downloading to a computer or personal audio player.

podgy *adjective* (**podgier**, **podgiest**) short and fat.

podiatry *noun* (*say* po-**dy**-a-tree) chiropody. **podiatrist** *noun*

podium (*say* **poh**-dee-um) *noun* (*plural* **podia**) a platform or pedestal. [from Greek *podion* = little- foot]

podocarp *noun* any of several kinds of Southern hemisphere fir tree.

poem *noun* a composition in verse. [from Greek *poiema* = thing made]

poet *noun* a person who writes poems. **poetess** *noun*

Poet Laureate *noun* **1** (*Britain*) a poet appointed to write poems for special occasions. **2** (*NZ*) a renowned New Zealand poet awarded this title for a two-year period.

poetry *noun* poems. **poetic** *adjective*, **poetical** *adjective*, **poetically** *adverb*

pogrom *noun* an organised massacre. [Russian, = destruction]

pōhutukawa *noun* an evergreen tree with bright crimson flowers, the New Zealand Christmas tree. [Māori]

poi *noun* a small light ball on the end of a string used in Māori songs and dances. [Māori]
poi dance a dance using poi.

poignant (*say* **poin**-yant) *adjective* very distressing; affecting the feelings, *poignant memories.* **poignancy** *noun* [from French, = pricking]

point *noun* **1** the narrow or sharp end of something. **2** a dot, *the decimal point.* **3** a particular place or time, *At this point she was winning.* **4** a detail; a characteristic, *He has his good points.* **5** the important or essential idea, *Keep to the point!* **6** purpose; value, *There is no point in hurrying.* **7** an electrical socket. **8** a device for changing a train from one track to another. **9** (**points**) (*NZ & Australia*) the outside edges of a sheep's fleece.
point of view a way of looking at or thinking of something.

point *verb* **1** aim; direct, *She pointed a gun at me.* **2** show where something is, especially by holding out a finger etc. towards it. **3** fill in the parts between bricks with mortar or cement.
point out draw attention to something. [from Latin *punctum* = pricked]

point-blank *adjective* **1** aimed or fired from close to the target. **2** direct; straightforward, *a point-blank refusal.*

point-blank *adverb* in a point-blank manner, *He refused point-blank.*

point-duty *noun* being stationed at a road junction to control the movement of traffic.

pointed *adjective* **1** with a point at the end. **2** clearly directed at a person, *a pointed remark.* **pointedly** *adverb*

pointer *noun* **1** a stick, rod, or mark etc. used to point at something. **2** a dog that points with its muzzle towards birds that it scents. **3** an indication or hint.

pointless *adjective* without a point; with no purpose. **pointlessly** *adverb*

poise *verb* (**poised**, **poising**) balance.

poise *noun* **1** balance; the way something is poised. **2** a dignified self-confident manner.

poison *noun* a substance that can harm or kill a living thing. **poisonous** *adjective*

poison *verb* **1** give poison to; kill with poison. **2** put poison in something. **3** corrupt; fill with prejudice, *He poisoned their minds.* **poisoner** *noun* [same origin as *potion*]

poke[1] *verb* (**poked**, **poking**) **1** prod; jab. **2** push out or forward; stick out. **3** search, *I was poking about in the attic.*
poke fun at ridicule.

poke[1] *noun* a poking movement; a prod.

poke[2] *noun* (*dialect*) a bag.
buy a pig in a poke buy something without seeing it. [compare *pouch*]

poker[1] *noun* a stiff metal rod for poking a fire.

poker[2] *noun* a card-game in which players bet on who has the best cards.

poky *adjective* (**pokier**, **pokiest**) small and cramped, *poky little rooms.* [from *poke*[1]]

polar *adjective* **1** of or near the North Pole or South Pole. **2** of either pole of a magnet. **polarity** *noun*
polar bear a white bear living in Arctic regions.

polarise *verb* (**polarised**, **polarising**) **1** keep vibrations of light-waves etc. to a single direction. **2** set at opposite extremes of feeling, *Opinions had polarised.* **polarisation** *noun*

pole[1] *noun* a long slender rounded piece of wood or metal. [same origin as *pale*[2]]

pole[2] *noun* **1** a point on the earth's surface that is as far north (**North Pole**) or as far south (**South Pole**) as possible. **2** either of the ends of a magnet. **3** either terminal of an electric cell or battery. [from Greek *polos* = axis]
pole-axe *noun* a butcher's axe with a hammer at the back.
pole-axe *verb* hit or slaughter with a pole-axe.
polecat *noun* an animal of the weasel family with an unpleasant smell.
pole-star *noun* the star above the North Pole.
pole-vault *noun* a jump over a high bar done with the help of a long pole.

polemic (*say* pol-**em**-ik) *noun* an attack in words against someone's opinion or actions. **polemical** *adjective* [from Greek *polemos* = war]

police *noun* the people whose job is to catch criminals and make sure that the law is kept. **policeman** *noun*, **policewoman** *noun*

police *verb* (**policed**, **policing**) keep order in a place by means of police.

policy[1] *noun* (*plural* **policies**) the aims or plan of action of a person or group. [same origin as *political*]

policy[2] *noun* (*plural* **policies**) a document stating the terms of a contract of insurance. [from Greek, = evidence]

polio *noun* poliomyelitis.

poliomyelitis (*say* poh-lee-oh-my-il-**I**-tiss) *noun* a disease that can cause paralysis.

polish *verb* **1** make a thing smooth and shiny by rubbing. **2** make a thing better by making corrections and alterations. **polisher** *noun*
polish off finish off.

polish *noun* (*plural* **polishes**) **1** a substance used in polishing. **2** a shine. **3** elegance of manner.

polite *adjective* having good manners. **politely** *adverb*, **politeness** *noun* [from Latin *politus* = polished]

politic (*say* **pol**-it-ik) *adjective* prudent.

political *adjective* connected with the governing of a country, city, etc. **politically** *adverb*
political correctness the avoidance of words or actions that may be thought to discriminate against or insult any minority group. **politically correct** *adjective* [from Greek *politeia* = government]

politician *noun* a person who is involved in politics.

politics *noun* political matters.

polka *noun* a lively dance for couples.
polka dots round dots evenly spaced to form a pattern on fabric.

poll (*say as* pole) *noun* **1** voting or votes at an election. **2** an opinion poll (see *opinion*). **3** (*old use*) the head.

poll *verb* **1** vote at an election. **2** receive a stated number of votes. **3** cut the top off a tree or the horns off cattle. **polling-booth** *noun*, **polling-station** *noun*

pollarded *adjective* (of trees) with the tops trimmed so that young shoots start to grow thickly there. [from *poll* 3]

polled *adjective* (of cattle) with the horns trimmed. [from *poll* 3]

pollen *noun* powder produced by the anthers of flowers, containing male cells for fertilising other flowers. [Latin, = fine flour]

pollinate *verb* (**pollinated, pollinating**) fertilise with pollen. **pollination** *noun*

pollster *noun* a person who conducts an opinion poll.

pollute *verb* (**polluted, polluting**) make a place or thing dirty or impure. **pollutant** *noun*, **pollution** *noun*

polo *noun* a game rather like hockey, with players on horseback.
polo neck a high round turned-over collar. **polo-necked** *adjective*

poltergeist *noun* a ghost or spirit that throws things about noisily. [from German *poltern* = make a disturbance, + *geist* = ghost]

poly *noun* (*informal*) a polytechnic.

poly- *prefix* many (as in *polytechnic*). [from Greek *polys* = much]

polyanthus *noun* (*plural* **polyanthuses**) a kind of cultivated primrose. [from *poly-*, + Greek *anthos* = flower]

polychromatic or **polychrome** *adjective* having many colours. [from *poly-*, + Greek *chroma* = colour]

polyester *noun* a kind of synthetic substance.

polygamy (*say* pol-**ig**-a-mee) *noun* the system of having more than one wife (or sometimes husband) at a time. **polygamous** *adjective* [from *poly-*, + Greek *gamos* = marriage]

polyglot *adjective* knowing or using several languages. [from *poly-*, + Greek *glotta* = language]

polygon *noun* a shape with many sides, *Hexagons and octagons are polygons.* **polygonal** *adjective* [from *poly-*, + Greek *gonia* = corner]

polyhedron *noun* a solid shape with many sides. [from *poly-*, + Greek *hedra* = base]

polymer *noun* a substance whose molecule is formed from a large number of simple molecules combined. [from *poly-*, + Greek *meros* = part]

Polynesian *noun* **1** a person whose ancestors came from Polynesia, a group of islands in the Pacific. **2** a Pacific Islander. **3** a group of similar languages spoken in many Pacific islands. **Polynesian** *adjective* [from *poly-*, + Greek *nesos* = island]

polyp (*say* **pol**-ip) *noun* **1** a tiny creature with a tube-shaped body. **2** a small abnormal growth.

polystyrene *noun* a kind of plastic used for insulating or packing things.

polytechnic *noun* a college giving instruction in many subjects at an advanced level. [from *poly-*, + Greek *techne* = skill]

polytheism (*say* **pol**-ith-ee-izm) *noun* belief in more than one god. **polytheist** *noun* [from *poly-*, + Greek *theos* = god]

polythene *noun* a lightweight plastic used to make bags, wrappings, etc.

polyunsaturated *adjective* (of a fat or oil) reacting with other compounds, so not adding to cholesterol levels in the blood.

polyvinyl chloride *noun* a kind of plastic used as a fabric and for electrical insulation etc.

pom or **pommy** *noun* (*NZ, slang*) a British person.

pomegranate *noun* a hard red fruit with many seeds. [from Latin *pomum* = apple, + *granatum* = having many seeds]

pomelo (*plural* **pomelos**) *noun* a kind of large citrus fruit.

pommel *noun* **1** a knob on the handle of a sword. **2** the raised part at the front of a saddle. [from Latin *pomum* = apple]

pomp *noun* stately and splendid ceremonial. [from Greek, = procession]

pompom or **pompon** *noun* a ball of coloured threads used as a decoration.

pompous *adjective* full of great dignity and self-importance. **pompously** *adverb*, **pomposity** *noun* [from *pomp*]

pond *noun* a small lake.

ponder *verb* think deeply and seriously; muse. [from Latin *ponderare* = weigh]

ponderous *adjective* **1** heavy and awkward. **2** laborious, *He writes in a ponderous style.* **ponderously** *adverb* [from Latin *ponderis* = of weight]

Pōneke *noun* a Māori name for Wellington. [Māori form of *Port Nick* = *Port Nicholson*, an early European name for Wellington and its harbour]

ponga *noun* a kind of tree-fern, the silver fern. [Māori]

pontiff *noun* **1** the pope. **2** a bishop; a chief priest. [from Latin *pontifex* = chief priest]

pontifical *adjective* **1** of a pontiff. **2** speaking or writing pompously. **pontifically** *adverb*

pontificate *verb* (**pontificated, pontificating**) speak or write pompously. **pontification** *noun*

pontoon[1] *noun* a boat or float used to support a bridge (a **pontoon bridge**) over a river. [from Latin *pontis* = of a bridge]

pontoon[2] *noun* **1** a card-game in which players try to get cards whose value totals 21. **2** a score of 21 from two cards in this game. [from French *vingt-et-un* = 21]

pony *noun* (*plural* **ponies**) a small horse.

pony-tail *noun* a bunch of long hair tied at the back of the head.

poodle *noun* a dog with thick curly hair.

poof (also **poofter**) *noun* (*slang*) **1** a homosexual male. **2** a boaster or skite.

pooh *interjection* an exclamation of contempt, or of disgust at a bad smell.

pooh-pooh *verb* (*informal*) dismiss (a suggestion etc.) scornfully.

pool[1] *noun* **1** a pond. **2** a puddle. **3** a swimming-pool.

pool[2] *noun* **1** the fund of money staked in a gambling game. **2** a group of things shared by several people.

pool[2] *verb* put money or things together for sharing.

poop *noun* the stern of a ship.

poor *adjective* **1** have very little money or other resources. **2** not good; inadequate, *a poor piece of work.* **3** unfortunate; deserving pity, *Poor fellow!* **poorness** *noun*

poorly *adverb* **1** in a poor way, *She was poorly dressed.* **2** rather ill.

poozle *verb* (*NZ, informal*) fossick or scavenge. **poozler** *noun.*

pop[1] *noun* **1** a small explosive sound. **2** a fizzy drink.

pop[1] *verb* (**popped**, **popping**) **1** make a pop. **2** (*informal*) put or go quickly, *Pop down to the shop.*

pop[2] *noun* modern popular music. [short for *popular*]

popcorn *noun* maize heated to burst and form fluffy balls.

pope *noun* the bishop of Rome, leader of the Roman Catholic Church. [from Greek *papas* = father]

popery *noun* (*contemptuous*) the papal system.

pop-eyed *adjective* with bulging eyes.

popgun *noun* a toy that shoots a cork etc. with a popping sound.

poplar *noun* a tall slender tree.

poplin *noun* a plain woven cotton material.

poppy *noun* (*plural* **poppies**) a plant with showy flowers, often red.

populace *noun* the general public.

popular *adjective* **1** liked or enjoyed by many people. **2** of or for the general public. **popularly** *adverb*, **popularity** *noun* [from Latin *populus* = people]

popularise *verb* (**popularised**, **popularising**) make a thing generally liked or known. **popularisation** *noun*

populate *verb* (**populated**, **populating**) supply with a population; inhabit.

population *noun* the people who live in a district or country; inhabitants.

pop-up *noun* a menu, item, or utility that can be quickly brought to a computer screen.

pōrae *noun* a fish rather like tarakihi. [Māori]

pōrangi *adjective* (*informal*) crazy, perverse. [Māori]

porcelain *noun* the finest kind of china.

porch *noun* (*plural* **porches**) a shelter outside the entrance to a building. [from Latin *porticus* (compare *portico*)]

porcupine *noun* a small animal covered with long prickles. [from Latin *porcus* = pig, + *spine*]

pore[1] *noun* a tiny opening on the skin through which moisture can pass in or out. [from Greek *poros* = passage]

pore[2] *verb* (**pored**, **poring**) **pore over** study with close attention, *He was poring over his books.* [related to *peer*[1]]

pork *noun* meat from a pig. [from Latin *porcus* = pig]

porker *noun* a pig raised for pork.

pornography (*say* porn-**og**-ra-fee) *noun* obscene pictures or writings. **pornographic** *adjective* [from Greek *porne* = prostitute, + *-graphy*]

poroporo *noun* a flowering shrub with edible fruit. [Māori]

porous *adjective* allowing liquid or air to pass through. **porosity** *noun* [same origin as *pore*[1]]

porphyry (*say* **por**-fir-ee) *noun* a kind of rock containing crystals of minerals. [from Latin, = purple stone]

porpoise (*say* **por**-pus) *noun* a sea-mammal rather like a small whale. [from Latin *porcus* = pig, + *piscis* = fish]

porridge *noun* a food made by boiling oatmeal to a thick paste.

port[1] *noun* **1** a harbour. **2** a place where goods pass in and out of a country by ship or aircraft. **3** the left-hand side of a ship or aircraft when you are facing forward. (Compare *starboard.*) [from Latin *portus* = harbour]

port[2] *noun* a strong red Portuguese wine. [from the city of Oporto in Portugal]

portable *adjective* able to be carried. [from Latin *portare* = carry]

portal *noun* **1** a doorway or gateway. **2** an Internet site providing a menu of links to other sites. [from Latin *porta* = gate]

portend *verb* foreshadow; be a sign that something will happen, *Dark clouds portend a storm.* [from Latin *pro-* = forwards, + *tendere* = stretch]

portent *noun* an omen; a sign that something will happen. **portentous** *adjective*

porter[1] *noun* a person whose job is to carry luggage or other goods. [from Latin *portare* = carry]

porter[2] *noun* a person whose job is to look after the entrance to a large building. [from Latin *porta* = gate]

portfolio *noun* (*plural* **portfolios**) **1** a case for holding documents or drawings. **2** a government minister's special responsibility. **3** the investments held by a person, company, etc. [from Italian *portare* = carry, + *foglio* = sheet of paper]

porthole *noun* a small window in the side of a ship or aircraft (formerly a hole for pointing a ship's cannon through).

portico *noun* (*plural* **porticoes**) a roof supported on columns, usually forming a porch to a building. [from Latin *porticus* = porch]

portion *noun* a part or share given to somebody.

portion *verb* divide into portions, *Portion it out.*

portly *adjective* (**portlier**, **portliest**) stout and dignified. **portliness** *noun*

portmanteau (*say* port-**mant**-oh) *noun* a trunk that opens into two equal parts for holding clothes etc.
portmanteau word a word made from the sounds and meanings of two others, e.g. *motel* (from *motor* + *hotel*).
[from French *porter* = carry, + *manteau* = coat]

portrait *noun* a picture of a person or animal.

portray *verb* **1** make a picture of a person or scene etc. **2** describe or show, *The play portrays the king as a kindly man.* **portrayal** *noun*

Portuguese man-of-war *noun* a marine animal related to the jellyfish, having a painful sting.

pose *noun* **1** a position or posture of the body, e.g. for a portrait or photograph. **2** a pretence; unnatural behaviour to impress people.

pose *verb* (**posed**, **posing**) **1** take up a pose. **2** put someone into a pose. **3** pretend. **4** put forward, *It poses several problems for us.*

poser *noun* **1** a puzzling question or problem. **2** a person who poses.

posh *adjective* (*slang*) very smart; high-class; luxurious.

position *noun* **1** the place where something is or should be. **2** the way a person or thing is placed or arranged, *in a sitting position.* **3** a situation or condition, *I am in no position to help you.* **4** paid employment; a job. **positional** *adjective*

position *verb* place a person or thing in a certain position. [from Latin *positum* = placed]

positive *adjective* **1** definite; certain, *We have positive proof that he is guilty.* **2** agreeing; saying 'yes', *We received a positive reply.* **3** greater than nought. **4** of the kind of electric charge that lacks electrons. **5** (of an adjective or adverb) in the simple form, not comparative or superlative, *The positive form is 'big', the comparative is 'bigger', the superlative is 'biggest'.* **6** affirming of a test or condition, *His test results were positive.* **7** showing progress or improvement, *It showed positive growth.* **positively** *adverb.*
positive discrimination the policy of giving preference to disadvantaged groups in allocating resources and jobs, etc.

USAGE The opposite of senses 1–4 is *negative.*

positive *noun* a photograph with the light and dark parts or colours as in the thing photographed. (Compare *negative.*)

positron *noun* a particle of matter with a positive electric charge. [from *positive*]

posse (*say* **poss**-ee) *noun* (*informal*) a group of people.

possess *verb* **1** have or own something. **2** control someone's thoughts or behaviour, *I don't know what possessed you to do such a thing!* **possessor** *noun*

possessed *adjective* seeming to be controlled by strong emotion or an evil spirit, *He fought like a man possessed.*

possession *noun* **1** something you possess or own. **2** possessing.

possessive *adjective* **1** wanting to possess and keep things for yourself. **2** showing that somebody owns something, *a possessive pronoun* (see *pronoun*).

possibility *noun* (*plural* **possibilities**) **1** being possible. **2** something that may exist or happen etc.

possible *adjective* able to exist, happen, be done, or be used. [from Latin *posse* = be able]

possibly *adverb* **1** in any way, *I can't possibly do it.* **2** perhaps.

possie *noun* (also **pozzie**) (*NZ, slang*) a position.

possum *noun* a furry, long-tailed marsupial that lives in trees. It was introduced into New Zealand from Australia.

post[1] *noun* **1** an upright piece of wood, concrete, or metal etc. set in the ground. **2** the starting-point or finishing-point of a race, *He was left at the post.*
post and rail fence (*NZ*) a simple kind of fence.

post[1] *verb* **1** put up a notice or poster to announce something. **2** send a message electronically, *Post it on the Internet.* [from Latin *postis* = post]

post[2] *noun* **1** the official collecting and delivering of letters, parcels, etc. **2** these letters and parcels etc. **3** an Internet posting.
post shop *noun* (*NZ*) an office providing postal services.

post[2] *verb* send a letter or parcel etc. by post.
keep me posted keep me informed.
[same origin as *position*]

post[3] *noun* **1** a position of paid employment; a job. **2** the place where someone is on duty, *a sentry-post.* **3** a place occupied by soldiers, traders, etc.
Last Post a military bugle-call sounded at sunset and at military funerals etc.

post[3] *verb* place someone on duty, *We posted sentries.*

post- *prefix* after (as in *post-war*). [from Latin *post* = after]

postage *noun* the charge for sending something by post.
postage stamp a stamp for sticking on things to be posted, showing the amount paid.

postal *adjective* of or by the post.

postcard *noun* a card for sending messages by post without an envelope.
postcode *noun* a group of figures included in a postal address to assist the sorting of mail.

poster *noun* a large sheet of paper announcing or advertising something, for display in a public place. [from *post*[1]]

posterior *adjective* situated at the back of something. (The opposite is *anterior.*)

posterior *noun* the buttocks. [Latin, = further back]

posterity *noun* future generations of people.

post-haste *adverb* with great speed or haste. [from *post*[2] + *haste*]

posthumous (*say* **poss**-tew-mus) *adjective* happening after a person's death. [from Latin *postumus-* = last]

postie *noun* (*informal*) a person who delivers the post.

postman *noun* (*plural* **postmen**) a person who delivers or collects letters etc.
postwoman *noun* (*plural* **postwomen**)

postmark *noun* an official mark put on something sent by post to show where and when it was posted.

post-mortem *noun* an examination of a dead body to discover the cause of death. [Latin, = after death]

postpone *verb* (**postponed**, **postponing**) fix a later time for something, *They postponed the meeting for a fortnight.* **postponement** *noun* [from *post-*, + Latin *ponere* = to place]

post-primary *adjective* teaching pupils after they have finished primary school.

postscript *noun* something extra added at the end of a letter (after the writer's signature) or at the end of a book. [from *post-*, + Latin *scriptum* = written]

postulant *noun* a person who applies to be admitted to an order of monks or nuns.

postulate *verb* (**postulated**, **postulating**) assume that something is true and use it in reasoning. **postulation** *noun*

postulate *noun* something postulated. [from Latin *postulare* = to claim]

posture *noun* the way a person stands, sits, or walks; a pose.

posture *verb* (**postured**, **posturing**) pose, especially to impress people. [same origin as *position*]

post-war *adjective* of the time after a war.

posy *noun* (*plural* **posies**) a small bunch of flowers.

pot[1] *noun* **1** a deep usually round container. **2** (*slang*) a lot of something, *He has got pots of money.*
go to pot (*slang*) lose quality; be ruined.
take pot luck (*informal*) take whatever is available.

pot[1] *verb* (**potted**, **potting**) **1** put into a pot. **2** (*informal*) abridge, *a potted version of the story.*

pot[2] *noun* (*slang*) marijuana. [short for Spanish *potiguaya* = drink of grief]

pōtae *noun* a hat. [Māori]

potash *noun* potassium carbonate. [from *pot*[1] + *ash*[1] (because it was first obtained from vegetable ashes washed in a pot)]

potassium *noun* a soft silvery-white metal substance that is essential for living things. [from *potash*]

potato *noun* (*plural* **potatoes**) a starchy white tuber growing underground, used as a vegetable. [from South American *batata* (potatoes were first taken to Europe from South America)]

potent (*say* **poh**-tent) *adjective* powerful.
potency *noun* [from Latin *potens* = able]

potentate (*say* **poh**-ten-tayt) *noun* a powerful monarch or ruler. [from *potent*]

potential (*say* po-**ten**-shal) *adjective* capable of happening or being used or developed, *a potential winner.* **potentially** *adverb*, **potentiality** *noun*

potential *noun* an ability or resources etc. available for use or development. [from Latin *potentia* = power]

pothole *noun* **1** a deep natural hole in the ground. **2** a hole in a road.

potholing *noun* exploring underground potholes. **potholer** *noun*

potion *noun* a liquid for drinking as a medicine etc. [from Latin *potus* = having drunk something]

pot-pourri (*say* **poh**-poor-ee) *noun* a scented mixture of dried petals and spices. [French, = rotten pot]

potter[1] *noun* a person who makes pottery.

potter[2] *verb* work or move about in a leisurely way.

pottery *noun* (*plural* **potteries**) **1** cups, plates, ornaments, etc. made of baked clay. **2** a place where a potter works.

pottle *noun* (*NZ*) a small container for food.

potty *adjective* (*slang*) crazy, silly.

pouch *noun* (*plural* **pouches**) **1** a small bag. **2** something shaped like a bag. [from French *poche* = bag or pocket]

pouffe (*say* poof) *noun* a low padded stool. [French]

poultice *noun* a soft hot dressing put on a sore or inflamed place.

poultry *noun* birds (e.g. chickens, geese, turkeys) kept for their eggs and meat.

pounamu *noun* greenstone. [Māori]

pounce *verb* (**pounced**, **pouncing**) jump or swoop down quickly on something. **pounce** *noun*

pound[1] *noun* **1** a unit of money in Britain (= 100 pence). **2** an imperial unit of weight, equivalent to about 0.45 of a kilogram.

pound[2] *noun* **1** a place where stray animals are taken. **2** a public enclosure for vehicles officially removed.

pound[3] *verb* **1** hit something often, especially so as to crush it. **2** run or go heavily, *pounding along*. **3** thump, *My heart was pounding*.

pour *verb* **1** flow; cause to flow. **2** rain heavily, *It poured all day*. **3** come or go in large amounts, *Letters poured in*. **pourer** *noun*

pout *verb* push out your lips when you are annoyed or sulking. **pout** *noun*

poverty *noun* being poor.

POW *abbreviation* prisoner of war.

powder *noun* **1** a mass of fine dry particles of something. **2** a medicine or cosmetic etc. made as a powder. **3** gunpowder, *Keep your powder dry*. **powdery** *adjective*

powder *verb* **1** put powder on something. **2** make into powder. [from Latin *pulveris* = of dust]

power *noun* **1** strength; energy; vigour. **2** the ability to do something; authority. **3** a powerful country, person, or organisation. **4** mechanical or electrical energy; the electricity supply, *There was a power failure after the storm*. **5** (in mathematics) the product of a number multiplied by itself a given number of times, *The third power of 2 = 2 × 2 × 2 = 8*. **powered** *adjective*, **powerless** *adjective*

powerful *adjective* having great power, strength, or influence. **powerfully** *adverb*

powerhouse *noun* a power-station.

power-station *noun* a building where electricity is produced.

pōwhiri *noun* a ceremonial welcome or greeting. [Maori, = beckon forward]

powwow *noun* (*informal*) a meeting for discussion.

pp. *abbreviation* pages.

PR *abbreviation* public relations; proportional representation.

practicable *adjective* able to be done.

practical *adjective* **1** able to do useful things, *a practical person*. **2** likely to be useful, *a very practical invention*. **3** actually doing something, *She has had practical experience*. **practicality** *noun*
practical joke a trick played on somebody. [from Greek *prattein* = do]

practically *adverb* **1** in a practical way. **2** almost, *I've practically finished*.

practice *noun* **1** practising, *Have you done your piano practice?* **2** actually doing something; action, not theory, *It works well in practice*. **3** the professional business of a doctor, dentist, lawyer, etc. **4** a habit or custom, *It is his practice to work until midnight*.
out of practice no longer skilful because you have not practised recently.

USAGE See the note on *practise*.

practise *verb* (**practised**, **practising**) **1** do something repeatedly in order to become better at it. **2** do something actively or habitually, *Practise what you preach*. **3** work as a doctor, dentist, or lawyer. [same origin as *practical*]

USAGE Note the spelling: *practice* is a noun, *practise* is a verb.

practised *adjective* experienced; expert.

practitioner *noun* a professional worker, especially a doctor.

pragmatic *adjective* treating things in a practical way, *Take a pragmatic approach to the problem.* **pragmatically** *adverb,* **pragmatism** *noun,* **pragmatist** *noun* [from Greek, = businesslike]

prairie *noun* a large area of flat grass-covered land in North America. [from Latin *pratum* = meadow]

praise *verb* (**praised, praising**) **1** say that somebody or something is very good. **2** honour God in words.

praise *noun* words that praise somebody or something. **praiseworthy** *adjective* [from Latin *pretium* = value]

pram *noun* a four-wheeled carriage for a baby, pushed by a person walking. [short for *perambulator*]

prance *verb* (**pranced, prancing**) move about in a lively or happy way.

prang *noun* (*slang*) a car crash. **prang** *verb*

prank *noun* a piece of mischief; a practical joke. **prankster** *noun*

prattle *verb* (**prattled, prattling**) chatter like a young child. **prattle** *noun*

prawn *noun* an edible shellfish like a large shrimp.

pray *verb* **1** talk to God. **2** ask earnestly for something; entreat. **3** (*formal*) please, *Pray be seated.*

prayer *noun* praying; words used in praying.

PRC *abbreviation* People's Republic of China.

pre- *prefix* before (as in *prehistoric*). [from Latin *prae* = before]

preach *verb* give a religious or moral talk. **preacher** *noun*

preamble *noun* the introduction to a speech or book or document etc. [from *pre-*, + Latin *ambulare* = go]

prearranged *adjective* arranged beforehand. **prearrangement** *noun*

precarious (*say* pri-**kair**-ee-us) *adjective* not very safe or secure. **precariously** *adverb* [from Latin *precarius* = uncertain]

precaution *noun* something done to prevent future trouble or danger. **precautionary** *adjective* [from *pre-* + *caution*]

precede *verb* (**preceded, preceding**) come or go in front of or before a person or thing. [from *pre-*, + Latin *cedere* = go]

precedence (*say* **press**-i-dens) *noun* priority; a first or earlier place.

precedent (*say* **press**-i-dent) *noun* a previous case that is taken as an example to be followed.

precept (*say* **pree**-sept) *noun* a rule for action or conduct; an instruction.

precinct (*say* **pree**-sinkt) *noun* **1** a part of a town where traffic is not allowed, *a pedestrian precinct.* **2** (**precincts**) the area surrounding a place. [from *pre-*, + Latin *cinctum* = surrounded]

precious *adjective* **1** very valuable. **2** greatly loved. **preciousness** *noun*

precious *adverb* (*informal*) very, *We have precious little time.* [from Latin *pretium* = value]

precipice *noun* a very steep place, such as the face of a cliff. [from Latin *praeceps* = headlong]

precipitate *verb* (**precipitated, precipitating**) **1** make something happen suddenly or soon, *The insult precipitated a quarrel.* **2** throw or send down; cause to fail, *The push precipitated him through the window.* **3** cause a solid substance to separate chemically from a solution. **precipitation** *noun*

precipitate *noun* a substance precipitated from a solution.

precipitate *adjective* hurried; hasty, *a precipitate departure.* [from Latin *praeceps* = headlong]

precipitous *adjective* like a precipice; steep. **precipitously** *adverb*

précis (*say* **pray**-see) *noun* (*plural* **précis**, *say* **pray**-seez) a summary. [French, = precise]

precise *adjective* exact; clearly stated. **precisely** *adverb,* **precision** *noun* [from Latin *praecisum* = cut short]

preclude *verb* (**precluded, precluding**) prevent. [from *pre-*, + Latin *claudere* = shut]

precocious (*say* prik-**oh**-shus) *adjective* developed or having abilities earlier than is usual, *a precocious child.* **precociously** *adverb,* **precocity** *noun* [from Latin *praecox* = ripe very early]

preconceived *adjective* (of an idea) formed in advance, before full information is available, **preconception** *noun*

precursor *noun* a forerunner.

predator (*say* **pred**-a-ter) *noun* an animal that hunts or preys upon others. **predatory** *adjective* [from Latin, = plunderer]

predecessor (*say* **pree**-dis-ess-er) *noun* an earlier person or thing, e.g. an ancestor or the former holder of a job. [from *pre-*, + Latin *decessor* = person departed]

predestine *verb* (**predestined, predestining**) destine beforehand. **predestination** *noun*

predicament (*say* prid-**ik**-a-ment) *noun* a difficult or unpleasant situation.

predicate *noun* the part of a sentence that says something about the subject, e.g. 'is short' in *life is short.* [from Latin *praedicare* = proclaim]

predicative (*say* prid-**ik**-a-tiv) *adjective* forming part of the predicate, e.g. *old* in *The dog is old.* (Compare *attributive.*) **predicatively** *adverb*

predict *verb* forecast; prophesy. **predictable** *adjective*, **prediction** *noun*, **predictor** *noun* [from *pre-*, + Latin *dicere* = to say]

predispose *verb* (**predisposed**, **predisposing**) cause a tendency; influence in advance, *We are predisposed to pity the refugees.* **predisposition** *noun*

predominate *verb* (**predominated**, **predominating**) be the largest or most important or most powerful. **predominant** *adjective*, **predominance** *noun*

pre-eminent *adjective* excelling others; outstanding. **pre-eminently** *adverb*, **pre-eminence** *noun*

pre-empt *verb* **1** take action to prevent a happening. **2** acquire or gain early.

preen *verb* **1** (of a bird) smooth its feathers with its beak. **2** (of a person) smarten. **preen yourself** congratulate yourself.

prefab *noun* (*informal*) a prefabricated building.

prefabricated *adjective* made in sections ready to be assembled on a site. **prefabrication** *noun*

preface (*say* **pref**-as) *noun* an introduction at the beginning of a book or speech. **preface** *verb*

prefect *noun* **1** a school pupil given authority to help to keep order. **2** a district official in France, Japan, and other countries. [from Latin *praefectus* = overseer]

prefer *verb* (**preferred**, **preferring**) **1** like one person or thing more than another. **2** put forward, *They preferred charges of forgery against him.* **preference** *noun* [from Latin *pine* = before, + *ferre* = carry]

preferable (*say* **pref**-er-a-bul) *adjective* liked better; more desirable. **preferably** *adverb*

preferential (*say* pref-er-**en**-shal) *adjective* being favoured above others, *preferential treatment.*

preferment *noun* promotion.

prefix *noun* (*plural* **prefixes**) a word or syllable joined to the front of a word to change or add to its meaning, as in *dis*order, *out*stretched, *un*happy.

pregnant *adjective* having a baby developing in the womb. **pregnancy** *noun* [from *pre-*, + Latin *gnasci* = be born]

prehensile *adjective* (of an animal's foot or tail etc.) able to grasp things. [from Latin *prehendere* = seize]

prehistoric *adjective* belonging to very ancient times, before written records of events were made. **prehistory** *noun*

prejudice *noun* a fixed opinion formed without examining the facts fairly. **prejudiced** *adjective* [from Latin *prae* = before, + *judicium* = judgement]

prelate (*say* **prel**-at) *noun* an important member of the clergy.

preliminary *adjective* coming before an important action or event and preparing for it. [from *pre-*, + Latin *limen* = threshold]

prelude *noun* **1** a thing that introduces or leads up to something else. **2** a short piece of music. [from *pre-*, + Latin *ludere* = to play]

premature *adjective* too early; coming before the usual or proper time. **prematurely** *adverb*

premeditated *adjective* planned beforehand, *a premeditated crime.*

premier (*say* **prem**-ee-er) *adjective* first in importance, order, or time.

premier *noun* **1** a prime minister. **2** (**premiers**) (*NZ & Australia*) a team which wins a major sporting championship. **premiership** *noun* [French, = first]

première (*say* prem-**yair**) *noun* the first public performance of a play or film. [French, = first]

premises *plural noun* a building and its grounds.

premiss (*say* **prem**-iss) *noun* (*plural* **premisses**) a statement used as the basis for a piece of reasoning.

premium *noun* **1** an amount or instalment paid to an insurance company. **2** an extra payment; a bonus.
at a premium above the normal price; highly valued.
[from Latin *praemium* = reward]

premix *verb* mix beforehand, *premixed concrete.*

premonition *noun* a presentiment. [from *pre-*, + Latin *monere* = warn]

preoccupied *adjective* having your thoughts completely busy with something. **preoccupation** *noun*

prep *noun* (*informal*) **1** preparation. **2** school homework.

preparation *noun* **1** preparing. **2** something prepared.

preparatory *adjective* preparing for something.

prepare *verb* (**prepared**, **preparing**) make ready; get ready.
be prepared to be ready and willing to do something.
[from *pre-*, + Latin *parare* = make ready]

preponderate *verb* (**preponderated**, **preponderating**) be more than others or more powerful. **preponderance** *noun*, **preponderant** *adjective* [from Latin *praeponderare* = outweigh]

preposition *noun* a word used with a noun or pronoun to show place, position, time, or means, e.g. *at* home, *in* the hall, *on* Sunday, *by* train. [from *pre-*, + Latin *positum* = placed]

prepossessing *adjective* attractive, *Its appearance is not very prepossessing.*

preposterous *adjective* very absurd; outrageous. [from Latin, = back to front (from *prae* = before, + *posterus* = behind)]

prerequisite *noun* something required as a condition or in preparation for something else, *The ability to swim is a prerequisite for learning to sail.* **prerequisite** *adjective*

prerogative *noun* a right or privilege that belongs to one person or group. [from Latin, = people voting first]

Presbyterian (*say* prez-bit-**eer**-ee-an) *noun* a member of a Church that is governed by people called *elders* or *presbyters* who are chosen by the congregation. [from Greek *presbyteros* = elder]

presbytery *noun* **1** a group of presbyters. **2** the house of a Roman Catholic priest.

preschool *adjective* of the time before a child is old enough to attend school.

preschool *noun* a kindergarten or playcentre.

prescribe *verb* (**prescribed**, **prescribing**) **1** advise a person to use a particular medicine or treatment etc. **2** say what should be done. [from *pre-*, + Latin *scribere* = write]

USAGE Do not confuse with *proscribe.*

prescription *noun* **1** a doctor's written order for a medicine. **2** the medicine prescribed. **3** prescribing.

presence *noun* being present in a place, *Your presence is required.*
presence of mind the ability to act quickly and sensibly in an emergency.

present[1] *adjective* **1** in a particular place, *No one else was present.* **2** belonging or referring to what is happening now; existing now, *the present Queen.*
present tense a tense of a verb showing that an action is now going on, will shortly happen, or occurs regularly, e.g. He *arrives*, he *is arriving.*

present[1] *noun* present times or events. [from Latin *praesens* = being at hand]

present[2] *noun* something given or received without payment; a gift.

present[2] (*say* priz-**ent**) *verb* **1** give, especially with a ceremony, *Who is to present the prizes?* **2** introduce someone to another person or to an audience. **3** put on a play or other entertainment. **4** show. **5** cause, *Writing a dictionary presents many problems.* **presentation** *noun*, **presenter** *noun*

presentable *adjective* fit to be presented to someone; looking good.

presentiment *noun* a feeling that something is about to happen; a foreboding.

presently *adverb* **1** soon, *I shall be with you presently.* **2** now, *the person who is presently in charge.*

preserve *verb* (**preserved**, **preserving**) keep something safe or in good condition. **preserver** *noun*, **preservation** *noun*, **preservative** *adjective & noun*

preserve *noun* **1** jam. **2** an activity that belongs to a particular person or group. [from *pre-*, + Latin *servare* = keep]

preside *verb* (**presided**, **presiding**) be in charge of a meeting etc. [from Latin *prae* = in front, + *-sidere* = sit]

president *noun* **1** the person in charge of a club, society, or council etc. **2** the head of a republic. **presidency** *noun*, **presidential** *adjective* [from *preside*]

press *verb* **1** put weight or force steadily on something; squeeze. **2** make something by pressing. **3** flatten; smooth; iron. **4** urge; make demands, *They pressed for an increase in wages.*

press *noun* (*plural* **presses**) **1** the action of pressing something. **2** a device for pressing things. **3** a device for printing things. **4** a firm that prints or publishes books etc., *Oxford University Press.* **5** newspapers; journalists.
press conference an interview with a group of journalists.
[from Latin *pressum* = squeezed]

press-gang *noun* (in history) a group of men whose job was to force people to serve in the army or navy.

pressing *noun* **1** the applying of force, *The olives have had their first pressing.* **2** an object made by moulding under pressure. **3** a series of objects pressed at one time.

pressure *noun* **1** continuous pressing. **2** the force with which something presses. **3** an influence that persuades or compels you to do something.

pressurise *verb* (**pressurised**, **pressurising**) **1** keep a compartment at the same air pressure all the time. **2** try to compel a person to do something. **pressurisation** *noun*

prestige (*say* pres-**teej**) *noun* good reputation. **prestigious** *adjective* [from Latin, = an illusion]

presumably *adverb* according to what you may presume.

presume *verb* (**presumed**, **presuming**) **1** suppose; assume something to be true. **2** take the liberty of doing something; venture, *May we presume to advise you?* **presumption** *noun*

presumptive *adjective* presuming something. **heir presumptive** see *heir*.

presumptuous *adjective* too bold or confident. **presumptuously** *adverb*

presuppose *verb* (**presupposed**, **presupposing**) suppose or assume something beforehand. **presupposition** *noun*

pre-tax *adjective* before tax is deducted, *pre-tax profits*.

pretence *noun* **1** pretending. **2** a pretext. **false pretences** pretending to be something that you are not, in order to deceive people.

pretend *verb* **1** behave as if something is true or real when you know that it is not, either in play or so as to deceive people. **2** put forward a claim, *The son of King James II was called the Old Pretender because he pretended to the British throne.* **pretender** *noun* [from Latin *prae* = in front, + *tendere* = offer]

pretension *noun* **1** a doubtful claim. **2** pretentious or showy behaviour.

pretentious *adjective* **1** showy; ostentatious. **2** claiming to have great merit or importance. **pretentiously** *adverb*, **pretentiousness** *noun*

pretext *noun* a reason put forward to conceal the true reason. [from Latin *praetextus* = an outward display]

pretty *adjective* (**prettier**, **prettiest**) attractive in a delicate way. **prettily** *adverb*, **prettiness** *noun*

pretty *adverb* quite, *It's pretty cold.*

prevail *verb* **1** be the most frequent or general, *The prevailing wind is from the south-west.* **2** be victorious. [from *pre-*, + Latin *valere* have power]

prevalent (*say* **prev**-a-lent) *adjective* most frequent or common; widespread. **prevalence** *noun* [same origin as *prevail*]

prevaricate *verb* (**prevaricated**, **prevaricating**) say something that is not actually a lie but is evasive or misleading. **prevarication** *noun* [from Latin, = walk crookedly]

prevent *verb* **1** stop something from happening. **2** stop a person from doing something. **preventable** *adjective*, **prevention** *noun*, **preventive** or **preventative** *adjective & noun* [from *pre-*, + Latin *ventum* = come]

preview *noun* a showing of a film or play etc. before it is shown to the general public.

previous *adjective* coming before this; preceding. **previously** *adverb* [from *pre-*, + Latin *via* = way]

prey (*say as* pray) *noun* an animal that is hunted or killed by another for food; a victim.
bird or **beast of prey** one that kills and eats other birds or four-footed animals.

prey *verb* **prey on** hunt or take as prey; cause to worry, *The problem preyed on his mind.* [from Latin *praeda* = booty]

price *noun* **1** the amount of money for which something is bought or sold. **2** what must be given or done in order to achieve something.

price *verb* (**priced**, **pricing**) decide the price of something.

price-fixing *noun* the fixing of prices of goods at a particular level by agreement between sellers or producers.

priceless *adjective* **1** very valuable. **2** (*informal*) very amusing.

prick *verb* **1** make a tiny hole in something. **2** hurt somebody with a pin or needle etc. **prick** *noun*
prick up your ears start listening suddenly.

pricker *noun* (*NZ, informal*) a nuisance or hindrance.

prickle *noun* **1** a small thorn. **2** a sharp-pointed projection on a hedgehog or cactus etc. **3** a feeling that something is pricking you. **prickly** *adjective*

prickle *verb* (**prickled**, **prickling**) feel or cause a pricking feeling.

pride *noun* **1** being proud. **2** something that makes you feel proud. **3** a group of lions.
pride of place the most important or most honoured position.

pride *verb* (**prided**, **priding**) **pride yourself on** be proud of.

priest *noun* **1** a member of the clergy. **2** a person who conducts religious ceremonies. **priestess** *noun*, **priesthood** *noun*, **priestly** *adjective*

prig *noun* a self-righteous person. **priggish** *adjective*

prim *adjective* (**primmer**, **primmest**) formal and correct in manner; disliking anything rough or rude. **primly** *adverb*, **primness** *noun*

prima ballerina (*say* **preem**-a) the chief female dancer in a ballet company.

primacy (*say* **pry**-ma-see) *noun* **1** being the first or most important. **2** the position of primate (= archbishop).

prima donna (*say* **preem**-a) the chief female singer in an opera. [Italian, = first lady]

primary *adjective* first; most important. (Compare *secondary*.) **primarily** (*say* **pry**-mer-il-ee) *adverb*
primary colours the colours from which all others can be made by mixing (red, yellow, and blue for paint; red, green, and violet for light).
primary school a school for the first stage of a child's education.
[same origin as *prime*]

primate (*say* **pry**-mat) *noun* **1** an archbishop. **2** an animal of the group that includes human beings, apes, and monkeys.

prime *adjective* **1** chief; most important, *the prime cause.* **2** excellent; first-rate, *prime beef.*
prime minister the leader of a government.
prime number a number (e.g. 2, 3, 5, 7, 11) that can be divided exactly only by itself and one.
prime stock (*NZ*) livestock that is ready to be killed for meat.
prime time the time at which a television audience is expected to be largest.

prime *noun* the best time or stage of something, *in the prime of life.*

prime *verb* (**primed**, **priming**) **1** prepare something for use or action. **2** put a coat of liquid on something to prepare it for painting. **3** equip a person with information. [from Latin *primus* = first]

primer *noun* **1** a liquid for priming a surface. **2** an elementary textbook.

primeval (*say* pry-**mee**-val) *adjective* of the earliest times of the world. [from Latin *primus* = first, + *aevum* = age]

primitive *adjective* of or at an early stage of development or civilisation; not complicated or sophisticated.
primo *adjective* (*informal*) outstanding, great.

primogeniture *noun* being a first-born child; the custom by which an eldest son inherits all his parents' property. [from Latin *primo* = first, + *genitus* = born]

primordial *adjective* primeval.

primrose *noun* a pale-yellow flower that blooms in spring. [from Latin *prima rosa* first rose]

prince *noun* **1** the son of a king or queen. **2** a man or boy in a royal family. **princely** *adjective* [from Latin *princeps* = chieftain]

princess *noun* (*plural* **princesses**) **1** the daughter of a king or queen. **2** a woman or girl in a royal family. **3** the wife of a prince.

principal *adjective* chief; most important. **principally** *adverb*

principal *noun* **1** the head of a college or school. **2** a sum of money that is invested or lent, *Interest is paid on the principal.* [same origin as *prince*]

> USAGE Do not confuse with *principle* (which is never used of a person).

principality *noun* a country ruled by a prince.

principle *noun* **1** a general truth, belief, or rule, *She taught me the principles of geometry.* **2** a rule of conduct, *Cheating is against his principles.*
in principle in general, not in details.
on principle because of your principles of behaviour.
[from Latin *principium* = source]

> USAGE See the note on *principal.*

print *verb* **1** put words or pictures on paper by using a machine. **2** write with letters that are not joined together. **3** press a mark or design etc. on a surface. **4** make a picture from the negative of a photograph. **printer** *noun*
printed circuit an electric circuit made by pressing thin metal strips on to a surface.

print *noun* **1** printed lettering or words. **2** a mark made by something pressing on a surface. **3** a printed picture, photograph, or design.

printout *noun* information etc. produced in printed form from a computer's printer.

prior *adjective* earlier or more important than something else.

prior *noun* a monk who is the head of a religious house or order. **prioress** *noun* [Latin, = former, more important]

priority *noun* (*plural* **priorities**) **1** being earlier or more important than something else; precedence. **2** something considered more important than other things, *Safety is a priority.* [from *prior*]

priory *noun* (*plural* **priories**) a religious house governed by a prior or prioress.

prise *verb* (**prised**, **prising**) lever something out or open, *Prise the lid off the crate.*

prism (*say* prizm) *noun* **1** a solid shape with ends that are triangles or polygons which are equal and parallel. **2** a glass prism that breaks up light into the colours of the rainbow. **prismatic** *adjective*

prison *noun* a place where criminals are kept as a punishment.

prisoner *noun* **1** a person kept in prison. **2** a captive.

pristine *adjective* ancient and unspoilt; original, *in its pristine form.* [from Latin *pristinus* = former]

private *adjective* **1** belonging to a particular person or group, *private property.* **2** confidential. **3** secluded. **4** not holding public office, *a private citizen.* **5** independent; not organised by a government, *private medicine; a private detective.* **privately** *adverb*, **privacy** (*say* **priv**-a-see) *noun*
in private where only particular people can see or hear; not in public.
private bag (*NZ*) a bag at a postal centre in which all the mail addressed to a particular organisation etc. is kept for collection or delivery.
private parts the genitals.
private school (also **independent school**) (*NZ*) a school not owned by the government, where fees are charged for attendance.

private *noun* a soldier of the lowest rank.

privation *noun* loss or lack of something; lack of necessities. [from Latin *privatus* = deprived]

privatise *verb* (**privatised, privatising**) transfer a nationalised industry etc. to a private organisation. **privatisation** *noun*

privet *noun* an evergreen shrub or tree with poisonous leaves, sometimes used to make hedges.

privilege *noun* a special right or advantage given to one person or group. **privileged** *adjective* [from Latin *privus* = of an individual, + *legis* = of law]

privy *adjective* (*old use*) hidden; secret.
be privy to be sharing in the secret of someone's plans etc.
[from Latin, = private]

Privy Council a group of distinguished people who advise the sovereign.

prize *noun* an award given to the winner of a game or competition etc.

prize *verb* (**prized, prizing**) value something greatly. [from *price*]

pro *noun* (*plural* **pros**) (*informal*) a professional.

pro- *prefix* **1** favouring or supporting (as in *pro-British*). **2** deputising or substituted for (as in *pronoun*). **3** onwards; forwards (as in *proceed*). [from Latin *pro* = for; in front of]

pro and con for and against.
pros and cons reasons for and against something.
[from Latin *pro* = for, + *contra* = against]

probable *adjective* likely to happen or be true. **probably** *adverb*, **probability** *noun* [same origin as *prove*]

probate *noun* the official process of proving that a person's will is valid. [from Latin *probatum* = tested, proved]

probation *noun* the testing of a person's character and abilities. **probationary** *adjective*
on probation being supervised by an official (a **probation officer**) instead of being sent to prison.
[same origin as *prove*]

probationer *noun* a person at an early stage of training.

probe *noun* **1** an instrument for exploring something. **2** an investigation.

probe *verb* (**probed, probing**) **1** explore with a probe. **2** investigate. [from Latin *probare* = to test]

probity (*say* **proh**-bit-ee) *noun* honesty. [from Latin *probus* = good]

problem *noun* **1** something difficult to deal with or understand. **2** something that has to be done or answered. **problematic** or **problematical** *adjective* [from Greek, = an exercise]

proboscis (*say* pro-**boss**-iss) *noun* (*plural* **proboscises**) **1** a long flexible snout. **2** an insect's long mouth-part. [from Greek *pro* = in front, + *boskein* = feed]

procedure *noun* an orderly way of doing something.

proceed *verb* **1** go forward or onward. **2** continue; go on with an action, *She proceeded to explain the plan.* [from *pro-*, + Latin *cedere* go]

proceedings *plural noun* **1** things that happen; activities. **2** a lawsuit.

proceeds *plural noun* the money made from a sale or show etc.; profit.

process[1] (*say* **proh**-sess) *noun* (*plural* **processes**) a series of actions for making or doing something.

process[1] *verb* put something through a manufacturing or other process, *processed cheese.* [same origin as *proceed*]

process[2] (*say* pro-**sess**) *verb* go in procession. [from *procession*]

procession *noun* a number of people or vehicles etc. moving steadily forward following each other.

processor *noun* a machine that processes things.

proclaim *verb* announce officially or publicly. **proclamation** *noun*

procrastinate *verb* (**procrastinated, procrastinating**) put off doing something. **procrastination** *noun*, **procrastinator** *noun* [from *pro-*, + Latin *crastinus* = of tomorrow]

procreate *verb* (**procreated**, **procreating**) produce offspring by the natural process of reproduction. **procreation** *noun*

procure *verb* (**procured**, **procuring**) obtain; acquire. **procurement** *noun* [from *pro-*, + Latin *curare* = look after]

prod *verb* (**prodded**, **prodding**) **1** poke. **2** stimulate into action. **prod** *noun*

prodigal *adjective* wasteful; extravagant. **prodigally** *adverb*, **prodigality** *noun* [from Latin *prodigus* = generous]

prodigious *adjective* wonderful; enormous. **prodigiously** *adverb*

prodigy *noun* (*plural* **prodigies**) **1** a person with wonderful abilities. **2** a wonderful thing. [from Latin *prodigium* = good omen]

produce *verb* (**produced**, **producing**) **1** make or create something; bring into existence. **2** bring out so that it can be seen. **3** organise the performance of a play, making of a film, etc. **4** extend a line further, *Produce the base of the triangle.* **producer** *noun*

produce (*say* **prod**-yooss) *noun* things produced, especially by farmers. [from *pro-*, + Latin *ducere* = to lead]

product *noun* **1** something produced. **2** the result of multiplying two numbers. (Compare *quotient.*)

production *noun* **1** producing. **2** the thing or amount produced.

productive *adjective* producing a lot of things. **productivity** *noun*

prof *noun* (*informal*) a professor.

profane *adjective* irreverent; blasphemous. **profanely** *adverb*, **profanity** *noun*

profane *verb* (**profaned**, **profaning**) treat irreverently. [from Latin *profanus* = outside the temple]

profess *verb* **1** declare. **2** claim; pretend, *She professed interest in our work.* **professedly** *adverb*

profession *noun* **1** an occupation that needs special education and training, *The professions include being a doctor, nurse, or lawyer.* **2** a declaration, *They made professions of loyalty.*

professional *adjective* **1** of a profession. **2** doing a certain kind of work as a full-time job for payment, not as an amateur, *a professional golfer.* **professional** *noun*, **professionally** *adverb*

professor *noun* a university lecturer of the highest rank. **professorship** *noun*

proffer *verb & noun* offer. [from *pro-* + *offer*]

proficient *adjective* doing something properly because of training or practice; skilled. **proficiency** *noun* [from Latin *proficiens* = making progress]

profile *noun* **1** a side view of a person's face. **2** a short description of a person's character or career. **3** a public reputation or significance, *Raising the profile of women in sport.*
keep a low profile not make yourself noticeable.

profit *noun* **1** the extra money obtained by selling something for more than it cost to buy or make. **2** an advantage gained by doing something. **profitable** *adjective*, **profitably** *noun*

profit *verb* (**profited**, **profiting**) get a profit.

profiteer *noun* a person who makes a great profit unfairly. **profiteering** *noun*

profligate *adjective* wasteful; unrestrained. **profligacy** *noun*

profound *adjective* **1** very deep or intense, *We take a profound interest in it.* **2** showing or needing great study. **profoundly** *adverb*, **profundity** *noun* [from Latin *profundus* = deep]

profuse *adjective* lavish; plentiful. **profusely** *adverb*, **profuseness** *noun*, **profusion** *noun* [from *pro-*, + Latin *fusum* = poured]

progenitor *noun* an ancestor.

progeny (*say* **proj**-in-ee) *noun* offspring; descendants.

prognosis (*say* prog-**noh**-sis) *noun* (*plural* prognoses) a forecast or prediction, especially about a disease. **prognostication** *noun* [from Greek *pro-* = before, + *gnosis* = knowing]

program *noun* a series of coded instructions for a computer to carry out.

program *verb* (**programmed**, **programming**) prepare a computer, instrument, or machine by means of a program. **programmer** *noun*

programme *noun* **1** a list of planned events; a leaflet giving details of a play, concert, etc. **2** a show, play or talk etc. on radio or television. [from Greek *programma* = public notice]

progress (*say* **proh**-gress) *noun* **1** forward movement; an advance. **2** a development or improvement.

progress (*say* pro-**gress**) *verb* make progress. **progression** *noun*, **progressive** *adjective* [from *pro-*, + Latin *gressus* = going]

prohibit *verb* (**prohibited**, **prohibiting**) forbid; ban, *Smoking is prohibited.* **prohibition** *noun* [from Latin, = keep off]

prohibitive *adjective* **1** prohibiting. **2** (of prices) so high that people will not buy things.

project (*say* **proh**-jekt or **proj**-ekt) *noun* **1** a plan or scheme. **2** the task of finding out as much as you can about something and writing about it.

project (*say* pro-**jekt**) *verb* **1** stick out. **2** throw outwards. **3** show a picture on a screen. **projection** *noun* [from *pro-*, + Latin *-jectum* = thrown]

projectile *noun* a missile.

projectionist *noun* a person who works a projector.

projector *noun* a machine for showing films or photographs on a screen.

proletariat (*say* proh-lit-**air**-ee-at) *noun* working people.

proliferate *verb* (**proliferated**, **proliferating**) increase rapidly in numbers. **proliferation** *noun* [from Latin *proles* = offspring, + *ferre* = to bear]

prolific *adjective* producing much fruit or many flowers or other things. **prolifically** *adverb*

prologue (*say* **proh**-log) *noun* an introduction to a poem or play etc. [from Greek *pro-* = before, + *logos* = speech]

prolong *verb* make a thing longer or make it last for a long time. **prolongation** *noun*

promenade (*say* prom-in-**ahd**) *noun* **1** a place suitable for walking, especially beside the sea. **2** a leisurely walk. **promenade** *verb* [from French *se promener* = to walk]

prominent *adjective* **1** sticking out; projecting. **2** conspicuous. **3** important. **prominently** *adverb*, **prominence** *noun*

promiscuous *adjective* **1** indiscriminate. **2** having many casual sexual relationships. **promiscuously** *adverb*, **promiscuity** *noun*

promise *noun* **1** a statement that you will definitely do or not do something. **2** an indication of future success or good results, *His work shows promise.*

promise *verb* (**promised**, **promising**) make a promise.

promising *adjective* likely to be good or successful, *a promising pianist.*

promo *noun* (*informal*) a filmed or other item of publicity for a coming event or programme. [abbreviation of *promotion*]

promontory *noun* (*plural* **promontories**) a piece of high land that sticks out into a sea or lake.

promote *verb* (**promoted**, **promoting**) **1** move a person to a higher rank or position. **2** help the progress or sale of something. **promoter** *noun*, **promotion** *noun* [from *pro-*, + Latin *motum* = moved]

prompt *adjective* **1** without delay, *a prompt reply.* **2** punctual. **promptly** *adverb*, **promptness** *noun*, **promptitude** *noun*

prompt *verb* **1** cause or encourage a person to do something. **2** remind an actor or speaker of words when he or she has forgotten them.

prompter *noun* [from Latin *promptum* = produced]

promulgate *verb* (**promulgated**, **promulgating**) make known to the public; proclaim. **promulgation** *noun*

prone *adjective* lying face downwards. (The opposite is *supine.*)
be prone to be likely to do or suffer something, *He is prone to jealousy.*

prong *noun* a spike of a fork. **pronged** *adjective*

pronoun *noun* a word used instead of a noun. **demonstrative pronouns** are *this, that, these, those*; **interrogative pronouns** are *who? what? which?*, etc.; **personal pronouns** are *I, me, we, us, thou, thee, you, ye, he, him, she, her, it, they, them*; **possessive pronouns** are *mine, yours, theirs*, etc.; **reflexive pronouns** are *myself, yourself*, etc.; **relative pronouns** are *who, what, which, that.*

pronounce *verb* (**pronounced**, **pronouncing**) **1** say a sound or word in a particular way, *'Two' is pronounced like 'too'.* **2** declare formally, *I now pronounce you man and wife.* [from *pro-*, + Latin *nuntiare* = announce]

pronounced *adjective* noticeable, *She walks with a pronounced limp.*

pronouncement *noun* a declaration.

pronunciation *noun* **1** the way a word is pronounced. **2** the way a person pronounces words.

> USAGE Note the spelling; this word should not be written or spoken as 'pronounciation'.

proof *noun* **1** a fact or thing that shows something is true. **2** a printed copy of a book or photograph etc. made for checking before other copies are printed. **3** a standard of the strength of whisky etc., *40% proof.*

proof *adjective* able to resist something or not be penetrated, *a bullet-proof jacket.*

prop *noun* **1** a support, especially one made of a long piece of wood or metal. **2** (in rugby) either of two front-row forwards on either side of the hooker in the scrum.

prop *verb* (**propped**, **propping**) support something by leaning it against something else.

propaganda *noun* publicity intended to make people believe something.

propagate *verb* (**propagated**, **propagating**) **1** breed; reproduce. **2** send out or transmit sound, light, etc. **propagation** *noun*, **propagator** *noun*

propel *verb* (**propelled**, **propelling**) push something forward. [from *pro-*, + Latin *pellere* = to drive]

propellant *noun* a substance that propels things, *Liquid fuel is the propellant used in these rockets.*

propeller *noun* a device with blades that spin round to drive an aircraft or ship.

propensity *noun* (*plural* **propensities**) a tendency.

proper *adjective* **1** suitable; right, *the proper way to hold a bat.* **2** respectable, *prim and proper.* **3** (*informal*) complete; great, *You're a proper nuisance!* **properly** *adverb*
proper fraction a fraction that is less than unity, with the numerator less than the denominator, e.g. 3/5.
proper noun see **noun**
[from Latin *proprius* = your own]

property *noun* (*plural* **properties**) **1** a thing or things that belong to somebody. **2** a building or someone's land. **3** a quality or characteristic, *It has the property of becoming soft when heated.* [same origin as *proper*]

prophecy *noun* (*plural* **prophecies**) **1** a statement that prophesies something. **2** the action of prophesying.

prophesy *verb* (**prophesied**, **prophesying**) forecast; foretell. [from Greek *pro* = before, + *phanai* = speak]

prophet *noun* **1** a person who makes prophecies. **2** a religious teacher who is believed to be inspired by God. **prophetess** *noun*, **prophetic** *adjective*
the Prophet Muhammad, who founded the Muslim faith.

propinquity *noun* nearness.

propitiate (*say* pro-**pish**-ee-ayt) *verb* (**propitiated**, **propitiating**) win a person's favour or forgiveness. **propitiation** *noun*, **propitiatory** *adjective*

propitious (*say* pro-**pish**-us) *adjective* favourable.

proponent (*say* prop-**oh**-nent) *noun* the person who puts forward a proposal. [from *pro-*, + Latin *ponere* = to place]

proportion *noun* **1** a part or share of a whole thing. **2** a ratio. **3** the correct relationship in size, amount, or importance between two things. **proportional** *adjective*, **proportionally** *adverb*, **proportionate** *adjective*
proportions *plural noun* size, *a ship of large proportions.*
proportional representation a system in which each political party has a number of Members of Parliament in proportion to the number of votes for all its candidates.
[from *pro-* + *portion*]

propose *verb* (**proposed**, **proposing**) **1** suggest an idea or plan etc. **2** ask a person to marry you. **proposal** *noun* [from *pro-*, + Latin *positum* = put]

proposition *noun* **1** a suggestion. **2** a statement. **3** (*informal*) an undertaking; a matter, *a difficult proposition.*

propound *verb* put forward an idea for consideration. [same origin as *propose*]

proprietary (*say* pro-**pry**-it-er-ee) *adjective* **1** made or sold by one firm; branded, *proprietary medicines.* **2** of an owner or ownership. [same origin as *property*]

proprietor *noun* the owner of a shop or business. **proprietress** *noun*

propriety (*say* pro-**pry**-it-ee) *noun* (*plural* **proprieties**) **1** being proper. **2** correct behaviour.

propulsion *noun* propelling something.

prorogue *verb* (**prorogued**, **proroguing**) stop the meetings of Parliament temporarily without dissolving it. **prorogation** *noun* [from Latin *prorogare* = prolong]

prosaic *adjective* plain or dull and ordinary. **prosaically** *adverb* [from *prose*]

proscribe *verb* (**proscribed**, **proscribing**) forbid by law. [from Latin *proscribere* = to outlaw]

USAGE Do not confuse with *prescribe.*

prose *noun* writing or speech that is not in verse.

prosecute *verb* (**prosecuted**, **prosecuting**) **1** make someone go to a lawcourt to be tried for a crime. **2** perform; carry on, *prosecuting their trade.* **prosecution** *noun*, **prosecutor** *noun* [from Latin *prosecutus* = pursued]

proselyte *noun* a person who has been converted to the Jewish faith or from one religion, opinion, etc. to another.

proselytise *verb* (**proselytised**, **proselytising**) to seek to make converts.

prosody (*say* **pross**-od-ee) *noun* the study of verse and its structure.

prospect *noun* **1** a possibility, *There is no prospect of success.* **2** a wide view.

prospect (*say* pro-**spekt**) *verb* explore in search of something, *prospecting for gold.* **prospector** *noun* [from Latin *pro* = forward, + *specere* = to look]

prospective *adjective* expected to be or to happen; possible, *prospective customers.*

prospectus *noun* (*plural* **prospectuses**) a booklet describing and advertising a school, business company, etc.

prosper *verb* be successful.

prosperous *adjective* successful; rich. **prosperity** *noun*

prostitute *noun* a person who takes part in sexual acts for payment. **prostitution** *noun* [from Latin, = for sale]

prostrate *adjective* lying face downwards.

prostrate *verb* (**prostrated**, **prostrating**) cause to be prostrate. **prostration** *noun* [from Latin *prostratum* = laid flat]

protagonist *noun* **1** the main character in a play. **2** a person competing against another. [from *proto-*, + Greek *agonistes* = actor]

protect *verb* keep safe from harm or injury. **protection** *noun*, **protective** *adjective*, **protector** *noun* [from *pro-*, + Latin *tectum* = covered]

protectorate *noun* a country that is under the official protection of a stronger country.

protégé (*say* **prot**-ezh-ay) *noun* a person who is given helpful protection or encouragement by another. [French, = protected]

protein *noun* a substance that is found in all living things and is an essential part of the food of animals.

protest (*say* **proh**-test) *noun* a statement or action showing that you disapprove of something.

protest (*say* pro-**test**) *verb* **1** make a protest (against). **2** declare firmly, *They protested their innocence.* **3** make a public declaration, *They were protesting the raising of student fees.* **4** make a strong response to an accusation or criticism. **protestation** *noun*, **protestor** *noun* [from *pro-*, + Latin *testari* = say on oath]

Protestant *noun* a member of any of the western Christian Churches separated from the Roman Catholic Church. [because in the 16th century many people protested (= declared firmly) their opposition to the Catholic Church]

proto- *prefix* first. [from Greek *protos* = first or earliest]

protocol *noun* **1** behaviour connected with one's rank. **2** a set of rules in computing that govern the transmission of data between devices.

proton *noun* a particle of matter with a positive electric charge.

prototype *noun* the first model of something, from which others are copied or developed. [from *proto-* + *type*]

protract *verb* prolong in time; lengthen. **protraction** *noun* [from *pro-*, + Latin *tractum* = drawn out]

protractor *noun* a device for measuring angles, usually a semicircle marked off in degrees.

protrude *verb* (**protruded**, **protruding**) project; stick out. **protrusion** *noun* [from *pro-*, + Latin *trudere* = push]

protuberance *noun a* protuberant part. **protuberant** *adjective* sticking out from a surface. [from *pro-*, + Latin *tuber* = a swelling]

proud *adjective* **1** very pleased with yourself or with someone else who has done well. **2** causing pride, *This is a proud moment for us.* **3** full of self-respect and independence, *They were too proud to ask for help.* **4** (of things) imposing, splendid; slightly projecting. **proudly** *adverb* [from Old French *prud* = brave]

prove *verb* (**proved**, **proved** or **proven**, **proving**) **1** show that something is true. **2** turn out, *The forecast proved to be correct.* **provable** *adjective* [from Latin *probare* = to test]

proven (*say* **proh**-ven) *adjective* proved, *a man of proven ability.*

provender *noun* fodder; food.

proverb *noun* a short well-known saying that states a truth, e.g. 'Many hands make light work'. [from *pro-*, + Latin *verbum* = word]

proverbial *adjective* **1** of or in a proverb. **2** well-known.

provide *verb* (**provided**, **providing**) **1** make something available; supply. **2** prepare for something, *Try to provide against emergencies.* **provider** *noun* [from Latin *providere* = foresee]

provided *conjunction* on condition, *You can stay provided that you help.*

providence *noun* **1** being provident. **2** God's or nature's care and protection.

provident *adjective* wisely providing for the future; thrifty. [same origin as *provide*]

providential *adjective* happening very luckily. **providentially** *adverb*

providing *conjunction* provided.

province *noun* **1** a section of a country or other territory. **2** the area of a person's special knowledge or responsibility, *Teaching you to swim is not my province.* **provincial** *adjective*
the provinces the parts of a country outside its capital city or main centres.

provision *noun* **1** providing something. **2** a statement in a document, *the provisions of the treaty.*
provisions *plural noun* supplies of food and drink.

provisional *adjective* arranged or agreed upon temporarily but possibly to be altered later. **provisionally** *adverb*

proviso (*say* prov-**I**-zoh) *noun* (*plural* **provisos**) a stipulation.

provoke *verb* (**provoked**, **provoking**) **1** make a person angry. **2** arouse; stimulate, *The joke provoked laughter.* **provocation** *noun*, **provocative** *adjective* [from *pro-*, + Latin *vocare* = summon]

prow *noun* the front end of a ship.

prowess *noun* great ability or daring.

prowl *verb* move about quietly or cautiously. **prowl** *noun*, **prowler** *noun*

proximity *noun* **1** nearness. **2** the part near something, *in the proximity of the station.* [from Latin *proximus* = nearest]

proxy *noun* (*plural* **proxies**) a person authorised to represent or act for another person.

prude *noun* a person who is easily shocked. **prudish** *adjective*, **prudery** *noun*

prudent *adjective* careful, not rash or reckless. **prudently** *adverb*, **prudence** *noun*, **prudential** *adjective* [same origin as *provide*]

prune[1] *noun* a dried plum.

prune[2] *verb* (**pruned**, **pruning**) cut off unwanted parts of a tree or bush etc.

pry *verb* (**pried**, **prying**) look or ask inquisitively.

PS *abbreviation* postscript.

PSA *abbreviation* (*NZ*) Public Service Association.

psalm (*say* sahm) *noun* a religious song, especially one from the Book of Psalms in the Bible. **psalmist** *noun* [from Greek, = song sung to the harp]

pseudo- (*say* s'**yood**-oh) *prefix* false; pretended. [Greek, = false]

pseudonym *noun* a false name used by an author. [from *pseudo-*, + Greek *onyma* = name]

psychiatrist (*say* sy-**ky**-a-trist) *noun* a doctor who treats mental illnesses. **psychiatry** *noun*, **psychiatric** *adjective* [from *psycho-*, + Greek *iatreia* = healing]

psychic (*say* **sy**-kik) *adjective* **1** of powers or events that seem to be supernatural. **2** of the mind or soul. **psychical** *adjective* [same origin as *psycho-*]

psycho- *prefix* of the mind. [from Greek *psyche* = life or soul]

psychoanalysis *noun* investigation of a person's mental processes, especially in psychotherapy.

psychology *noun* the study of the mind and how it works. **psychological** *adjective*, **psychologist** *noun* [from *psycho-* + *-logy*]

psychopath *noun* a mentally ill person whose behaviour harms or endangers other people.

psychotherapy *noun* treatment of mental illness by psychological methods.

PT *abbreviation* physical training.

PTA *abbreviation* Parent-Teacher Association.

ptarmigan (*say* **tar**-mig-an) *noun* a bird of the grouse family.

pterodactyl (*say* te-ro-**dak**-til) *noun* an extinct reptile with wings. [from Greek *pteron* = wing, + *daktylos* = finger]

PTO *abbreviation* please turn over.

pub *noun* (*informal*) a public house. [abbreviation]

puberty (*say* **pew**-ber-tee) *noun* the time when a young person is developing physically into an adult.

pubic (*say* **pew**-bik) *adjective* of the lower front part of the abdomen.

public *adjective* belonging to or known by everyone, not private. **publicly** *adverb*
public house a place where alcoholic drinks are sold and consumed.
public relations the cultivation, by an organisation or company etc., of a favourable public image.
public school in New Zealand and elsewhere, a school maintained by the state; in England = *private school.*
public service the departments that administer government policies.
public servant *noun*

public *noun* all the people.
in public openly, not in private.
[from Latin *publicus* = of the people]

publican *noun* the person in charge of a public house.

publication *noun* **1** publishing. **2** a published book or newspaper etc.

publicise *verb* (**publicised**, **publicising**) bring something to people's attention; advertise.

publicity *noun* public attention; doing things (e.g. advertising) to draw people's attention to something.

publish *verb* **1** have something printed and sold to the public. **2** announce something in public. **publisher** *noun* [from *public*]

puce *noun* brownish-purple colour. [French, = flea-colour]

puck *noun* a hard rubber disc used in ice hockey.

pucker *verb* wrinkle.

puckeroo *adjective* useless, broken. [from Māori *pakaru* = broken]

pudding *noun* **1** a food made in a soft mass, especially in a mixture of flour and other ingredients. **2** the sweet course of a meal.

puddle *noun* a shallow patch of liquid, especially of rainwater on a road.

pudgy *adjective* podgy.

puerile (*say* **pew**-er-I'll) *adjective* silly and childish. **puerility** *noun* [from Latin *puer* = boy]

puff *noun* **1** a short blowing of breath, wind, or smoke etc. **2** a soft pad for putting powder on the skin. **3** a cake of very light pastry filled with cream.

puff *verb* **1** blow out puffs of smoke etc. **2** breathe with difficulty; pant. **3** inflate or swell something, *He puffed out his chest.*

puffin *noun* a North Atlantic sea-bird with a large striped beak.

puffy *adjective* puffed out; swollen. **puffiness** *noun*

pug *noun* a small dog with a flat face like a bulldog.

pugilist (*say* **pew**-jil-ist) *noun* a boxer.

pugnacious *adjective* wanting to fight; aggressive. **pugnaciously** *adverb*, **pugnacity** *noun* [from Latin *pugnare* = to fight]

pūhā *noun* an edible plant, the sow thistle or rauriki. [Māori]

pukatea *noun* a tall timber tree of the laurel family. [Māori]

pūkeko *noun* a common black and purple New Zealand rail, also called *swamp-hen.* [Māori]

puku *noun* the stomach. [Māori]

pull *verb* **1** make a thing come towards or after you by using force on it. **2** move by a driving force, *The car pulled out into the road.* **pull** *noun*
pull a face make a strange face.
pull off achieve something.
pull somebody's leg tease him or her.
pull through recover from an illness.
pull yourself together become calm or sensible.

pullet *noun* a young hen.

pulley *noun* (*plural* **pulleys**) a wheel with a rope, chain, or belt over it, used for lifting or moving heavy things.

pullover *noun* a knitted garment (with no fastenings) for the top half of the body.

pulmonary (*say* **pul**-mon-er-ee) *adjective* of the lungs. [from Latin *pulmo* = lung]

pulp *noun* **1** the soft moist part of fruit. **2** any soft moist mass. **pulpy** *adjective*

pulpit *noun* a small enclosed platform for the preacher in a church or chapel.

pulsar *noun* a kind of star that emits powerful radiation in regular pulses. [from *pulsating star*]

pulsate *verb* (**pulsated**, **pulsating**) expand and contract rhythmically; vibrate. **pulsation** *noun*

pulsator *noun* a part of a milking machine.

pulse[1] *noun* **1** the rhythmical movement of the arteries as blood is pumped through them by the beating of the heart, *The pulse can be felt in a person's wrists.* **2** a throb.

pulse[1] *verb* (**pulsed**, **pulsing**) throb. [from Latin *pulsum* = driven, beaten]

pulse[2] *noun* the edible seed of peas, beans, lentils, etc.

pulverise *verb* (**pulverised**, **pulverising**) crush into powder. **pulverisation** *noun* [from Latin *pulveris* = of dust]

puma (*say* **pew**-ma) **1** a large brown animal of western America, a cougar or mountain lion. **2** (**Puma**) a member of the Pumas international rugby team of Argentina.

pumice *noun* a kind of porous stone used for rubbing stains from the skin or as powder for polishing things.

pummel *verb* (**pummelled**, **pummelling**) keep on hitting something.

pump[1] *noun* a device that pushes air or liquid into or out of something, or along pipes.

pump[1] *verb* **1** move air or liquid with a pump. **2** (*informal*) question a person to obtain information.
pump up inflate.

pump[2] *noun* a lightweight shoe.

pumpkin *noun* a very large round vegetable with a hard skin.

pun *noun* a joking use of a word sounding the same as another, e.g. 'Deciding where to bury him was a *grave* decision.'

punch[1] *verb* **1** hit with a fist. **2** make a hole in something.

punch[1] *noun* (*plural* **punches**) **1** a hit with a fist. **2** a device for making holes in paper, metal, leather, etc. **3** vigour.
punch line words that give the climax of a joke or story.
[same origin as *puncture*]

punch[2] *noun* a drink made by mixing wine or spirits and fruit-juice in a bowl.

punch-up *noun* (*informal*) a fight.

punctilious *adjective* very careful about details; conscientious. **punctiliously** *adverb*, **punctiliousness** *noun* [from Latin *punctillum* = little point]

punctual *adjective* doing things exactly at the time arranged; not late. **punctually** *adverb*, **punctuality** *noun*

punctuate *verb* (**punctuated**, **punctuating**) **1** put punctuation marks into something. **2** put in at intervals, *His speech was punctuated with cheers.* [from Latin *punctum* = a point]

punctuation *noun* **1** marks such as commas, full stops, and brackets put into a piece of writing to make it easier to read. **2** the action of punctuating.

puncture *noun* a small hole made by something sharp, especially in a tyre.

puncture *verb* (**punctured**, **puncturing**) make a puncture in something. [from Latin *punctum* = pricked]

pundit *noun* a person who is an authority on something. [from Hindi *pandit* = learned (person)]

punga *noun* = **ponga**.

pungent (*say* **pun**-jent) *adjective* **1** having a strong taste or smell. **2** (of remarks) sharp. **pungently** *adverb*, **pungency** *noun* [from Latin *pungens* = pricking]

punish *verb* make a person suffer because he or she has done something wrong. **punishable** *adjective*, **punishment** *noun* [from Latin *poena* = penalty]

punitive (*say* **pew**-nit-iv) *adjective* inflicting punishment.

punk *noun* (*slang*) a young person who dresses or behaves in a way that is meant to shock; a follower of punk rock.
punk rock a loud and aggressive form of rock music, popular in the late 1970s.

punk *adjective* (*slang*) of poor quality, worthless.

punnet *noun* a small container for soft fruit such as strawberries, or for ice-cream, seedlings, etc.

punt[1] *verb* kick a football after dropping it from your hands and before it touches the ground.

punt[2] *verb* gamble; bet on a horse-race. **punter** *noun*

puny (*say* **pew**-nee) *adjective* small or undersized; feeble.

pup *noun* **1** a puppy. **2** a young seal.

pupa (*say* **pew**-pa) *noun* (*plural* **pupae**) a chrysalis.

pupate (*say* pew-**payt**) *verb* (**pupated**, **pupating**) become a pupa. **pupation** *noun*

pupil *noun* **1** someone who is being taught by another person. **2** the opening in the centre of the eye. [from Latin *pupilla* = little girl or doll (the use in sense 2 refers to the tiny images of people and things that can be seen in the eye)]

puppet *noun* **1** a kind of doll that can be made to move by fitting it over your hand or working it by strings or wires. **2** a person whose actions are controlled by someone else. **puppetry** *noun*

puppy *noun* (*plural* **puppies**) a young dog.

purchase *verb* (**purchased**, **purchasing**) buy. **purchaser** *noun*

purchase *noun* **1** something bought. **2** buying. **3** a firm hold to pull or raise something.

purdah *noun* the Muslim or Hindu custom of keeping women from the sight of men or strangers. [Urdu, = veil]

pure *adjective* **1** not mixed with anything else; clean. **2** mere; nothing but, *pure nonsense.* **purely** *adverb*, **pureness** *noun*

purée (*say* **pewr**-ay) *noun* fruit or vegetables made into pulp. [French, = squeezed]

purgative *noun* a strong laxative.

purgatory *noun* (in Roman Catholic belief) a place or condition in which souls are purified by punishment. [same origin as *purge*]

purge *verb* (**purged**, **purging**) get rid of unwanted people or things.

purge *noun* **1** purging. **2** a purgative. [from Latin *purgare* = make pure]

purify *verb* (**purified**, **purifying**) make a thing pure. **purification** *noun*, **purifier** *noun*

pūriri *noun* a timber tree.
pūriri moth the largest moth in New Zealand, with larvae that bore into wood. [Māori]

purist *noun* a person who likes things to be exactly right, especially in people's use of words.

Puritan *noun* a Protestant in England in the 16th and 17th centuries who wanted simpler religious ceremonies and strictly moral behaviour.

puritan *noun* a person with very strict morals. **puritanical** *adjective* [from Latin *puritas* = purity]

purity *noun* pureness.

purl[1] *noun* a knitting-stitch that makes a ridge towards the knitter. **purl** *verb* [from Scottish *pirl* = twist]

purl[2] *verb* (of a stream) ripple with a murmuring sound.

purloin *verb* take something without permission.

purple *noun* deep reddish-blue colour.

purport (*say* per-**port**) *verb* claim, *The letter purports to be from the council.* **purportedly** *adverb*

purport (*say* **per**-port) *noun* meaning.

purpose *noun* **1** what you intend to do; a plan or aim. **2** determination. **purposeful** *adjective*, **purposefully** *adverb*
on purpose by intention, not by accident. [same origin as *propose*]

purposely *adverb* on purpose.

purr *verb* make the low murmuring sound that a cat does when it is pleased. **purr** *noun*

purse *noun* a small pouch for carrying money.

purse *verb* (**pursed**, **pursing**) draw into folds. *She pursed up her lips.* [from Latin *bursa* = a bag]

purser *noun* a ship's officer in charge of accounts. [from *purse*]

pursuance *noun* performing or carrying out an intention etc., *in pursuance of my duties.*

pursue *verb* (**pursued, pursuing**) **1** chase in order to catch or kill. **2** continue with something; work at, *We are pursuing our inquiries.* **pursuer** *noun*

pursuit *noun* **1** the action of pursuing. **2** a regular activity.

purvey *verb* (**purveyed, purveying**) supply food etc. as a trade. **purveyor** *noun* [same origin as *provide*]

pus *noun* a thick yellowish substance produced in inflamed or infected tissue, e.g. in an abscess or boil.

push *verb* **1** make a thing go away from you by using force on it. **2** move yourself by using force, *He pushed in front of me.* **3** try to force someone to do or use something; urge.
push off (*slang*) go away.

push *noun* (*plural* **pushes**) a pushing movement or effort.
at a push if necessary but only with difficulty.

push-chair *noun* a folding chair on wheels, in which a child can be pushed along.

pusher *noun* a person who sells illegal drugs.

Push Play *noun* (*NZ*) a national exercise programme for people of all ages.

pushy *adjective* unpleasantly self-confident and eager to do things.

pusillanimous (*say* pew-sil-**an**-im-us) *adjective* timid; cowardly. [from Latin *pusillus* = small, + *animus* = mind]

puss *noun* (*informal*) a cat.

pussy *noun* (*plural* **pussies**) (*informal*) a cat.
pussy willow a willow with furry catkins.

pustule *noun* a pimple containing pus.

put *verb* (**put, putting**) This word has many uses, including (**1**) move a person or thing to a place or position (*Put the lamp on the table*), (**2**) cause a person or thing to do or experience something or be in a certain condition (*Put the light on. Put her in a good mood*), (**3**) express in words (*She put it tactfully*).
be hard put have difficulty in doing something.
put off postpone; dissuade; stop someone wanting something, *The smell puts me off.*
put out stop a fire from burning or a light from shining; annoy or inconvenience, *Our lateness has put her out.*
put up build; raise; give someone a place to sleep; provide, *Who will put up the money?*
put up with endure; tolerate.

pūtangitangi *noun* the paradise duck. [Māori]

putrefy (*say* **pew**-trif-I) *verb* (**putrefied, putrefying**) decay; rot. **putrefaction** *noun* [from Latin *puter* = rotten]

putrid (*say* **pew**-trid) *adjective* **1** decomposed; rotting. **2** smelling bad.

putt *verb* hit a golf-ball along the ground towards the hole. **putt** *noun*, **putter** *noun*, **putting-green** *noun*

putty *noun* a soft paste that sets hard, used for fitting the glass into a window-frame.

puzzle *noun* **1** a difficult question; a problem. **2** a game or toy that sets a problem or difficult task.

puzzle *verb* (**puzzled, puzzling**) **1** give someone a problem so that they have to think hard. **2** think patiently about how to solve something. **puzzlement** *noun*

PVC *abbreviation* polyvinyl chloride.

pygmy (*say* **pig**-mee) *noun* (*plural* **pygmies**) **1** a very small person or thing. **2** a member of a Black people in Central Africa who are very short.

pyjamas *plural noun* a loose jacket and trousers worn in bed. [from Urdu *pay jama* = leg-clothes]

pylon *noun* a tall framework made of strips of steel, supporting electric cables. [from Greek *pyle* = gate]

PYO *abbreviation* (*NZ*) pick your own (fruit etc.).

pyramid *noun* **1** a structure with a square base and with sloping sides that meet in a point at the top. **2** an ancient Egyptian tomb shaped like this. **pyramidal** (*say* pir-**am**-id-al) *adjective*

pyre *noun* a pile of wood etc. for burning a dead body as part of a funeral ceremony. [from Greek *pyr* = fire]

pyrites *noun* a kind of yellow mineral.

python *noun* a large snake that squeezes its prey so as to suffocate it.

Qq

QC *abbreviation* Queen's Counsel.

QED *abbreviation* quod erat demonstrandum (Latin, = which was the thing that had to be proved).

quack[1] *verb* make the harsh cry of a duck.
quack *noun* [imitation of the sound]

quack[2] *noun* a person who falsely claims to have medical skill or have remedies to cure diseases. [from Dutch *quacken* = to boast]

quad (*say* kwod) *noun* **1** a quadrangle. **2** a quadruplet.

quadrangle *noun* a rectangular courtyard with large buildings round it. [from *quadri-* + *angle*]

quadrant *noun* a quarter of a circle.

quadri- *prefix* four. [from Latin *quattuor* = four]

quadrilateral *noun* a flat geometric shape with four sides. [from quadrilateral]

quadriplegic *noun* a person with paralysis of all four limbs.

quadruped *noun* an animal with four feet. [from *quadri-*, + Latin *pedis* = of a foot]

quadruple *adjective* **1** four times as much or as many. **2** having four parts.

quadruple *verb* (**quadrupled**, **quadrupling**) make or become four times as much or as many. [from *quadri-*]

quadruplet *noun* each of four children born to the same mother at one time.

quadruplicate *noun* each of four things that are exactly alike.

quaff (*say* kwof) *verb* drink.

quagmire *noun* a bog or marsh.

quail[1] *noun* (*plural* **quail** or **quails**) a bird related to the partridge.
quail-hawk *noun* the New Zealand falcon, kārearea.

quail[2] *verb* flinch; feel or show fear.

quaint *adjective* attractive through being unusual or old-fashioned. **quaintly** *adverb*, **quaintness** *noun*

quake *verb* (**quaked**, **quaking**) tremble; shake with fear.

Quaker *noun* a member of a religious group called the Society of Friends, founded by George Fox in England in the 17th century.

qualify *verb* (**qualified**, **qualifying**) **1** make or become able to do something through having certain qualities or training, or by passing a test. **2** make a statement less extreme, limit its meaning. **3** (of an adjective) add meaning to a noun. **qualification** *noun*

quality *noun* (*plural* **qualities**) **1** how good or bad something is. **2** a characteristic; something that is special in a person or thing. [from Latin *qualis* = of what kind]

qualm (*say* kwahm) *noun* a misgiving; a scruple.

quandary *noun* (*plural* **quandaries**) a difficult situation where you are uncertain what to do.

quantify *verb* to measure.

quantity *noun* (*plural* **quantities**) **1** how much there is of something; how many things there are of one sort. **2** a large amount. [from Latin *quantus* = how much]

quantum *noun* (*plural* **quanta**) a quantity or amount.
quantum leap a sudden large increase or improvement in something.

quarantine *noun* keeping a person or animal isolated in case they have a disease which could spread to others. [from Italian *quaranta* = forty (the original period of isolation was 40 days)]

quark[1] *noun* (physics) a particle in the composition of an atom.

quark[2] *noun* a type of soft, unripened cow's milk cheese with a low fat content.

quarrel *noun* an angry disagreement.

quarrel *verb* (**quarrelled**, **quarrelling**) have a quarrel. **quarrelsome** *adjective* [from Latin *querela* = complaint]

quarry[1] *noun* (*plural* **quarries**) an open place where stone or slate is dug or cut out of the ground.

quarry[1] *verb* (**quarried**, **quarrying**) dig or cut from a quarry.

quarry[2] *noun* (*plural* **quarries**) an animal etc. being hunted or pursued.

quart *noun* an imperial unit of volume for liquids, equivalent to about 1.14 litres.

quarter *noun* **1** each of four equal parts into which a thing is or can be divided. **2** three months, one-fourth of a year. **3** a district or region, *People came from every quarter.* **4** mercy towards an enemy, *They gave no quarter.*
quarters *plural noun* lodgings.
at close quarters very close together.

quarter *verb* **1** divide something into quarters. **2** put soldiers etc. into lodgings. [from Latin *quartus* = fourth]

quarterdeck *noun* the part of a ship's upper deck nearest the stern, usually reserved for the officers.

quarterly *adjective & adverb* happening or produced once in every three months.

quarterly *noun* (*plural* **quarterlies**) a quarterly magazine etc.

quartet *noun* **1** a group of four musicians. **2** a piece of music for four musicians. **3** a set of four people or things.

quartz *noun* a hard mineral.

quasar *noun* a very distant star-like object. [from *quasi-stellar*]

quash *verb* cancel or forego something, *The judges quashed his conviction.*

quasi- (*say* **kwayz**-I) *prefix* seeming to be something but not really so, *a quasi-scientific explanation.* [from Latin *quasi* = as if]

quatrain *noun* a stanza with four lines. [from French *quatre* = four]

quaver *verb* tremble; quiver.

quaver *noun* **1** a quavering sound. **2** a note in music (♪) lasting half as long as a crotchet.

quay (*say* kee) *noun* a landing-place where ships can be tied up for loading and unloading; a wharf. **quayside** *noun*

queasy *adjective* feeling slightly sick. **queasily** *adverb*, **queasiness** *noun*

queen *noun* **1** a woman who is the ruler of a country through inheriting the position. **2** the wife of a king. **3** a female bee or ant that produces eggs. **4** an important piece in chess. **5** a playing-card with a picture of a queen on it. **queenly** *adjective*
Queen's chain (*NZ*) a 20-metre wide strip of land along the coastline and river-bank etc. that is for public access and use.
Queen City a name for Auckland.
queen mother a king's widow who is the mother of the present king or queen.
Queen's Counsel a senior barrister.

queer *adjective* **1** strange; eccentric. **2** slightly ill or faint. **queerly** *adverb*, **queerness** *noun*

queer *verb* **queer a person's pitch** spoil his or her chances beforehand.

quell *verb* suppress; subdue.

quench *verb* **1** satisfy your thirst by drinking. **2** put out a fire or flame.

quern *noun* a hand-operated device for grinding corn or pepper.

querulous (*say* **kwe**-rew-lus) *adjective* complaining peevishly. **querulously** *adverb* [same origin as *quarrel*]

query (*say* **kweer**-ee) *noun* (*plural* **queries**) **1** a question. **2** a question mark. [from Latin *quaere* = ask]

quest *noun* a search, *the quest for gold.*

question *noun* **1** a sentence asking something. **2** a problem to be discussed or solved, *Parliament debated the question of immigration.* **3** doubt, *Whether we shall win is open to question.*
in question being discussed or disputed, *His honesty is not in question.*
out of the question impossible.
question mark the punctuation mark ? placed after a question.

question *verb* **1** ask someone questions. **2** say that you are doubtful about something. **questioner** *noun* [from Latin *quaesitum* = sought for]

questionable *adjective* causing doubt; not certainly true or honest or advisable.

questionnaire *noun* a list of questions.

queue (*say* kew) *noun* a line of people or vehicles waiting for something.

queue *verb* (**queued**, **queuing**) wait in a queue. [from Latin *cauda* = tail]

quibble *noun* a petty objection.

quibble *verb* (**quibbled**, **quibbling**) make petty objections.

quiche (*say* keesh) *noun* an open tart with a savoury filling. [French]

quick *adjective* **1** taking only a short time to do something. **2** done in a short time. **3** able to notice or learn or think quickly. **4** (*old use*) alive, *the quick and the dead.* **quickly** *adverb*, **quickness** *noun*

quicken *verb* **1** make or become quicker. **2** stimulate; make or become livelier.

quicksand *noun* an area of loose wet sand which is so deep that heavy objects sink into it.

quicksilver *noun* mercury.

quiescent (*say* kwee-**ess**-ent) *adjective* inactive; quiet. **quiescence** *noun* [from Latin *quiescens* = becoming quiet]

quiet *adjective* **1** silent, *Be quiet!* **2** with little sound; not loud or noisy. **3** calm; without disturbance; peaceful, *a quiet life.* **4** (of colours) not bright. **quietly** *adverb*, **quietness** *noun*

quiet *noun* quietness. [from Latin *quietus* = calm]

quieten *verb* make or become quiet.

quiff *noun* an upright tuft of hair.

quill *noun* **1** a large feather. **2** a pen made from a large feather. **3** one of the spines on a hedgehog.

quilt *noun* a padded bed-cover.

quilt *verb* line material with padding and fix it with lines of stitching.

quin *noun* a quintuplet.

quince *noun* a hard pear-shaped fruit used for making jam.

quinella *noun* a kind of bet where a person tries to forecast the first two finishers.

quinine (*say* kwin-**een**) *noun* a bitter-tasting medicine used to cure malaria.

quinquennial *adjective* lasting or occurring every five years.

quintessence *noun* **1** the essence of something. **2** a perfect example of a quality.

quintet *noun* **1** a group of five musicians. **2** a piece of music for five musicians. [from Latin *quintus* = fifth]

quintuplet *noun* each of five children born to the same mother at one time. [from Latin *quintus* = fifth]

quip *noun* a witty remark.

quirk *noun* **1** a peculiarity of a person's behaviour. **2** a trick of fate.

quit *verb* (**quitted** or **quit**, **quitting**) **1** leave; abandon. **2** (*informal*) stop doing something. **quitter** *noun*

quite *adverb* **1** completely; entirely, *I am quite all right.* **2** somewhat; rather, *She is quite a good swimmer.* **3** really, *It's quite a change.*

quits *adjective* even or equal after retaliating or paying someone.

quiver[1] *noun* a container for arrows.

quiver[2] *verb* tremble. **quiver** *noun*

quixotic (*say* kwiks-**ot**-ik) *adjective* very chivalrous and unselfish, often to an impractical extent. **quixotically** *adverb* [named after Don Quixote, hero of a Spanish story]

quiz (*plural* **quizzes**) *noun* a series of questions, especially as an entertainment or competition.

quiz *verb* (**quizzed**, **quizzing**) question someone closely.

quizzical *adjective* **1** in a questioning way. **2** gently amused. **quizzically** *adverb* [from *quiz*]

quoit *noun* a ring thrown at a peg in the game of **quoits**.

quorum *noun* the smallest number of people needed to make a meeting of a committee etc. valid. [Latin, = of which people]

quota *noun* **1** a fixed share that must be given or received or done. **2** a limited amount. [from Latin *quot* = how many]

quotation *noun* **1** quoting. **2** something quoted. **3** a statement of the price. **quotation marks** inverted commas (see *invert*).

quote *verb* (**quoted**, **quoting**) **1** repeat words that were first written or spoken by someone else. **2** mention something as proof. **3** state the price of goods or services that you can supply.

quoth *verb* (*old use*) said.

quotient (*say* **kwoh**-shent) *noun* the result of dividing one number by another. (Compare *product*.) [from Latin, = how many times]

q.v. *abbreviation* which see. [from Latin *quid vide*]

Rr

rabbi (*say* **rab**-I) *noun* (*plural* **rabbis**) a Jewish religious leader. [Hebrew, = my master]

rabbit *noun* a furry animal with long ears that digs burrows.

rabbiter *noun* (*NZ*) a person employed to kill rabbits.

rabble *noun* a disorderly crowd; a mob.

rabid (*say* **rab**-id) *adjective* **1** fanatical, *a rabid tennis fan.* **2** suffering from rabies. [from Latin *rabidus* = raving]

rabies (*say* **ray**-beez) *noun* a fatal disease that affects dogs, cats, etc. and can infect people.

race[1] *noun* **1** a competition to be the first to reach a particular place or to do something. **2** a strong fast current of water, *the tidal race.* **3** (*NZ*) a fenced passageway for driving sheep etc. through.

race[1] *verb* (**raced**, **racing**) **1** compete in a race. **2** move very fast. **racer** *noun*

race[2] *noun* a very large group of people thought to have the same ancestors and with physical characteristics (e.g. colour of skin and hair, shape of eyes and nose) that differ from those of other groups. **racial** *adjective*
race relations relationships between people of different races in the same country or community.

racecourse *noun* a place where horse-races are run.

racehorse *noun* a horse bred or kept for racing.

racetrack *noun* **1** a racecourse. **2** a motor-racing track.

racialism (*say* **ray**-shal-izm) *noun* racism. **racialist** *noun*

racism (*say* **ray**-sizm) *noun* **1** belief that a particular race of people is better than others. **2** hostility towards people of other races. **racist** *noun*

rack[1] *noun* **1** a framework used as a shelf or container. **2** a bar or rail with cogs into which the cogs of a gear or wheel etc. fit. **3** (in history) a device for torturing people by stretching them.

rack[1] *verb* torment, *He was racked with pain.*
rack your brains think hard in trying to solve a problem.
rack up tally or achieve numerically, *He racked up three wins.*

rack[2] *noun* destruction, *The place has gone to rack and ruin.*

racket[1] *noun* a bat with strings stretched across a frame, used in tennis and similar games. [from Arabic *rahat* = palm of the hand]

racket[2] *noun* **1** a loud noise; a din. **2** a dishonest business; a swindle.

racketeer *noun* a person involved in a dishonest business. **racketeering** *noun*

racoon *noun* an American animal with a bushy tail.

racy *adjective* lively in style, *She gave a racy account of her travels.*

radar *noun* a system or apparatus that uses radio waves to show on a screen etc. the position of objects that cannot be seen because of darkness, fog, distance, etc. [from the initial letters of *radio detection and ranging*]

radial *adjective* **1** of rays or radii. **2** having spokes or lines that radiate from a central point. **radially** *adverb*

radiant *adjective* **1** radiating light or heat etc.; radiated. **2** looking very bright and happy. **radiantly** *adverb*, **radiance** *noun*

radiata pine (**radiata** for short) the main exotic pine tree grown in New Zealand.

radiate *verb* (**radiated**, **radiating**) **1** send out light, heat, or other energy in rays. **2** spread out from a central point like the spokes of a wheel. [from Latin *radius* = ray]

radiation *noun* **1** the process of radiating. **2** light, heat, or other energy radiated. **3** radioactivity.

radiator *noun* **1** a device that gives out heat, especially a metal case that is heated electrically or through which steam or hot water flows. **2** a device that cools the engine of a motor vehicle.

radical *adjective* **1** basic; thorough, *radical changes.* **2** wanting to make great reforms, a *radical politician.* **radically** *adverb*

radical *noun* a person who wants to make great reforms. [from Latin *radicis* = of a root]

radicle *noun* a root that forms in the seed of a plant. [from Latin, = little root]

radio *noun* (*plural* **radios**) **1** the process of sending and receiving sound or pictures by means of electromagnetic waves without a connecting wire. **2** an apparatus for receiving sound (a *receiver*) or sending it out (a *transmitter*) in this way. **3** sound-broadcasting. [from Latin *radius* = ray]

radio- *prefix* **1** of rays or radiation. **2** of radio.

radioactive *adjective* having atoms that break up and send out radiation which produces electrical and chemical effects and penetrates things. **radioactivity** *noun*

radiography *noun* the production of X-ray photographs. **radiographer** *noun* [from *radio-* + *-graphy*]

radiology *noun* the study of X-rays and similar radiation. **radiologist** *noun* [from *radio-* + *-logy*]

radish *noun* (*plural* **radishes**) a small hard round red vegetable, eaten raw in salads. [from Latin *radix* = root]

radium *noun* a radioactive substance found in pitchblende. [from Latin *radius* = ray]

radius *noun* (*plural* **radii** or **radiuses**) **1** a straight line from the centre of a circle or sphere to the circumference; the length of this line. **2** a range or distance from a central point, *The school takes pupils living within a radius of ten kilometres.* [from Latin *radius* = a spoke or ray]

raffia *noun* soft fibre from the leaves of a kind of palm-tree.

raffish *adjective* looking disreputable.

raffle *noun* a kind of lottery, usually to raise money for a charity.

raffle *verb* (**raffled**, **raffling**) offer something as a prize in a raffle.

raft *noun* a flat floating structure made of wood etc., used as a boat.

rafter *noun* any of the long sloping pieces of wood that hold up a roof.

rag[1] *noun* an old or torn piece of cloth.

rag[2] *verb* (**ragged**, **ragging**) (*slang*) tease.

ragamuffin *noun* a person in ragged dirty clothes.

rage *noun* **1** great or violent anger. **2** a craze, *Skateboarding was all the rage.* **3** a conflict in a specific situation, *road rage.* **4** a natural force, *the rage of the wind.*

rage *verb* (**raged**, **raging**) **1** be very angry. **2** be violent or noisy, *A storm was raging.*

ragged *adjective* **1** torn or frayed. **2** wearing torn clothes. **3** jagged. **4** irregular; uneven, *a ragged performance.*

raglan *noun* a sleeve joined to a garment by sloping seams. [named after Lord Raglan, British military commander (died 1855)]

ragtime *noun* a kind of jazz music.

ragwort *noun* a noxious weed with yellow flowers.

rāhui *noun* a sign or mark to warn people against trespassing. [Māori]

raid *noun* **1** a sudden attack. **2** a surprise visit by police etc. to arrest people or seize illegal goods.

raid *verb* make a raid on a place. **raider** *noun*

rail[1] *noun* **1** a level or sloping bar for hanging things on or forming part of a fence, banisters, etc. **2** a long metal bar forming part of a railway track.
by rail on a train.

rail[2] *noun* a marshland bird.

rail[3] *verb* protest angrily.

railings *plural noun* a fence made of metal bars.

railway *noun* **1** the parallel metal bars that trains travel on. **2** a system of transport using rails.

raiment *noun* (*old use*) clothing.

rain *noun* drops of water that fall from the sky. **rainy** *adjective*

rain *verb* **1** fall as rain or like rain. **2** send down like rain, *They rained blows on him.*

rainbird *noun* a bird whose call is thought to foretell rain, e.g. the riroriro.

rainbow *noun* a curved band of colours seen in the sky when the sun shines through rain.

raincoat *noun* a waterproof coat.

raindrop *noun* a single drop of rain.

rainfall *noun* the amount of rain that falls in a particular place or time.

rainforest *noun* thick forest in regions (especially in the tropics) where there is heavy rainfall.

rainwater *noun* water that has fallen as rain.

raise *verb* (**raised**, **raising**) **1** move something to a higher place or an upright position. **2** increase the amount or level of something. **3** collect; manage to obtain, *They raised $100 for CORSO.* **4** bring up young children or animals, *raise a family.* **5** rouse; cause, *She raised a laugh with her joke.* **6** put forward, *We raised objections.* **7** end a siege.

raisin *noun* a dried grape.

raj (*say* rahj) *noun* the period of Indian history when the country was ruled by Britain. [Hindi, = reign]

rajah *noun* an Indian king or prince. (Compare *ranee*.) [Hindi]

rake[1] *noun* a gardening tool with a row of short spikes fixed to a long handle.

rake[1] *verb* (**raked**, **raking**) **1** gather or smooth with a rake. **2** search. **3** gather; collect, *raking it in.*
rake up collect; remind people of an old scandal etc., *Don't rake that up.*

rake[2] *noun* a man who lives an irresponsible and immoral life.

rakish (*say* **ray**-kish) *adjective* like a rake (= *rake*[2]); jaunty.

Rakiura *noun* a Māori name for Stewart Island.

raku *noun* a kind of pottery. [Japanese]

rally *noun* (*plural* **rallies**) **1** a large meeting to support something or share an interest. **2** a competition to test skill in driving. **3** a series of strokes in tennis before a point is scored. **4** a recovery.

rally *verb* (**rallied**, **rallying**) **1** bring or come together for a united effort, *They rallied support. People rallied round.* **2** revive; recover strength.

RAM *abbreviation* random-access memory (in a computer), with contents that can be retrieved or stored directly without having to read through items already stored.

ram *noun* **1** a male sheep. **2** a device for ramming things.

ram *verb* (**rammed**, **ramming**) push one thing hard against another.

Ramadan *noun* the ninth month of the Muslim year, when Muslims fast between sunrise and sunset.

ramarama *noun* a kind of myrtle. [Māori]

ramble *noun* a walk in the countryside.

ramble *verb* (**rambled**, **rambling**) **1** go for a ramble; wander. **2** talk or write a lot without keeping to the subject. **rambler** *noun*

ramifications *plural noun* **1** the branches of a structure. **2** the many effects of a plan or action. [from Latin *ramus* = branch]

ramp[1] *noun* a slope joining two different levels.

ramp[2] *noun* a swindle.

rampage *verb* (**rampaged**, **rampaging**) rush about wildly or destructively. **rampage** *noun*

rampant *adjective* **1** growing or increasing unrestrained, *Disease was rampant in the poorer districts.* **2** (of an animal on coats of arms) standing upright on a hind leg, *a lion rampant.* [from *ramp*[1]]

rampart *noun* a wide bank of earth built as a fortification; a wall on top of this.

ramrod *noun* a straight rod formerly used for ramming an explosive into a gun.

ramshackle *adjective* badly made and rickety, *a ramshackle hut.*

ranch *noun* (*plural* **ranches**) a large cattle-farm in America.

ranchslider *noun a* sliding glass door that opens onto a patio or garden.

rancid *adjective* smelling or tasting unpleasant like stale fat.

rancour (*say* **rank**-er) *noun* bitter resentment or ill will. **rancorous** *adjective*

random *noun* **at random** using no particular order or method, *In housie, numbers are chosen at random.*

random *adjective* done or taken at random, *a random sample.*

ranee (*say* **rah**-nee) *noun* a rajah's wife or widow. [Hindi]

Ranfurly Shield *noun* (*NZ*) an interprovincial rugby union trophy, competed for in games between the holder and its challengers. [donated by the Earl of Ranfurly in 1902]

rangatahi *noun* young people. [Māori]

rangatira *noun* a chief or noble person. [Māori]

rangatiratanga *noun* chieftainship; sovereignty. [Māori]

range *noun* **1** a line or series of things, *a range of mountains.* **2** the limits between which things exist or are available; an extent, *a wide range of goods.* **3** the distance that a gun can shoot, an aircraft can travel, a sound can be heard, etc. **4** a place with targets for shooting-practice. **5** a large open area of grazing-land or hunting-ground. **6** a kitchen fireplace with ovens.

range *verb* (**ranged**, **ranging**) **1** exist between two limits; extend, *Prices ranged from $20 to $50.* **2** arrange. **3** move over a wide area; wander.

ranger *noun* someone who looks after or patrols a park, forest, etc.

rangi *noun* the sky; heaven. [Māori]

rangiora *noun* an evergreen shrub with white downy shoots. [Māori]

rank[1] *noun* **1** a line of people or things. **2** a place where taxis stand to await customers. **3** a position in a series of different levels. *He holds the rank of sergeant.*
the rank and file ordinary people.

rank[1] *verb* **1** arrange in a rank or ranks. **2** have a certain rank or place, *She ranks among the greatest novelists.*

rank[2] *adjective* **1** growing too thickly and coarsely. **2** smelling very unpleasant. **3** unmistakably bad, *rank injustice.* **rankly** *adverb*, **rankness** *noun*

rankle *verb* (**rankled**, **rankling**) cause lasting annoyance or resentment.

ransack *verb* **1** search thoroughly or roughly. **2** rob or pillage a place.

ransom *noun* money that has to be paid for a prisoner to be set free.
hold to ransom hold someone captive or in your power and demand ransom.

ransom *verb* **1** free someone by paying a ransom. **2** get a ransom for someone. [same origin as *redeem*]

rant *verb* speak loudly and violently.

rap *verb* (**rapped**, **rapping**) **1** knock loudly. **2** (*informal*) reprimand. **3** (*slang*) chat. **4** speak rhymes with a backing of rock music.

rap *noun* **1** a rapping movement or sound. **2** (*informal*) blame; punishment, *take the rap*. **3** (*slang*) a chat. **4** rhymes spoken with a backing of rock music.

rapacious (*say* ra-**pay**-shus) *adjective* greedy; plundering. **rapaciously** *adverb*, **rapacity** *noun* [from Latin *rapax* = grasping]

rape[1] *noun* the act of having sexual intercourse with a person without her or his consent.

rape[1] *verb* (**raped**, **raping**) commit rape on a person. **rapist** *noun* [from Latin *rapere* = seize]

rape[2] *noun* a plant grown as food for sheep and for its seed from which oil is obtained.

rapid *adjective* quick; swift. **rapidly** *adverb*, **rapidity** *noun*

rapids *plural noun* part of a river where the water flows very quickly.

rapier *noun* a thin lightweight sword.

rapt *adjective* **1** very intent and absorbed; enraptured. **2** (*slang*) very pleased. **raptly** *adverb* [from Latin *raptum* = seized]

rapture *noun* very great delight. **rapturous** *adjective*, **rapturously** *adverb*

rare *adjective* **1** unusual; not often found or happening. **2** (of air) thin; below normal pressure. **rarely** *adverb*, **rareness** *noun*, **rarity** *noun*

rarefied *adjective* **1** (of air) thin; rare. **2** (of an idea etc.) very subtle.

Rarotongan *noun* **1** a person from Rarotonga, the largest of the Cook Islands. **2** the language of Rarotonga. **Rarotongan** *adjective*

rascal *noun* a dishonest or mischievous person; a rogue. **rascally** *adjective*

rash[1] *adjective* doing something or done without thinking of the possible risks or effects. **rashly** *adverb*, **rashness** *noun*

rash[2] *noun* (*plural* **rashes**) an outbreak of spots or patches on the skin.

rasher *noun* a slice of bacon.

rasp *noun* **1** a file with sharp points on its surface. **2** a rough grating sound.

rasp *verb* **1** scrape roughly. **2** make a rough grating sound or effect.

raspberry *noun* (*plural* **raspberries**) a small soft red fruit.

Rastafarian *noun* a member of a religious group that started in Jamaica. [from *Ras Tafari* (*ras* = chief), the title of a former Ethiopian king whom the group reveres]

rat *noun* **1** an animal like a large mouse. **2** an unpleasant or treacherous person.
rat race a continuous struggle for success in a career, business, etc.

rātā *noun* a large tree with crimson flowers. [Māori]

Rātana *noun* a Māori religious movement founded in 1918 by Tahupōtiki Wiremu Rātana.

ratbag *noun* (*informal*) an irritating or unreliable person.

ratchet *noun* a row of notches on a bar or wheel in which a device (a *pawl*) catches to prevent it running backwards.

rate *noun* **1** speed, *The train travelled at a great rate*. **2** a measure of cost, value, etc., *Postage rates went up*. **3** quality; standard, *first-rate*. **4** a tax paid by householders to the local council.
at any rate anyway.

rate *verb* (**rated**, **rating**) **1** put a value on something. **2** regard as, *He rated me among his friends*. [from Latin *ratum* = reckoned]

rather *adverb* **1** slightly; somewhat, *It's rather dark*. **2** more willingly; preferably, *I would rather not go*. **3** more exactly, *He is lazy rather than stupid*. **4** (*informal*) definitely; yes, *'Will you come?' 'Rather!'*

ratify *verb* (**ratified**, **ratifying**) confirm or agree to something officially, *They ratified the treaty*. **ratification** *noun*

rating *noun* **1** the way something is rated. **2** a sailor who is not an officer.

ratio (*say* **ray**-shee-oh) *noun* (*plural* **ratios**) **1** the relationship between two numbers, given by the quotient, *The ratio of 2 to 10 = 2:10* = 2/10 = 1/5. **2** proportion, *Mix flour and butter in the ratio of two to one* (= two measures of flour to one measure of butter). [from Latin, = reckoning]

ration *noun* an amount allowed to one person.

ration *verb* share something out in fixed amounts. [same origin as *ratio*]

rational *adjective* **1** reasonable; sane. **2** able to reason, *Plants are not rational*. **rationally** *adverb*, **rationality** *noun*

rationalise *verb* (**rationalised**, **rationalising**) **1** make a thing logical and consistent, *Attempts to rationalise English spelling have failed*. **2** invent a reasonable explanation of something, *She rationalised her meanness* *by calling it economy.* **3** make an industry etc. more efficient by reorganising it. **rationalisation** *noun*

rattle *verb* (**rattled**, **rattling**) **1** make a series of short sharp hard sounds. **2** say something quickly, *She rattled off the poem.* **3** (*informal*) make a person nervous or flustered. **rattle your dags** (*NZ, slang*) hurry up!

rattle *noun* **1** a rattling sound. **2** a device or baby's toy that rattles.

rattlesnake *noun* a poisonous American snake with a tail that rattles.

rattling *adjective* **1** that rattles. **2** vigorous; brisk, *a rattling pace.*

ratty *adjective* (*slang*) angry.

raucous (*say* **raw**-kus) *adjective* loud and harsh, *a raucous voice.*

Raukawa *noun* a Māori name for Cook Strait.

raupatu *noun* confiscation. [Māori]

raupō *noun* a kind of bulrush. [Māori]

rauriki *noun* pūhā. [Māori]

ravage *verb* (**ravaged**, **ravaging**) do great damage to something; devastate. **ravages** *plural noun*

rave *verb* (**raved**, **raving**) **1** talk wildly or angrily or madly. **2** talk rapturously about something. **rave** *noun*

ravel *verb* (**ravelled**, **ravelling**) tangle.

raven *noun* a large black bird.

ravenous *adjective* very hungry. **ravenously** *adverb*

ravine (*say* ra-**veen**) *noun* a deep narrow gorge or valley.

ravish *verb* **1** rape. **2** enrapture.

ravishing *adjective* very beautiful.

raw *adjective* **1** not cooked. **2** in the natural state; not yet processed, *raw materials.* **3** without experience, *raw recruits.* **4** with the skin removed, *a raw wound.* **5** cold and damp, *a raw morning.* **rawness** *noun* **raw deal** (*informal*) unfair treatment.

ray[1] *noun* **1** a thin line of light, heat, or other radiation. **2** each of a set of lines or parts extending from a centre. [from Latin *radius* = ray]

ray[2] *noun* a large sea-fish related to the shark.

rayon *noun* a synthetic fibre or cloth made from cellulose.

raze *verb* (**razed**, **razing**) destroy a building or town completely, *raze it to the ground.* [from Latin *rasum* = scraped]

razoo *noun* (*NZ, slang*) an imaginary small coin (in negative contexts only), *He didn't have a brass razoo,* i.e. he had no money at all.

razor *noun* a device with a very sharp blade, especially one used for shaving. [from *raze*]

razzamatazz *noun* (*informal*) showy publicity.

RC *abbreviation* Roman Catholic.

RD *abbreviation* (*NZ*) rural delivery.

re- *prefix* **1** again (as in *rebuild*). **2** back again, to an earlier condition (as in *reopen*). **3** in return; to each other (as in *react*). **4** against (as in *rebel*). **5** away or down (as in *recede*). [Latin]

reach *verb* **1** go as far as; arrive at a place or thing. **2** stretch out your hand to get or touch something. **reachable** *adjective*

reach *noun* (*plural* **reaches**) **1** the distance a person or thing can reach. **2** a distance you can easily travel, *We live within reach of the sea.* **3** a straight stretch of a river or canal.

react *verb* have a reaction.

reaction *noun* **1** an effect or feeling etc. produced in one person or thing by another. **2** a chemical change caused when substances act upon each other.

reactionary *adjective* opposed to progress or reform.

reactor *noun* an apparatus for producing nuclear power in a controlled way.

read *verb* (**read** (*say as* red), **reading**) **1** look at something written or printed and understand it or say it aloud. **2** (of a computer) copy, search, or extract data. **3** indicate; register, *The thermometer reads 20° Celsius.* **readable** *adjective*

reader *noun* **1** a person who reads. **2** a book that helps you learn to read.

readily (*say* **red**-il-ee) *adverb* **1** willingly. **2** easily; without any difficulty.

ready *adjective* (**readier**, **readiest**) able or willing to do something or be used immediately; prepared. **readiness** *noun* **at the ready** ready for use or action.

ready *adverb* beforehand, *This meat is ready cooked.* **ready-made** *adjective*

real *adjective* **1** existing; true; not imaginary. **2** genuine; not an imitation, *real pearls.*

realise *verb* (**realised**, **realising**) **1** be fully aware of something; accept something as true. **2** make a hope or plan etc. happen, *She realised her ambition to become a racing driver.* **3** obtain money in exchange for something by selling it. **realisation** *noun*

realism *noun* seeing or showing things as they really are. **realist** *noun*, **realistic** *adjective*, **realistically** *adverb*

reality *noun* (*plural* **realities**) what is real; something real.

really *adverb* truly; certainly; in fact.

realm (*say* relm) *noun* **1** a kingdom. **2** an area of knowledge, interest, etc., *in the realms of science.*

ream *noun* 500 (originally 480) sheets of paper.
reams *plural noun* a large quantity of writing.

reap *verb* **1** cut down and gather grain etc. when it is ripe. **2** obtain as the result of something done, *They reaped great benefit from their training.* **reaper** *noun*

reappear *verb* appear again.

rear[1] *noun* the back part.

rear[1] *adjective* placed at the rear.

rear[2] *verb* **1** bring up young children or animals. **2** rise up; raise itself on hind legs, *The horse reared in fright.* **3** build or set up a monument etc.

rearguard *noun* troops protecting the rear of an army.

rearrange *verb* (**rearranged**, **rearranging**) arrange in a different way or order. **rearrangement** *noun*

reason *noun* **1** a cause or explanation of something. **2** reasoning; common sense, *Listen to reason.*

USAGE Do not use the phrase *the reason is* with the word *because* (which means the same thing). Correct usage is *We cannot come. The reason is that we both have flu* (not 'The reason is because ...').

reason *verb* **1** use your ability to think and draw conclusions. **2** try to persuade someone by giving reasons, *We reasoned with the rebels.*

reasonable *adjective* **1** ready to use or listen to reason; sensible; logical. **2** fair; moderate; not expensive, *reasonable prices.* **reasonably** *adverb*

reassure *verb* (**reassured**, **reassuring**) restore someone's confidence by removing doubts and fears. **reassurance** *noun*

rebate *noun* a reduction in the amount to be paid; a partial refund. [from *re-* + *abate*]

rebel (*say* rib-**el**) *verb* (**rebelled**, **rebelling**) refuse to obey someone in authority, especially the government; fight against the rulers of your own country.

rebel (*say* **reb**-el) *noun* someone who rebels. **rebellion** *noun*, **rebellious** *adjective* [from *re-*, + Latin *bellare* = fight]

rebirth *noun* a return to life or activity; a revival of something.

rebound *verb* bounce back after hitting something. **rebound** *noun*

rebuff *noun* an unkind refusal; a snub. **rebuff** *verb*

rebuild *verb* (**rebuilt**, **rebuilding**) build something again after it has been destroyed.

rebuke *verb* (**rebuked**, **rebuking**) speak severely to a person who has done wrong. **rebuke** *noun*

rebut *verb* (**rebutted**, **rebutting**) refute; disprove. **rebuttal** *noun* [from *re-* + *butt*]

recalcitrant *adjective* disobedient. **recalcitrance** *noun* [from Latin, = kicking back]

recall *verb* **1** ask a person to come back. **2** bring back into the mind; remember.

recall *noun* recalling.

recant *verb* withdraw something you have said. **recantation** *noun* [from *re-*, + Latin *cantare* = sing]

recap *verb* (**recapped**, **recapping**) (*informal*) recapitulate. **recap** *noun*

recapitulate *verb* (**recapitulated**, **recapitulating**) state again the main points of what has been said. **recapitulation** *noun* [from *re-*, + Latin *capitulum* = chapter]

recapture *verb* (**recaptured**, **recapturing**) capture again; recover. **recapture** *noun*

recede *verb* (**receded**, **receding**) go back from a certain point, *The floods receded.* [from *re-*, + Latin *cedere* = go]

receipt (*say* ris-**eet**) *noun* **1** a written statement that money has been paid or something has been received. **2** receiving something.

receive *verb* (**received**, **receiving**) **1** take or get something that is given or sent. **2** greet someone who comes. [from *re-* = back again, + Latin *capere* take]

received pronunciation *noun* standard form of British English pronunciation.

receiver *noun* **1** a person or thing that receives something. **2** a person who buys and sells stolen goods. **3** an official who takes charge of a bankrupt person's property. **4** a radio or television set that receives broadcasts. **5** the part of a telephone that receives the sound and is held to a person's ear.

recent *adjective* not long past; happening or made a short time ago. **recently** *adverb*, **recency** *noun*

receptacle *noun* something for holding or containing what is put into it.

reception *noun* **1** the way a person or thing is received. **2** a *formal* party to receive guests, *a wedding reception.* **3** a place in a hotel or office etc. where visitors are received and registered.

receptionist *noun* a person whose job is to receive and direct visitors, patients, etc.

receptive *adjective* quick or willing to receive ideas etc.

recess (*say* ris-**ess**) *noun* (*plural* **recesses**) **1** an alcove. **2** a time when work or business is stopped for a while. [same origin as *recede*]

recession *noun* **1** receding from a point. **2** a reduction in trade or prosperity.

recharge *verb* (**recharged**, **recharging**) charge again. **rechargeable** *adjective*

recipe (*say* **ress**-ip-ee) *noun* instructions for preparing or cooking food. [Latin, = take!]

recipient *noun* a person who receives something.

reciprocal (*say* ris-**ip**-rok-al) *adjective* given and received; mutual, *reciprocal help.* **reciprocally** *adverb*, **reciprocity** *noun*

reciprocal *noun* a reversed fraction, $^3/_2$ *is the reciprocal of* $^2/_3$. [from Latin, = moving backwards and forwards]

reciprocate *verb* (**reciprocated**, **reciprocating**) give and receive; do the same thing in return, *She did not reciprocate his love.* **reciprocation** *noun*

recital *noun* **1** reciting something. **2** a musical entertainment given by one performer or group.

recitative (*say* res-it-a-**teev**) *noun* a speech sung to music in an oratorio or opera.

recite *verb* (**recited**, **reciting**) say a poem etc. aloud from memory. **recitation** *noun* [from Latin, = read aloud]

reckless *adjective* rash; heedless, **recklessly** *adverb*, **recklessness** *noun* [from *reck* = heed, + *-less* = without]

reckon *verb* **1** calculate; count up. **2** have as an opinion; feel confident, *I reckon we shall win.*

reclaim *verb* **1** claim or get something back. **2** make a thing usable again, *reclaimed land.* **reclamation** *noun*

recline *verb* (**reclined**, **reclining**) lean or lie back. [from *re-*, + Latin *-clinare* = to lean]

recluse *noun* a person who lives alone and avoids mixing with people. [from *re-* = away, + Latin *clausum* = shut]

recognise *verb* (**recognised**, **recognising**) **1** know who someone is or what something is because you have seen that person or thing before. **2** realise, *We recognise the truth of what you said.* **3** accept something as genuine, welcome, or lawful etc., *Nine countries recognised the island's new government.* **recognition** *noun*, **recognisable** *adjective* [from *re-*, + Latin *cognoscere* = know]

recollect *verb* remember. **recollection** *noun*

recommend *verb* say that a person or thing would be a good one to do a job or achieve something. **recommendation** *noun*

recompense *verb* (**recompensed**, **recompensing**) repay or reward someone; compensate. **recompense** *noun*

reconcile *verb* (**reconciled**, **reconciling**) **1** make people who have quarrelled become friendly again. **2** persuade a person to put up with something, *New frames reconciled him to wearing glasses.* **3** make things agree, *I cannot reconcile what you say with what you do.* **reconciliation** *noun* [from *re-* + *conciliate*]

recondition *verb* overhaul and repair.

reconnaissance (*say* rik-**on**-i-sans) *noun* an exploration of an area, especially in order to gather information about it for military purposes. [French, = recognition]

reconnoitre *verb* (**reconnoitred**, **reconnoitring**) make a reconnaissance of an area.

reconsider *verb* consider something again and perhaps change an earlier decision. **reconsideration** *noun*

reconstitute *verb* (**reconstituted**, **reconstituting**) put together again; reconstruct; reorganise.

reconstruct *verb* **1** construct or build something again. **2** create or act past events again, *Police reconstructed the robbery.* **reconstruction** *noun*

record (*say* **rek**-ord) *noun* **1** information kept in a permanent form, e.g. written or printed. **2** a disc on which sound has been recorded. **3** facts known about a person's past life or career etc., *She has a good school record.* **4** the best performance in a sport etc., or the most remarkable event of its kind, *He holds the record for the high jump.*

record (*say* rik-**ord**) *verb* **1** put something down in writing or other permanent form. **2** store sounds or scenes (e.g. television pictures) on a disc or magnetic tape etc. so that you can play or show them later.

recorder *noun* **1** a kind of flute held downwards from the player's mouth. **2** a person or thing that records something.

record-player *noun* a device for reproducing sound from records.

recount *verb* give an account of, *We recounted our adventures.* [from Old French *reconter* = tell]

re-count *verb* count something again.

recoup (*say* ri-**koop**) *verb* recover the cost of an investment etc. or of a loss.

recourse *noun* a source of help. **have recourse to** go to a person or thing for help.

recover *verb* **1** get something back again after losing it; regain. **2** get well again after being ill or weak. **recovery** *noun*

recreation *noun* **1** refreshing your mind or body after work through an enjoyable pastime. **2** a game or hobby etc. that is an enjoyable pastime. **recreational** *adjective* [from *re-* + *creation*]

recrimination *noun* an angry retort or accusation made against a person who has criticised or blamed you. [from *re-*, + Latin *criminare* = accuse]

recrudescence (*say* rek-roo-**dess**-ens) *noun* a fresh outbreak of a disease or trouble etc. [from *re-*, + Latin *crudescens* = becoming raw]

recruit *noun* **1** a person who has just joined the armed forces. **2** a new member of a society or group etc.

recruit *verb* enlist recruits. **recruitment** *noun*

rectangle *noun* a shape with four sides and four right angles. **rectangular** *adjective* [from Latin *rectus* = straight or right, + *angle*]

rectify *verb* (**rectified**, **rectifying**) correct or put something right. **rectification** *noun* [from Latin *rectus* = right]

rectilinear *adjective* with straight lines, *Squares and triangles are rectilinear figures.* [from Latin *rectus* = straight, + *linear*]

rectitude *noun* moral goodness; rightness of behaviour or procedure. [from Latin *rectus* = right]

rector *noun* **1** a member of the Anglican clergy in charge of a parish. **2** the parish priest of a Roman Catholic church. [Latin, = ruler]

rectory *noun* (*plural* **rectories**) the house of a rector.

rectum *noun* the last part of the large intestine, ending at the anus. [Latin, = straight (intestine)]

recumbent *adjective* lying down. [from *re-*, + Latin *cumbens* = lying]

recuperate *verb* (**recuperated**, **recuperating**) get better after an illness. **recuperation** *noun*

recur *verb* (**recurred**, **recurring**) happen again; keep on happening. **recurrent** *adjective*, **recurrence** *noun* [from *re-*, + Latin *currere* = to run]

recycle *verb* (**recycled**, **recycling**) convert waste material into a form in which it can be reused.

red *adjective* (**redder**, **reddest**) **1** of the colour of blood or a colour rather like this. **2** of Communists; favouring Communism. **redness** *noun*
red admiral a common New Zealand butterfly.
red card a card shown by a referee to a player who is being sent off.
red herring something that draws attention away from the main subject; a misleading clue.
red pine (*old use*) a New Zealand tree, the rimu.
red tape use of too many rules and forms in official business.

red *noun* **1** red colour. **2** a Communist.
in the red in debt (debts were entered in red in account-books).

redden *verb* make or become red.

reddish *adjective* rather red.

redeem *verb* **1** buy something back; pay off a debt. **2** save a person from damnation, *Christians believe that Christ redeemed us all.* **3** make up for faults, *His one redeeming feature is his kindness.* **redeemer** *noun*, **redemption** *noun* [from *re-*, + Latin *emere* = buy]

redevelop *verb* (**redeveloped**, **redeveloping**) develop land etc. in a different way. **redevelopment** *noun*

red-handed *adjective* while actually committing a crime, *He was caught red-handed.*

redhead *noun* a person with reddish hair.

redneck *noun* a person of extremely conservative views.

redolent (*say* **red**-ol-ent) *adjective* **1** having a strong smell, *redolent of onions.* **2** full of memories, *a castle redolent of romance.* [from *re-*, + Latin *olens* = smelling]

redoubtable *adjective* formidable. [from French *redouter* = to fear]

redound *verb* come back as an advantage or disadvantage. *This will redound to our credit.* [from Latin *redundare* = overflow]

redress *verb* set right; rectify, *redress the balance.*

redress *noun* redressing; compensation, *You should seek redress for this damage.*

reduce *verb* (**reduced**, **reducing**) **1** make or become smaller or less. **2** force someone into a condition or situation, *He was reduced to borrowing the money.* **reduction** *noun* [from *re-*, + Latin *ducere* = bring]

redundant *adjective* not needed, especially for a particular job. **redundancy** *noun* [same origin as *redound*]

redwood *noun* a tall Californian conifer.

re-echo *verb* (**re-echoed**, **re-echoing**) echo; go on echoing.

reed *noun* **1** a tall plant that grows in water or marshy ground. **2** a thin strip that vibrates to make the sound in a clarinet, saxophone, oboe, etc.

reedy *adjective* **1** full of reeds. **2** (of a voice) having a thin high tone like a reed instrument. **reediness** *noun*

reef[1] *noun* a ridge of rock or sand etc., especially one near the surface of the sea.

reef[2] *verb* shorten a sail by drawing in a strip (called a *reef*) at the top or bottom to reduce the area exposed to the wind.

reef-knot *noun* a symmetrical double knot that is very secure.

reek *verb* smell strongly or unpleasantly.
reek *noun*

reel *noun* **1** a spool. **2** a lively Scottish dance.

reel *verb* **1** wind something on to or off a reel. **2** stagger.
reel off say something quickly.

re-elect *verb* elect again.

re-enter *verb* enter again.

re-examine *verb* examine again.

ref *noun & verb* (*informal*) referee.

refectory *noun* (*plural* **refectories**) the dining-room of a monastery etc. [from Latin *refectum* = refreshed]

refer *verb* (**referred**, **referring**) pass a problem etc. to someone else, *My doctor referred me to a specialist.* **referral** *noun*
refer to mention; speak about, *I wasn't referring to you*; look in a book etc. for information, *We referred to our dictionary.* [from *re-* = back, + Latin *ferre* = bring]

referee *noun* someone appointed to see that people keep to the rules of a game.

referee *verb* (**refereed**, **refereeing**) act as a referee; umpire.

reference *noun* **1** referring to something, *There was no reference to recent events.* **2** a direction to a book or page or file etc. where information can be found. **3** a testimonial.
in or **with reference to** concerning; about.
reference book a book (such as a dictionary or encyclopedia) that gives information systematically.
reference library a library where books can be used but not taken away.

referendum *noun* (*plural* **referendums**) voting by all the people of a country (not by Parliament) to decide whether something shall be done. [Latin, = referring]

refill *verb* fill again. **refill** *noun*

refine *verb* (**refined**, **refining**) **1** purify. **2** improve something, especially by making small changes.

refined *adjective* **1** purified. **2** cultured; with good manners.

refinement *noun* **1** the action of refining. **2** being refined. **3** something added to improve a thing.

refinery *noun* (*plural* **refineries**) a factory for refining something, *an oil refinery.*

reflect *verb* **1** send back light, heat, or sound etc. from a surface. **2** form an image of something as a mirror does. **3** think something over; consider. **4** be influenced by something, *Prices reflect the cost of producing things.* **reflection** *noun*, **reflective** *adjective*, **reflector** *noun* [from *re-*, + Latin *flectere* = to bend]

reflex *noun* (*plural* **reflexes**) a movement or action done without any conscious thought.
reflex angle an angle of more than 180°. [from *reflect*]

reflexive *adjective* referring back.
reflexive pronoun any of the pronouns *myself, herself, himself,* etc. (as in 'She cut *herself*'), which refer back to the subject of the verb.
reflexive verb a verb where the subject and the object are the same person or thing, as in 'She *cut herself*', 'The cat *washed itself*'.

reform *verb* make or become better by removing faults. **reformer** *noun*, **reformative** *adjective*, **reformatory** *adjective*

reform *noun* **1** reforming. **2** a change made in order to improve something.

reformation *noun* reforming.
the Reformation a religious movement in Europe in the 16th century to reform certain teachings and practices of the Church, which resulted in the establishment of the Reformed or Protestant Churches.

refract *verb* bend a ray of light at the point where it enters water or glass etc. at an angle. **refraction** *noun*, **refractor** *noun*, **refractive** *adjective* [from *re-*, + Latin *fractum* = broken]

refractory *adjective* **1** difficult to control; stubborn. **2** (of substances) resistant to heat.

refrain[1] *verb* stop yourself from doing something, *Refrain from talking.*

refrain[2] *noun* the chorus of a song.

refresh *verb* make a tired person etc. feel fresh and strong again.

refreshment *noun* refreshing.
refreshments *plural noun* drinks and snacks.

refrigerate *verb* (**refrigerated**, **refrigerating**) make a thing extremely cold, especially in order to preserve it and keep it fresh. **refrigeration** *noun* [from *re-*, + Latin *frigus* = cold]

refrigerator *noun* a cabinet or room in which food is stored at a very low temperature.

refuel *verb* (**refuelled**, **refuelling**) supply a ship or aircraft with more fuel.

refuge *noun* a place where a person is safe from pursuit or danger. [from *re-*, + Latin *fugere* = flee]

refugee *noun* a person who has had to leave home and seek refuge somewhere, e.g. because of war or persecution or famine.

refund *verb* pay money back.

refund *noun* money paid back.

refurbish *verb* freshen something up; redecorate.

refuse (*say* ri-**fewz**) *verb* (**refused**, **refusing**) **1** say that you are unwilling to do or give or accept something. **refusal** *noun*

refuse (*say* **ref**-yooss) *noun* waste material, *Trucks collected the refuse.*

refute *verb* (**refuted**, **refuting**) **1** prove that a person or statement etc. is wrong. **2** deny, reject as untrue. **refutation** *noun*

regain *verb* **1** get something back after losing it. **2** reach a place again.

regal (*say* **ree**-gal) *adjective* of or by a monarch; fit for a king or queen. [from Latin *regis* = of a king]

regale (*say* rig-**ayl**) *verb* (**regaled**, **regaling**) feed or entertain well, *They regaled us with stories.*

regalia *plural noun* the emblems of royalty or rank, *The royal regalia include the crown, sceptre, and orb.*

regard *verb* **1** look or gaze at. **2** think of in a certain way; consider to be, *We regard the matter as serious.*

regard *noun* **1** a gaze. **2** consideration; heed, *You acted without regard to people's safety.* **3** respect, *We have a great regard for her.*
regards *plural noun* kind wishes sent in a message. *Give him my regards.*
with regard to concerning.

regarding *preposition* concerning, *There are laws regarding drugs.*

regardless *adverb* without considering something, *Do it, regardless of the cost.*

regatta *noun* a meeting for boat or yacht races. [from Italian]

regency *noun* being a regent.

regenerate *verb* (**regenerated**, **regenerating**) give new life or strength to something. **regeneration** *noun*

regent *noun* a person appointed to rule a country while the monarch is too young or unable to rule. [from Latin *regens* = ruling]

reggae (*say* **reg**-ay) *noun* a West Indian style of music with a strong beat.

regime (*say* ray-*zh***eem**) *noun* a system of government or organisation, *a Communist regime.*

regiment *noun* an army unit, usually divided into battalions or companies. **regimental** *adjective*

region *noun* an area; a part of a country or of the world, *in tropical regions.* **regional** *adjective*, **regionally** *adverb*
in the region of near, *The cost will be in the region of $100.*

register *noun* **1** an official list of things or names etc. **2** a book in which information about school attendances is recorded. **3** a device that records the amount of something automatically, *a cash register.* **4** the range of a voice or musical instrument. **5** the use of language associated with a particular field or profession, e.g. law, medicine.

register *verb* **1** list something in a register. **2** indicate; show, *The thermometer registered 35°.* **3** make an impression on someone's mind. **4** pay extra for a letter or parcel to be sent with special care.
registration *noun*

registrar *noun* an official whose job is to keep written records or registers.

registry *noun* (*plural* **registries**) a place where registers are kept.
registry office an office where marriages are performed and records of births, marriages, and deaths are kept.

regression *noun* **1** a backward movement. **2** reversion; returning to an earlier condition. **regressive** *adjective* [from *re-*, + Latin *gressus* = gone]

regret *noun* a feeling of sorrow or disappointment about something that has happened or been done. **regretful** *adjective*, **regretfully** *adverb*

regret *verb* (**regretted**, **regretting**) feel regret about something. **regrettable** *adjective*, **regrettably** *adverb*

regular *adjective* **1** always happening or doing something at certain times. **2** even; symmetrical, *regular teeth.* **3** normal; standard; correct, *the regular procedure.* **4** of a country's permanent armed forces, *a regular soldier.* **regularly** *adverb*, **regularity** *noun* [from Latin *regula* = a rule]

regulate *verb* (**regulated**, **regulating**) **1** adjust. **2** control. **regulator** *noun*

regulation *noun* **1** regulating. **2** a rule or law. [same origin as *regular*]

regurgitate *verb* (**regurgitated**, **regurgitating**) bring swallowed food up again into the mouth.
regurgitation *noun*

rehab *noun* rehabilitation.

rehabilitation *noun* restoring a person to a normal life or a building etc. to a good condition. **rehabilitate** *verb*

rehash *verb* (*informal*) repeat something without changing it very much.

rehearse *verb* (**rehearsed**, **rehearsing**) practise something before performing to an audience. **rehearsal** *noun*

reign *verb* **1** rule a country as king or queen. **2** be supreme; be the strongest influence, *Silence reigned.*

reign *noun* the time when someone reigns. [from Latin *regnum* = royal authority]

reimburse *verb* (**reimbursed**, **reimbursing**) repay. **reimbursement** *noun*

rein *noun* a strap used to guide a horse. [same origin as *retain*]

reincarnation *noun* being born again into a new body.

reindeer *noun* (*plural* **reindeer**) a kind of deer that lives in Arctic regions.

reinforce *verb* (**reinforced**, **reinforcing**) strengthen by adding extra people or supports etc.

reinforcement *noun* **1** reinforcing. **2** something that reinforces.
reinforcements *plural noun* extra troops or ships etc. sent to strengthen a force.

reinsman *noun* a harness-racing driver.

reinstate *verb* (**reinstated**, **reinstating**) put a person or thing back into a former position. **reinstatement** *noun*

reiterate *verb* (**reiterated**, **reiterating**) say something again and again. **reiteration** *noun* [from *re-*, + Latin *iterum* = again]

reject *verb* **1** refuse to accept a person or thing. **2** throw away; discard. **rejection** *noun* [from *re-* = away, + Latin *-jectum* = thrown]

rejoice *verb* (**rejoiced**, **rejoicing**) feel or show great joy.

rejoin *verb* **1** join again. **2** answer; retort.

rejoinder *noun* an answer; a retort.

rejuvenate *verb* (**rejuvenated**, **rejuvenating**) make a person seem young again. **rejuvenation** *noun* [from *re-*, + Latin *juvenis* = young]

relapse *verb* (**relapsed**, **relapsing**) return to a previous condition; become worse after improving. **relapse** *noun* [from *re-*, + Latin *lapsum* = slipped]

relate *verb* (**related**, **relating**) **1** narrate. **2** connect or compare one thing with another. **3** behave happily towards people or animals. *Some people cannot relate to animals.*

related *adjective* belonging to the same family.

relation *noun* **1** a relative. **2** the way one thing is related to another.

relationship *noun* **1** how people or things are related. **2** how people get on with each other. **3** an emotional and sexual association between two people, *They're in a relationship.*

relative *noun* a person who is related to another.

relative *adjective* connected or compared with something; compared with the average. *They live in relative comfort.* **relatively** *adverb*
relative pronoun see *pronoun.*

relax *verb* **1** become less strict or stiff. **2** stop working; rest. **relaxation** *noun* [from *re-* = back, +Latin *laxus* = loose]

relay *verb* pass on a message or broadcast.

relay *noun* **1** a fresh group taking the place of another, *The firemen worked in relays.* **2** a relay race. **3** an electronic device for relaying a message or broadcast.
relay race a race between teams in which each person covers part of the distance.

release *verb* (**released**, **releasing**) **1** set free; unfasten. **2** let a thing fall or fly or go out. **3** make a movie or record etc. available to the public.

release *noun* **1** being released. **2** something released. **3** a device that unfastens something.

relegate *verb* (**relegated**, **relegating**) **1** put into a less important place. **2** put a sports team into a lower division of a league. **relegation** *noun* [from *re-* = back, + Latin *legatum* = sent]

relent *verb* become less severe or more merciful. [from *re-* = back, + Latin *lentus* = flexible]

relentless *adjective* not relenting; pitiless. **relentlessly** *adverb*

relevant *adjective* connected with what is being discussed or dealt with. (The opposite is *irrelevant.*) **relevance** *noun*

reliable *adjective* able to be relied on; trustworthy. **reliably** adverb, **reliability** *noun*

reliance *noun* relying; trust. **reliant** *adjective*

relic *noun* something that has survived from an earlier time. [same origin as *relinquish*]

relief *noun* **1** the ending or lessening of pain, trouble, boredom, etc. **2** something that gives relief or help. **3** a person who takes over a turn of duty when another finishes. **4** a method of making a design etc. that stands out from a surface.
relief map a map that shows hills and valleys by shading or moulding.
[from *re-*, + Latin *levis* = lightweight]

relieve *verb* (**relieved**, **relieving**) give relief to a person or thing.
relieve of take something from a person, *The thief relieved him of his wallet.*

religion *noun* what people believe about God or gods, and how they worship. [from Latin *religio* = reverence]

religious *adjective* **1** of religion. **2** believing firmly in a religion and taking part in its customs. **religiously** *adverb*

relinquish *verb* give up; let go. **relinquishment** *noun* [from *re-* = behind, + Latin *linquere* = leave]

relish *noun* **1** great enjoyment. **2** something tasty that adds flavour to plainer food.

relish *verb* enjoy greatly.

rellie *noun* (*NZ, slang*) a relative.

reluctant *adjective* unwilling; not keen. **reluctantly** *adverb*, **reluctance** *noun* [from Latin, = struggling against something]

rely *verb* (**relied**, **relying**) **rely on** trust a person or thing to help or support you.

remain *verb* **1** be there after other parts have gone or been dealt with; be left over. **2** continue to be in the same place or condition; stay. [from *re-* = behind, Latin *manere* = stay]

remainder *noun* **1** the remaining part or people or things. **2** the number left after subtraction or division.

remains *plural noun* **1** all that is left over after other parts have been removed or destroyed. **2** ancient ruins or objects; relics. **3** a dead body.

remand *verb* send back a prisoner into custody while further evidence is sought. **remand** *noun* [from *re-*, + Latin *mandare* = entrust]

remark *noun* something said; a comment.

remark *verb* **1** make a remark; say. **2** notice.

remarkable *adjective* unusual; extraordinary. **remarkably** *adverb*

remedial *adjective* helping to cure an illness or deficiency.

remedy *noun* (*plural* **remedies**) something that cures or relieves a disease etc. or that puts a matter right.

remedy *verb* (**remedied**, **remedying**) be a remedy for something; put right. [from *re-*, + Latin *mederi* = heal]

remember *verb* **1** keep something in your mind. **2** bring something back into your mind. **remembrance** *noun* [from *re-*, + Latin *memor* = mindful]

remind *verb* help or cause a person to remember something. **reminder** *noun*

reminisce (*say* rem-in-**iss**) *verb* (**reminisced**, **reminiscing**) think or talk about things that you remember. **reminiscence** *noun*, **reminiscent** *adjective*

remiss *adjective* negligent; careless about doing what you ought to do.

remit (*say* **ree**-mit) *noun* a proposal put forward for adoption at a political conference etc.

remit (*say* re-**mit**) *verb* (**remitted**, **remitting**) **1** send, especially money. **2** forgive; reduce or cancel a punishment etc. **3** make or become less intense; slacken, *We must not remit our efforts.* **remission** *noun* [from *re-* = back, + Latin *mittere* = send]

remittance *noun* **1** sending money. **2** the money sent.

remnant *noun* a part or piece left over from something. [compare *remain*]

remonstrate *verb* (**remonstrated**, **remonstrating**) make a protest, *We remonstrated with him about his behaviour.* [from *re-* = against, + Latin *monstrare* = to show]

remorse *noun* deep regret for having done wrong. **remorseful** *adjective*, **remorsefully** *adverb* [from *re-* = back, + Latin *morsum* = bitten]

remorseless *adjective* relentless.

remote *adjective* **1** far away. **2** some but very little; unlikely, *a remote chance.* **remotely** *adverb*, **remoteness** *noun*
remote control controlling something from a distance, usually by signals transmitted from a radio or electronic device; (also **remote**) such a device.
[from Latin *remotum* = removed]

removable *adjective* able to be removed.

removal *noun* removing or moving something.

remove *verb* (**removed**, **removing**) take something away or off.

remove *noun* a distance or degree away from something, *That is several removes from the truth.*

remunerate *verb* (**remunerated**, **remunerating**) pay or reward someone. **remuneration** *noun*, **remunerative** *adjective* [from re-, + Latin *muneris* of a gift]

Renaissance (*say* ren-**ay**-sans) *noun* the revival of classical styles of art and literature in Europe in the 14th–16th centuries. [French, = rebirth]

renal (*say* **reen**-al) *adjective* of the kidneys.

rend *verb* (**rent**, **rending**) rip; tear.

render *verb* **1** give or perform something, *render help to the victims.* **2** cause to become, *The shock rendered us speechless.* [from Latin *reddere* = give back]

rendezvous (*say* **rond**-ay-voo) *noun* (*plural* **rendezvous**, *say* **rond**-ay-vooz) a meeting with somebody; a place arranged for this. [from French *rendezvous* = present yourselves]

renegade (*say* **ren**-ig-ayd) *noun* a person who deserts a group or religion etc. [from *re-* = back, + Latin *negare* = deny]

renew *verb* **1** restore something to its original condition or replace it with something new. **2** begin or make or give again, *We renewed our request.* **renewal** *noun*

renewable *adjective* able to be renewed.

rennet *noun* a substance used to curdle milk in making cheese.

renounce *verb* (**renounced**, **renouncing**) give up; reject. **renunciation** *noun* [from *re-* = back, + Latin *nuntiare* = announce]

renovate *verb* (**renovated**, **renovating**) repair a thing and make it look new. **renovation** *noun* [from *re-*, + Latin *novus* = new]

renown *noun* fame. **renowned** *adjective*

rent[1] *noun* a regular payment for the use of something, especially a house that belongs to another person.

rent[1] *verb* have or allow the use of something in return for rent.

rent[2] *past tense* of **rend**.

rent[2] *noun* a torn place; a split.

rental *noun* **1** a payment for rent. **2** a rented house, car, television, etc.

renunciation *noun* renouncing something.

reo *noun* (a) language. **te reo Māori** the Māori language. [Māori]

reorganise *verb* (**reorganised**, **reorganising**) organise in a new way.

rep *noun* (*informal*) *a* representative, *He's a Wellington rugby rep.* [abbreviation]

repair[1] *verb* put something into good condition after it has been damaged or broken etc. **repairable** *adjective*

repair[1] *noun* repairing; being repaired. [from *re-*, + Latin *parare* = make ready]

repair[2] *verb* (*formal*) go, *The guests repaired to the dining-room.* [same origin as *repatriate*]

reparation *noun* compensation; amends.

repartee *noun* a witty reply.

repast *noun* (*formal*) *a* meal.

repatriate *verb* (**repatriated**, **repatriating**) send a person back to his or her own country. **repatriation** *noun* [from *re-*, + Latin *patria* = native country]

repay *verb* (**repaid**, **repaying**) pay back, especially money. **repayable** *adjective*, **repayment** *noun*

repeal *verb* cancel a law officially. **repeal** *noun*

repeat *verb* say or do the same thing again. **repeatedly** *adverb*

repeat *noun* **1** the action of repeating. **2** something that is repeated. **repeat offender** a person who commits the same or similar crime again. [from *re-*, + Latin *petere* = seek]

repel *verb* (**repelled**, **repelling**) **1** drive away; repulse, *repel the attack.* **2** disgust somebody. **repellent** *adjective & noun* [from *re-*, + Latin *pellere* = to drive]

repent *verb* be sorry for what you have done. **repentance** *noun*, **repentant** *adjective* [*from re- + penitent*]

repercussion *noun* a result or reaction produced indirectly by something.

repertoire (*say* **rep**-er-twahr) *noun* a stock of songs or plays etc. that a person or company knows and can perform.

repertory *noun* a repertoire. **repertory company** or **theatre** a company or theatre giving performances of various plays for short periods.

repetition *noun* repeating; something repeated. **repetitious** *adjective*

repetitive *adjective* full of repetitions. **repetitively** *adverb*

replace *verb* (**replaced**, **replacing**) **1** put a thing back in its place. **2** take the place of another person or thing. **3** put a new or different thing in place of something. **replacement** *noun*

replay *verb* play a sports match or a recording again. **replay** *noun*

replenish *verb* fill again; add a new supply of something. **replenishment** *noun* [from *re-*, + Latin *plenus* = full]

replete *adjective* **1** well supplied. **2** feeling full after eating. [from *re-*, + Latin *-pletum* = filled]

replica *noun* an exact copy.

reply *noun* (*plural* **replies**) something said or written to deal with a question, letter, etc.; an answer.

reply *verb* (**replied**, **replying**) give a reply to; answer.

report *verb* **1** describe something that has happened or that you have done or studied. **2** make a complaint or accusation against somebody. **3** go and tell somebody that you have arrived or are ready for work.

report *noun* **1** a description or account of something. **2** a regular statement of how someone has worked or behaved, e.g. at school. **3** an explosive sound. [from *re-* = back, + Latin *portare* = carry]

reporter *noun* a person whose job is to collect and report news for a newspaper, radio or television programme, etc.

repose *noun* rest; sleep.

repose *verb* (**reposed**, **reposing**) rest or lie somewhere.

repository *noun* (*plural* **repositories**) a place where things are stored.

reprehensible *adjective* deserving blame or rebuke.

represent *verb* **1** show a person or thing in a picture or play etc. **2** symbolise; stand for, *In Roman numerals, V represents 5.* **3** be an example or equivalent of something. **4** help someone by speaking or doing something on their behalf. **5** (*NZ*) be selected to play for (one's province or country etc.). **6** be elected as a member of parliament etc., *He represented Auckland Central.* **representation** *noun*

representative *noun* a person or thing that represents another or others.

representative *adjective* **1** representing others. **2** typical of a group.

repress *verb* keep down; restrain; suppress. **repression** *noun*, **repressive** *adjective*

reprieve *noun* postponement or cancellation of a punishment etc., especially the death penalty.

reprieve *verb* (**reprieved**, **reprieving**) give a reprieve to.

reprimand *noun* a rebuke, especially a *formal* or official one.

reprimand *verb* give someone a reprimand.

reprisal *noun* an act of revenge.

reproach *verb* rebuke. **reproach** *noun*, **reproachful** *adjective*, **reproachfully** *adverb*

reproduce *verb* (**reproduced**, **reproducing**) **1** cause to be seen or heard or happen again. **2** make a copy of something. **3** produce offspring. **reproduction** *noun*, **reproductive** *adjective*

reprove *verb* (**reproved**, **reproving**) rebuke; reproach. **reproof** *noun*

reptile *noun* a cold-blooded animal that has a backbone and very short legs or no legs at all, e.g. a snake, lizard, crocodile, or tuatara. [from Latin *reptilis* = crawling]

republic *noun* a country that has a president, especially one who is elected. (Compare *monarchy*.) **republican** *adjective* [from Latin *res publica* = public affairs]

repudiate *verb* (**repudiated**, **repudiating**) reject; deny. **repudiation** *noun*

repugnant *adjective* distasteful; objectionable. **repugnance** *noun* [from *re-* = against, + Latin *pugnans* = fighting]

repulse *verb* (**repulsed**, **repulsing**) **1** drive away; repel. **2** reject an offer etc.; rebuff. [same origin as *repel*]

repulsion *noun* **1** repelling; repulsing. **2** a feeling of disgust. (The opposite is *attraction*.)

repulsive *adjective* **1** disgusting. **2** repelling things. (The opposite is *attractive*.) **repulsively** *adverb*, **repulsiveness** *noun*

reputable (*say* **rep**-yoo-ta-bul) *adjective* having a good reputation; respected. **reputably** *adverb*

reputation *noun* what people say about a person or thing. [from Latin *reputare* = consider]

repute *noun* reputation.

reputed *adjective* said or thought to be something, *This is reputed to be the best hotel.* **reputedly** *adverb*

request *verb* ask for a thing; ask a person to do something.

request *noun* **1** asking for something. **2** a thing asked for. [same origin as *require*]

requiem (*say* **rek**-wee-em) *noun* a special Mass for someone who has died; music for the words of this. [Latin, = rest]

require *verb* (**required**, **requiring**) **1** need. **2** make somebody do something; oblige, *Drivers are required to pass a test.* [from *re-*, + Latin *quaerere* = seek]

requirement *noun* what is required; a need.

requisite (*say* **rek**-wiz-it) *adjective* required; needed.

requisite *noun* a thing needed for something. [same origin as *require*]

requisition *verb* take something over for official use.

rescue *verb* (**rescued**, **rescuing**) save from danger, harm, etc.; bring away from captivity. **rescuer** *noun*

rescue *noun* the action of rescuing.

research (*say* ri-**serch**) *noun* careful study or investigation to discover facts or information.

research (*say* ri-**serch**) *verb* do research into something. **researcher** *noun*

resemblance *noun* likeness.

resemble *verb* (**resembled**, **resembling**) be like another person or thing. [from *re-*, + Latin *similis* = *like*]

resent *verb* feel indignant about or insulted by something. **resentful** *adjective*, **resentfully** *adverb*, **resentment** *noun* [*from re-* = against, + Latin *sentire* = feel]

reservation *noun* **1** reserving. **2** something reserved. **3** an area of land kept for a special purpose. **4** a limit on how far you agree with something, *I believe most of his story, but I have some reservations.*

reserve *verb* (**reserved**, **reserving**) **1** keep or order something for a particular person or a special use. **2** postpone, *reserve judgement.*

reserve *noun* **1** a person or thing kept ready to be used if necessary. **2** an area of land kept for a special purpose, *a nature reserve.* **3** shyness; keeping your thoughts and feelings private. [from *re-* = *back*, + Latin *servare* = keep]

reserved *adjective* (of a person) showing reserve of manner (see *reserve* 3).

reservoir (*say* **rez**-er-vwar) *noun* a place where water is stored, especially an artificial lake.

reshuffle *noun* a rearrangement, especially an exchange of jobs between members of a group, *a Cabinet reshuffle.* **reshuffle** *verb*

reside *verb* (**resided**, **residing**) live in a particular place; dwell. [from *re-*, + Latin *-sidere* = sit]

residence *noun* **1** a place where a person lives. **2** residing.

resident *noun* a person living or residing in a particular place. **resident** *adjective* [from *re-*, + Latin *-sidens* = sitting]

residential *adjective* containing people's homes, *a residential area.*

residue *noun* what is left over. **residual** *adjective*

resign *verb* give up your job or position. **resignation** *noun*
be resigned or **resign yourself to something** accept that you must put up with it.
[from Latin *resignare* = unseal]

resilient *adjective* **1** springy. **2** recovering quickly from illness or trouble. **resilience** *noun* [from *re-* = back, + Latin *-siliens* = jumping]

resin *noun* a sticky substance that comes from plants or is manufactured, used in varnish, plastics, etc. **resinous** *adjective*

resist *verb* oppose; fight or act against something. **resistance** *noun*, **resistant** *adjective* [from *re-* = against, + Latin *sistere* = stand firmly]

resistor *noun* a device that increases the resistance to an electric current.

resolute *adjective* showing great determination. **resolutely** *adverb* [same origin as *resolve*]

resolution *noun* **1** being resolute. **2** something you have resolved to do, *New Year resolutions.* **3** a *formal* decision made by a committee etc. **4** the solving of a problem etc. **5** the degree of detail in a photographic, electronic, or television image.

resolve *verb* (**resolved**, **resolving**) **1** decide firmly or formally. **2** solve a problem etc. **3** overcome doubts or disagreements.

resolve *noun* **1** something you have decided to do; a resolution. **2** great determination. [from *re-*, + Latin *solvere* = loosen]

resonant *adjective* resounding; echoing. **resonance** *adjective* [from *re-*, + Latin *sonans* = sounding]

resort *verb* turn to or make use of something, *They resorted to violence.*

resort *noun* **1** a place where people go for relaxation or holidays. **2** resorting, *without resort to cheating.*
the last resort something to be tried when everything else has failed.

resound *verb* fill a place with sound; echo.

resounding *adjective* very great; outstanding, *a resounding victory.*

resource *noun* **1** something that can be used; an asset, *The country's natural resources include coal and oil.* **2** an ability; ingenuity.

resourceful *adjective* clever at finding ways of doing things. **resourcefully** *adverb*, **resourcefulness** *noun*

respect *noun* **1** admiration for a person's or thing's good qualities. **2** politeness; consideration, *Have respect for people's feelings.* **3** a detail or aspect, *In this respect he is like his sister.* **4** reference, *The rules with respect to bullying are quite clear.*

respect *verb* have respect for a person or thing. [from *re-* = back, + Latin *specere* = to look]

respectable *adjective* **1** having good manners and character etc. **2** fairly good, *a respectable score.* **respectably** *adverb*, **respectability** *noun*

respectful *adjective* showing respect. **respectfully** *adverb*

respecting *preposition* concerning.

respective *adjective* of or for each individual, *We went to our respective rooms.* **respectively** *adverb*

respiration *noun* breathing. **respiratory** *adjective*

respirator *noun* **1** a device that fits over a person's nose and mouth to purify air before it is breathed. **2** an apparatus for giving artificial respiration.

respire *verb* (**respired**, **respiring**) breathe. [from *re-*, + Latin *spirare* = breathe]

respite *noun* an interval of rest, relief, or delay.

resplendent *adjective* brilliant with colour or decorations. [from *re-*, + Latin *splendens* = glittering]

respond *verb* **1** reply. **2** react. [from *re-*, + Latin *spondere* = promise]

respondent *noun* the person answering.

response *noun* **1** a reply. **2** a reaction.

responsibility *noun* (*plural* **responsibilities**) **1** being responsible. **2** something for which a person is responsible.

responsible *adjective* **1** looking after a person or thing and having to take the blame if something goes wrong. **2** reliable; trustworthy. **3** with important duties, *a responsible job.* **4** causing something, *His carelessness was responsible for their deaths.* **responsibly** *adverb*

responsive *adjective* responding well.

rest[1] *noun* **1** a time of sleep or freedom from work as a way of regaining strength. **2** a support, *an arm-rest.* **3** an interval of silence between notes in music.

rest[1] *verb* **1** have a rest; be still. **2** allow to rest, *Sit down and rest your feet.* **3** support; be supported. **4** be left without further investigation etc., *And there the matter rests.* [from Old English *raest* = bed]

rest[2] *noun* **the rest** the remaining part; the others.

rest[2] *verb* remain, *Rest assured, it will be a success.*
rest with be left to someone to deal with, *It rests with you to suggest a date.*
[from Latin *restare* = stay behind]

restaurant *noun* a place where you can buy a meal and eat it.

restful *adjective* giving rest or a feeling of rest.

restitution *noun* **1** restoring something. **2** compensation. [from *re-*, + Latin *statutum* = established]

restive *adjective* restless or impatient because of delay, boredom, etc.

restless *adjective* unable to rest or keep still. **restlessly** *adverb*

restore *verb* (**restored**, **restoring**) put something back to its original place or condition. **restoration** *noun*

restrain *verb* hold a person or thing back; keep under control. **restraint** *noun*

restrict *verb* limit. **restriction** *noun*, **restrictive** *adjective*

restructure *verb* rebuild, reorganise (especially a country's economy and government services). **restructuring** *noun*

result *noun* **1** something produced by an action or condition etc.; an effect or consequence. **2** the final score or situation in a game, competition, race, or test. **3** the answer to a sum or calculation.

result *verb* **1** happen as a result. **2** have a particular result. **resultant** *adjective*

resume *verb* (**resumed**, **resuming**) **1** begin again after stopping for a while. **2** take or occupy again, *After the interval we resumed our seats.* **resumption** *noun* [from *re-*, + Latin *sumere* = take up]

résumé (*say* **rez**-yoo-may) *noun* a summary. [French, = summed up]

resurgence *noun* a rise or revival of something, *a resurgence of interest in grammar.* [from *re-*, + Latin *surgens* = rising]

resurrect *verb* bring back into use or existence, *resurrect an old custom.*

resurrection *noun* **1** coming back to life after being dead. **2** the revival of something. [same origin as *resurgence*]

resuscitate *verb* (**resuscitated**, **resuscitating**) revive a person from unconsciousness or a custom etc. from disuse. **resuscitation** *noun*

retail *verb* **1** sell goods to the general public. **2** tell what happened; recount; relate. **retailer** *noun*

retail *noun* selling to the general public. (Compare *wholesale.*)

retain *verb* **1** continue to have something; keep in your possession or memory etc. **2** hold something in place. [from *re-*, + Latin *tenere* = to hold]

retainer *noun* (*old use*) an attendant of a person of high rank.

retaliate *verb* (**retaliated**, **retaliating**) repay an injury or insult etc. with a similar one; counter-attack. **retaliation** *noun* [from *re-*, + Latin *talis* = the same kind]

retard *verb* slow down or delay the progress or development of something. **retarded** *adjective*, **retardation** *noun* [from *re-*, + Latin *tardus* = slow]

retch *verb* strain your throat as if being sick.

retention *noun* retaining; keeping. **retentive** *adjective*

reticent (*say* **ret**-i-sent) *adjective* not telling people what you feel or think; discreet. **reticence** *noun*

reticulate *verb* supply a network of water, gas, electricity, sewerage pipes, etc.

retina *noun* a layer of membrane at the back of the eyeball, sensitive to light.

retinue *noun* a group of people accompanying an important person.

retire *verb* (**retired**, **retiring**) **1** give up your regular work because you are getting old. **2** retreat. **3** go to bed or to your private room. **retirement** *noun* [from French *retirer* = draw back]

retiring *adjective* shy; avoiding company.

retort *noun* **1** a quick or witty or angry reply. **2** a glass bottle with a long downward-bent neck, used in distilling liquids. **3** a receptacle used in making steel etc.

retort *verb* make a quick, witty, or angry reply. [from *re-*, + Latin *tortum* = twisted]

retrace *verb* (**retraced**, **retracing**) go back over something, *We retraced our steps and returned to the ferry.*

retract *verb* **1** pull back or in, *The snail retracts its horns.* **2** withdraw, *She refused to retract her threat.* **retraction** *noun*, **retractable** *adjective*, **retractile** *adjective* [from *re-*, + Latin *tractum* = pulled]

retreat *verb* go back after being defeated or to avoid danger or difficulty etc.; withdraw.

retreat *noun* **1** retreating. **2** a quiet place to which someone can withdraw. [same origin as *retract*]

retrench *verb* reduce the amount of something; economise. **retrenchment** *noun*

retribution *noun* a deserved punishment. [from *re-*, + Latin *tributum* = assigned]

retrieve *verb* (**retrieved**, **retrieving**) get something back; rescue. **retrievable** *adjective*, **retrieval** *noun* [from Old French *retrover* = find again]

retriever *noun* a kind of dog that is often trained to retrieve game.

retro- *prefix* back; backward (as in *retrograde*). [from Latin *retro* = backwards]

retrograde *adjective* **1** going backwards. **2** becoming less good.

retrogress *verb* **1** move backwards. **2** deteriorate. **retrogression** *noun*, **retrogressive** *adjective* [from *retro-* + *progress*]

retrospect *noun* a survey of past events.
in retrospect when you look back at what has happened.
[from *retro-* + *prospect*]

retrospective *adjective* **1** looking back on the past. **2** applying to the past as well as the future, *The law could not be made retrospective.* **retrospection** *noun*

return *verb* **1** come back or go back. **2** bring, give, put, or send back.
returned serviceman (*NZ*) a member of the armed forces who has fought in a war overseas.

return *noun* **1** returning. **2** something returned. **3** profit, *He gets a good return on his savings.* **4** a return ticket.
return match a second match played between the same teams.
return ticket a ticket for a journey to a place and back again.

reunion *noun* **1** reuniting. **2** a meeting of people who have not met for some time.

reunite *verb* (**reunited**, **reuniting**) unite again after being separated.

reuse *verb* (**reused**, **reusing**) use again. **reusable** *adjective*

reuse *noun* using again.

rev *verb* (**revved**, **revving**) (*informal*) make an engine run quickly, especially when starting.

rev *noun* (*informal*) *a* revolution of an engine. [short for *revolution*]

Rev. *abbreviation* Reverend.

revalue *verb* **1** reassess the value of something. **2** give a new value to a nation's currency.

revamp *verb* renovate, redesign, or renew.

reveal *verb* let something be seen or known. [from Latin *revelare* = unveil]

reveille (*say* riv-**al**-ee) *noun* a military waking-signal sounded on a bugle or drums. [from French *réveillez* = wake up!]

revel *verb* (**revelled**, **revelling**) **1** take great delight in something. **2** hold revels. **reveller** *noun*
revels *plural noun* noisy festivities.

revelation *noun* **1** revealing. **2** something revealed, especially something surprising.

revelry *noun* revelling; revels.

revenge *noun* harming somebody in return for harm that they have caused.

revenge *verb* (**revenged**, **revenging**) avenge; take vengeance.

revenue *noun* any large income, such as a government receives from taxes or a company from its sales. [French, = returned]

reverberate *verb* (**reverberated**, **reverberating**) resound; re-echo. **reverberation** *noun* [from *re-*, + Latin *verberare* = to lash]

revere (*say* riv-**eer**) *verb* (**revered**, **revering**) respect deeply or with reverence.

reverence *noun* a feeling of awe and deep or religious respect.

Reverend *noun* the title of a member of the clergy, *the Reverend John Smith.* [from Latin, = person to be revered]

reverent *adjective* feeling or showing reverence. **reverently** *adverb* [from Latin, = revering]

reverie (*say* **rev**-er-ee) *noun* a daydream.

revers (*say* riv-**eer**) *noun* (*plural* **revers**, *say* riv-**eerz**) a folded-back part of a garment, as in a lapel.

reversal *noun* reversing.

reverse *adjective* opposite in direction, order, or manner etc.
reverse gear a gear that allows a vehicle to be driven backwards.

reverse *noun* **1** the reverse side, order, manner. etc. **2** a piece of misfortune, *They suffered several reverses.*
in reverse the opposite way round.

reverse *verb* (**reversed**, **reversing**) **1** turn in the opposite direction or order etc.; turn something inside out or upside down. **2** move backwards. **3** cancel a decision or decree. **reversible** *adjective* [same origin as *revert*]

revert *verb* return to a former condition, habit, or subject etc. **reversion** *noun* [from *re-* = back, + Latin *vertere* = to turn]

review *noun* **1** an inspection or survey. **2** a published description and opinion of a book, movie, play, etc.

review *verb* make a review of something. **reviewer** *noun*

revile *verb* (**reviled**, **reviling**) criticise angrily. **revilement** *noun*

revise *verb* (**revised**, **revising**) **1** go over work that you have already done, especially in preparing for an examination. **2** alter or correct something. **revision** *noun* [from *re-*, + Latin *visere* = examine]

revive *verb* (**revived**, **reviving**) come or bring back to life, strength, activity, or use etc. **revival** *noun* [from *re-*, + Latin *vivere* = to live]

revoke *verb* (**revoked**, **revoking**) withdraw or cancel a decree or licence etc. [from *re-*, + Latin *vocare* = to call]

revolt *verb* **1** rebel. **2** disgust somebody.

revolt *noun* **1** a rebellion. **2** a feeling of disgust. [same origin as *revolve*]

revolting *adjective* disgusting.

revolution *noun* **1** a rebellion that overthrows the government. **2** a complete change. **3** revolving; rotation; one complete turn of a wheel, engine, etc. [same origin as *revolve*]

revolutionary *adjective* **1** involving a great change. **2** of a political revolution.

revolutionise *verb* (**revolutionised**, **revolutionising**) make a great change in something.

revolve *verb* (**revolved**, **revolving**) turn or keep on turning round. [from *re-*, + Latin *volvere* = to roll]

revolver *noun* a pistol with a revolving mechanism that makes it possible to fire it a number of times without reloading.

revue *noun* an entertainment consisting of a number of items. [French]

revulsion *noun* **1** strong disgust. **2** a sudden violent change of feeling.

reward *noun* something given in return for a useful action or a merit.

reward *verb* give a reward to someone.

rewarewa *noun* a tall tree with red flowers. [Māori]

rewrite *verb* (**rewrote**, **rewritten**, **rewriting**) write something again or differently.

rhapsody (*say* **rap**-so-dee) *noun* (*plural* **rhapsodies**) **1** a statement of great delight about something. **2** a romantic piece of music. **rhapsodise** *verb* [from Greek *rhapsoidos* = one who stitches songs together]

rhetoric (*say* **ret**-er-ik) *noun* **1** the act of using words impressively, especially in public speaking. **2** affected or exaggerated expressions used because they sound impressive. **rhetorical** *adjective*, **rhetorically** *adverb*
rhetorical question something put as a question so that it sounds dramatic, not to get an answer, e.g. 'Who cares?' (= nobody cares).
[from Greek *rhetor* = orator]

rheumatism *noun* a disease that causes pain and stiffness in joints and muscles. **rheumatic** *adjective*, **rheumatoid** *adjective*

rhinoceros *noun* (*plural* **rhinoceroses**) a large heavy animal with a horn or two horns on its nose. [from Greek *rhinos* = of the nose, + *keras* = horn]

rhododendron *noun* an evergreen shrub with large trumpet-shaped flowers. [from Greek *rhodon* = rose, + *dendron* = tree]

rhombus *noun* (*plural* **rhombuses**) a quadrilateral with equal sides but no right angles, like the diamond on playing-cards.

rhubarb *noun* a plant with thick reddish stalks that are used as fruit.

rhyme *noun* **1** a similar sound in the endings of words, e.g. *bat/fat/mat, batter/fatter/matter*. **2** a poem with rhymes. **3** a word that rhymes with another.

rhyme *verb* (**rhymed**, **rhyming**) form a rhyme; have rhymes.

rhythm *noun* a regular pattern of beats, sounds, or movements. **rhythmic** *adjective*, **rhythmical** *adjective*, **rhythmically** *adverb*

rib *noun* **1** each of the curved bones round the chest. **2** a curved part that looks like a rib or supports something, *the ribs of an umbrella*. **ribbed** *adjective*

ribald (*say* **rib**-ald) *adjective* funny in a vulgar or disrespectful way. **ribaldry** *noun*

riband *noun* a ribbon.

ribbon *noun* **1** a narrow strip of silk or nylon etc. used for decoration or for tying something. **2** a long narrow strip of inked material used in a typewriter etc.

ribbonwood *noun* a New Zealand tree, the lacebark.

rice *noun* the white seeds of a plant that is grown in marshes in hot countries, used as food.

rich *adjective* **1** having a lot of money or property or resources etc.; wealthy. **2** full of goodness, quality, etc. **3** costly; luxurious. **richly** *adverb*, **richness** *noun*

riches *plural noun* wealth.

Richter scale a scale that measures the strength of earthquakes.

rick[1] *noun* a large neat stack of hay or straw.

rick[2] *verb* sprain; wrench.

rickets *noun* a disease caused by lack of vitamin D, causing deformed bones.

rickety *adjective* unsteady.

rickshaw *noun* a two-wheeled carriage pulled by one or more people, used in the Far East. [from Japanese *jin-riki-sha* = person-power-vehicle]

ricochet (*say* **rik**-osh-ay) *verb* (**ricocheted**, **ricocheting**) bounce off something; rebound, *The bullets ricocheted off the wall.* **ricochet** *noun*

rid *verb* (**rid**, **ridding**) make a person or place free from something unwanted, *He rid the town of rats.* **riddance** *noun*
get rid of cause to go away.

riddle[1] *noun* a puzzling question. especially as a joke.

riddle[2] *noun* a coarse sieve.

riddle[2] *verb* (**riddled**, **riddling**) **1** pass gravel etc. through a riddle. **2** pierce with many holes, *They riddled the target with bullets.*

ride *verb* (**rode**, **ridden**, **riding**) **1** sit on a horse, bicycle, etc., and be carried along on it. **2** travel in a car, bus, train, etc. **3** float or be supported on something, *The ship rode the waves.*

ride *noun* riding; a journey on a horse, bicycle, etc. in a vehicle, or at a sideshow or fair.

rider *noun* **1** someone who rides. **2** an extra comment or statement.

ridge *noun* a long narrow part higher than the rest of something. **ridged** *adjective*

ridicule *verb* (**ridiculed**, **ridiculing**) make fun of a person or thing. **ridicule** *noun* [from Latin *ridere* = to laugh]

ridiculous *adjective* so silly that it makes people laugh or despise it. **ridiculously** *adverb*

rife *adjective* widespread; happening frequently, *Crime was rife in the town.*

riff-raff *noun* the rabble; disreputable people.

rifle *noun* a long gun with spiral grooves (called *rifling*) inside the barrel that make the bullet spin and so travel more accurately.

rifle *verb* (**rifled**, **rifling**) search and rob, *They rifled his desk.*

rifleman *noun* (*plural* **riflemen**) **1** a soldier armed with a rifle. **2** a small New Zealand forest bird.

rift *noun* **1** a crack or split. **2** a disagreement that separates friends.

rift-valley *noun* a steep-sided valley formed where the land has sunk.

rig *verb* (**rigged**, **rigging**) **1** provide a ship with ropes, spars, sails, etc. **2** set something up quickly or out of makeshift materials.
rig out provide with clothes or equipment.
rig-out *noun*

rig *noun* **1** a framework supporting the machinery for drilling an oil-well. **2** the way a ship's masts and sails etc. are arranged.

rigger[1] *noun* a person who works on an oil rig.

rigger[2] *noun* (*NZ*) a container for beer etc.

rigging *noun* the ropes etc. that support a ship's mast and sails.

right *adjective* **1** of the right-hand side. **2** correct; true, *the right answer.* **3** morally good; fair; just, *Is it right to cheat?* **rightly** *adverb*, **rightness** *noun*
right angle an angle of 90°.
right hand the hand that most people use more than the left, on the side of the body opposite the left hand.
right-hand *adjective*
right-handed *adjective* using the right hand in preference to the left hand.
she'll be right (*NZ, informal*) it will do; all will be well.
too right yes, definitely.

right *adverb* **1** on or towards the right-hand side, *Turn right.* **2** straight, *Go right on.* **3** completely, *Go right round it.* **4** exactly, *right in the middle.* **5** rightly, *You did right to tell me.*
right away immediately.

right *noun* **1** the right-hand side or part etc. **2** what is morally good or fair or just. **3** something that people are allowed to do or have, *People over 18 have the right to vote in elections.* **4** (**Right**) the right wing of a political party or other group.
Right Honourable title given to high officials such as Chief Justice, principal judges and the Prime Minister.
right of way a path or driveway that passes over someone else's land.

right *verb* make a thing right or upright, *They righted the boat.*

righteous *adjective* doing what is right; virtuous. **righteously** *adverb*, **righteousness** *noun*

rightful *adjective* deserved; proper, *in her rightful place.* **rightfully** *adverb*

right wing *noun* **1** the more conservative side of a political party or system. **2** (rugby etc.) the right-hand side of the field; a player positioned there. **right-wing** *adjective*, **right-winger** *noun*

rigid *adjective* **1** stiff; firm; not bending, *a rigid support.* **2** strict, *rigid rules.* **rigidly** *adverb*, **rigidity** *noun*

rigmarole *noun* **1** a long rambling statement. **2** a complicated procedure.

rigorous *adjective* strict; severe. **rigorously** *adverb*

rigour *noun* **1** strictness; severity. **2** harshness of weather or conditions, *the rigours of winter.*

rile *verb* (**riled**, **riling**) (*informal*) annoy.

rim *noun* the outer edge of a cup, wheel, or other round object.

rimmed *adjective* edged.

rimu *noun* **1** the principal softwood timber tree in New Zealand. **2** its wood. [Māori]

rind *noun* the tough skin on bacon, cheese, or fruit.

ring[1] *noun* **1** a circle. **2** a thin circular piece of metal worn on a finger. **3** the space where a circus performs. **4** a square area in which a boxing-match or wrestling-match takes place.
ring road a bypass that encircles a town or city.
run rings around be clearly superior to or easily outwit (someone).

ring[1] *verb* put a ring round something; encircle.

ring[2] *verb* (**rang**, **rung**, **ringing**) **1** cause a bell to sound. **2** make a loud clear sound like that of a bell. **3** be filled with sound, *The hall rang with cheers.* **4** telephone, *Please ring me tomorrow.*
ring a bell (*informal*) sound familiar; stir a vague memory.

ring[2] *noun* **1** the act or sound of ringing. **2** a telephone call.

Ringatū *noun* a Māori religious movement founded in the 1860s. [Māori, = upraised hand]

ringbark *verb* kill (a tree) by cutting a circle of bark around the trunk.

ringer *noun* (*NZ*) the fastest shearer in a shearing gang.

ringleader *noun* a person who leads others in rebellion, mischief, crime, etc.

ringlet *noun* a tube-shaped curl.

ringmaster *noun* the person in charge of a performance in a circus ring.

ringtail *noun* a kind of possum.

ringworm *noun* a skin disease in animals and human beings, caused by a fungus forming circular patches.

rink *noun* a place made for skating.

rinse *verb* (**rinsed**, **rinsing**) **1** wash something lightly. **2** wash in clean water to remove soap. **rinse** *noun*

riot *noun* wild or violent behaviour by a crowd of people.

riot *verb* (**rioted**, **rioting**) take part in a riot.

riotous *adjective* **1** disorderly; unruly. **2** boisterous, *riotous laughter.*

rip *verb* (**ripped**, **ripping**) **1** tear roughly. **2** rush.
rip off (*slang*) swindle. **rip-off** *noun*

rip *noun* a torn place.

ripe *adjective* **1** ready to be harvested or eaten. **2** ready and suitable, *The time is ripe for revolution.* **3** mature; advanced, *She lived to a ripe old age.* **ripeness** *noun*

ripen *verb* make or become ripe.

riposte (*say* rip-**ost**) *noun* **1** a quick counterstroke in fencing. **2** a quick retort.

ripple *noun* a small wave or series of waves.

ripple *verb* (**rippled**, **rippling**) form ripples.

riri *adjective* angry. [Māori]

riroriro *noun* the grey warbler. [Māori]

rise *verb* (**rose**, **risen**, **rising**) **1** go upwards. **2** get up from lying, sitting, or kneeling; get out of bed. **3** come to life again after death, *Christ is risen.* **4** rebel, *They rose in revolt against the tyrant.* **5** (of a river) begin its course. **6** (of the wind) begin to blow more strongly.

rise *noun* **1** the action of rising; an upward movement. **2** an increase in amount etc. or in wages. **3** an upward slope.
give rise to cause.

rising *noun* a revolt.

risk *noun* a chance of danger or loss.

risk *verb* take the chance of damaging or losing something.

risky *adjective* (**riskier**, **riskiest**) full of risk.

rissole *noun* a fried cake of minced meat or fish.

rite *noun* a religious ceremony; a solemn ritual.

ritual *noun* the series of actions used in a religious or other ceremony. **ritual** *adjective*, **ritually** *adverb*

rival *noun* a person or thing that competes with another or tries to do the same thing. **rivalry** *noun*

rival *verb* (**rivalled**, **rivalling**) be a rival of a person or thing. [from Latin *rivalis* = person using the same stream (*rivus* = stream)]

riven *adjective* split; torn apart.

river *noun* a large stream of water flowing in a natural channel. [from Latin *ripa* = bank]

rivet *noun* a strong nail or bolt for holding pieces of metal together. The end opposite the head is flattened to form another head when it is in place.

rivet *verb* (**riveted**, **riveting**) **1** fasten with rivets. **2** hold firmly, *He stood riveted to the spot.* **3** fascinate, *The concert was riveting.* **riveter** *noun*

rivulet *noun* a small stream.

RNA *abbreviation* ribonucleic acid, a substance in living cells that carries instructions from DNA.

RNZ *abbreviation* Radio New Zealand.

RNZAF *abbreviation* Royal New Zealand Air Force.

RNZN *abbreviation* Royal New Zealand Navy.

road *noun* **1** a level way with a hard surface made for traffic to travel on. **2** a way or course, *the road to success.* **road rage** anger provoked by another driver's actions. **roadside** *noun*, **roadway** *noun*

Road Code *noun* (*NZ*) official guide for traffic laws and driving safety.

road-metal *noun* broken stone for road-making.

roadworthy *adjective* safe to be used on roads.

roam *verb* wander. **roam** *noun*

roan *adjective* (of a horse) brown or black with many white hairs.

roar *noun* a loud deep sound like that made by a lion.

roar *verb* make a roar.
a roaring trade brisk selling of something.

ROAR *abbreviation* right of admission reserved.

roast *verb* **1** cook meat etc. in an oven or by exposing it to heat. **2** make or be very hot.

roast *adjective* roasted, *roast beef.*

roast *noun* meat for roasting; roast meat.

rob *verb* (**robbed**, **robbing**) take or steal from somebody, *He robbed me of my watch.* **robber** *noun*, **robbery** *noun* [from Old French *robe* = booty]

robe *noun* a long loose garment.

robe *verb* (**robed**, **robing**) dress in a robe or ceremonial robes.

robin *noun* **1** a small bird with a red breast. **2** (*NZ*) a small, friendly bush bird.

robot *noun* **1** a machine that looks and acts like a person. **2** a machine operated by remote control. [from Czech *robota* = compulsory labour]

robust *adjective* strong; vigorous. **robustly** *adverb*, **robustness** *noun* [from Latin *robur* = strength]

rock[1] *noun* **1** a large stone or boulder. **2** the hard part of the earth's crust, under the soil. **rock lobster** (*NZ*) a commercial name for marine crayfish.

rock[2] *verb* **1** move gently backwards and forwards while supported on something. **2** shake violently, *The earthquake rocked the city.*

rock[2] *noun* **1** a rocking movement. **2** rock music.
rock music popular music with a heavy beat.

rocker *noun* **1** a thing that rocks something or is rocked. **2** a rocking-chair.
off your rocker (*slang*) mad.

rockery *noun* (*plural* **rockeries**) a mound or bank in a garden, where plants are made to grow between large rocks.

rocket *noun* **1** a firework that shoots high into the air. **2** a structure that flies by expelling burning gases, used to send up a missile or a spacecraft. **rocketry** *noun*

rocket *verb* (**rocketed**, **rocketing**) move quickly upwards or away.

rocking-chair *noun* a chair that can be rocked by a person sitting in it.

rocking-horse *noun* a model of a horse that can be rocked by a child sitting on it.

rocky[1] *adjective* (**rockier**, **rockiest**) like rock; full of rocks.

rocky[2] *adjective* (**rockier**, **rockiest**) unsteady. **rockiness** *noun*

rod *noun* **1** a long thin stick or bar. **2** a stick with a line attached for fishing.

rodent *noun* an animal that has large front teeth for gnawing things, *Rats, mice, and squirrels are rodents.* [from Latin *rodens* = gnawing]

rodeo (*say* roh-**day**-oh) *noun* (*plural* **rodeos**) a display of cowboys' skill in riding, controlling horses, etc.

roe[1] *noun* a mass of eggs or reproductive cells in a fish's body.

roe[2] *noun* (*plural* **roes** or **roe**) a kind of small deer. The male is called a **roebuck**.

rogue *noun* **1** a dishonest person. **2** a mischievous person. **roguery** *noun*

roguish *adjective* playful.

roister *verb* make merry noisily.

role *noun* a performer's part in a play or film etc.

roll *verb* **1** move along by turning over and over, like a ball or wheel. **2** form something into the shape of a cylinder or ball. **3** flatten something by rolling a rounded object over it. **4** rock from side to side. **5** pass steadily,

The years rolled on. **6** make a long vibrating sound, *The thunder rolled.* **7** move forward with an undulating motion.

roll *noun* **1** a cylinder made by rolling something up. **2** a small individual portion of bread baked in a rounded shape. **3** an official list of names. **4** a long vibrating sound, *a drum roll.* [from Latin *rotula* = little wheel]

roll-call *noun* the calling of a list of names to check that everyone is present.

roller *noun* **1** a cylinder for rolling over things, or on which something is wound. **2** a long, swelling sea-wave.

rollerblade *noun* (*trade mark*) an in-line skate. **rollerblader** *noun*

roller-coaster *noun* an undulating or steep ride.
roller-coaster ride a difficult or dramatic experience.

roller-skate *noun* a skate fitted with wheels.
roller-skating *noun*

rollicking *adjective* boisterous and full of fun. [from *romp* + *frolic*]

rolling-pin *noun* a heavy cylinder for rolling over pastry to flatten it.

rolling-stock *noun* railway engines and carriages and wagons etc.

roly-poly *noun* a pudding of paste covered with jam, rolled up and boiled.

ROM *abbreviation* read-only memory (in a computer), with contents that can be searched or copied but not changed.

Roman *adjective* **1** of ancient or modern Rome or its people. **2** Roman Catholic.
Roman *noun*
Roman candle a tubular firework that sends out coloured fire-balls.
Roman Catholic of the Church that has the pope (bishop of Rome) as its leader; a member of this Church.
Roman numerals letters that represent numbers (I = 1, V = 5, X = 10, etc.), used by the ancient Romans.

romance *noun* **1** tender feelings, experiences, and qualities connected with love. **2** a love story. **3** a love affair. **4** an imaginative story about the adventures of heroes, *a romance of King Arthur's court.* **romantic** *adjective*, **romantically** *adverb*

Romney *noun* the most common breed of sheep in New Zealand, with long fleece, farmed for wool and meat. [from Romney Marsh in Kent, England]

romp *verb* play in a lively way.
romp *noun*

rompers *plural noun* a one-piece garment for babies.

rondo *noun* (*plural* **rondos**) a piece of music whose first part recurs several times.

RONZ *abbreviation* rest of New Zealand (other than Auckland).

rood *noun* a crucifix in a church, especially one placed on top of a screen (the **rood-screen**) separating the nave from the chancel.

roof *noun* (*plural* **roofs**) **1** the part that covers the top of a building, shelter, or vehicle. **2** the upper part of the mouth.

rook[1] *noun* a black crow that nests in large groups. [from Old English *hroc*]

rook[1] *verb* (*informal*) swindle; charge people an unnecessarily high price.

rook[2] *noun* a chess piece shaped like a castle. [from Arabic *rukk*]

rookery *noun* (*plural* **rookeries**) a place where many rooks nest.

rookie *noun* (*informal*) a new recruit, novice.

room *noun* **1** a part of a building with its own walls and ceiling. **2** enough space, *Is there room for me?* **roomful** *noun*

roomy *adjective* (**roomier**, **roomiest**) containing plenty of room; spacious.

roost *noun* a place where birds perch or settle for sleep.

roost *verb* perch; settle for sleep.

rooster *noun* **1** a cockerel. **2** (*NZ, slang*) a fellow, chap.

root[1] *noun* **1** that part of a plant that grows under the ground and absorbs water and nourishment from the soil. **2** a source or basis, *The love of money is the root of all evil.* **3** a number in relation to the number it produces when multiplied by itself, *9 is the square root of 81* (9 × 9 = 81).
take root grow roots; become established.

root[1] *verb* **1** take root; cause something to take root. **2** fix firmly, *Fear rooted us to the spot.*
root out get rid of something.

root[2] *verb* rummage; (of an animal) turn up ground in search of food.

rope *noun* a strong thick cord made of twisted strands of fibre.
show someone the ropes show him or her how to do something.

rope *verb* (**roped**, **roping**) fasten with a rope.
rope in persuade a person to take part in something.

ropeable *adjective* (*NZ, informal*) angry.

rosary *noun* (*plural* **rosaries**) a string of beads for keeping count of a set of prayers as they are said.

rose[1] *noun* **1** a shrub that has showy flowers often with thorny stems. **2** deep pink colour. **3** a sprinkling-nozzle with many holes, e.g. on a watering-can.

rose[2] *past tense* of **rise**.

roseate *adjective* deep pink; rosy.

rosebud *noun* the bud of a rose.

rosella *noun* a brightly-coloured Australian parakeet.

rosemary *noun* an evergreen shrub with fragrant leaves used in cooking.

rosette *noun* a large circular badge or ornament. [French, = little rose]

roster *noun* a list showing people's turns to be on duty etc.

roster *verb* place on a roster.

rostrum *noun* (*plural* **rostra**) a platform for one person.

rosy *adjective* (**rosier**, **rosiest**) **1** deep pink. **2** hopeful; cheerful, *a rosy future*. **rosiness** *noun*

rot *verb* (**rotted**, **rotting**) go soft or bad and become useless; decay.

rot *noun* **1** rotting; decay. **2** (*slang*) nonsense.

rota (*say* **roh**-ta) *noun* a list of people to do things or of things to be done in turn. [Latin, = wheel]

Rotary *noun a* world-wide organisation for businessmen. [short for Rotary International]

rotate *verb* (**rotated**, **rotating**) **1** go round like a wheel; revolve. **2** arrange or happen in a series; take turns at doing something. **rotation** *noun*, **rotary** *adjective*, **rotatory** *adjective* [same origin as *rota*]

rote *noun* **by rote** from memory or by routine, without full understanding of the meaning, *We used to learn French songs by rote*.

rotor *noun* a rotating part of a machine or helicopter.

rotten *adjective* **1** rotted, *rotten apples*. **2** (*informal*) worthless; unpleasant. **rottenness** *noun*

Rottweiler (*say* **rot**-wy-ler) *noun* a kind of large fierce black dog.

rotund *adjective* rounded; plump. **rotundity** *noun* [from Latin, = round]

rouble (*say* **roo**-bul) *noun* the unit of money in Russia.

rouge (*say* roozh) *noun* a reddish cosmetic for colouring the cheeks. **rouge** *verb* [French, = red]

rough *adjective* **1** not smooth; uneven. **2** not gentle or careful; violent, *a rough push*. **3** not exact, *a rough guess*. **roughly** *adverb*, **roughness** *noun*

rough *verb* **rough it** do without ordinary comforts.
rough out draw or plan something roughly.
rough up (*slang*) treat a person violently.

roughage *noun* fibre in food, which helps digestion.

roughen *verb* make or become rough.

roulette (*say* roo-**let**) *noun* a gambling game where players bet on where the ball in a rotating disc will come to rest. [French, = little wheel]

round *adjective* **1** shaped like a circle or ball or cylinder; curved. **2** full; complete, *a round dozen*. **3** returning to the stars, *a round trip*, **roundness** *noun*
in round figures approximately, without giving exact units.

round *adverb* **1** in a circle or curve; round something, *Go round to the back of the house*. **2** in every direction, *Hand the cakes round*. **3** in a new direction, *Turn your chair round*. **4** to someone's house or office etc., *Go round after dinner*. **5** into being conscious again, *Has she come round from the anaesthetic yet?*
round about nearby; approximately.

round *preposition* **1** on all sides of, *Put a fence round the paddock*. **2** in a curve or circle at an even distance from, *The earth moves round the sun*. **3** to all parts of, *Show them round the house*. **4** on the further side of, *The shop is round the corner*.

round *noun* **1** a round object. **2** a whole slice of bread; a sandwich made with two slices of bread. **3** a series of visits made by a doctor, postman, etc. **4** one section or stage in a competition, *Winners go on to the next round*. **5** a shot or volley of shots from a gun; ammunition for this. **6** a song in which people sing the same words but start at different times.

round *verb* **1** make or become round. **2** travel round, *The car rounded the corner*.
round off finish something.
round up gather people or animals together.
round-up *noun*

roundabout *noun* **1** a road junction where traffic has to pass round a circular structure in the road. **2** a merry-go-round.

roundabout *adjective* indirect; not using the shortest way of going or of saying or doing something, *I heard the news in a roundabout way*.

rounders *noun* a game in which players try to hit a ball and run round a circuit.

roundly *adverb* **1** thoroughly; severely, *We were roundly told off for being late*. **2** in a rounded shape.

rouse *verb* (**roused**, **rousing**) **1** make or become awake. **2** cause to become active or excited.

rouseabout *noun* (*NZ*) an odd-job person on a sheep station, especially one who works in the shearing shed.

rousing *adjective* loud, *three rousing cheers.*

rout *verb* defeat and chase away an enemy. **rout** *noun*

route (*say as* root) *noun* the way taken to get to a place.

routine (*say* roo-**teen**) *noun* **1** a regular way of doing things. **2** a sequence of instructions for performing a computer task. **routinely** *adverb*

rove *verb* (**roved**, **roving**) roam. **rover** *noun*

Rover *noun* a member of a Scout Association group for people aged 18 to 26.

row[1] (*rhymes with* go) *noun* a line of people or things.

row[2] (*rhymes with* go) *verb* make a boat move by using oars. **rower** *noun*, **rowing-boat** *noun*

row[3] (*rhymes with* cow) *noun* (*informal*) **1** a loud noise. **2** a quarrel.

rowan (*say* **roh**-an) *noun* a tree that bears hanging bunches of red berries.

rowdy *adjective* (**rowdier**, **rowdiest**) noisy and disorderly. **rowdiness** *noun*

rowlock (*say* **rol**-ok) *noun* a device on the side of a boat, keeping an oar in place.

royal *adjective* of or connected with a king or queen. **royally** *adverb* [from Latin *regalis* = regal]

royalty *noun* (*plural* **royalties**) **1** being royal. **2** a royal person or persons, *in the presence of royalty.* **3** a payment made to an author or composer etc. for each copy of a work sold or for each performance.

r.p.m. *abbreviation* revolutions per minute.

RSA *abbreviation* (*NZ*) Returned Services Association.

RSI *abbreviation* repetitive strain injury (caused by long periods of keyboard work especially).

RSVP *abbreviation* répondez s'il vous plaît (French, = please reply).

rua[1] *noun* a pit. [Māori]

rua[2] *noun* a variety of potato. [Māori = two]

rub *verb* (**rubbed**, **rubbing**) move something backwards and forwards while pressing it on something else. **rub** *noun*
rub out remove something by rubbing.

rubber *noun* **1** a strong elastic substance used for making tyres, balls, hoses, etc. **2** a piece of rubber for rubbing out pencil or ink marks. **rubbery** *adjective*

rubbish *noun* **1** things that are worthless or not wanted. **2** nonsense.

rubbish *verb* criticise as worthless; belittle, *She rubbished his efforts.*

rubble *noun* broken pieces of brick or stone.

rubella *noun* a contagious disease like mild measles (also called *German measles*).

rubicund *adjective* ruddy; red-faced. [same origin as *ruby*]

ruby *noun* (*plural* **rubies**) a red jewel. [from Latin *rubeus* = red]

ruck *noun* **1** a dense crowd. **2** a loose scrum in rugby union, with the ball on the ground.

rucksack *noun* a backpack. [from German *rücken* = back, + *sack*]

ructions *plural noun* (*informal*) protests and noisy argument.

rudder *noun* a hinged upright piece at the back of a ship or aircraft, used for steering.

ruddy *adjective* red and healthy-looking, *a ruddy complexion.*

rude *adjective* **1** impolite. **2** indecent; improper. **3** roughly made; crude, *a rude shelter.* **4** vigorous; hearty, *in rude health.*
a bit rude (*informal*) unfair, unexpected.
rudely *adverb*, **rudeness** *noun* [from Latin *rudis* = raw, wild]

rudimentary *adjective* **1** of rudiments; elementary. **2** not fully developed, *Penguins have rudimentary wings.*

rudiments (*say* **rood**-i-ments) *plural noun* the elementary principles of a subject, *Learn the rudiments of chemistry.*

rue *verb* (**rued**, **ruing**) regret, *I rue the day I started this!*

rueful *adjective* regretful. **ruefully** *adverb*

ruff *noun* **1** a starched pleated frill worn round the neck in Europe in the 16th century. **2** a collar-like ring of feathers or fur round a bird's or animal's neck.

ruffian *noun* a violent lawless person. **ruffianly** *adjective*

ruffle *verb* (**ruffled**, **ruffling**) **1** disturb the smoothness of a thing. **2** upset or annoy someone.

ruffle *noun* a gathered ornamental frill.

rug *noun* **1** a thick mat for the floor. **2** a piece of thick fabric used as a blanket.

rugby *noun* (in full **rugby football**) a kind of football game using an oval ball that players may carry or kick.
rugby league a form of rugby with 13 players on each side.
rugby union a form of rugby with 15 players on each side.
[named after Rugby School in Warwickshire, England, where it was first played]

rugged *adjective* **1** having an uneven surface or outline; craggy. **2** sturdy.

ruin *noun* **1** severe damage or destruction to something. **2** a building that has fallen down.

ruin *verb* damage a thing so severely that it is useless; destroy. **ruination** *noun* [from Latin *ruere* = to fall]

ruinous *adjective* **1** causing ruin. **2** in ruins; ruined.

rule *noun* **1** something that people have to obey. **2** ruling; governing, *under French rule.* **3** a carpenter's ruler.
as a rule usually; more often than not.

rule *verb* (**ruled**, **ruling**) **1** govern; reign. **2** make a decision, *The referee ruled that it was a foul.* **3** draw a straight line with a ruler or other straight edge. [from Latin *regula* = rule]

ruler *noun* **1** a person who governs. **2** a strip of wood, metal, or plastic with straight edges, used for measuring and drawing straight lines.

ruling *noun* a judgement.

rum *noun* a strong alcoholic drink made from sugar or molasses.

rumble *verb* (**rumbled**, **rumbling**) **1** make a deep continuous sound like thunder. **2** (*informal*) take part in a fight. **3** (*informal*) discover or report wrongdoing.

rumble *noun* **1** a rumbling sound. **2** (*informal*) a gang fight. **3** (*informal*) a report of a wrongdoing.

ruminant *adjective* ruminating.

ruminant *noun* an animal that chews the cud (see *cud*).

ruminate *verb* (**ruminated**, **ruminating**) **1** chew the cud. **2** meditate; ponder. **rumination** *noun*, **ruminative** *adjective*

rummage *verb* (**rummaged**, **rummaging**) turn things over or move them about while looking for something. **rummage** *noun*

rummy *noun* a card-game in which players try to form sets or sequences of cards.

rumour *noun* information that spreads to a lot of people but may not be true.

rumour *verb* **be rumoured** be spread as a rumour. [from Latin *rumor* = noise]

rump *noun* the hind part of an animal.

rumple *verb* (**rumpled**, **rumpling**) crumple; make a thing untidy.

rumpus *noun* (*plural* **rumpuses**) (*slang*) an uproar; an angry protest.

run *verb* (**ran**, **run**, **running**) **1** move with quick steps so that both or all feet leave the ground at each stride. **2** go or travel; flow, *Tears ran down his cheeks.* **3** produce a flow of liquid, *Run some water into it.* **4** work or function, *The engine was running smoothly.* **5** manage; organise, *She runs a clothes shop.* **6** compete in a contest, *He ran for President.* **7** extend, *A fence runs round the property.* **8** go or take in a vehicle, *I'll run you to the station.* **9** (*NZ*) have animals on your farm, *run sheep.*
run away leave a place secretly or quickly.
run into collide with; happen to meet.
run out have used up your stock of something; knock over the wicket of a running batsman.
run over knock down or crush with a moving vehicle.

run *noun* **1** the action of running; a time spent running, *Go for a run.* **2** a point scored in cricket or baseball. **3** a continuous series of events, etc., *She had a run of good luck.* **4** an enclosure for animals, *a chicken run.* **5** (*NZ*) a sheep station or a cattle station. **6** a track, *a ski-run.*
on the run running away from pursuit or capture.

rūnanga *noun* an assembly or council. [Māori]

runaway *noun* someone who has run away

runaway *adjective* **1** having run away or out of control. **2** won easily, *a runaway victory.*

rung[1] *noun* a cross-piece in a ladder.

rung[2] *past participle* of **ring**[2].

runholder *noun* (*NZ*) the owner or manager of a sheep or cattle station.

runner *noun* **1** a person or animal that runs, especially in a race. **2** a stem that grows away from a plant and roots itself. **3** a groove, rod, or roller for a thing to move on; each of the long strips under a sledge. **4** a long narrow strip of carpet or covering.
runner bean a kind of climbing bean.

runner-up *noun* (*plural* **runners-up**) someone who comes second in a competition.

running *present participle* of **run**.
in the running competing and with a chance of winning.

running *adjective* continuous; consecutive; without an interval, *It rained for four days running.*

runny *adjective* flowing like liquid; producing a flow of liquid.

run-off *noun* (*NZ*) a separate area of land for keeping young animals etc.

runway *noun* a long hard surface on which aircraft take off and land.

rupee *noun* the unit of money in India and Pakistan. [from Urdu *rupiyah*]

rupture *verb* (**ruptured**, **rupturing**) break; burst. **rupture** *noun* [from Latin *ruptum* = broken]

rural *adjective* of or like the countryside. [from Latin *ruris* = of the country]

ruru *noun* the morepork. [Māori]

rusa *noun* a kind of deer.

ruse *noun* a deception or trick.

rush[1] *verb* **1** hurry. **2** move or flow quickly. **3** attack or capture by rushing.

rush[1] *noun* (*plural* **rushes**) **1** a hurry. **2** a sudden movement towards something. **3** a sudden great demand for something.

rush[2] *noun* (*plural* **rushes**) a plant with a thin stem that grows in marshy places.

rush-hour *noun* the time when traffic is busiest.

rusk *noun* a kind of biscuit, especially for feeding babies.

russet *noun* reddish-brown colour. [from Latin *russus* = red]

rust *noun* **1** a red or brown substance that forms on iron or steel exposed to damp and corrodes it. **2** reddish-brown colour.

rust *verb* make or become rusty.

rustic *adjective* **1** rural. **2** made of rough timber or branches, *a rustic bridge.* **3** rough-hewn or rough-surfaced.

rusticate *verb* (**rusticated**, **rusticating**) settle in the country. **rusticated weatherboard** (*NZ*) a style of weatherboard in which boards are lapped together in order to cover joints. **rustication** *noun* [from *rustic*]

rustle *verb* (**rustled**, **rustling**) **1** make a sound like paper being crumpled. **2** steal horses or cattle, *cattle rustling.* **rustle** *noun*, **rustler** *noun*

rustle up (*informal*) produce, *rustle up a meal.*

rusty *adjective* (**rustier**, **rustiest**) **1** coated with rust. **2** weakened by lack of use or practice, *My Māori is a bit rusty.* **rustiness** *noun*

rut *noun* **1** a deep track made by wheels in soft ground. **2** a settled and usually dull way of life, *We are getting into a rut.* **rutted** *adjective*

ruthless *adjective* pitiless; merciless; cruel. **ruthlessly** *adverb*, **ruthlessness** *noun* [from *ruth* = pity]

rye *noun* a cereal used to make bread, biscuits, etc.

Ss

S. *abbreviation* south; southern.

Saanen *noun* a kind of goat kept for milking. [from Saanen in Switzerland]

sabbath *noun* a weekly day for rest and prayer, Saturday for Jews, Sunday for Christians. [from Hebrew, = rest]

sable *noun* **1** a kind of dark fur. **2** (*poetic*) black.

sabotage *noun* deliberate damage or disruption to hinder an enemy, employer, etc. **sabotage** *verb*, **saboteur** *noun*

sabre *noun* **1** a heavy sword with a curved blade. **2** a light fencing-sword.

sac *noun* a bag-shaped part in an animal or plant.

saccharin (*say* **sak**-er-in) *noun* a very sweet substance used as a substitute for sugar. [from Greek *saccharom* = sugar]

saccharine (*say* **sak**-er-een) *adjective* unpleasantly sweet, *a saccharine smile.*

sachet (*say* **sash**-ay) *noun a* small sealed bag or packet holding a scented substance or a single portion of something. [French, = little sack]

sack[1] *noun* a large bag made of strong material. **sacking** *noun*
the sack (*informal*) dismissal from a job, *He got the sack.*

sack[1] *verb* (*informal*) dismiss someone from a job.

sack[2] *verb* plunder a captured town in a violent destructive way. **sack** *noun*

sacrament *noun* an important Christian religious ceremony such as baptism or Holy Communion. [same origin as *sacred*]

sacred *adjective* holy; of God or a god. [from Latin *sacer* = holy]

sacrifice *noun* **1** giving something that you think will please a god. **2** giving up a thing you value, so that something good may happen. **3** a thing sacrificed. **sacrificial** *adjective*

sacrifice *verb* (**sacrificed**, **sacrificing**) give something as a sacrifice. [from Latin, = make a thing sacred]

sacrilege (*say* **sak**-ril-ij) *noun* disrespect or damage to something people regard as sacred. **sacrilegious** *adjective* [from Latin *sacer* = sacred, + *legere* = take away]

sacrosanct *adjective* sacred or respected and therefore not to be harmed. [from Latin *sacro* = by a sacred rite, + *sanctus* = holy]

sad *adjective* (**sadder**, **saddest**) unhappy; showing or causing sorrow. **sadly** *adverb*, **sadness** *noun*

sad *noun* **pack a sad** (*NZ, slang*) be depressed.

sadden *verb* make a person sad.

saddle *noun* **1** a seat for putting on the back of a horse or other animal. **2** the seat of a bicycle. **3** a ridge of high land between two peaks.

saddle *verb* (**saddled**, **saddling**) put a saddle on a horse etc.

saddleback *noun* **1** a black New Zealand bird with brown plumage on its back and wings. **2** a black pig with a white stripe across its back.

sadist (*say* **say**-dist) *noun* a person who enjoys hurting other people. **sadism** *noun*, **sadistic** *adjective* [named after a French novelist, the Marquis de Sade, noted for his crimes]

s.a.e. *abbreviation* stamped addressed envelope.

safari *noun* (*plural* **safaris**) an expedition to see or hunt wild animals. [from Arabic *safara* = travel]

safe *adjective* free from risk or danger; not dangerous. **safely** *adverb*, **safeness** *noun*, **safety** *noun*
safe sex sexual activity in which condoms are used as a precaution against disease.

safe *noun* a strong cupboard or box in which valuables can be locked safely. [from Latin *salvus* = uninjured]

safeguard *noun* a protection.

safeguard *verb* protect.

safety-pin *noun* a U-shaped pin with a clip fastening over the point.

saffron *noun* **1** deep yellow colour. **2** a kind of crocus with orange-coloured stigmas. **3** these stigmas dried and used to colour or flavour food.

sag *verb* (**sagged**, **sagging**) go down in the middle because something heavy is pressing on it; droop. **sag** *noun*

saga (*say* **sah**-ga) *noun* a long story with many episodes.

sagacious (*say* sa-**gay**-shus) *adjective* shrewd and wise. **sagaciously** *adverb*, **sagacity** *noun* [from Latin *sagax* = wise]

sage[1] *noun* a kind of herb.

sage[2] *adjective* wise. **sagely** *adverb*

sage[2] *noun* a wise and respected person.

sago *noun* a starchy white food used to make puddings.

sail *noun* **1** a large piece of strong cloth attached to a mast etc. to catch the wind and make a ship or boat move. **2** a short voyage. **3** an arm of a windmill.

sail *verb* **1** travel in a ship or boat. **2** start a voyage, *We sail at noon.* **3** control a ship or boat. **4** move quickly and smoothly. **sailing-ship** *noun*

sailor *noun* a person who sails; a member of a ship's crew or of a navy.

saint *noun* a holy or very good person. **saintly** *adverb*, **saintliness** *noun* [from Latin *sanctus* = holy]

sake[1] *noun* **for the sake of** so as to help or please a person, get a thing, etc.

sake[2] (*say* **sak**-ay) a Japanese alcoholic drink made from rice. [Japanese]

salaam *noun* a low bow with the right hand on the forehead. [from Arabic *salam* = peace]

salad *noun* a mixture of vegetables eaten raw or cold.

salamander *noun* a lizard-like animal formerly thought to live in fire.

salami *noun* a spiced sausage.

salary *noun* (*plural* **salaries**) a regular wage, usually for a year's work, paid in monthly instalments. **salaried** *adjective* [from Latin *salarium* = salt-money, money given to Roman soldiers to buy salt]

sale *noun* **1** selling. **2** a time when things are sold at reduced prices.

salesman *noun* (*plural* **salesmen**), **saleswoman** *noun* (*plural* **saleswomen**) a person employed to sell goods.

saleyard *noun* (*NZ*) a place where livestock, cars, etc., are sold.

salient (*say* **say**-lee-ent) *adjective* **1** projecting. **2** most noticeable, *the salient features of the plan.*

salient *noun* a part of a fortification or battle-line that juts out. [from Latin *saliens* = leaping]

saline *adjective* containing salt.

saliva *noun* the natural liquid in a person's or animal's mouth. **salivary** *adjective*

salivate (*say* **sal**-iv-ayt) *verb* (**salivated**, **salivating**) form saliva. **salivation** *noun*

sallow *adjective* slightly yellow, *a sallow complexion.* **sallowness** *noun*

sally *noun* (*plural* **sallies**) **1** a sudden rush forward. **2** an excursion. **3** a lively or witty remark.

sally *verb* (**sallied**, **sallying**) make a sudden attack or an excursion. [same origin as *salient*]

salmon (*say* **sam**-on) *noun* (*plural* **salmon**) a large edible fish with pink flesh.

salmonella (*say* sal-mon-**el**-a) *noun* a bacterium that can cause food-poisoning and various diseases.

salon *noun* **1** a large elegant room. **2** a room or shop where a hairdresser etc. receives customers.

saloon *noun* **1** a car with a hard roof. **2** a room where people can sit, drink, etc.

salsa *noun* a spicy sauce. [Spanish]

salt *noun* **1** sodium chloride, the white substance that gives sea-water its taste and is used for flavouring food. **2** a chemical compound of a metal and an acid. **salty** *adjective*

salts *plural noun* a substance that looks like salt, especially a laxative.

salt *verb* flavour or preserve food with salt.

salt-cellar *noun* a small dish or perforated pot holding salt for use at meals.

salt-lick *noun* a block of salt provided for farm animals to lick.

salubrious *adjective* good for people's health. **salubrity** *noun* [from Latin *salus* = health]

salutary *adjective* beneficial; having a good effect, *She gave us some salutary advice.* [from Latin *salus* = health]

salutation *noun* a greeting.

salute *verb* (**saluted**, **saluting**) **1** raise your right hand to your forehead as a sign of respect. **2** greet. **3** say that you respect or admire something, *We salute this achievement.*

salute *noun* **1** the act of saluting. **2** the firing of guns as a sign of greeting or respect. [from Latin *salus* = health]

salvage *verb* (**salvaged**, **salvaging**) save or rescue something so that it can be used again. **salvage** *noun* [from Latin *salvare* = save]

salvation *noun* **1** saving from loss or damage etc. **2** (in Christian teaching) saving the soul from sin and its consequences.

salve *noun* **1** a soothing ointment. **2** something that soothes.

salve *verb* (**salved**, **salving**) soothe a person's conscience or wounded pride.

salver *noun* a small tray, usually of metal.

salvo *noun* (*plural* **salvoes**) a volley of shots or of applause.

sambar *noun* a kind of elk.

same *adjective* of one kind, exactly alike or equal; not changing; not different. **sameness** *noun*

sammie *noun* (*NZ, informal*) a sandwich.

Samoan *noun* **1** a person from Samoa. **2** the language of Samoa. **Samoan** *adjective*

samovar *noun* a Russian tea-urn. [Russian, = self-boiler]

sampan *noun* a small flat-bottomed boat used in China. [from Chinese *sanpan* (*san* = three, *pan* = boards)]

sample *noun* a small amount that shows what something is like; a specimen.

sample *verb* (**sampled**, **sampling**) take a sample of something.

sampler *noun* a piece of embroidery worked in various stitches to show skill in needlework.

samurai *noun* (*plural* **samurai**) a Japanese army officer. [Japanese]

sanatorium *noun* a hospital for treating chronic diseases (e.g. tuberculosis) or convalescents. [from Latin *sanare* = heal]

sanctify *verb* (**sanctified**, **sanctifying**) make holy or sacred. **sanctification** *noun* [from Latin *sanctus* = holy]

sanctimonious *adjective* making a show of being virtuous or pious.

sanction *noun* **1** permission; authorisation. **2** action taken against a nation that is considered to have broken an international law etc., *Sanctions against that country include refusing to trade with it.*

sanction *verb* **1** permit; authorise. **2** penalise. [from Latin *sancire* = make holy]

sanctity *noun* being sacred; holiness.

sanctuary *noun* (*plural* **sanctuaries**) **1** a safe place; a refuge. **2** a sacred place; the part of a church where the altar stands. [from Latin *sanctus* = holy]

sanctum *noun* a person's private room. [Latin, = holy thing]

sand *noun* the tiny particles that cover the ground in deserts, sea-shores, etc. **sands** *plural noun* a sandy area.

sand *verb* smooth or polish with sandpaper or some other rough material. **sander** *noun*

sandal *noun* a lightweight shoe with straps over the foot. **sandalled** *adjective*

sandalwood *noun* **1** a scented wood from a tropical tree. **2** perfume or incense from a sandalwood tree.

sandbag *noun* a bag filled with sand, used to build defences.

sandbank *noun* a bank of sand under water.

sandfly *noun* (*plural* **sandflies**) a very small biting insect.

sandpaper *noun* strong paper coated with sand or a similar substance, rubbed on rough surfaces to make them smooth.

sandshoe *noun* (*NZ*) a light shoe, usually made of canvas.

sandstone *noun* rock made of compressed sand.

sandwich *noun* (*plural* **sandwiches**) two or more slices of bread with jam, meat, or cheese etc. between them. [invented by the Earl of Sandwich (1718–92) so that he could eat while gambling]

sandwich *verb* put a thing between two other things.

sandy *adjective* **1** like sand; covered with sand. **2** yellowish-red, *sandy hair*. **sandiness** *noun*

sane *adjective* **1** having a healthy mind; not mad. **2** sensible. **sanely** *adverb*, **sanity** *noun* [from Latin *sanus* = healthy]

sanguinary *adjective* bloodstained. [from Latin *sanguis* = blood]

sanguine (*say* **sang**-gwin) *adjective* hopeful; optimistic.

sanitary *adjective* **1** free from germs and dirt; hygienic. **2** of sanitation.
sanitary towel an absorbent pad worn during menstruation.
[from Latin *sanus* = healthy]

sanitation *noun* arrangements for drainage and the disposal of sewage.

sanity *noun* being sane.

sap *noun* the liquid inside a plant, carrying food to all its parts.

sap *verb* (**sapped**, **sapping**) take away a person's strength gradually.

sapling *noun* a young tree. [from *sap*]

sapphire *noun* a bright-blue jewel.

sarcastic *adjective* saying amusing or contemptuous things that hurt someone's feelings; using irony. **sarcastically** *adverb*, **sarcasm** *noun* [from Greek *sarkazein* = tear the flesh]

sarcophagus *noun* (*plural* **sarcophagi**) a stone coffin, often decorated with carvings. [from Greek *sarkos* = of flesh, + *phagos* = eating]

sardine *noun* a small sea-fish, usually sold in tins, packed tightly in oil.

sardonic *adjective* funny in a grim or sarcastic way. **sardonically** *adverb*

sari *noun* (*plural* **saris**) a length of cloth worn wrapped round the body as a garment, especially by Indian women and girls. [Hindi]

sarong *noun* a strip of cloth worn tucked round the waist or under the armpits by men and women of Malaya and Java.

sartorial *adjective* of clothes. [from Latin *sartor* = tailor]

sash *noun* (*plural* **sashes**) a strip of cloth worn round the waist or over one shoulder. [from Arabic *shash* = turban]

sash window a window that slides up and down. [from French *châssis* = frame]

satanic (*say* sa-**tan**-ik) *adjective* of or like Satan. [from *Satan*, the Devil in Jewish and Christian teaching]

satchel *noun* a bag worn on the shoulder or over the back, especially for carrying books to and from school. [from Latin *saccellus* = little sack]

sate *verb* (**sated**, **sating**) satiate.

sateen *noun* a cotton material that looks like satin.

satellite *noun* **1** a planet or spacecraft etc. that moves in an orbit round a planet, *The moon is a satellite of the earth.* **2** a country that is under the influence of a more powerful country. [from Latin *satelles* = guard]
satellite dish a dish-shaped aerial for receiving broadcasts from a satellite.

satiate (*say* **say**-shee-ayt) *verb* (**satiated**, **satiating**) satisfy an appetite or desire etc. fully; glut. [from Latin *satis* = enough (compare *satisfaction*)]

satiety (*say* sat-**I**-it-ee) *noun* being or feeling satiated.

satin *noun* a silky material that is shiny on one side. **satiny** *adjective*

satinwood *noun* **1** a glossy yellow wood used for furniture-making. **2** a tree producing satinwood.

satire *noun* using humour or exaggeration to make fun of a person or thing; a play or poem etc. that does this. **satirical** *adjective*, **satirically** *adverb*, **satirist** *noun*, **satirise** *verb*

satisfaction *noun* **1** satisfying. **2** being satisfied and pleased because of this. **3** something that satisfies a desire etc. [from Latin *satis* = enough, + *facere* = make]

satisfactory *adjective* good enough; sufficient. **satisfactorily** *adverb*

satisfy *verb* (**satisfied**, **satisfying**) **1** give a person etc. what is needed or wanted. **2** make someone feel certain; convince, *The firemen were satisfied that the fire was out.* [same origin as *satisfaction*]

satsuma *noun* **1** a variety of mandarin orange originally from Japan. **2** a Japanese variety of plum. **3** a variety of Japanese pottery. [named after Satsuma, a Japanese province]

saturate *verb* (**saturated**, **saturating**) **1** make a thing very wet. **2** make something take in as much as possible of a substance or goods etc. **saturation** *noun*

Saturday *noun* the day after Friday.

saturnine *adjective* looking gloomy and forbidding, *a saturnine face.*

satyr (*say* **sat**-er) *noun* (in Greek myths) a woodland god with a man's body and a goat's ears, tail, and legs.

sauce *noun* **1** a thick liquid served with food to add flavour. **2** (*informal*) being cheeky; impudence.

saucepan *noun* a metal cooking-pan with a handle at the side.

saucer *noun* a small shallow object on which a cup etc. is placed.

saucy *adjective* (**saucier**, **sauciest**) cheeky; impudent. **saucily** *adverb*, **sauciness** *noun*

sauna *noun* a room or compartment filled with steam, used as a kind of bath (originally in Finland). [Finnish]

saunter *verb* walk slowly and casually. **saunter** *noun*

sausage *noun* a tube of edible skin stuffed with minced meat and other filling.
sausage sizzle (*NZ*) the outdoor cooking and selling of sausages to raise funds.

savage *adjective* wild and fierce; cruel. **savagely** *adverb*, **savageness** *noun*, **savagery** *noun*

savage *noun* a primitive or savage person. [from Latin *silvaticus* = of the woods, wild]

savannah *noun* a grassy plain in a hot country, with few or no trees.

save *verb* (**saved**, **saving**) **1** keep safe; free a person or thing from danger or harm. **2** keep something, such as money, computer data, so that it can be used later. **3** avoid wasting something, *This will save time.* **4** (in sports) prevent an opponent from scoring. **save** *noun*, **saver** *noun*

save *preposition* except, *All the men save one were killed.* [from Latin *salvus* = safe]

saveloy *noun* a kind of red spicy sausage.

savings *plural noun* money saved.

saviour *noun* a person who saves someone. **our Saviour** Jesus Christ as the saviour of mankind.

savour *noun* the taste or smell of something.

savour *verb* **1** taste or smell. **2** enjoy; relish. [from Latin *sapor* = flavour]

savoury *adjective* **1** tasty but not sweet. **2** having an appetising taste or smell.

savoury *noun* (*plural* **savouries**) a savoury dish.

savoy *noun* a kind of cabbage.

saw[1] *noun* a tool with a zigzag edge for cutting wood or metal etc.

saw[1] *verb* (**sawed**, **sawn**, **sawing**) **1** cut with a saw. **2** move to and fro as a saw does.

saw[2] *past tense* of **see**[1].

sawdust *noun* powder that comes from wood cut by a saw.

sawmill *noun* a mill where timber is cut into planks etc. by machinery.

sawyer *noun* a person whose job is to saw timber.

Saxon *noun* a member of a people who came from Europe and occupied parts of England in the 5th–6th centuries.

saxophone *noun* a brass wind instrument with a reed in the mouthpiece. **saxophonist** *noun* [from the name of A. Sax, its Belgian inventor]

say *verb* (**said**, **saying**) **1** speak or express something in words. **2** give an opinion.

say *noun* the power to decide something, *I have no say in the matter.*

saying *noun* a well-known phrase or proverb or other statement.

scab *noun* **1** a hard crust that forms over a cut or graze while it is healing. **2** (*informal*) a blackleg.

scabbard *noun* the sheath of a sword or dagger.

scabby *adjective* covered in scabs.
scabby mouth (*NZ*) a contagious disease of sheep and goats.

scabies (*say* **skay**-beez) *noun* a contagious skin-disease that causes itching.

scaffold *noun* **1** (in history) a platform on which criminals were executed. **2** scaffolding.

scaffolding *noun* a structure of poles or tubes and planks making platforms for workers to stand on while building or repairing a house etc.

scald *verb* **1** burn yourself with very hot liquid or steam. **2** heat milk until it is nearly boiling. **3** clean pans etc. with boiling water. **scald** *noun*

scale[1] *noun* **1** a series of units, degrees, or qualities etc. for measuring something. **2** a series of musical notes going up or down in a fixed pattern. **3** proportion; ratio, *The scale of this map is one centimetre to the kilometre.* **4** the relative size or importance of something, *They entertain friends on a large scale.*

scale[1] *verb* (**scaled**, **scaling**) **1** climb, *She scaled the ladder.* **2** alter or arrange something in proportion to something else, *Scale your spending according to your income!* [from Latin *scala* = ladder]

scale[2] *noun* **1** each of the thin overlapping parts on the outside of fish, snakes, etc.; a thin flake or part like this. **2** a hard substance formed in a kettle or boiler by hard water, or on teeth.

scale[2] *verb* (**scaled**, **scaling**) remove scales or scale from something. [from Old French *escale* = flake, from an old Germanic word *skalo*]

scale[3] *noun* the pan of a balance.
scales *plural noun* a device for weighing things. [from Old Norse *skul* = bowl, from *skalo* (see *scale*[2])]

scale[3] *verb* adjust an amount according to a fixed scale.

scallop *noun* **1** a shellfish with two hinged fan-shaped shells. **2** each curve in an ornamental wavy border. **scalloped** *adjective*

scallywag *noun* (*slang*) a rascal.

scalp *noun* the skin on the top of the head.

scalp *verb* **1** cut or tear the scalp from. **2** to resell admission tickets to a concert, game, etc.

scalpel *noun* a small straight knife used by a surgeon or artist.

scaly *adjective* covered in scales or scale. [from *scale*[2]]

scamp *noun* a rascal.

scamp *verb* do work hastily and without proper care.

scamper *verb* run hurriedly. **scamper** *noun*

scan *verb* (**scanned**, **scanning**) **1** look at every part of something. **2** glance at something. **3** count the beats of a line of poetry; be correct in rhythm, *This line doesn't scan.* **4** sweep a radar or electronic beam over an area in search of something. **5** obtain an image of (part of the body) using an X-ray machine etc. **6** read a barcode on packaging etc. **7** convert (a document or picture) into digital form for reading and storing on a computer. **scan** *noun*, **scanner** *noun*

scandal *noun* **1** something shameful or disgraceful. **2** gossip about people's faults and wrongdoing. **scandalous** *adjective* [from Greek, = stumbling-block]

scandalise *verb* (**scandalised**, **scandalising**) shock a person by something considered shameful or disgraceful.

scandalmonger *noun* a person who invents or gossips about scandal.

Scandinavian *adjective* of Scandinavia (= Norway, Sweden, and Denmark; sometimes also Finland and Iceland). **Scandinavian** *noun*

scansion *noun* the scanning of verse.

scant *adjective* scanty.

scanty *adjective* (**scantier**, **scantiest**) small in amount or extent; meagre, *a scanty harvest.* **scantily** *adverb*, **scantiness** *noun*

scapegoat *noun* a person who is made to bear the blame or punishment for what others have done. [named after the *goat* which the ancient Jews allowed to *escape* into the desert after the priest had symbolically laid the people's sins upon it]

scar[1] *noun* the mark left by a cut or burn etc. after it has healed.

scar[1] *verb* (**scarred**, **scarring**) make a scar or scars on skin etc.

scar[2] *noun* a steep craggy place.

scarab *noun* an ancient Egyptian ornament or symbol carved in the shape of a beetle.

scarce *adjective* not enough to supply people; rare. **scarcity** *noun*
make yourself scarce (*informal*) go away; keep out of the way.

scarcely *adverb* only just; only with difficulty. *She could scarcely walk.*

scare *verb* (**scared**, **scaring**) frighten.

scare *noun* a fright; alarm. **scary** *adjective*

scarecrow *noun* a figure of a person dressed in old clothes, set up to frighten birds away from crops.

scarf *noun* (*plural* **scarves**) a strip of material worn round the neck or head.

scarifier *noun* a tool used for treating surfaces of a road, soil, lawn, or skin.

scarify *verb* **1** resurface or treat a surface. **2** criticise strongly.

scarlet *adjective & noun* bright red.
scarlet fever an infectious fever producing a scarlet rash.

scarp *noun* a steep slope on a hill.

scarper *verb* (*slang*) run away.

scathing (*say* **skay***th*-ing) *adjective* severely criticising a person or thing.

scatter *verb* throw or send or move in various directions.

scatterbrain *noun* a careless forgetful person. **scatterbrained** *adjective*

scaup *noun* a kind of diving duck.

scavenge *verb* (**scavenged**, **scavenging**) **1** search for useful things amongst rubbish. **2** (of a bird or animal) search for decaying flesh as food. **scavenger** *noun*

scenario *noun* (*plural* **scenarios**) **1** a summary of the plot of a play etc. **2** a possible way in which events etc. may develop in the future. [Italian]

scene *noun* **1** the place where something happens, *the scene of the crime*. **2** a part of a play or film. **3** a view as seen by a spectator. **4** an angry or noisy outburst, *He made a scene about the money*. **5** stage scenery. [from Greek *skene* = stage]

scenery *noun* **1** the natural features of a landscape. **2** things put on a stage to make it look like a place.

scenic *adjective* having fine natural scenery, *a scenic road along the coast.*

scent *noun* **1** a pleasant smell. **2** a liquid perfume. **3** an animal's smell that other animals can detect.

scent *verb* **1** discover something by its scent; detect. **2** put scent on something; make fragrant. **scented** *adjective* [from Latin *sentire* = perceive]

sceptic (*say* **skep**-tik) *noun* a sceptical person.

sceptical (*say* **skep**-tik-al) *adjective* not believing things. **sceptically** *adverb*, **scepticism** *noun* [from Greek *skeptikos* = thoughtful]

sceptre *noun* a rod carried by a king or queen as a symbol of sovereignty.

SCF *abbreviation* Save the Children Fund.

schedule (*say* **shed**-yool or **sked**-yool) *noun* a programme or timetable of planned events or work.

schedule *verb* (**scheduled**, **scheduling**) put into a schedule; plan. [from Latin *scedula* = little piece of paper]

schematic (*say* skee-**mat**-ik) *adjective* in the form of a diagram or chart.

scheme *noun* a plan of action.

scheme *verb* (**schemed**, **scheming**) make plans; plot. **schemer** *noun* [from Greek *schema* = form]

scherzo (*say* **skairts**-oh) *noun* (*plural* **scherzos**) a lively piece of music. [Italian, = joke]

schism (*say* sizm or skizm) *noun* the splitting of a group into two opposing sections because they disagree about something important. [from Greek *schisma* = split]

schizophrenia (*say* skid-zo-**free**-nee-a) *noun* a kind of mental illness. **schizophrenic** *adjective & noun* [from Greek *schizein* = to split, + *phren* = mind]

schnitzel *noun* a thin slice of meat, especially veal.

scholar *noun* **1** a person who has studied a subject thoroughly. **2** a person who has been awarded a scholarship. **scholarly** *adjective* [same origin as *school*[1]]

scholarship *noun* **1** a grant of money given to someone to help to pay for his or her education. **2** scholars' knowledge or methods; advanced study.

scholastic *adjective* of schools or education; academic.

school[1] *noun* **1** a place where teaching is done, especially of children. **2** the pupils in a school. **3** the time when teaching takes place in a school, *School begins at 9 a.m.* **4** a group of people who have the same beliefs or style of work etc. **schoolboy** *noun*, **schoolchild** *noun*, **schoolgirl** *noun*, **schoolmaster** *noun*, **schoolmistress** *noun*, **schoolroom** *noun*, **schoolteacher** *noun*

School C., **School Cert**. (*informal*) School Certificate.
School Certificate (*NZ*) an examination usually taken after three years at a secondary school before 2002.
school trustee (*NZ*) a member of a school's Board of Trustees, which manages the school's finances, appoints its staff, etc.

school[1] *verb* train, *She was schooling her horse for the competition.* [from Greek *schole* = leisure, lecture-place]

school[2] *noun* a shoal of fish or whales etc. [from an old word *scolu* = troop]

schooling *noun* training; education, especially in a school.

schooner (*say* **skoon**-er) *noun* a sailing-ship with two or more masts and with sails rigged along its length, not crosswise.

sciatica (*say* sy-**at**-ik-a) *noun* pain in the sciatic nerve (a large nerve in the hip and thigh).

science *noun* **1** the systematic study of the phenomena of the physical universe. **2** any branch of that study, such as chemistry and physics. **3** any other subject that uses a scientific method. [from Latin *scientia* = knowledge]

science fiction stories about imaginary scientific discoveries or space travel and life on other planets.

scientific *adjective* **1** of science or scientists. **2** studying things systematically and testing ideas carefully. **scientifically** *adverb*

scientist *noun* an expert in science; someone who studies science.

scientology *noun* a religion based on self-knowledge through study.

sci fi *abbreviation* science fiction.

scimitar *noun* a curved oriental sword.

scintillate *verb* (**scintillated**, **scintillating**) sparkle; be brilliant. **scintillation** *noun* [from Latin *scintilla* = spark]

scion (*say* **sy**-on) *noun* a descendant, especially of a noble family. [from Old French *cion* = a twig]

scissors *plural noun* a cutting-instrument used with one hand, with two blades pivoted so that they can close against each other. [from Latin *scissum* = cut]

scoff *verb* jeer; speak contemptuously. **scoffer** *noun*

scold *verb* rebuke; find fault with someone angrily. **scolding** *noun*

scone (*say* skon or skohn) *noun* a soft flat cake, usually eaten with butter.

scoop *noun* **1** a kind of deep spoon for serving ice-cream etc. **2** a deep shovel for lifting grain, sugar, etc. **3** a scooping movement. **4** an important piece of news published by only one newspaper.

scoop *verb* lift or hollow something out with a scoop.

scoot *verb* run or go away quickly.

scooter *noun* **1** a kind of lightweight motorcycle. **2** a board for riding on, with wheels and a long handle.

scope *noun* **1** opportunity to work, *This job gives scope for your musical abilities.* **2** the range or extent of a subject. [from Greek *skopos* = target]

scorch *verb* **1** make something go brown by burning it slightly. **2** (*slang*) travel very fast, *scorching along.*

scorching *adjective* (*informal*) very hot.

score *noun* **1** the number of points or goals made in a game; a result. **2** twenty, *'Three score years and ten' means 3 × 20 + 10 = 70 years.* **3** written or printed music. **4** a reason, *We refused to go on the score of cost.*

score *verb* (**scored**, **scoring**) **1** get a point or goal in a game. **2** keep a count of the score. **3** mark with lines or cuts. **4** write out a musical score. **scorer** *noun*

scoria *noun* a mass of rough stony lava.

scorn *noun* contempt. **scornful** *adjective*, **scornfully** *adverb*

scorn *verb* treat or refuse scornfully.

scorpion *noun* an animal that looks like a tiny lobster, with a poisonous sting.

Scot *noun* a person born in Scotland.

scotch *verb* put an end to an idea or rumour etc.

Scotch, **Scots**, **Scottish** *adjective* of or from Scotland.

scot-free *adjective* **1** without harm or punishment. **2** free of charge. [from *scot* = tax, + *free*]

scour[1] *verb* **1** rub something until it is clean and bright. **2** clear a channel or pipe by the force of water flowing through it. **scourer** *noun*

scour[2] *verb* search thoroughly.

scourge (*say* skerj) *noun* **1** a whip for flogging people. **2** something that inflicts suffering or punishment.

scourge *verb* (**scourged**, **scourging**) **1** flog with a whip. **2** cause suffering or punishment.

Scout *noun* a member of the Scout Association, an organisation for boys and girls.

scout[1] *noun* someone sent out to collect information.

scout[1] *verb* act as a scout; search an area thoroughly.

scout[2] *verb* reject an idea scornfully.

scowl *noun* a bad-tempered frown.

scowl *verb* make a scowl.

Scrabble *noun* (*trade mark*) a game played on a board, in which words are built up from single letters.

scrabble *verb* (**scrabbled**, **scrabbling**) **1** scratch or claw at something with the hands or feet. **2** grope or struggle to get something.

scrag or **scrag-end** *noun* the less meaty end of a neck of mutton.

scraggy *adjective* thin and bony.

scram *verb* (*slang*) go away. [from *scramble*]

scramble *verb* (**scrambled**, **scrambling**) **1** move quickly and awkwardly. **2** struggle to do or get something. **3** (of aircraft or their crew) hurry and take off quickly. **4** cook eggs by mixing them up and heating them in a pan. **5** mix things together. **6** alter a telephone or television signal so that it cannot be used without a special receiver. **scrambler** *noun*

scramble *noun* **1** a climb or walk over rough ground. **2** a struggle to do or get something. **3** a motorcycle race over rough ground.

scrap[1] *noun* **1** a small piece. **2** rubbish; waste material, especially metal that is suitable for reprocessing.

scrap[1] *verb* (**scrapped**, **scrapping**) get rid of something that is useless or unwanted.

scrap[2] *noun* (*informal*) a fight.

scrap[2] *verb* (**scrapped**, **scrapping**) (*informal*) fight.

scrape *verb* (**scraped**, **scraping**) **1** clean or smooth or damage something by passing something hard over it. **2** remove by scraping, *Scrape the mud off your shoes.* **3** pass with difficulty, *We scraped through.* **4** get something by great effort or care, *They scraped together enough money for a holiday.* **scraper** *noun*

scrape *noun* **1** a scraping movement or sound. **2** a mark etc. made by scraping. **3** an awkward situation caused by mischief or foolishness.

scrapie *noun* a disease of sheep and goats.

scrappy *adjective* made of scraps or bits or disconnected things. **scrappiness** *noun*

scratch *verb* **1** mark or cut the surface of a thing with something sharp. **2** rub the skin with finger-nails or claws because it itches. **3** withdraw from a race or competition.

scratch *noun* (*plural* **scratches**) **1** a mark made by scratching. **2** the action of scratching. **scratchy** *adjective*
start from scratch start from the beginning or with nothing prepared.
up to scratch up to the proper standard.

scratch-ticket *noun* (also **scratchie** *informal*) a gambling card with areas to scratch the covering from to see if one has won a prize.

scrawl *noun* untidy handwriting.

scrawl *verb* write in a scrawl.

scrawny *adjective* scraggy.

scream *noun* **1** a loud cry of pain, fear, anger, or excitement. **2** a loud piercing sound. **3** (*slang*) a very amusing person or thing.

scream *verb* make a scream.

scree *noun* a mass of loose stones on the side of a mountain.

screech *noun* a harsh high-pitched scream or sound. **screech** *verb*

screed *noun* a very long piece of writing.

screen *noun* **1** a thing that protects, hides, or divides something. **2** a surface on which movies or television pictures are shown. **3** a visual display unit. **4** a windscreen.

screen *verb* **1** protect, hide, or divide with a screen. **2** show a movie or television pictures on a screen. **3** examine carefully, e.g. to check whether a person is suitable for a job or whether a substance is present in something. **4** sift gravel etc.

screw *noun* **1** a metal pin with a spiral ridge (the *thread*) round it, holding things together by being twisted in. **2** a twisting movement. **3** something twisted. **4** a propeller, especially for a ship or motor boat.

screw *verb* **1** fasten with a screw or screws. **2** twist.

screwdriver *noun* a tool for turning screws.

scribble *verb* (**scribbled**, **scribbling**) **1** write quickly or untidily or carelessly. **2** make meaningless marks. **scribble** *noun* [same origin as *scribe*]

scribe *noun* **1** a person who made copies of writings before printing was invented. **2** (in biblical times) a professional religious scholar. **scribal** *adjective* [from Latin *scribere* = write]

scrim *noun* a loosely woven cotton fabric used to line walls etc.

scrimmage *noun* a confused struggle.

scrimp *verb* skimp, *scrimp and save.*

script *noun* **1** handwriting. **2** a manuscript. **3** the text of a play, movie, broadcast talk, etc. **4** an alphabet or writing system. **5** a doctor's prescription. **6** a series of instructions that can be adapted by a computer program. [from Latin *scriptum* = written]

scripture *noun* sacred writings, especially the Bible. [same origin as *script*]

scroggin *noun* (*NZ*) a mix of dried fruit, nuts, etc., eaten as a snack by trampers.

scroll *noun* **1** a roll of paper or parchment used for writing on. **2** a spiral design.

scrotum (*say* **skroh**-tum) *noun* the pouch of skin behind the penis, containing the testicles. **scrotal** *adjective*

scrounge *verb* (**scrounged**, **scrounging**) (*slang*) cadge. **scrounger** *noun*

scrub[1] *verb* (**scrubbed**, **scrubbing**) **1** rub with a hard brush, especially to clean something. **2** (*slang*) cancel. **scrub** *noun*

scrub[2] *noun* low trees and bushes; land covered with these.

scrubby *adjective* undersized and shabby or wretched. [from *scrub*[2]]

scrub-cutter *noun* (*NZ*) **1** a person whose job is clearing the land of scrub. **2** a machine or tool for cutting scrub. **scrub-cutting** *noun*

scruff *noun* the back of the neck.

scruffy *adjective* shabby and untidy. **scruffily** *adverb*, **scruffiness** *noun*

scrum *noun* **1** (*old use* **scrummage**) a group of players from each side in rugby who push against each other and try to heel out the ball which is thrown between them. **2** a crowd pushing against each other.

scrumptious *adjective* delicious.

scrunch *verb* crunch.

scruple *noun* a feeling of doubt or hesitation when your conscience tells you that an action would be wrong.

scruple *verb* (**scrupled**, **scrupling**) have scruples, *He would not scruple to betray us.*

scrupulous *adjective* **1** very careful and conscientious. **2** strictly honest or honourable. **scrupulously** *adverb*

scrutinise *verb* (**scrutinised**, **scrutinising**) examine or look at something carefully. **scrutiny** *noun*

scuba *noun* a device for breathing under water. [from the initial letters of *self-contained underwater breathing apparatus*]

scud *verb* (**scudded**, **scudding**) move fast, *Clouds scudded across the sky.*

scuff *verb* **1** drag your feet while walking. **2** scrape with your foot; mark or damage something by doing this.

scuffle *noun* a confused fight or struggle.

scuffle *verb* (**scuffled**, **scuffling**) take part in a scuffle.

scull *noun* a small or lightweight oar.

scull *verb* row with sculls.

sculptor *noun* a person who makes sculptures.

sculpture *noun* making shapes by carving wood or stone or casting metal; a shape made in this way. **sculpture** *verb* [from Latin *sculpere* = carve]

scum *noun* **1** froth or dirt on top of a liquid. **2** worthless people.

scunge *noun* (*NZ, informal*) **1** dirt, mess. **2** a disagreeable person. **scungy** *adjective*

scupper *noun* an opening in a ship's side to let water drain away.

scupper *verb* **1** sink a ship deliberately. **2** (*informal*) wreck, *It scuppered our plans.*

scurf *noun* flakes of dry skin. **scurfy** *adjective*

scurrilous *adjective* **1** very insulting. **2** vulgar. **scurrilously** *adverb*

scurry *verb* (**scurried**, **scurrying**) run with short steps; hurry.

scurvy *noun* a disease caused by lack of vitamin C in food.

scut *noun* the short tail of a rabbit etc.

scutter *verb* scurry.

scuttle[1] *noun* a bucket or container for coal in a house. [from Latin *scutella* = dish]

scuttle[2] *verb* (**scuttled**, **scuttling**) scurry; hurry away. [from *scud*]

scuttle[3] *noun* a small opening with a lid in a ship's deck or side.

scuttle[3] *verb* (**scuttled**, **scuttling**) sink a ship deliberately by letting water into it. [from Spanish *escotar* = cut out]

scuzzy *adjective* (*slang*) dirty, disgusting.

scythe *noun* a tool with a long curved blade for cutting grass or corn.

scythe *verb* (**scythed**, **scything**) cut with a scythe.

SE *abbreviation* south-east; south-eastern.

se- *prefix* **1** apart; aside (as in *secluded*). **2** without (as in *secure*). [Latin]

sea *noun* **1** the salt water that covers most of the earth's surface; a part of this. **2** a lake, *the Sea of Galilee.* **3** a large area of something, *a sea of faces.*
at sea on the sea; not knowing what to do.
sea anemone a sea-creature with short tentacles round its mouth.
sea change a dramatic change.

seaboard *noun* the coast.

seafaring *adjective & noun* working or travelling on the sea. **seafarer** *noun*

seafood *noun* fish or shellfish from the sea eaten as food.

seagull *noun* a sea-bird with long wings.

sea-horse *noun* a small fish with a head rather like a horse's head.

seal[1] *noun* a sea-animal with thick fur or bristles, that eats fish.

seal[2] *noun* **1** a piece of metal with an engraved design for pressing on a soft substance to leave an impression. **2** this impression. **3** a tar-sealed surface or area. **4** something designed to close an opening and prevent air or liquid etc. from getting in or out. **5** a small decorative sticker, *Christmas seals.*

seal[2] *verb* **1** close something by sticking two parts together. **2** close securely; stop up. **3** tar-seal (a road etc.). **4** press a seal on something.
seal off prevent people getting to an area.

sea-level *noun* the level of the sea halfway between high and low tide.

sealing-wax *noun* a substance that is soft when heated but hardens when cooled, used for sealing documents or for marking with a seal.

sea-lion *noun* a kind of large seal.

seam *noun* **1** the line where two edges of cloth or wood etc. join. **2** a layer of coal in the ground.

seaman *noun* (*plural* **seamen**) a sailor.

seamanship *noun* skill in seafaring.

seamy *adjective* **seamy side** the less attractive side or part, *Police see a lot of the seamy side of life.*

seance (*say* **say**-ahns) *noun* a spiritualist meeting. [French, = a sitting]

seaplane *noun* an aeroplane that can land on and take off from water.

seaport *noun* a port on the coast.

sear *verb* scorch or burn the surface of something.

search *verb* look very carefully in a place etc. in order to find something. **search** *noun,* **searcher** *noun*
search engine (*Computing*) a program which helps you locate the information you want on the Internet.

searchlight *noun* a light with a strong beam that can be turned in any direction.

seascape *noun* a picture or view of the sea. (Compare *landscape.*)

seasick *adjective* sick because of the movement of a ship. **seasickness** *noun*

season *noun* **1** each of the four main parts of the year (spring, summer, autumn, winter). **2** the time of year when something happens, *the football season.*
in season available and ready for eating, *Apples are in season in the autumn.*

season *verb* **1** give extra flavour to food by adding salt, pepper, or other strong-tasting substances. **2** dry and treat timber etc. to make it ready for use.

seasonable *adjective* suitable for the season, *Hot weather is seasonable in summer.* **seasonably** *adverb*

seasonal *adjective* of or for a season; happening in a particular season. *Fruit-picking is seasonal work.* **seasonally** *adverb*

seasoning *noun* a substance used to season food.

season-ticket *noun* a ticket that can be used as often as you like throughout a period of time.

seat *noun* **1** a thing made or used for sitting on. **2** the right to be a member of a council, committee, parliament, etc., *She won the seat ten years ago.* **3** the buttocks; the part of a skirt or trousers covering these. **4** the place where something is based or located, *Wellington is the seat of our government.*

seat *verb* **1** place in or on a seat. **2** have seats for, *The theatre seats 3,000 people.*

seatbelt *noun* a strap to hold a person securely in a seat.

sea-urchin *noun* a sea-animal with a shell covered in sharp spikes.

seaward *adjective & adverb* towards the sea. **seawards** *adverb*

seaweed *noun* a plant or plants that grow in the sea.

seaworthy *adjective* (of a ship) fit for a sea voyage. **seaworthiness** *noun*

secateurs *plural noun* clippers held in the hand for pruning plants. [from Latin *secare* = to cut]

secede (*say* sis-**seed**) *verb* (**seceded, seceding**) withdraw from being a member of an organisation. **secession** *noun* [from *se-* = aside, + Latin *cedere* = go]

secluded *adjective* screened or sheltered from view. **seclusion** *noun* [from *se-* = aside, + Latin *claudere* = shut]

second[1] *adjective* **1** next after the first. **2** another, *a second chance.* **3** less good, *second quality.* **secondly** *adverb*
second nature behaviour that has become automatic or a habit, *Lying is second nature to him.*
second sight the ability to foresee the future.

second[1] *noun* **1** a person or thing that is second. **2** an attendant of a fighter in a boxing-match, duel, etc. **3** a product with minor defects. **4** one-sixtieth of a minute of time or of a degree used in measuring angles.

second[1] *verb* **1** assist someone. **2** support a proposal, motion, etc. **seconder** *noun* [from Latin *secundus* = next]

second[2] (*say* sik-**ond**) *verb* transfer a person temporarily to another job or department etc. **secondment** *noun*

secondary *adjective* **1** coming after or from something. **2** less important. **3** (of education etc.) for children of more than about 13 years old, *a secondary school.* (Compare *primary.*)
secondary colours colours made by mixing two primary colours.

second-hand *adjective* **1** bought or used after someone else has owned it. **2** selling used goods, *a second-hand shop.*

secret *adjective* **1** that must not be told or shown to other people. **2** not known by everybody. **3** working secretly. **secretly** *adverb*, **secrecy** *noun*

secret *noun* something secret. [from Latin *secretum* = set apart]

secretariat *noun* an administrative department of a large organisation such as the United Nations.

secretary (*say* **sek**-rit-ree) *noun* (*plural* **secretaries**) **1** a person whose job is to help with letters, answer the telephone, and make business arrangements for a person or organisation. **2** the chief assistant of a government minister or ambassador. **secretarial** *adjective*

secrete (*say* sik-**reet**) *verb* (**secreted**, **secreting**) **1** hide something. **2** produce a substance in the body, *Saliva is secreted in the mouth.* **secretion** *noun* [from *secret*]

secretive (*say* **seek**-rit-iv) *adjective* liking or trying to keep things secret. **secretively** *adverb*, **secretiveness** *noun*

sect *noun* a group whose beliefs differ from those of others in the same religion; a faction.

sectarian (*say* sekt-**air**-ee-an) *adjective* belonging to or supporting a sect.

section *noun* **1** a part of something. **2** a cross-section. **3** (*NZ*) a piece of land on which a house is or will be built. **4** (*NZ*) a division of a bus route, used in calculating fares, *It costs $1.80 for two sections.* **sectional** *adjective*
on section (*NZ*) (of a trainee teacher) working in a school.
[from Latin *sectum* = cut]

sector *noun* **1** one part of an area. **2** a part of something, *the private sector of industry.*

secular *adjective* of worldly affairs, not of spiritual or religious matters.

secure *adjective* **1** safe, especially against attack. **2** certain not to slip or fail. **3** reliable. **securely** *adverb*

secure *verb* (**secured**, **securing**) **1** make a thing secure. **2** obtain, *We secured two tickets for the show.* [from Latin, = free from worry (*se-* = apart, *cura* = care)]

security *noun* (*plural* **securities**) **1** being secure; safety. **2** precautions against theft or spying etc. **3** something given as a guarantee that a promise will be kept or a debt repaid. **4** investments such as stocks and shares.

sedate *adjective* calm and dignified. **sedately** *adverb*, **sedateness** *noun* [from Latin *sedatum* = made calm]

sedative (*say* **sed**-a-tiv) *noun* a medicine that makes a person calm. **sedation** *noun*

sedentary (*say* **sed**-en-ter-ee) *adjective* done sitting down, *sedentary work.* [from Latin *sedens* = sitting]

sedge *noun* a grass-like plant growing in marshes or near water.

sediment *noun* fine particles of solid matter that float in liquid or sink to the bottom of it. [from Latin *sedere* = sit]

sedimentary *adjective* formed from particles that have settled on a surface, *sedimentary rocks.*

sedition *noun* making people rebel against the authority of the State. **seditious** *adjective*

seduce *verb* (**seduced**, **seducing**) **1** persuade a person to have sexual intercourse. **2** attract or lead astray by offering temptations. **seducer** *noun*, **seduction** *noun*, **seductive** *adjective* [from *se-* = aside, + Latin *ducere* = to lead]

sedulous *adjective* diligent and persevering. **sedulously** *adverb*

see[1] *verb* (**saw**, **seen**, **seeing**) **1** perceive with the eyes. **2** meet or visit somebody, *See a doctor about your cough.* **3** understand, *She saw what I meant.* **4** imagine, *Can you see yourself as a teacher?* **5** consider, *I will see what can be done.* **6** make sure, *See that the windows are shut.* **7** discover, *See who is at the door.* **8** escort, *See her to the door.*
see through not be deceived by something.
see to attend to.

see[2] *noun* the district of which a bishop or archbishop is in charge, *the see of Canterbury.* [from Latin *sedes* = seat]

seed *noun* (*plural* **seeds** or **seed**) **1** a fertilised part of a plant, capable of growing into a new plant. **2** (*old use*) descendants. **3** a seeded player.

seed *verb* **1** plant or sprinkle seeds in something. **2** name the best players and arrange for them not to play against each other in the early rounds of a tournament.

seedling *noun* a very young plant growing from a seed.

seedy *adjective* (**seedier**, **seediest**) **1** full of seeds. **2** shabby and disreputable. **seediness** *noun*

seeing *conjunction* considering, *Seeing that we have all finished, let's go.*

seek *verb* (**sought**, **seeking**) search for; try to find or obtain.

seem *verb* give the impression of being something, *She seems worried about her work.* **seemingly** *adverb*

seemly *adjective* (of behaviour etc.) proper; suitable. **seemliness** *noun*

seep *verb* ooze slowly out or through something. **seepage** *noun*

seer *noun* a prophet. [from *see*[1]]

seersucker *noun* fabric woven with a puckered surface. [from Persian, = milk and sugar, or a striped garment]

see-saw *noun* a plank balanced in the middle so that two people can sit, one on each end, and make it go up and down.

seethe *verb* (**seethed**, **seething**) **1** bubble and surge like water boiling. **2** be very angry or excited.

segment *noun* a part that is cut off or separates naturally from other parts, *the segments of an orange.* **segmented** *adjective*

segregate *verb* (**segregated**, **segregating**) **1** separate people of different religions, races, etc. **2** isolate a person or thing. **segregation** *noun* [from *se-* = apart, + Latin *-gregatum* = herded]

seismic (*say* **sy**-zmik) *adjective* of earthquakes or other vibrations of the earth.
seismic remediation *noun* earthquake strengthening of a building.

seismograph (*say* **sy**-zmo-grahf) *noun* an instrument for measuring the strength of earthquakes. [from Greek *seismos* = earthquake, + *-graph*]

seize *verb* (**seized**, **seizing**) **1** take hold of a person or thing suddenly or forcibly. **2** take eagerly, *Seize your chance!* **3** have a sudden effect on, *Panic seized us.*
seize up become jammed, especially because of friction or overheating.

seizure *noun* **1** seizing. **2** a sudden fit, as in epilepsy or a heart attack.

seldom *adverb* rarely; not often.

select *verb* **1** choose a person or thing. **2** use a computer mouse or keystroke to define or highlight text. **selection** *noun*, **selector** *noun*

select *adjective* **1** carefully chosen, *a select group of pupils.* **2** (of a club etc.) choosing its members carefully; exclusive. [from *se-* = apart, + Latin *legere* = pick]

selective *adjective* choosing or chosen carefully. **selectively** *adverb*, **selectivity** *noun*

self *noun* (*plural* **selves**) **1** a person as an individual. **2** a person's particular nature, *She has recovered and is her old self again.* **3** a person's own advantage, *He always puts self first.*

self- *prefix* **1** of or to or done by yourself or itself. **2** automatic (as in *self-loading*).
self-addressed addressed to yourself.
self-assured self-confident.
self-catering catering for yourself (instead of having meals provided).
self-centred selfish.
self-confident confident of your own abilities.
self-conscious embarrassed or unnatural because you know that people are watching you.
self-contained complete in itself.
self-control the ability to control your own behaviour.
self-controlled having self-control.
self-defence defending yourself.
self-denial deliberately going without things you would like to have.
self-employed working independently, not for an employer.
self-evident obvious and not needing proof or explanation.
self-important pompous.
self-interest your own advantage.
self-possessed calm and dignified.
self-raising (of flour) making cakes rise without needing to have baking-powder etc. added.
self-respect your own proper respect for yourself.
self-righteous smugly sure that you are behaving virtuously.
self-satisfied very pleased with yourself.
self-seeking selfishly trying to benefit yourself.
self-service where customers help themselves to things and pay a cashier for what they have taken.
self-sufficient able to provide what you need without help from others.
self-willed obstinately doing what you want; stubborn.

selfish *adjective* doing what you want and not thinking of other people; keeping things for yourself. **selfishly** *adverb*, **selfishness** *noun*

selfless *adjective* unselfish.

selfsame *adjective* the very same.

sell *verb* (**sold**, **selling**) exchange something for money. **seller** *noun*
sell out sell all your stock of something; (*informal*) betray someone.

sell *noun* **1** the manner of selling something. **2** (*informal*) a deception.

sellotape *noun* (*trade mark*) adhesive tape.

selvage *noun* an edge of cloth woven so that it does not unravel. [from *self* + *edge*]

selves *plural* of **self**.

semantic *adjective* of or relating to the meaning of words.

semantics *noun* the study of meaning in language.

semaphore *noun* a system of signalling by holding the arms in positions that indicate letters of the alphabet. [from Greek *sema* = sign, + *phoros* = carrying]

semblance *noun* an outward appearance.

semen (*say* **seem**-en) *noun* a white liquid produced by males and containing sperm. [Latin, = seed]

semester (*say* sim-**est**-er) *noun* a half-year period in universities.

semi- *prefix* half; partly. [Latin, = half]

semibreve *noun* the longest musical note normally used (𝅝), equal to two minims in length.

semicircle *noun* half a circle. **semicircular** *adjective*

semicolon *noun* a punctuation mark (;) used to mark a break that is more than that marked by a comma.

semiconductor *noun* a substance that can conduct electricity but not as well as most metals do.

semi-detached *adjective* (of a house) joined to another house on one side only.

semifinal *noun* a match or round whose winner will take part in the final.

seminar *noun* a meeting for advanced discussion and research on a subject.

seminary *noun* (*plural* **seminaries**) a training college for priests.

semiquaver *noun* a note in music (𝅘𝅥𝅯), equal to half a quaver in length.

Semitic (*say* sim-**it**-ik) *adjective* of the Semites, the group of people that includes the Jews and Arabs. **Semite** (*say* **see**-my't) *noun*

semitone *noun* half a tone in music.

semolina *noun* hard round grains of wheat used to make milk puddings and pasta. [from Italian *semola* = bran]

senate *noun* **1** the governing council in ancient Rome. **2** the upper house of the parliament of the United States, Australia, and certain other countries. **senator** *noun* [from Latin *senatus* = council of elders]

send *verb* (**sent**, **sending**) **1** make a person or thing go somewhere. **2** cause to become, *It sent them mad.* **sender** *noun*
send for order a person or thing to come or be brought to you.
send up (*informal*) make fun of something by imitating it.

senile (*say* **seen**-I'll) *adjective* suffering from weakness of the body or mind because of old age. **senility** *noun* [from Latin *senilis* = old]

senior *adjective* **1** older in age. **2** higher in rank. **3** for older children, *a senior school.* **seniority** *noun*
senior citizen an elderly person.

senior *noun* **1** a person who is older or higher in rank than you are, *He is my senior.* **2** a member of a senior school. [Latin, = older]

senna *noun* the dried pods or leaves of a tropical tree, used as a laxative.

sensation *noun* **1** a feeling, *a sensation of warmth.* **2** a very excited condition; something causing this, *The news caused a great sensation.* **sensational** *adjective*, **sensationally** *adverb* [same origin as *sense*]

sensationalism *noun* deliberate use of dramatic words or style etc. to arouse excitement. **sensationalist** *noun*

sense *noun* **1** the ability to see, hear, smell, touch, or taste things. **2** the ability to feel or appreciate something; awareness, *a sense of humour.* **3** the power to think or make wise decisions, *He hasn't got the sense to come in out of the rain.* **4** meaning, *The word 'run' has many senses.*
senses *plural noun* sanity, *He is out of his senses.*
make sense have a meaning; be a sensible idea.

sense *verb* (**sensed**, **sensing**) **1** feel; get an impression, *I sensed that she did not like me.* **2** detect something, *This device senses radioactivity.* **sensor** *noun*

senseless *adjective* **1** stupid; not showing good sense. **2** unconscious.

sensibility *noun* (*plural* **sensibilities**) sensitiveness; feeling, *The criticism hurt the artist's sensibilities.*

sensible *adjective* **1** wise; having or showing good sense. **2** aware, *We are sensible of the honour you have done us.* **sensibly** *adverb*

sensitise *verb* (**sensitised**, **sensitising**) make a thing sensitive to something.

sensitive *adjective* **1** receiving impressions quickly and easily, *sensitive fingers.* **2** easily hurt or offended, *She is very sensitive about her height.* **3** affected by something, *Photographic paper is sensitive to light.* **sensitively** *adverb*, **sensitivity** *noun*

sensory *adjective* of the senses; receiving sensations, *sensory nerves.*

sensual *adjective* of the senses; pleasing the body, *sensual pleasures.*

sensuous *adjective* giving pleasure to the senses, especially by being beautiful or delicate.

sentence *noun* **1** a group of words that express a complete thought and form a statement, question, exclamation, or command. **2** the punishment announced to a convicted person in a lawcourt.

sentence *verb* (**sentenced**, **sentencing**) give someone a sentence in a lawcourt, *The judge sentenced him to a year in prison.* [from Latin *sententia* = opinion]

sententious *adjective* giving moral advice in a pompous way.

sentient *adjective* capable of feeling and perceiving things, *sentient beings.* [from Latin *sentiens* = feeling]

sentiment *noun* **1** an opinion. **2** sentimentality. [from Latin *sentire* = feel]

sentimental *adjective* showing or arousing tenderness or romantic feeling or foolish emotion. **sentimentally** *adverb*, **sentimentality** *noun*

sentinel *noun* a sentry.

sentry *noun* (*plural* **sentries**) a soldier guarding something.

sepal *noun* each of the leaves forming the calyx of a bud.

separable *adjective* able to be separated.

separate *adjective* not joined to anything; on its own; not shared. **separately** *adverb*

separate *verb* (**separated**, **separating**) **1** make or keep separate; divide. **2** become separate. **3** stop living together as a married couple. **separation** *noun*, **separator** *noun* [from *se-* = apart, + Latin *parare* = make ready]

separatism *noun* a policy of achieving political independence through separation.

sepia *noun* reddish-brown. [from Greek, = cuttlefish (from which the dye was originally obtained)]

sepsis *noun* a septic condition.

September the ninth month of the year. [from Latin *septem* = seven (in Roman times it was the seventh month)]

septet *noun* **1** a group of seven musicians. **2** a piece of music for seven musicians. [from Latin *septem* = seven]

septic *adjective* infected with harmful bacteria that cause pus to form. [from Greek *septikos* = made rotten]

sepulchral (*say* sep-**ul**-kral) *adjective* **1** of a sepulchre. **2** (of a voice) sounding deep and hollow.

sepulchre (*say* **sep**-ul-ker) *noun* a tomb. [from Latin *sepultum* = buried]

sequel *noun* **1** a book or movie etc. that continues the story of an earlier one. **2** something that follows or results from an earlier event.

sequence *noun* **1** the following of one thing after another; the order in which things happen. **2** a series of things. [from Latin *sequens* = following]

sequestrate *verb* (**sequestrated**, **sequestrating**) confiscate. **sequestration** *noun*

sequin *noun* a tiny bright disc sewn on clothes etc. to decorate them. **sequinned** *adjective*

seraph *noun* (*plural* **seraphim** or **seraphs**) a kind of angel.

seraphic (*say* ser-**af**-ik) *adjective* angelic, *a seraphic smile*. **seraphically** *adverb*

serenade *noun* a song or tune played by a lover to his lady.

serenade *verb* (**serenaded**, **serenading**) sing or play a serenade to someone.

serene *adjective* calm and cheerful. **serenely** *adverb*, **serenity** *noun*

serf *noun* a farm labourer who worked for a landowner in the Middle Ages. **serfdom** *noun* [same origin as *servant*]

serge *noun* a kind of strong woven fabric.

sergeant (*say* **sar**-jent) *noun* a soldier or policeman who is in charge of others.

sergeant-major *noun* a soldier who is one rank higher than a sergeant.

serial *noun* **1** a story or film that is presented in separate parts. **2** a periodical or journal. **serial killer** a person who murders a number of victims in succession.

serialise *verb* (**serialised**, **serialising**) produce a story or film etc. as a serial. **serialisation** *noun*

series *noun* (*plural* **series**) a number of things following or connected with each other. [Latin, = row or chain]

serious *adjective* **1** solemn and thoughtful; not smiling. **2** sincere; not casual; not light-hearted, *a serious attempt*. **3** causing anxiety, not trivial, *a serious accident*. **seriously** *adverb*, **seriousness** *noun*

sermon *noun* a talk given by a preacher, especially as part of a religious service.

serpent *noun* a snake. [from Latin *serpens* = creeping]

serpentine *adjective* twisting and curving like a snake, *a serpentine road*.

serrated *adjective* having a notched edge. [from Latin *serratum* = sawn]

serried *adjective* arranged in rows close together, *serried ranks of troops*.

serum (*say* **seer**-um) *noun* the thin pale-yellow liquid that remains from blood when the rest has clotted; this fluid used medically. [Latin, = whey]

servant *noun* a person whose job is to work or serve in someone else's house. [from Latin *servus* = slave]

serve *verb* (**served**, **serving**) **1** work for a person or organisation or country etc. **2** sell things to people in a shop. **3** give out food to people at a meal. **4** spend time in something; undergo, *He served a prison sentence*. **5** be suitable for something, *This will serve our purpose*. **6** start play in tennis etc. by hitting the ball.
it serves you right you deserve it.

serve *noun* a service in tennis etc.

server *noun* **1** a computer or program that manages access to a central resource or service in a network. **2** (in tennis etc.) the player who is serving.

service *noun* **1** working for a person or organisation or country etc. **2** something that helps people or supplies what they want, *a bus service*. **3** the army, navy, or air force, *the armed services*. **4** a religious ceremony. **5** providing people with goods, food, etc., *quick service*. **6** a set of dishes and plates etc. for a meal, *a dinner service*. **7** the servicing of a vehicle or machine etc. **8** the action of serving in tennis etc.
service road a temporary road used in road building etc.; a secondary access used by workers and tradesmen.

service *verb* (**serviced**, **servicing**) **1** repair or keep a vehicle or machine etc. in working order. **2** supply with services.

serviceable *adjective* usable; suitable for ordinary use or wear.

serviceman *noun* (*plural* **servicemen**), **servicewoman** *noun* (*plural* **servicewomen**) a member of the armed services.

serviette *noun* a piece of cloth or paper used to keep your clothes or hands clean at a meal.

servile *adjective* of or like a slave; slavish. **servility** *noun* [same origin as *servant*]

servitude *noun* the condition of being obliged to work for someone else and having no independence; slavery.

sesame (*say* **ses**-a-mee) *noun* **1** a plant with seeds that are used as food or as a source of oil. **2** its seeds.

sesquicentenary *noun* a 150th anniversary.

session *noun* **1** a meeting or series of meetings, *The Queen will open the next session of Parliament*. **2** a time spent doing one thing, *a recording session*. [from Latin *sessio* = sitting]

set *verb* (**set**, **setting**) This word has many uses, including (**1**) put or fix (*Set the vase on the table. Set a date for the wedding*), (**2**) make or become firm or hard (*Leave the jelly to set*), (**3**) give someone a task (*This sets us a problem*), (**4**) put into a condition (*Set them free*), (**5**) go down below the horizon (*The sun was setting*).
set about start doing something; (*informal*) attack somebody.
set off begin a journey; start something happening; cause to explode.
set out begin a journey; display or make known.
set sail begin a voyage.
set to begin doing something vigorously; begin fighting or arguing.
set up place in position; establish, *set up house*; cause or start, *set up a din*.

set *noun* **1** a group of people or things that belong together. **2** a radio or television receiver. **3** the way something is placed, *the set of his jaw*. **4** the scenery or stage for a play or movie. **5** a group of games in a tennis match.

set-back *noun* something that stops progress or slows it down.

set square a device shaped like a right-angled triangle, used in drawing lines parallel to each other etc.

settee *noun* a long soft seat with a back and arms.

setter *noun* a dog of a long-haired breed that can be trained to stand rigid when it scents game.

setting *noun* **1** the way or place in which something is set. **2** music for the words of a song etc.

settle[1] *verb* (**settled**, **settling**) **1** arrange; decide or solve something, *That settles the problem*. **2** make or become calm or comfortable or orderly; stop being restless, *Stop chattering and settle down!* **3** go and live somewhere, *They settled in Masterton*. **4** sink; come to rest on something, *Dust had settled on his books*. **5** pay a bill or debt. **settler** *noun*

settle[2] *noun* a long wooden seat with a high back and arms.

settlement *noun* **1** settling something. **2** the way something is settled. **3** a small number of people or houses established in a new area; a small rural community.

set-up *noun* (*informal*) the way something is organised or arranged.

seven *noun & adjective* the number 7; one more than six. **seventh** *adjective & noun*

Sevens *noun* a form of rugby union with seven players to a side.

seventeen *noun & adjective* the number 17; one more than sixteen. **seventeenth** *adjective & noun*

seventy *noun & adjective* (*plural* **seventies**) the number 70; seven times ten. **seventieth** *adjective & noun*

sever *verb* (**severed**, **severing**) cut or break off. **severance** *noun*

several *adjective & noun* more than two but not many.

severally *adverb* separately.

severe *adjective* **1** strict; not gentle or kind. **2** intense; forceful, *severe gales*. **3** very plain, *a severe style of dress*. **severely** *adverb*, **severity** *noun*

sew *verb* (**sewed**, **sewn** or **sewed**, **sewing**) **1** join things together by using a needle and thread. **2** work with a needle and thread or with a sewing-machine.
sew up (*informal*) complete or round off favourably.

sewage (*say* **soo**-ij) *noun* waste matter carried away in drains.

sewer (*say* **soo**-er) *noun* a drain for carrying away sewage.

sewing-machine *noun* a machine for sewing things.

sex *noun* (*plural* **sexes**) **1** each of the two groups (*male* and *female*) into which living things are placed according to their functions in the process of reproduction. **2** the instinct that causes members of the two sexes to be attracted to one another. **3** sexual intercourse. [from Latin *secus* = division]

sexism *noun* discrimination against people of a particular sex, especially women. **sexist** *adjective & noun*

sextant *noun* an instrument for measuring the angle of the sun and stars, used for finding your position when navigating. [from Latin *sextus* = sixth (because early sextants contained 60°, one-sixth of a circle)]

sextet *noun* **1** a group of six musicians. **2** a piece of music for six musicians. [from Latin *sextus* = sixth]

sexton *noun* a person whose job is to take care of a church and churchyard.

sextuplet *noun* each of six children born to the same mother at one time. [from Latin *sextus* = sixth]

sexual *adjective* **1** of sex or the sexes. **2** (of reproduction) happening by the fusion of male and female cells. **sexually** *adverb*, **sexuality** *noun*
sexual harassment unwanted sexual advances or remarks etc. made to a person, especially at a place of work.
sexual intercourse sexual contact involving penetration.

sexy *adjective* (**sexier**, **sexiest**) (*informal*) **1** sexually attractive. **2** concerned with sex.

SF *abbreviation* science fiction.

SGML *abbreviation* standard generalised markup language, a form of code used to produce print in electronic form.

shabby *adjective* (**shabbier**, **shabbiest**) **1** in a poor or worn-out condition; dilapidated. **2** poorly dressed. **3** unfair; dishonourable, *a shabby trick*. **shabbily** *adverb*, **shabbiness** *noun*

shack *noun* a roughly-built hut.

shackle *noun* an iron ring for fastening a prisoner's wrist or ankle to something.

shackle *verb* (**shackled**, **shackling**) put shackles on a prisoner.

shade *noun* **1** slight darkness produced where something blocks the sun's light. **2** a device that reduces or shuts out bright light. **3** a colour; how light or dark a colour is. **4** a slight difference, *The word had several shades of meaning*. **5** a ghost.

shade *verb* (**shaded**, **shading**) **1** shelter something from bright light. **2** make part of a drawing darker than the rest.

shadow *noun* **1** the dark shape that falls on a surface when something is between the surface and a light. **2** an area of shade.
shadowy *adjective*
Shadow Cabinet members of the Opposition in Parliament who act as spokespersons on important matters.

shadow *verb* **1** cast a shadow on something. **2** follow a person secretly.

shady *adjective* (**shadier**, **shadiest**) **1** giving shade, *a shady tree*. **2** in the shade, *a shady place*. **3** not completely honest; disreputable, *a shady deal*.

shaft *noun* **1** a long slender rod or straight part, *the shaft of an arrow*. **2** a ray of light. **3** a deep narrow hole, *a mine-shaft*.

shag *noun* a large sea-bird that dives for fish.

shaggy *adjective* (**shaggier**, **shaggiest**) **1** having long rough hair or fibre. **2** rough, thick, and untidy, *shaggy hair*.

shah *noun* the former ruler of Iran. [Persian, = king]

shake *verb* (**shook**, **shaken**, **shaking**) **1** move quickly up and down or from side to side. **2** disturb; shock; upset, *The news shook us*. **3** tremble; be unsteady, *His voice was shaking*. **shaker** *noun*
shake hands clasp a person's right hand with yours in greeting or parting or as a sign of agreement.

shake *noun* **1** shaking; a shaking movement. **2** an earthquake. **3** (*informal*) a moment, *I'll be there in two shakes*. **shaky** *adjective*, **shakily** *adverb*

shale *noun* a kind of stone that splits easily into layers. [same origin as *scale*[3]]

shall *auxiliary verb* **1** used with *I* and *we* to express the ordinary future tense, e.g. *I shall arrive tomorrow*, and in questions, e.g. *Shall I shut the door?* (but *will* is used with other words, e.g. *they will arrive*; *will you shut the door?*). **2** used with words other than *I* and *we* in promises, e.g. *Cinderella, you shall go to the ball!* (but *I will go* = I promise or intend to go).

> USAGE If you want to be strictly correct, keep to the rules given here, but nowadays many people use will after *I* and *we* and it is not usually regarded as wrong.

shallot *noun* a kind of small onion.

shallow *adjective* **1** not deep, *shallow water.* **2** not capable of deep feelings, *a shallow character.* **shallowness** *noun*

shallows *plural noun* a shallow part of a stretch of water.

sham *noun* something that is not genuine; a pretence. **sham** *adjective*

sham *verb* (**shammed**, **shamming**) pretend.

shamble *verb* (**shambled**, **shambling**) walk or run in a lazy or awkward way.

shambles *noun* a scene of great disorder or bloodshed. [the word originally meant 'slaughterhouse']

shambolic *adjective* chaotic, disorganised, or mismanaged.

shame *noun* **1** a feeling of great sorrow or guilt because you have done wrong. **2** something you regret, *It's a shame that it rained.* **shameful** *adjective*, **shamefully** *adverb*

shame *verb* (**shamed**, **shaming**) make a person feel ashamed.

shamefaced *adjective* looking ashamed.

shameless *adjective* not feeling or looking ashamed. **shamelessly** *adverb*

shampoo *noun* **1** a liquid substance for washing the hair. **2** a substance for cleaning a carpet etc. or washing a car.

shampoo *verb* wash or clean with a shampoo. [from Hindi *champo* = press!]

shamrock *noun* a plant rather like clover.

shandy *noun* (*plural* **shandies**) a mixture of beer and lemonade or some other soft drink.

shank *noun* **1** the leg, especially the part from knee to ankle. **2** a long narrow part, *the shank of a pin.*

shan't (*mainly spoken*) shall not.

shantung *noun* soft Chinese silk. [from Shantung, a province of China]

shanty[1] *noun* (*plural* **shanties**) a shack.
shanty town a settlement consisting of shanties.

shanty[2] *noun* (*plural* **shanties**) a sailors' song with a chorus. [from French *chantez* = sing!]

shape *noun* **1** a thing's outline; the appearance an outline produces. **2** proper form or condition, *Get it into shape.*

shape *verb* (**shaped**, **shaping**) **1** make into a particular shape. **2** develop, *It's shaping up nicely.*

shapeless *adjective* having no definite shape.

shapely *adjective* (**shapelier**, **shapeliest**) having an attractive shape.

share *noun* **1** a part given to one person or thing out of something that is being divided. **2** each of the equal parts forming a business company's capital, giving the person who holds it the right to receive a portion (a *dividend*) of the company's profits.
shareholder *noun*

share *verb* (**shared**, **sharing**) **1** give portions of something to two or more people. **2** have or use or experience something that others have too, *share a room*; *share the responsibility.*

sharemarket *noun* (*NZ*) = **stock market**.

share-milker *noun* (*NZ*) a tenant farmer on a dairy farm who receives a share of the profits. **share-milking** *noun*

shark *noun* a large sea-fish with sharp teeth.

sharp *adjective* **1** with an edge or point that can cut or make holes. **2** quick at noticing or learning things, *sharp eyes.* **3** steep or pointed; not gradual, *a sharp bend.* **4** forceful; severe, *a sharp frost.* **5** distinct; loud and shrill, *a sharp cry.* **6** slightly sour. **7** (in music) one semitone higher than the natural note, *C sharp.* **sharply** *adverb*, **sharpness** *noun*
sharp practice dishonest or barely honest dealings in business.

sharp *adverb* **1** sharply, *turn sharp right.* **2** punctually, *at six o'clock sharp.* **3** (in music) above the correct pitch, *You were singing sharp.*

sharp *noun* (in music) a note one semitone higher than the natural note; the sign (♯) that indicates this.

sharpen *verb* make or become sharp.
sharpener *noun*

sharpshooter *noun* a skilled marksman.

shatter *verb* **1** break violently into small pieces. **2** destroy, *It shattered our hopes.* **3** upset greatly, *We were shattered by the news.*

shave *verb* (**shaved**, **shaving**) **1** scrape growing hair off the skin. **2** cut or scrape a thin slice off something. **shaver** *noun*

shave *noun* the act of shaving the face.
close shave (*informal*) a narrow escape.

shavings *plural noun* thin strips shaved off a piece of wood or metal.

shawl *noun* a large piece of material worn round the shoulders or head or wrapped round a baby.

she *pronoun* the female person or animal being talked about.

sheaf *noun* (*plural* **sheaves**) **1** a bundle of corn-stalks tied together. **2** a bundle of arrows, papers, etc. held together.

shear *verb* (**sheared**, **shorn** or **sheared**, **shearing**) cut or trim; cut the wool off a sheep. **shear** *noun*, **shearer** *noun*

shears *plural noun* a shearing, clipping, or cutting tool shaped like a very large pair of scissors.

sheath *noun* a close-fitting cover; a cover for the blade of a knife or sword etc.

sheathe *verb* (**sheathed**, **sheathing**) **1** put into a sheath, *He sheathed his sword.* **2** put a close covering on something.

shed[1] *noun* a simply-made building used for storing things, for handling livestock, or as a workshop.

shed[2] *verb* (**shed**, **shedding**) **1** let something fall or flow, *The tree shed its leaves. We shed tears.* **2** give off, *A heater sheds warmth.* **3** (*NZ*) to separate a number of sheep etc. from a mob.

sheen *noun* a shine; a gloss.

sheep *noun* (*plural* **sheep**) an animal that eats grass and has a thick fleecy coat, kept in flocks for its wool and its meat.
sheep run or **sheep station** (*NZ*) a large property where sheep are farmed.

sheep-dip *noun* **1** a liquid used to kill lice etc. on sheep. **2** the place where sheep are dipped in this.

sheepdog *noun* a dog trained to guard and herd sheep.

sheepish *adjective* bashful; embarrassed.
sheepishly *adverb*, **sheepishness** *noun*

sheepmeat *noun* mutton or lamb.

sheepshank *noun* a knot used to shorten a rope.

sheepskin *noun* a sheep's skin with the wool on, used as a rug or to make clothes etc.

sheer[1] *adjective* **1** complete; thorough, *sheer stupidity*. **2** vertical, with almost no slope, *a sheer drop*. **3** (of material) very thin; transparent.

sheer[2] *verb* swerve; move sharply away.

sheet[1] *noun* **1** a large piece of lightweight material used on a bed in pairs for a person to sleep between. **2** a whole flat piece of paper, glass, or metal. **3** a wide area of water, ice, flame, etc.

sheet[2] *noun* a rope or chain fastening a sail.

sheikh (*say* shayk) *noun* the leader of an Arab tribe or village. [Arabic, = old man]

sheila *noun* (*NZ, slang*) a woman.

shelf *noun* (*plural* **shelves**) **1** a flat piece of wood, metal, or glass etc. fixed to a wall or in a piece of furniture so that things can be placed on it. **2** a flat level surface that sticks out; a ledge.

shell *noun* **1** the hard outer covering of a nut, egg, snail, tortoise, etc. **2** the walls or framework of a building, ship, etc. **3** a metal case filled with explosive, fired from a large gun. [from Old English *sciell*, which has the same origin as *scale*[2] and *scale*[3]]

shell *verb* **1** take something out of its shell. **2** fire explosive shells at something.
shell out (*slang*) pay out money.

shellfish *noun* (*plural* **shellfish**) a sea-animal that has a shell.

shelter *noun* **1** something that protects people from rain, wind, danger, etc. **2** protection, *Seek shelter from the rain.*

shelter *verb* **1** provide with shelter. **2** protect. **3** find a shelter, *They sheltered under the trees.*

shelter-belt *noun* a row of trees planted as a wind-break.

shelve *verb* (**shelved**, **shelving**) **1** put things on a shelf or shelves. **2** fit a wall or cupboard etc. with shelves. **3** postpone or reject a plan etc. **4** slope, *The bed of the river shelves steeply.*

shepherd *noun* a person whose job is to look after sheep. **shepherdess** *noun*
shepherd's pie cottage pie.

shepherd *verb* guide or direct people. [from *sheep* + *herd*]

sherang *noun* **head sherang** (*NZ*) the boss or person in charge. [Indian]

sherbet *noun* a fizzy sweet powder or drink. [from Arabic *sharab* = a drink]

sheriff *noun* (*American*) the chief law-enforcing officer of a county.

sherry *noun* (*plural* **sherries**) a kind of strong wine. [from *Jerez* in Spain]

shickered *adjective* (*NZ, slang*) drunk.

shield *noun* **1** a large piece of metal, wood, etc. carried to protect the body. **2** a model of a triangular shield used as a trophy. **3** a protection.
the Shield (*NZ*) the Ranfurly Shield.

shield *verb* protect from harm or from being discovered.

shift *verb* **1** move; change. **2** (*NZ*) move house. **3** manage, *Learn to shift for yourself.*

shift *noun* **1** a change of position or condition etc. **2** (*NZ*) a change of address. **3** a group of workers who start work as another group finishes; the time when they work, *the night shift*. **4** a straight dress.

shifty *adjective* evasive, not straightforward; untrustworthy. **shiftily** *adverb*, **shiftiness** *noun*

shilling *noun* a former British and New Zealand coin worth one twentieth of a pound.

shilly-shally *verb* (**shilly-shallied**, **shilly-shallying**) be unable to make up your mind. [from *shall I? shall I?*]

shimmer *verb* shine with a quivering light, *The sea shimmered in the moonlight.*
shimmer *noun*

shin *noun* the front of the leg between the knee and the ankle.

shin *verb* (**shinned**, **shinning**) climb by using the arms and legs, not on a ladder.

shindy *noun* (*plural* **shindies**) (*informal*) a din; a brawl.

shine *verb* (**shone** (in sense 4 **shined**), **shining**) **1** give out or reflect light; be bright. **2** be excellent, *He doesn't shine in maths.* **3** aim a light, *Shine your torch on it.* **4** polish, *Have you shined your shoes?*

shine *noun* **1** brightness. **2** a polish.

shingle *noun* **1** small smooth stones on a beach. **2** (*NZ*) loose road-metal or loose gravel on a mountain slope etc. **3** a wooden tile used on roofs etc.

Shinto *noun* a Japanese religion.

shiny *adjective* (**shinier**, **shiniest**) shining; glossy.

ship *noun* a large boat, especially one that goes to sea.

ship *verb* (**shipped**, **shipping**) send goods etc. by ship; transport.

shipment *noun* **1** the process of shipping goods. **2** the amount shipped.

shipping *noun* **1** ships. **2** transporting goods by ship.

shipshape *adjective* in good order; tidy.

shipwreck *noun* the wrecking of a ship. **shipwrecked** *adjective*

shipyard *noun* a ship-building yard; a dock.

shirk *verb* avoid a duty or work etc. selfishly or unfairly. **shirker** *noun*

shirr *verb* gather cloth into folds by rows of threads run through it.

shirt *noun* a loose-fitting garment of cotton or silk etc. for the top half of the body.
in your shirtsleeves not wearing a jacket over your shirt.

shirty *adjective* (*slang*) annoyed.

shiver[1] *verb* tremble with cold or fear. **shiver** *noun*, **shivery** *adjective*

shiver[2] *verb* shatter into pieces.

shoal[1] *noun* a large number of fish swimming together.

shoal[2] *noun* a shallow place; an underwater sandbank.

shock[1] *noun* **1** a sudden unpleasant surprise. **2** great weakness caused by pain or injury etc. **3** the effect of a violent shake or knock. **4** an effect caused by electric current passing through the body.

shock[1] *verb* **1** give someone a shock; surprise or upset a person greatly. **2** seem very improper or scandalous to a person.

shock[2] *noun* a bushy mass of hair.

shod *past tense* of **shoe**.

shoddy *adjective* (**shoddier**, **shoddiest**) of poor quality; badly made or done, *shoddy work.* **shoddily** *adverb*, **shoddiness** *noun*

shoe *noun* **1** a strong covering for the foot. **2** a horseshoe. **3** something shaped or used like a shoe. **shoelace** *noun*, **shoemaker** *noun*
be in somebody's shoes be in his or her situation.
on a shoe-string with only a small amount of money.

shoe *verb* (**shod**, **shoeing**) fit with a shoe or shoes.

shoehorn *noun* a curved piece of stiff material for easing your heel into the back of a shoe.

shonky *adjective* (*NZ, informal*) dishonest, shady, *a shonky deal.*

shoo *interjection* a word used to frighten animals away. **shoo** *verb*

shook *adjective* **be shook on** (*NZ, informal*) be keen on, like.

shoot *verb* (**shot**, **shooting**) **1** fire a gun or missile etc. **2** hurt or kill by shooting. **3** move or send very quickly, *The car shot past us.* **4** kick or hit a ball at a goal. **5** (of a plant) put out buds or shoots. **6** slide the bolt of a door into or out of its fastening. **7** film or photograph something, *They shot the movie in New Zealand.*
shooting star a meteor.
shoot through (*NZ, slang*) leave hurriedly.

shoot *noun* **1** a young branch or new growth of a plant. **2** an expedition for shooting animals.

shoot out *noun* a means in soccer of deciding a winner in a drawn game by the taking of penalty kicks.

shop *noun* **1** a building or room where goods or services are on sale to the public. **2** a workshop. **3** talk that is about your own work or job, *She is always talking shop.*
shop steward a trade-union official who represents his or her fellow workers.

shop *verb* (**shopped**, **shopping**) go and buy things at shops. **shopper** *noun*

shopkeeper *noun* a person who owns or manages a shop.

shoplifter *noun* a person who steals goods from a shop after entering as a customer. **shoplifting** *noun*

shopping *noun* **1** buying goods in shops. **2** the goods bought.

shore[1] *noun* the land along the edge of a sea or of a lake.

shore[2] *verb* (**shored**, **shoring**) prop something up with a piece of wood etc.

shorn *past participle* of **shear**.

short *adjective* **1** not long; occupying a small distance or time, *a short walk.* **2** not tall, *a short person.* **3** not enough; not having enough of something, *We are short of water.* **4** curt. **5** (of pastry) rich and crumbly because it contains a lot of fat.
shortness *noun*
for short as an abbreviation, *Raymond is called Ray for short.*
short circuit a fault in an electrical circuit in which current flows along a shorter route than the normal one.
short cut a route or method that is quicker than the usual one.
short for an abbreviation of, *'Ray' is short for Raymond.*

short *adverb* suddenly, *She stopped short.*

shortage *noun* lack or scarcity of something; insufficiency.

shortbread *noun* a rich sweet biscuit.

shortcake *noun* shortbread.

shortcoming *noun* a fault or failure to reach a good standard.

shorten *verb* make or become shorter.

shortfall *noun* a deficit.

shorthand *noun* a set of special signs for writing words down as quickly as people say them.

shortly *adverb* **1** in a short time; soon, *They will arrive shortly.* **2** in a few words. **3** curtly.

shorts *plural noun* trousers reaching to the knee or higher.

short-sighted *adjective* unable to see distant things clearly.

short-tempered *adjective* easily becoming angry.

shot *past tense* of **shoot**.

shot *noun* **1** the firing of a gun or missile etc.; the sound of this. **2** something fired from a gun; lead pellets for firing from small guns. **3** a person judged by skill in shooting, *He's a good shot.* **4** a heavy metal ball thrown as a sport. **5** a stroke in tennis, cricket, billiards, etc. **6** a photograph; a filmed scene. **7** an attempt, *Have a shot at the crossword.*

shot *adjective* (of fabric) woven so that different colours show at different angles, *shot silk.*

shotgun *noun* a gun for firing small shot at close range.

should *auxiliary verb* used to express (**1**) obligation or duty, = ought to (*You should have told me*), (**2**) something expected (*They should be here by ten o'clock*), (**3**) a possible event (*if you should happen to see him*), (**4**) with *I* and *we* to make a polite statement (*I should like to come*) or in a conditional clause (*If they had supported us we should have won*).

USAGE In sense 4, although should is strictly correct, many people nowadays use would and this is not regarded as wrong.

shoulder *noun* **1** the part of the body between the neck and the arm, foreleg, or wing. **2** a side that juts out, *the shoulder of the bottle.*

shoulder *verb* **1** take something on your shoulder or shoulders. **2** push with your shoulder. **3** accept responsibility or blame.

shoulder-blade *noun* either of the two large flat bones at the top of your back.

shouldn't (*mainly spoken*) should not.

shout *noun* **1** a loud cry or call. **2** (*NZ*) a person's turn to buy a round of drinks; any treat.

shout *verb* **1** give a shout; call loudly. **2** (*NZ*) buy something, e.g. a drink or meal, for someone else.

shove *verb* (**shoved**, **shoving**) push roughly.
shove *noun*
shove off (*informal*) go away.

shovel *noun* a tool like a spade with the sides turned up, used for lifting coal, earth, snow, etc.

shovel *verb* (**shovelled**, **shovelling**) **1** move or clear with a shovel. **2** scoop or push roughly, *He was shovelling food into his mouth.*

shoveler *noun* a type of duck.

show *verb* (**showed**, **shown**, **showing**) **1** allow or cause something to be seen, *Show me your new bike.* **2** make a person understand; demonstrate, *Show me how to use it.* **3** guide, *Show him in.* **4** treat in a certain way, *She showed us much kindness.* **5** be visible, *That scratch won't show.* **6** prove your ability to someone, *We'll show them!*
show off show something proudly; try to impress people.
show up make or be clearly visible; reveal a fault etc.; (*informal*) arrive.

show *noun* **1** a display or exhibition, *a flower show.* **2** an entertainment. **3** (*slang*) something that happens or is done, *He runs the whole show.* **4** (*informal*) an opportunity or chance, *They had no show of catching up.*
give the show away reveal a secret.
good show! well done!

showdown *noun* a final test or confrontation.

shower *noun* **1** a brief fall of rain or snow. **2** a lot of small things coming or falling like rain, *a shower of stones.* **3** a device or cabinet for spraying water to wash a person's body; a wash in this.

shower *verb* **1** fall or send things in a shower. **2** wash under a shower.

showery *adjective* (of weather) with many showers.

showjumping *noun* a competition in which riders make their horses jump over fences and other obstacles. **showjumper** *noun*

showman *noun* (*plural* **showmen**) **1** a person who presents entertainments. **2** someone who is good at attracting attention. **showmanship** *noun*

showroom *noun* a room where goods are displayed for people to look at.

showy *adjective* (**showier**, **showiest**) likely to attract attention; brightly or highly decorated. **showily** *adverb*, **showiness** *noun*

shrapnel *noun* pieces of metal scattered from an exploding shell. [named after H. Shrapnel, the British officer who invented it in about 1806]

shred *noun* **1** a tiny piece torn or cut off something. **2** a small amount, *There is not a shred of evidence.*

shred *verb* (**shredded**, **shredding**) cut into shreds. **shredder** *noun*

shrew *noun* **1** a small mouse-like animal. **2** a bad-tempered woman who is constantly scolding people. **shrewish** *adjective*

shrewd *adjective* having common sense and good judgement; clever. **shrewdly** *adverb*, **shrewdness** *noun*

shriek *noun* a shrill cry or scream.

shriek *verb* give a shriek.

shrift *noun* **short shrift** curt treatment.

shrill *adjective* sounding very high and piercing. **shrilly** *adverb*, **shrillness** *noun*

shrimp *noun* **1** a small shellfish, pink when boiled. **2** a small person.

shrimping *noun* fishing for shrimps.

shrine *noun* an altar, chapel, or other sacred place.

shrink *verb* (**shrank**, **shrunk**, **shrinking**) **1** make or become smaller. **2** move back to avoid something. **3** avoid doing something because of fear, conscience, embarrassment, etc. **shrinkage** *noun*

shrive *verb* (**shrove**, **shriven**, **shriving**) (*old use*) (of a priest) hear a person's confession and give absolution.

shrivel *verb* (**shrivelled**, **shrivelling**) make or become dry and wrinkled.

shroud *noun* **1** a cloth in which a dead body is wrapped. **2** each of a set of ropes supporting a ship's mast.

shroud *verb* **1** wrap in a shroud. **2** cover or conceal, *The town was shrouded in mist.*

shrove *past tense* of **shrive**.
Shrove Tuesday the day before Ash Wednesday, when it was formerly the custom to be shriven.

shrub *noun* a woody plant smaller than a tree; a bush. **shrubby** *adjective*

shrubbery *noun* (*plural* **shrubberies**) an area planted with shrubs.

shrug *verb* (**shrugged**, **shrugging**) raise your shoulders as a sign that you do not care, do not know, etc. **shrug** *noun*

shrunken *adjective* having shrunk.

shudder *verb* **1** shiver violently with horror, fear, or cold. **2** make a strong shaking movement. **shudder** *noun*

shuffle *verb* (**shuffled**, **shuffling**) **1** walk without lifting the feet from the ground. **2** slide playing-cards over each other to get them into random order. **3** shift; rearrange. **shuffle** *noun*

shun *verb* (**shunned**, **shunning**) avoid.

shunt *verb* move a train or wagons on to another track; divert. **shunt** *noun*, **shunter** *noun*

shut *verb* (**shut**, **shutting**) **1** move a door, lid, or cover etc. so that it blocks an opening; make or become closed. **2** bring or fold parts together, *Shut the book.*
shut down stop work; stop business.
shut up shut securely; (*informal*) stop talking or making a noise.

shutdown *noun* **1** closure of a production or system, sometimes for maintenance. **2** the turning off of a computer.

shutter *noun* **1** a panel or screen that can be closed over a window. **2** the device in a camera that opens and closes to let light fall on the film. **shuttered** *adjective* [from *shut*]

shuttle *noun* **1** a holder carrying the weft-thread across a loom in weaving. **2** a train, bus, or aircraft that makes frequent short journeys between two points. **3** a space shuttle (see *space*).

shuttle *verb* (**shuttled**, **shuttling**) move, travel, or send backwards and forwards.

shuttlecock *noun* a small rounded piece of cork or plastic with a crown of feathers, struck to and fro by players in badminton.

shy[1] *adjective* (**shyer**, **shyest**) afraid to meet or talk to other people; timid. **shyly** *adverb*, **shyness** *noun*

shy[1] *verb* (**shied, shying**) move suddenly in alarm, *The horse shied at the sound*

shy[2] *verb* (**shied, shying**) throw a stone etc.

shy[2] *noun* (*plural* **shies**) a throw.

SI *abbreviation* **1** Système International d'Unités (French, = International System of Units). Basic SI units include the metre, the kilogram, and the second. **2** (*NZ*) South Island.

Siamese *adjective* of Siam (now called Thailand) or its people. **Siamese** *noun*
Siamese cat a cat with short pale fur with darker face, ears, tail, and feet.
Siamese twins twins who are born with their bodies joined together.

sibilant *adjective* having a hissing sound, *a sibilant whisper.*

sibilant *noun* a speech-sound that sounds like hissing, e.g. *s, sh.* [from Latin *sibilans* hissing]

sibling *noun* a brother or sister.

sibyl *noun* a prophetess in ancient Greece or Rome.

sick *adjective* **1** ill; physically or mentally unwell. **2** vomiting or likely to vomit, *I feel sick.* **3** distressed; disgusted.
sick of tired of.

sicken *verb* **1** begin to be ill. **2** make or become distressed or disgusted, *Vandalism sickens us all.* **sickening** *adjective*

sickie *noun* (*NZ, informal*) a day off work because of sickness.

sickle *noun* **1** a tool with a narrow curved blade, used for cutting corn etc. **2** something shaped like this blade, e.g. the crescent moon.

sickly *adjective* **1** often ill; unhealthy. **2** making people feel sick, *a sickly smell.* **3** weak, *a sickly smile.*

sickness *noun* **1** illness. **2** a disease. **3** vomiting.

side *noun* **1** a surface, especially one joining the top and bottom of something. **2** a line that forms part of the boundary of a triangle, square, etc. **3** either of the two halves into which something can be divided by a line down its centre. **4** the part near the edge and away from the centre. **5** the place or region next to a person or thing, *He stood at my side.* **6** one aspect or view of something, *Study all sides of the problem.* **7** one of two groups or teams etc. who oppose each other.
on the side as a sideline.
side by side next to each other.

side *adjective* at or on a side, *the side door.*

side *verb* (**sided, siding**) take a person's side in an argument, *He sided with his son.*

sideboard *noun* a long piece of furniture with drawers and cupboards for china etc. and a flat top.

sidelight *noun* **1** a light at the side of a vehicle or ship. **2** light from one side.

sideline *noun* **1** something done in addition to the main work or activity. **2** a line at the side of a football pitch etc.; the area just outside this.

sidelong *adjective* towards one side; sideways, *a sidelong glance.*

sidereal (*say* sid-**eer**-ee-al) *adjective* of or measured by the stars. [from Latin *sideris* of a star]

sideshow *noun* a small entertainment forming part of a large one, e.g. at a fair.

sideways *adverb & adjective* **1** to or from one side, *Move it sideways.* **2** with one side facing forwards, *We sat sideways in the bus.*

siding *noun* a short railway line by the side of a main line.

sidle *verb* (**sidled, sidling**) **1** walk in a shy or nervous manner. **2** walk along or around the side of a hill or slope. [from *sidelong*]

SIDS *abbreviation* sudden infant death syndrome (also known as *cot death*).

siege *noun* the besieging of a place.
lay siege to begin besieging.

sienna *noun* a kind of clay used in making brownish paints. [from Siena, a town in Italy]

sierra *noun* a range of mountains with sharp peaks, in Spain or parts of America. [from Latin *serra* = a saw]

siesta (*say* see-**est**-a) *noun* an afternoon rest. [Spanish, from Latin *sexta* = sixth (hour)]

sieve (*say* siv) *noun* a device made of mesh or perforated metal or plastic, used to separate the smaller or soft parts of something from the larger or hard parts.

sieve *verb* (**sieved, sieving**) put something through a sieve.

sift *verb* **1** sieve. **2** examine and analyse facts or evidence etc. carefully. **sifter** *noun*

sigh *noun* a sound made by breathing out heavily when you are sad, tired, relieved, etc.

sigh *verb* make a sigh.

sight *noun* **1** the ability to see. **2** a thing that can be seen or is worth seeing, *Our roses are a wonderful sight.* **3** an unsightly thing, *You do look a sight in those clothes!* **4** a device looked through to help aim a gun or telescope etc.
at sight or **on sight** as soon as a person or thing has been seen.
in sight visible; clearly near, *Victory was in sight.*

sight *verb* **1** see or observe something. **2** aim a gun or telescope etc.

sightless *adjective* blind.

sight-reading *noun* playing or singing music at sight, without preparation.

sightseeing *noun* visiting interesting places in a town etc. **sightseer** *noun*

sign *noun* **1** something that shows that a thing exists, *There are signs of decay.* **2** a mark, device, or notice etc. that gives a special meaning, *a road sign.* **3** an action or movement giving information or a command etc. **4** any of the twelve divisions of the zodiac, represented by a symbol.

sign *verb* **1** make a sign or signal. **2** write your signature on something; accept a contract etc. by doing this. [from Latin *signum* = a mark]

signal *noun* **1** a device, gesture, or sound etc. that gives information or a command; a message made up of such things. **2** a sequence of electrical impulses or radio waves.

signal *verb* (**signalled**, **signalling**) make a signal to somebody. **signaller** *noun*

signal *adjective* remarkable, a *signal success.* **signally** *adverb* [same origin as *sign*]

signal-box *noun* a building from which railway signals are controlled.

signatory *noun* (*plural* **signatories**) a person who signs an agreement etc.

signature *noun* a person's name written by himself or herself.
signature tune a special tune always used to announce a particular programme, performer, etc. [same origin as *sign*]

signet *noun* a seal with an engraved design, especially one set in a person's ring (a **signet-ring**). [same origin as *sign*]

significant *adjective* **1** having a meaning; full of meaning. **2** important, *a significant event.* **significantly** *adverb*, **significance** *noun*

signification *noun* meaning.

signify *verb* (**signified**, **signifying**) **1** be a sign or symbol of; mean. **2** indicate, *She signified her approval.* **3** be important; matter. [from Latin *signum* = sign]

sign language *noun* a system of communication used mainly amongst deaf and autistic people, usually consisting of facial, hand, and body language.

signpost *noun* a sign at a road junction etc. showing the names and distances of places down each road.

sika *noun* a kind of deer. [Japanese]

Sikh (*say* **as** seek) *noun* a member of an Indian religion believing in one God and accepting some Hindu and some Islamic beliefs. **Sikhism** *noun* [Hindi, = disciple]

silage *noun* fodder made from green crops stored in a silo.

silence *noun* absence of sound or talk.

silence *verb* (**silenced**, **silencing**) make a person or thing silent. [from Latin *silere* = to be silent]

silencer *noun* a device for reducing the sound made by a gun or a vehicle's exhaust system etc.

silent *adjective* without any sound; not speaking. **silently** *adverb*

silhouette (*say* sil-oo-**et**) *noun* a dark shadow seen against a light background. **silhouette** *verb* [named after a French author, E. de Silhouette, who made paper cut-outs of people's profiles from their shadows]

silica *noun* a hard white mineral that is a compound of silicon. [from Latin *silicis* = of flint]

silicon *noun* a substance found in many rocks, used in making transistors, chips for microprocessors, etc.

silicone *noun* a compound of silicon used in paints, varnish, and lubricants.

silk *noun* a fine soft thread or cloth made from the fibre produced by silkworms for making their cocoons. **silken** *adjective*, **silky** *adjective*

silkworm *noun* the caterpillar of a kind of moth, which feeds on mulberry leaves and spins itself a cocoon.

sill *noun* a strip of stone, wood, or metal underneath a window or door.

silly *adjective* (**sillier**, **silliest**) foolish; unwise. **silliness** *noun* [the word originally meant 'feeble' (from an older word *seely* = happy or fortunate)]

silo (*say* **sy**-loh) *noun* (*plural* **silos**) **1** a pit or tower for storing green crops (see *silage*) or corn or cement etc. **2** an underground place for storing a missile ready for firing.

silt *noun* sediment laid down by a river or sea etc.

silt *verb* block or clog or become blocked with silt, *The harbour had silted up.*

silvan *adjective* of the woods; having woods, rural. [from Latin *silva* = a wood]

silver *noun* **1** a shiny white precious metal. **2** the colour of silver. **3** coins or objects made of silver or silver-coloured metal. **4** a silver medal, usually given as second prize. **silvery** *adjective*

silver *adjective* **1** made of silver. **2** coloured like silver.
silver beech (also called **silver birch**) (*NZ*) a beech tree with silvery bark.
silver beet (*NZ*) a kind of beet with large crinkly leaves that are eaten as a vegetable.
silver fern (*NZ*) ponga.
Silver Fern a New Zealand national netball representative.
silver wedding the 25th anniversary of a wedding.

silver *verb* make or become silvery.

silverbelly *noun* a New Zealand freshwater eel.

silvereye *noun* a small Australian and New Zealand bird with a distinctive white ring around the eye.

silverfish *noun* **1** a silvery insect that feeds on paper etc. **2** any of various silver-coloured fish.

silverside *noun* **1** a cut of beef from the haunch, usually corned and boiled. **2** a silver-coloured marine fish.

SIM *abbreviation* subscriber identification module, a smart card inside a mobile phone.

simian *adjective* like a monkey. [from Latin *simia* = monkey]

similar *adjective* nearly the same as another person or thing; of the same kind. **similarly** *adverb*, **similarity** *noun* [from Latin *similis* = like]

simile (*say* **sim**-il-ee) *noun* a comparison of one thing with another, e.g. *He is as strong as a horse. We ran like the wind.* [from Latin *similis* = like]

similitude *noun* similarity.

simmer *verb* boil very gently.
simmer down calm down.

simper *verb* smile in a silly affected way.
simper *noun*

simple *adjective* **1** easy, *a simple question.* **2** not complicated or elaborate; plain, not showy, *a simple bach.* **3** without much sense or intelligence. **4** not of high rank; ordinary, *a simple countryman.* **simplicity** *noun*

simpleton *noun* a foolish person.

simplify *verb* (**simplified**, **simplifying**) make a thing simple or easy to understand. **simplification** *noun*

simply *adverb* **1** in a simple way, *Explain it simply.* **2** without doubt; completely, *It's simply marvellous.* **3** only; merely, *It's simply a question of time.*

simulate *verb* (**simulated**, **simulating**) **1** reproduce the appearance or conditions of something; imitate, *This device simulates a space flight.* **2** pretend, *They simulated fear.* **simulation** *noun*, **simulator** *noun* [from Latin *similis* = like]

simultaneous (*say* sim-ul-**tay**-nee-us) *adjective* happening at the same time. **simultaneously** *adverb*

sin *noun* the breaking of a religious or moral law; a very bad action.
sin bin (in sport) a bench etc. to which players may be sent for a period as a penalty during a game. **sin-bin** *verb* (**sin-binned**, **sin-binning**)

sin *verb* (**sinned**, **sinning**) commit a sin.
sinner *noun*

since *conjunction* **1** from the time when, *Where have you been since I last saw you?* **2** because, *Since we have missed the bus we must walk home.*

since *preposition* from a certain time, *She has been here since Christmas.*

since *adverb* between then and now, *He ran away and hasn't been seen since.*

sincere *adjective* without pretence; truly felt or meant, *my sincere thanks.* **sincerely** *adverb*, **sincerity** *noun*
Yours sincerely see *yours.*
[from Latin *sincerus* = pure]

sine *noun* (in a right-angled triangle) the ratio of the length of a side opposite one of the acute angles to the length of the hypotenuse. (Compare *cosine.*)

sinecure (*say* **sy**-nik-yoor) *noun* a paid job that requires no work. [from Latin *sine cura* = without care]

sinew *noun* **1** a tendon. **2** strength; muscular power. **sinewy** *adjective*

sinful *adjective* guilty of sin; wicked. **sinfully** *adverb*, **sinfulness** *noun*

sing *verb* (**sang**, **sung**, **singing**) **1** make musical sounds with the voice. **2** perform a song. **3** make a humming or whistling sound.
singer *noun*

singe (*say* sinj) *verb* (**singed**, **singeing**) burn something slightly.

single *adjective* **1** one only; not double or multiple. **2** suitable for one person, *single beds.* **3** separate, *We sold every single thing.* **4** not married. **5** for the journey to a place but not back again, *a single ticket.* **singly** *adverb*
single file a line of people one behind the other.

single *noun* **1** a single person or thing. **2** a single ticket. **3** a CD containing a new release and two or three other tracks.

single *verb* (**singled**, **singling**) **single out** pick out or distinguish from other people or things.

single-handed *adjective* without help.

single-minded *adjective* with your mind set on one purpose only.

singlet *noun* a man's garment worn under or instead of a shirt; a vest.

singsong *adjective* having a monotonous tone or rhythm, *a singsong voice.*

singsong *noun* **1** *informal* singing by a gathering of people. **2** a singsong tone.

singular *noun* the form of a *noun* or verb used when it stands for only one person or thing, *The singular is 'man', the plural is 'men'.*

singular *adjective* **1** of the singular. **2** uncommon; extraordinary, *a woman of singular courage.* **singularly** *adverb,* **singularity** *noun*

sinister *adjective* looking evil or harmful; wicked. [from Latin, = on the left (which was thought to be unlucky)]

sink *verb* (**sank**, **sunk**, **sinking**) **1** go or cause to go under the surface or to the bottom of the sea etc., *The ship sank. They sank the ship.* **2** go or fall slowly downwards, *He sank to his knees.* **3** dig or drill, *They sank a well.* **4** invest money in something.
sink in become understood.

sink *noun* a fixed basin with a drainpipe and a tap or taps to supply water.

sinkhole *noun* an underground cavity caused by the action of water.

sinuous *adjective* with many bends or curves. [same origin as *sinus*]

sinus (*say* **sy**-nus) *noun* (*plural* **sinuses**) a hollow part in the bones of the skull, connected with the nose, *My sinuses are blocked.* [Latin, = curve]

sip *verb* (**sipped**, **sipping**) drink in small mouthfuls. **sip** *noun*

siphon *noun* **1** a pipe or tube in the form of an upside-down U, arranged so that liquid is forced up it and down to a lower level. **2** a bottle containing soda-water which is released through a tube.

siphon *verb* flow or draw out through a siphon. [Greek, = pipe]

sir *noun* **1** a word used when speaking politely to a man, *Please sir, may I go?* **2** **Sir** the title given to a knight or baronet, *Sir Edmund Hillary.* [from *sire*]

sire *noun* **1** the male parent of a horse or dog etc. (Compare *dam*[2].) **2** a word formerly used when speaking to a king. [same origin as *senior*]

siren *noun* **1** a device that makes a long loud sound as a signal. **2** a dangerously attractive woman. [named after the Sirens in Greek legend, women who by their sweet singing lured seafarers to shipwreck on the rocks]

sirloin *noun* beef from the upper part of the loin. [from *sur-* = over, + *loin*]

sirocco *noun* a hot dry wind that reaches Italy from Africa. [from Arabic *shark* = east wind]

SIS *abbreviation* (*NZ*) Security Intelligence Service.

sisal (*say* **sy**-sal) *noun* fibre from a tropical plant, used for making ropes.

sissy *noun* (*plural* **sissies**) a timid or cowardly person. [from *sis* = sister]

sister *noun* **1** a daughter of the same parents as another person. **2** a woman who is a fellow member of an association etc. **3** a nun. **4** a female hospital nurse in charge of others. **sisterhood** *noun,* **sisterly** *adjective*

sister-in-law *noun* (*plural* **sisters-in-law**) the sister of a married person's husband or wife; the wife of a person's brother.

sit *verb* (**sat**, **sitting**) **1** rest with the body supported on the buttocks; occupy a seat, *We were sitting in the front row.* **2** seat; cause someone to sit. **3** (of birds) perch; stay on the nest to hatch eggs. **4** be a candidate for an examination. **5** be situated; stay. **6** (of Parliament or a lawcourt etc.) be assembled for business. **sitter** *noun*

sitar *noun* an Indian musical instrument that is like a guitar. [Hindi, = three-stringed]

site *noun* **1** the place where something happens or happened or is built etc., *a camping site.* **2** a website.

site *verb* (**sited**, **siting**) provide with a site; locate. [from Latin *situs* = position]

sitting room *noun* a room with comfortable chairs for sitting in.

situated *adjective* in a particular place or situation.

situation *noun* **1** a position, with its surroundings. **2** a state of affairs at a certain time, *The police faced a difficult situation.* **3** a job. [same origin as *site*]

six *noun* (*plural* **sixes**) & *adjective* the number 6; one more than five.
at sixes and sevens in disorder.

sixteen *noun & adjective* the number 16; one more than fifteen. **sixteenth** *adjective & noun*

sixth *adjective & noun* next after the fifth.

sixty *noun & adjective* (*plural* **sixties**) the number 60; six times ten. **sixtieth** *adjective & noun*

size[1] *noun* **1** the measurements or extent of something. **2** any of the series of standard measurements in which certain things are made, *a size eight shoe.*

size[1] *verb* (**sized**, **sizing**) arrange things according to their size.
size up estimate the size of something; (*informal*) form an opinion or judgement about a person or thing.

size[2] *noun* a gluey substance used to glaze paper or stiffen cloth etc.

size[2] *verb* (**sized**, **sizing**) treat with size.

sizeable *adjective* large; fairly large.

sizzle *verb* (**sizzled**, **sizzling**) make a crackling or hissing sound.

skate[1] *noun* a boot with a blade or wheels attached, for gliding over ice or a hard surface.

skate[1] *verb* (**skated**, **skating**) move on skates. **skater** *noun*

skate[2] *noun* (*plural* **skate**) a large flat edible sea-fish.

skateboard *noun* a small board with wheels, used for riding on (as a sport) while standing. **skateboarding** *noun*

skein *noun* a coil of yarn or thread.

skeleton *noun* **1** the framework of bones of the body. **2** the shell or other hard part of a crab etc. **3** a framework, e.g. of a building. **skeletal** *adjective* [from Greek *skeletos* = dried-up]

skerrick *noun* (*NZ, informal*) a scrap or small amount, *there wasn't a skerrick left.*

sketch *noun* (*plural* **sketches**) **1** a rough drawing or painting. **2** a short account of something. **3** a short amusing play.

sketch *verb* make a sketch. [from Greek *schedios* = impromptu]

sketchy *adjective* rough and not detailed or careful.

skew *adjective* askew; slanting.

skew *verb* make a thing askew.

skewer *noun* a long pin pushed through meat to hold it together while it is being cooked. **skewer** *verb*

ski (*say* skee) *noun* (*plural* **skis**) each of a pair of long narrow strips of wood, metal, or plastic fixed under the feet for moving quickly over snow.

ski *verb* (**skied**, **skiing**) travel on skis. **skier** *noun* [Norwegian]

skid *verb* (**skidded**, **skidding**) slide accidentally.

skid *noun* **1** a skidding movement. **2** a runner on a helicopter, for use in landing.

skilful *adjective* having or showing great skill. **skilfully** *adverb*

skill *noun* the ability to do something well. **skilled** *adjective*

skim *verb* (**skimmed**, **skimming**) **1** remove something from the surface of a liquid; take the cream off milk. **2** move quickly over a surface or through the air. **3** read something quickly.

skimp *verb* supply or use less than is needed, *Don't skimp on the food.*

skimpy *adjective* (**skimpier**, **skimpiest**) scanty; too small.

skin *noun* **1** the flexible outer covering of a person's or animal's body. **2** an outer layer or covering, e.g. of a fruit. **3** a skin-like film formed on the surface of a liquid. **4** a customised visual interface for a computer application or operating system.

skin *verb* (**skinned**, **skinning**) take the skin off something.

skin-diving *noun* swimming under water with flippers and breathing-apparatus but without a diving-suit. **skin-diver** *noun*

skinflint *noun* a miserly person.

skinhead *noun* a youth with very closely cropped hair.

skink *noun* a small lizard.

skinny *adjective* (**skinnier**, **skinniest**) **1** very thin. **2** (*informal*) miserly.

skip[1] *verb* (**skipped**, **skipping**) **1** move along lightly, especially by hopping on each foot in turn. **2** jump with a skipping-rope. **3** go quickly from one subject to another. **4** miss something out, *You can skip chapter six.*

skip[1] *noun* a skipping movement.

skip[2] *noun* a large metal container for taking away builders' rubbish etc.

skipper *noun* a captain.

skipping-rope *noun* a rope, usually with a handle at each end, that is swung over your head and under your feet as you jump.

skirmish *noun* (*plural* **skirmishes**) a small fight or conflict. **skirmish** *verb*

skirt *noun* a woman's or girl's garment that hangs down from the waist.

skirt *verb* **1** go round the edge of something. **2** (*NZ*) remove skirtings from (a fleece).

skirting *noun* (*also* **skirting-board**) a narrow board round the wall of a room, close to the floor.

skirtings *plural noun* (*NZ*) the inferior parts trimmed from a shorn fleece.

skit *noun* a parody, *He wrote a skit on 'Hamlet'.*

skite *noun* (*NZ, informal*) a boaster or show-off.

skite *verb* (**skited**, **skiting**) (*NZ, informal*) boast. **skiter** *noun*

skittish *adjective* frisky.

skittle *noun* a wooden pin that people try to knock down by bowling a ball in the game of **skittles**.

skive *verb* (**skived**, **skiving**) (*slang*) dodge work etc. **skiver** *noun*

skulk *verb* loiter stealthily.

skull *noun* the framework of bones of the head.

skunk *noun* a black furry American animal that can spray a bad-smelling fluid.

sky *noun* (*plural* **skies**) the space above the earth, appearing blue in daylight on fine days.

sky *verb* (**skied**, **skying**) hit a ball very high.

skylark *noun* a lark that sings while it hovers high in the air.

skylark *verb* play about light-heartedly.

skylight *noun* a window in a roof.

skyline *noun* **1** the horizon, where earth and sky appear to meet. **2** the outline of buildings etc. against the sky.

skyscraper *noun* a very tall building.

slab *noun* a thick flat piece.

slack *adjective* **1** not pulled tight. **2** not busy; not working hard. **3** (*NZ, informal*) poor, bad, or unattractive, *He did a real slack job.* **slackly** *adverb*, **slackness** *noun*

slack *verb* avoid work. **slacker** *noun*

slacken *verb* make or become slack.

slacks *plural noun* trousers for informal occasions.

slag *noun* waste material separated from metal in smelting.

slag-heap *noun* a mound of waste matter from a mine etc.

slain *past participle* of **slay**.

slake *verb* (**slaked**, **slaking**) quench, *slake your thirst.*

slam *verb* (**slammed**, **slamming**) **1** shut loudly. **2** hit violently. **slam** *noun*

slander *noun* a spoken statement that damages a person's reputation and is untrue. (Compare *libel.*) **slanderous** *adjective*

slander *verb* make a slander against someone. **slanderer** *noun*

slang *noun* words that are used very informally to add vividness or humour to what is said. **slangy** *adjective*

slang *verb* speak insultingly to somebody.

slant *verb* **1** slope. **2** present news or information etc. from a particular point of view. **slant** *noun*

slap *verb* (**slapped**, **slapping**) **1** hit with the palm of the hand or with something flat. **2** put forcefully or carelessly, *We slapped paint on the walls.* **slap** *noun*

slapdash *adjective* hasty and careless.

slapstick *noun* comedy with people hitting each other, falling over, etc.

slash *verb* **1** make large cuts in something; cut or strike with a long sweeping movement. **2** reduce greatly, *Prices were slashed.*

slash *noun* (*plural* **slashes**) **1** a slashing cut. **2** a stroke used in print between alternatives (*and/or*), in web page addresses, etc.

slat *noun* each of the thin strips of wood or metal or plastic arranged so that they overlap and form a screen, e.g. in a venetian blind.

slate *noun* **1** a kind of grey rock that is easily split into flat plates. **2** a piece of this rock used in covering a roof or (formerly) for writing on. **slaty** *adjective*

slate *verb* (**slated**, **slating**) **1** cover a roof with slates. **2** (*informal*) criticise severely; reprimand.

slater *noun* a kind of louse.

slather *noun* **open slather** (*NZ, informal*) a situation where people may act or do act without restraint.

slattern *noun* a slovenly woman. **slatternly** *adjective*

slaughter *verb* **1** kill an animal for food. **2** kill people or animals ruthlessly or in great numbers. **slaughter** *noun*

slaughterhouse *noun* a place where animals are killed for food.

slave *noun* a person who is owned by another and obliged to work for him or her without being paid. **slavery** *noun*

slave *verb* (**slaved**, **slaving**) work very hard.

slave-driver *noun* a person who makes others work very hard.

slaver (*say* **slav**-er or **slay**-ver) *verb* have saliva flowing from the mouth, *a slavering dog.*

slavish *adjective* like a slave; showing no independence or originality.

slay *verb* (**slew**, **slain**, **slaying**) kill.

sleazy *adjective* squalid, disreputable.

sled *noun* a sledge.

sledge *noun* a vehicle for travelling over snow, with strips of metal or wood instead of wheels. **sledging** *noun*

sledgehammer *noun* a very large heavy hammer.

sleek *adjective* smooth and shiny.

sleep *noun* the condition or time of rest in which the eyes are closed, the body relaxed, and the mind unconscious. **sleepy** *adjective*, **sleepily** *adverb*, **sleepiness** *noun*

sleep *verb* (**slept**, **sleeping**) have a sleep.

sleeper *noun* **1** someone who is asleep. **2** each of the wooden or concrete beams on which the rails of a railway rest. **3** a railway carriage with beds or berths for passengers to sleep in; a place in this.

sleepless *adjective* unable to sleep.

sleep-out *noun* (*NZ*) an extra room for sleeping in, separate from the main house.

sleepwalker *noun* a person who walks about while asleep. **sleepwalking** *noun*

sleet *noun* a mixture of rain and snow or hail.

sleeve *noun* **1** the part of a garment that covers the arm. **2** the cover of a record. **up your sleeve** hidden but ready for you to use.

sleeveless *adjective* without sleeves.

sleigh (*say* as slay) *noun* a sledge, especially a large one pulled by horses. **sleighing** *noun*

sleight (*say as* slight) *noun* **sleight of hand** skill in using the hands to do conjuring tricks etc. [from Norse *slaegth* = slyness]

slender *adjective* slim. **slenderness** *noun*

sleuth (*say* slooth) *noun* a detective.

slew *past tense* of **slay**.

slice *noun* **1** a thin piece cut off something. **2** a portion.

slice *verb* (**sliced**, **slicing**) **1** cut into slices. **2** cut from a larger piece, *Slice the top off the egg.* **3** cut cleanly, *The knife sliced through the apple.*

slick *adjective* **1** quick and clever or cunning. **2** slippery.

slick *noun* **1** a large patch of oil floating on water. **2** a slippery place.

slide *verb* (**slid**, **sliding**) **1** move or cause to move smoothly on a surface. **2** move quietly or secretly, *The thief slid behind a bush.*

slide *noun* **1** a sliding movement. **2** a smooth surface or structure on which people or things can slide. **3** a photograph that can be projected on a screen. **4** a small glass plate on which things are placed to be examined under a microscope. **5** a fastener to keep hair tidy.

slight *adjective* very small; not serious or important. **slightly** *adverb*, **slightness** *noun*

slight *verb* insult a person by treating him or her without respect.

slim *adjective* (**slimmer**, **slimmest**) **1** thin and graceful. **2** small, *a slim chance.* **slimness** *noun*

slim *verb* (**slimmed**, **slimming**) make yourself thinner. **slimmer** *noun*

slime *noun* unpleasant wet slippery stuff. **slimy** *adjective*, **sliminess** *noun*

sling *noun* **1** a loop or band placed round something to support or lift it. **2** a looped strap used to throw a stone etc.

sling *verb* (**slung**, **slinging**) **1** support or lift with a sling. **2** (*informal*) throw.
sling off at (*NZ, informal*) scoff at, criticise.

slink *verb* (**slunk**, **slinking**) move in a stealthy or guilty way. **slinky** *adjective*

slink *noun* (*NZ*) a lamb or calf that is born dead or dies soon after birth; its skin.

slip *verb* (**slipped**, **slipping**) **1** slide accidentally; lose your balance by sliding. **2** move or put quickly and quietly, *Slip it in your pocket. We slipped away from the party.* **3** escape from, *The dog slipped its leash. It slipped my memory.*
slip up make a mistake.

slip *noun* **1** an accidental slide or fall. **2** a landslip. **3** a mistake. **4** a small piece of paper. **5** a petticoat. **6** a pillowcase.
give someone the slip escape or avoid him or her skilfully.

slipper *noun* a soft comfortable shoe to wear indoors.

slippery *adjective* smooth or wet so that it is difficult to stand on or hold. **slipperiness** *noun*

slipshod *adjective* careless; not systematic.

slit *noun* a narrow straight cut or opening.

slit *verb* (**slitted**, **slitting**) make a slit or slits in something.

slither *verb* slip or slide unsteadily.

sliver (*say* **sliv**-er) *noun* a thin strip of wood or glass etc.

slobber *verb* slaver; dribble.

slog *verb* (**slogged**, **slogging**) **1** hit hard. **2** work or walk hard and steadily. **slog** *noun*, **slogger** *noun*

slogan *noun* a phrase used to advertise something or to sum up the aims of a campaign etc., as in *'Christchurch, the city that shines'.*

sloop *noun* a small sailing-ship with one mast.

slop *verb* (**slopped**, **slopping**) spill liquid over the edge of its container.

slops *plural noun* slopped liquid; liquid waste matter.

slope *verb* (**sloped**, **sloping**) lie or turn at an angle; slant.
slope off (*slang*) go away.

slope *noun* **1** a sloping surface. **2** the amount by which something slopes.

sloppy *adjective* (**sloppier**, **sloppiest**) **1** liquid and splashing easily. **2** careless; slipshod, *sloppy work.* **3** weakly sentimental, *a sloppy story.* **sloppily** *adverb*, **sloppiness** *noun*

slosh *verb* (*slang*) **1** splash; slop; pour liquid carelessly. **2** hit.

slot *noun* a narrow opening to put things in. **slotted** *adjective*

sloth (*rhymes with* both) *noun* **1** laziness. **2** a South American animal that lives in trees and moves very slowly. **slothful** *adjective*

slot-machine *noun* a machine worked by putting a coin in the slot.

slouch *verb* stand, sit, or move in a lazy awkward way, not with an upright posture. **slouch** *noun*

slough[1] (*rhymes with* cow) *noun* a swamp or marshy place.

slough[2] (*say* sluf) *verb* shed, *A snake sloughs its skin periodically.*

slovenly (*say* **sluv**-en-lee) *adjective* carelessly; untidy. **slovenliness** *noun*

slow *adjective* **1** not quick; taking more time than is usual. **2** showing a time earlier than the correct time, *Your watch is slow.* **slowly** *adverb*, **slowness** *noun*

slow *adverb* slowly, *Go slow.*

slow *verb* go more slowly; cause to go more slowly, *The storm slowed us down.*

slow food *noun* food that is carefully produced or prepared in accordance with local culinary traditions.

sludge *noun* thick mud.

slug *noun* **1** a small slimy animal like a snail without a shell. **2** a pellet for firing from a gun.

sluggard *noun* a slow or lazy person.

sluggish *adjective* slow-moving; not alert or lively.

sluice (*say* slooss) *noun* **1** a sliding barrier for controlling a flow of water. **2** a channel carrying off water.

sluice *verb* (**sluiced**, **sluicing**) **1** wash with a flow of water. **2** let out water.

slum *noun* an area of dirty overcrowded houses.

slumber *noun & verb* sleep. **slumberer** *noun*, **slumberous** or **slumbrous** *adjective*

slump *verb* fall heavily or suddenly.

slump *noun* a sudden great fall in prices or trade.

slur *verb* (**slurred**, **slurring**) **1** pronounce words indistinctly by running the sounds together. **2** mark with a slur in music.

slur *noun* **1** a slurred sound. **2** discredit, *It casts a slur on his reputation.* **3** a curved line placed over notes in music to show that they are to be sung or played smoothly without a break.

slush *noun* partly melted snow on the ground. **slushy** *adjective*

sly *adjective* (**slyer**, **slyest**) **1** unpleasantly cunning or secret. **2** mischievous, *a sly smile.* **slyly** *adverb*, **slyness** *noun*

smack[1] *noun* a slap; a hard hit.

smack[1] *verb* slap; hit hard.
smack your lips close and then part them noisily in enjoyment.

smack[1] *adverb* (*informal*) with a smack; directly, *The ball went smack through the window.*

smack[2] *noun* a slight flavour of something; a trace.

smack[2] *verb* have a slight flavour or trace, *His manner smacks of conceit.*

smack[3] *noun* a small sailing-boat used for fishing etc.

small *adjective* not large; less than the usual size. **smallness** *noun*
small talk polite conversation on trivial subjects.
the small of the back the smallest part of the back (at the waist).

smallgoods *plural noun* (*NZ*) bacon, sausages, etc.

small-minded *adjective* selfish; petty.

smallpox *noun* a former contagious disease with spots that often left bad scars on the skin.

smart *adjective* **1** neat and elegant; dressed well. **2** clever. **3** forceful; brisk, *She ran at a smart pace.* **4** (of a device) programmed to perform action independently. **smartly** *adverb*, **smartness** *noun*
smart card a plastic card with a microprocessor built in.

smart *verb* **1** feel a stinging pain. **2** feel insulted. **smart** *noun*

smarten *verb* make or become smarter.

smartphone *noun* a mobile phone on which one can display photos, play videos, check and send e-mails, and surf the web.

smash *verb* **1** break noisily into pieces. **2** hit or move with great force. **3** destroy or defeat completely.

smash *noun* (*plural* **smashes**) **1** the action or sound of smashing. **2** a collision. **3** a disaster.
smash hit (*slang*) something very successful.

smashing *adjective* (*informal*) excellent; beautiful. **smasher** *noun*

smattering *noun* a slight knowledge of a subject or a foreign language.

smear *verb* **1** rub something greasy or sticky or dirty on a surface. **2** try to damage someone's reputation. **smear** *noun*, **smeary** *adjective*

smell *verb* (**smelt**, **smelling**) **1** be aware of something by means of the sense-organs of the nose, *I can smell smoke.* **2** give out a smell.

smell *noun* **1** something you can smell; a quality in something that makes people able to smell it. **2** an unpleasant quality of this kind. **3** the ability to smell things. **smelly** *adjective*

smelt *verb* melt ore to get the metal it contains.

smile *noun* an expression on the face that shows pleasure or amusement, with the lips stretched and turning upwards at the ends.

smile *verb* (**smiled**, **smiling**) give a smile.

smirch *verb* **1** soil. **2** disgrace or dishonour a reputation. **smirch** *noun*

smirk *noun* a self-satisfied smile.

smirk *verb* give a smirk.

smite *verb* (**smote**, **smitten**, **smiting**) hit hard.
be smitten with be affected by a disease or desire or fascination etc.

smith *noun* a person who makes things out of metal; a blacksmith.

smithereens *plural noun* (*informal*) small fragments.

smithy *noun* a blacksmith's workshop.

smitten *past participle* of **smite**.

smock *noun* an overall shaped like a very long shirt.

smock *verb* stitch into close gathers with embroidery. **smocking** *noun*

smog *noun* a mixture of smoke and fog. [from *smoke* + *fog*]

smoke *noun* **1** the mixture of gas and solid particles given off by a burning substance. **2** a period of smoking tobacco, *He wanted a smoke.* **smoky** *adjective*

smoke *verb* (**smoked**, **smoking**) **1** give out smoke. **2** have a lighted cigarette, cigar, or pipe between your lips and draw its smoke into your mouth; do this as a habit. **3** preserve meat or fish by treating it with smoke, *smoked salmon.* **smoker** *noun*

smokeless *adjective* without smoke.

smokescreen *noun* **1** a mass of smoke used to hide the movement of troops. **2** something that conceals what is happening.

smoko *noun* (*plural* **smokos**) (*NZ, informal*) a break from work.

smooth *adjective* **1** having a surface without any lumps, wrinkles, roughness, etc. **2** moving without bumps or jolts etc. **3** not harsh, *a smooth flavour.* **smoothly** *adverb,* **smoothness** *noun*

smooth *verb* make a thing smooth.

smote *past tense* of **smite**.

smother *verb* **1** suffocate. **2** cover thickly, *The cakes were smothered in sugar.* **3** restrain; conceal, *She smothered a smile.* **4** (*NZ*) (of sheep in a mob) die of suffocation. **5** stop the motion of a ball or shot in sport.

smoulder *verb* **1** burn slowly without a flame. **2** continue to exist inwardly, *Their anger smouldered.*

smudge *noun* a dirty mark made by rubbing something. **smudgy** *adjective*

smudge *verb* (**smudged**, **smudging**) make a smudge on something; become smudged.

smug *adjective* self-satisfied. **smugly** *adverb,* **smugness** *noun*

smuggle *verb* (**smuggled**, **smuggling**) bring something into a country etc. secretly or illegally. **smuggler** *noun*

smut *noun* **1** a small piece of soot or dirt. **2** indecent talk or pictures etc. **smutty** *adjective*

snack *noun* a small meal; food eaten between meals.

snag *noun* **1** a difficulty. **2** a sharp projection. **3** a tear in material that has been caught on something sharp.

snail *noun* a small animal with a soft body and a shell.
snail mail *noun* regular postal mail, which takes considerably longer than e-mail.
snail's pace a very slow pace.

snake *noun* a reptile with a long narrow body and no legs. [from Old English *snaca*]

snaky *adjective* **1** like a snake. **2** (*NZ, slang*) angry, irritable.

snap *verb* (**snapped**, **snapping**) **1** break suddenly or with a sharp sound. **2** bite suddenly or quickly. **3** say something quickly and angrily. **4** take something or move quickly. **5** take a snapshot of something.

snap *noun* **1** the action or sound of snapping. **2** a snapshot. **3** (**Snap**) a card-game in which players shout 'Snap!' when they see two similar cards.

snap *adjective* sudden, *a snap decision.*

snapdragon *noun* a plant with flowers that have a mouth-like opening.

snapper *noun* a large pink edible fish.

snappy *adjective* **1** snapping at people. **2** quick; lively. **snappily** *adverb*

snapshot *noun* an informal photograph.

snare *noun* a trap for catching birds or animals.

snare *verb* (**snared**, **snaring**) catch in a snare.

snarl[1] *verb* **1** growl angrily. **2** speak in a bad-tempered way. **snarl** *noun*

snarl[2] *verb* make or become tangled or jammed, *Traffic was snarled up.*

snatch *verb* seize; take quickly.

sneak *verb* **1** move quietly and secretly. **2** (*slang*) take secretly, *He sneaked a biscuit from the tin.* **3** (*slang*) tell tales.

sneak *noun* a tell-tale. **sneaky** *adjective,* **sneakily** *adverb*

sneakers *plural noun* soft-soled running-shoes.

sneer *verb* speak or behave in a scornful way. **sneer** *noun*

sneeze *verb* (**sneezed**, **sneezing**) send out air suddenly and uncontrollably through the nose and mouth in order to get rid of something irritating the nostrils. **sneeze** *noun*
not to be sneezed at (*informal*) worth having.

sniff *verb* **1** make a sound by drawing in air through the nose. **2** smell something. **sniff** *noun,* **sniffer** *noun*

sniffle *verb* (**sniffled**, **sniffling**) sniff slightly; keep on sniffing. **sniffle** *noun*

snig *noun* (*NZ*) a load to be dragged or hauled. **snigchain** *noun*

snig *verb* (*NZ*) drag or haul.

snigger *verb* giggle slyly. **snigger** *noun*

snip *verb* (**snipped**, **snipping**) cut with scissors or shears in small quick cuts. **snip** *noun*

snipe *verb* (**sniped**, **sniping**) **1** shoot at people from a hiding-place. **2** make a sly verbal attack. **sniper** *noun*

snippet *noun* a small piece of news, information, etc. [from *snip*]

snivel *verb* (**snivelled**, **snivelling**) cry or complain in a whining way.

snob *noun* a person who despises those who have not got wealth, power, or particular tastes or interests. **snobbery** *noun*, **snobbish** *adjective*

snooker *noun* a game played with cues and 21 balls on a special cloth-covered table.

snoop *verb* (*informal*) pry. **snooper** *noun*

snooze *noun* a nap. **snooze** *verb*

snore *verb* (**snored**, **snoring**) breathe very noisily while sleeping. **snore** *noun*

snorkel *noun* a tube through which a person swimming under water can take in air. **snorkelling** *noun*

snort *verb* make a rough sound by breathing forcefully through the nose. **snort** *noun*

snout *noun* an animal's projecting nose, or nose and jaws.

snow *noun* frozen drops of water that fall from the sky in small white flakes.

snow *verb* send down snow.
be snowed under be overwhelmed with a mass of letters or work etc.

snowball *noun* snow pressed into a ball for throwing. **snowballing** *noun*

snowboard *noun* a single wide and short ski for sliding downhill on snow. **snowboarder** *noun*, **snowboarding** *noun*

snowdrop *noun* a small white flower that blooms in early spring.

snowflake *noun* a flake of snow.

snow-grass *noun* (*NZ*) a kind of tall coarse grass that grows on mountains.

snowman *noun* (*plural* **snowmen**) a figure made of snow.

snowplough *noun* a vehicle or device for clearing a road or railway track etc. by pushing snow aside.

snowstorm *noun* a storm in which snow falls.

snow-white *adjective* pure white.

snowy *adjective* **1** with snow falling, snowy weather. **2** covered with snow, snowy roofs. **3** pure white.

snub *verb* (**snubbed**, **snubbing**) treat in a scornful or unfriendly way.

snub *noun* scornful or unfriendly treatment.

snub-nosed *adjective* having a short thick nose.

snuff[1] *noun* powdered tobacco for taking into the nose by sniffing.

snuff[2] *verb* put out a candle by covering or pinching the flame. **snuffer** *noun*

snuffle *verb* (**snuffled**, **snuffling**) sniff in a noisy way. **snuffle** *noun*

snug *adjective* (**snugger**, **snuggest**) cosy. **snugly** *adverb*, **snugness** *noun*

snuggle *verb* (**snuggled**, **snuggling**) press closely and comfortably; nestle.

so *adverb* **1** in this way; to such an extent, *Why are you so cross?* **2** very, *Cricket is so boring.* **3** also, *I was wrong but so were you.*
or so or about that number.
so far up to now.
so long! (*informal*) goodbye.
so what? (*informal*) that is not important.

so *conjunction* for that reason, *They threw me out, so I came here.*

soak *verb* make a person or thing very wet. **soak** *noun*
soak up take in a liquid in the way that a sponge does.

so-and-so *noun* (*plural* **so-and-sos**) a person or thing that need not be named.

soap *noun* a substance used with water for washing and cleaning things. **soapy** *adjective*

soap *verb* put soap on something.

soar *verb* **1** rise high in the air. **2** rise very high, *Prices were soaring.*

sob *verb* (**sobbed**, **sobbing**) make a gasping sound when crying. **sob** *noun*

sober *adjective* **1** not intoxicated. **2** serious and calm. **2** (of colour) not bright. **soberly** *adverb*, **sobriety** (*say* so-**bry**-it-ee) *noun*

sober *verb* make or become sober.

so-called *adjective* named in what may be the wrong way, *This so-called gentleman slammed the door.*

soccer *noun* a kind of football game played by teams of eleven with a round ball.

sociable *adjective* liking to be with other people; friendly. **sociably** *adverb*, **sociability** *noun*

social *adjective* **1** living in a community, not alone, *Bees are social insects.* **2** of life in a community, *social science.* **3** concerned with people's welfare, *social worker.* **4** helping people to meet each other, *a social club.* **5** sociable. **socially** *adverb*

social network service Internet social chatroom or facility such as Twitter where participants can make postings.

social security or **social welfare** money and other assistance provided by the government for those in need through being ill, disabled, unemployed, etc.
social services welfare services provided by the government, including schools, hospitals, and pensions. [from Latin *socius* = companion]

socialism *noun* a political system where wealth is shared equally between people, and the main industries and trade etc. are controlled by the government. (Compare *capitalism*.)

socialist *noun* a person who believes in socialism.

society *noun* (*plural* **societies**) **1** a community; people living together in a group or nation. **2** a group of people organised for a particular purpose, *the school dramatic society*. **3** company; companionship, *We enjoy the society of our friends*. [same origin as *social*]

sociology (*say* soh-see-**ol**-o-jee) *noun* the study of human society and social behaviour. **sociological** *adjective*, **sociologist** *noun* [from *socio-* = of society, + *-logy*]

sock[1] *noun* **1** a short stocking reaching only to the ankle or below the knee. **2** wool on a sheep's lower leg.

sock[2] *verb* (*slang*) hit hard; punch. *He socked me on the jaw*. **sock** *noun*

socket *noun* **1** a hollow into which something fits, *a tooth-socket*. **2** a device into which an electric plug or bulb is put to make a connection.

sod *noun* a piece of turf.

soda *noun* **1** a compound of sodium used in washing, cooking, etc. **2** soda-water.

soda-water *noun* water made fizzy with carbon dioxide, used in drinks.

sodden *adjective* made very wet.

sodium *noun* a soft white metal.

SOE *abbreviation* (*NZ*) State-owned enterprise.

sofa *noun* a kind of settee.

soft *adjective* **1** not hard or firm; easily pressed. **2** smooth, not rough or stiff. **3** gentle; not loud. **4** falling in value. **softly** *adverb*, **softness** *noun*
soft drink a drink that is not alcoholic.

softball *noun* **1** a game like baseball but played with a larger, softer ball. **2** the ball used in this game.

soften *verb* make or become soft or softer. **softener** *noun*

software *noun* computer programs, tapes, etc. (Compare *hardware*.)

softwood *noun* the wood of evergreen trees with cones. **softwood** *adjective*

soggy *adjective* (**soggier**, **soggiest**) very wet and heavy, *soggy ground*.

soil[1] *noun* **1** the loose earth in which plants grow. **2** territory, *on New Zealand soil*.

soil[2] *verb* make a thing dirty.

sojourn (*say* **soj**-ern) *verb* stay at a place temporarily.

sojourn *noun* a temporary stay.

solace (*say* **sol**-as) *verb* (**solaced**, **solacing**) comfort someone who is unhappy or disappointed. **solace** *noun* [from Latin *solari* = to console]

solar *adjective* of or from the sun.
solar system the sun and the planets that revolve round it.
[from Latin *sol* = sun]

solder *noun* a soft alloy that is melted to join pieces of metal together. **solder** *verb* [from Latin *solidare* = make firm or solid]

soldier *noun* a member of an army.

sole[1] *noun* **1** the bottom surface of a foot or shoe. **2** an edible flatfish.

sole[1] *verb* (**soled**, **soling**) put a sole on a shoe.

sole[2] *adjective* single; only, *She was the sole survivor*. **solely** *adverb*

sole-charge *adjective* (*NZ*) **1** (of a teacher) having sole charge of a school. **2** (of a school) with only one teacher.

solecism (*say* **sol**-uh-siz-uhm) *noun* **1** grammatical mistake, e.g. *Yous people will win*. **2** a social gaffe or lapse in manners.

solemn *adjective* **1** not smiling; not cheerful. **2** dignified; *formal*. **solemnly** *adverb*, **solemnity** *noun*

solemnise *verb* (**solemnised**, **solemnising**) celebrate a festival; perform a marriage ceremony. **solemnisation** *noun*

solenoid *noun* a coil of wire that becomes magnetic when an electric current is passed through it.

sol-fa *noun* a system of syllables (*doh, ray, me, fah, soh, la, te*) used to represent the notes of the musical scale.

solicit *verb* (**solicited**, **soliciting**) ask for; try to obtain, *solicit votes* or *solicit for votes*. **solicitation** *noun*

solicitor *noun* a lawyer who advises clients, prepares legal documents, etc.

solicitous *adjective* anxious and concerned about a person's comfort, welfare, etc. **solicitously** *adverb*, **solicitude** *noun* [from Latin *sollicitus* = worrying]

solid *adjective* **1** not hollow; with no space inside. **2** keeping its shape; not liquid or gas. **3** continuous, *for two solid hours*. **4** firm or strongly made; not flimsy, *a solid foundation*. **5** showing solidarity; unanimous. **solidly** *adverb*, **solidity** *noun*

solid *noun* **1** a solid thing; solid food. **2** a shape that has three dimensions (length, width, and height or depth).

solidarity *noun* **1** being solid. **2** unity and support for each other because of agreement in opinions, interests, etc.

solidify *verb* (**solidified, solidifying**) make or become solid.

soliloquy (*say* sol-**il**-ok-wee) *noun* (*plural* **soliloquies**) a speech in which a person speaks his or her thoughts aloud without addressing anyone. **soliloquise** *verb* [from Latin *solus* = alone, + *loqui* = speak]

solipsism (*say* **sol**-uhp-siz-uhm) *noun* **1** the view that the self is all that can be known to exist. **2** self-centredness. **solipsistic** *adjective*

solitaire *noun* **1** a game for one person, in which marbles are moved on a special board until only one is left. **2** a diamond or other precious stone set by itself.

solitary *adjective* **1** alone, without companions. **2** single, *a solitary example.* **3** lonely, *a solitary valley.* [from Latin *solus* = alone]

solitude *noun* being solitary.

solo *noun* (*plural* **solos**) something sung, played, danced, or done by one person. **solo** *adjective & adverb*, **soloist** *noun*
solo parent (*NZ*) a person bringing up a child on his or her own. **solo mother, solo father**
[Italian, = alone]

solstice (*say* **sol**-stiss) *noun* either of the two times in each year when the sun is at its furthest point north or south of the equator. **summer solstice** about 22 December. **winter solstice** about 21 June. [from Latin *sol* = sun, + *sistere* = stand still]

soluble *adjective* **1** able to be dissolved. **2** able to be solved. **solubility** *noun* [same origin as *solve*]

solution *noun* **1** a liquid in which something is dissolved. **2** the answer to a problem or puzzle. [same origin as *solve*]

solve *verb* (**solved, solving**) find the answer to a problem or puzzle. [from Latin *solvere* = unfasten]

solvent *adjective* **1** having enough money to pay all your debts. **2** able to dissolve another substance. **solvency** *noun*

solvent *noun* a liquid used for dissolving something.

sombre *adjective* dark and gloomy. [from Latin *sub* = under, + *umbra* = shade]

sombrero (*say* som-**brair**-oh) *noun* (*plural* **sombreros**) a hat with a very wide brim. [from Spanish *sombra* = shade (same origin as *sombre*)]

some *adjective* **1** a few; a little, *some apples; some sugar.* **2** an unknown person or thing, *Some fool left the door open.* **3** about, *We waited some 20 minutes.*

some *pronoun* a certain number or amount that is less than the whole, *Some of them were late.*

somebody *pronoun* some person.

somehow *adverb* in some way.

someone *pronoun* somebody.

somersault *noun* a movement in which you turn head over heels before landing on your feet. **somersault** *verb* [from Latin *supra* = above, + *saltus* = a leap]

something *noun* some thing.
something like rather like, *It's something like a rabbit*; approximately, *It cost something like $10.*

sometime *adjective* former, *her sometime friend.*

sometimes *adverb* at some times but not always, *We sometimes walk to school.*

somewhat *adverb* to some extent. *He was somewhat annoyed.*

somewhere *adverb* in or to some place.

somnambulist *noun* a sleepwalker. [from Latin *somnus* = sleep, + *ambulare* = to walk]

somnolent *adjective* sleeping; sleepy. **somnolence** *noun* [from Latin *somnus* = sleep]

son *noun* a boy or man who is someone's child.

sonar *noun* a device for finding objects under water by the reflection of sound-waves. [from *so*und *na*vigation and *r*anging]

sonata *noun* a musical composition for one instrument or two, in several movements. [from Italian *sonare* = to sound]

song *noun* **1** a tune for singing. **2** singing, *He burst into song.*
a song and dance (*informal*) a great fuss.
for a song bought or sold very cheaply.

songbird *noun* a bird that sings sweetly.

songster *noun* **1** a singer. **2** a songbird.

sonic *adjective* of sound or sound-waves. [from Latin *sonus* = sound]

son-in-law *noun* (*plural* **sons-in-law**) a daughter's husband.

sonnet *noun* a kind of poem with 14 lines.

sonny *noun* (*informal*) boy, young man, *Come on, sonny!*

sonorous (*say* **sonn**-er-us) *adjective* giving a loud deep sound; resonant. [from Latin *sonor* = sound]

sook *noun* (also **sookie**) (*NZ*) **1** a hand-reared calf. **2** (*informal*) a sissy.

sool *verb* (*NZ*) **1** urge on (a dog) to chase or attack. **2** (of a dog) pursue or attack.

soon *adverb* **1** in a short time from now. **2** not long after something.
as soon as willingly, *I'd just as soon stay here.*
as soon as at the moment that.
sooner or later at some time in the future.

soot *noun* the black powder left by smoke in a chimney or on a building etc. **sooty** *adjective*

soothe *verb* (**soothed**, **soothing**) calm; ease pain or distress. **soothingly** *adverb*

soothsayer *noun* a prophet. [from an old word *sooth* = truth, + *say*]

sop *noun* **1** a piece of bread dipped in liquid before being eaten or cooked. **2** something unimportant given to pacify or bribe a troublesome person.

sophisticated *adjective* **1** of or accustomed to fashionable life and its ways. **2** complicated, *a sophisticated machine.* **sophistication** *noun*

sophistry (*say* **sof**-ist-ree) *noun* (*plural* **sophistries**) a piece of reasoning that is clever but false or misleading. [from Greek *sophos* = wise]

soporific *adjective* causing sleep. [from Latin *sopor* = sleep, + *facere* = make]

sopping *adjective* very wet; drenched.

soppy *adjective* **1** very wet. **2** (*informal*) sentimental in a sickly way.

soprano *noun* (*plural* **sopranos**) a woman, girl, or boy with a high singing-voice. [from Italian *sopra* = above]

sorcerer *noun* a wizard. **sorceress** *noun*, **sorcery** *noun*

sordid *adjective* **1** dirty; squalid. **2** dishonourable; selfish and mercenary, *sordid motives.* **sordidly** *adverb*, **sordidness** *noun*

sore *adjective* **1** painful; smarting. **2** (*informal*) annoyed; offended. **3** serious; distressing, *in sore need.* **soreness** *noun*

sore *noun* a sore place.

sorely *adverb* seriously; very, *I was sorely tempted to run away.*

sorghum *noun* a kind of tropical cereal grass.

sorrel[1] *noun* a herb with sharp-tasting leaves.

sorrel[2] *noun* a reddish-brown horse.

sorrow *noun* unhappiness or regret caused by loss or disappointment. **sorrowful** *adjective*, **sorrowfully** *adverb*

sorrow *verb* feel sorrow; grieve.

sorry *adjective* (**sorrier**, **sorriest**) **1** feeling pity, regret, or sympathy. **2** wretched, *His clothes were in a sorry state.*

sort *noun* **1** a group of things or people that are similar; a kind or variety. **2** (*informal*) a person, *He's quite a good sort.*
out of sorts slightly unwell or depressed.
sort of (*informal*) rather; to some extent, *I sort of expected it.*

sort *verb* arrange things in groups according to their size, kind, etc. **sorter** *noun*
sort out disentangle; select; (*slang*) deal with and punish someone.

sortie *noun* **1** an attack by troops coming out of a besieged place. **2** an attacking expedition by a military aircraft. [from French *sortir* = go out]

SOS *noun* an urgent appeal for help. [the international Morse code-signal of extreme distress]

soul *noun* **1** the invisible part of a person that is believed to go on living after the body has died. **2** a person's mind and emotions etc. **3** a person, *There isn't a soul about.*

soulful *adjective* having or showing deep feeling. **soulfully** *adverb*

sound[1] *noun* **1** vibrations that travel through the air and can be detected by the ear; the sensation they produce. **2** sound reproduced in a movie etc. **3** a mental impression, *We don't like the sound of his plans.*
sound barrier the resistance of the air to objects moving at nearly supersonic speed.

sound[1] *verb* **1** produce or cause to produce a sound. **2** give an impression when heard, *He sounds angry.* **3** test by noting the sounds heard, *A doctor sounds a patient's lungs with a stethoscope.* [from Latin *sonus* = a sound]

sound[2] *verb* test the depth of water beneath a ship.
sound out try to find out what a person thinks or feels about something.
[from Latin *sub* = under, + *unda* wave]

sound[3] *adjective* **1** in good condition; not damaged. **2** healthy; not diseased. **3** reasonable; correct, *His ideas are sound.* **4** reliable; secure, *a sound investment.* **5** thorough; deep, *a sound sleep.* **soundly** *adverb*, **soundness** *noun* [from Old English *gesund* = healthy]

sound[4] *noun* a strait or long inlet of the sea, *Milford Sound.* [from Old English *sund* = swimming or sea]

soundtrack *noun* the sound that goes with a cinema film.

soup *noun* liquid food made from stewed bones, meat, fish, vegetables, etc.
in the soup (*slang*) in trouble.

sour *adjective* **1** tasting sharp like unripe fruit. **2** stale and unpleasant, not fresh, *sour milk.* **3** bad-tempered. **sourly** *adverb*, **sourness** *noun*

sour *verb* make or become sour.

source *noun* the place from which something comes.

souse *verb* (**soused**, **sousing**) **1** soak; drench. **2** soak fish in pickle.

south *noun* **1** the direction to the right of a person who faces east. **2** the southern part of a country, city, etc.

south *adjective & adverb* towards or in the south. **southerly** (*say* **su***th*-er-lee) *adjective*, **southern** *adjective*, **southerner** *noun*, **southernmost** *adjective*

Southdown *noun* a kind of sheep bred for its meat. [from South Downs in England]

south-east *noun, adjective, & adverb* midway between south and east. **south-easterly** *adjective*, **south-eastern** *adjective*

Southern Cross a constellation in the southern sky, that is represented on the New Zealand flag.

South Islander (*NZ*) a person born in or who lives in the South Island.

southward *adjective & adverb* towards the south. **southwards** *adverb*

south-west *noun, adjective, & adverb* midway between south and west. **south-westerly** *adjective*, **south-western** *adjective*

souvenir (*say* soo-ven-**eer**) *noun* something that you keep to remind you of a person, place, or event. [from French *se souvenir* remember]

souvlaki *noun* (*say* soov-**lah**-kee) a meal of meat pieces cooked on a skewer and served in pitta bread. [Greek]

sou'wester *noun* **1** (*NZ*) a cold wind, often with rain. **2** a waterproof hat with a wide flap at the back.

sovereign *noun* **1** a king or queen who is the ruler of a country; a monarch. **2** an old British gold coin.

sovereign *adjective* **1** supreme, *sovereign power*. **2** having sovereign power; independent, *sovereign states*. [from Latin *super* = over]

sovereignty *noun* supreme authority; complete power.

sow[1] (*rhymes with* go) *verb* (**sowed**, **sown** or **sowed**, **sowing**) put seeds into the ground so that they will grow into plants. **sower** *noun*

sow[2] (*rhymes with* cow) *noun* a female pig. **sow thistle** (*NZ*) pūhā, a plant with thistle-like leaves.

soy or **soya bean** a kind of bean from which edible oil and flour are made.

spa *noun* **1** a health resort where there is a spring of water containing mineral salts. **2** a (usually hot) bath or pool with jets to agitate the water for body massage. [from Spa, a town in Belgium with a mineral spring]

space *noun* **1** the whole area outside the earth, where the stars and planets are. **2** an area or volume, *This table takes too much space.* **3** an empty area; a gap. **4** an interval of time, *within the space of an hour.*
space shuttle a spacecraft for repeated use to and from outer space.

space *verb* (**spaced**, **spacing**) arrange things with spaces between, *Space them out.* [from Latin *spatium* = a space]

spacecraft *noun* (*plural* **spacecraft**) a vehicle for travelling in outer space.

spaceman *noun* (*plural* **spacemen**) an astronaut. **spacewoman** *noun* (*plural* **spacewomen**)

spaceship *noun* a spacecraft.

space shuttle *noun* a rocket-launched spacecraft, used to make return journeys into space.

spacious *adjective* providing a lot of space; roomy. **spaciousness** *noun*

spade[1] *noun* a tool with a long handle and a wide blade for digging. [from Old English *spadu*]

spade[2] *noun* a playing-card with black shapes like upside-down hearts on it, each with a short stem. [from Italian *spada* = sword]

spaghetti *noun* pasta made in long thin sticks. [from Italian, = little strings]

span *noun* **1** the length from end to end or across something. **2** the distance from the tip of the thumb to the tip of the little finger when the hand is spread out. **3** the part between two uprights of an arch or bridge. **4** the length of a period of time.

span *verb* (**spanned**, **spanning**) reach across, *A bridge spans the river.*

spangle *noun* a small piece of glittering material. **spangled** *adjective*

spaniel a kind of dog with long ears and silky fur. [from French, = Spanish dog]

spank *verb* **1** smack a person on the bottom as a punishment. **2** (*NZ, informal*) milk cows.

spanking *adjective* (*informal*) brisk; lively, *at a spanking pace.*

spanner *noun* a tool for gripping and turning the nut on a bolt etc.

spar[1] *noun* a strong pole used for a mast or boom etc. on a ship.

spar[2] *verb* (**sparred**, **sparring**) **1** practise boxing. **2** quarrel or argue.

spare *verb* (**spared**, **sparing**) **1** afford to give something, *Can you spare a moment?* **2** be merciful towards someone; not hurt or harm a person or thing. **3** use or treat economically, *No expense will be spared.*

spare *adjective* **1** not used but kept ready in case it is needed; extra, *a spare wheel.* **2** thin; lean. **sparely** *adverb*, **spareness** *noun*
go spare (*slang*) become very annoyed.
spare time time not needed for work.

sparing (*say* **spair**-ing) *adjective* economical; grudging. **sparingly** *adverb*

spark *noun* **1** a tiny glowing particle. **2** a flash produced electrically.

spark *verb* give off a spark or sparks.

sparkle *verb* (**sparkled**, **sparkling**) **1** shine with tiny flashes of light. **2** show brilliant wit or liveliness.

sparkler *noun* a sparking firework.

spark-plug *noun* a device that makes a spark to ignite the fuel in an engine.

sparrow *noun* a small brown bird.

sparse *adjective* thinly scattered; not numerous, *a sparse population*. **sparsely** *adverb*, **sparseness** *noun* [from Latin *sparsum* = scattered]

spartan *adjective* simple and without comfort or luxuries. [named after the people of Sparta in ancient Greece, famous for their hardiness]

spasm *noun* **1** a sudden involuntary movement of a muscle. **2** a sudden brief spell of activity etc.

spasmodic *adjective* in spasms; happening or done at irregular intervals. **spasmodically** *adverb*

spastic *adjective* suffering from spasms of the muscles and jerky movements, especially caused by a condition called *cerebral palsy*.

spat *past tense* of **spit**[1].

spate *noun* a sudden flood or rush.

spathe (*rhymes with* bathe) *noun* a large petal-like part of a flower, round a central spike.

spatial *adjective* of or in space. [same origin as *space*]

spatter *verb* scatter in small drops; splash. **spatter** *noun*

spatula *noun* a tool like a knife with a broad blunt flexible blade, used for spreading things.

spawn *noun* **1** the eggs of fish, frogs, toads, or shellfish. **2** the thread-like matter from which fungi grow.

spawn *verb* **1** put out spawn; produce from spawn. **2** produce something in great quantities.

spay *verb* sterilise a female animal by removing the ovaries.

SPCA *abbreviation* (*NZ*) Society for the Prevention of Cruelty to Animals.

speak *verb* (**spoke**, **spoken**, **speaking**) **1** say something; talk. **2** talk or be able to talk in a foreign language, *Do you speak French?* **3** present as evidence or signify, *Her outfit spoke of money.*
speak for represent or substitute for somebody.
speak up speak more loudly; give your opinion.

speaker *noun* **1** a person who is speaking; someone who makes a speech. **2** a loudspeaker.
the Speaker the person who controls the debates in Parliament or a similar assembly.

spear *noun* a weapon for throwing or stabbing, with a long shaft and a pointed tip.

spear *verb* pierce with a spear or with something pointed.

speargrass *noun* (*NZ*) a plant with stiff narrow leaves.

spearmint *noun* mint used in cookery and for flavouring chewing-gum.

spec *noun* (*informal*) speculation.

special *adjective* **1** of a particular kind; for some purpose, not general, *special training.* **2** exceptional, *Take special care of it.*

special *noun* **1** an item being sold at a reduced price in a supermarket etc. **2** a concession fare. **3** a particular edition, event, etc. **4** (*NZ*) an extraordinary electoral vote.
on special of an item so reduced, *bread is on special.*

specialise *verb* (**specialised**, **specialising**) give particular attention or study to one subject or thing, *She specialised in biology.* **specialisation** *noun*

specialist *noun* an expert in one subject or branch of medicine etc., *a skin specialist.*

speciality *noun* (*plural* **specialities**) a special quality or product; something in which a person specialises.

specially *adverb* in a special way; for a special purpose.

species (*say* **spee**-seez or **spee**-sheez) *noun* (*plural* **species**) **1** a group of animals or plants that are very similar. **2** a kind or sort, *a species of sledge.* [Latin, = appearance]

specific *adjective* definite; precise; of or for a particular thing, *The money was given for a specific purpose.* **specifically** *adverb*
specific gravity the weight of something as compared with the same volume of water or air.

specify *verb* (**specified**, **specifying**) name or list things precisely, *The recipe specified cream, not milk.* **specification** *noun*

specimen *noun* **1** a sample. **2** an example, *a fine specimen of New Zealand wine.*

specious (*say* **spee**-shus) *adjective* seeming good but lacking real merit, *specious reasoning.* [from Latin *speciosus* = attractive]

speck *noun* a small spot or particle.

speckle *noun* a small spot or mark. **speckled** *adjective*

specs *plural noun* (*informal*) spectacles.

spectacle *noun* **1** an impressive sight or display. **2** a ridiculous sight.
spectacles *plural noun* a pair of lenses set in a frame, worn in front of the eyes to help the wearer to see clearly. **spectacled** *adjective* [from Latin *spectare* = look at]

spectacular *adjective* impressive.

spectator *noun* a person who watches a game, show, incident, etc.

spectre *noun* a ghost. **spectral** *adjective* [same origin as *spectrum*]

spectrum *noun* (*plural* **spectra**) **1** the bands of colours seen in a rainbow. **2** a wide range of things, ideas, etc. [Latin, = image]

speculate *verb* (**speculated**, **speculating**) **1** form opinions without having any definite evidence. **2** make investments in the hope of making a profit but risking a loss. **speculation** *noun*, **speculator** *noun*, **speculative** *adjective* [from Latin *speculari* = spy out]

sped *past tense* of **speed**.

speech *noun* (*plural* **speeches**) **1** the action or power of speaking. **2** words spoken; a talk to an audience.

speechless *adjective* unable to speak because of great emotion.

speed *noun* **1** a measure of the time in which something moves or happens. **2** quickness; swiftness.
at speed quickly.
up to speed (*informal*) up to date or at full speed.

speed *verb* (**sped** (in senses 3 and 4 **speeded**), **speeding**) **1** go quickly, *The train sped by.* **2** send quickly, *to speed you on your way.* **3** travel too fast. **4** make or become quicker, *This will speed things up.*

speedboat *noun* a fast motor-boat.

speedometer *noun* a device in a vehicle, showing its speed. [from *speed* + *meter*]

speedway *noun* a track for motorcycle racing.

speedwell *noun* a wild plant with small blue flowers.

speedy *adjective* (**speedier**, **speediest**) quick; swift. **speedily** *adverb*

speleology (*say* spel-ee-**ol**-o-jee) *noun* the exploration and study of caves. [from Greek *spelaion* = cave, + *-logy*]

spell[1] *noun* a saying or action etc. supposed to have magical power.

spell[2] *noun* **1** a period of time. **2** a period of a certain work or activity etc. **3** (*NZ*) a period of rest from work. **4** a series of cricket overs bowled by a single bowler.

spell[3] *verb* (**spelt**, **spelling**) **1** put letters in the right order to make a word or words. **2** have as a result, *Wet weather spells ruin for crops.* **3** (*NZ & Australia*) rest; allow a person, animal, land, etc. to rest. **speller** *noun*

spellbound *adjective* entranced as if by a magic spell.

spend *verb* (**spent**, **spending**) **1** use money to pay for things. **2** use up, *Don't spend too much time on it.* **3** pass time, *We spent a holiday in Norfolk Island.*

spendthrift *noun* a person who spends money extravagantly and wastefully.

sperm *noun* (*plural* **sperms** or **sperm**) the male cell that fuses with an ovum.
sperm whale a kind of large whale.
[from Greek *sperma* = seed]

spew *verb* **1** vomit. **2** cast out in a stream, *The volcano spewed out lava.*

sphere *noun* **1** a perfectly round solid shape; the shape of a ball. **2** a field of action or interest etc., *That country is in Russia's sphere of influence.* **spherical** *adjective* [from Greek *sphaira* = ball]

spheroid *noun* a sphere-like but not perfectly spherical solid.

sphinx *noun* (*plural* **sphinxes**) a stone statue with the body of a lion and a human head, especially the huge one (almost 5,000 years old) in Egypt.

spice *noun* a substance used to flavour food, often made from dried parts of plants. **spicy** *adjective*

spick and span neat and clean.

spider *noun* a small animal with eight legs that spins webs to catch insects on which it feeds. **spidery** *adjective*

spike *noun* **1** a pointed piece of metal; a sharp point. **2** a long narrow projecting part. **spiky** *adjective*

spike *verb* (**spiked**, **spiking**) **1** put spikes on something. **2** pierce with a spike.
spike a person's guns spoil his or her plans.

spill[1] *verb* (**spilt** or **spilled**, **spilling**) **1** let something fall out of a container. **2** become spilt, *The coins came spilling out.* **spillage** *noun*

spill[1] *noun* **1** spilling. **2** a fall.

spill[2] *noun* a thin strip of wood or rolled paper used to carry a flame, e.g. to light a pipe.

spin *verb* (**spun**, **spinning**) **1** turn round and round quickly. **2** make raw wool or cotton into threads by pulling and twisting its fibres. **3** (of a spider or silkworm) make a web or cocoon out of threads from its body.
spin a yarn tell a story.
spin out cause to last a long time.

spin *noun* **1** a spinning movement. **2** (*informal*) a short excursion in a vehicle. **3** a favourable emphasis or slant on a news story.
spin doctor a person whose job is to present a favourable impression of political events to the media.

spinach *noun* a vegetable with dark-green leaves.

spinal *adjective* of the spine.

spindle *noun* **1** a thin rod on which thread is wound. **2** a pin or bar that turns round or on which something turns.

spindly *adjective* thin and long or tall.

spin-drier *noun* a machine in which washed clothes are spun round and round to dry them.

spindrift *noun* spray blown along the surface of the sea.

spine *noun* **1** the line of bones down the middle of the back. **2** a thorn or prickle. **3** the back part of a book where the pages are joined together.

spineless *adjective* **1** without a backbone. **2** lacking in determination or strength of character.

spinet *noun* a small harpsichord.

spinnaker *noun* a large triangular extra sail on a racing yacht.

spinney *noun* (*plural* **spinneys**) (*British*) a small wood; a thicket.

spinning-wheel *noun* a household device for spinning fibre into thread.

spin-off *noun* (*plural* **spin-offs**) a by-product.

spinster *noun* a woman who has not married. [the original meaning was 'one who spins']

spiny *adjective* full of spines; prickly.

spiral *adjective* going round and round a central point and becoming gradually closer to it or further from it; twisting continually round a central line or cylinder etc.
spirally *adverb*

spiral *noun* a spiral line or course.

spiral *verb* (**spiralled**, **spiralling**) move in a spiral.

spire *noun* a tall pointed part on top of a church tower.

spirit *noun* **1** the soul. **2** a person's mood or mind and feelings, *He was in good spirits.* **3** a ghost; a supernatural being. **4** courage; liveliness, *She answered with spirit.* **5** a kind of quality in something, *the romantic spirit of the book.* **6** a strong distilled alcoholic drink.

spirit *verb* carry off quickly and secretly, *They spirited her away.* [from Latin *spiritus* = breath]

spirited *adjective* brave; lively.

spiritual *adjective* **1** of the human soul; not physical. **2** of the Church or religion.
spiritually *adverb*, **spirituality** *noun*

spiritual *noun* a religious folk-song, especially of Black people in America.

spiritualism *noun* the belief that the spirits of dead people communicate with living people. **spiritualist** *noun*

spirituous *adjective* containing a lot of alcohol; distilled, *spirituous liquors.*

spirulina *noun* **1** blue-green algae used in a health drink. **2** a health drink made from this.

spit[1] *verb* (**spat** or **spit**, **spitting**) **1** send out drops of liquid etc. forcibly from the mouth, *He spat at me.* **2** fall lightly, *It's spitting with rain.*

spit[1] *noun* saliva; spittle.

spit[2] *noun* **1** a long thin metal spike put through meat to hold it while it is being roasted. **2** a narrow strip of land sticking out into the sea.

spite *noun* a desire to hurt or annoy somebody. **spiteful** *adjective*, **spitefully** *adverb*, **spitefulness** *noun*
in spite of not being prevented by, *We went out in spite of the rain.*

spitfire *noun* a fiery-tempered person.

spitting image an exact likeness.

spittle *noun* saliva, especially that spat out.

spittoon *noun* a receptacle for people to spit into.

splash *verb* **1** make liquid fly about in drops. **2** (of liquid) be splashed. **3** wet by splashing, *The bus splashed us.*

splash *noun* (*plural* **splashes**) **1** the action or sound or mark of splashing. **2** a striking display or effect.

splatter *verb* splash noisily.

splay *verb* spread or slope apart.

spleen *noun* **1** an organ of the body, close to the stomach, that helps to keep the blood in good condition. **2** bad temper; spite, *He vented his spleen on us.*

splendid *adjective* **1** magnificent; full of splendour. **2** excellent. **splendidly** *adverb* [from Latin *splendidus* = shining]

splendour *noun* a brilliant display or appearance.

splice *verb* (**spliced**, **splicing**) **1** join pieces of rope etc. by twisting their strands together. **2** join pieces of film or wood etc. by overlapping the ends.

splint *noun* a straight piece of wood or metal etc. tied to a broken arm or leg to hold it firm.

splint *verb* hold with a splint.

splinter *noun* a thin sharp piece of wood, glass, stone, etc. broken off a larger piece.

splinter *verb* break into splinters.

split *verb* (**split**, **splitting**) **1** break into parts; divide. **2** (*slang*) reveal a secret.

split *noun* **1** the splitting or dividing of something. **2** a place where something has split.
the splits an acrobatic position in which the legs are stretched widely in opposite directions.

split screen *noun* a screen on which two or more images are displayed at one time.

splutter *verb* **1** make a quick series of spitting sounds. **2** speak quickly but not clearly. **splutter** *noun*

spoil *verb* (**spoilt** or **spoiled**, **spoiling**) **1** damage something and make it useless or unsatisfactory. **2** make someone selfish by always letting them have what they want.

spoil *noun* (also **spoils**) plunder or other things gained by a victor, *the spoils of war.* [from Latin *spolium* = plunder]

spoilsport *noun* a person who spoils other people's enjoyment of things.

spoke[1] each of the bars or rods that go from the centre of a wheel to its rim.

spoke[2] *past tense* of **speak**.

spokesman *noun* (*plural* **spokesmen**) a person who speaks on behalf of a group of people. **spokeswoman** *noun* (*plural* **spokeswomen**), **spokesperson** *noun*

spoliation *noun* pillaging.

sponge *noun* **1** a sea-creature with a soft porous body. **2** the skeleton of this creature, or a piece of a similar substance, used for washing or padding things. **3** a soft lightweight cake or pudding. **spongy** *adjective*

sponge *verb* (**sponged**, **sponging**) **1** wipe or wash something with a sponge. **2** (*informal*) live by cadging from people, *He sponged on his friends.* **sponger** *noun*

sponsor *noun* someone who provides money or help etc. for a person or thing, or who gives money to a charity in return for something achieved by another person. **sponsorship** *noun*

sponsor *verb* be a sponsor for a person or thing. [from Latin *sponsum* = promised]

spontaneous (*say* spon-**tay**-nee-us) *adjective* happening or done naturally; not forced or suggested by someone else. **spontaneously** *adverb*, **spontaneity** *noun* [from Latin *sponte* = of your own accord]

spoof *noun* (*slang*) a hoax; a parody.

spook *noun* (*informal*) a ghost. **spooky** *adjective*, **spookiness** *noun*

spool *noun* a rod or cylinder on which something is wound.

spoon *noun* a small device with a rounded bowl on a handle, used for lifting things to the mouth or for stirring or measuring things. **spoonful** *noun* (*plural* **spoonfuls**)

spoon *verb* take or lift something with a spoon.

spoonerism *noun* an accidental exchange of the initial letters of two words, e.g. by saying *a boiled sprat* instead of *a spoiled brat.* [named after Canon Spooner (1844–1930), who made mistakes of this kind]

spoor *noun* the track left by an animal.

sporadic *adjective* happening or found at irregular intervals; scattered. **sporadically** *adverb* [from Greek *sporas* = scattered]

spore *noun* a tiny reproductive cell of a plant such as a fungus or fern. [from Greek *spora* = seed]

sporran *noun* a pouch worn in front of a kilt.

sport *noun* **1** an athletic activity; a game or pastime, especially outdoors. **2** games of this kind, *Are you keen on sport?* **3** (*informal*) a person who behaves fairly and generously, *Come on, be a sport!* **4** (*informal*) a term of address, = mate, *No way, sport!*
sports car an open low-built fast car.
sports coat or **jacket** a man's jacket for *informal* wear (not part of a suit).

sport *verb* **1** play; amuse yourself. **2** wear, *He sported a gold tie-pin.*

sporting *adjective* **1** connected with sport; interested in sport. **2** behaving fairly and generously.
a sporting chance a reasonable chance of success.

sportive *adjective* playful.

sportsman *noun* (*plural* **sportsmen**) a sporting man. **sportsmanship** *noun*

sportswoman *noun* (*plural* **sportswomen**) a sporting woman.

sporty *adjective* **1** fond of sport. **2** energetic and healthy. **3** casual in clothes. **4** with rapid acceleration.

spot *noun* **1** a small round mark. **2** a pimple. **3** a small amount, *We had a spot of trouble.* **4** a place. **5** a drop, *a few spots of rain.*
on the spot without delay or change of place; under pressure to take action, *This really puts him on the spot!*

spot *verb* (**spotted**, **spotting**) **1** mark with spots. **2** (*informal*) notice, *We spotted her in the crowd.* **3** watch for and take note of, *train-spotting.* **spotter** *noun*

spotless *adjective* perfectly clean.

spotlight *noun* a strong light that can shine on one small area.

spotty *adjective* marked with spots.

spouse *noun* a person's husband or wife. [from Latin *sponsus* = betrothed]

spout *noun* **1** a pipe or similar opening from which liquid can pour. **2** a jet of liquid.

spout *verb* **1** come or send out as a jet of liquid. **2** (*informal*) speak for a long time.

sprain *verb* injure a joint by twisting it. **sprain** *noun*

sprat *noun* a small edible fish.

sprawl *verb* **1** sit or lie with the arms and legs spread out loosely. **2** spread out loosely or untidily. **sprawl** *noun*

spray[1] *verb* scatter tiny drops of liquid over something.

spray[1] *noun* **1** tiny drops of liquid sprayed. **2** a device for spraying liquid.

spray[2] *noun* **1** a single shoot with its leaves and flowers. **2** a small bunch of flowers.

spread *verb* (**spread**, **spreading**) **1** open or stretch something out to its full size, *The bird spread its wings.* **2** make something cover a surface, *We spread jam on the bread.* **3** become longer or wider, *The stain was spreading.* **4** make or become more widely known or felt or distributed etc., *We spread the news. Panic spread.*

spread *noun* **1** the action or result of spreading. **2** a thing's breadth or extent. **3** a paste for spreading on bread. **4** (*informal*) a huge meal.

spread-eagle *verb* (**spread-eagled**, **spread-eagling**) spread out a person's body with arms and legs stretched out.

spreadsheet *noun* a computer program used for accounting and recording of figures.

spree *noun* (*informal*) a lively outing.

sprig *noun* **1** a small branch; a shoot. **2** (*NZ*) one of a set of studs on the sole of a rugby boot, etc.

sprightly *adjective* (**sprightlier**, **sprightliest**) lively; full of energy.

spring *verb* (**sprang**, **sprung**, **springing**) **1** jump; move quickly or suddenly, *He sprang to his feet.* **2** originate; arise, *The trouble has sprung from carelessness.* **3** present or produce suddenly, *They sprang a surprise on us.*

spring *noun* **1** a springy coil or bent piece of metal. **2** a springing movement. **3** a place where water comes up naturally from the ground. **4** the season when most plants begin to grow.

springboard *noun* a springy board from which people jump in diving and gymnastics.

springbok *noun* a South African gazelle.

Springbok *noun* a South African national rugby union representative.

spring-clean *verb* clean a house thoroughly in springtime.

springtime *noun* the season of spring.

springy *adjective* (**springier**, **springiest**) able to spring back easily after being bent or squeezed. **springiness** *noun*

sprinkle *verb* (**sprinkled**, **sprinkling**) make tiny drops or pieces fall on something. **sprinkler** *noun*

sprinkling *noun* a few here and there.

sprint *verb* run very fast for a short distance. **sprint** *noun*, **sprinter** *noun*

sprite *noun* an elf, fairy, or goblin.

sprocket *noun* each of the row of teeth round a wheel, fitting into links on a chain.

sprout *verb* start to grow; put out shoots.

sprout *noun* **1** a shoot of a plant. **2** a Brussels sprout.

spruce[1] *noun* a kind of fir-tree.

spruce[2] *adjective* neat and trim; smart.

spruce[2] *verb* (**spruced**, **sprucing**) smarten, *Spruce yourself up.*

spry *adjective* (**spryer**, **spryest**) active; nimble; lively.

SPUC *abbreviation* (*NZ*) Society for the Protection of the Unborn Child.

spud *noun* (*slang*) a potato.

spume *noun* froth; foam.

spur *noun* **1** a sharp device worn on the heel of a rider's boot to urge a horse to go faster. **2** a stimulus or incentive. **3** a projecting part. **on the spur of the moment** on an impulse; without planning.

spur *verb* (**spurred**, **spurring**) urge on; encourage.

spurious *adjective* not genuine.

spurn *verb* reject scornfully.

spurt *verb* **1** gush out. **2** increase your speed suddenly.

spurt *noun* **1** a sudden gush. **2** a sudden increase in speed or effort.

sputter *verb* splutter. **sputter** *noun*

spy *noun* (*plural* **spies**) someone who works secretly to find out things about another country, person, etc.

spy *verb* (**spied**, **spying**) **1** be a spy; keep watch secretly. **2** see; notice, *She spied a house.* **3** pry.

spyware *noun* computing software enabling a user to obtain information from another computer undetected.

SQL *abbreviation* Structured Query Language, an international standard language for database manipulation.

squab *noun* a thick seat cushion.

squabble *verb* (**squabbled**, **squabbling**) quarrel; bicker. **squabble** *noun*

squad *noun* a small group of people working or being trained together.

squadron *noun* part of an army, navy, or air force.

squalid *adjective* dirty and unpleasant. **squalidly** *adverb*, **squalor** *noun* [from Latin *squalidus* = rough, dirty]

squall *noun* **1** a sudden storm or gust of wind. **2** a baby's loud cry.

squall *verb* (of a baby) cry loudly.

squander *verb* spend money or time etc. wastefully.

square *noun* **1** a flat shape with four equal sides and four right angles. **2** an area surrounded by buildings, *Cathedral Square.* **3** the number produced by multiplying something by itself, *9 is the square of 3* (*9 = 3 × 3*). **4** (*informal*) a person who is considered too conservative or conventional.

square *adjective* **1** having the shape of a square. **2** forming a right angle, *The desk has square corners.* **3** equal; even, *The teams are all square with six points each.* **4** honest; fair, *a square deal.* **5** (*informal*) old-fashioned, conventional. **squarely** *adverb*, **squareness** *noun*
square meal a good satisfying meal.
square metre the area of a surface with sides that are one metre long.
square root the number that gives a particular number if it is multiplied by itself, *3 is the square root of 9* (*3 × 3 = 9*).

square *verb* (**squared**, **squaring**) **1** make a thing square. **2** multiply a number by itself, *5 squared is 25.* **3** match; make or be consistent, *His story doesn't square with yours.* **4** (*informal*) bribe. [from Latin *quadra* = square]

square-rigged *adjective* with the sails set across the ship, not lengthways.

squash[1] *verb* **1** press something so that it loses its shape; crush. **2** pack tightly. **3** suppress; quash.

squash[1] *noun* (*plural* **squashes**) **1** a crowded condition. **2** a fruit-flavoured soft drink. **3** a game played with rackets and a soft ball in a special indoor court.

squash[2] *noun* (*plural* **squashes**) a kind of gourd used as a vegetable.

squat *verb* (**squatted**, **squatting**) **1** sit on your heels; crouch. **2** use an unoccupied house for living in without permission. **squat** *noun*, **squatter** *noun*

squat *adjective* short and fat.

squaw *noun* a North American Indian woman or wife.

squawk *verb* make a loud harsh cry. **squawk** *noun*

squeak *verb* make a short high-pitched cry or sound. **squeak** *noun*, **squeaky** *adjective*, **squeakily** *adverb*

squeal *verb* make a long shrill cry or sound. **squeal** *noun*

squeamish *adjective* easily disgusted or shocked. **squeamishness** *noun*

squeeze *verb* (**squeezed**, **squeezing**) **1** press from opposite sides; press something so as to get liquid out of it. **2** force into or through a place, *We squeezed through a gap in the hedge.* **squeezer** *noun*

squeeze *noun* **1** the action of squeezing. **2** a drop of liquid squeezed out, *Add a squeeze of lemon.* **3** a time when money is difficult to get or borrow.

squelch *verb* make a sound like someone treading in thick mud. **squelch** *noun*

squib *noun* a small firework that hisses and then explodes.

squid *noun* a sea-animal with eight short tentacles and two long ones.

squiggle *noun* a short curly line.

squint *verb* **1** be cross-eyed. **2** peer; look with half-shut eyes at something. **squint** *noun*

squirm *verb* wriggle.

squirrel *noun* a small animal with a bushy tail and red or grey fur, living in trees.

squirt *verb* send or come out in a jet of liquid.

squiz *noun* (*NZ, informal*) a look, a glance.

St *abbreviation* **1** Saint. **2** Street.

stab *verb* (**stabbed**, **stabbing**) pierce or wound with something sharp.

stab *noun* **1** the action of stabbing. **2** a sudden sharp pain, *She felt a stab of fear.* **3** (*informal*) an attempt, *I'll have a stab at it.*

stabilise *verb* (**stabilised**, **stabilising**) make or become stable. **stabilisation** *noun*, **stabiliser** *noun*

stability *noun* being stable.

stable[1] *adjective* steady; firmly fixed. **stably** *adverb* [from Latin *stabilis* = standing firm]

stable[2] *noun* a building where horses are kept.

stable[2] *verb* (**stabled**, **stabling**) put or keep in a stable.

staccato *adverb & adjective* (in music) played with each note short and separate. [Italian, = detached]

stack *noun* **1** a neat pile. **2** a haystack. **3** (*informal*) a large amount, *a stack of work.* **4** a single tall chimney; a group of chimneys.

stack *verb* pile things up.

stadium *noun* a sports ground surrounded by seats for spectators.

staff *noun* **1** the people who work in an office, shop, etc. **2** the teachers in a school or college. **3** a stick or pole used as a weapon or support or as a symbol of authority. **4** (*plural* **staves**) a set of five horizontal lines on which music is written.

staff *verb* provide with a staff of people.

stag *noun* a male deer.

stage *noun* **1** a platform for performances in a theatre or hall. **2** a point or part of a process, journey, etc., *the final stage.*

stage *verb* (**staged**, **staging**) **1** present a performance on a stage. **2** organise, *We decided to stage a protest.*

stage-coach *noun* a horse-drawn coach that formerly ran regularly from one point to another along the same route.

stagger *verb* **1** walk unsteadily. **2** shock deeply; amaze, *We were staggered at the price.* **3** arrange things so that they do not coincide, *Please stagger your holidays so that there is always someone here.*
stagger *noun*

stagnant *adjective* not flowing or not changing, *a pool of stagnant water.*

stagnate *verb* (**stagnated**, **stagnating**) **1** be stagnant. **2** be dull through lack of activity or variety. **stagnation** *noun* [from Latin *stagnum* = a pool]

staid *adjective* steady and serious in manner; sedate.

stain *noun* **1** a dirty mark on something. **2** a blemish on someone's character or past record. **3** a liquid used for staining things.

stain *verb* **1** make a stain on something. **2** colour with a liquid that sinks into the surface.

stainless *adjective* without a stain.
stainless steel steel that does not rust easily.

stair *noun* each of the fixed steps in a series that lead from one level or floor to another in a building.

staircase *noun* a flight of stairs.

stake *noun* **1** a thick pointed stick to be driven into the ground. **2** the post to which people used to be tied for execution by being burnt alive. **3** an amount of money bet on something. **4** an investment that gives a person a share or interest in an enterprise.
at stake being risked.

stake *verb* (**staked**, **staking**) **1** fasten, support, or mark out with stakes. **2** bet or risk money etc. on an event.
stake a claim claim or obtain a right to something.

stalactite *noun* a stony spike hanging like an icicle from the roof of a cave. [from Greek *stalaktos* = dripping]

stalagmite *noun* a stony spike standing like a pillar on the floor of a cave. [from Greek *stalagma* = a drop]

stale *adjective* not fresh. **staleness** *noun*

stalemate *noun* **1** a drawn position in chess when a player cannot make a move without putting his or her king in check. **2** a deadlock; a draw in a contest that was held to decide something.

stalk[1] *noun* a stem of a plant etc.

stalk[2] *verb* **1** track or hunt stealthily. **2** walk in a stiff or dignified way.

stall[1] *noun* **1** a stand from which things are sold. **2** a place for one animal in a stable or shed. **3** a seat in the part of a theatre (*the stalls*) nearest the stage.

stall[1] *verb* **1** stop suddenly, *The car engine stalled.* **2** put an animal into a stall.

stall[2] *verb* delay things deliberately so as to avoid having to take action. [from *stall* = pickpocket's helper]

stallion *noun* a male horse.

stalwart *adjective* sturdy; strong and faithful, *my stalwart supporters.*

stamen *noun* the part of a flower bearing pollen.

stamina *noun* strength and ability to endure things for a long time.

stammer *verb* keep repeating the same syllables when you speak. **stammer** *noun*

stamp *noun* **1** a postage stamp; a small piece of gummed paper with a special design on it. **2** a small device for pressing words or marks on something; the words or marks made by this. **3** a distinctive characteristic, *His story bears the stamp of truth.*

stamp *verb* **1** bang a foot heavily on the ground. **2** walk with loud heavy steps. **3** stick a stamp on something. **4** press a mark or design etc. on something.
stamp out put out a fire etc. by stamping; stop something, *stamp out cruelty.*

stampede *noun* a sudden rush by animals or people. **stampede** *verb*

stance *noun* the way a person or animal stands; an attitude.

stanchion *noun* an upright bar or post forming a support.

stand *verb* (**stood**, **standing**) **1** be on your feet without moving, *We were standing at the back of the hall.* **2** set or be upright; place, *We stood the vase on the table.* **3** stay the same, *My offer still stands.* **4** be a candidate for election, *She stood for Parliament.* **5** tolerate; endure, *I can't stand that noise.* **6** provide and pay for, *I'll stand you a drink.*
it stands to reason it is reasonable or obvious.
stand by be ready for action.
stand for represent; tolerate.
stand up for support; defend.
stand up to resist bravely; stay in good condition in hard use.

stand *noun* **1** something made for putting things on, *a music-stand.* **2** a stall where things are sold or displayed. **3** a grandstand. **4** a stationary condition or position, *He took his stand near the door.* **5** resistance to attack, *We made a stand.*

standard *noun* **1** how good something is, *a high standard of work.* **2** a thing used to measure or judge something else. **3** a special flag, *the royal standard.* **4** an upright support.
standard lamp a lamp on an upright pole that stands on the floor.

standard *adjective* **1** of the usual or average quality or kind. **2** regarded as the best and widely used, *the standard book on spiders.*

standardbred *noun & adjective* (a racehorse) bred for pacing or trotting.

standardise *verb* (**standardised, standardising**) make things be of a standard size, quality, etc. **standardisation** *noun*

standpoint *noun* a point of view.

standstill *noun* a stop; an end to movement or activity.

stanza *noun* a verse of poetry.

staple[1] *noun* **1** a small piece of metal pushed through papers and clenched to fasten them together. **2** a U-shaped nail. **staple** *verb,* **stapler** *noun*

staple[2] *adjective* main; usual, *Rice is their staple food.* **staple** *noun*

star *noun* **1** a heavenly body that is seen as a speck of light in the sky at night. **2** a shape with rays from it; an asterisk; a mark of this shape showing that something is good, *a five-star hotel.* **3** a famous performer; one of the chief performers in a play or show etc.

star *verb* (**starred, starring**) **1** perform or present as a star in a show etc. **2** mark with an asterisk or star symbol.

starboard *noun* the right-hand side of a ship or aircraft when you are facing forward. (Compare *port*[1].)

starch *noun* (*plural* **starches**) **1** a white carbohydrate in bread, potatoes, etc. **2** this or a similar substance used to stiffen clothes. **starchy** *adjective*

starch *verb* stiffen with starch.

stardom *noun* being a star performer.

stare *verb* (**stared, staring**) look at something intensely. **stare** *noun*

starfish *noun* (*plural* **starfish** or **starfishes**) a sea-animal shaped like a star with five points.

stark *adjective* **1** complete; unmistakable, *stark nonsense.* **2** desolate; without cheerfulness, *the stark lunar landscape.* **starkly** *adverb,* **starkness** *noun*

stark *adverb* completely, *stark naked.*

starlight *noun* light from the stars.

starling *noun* a noisy black bird with speckled feathers.

starry *adjective* full of stars.

start *verb* **1** begin or cause to begin. **2** begin a journey. **3** make a sudden movement because of pain or surprise. **starter** *noun*

start *noun* **1** the beginning; the place where a race starts. **2** an advantage that someone starts with, *We gave the young ones ten minutes' start.* **3** a sudden movement.

startle *verb* (**startled, startling**) surprise or alarm someone.

starve *verb* (**starved, starving**) **1** suffer or die from lack of food; cause to do this. **2** (*informal*) be very hungry. **starvation** *noun*

state *noun* **1** the quality of a person's or thing's characteristics or circumstances; condition. **2** a grand style, *She arrived in state.* **3** an organised community under one government (*the State of Israel*) or forming part of a republic (*the 50 States of the USA*). **4** a country's government, *Help for the earthquake victims was provided by the state.* **5** (*informal*) an excited or upset condition, *Don't get into a state about the robbery.*
state forest (*NZ*) a forest planted on Crown land.
state house (*NZ*) a house built and owned by the state and rented to a tenant.
state school (*NZ*) any school providing free education from government funds.

state *verb* (**stated, stating**) express something in spoken or written words. [same origin as *status*]

stately *adjective* (**statelier, stateliest**) dignified; imposing; grand. **stateliness** *noun*

statement *noun* **1** words stating something. **2** a *formal* account of facts, *The witness made a statement to the police.* **3** a written report of a financial account, *a bank statement.*

state-of-the-art *adjective* completely up to date.

State-owned enterprise a government department or ministry that has been corporatised.

stateroom *noun* a large room in a palace, public building, or ship.

statesman *noun* (*plural* **statesmen**) a person who is important or skilled in governing a country. **statesmanship** *noun,* **stateswoman** *noun*

static *adjective* not moving; not changing. **static electricity** electricity that is present in something, not flowing as current. [from Greek *statikos* = standing]

station *noun* **1** a place where a person or thing stands or is stationed; a position. **2** a stopping-place on a railway with buildings for passengers and goods. **3** a building equipped for people who serve the public or for certain activities, *the police station.* **4** a broadcasting establishment with its own frequency. **5** (*NZ*) a large sheep or cattle farm. **station wagon** (*NZ*) a motor car with a lengthened body giving extra room for carrying passengers and goods.

station *verb* put someone in a certain place for a purpose, *He was stationed at the door to take the tickets.* [from Latin *statio* = a standing]

stationary *adjective* not moving, *The car was stationary when the van hit it.*

USAGE Do not confuse with stationery.

stationer *noun* a shopkeeper who sells stationery.

stationery *noun* paper, envelopes, and other articles used in writing or typing.

USAGE Do not confuse with stationary.

statistic *noun* a piece of information expressed as a number, *These statistics show that the population has doubled.* **statistical** *adjective*, **statistically** *adverb* **statistics** *noun* the study of information based on the numbers of things.

statistician (*say* stat-is-**tish**-an) *noun* an expert in statistics.

statuary *noun* statues.

statue *noun* a model made of stone or metal etc. to look like a person or animal.

statuesque (*say* stat-yoo-**esk**) *adjective* like a statue in stillness or dignity.

statuette *noun* a small statue.

stature *noun* **1** the natural height of the body. **2** greatness because of ability or achievement.

status (*say* **stay**-tus) *noun* (*plural* **statuses**) **1** a person's or thing's position or rank in relation to others. **2** high rank or prestige. [from Latin *status* = a standing]

statute *noun* a law passed by a parliament. **statutory** *adjective* [from Latin *statutum* = set up]

staunch *adjective* firm and loyal, *our staunch supporters.* **staunchly** *adverb*

stave *noun* **1** each of the curved strips of wood forming the side of a cask or tub. **2** a staff in music (see *staff 4*).

stave *verb* (**staved** or **stove**, **staving**) dent or break a hole in something, *The collision stove in the front of the ship.* **stave off** keep something away, *We staved off the disaster.*

stay[1] *verb* **1** continue to be in the same place or condition; remain. **2** spend time in a place as a visitor. **3** satisfy temporarily, *We stayed our hunger with a sandwich.* **4** pause. **5** show endurance in a race or task. **stay put** (*informal*) remain in place.

stay[1] *noun* **1** a time spent somewhere, *We made a short stay in Tawa.* **2** a postponement, *a stay of execution.*

stay[2] *noun* a support, especially a rope or wire holding up a mast etc.

STD *abbreviation* **1** sexually transmitted disease. **2** subscriber trunk dialling.

stead *noun* **in a person's** or **thing's stead** instead of this person or thing. **stand a person in good stead** be very useful to him or her.

steadfast *adjective* firm and not changing, *a steadfast refusal.*

steady *adjective* (**steadier**, **steadiest**) **1** not shaking or moving; firm. **2** regular; continuing the same, *a steady pace.* **steadily** *adverb*, **steadiness** *noun*

steak *noun* a thick slice of meat or fish.

steal *verb* (**stole**, **stolen**, **stealing**) **1** take and keep something that does not belong to you; take secretly or dishonestly. **2** move secretly or without being noticed, *He stole out of the room.*

stealthy (*say* **stel**th-ee) *adjective* (**stealthier**, **stealthiest**) quiet and secret, so as not to be noticed. **stealth** *noun*, **stealthily** *adverb*, **stealthiness** *noun*

steam *noun* **1** the gas or vapour that comes from boiling water; this used to drive machinery. **2** energy, *He ran out of steam.* **steamy** *adjective*

steam *verb* **1** give out steam. **2** cook or treat by steam, *a steamed pudding.* **3** move by the power of steam, *The ship steamed down the river.*

steam-engine *noun* an engine driven by steam.

steamer *noun* **1** a steamship. **2** a container in which things are steamed.

steamroller *noun* a heavy vehicle with a large roller used to flatten surfaces when making roads.

steamship *noun* a ship driven by steam.

steed *noun* (*poetical*) a horse.

steel *noun* **1** a strong metal made from iron and carbon. **2** a steel rod for sharpening knives. **steely** *adjective*
steel band a West Indian band of musicians with instruments usually made from oil-drums.

steep[1] *adjective* **1** sloping very sharply, not gradually. **2** (*informal*) unreasonably high, *a steep price*. **steeply** *adverb*, **steepness** *noun*

steep[2] *verb* soak thoroughly; saturate.

steepen *verb* make or become steeper.

steeple *noun* a church tower with a spire on top.

steeplechase *noun* a race across country or over hedges or fences. [so called because the race originally had a distant church steeple in view as its goal]

steeplejack *noun* a person who climbs tall chimneys or steeples to do repairs.

steer[1] *verb* make a car, ship, or bicycle etc. go in the direction you want; guide. **steersman** *noun*

steer[2] *noun* a young bull kept for its beef.

steering-wheel *noun* a wheel for steering a car, boat, etc.

stellar *adjective* of a star or stars. [from Latin *stella* = star]

stem[1] *noun* **1** the main central part of a tree, shrub, or plant. **2** a thin part on which a leaf, flower, or fruit is supported. **3** a thin upright part; the thin part of a wine glass between the bowl and the foot. **4** the main part of a verb or other word, to which endings are attached. **5** the front part of a ship, *from stem to stern*.

stem[1] *verb* (**stemmed**, **stemming**) **stem from** arise from; have as its source.

stem[2] *verb* (**stemmed**, **stemming**) stop the flow of something.

stench *noun* (*plural* **stenches**) a very unpleasant smell.

stencil *noun* a piece of card, metal, or plastic with pieces cut out of it, used to produce a picture, design, etc.

stencil *verb* (**stencilled**, **stencilling**) produce or decorate with a stencil.

stentorian *adjective* very loud, *a stentorian voice*. [from the name of Stentor, a herald in ancient Greek legend]

step *noun* **1** a movement made by lifting the foot and setting it down. **2** the sound or rhythm of stepping. **3** a level surface for placing the foot on in climbing up or down. **4** each of a series of things done in some process or action, *The first step is to find somewhere to practise*.
steps *plural noun* a stepladder.
in step stepping in time with others in marching or dancing; in agreement.
watch your step be careful.

step *verb* (**stepped**, **stepping**) tread; walk.
step in intervene.
step on it (*slang*) hurry.
step up increase something.

step- *prefix* related through remarriage of one parent.

stepchild *noun* (*plural* **stepchildren**) a child that a person's husband or wife has from an earlier marriage. **stepbrother**, **stepdaughter**, **stepsister**, **stepson** *nouns*

stepfather *noun* a man who is married to your mother but was not your natural father.

stepladder *noun* a folding ladder with flat treads.

stepmother *noun* a woman who is married to your father but was not your natural mother.

steppe *noun* a grassy plain with few trees, especially in Russia.

stepping-stone *noun* each of a line of stones put into a shallow stream so that people can walk across.

stereo *adjective* stereophonic.

stereo *noun* (*plural* **stereos**) **1** stereophonic sound or recording. **2** a music system with two or more speakers that produces stereophonic sound.

stereophonic *adjective* using sound that comes from two different directions so as to give a natural effect. [from Greek *stereos* = solid, + *phone* = sound]

stereoscopic *adjective* giving the effect of being three-dimensional, e.g. in photographs. [from Greek *stereos* = solid, *skopein* = look at]

stereotype *noun* a standardised character; a fixed idea etc., *The stereotype of a hero is one who is tall, strong, brave, and good-looking*. [from Greek *stereos* = solid, + *type* (= fixed type formerly used in printing)]

sterile *adjective* **1** not fertile; barren. **2** free from germs. **sterility** *noun*

sterilise *verb* (**sterilised**, **sterilising**) **1** make a thing free from germs, e.g. by heating it. **2** make a person or animal unable to reproduce. **sterilisation** *noun*, **steriliser** *noun*

sterling *noun* British money. [from *steorling* = Norman coin with a star on it]

sterling *adjective* **1** genuine, *sterling silver*. **2** excellent; of great worth, *her sterling qualities*.

stern[1] *adjective* strict and severe, not lenient or kindly. **sternly** *adverb*, **sternness** *noun*

stern[2] *noun* the back part of a ship.

steroid *noun* a substance of a kind that includes certain hormones and other natural secretions.

stethoscope *noun* a device used for listening to sounds in a person's body, e.g. heart-beats and breathing. [from Greek *stethos* = breast, + *skopein* = look at]

stevedore *noun* a man employed in loading and unloading ships; a watersider.

stew *verb* cook slowly in liquid.

stew *noun* a dish of stewed food, especially meat and vegetables.
in a stew (*informal*) very worried or agitated.

steward *noun* **1** a person whose job is to look after the passengers on a ship or aircraft. **2** an official who looks after something. **stewardess** *noun*

stick[1] *noun* **1** a long thin piece of wood. **2** a walking-stick. **3** the implement used to hit the ball in hockey, polo, etc. **4** a long thin piece of something, *a stick of liquorice.*
stick insect an insect with a body like a twig.
the sticks (*informal*) **1** remote rural areas, the backblocks. **2** the goalposts (in rugby etc.); the stumps (in cricket).

stick[2] *verb* (**stuck**, **sticking**) **1** push a thing into something, *Stick a pin in it.* **2** fix or be fixed by glue or as if by this, *Stick stamps on the parcel.* **3** become fixed and unable to move, *The boat stuck on a sandbank.* **4** (*informal*) stay, *We must stick together.* **5** (*informal*) endure; tolerate, *I can't stick that noise!* **6** (*informal*) impose a task on someone, *We were stuck with the clearing up.*
stick out come or push out from a surface; stand out from the surrounding area; be very noticeable.
stick to remain faithful to a friend or promise etc.; keep to and not alter, *He stuck to his story.*
stick up for (*informal*) stand up for.
get stuck in (**to**) (*informal*) assault (a person) with blows or words; attack a task or a meal etc.

sticker *noun* an adhesive label or sign for sticking to something.

sticking-plaster *noun* a strip of adhesive material for covering cuts.

stickleback *noun* a small fish with sharp spines on its back.

stickler *noun* a person who insists on something, *a stickler for punctuality.*

sticky *adjective* (**stickier**, **stickiest**) **1** able or likely to stick to things. **2** (of weather) hot and humid, causing perspiration. **3** (*informal*) unpleasant, *He'll come to a sticky end.* **4** (*informal*) uncooperative, *She was very sticky about giving me leave.* **stickily** *adverb*, **stickiness** *noun*

sticky *noun* **1** a dessert or ice wine. **2** madeira, port, or sherry. **3** a small piece of paper with an adhesive strip.

stickybeak *noun* (*NZ*) a nosy or prying person.

stiff *adjective* **1** not bending or moving or changing its shape easily. **2** not fluid; hard to stir, *a stiff dough.* **3** difficult, *a stiff examination.* **4** *formal* in manner; not friendly. **5** strong, *a stiff breeze.* **stiffly** *adverb*, **stiffness** *noun*

stiffen *verb* make or become stiff. **stiffener** *noun*

stifle *verb* (**stifled**, **stifling**) **1** suffocate. **2** suppress, *She stifled a yawn.*

stigma *noun* **1** a mark of disgrace; a stain on a reputation. **2** the part of a pistil that receives the pollen in pollination. [Greek, = a mark]

stigmatise *verb* (**stigmatised**, **stigmatising**) brand as something disgraceful, *He was stigmatised as a coward.*

stile *noun* an arrangement of steps or bars for people to climb over a fence.

stiletto *noun* (*plural* **stilettos**) a dagger with a narrow blade. [Italian, = little dagger]
stiletto heel a high pointed shoe-heel.

still[1] *adjective* **1** not moving, *still water.* **2** silent. **3** not fizzy. **stillness** *noun*

still[1] *adverb* **1** without moving, *Stand still.* **2** up to this or that time, *He was still there.* **3** in a greater amount or degree, *You can do still better.* **4** nevertheless, *They've lost. Still, they tried, and that was good.*
still life a painting of lifeless things such as ornaments and fruit.

still[1] *verb* make or become still.

still[2] *noun* an apparatus for distilling alcohol or other liquid. [from *distil*]

stillborn *adjective* born dead.

stilt *noun* a long-legged bird found in swamps or mud-flats.

stilted *adjective* stiffly formal.

stilts *plural noun* **1** a pair of poles with supports for the feet so that the user can walk high above the ground. **2** posts for supporting a house etc. above marshy ground.

stimulant *noun* something that stimulates.

stimulate *verb* (**stimulated**, **stimulating**) make more lively or active; excite or interest. **stimulation** *noun*

stimulus *noun* (*plural* **stimuli**) something that stimulates or produces a reaction. [Latin, = goad]

sting *noun* **1** a sharp-pointed part of an animal or plant that can cause a wound. **2** a painful wound caused by this part.

sting *verb* (**stung**, **stinging**) **1** wound or hurt with a sting. **2** feel a sharp pain. **3** stimulate sharply, *I was stung into answering rudely.* **4** (*slang*) cheat a person by over-charging; extort money from someone.

stingray *noun* a large, flat fish with a stinging tail.

stingy (*say* **stin**-jee) *adjective* (**stingier**, **stingiest**) mean, not generous; giving or given in small amounts. **stingily** *adverb*, **stinginess** *noun*

stink *noun* **1** an unpleasant smell. **2** (*slang*) an unpleasant fuss or protest.

stink *verb* (**stank** or **stunk**, **stunk**, **stinking**) have an unpleasant smell.

stint *noun* **1** a fixed amount of work to be done. **2** limitation of a supply or effort, *They gave help without stint.*

stint *verb* limit; be niggardly, *Don't stint them of food.*

stipend (*say* **sty**-pend) *noun* a salary. [from Latin *stips* = wages, + *pendere* = to pay]

stipple *verb* (**stippled**, **stippling**) paint, draw, or engrave in small dots.

stipulate *verb* (**stipulated**, **stipulating**) insist on something as part of an agreement. **stipulation** *noun*

stir *verb* (**stirred**, **stirring**) **1** mix a liquid or soft mixture by moving a spoon etc. round and round in it. **2** move slightly; start to move. **3** excite; stimulate, *They stirred up trouble.*

stir *noun* **1** the action of stirring. **2** a disturbance; excitement, *The news caused a stir.*

stirrer *noun* (*informal*) a troublemaker.

stirrup *noun* a metal part that hangs from each side of a horse's saddle, for a rider to put his or her foot in.

stitch *noun* (*plural* **stitches**) **1** a loop of thread made in sewing or knitting. **2** a method of arranging the threads, *cross-stitch.* **3** a sudden sharp pain in the side of the body, caused by running.

stitch *verb* sew or fasten with stitches.

stitchbird *noun* a rare New Zealand bird that feeds on honey.

stoat *noun* a kind of weasel also called an ermine.

stock *noun* **1** a number of things kept ready to be sold or used. **2** livestock. **3** a line of ancestors, *a man of Irish stock.* **4** liquid made by stewing meat, fish, or vegetables, used for making soup etc. **5** a garden flower with a sweet smell. **6** shares in a business company's capital (see *share* 2). **7** the main stem of a tree or plant. **8** the base, holder, or handle of an implement etc.
stock and station agent (*NZ*) a person or company that sells farm products and supplies, or provides money for farming.
stock exchange a place where stocks and shares are bought and sold.
stock market the stock exchange; the business conducted there.

stock *verb* **1** keep goods in stock. **2** provide a place with a stock of something.

stockade *noun* a fence made of stakes.

stockbreeder *noun* a farmer who raises livestock.

stockbroker *noun* a broker who deals in stocks and shares.

stock-car *noun* an ordinary car strengthened for use in races where deliberate bumping is allowed.

stockholder *noun* **1** an owner of stocks or shares. **2** (*NZ*) an owner of large herds of cattle, sheep, etc.

stocking *noun* a garment covering the foot and part or all of the leg.

stockist *noun* a shopkeeper who stocks a certain kind of goods.

stockman *noun* (*plural* **stockmen**) (*NZ*) a man employed to look after cattle, sheep, etc.

stockpile *noun* a large stock of things kept in reserve. **stockpile** *verb*

stock-proof *adjective* that prevents cattle etc. from straying.

stocks *plural noun* a wooden framework with holes for a seated person's legs, used like the pillory.

stock-still *adjective* quite still.

stocky *adjective* (**stockier**, **stockiest**) short and solidly built, *a stocky man.*

stockyard *noun* (*NZ*) an enclosed area where livestock is held for drafting, killing, etc.

stodge *noun* stodgy food.

stodgy *adjective* (**stodgier**, **stodgiest**) **1** (of food) heavy and filling. **2** dull and boring, *a stodgy book.* **stodginess** *noun*

stoical (*say* **stoh**-ik-al) *adjective* bearing pain or difficulties etc. calmly without complaining. **stoically** *adverb*, **stoicism** *noun* [named after ancient Greek philosophers called *Stoics*]

stoke *verb* (**stoked**, **stoking**) put fuel in a furnace or on a fire. **stoker** *noun*

stoked *adjective* (*informal*) thrilled.

stole[1] *noun* a wide piece of material worn round the shoulders.

stole[2] *past tense* of **steal**.

stolid *adjective* not excitable; not feeling or showing emotion. **stolidly** *adverb*, **stolidity** *noun*

stomach *noun* **1** the part of the body where food starts to be digested. **2** the abdomen.

stomach *verb* endure; tolerate.

stone *noun* **1** a piece of rock. **2** stones or rock as material, e.g. for building. **3** a jewel. **4** the hard case round the kernel of plums, cherries, etc. **5** an imperial unit of weight, equivalent to about 6.35 kilograms.

stone *verb* (**stoned**, **stoning**) **1** throw stones at somebody. **2** remove the stones from fruit.

stone- *prefix* completely, *stone-cold*.

stone-fruit *noun* a fruit with flesh that surrounds a stone.

stoneware *noun* a kind of pottery.

stonkered *adjective* (*NZ, slang*) **1** exhausted. **2** beaten, at a loss. **3** drunk.

stony *adjective* **1** full of stones. **2** like stone; hard. **3** not answering, *a stony silence*.

stony-broke *adjective* (*slang*) having spent all your money.

stooge *noun* (*informal*) **1** a comedian's assistant, used as a target for jokes. **2** an assistant who does dull or routine work.

stool *noun* a movable seat without arms or a back; a footstool.

stoop *verb* **1** bend your body forwards and down. **2** lower yourself, *He would not stoop to cheating*. **stoop** *noun*

stop *verb* (**stopped**, **stopping**) **1** bring or come to an end; not continue working or moving. **2** stay. **3** prevent or obstruct something. **4** fill a hole. **stoppage** *noun*

stop *noun* **1** stopping; a pause or end. **2** a place where a bus or train etc. regularly stops. **3** a punctuation mark, especially a full stop. **4** a lever or knob that controls pitch in a wind instrument or allows organ-pipes to sound.

stopbank *noun* (*NZ*) an embankment to stop a river overflowing.

stopcock *noun* a valve controlling the flow of liquid or gas in a pipe.

stopgap *noun* a temporary substitute.

stopper *noun* a plug for closing a bottle etc.

stop-press *noun* late news put into a newspaper after printing has started.

stopwatch *noun* a watch that can be started and stopped when you wish, used for timing races etc.

stop-work meeting (*NZ*) a meeting of workers held during work time.

storage *noun* the storing of things.
storage heater an electric heater that gives out heat that it has stored.

store *noun* **1** a stock of things kept for future use; a place where these are kept. **2** a shop, especially a large one.
in store being stored; going to happen, *There's a surprise in store for you*.
set store by something value it greatly.

store *verb* (**stored**, **storing**) keep things until they are needed.

storey *noun* (*plural* **storeys**) one whole floor of a building.

stork *noun* a large bird with long legs and a long beak.

storm *noun* **1** a very strong wind usually with rain, snow, etc. **2** a violent attack or outburst, *a storm of protest*. **stormy** *adjective*
storm in a teacup a great fuss over something unimportant.

storm *verb* **1** move or behave violently or angrily, *He stormed out of the room*. **2** attack or capture by a sudden assault, *They stormed the castle*.

story *noun* (*plural* **stories**) **1** an account of a real or imaginary event. **2** the plot of a play or novel etc. **3** (*informal*) a lie, *Don't tell stories!* **4** the correct information, *You can get the story from the landlord*.
that's the story (*NZ*) that's right, that's well done.
what's the story? (*NZ*) what's going on?
[same origin as *history*]

stoush *noun* (*NZ, informal*) a fight or quarrel.

stout *adjective* **1** rather fat. **2** thick and strong. **3** brave. **stoutly** *adverb*, **stoutness** *noun*

stout *noun* a kind of dark beer.

stove[1] *noun* **1** a device containing an oven or ovens. **2** a device for heating a room.

stove[2] *past tense* of **stave**.

stow *verb* pack or store something away.
stowage *noun*
stow away hide on a ship or aircraft so as to travel without paying. **stowaway** *noun*
[from *bestow*]

straddle *verb* (**straddled**, **straddling**) be astride; sit or stand across something, *A long bridge straddles the river*.

straggle *verb* (**straggled**, **straggling**) **1** grow or spread in an untidy way. **2** lag behind; wander on your own. **straggler** *noun*, **straggly** *adjective*

straight *adjective* **1** going continuously in one direction; not curving or bending. **2** tidy; in proper order. **3** honest; frank, *a straight answer*. **straightness** *noun*

straight *adverb* **1** in a straight line or manner. **2** directly; without delay, *Go straight home*.
straight away immediately.

straighten *verb* make or become straight.

straightforward *adjective* **1** easy, not complicated. **2** honest; frank.

strain[1] *verb* **1** stretch tightly. **2** injure or weaken something by stretching or working it too hard. **3** make a great effort. **4** put something through a sieve or filter to separate liquid from solid matter.

strain[1] *noun* **1** straining; the force of straining. **2** an injury caused by straining. **3** something that uses up strength, patience, resources, etc. **4** exhaustion. **5** a part of a tune.

strain[2] *noun* **1** a breed or variety of animals, plants, etc.; a line of descent. **2** an inherited characteristic, *There's an artistic strain in the family.*

strainer *noun* **1** a device for straining liquids, *a tea-strainer.* **2** (*NZ*) a large post against which the wire of a fence is tightened.

strait *adjective* (*old use*) narrow; restricted.

strait *noun* a narrow stretch of water connecting two seas.
straits *plural noun* **1** a strait. **2** a difficult condition, *We were in dire straits when we lost our money.*

straitened *adjective* restricted; made narrow.
in straitened circumstances short of money.
[from *strait*]

strait-jacket *noun* a strong jacket-like garment put round a violent person to restrain his or her arms.

strait-laced *adjective* very prim and proper.

strand[1] *noun* **1** each of the threads or wires etc. twisted together to form a rope, yarn, or cable. **2** a single thread. **3** a lock of hair.

strand[2] *noun* a shore.

strand[2] *verb* **1** run or cause to run on to sand or rocks in shallow water. **2** leave in a difficult or helpless position, *We were stranded when our car broke down.*

strange *adjective* unusual; not known or seen or experienced before. **strangely** *adverb,* **strangeness** *noun*

stranger *noun* **1** a person you do not know. **2** a person who is in a place or company that he or she does not know.

strangle *verb* (**strangled**, **strangling**) kill by squeezing the throat to prevent breathing. **strangler** *noun* [from Greek *strangale* = a halter]

strangulate *verb* (**strangulated**, **strangulating**) strangle; squeeze so that nothing can pass through. **strangulation** *noun*

strap *noun* a flat strip of leather or cloth etc. for fastening things or holding them in place.

strap *verb* (**strapped**, **strapping**) fasten with a strap or straps; bind.

strapping *adjective* tall and healthy-looking, *a strapping lad.*

strata *plural* of **stratum**.

stratagem *noun* a cunning method of achieving something; a trick.

strategic *adjective* **1** of strategy. **2** giving an advantage. **strategical** *adjective,* **strategically** *adverb*

strategist *noun* an expert in strategy.

strategy *noun* (*plural* **strategies**) **1** a plan or policy to achieve something, *our economic strategy.* **2** the planning of a war or campaign. (Compare *tactics.*) [from Greek *strategos* = a general]

stratified *adjective* arranged in strata. **stratification** *noun*

stratosphere *noun* a layer of the atmosphere between about 10 and 60 kilometres above the earth's surface. [from *stratum* + *sphere*]

stratum (*say* **strah**-tum or **stray**-tum) *noun* (*plural* **strata**) a layer. [Latin, = thing spread]

> USAGE The word *strata* is a *plural.* It is incorrect to say 'a strata' or 'this strata'; correct use is *this stratum* or *these strata.*

straw *noun* **1** dry cut stalks of corn. **2** a narrow tube for drinking through.

strawberry *noun* (*plural* **strawberries**) a small red juicy fruit.

stray *verb* leave a group or proper place and wander; get lost.

stray *adjective* that has strayed, *a stray cat.* **stray** *noun*

streak *noun* **1** a long thin line or mark. **2** a trace, *a streak of cruelty.* **streaky** *adjective*

streak *verb* **1** mark with streaks. **2** move very quickly.

stream *noun* **1** water flowing in a channel; a small river. **2** a flow of liquid or of things or people. **3** a group in which children of similar ability are placed in a school.

stream *verb* **1** move in or like a stream. **2** produce a stream of liquid. **3** arrange schoolchildren in streams according to their ability.

streamer *noun* a long narrow ribbon or strip of paper etc.

streamline *verb* (**streamlined**, **streamlining**) **1** give something a smooth shape that helps it to move easily through air or water. **2** organise something so that it works more efficiently.

street *noun* a road with houses beside it in a city or town. [from Latin *strata via* = paved way]

strength *noun* how strong a person or thing is; being strong.

strengthen *verb* make or become stronger.

strenuous *adjective* needing or using great effort. **strenuously** *adverb*

stress *noun* (*plural* **stresses**) **1** a force that acts on something, e.g. by pressing, pulling, or twisting it; strain. **2** emphasis, especially the extra force with which you pronounce part of a word or phrase.

stress *verb* put a stress on something; emphasise. [from *distress*]

stretch *verb* **1** pull something or be pulled so that it becomes longer or wider or larger. **2** be continuous, *The wall stretches right round the estate.* **3** push out your arms and legs etc. **4** be sufficient for a purpose, *Our money stretched to a first class ticket.*

stretch *noun* (*plural* **stretches**) **1** the action of stretching. **2** a continuous period of time or area of land or water.

stretcher *noun* a framework for carrying a sick or injured person.

strew *verb* (**strewed**, **strewn** or **strewed**, **strewing**) scatter things over a surface.

striated (*say* stry-**ay**-tid) *adjective* marked with lines or ridges. **striation** *noun*

stricken *adjective* overcome or strongly affected by an illness, grief, fear, etc.

strict *adjective* **1** demanding obedience and good behaviour, *a strict teacher.* **2** complete; exact, *the strict truth.* **strictly** *adverb*, **strictness** *noun*

stricture *noun* **1** criticism. **2** constriction.

stride *verb* (**strode**, **stridden**, **striding**) **1** walk with long steps. **2** stand astride something.

stride *noun* **1** a long step when walking or running. **2** progress.
get into your stride settle into a fast and steady pace of working.

strident (*say* **stry**-dent) *adjective* loud and harsh. **stridently** *adverb*, **stridency** *noun* [from Latin *stridens* = creaking]

strife *noun* a conflict; fighting or quarrelling.

strike *verb* (**struck**, **striking**) **1** hit. **2** attack suddenly. **3** produce by pressing or stamping something, *They are striking some special coins.* **4** light a match by rubbing it against a rough surface. **5** sound, *The clock struck ten.* **6** make an impression on someone's mind, *She strikes me as truthful.* **7** find gold or oil etc. by digging or drilling. **8** stop work until the people in charge agree to improve wages or conditions etc. **9** go in a certain direction. *We struck north through the forest.*
strike off or **out** cross out.
strike up begin playing or singing; start a friendship etc.

strike *noun* **1** a hit. **2** an attack. **3** a stoppage of work, as a way of making a protest (see sense 8 of the verb). **4** a sudden discovery of gold or oil etc.
on strike (of workers) striking.

striker *noun* **1** a person or thing that strikes something. **2** a worker who is on strike. **3** a soccer player whose function is to try to score goals.

striking *adjective* **1** that strikes. **2** noticeable. **strikingly** *adverb*

Strine *noun* (*slang*) Australian English.

string *noun* **1** cord used to fasten or tie things; a piece of this or similar material. **2** a piece of wire or cord etc. stretched and vibrated to produce sounds in a musical instrument. **3** a line or series of things, *a string of buses.* **strings** *plural noun* stringed instruments.

string *verb* (**strung**, **stringing**) **1** fit or fasten with string. **2** thread on a string. **3** remove the tough fibre from beans.
string out spread out in a line; cause something to last a long time.

stringed *adjective* (of musical instruments) having strings.

stringent (*say* **strin**-jent) *adjective* strict, *There are stringent rules.* **stringently** *adverb*, **stringently** *noun*

stringy *adjective* **1** like string. **2** containing tough fibres.

strip[1] *verb* (**stripped**, **stripping**) **1** take a covering or layer off something. **2** undress. **3** deprive a person of something. **stripper** *noun*

strip[2] *noun* **1** a long narrow piece or area. **2** a sports team's distinctive outfit, *Auckland's blue and white strip.*
strip cartoon a comic strip (see *comic*).

stripe *noun* **1** a long narrow band of colour. **2** a strip of cloth worn on the sleeve of a uniform to show the wearer's rank. **striped** *adjective*, **stripy** *adjective*

stripling *noun* a youth.

striptease *noun* an entertainment in which a person slowly undresses.

strive *verb* (**strove**, **striven**, **striving**) **1** try hard to do something. **2** carry on a conflict.

strobe *noun* (short for **stroboscope**) a light that flashes on and off continuously. [from Greek *strobos* = whirling]

stroke[1] *noun* **1** a hit; a movement or action. **2** the sound made by a clock striking. **3** a sudden illness that often causes paralysis.

stroke[2] *verb* (**stroked**, **stroking**) move your hand gently along something. **stroke** *noun*

stroll *verb* walk in a leisurely way. **stroll** *noun*, **stroller** *noun*

strong *adjective* **1** having great power, energy, effect, flavour, etc. **2** not easy to break, damage, or defeat. **3** having a certain number of members, *an army 5,000 strong.* **strongly** *adverb*

strong *adverb* strongly, *going strong.*

stronghold *noun* a fortified place.

strontium *noun* a soft silvery metal.

strop *noun* a strip of leather or canvas on which a razor is sharpened.

strop *verb* (**stropped**, **stropping**) sharpen on a strop.

strove *past tense* of **strive**.

structure *noun* **1** something that has been constructed or built. **2** the way something is constructed or organised. **structural** *adjective*, **structurally** *adverb* [from Latin *structura* = thing built]

struggle *verb* (**struggled**, **struggling**) **1** move your arms, legs, etc. in trying to get free. **2** make strong efforts to do something. **3** try to overcome an opponent or a problem etc.

struggle *noun* the action of struggling.

strum *verb* (**strummed**, **strumming**) **1** sound a guitar by running your fingers across its strings. **2** play badly or casually on a musical instrument.

strut *verb* (**strutted**, **strutting**) walk proudly or stiffly.

strut *noun* **1** a bar of wood or metal strengthening a framework. **2** a strutting walk.

strychnine (*say* **strik**-neen) *noun* a bitter poisonous substance.

stub *noun* **1** a short stump left when the rest has been used or worn down. **2** a counterfoil.

stub *verb* (**stubbed**, **stubbing**) bump your toe painfully.
stub out put out a cigarette by pressing it against something hard.

stubble *noun* **1** the short stalks of corn left in the ground after the harvest is cut. **2** short hairs growing after shaving.

stubborn *adjective* obstinate. **stubbornly** *adverb*, **stubbornness** *noun*

stubby *adjective* short and thick.

stucco *noun* plaster or cement used for coating walls and ceilings, often moulded into decorations. **stuccoed** *adjective* [from Italian]

stuck-up *adjective* (*slang*) conceited; snobbish.

stud[1] *noun* **1** a small curved lump or knob. **2** a device like a button on a stalk, used to fasten a detachable collar to a shirt. **3** the upright part of the wooden framework of a wall.

stud[1] (**studded**, **studding**) set or decorate with studs etc., *The necklace was studded with jewels.*

stud[2] *noun* horses kept for breeding.

student *noun* a person who studies a subject, especially at a college or university. [from Latin *studens* = studying]

studio *noun* (*plural* **studios**) **1** the room where a painter or photographer etc. works. **2** a place where cinema films are made. **3** a room from which radio or television broadcasts are made or recorded. **4** a one-roomed apartment or motel unit. [same origin as *study*]

studious *adjective* **1** keen on studying. **2** deliberate, *with studious politeness.* **studiously** *adverb*, **studiousness** *noun*

study *verb* (**studied**, **studying**) **1** spend time learning about something. **2** look at something carefully.

study *noun* (*plural* **studies**) **1** the process of studying. **2** a subject studied; a piece of research. **3** a room where someone studies. **4** a piece of music for playing as an exercise. **5** a detailed investigation. [from Latin *studium* = zeal]

stuff *noun* **1** a substance or material. **2** things, *Leave your stuff outside.* **3** (*slang*) valueless matter, *stuff and nonsense!*

stuff *verb* **1** fill tightly. **2** fill with stuffing. **3** push a thing into something, *He stuffed the catapult into his pocket.* **4** (*informal*) eat greedily. **5** (*NZ* & *Australia, informal*) defeat, overcome, exhaust. **stuff up** (*informal*) blunder, fail, ruin.

stuffing *noun* **1** material used to fill the inside of something; padding. **2** a savoury mixture put into meat or poultry etc. before cooking.

stuffy *adjective* (**stuffier**, **stuffiest**) **1** badly ventilated; without fresh air. **2** with blocked breathing passages, *a stuffy nose.* **3** *formal*; boring. **stuffily** *adverb*, **stuffiness** *noun*

stultify *verb* (**stultified**, **stultifying**) prevent from being effective, *Their stubbornness stultified the discussions.* **stultification** *noun* [from Latin *stultus* = foolish]

stumble *verb* (**stumbled**, **stumbling**) **1** trip and lose your balance. **2** speak or do something hesitantly or uncertainly. **stumble** *noun*
stumble across or **on** find accidentally.

stumbling-block *noun* an obstacle; something that causes difficulty.

stump *noun* **1** the bottom of a tree-trunk left in the ground when the rest has fallen or been cut down. **2** something left when the main part is cut off or worn down. **3** each of the three upright sticks of a wicket in cricket.

stump *verb* **1** walk stiffly or noisily. **2** put a batter out by knocking the bails off the stumps while he or she is out of the crease. **3** (*informal*) be too difficult for somebody, *The question stumped him.*
stump up (*slang*) produce the money to pay for something.

stumpy *adjective* short and thick. **stumpiness** *noun*

stun *verb* (**stunned**, **stunning**) **1** knock a person unconscious. **2** daze or shock, *She was stunned by the news.*

stunt[1] *verb* prevent a thing from growing or developing normally, *a stunted tree.*

stunt[2] *noun* something unusual or difficult done as a performance or to attract attention.

stupefy *verb* (**stupefied**, **stupefying**) make a person dazed. **stupefaction** *noun* [from Latin *stupere* = be amazed]

stupendous *adjective* amazing; tremendous. **stupendously** *adverb*

stupid *adjective* not clever or thoughtful; without reason or common sense. **stupidly** *adverb*, **stupidity** *noun* [from Latin *stupidus* = dazed]

stupor (*say* **stew**-per) *noun* a dazed condition. [same origin as *stupefy*]

sturdy *adjective* (**sturdier**, **sturdiest**) strong and vigorous or solid. **sturdily** *adverb*, **sturdiness** *noun*

sturgeon *noun* (*plural* **sturgeon**) a large edible fish.

stutter *verb & noun* stammer.

sty[1] *noun* (*plural* **sties**) a pigsty.

sty[2] or **stye** *noun* (*plural* **sties** or **styes**) a sore swelling on an eyelid.

style *noun* **1** the way something is done, made, said, or written etc. **2** elegance. **3** the part of a pistil that supports the stigma in a plant. **stylistic** *adjective*

style *verb* (**styled**, **styling**) design or arrange something, especially in a fashionable style. **stylist** *noun* [same origin as *stylus*]

stylish *adjective* in a fashionable style.

stylus *noun* an instrument for engraving or writing.

suave (*say* swahv) *adjective* smoothly polite. **suavely** *adverb*, **suavity** *noun* [from Latin *suavis* = agreeable]

sub *noun* (*informal*) **1** a submarine. **2** a subscription. **3** a substitute.

sub- *prefix* (often changing to **suc-**, **suf-**, **sum-**, **sup-**, **sur-**, **sus-** before certain consonants) **1** under (as in *submarine*). **2** subordinate, secondary (as in *subsection*). [from Latin *sub* = under]

subaltern *noun* an army officer ranking below a captain.

subantarctic *adjective* of regions bordering on the Antarctic.

subarctic *adjective* of regions bordering on the Arctic.

subconscious *adjective* of our own mental activities of which we are not fully aware. **subconscious** *noun*

subcontinent *noun* a large mass of land not large enough to be called a continent, *the Indian subcontinent.*

subdivide *verb* (**subdivided**, **subdividing**) divide again or into smaller parts.

subdivision *noun* an area of land divided into blocks or sections; a housing area.

subdue *verb* (**subdued**, **subduing**) **1** overcome; bring under control. **2** make quieter or gentler.

subject *noun* **1** the person or thing being talked about or written about etc. **2** something that is studied. **3** (in grammar) the word or words naming who or what does the action of a verb, e.g. *'the book'* in *the book fell off the table.* **4** someone who is ruled by a particular king, government, etc.

subject *adjective* ruled by a king or government etc.; not independent. **subject to** having to obey; liable to, *Flights are subject to delays during fog*; depending upon, *Our decision is subject to your approval.*

subject (*say* sub-**jekt**) *verb* **1** make a person or thing undergo something, *They subjected him to torture.* **2** bring a country under your control. **subjection** *noun* [from *sub-*, + Latin *-jectum* = thrown]

subjective *adjective* **1** existing in a person's mind and not produced by things outside it. **2** depending on a person's own taste or opinions etc. (Compare *objective.*)

subjugate *verb* (**subjugated**, **subjugating**) bring under your control; conquer. **subjugation** *noun* [from Latin *sub* = under, + *jugum* = a yoke]

subjunctive *noun* the form of a verb used to indicate what is imagined or wished or possible. There are only a few cases where it is commonly used in English, e.g. *'were'* in *if I were you* and *'save'* in *God save the Queen.* [from *sub-*, + Latin *junctum* = joined]

sublet *verb* (**sublet**, **subletting**) let to another person a house etc. that is let to you by a landlord.

sublime *adjective* **1** noble; impressive. **2** extreme; not caring about the consequences, *with sublime carelessness.*

submarine *adjective* under the sea, *We laid a submarine cable.*

submarine *noun* a ship that can travel under water.

submerge *verb* (**submerged**, **submerging**) go under or put under water or other liquid. **submergence** *noun*, **submersion** *noun* [from *sub-*, + Latin *mergere* = dip]

submissive *adjective* willing to obey.

submit *verb* (**submitted, submitting**) **1** let someone have authority over you; surrender. **2** put forward for consideration, testing, etc., *Submit your plans to the committee.* **submission** *noun* [from *sub-*, + Latin *mittere* = send]

subnormal *adjective* below normal.

subordinate *adjective* less important; lower in rank.
subordinate clause a clause that is not the main clause in a sentence.

subordinate *noun* a person working under someone's authority or control.

subordinate *verb* (**subordinated, subordinating**) treat as being less important than another person or thing. **subordination** *noun* [from *sub-*, + Latin *ordinare* = arrange]

suborn *verb* bribe; incite someone secretly.

sub-plot *noun* a secondary plot in a play etc.

subpoena (*say* sub-**peen**-a) *noun* an official document ordering a person to appear in a lawcourt.

subpoena *verb* (**subpoenaed, subpoenaing**) summon by a subpoena. [from Latin *sub poena* = under a penalty (because there is a punishment for not obeying)]

subscribe *verb* (**subscribed, subscribing**) **1** contribute money; pay regularly so as to be a member of a society, get a periodical, have the use of a telephone, etc. **2** sign, *subscribe your name.* **3** say that you agree, *We cannot subscribe to this theory.* **subscriber** *noun*, **subscription** *noun* [from *sub-*, + Latin *scribere* = write]

subsequent *adjective* coming after in time or order; later. **subsequently** *adverb* [from *sub-*, + Latin *sequens* = following]

subservient *adjective* under someone's power; submissive. **subservience** *noun* [from *sub-*, + Latin *serviens* = serving]

subside *verb* (**subsided, subsiding**) **1** sink. **2** become less intense, *Her fear subsided.* **subsidence** *noun* [from *sub-*, + Latin *sidere* = settle]

subsidiary *adjective* **1** less important; secondary. **2** (of a business) controlled by another, *a subsidiary company.* [same origin as *subsidy*]

subsidise *verb* (**subsidised, subsidising**) pay a subsidy to a person or firm etc.

subsidy *noun* (*plural* **subsidies**) money paid to an industry etc. that needs help, or to keep down the price at which its goods etc. are sold to the public. [from Latin *subsidium* = assistance]

subsist *verb* exist; keep yourself alive, *We subsisted on nuts.* **subsistence** *noun* [from Latin *subsistere* = stand firm]

subsoil *noun* soil lying just below the surface layer.

subsonic *adjective* not as fast as the speed of sound. (Compare supersonic.)

substance *noun* **1** matter of a particular kind. **2** the main or essential part of something, *We agree with the substance of your report but not with its details.* [from Latin *substantia* = essence]

substantial *adjective* **1** of great size, value, or importance, *a substantial fee.* **2** solidly built, *substantial houses.* **3** actually existing. **substantially** *adverb*

substantiate *verb* (**substantiated, substantiating**) produce evidence to prove something. **substantiation** *noun*

substation *noun* a subsidiary station for distributing electric current.

substitute *noun* a person or thing that acts or is used instead of another.

substitute *verb* (**substituted, substituting**) **1** put or use a person or thing as a substitute. **2** replace a person or thing with a substitute, *The injured player was substituted at halftime.* **substitution** *noun* [from *sub-*, + Latin *statuere* = to set up]

subterfuge *noun* a deception.

subterranean *adjective* underground. [from *sub-*, + Latin *terra* = ground]

subtitle *noun* **1** a subordinate title. **2** words shown on the screen during a film, e.g. to translate a foreign language.

subtle (*say* **sut**-el) *adjective* **1** slight and delicate, *a subtle perfume.* **2** ingenious; not immediately obvious, *a subtle joke.* **subtly** *adverb*, **subtlety** *noun*

subtotal *noun* the total of part of a group of figures.

subtract *verb* deduct; take away a part, quantity, or number from a greater one. **subtraction** *noun* [from *sub-*, + Latin *tractum* = pulled]

subtropical *adjective* of regions that border on the tropics.

suburb *noun* a district with houses that is outside the central part of a city. **suburban** *adjective*, **suburbia** *noun* [from *sub-*, + Latin *urbs* = city]

subvert *verb* get someone to be disloyal to their government, religion, standards of behaviour, etc.; overthrow a government etc. in this way. **subversion** *noun*, **subversive** *adjective* [from *sub-*, + Latin *vertere* = to turn]

subway *noun* an underground passage.

suc- *prefix* see **sub-**.

succeed *verb* **1** be successful. **2** come after another person or thing; become the next king or queen, *She succeeded to the throne; Edward VII succeeded Queen Victoria.* [from *suc-*, + Latin *cedere* = go]

success *noun* (*plural* **successes**) **1** doing or getting what you wanted or intended. **2** a person or thing that does well, *The show was a great success.*

successful *adjective* having success; being a success. **successfully** *adverb*

succession *noun* **1** a series of people or things. **2** the process of following in order. **3** succeeding to the throne; the right of doing this.

successive *adjective* following one after another, *on five successive days.* **successively** *adverb*

successor *noun* a person or thing that succeeds another.

succinct (*say* suk-**sinkt**) *adjective* concise. **succinctly** *adverb* [from Latin *succinctum* = tucked up]

succour (*say* **suk**-er) *noun & verb* help. [from Latin *succurrere* = run to a person's aid]

succulent *adjective* juicy.

succumb (*say* suk-**um**) *verb* give way to something overpowering. [from *suc-*, + Latin *cumbere* = to lie]

such *adjective* **1** of the same kind; similar, *Cakes, biscuits, and all such foods are fattening.* **2** of the kind described, *There's no such person.* **3** so great or intense, *It gave me such a fright!*

such-and-such *adjective* particular but not now named, *He promises to come at such-and-such a time but is always late.*

suchlike *adjective* of that kind.

suck *verb* **1** take in liquid or air through almost-closed lips. **2** squeeze something in your mouth by using your tongue, *sucking a toffee.* **3** draw in, *The canoe was sucked into the whirlpool.* **suck** *noun*
suck up to (*slang*) flatter someone in the hope of winning their favour.

sucker *noun* **1** a thing that sucks something. **2** something that can stick to a surface by suction. **3** a shoot coming up from a root or underground stem. **4** (*slang*) a person who is easily deceived.

suckle *verb* (**suckled**, **suckling**) feed on milk at the mother's breast or udder.

suckling *noun* a child or animal that has not yet been weaned.

suction *noun* **1** sucking. **2** producing a vacuum so that things are sucked into the empty space, *Vacuum cleaners work by suction.*

sudden *adjective* happening or done quickly or without warning. **suddenly** *adverb*, **suddenness** *noun*

sudden death *noun* (*informal*) a means of deciding a winner in a tied sports match in which play resumes and the first scorer is the winner.

suds *plural noun* froth on soapy water.

sue *verb* (**sued**, **suing**) start a lawsuit to claim money from somebody.

suede (*say* swayd) *noun* leather with one side rubbed to make it velvety. [from *Suède*, the French name for Sweden, where it was first made]

suet *noun* hard fat from cattle and sheep, used in cooking.

suf- *prefix* see **sub-**.

suffer *verb* **1** feel pain or sadness. **2** experience something bad, *suffer damage.* **3** (*old use*) allow; tolerate. **sufferer** *noun*, **suffering** *noun* [from *suf-*, + Latin *ferre* = to bear]

sufferance *noun* **on sufferance** allowed but only reluctantly.

suffice *verb* (**sufficed**, **sufficing**) be enough for someone's needs.

sufficient *adjective* enough. **sufficiently** *adverb*, **sufficiency** *noun*

suffix *noun* (*plural* **suffixes**) a letter or set of letters joined to the end of a word to make another word (e.g. in forget*ful*, lion*ess*, rust*y*) or a form of a verb (e.g. sing*ing*, wait*ed*). [from *suf-* + *fix*]

suffocate *verb* (**suffocated**, **suffocating**) **1** make it difficult or impossible for someone to breathe. **2** suffer or die because breathing is prevented. **suffocation** *noun* [from *suf-*, + Latin *fauces* = throat]

suffrage *noun* the right to vote in political elections. [from Latin, = vote]

suffragette *noun* a woman who campaigned in the early 20th century for British women to have the right to vote.

suffuse *verb* (**suffused**, **suffusing**) spread through or over something, *A blush suffused her cheeks.* [from *suf-*, + Latin *fusum* = poured]

sugar *noun* a sweet food obtained from the juices of various plants (e.g. sugar-cane, sugar-beet). **sugar** *verb*, **sugary** *adjective* [from Arabic *sukkar*]

suggest *verb* **1** give somebody an idea that you think is useful. **2** cause an idea or possibility to come into the mind. **suggestion** *noun*, **suggestive** *adjective*

suggestible *adjective* easily influenced by people's suggestions.

suicide *noun* **1** killing yourself deliberately, *commit suicide.* **2** a person who deliberately kills himself or herself. **suicidal** *adjective* [from Latin *sui* = of yourself, + *caedere* = kill]

suit *noun* **1** a matching jacket and trousers, or a jacket and skirt, that are meant to be worn together. **2** clothing for a particular activity, *a diving-suit.* **3** any of the four sets of cards (clubs, hearts, diamonds, spades) in a pack of playing-cards. **4** a lawsuit.

suit *verb* **1** be suitable or convenient for a person or thing. **2** make a person look attractive.

suitable *adjective* satisfactory or right for a particular person, purpose, or occasion etc. **suitably** *adverb*, **suitability** *noun*

suitcase *noun* a rectangular container for carrying clothes, usually with a hinged lid and a handle.

suite (*say* as sweet) *noun* **1** a set of furniture. **2** a set of rooms. **3** a set of attendants. **4** a set of short pieces of music.

suitor *noun* **1** a man who courts a woman. **2** a prospective buyer of a business. **3** a candidate or contestant, *He was a suitor for that new position.* [from Latin *secutor* = follower]

sulk *verb* be silent and bad-tempered because you are not pleased. **sulks** *plural noun*, **sulky** *adjective*, **sulkily** *adverb*, **sulkiness** *noun*

sulky *noun* a two-wheeled vehicle for one, pulled by a horse in trotting races.

sullen *adjective* sulking and gloomy. **sullenly** *adverb*, **sullenness** *noun*

sully *verb* (**sullied**, **sullying**) soil or stain something; blemish, *The scandal sullied his reputation.*

sulphur *noun* a yellow chemical used in industry and in medicine. **sulphurous** *adjective*

sulphuric acid a strong colourless acid containing sulphur.

sultan *noun* the ruler of certain Muslim countries. [from Arabic, = ruler]

sultana *noun* **1** a small raisin. **2** the wife of a sultan.

sultry *adjective* hot and humid, *sultry weather.* **sultriness** *noun*

sum *noun* **1** a total. **2** a problem in arithmetic. **3** an amount of money.

sum *verb* (**summed**, **summing**) **sum up** summarise, especially at the end of a talk etc.; form an opinion of a person, *sum him up.* [from Latin *summa* = main thing]

sum- *prefix* see **sub-**.

summarise *verb* (**summarised**, **summarising**) make or give a summary of something.

summary *noun* (*plural* **summaries**) a statement of the main points of something said or written.

summary *adjective* **1** brief. **2** done or given hastily, without delay, *summary punishment.* **summarily** *adverb* [same origin as *sum*]

summer *noun* the warm season between spring and autumn. **summery** *adjective*

summit *noun* **1** the top of a mountain or hill. **2** a meeting between the leaders of powerful countries, *a summit conference.* [from Latin *summus* = highest]

summon *verb* **1** order someone to come or appear. **2** request firmly, *He summoned the rebels to surrender.*
summon up gather or prepare, *Can you summon up the energy to get out of bed?* [from *sum-*, + Latin *monere* = warn]

summons *noun* (*plural* **summonses**) a command to appear in a lawcourt.

sump *noun* a metal case that holds oil round an engine.

sumptuous *adjective* splendid and expensive-looking. **sumptuously** *adverb* [from Latin *sumptus* = cost]

sun *noun* **1** the large ball of fire round which the earth travels. **2** light and warmth from the sun, *Go and sit in the sun.*

sun *verb* (**sunned**, **sunning**) warm something in the sun, *sunning ourselves on the beach.*

sunbathe *verb* (**sunbathed**, **sunbathing**) expose your body to the sun.

sunbeam *noun* a ray of sun.

sunburn *noun* redness of the skin caused by the sun. **sunburnt** *adjective*

sundae (*say* **sun**-day) *noun* a mixture of ice-cream and fruit, nuts, cream, etc.

Sunday *noun* the day after Saturday, traditionally observed by Christians as a day of religious worship.

sunder *verb* (*poetical*) break apart; sever.

sundial *noun* a device that shows the time by a shadow on a dial.

sundown *noun* sunset.

sundries *plural noun* various small things.

sundry *adjective* various; several.
all and sundry everyone.

sunflower *noun* a very tall flower with golden petals round a dark centre.

sunglasses *plural noun* dark glasses to protect your eyes from strong sunlight.

sunken *adjective* sunk deeply into a surface, *Their cheeks were pale and sunken.*

sunlight *noun* light from the sun. **sunlit** *adjective*

sunny *adjective* (**sunnier**, **sunniest**) **1** full of sunshine. **2** cheerful, *She was in a sunny mood.* **sunnily** *adverb*

sunrise *noun* the rising of the sun; dawn.

sunscreen *noun* a cream that protects your skin from the sun.

sunset *noun* the setting of the sun.

sunshade *noun* a parasol or other device to protect people from the sun.

sunshine *noun* sunlight with no cloud between the sun and the earth.

sunspot *noun* **1** a dark place on the sun's surface. **2** (*informal*) a sunny place.

sunstroke *noun* illness caused by being in the sun too long.

sup *verb* (**supped**, **supping**) **1** drink liquid in sips or spoonfuls. **2** eat supper.

sup- *prefix* see **sub-**.

super *noun* **1** short for *superintendent.* **2** (*NZ*) short for *superannuation.* **3** short for *superphosphate.*

super *adjective* (*slang*) excellent; superb.

super- *prefix* **1** over; on top (as in *superstructure*). **2** of greater size or quality etc. (as in *supermarket*). **3** extremely (as in *superabundant*). **4** beyond (as in *supernatural*). [from Latin *super* = over]

superannuation *noun* **1** a pension for a retired person. **2** regular payments made by an employee towards this. [from *super-*, + Latin *annus* = a year]

superannuitant *noun* (*NZ*) a person who receives superannuation.

superb *adjective* magnificent; excellent. **superbly** *adverb* [from Latin *superbus* = proud]

supercilious *adjective* haughty and scornful. **superciliously** *adverb* [from Latin *supercilium* = eyebrow]

superette *noun* a small self-service shop selling a wide range of goods.

superficial *adjective* on the surface; not deep or thorough. **superficially** *adverb*, **superficiality** *noun* [from *super-*, + Latin *facies* = face]

superfluous *adjective* more than is needed. **superfluity** *noun* [from *super-*, + Latin *fluere* = flow]

Super 14 (previously **Super 12**) *noun* an annual rugby union competition between teams from New Zealand, Australia, and South Africa.

superhuman *adjective* **1** beyond ordinary human ability, *superhuman strength.* **2** higher than human; divine.

superimpose *verb* (**superimposed**, **superimposing**) place a thing on top of something else. **superimposition** *noun*

superintend *verb* supervise. **superintendent** *noun*

superior *adjective* **1** higher in position or rank, *She is your superior officer.* **2** better than another person or thing. **3** conceited. **superiority** *noun*

superior *noun* a person or thing that is superior to another. [Latin, = higher]

superlative *adjective* of the highest degree or quality, *superlative skill.* **superlatively** *adverb*

superlative *noun* the form of an *adjective* or adverb that expresses 'most', *The superlative of 'great' is 'greatest'.* (Compare *positive* and *comparative.*) [from Latin *superlatum* = carried above]

superman *noun* (*plural* **supermen**) a man with superhuman powers.

supermarket *noun* a large self-service shop that sells food and other goods.

supernatural *adjective* not belonging to the natural world, *supernatural beings such as ghosts.*

superphosphate *noun* a fertiliser made from phosphate rock.

superpower *noun* one of the most powerful nations in the world.

supersede *verb* (**superseded**, **superseding**) take the place of something, *Cars superseded horse-drawn carriages.* [from *super-*, + Latin *sedere* = sit]

supersonic *adjective* faster than the speed of sound. (Compare *subsonic.*)

superstition *noun* a belief or action that is not based on reason or evidence, e.g. the belief that it is unlucky to walk under a ladder. **superstitious** *adjective*

superstructure *noun* a structure that rests on something else; a building as distinct from its foundations.

supertanker *noun* a very large tanker.

supervene *verb* (**supervened**, **supervening**) happen and interrupt or change something, *The country was prosperous until an earthquake supervened.* [from *super-*, + Latin *venire* = come]

supervise *verb* (**supervised**, **supervising**) be in charge of a person or thing and inspect what is done. **supervision** *noun*, **supervisor** *noun*, **supervisory** *adjective* [from *super-*, + Latin *visum* = seen]

supine (*say* **soop**-I'n) *adjective* **1** lying face upwards. (The opposite is *prone.*) **2** not taking action.

supper *noun* a meal or snack eaten in the evening.

supplant *verb* take the place of a person or thing that has been ousted.

supple *adjective* bending easily; flexible. **supplely** *adverb*, **suppleness** *noun*

supplejack *noun* a woody climbing plant.

supplement *noun* **1** something added as an extra. **2** an extra section added to a book or newspaper, *the fashion supplement.* **supplementary** *adjective*

supplement *verb* add to something, *She supplements her pocket-money by working on Saturdays.* [same origin as *supply*]

suppliant (*say* **sup**-lee-ant) *noun* a person who asks humbly for something.

supplicate *verb* (**supplicated**, **supplicating**) beg humbly; beseech. **supplication** *noun* [from Latin, = kneel]

supply *verb* (**supplied**, **supplying**) give or sell or provide what is needed or wanted. **supplier** *noun*

supply *noun* (*plural* **supplies**) **1** an amount of something that is available for use when needed. **2** the action of supplying something; the thing supplied. [from *sup-*, + Latin *-plere* = fill]

support *verb* **1** keep a person or thing from falling or sinking. **2** give strength, help, or encouragement to someone, *Support your local team.* **3** provide with the necessities of life, *She has two children to support.* **supporter** *noun*, **supportive** *adjective*

support *noun* **1** the action of supporting. **2** a person or thing that supports. [from *sup-*, + Latin *portare* = carry]

suppose *verb* (**supposed**, **supposing**) think that something is likely to happen or be true. **supposedly** *adverb*, **supposition** *noun*
be supposed to be expected to do something; have as a duty.

suppress *verb* **1** put an end to something forcibly or by authority, *Troops suppressed the rebellion.* **2** keep something from being known or seen, *They suppressed the truth.* **suppression** *noun*, **suppressor** *noun*

supreme *adjective* highest in rank; most important; greatest, *supreme courage.* **supremely** *adverb*, **supremacy** *noun* [from Latin *supremus* = highest]

sur-[1] *prefix* see **sub-**.

sur-[2] *prefix* = super- (as in *surcharge, surface*).

surcharge *noun* an extra charge or tax.

sure *adjective* **1** convinced; feeling no doubt. **2** certain to happen or do something, *Our team is sure to win.* **3** reliable; undoubtedly true. **sureness** *noun*
for sure definitely.
make sure find out exactly; make something happen or be true, *Make sure the door is locked.*

sure *adverb* (*informal*) surely.
sure enough certainly; in fact.
[from Latin *securus* = secure]

surely *adverb* **1** in a sure way; certainly; securely. **2** it must be true; I feel sure, *Surely we met last year?*

surety *noun* (*plural* **sureties**) **1** a guarantee. **2** a person who promises to pay a debt or fulfil a contract etc. if another person fails to do so.

surf *noun* the white foam of waves breaking on a rock or shore.

surf *verb* **1** ride waves on a surfboard. **2** move from site to site on the Internet in search of information. **surfer** *noun*, **surfing** *noun*

surface *noun* **1** the outside of something. **2** any of the sides of an object, especially the top part. **3** an outward appearance, *On the surface he was a kindly man.*

surface *verb* (**surfaced**, **surfacing**) **1** put a surface on a road, path, etc. **2** come up to the surface from under water.

surfboard *noun* a board used in surfing.

surfeit (*say* **ser**-fit) *noun* too much of something. **surfeited** *adjective*

surfie *noun* (*NZ, informal*) a person who goes surfing.

surf-lifesaver *noun* (*NZ*) a member of a group trained to rescue swimmers in danger.

surf-riding *noun* balancing yourself on a board that is carried to the shore on the waves. **surf-rider** *noun*

surge *verb* (**surged**, **surging**) move forwards or upwards like waves. **surge** *noun* [from Latin *surgere* = rise]

surgeon *noun* a doctor who treats disease or injury by cutting or repairing the affected parts of the body.

surgery *noun* (*plural* **surgeries**) **1** the place where a doctor or dentist etc. regularly gives advice and treatment to patients. **2** the time when patients can visit the doctor etc. **3** the work of a surgeon. **surgical** *adjective*, **surgically** *adverb* [from Greek, = handiwork]

surimi *noun* (*NZ*) a fish product used in crabsticks etc. [from Japanese]

surly *adjective* (**surlier**, **surliest**) bad-tempered and unfriendly. **surliness** *noun*

surmise *noun* a guess. **surmise** *verb*

surmount *verb* **1** overcome a difficulty. **2** get over an obstacle. **3** be on top of something, *The church tower is surmounted by a steeple.*

surname *noun* the name held by all members of a family.

surpass *verb* do or be better than all others; excel.

surplice *noun* a loose white garment worn over a cassock by clergy and choir at a religious service.

surplus *noun* (*plural* **surpluses**) an amount left over after spending or using all that was needed.

surprise *noun* **1** something unexpected. **2** the feeling caused by something that was not expected.

surprise *verb* (**surprised**, **surprising**) **1** be a surprise to somebody. **2** come upon or attack somebody unexpectedly. **surprisingly** *adverb*

surrealism *noun* a style of art and literature that aims to depict the strange features of dreams and fantasies. **surrealist** *noun*, **surrealistic** *adjective* [from *sur-*[2] + *real*]

surrender *verb* **1** give yourself up to an enemy. **2** hand something over to another person, especially when compelled to do so. **surrender** *noun* [from *sur-*[2] + *render*]

surreptitious (*say* su-rep-**tish**-us) *adjective* stealthy. **surreptitiously** *adverb* [from Latin, = seized secretly]

surrogate (*say* **su**-rog-at) *noun* a deputy or substitute.
surrogate mother a woman who bears a child for another woman, by having her egg fertilised by the other woman's partner.

surround *verb* come or be all round a person or thing; encircle.

surroundings *plural noun* the things or conditions round a person or thing.

surveillance (*say* ser-**vay**-lans) *noun* a close watch kept on a person or thing, *Police kept him under surveillance.*

survey (*say* **ser**-vay) *noun* **1** a general look at something. **2** an inspection of an area, building, etc. **3** an investigation of people's opinions or experience.

survey (*say* ser-**vay**) *verb* make a survey of something; inspect. **surveyor** *noun* [from *sur-*[2], + Latin *videre* = see]

survive *verb* (**survived**, **surviving**) stay alive; go on living or existing after someone has died or after a disaster. **survival** *noun*, **survivor** *noun* [from *sur-*[2], + Latin *vivere* = to live]

sus- *prefix* see **sub-**.

susceptible (*say* sus-**ept**-ib-ul) *adjective* likely to be affected by something, *She is susceptible to colds.* **susceptibility** *noun* [from Latin *susceptum* = caught up]

suspect (*say* sus-**pekt**) *verb* **1** think that a person is not to be trusted or has committed a crime; distrust. **2** have a feeling that something is likely or possible.

suspect (*say* **sus**-pekt) *noun* a person who is suspected of a crime etc. **suspect** *adjective*

suspend *verb* **1** hang something up. **2** postpone; stop something temporarily. **3** deprive a person of a job or position etc. for a time. [from *sus-*, + Latin *pendere* = hang]

suspender *noun* a fastener to hold up a sock or stocking by its top.

suspense *noun* an anxious or uncertain feeling while waiting for something to happen or become known.

suspension *noun* suspending.
suspension bridge a bridge supported by cables.

suspicion *noun* **1** suspecting a person or thing; being suspected; distrust. **2** a slight belief.

suspicious *adjective* feeling or causing suspicion. **suspiciously** *adverb*

sustain *verb* **1** support. **2** keep someone alive. **3** keep something happening. **4** undergo; suffer, *We sustained a defeat.* [from *sus-*, + Latin *tenere* = hold]

sustenance *noun* food; nourishment.

suture (*say* **soo**-cher) *noun* surgical stitching of a cut. [from Latin *sutura* = sewing]

suzerainty (*say* **soo**-zer-en-tee) *noun* **1** the partial control of a weaker country by a stronger one. **2** the power of an overlord in feudal times.

svelte *adjective* slim and graceful.

SW *abbreviation* south-west; southwestern.

swab (*say* swob) *noun* a mop or pad for cleaning or wiping something.

swab *verb* (**swabbed**, **swabbing**) clean or wipe with a swab.

swaddle *verb* (**swaddled**, **swaddling**) wrap in warm clothes or blankets etc.

swag *noun* **1** loot. **2** (*NZ*) a bundle of personal belongings, carried by a tramp etc. **3** (*NZ, slang*) a lot.

swagger *verb* walk or behave in a conceited way; strut. **swagger** *noun*

swagman *noun* (*plural* **swagmen**) (*NZ*) a tramp.

swain *noun* (*old use*) **1** a country lad. **2** a suitor.

swallow[1] *verb* **1** make something go down your throat. **2** believe something that ought not to be believed. **swallow** *noun*
swallow up take in and cover; engulf, *She was swallowed up in the crowd.*

swallow[2] *noun* a small bird with a forked tail and pointed wings.

swamp *noun* a marsh. **swampy** *adjective*

swamp *verb* **1** flood. **2** overwhelm with a great mass or number of things.

swamp-hen *noun* (*NZ*) pukeko.

swan *noun* a large white or black swimming bird with a long neck.

swank *verb* (*informal*) boast; swagger.

swank *noun* (*informal*) **1** swanking; boasting. **2** a boastful person.

swannie *noun* (*NZ, informal*) a woollen jacket. [from *Swanndri* (trade mark)]

swansong *noun* a person's last performance or work. [from the old belief that a swan sang sweetly when about to die]

swap *verb* (**swapped**, **swapping**) (*informal*) exchange. **swap** *noun*

swarm[1] *noun* a large number of insects or birds etc. flying or moving about together.

swarm[1] *verb* **1** gather or move in a swarm. **2** be crowded or overrun with insects, people, etc.

swarm[2] *verb* climb by gripping with the hands or arms and legs.

swarthy *adjective* having a dark complexion. **swarthiness** *noun*

swashbuckling *adjective* swaggering aggressively.

swastika *noun* an ancient symbol formed by a cross with its ends bent at right angles, adopted by the Nazis as their sign.

swat *verb* (**swatted**, **swatting**) hit or crush a fly etc. **swatter** *noun*

swathe *verb* (**swathed**, **swathing**) wrap in layers of bandages, paper, or clothes etc.

sway *verb* **1** swing gently; move from side to side. **2** influence, *His speech swayed the crowd.* **sway** *noun*

swear *verb* (**swore**, **sworn**, **swearing**) **1** make a solemn promise, *She swore to tell the truth.* **2** make a person take an oath, *We swore him to secrecy.* **3** use curses or coarse **words in anger or** surprise etc. **swear-word** *noun*
swear by have great confidence in something.

sweat (*say* swet) *noun* moisture given off by the body through the pores of the skin; perspiration. **sweaty** *adjective*

sweat *verb* give off sweat; perspire.

sweater *noun* a jersey or pullover.

sweatshirt *noun* a cotton sweater with a soft lining.

swede *noun* a large yellow kind of turnip.

sweep *verb* (**swept**, **sweeping**) **1** clean or clear with a broom or brush etc. **2** move or remove quickly, *The floods swept away the bridge.* **3** go smoothly, quickly, or proudly, *She swept out of the room.* **4** defend or patrol an area in sport. **sweeper** *noun*

sweep *noun* **1** the process of sweeping, *Give this room a good sweep.* **2** a chimney-sweep. **3** a sweepstake.

sweeping *adjective* general; wide-ranging, *He made sweeping changes.*

sweepstake *noun* a kind of lottery used in gambling on the result of a horse-race etc.

sweet *adjective* **1** tasting as if it contains sugar; not bitter. **2** very pleasant, *a sweet smell.* **3** (*informal*) charming. **sweetly** *adverb*, **sweetness** *noun*
sweet as (*NZ, informal*) excellent.
sweet corn the seeds of maize.
sweet pea a climbing plant with fragrant flowers.

sweet *noun* **1** a small shaped piece of sweet food made with sugar, chocolate, etc. **2** a pudding; the sweet course in a meal. **3** a beloved person.

sweetbread *noun* an animal's pancreas used as food.

sweeten *verb* make or become sweet. **sweetener** *noun*

sweetheart *noun* a person you love very much.

sweetmeat *noun* a sweet.

swell *verb* (**swelled**, **swollen** or **swelled**, **swelling**) make or become larger in size or amount or force.
a swollen head (*slang*) conceit.

swell *noun* **1** the process of swelling. **2** the rise and fall of the sea's surface.

swell *adjective* (*American, informal*) very good.

swelling *noun* a swollen place.

swelter *verb* feel uncomfortably hot.

swerve *verb* (**swerved**, **swerving**) turn to one side suddenly. **swerve** *noun*

swift *adjective* quick; rapid. **swiftly** *adverb*, **swiftness** *noun*

swift *noun* a small bird rather like a swallow.

swiftie *noun* (*NZ, slang*) a piece of trickery or deception, *to pull a swiftie.*

swig *verb* (**swigged**, **swigging**) (*slang*) drink; swallow. **swig** *noun*

swill *verb* pour water over or through something; wash or rinse.

swill *noun* **1** the process of swilling, *Give it a swill.* **2** a sloppy mixture of waste food given to pigs.

swim *verb* (**swam**, **swum**, **swimming**) **1** move the body through the water; be in the water for pleasure. **2** cross by swimming, *She swam Cook Strait.* **3** float. **4** be covered with or full of liquid, *Our eyes were swimming in tears.* **5** feel dizzy, *His head swam.* **swimmer** *noun*

swim *noun* the action of swimming, *We went for a swim.* **swimsuit** *noun*

swimming-bath or **swimming-pool** *noun* an artificial pool for swimming in.

swindle *verb* (**swindled**, **swindling**) cheat a person in business etc. **swindle** *noun*, **swindler** *noun*

swine *noun* (*plural* **swine**) **1** a pig. **2** a very unpleasant person or thing.

swing *verb* (**swung**, **swinging**) **1** move to and fro while hanging; move or turn in a curve, *The door swung open.* **2** change from one opinion or mood etc. to another.

swing *noun* **1** a swinging movement. **2** a seat hung on chains or ropes etc. so that it can be moved backwards and forwards. **3** the amount by which votes or opinions etc. change from one side to another. **4** a kind of jazz music.
in full swing full of activity; working fully.

swingeing (*say* **swin**-jing) *adjective* **1** (of a blow) very powerful. **2** huge in amount, *a swingeing increase in taxes.*

swipe *verb* (**swiped**, **swiping**) (*informal*) **1** hit hard. **2** steal something. **3** slide a swipe card through the device that reads it. **swipe** *noun*
swipe card a credit card etc. on which information is stored for reading by an electronic device.

swirl *verb* move round quickly in circles; whirl. **swirl** *noun*

swish *verb* move with a hissing sound. **swish** *noun*

swish *adjective* (*informal*) smart; fashionable.

Swiss roll a thin sponge-cake spread with jam or cream and rolled up.

switch *noun* (*plural* **switches**) **1** a device that is pressed or turned to start or stop something working, especially by electricity. **2** a change of opinion, policy, or methods. **3** mechanism for moving the points on a railway track. **4** a flexible rod or whip.

switch *verb* **1** turn something on or off by means of a switch. **2** change or transfer or divert something.

switchback *noun* **1** a road with sharp or hairpin bends. **2** a roller-coaster.

switchboard *noun* a panel with switches etc. for making telephone connections or operating electric circuits.

swivel *verb* (**swivelled**, **swivelling**) turn round. **swivel** *noun*

swollen *past participle* of **swell**.

swoon *verb* faint. **swoon** *noun*

swoop *verb* come down with a rushing movement; make a sudden attack. **swoop** *noun*

swop *verb* (**swopped**, **swopping**) swap.

sword (*say* sord) *noun* a weapon with a long pointed blade fixed in a handle or hilt. **swordsman** *noun*

swordfish *noun* a large sea-fish with a long upper jaw like a sword.

swot *verb* (**swotted**, **swotting**) (*slang*) study hard. **swot** *noun* [a dialect word for *sweat*]

sycamore *noun* a kind of maple-tree.

sycophant (*say* **sik**-o-fant) *noun* a person who tries to win people's favour by flattering them. **sycophantic** *adjective*, **sycophantically** *adverb*, **sycophancy** *noun*

syl- *prefix* see **syn-**.

syllable *noun* a word or part of a word that has one sound when you say it, *'Cat' has one syllable, 'el-e-phant' has three syllables.* **syllabic** *adjective* [from *syl-*, + Greek *lambanein*= take]

syllabus *noun* (*plural* **syllabuses**) a summary of the things to be studied by a class or for an examination etc.

sylph *noun* a slender girl or woman.

sym- *prefix* see **syn-**.

symbol *noun* **1** a thing that suggests something, *The cross is a symbol of Christianity.* **2** a mark or sign with a special meaning (e.g. +, –, and ÷ in mathematics). **symbolic** *adjective*, **symbolical** *adjective*, **symbolically** *adverb* [from Greek *symbolon* = token]

symbolise *verb* (**symbolised**, **symbolising**) make or be a symbol of something.

symbolism *noun* the use of symbols to represent things.

symmetrical *adjective* able to be divided into two halves which are exactly the same but the opposite way round, *Wheels and butterflies are symmetrical.* **symmetrically** *adverb*, **symmetry** *noun* [from *sym-*,+ *metrical*]

sympathise *verb* (**sympathised**, **sympathising**) show or feel sympathy. **sympathiser** *noun*

sympathy *noun* (*plural* **sympathies**) **1** the sharing or understanding of other people's feelings, opinions, etc. **2** a feeling of pity or tenderness towards someone who is hurt, sad, or in trouble. **sympathetic** *adjective*, **sympathetically** *adverb* [from *sym-*, + Greek *pathos* feeling]

symphony *noun* (*plural* **symphonies**) a long piece of music for an orchestra. **symphonic** *adjective* [from *sym-*, + Greek *phone* = sound]

symptom *noun* a sign that a disease or condition exists, *Red spots are a symptom of measles.* **symptomatic** *adjective*

syn- *prefix* (changing to **syl-** or **sym-** before certain consonants) **1** with, together (as in *synchronise*). **2** alike (as in *synonym*). [from Greek *syn* = with]

synagogue (*say* **sin**-a-gog) *noun* a place where Jews meet for worship. [from Greek, = assembly]

synchronise (*say* **sink**-ron-I'z) *verb* (**synchronised**, **synchronising**) **1** make things happen at the same time. **2** make watches or clocks show the same time. **3** happen at the same time. **synchronisation** *noun* [from *syn-*, + Greek *chronos* = time]

syncopate (*say* **sink**-o-payt) *verb* (**syncopated**, **syncopating**) change the strength of beats in a piece of music. **syncopation** *noun*

syndicate *noun* a group of people or firms who work together in business.

syndrome *noun* a set of symptoms.

synod (*say* **sin**-od) *noun* a council of senior members of the clergy. [from Greek, = meeting]

synonym (*say* **sin**-o-nim) *noun* a word that means the same or almost the same as another word, *'Large' and 'great' are synonyms of 'big'.* **synonymous** (*say* sin-**on**-im-us) *adjective* [from *syn-*, + Greek *onyma* = name]

synopsis (*say* sin-**op**-sis) *noun* (*plural* **synopses**) a summary. [from *syn-*, + Greek *opsis* = seeing]

syntax (*say* **sin**-taks) *noun* **1** the way words are arranged to make phrases or sentences. **2** the set of rules of word order in a sentence. **3** analysis of the word order in a sentence. **syntactic** *adjective*, **syntactically** *adverb* [from *syn-*, + Greek *taxis* = arrangement.]

synthesis (*say* **sin**-thi-sis) *noun* (*plural* **syntheses**) combining different things to make something. **synthesise** *verb* [from *syn-*, + Greek *thesis* = placing]

synthesiser *noun* an electronic musical instrument that can make a large variety of sounds.

synthetic *adjective* artificially made; not natural. **synthetically** *adverb*

syringe *noun* a device for sucking in a liquid and squirting it out.

syrup *noun* a thick sweet liquid. **syrupy** *adjective* [from Arabic *sharab* = a drink]

system *noun* **1** a set of parts, things, or ideas that are organised to work together. **2** a way of doing something, *a new system of voting.* [from Greek, = setting up]

systematic *adjective* methodical; carefully planned. **systematically** *adverb*

Tt

TAB *abbreviation* (*NZ*) Totalisator Agency Board (the government agency which controls legal betting on horse-racing and other sports).

tab[1] *noun* a small flap or strip that sticks out.

tab[2] *noun* a tabulator.

tabard *noun* **1** a kind of tunic decorated with a coat of arms. **2** a piece of clothing of the same shape, worn by women or children.

tabby *noun* (*plural* **tabbies**) a grey or brown cat with dark stripes.

tabernacle *noun* (in the Bible) the portable shrine used by the ancient Jews during their wanderings in the desert.

table *noun* **1** a piece of furniture with a flat top supported on legs. **2** a list of facts or figures arranged in order; a list of the results of multiplying a number by other numbers, *multiplication tables.*

table *verb* (**tabled, tabling**) put forward a proposal etc. for discussion, e.g. in Parliament. [from Latin *tabula* = plank]

tableau (*say* **tab**-loh) *noun* (*plural* **tableaux**, *say* **tab**-lohz) a dramatic or picturesque scene, especially one posed on a stage by a group of people who do not speak or move. [French, = little table]

tablecloth *noun* a cloth for covering a table, especially at meals.

tablespoon *noun* a large spoon for serving food. **tablespoonful** *noun*

tablet *noun* **1** a pill. **2** a solid piece of soap. **3** a flat piece of stone or wood etc. with words carved or written on it.

tabloid *noun* a newspaper with pages that are half the size of larger newspapers.

taboo *adjective* not to be touched or done or used. **taboo** *noun* [Tongan]

tabor (*say* **tay**-ber) *noun* a small drum.

tabular *adjective* arranged in a table or in columns.

tabulate *verb* (**tabulated, tabulating**) arrange information or figures in a table or list. **tabulation** *noun*

tabulator *noun* a device on a keyboard that automatically sets the positions for columns.

tachometer *noun* an instrument used to measure the working speed of an engine.

tacit (*say* **tas**-it) *adjective* implied or understood without being put into words; silent, *tacit approval.* [from Latin *tacitus* = not speaking]

taciturn (*say* **tas**-i-tern) *adjective saying very little.* **taciturnity** *noun*

tack[1] *noun* **1** a short nail with a flat top. **2** a tacking stitch. **3** (in sailing) the direction taken when tacking.

tack[1] *verb* **1** nail down with tacks. **2** fasten material together with long stitches. **3** sail a zigzag course so as to use what wind there is. **tack on** (*informal*) add an extra thing.

tack[2] *noun* harness, saddles, etc. [from *tackle* = equipment]

tackle *verb* (**tackled, tackling**) **1** try to do something that needs doing. **2** seize and stop a player running with the ball in rugby. **3** try to get the ball from someone else in soccer or hockey.

tackle *noun* **1** equipment, especially for fishing. **2** a set of ropes and pulleys. **3** the action of tackling someone in rugby etc.

tacky *adjective* **1** sticky, not quite dry, *The paint is still tacky.* **2** (*informal*) cheap, shabby, in poor taste. **tackiness** *noun*

taco *noun* (*plural* **tacos**) a dish of meat etc. in a folded maize pancake. [Mexican Spanish]

tact *noun* skill in not offending people. **tactful** *adjective*, **tactfully** *adverb*, **tactless** *adjective*, **tactlessly** *adverb* [from Latin *tactus* = sense of touch]

tactics *noun* the method of arranging troops etc. skilfully for a battle, or of doing things to achieve something. **tactical** *adjective*, **tactically** *adverb*, **tactician** *noun* [from Greek *taktika* = things arranged]

> USAGE *Strategy* is a general plan for a whole campaign, *tactics* is for one part of this.

tactile *adjective* of or using the sense of touch. [from Latin *tactum* = touched]

tadpole *noun* a young frog or toad that has developed from the egg and lives entirely in water. [from old words *tad* = toad, + *poll* = head]

taffeta *noun* a stiff silky material.

tag[1] *noun* **1** a label tied on or stuck into something. **2** a metal or plastic point at the end of a shoelace. **3** monitoring of an electronic device. **4** a loose flap or end. **5** the work of a graffiti artist.

tag[1] *verb* (**tagged**, **tagging**) **1** label something with a tag. **2** add as an extra thing, *A postscript was tagged on to her letter.* **3** (*informal*) go with other people, *Her sister tagged along.* **4** mark with graffiti.

tag[2] *noun* a game in which one person chases the others.

tagging *noun* the marking of walls etc. with graffiti. **tagger** *noun*

taha Māori the Māori side of New Zealand life and culture. [Māori]

Tahitian *noun* **1** a person from Tahiti. **2** the language of Tahiti. **Tahitian** *adjective*

taiaha *noun* a wooden weapon with a long handle. [Māori]

taihoa *interjection* wait! [Māori]

tail *noun* **1** the part that sticks out from the rear end of the body of a bird, fish, or animal. **2** the part at the end or rear of something. **3** the side of a coin opposite the head, *Heads or tails?*

tail *verb* **1** remove stalks etc. from fruit, *top and tail gooseberries.* **2** (*NZ*) dock a lamb's tail. **3** (*informal*) follow a person or thing.
tail off become fewer, smaller, or slighter etc.; cease gradually.

tailless *adjective* without a tail.

tailor *noun* a person who makes men's clothes.

tailor *verb* **1** make or fit clothes. **2** adapt or make something for a special purpose.

taint *noun* a small amount of decay, pollution, or a bad quality that spoils something.

taint *verb* give something a taint. [same origin as *tint*]

taipo *noun* an evil spirit. [Māori]

takahē *noun* a rare blue-green flightless bird. [Māori]

tākapu *noun* a kind of sea-bird. [Māori]

take[1] *noun* a cause or case. [Māori]

take[2] *verb* (**took**, **taken**, **taking**) This word has many uses, including (**1**) get something into your hands or possession or control etc. (*take this cup*; *we took many prisoners*), (**2**) make use of (*take a taxi*) or indulge in (*take a holiday*), (**3**) carry or convey (*Take this parcel to the post*), (**4**) perform or deal with (*When do you take your music exam?*), (**5**) study or teach a subject (*Who takes you for maths?*), (**6**) make an effort (*take trouble*) or experience a feeling (*Don't take offence*), (**7**) accept; endure (*I'll take a risk*), (**8**) require (*It takes a strong man to lift this*), (**9**) write down (*take notes*), (**10**) make a photograph, (**11**) subtract (*take 4 from 10*), (**12**) assume (*I take it that you agree*). **taker** *noun*
take after be like a parent etc.
take in deceive somebody.
take leave of say goodbye to.
take off (of an aircraft) leave the ground and become airborne. **take-off** *noun*
take on begin to employ someone; play or fight against someone; (*informal*) show that you are upset.
take over take control. **take-over** *noun*
take place happen; occur.
take up start something; occupy space or time etc.; accept an offer.

takeaway *noun* a place that sells cooked meals for customers to take away; a meal from this.

takings *plural noun* money received.

talcum powder a scented powder put on the skin to make it feel smooth and dry.

tale *noun* a story.

talent *noun* a special or very great ability. **talented** *adjective* [from Greek *talanton* = sum of money]

talisman *noun* (*plural* **talismans**) an object supposed to bring good luck. [from Greek *telesma* = consecrated object]

talk *verb* speak; have a conversation. **talker** *noun*

talk *noun* **1** talking; a conversation. **2** an informal lecture.
talk show a radio or television programme consisting of discussion or interviews.

talkative *adjective* talking a lot.

talkback *noun* a broadcast in which people phone the studio and take part.

tall *adjective* **1** higher than the average, *a tall tree.* **2** measured from the bottom to the top, *It is 10 metres tall.* **tallness** *noun*
Tall Black a New Zealand national men's basketball representative.
tall poppy (*NZ*) a person whose success makes some people want to cut them down to size.
tall story (*informal*) a story that is hard to believe. [the original meaning was 'swift']

tallboy *noun* a tall chest of drawers.

tallow *noun* animal fat used to make candles, soap, lubricants, etc.

tally *noun* (*plural* **tallies**) **1** the total amount of a debt or score. **2** (*NZ*) the number of sheep shorn by a shearer in a day etc.

tally *verb* (**tallied**, **tallying**) correspond or agree with something else, *Does your list tally with mine?*

talofa *interjection* a Samoan greeting.

talon *noun* a strong claw.

tama *noun* (*NZ*) boy. [Māori]

Tamaki-Makau-Rau *noun* a Māori name for Auckland.

tamariki *plural noun* children; young people. [Māori]

tamarillo *noun* an egg-shaped red fruit, formerly called *tree-tomato.*

tambourine *noun* a circular musical instrument with metal discs round it, tapped or shaken to make it jingle.

tame *adjective* **1** (of animals) gentle and not afraid of people; not wild or dangerous. **2** not exciting; dull. **tamely** *adverb,* **tameness** *noun*

tame *verb* (**tamed, taming**) make an animal become tame. **tamer** *noun*

Tamil *noun* **1** a member of a people of southern India and Sri Lanka. **2** their language.

tam-o'-shanter *noun* a beret with a wide top. [named after Tam o' Shanter, hero of a poem by the Scottish poet Robert Burns]

tamp *verb* pack or ram down tightly.

tamper *verb* meddle or interfere with something.

tampon *noun* a plug of absorbent material.

tan *noun* **1** light-brown colour. **2** brown colour in skin that has been exposed to sun.

tan *verb* (**tanned, tanning**) **1** make or become brown by exposing skin to the sun. **2** make an animal's skin into leather by treating it with chemicals.

tandem *noun* a bicycle for two riders, one behind the other. [Latin, = at length]

tanekaha *noun* celery pine. [Māori]

tang *noun* a strong flavour or smell.

tangata whenua *noun* **1** the local people, the hosts. **2** the indigenous people of a country. [Māori]

tangelo *noun* a fruit that is a cross between a tangerine and a grapefruit.

tangent *noun* a straight line that touches the outside of a curve or circle. [from Latin *tangens* = touching]

tangerine *noun* a kind of small orange from Tangier in Morocco. [named after *Tangier*]

tangi *noun* a gathering to mourn a person's death, with lamentation and speeches, followed by feasting.

tangi *verb* lament; cry. [Māori]

tangible *adjective* able to be touched; real. **tangibly** *adverb,* **tangibility** *noun* [from Latin *tangere* = touch]

tangle *verb* (**tangled, tangling**) make or become twisted into a confused mass. **tangle** *noun*

tango *noun* (*plural* **tangos**) a ballroom dance with gliding steps.

taniwha *noun* a mythical monster that lives in water. [Māori]

tank *noun* **1** a large container for a liquid or gas. **2** a heavy armoured vehicle used in war.

tankard *noun* a large mug for drinking from, usually made of silver or pewter.

tanker *noun* **1** a large ship for carrying oil. **2** a large truck for carrying a liquid.

tanner *noun* a person who tans animal skins into leather. **tannery** *noun*

tannin *noun* a substance obtained from the bark or fruit of various trees (also found in tea), used in tanning and dyeing things.

tantalise *verb* (**tantalised, tantalising**) tease or torment a person by showing him or her something good but keeping it out of reach. [from the name of Tantalus in Greek mythology, who was punished by being made to stand near water and fruit which moved away when he tried to reach them]

tantamount *adjective* equivalent, *The Queen's request was tantamount to a command.* [from Italian *tanto montare* = amount to so much]

tantrum *noun* an outburst of bad temper.

taonga *noun* a treasure, a prized possession. [Māori]

tap[1] *noun* a device for letting out liquid or gas in a controlled flow.

tap[1] *verb* (**tapped, tapping**) **1** take liquid out of something, especially through a tap. **2** obtain supplies or information etc. from a source. **3** fix a device to a telephone cable etc. so that you can overhear conversations on it.

tap[2] *noun* **1** a quick light hit; the sound of this. **2** tap-dancing.

tap[2] *verb* (**tapped, tapping**) hit a person or thing quickly and lightly.

tapa *noun* a cloth made from bark in the Pacific Islands. [Polynesian]

tap-dancing *noun* dancing with shoes that make elaborate tapping sounds on the floor. **tap-dance** *noun & verb,* **tap-dancer** *noun*

tape *noun* **1** a narrow strip of cloth, paper, plastic, etc. **2** a narrow plastic strip coated with a magnetic substance and used for making recordings. **3** a tape-recording. **4** a tape-measure.

tape *verb* (**taped, taping**) **1** fix, cover, or surround something with tape. **2** record something on magnetic tape.
get or **have something taped** (*slang*) know or understand it; be able to deal with it.

tape-measure *noun* a long strip marked in centimetres etc. for measuring things.

taper *verb* make or become narrower gradually.

taper *noun* a very thin candle.

tape-recorder *noun* a device for recording sounds or computer data on magnetic tape and reproducing them. **tape-recording** *noun*

tapestry *noun* (*plural* **tapestries**) a piece of strong cloth with pictures or patterns woven or embroidered on it. [from French *tapis* = carpet]

tapeworm *noun* a long flat worm that can live as a parasite in the intestines of people and animals.

tapioca *noun* a starchy substance in hard white grains obtained from cassava, used for making puddings.

tapir (*say* **tay**-per) *noun* a pig-like animal with a long flexible snout.

tapu *noun* a solemn restriction.

tapu *adjective* **1** solemnly forbidden. **2** sacred.

tapu *verb* place under a tapu. [Māori; compare *taboo*]

tar *noun* a thick black liquid made from coal or wood etc. and used in making roads.

tar *verb* (**tarred**, **tarring**) coat something with tar.

tara *noun* a kind of black and grey tern. [Māori]

taraire *noun* a large tree with white wood. [Māori]

tarakihi *noun* an edible fish. [Māori]

Taranaki gate (*NZ*) a temporary gate made from wires attached to upright battens.

tarantula *noun* a large kind of spider found in southern Europe and in tropical countries.

tarata *noun* lemonwood. [Māori]

tardy *adjective* (**tardier**, **tardiest**) slow; late. **tardily** *adverb*, **tardiness** *noun* [from Latin *tardus* = slow]

target *noun* something aimed at; a thing that someone tries to hit or reach.

target *verb* (**targeted**, **targeting**) aim at or have as a target.

tariff *noun* a list of prices or charges.

tarmac *noun* an area surfaced with tar macadam, especially on an airport runway. [*Tarmac* is a trade mark]

tar macadam a mixture of tar and broken stone, used for making a hard surface on roads, paths, playgrounds, etc.

tarn *noun* a small mountain lake.

tarnish *verb* **1** make or become less shiny, *The silver had tarnished.* **2** spoil; blemish, *The scandal tarnished his reputation.* **tarnish** *noun*

taro *noun* a plant whose root is used for food. [Māori]

tarpaulin *noun* a large sheet of waterproof canvas. [from *tar* + *pall*[1]]

tarragon *noun* a plant with leaves that are used to flavour salads etc.

tarry[1] (*say* **tar**-ee) *adjective* of or like tar.

tarry[2] (*say* **ta**-ree) *verb* (**tarried**, **tarrying**) (*old use*) linger.

tar-seal *verb* (*NZ*) surface a road etc. with tar macadam.

tar-seal *noun* a tar-sealed road or area.

tart[1] *noun* **1** a pie containing fruit or sweet filling. **2** a piece of pastry with jam etc. on top.

tart[2] *adjective* **1** sour. **2** sharp in manner, *a tart reply.* **tartly** *adverb*, **tartness** *noun*

tartan *noun* a pattern with coloured stripes crossing each other, especially one associated with a Scottish clan.

tartar[1] *noun* a person who is fierce or difficult to deal with. [named after the Tartars, warriors from central Asia in the 13th century]

tartar[2] *noun* a hard chalky deposit that forms on teeth. [medieval Latin from Greek]

tartlet *noun* a small pastry tart.

task *noun* a piece of work to be done. **take a person to task** rebuke him or her. **task force** a group specially organised for a particular task.

taskmaster *noun* a person imposing tasks on others, *a hard taskmaster.*

Tasman *noun* **the Tasman** the Tasman Sea. **across the Tasman** to or in Australia.

Tasmanian devil a black Australian marsupial rather like a bear.

tassel *noun* a bundle of threads tied together at the top and used to decorate something. **tasselled** *adjective*

Tassie *abbreviation* (*NZ & Australia, informal*) **1** Tasmania. **2** Tasmanian. **3** Tasman Sea.

taste *verb* (**tasted**, **tasting**) **1** take a small amount of food or drink to try its flavour. **2** be able to perceive flavours. **3** have a certain flavour.

taste *noun* **1** the feeling caused in the tongue by something placed on it. **2** the ability to taste things. **3** the ability to enjoy beautiful things or to choose what is suitable, *Her choice of clothes shows her good taste.* **4** a liking, *He always had a taste for camping.* **5** a very small amount of food or drink.

tasteful *adjective* showing good taste. **tastefully** *adverb*, **tastefulness** *noun*

tasteless *adjective* **1** having no flavour. **2** showing poor taste. **tastelessly** *adverb*, **tastelessness** *noun*

tasty *adjective* (**tastier**, **tastiest**) having a strong pleasant taste.

tattered *adjective* badly torn; ragged.

tatters *plural noun* rags; badly torn pieces, *My coat was in tatters.*

tatting *noun* a kind of hand-made lace.

tattle *verb* (**tattled**, **tattling**) gossip. **tattle** *noun*

tattoo[1] *verb* mark a person's skin with a picture or pattern by using a needle and some dye.

tattoo[1] *noun* a tattooed mark. [Polynesian]

tattoo[2] *noun* **1** a drumming or tapping sound. **2** an entertainment consisting of military music, marching, etc.

tatty *adjective* **1** ragged; shabby and untidy. **2** cheap and gaudy. **tattily** *adverb*, **tattiness** *noun*

tauhinu *noun* a shrub with white flowers, also called tawhini. [Māori]

tauiwi *noun* a foreigner. [Māori]

taunt *verb* jeer at or insult someone. **taunt** *noun* [from French *tant pour tant* = tit for tat]

taupata *noun* a shrub often used as a hedge. [Māori]

taut *adjective* stretched tightly. **tautly** *adverb*, **tautness** *noun*

tauten *verb* make or become taut.

tautology *noun* (*plural* **tautologies**) saying the same thing again in different words, e.g. *You can get the book free for nothing* (where *free* and *for nothing* mean the same). [from Greek *tauto* = the same, + *logos* = word]

tavern *noun* a public house (without accommodation). [from Latin *taberna* = hut]

tawa *noun* a tree with purple berries. [Māori]

tawai *noun* = **tawhai**.

tawdry *adjective* cheap and gaudy. **tawdriness** *noun* [from *St Audrey's lace* (cheap finery formerly sold at St Audrey's fair at Ely, England)]

tawhai *noun* a New Zealand beech tree. [Māori]

tawhini *noun* = **tauhinu**.

tāwhiri *noun* a tree of the pittosporum family, with fragrant white blossoms. [Māori, = beckon, welcome]

tawny *adjective* brownish-yellow.

tax *noun* (*plural* **taxes**) **1** money that people or business firms have to pay to the government, to be used for public purposes. **2** a strain or burden, *The long walk was a tax on his strength.*

tax *verb* **1** put a tax on something. **2** charge someone a tax. **3** put a strain or burden on a person or thing, *Will it tax your strength?* **4** accuse, *I taxed him with leaving the door open.* **taxable** *adjective*, **taxation** *noun* [from Latin *taxare* = calculate]

taxi *noun* (*plural* **taxis**) a car that carries passengers for payment, usually with a meter to record the fare payable. **taxi-cab** *noun* [short for *taxi-meter cab*]

taxi *verb* (**taxied**, **taxiing**) (of an aircraft) move along the ground, especially before or after flying.

taxidermist *noun* a person who prepares and stuffs the skins of animals in a lifelike form. **taxidermy** *noun* [from Greek *taxis* = arrangement, + *derma* = skin]

taxpayer *noun* a person who pays tax.

TB *abbreviation* tuberculosis.

tea *noun* **1** a drink made by pouring hot water on the dried leaves of an evergreen shrub (the *tea-plant*). **2** these dried leaves. **3** the main evening meal. **teacup** *noun*, **tea-leaf** *noun*, **teatime** *noun* [from Chinese *t'e*]

tea-bag *noun* a small bag holding about a teaspoonful of tea.

teacake *noun* a kind of bun usually served toasted and buttered.

teach *verb* (**taught**, **teaching**) **1** give a person knowledge or skill; train. **2** give lessons, especially in a particular subject. **3** show someone what to do or avoid, *That will teach you not to meddle!*

teachable *adjective* able to be taught.

teacher *noun* a person who teaches others, especially in a school.

tea-chest *noun* a large light wooden box lined with metal.

tea-cloth *noun* a tea-towel.

teak *noun* the hard strong wood of an evergreen Asian tree.

teal *noun* (*plural* **teal**) a kind of duck.

team *noun* **1** a set of players forming one side in certain games and sports. **2** a set of people working together. **3** two or more animals harnessed to pull a vehicle or a plough etc.

team *verb* put together in a team; combine.

teapot *noun* a pot with a lid and a handle, for making and pouring tea.

tear[1] (*say* teer) *noun* a drop of the water that comes from the eyes when a person cries. **tear-drop** *noun*
in tears crying.

tear[2] (*say* tair) *verb* (**tore**, **torn**, **tearing**) **1** pull something apart, away, or into pieces. **2** become torn, *Newspaper tears easily.* **3** run or travel hurriedly.

tear[2] *noun* a split made by tearing.

tearaway *noun* a reckless hooligan.

tearful *adjective* in tears; crying easily. **tearfully** *adverb*

tear-gas *noun* a gas that makes people's eyes water painfully.

tease *verb* (**teased**, **teasing**) **1** amuse yourself by deliberately annoying or making fun of someone. **2** pick threads apart into separate strands.

tease *noun* a person who often teases others.

teasel *noun* a plant with bristly heads formerly used to brush up the surface of cloth. [from *tease*[2]]

teaser *noun* a difficult problem.

teaspoon *noun* a small spoon for stirring tea etc. **teaspoonful** *noun*

teat *noun* **1** a nipple through which a baby sucks milk. **2** the cap of a baby's feeding-bottle.

tea-towel *noun* a cloth for drying washed dishes, cutlery, etc.

tea-tree *noun* one of several kinds of New Zealand shrubs, including manuka.

tech *noun* (*informal*) **1** a technical college or polytechnic. **2** technology. **3** a technician.

technical *adjective* **1** concerned with technology. **2** of a particular subject and its methods, *the technical terms of chemistry.* **technically** *adverb* [from Greek *technikos* = skilful]

technicality *noun* (*plural* **technicalities**) **1** being technical. **2** a technical word or phrase; a special detail.

technician *noun* a skilled mechanic.

technique *noun* the method of doing something skilfully.

technology *noun* (*plural* **technologies**) the study of machinery, engineering, and how things work. **technological** *adjective*, **technologist** *noun* [from Greek *techne* = skill, + *-logy*]

teddy-bear *noun* a soft furry toy bear. [named after US President Theodore ('Teddy') Roosevelt in about 1906]

tedious *adjective* annoyingly slow or long; boring. **tediously** *adverb*, **tediousness** *noun*, **tedium** *noun* [from Latin *taedium* = tiredness]

tee *noun* **1** the flat area from which golfers strike the ball at the start of play for each hole. **2** a small piece of wood or plastic on which the ball is placed for being struck.

tee *verb* place on a tee.
tee off hit a ball from the tee.

teem *verb* **1** be full of something, *The river was teeming with fish.* **2** rain very hard; pour.

teenage *adjective* of teenagers.

teenaged *adjective* in your teens.

teenager *noun* a person in his or her teens.

teens *plural noun* the time of life between 13 and 19 years of age.

teeny *adjective* (**teenier**, **teeniest**) (*informal*) tiny.

teeter *verb* stand or move unsteadily.

teething *noun* (of a baby) having its first teeth beginning to grow through the gums.

teetotal *adjective* never drinking alcohol.
teetotaller *noun*

Te Ika a Māui the Māori name for the North Island. [= the fish of Maui]

tele- *prefix* far; at a distance (as in *telescope*). [from Greek *tele* = far off]

telecast *noun* a television broadcast.

telecommunications *plural noun* communications over a long distance, e.g. by telephone, telegraph, radio, or television.

telegenic *adjective* looking attractive on television. [compare *photogenic*]

telegram *noun* a message sent by telegraph. [from *tele-* + *-gram*]

telegraph *noun* a way of sending messages by using electric current along wires or by radio. **telegraphic** *adjective*, **telegraphy** *noun* [from *tele-* + *-graph*]

telemarketing *noun* the selling of goods and services by means of telephone calls to possible customers.

telepathy (*say* til-**ep**-ath-ee) *noun* communication of thoughts from one person's mind to another without speaking, writing, or gestures. **telepathic** *adjective* [from *tele-*, + Greek *pathos* = feeling]

telephone *noun* a device or system using electric wires or radio etc. to enable one person to speak to another who is some distance away.

telephone *verb* (**telephoned**, **telephoning**) speak to a person on the telephone. [from *tele-*, + Greek *phone* = voice]

telephonist (*say* til-**ef**-on-ist) *noun* a person who operates a telephone switchboard.

telephoto lens *noun* a magnifying lens used in photographing distant objects.

telescope *noun* an instrument using lenses to magnify distant objects. **telescopic** *adjective* [from *tele-*, + Greek *skopein* = look at]

telescope *verb* (**telescoped**, **telescoping**) **1** make or become shorter by sliding overlapping sections into each other. **2** compress or condense so as to take less space or time.

teletext *noun* a system in which news etc. is transmitted in written form to a television screen.

telethon *noun* a marathon fund-raising television programme. [from *tele*vision + mara*thon*]

televise *verb* (**televised**, **televising**) broadcast something by television.

television *noun* **1** a system using radio waves to reproduce a view of scenes, events, or plays etc. on a screen. **2** an apparatus for receiving these pictures. **3** televised programmes. [from *tele-* + *vision*]

telex *noun* a system for sending printed messages by telegraphy. **telex** *verb*

tell *verb* (**told**, **telling**) **1** make a thing known to someone, especially by words. **2** speak, *Tell the truth.* **3** order, *Tell them to wait.* **4** reveal a secret, *Promise you won't tell.* **5** decide; distinguish, *Can you tell the difference between butter and margarine?* **6** produce an effect, *The strain began to tell on him.* **7** count, *There are ten of them, all told.*
tell off (*informal*) reprimand.
tell tales report what someone has done.

teller *noun* an employee receiving or paying out money at a bank-counter.

telling *adjective* having a strong effect, *a very telling reply.*

tell-tale *noun* a person who tells tales.

tell-tale *adjective* revealing or indicating something, *There was a tell-tale spot of jam on his chin.*

telly *noun* (*plural* **tellies**) (*informal*) **1** television. **2** a television set.

Te Māngai Pāho *noun* (*NZ*) Māori broadcasting authority. [Māori]

temerity (*say* tim-**e**rri-tee) *noun* rashness; boldness.

temper *noun* **1** a person's mood, *He is in a good temper.* **2** an angry mood, *She was in a temper.*
lose your temper lose your calmness and become angry.

temper *verb* **1** harden or strengthen metal etc. by heating and cooling it. **2** moderate or soften the effects of something, *tempering justice with mercy.* [from Latin *temperare* = mix]

temperament *noun* a person's nature as shown in the way he or she usually behaves, *a nervous temperament.*

temperamental *adjective* **1** of a person's temperament. **2** likely to become excitable or moody suddenly. **temperamentally** *adverb*

temperance *noun* **1** moderation; self-restraint. **2** drinking little or no alcohol.

temperate *adjective* **1** neither extremely hot nor extremely cold, *New Zealand has a temperate climate.* **2** moderate; reasonable.

temperature *noun* **1** how hot or cold a person or thing is. **2** an abnormally high temperature of the body.

tempest *noun* a violent storm. [from Latin *tempestas* = weather]

tempestuous *adjective* stormy; full of commotion.

temple[1] *noun* a building where a god is worshipped. [from Latin *templum* = consecrated place]

temple[2] *noun* the part of the head between the forehead and the ear. [from Latin *tempora* = sides of the head]

tempo *noun* (*plural* **tempi** or **tempos**) the speed or rhythm of something, especially of a piece of music. [Italian, from Latin *tempus* = time]

temporary *adjective* lasting for a limited time only; not permanent. **temporarily** *adverb* [from Latin *temporis* = of a time]

temporise *verb* (**temporised**, **temporising**) avoid giving a definite answer, in order to postpone something.

tempt *verb* try to persuade or attract someone, especially into doing something wrong or unwise. **temptation** *noun*, **tempter** *noun*, **temptress** *noun* [from Latin *temptare* = test]

ten *noun & adjective* the number 10; one more than nine.

tenable *adjective* able to be held, *a tenable theory; the job is tenable for one year only.* [from Latin *tenere* = to hold]

tenacious (*say* ten-**ay**-shus) *adjective* holding or clinging firmly to something. **tenaciously** *adverb*, **tenacity** *noun*

tēnā koe *interjection* hello (said to one person). [Māori]

tēnā kōrua *interjection* hello (said to two people). [Māori]

tēnā koutou *interjection* hello (said to three or more people). [Māori]

tenant *noun* a person who rents a house, building, or land etc. from a landlord. **tenancy** *noun* [from Latin *tenens* = holding]

tend[1] *verb* have a certain tendency, *Prices tend to rise.* [from Latin *tendere* = stretch]

tend[2] *verb* look after, *Shepherds were tending their sheep.* [from *attend*]

tendency *noun* (*plural* **tendencies**) the way a person or thing is likely to behave, *She has a tendency to be lazy.*

tender[1] *adjective* **1** easy to chew; not tough or hard. **2** easily hurt or damaged; sensitive; delicate, *tender plants.* **3** gentle and loving, *a tender smile.* **tenderly** *adverb*, **tenderness** *noun* [from Latin *tener* = soft]

tender[2] *verb* offer something formally, *He tendered his resignation.*

tender[2] *noun* a formal offer to supply goods or carry out work at a stated price, *The council asked for tenders to build the gallery.* **legal tender** kinds of money that are legal for making payments, *Are $1 notes still legal tender?* [same origin as *tend*[1]]

tender[3] *noun* **1** a truck attached to a steam locomotive to carry its coal and water. **2** a small boat carrying stores or passengers to and from a larger one. [from *tend*[2]]

tendon *noun* a strong strip of tissue that joins muscle to bone.

tendril *noun* **1** a thread-like part by which a climbing plant clings to a support. **2** a thin curl of hair etc.

tenement *noun* (*American*) a large house or building divided into flats or rooms that are let to separate tenants.

tenet (*say* **ten**-it) *noun* a firm belief held by a person or group. [Latin, = he or she holds]

tennis *noun* a game played with rackets and a ball on a court with a net across the middle. [from French *tenez!* = receive (called by the person serving)]

tenon *noun* a projecting piece of wood etc. shaped to fit into a mortise.

tenor *noun* a male singer with a high voice.

tense[1] *noun* the form of a verb that shows when something happens, e.g. he *came* (**past tense**), he *comes* or *is coming* (**present tense**), he *will come* (**future tense**). [from Latin *tempus* = time]

tense[2] *adjective* **1** tightly stretched. **2** with muscles tight because you are nervous or excited. **tensely** *adverb*, **tenseness** *noun*

tense[2] *verb* (**tensed**, **tensing**) make or become tense. [from Latin *tensum* = stretched]

tensile *adjective* **1** of tension. **2** able to be stretched.

tension *noun* **1** pulling so as to stretch something; being stretched. **2** tenseness; the condition when feelings are tense. **3** voltage, *high-tension cables.*

tent *noun* a shelter made of canvas or other material. [same origin as *tense*[2]]

tentacle *noun* a long flexible part of the body of certain animals (e.g. snails, octopuses), used for feeling or grasping things or for moving.

tentative *adjective* cautious; trying something out, *a tentative suggestion.* **tentatively** *adverb* [same origin as *tempt*]

tenterhooks *plural noun* **on tenterhooks** tense and anxious. [from *tenter* = a machine with hooks for stretching cloth to dry]

tenth *adjective & noun* next after the ninth.

tenuous *adjective* very slight or thin, *tenuous threads.* [from Latin *tenuis* = thin]

tenure (*say* **ten**-yoor) *noun* the holding of office or of land, accommodation, etc.

Te Papa (or **Te Papa Tongarewa**) *noun* (*NZ*) the national museum of New Zealand, translated as 'the treasure trove'. [Māori]

tepee (*say* **tee**-pee) *noun* a wigwam.

tepid *adjective* only slightly warm; lukewarm, *tepid water.*

Te Puni Kōkiri *noun* (*NZ*) Ministry of Māori Affairs. [Māori]

terakihi *noun* = **tarakihi**.

term *noun* **1** the period of weeks when a school or college is open. **2** a definite period, *a term of imprisonment.* **3** a word or expression, *technical terms.* **terms** *plural noun* a relationship between people, *They are on friendly terms*; conditions offered or accepted, *peace terms.*

term *verb* name; call by a certain term, *This music is termed jazz.* [from Latin *terminus* = boundary]

termagant *noun* a shrewish bullying woman.

terminable *adjective* able to be terminated.

terminal *noun* **1** the place where something ends; a terminus. **2** a building where air passengers arrive or depart. **3** a place where a wire is connected in an electric circuit or battery etc. **4** a device for sending information to a computer, or for receiving it.

terminal *adjective* **1** of or at the end or boundary of something. **2** of or in the last stage of a fatal disease, *terminal cancer.* **terminally** *adverb*

terminate *verb* (**terminated**, **terminating**) end; stop finally. **termination** *noun* [same origin as *terminus*]

terminology *noun* the technical terms of a subject. **terminological** *adjective* [from *term* + *-logy*]

terminus *noun* (*plural* **termini**) the end of something; the last station on a railway or bus route. [Latin, = the end]

termite *noun* a small insect that is very destructive to timber.

tern *noun* a sea-bird with long wings.

terrace *noun* **1** a level area on a slope or hillside. **2** a paved area beside a house. **terraced** *adjective* [from Latin *terra* = earth]

terracotta *noun* **1** a kind of pottery. **2** the brownish-red colour of flowerpots. [Italian, = baked earth]

terrain *noun* a stretch of land, *hilly terrain.* [from Latin *terra* = earth]

terrapin *noun* an edible freshwater turtle of North America.

terrestrial *adjective* **1** of the earth. **2** of land; living on land. [from Latin *terra* = earth]

terrible *adjective* very bad; distressing. **terribly** *adverb* [from Latin *terrere* = frighten]

terrier *noun* a kind of small lively dog.

terrific *adjective* (*informal*) **1** very great, *a terrific storm*. **2** excellent. **terrifically** *adverb*

terrify *verb* (**terrified**, **terrifying**) fill someone with terror.

territory *noun* (*plural* **territories**) an area of land, especially one that belongs to a country or person. **territorial** *adjective* [from Latin *terra* = earth]

terror *noun* **1** very great fear. **2** a terrifying person or thing. [from Latin *terrere* = frighten]

terrorise *verb* (**terrorised**, **terrorising**) fill someone with terror; control or compel someone by frightening them. **terrorisation** *noun*

terrorist *noun* a person who uses violence for political purposes. **terrorism** *noun*

terse *adjective* concise; curt. **tersely** *adverb*, **terseness** *noun* [from Latin *tersum* = polished]

tertiary (*say* **ter**-sher-ee) *adjective* of the third stage of something; coming after secondary. [from Latin *tertius* = third]

tessellate *verb* (**tessellated**, **tessellating**) fit shapes into a pattern without overlapping. **tessellation** *noun*

test *noun* **1** a short examination; a way of discovering the qualities or abilities etc. of a person or thing. **2** a test match. **3** a medical analysis of blood or body parts.
test match a game of cricket, netball, etc. between teams from different countries.

test *verb* **1** make an examination of a person or thing. **2** carry out a trial. **3** carry out a medical analysis. **tester** *noun*

testament *noun* **1** a written statement. **2** either of the two main parts of the Bible, the Old Testament or the New Testament. [from Latin *testis* = witness]

testator *noun* a person who has made a will.

testicle *noun* either of the two glands in the scrotum where semen is produced.

testify *verb* (**testified**, **testifying**) give evidence; swear that something is true. [from Latin *testis* = witness]

testimonial *noun* **1** a letter describing someone's abilities, character, etc. **2** a gift presented to someone as a mark of respect.

testimony *noun* (*plural* **testimonies**) evidence; what someone testifies.

test-tube *noun* a tube of thin glass with one end closed, used for experiments in chemistry etc.

testy *adjective* easily annoyed; irritable.

tetanus *noun* a disease that makes the muscles become stiff, caused by bacteria. [from Greek *tetanos* = a spasm]

tether *verb* tie an animal so that it cannot move far.

tether *noun* a rope for tethering an animal. **at the end of your tether** unable to endure something any more.

tetra- *prefix* four. [Greek, = four]

tetrahedron *noun* a solid with four sides (e.g. a pyramid with a triangular base). [from *tetra-*, + Greek *hedra* = base]

Te Waipounamu a Māori name for the South Island. [= the water (of) greenstone]

Te Whanga-Nui-a-Tara *noun* a Māori name for Wellington.

text *noun* **1** the words of something written or printed. **2** a sentence from the Bible used as the subject of a sermon etc. **3** written words or computer data. **4** a text message. [from Latin *textus* = literary style]

text message *noun* a written communication on a mobile phone.

textbook *noun* a book that teaches you about a subject.

textiles *plural noun* kinds of cloth; fabrics. [from Latin *textum* = woven]

texture *noun* the way that the surface of something feels.

thalidomide *noun* a medicinal drug that was found (in 1961) to cause babies to be born with deformed arms and legs. [from its chemical name]

than *conjunction* compared with another person or thing, *His brother is taller than he is* or *taller than him.*

thank *verb* tell someone that you are grateful to him or her.
thank you I thank you.

thankful *adjective* grateful. **thankfully** *adverb*

thankless *adjective* not likely to win thanks from people, *a thankless task.*

thanks *plural noun* **1** statements of gratitude. **2** (*informal*) thank you.
thanks to as a result of; because of, *Thanks to your help, we succeeded.*

thanksgiving *noun* an expression of gratitude, especially to God.

thar *noun* a Himalayan goat classed as a noxious animal in New Zealand.

that *adjective & pronoun* (*plural* **those**) the one there, *That book is mine. Whose is that?*

that *adverb* to such an extent, *I'll come that far but no further.*

that *relative pronoun* which, who, or whom, *This is the record that I wanted. We liked the people that we met on holiday.*

that *conjunction* used to introduce a wish, reason, result, etc., *I hope that you are well. The puzzle was so hard that no one could solve it.*

thatch *noun* straw or reeds used to make a roof.

thatch *verb* make a roof with thatch.
thatcher *noun*

thaw *verb* melt; stop being frozen.

thaw *noun* the process of thawing; weather that thaws ice.

the *adjective* (called the *definite article*) a particular one; that or those.

theatre *noun* **1** a building where plays etc. are performed to an audience. **2** an operating theatre. [from Greek *theatron* = place for seeing things]

theatrical *adjective* of plays or acting.
theatrically *adverb*

theatricals *plural noun* performances of plays etc.

thee *pronoun* (*old use*) the form of *thou* used as the object of a verb or after a preposition.

theft *noun* stealing.

their *adjective* **1** belonging to them, *Their coats are over there.* **2** (*informal*) belonging to a person, *Somebody has left their coat on the bus.*

theirs *possessive pronoun* belonging to them, *These coats are theirs.*

USAGE It is incorrect to write *their's*.

them *pronoun* the form of *they* used as the object of a verb or after a preposition, *We saw them.*

theme *noun* **1** the subject about which a person speaks, writes, or thinks. **2** a melody.

themselves *pronoun* they or them and nobody else. (Compare *herself*.)

then *adverb* **1** at that time, *We were younger then.* **2** after that; next, *Make the tea, then pour it out.* **3** in that case, *If this is yours, then this must be mine.*

thence *adverb* **1** from a place already mentioned. **2** consequently.

theology *noun* the study of religion.
theological *adjective*, **theologian** *noun* [from Greek *theos* = a god, + *-logy*]

theorem *noun* a mathematical statement that can be proved by reasoning. [from Greek *theorema* = theory]

theoretical *adjective* based on theory not on experience. **theoretically** *adverb*

theorise *verb* (**theorised**, **theorising**) form a theory or theories.

theory *noun* (*plural* **theories**) **1** an idea or set of ideas put forward to explain something. **2** ideas (contrasted with *practice*). **3** the principles of a subject.

therapeutic (*say* therra-**pew**-tik) *adjective* treating or curing a disease etc., *Sunshine can have a therapeutic effect.*

therapy *noun* treatment to cure a disease etc. [from Greek *therapeia* = healing]

there *adverb* **1** in or to that place etc. **2** used to call attention to something (*There's a good boy!*) or to introduce a sentence where the verb comes before its subject (*There was plenty to eat*).
go there talk about, *Let's not go there.*

thereabouts *adverb* near there.

thereafter *adverb* from then or there onwards.

thereby *adverb* by that means; because of that.

therefore *adverb* for that reason.

thereupon *adverb* after that.

therm *noun* a unit for measuring heat, especially from gas. [from Greek *therme* = heat]

thermal *adjective* **1** of heat; worked by heat. **2** producing heat, *thermal springs.*

thermo- *prefix* heat.

thermodynamics *noun* the science dealing with the relation between heat and other forms of energy.

thermometer *noun* a device for measuring temperature. [from *thermo-* + *meter*]

thermos *noun* (*trade mark*) a vacuum flask.

thermostat *noun* a device that automatically keeps the temperature of a room or device steady. **thermostatic** *adjective*, **thermostatically** *adverb* [from *thermo-*, + Greek *statos* = standing]

thesaurus (*say* thi-**sor**-us) *noun* (*plural* **thesauri**) a kind of dictionary containing sets of words grouped according to their meaning. [from Greek, = treasury]

these *plural* of **this**.

thesis *noun* (*plural* **theses**) a theory put forward, especially a long essay written by a candidate for a university degree. [from Greek, = placing]

thews *plural noun* (*literary*) muscles; muscular strength.

they *pronoun* **1** the people or things being talked about. **2** people in general, *They say the show is a great success.* **3** (*informal*) he or she; a person, *I am never angry with anyone unless they deserve it.*

they're (*mainly spoken*) they are.

thick *adjective* **1** measuring a lot or a certain amount between opposite surfaces. **2** (of a line) broad, not fine. **3** crowded with things; dense, *a thick forest; thick fog.* **4** fairly stiff, *thick cream.* **5** (*informal*) stupid. **thickly** *adverb*, **thickness** *noun*

thicken *verb* make or become thicker.

thicket *noun* a number of shrubs and small trees etc. growing close together.

thickset *adjective* **1** with parts placed or growing close together. **2** having a stocky or burly body.

thief *noun* (*plural* **thieves**) a person who steals things. **thievish** *adjective*, **thievery** *noun*, **thieving** *noun*

thigh *noun* the part of the leg between the hip and the knee.

thimble *noun* a small metal or plastic cap worn on the end of the finger to push the needle in sewing.

thin *adjective* (**thinner**, **thinnest**) **1** not thick; not fat. **2** feeble, *a thin excuse.* **thinly** *adverb*, **thinness** *noun*

thin *verb* (**thinned**, **thinning**) make or become less thick. **thinner** *noun*

thine *adjective & possessive pronoun* (*old use*) belonging to thee.

thing *noun* an object; that which can be seen, touched, thought about, etc.

think *verb* (**thought**, **thinking**) **1** use your mind; form connected ideas. **2** have as an idea or opinion, *We think we shall win.* **thinker** *noun*

think-tank *noun* a group of experts advising the government or some other body.

third *adjective* next after the second. **thirdly** *adverb*

third *noun* **1** the third person or thing. **2** one of three equal parts of something.

Third World the poorest and underdeveloped countries of Asia, Africa, and South America (originally called 'third' because they were not considered to be politically connected with either the USA or the former Soviet Union).

thirst *noun* **1** a feeling of dryness in the mouth and throat, causing a desire to drink. **2** a strong desire, *a thirst for adventure.* **thirsty** *adjective*, **thirstily** *adverb*

thirteen *noun & adjective* the number 13; one more than twelve. **thirteenth** *adjective & noun*

thirty *noun & adjective* (*plural* **thirties**) the number 30; three times ten. **thirtieth** *adjective & noun*

this *adjective & pronoun* (*plural* **these**) the one here, *This house is ours. Whose is this?*

this *adverb* to such an extent, *I'm surprised he got this far.*

thistle *noun* a prickly wild plant with purple, white, or yellow flowers.

thistledown *noun* the very light fluff on thistle seeds.

thither *adverb* (*old use*) to that place.

thong *noun* **1** a narrow strip of leather etc. used for fastening things. **2** skimpy underpants or bathing suit bottom. **thongs** *plural noun* jandals.

thorax *noun* (*plural* **thoraxes**) the part of the body between the head or neck and the abdomen. **thoracic** *adjective* [Greek, = breastplate]

thorn *noun* **1** a small pointed growth on the stem of a plant. **2** a thorny tree or shrub.

thorny *adjective* (**thornier**, **thorniest**) **1** having many thorns. **2** like a thorn. **3** difficult, *a thorny problem.*

thorough *adjective* **1** done or doing things carefully and in detail. **2** complete in every way, *a thorough mess.* **thoroughly** *adverb*, **thoroughness** *noun*

thoroughbred *adjective* bred of pure or pedigree stock. **thoroughbred** *noun*

thoroughfare *noun* a public road or path that is open at both ends.

those *plural* of **that**.

thou *pronoun* (*old use*, in speaking to one person) you.

though *conjunction* in spite of the fact that; even if, *We must look for it, though we probably shan't find it.*

though *adverb* however, *She's right, though.*

thought *noun* **1** something that you think; an idea or opinion. **2** the process of thinking, *She was deep in thought.*

thought *past tense* of **think**.

thoughtful *adjective* **1** thinking a lot. **2** showing thought for other people's needs; considerate. **thoughtfully** *adverb*, **thoughtfulness** *noun*

thoughtless *adjective* **1** careless, not thinking of what may happen. **2** inconsiderate. **thoughtlessly** *adverb*, **thoughtlessness** *noun*

thousand *noun & adjective* the number 1,000; ten hundred. **thousandth** *adjective & noun*

USAGE Say a *few thousand* (not 'a few thousands').

thrall *noun* slavery; servitude, *in thrall.*

thrash *verb* **1** beat with a stick or whip; keep hitting very hard. **2** defeat someone thoroughly. **3** move violently, *The crocodile thrashed its tail.* **4** (*informal*) overwork.

thread *noun* **1** a thin length of any substance. **2** a length of spun cotton, wool, or nylon etc. used for making cloth or in sewing or knitting. **3** the spiral ridge round a screw. **threads** (*plural noun*) (*informal*) clothes.

thread *verb* **1** put a thread through the eye of a needle. **2** pass a strip of film etc. through or round something. **3** put beads on a thread.

threadbare *adjective* (of cloth) with the surface worn away so that the threads show.

threat *noun* **1** a warning that you will punish, hurt, or harm a person or thing. **2** a sign of something undesirable. **3** a person or thing causing danger.

threaten *verb* **1** make threats against someone. **2** be a threat or danger to a person or thing.

three *noun & adjective* the number 3; one more than two.

three-dimensional *adjective* having three dimensions (length, width, and height or depth).

three-quarter *noun* (in a New Zealand rugby team) any of the players positioned between the five-eighths and the full-back.

thresh *verb* beat corn so as to separate the grain from the husks.

thresher shark a shark with a long upper lobe to its tail.

threshold *noun* **1** a slab of stone or board etc. forming the bottom of a doorway; the entrance. **2** the beginning, *We are on the threshold of a great discovery.*

thrice *adverb* (*old use*) three times.

thrift *noun* being economical with money or resources. **thrifty** *adjective*, **thriftily** *adverb* [same origin as *thrive*]

thrill *noun* **1** a feeling of excitement. **2** an exciting experience. **3** a wave of emotion.

thrill *verb* **1** feel excitement. **2** cause someone to feel excitement.

thriller *noun* an exciting story, play, or movie, usually about crime.

thrive *verb* (**thrived** or **throve**, **thriving**) grow strongly; prosper or be successful. [from Old Norse *thrifask* = prosper]

throat *noun* **1** the tube in the neck that takes food and drink down into the body. **2** the front of the neck.

throaty *adjective* **1** produced deep in the throat, *a throaty chuckle.* **2** hoarse. **throatily** *adverb*

throb *verb* (**throbbed**, **throbbing**) beat or vibrate with a strong rhythm, *My heart throbbed.* **throb** *noun*

throes *plural noun* severe pangs of pain. **in the throes of** (*informal*) struggling with, *We are in the throes of exams.*

thrombosis *noun* the formation of a clot of blood in the body. [from Greek *thrombos* = lump]

throne *noun* a special chair for a king, queen, or bishop at ceremonies. [from Greek *thronos* = high seat]

throng *noun* a crowd of people.

throng *verb* crowd, *People thronged the streets.*

throttle *noun* a device controlling the flow of fuel to an engine; an accelerator.

throttle *verb* (**throttled**, **throttling**) strangle. **throttle back** or **down** reduce the speed of an engine by partially closing the throttle.

through *preposition* **1** from one end or side to the other end or side of, *Climb through the window.* **2** by means of; because of, *We lost it through carelessness.* **3** at the end of; having finished successfully, *He is through his exam.* **4** (mainly American) up to and including, *They discussed items one through four.*

through *adverb* **1** through something, *We squeezed through.* **2** with a telephone connection made, *I'll put you through to the president.* **3** finished, *Wait till I'm through with these papers.*

through *adjective* going through something, *No through road.*

throughout *preposition & adverb* all the way through.

throve *past tense* of **thrive**.

throw *verb* (**threw**, **thrown**, **throwing**) **1** send a person or thing through the air. **2** put carelessly or hastily. **3** move part of your body quickly, *He threw his head back.* **4** cause to be in a certain condition etc., *It threw us into confusion.* **5** move a switch or lever so as to operate it. **6** shape a pot on a potter's wheel. **throw** *noun*, **thrower** *noun* **throw away** put something out as being useless or unwanted; waste, *You threw away an opportunity.*

thrum *verb* (**thrummed**, **thrumming**) sound monotonously; strum. **thrum** *noun*

thrush[1] *noun* (*plural* **thrushes**) a songbird with a speckled breast.

thrush[2] *noun* a disease causing tiny white patches in the mouth and throat.

thrust *verb* (**thrust**, **thrusting**) push hard. **thrust** *noun*

thud *verb* (**thudded**, **thudding**) make the dull sound of a heavy knock or fall. **thud** *noun*

thug *noun* a violent ruffian. **thuggery** *noun* [the Thugs were robbers in India in the 17th–19th centuries]

thumb *noun* the short thick finger set apart from the other four.
be under a person's thumb be completely under his or her influence.

thumb *verb* turn the pages of a book etc. quickly with your thumb.
thumb a lift hitchhike.

thumbnail *noun* **1** a nail of a thumb. **2** a concise form. **3** a small version of a computer image or layout.

thumbscrew *noun* a former instrument of torture for squeezing the thumb.

thumb stick *noun* a small, portable memory storage device about the size of a thumb. A thumb stick is also known as a flash drive, a flash stick, a memory stick, a pen drive, a thumb drive or USB drive.

thump *verb* **1** hit or knock something heavily. **2** punch. **3** thud. **thump** *noun*

thunder *noun* **1** the loud noise that goes with lightning. **2** a similar noise, *thunders of applause.* **thunderous** *adjective,* **thunderstorm** *noun,* **thundery** *adjective*

thunder *verb* **1** sound with thunder. **2** make a noise like thunder; speak loudly.

thunderbolt *noun* a lightning-flash thought of as a destructive missile.

thunderstruck *adjective* amazed.

Thursday *noun* the day after Wednesday.

thus *adverb* **1** in this way, *Hold the wheel thus.* **2** therefore.

thwart *verb* frustrate.

thy *adjective* (*old use*) belonging to thee.

thyme (*say as* time) *noun* a herb with fragrant leaves. [from Greek *thymon*]

thyroid gland a large gland at the front of the neck. [from Greek *thyreos* = shield]

thyself *pronoun* (*old use*) thou or thee and nobody else. (Compare *herself.*)

tī *noun* the cabbage-tree. [Māori]

tiara (*say* tee-**ar**-a) *noun* a woman's jewelled crescent-shaped ornament worn like a crown.

tic *noun* an unintentional twitch of a muscle, especially of the face. [French]

tick[1] *noun* **1** a small mark (usually ✓) put by something to show that it is correct or has been checked. **2** a regular clicking sound, especially that made by a clock or watch. **3** (*informal*) a moment.

tick[1] *verb* **1** put a tick by something. **2** make the sound of a tick.
tick off (*slang*) reprimand someone.

tick[2] *noun* a blood-sucking insect.

ticket *noun* **1** a printed piece of paper or card that allows a person to travel on a bus or train, see a show, etc. **2** a label showing a thing's price.

tickle *verb* (**tickled, tickling**) **1** touch a person's skin lightly so as to cause a slight tingling feeling. **2** (of a part of the body) have a slight tingling or itching feeling. **3** amuse or please somebody.

ticklish *adjective* **1** likely to laugh or wriggle when tickled. **2** awkward; difficult, *a ticklish situation.*

tidal *adjective* of or affected by tides.
tidal wave a huge sea-wave.

tiddler *noun* (*informal*) a very small fish.

tiddly-wink *noun* a small counter flicked into a cup by pressing with another counter in the game of **tiddly-winks**.

tide *noun* **1** the regular rise and fall in the level of the sea which usually happens twice a day. **2** (*old use*) a time or season, *Christmas-tide.*

tide *verb* (**tided, tiding**) **tide a person over** provide him or her with what is needed, for a short time.

tidings *plural noun* news.

tidy *adjective* (**tidier, tidiest**) **1** with everything in its right place; orderly. **2** (*informal*) fairly large, *It costs a tidy amount.* **tidily** *adverb,* **tidiness** *noun*

tidy *verb* (**tidied, tidying**) make a thing tidy.

tie *verb* (**tied, tying**) **1** fasten with string, ribbon, etc. **2** arrange something into a knot or bow. **3** make the same score as another competitor.

tie *noun* **1** a necktie. **2** a result when two or more competitors have equal scores.

tīeke *noun* a New Zealand bird, the saddleback. [Māori]

tier (*say* teer) *noun* each of a series of rows or levels etc. placed one above the other. **tiered** *adjective*

tiff *noun* a slight quarrel.

tiger *noun* a large wild animal of the cat family, with yellow and black stripes.

tight *adjective* **1** fitting very closely. **2** firmly fastened. **3** fully stretched; tense. **4** in short supply, *Money is tight at the moment.* **5** stingy, *He is very tight with his money.* **6** (*slang*) drunk. **tightly** *adverb,* **tightness** *noun*

tighten *verb* make or become tighter.

tightrope *noun* a tightly stretched rope high above the ground, on which acrobats perform.

tights *plural noun* a garment that fits tightly over the feet, legs, and lower part of the body.

tigress *noun* a female tiger.

tika *adjective* correct, proper. [Māori]
tikanga Māori Māori customs and procedures.

tiki *noun* a carved human figure; this as a pendant, heitiki. [Māori]

tile *noun* a thin piece of baked clay or other hard material, used in rows for covering roofs, walls, or floors. **tiled** *adjective*

till[1] *preposition & conjunction* until. [from Old English *til* = to]

> USAGE It is better to use *until* rather than *till* when the word stands first in a sentence (e.g. *Until last year we had never been abroad*) or when you are speaking or writing formally.

till[2] *noun* a drawer or box for money in a shop; a cash register. [origin unknown]

till[3] *verb* cultivate land. [from Old English *tilian* = try]

tiller *noun* a handle used to turn a boat's rudder.

tilt *verb* move into a sloping position.

tilt *noun* a sloping position.
at full tilt at full speed or force.

timber *noun* **1** wood for building or making things. **2** a wooden beam. **3** the framework of deer antlers.

timbered *adjective* made of wood or with a wooden framework, *timbered houses.*

timbre (*say* tambr) *noun* the quality of a voice or musical sound. [French]

time *noun* **1** all the years of the past, present, and future; the continuous existence of the universe. **2** a particular point or portion of time. **3** an occasion, *the first time I saw him.* **4** a period suitable or available for something, *Is there time for a cup of tea?* **5** a system of measuring time, *Greenwich Mean Time.* **6** (in music) rhythm depending on the number and accentuation of beats in the bar. **7** (in mathematics) **times** multiplied by, *Five times three is 15* ($5 \times 3 = 15$).
in time not late; eventually.
on time punctual.

time *verb* (**timed, timing**) **1** measure how long something takes. **2** arrange when something is to happen. **timer** *noun*

timeless *adjective* not affected by the passage of time; eternal.

time-limit *noun* a fixed amount of time within which something must be done.

timely *adjective* happening at a suitable or useful time, *a timely warning.*

time-share *noun* **1** a system of multiple ownership of a holiday apartment, with each owner using the property for a specified time each year. **2** a property owned in this way.

timetable *noun* a list showing the times when things will happen, e.g. when buses or trains will arrive and depart, or when school lessons will take place.

timid *adjective* easily frightened.
timidly *adverb*, **timidity** *noun* [from Latin *timidus* = nervous]

timing *noun* the way something is timed.

timorous *adjective* timid. [from Latin *timor* = fear]

timpani *plural noun* kettledrums. [Italian]

tin *noun* **1** a silvery-white metal. **2** a metal container for food.

tin *verb* (**tinned, tinning**) seal food in a tin to preserve it.

tincture *noun* **1** a solution of medicine in alcohol. **2** a slight trace of something. [same origin as *tint*]

tinder *noun* any dry substance that catches fire easily.

tine *noun* a point or prong of a fork, harrow, or antler.

tinge *verb* (**tinged, tingeing**) colour something slightly; tint. **tinge** *noun* [same origin as *tint*]

tingle *verb* (**tingled, tingling**) have a slight pricking or stinging feeling.
tingle *noun*

tinker *noun* (*old use*) a person travelling about to mend pots and pans etc.

tinker *verb* work at something casually, trying to improve or mend it.

tinkle *verb* (**tinkled, tinkling**) make a gentle ringing sound. **tinkle** *noun*

tinny *adjective* **1** of tin; like tin. **2** flimsy, poorly made. **3** (*NZ, informal*) lucky.

tinny *noun* **1** (*NZ & Australia, informal*) a can of beer. **2** (*NZ, informal*) a cannabis leaf wrapped in foil. **3** (*NZ, informal*) an aluminium boat.

tino pai *adjective* (*NZ*) excellent. [Māori]

tino rangatiratanga *noun* (*NZ*) sovereignty or self-determination.

tinpot *adjective* (*NZ, informal*) **1** cheap. **2** small; pathetic.

tinsel *noun* strips of glittering material used for decoration.

tint *noun* a shade of colour, especially a pale one.

tint *verb* colour something slightly. [from Latin *tinctum* = stained]

tiny *adjective* (**tinier, tiniest**) very small.

tip[1] *noun* the part right at the top or end of something.

tip[1] *verb* (**tipped, tipping**) put a tip on something.

tip² *noun* **1** a small present of money given to someone who has helped you. **2** a small but useful piece of advice; a hint. **3** a slight push.

tip² *verb* (**tipped**, **tipping**) **1** give a person a tip. **2** name as a likely winner, *Which team would you tip to win the championship?*
tipper *noun*

tip³ *verb* (**tipped**, **tipping**) **1** tilt; topple. **2** empty rubbish somewhere.

tip³ *noun* **1** the action of tipping something. **2** a place where rubbish etc. is tipped.

tipple *verb* (**tippled**, **tippling**) drink alcohol.
tipple *noun*, **tippler** *noun*

tipsy *adjective* drunk. [from *tip³*]

tiptoe *verb* (**tiptoed**, **tiptoeing**) walk on your toes very quietly or carefully.
on tiptoe walking or standing on your toes.

tiptop *adjective* (*informal*) excellent; very best, *in tiptop condition.* [from *tip¹*]

tipuna *noun* = **tupuna**.

tirade (*say* ty-**rayd**) *noun* a long angry or violent speech.

tire *verb* (**tired**, **tiring**) make or become tired.

tired *adjective* feeling that you need to sleep or rest.
tired of having had enough of something and impatient or bored with it.

tiresome *adjective* annoying.

tiriti *noun* the Treaty of Waitangi. [Māori]

tiro *noun* (*plural* **tiros**) a beginner. [Latin, = recruit]

tissue *noun* **1** tissue-paper. **2** a paper handkerchief. **3** the substance forming any part of the body of an animal or plant, *bone-tissue.*

tissue-paper *noun* very thin soft paper used for wrapping and packing things.

tit¹ *noun* a kind of small bird.

tit² *noun* **tit for tat** something equal given in return; retaliation.

titanic (*say* ty-**tan**-ik) *adjective* huge. [from the Titans, gods and goddesses in Greek mythology]

titbit *noun* a nice little piece of something, e.g. of food, gossip, or information.

tithe *noun* one-tenth of a year's output from a farm etc., formerly paid as tax to support the clergy and church. [from Old English *teotha* = tenth]

tītī *noun* the mutton-bird. [Māori]

titillate *verb* (**titillated**, **titillating**) stimulate something pleasantly. **titillation** *noun*

titipounamu *noun* a New Zealand bird, the rifleman. [Māori]

titivate *verb* (**titivated**, **titivating**) put the finishing touches to something; smarten up.
titivation *noun*

title *noun* **1** the name of a book, film, song, etc. **2** a word used to show a person's rank or position, e.g. *Dr, Lord, Mrs.* **3** a championship in sport, *the world heavyweight title.* **4** a legal right to something. [from Latin *titulus* = title]

titled *adjective* having a title as a noble.

tītoki *noun* a timber tree with red flowers. [Māori]

tī-tree *noun* **1** the ti. **2** an incorrect form of *tea-tree.*

titter *verb & noun* giggle.

TNT *abbreviation* trinitrotoluene, a powerful explosive.

to *preposition* This word is used to show (**1**) direction or arrival at a position (*We walked to school. He rose to power*), (**2**) limit (*from noon to two o'clock*), (**3**) comparison (*We won by six goals to three*), (**4**) receiving or being affected by something (*Give it to me. Be kind to animals*).

to used before a verb to form an infinitive (*I want to see him*) or to show purpose etc. (*He does that to annoy us*), or alone when the verb is understood (*We meant to go but forgot to*).

to *adverb* **1** to or in the proper or closed position or condition, *Push the door to.* **2** into a state of activity, *We set to and cleaned the kitchen.*
to and fro backwards and forwards.

toad *noun* a frog-like animal that lives chiefly on land.

toadstool *noun* a fungus (usually poisonous) with a round top on a stalk.

toady *verb* (**toadied**, **toadying**) flatter someone so as to make them want to like or help you. **toady** *noun*

toast *verb* **1** heat bread etc. to make it brown and crisp. **2** warm something in front of a fire etc. **3** drink in honour of someone.

toast *noun* **1** toasted bread. **2** the call to drink in honour of someone; the person honoured in this way. [from Latin *tostum* = dried up]

toaster *noun* an electrical device for toasting bread.

toatoa *noun* a kind of small tree. [Māori]

tobacco *noun* the dried leaves of certain plants prepared for smoking or making snuff.

tobacconist *noun* a shopkeeper who sells cigarettes, cigars, etc.

toboggan *noun* a small sledge used for sliding downhill. **tobogganing** *noun*

tocsin *noun* a bell rung as an alarm-signal.

today *noun* this present day, *Today is Monday.*

today *adverb* on this day, *Have you seen him today?*

toddler *noun* a young child who has only recently learnt to walk. **toddle** *verb*

toddy *noun* a sweetened drink made with spirits and hot water.

to-do *noun* a fuss; a commotion.

toe *noun* **1** any of the separate parts (five in humans) at the end of each foot. **2** the part of a shoe or sock etc. that covers the toes.

toetoe *noun* a New Zealand grass with tall feathery flowerheads. [Māori]

toey *adjective* (*NZ, informal*) tense, eager to go.

toffee *noun* a sticky sweet made from heated butter and sugar.

tofu *noun* a product made from soya beans, used as a meat substitute. [Japanese]

toga (*say* **toh**-ga) *noun* a long loose garment worn by men in ancient Rome.

together *adverb* with another person or thing; with each other, *They went to the party together*. [from *to* + *gather*]

toggle *noun* a short piece of wood or metal etc. used like a button.

togs *plural noun* (*NZ, informal*) a swimming costume.

toheroa *noun* an edible shellfish. [Māori]

tohunga *noun* a priest or learned person. [Māori]

toil *verb* **1** work hard. **2** move slowly and with difficulty. **toiler** *noun*

toil *noun* hard work.

toilet *noun* **1** a bowl-like fitment in which the body can get rid of its waste matter. **2** a room containing a toilet. **3** the process of washing, dressing, and tidying yourself.

toilet-paper *noun* paper for use in a toilet.

toitoi *noun* toetoe.

Tokelauan *noun* a person who lives in or comes from Tokelau, a group of three small South Pacific Islands.

token *noun* **1** a piece of metal or plastic bought for use instead of money, *milk tokens*. **2** a voucher or coupon that can be exchanged for goods. **3** a sign or signal of something, *a token of our friendship*.

tokenism *noun* granting only small concessions, especially to a minority or oppressed group.

toki *noun* an adze or axe. [Māori]

tokotoko *noun* a walking-stick. [Māori]

tolerable *adjective* able to be tolerated. **tolerably** *adverb*

tolerant *adjective* tolerating things, especially other people's behaviour, beliefs, etc. **tolerantly** *adverb*, **tolerance** *noun*

tolerate *verb* (**tolerated**, **tolerating**) allow something without protesting or interfering. **toleration** *noun* [from Latin *tolerare* = endure]

toll[1] *noun* **1** a charge made for using a road, bridge, etc. **2** loss or damage caused, *The death toll in the earthquake is rising*. **3** a charge for a toll call.
toll call a long-distance telephone call. [from Greek *telos* = tax]

toll[2] *verb* ring a bell slowly. **toll** *noun*

tom *noun* a male cat. **tomcat** *noun* [short for *Thomas*, a man's name]

tomahawk *noun* a small axe used by American Indians. [from an American Indian word, = he cuts]

tomato *noun* (*plural* **tomatoes**) a soft round red or yellow fruit eaten as a vegetable.

tomb (*say* toom) *noun* a place where someone is buried; a monument built over this.

tomboy *noun* a girl who enjoys rough noisy games etc.

tombstone *noun* a memorial stone set up over a grave.

tome *noun* a large heavy book.

tommygun *noun* a small machine-gun. [from the name of its American inventor, J. T. Thompson (died 1940)]

tomo *noun* a dip or hole in limestone areas. [Māori *tomo* = be filled]

tomorrow *noun & adverb* the day after today.

tomtit *noun* a small songbird.

tom-tom *noun* a drum with a low sound; a small drum beaten with the hands.

ton *noun* **1** an imperial unit of mass or weight, equivalent to about 1,016 kilograms. **2** a large amount, *There's tons of room*. **3** (*slang*) a speed of 100 miles per hour. **4** (*informal*) a century in cricket.
metric ton 1,000 kilograms.

tone *noun* **1** a sound in music or of the voice. **2** each of the five larger intervals between notes in a musical scale (the smaller intervals are *semitones*). **3** a shade of a colour. **4** the quality or character of something, *a cheerful tone*. **tonal** *adjective*, **tonally** *adverb*

tone *verb* (**toned**, **toning**) **1** give a particular tone or quality to something. **2** be harmonious in colour.
tone down make a thing quieter or less bright or less harsh.
tone up make a thing brighter or stronger. [from Greek *tonos* = tension]

toner *noun* **1** an ink-like substance used in printers and photocopiers. **2** a cosmetic for tightening the pores of the skin.

Tongan *noun* **1** a person born in or living in Tonga. **2** the language of Tonga. **Tongan** *adjective*

tongs *plural noun* a tool with two arms joined at one end, used to pick up or hold things.

tongue *noun* **1** the long soft muscular part that moves about inside the mouth. **2** a language. **3** a projecting strip or flap. **4** a pointed flame.

tongue-tied *adjective* too shy to speak.

tongue-twister *noun* something that is difficult to say quickly and correctly, e.g. 'She sells sea shells'.

tonic *noun* **1** a medicine etc. that makes a person healthier or stronger. **2** a keynote in music. **tonic** *adjective* [same origin as *tone*]

tonight *noun & adverb* this evening or night.

tonnage *noun* the amount a ship or ships can carry, expressed in tons.

tonne *noun* a unit of mass or weight equal to 1,000 kilograms.

tonsil *noun* either of two small masses of soft tissue at the sides of the throat.

tonsillitis *noun* inflammation of the tonsils.

too *adverb* **1** also, *Take the others too.* **2** more than is wanted or allowed etc., *That's too much sugar for me.*

tool *noun* an object that helps you to do a particular job, *A saw is a tool for cutting wood or metal.*

toot[1] *noun* a short sound produced by a horn. **toot** *verb*

toot[2] *noun* = **tutu**[2].

tooth *noun* (*plural* **teeth**) **1** any of the hard white bony parts that are rooted in the gums, used for biting and chewing things. **2** each of a row of sharp parts or projections, *the teeth of a saw.* **toothache** *noun,* **toothbrush** *noun,* **toothed** *adjective*
fight tooth and nail fight very fiercely.

toothpaste *noun* a paste for cleaning your teeth.

toothpick *noun* a small pointed piece of wood etc. for removing bits of food from between your teeth.

toothy *adjective* having large teeth.

top[1] *noun* **1** the highest part of something. **2** the upper surface. **3** the covering or stopper of a bottle, jar, etc. **4** a garment for the upper part of the body.
on top of in addition to something.
over the top (*informal*) excessive.

top[1] *adjective* highest, *at top speed.*
top hat a man's tall stiff black or grey hat worn with formal clothes.

top[1] *verb* (**topped, topping**) **1** put a top on something. **2** be at the top of something, *She tops the list.* **3** remove the top of something.
top up fill up something that is half empty.

top[2] *noun* a toy that can be made to spin on its point.

topaz *noun* a kind of gem, often yellow.

top-dress *verb* apply fertiliser to the ground without digging it in.

top-heavy *adjective* too heavy at the top and likely to overbalance.

topic *noun* a subject to write, learn, or talk about. [from Greek *topos* = place]

topical *adjective* connected with things that are happening now, *a topical film.* **topically** *adverb,* **topicality** *noun*

topless *adjective* not wearing any clothes on the top half of the body.

topmost *adjective* highest.

topography (*say* top-**og**-ra-fee) *noun* the position of the rivers, mountains, roads, buildings, etc. in a place. **topographical** *adjective* [from Greek *topos* = place, + *-graphy*]

topple *verb* (**toppled, toppling**) **1** fall over; totter and fall. **2** cause to fall; overthrow. [from *top*[1]]

topsy-turvy *adverb & adjective* upside-down; muddled.

torch *noun* (*plural* **torches**) **1** a small electric lamp for carrying in the hand. **2** a stick with burning material on the end, used as a light.

toreador (*say* **to**rree-a-dor) *noun* a bullfighter. [from Spanish *toro* = bull]

torment *verb* **1** cause a person to suffer greatly. **2** tease; keep annoying someone. **tormentor** *noun*

torment *noun* great suffering. [from Latin *tortum* = twisted]

tornado (*say* tor-**nay**-doh) *noun* (*plural* **tornadoes**) a violent storm or whirlwind. [from Spanish, = thunderstorm]

torpedo *noun* (*plural* **torpedoes**) a long tubular missile that can be sent under water to destroy ships. [Latin, = large sea-fish that can give an electric shock which causes numbness]

torpedo *verb* (**torpedoed, torpedoing**) attack or destroy with a torpedo.

torpid *adjective* slow-moving, not lively. **torpidly** *adverb,* **torpidity** *noun,* **torpor** *noun* [from Latin *torpidus* = numb]

torrent *noun* **1** a rushing stream; a great flow. **2** a great downpour. **torrential** *adjective*

torrid *adjective* very hot and dry. [from Latin *torridus* = parched]

torsion *noun* twisting, especially of one end of a thing while the other is held in a fixed position. [same origin as *torture*]

torso *noun* (*plural* **torsos**) the trunk of the human body. [Italian, = stump]

tortoise *noun* a slow-moving animal with a shell over its body.

tortoiseshell *noun* **1** the mottled brown and yellow shell of certain turtles, used for making combs etc. **2** a cat or butterfly with mottled brown colouring.

tortuous *adjective* full of twists and turns. **tortuosity** *noun* [from Latin *tortum* = twisted]

torture *verb* (**tortured**, **torturing**) make a person feel great pain or worry. **torture** *noun*, **torturer** *noun* [from Latin *tortum* = twisted]

toss *verb* **1** throw, especially up into the air. **2** spin a coin to decide something according to which side of it is upwards after it falls. **3** move restlessly or unevenly from side to side. **toss** *noun*
not give a toss (*slang*) not care.

toss-up *noun* **1** the tossing of a coin. **2** an even chance.

tot[1] *noun* **1** a small child. **2** (*informal*) a small amount of spirits, *a tot of rum.*

tot[2] *verb* (**totted**, **totting**) **tot up** (*informal*) add up. [short for *total*]

total *adjective* **1** including everything, *the total amount.* **2** complete, *total darkness.* **totally** *adverb*

total *noun* the amount you get by adding everything together.

total *verb* (**totalled**, **totalling**) **1** reckon up the total. **2** amount to something. **3** (*informal*) wreck a car completely. [from Latin *totum* = the whole]

totalitarian *adjective* using a form of government where people are not allowed to form rival political parties.

totality *noun* **1** being total. **2** a total.

tōtara *noun* **1** a large timber tree. **2** its wood. [Māori]

totem-pole *noun* a pole carved or painted by North American Indians with the emblems (*totems*) of their tribes or families.

totter *verb* walk unsteadily; wobble. **tottery** *adjective*

toucan (*say* **too**-kan) *noun* a tropical American bird with a huge beak.

touch *verb* **1** put your hand or fingers etc. on something lightly. **2** be or come together so that there is no space between. **3** hit gently. **4** move or meddle with something. **5** reach, *The thermometer touched 30° Celsius.* **6** arouse sympathy etc. in someone, *The sad story touched our hearts.* **7** (*slang*) persuade someone to give or lend money.
touch and go an uncertain situation.
touch down (of an aircraft) land.
touch up improve something by making small additions or changes.

touch *noun* (*plural* **touches**) **1** the action of touching. **2** the ability to feel things by touching them. **3** a small amount; a small thing done, *the finishing touches.* **4** a special skill or style of workmanship, *She hasn't lost her touch.* **5** communication with someone, *We lost touch with him.* **6** (in rugby, hockey, etc.) the area beyond the touchlines, where the ball is out of play. **7** (in full **touch football**) a game based on rugby played by teams of seven, with touching instead of tackling.
touch judge an official in rugby who indicates where the ball has gone into touch.

touchable *adjective* able to be touched.

touchdown *noun* **1** a landing. **2** (rugby) a try.

touching *adjective* arousing kindly feelings such as pity or sympathy.

touchline *noun* (in rugby, soccer, etc.) a line on each side of the field marking the boundary of the playing area.

touchstone *noun* a test by which the quality of something is judged. [formerly, a kind of stone against which gold and silver were rubbed to test their purity]

touchy *adjective* (**touchier**, **touchiest**) easily offended. **touchily** *adverb*, **touchiness** *noun*

tough *adjective* **1** strong; difficult to break or damage. **2** difficult to chew. **3** firm; stubborn; rough or violent, *tough criminals.* **4** difficult, *a tough job.* **toughly** *adverb*, **toughness** *noun*

toughen *verb* make or become tough.

tour *noun* a journey visiting several places.

tour *verb* make a tour. [same origin as *turn*]

tourist *noun* a person who makes a tour or visits a place for pleasure. **tourism** *noun*

tournament *noun* a series of contests.

tourniquet (*say* **toor**-nik-ay) *noun* a strip of material etc. pulled tightly round an arm or leg to stop bleeding from an artery.

tousle (*say* **how**-zel) *verb* (**tousled**, **tousling**) ruffle someone's hair.

tout (*rhymes with* scout) *verb* **1** solicit; try to obtain orders for goods or services. **2** onsell a ticket or a product at a profit.

tout *noun* a person who touts things, *ticket touts.*

tow[1] (*rhymes with* go) *verb* pull something along behind you. **tow** *noun*

tow[2] (*rhymes with* go) *noun* short light-coloured fibres of flax or hemp.

tōwai *noun* a large timber tree. [Māori]

toward *preposition* towards.

towards *preposition* **1** in the direction of, *She walked towards the sea.* **2** in relation to; regarding, *He behaved kindly towards his children.* **3** as a contribution to, *Put the money towards a new bicycle.* **4** near, *towards four o'clock.*

towel *noun* a piece of absorbent cloth for drying things. **towelling** *noun*

tower *noun* a tall narrow building.

tower *verb* be very high; be taller than others, *Skyscrapers towered over the city.* [from Latin *turris* = tower]

town *noun* a place with many houses, shops, offices, and other buildings.
town hall a building with offices for the local council and/or a hall for public events.
town house a city or suburban dwelling of a modern type, often semi-detached and of two storeys, with only a small amount of garden. [from Old English *tun* = enclosure]

townie *noun* (*informal*) a country person's name for someone living in a town or city.

township *noun* (*NZ*) a small town or settlement.

toxic *adjective* poisonous; caused by poison. **toxicity** *noun* [from Greek, = poison for arrows (*toxa* = arrows)]

toxicology *noun* the study of poisons. **toxicologist** *noun* [from *toxic* + *-logy*]

toxin *noun* a poisonous substance, especially one formed in the body by germs. [from *toxic*]

toy *noun* a thing to play with.

toy *adjective* **1** made as a toy. **2** (of a dog) of a very small breed kept as a pet, *a toy poodle.*

toy *verb* **toy with** handle a thing or consider an idea casually.

toyshop *noun* a shop that sells toys.

trace[1] *noun* **1** a mark left by a person or thing; a sign, *There was no trace of the thief.* **2** a very small amount.

trace[1] *verb* (**traced**, **tracing**) **1** copy a picture or map etc. by drawing over it on transparent paper. **2** follow the traces of a person or thing; find. **tracer** *noun*

trace[2] *noun* each of the two straps or ropes etc. by which a horse pulls a cart.
kick over the traces (of a person) become disobedient or reckless.

traceable *adjective* able to be traced.

tracery *noun* a decorative pattern of holes in stone, e.g. in a church window. [from *trace*[1]]

track *noun* **1** a mark or marks left by a moving person or thing. **2** a rough path made by being used. **3** a road or area of ground specially prepared for something (e.g. racing). **4** a set of rails for trains or trams etc. **5** a section of a record or along the length of a magnetic tape etc. **6** a continuous band round the wheels of a tank or tractor etc.
down the track (*NZ & Australia, informal*) in the future.
keep track of keep yourself informed about where something is or what someone is doing.
track suit a warm loose suit of the kind worn by athletes etc. before and after contests or for jogging.

track *verb* **1** follow the tracks left by a person or animal. **2** follow or observe something as it moves. **tracker** *noun*
track down find by searching.

tract[1] *noun* **1** an area of land. **2** a series of connected parts along which something passes, *the digestive tract.*

tract[2] *noun* a pamphlet containing a short essay, especially about religion.

traction *noun* **1** pulling a load. **2** a continuous pull on a limb etc. in medical treatment, *her leg is in traction.* **3** the grip of a tyre on a road. **4** (*informal*) attraction or appeal; momentum, *Her ideas gained some traction.* [from Latin *tractum* = pulled]

traction engine *noun* a steam or diesel engine for pulling a heavy load along a road or across a field etc.

tractor *noun* a motor vehicle for pulling farm machinery or other heavy loads. [same origin as *traction*]

trade *noun* **1** buying, selling, or exchanging goods. **2** business of a particular kind; the people working in this. **3** an occupation, especially a skilled craft.
trade mark a firm's registered emblem or name used to distinguish its goods etc. from those of other firms.
trade union (*plural* **trade unions**) a group of workers organised to help and protect workers in their own trade.

trade *verb* (**traded**, **trading**) buy, sell, or exchange things. **trader** *noun*
trade in give a thing as part of the payment for something new, *He traded in his motorcycle for a car.*

TradeMe *noun* (*NZ*) a large New Zealand Internet auction operator.

tradesman *noun* (*plural* **tradesmen**) a person employed in trade, especially one who sells or delivers goods.

tradition *noun* **1** the passing down of beliefs or customs etc. from one generation to another. **2** something passed on in this way. **traditional** *adjective*, **traditionally** *adverb* [from Latin *traditum* = handed on]

traffic *noun* **1** vehicles, ships, or aircraft moving along a route. **2** trading, especially when it is illegal or wrong, *drug traffic.*

traffic *verb* (**trafficked**, **trafficking**) trade. **trafficker** *noun*

traffic lights *plural noun* coloured lights used as a signal to traffic at road junctions etc.

tragedian (*say* tra-**jee**-dee-an) *noun* **1** a person who writes tragedies. **2** an actor in tragedies.

tragedy *noun* (*plural* **tragedies**) **1** a play with unhappy events or a sad ending. **2** a very sad event. [from Greek *tragos* = goat, + *oide* = song]

tragic *adjective* **1** very sad; causing sadness. **2** of tragedies, *a great tragic actor.* **tragically** *adverb*

trail *noun* **1** a track, scent, or other sign left where something has passed. **2** a path or track made through a wild region.
trail bike a light motorcycle used in rough country.

trail *verb* **1** follow the trail of something; track. **2** drag or be dragged along behind; lag behind. **3** hang down or float loosely. [from Latin *tragula* = net for dragging a river]

trailer *noun* **1** a truck or other container pulled along by a vehicle. **2** a short piece from a movie or television programme, shown in advance to advertise it.

train *noun* **1** a railway engine pulling a line of carriages or trucks that are linked together. **2** a number of people or animals moving in a line, *a camel train.* **3** a series of things, *a train of events.* **4** part of a long dress or robe that trails on the ground at the back.

train *verb* **1** give a person instruction or practice so that he or she becomes skilled. **2** practise, *She was training for the race.* **3** make something grow in a particular direction. **4** aim a gun etc., *Train that gun on the bridge.* [same origin as *traction*]

trainee *noun a* person being trained.

trainer *noun* **1** a person who trains people or animals. **2** (*mainly British*) a soft rubber-soled shoe of the kind worn for running or by athletes etc. while exercising.

traipse *verb* (**traipsed**, **traipsing**) trudge.

trait *noun* a characteristic. [from French]

traitor *noun* a person who betrays his or her country or friends. **traitorous** *adjective* [same origin as *tradition*]

trajectory *noun* (*plural* **trajectories**) the path taken by a moving object such as a bullet or rocket. [from *trans-*, + Latin *jactum* = thrown]

tram *noun* a public passenger vehicle running on rails in the road.

tramlines *plural noun* **1** rails for a tram. **2** the pair of parallel lines at the side of a tennis court.

tramp *noun* **1** a person without a home or job who walks from place to place. **2** (*NZ*) a long walk in bush or mountain country. **3** the sound of heavy footsteps.

tramp *verb* **1** walk with heavy footsteps. **2** (*NZ*) go on a lengthy walk in bush or mountain country. **tramper** *noun*, **tramping** *noun*

trample *verb* (**trampled**, **trampling**) tread heavily on something; crush something by treading on it.

trampoline *noun* a large piece of canvas joined to a frame by springs, used for jumping on in acrobatics. [from Italian *trampoli* = stilts]

trance *noun* a dreamy or unconscious condition rather like sleep. [same origin as *transit*]

tranquil *adjective* calm and quiet. **tranquilly** *adverb*, **tranquillity** *noun*

tranquilliser *noun* a medicine used to make a person feel calm.

trans- *prefix* across; through; beyond. [from Latin *trans* = across]

transact *verb* carry out business. **transaction** *noun*

transatlantic *adjective* across or on the other side of the Atlantic Ocean.

transcend *verb* go beyond something; surpass. [from *trans-*, + Latin *scandere* = climb]

transcribe *verb* (**transcribed**, **transcribing**) copy or write something out. **transcription** *noun* [from *trans-*, + Latin *scribere* = write]

transcript *noun* a written copy.

transept *noun* the part that is at right angles to the nave in a cross-shaped church. [from *trans-*, + Latin *septum* = partition]

transfer *verb* (**transferred**, **transferring**) **1** move a person or thing to another place. **2** hand over. **transferable** *adjective*, **transference** *noun*

transfer *noun* **1** the transferring of a person or thing. **2** a picture or design that can be transferred on to another surface. [from *trans-*, + Latin *ferre* = carry]

transfigure *verb* (**transfigured**, **transfiguring**) change the appearance of something greatly. **transfiguration** *noun*

transfix *verb* **1** pierce and fix with something pointed. **2** make a person or animal unable to move because of fear or surprise etc.

transform *verb* change the form or appearance or character of a person or thing. **transformation** *noun*

transformer *noun* a device used to change the voltage of an electric current.

transfusion *noun* putting blood taken from one person into another person's body. **transfuse** *verb* [from *trans-*, + Latin *fusum* = poured]

transgender *noun* a person whose gender identity does not match his or her original or assigned identity.

transgress *verb* break a rule or law etc. **transgression** *noun* [from *trans-*, + Latin *gressus* = gone]

transient *adjective* passing away quickly; not lasting. **transience** *noun* [from *trans-*, + Latin *iens* = going]

transistor *noun* **1** a tiny semiconductor device controlling a flow of electricity. **2** (also **transistor radio**) a radio receiver using transistors. **transistorised** *adjective* [from *transfer* + *resistor*]

transit *noun* the process of travelling across or through. [from *trans-*, + Latin *itum* = gone]

transition *noun* the process of changing from one condition or style etc. to another. **transitional** *adjective*

transitive *adjective* (of a verb) used with a direct object after it, e.g. *change* in *change your shoes* (but not in *change into dry shoes*). Compare *intransitive*. **transitively** *adverb*

Transit New Zealand *noun* (*NZ*) a Crown entity responsible for management, maintenance, and development of roads.

transitory *adjective* existing for a time but not lasting.

translate *verb* (**translated**, **translating**) **1** put something into another language. **2** change or convert to another form. **3** move from one place to another. **translatable** *adjective*, **translation** *noun*, **translator** *noun* [from *trans-*, + Latin *latum* = carried]

transliterate *verb* (**transliterated**, **transliterating**) put letters or words into letters of a different alphabet. **transliteration** *noun* [from *trans-*, + Latin *littera* = letter]

translucent (*say* tranz-**loo**-sent) *adjective* allowing light to shine through but not transparent. [from *trans-*, + Latin *lucens* = shining]

transmigration *noun* **1** migration. **2** the passing of a person's soul into another body after his or her death.

transmission *noun* **1** transmitting something. **2** a broadcast. **3** the gears by which power is transmitted from the engine to the wheels of a vehicle.

transmit *verb* (**transmitted**, **transmitting**) **1** send or pass on from one person or place to another. **2** send out a signal or broadcast etc. **transmitter** *noun* [from *trans-*, + Latin *mittere* = send]

transmutation *noun* the process of changing or being changed from one form or substance into another.

transom *noun* **1** a horizontal bar of wood or stone dividing a window or separating a door from a window above it. **2** a small window above a door.

transparency *noun* (*plural* **transparencies**) **1** being transparent. **2** a transparent photograph that can be projected on to a screen.

transparent *adjective* able to be seen through. [from *trans-*, + Latin *parens* = appearing]

transpire *verb* (**transpired**, **transpiring**) **1** (of information) become known; leak out. **2** (of plants) give off watery vapour from leaves etc. **transpiration** *noun* [from *trans-*, + Latin *spirare* = breathe]

transplant *verb* **1** remove a plant and put it to grow somewhere else. **2** transfer a part of the body to another person or animal. **transplantation** *noun*

transplant *noun* **1** the process of transplanting. **2** something transplanted.

transport *verb* take a person, animal, or thing from one place to another. **transportation** *noun*, **transporter** *noun*

transport *noun* the action or means of transporting people, animals, or things. [from *trans-*, + Latin *portare* = carry]

transpose *verb* (**transposed**, **transposing**) **1** change the position or order of something. **2** put a piece of music into a different key. **transposition** *noun* [from *trans-*, + Latin *positum* = placed]

trans-Tasman *adjective* between New Zealand and Australia, *trans-Tasman rivalry.*

transverse *adjective* lying across something. **transversely** *adverb* [from *trans-*, + Latin *versum* = turned]

trap *noun* **1** a device for catching and holding animals. **2** an arrangement for capturing, detecting, or cheating someone. **3** a device for collecting water etc. or preventing it from passing. **4** a two-wheeled carriage pulled by a horse.

trap *verb* (**trapped**, **trapping**) catch or hold in a trap. **trapper** *noun*

trapdoor *noun* a door in a floor, ceiling, or roof.

trapeze *noun* a bar hanging from two ropes as a swing for acrobats.

trapezium *noun* a quadrilateral in which two opposite sides are parallel and the other two are not. [from Greek *trapeza* = table]

trapezoid *noun* a quadrilateral in which no sides are parallel.

trappings *plural noun* **1** ornamental accessories or equipment etc., e.g. for officials. **2** ornamental harness for a horse.

trash *noun* rubbish; nonsense. **trashy** *adjective*

trauma (*say* **traw**-ma) *noun* a shock that produces a lasting effect on a person's mind. **traumatic** *adjective*, **traumatise** *verb* [Greek, = a wound]

travail *noun* (*old use*) hard or laborious work. **travail** *verb*

travel *verb* (**travelled**, **travelling**) move from place to place. **travel** *noun*, **traveller** *noun* [the original meaning was *travail*]

traverse *verb* (**traversed**, **traversing**) go across something. **traverse** *noun*, **traversal** *noun* [same origin as *transverse*]

travesty *noun* (*plural* **travesties**) a bad or ridiculous form of something, *His story is a travesty of the truth.* [from French *travesti* = having changed clothes]

trawl *verb* fish by dragging a large net along the sea-bed.

trawler *noun* a boat used in trawling.

tray *noun* **1** a flat piece of wood, metal, or plastic, usually with raised edges, for carrying cups, plates, food, etc. **2** an open container for holding letters etc. in an office.

treacherous *adjective* **1** betraying someone; disloyal. **2** not to be trusted. **treacherously** *adverb*, **treachery** *noun*

treacle *noun* a thick sticky liquid produced when sugar is purified. **treacly** *adjective*

tread *verb* (**trod**, **trodden**, **treading**) walk or put your foot on something.

tread *noun* **1** a sound or way of walking. **2** the top surface of a stair; the part you put your foot on. **3** the part of a tyre that touches the ground.

treadle *noun* a lever that you press with your foot to turn a wheel that works a machine.

treadmill *noun* **1** a wide mill-wheel turned by people or animals. **2** a fitness device. **3** a tedious or lengthy task.

treason *noun* the action of betraying your country. **treasonable** *adjective*, **treasonous** *adjective* [same origin as *tradition*]

treasure *noun* **1** a store of precious metals or jewels. **2** a precious thing or person.
treasure trove gold or silver etc. found hidden and with no known owner.

treasure *verb* (**treasured**, **treasuring**) value greatly something that you have. [from Greek *thesauros* = treasury]

treasure-hunt *noun* a game in which people try to find a hidden object.

treasurer *noun* a person in charge of the money of a club, society, etc.

treasury *noun* (*plural* **treasuries**) a place where money and valuables are kept.
the Treasury the government department in charge of a country's income.

treat *verb* **1** behave in a certain way towards a person or thing. **2** deal with a subject etc. **3** give medical care in order to cure a person or animal. **4** put something through a chemical or other process, *The fabric has been treated to make it waterproof.* **5** pay for someone else's food, drink, or entertainment, *I'll treat you to an ice-cream.*

treat *noun* **1** something special that gives pleasure. **2** the process of treating someone to food, drink, or entertainment. [from Latin *tractare* = to handle]

treatise *noun* a book or long essay on a subject. [same origin as *treat*]

treatment *noun* the process or manner of dealing with a person, animal, or thing.

treaty *noun* (*plural* **treaties**) a formal agreement between two or more countries. [same origin as *treat*]

Treaty of Waitangi a document setting out an agreement between certain Māori tribes and the British Crown, by which New Zealand became a British colony in February 1840. [Waitangi, a settlement in Northland where the first signatures and marks were put to the treaty]

treble *adjective* three times as much or as many.

treble *noun* **1** a treble amount. **2** a bet picking the winners of three selected races. **3** a person with a high-pitched or soprano voice.

treble *verb* (**trebled**, **trebling**) make or become three times as much or as many. [same origin as *triple*]

tree *noun* a tall plant with a single very thick hard stem or trunk that is usually without branches for some distance above the ground.
out of one's tree (*informal*) angry; silly; drunk.

tree-fern *noun* (*NZ*) a large fern with a straight woody stem.

tree-tomato *noun* (*NZ*) an older name for the tamarillo.

trefoil *noun* a plant with three small leaves (e.g. clover). [from Latin *tres* = three, + *folium* = leaf]

trek *noun* a long walk or ride.

trek *verb* (**trekked**, **trekking**) make a trek. [from Dutch *trekken* = pull]

trellis *noun* (*plural* **trellises**) a framework with crossing bars of wood or metal etc. to support climbing plants.

tremble *verb* (**trembled**, **trembling**) shake gently, especially with fear. **tremble** *noun*

tremendous *adjective* **1** very large; huge. **2** (*informal*) excellent. **tremendously** *adverb* [from Latin, = causing people to tremble]

tremor *noun* a shaking or trembling movement.

tremulous *adjective* trembling from nervousness or weakness. **tremulously** *adverb* [from Latin *tremulus* = trembling]

trench *noun* (*plural* **trenches**) a long narrow hole cut in the ground.

trench *verb* dig a trench or trenches.

trenchant *adjective* strong and effective, *trenchant criticism*.

trend *noun* the general direction in which something is going.

trendy *adjective* (*informal*) fashionable; following the latest trends. **trendily** *adverb*, **trendiness** *noun*

trepidation *noun* fear and anxiety; nervousness. [from Latin *trepidare* = be afraid]

trespass *verb* **1** go on someone's land or property unlawfully. **2** (*old use*) do wrong; sin. **trespasser** *noun*

trespass *noun* (*plural* **trespasses**) (*old use*) wrongdoing; sin. [from Old French *trespasser* = pass over (same origin as *trans-* + *pass*)]

tress *noun* (*plural* **tresses**) a lock of hair.

trestle *noun* each of a set of supports on which a board is rested to form a table. **trestle-table** *noun*

trevally *noun* (*NZ*) an edible fish.

tri- *prefix* three (as in *triangle*). [from Latin *tres* or Greek *treis* = three]

trial *noun* **1** testing a thing to see how good it is. **2** a test of qualities or ability. **3** the trying of a person in a lawcourt. **4** an annoying person or thing; a hardship.
on trial being tried. [from *try*]

trial *verb* **1** test a new product or process. **2** test something for suitability or performance.

triangle *noun* **1** a flat shape with three sides and three angles. **2** a percussion instrument made from a metal rod bent into a triangle. **triangular** *adjective* [from *tri-* + *angle*]

triathlon *noun* a three-part athletic contest in which competitors swim, then cycle, then run. **triathlete** *noun* [from *tri-* + Greek *athlon* = contest]

tribe *noun* **1** a group of families living in one area as a community, ruled by a chief. **2** a set of people. **tribal** *adjective*, **tribally** *adverb*, **tribesman** *noun*

tribulation *noun* great troubles.

tribunal (*say* try-**bew**-nal) *noun* a committee appointed to hear evidence and give judgements when there is a dispute.

tribune *noun* an official chosen by the people in ancient Rome.

tributary *noun* (*plural* **tributaries**) a river or stream that flows into a larger one or into a lake.

tribute *noun* **1** something said, done, or given to show respect or admiration. **2** payment that one country or ruler was formerly obliged to pay to a more powerful one. [from Latin *tributum* = assigned]

trice *noun* (*old use*) **in a trice** in a moment.

trick *noun* **1** a crafty or deceitful action; a practical joke. **2** a skilful action, especially one done for entertainment. **3** one round of a card-game such as whist. **4** (*informal*) a crafty or amusing person.

trick *verb* **1** deceive or cheat someone by a trick. **2** decorate, *The building was tricked out with little flags*.

trickery *noun* the use of tricks.

trickle *verb* flow or move slowly. **trickle** *noun*

trickster *noun* a person who tricks or cheats people.

tricky *adjective* (**trickier**, **trickiest**) **1** difficult; needing skill, *a tricky job*. **2** cunning; deceitful. **trickiness** *noun*

tricolour (*say* **trik**-ol-er) *noun* a flag with three coloured stripes, e.g. the national flag of France or Ireland. [from *tri-* + *colour*]

tricycle *noun* a vehicle like a bicycle but with three wheels.

trident *noun* a spear with three prongs for spearing fish, carried by Neptune and Britannia as a symbol of their power over the sea. [from *tri-*, + Latin *dens* = tooth]

triennial (*say* try-**en**-ee-al) *adjective* happening every third year. [from *tri-*, + Latin *annus* = year]

trier *noun* a person who tries hard.

trifecta *noun* a kind of bet where a person tries to forecast the first three finishers in order.

trifle *noun* **1** a pudding made of sponge-cake covered in custard, fruit, cream, etc. **2** a very small amount. **3** something that has very little importance or value.

trifle *verb* (**trifled**, **trifling**) behave frivolously; toy with something.

trifling *adjective* trivial.

trig *noun* (*slang*) trigonometry.
trig station (*NZ*) a landmark used by surveyors.

trigger *noun* a lever that is pulled to fire a gun.

trigger *verb* **trigger off** start something happening.

trigonometry (*say* trig-on-**om**-it-ree) *noun* the calculation of distances and angles by using triangles. [from Greek *trigonon* = triangle, + *metria* = measurement]

trilateral *adjective* having three sides. [from *tri-* + *lateral*]

trilby *noun* (*plural* **trilbies**) a man's soft felt hat.

trill *verb* make a quivering musical sound. **trill** *noun*

trillion *noun* **1** a million million. **2** (*old use*) a million million million. [from *tri-* + million]

trilogy *noun* (*plural* **trilogies**) a group of three stories, poems, or plays etc. about the same people or things. [from *tri-*, + Greek *-logia* = writings]

trim *adjective* neat and orderly. **trimly** *adverb*, **trimness** *noun*

trim *verb* (**trimmed**, **trimming**) **1** cut the edges or unwanted parts off something. **2** ornament a piece of clothing etc. **3** arrange sails to suit the wind. **4** balance a boat or aircraft evenly by arranging the people or cargo in it.

trim *noun* **1** condition, *in good trim.* **2** cutting or trimming, *Your beard needs a trim.* **3** ornamentation. **4** the balance of a boat or aircraft.

trimaran *noun* a vessel rather like a catamaran, with three hulls side by side.

Trinity *noun* God regarded as three persons (Father, Son, and Holy Spirit).

trinket *noun* a small ornament or piece of jewellery.

trio *noun* (*plural* **trios**) **1** a group of three people or things. **2** a group of three musicians or singers. **3** a piece of music for three musicians. [from Latin *tres* = three]

trip *verb* (**tripped**, **tripping**) **1** catch your foot on something and fall; cause a person to do this. **2** move with quick light steps. **3** operate a switch.
trip up stumble; make a slip or blunder; cause a person to do this.

trip *noun* **1** a journey or excursion. **2** the action of tripping; a stumble.

tripartite *adjective* having three parts; involving three groups, *tripartite talks.*

tripe *noun* **1** part of an ox's stomach used as food. **2** (*slang*) nonsense.

triple *adjective* **1** consisting of three parts. **2** involving three people or groups, *a triple alliance.* **3** three times as much or as many. **triply** *adverb*

triple *verb* (**tripled**, **tripling**) treble. [from Latin *triplus* = three times as much]

triplet *noun* each of three children or animals born to the same mother at one time. [from *triple*]

triplicate *noun* **in triplicate** as three identical copies. [from Latin *triplex* = triple]

tripod (*say* **try**-pod) *noun* a stand with three legs, e.g. to support a camera. [from *tri-*, + Greek *podos* = of a foot]

trisect *verb* divide into three equal parts. **trisection** *noun* [from *tri-*, + Latin *sectum* = cut]

trite (*rhymes with* kite) *adjective* commonplace; hackneyed, *a few trite remarks.* [from Latin *tritum* = worn by use]

triumph *noun* **1** a great success or victory; a feeling of joy at this. **2** a celebration of a victory. **triumphal** *adjective*, **triumphant** *adjective*, **triumphantly** *adverb*

triumph *verb* **1** be successful or victorious. **2** rejoice in success or victory.

triumvirate *noun* a ruling group of three people. [from Latin *trium virorum* = of three men]

trivet *noun* an iron stand for a pot or kettle etc., placed over a fire. [from Latin, = three-footed (compare *tripod*)]

trivial *adjective* of only small value or importance. **trivially** *adverb*, **triviality** *noun* [from Latin, = commonplace]

troglodyte *noun* a person living in a cave in ancient times. [from Greek *trogle* = hole]

troll *noun* (in Scandinavian mythology) a supernatural being, either a giant or a friendly but mischievous dwarf.

trolley *noun* (*plural* **trolleys**) **1** a small table on wheels or castors. **2** a small cart or truck.

trolley-bus *noun* (*plural* **trolley-buses**) a bus powered by electricity from an overhead wire to which it is connected.

trombone *noun* a large brass musical instrument with a sliding tube. [from Italian *tromba* = trumpet]

troop *noun* **1** an organised group of soldiers, Scouts, etc. **2** a number of people moving along together.
troops *plural noun* armed forces.

troop *verb* move along as a group or in large numbers, *They all trooped in.*

trooper *noun* a soldier in the cavalry or in an armoured unit.

trophy *noun* (*plural* **trophies**) a prize or souvenir for a victory or other success.

tropic *noun* a line of latitude $23^1/_2°$ about north of the equator (**tropic of Cancer**) or $23^1/_2°$ south of the equator (**tropic of Capricorn**). **tropical** *adjective*
the tropics the region between these two latitudes. [from Greek *trope* = turning (because the sun seems to turn back when it reaches these points)]

troposphere *noun* the layer of the atmosphere extending about 6–10 kilometres upwards from the earth's surface. [from Greek *tropos* = turning, + *sphere*]

trot *verb* (**trotted**, **trotting**) **1** (of a horse) run, going faster than when walking but more slowly than when cantering. **2** (*informal*) go, *Trot round to the chemist.*
trot out (*informal*) produce, *He trotted out the usual excuses.*

trot *noun* a trotting run.
on the trot (*informal*) one after the other without a break, *She worked for ten days on the trot.*
the trots (*NZ, informal*) harness racing.

troth (*rhymes with* both) *noun* (*old use*) loyalty; a solemn promise. [from *truth*]

trotter *noun* **1** an animal's foot as food, *pigs' trotters.* **2** a horse bred or trained for trotting-races.

trotting *noun* harness racing.

troubadour (*say* **troo**-bad-oor) *noun* a poet and singer in southern France in the 11th–13th centuries.

trouble *noun* **1** difficulty, inconvenience, or distress. **2** a cause of any of these.
take trouble take great care in doing something.

trouble *verb* (**troubled**, **troubling**) **1** cause trouble to someone. **2** give yourself trouble or inconvenience etc., *Don't trouble to reply.* [same origin as *turbid*]

troublesome *adjective* causing trouble or annoyance.

trough (*say* trof) *noun* **1** a long narrow open container, especially one holding water or food for animals. **2** a channel for liquid. **3** the low part between two waves or ridges. **4** a long region of low air-pressure.

trounce *verb* (**trounced**, **trouncing**) **1** thrash. **2** defeat someone heavily.

troupe (*say* as troop) *noun* a company of actors or other performers.

trousers *plural noun* a garment worn over the lower half of the body, with a separate part for each leg.

trousseau (say **troo**-soh) *noun* a bride's collection of clothing etc. to begin married life. [from French, = bundle]

trout *noun* (*plural* **trout**) a freshwater fish that is caught as a sport and for food.

trowel *noun* **1** a small garden tool with a curved blade for lifting plants or scooping things. **2** a small tool with a flat blade for spreading mortar etc. [from Latin *trulla* = scoop]

truant *noun* a child who stays away from school without permission. **truancy** *noun*
play truant be a truant. [the word originally meant 'idle rogue', from a Celtic word related to Welsh *truan* = miserable]

truce *noun* an agreement to stop fighting for a while.

truck[1] **1** a large powerful motor vehicle for transporting goods etc. **2** an open railway wagon for freight.

truck[2] *noun* dealings, *I'll have no truck with fortune-tellers!*

truckie *noun* (*NZ, informal*) a truck-driver.

truculent (*say* **truk**-yoo-lent) *adjective* defiant and aggressive. **truculently** *adverb*, **truculence** *noun*

trudge *verb* (**trudged**, **trudging**) walk slowly and heavily.

true *adjective* (**truer**, **truest**) **1** representing what has happened or exists, *a true story.* **2** genuine, not false, *He was the true heir.* **3** accurate. **4** loyal; faithful, *Be true to your friends.* **trueness** *noun*

truffle *noun* **1** a soft sweet made with chocolate. **2** a fungus that grows underground and is valued as food because of its rich flavour.

truism *noun* a statement that is obviously true, especially one that is hackneyed, e.g. 'Nothing lasts for ever'.

truly *adverb* **1** truthfully. **2** sincerely; genuinely, *We are truly grateful.* **3** accurately. **4** loyally; faithfully.
Yours truly see *yours.*

trump[1] *noun* a playing-card of a suit that ranks above the others for one game.

trump[1] *verb* defeat a card by playing a trump.
trump up invent an excuse or an accusation etc. [from *triumph*]

trump[2] *noun* (*old use*) the sound of a trumpet.

trumpery *adjective* showy but worthless, *trumpery ornaments.* [from French *tromper* = deceive]

trumpet *noun* **1** a metal wind instrument with a narrow tube that widens near the end. **2** something shaped like this.

trumpet *verb* (**trumpeted**, **trumpeting**) **1** blow a trumpet. **2** (of an elephant) make a loud sound with its trunk. **3** shout or announce something loudly.

trumpeter *noun* **1** a person who plays the trumpet. **2** (*NZ*) a kind of edible fish.

truncate *verb* (**truncated**, **truncating**) shorten something by cutting off its top or end. **truncation** *noun*

truncheon *noun* a short thick stick carried as a weapon, especially by police. [from Latin *truncus* = tree-trunk]

trundle *verb* (**trundled**, **trundling**) roll along heavily, *He was trundling a wheelbarrow. A bus trundled up.*

trundler *noun* (*NZ*) **1** a wire basket on wheels, used to carry food etc. bought at a supermarket. **2** a collapsible trolley for carrying a golf bag and clubs.

trunk *noun* **1** the main stem of a tree. **2** an elephant's long flexible nose. **3** a large box with a hinged lid for transporting or storing clothes etc. **4** the human body except for the head, arms, and legs.
trunks *plural noun* shorts worn by men and boys for swimming, boxing, etc.

trunk line *noun* the main line of a railway.

truss *noun* (*plural* **trusses**) **1** a framework of beams or bars supporting a roof or bridge etc. **2** a bundle of hay etc.

truss *verb* **1** tie up a person or thing securely. **2** support a roof or bridge etc. with trusses.

trust *verb* **1** believe that a person or thing is good, truthful, or strong. **2** entrust. **3** hope, *I trust that you are well.*
trust to rely on, *trusting to luck.*

trust *noun* **1** the belief that a person or thing can be trusted. **2** responsibility; being trusted, *Being a prefect is a position of trust.* **3** money legally entrusted to a person with instructions about how to use it. **trustful** *adjective*, **trustfully** *adverb*, **trustworthy** *adjective* [from Norse *traustr* = strong]

trustee *noun* a person who looks after money or property entrusted to him or her. **trusteeship** *noun*

trusty *adjective* (*old use*) trustworthy; reliable, *my trusty sword.*

truth *noun* **1** something that is true. **2** the quality of being true.

truthful *adjective* **1** telling the truth, *a truthful boy.* **2** true, *a truthful account of what happened.* **truthfully** *adverb*, **truthfulness** *noun*

try *verb* (**tried**, **trying**) **1** attempt. **2** test something by using or doing it, *Try sleeping on your back.* **3** examine the accusations against someone in a lawcourt. **4** be a strain on, *Very small print tries your eyes.*
try on put on clothes etc. to see if they fit.

try *noun* (*plural* **tries**) **1** an attempt. **2** (in rugby) putting the ball down behind the opponents' goal-line so as to score points. [the original meaning was 'to separate or distinguish things']

trying *adjective* putting a strain on someone's patience; annoying.

tsar (*say* zar) *noun* the title of the former ruler of Russia. [Russian, from Latin *Caesar*]

tsetse fly (say **tet**-see) a tropical African fly that can transmit sleeping sickness to people whom it bites.

T-shirt *noun* a short-sleeved shirt shaped like a T.

tsunami (*say* soo-**nar**-mee) *noun* an extensive high sea wave, often caused by undersea earthquakes.

tuatara *noun* a large primitive reptile rather like an iguana. [Māori]

tuatua *noun* a kind of edible mollusc. [Māori]

tub *noun* a round open container holding liquid, ice-cream, soil for plants, etc.

tuba (*say* tew-ba) *noun* a large brass wind instrument with a deep tone. [Latin, = trumpet]

tubby *adjective* (**tubbier**, **tubbiest**) short and fat. **tubbiness** *noun* [from *tub*]

tube *noun* **1** a long hollow piece of metal, plastic, rubber, glass, etc., especially for liquids or air etc. to pass along. **2** a container made of flexible material with a screw-cap, *a tube of toothpaste.*
down the tube (*informal*) lost or wasted.

tuber *noun* a short thick rounded root (e.g. of a dahlia) or underground stem (e.g. of a potato) that produces buds from which new plants will grow. [Latin, = a swelling]

tuberculin-tested *adjective* (of cows or their milk) tested and known to be free of tuberculosis.

tuberculosis *noun* a disease of people and animals, producing small swellings in the parts affected by it, especially in the lungs. **tubercular** *adjective* [from Latin *tuberculum* = little swelling]

tubing *noun* tubes; a length of tube.

tubular *adjective* shaped like a tube.

tuck *verb* **1** push a loose edge into something so that it is hidden or held in place. **2** put something away in a small space, *Tuck this in your pocket.*
tuck in (*informal*) eat heartily.

tuck *noun* **1** a flat fold stitched into a garment. **2** an operation to reduce fat, *tummy tuck.* **3** a position with knees bent and held close to the chest.

tucker *noun* (*NZ, slang*) food.

tuck-shop *noun* a shop in a school selling snacks and drinks etc.

Tuesday *noun* the day after Monday.

tuft *noun* a bunch of threads, grass, hair, or feathers etc. growing close together. **tufted** *adjective*

tug *verb* (**tugged**, **tugging**) **1** pull hard or suddenly. **2** tow.

tug *noun* **1** a hard or sudden pull. **2** a small powerful boat used for towing others.
tug of war a contest between two teams pulling a rope from opposite ends.

tūī *noun* a bird with dark feathers and a white tuft on the throat. [Māori]

tuition *noun* teaching. [from Latin *tuitio* = looking after something]

tukutuku *noun* a kind of ornamental lattice-work used as wall panelling. [Māori]

tulip *noun* a large cup-shaped flower on a tall stem growing from a bulb. [from old Turkish *tuliband* = turban (because the flowers are this shape)]

tulle (*say* **tewl**) *noun* a very fine silky net material used for veils, wedding-dresses, etc.

tumble *verb* (**tumbled, tumbling**) **1** fall. **2** cause to fall. **3** move or push quickly and carelessly. **tumble** *noun*
tumble to (*informal*) realise what something means.

tumbledown *adjective* falling into ruins.

tumbler *noun* **1** a drinking-glass with no stem or handle. **2** a part of a lock that is lifted when a key is turned to open it.

tumbrel or **tumbril** *noun* (*old use*) an open cart of the kind used to carry condemned people to the guillotine during the French Revolution.

tummy *noun* (*plural* **tummies**) (*informal*) the stomach.

tumour (*say* **tew**-mer) *noun* an abnormal lump growing on or in the body.

tumult (*say* **tew**-mult) *noun* an uproar; a state of confusion and agitation.

tumultuous (*say* tew-**mul**-tew-us) *adjective* making a tumult; noisy.

tun *noun* a large cask or barrel.

tuna[1] (*say* **tew**-na) *noun* (*plural* **tuna**) a large edible sea-fish with pink flesh.

tuna[2] *noun* the freshwater eel. [Māori]

tundra *noun* the vast level Arctic regions of Europe, Asia, and America where there are no trees and the subsoil is always frozen.

tune *noun* a short piece of music; a pleasant series of musical notes. **tuneful** *adjective*, **tunefully** *adverb*
in tune at the correct musical pitch.

tune *verb* (**tuned, tuning**) **1** put a musical instrument in tune. **2** adjust a radio or television set to receive a certain channel. **3** adjust an engine so that it runs smoothly.
tune in 1 watch or listen to a broadcast. **2** pay attention. **tuner** *noun*

tungsten *noun* a grey metal used to make a kind of steel. [from Swedish *tung* = heavy, + *sten* = stone]

tunic *noun* **1** a jacket worn as part of a uniform. **2** a garment reaching from the shoulders to the hips or knees.

tunnel *noun* an underground passage.

tunnel *verb* (**tunnelled, tunnelling**) make a tunnel.

tupuna *noun* (*plural* **tupuna**) an ancestor, a grandparent. [Māori]

tūrangawaewae *noun* a place where you belong, a permanent home. [from Māori *tūranga* = standing-place, + *waewae* = feet]

turban *noun* a covering for the head made by wrapping a strip of cloth round a cap. [from old Turkish *tuliband* (compare *tulip*)]

turbid *adjective* (of water, etc.) muddy, not clear. **turbidly** *adverb*, **turbidity** *noun* [from Latin *turba* = crowd, disturbance]

turbine *noun* a machine or motor driven by a flow of water, steam, or gas. [from Latin *turbinis* = of a whirlwind]

turbo-jet *noun* a jet engine or aircraft with turbines.

turbulent *adjective* **1** moving violently and unevenly, *turbulent seas.* **2** unruly. **turbulently** *adverb*, **turbulence** *noun* [same origin as *turbid*]

tureen *noun* a deep dish with a lid, from which soup is served at the table.

turf *noun* (*plural* **turves**) **1** short grass and the earth around it. **2** (*informal*) a person's territory or patch.

turf *verb* cover ground with turf.
turf out (*slang*) throw out.

turgid (*say* **ter**-jid) *adjective* swollen and not flexible.

turkey *noun* (*plural* **turkeys**) a large bird kept for its meat. [the name was originally used of a kind of fowl imported through Turkey in the 16th century]

turmoil *noun* a disturbance; confusion.

turn *verb* **1** move round; move to a new direction. **2** change in appearance etc.; become, *He turned pale.* **3** make something change, *You can turn milk into butter.* **4** move a switch or tap etc. to control something, *Turn that radio off.* **5** pass a certain time, *It has turned midnight.* **6** shape something on a lathe.
turn down fold down; reduce the flow or sound of something; reject, *We offered her a job but she turned it down.*
turn on organise or provide for an event.
turn out send out, expel; empty something, especially to search or clean it; happen; go to a meeting, or to vote, etc.; prove to be, *The visitor turned out to be my uncle.*
turn up appear or arrive; increase the flow or sound of something.

turn *noun* **1** the action of turning; a turning movement. **2** a change; the point where something turns. **3** an opportunity or duty etc. that comes to each person etc. in succession, *It's your turn to wash up.* **4** a short performance in an entertainment. **5** (informal) an attack of illness; a nervous shock, *It gave me a nasty turn.*
good turn a helpful action.
in turn in succession; one after another.
turn-off (*informal*) a deterrent; something that is off-putting.
turn-on (*informal*) an attraction or boost. [from Greek *tornos* = lathe]

turncoat *noun* a person who changes his or her principles or beliefs.

turner *noun* a person who makes things on a lathe.

turning *noun* a place where one road meets another, forming a corner.

turning-point *noun* a point where an important change takes place.

turnip *noun* a plant with a large round white root used as a vegetable.

turnout *noun* the number of people attending a meeting etc., *there was a good turnout.*

turnover *noun* **1** a small pie made by folding pastry over fruit, jam, etc. **2** the amount of money received by a firm selling things. **3** the rate at which goods are sold or workers leave and are replaced.

turnstile *noun* a revolving gate that admits one person at a time.

turntable *noun* a circular revolving platform or support.

turn-up *noun* **1** (*informal*) an unexpected event. **2** the end of a trouser leg folded upwards on the outside.

turpentine *noun* a kind of oil used for thinning paint, cleaning paintbrushes, etc.

turpitude *noun* wickedness. [from Latin *turpis* = shameful]

turps *noun* (*informal*) turpentine.

turquoise *noun* **1** a sky-blue or greenish-blue colour. **2** a blue jewel. [French, = Turkish stone]

turret *noun* **1** a small tower on a castle or other building. **2** a revolving structure containing a gun. **turreted** *adjective* [from French *tour* = tower]

turtle *noun* a sea-animal that looks like a tortoise.
turn turtle capsize.

turtle-dove *noun* a wild dove.

tusk *noun* a long pointed tooth projecting outside the mouth of an elephant, walrus, etc.

tussle *noun* a struggle; a conflict.

tussle *verb* (**tussled**, **tussling**) take part in a tussle.

tussock *noun* **1** a tuft or clump of grass. **2** (also **tussock-grass**) a pasture-grass that grows in clumps.

tutor *noun* **1** a teacher who teaches one person or a small group, not in a school. **2** a teacher of students in a college or university. [Latin, = guardian]

tutu[1] (*say* too-**too**) *noun* a ballet-dancer's short stiff frilled skirt. [French]

tutu[2] *noun* a shrub with black berries containing poisonous seeds. [Māori]

TV *abbreviation* television.

TVNZ *abbreviation* Television New Zealand.

twaddle *noun* nonsense.

twain *noun & adjective* (*old use*) two.

twang *verb* **1** play a guitar etc. by plucking its strings. **2** make a sharp sound like that of a wire when plucked. **twang** *noun*

tweak *verb* pinch and twist or pull something sharply. **tweak** *noun*

tweed *noun* thick woollen twill, often woven of mixed colours. [originally a mistake; the Scottish word *tweel* (= twill) was wrongly read as *tweed* by being confused with the River Tweed]

tweeds *plural noun* (informal) trousers.

tweet *noun & verb* **1** the chirping sound made by a small bird; to make a chirping sound. **2** a posting made on the social network service Twitter; to make a posting on the social network service Twitter.

tweezers *plural noun* small pincers for picking up or pulling very small things.

twelve *noun & adjective* the number 12; one more than eleven. **twelfth** *adjective & noun*

twenty *noun & adjective* (*plural* **twenties**) the number 20; two times ten. **twentieth** *adjective & noun*

twenty-four-seven *adverb* each hour of the day, every day of the week.

twenty-two *noun* a line marked on a rugby field twenty-two metres from each goal line.

twerp *noun* (*informal*) a silly person.

twice *adverb* **1** two times; on two occasions. **2** double the amount.

twiddle *verb* (**twiddled**, **twiddling**) twirl or finger something in an idle way; twist something quickly to and fro. **twiddle** *noun*, **twiddly** *adjective* [from *twirl* and *fiddle*]

twig[1] *noun* a small shoot on a branch or stem of a tree or shrub.

twig[2] *verb* (**twigged**, **twigging**) (*informal*) realise what something means.

twilight *noun* dim light from the sky just after sunset or just before sunrise.

twill *noun* material woven so that there is a pattern of diagonal lines.

twin *noun* **1** either of two children or animals born to the same mother at one time. **2** either of two things that are exactly alike.

twin *verb* (**twinned**, **twinning**) put things together as a pair. [from Old English *twinn* = double]

twine *noun* strong thin string.

twine *verb* (**twined**, **twining**) twist or wind together or round something.

twinge *noun* a sudden pain; a pang.

twinkle *verb* (**twinkled**, **twinkling**) sparkle. **twinkle** *noun*

twirl *verb* twist quickly. **twirl** *noun*

twist *verb* **1** pass threads or strands round something or round each other. **2** turn the ends of something in opposite directions. **3** turn round or from side to side, *The road twisted through the hills.* **4** bend something out of its proper shape. **5** (*informal*) swindle somebody. **twister** *noun*

twist *noun* a twisting movement or action. **twisty** *adjective*

twit *verb* (**twitted**, **twitting**) taunt.

twit *noun* (*slang*) a silly person.

twitch *verb* pull or move with a slight jerk. **twitch** *noun*

twitter *verb* **1** make quick chirping sounds. **2** make a posting on the social network Twitter. **twitter** *noun*

two *noun & adjective* (*plural* **twos**) the number 2; one more than one.
be in two minds be undecided about something.

two-tooth *noun* (*NZ*) a sheep between 18 and 22 months old.

tycoon *noun* a rich and influential business person. [from Japanese *taikun* = great prince]

tying *present participle* of **tie**.

type *noun* **1** a kind or sort. **2** letters or figures etc. designed for use in printing.

type *verb* (**typed**, **typing**) write something by using a typewriter or keyboard. [from Greek *typos* = impression]

typescript *noun* a typewritten document.

typewriter *noun* a machine with keys that are pressed to print letters or figures etc. on a piece of paper. **typewritten** *adjective* [the word *typewriter* at first meant the person using the machine, as well as the machine itself]

typhoid fever a serious infectious disease with fever, caused by harmful bacteria in food or water etc. [from *typhus*]

typhoon *noun* a violent hurricane in the western Pacific or East Asian seas. [from Chinese *tai fung* = great wind]

typhus *noun* an infectious disease causing fever, weakness, and a rash. [from Greek *typhos* = vapour]

typical *adjective* **1** having the qualities of a particular type of person or thing, *a typical school playground.* **2** usual in a particular person or thing, *He worked with typical carefulness.* **typically** *adverb* [same origin as type]

typify (*say* **tip**-if-I) *verb* (**typified**, **typifying**) be a typical example of something.

typist *noun* a person who types.

typography (*say* ty-**pog**-ra-fee) *noun* the style or appearance of the letters and figures etc. in printed material. [from *type* + *-graphy*]

tyrannise (*say* tirran-I'z) *verb* (**tyrannised**, **tyrannising**) rule or behave like a tyrant.

tyranny (*say* tirran-ee) *noun* (*plural* **tyrannies**) **1** government by a tyrant. **2** the way a tyrant behaves towards people. **tyrannical** *adjective*, **tyrannous** *adjective*

tyrant (*say* **ty**-rant) *noun* a person who rules cruelly and unjustly; someone who insists on being obeyed. [from Greek *tyrannos* = ruler with full power]

tyre *noun* a covering of rubber fitted round a wheel to make it grip the road and run more smoothly.

tyro *noun* = **tiro**.

Uu

U *abbreviation* (of usage or habit) upper class.

ubiquitous (*say* yoo-**bik**-wit-us) *adjective* found everywhere, *The ubiquitous television aerials spoil the view.* **ubiquity** *noun* [from Latin *ubique* = everywhere]

U-boat *noun* a German submarine of the kind used in the Second World War. [short for German *Unterseeboot* = under-sea boat]

udder *noun* the bag-like part of a cow, ewe, female goat, etc. from which milk is taken.

UFO *abbreviation* unidentified flying object. **ufo** *noun* (*plural* **ufos**)

ugly *adjective* (**uglier**, **ugliest**) **1** unpleasant to look at; not beautiful. **2** hostile and threatening, *The crowd was in an ugly mood.* **ugliness** *noun* [from Old Norse *uggligr* = frightening]

UHF *abbreviation* ultra-high frequency (between 300 and 3000 megahertz).

UK *abbreviation* United Kingdom.

ukulele (*say* yoo-kul-**ay**-lee) *noun* a small guitar with four strings.

ulcer *noun* an open sore. **ulcerated** *adjective*, **ulceration** *noun*

ulterior *adjective* beyond what is obvious or stated, *an ulterior motive.* [Latin, = further (compare *ultra-*)]

ultimate *adjective* furthest in a series of things; final, *Our ultimate destination is London.* **ultimately** *adverb* [from Latin *ultimus* = last]

ultimate *noun* the final, best, or most typical of a kind.

ultimatum (*say* ul-tim-**ay**-tum) *noun* a final demand; a statement that unless something is done by a certain time action will be taken or war will be declared. [same origin as *ultimate*]

ultra- *prefix* **1** beyond (as in *ultraviolet*). **2** extremely; excessively (as in *ultra-modern*). [from Latin *ultra* = beyond]

ultramarine *noun* deep bright blue.

ultrasonic *adjective* (of sound) beyond the range of human hearing.

ultraviolet *adjective* (of light-rays) beyond the violet end of the spectrum.

umber *noun* a kind of brown pigment.

umbilical (*say* um-**bil**-ik-al) *adjective* of the navel.
umbilical cord the tube through which a baby receives nourishment before it is born, connecting its body with the mother's womb.

umbrage *noun* **take umbrage** take offence. [from Latin *umbra* = shadow]

umbrella *noun* **1** a circular piece of material stretched over a folding frame with a central stick used as a handle, or a central pole, opened to protect the user from rain or sun. **2** a general protection. [from Italian *ombrella* = a little shade]

umpire *noun* a referee in cricket, tennis, and some other games.

umpire *verb* (**umpired**, **umpiring**) act as an umpire.

umu *noun* an earth oven. [Māori]

UN *abbreviation* United Nations.

un- *prefix* **1** not (as in *uncertain*). **2** (before a verb) reversing the action (as in *unlock* = release from being locked).

> NOTE Many words beginning with this prefix are not listed here if their meaning is obvious.

unable *adjective* not able to do something.

unaccountable *adjective* **1** unable to be explained. **2** not accountable for what you do. **unaccountably** *adverb*

unadulterated *adjective* pure; not mixed with things that are less good.

unaided *adjective* without help.

unanimous (*say* yoo-**nan**-im-us) *adjective* with everyone agreeing, *a unanimous decision.* **unanimously** *adverb*, **unanimity** (*say* yoo-nan-**im**-it-ee) *noun* [from Latin *unus* = one, + *animus* = mind]

unassuming *adjective* modest; not arrogant or pretentious.

unavoidable *adjective* not able to be avoided.

unaware *adjective* not aware.

unawares *adverb* unexpectedly; without noticing.

unbearable *adjective* not able to be endured. **unbearably** *adverb*

unbeatable *adjective* unable to be defeated or surpassed.

unbeaten *adjective* not defeated; not surpassed.

unbecoming *adjective* not making a person look attractive; not suitable.

unbeknown *adjective* without someone knowing about it, *Unbeknown to us, they were working for our enemies.*

unbelievable *adjective* not able to be believed; incredible. **unbelievably** *adverb*

unbend *verb* (**unbent**, **unbending**) **1** change or become changed from a bent position. **2** relax and become friendly.

unbiased *adjective* not biased.

unbidden *adjective* not commanded; not invited.

unblock *verb* remove an obstruction from something.

unborn *adjective* not yet born.

unbridled *adjective* unrestrained.

unbroken *adjective* not broken; not interrupted.

unburden *verb* remove a burden from the person etc. carrying it.
unburden yourself tell someone what you know.

uncalled-for *adjective* not justified; impertinent.

uncanny *adjective* (**uncannier**, **uncanniest**) **1** strange and rather frightening. **2** extraordinary, *They forecast the exam results with uncanny accuracy.* **uncannily** *adverb*, **uncanniness** *noun*

unceremonious *adjective* without proper formality or dignity.

uncertain *adjective* **1** not certain. **2** not reliable, *His aim is rather uncertain.* **uncertainly** *adverb*, **uncertainty** *noun*
in no uncertain terms clearly and forcefully.

uncharitable *adjective* making unkind judgements of people or actions. **uncharitably** *adverb*

uncle *noun* the brother of your father or mother; your aunt's husband. [from Latin *avunculus* uncle]

unclothed *adjective* naked.

uncomfortable *adjective* not comfortable. **uncomfortably** *adverb*

uncommon *adjective* not common; unusual.

uncompromising (*say* un-**komp**-rom-I-zing) *adjective* not allowing a compromise; inflexible.

unconcerned *adjective* **1** not caring about something; not worried. **2** not involved, not taking part in something.

unconditional *adjective* without any conditions; absolute, *unconditional surrender.* **unconditionally** *adverb*

unconscious *adjective* not conscious; not aware of things. **unconsciously** *adverb*, **unconsciousness** *noun*

uncontrollable *adjective* unable to be controlled or stopped. **uncontrollably** *adverb*

uncooperative *adjective* not cooperative.

uncouple *verb* (**uncoupled**, **uncoupling**) disconnect.

uncouth (*say* on-**koo**th) *adjective* rude and awkward in manner; boorish. [from *un-* + Old English *cuth* = known]

uncover *verb* **1** remove the covering from something. **2** reveal; expose, *They uncovered a plot to kill the king.*

unction *noun* **1** anointing with oil, especially in a religious ceremony. **2** unctuousness. [from Latin *unctum* = oiled]

unctuous (*say* **unk**-tew-us) *adjective* having an oily manner; polite in an exaggerated way. **unctuously** *adverb*, **unctuousness** *noun* [same origin as *unction* and *unguent*)]

undecided *adjective* **1** not yet settled; not certain. **2** not having made up your mind yet.

undeniable *adjective* impossible to deny; undoubtedly true. **undeniably** *adverb*

under *preposition* **1** below; beneath, *Hide it under the desk.* **2** less than, *under 5 years old.* **3** governed or controlled by, *The country prospered under his rule.* **4** in the process of; undergoing, *The road is under repair.* **5** using, *He writes under the name of 'Lewis Carroll'.* **6** according to the rules of, *This is permitted under our agreement.*
under way moving on water; in progress.

under *adverb* in or to a lower place or level or condition, *Slowly the diver went under.*

under *adjective* lower, *the under layers.*

under- *prefix* **1** below, beneath (as in *underwear*). **2** lower; subordinate (as in *under-manager*). **3** not enough; incompletely (as in *undercooked*).

underarm *adjective & adverb* **1** moving the hand and arm forward and upwards. **2** in or for the armpit.

undercarriage *noun* an aircraft's landing-wheels and their supports.

underclothes *plural noun* underwear. **underclothing** *noun*

undercover *adjective* done or doing things secretly, *an undercover agent.*

undercurrent *noun* **1** a current that is below the surface or below another current. **2** an underlying feeling or influence, *an undercurrent of fear.*

undercut *verb* (**undercut, undercutting**) **1** cut away the part below something. **2** sell something for a lower price than someone else sells it.

underdog *noun* a person or team etc. that is expected to lose a contest or struggle.

underdone *adjective* not thoroughly done; undercooked.

underestimate *verb* (**underestimated, underestimating**) make too low an estimate of a person or thing.

underfoot *adverb* on the ground; under your feet.

undergarment *noun* a piece of underwear.

undergo *verb* (**underwent, undergone, undergoing**) experience or endure something; be subjected to, *The new aircraft underwent intensive tests.*

undergraduate *noun* a student at a university who is studying for his or her first degree.

underground *adjective & adverb* **1** under the ground. **2** done or working in secret.

undergrowth *noun* bushes and other plants growing closely, especially under trees.

underhand *adjective* done or doing things in a sly or secret way.

underlie *verb* (**underlay, underlain, underlying**) **1** be or lie under something. **2** be the basis or explanation of something.

underline *verb* (**underlined, underlining**) **1** draw a line under a word etc. **2** emphasise something.

underling *noun* a subordinate.

underlying *adjective* **1** lying under something, *the underlying rocks.* **2** forming the basis or explanation of something, *the underlying causes of the trouble.*

undermine *verb* (**undermined, undermining**) **1** make a hollow or tunnel beneath something, especially one causing weakness at the base. **2** weaken something gradually.

underneath *preposition & adverb* below; beneath; under.

underpants *plural noun* an undergarment covering the lower part of the body.

underpass *noun* (*plural* **underpasses**) a road that goes underneath another.

underpay *verb* (**underpaid, underpaying**) pay someone too little.

underprivileged *adjective* having less than the normal standard of living or rights in a community.

underrate *verb* (**underrated, underrating**) have too low an opinion of a person or thing.

undersell *verb* (**undersold, underselling**) sell at a lower price than another person.

undersigned *adjective* who has or have signed at the bottom of this document, *We, the undersigned, wish to protest.*

undersized *adjective* of less than the normal size.

understand *verb* (**understood, understanding**) **1** know what something means or how it works or why it exists. **2** know and tolerate a person's ways. **3** have been told. **4** take something for granted, *Your expenses will be paid, that's understood.* **understandable** *adjective,* **understandably** *adverb*

understanding *noun* **1** the power to understand or think; intelligence. **2** sympathy; tolerance. **3** agreement in opinion or feeling, *a better understanding between nations.*

understatement *noun* an incomplete or very restrained statement of facts or truth, *To say they disagreed is an understatement; they had a violent quarrel.*

understudy *noun* (*plural* **understudies**) an actor who studies a part in order to be able to play it if the usual performer is absent.

understudy *verb* (**understudied, understudying**) be an understudy for an actor or part.

undertake *verb* (**undertook, undertaken, undertaking**) agree or promise to do something.

undertaker *noun* a person whose job is to arrange funerals and burials or cremations.

undertaking *noun* **1** work etc. undertaken. **2** a promise or guarantee. **3** the business of an undertaker.

undertone *noun* **1** a low or quiet tone, *They spoke in undertones.* **2** an underlying quality or feeling etc., *His letter has a threatening undertone.*

undertow *noun* a current below that of the surface of the sea and moving in the opposite direction.

underwater *adjective & adverb* placed, used, or done beneath the surface of water.

underwear *noun* clothes worn next to the skin, under indoor clothing.

underweight *adjective* not heavy enough.

underwent *past tense* of **undergo**.

underworld *noun* **1** (in myths and legends) the place for the spirits of the dead, under the earth. **2** the people who are regularly engaged in crime.

underwrite *verb* (**underwrote, underwritten, underwriting**) guarantee to finance something, or to pay for any loss or damage etc. **underwriter** *noun*

undesirable *adjective* not desirable; objectionable. **undesirably** *adverb*

undignified *adjective* not dignified.

undo *verb* (**undid**, **undone**, **undoing**) **1** unfasten; unwrap. **2** cancel the effect of something, *He has undone all our careful work.*

undoubted *adjective* certain; not regarded as doubtful. **undoubtedly** *adverb*

undress *verb* take clothes off.

undue *adjective* excessive; too great. **unduly** *adverb*

undulate *verb* (**undulated**, **undulating**) move like a wave or waves; have a wavy appearance. **undulation** *noun* [from Latin *unda* = a wave]

undying *adjective* everlasting.

unearth *verb* **1** dig something up; uncover by digging. **2** find something by searching.

unearthly *adjective* **1** not earthly; supernatural; strange and frightening. **2** (*informal*) very early or inconvenient, *We had to get up at an unearthly hour.*

uneasy *adjective* **1** uncomfortable. **2** worried; worrying about something. **uneasily** *adverb*, **uneasiness** *noun*

uneatable *adjective* not fit to be eaten.

uneconomic *adjective* not profitable.

unemployed *adjective* without a job. **unemployment** *noun*

unending *adjective* not coming to an end.

UNESCO *abbreviation* United Nations Educational, Scientific, and Cultural Organisation.

unequal *adjective* not equal. **unequalled** *adjective*, **unequally** *adverb*

unerring (*say* un-**er**-ing) *adjective* making no mistake, *unerring accuracy.*

uneven *adjective* **1** not level; not regular. **2** unequal. **unevenly** *adverb*, **unevenness** *noun*

unexampled *adjective* unprecedented; exceptional, *an unexampled opportunity.*

unexceptionable *adjective* not in any way objectionable.

unexceptional *adjective* not exceptional; quite ordinary.

unexpected *adjective* not expected. **unexpectedly** *adverb*, **unexpectedness** *noun*

unfair *adjective* not fair; unjust. **unfairly** *adverb*, **unfairness** *noun*

unfaithful *adjective* not faithful; disloyal.

unfamiliar *adjective* not familiar. **unfamiliarity** *noun*

unfasten *verb* open the fastenings of something.

unfavourable *adjective* not favourable. **unfavourably** *adverb*

unfeeling *adjective* **1** not able to feel things. **2** not caring about other people's feelings; unsympathetic.

unfit *adjective* **1** unsuitable. **2** not in perfect health.

unfit *verb* (**unfitted**, **unfitting**) make a person or thing unsuitable.

unfold *verb* **1** open; spread out. **2** make or become known slowly, *as the story unfolds.*

unforeseen *adjective* not foreseen; unexpected.

unforgettable *adjective* not able to be forgotten.

unforgivable *adjective* not able to be forgiven.

unfortunate *adjective* **1** unlucky. **2** unsuitable; regrettable, *an unfortunate remark.* **unfortunately** *adverb*

unfounded *adjective* not based on facts.

unfreeze *verb* (**unfroze**, **unfrozen**, **unfreezing**) thaw; cause something to thaw.

unfriendly *adjective* not friendly. **unfriendliness** *noun*

unfrock *verb* dismiss a person from being a priest.

unfurl *verb* unroll; spread out.

unfurnished *adjective* without furniture.

ungainly *adjective* awkward-looking; clumsy; ungraceful. **ungainliness** *noun* [from *un-*, + *gainly* = graceful]

ungodly *adjective* **1** not giving reverence to God; not religious. **2** (*informal*) outrageous; very inconvenient, *She woke me at an ungodly hour.* **ungodliness** *noun*

ungovernable *adjective* uncontrollable.

ungracious *adjective* not kindly; not courteous. **ungraciously** *adverb*

ungrateful *adjective* not grateful. **ungratefully** *adverb*

unguarded *adjective* **1** not guarded. **2** without thought or caution; indiscreet, *He said this in an unguarded moment.*

unguent (*say* **ung**-went) *noun* an ointment or lubricant. [from Latin *unguere* = to oil or anoint]

unhappy *adjective* **1** not happy; sad. **2** unfortunate; unsuitable. **unhappily** *adverb*, **unhappiness** *noun*

UNHCR *abbreviation* United Nations High Commission for Refugees.

unhealthy *adjective* not healthy. **unhealthiness** *noun*

unheard-of *adjective* never known or done before; extraordinary.

unhinge *verb* (**unhinged**, **unhinging**) cause a person's mind to become unbalanced.

uni *noun* (*informal*) university.

uni- *prefix* one; single (as in *unicorn*). [from Latin *unus* = one]

UNICEF *abbreviation* United Nations International Children's Emergency Fund.

unicorn *noun* (in legends) an animal that is like a horse with one long straight horn growing from its forehead. [from *uni-*, + Latin *cornu* = horn]

uniform *noun* special clothes showing that the wearer is a member of a certain organisation, school, etc.

uniform *adjective* always the same; not varying, *The desks are of uniform size.* **uniformly** *adverb*, **uniformity** *noun* [from *uni-* + *form*]

uniformed *adjective* wearing a uniform.

unify *verb* (**unified**, **unifying**) make into one thing; unite. **unification** *noun*

unilateral *adjective* of or done by one person or group or country etc. [from *uni-* + *lateral*]

unimpeachable *adjective* completely trustworthy, *unimpeachable honesty.*

uninhabitable *adjective* not suitable for habitation.

uninhabited *adjective* not inhabited.

uninhibited *adjective* not inhibited; having no inhibitions.

uninterested *adjective* not interested; showing or feeling no concern.

USAGE See the note on *disinterested.*

union *noun* **1** the joining of things together; uniting. **2** a trade union (see *trade*). **Union Jack** the British flag. [from Latin *unio* = unity]

unionist *noun* **1** a member of a trade union. **2** a person who wishes to unite one country with another.

unique (*say* yoo-**neek**) *adjective* being the only one of its kind, *This jewel is unique.* **uniquely** *adverb* [from Latin *unus* = one]

unison *noun* **in unison** with all sounding or singing the same tune etc. together, or speaking in chorus; in agreement. [from *uni-*, + Latin *sonus* = sound]

unit *noun* **1** an amount used as a standard in measuring or counting things, *Centimetres are units of length; cents are units of money.* **2** a group, device, piece of furniture, etc. regarded as a single thing but forming part of a larger group or whole, *an army unit; a sink unit.* **3** one dwelling or accommodation unit in a block of flats or motel etc. **4** (*NZ*) a suburban electric train. **5** a complete section of a school or university course. [from Latin *unus* = one]

unite *verb* (**united**, **uniting**) join together; make or become one thing.

United Kingdom the country comprising England, Scotland, Wales and Northern Ireland.

unity *noun* **1** being united; being in agreement. **2** something whole that is made up of parts. **3** (in mathematics) the number one.

universal *adjective* of or including or done by everyone or everything. **universally** *adverb*

universe *noun* everything that exists, including the earth and living things and all the heavenly bodies. [from Latin *universus* = combined into one]

university *noun* (*plural* **universities**) a place where people go to study at an advanced level after leaving school. [same origin as *universe*]

unjust *adjective* not fair; not just.

unkempt *adjective* looking untidy or neglected. [from *un-*, + an old word *kempt* = combed]

unkind *adjective* not kind. **unkindly** *adverb*, **unkindness** *noun*

unknown *adjective* not known.

unleaded *adjective* (of petrol) without added lead.

unleash *verb* set free from a leash; let loose.

unleavened (*say* un-**lev**-end) *adjective* (of bread) made without yeast or other substances that would make it rise.

unless *conjunction* except when; if ... not, *We cannot go unless we are invited.*

unlike *preposition* not like, *Unlike me, she enjoys cricket.*

unlike *adjective* not alike; different, *The two children are very unlike.*

unlikely *adjective* (**unlikelier**, **unlikeliest**) not likely to happen or be true.

unlimited *adjective* not limited; very great or very many.

unload *verb* remove the load of things carried by a ship, aircraft, vehicle, etc.

unlock *verb* open something by undoing a lock.

unlucky *adjective* not lucky; having or bringing bad luck. **unluckily** *adverb*

unmanageable *adjective* unable to be managed.

unmarried *adjective* not married.

unmask *verb* **1** remove a person's mask. **2** reveal what a person or thing really is.

unmentionable *adjective* too bad to be spoken of.

unmistakable *adjective* not able to be mistaken for another person or thing. **unmistakably** *adverb*

unmitigated *adjective* absolute, *an unmitigated disaster.*

unnatural *adjective* not natural; not normal. **unnaturally** *adverb*

unnecessary *adjective* not necessary; more than is necessary.

unnerve *verb* (**unnerved**, **unnerving**) cause someone to lose courage or determination.

unoccupied *adjective* not occupied.

unofficial *adjective* not official. **unofficially** *adverb*

unpack *verb* take things out of a suitcase, bag, box, etc.

unparalleled *adjective* having no parallel or equal.

unparliamentary *adjective* impolite; abusive.

> USAGE It is a rule of debates in Parliament that speakers must be polite to each other. Impolite language is 'unparliamentary'.

unpick *verb* undo the stitching of something.

unpleasant *adjective* not pleasant. **unpleasantly** *adverb*, **unpleasantness** *noun*

unpopular *adjective* not popular.

unprecedented (*say* un-**press**-id-en-tid) *adjective* that has never happened before.

unprejudiced *adjective* impartial.

unprepared *adjective* not prepared beforehand; not ready, not equipped.

unprepossessing *adjective* not attractive; not making a good impression.

unprincipled *adjective* without good moral principles; unscrupulous.

unprintable *adjective* too rude or indecent to be printed.

unprofessional *adjective* not professional; not worthy of a member of a profession.

unprofitable *adjective* not producing a profit or advantage. **unprofitably** *adverb*

unqualified *adjective* **1** not officially qualified to do something. **2** not limited, *We gave it our unqualified approval.*

unravel *verb* (**unravelled**, **unravelling**) **1** disentangle. **2** undo something that is knitted. **3** investigate and solve a mystery etc. **4** lose composure.

unready *adjective* not ready; hesitating.

unreal *adjective* **1** not real, existing in the imagination only. **2** (*informal*) incredible. **unreality** *noun*

unreasonable *adjective* **1** not reasonable. **2** excessive; unjust. **unreasonably** *adverb*

unreel *verb* unwind from a reel.

unrelieved *adjective* without anything to vary it, *unrelieved gloom.*

unremitting *adjective* not stopping, not relaxing; persistent.

unrequited (*say* un-ri-**kwy**-tid) *adjective* (of love) not returned or rewarded. [from *un-* + *requited* = paid back]

unreserved *adjective* **1** not reserved. **2** without restriction; complete, *unreserved loyalty.* **unreservedly** *adverb*

unrest *noun* restlessness; trouble caused because people are dissatisfied.

unripe *adjective* not yet ripe.

unrivalled *adjective* having no equal; better than all others.

unroll *verb* open something that has been rolled up.

unruly *adjective* difficult to control; disorderly. **unruliness** *noun* [from *un-* + *rule*]

unsavoury *adjective* unpleasant; disgusting.

unscathed *adjective* uninjured. [from *un-*, + an old word *scathed* = harmed]

unscrew *verb* undo something that has been screwed up.

unscrupulous *adjective* having no scruples about wrongdoing.

unseat *verb* throw a person from horseback or from a seat on a bicycle etc.

unseemly *adjective* not seemly; improper.

unseen *adjective* not seen; invisible.

unseen *noun* a passage for translation without previous preparation.

unselfish *adjective* not selfish.

unsettled *adjective* not settled; not calm; likely to change.

unshakeable *adjective* not able to be shaken; firm.

unsightly *adjective* not pleasant to look at; ugly. **unsightliness** *noun*

unskilled *adjective* not having or not needing special skill or training.

unsociable *adjective* not sociable.

unsolicited *adjective* not asked for.

unsound *adjective* not sound; damaged, unhealthy, unreasonable, or unreliable. [from *un-* + *sound*[3]]

unspeakable *adjective* too bad to be described; very objectionable.

unstable *adjective* not stable; likely to change or become unbalanced.

unsteady *adjective* not steady.

unstinted *adjective* given generously.

unstuck *adjective* **come unstuck** cease to stick; (*informal*) fail, go wrong.

unsuccessful *adjective* not successful.

unsuitable *adjective* not suitable.

untenable *adjective* not tenable.

unthinkable *adjective* too bad or too unlikely to be worth considering.

unthinking *adjective* thoughtless.

untidy *adjective* (**untidier**, **untidiest**) not tidy. **untidily** *adverb*, **untidiness** *noun*

untie *verb* (**untied**, **untying**) undo something that has been tied.

until *preposition & conjunction* up to a particular time or event.

untimely *adjective* happening too soon or at an unsuitable time.

unto *preposition* (*old use*) to.

untold *adjective* **1** not told. **2** too much or too many to be counted, *untold wealth* or *wealth untold.*

untouchable *adjective* **1** unable to be touched or affected. **2** unable to be beaten. **3** repellent.

untoward *adjective* inconvenient; awkward, *If nothing untoward happens.*

untraceable *adjective* unable to be traced.

untrue *adjective* not true.

untruth *noun* an untrue statement; a lie. **untruthful** *adjective*, **untruthfully** *adverb*

unused *adjective* **1** (*say* un-**yoozd**) not yet used, *an unused stamp.* **2** (*say* un-**yoost**) not accustomed, *He is unused to eating meat.*

unusual *adjective* not usual; exceptional; strange. **unusually** *adverb*

unutterable *adjective* too great to be described, *unutterable joy.*

unvarnished *adjective* **1** not varnished. **2** plain and straightforward, *the unvarnished truth.*

unveil *verb* **1** remove a veil or covering from something. **2** reveal.

unwaged *adjective & noun* (a person) not in paid employment.

unwanted *adjective* not wanted.

unwarrantable *adjective* not justifiable. **unwarrantably** *adverb*

unwarranted *adjective* not justified; not authorised.

unwary *adjective* not cautious. **unwarily** *adverb*, **unwariness** *noun*

unwell *adjective* not in good health.

unwholesome *adjective* not wholesome.

unwieldy *adjective* awkward to move or control because of its size, shape, or weight. **unwieldiness** *noun*

unwilling *adjective* not willing. **unwillingly** *adverb*

unwind *verb* (**unwound**, **unwinding**) **1** unroll. **2** (*informal*) relax after a time of work or strain.

unwise *adjective* not wise; foolish. **unwisely** *adverb*

unwitting *adjective* **1** unaware. **2** unintentional. **unwittingly** *adverb*

unwonted (*say* un-**wohn**-tid) *adjective* not customary; not usual, *She spoke with unwonted rudeness.* **unwontedly** *adverb* [from un- + wont]

unworn *adjective* not yet worn.

unworthy *adjective* not worthy.

unwrap *verb* (**unwrapped**, **unwrapping**) open something that is wrapped.

up *adverb* **1** to or in a higher place or position or level, *Prices went up.* **2** so as to be upright, *Stand up.* **3** out of bed, *It's time to get up.* **4** completely, *Eat up your carrots.* **5** finished, *Your time is up.* **6** (*informal*) happening, *Something is up.*
up against close to; (*informal*) faced with difficulties, dangers, etc.
ups and downs ascents and descents; alternate good and bad luck.
up to until; busy with or doing something; capable of; needed from, *It's up to us to help her.*
up to date modern; fashionable; giving recent information etc.

> USAGE Use hyphens when this is used as an *adjective* before a noun, e.g. *up-to-date information* (but *The information is up to date*).

up *preposition* upwards through or along or into, *Water came up the pipes.*

upbraid *verb* (*formal*) reproach.

upbringing *noun* the way someone is trained during childhood.

update *verb* (**updated**, **updating**) bring a thing up to date.

upheaval *noun* a sudden violent change or disturbance.

uphill *adverb* up a slope.

uphill *adjective* **1** going up a slope. **2** difficult, *It was uphill work.*

uphold *verb* (**upheld**, **upholding**) **1** support, keep something from falling. **2** support a decision or belief etc.

upholster *verb* put covers, padding, and springs etc. on furniture. **upholstery** *noun* [from *uphold* = maintain and repair]

upkeep *noun* keeping something in good condition; the cost of this.

uplands *plural noun* the higher parts of a country or region. **upland** *adjective*

upload *verb* (*Computing*) transfer data to a larger system.

up-market *adjective* superior, stylish.

upon *preposition* on.

upper *adjective* higher in place or rank etc.
upper case capital letters in printing or typing.

uppermost *adjective* highest.

uppermost *adverb* on or to the top or the highest place, *Keep the painted side uppermost.*

upright *adjective* **1** vertical; erect. **2** strictly honest or honourable.

upright *noun* a post or rod etc. placed upright, especially as a support.

uprising *noun* a rebellion; a revolt.

uproar *noun* an outburst of noise or excitement or anger.

uproarious *adjective* very noisy.

uproot *verb* **1** remove a plant and its roots from the ground. **2** make someone leave the place where he or she has lived for a long time.

upset *verb* (**upset**, **upsetting**) **1** overturn; knock something over. **2** make a person unhappy. **3** disturb the normal working of something.

upset *noun* upsetting something; being upset.

upshot *noun* an outcome.

upside-down *adverb & adjective* **1** with the upper part underneath instead of on top. **2** in great disorder; very untidy.

upstairs *adverb & adjective* to or on a higher floor.
go upstairs request a decision from the third umpire or video referee in a sports game.

upstart *noun* a person who has risen suddenly to a high position, especially one who then behaves arrogantly.

upstream *adjective & adverb* in the direction from which a stream flows.

uptake *noun* (*informal*) understanding, *She is quick on the uptake.*

uptight *adjective* (*informal*) tense and nervous or annoyed.

upturn *noun* an upward trend; an improvement.

upward *adjective & adverb* going towards what is higher. **upwards** *adverb*

uranium *noun* a heavy radioactive grey metal used as a source of nuclear energy. [named after the planet Uranus]

urban *adjective* of a town or city. [from Latin *urbis* = of a city]

urbane *adjective* having smoothly polite manners. **urbanely** *adverb*, **urbanity** *noun* [same origin as *urban*]

urbanise *verb* (**urbanised**, **urbanising**) change a place into a town-like area. **urbanisation** *noun*

urchin *noun* **1** a poorly dressed or mischievous boy. **2** a sea-urchin. [from Latin *ericius* = hedgehog]

Urdu *noun* the official language of Pakistan, also widely used in India.

urge *verb* (**urged**, **urging**) **1** try to persuade a person to do something. **2** drive people or animals onward.

urge *noun* a strong desire.

urgent *adjective* needing to be done or dealt with immediately. **urgently** *adverb*, **urgency** *noun* [from Latin *urgens* = urging]

urinate (*say* **yoor**-in-ayt) *verb* (**urinated**, **urinating**) pass urine out of your body. **urination** *noun*

urine (*say* **yoor**-in) *noun* waste liquid that collects in the bladder and is passed out of the body. **urinary** *adjective*

URL *abbreviation* (*Computing*) uniform resource locator (the 'address' of a web page).

urn *noun* **1** a large metal container with a tap. **2** a container shaped like a vase, usually with a base; a container for holding the ashes of a cremated person.

US *abbreviation* United States (of America).

us *pronoun* the form of *we* used when it is the object of a verb or after a preposition.

USA *abbreviation* United States of America.

usable *adjective* able to be used.

usage *noun* **1** use; the way something is used. **2** the way words are used in a language, *New Zealand usage often differs from British usage.*

USB *abbreviation* universal serial bus, a way of connecting a printer, keyboard, or other piece of equipment to a computer using a special cable and without having to turn the computer off and on again.

use (*say* yooz) *verb* (**used**, **using**) perform an action or job with something, *Use soap for washing.* **user** *noun*
used to (*say* yoost) was or were accustomed to, *We used to go by train.*
use up use all of something.

use (*say* yooss) *noun* **1** the action of using something; being used. **2** the purpose for which something is used. **3** the quality of being useful.

use-by date *noun* a date marked on a package of food or other product, showing how long it can be kept or used.

used (*say* yoozd) *adjective* not new; second-hand.

useful *adjective* able to be used a lot or to do something that needs doing. **usefully** *adverb*, **usefulness** *noun*

useless *adjective* not useful; producing no effect, *Their efforts were useless.* **uselessly** *adverb*, **uselessness** *noun*

user-friendly *adjective* (of a computer etc.) designed to be easy for a non-technical person to operate.

usher *noun* a person who shows people to their seats in a public hall or church etc.

usher *verb* lead in or out; escort someone as an usher.

usherette *noun* a woman who shows people to their seats in a cinema or theatre.

usual *adjective* such as happens or is done or used etc. always or most of the time. **usually** *adverb* [from Latin *usum* = used]

usurp (*say* yoo-**zerp**) *verb* take power or a position or right etc. wrongfully or by force. **usurpation** *noun*, **usurper** *noun*

usury (*say* **yoo**-*zh*er-ee) *noun* the lending of money at an excessively high rate of interest. **usurer** *noun*

ute *noun* (*NZ, informal*) a utility truck.

utensil (*say* yoo-**ten**-sil) *noun* a device or container, especially one for use in the house, *cooking utensils.*

uterus (*say* **yoo**-ter-us) *noun* the womb. [Latin, = womb]

utilise *verb* (**utilised**, **utilising**) use; find a use for something. **utilisation** *noun*

utilitarian *adjective* designed to be useful rather than decorative or luxurious; practical. [from *utility*]

utility *noun* (*plural* **utilities**) **1** usefulness. **2** a useful thing. **3** (*NZ*) a utility truck. **4** a computer program for routine functions. **utility truck** a small truck or van with an open deck at the back for carrying loads. [from Latin *utilis* = useful]

utmost *adjective* extreme; greatest, *Look after it with the utmost care.* **utmost** *noun* [from Old English, = furthest out]

Utopia (*say* yoo-**toh**-pee-a) *noun* an imaginary place or state of things where everything is perfect. **Utopian** *adjective* [named after *Utopia*, the title of a book by Sir Thomas More (1516), meaning 'Nowhere']

utter[1] *verb* say or speak; make a sound with your mouth. **utterance** *noun*

utter[2] *adjective* complete; absolute, *utter misery.* **utterly** *adverb*

uttermost *adjective & noun* utmost.

utu *noun* **1** compensation paid for injuries that have been suffered. **2** a payment or price. **3** revenge. [Māori]

U-turn *noun* **1** a U-shaped turn made in a vehicle so that it then travels in the opposite direction. **2** a complete change of policy.

UV *abbreviation* ultraviolet.

Vv

v. *abbreviation* versus.

vacant *adjective* **1** empty; not filled or occupied. **2** without expression; blank, a *vacant stare*. **vacantly** *adverb*, **vacancy** *noun* [from Latin *vacans* = being empty]

vacate *verb* (**vacated**, **vacating**) leave or give up a place or position. [from Latin *vacare* = be empty or free from work]

vacation (*say* vak-**ay**-shon) *noun* **1** a holiday. **2** the period between terms at a university etc. **3** vacating a place or position. [same origin as *vacate*]

vaccinate (*say* **vak**-sin-ayt) *verb* (**vaccinated**, **vaccinating**) inoculate someone with a vaccine. **vaccination** *noun*

vaccine (*say* **vak**-seen) *noun* a substance used to immunise a person against a disease. [from Latin *vacca* = cow (because serum from cows was used to protect people from smallpox)]

vacillate (*say* **vass**-il-ayt) *verb* (**vacillated**, **vacillating**) keep changing your mind; waver. **vacillation** *noun* [from Latin *vacillare* = sway]

vacuous (*say* **vak**-yoo-us) *adjective* empty-headed; without expression, *a vacuous stare*. **vacuously** *adverb*, **vacuousness** *noun*, **vacuity** *noun* [same origin as *vacuum*]

vacuum *noun* **1** a completely empty space; a space without any air in it. **2** (*informal*) a vacuum cleaner. **vacuum** *verb*
vacuum cleaner an electrical device that sucks up dust and dirt etc.
vacuum flask a container with double walls that have a vacuum between them, used for keeping liquids hot or cold.
[from Latin *vacuus* = empty]

vagabond *noun* a wanderer; a vagrant. [from Latin *vagari* = wander]

vagary (*say* **vay**-ger-ee) *noun* (*plural* **vagaries**) an impulsive change or whim, *the vagaries of fashion*. [from Latin *vagari* = wander]

vagina (*say* va-**jy**-na) *noun* the passage that leads from the vulva to the womb. [from Latin *vagina* = sheath]

vagrant (*say* **vay**-grant) *noun* a person with no settled home or regular work; a tramp. **vagrancy** *noun* [from Latin *vagans* = wandering]

vague *adjective* not definite; not clear. **vaguely** *adverb*, **vagueness** *noun* [from Latin *vagus* = wandering]

vain *adjective* **1** conceited, especially about your appearance. **2** useless, *They made vain attempts to save her*. **vainly** *adverb*
in vain with no result; uselessly.
[from Latin *vanus* = empty]

valance *noun* a short curtain round the frame of a bed or above a window.

vale *noun* (*old use*) a valley. [from Latin *vallis* = valley]

valediction (*say* val-id-**ik**-shon) *noun* saying farewell. **valedictory** *adjective* [from Latin *vale* = farewell, + *dicere* = say (compare *benediction*)]

valentine *noun* **1** a card sent on St Valentine's day (14 February) to the person you love. **2** the person to whom you send this card.

valet (*say* **val**-ay or **val**-it) *noun* a man's servant who looks after his clothes etc.

valetudinarian *noun* a person who is excessively concerned about keeping healthy. [from Latin *valetudo* = health]

valiant *adjective* brave; courageous. **valiantly** *adverb* [same origin as *value*]

valid *adjective* **1** legally able to be used or accepted. *This passport is out of date and not valid*. **2** (of reasoning) sound and logical. **validity** *noun* [from Latin *validus* = strong]

valley *noun* (*plural* **valleys**) **1** a long low area between hills. **2** an area through which a river flows, *the Nile valley*. [same origin as *vale*]

valour *noun* bravery. **valorous** *adjective* [from Latin *valor* = strength]

valuable *adjective* worth a lot of money; of great value. **valuably** *adverb*
valuables *plural noun* valuable things.

value *noun* **1** the amount of money etc. that is considered to be the equivalent of something, or for which it can be exchanged. **2** how useful or important something is, *They learnt the value of regular exercise*.

value *verb* (**valued**, **valuing**) **1** think that something is valuable. **2** estimate the value of a thing. **valuation** *noun*, **valuer** *noun* [from Latin *valere* = be strong]

valueless *adjective* having no value.

valve *noun* **1** a device for controlling the flow of gas or liquid through a pipe or tube. **2** each piece of the shell of oysters etc. **valvular** *adjective* [from Latin *valva* = section of a folding door]

vamp *noun* **1** the front part of a shoe that goes over the foot. **2** a short introductory musical piece, often repeated.

vamp *verb* **1** make from odds and ends, *We'll vamp something up.* **2** improvise a musical accompaniment. **3** attach a new shoe upper. **4** (*informal*) repair or improve something.

vampire *noun* a ghost or revived corpse supposed to leave a grave at night and suck blood from living people.

van[1] *noun* **1** a covered vehicle for carrying goods or horses etc. or prisoners. **2** a railway carriage for luggage or goods, or for the use of the guard. [short for *caravan*]

van[2] *noun* the vanguard; the forefront.

vandal *noun* a person who deliberately breaks or damages things. **vandalism** *noun* [named after the Vandals, a Germanic tribe who invaded the Roman Empire in the 5th century, destroying many books and works of art]

vandalise *verb* (**vandalised**, **vandalising**) damage things as a vandal.

vane *noun* **1** a weather-vane. **2** the blade of a propeller, sail of a windmill, or other device that acts on or is moved by wind or water.

vanguard *noun* **1** the leading part of an army or fleet. **2** the first people to adopt a fashion or idea etc. [from French *avant* = before, + *garde* = guard]

vanilla *noun* a flavouring obtained from the pods of a tropical plant. [from Spanish *vainilla* = little pod]

vanish *verb* disappear completely.

vanity *noun* conceit; being vain.

vanquish *verb* conquer. [from Latin *vincere* = conquer]

vantage-point *noun* a place from which you have a good view of something. [from *vantage* = advantage]

vapid *adjective* not lively, not interesting.

vaporise *verb* (**vaporised**, **vaporising**) change or be changed into vapour. **vaporisation** *noun*, **vaporiser** *noun*

vapour *noun* a visible gas to which some substances can be converted by heat; steam or mist. [from Latin *vapor* = steam]

variable *adjective* varying; changeable. **variably** *adverb*, **variability** *noun*

variable *noun* something that varies or can vary; a variable quantity.

variance *noun* the amount by which things differ.
at variance differing; conflicting.

variant *adjective* differing from something, *'Gipsy' is a variant spelling of 'gypsy'.* **variant** *noun*

variation *noun* **1** varying; the amount by which something varies. **2** a different form of something.

varicose *adjective* (of veins) permanently swollen.

varied *adjective* of different sorts; full of variety.

variegated (*say* **vair**-ig-ay-tid) *adjective* with patches of different colours. **variegation** *noun* [same origin as *various*]

variety *adjective* (*plural* **varieties**) **1** a quantity of different kinds of things. **2** the quality of not always being the same; variation. **3** a particular kind of something, *There are several varieties of spaniel.* **4** an entertainment that includes short performances of various kinds.

various *adjective* **1** of several kinds; unlike one another, *for various reasons.* **2** several, *We met various people.* **variously** *adverb* [from Latin *varius* = changing]

varnish *noun* (*plural* **varnishes**) a liquid that dries to form a hard shiny usually transparent coating.

varnish *verb* coat something with varnish.

varsity *noun* (*NZ, informal*) university.

vary *verb* (**varied**, **varying**) **1** make or become different; change. **2** be different.

vascular *adjective* consisting of tubes or similar vessels for circulating blood, sap, or water in animals or plants, *the vascular system.* [from Latin *vasculum* = little vessel]

vase *noun* an open usually tall container used for holding cut flowers or as an ornament. [from Latin *vas* = vessel]

vaseline *noun* (*trade mark*) petroleum jelly for use as an ointment. [from German *Wasser* = water, + Greek *elaion* = oil]

vassal *noun* a humble servant or subordinate.

vast *adjective* very great, especially in area, *a vast expanse of water.* **vastly** *adverb*, **vastness** *noun* [from Latin *vastus* = unoccupied, desert]

vat *noun* a very large container for holding liquid.

vaudeville (*say* **vawd**-vil) *noun* a kind of variety entertainment.

vault *verb* jump over something, especially while supporting yourself on your hands or with the help of a pole.

vault *noun* **1** a vaulting jump. **2** an arched roof. **3** an underground room used to store things. **4** a room for storing money or valuables. **5** a burial chamber. [from Latin *volvere* = to roll]

vaulted *adjective* having an arched roof.

vaulting-horse *noun* a padded structure for vaulting over in gymnastics.

vaunt *verb & noun* (*old use* or *poetical*) boast. [from Latin *vanus* = vain]

VC *abbreviation* Victoria Cross.

VCR *abbreviation* video cassette recorder.

VDU *abbreviation* visual display unit.

veal *noun* calf's flesh used as food. [from Latin *vitulus* = calf]

vector *noun* (in mathematics) a quantity that has size and direction (e.g. velocity, = speed in a certain direction). **vectorial** *adjective*

veer *verb* change direction; swerve.

vegan *noun* a person who does not eat meat or any animal products (e.g. eggs, cheese). **vegan** *adjective*

Vegemite *noun* (*NZ, trade mark*) a spread made from yeast and vegetable extracts.

vege(s) *noun* (*NZ, informal*) vegetable(s).

vegetable *noun* a plant that can be used as food.
vegetable caterpillar (*NZ*) the āwhato.
vegetable sheep (*NZ*) a plant with white leaves that from a distance looks like sheep.

vegetarian *noun* a person who does not eat meat. **vegetarianism** *noun*

vegetate *verb* (**vegetated, vegetating**) live a dull or inactive life.

vegetation *noun* **1** plants that are growing. **2** vegetating.

vehement (*say* **vee**-im-ent) *adjective* showing strong feeling, *a vehement refusal.* **vehemently** *adverb*, **vehemence** *noun*

vehicle *noun* a device for transporting people or goods on land or in space. [from Latin *vehere* = carry]

veil *noun* a piece of thin material worn to cover the face or head.
take the veil become a nun.

veil *verb* cover with a veil or as if with a veil; conceal partially.

vein *noun* **1** any of the tubes that carry blood from all parts of the body to the heart. (Compare *artery.*) **2** a line or streak on a leaf, rock, insect's wing, etc. **3** a long deposit of mineral or ore in the middle of a rock. **4** a mood or manner, *She spoke in a serious vein.* [from Latin *vena* = vein]

veld (*say* velt) *noun* an area of open grassland in South Africa. [Afrikaans, = field]

vellum *noun* smooth parchment or writing-paper. [same origin as *veal* (because parchment was made from animals' skins)]

velocity *noun* (*plural* **velocities**) speed. [from Latin *velox* = swift]

velour (*say* vil-**oor**) *noun* a thick velvety material. [from French *velours* = velvet]

velvet *noun* **1** a woven material with very short soft furry fibres on one side. **2** the furry skin that grows on a deer's antler. **velvety** *adjective* [from Latin *villus* = soft fur]

venal (*say* **veen**-al) *adjective* able to be bribed. **venality** *noun* [from Latin *venalis* = for sale]

vend *verb* offer something for sale. [from Latin *vendere* = sell]

vendetta *noun* a feud. [Italian, from Latin *vindicta* = vengeance]

vending-machine *noun* a slot-machine where small articles can be obtained.

vendor *noun* a seller. [from *vend*]

veneer *noun* **1** a thin layer of good wood covering the surface of a cheaper wood in furniture etc. **2** an outward show of some good quality, *a veneer of politeness.*

venerable *adjective* worthy of being venerated, especially because of great age.

venerate *verb* (**venerated, venerating**) honour with great respect or reverence. **veneration** *noun* [from Latin *venerari* = revere]

venereal (*say* vin-**eer**-ee-al) *adjective* of sexual intercourse; caused by sexual intercourse with an infected person, *venereal diseases.* [from *Venus*, the Roman goddess of love]

venetian blind a window blind consisting of horizontal strips that can be adjusted to let light in or shut it out. [from Latin *Venetia* = Venice]

vengeance *noun* revenge.
with a vengeance very strongly or effectively. [same origin as *vindictive*]

vengeful *adjective* seeking vengeance. **vengefully** *adverb*, **vengefulness** *noun*

venial (*say* **veen**-ee-al) *adjective* (of sins or faults) pardonable, not serious. [from Latin *venia* = forgiveness]

venison *noun* deer's flesh as food. [from Latin *venatio* = hunting]

venom *noun* **1** the poisonous fluid produced by snakes, scorpions, etc. **2** very bitter feeling towards somebody; hatred. **venomous** *adjective* [from Latin *venenum* = poison]

vent *noun* an opening in something, especially to let out smoke or gas etc.
give vent to express your feelings etc. openly.

vent *verb* **1** make a vent in something. **2** give vent to feelings. [from Latin *ventus* = wind]

ventilate *verb* (**ventilated**, **ventilating**) let air move freely in and out of a room etc. **ventilation** *noun*, **ventilator** *noun* [same origin as *vent*]

ventral *adjective* of or on the abdomen, *This fish has a ventral fin.* [from Latin *venter* = abdomen]

ventriloquist *noun* an entertainer who makes his or her voice sound as if it comes from another source. **ventriloquism** *noun* [from Latin *venter* = abdomen, + *loqui* = speak]

venture *noun* something you decide to do that is risky.

venture *verb* (**ventured**, **venturing**) risk; dare to do or say something or to go somewhere, *We ventured out into the snow.* [compare *adventure*]

Venture Scout a member of a senior branch of the Scout Association.

venturesome *adjective* ready to take risks; daring.

venue (*say* **ven**-yoo) *noun* the place where a meeting, sports match, etc. is held. [from French *venir* = come]

veracity (*say* ver-**as**-it-ee) *noun* truth. **veracious** (*say* ver-**ay**-shus) *adjective* [from Latin *verus* = true]

veranda *noun* (also **verandah**) **1** a terrace with a roof along the side of a house. **2** (*NZ*) a roof over the footpath outside a shop or row of shops. [from Hindi *varanda*]

verb *noun* a word that shows what a person or thing is doing, e.g. *bring, came, sing, were.* [from Latin *verbum* = word]

verbal *adjective* **1** of or in words; spoken, not written, a *verbal statement.* **2** of verbs. **verbally** *adverb* [same origin as *verb*]

verbatim (*say* ver-**bay**-tim) *adverb & adjective* in exactly the same words, *He copied his friend's essay verbatim.*

verbose *adjective* using more words than are needed. **verbosely** *adverb*, **verbosity** (*say* ver-**boss**-it-ee) *noun*

verdant *adjective* (of grass or fields) green. [compare *verdure*]

verdict *noun* a judgement or decision made after considering something, especially that made by a jury. [from Latin *verus* = true, + *dictum* = said]

verdigris (*say* **verd**-i-grees) *noun* green rust on copper or brass. [from French, = green (*vert*) of Greece]

verdure *noun* green vegetation; its greenness. [from Old French *verd* = green]

verge *noun* **1** the extreme edge or brink of something. **2** a strip of grass along the edge of a road or path etc.

verge *verb* (**verged**, **verging**) **verge on** border on something; be close to.

verger *noun* a person who is caretaker and attendant in a church.

verify *verb* (**verified**, **verifying**) check or show that something is true or correct. **verifiable** *adjective*, **verification** *noun* [from Latin *verus* = true]

verisimilitude *noun* an appearance of being true or lifelike. [from Latin *verus* = true, + *similis* = like]

veritable *adjective* real; rightly named, *a veritable villain.* **veritably** *adverb* [same origin as *verity*]

verity *noun* (*plural* **verities**) truth. [from Latin *veritas* = truth]

vermicelli (*say* verm-i-**sel**-ee) *noun* pasta made in long thin threads. [Italian, = little worms]

vermilion *noun & adjective* bright red. [from Latin *vermiculus* = little worm]

vermin *plural noun* **1** pests (e.g. possums, rats, mice) regarded as harmful to other animals, crops, or food. **2** unpleasant or parasitic insects, e.g. lice. **verminous** *adjective* [from Latin *vermis* = worm]

vernacular (*say* ver-**nak**-yoo-ler) *noun* the language of a country or district, as distinct from an official or *formal* language. [from Latin *vernaculus* = domestic]

vernal *adjective* of the season of spring. [from Latin *ver* = spring]

verruca (*say* ver-**oo**-ka) *noun* a kind of wart on the sole of the foot.

versatile *adjective* able to do or be used for many different things. **versatility** *noun* [from Latin *versare* = to turn]

verse *noun* **1** writing arranged in short lines, usually with a particular rhythm and often with rhymes. **2** a group of lines forming a unit in a poem or hymn. **3** each of the short numbered sections of a chapter in the Bible. [from Latin *versus* = line of writing]

versed *adjective* **versed in** experienced or skilled in something. [from Latin *versatus* = engaged in something]

version *noun* **1** a particular person's account of something that happened. **2** a translation, *modern versions of the Bible.* **3** a special or different form of something, *the latest version of this car.* [from Latin *versum* = turned]

versus *preposition* against; competing with, *Waikato versus Bay of Plenty.* [Latin, = against]

vertebra *noun* (*plural* **vertebrae**) each of the bones that form the backbone.

vertebrate *noun* an animal that has a backbone. (The opposite is *invertebrate.*) [from *vertebra*]

vertex *noun* (*plural* **vertices**, (*say* **ver**-tis-eez) the highest point (*apex*) of a cone or triangle, or of a hill etc. [from Latin *vertex* = top of the head]

vertical *adjective* at right angles to something horizontal; upright. **vertically** *adverb* [from *vertex*]

vertigo *noun* a feeling of dizziness and loss of balance, especially when you are very high up. [Latin, = whirling (*vertere* = to turn)]

verve (*say* verv) *noun* enthusiasm; liveliness.

very *adverb* **1** to a great amount or intensity; extremely, *It was very cold.* **2** (used to emphasise something), *on the very next day; the very last drop.*

very *adjective* **1** exact; actual, *It's the very thing we need.* **2** extreme, *at the very end.* [from Latin *verus* = true]

vespers *plural noun* a church service held in the evening. [from Latin *vesper* = evening]

vessel *noun* **1** a ship or boat. **2** a container, especially for liquid. **3** a tube carrying blood or other liquid in the body of an animal or plant. [same origin as *vase*]

vest *noun* **1** an undergarment covering the trunk of the body; a singlet. **2** (*American*) a waistcoat.

vest *verb* **1** confer something as a right, *The power to make laws is vested in Parliament.* **2** (*old use*) to clothe.
vested interest a right that benefits a person or group and is securely held by them. [from Latin *vestis* = garment]

vestibule *noun* **1** an entrance hall or lobby. **2** a church porch.

vestige *noun* a trace; a very small amount, especially of something that formerly existed. **vestigial** *adjective* [from Latin *vestigium* = footprint]

vestment *noun* a ceremonial garment, especially one worn by clergy or choir at a service. [same origin as *vest*]

vestry *noun* (*plural* **vestries**) a room in a church where vestments are kept and where clergy and choir put these on.

vet[1] *noun* a person trained to give medical and surgical treatment to animals. [short for *veterinary surgeon*]

vet[2] *noun* a veteran. [abbreviation]

vet[1] *verb* (**vetted**, **vetting**) check a thing to see if it has any mistakes or faults.

vetch *noun* a plant of the pea family.

veteran *noun* **1** a person who has had long service or experience in something. **2** an ex-serviceman or woman, *a Vietnam War veteran.*
veteran car a motor vehicle built before 1918.
[from Latin *vetus* = old]

veterinary (*say* **vet**-rin-ree) *adjective* of the medical and surgical treatment of animals, *a veterinary surgeon.* [from Latin *veterinae* = cattle]

veto (*say* **vee**-toh) *noun* (*plural* **vetoes**) **1** a refusal to let something happen. **2** the right to prohibit something.

veto *verb* (**vetoed**, **vetoing**) refuse or prohibit something. [Latin, = I forbid]

vex *verb* annoy; cause somebody worry.
vexation *noun*, **vexatious** *adjective*
vexed question a problem that is difficult or much discussed. [from Latin *vexare* = to shake]

VHF *abbreviation* very high frequency.

via (*say* **vy**-a) *preposition* through, *The train goes from Auckland to Wellington via Palmerston North.* [Latin, = by way]

viable *adjective* able to exist successfully; practicable. **viability** *noun* [from French *vie* = life]

viaduct *noun* a long bridge, usually with many arches, carrying a road or railway over a valley or low ground. [from Latin *via* = way, + *ducere* = to lead (compare *aqueduct*)]

vial *noun* a small glass bottle. [compare *phial*]

viands (*say* **vy**-andz) *plural noun* food.

vibrant *adjective* vibrating; lively.

vibraphone *noun* a musical instrument like a xylophone with metal bars under which there are tiny electric fans making a vibrating effect. [from *vibrate*, + Greek *phone* = voice]

vibrate *verb* (**vibrated**, **vibrating**) **1** shake very quickly to and fro. **2** make a throbbing sound. **vibration** *noun* [from Latin *vibrare* = shake]

vicar *noun* a member of the Anglican clergy who is in charge of a parish.

vicarage *noun* the house of a vicar.

vicarious (*say* vik-**air**-ee-us) *adjective* felt by imagining you share someone else's activities, *We felt a vicarious thrill by watching people skiing.* [from Latin *vicarius* = substitute]

vice[1] *noun* **1** evil; wickedness. **2** an evil or bad habit; a bad fault. [from Latin *vitium* = fault]

vice[2] *noun* a device for gripping something and holding it firmly while you work on it. [from Latin *vitis* = vine]

vice- *prefix* **1** authorised to act as a deputy or substitute (as in *vice-captain*, *vice-president*). **2** next in rank to someone (as in *vice-admiral*). [from Latin *vice* = by a change]

vice versa *adverb* the other way round. [Latin]

vicinity *noun* the area near or round something.

vicious *adjective* evil; brutal; dangerously wicked or strong. **viciously** *adverb*, **viciousness** *noun*
vicious circle a situation where a problem produces an effect which itself produces the original problem or makes it worse.
[same origin as *vice*[1]]

vicissitude (*say* viss-**iss**-i-tewd) *noun* a change of circumstances. [from Latin *vicissim* = in turn]

victim *noun* someone who is injured, killed, robbed, etc.

victimise *verb* (**victimised**, **victimising**) make a victim of someone; punish a person unfairly. **victimisation** *noun*

victor *noun* the winner.

Victorian *adjective* **1** of the time of Queen Victoria (1837–1901). **2** of the Australian State of Victoria. **Victorian** *noun*

victory *noun* (*plural* **victories**) success won against an opponent in a battle, contest, or game. **victorious** *adjective* [from Latin *victum* = conquered]

victualler (*say* **vit**-ler) *noun* a person who supplies victuals.
licensed victualler a person who holds the licence of a public house.

victuals (*say* **vit**-alz) *plural noun* food; provisions. [from Latin *victus* = food]

video *noun* (*plural* **videos**) **1** recorded or broadcast pictures. **2** a video recorder or recording.
video cassette a cassette of videotape.
video recorder or **video cassette recorder** a device for recording a television programme etc. on magnetic tape for playing back later.
[Latin, = I see]

video *verb* make a video recording.

videotape *noun* magnetic tape suitable for recording television programmes.

vie *verb* (**vied**, **vying**) compete; carry on a rivalry, *vying with each other*.

view *noun* **1** what can be seen from one place; beautiful scenery. **2** sight; range of vision, *The ship sailed into view*. **3** an opinion, *She has strong views about politics*.
in view of because of.
on view displayed for inspection.
with a view to with the hope or intention of.

view *verb* **1** look at something. **2** consider.
viewer *noun*

viewpoint *noun* a point of view.

vigil (*say* **vij**-il) *noun* **1** staying awake to keep watch or pray, *a long vigil*. **2** a silent protest or demonstration. [from Latin *vigil* = wakeful]

vigilant (*say* **vij**-il-ant) *adjective* watchful. **vigilantly** *adverb*, **vigilance** *noun* [from Latin *vigilans* = keeping watch]

vigilante (*say* vij-il-**an**-tee) *noun* a member of a group who organise themselves, without authority, to try to prevent crime and disorder in a small area. [Spanish, = vigilant]

vigorous *adjective* full of vigour. **vigorously** *adverb*

vigour *noun* strength; energy; liveliness. [from Latin *vigor* = strength]

Viking *noun* a Scandinavian trader and pirate in the 8th–11th centuries.

vile *adjective* **1** extremely disgusting. **2** very bad or wicked. **vilely** *adverb*, **vileness** *noun* [from Latin *vilis* = cheap, unworthy]

vilify (*say* **vil**-if-I) *verb* (**vilified**, **vilifying**) say unpleasant things about a person or thing. **vilification** *noun* [same origin as *vile*]

villa *noun* **1** (in Europe) a large country house or mansion. **2** (in New Zealand) a large wooden house typical of the late 19th–early 20th centuries. **3** (*NZ*) a home unit in a retirement village. [Latin, = country house]

village *noun* **1** a group of houses and other buildings in a country district, smaller than a town. **2** (*NZ*) a suburban shopping centre, *Parnell village*. **3** an accommodation complex for the elderly, athletes, etc., *retirement village, Olympic village*. **villager** *noun* [from *villa*]

villain *noun* a wicked person; a criminal. **villainous** *adjective*, **villainy** *noun*

villein (*say* **vil**-in) *noun* a tenant in feudal times.

vim *noun* (*informal*) vigour.

vinaigrette *noun* a salad dressing made from oil and vinegar.

vindicate *verb* (**vindicated**, **vindicating**) **1** clear a person of blame or suspicion etc. **2** prove something to be true or worth while. **vindication** *noun* [from Latin *vindicare* = set free]

vindictive *adjective* showing a desire for revenge. **vindictively** *adverb*, **vindictiveness** *noun* [from Latin *vindicta* = vengeance]

vine *noun* a climbing or trailing plant whose fruit is the grape. [from Latin *vinum* = wine]

vinegar *noun* a sour liquid used to flavour food or in pickling. [from Latin *vinum* = wine, + *acer* = sour]

vineyard (*say* **vin**-yard) *noun* a plantation of vines producing grapes for making wine.

vintage *noun* **1** the harvest of a season's grapes; the wine made from this. **2** the period from which something comes.
vintage car an early model of car, especially one made between 1917 and 1930.

vinyl *noun* a kind of plastic.

viola[1] (*say* vee-**oh**-la) *noun* a musical instrument like a violin but slightly larger and with a lower pitch.

viola[2] (*say* **vy**-ol-a) *noun* a plant of the kind that includes violets and pansies.

violate *verb* (**violated**, **violating**) **1** break a promise, law, or treaty etc. **2** break into somewhere; treat a person or place without respect. **3** rape. **violation** *noun*, **violator** *noun* [from Latin *violare* = treat violently]

violence *noun* force that does harm or damage. **violent** *adjective*, **violently** *adverb*

violet *noun* **1** a small plant that often has purple flowers. **2** purple.

violin *noun* a musical instrument with four strings, played with a bow. **violinist** *noun*

VIP *abbreviation* very important person.

viper *noun* a small poisonous snake.

virago (*say* vir-**ah**-goh) *noun* (*plural* **viragos**) a fierce or bullying woman. [Latin, = female soldier]

virgin *noun* a person, especially a girl or woman, who has never had sexual intercourse. **virginal** *adjective*, **virginity** *noun*

virgin *adjective* **1** of a virgin. **2** spotless. **3** not yet touched, *virgin snow.*

virginals *plural noun* an instrument rather like a harpsichord, used in Europe in the 16th–17th centuries.

virile (*say* **vir**-I'l) *adjective* having masculine strength or vigour. **virility** *noun* [from Latin *vir* = man]

virology *noun* the study of viruses. **virological** *adjective*, **virologist** *noun* [from *virus* + *-logy*]

virtual *adjective* **1** appearing as real. **2** almost or nearly. **virtually** *adverb*
virtual reality the simulation of reality by computerised means.

virtue *noun* **1** moral goodness; a particular form of this, *Honesty is a virtue.* **2** a good quality; an advantage. **virtuous** *adjective*, **virtuously** *adverb*
by virtue of because of.
[from Latin *virtus* = worth]

virtuoso (*say* ver-tew-**oh**-soh) *noun* (*plural* **virtuosos** or **virtuosi**) a person with outstanding skill, especially in singing or playing music. **virtuosity** *noun* [Italian, = skilful]

virulent (*say* **vir**-oo-lent) *adjective* **1** strongly poisonous or harmful, *a virulent disease.* **2** bitterly hostile, *virulent criticism.* **virulence** *noun* [same origin as *virus*]

virus *noun* (*plural* **viruses**) **1** a very tiny living thing, smaller than a bacterium, that can cause disease. **2** a self-duplicating program intended to sabotage a computer system by destroying data as it spreads. [Latin, = poison]

visa (*say* **vee**-za) *noun* an official mark put on someone's passport by officials of a country to show that the holder has permission to enter that country. [Latin, = things seen]

visage (*say* **viz**-ij) *noun* a person's face. [from Latin *visus* = sight]

viscera (*say* **vis**-er-a) *plural noun* the intestines and other internal organs of the body. [Latin, = soft parts]

viscid (*say* **vis**-id) *adjective* thick and gluey. **viscidity** *noun*

viscose (*say* **vis**-kohs) *noun* fabric made from viscous cellulose.

viscous (*say* **visk**-us) *adjective* thick and gluey, not pouring easily. **viscosity** *noun*

visible *adjective* able to be seen or noticed, *The ship was visible on the horizon.* **visibly** *adverb*, **visibility** *noun* [same origin as *vision*]

vision *noun* **1** the ability to see; sight. **2** something seen in a person's imagination or in a dream. **3** foresight and wisdom in planning things. **4** a person or thing that is beautiful to see. **5** the picture on a television screen. [from Latin *visum* = seen]

visionary *adjective* imaginary; fanciful.

visionary *noun* (*plural* **visionaries**) a person with visionary ideas.

visit *verb* **1** go to see a person or place. **2** stay somewhere for a while. **3** access and view (a website). **visitor** *noun*

visit *noun* the action of visiting. [from Latin *visitare* = go to see]

visitant *noun* **1** a visitor, especially a supernatural one. **2** a bird that is a visitor to an area while migrating.

visitation *noun* an official visit, especially to inspect something.

visor (*say* **vy**-zer) *noun* **1** the part of a helmet that covers the face. **2** a shield to protect the eyes from bright light or sunshine. [same origin as *visage*]

vista *noun* a long view. [Italian, = view]

visual *adjective* of or used in seeing; of sight. **visually** *adverb*
visual aids pictures and films etc. used as an aid in teaching.
visual display unit a device that looks like a television screen and displays data being received from a computer or fed into it.
[same origin as *vision*]

visualise *verb* (**visualised, visualising**) form a mental picture of something. **visualisation** *noun*

vital *adjective* **1** connected with life; necessary for life to continue, *vital functions such as breathing.* **2** essential; very important. **vitally** *adverb* [from Latin *vita* = life]

vitalise *verb* (**vitalised, vitalising**) put life or vitality into something.

vitality *noun* liveliness; energy.

vitamin (*say* **vit**-a-min or **vy**-ta-min) *noun* any of a number of substances that are present in various foods and are essential to keep people and animals healthy. [same origin as *vital*]

vitiate (*say* **vish**-ee-ayt) *verb* (**vitiated, vitiating**) spoil something by making it imperfect. **vitiation** *noun* [from Latin *vitium* = fault]

vitreous (*say* **vit**-ree-us) *adjective* like glass in being hard, transparent, or brittle, *vitreous enamel.* [from Latin *vitrum* = glass]

vitriol (*say* **vit**-ree-ol) *noun* **1** sulphuric acid or one of its compounds. **2** savage criticism. **vitriolic** *adjective*

vituperation *noun* abusive words.

vivacious (*say* viv-**ay**-shus) *adjective* happy and lively. **vivaciously** *adverb*, **vivacity** *noun* [from Latin *vivere* = to live]

vivid *adjective* **1** bright and strong or clear, *vivid colours; a vivid description.* **2** active and lively, *a vivid imagination.* **vividly** *adverb*, **vividness** *noun* [from Latin *vividus* = full of life]

vivisection *noun* doing surgical experiments on live animals. [from Latin *vivus* = alive, + *dissection*]

vixen *noun* a female fox.

viz. *abbreviation* namely. [from Latin *videlicet*]

vizier (*say* viz-**eer**) *noun* (in former times) an important Muslim official. [from Arabic *wazir* = chief counsellor]

vocabulary *noun* (*plural* **vocabularies**) **1** the words used by a particular language. **2** the words known to a person or used in a particular book or subject etc. [from Latin *vocabulum* = name]

vocal *adjective* of or producing or using the voice. **vocally** *adverb*
vocal cords two strap-like membranes in the throat that can be made to vibrate and produce sounds.
[from Latin *vocis* = of the voice]

vocalist *noun* a singer, especially in a pop group.

vocation *noun* **1** a person's job or occupation. **2** a strong desire to do a particular kind of work, or feeling of being called by God to do something. **vocational** *adjective* [from Latin *vocare* = to call]

vociferate (*say* vo-**sif**-er-ayt) *verb* (**vociferated, vociferating**) say something loudly or noisily. **vociferation** *noun* [from Latin *vocis* = of the voice, + *ferre* = carry]

vociferous (*say* vo-**sif**-er-us) *adjective* making an outcry; shouting.

vodka *noun* a strong alcoholic drink very popular in Russia [from Russian *voda* = water]

vogue *noun* the current fashion.

voice *noun* **1** sounds formed by the vocal cords and uttered by the mouth, especially in speaking, singing, etc. **2** the ability to speak or sing, *She has lost her voice.* **3** an opinion expressed. **4** the right to express an opinion or desire, *I have no voice in this matter.*

voice *verb* (**voiced, voicing**) say something, *We voiced our opinions.* [from Latin *vox* = voice]

voice-over *noun* narration by an unseen speaker in a television documentary or advertisement etc.

void *adjective* **1** empty. **2** having no legal validity.

void *noun* an empty space.

voile (*say* voil) *noun* a very thin almost transparent material. [French, = veil]

volatile (*say* **vol**-a-tyl) *adjective* **1** evaporating quickly, a *volatile liquid.* **2** changing quickly from one mood or interest to another. **volatility** *noun* [from Latin *volatilis* = flying]

volcano *noun* (*plural* **volcanoes**) a mountain with an opening at the top from which lava and hot gases etc. flow. **volcanic** *adjective* [from the name of Vulcan, the ancient Roman god of fire]

volition *noun* using your own will in choosing to do something, *She left of her own volition.* [from Latin *volo* = I wish]

volley *noun* (*plural* **volleys**) **1** a number of bullets or shells etc. fired at the same time. **2** hitting back the ball in tennis etc. before it touches the ground.

volley *verb* send or hit something in a volley or volleys. [from Latin *volare* = to fly]

volleyball *noun* a game in which two teams hit a large ball to and fro over a net with their hands.

volt *noun* a unit for measuring electric force. [named after an Italian scientist, Alessandro Volta]

voltage *noun* electric force measured in volts.

voluble *adjective* talking very much. **volubly** *adverb*, **volubility** *noun* [from Latin *volubilis* = rolling]

volume *noun* **1** the amount of space filled by something. **2** an amount or quantity, *The volume of work has increased.* **3** the strength or power of sound. **4** a book, especially one of a set. [from Latin *volumen* = a roll (because ancient books were made in a rolled form)]

voluminous (*say* vol-**yoo**-min-us) *adjective* **1** bulky; large and full, *a voluminous skirt.* **2** numerous; filling many volumes, *a voluminous writer.*

voluntary *adjective* **1** done or doing something willingly, not by being compelled. **2** unpaid. **voluntarily** *adverb*

voluntary *noun* (*plural* **voluntaries**) an organ solo, often improvised, played before or after a church service. [from Latin *voluntas* = the will]

volunteer *verb* give or offer something of your own accord.

volunteer *noun* a person who volunteers to do something, e.g. to serve in the armed forces.

voluptuous *adjective* giving a luxurious or sensual feeling, *voluptuous furnishings.* [from Latin *voluptas* = pleasure]

vomit *verb* bring up food etc. from the stomach and out through the mouth; be sick. **vomit** *noun*

voodoo *noun* a form of witchcraft and magical rites, especially in the West Indies.

voracious (*say* vor-**ay**-shus) *adjective* greedy; devouring things eagerly. **voraciously** *adverb*, **voracity** *noun* [from Latin *vorare* = devour]

vortex *noun* (*plural* **vortices**) a whirlpool or whirlwind. [Latin]

vote *verb* (**voted**, **voting**) show which person or thing you prefer by putting up your hand, making a mark on a paper, etc. **voter** *noun*

vote *noun* **1** the action of voting. **2** the right to vote. [from Latin *votum* = a wish or vow]

votive *adjective* given in fulfilment of a vow, *votive offerings at the shrine.*

vouch *verb* **vouch for** guarantee that something is true or certain, *I will vouch for his honesty.*

voucher *noun* a piece of paper that can be exchanged for certain goods or services; a receipt.

vouchsafe *verb* (**vouchsafed**, **vouchsafing**) grant something in a gracious or condescending way, *She did not vouchsafe a reply.*

vow *noun* a solemn promise, especially to God or a saint.

vow *verb* make a vow.

vowel *noun* **1** any of the sounds of speech in which there is no obstruction of the breath, e.g. the central sounds in *dog, cheese, thing.* **2** any of the letters of the alphabet used to represent these sounds, i.e. *a, e, i, o, u*, and sometimes *y*. (Compare *consonant.*) [from Latin *vocalis littera* = vocal letter]

voyage *noun* a long journey on water or in space.

voyage *verb* (**voyaged**, **voyaging**) make a voyage. **voyager** *noun*

VSA *abbreviation* Volunteer Service Abroad.

vulcanise *verb* (**vulcanised**, **vulcanising**) treat rubber with sulphur to strengthen it. **vulcanisation** *noun* [same origin as *volcano*]

vulgar *adjective* rude; without good manners. **vulgarly** *adverb*, **vulgarity** *noun*
vulgar fraction a fraction shown by numbers above and below a line (e.g. 2/3, 5/8), not a decimal fraction.
[from Latin *vulgus* = the ordinary people]

vulnerable *adjective* able to be hurt or harmed or attacked. **vulnerability** *noun* [from Latin *vulnus* = wound]

vulture *noun* a large bird that feeds on dead animals.

vulva *noun* the outer parts of the female genitals. [Latin]

vying *present participle* of **vie**.

Ww

W. *abbreviation* west; western.

wad (*say* wod) *noun* a pad or bundle of soft material or pieces of paper etc.

wad *verb* (**wadded**, **wadding**) pad something with soft material.

waddle *verb* (**waddled**, **waddling**) walk with short steps, swaying from side to side.
waddle *noun*

wade *verb* (**waded**, **wading**) walk through water or mud etc. **wader** *noun*

wafer *noun a* kind of thin biscuit.

waffle[1] (*say* **wof**-el) *noun a* small cake made of batter and eaten hot.

waffle[2] (*say* **wof**-el) *noun* (*informal*) vague wordy talk or writing. **waffle** *verb* [from a dialect word *waff* = yelp]

waft (*say* woft) *verb* carry or float gently through the air or over water.

wag[1] *verb* (**wagged**, **wagging**) move quickly to and fro. **wag** *noun*

wag[2] *noun* a person who makes jokes.

wage[1] *noun* or **wages** *plural noun* a regular payment to someone in return for his or her work.

wage[2] *verb* (**waged**, **waging**) carry on a war or campaign.

wager (*say* **way**-jer) *noun & verb* bet.

waggle *verb* (**waggled**, **waggling**) **1** move with short quick vertical or horizontal movements. **2** swing a golf club before playing a shot. **waggle** *noun*

wagon *noun* **1** a cart with four wheels, pulled by a horse or an ox. **2** an open railway truck, e.g. for coal. **3** a trolley for carrying food etc.

wagtail *noun* a small bird with a long tail that it moves up and down.

wahine *noun* (*plural* **wahine**) a woman; a wife. [Māori]

wai *noun* water. [Māori]

waiata *noun* a song. [Māori]

waif *noun* a homeless and helpless person, especially a child.

wail *verb* make a long sad cry. **wail** *noun*

wainscoting *noun* wooden panelling on the wall of a room.

wairua *noun* a spirit or soul; spirituality. [Māori]

waist *noun* the narrow part in the middle of the body.

waistcoat *noun* a short close-fitting jacket without sleeves, worn over a shirt and under a jacket.

wait *verb* **1** stay somewhere or postpone an action until something happens; pause. **2** be postponed, *This question must wait until our next meeting.* **3** wait on people.
wait on hand food and drink to people at a meal; be an attendant to someone.

wait *noun* an act or time of waiting, *We had a long wait for the train.*

Waitangi Day (*NZ*) 6 February, a public holiday that commemorates the signing of the Treaty of Waitangi in 1840.

waiter *noun* a man employed to serve people with food. **waitress** *noun*

waiting-list *noun* a list of people waiting for something to become available.

waiting-room *noun* a room provided for people who are waiting for something.

waive *verb* (**waived**, **waiving**) not insist on having something, *She waived her right to travel first class.* [from Old French, = abandon (compare *waif*)]

waka *noun* **1** a traditional Māori canoe. **2** a group of tribes, all descended from the occupants of one of the first canoes to reach New Zealand. **3** a common situation, enterprise, vessel, or vehicle, *We're all in the same waka.*
waka ama outrigger canoe.
waka-jump leave a political party.
[Māori]

wake[1] *verb* (**woke**, **woken**, **waking**) **1** stop sleeping, *Wake up! I woke when I heard the bell.* **2** cause someone to stop sleeping, *You have woken the baby.*

wake[1] *noun* (in Ireland) festivities held in connection with a funeral.

wake[2] *noun* **1** the track left on the water by a moving ship. **2** currents of air left behind a moving aircraft.
in the wake of following.

wakeful *adjective* unable to sleep.

waken *verb* wake.

walk *verb* move along on your feet at an ordinary speed. **walker** *noun*

walk *noun* **1** a journey on foot. **2** the manner of walking. **3** a path or route for walking.
walk of life a person's occupation or social level.

walkabout *noun* an informal stroll among a crowd by an important visitor.
go walkabout (of Australian Aborigines) journey for a time in the bush.

walkie-talkie *noun* a small portable radio transmitter and receiver.

walking-stick *noun* a stick for use as a support while walking.

walkover *noun* an easy victory.

walkway *noun* **1** a passage for walking along. **2** a public path or track.

wall *noun* **1** a continuous upright structure, usually made of brick, wood, or stone, forming one of the sides of a building or room or supporting something or enclosing an area. **2** the outside part of something.

wall *verb* enclose or block with a wall.

wallaby *noun* (*plural* **wallabies**) a kind of small kangaroo.

Wallaby *noun* an Australian national rugby union representative.

wallet *noun* a small flat folding case for holding banknotes, documents, etc.

wallflower *noun* a garden plant with fragrant flowers, blooming in spring.

wallop *verb* (**walloped**, **walloping**) (*slang*) thrash. **wallop** *noun*

wallow *verb* **1** roll about in water, mud, etc. **2** get great pleasure by being surrounded by something, *wallowing in luxury*.
wallow *noun*

wallpaper *noun* paper used to cover the inside walls of rooms.

walnut *noun* an edible nut with a wrinkled surface.

walrus *noun* (*plural* **walruses**) a large Arctic sea-animal with two long tusks.

waltz *noun* (*plural* **waltzes**) a dance with three beats to a bar.

waltz *verb* dance a waltz. [from German *walzen* = revolve]

wan (*say* wonn) *adjective* pale from being ill or tired. **wanly** *adverb*, **wanness** *noun*

wananga *noun* (*NZ*) a tertiary institute. [Māori]

wand *noun* a thin rod, especially one used by a magician.

wander *verb* **1** go about without trying to reach a particular place. **2** leave the right path or direction; stray. **wanderer** *noun*

wander *noun* a wandering journey.

wanderlust *noun* a strong desire to travel.

wane *verb* (**waned**, **waning**) **1** (of the moon) show a bright area that becomes gradually smaller after being full. (The opposite is *wax*.) **2** become less or smaller, *His popularity waned*. **wane** *noun* [from Old English *wanian* = reduce]

wangle *verb* (**wangled**, **wangling**) (*slang*) get or arrange something by using trickery, special influence, etc. **wangle** *noun*

wannabe *noun* (*informal*) one who aspires to be something or somebody specific.

want *verb* **1** wish to have something. **2** need, *Your hair wants cutting*. **3** be without something; lack. **4** be without the necessaries of life, *Waste not, want not*.

want *noun* **1** a wish to have something. **2** lack or need of something. [same origin as *wane*]

wanted *adjective* (of a suspected criminal) that the police wish to find or arrest.

wanton (*say* **wonn**-ton) *adjective* irresponsible; without a motive, *wanton damage*.

wapiti (*say* **wop**-it-ee) *noun* a large deer, originally from North America, now farmed in New Zealand.

war *noun* **1** fighting between nations or groups, especially using armed forces. **2** a serious struggle or effort against crime, disease, poverty, etc.
at war engaged in a war.

warble *verb* (**warbled**, **warbling**) sing with a trilling sound, as some birds do.
warble *noun*

warbler *noun* a kind of small bird.

ward *noun* **1** a room with beds for patients in a hospital. **2** a child looked after by a guardian. **3** an area electing a councillor to represent it.

ward *verb* **ward off** keep something away. [from Old English *weard* = guard]

warden *noun* an official who is in charge of a hostel, college, etc., or who supervises something.

warder *noun* an official in charge of prisoners in a prison.

wardrobe *noun* **1** a cupboard to hang clothes in. **2** a stock of clothes or costumes. [from *guard* + *robe*]

ware *noun* manufactured goods of a certain kind, *hardware*; *silverware*.
wares *plural noun* goods offered for sale.

warehou *noun* a sea-fish used as food. [Māori]

warehouse *noun* a large building where goods are stored. [from *ware* + *house*]

warfare *noun* war; fighting.

warhead *noun* the head of a missile or torpedo etc., containing explosives.

warlike *adjective* **1** fond of making war. **2** of or for war.

warm *adjective* **1** fairly hot; not cold or cool. **2** loving; enthusiastic, *a warm welcome.* **warmly** *adverb,* **warmness** *noun,* **warmth** *noun*

warm *verb* make or become warm.

warm-blooded *adjective* having blood that remains warm permanently.

warn *verb* tell someone about a danger etc. that may affect them, or about what they should do, *I warned you to take your raincoat.* **warning** *noun*

warp (*say* worp) *verb* **1** bend out of shape, e.g. by dampness. **2** distort a person's ideas etc., *Jealousy warped his mind.*

warp *noun* **1** a warped condition. **2** the lengthwise threads in weaving, crossed by the weft.

warrant *noun* a document that authorises a person to do something (e.g. to search a place) or to receive something.
warrant of fitness (*NZ*) a certificate that a car is roadworthy.

warrant *verb* **1** justify, *Nothing can warrant such rudeness.* **2** guarantee.

warranty *noun* a guarantee.

warren *noun* **1** a piece of ground where there are many burrows in which rabbits live and breed. **2** a building or place with many winding passages.

warring *adjective* occupied in war.

warrior *noun* a person who fights in battle; a soldier.

warship *noun* a ship for use in war.

wart *noun* a small hard lump on the skin, caused by a virus.

wartime *noun* a time of war.

wary (*say* **wair**-ee) *adjective* cautious; looking carefully for possible danger or difficulty. **warily** *adverb,* **wariness** *noun* [compare *aware*]

wash *verb* **1** clean something with water or other liquid. **2** be washable, *Cotton washes easily.* **3** flow against or over something, *Waves washed over the deck.* **4** carry along by a moving liquid, *A wave washed him overboard.* **5** (*informal*) be accepted or believed, *That excuse won't wash.*
wash out (*informal*) cancel something.
wash up wash dishes and cutlery etc. after use.
washing-up *noun*

wash *noun* (*plural* **washes**) **1** the action of washing. **2** clothes etc. being washed. **3** the disturbed water or air behind a moving ship or aircraft. **4** a thin coating of colour.

washable *adjective* able to be washed without becoming damaged.

washbasin *noun* a small sink for washing your hands etc.

washer *noun* **1** a small ring of rubber or metal etc. placed between two surfaces (e.g. under a bolt or screw) to fit them tightly together. **2** a washing-machine.

washing *noun* clothes etc. being washed.

washing-machine *noun* a machine for washing clothes etc.

wash-out *noun* (*slang*) a complete failure.

wasn't (*mainly spoken*) was not.

wasp *noun* a stinging insect with black and yellow stripes round its body.

wastage *noun* loss of something by waste.

waste *verb* (**wasted**, **wasting**) **1** use something in an extravagant way or without getting enough results. **2** fail to use something, *You wasted an opportunity.* **3** make or become gradually weaker or useless.

waste *adjective* **1** left over or thrown away because it is not wanted. **2** not used; not usable, *waste land.*
lay waste destroy the crops and buildings etc. of a district.

waste *noun* **1** the action of wasting a thing, not using it well, *a waste of time.* **2** things that are not wanted or not used. **3** an area of waste land, *the wastes of the Sahara Desert.* **wasteful** *adjective,* **wastefully** *noun,* **wastefulness** *noun* [from Latin *vastus* = empty]

wastrel (*say* **way**-strel) *noun* a person who wastes his or her life and does nothing useful.

watch *verb* **1** look at a person or thing for some time. **2** be on guard or ready for something to happen, *Watch for the traffic lights to turn green.* **3** take care of something. **watcher** *noun*

watch *noun* (*plural* **watches**) **1** the action of watching. **2** a turn of being on duty in a ship. **3** a device like a small clock, usually worn on the wrist.

watchful *adjective* watching closely; alert. **watchfully** *adverb,* **watchfulness** *noun*

watching brief *noun* **1** interest in a proceeding of indirect concern. **2** a barrister's brief to follow a case of indirect concern.

watchman *noun* (*plural* **watchmen**) a person employed to look after an empty building etc., especially at night.

watchword *noun* a word or phrase that sums up a group's policy; a slogan, *Our watchword is 'safety first'.*

water *noun* **1** a colourless odourless tasteless liquid that is a compound of hydrogen and oxygen. **2** a lake or sea etc. **3** the tide, *at high water.* **4** urine; sweat; saliva.

water *verb* **1** sprinkle or supply something with water. **2** produce tears or saliva, *It makes my mouth water.*
water down dilute.

water-colour *noun* **1** paint made with pigment and water (not oil). **2** a painting done with this kind of paint.

watercress *noun* a kind of cress that grows in water.

waterfall *noun* a stream flowing over the edge of a cliff or large rock.

watering-can *noun* a container with a long spout, for watering plants.

water-lily *noun* a plant that grows in water, with broad floating leaves and large flowers.

waterlogged *adjective* completely soaked or swamped in water.

watermark *noun* **1** a mark showing how high a river or tide rises or how low it falls. **2** a design that can be seen in some kinds of paper when they are held up to the light.

waterproof *adjective* that keeps out water. **waterproof** *verb*

watershed *noun* **1** a line of high land from which streams flow down on each side. **2** a turning-point in the course of events.

watersider *noun* (*NZ*) a person who loads and unloads ships at a port.

water-skiing *noun* skimming over the surface of water on a pair of flat boards (**water-skis**) while being towed by a motor boat.

waterspout *noun* a column of water formed when a whirlwind draws up a whirling mass of water from the sea.

water-table *noun* the level below which the ground is saturated with water.

watertight *adjective* **1** made or fastened so that water cannot get in or out. **2** that cannot be changed or set aside or proved to be untrue, *a watertight excuse.*

waterway *noun* a river or canal that ships can travel on.

waterworks *noun* a place with pumping machinery etc. for supplying water to a district.

watery *adjective* **1** of or like water. **2** full of water. **3** containing too much water.

watt *noun* a unit of electric power. [named after James Watt, a Scottish engineer]

wattage *noun* electric power measured in watts.

wattle[1] *noun* **1** sticks and twigs woven together to make fences, walls. etc. **2** an Australian tree with golden flowers.

wattle[2] *noun* a red fold of skin hanging from the throat of turkeys and some other birds.

wattle-bird *noun* (*NZ*) the huia, kokako, or saddleback.

wave *noun* **1** a ridge moving along the surface of the sea etc. or breaking on the shore. **2** a wave-like curve, e.g. in hair. **3** the wave-like movement by which heat, light, sound, or electricity etc. travels. **4** the action of waving.

wave *verb* (**waved**, **waving**) **1** move loosely to and fro or up and down. **2** move your hand to and fro as a signal or greeting etc. **3** make a thing wavy. **4** be wavy.

waveband *noun* the wavelengths between certain limits.

wavelength *noun* the size of a sound-wave or electromagnetic wave.

wavelet *noun* a small wave.

waver *verb* **1** be unsteady; move unsteadily. **2** hesitate; be uncertain.

wavy *adjective* full of waves or curves. **wavily** *adverb*, **waviness** *noun*

wax[1] *noun* (*plural* **waxes**) **1** a soft substance that melts easily, used to make candles, crayons, and polish. **2** beeswax. **waxy** *adjective*

wax[1] *verb* coat or polish something with wax.

wax[2] *verb* **1** (of the moon) show a bright area that becomes gradually larger. (The opposite is *wane.*) **2** become stronger or more important.

waxen *adjective* **1** made of wax. **2** like wax.

waxeye *noun* (*NZ*) the silvereye.

waxwork *noun* a model of a person etc. made in wax.

way *noun* **1** a line of communication between places, e.g. a path or road. **2** a route or direction. **3** a distance to be travelled. **4** how something is done; a method or style. **5** a respect, *It's a good idea in some ways.* **6** a condition or state, *Things were in a bad way.*
get or **have your own way** make people let you do what you want.
give way collapse; let somebody else move first; yield.
in the way forming an obstacle or hindrance.
no way (*informal*) that is impossible!
under way see *under.*

way *adverb* (*informal*) far, *That is way beyond what we can afford.*

wayfarer *noun* a traveller, especially someone who is walking.

waylay *verb* (**waylaid**, **waylaying**) lie in wait for a person or people, especially so as to talk to them or rob them.

wayside *noun* the land beside a road or path.

wayward *adjective* disobedient; wilfully doing what you want.

we *pronoun* a word used by a person to refer to himself or herself and another or others.

WEA *abbreviation* Workers' Educational Association.

weak *adjective* not strong; easy to break, bend, defeat, etc. **weakness** *noun*

weaken *verb* make or become weaker.

weakling *noun* a weak person or animal.

weakly *adverb* in a weak manner.

weakly *adjective* sickly; not strong.

weal *noun* a ridge raised on the flesh by a cane or whip etc.

wealth *noun* **1** much money or property; riches. **2** a large quantity, *The book has a wealth of illustrations.* [from *well*[2]]

wealthy *adjective* (**wealthier**, **wealthiest**) having wealth; rich. **wealthiness** *noun*

wean *verb* make a baby or young animal take food other than its mother's milk.

weaner *noun* a calf, pig, or lamb in the year in which it has been weaned.

weapon *noun* something used to do harm in a battle or fight. **weaponry** *noun*

wear *verb* (**wore**, **worn**, **wearing**) **1** have something on your body as clothes, ornaments, etc. **2** damage something by rubbing or using it often; become damaged in this way, *The carpet has worn thin.* **3** last while in use, *It has worn well.* **wearable** *adjective*, **wearer** *noun*
wear off be removed by wear or use; become less intense.
wear on pass gradually, *The night wore on.*
wear out use or be used until it becomes weak or useless; exhaust.

wearisome *adjective* causing weariness.

weary *adjective* (**wearier**, **weariest**) **1** tired. **2** tiring, *It's weary work.* **wearily** *adverb*, **weariness** *noun*

weary *verb* (**wearied**, **wearying**) tire.

weasel *noun* a small fierce animal with a slender body and reddish-brown fur.
weasel words words that are deliberately misleading.

weather *noun* the rain, snow, wind, sunshine, etc. at a particular time or place.
under the weather feeling ill or depressed.

weather *verb* **1** expose something to the effects of the weather. **2** come through something successfully, *The ship weathered the storm.*

weatherboard *adjective* (of a house) having outside walls of weatherboard.

weatherboard *noun* one of a series of overlapping horizontal boards used on the outside walls of a house.

weathercock or **weather-vane** *noun* a pointer, often shaped like a cockerel, that turns in the wind and shows from which direction it is blowing.

weave *verb* (**wove**, **woven**, **weaving**) **1** make material or baskets etc. by passing crosswise threads or strips under and over lengthwise ones. **2** put a story together, *She wove a thrilling tale.* **3** (*past tense & past participle* **weaved**) twist and turn, *He weaved through the traffic.* **weaver** *noun*

weave *noun* a style of weaving, *a loose weave.*

web *noun* **1** a cobweb. **2** a network. **3** (**the Web**) the World Wide Web.
web page (*Computing*) a document that can be accessed by using the World Wide Web.

webbed or **web-footed** *adjective* having toes joined by pieces of skin, *Ducks have webbed feet; they are web-footed.*

weblog *noun* a personal website on which correspondents can write opinions or information.

website *noun* a location connected to the Internet that maintains web pages.

wed *verb* (**wedded**, **wedding**) **1** marry. **2** unite two different things.

wedding *noun* the ceremony when a man and woman get married.

wedge *noun* **1** a piece of wood or metal etc. that is thick at one end and thin at the other. It is pushed between things to force them apart or prevent something from moving. **2** a wedge-shaped thing.

wedge *verb* (**wedged**, **wedging**) **1** keep something in place with a wedge. **2** pack tightly together, *Ten of us were wedged in the lift.*

wedlock *noun* the condition of being married; matrimony. [from Old English, = marriage vow]

Wednesday (*say* **wenz**-day) *noun* the day after Tuesday.

wee *adjective* (*Scottish and New Zealand*) little.

weed *noun* **1** a wild plant that grows where it is not wanted. **2** (*slang*) marijuana.

weed *verb* remove weeds from the ground.

weeds *plural noun* the black clothes formerly worn by a widow in mourning.

weedy *adjective* (**weedier**, **weediest**) **1** full of weeds. **2** thin and weak.

week *noun* a period of seven days, especially from Monday to the following Sunday.

weekday *noun* a day other than Saturday or Sunday.

weekend *noun* Saturday and Sunday.

weekly *adjective & adverb* happening or done once a week.

weeny *adjective* (*informal*) tiny.

weep *verb* (**wept**, **weeping**) **1** shed tears; cry. **2** ooze moisture in drops. **weep** *noun*, **weepy** *adjective*

weeping *adjective* (of a tree) having drooping branches, *a weeping willow.*

weevil *noun* a kind of small beetle.

weft *noun* the crosswise threads in weaving, passing through the warp.

weigh *verb* **1** measure the weight of something. **2** have a certain weight. **3** be important; have influence, *Her evidence weighed with the jury.*
weigh anchor raise the anchor and start a voyage.
weigh down keep something down by its weight; depress or trouble somebody.
weigh up estimate; assess.

weight *noun* **1** how heavy something is; an object's mass expressed as a number according to a scale of units. (Compare *mass*[1] 3.) **2** a piece of metal of known weight, especially one used on scales to weigh things. **3** a heavy object. **4** importance; influence. **weighty** *adjective*, **weightless** *adjective*

weight *verb* put a weight on something.

weir (*say* weer) *noun* a small dam across a river or canal to control the flow of water.

weird *adjective* very strange; uncanny. **weirdly** *adverb*, **weirdness** *noun*

weka *noun* a flightless brown rail, also called *woodhen.* [Māori]

WEL *abbreviation* (*NZ*) Women's Electoral Lobby.

welcome *noun* a greeting or reception, especially a kindly one.

welcome *adjective* **1** that you are glad to receive or see, *a welcome gift.* **2** gladly allowed, *You are welcome to come.*

welcome *verb* (**welcomed**, **welcoming**) show that you are pleased when a person or thing arrives. [from *well*[2] + *come*]

weld *verb* **1** join pieces of metal or plastic by heating and pressing or hammering them together. **2** unite people or things into a whole.

welfare *noun* people's health, happiness, and comfort.
welfare state a country that looks after the welfare of its people by social services run by the government.
[from *well*[2] + *fare*]

well[1] *noun* **1** a deep hole dug to bring up water or oil from underground. **2** a deep space, e.g. containing a staircase.

well[1] *verb* rise or flow up, *Tears welled up in our eyes.* [from Old English *wella* = spring of water]

well[2] *adverb* (**better**, **best**) **1** in a good or suitable way, *She swims well.* **2** thoroughly, *Polish it well.* **3** easily; probably, *This may well be our last chance.*
well off fairly rich; in a good situation.

well[2] *adjective* **1** in good health, *He is not well.* **2** satisfactory, *All is well.* [from Old English *wel* = prosperously]

well-being *noun* good health, happiness, and comfort.

well-known *adjective* **1** known to many people. **2** known thoroughly.

well-mannered *adjective* having good manners.

wellnigh *adverb* almost.

well-read *adjective* having read much literature.

well-to-do *adjective* fairly rich.

welsh *verb* cheat someone by avoiding paying what you owe them or by breaking an agreement. **welsher** *noun*

welt *noun* **1** a strip or border. **2** a weal.

welter *verb* (of a ship) be tossed to and fro by waves.

welter *noun* a confused mixture.

wen *noun* a large but harmless tumour on the head or neck.

wench *noun* (*plural* **wenches**) (*old use*) a girl or young woman.

wend *verb* **wend your way** go.

weren't (*mainly spoken*) were not.

werewolf *noun* (*plural* **werewolves**) (in legends) a person who sometimes changes into a wolf. [from Old English *wer* = man, + *wolf*]

wero *noun* a challenge. [Māori]

west *noun* **1** the direction where the sun sets, opposite east. **2** the western part of a country, city, etc.
the West Europe in contrast to Asian countries; the countries of western Europe and North America; the Occident.

west *adjective* **1** situated in the west, *the west coast.* **2** coming from the west, *a west wind.*

west *adverb* towards the west, *We sailed west.*

westerly *adjective* to or from the west.

western *adjective* of or in the west.

western *noun* a movie or story about cowboys or American Indians in western North America.

Westie *noun* (*NZ, informal*) a person from West Auckland.

westward *adjective & adverb* towards the west. **westwards** *adverb*

wet *adjective* (**wetter**, **wettest**) **1** soaked or covered in water or other liquid. **2** not yet dry, *wet paint.* **3** rainy, *wet weather.* **wetly** *adverb*, **wetness** *noun*
wet suit a rubber suit worn by skin-divers, water-skiers, etc. to keep warm.

wet *verb* (**wetted**, **wetting**) make a thing wet. [from Old English *waet* = wet]

weta *noun* a large grasshopper without wings. [Māori]

wetback *noun* (*NZ*) a domestic hot-water system using heat from a fire or stove.

wether *noun* a castrated male goat or sheep.

whack *verb* hit hard, especially with a stick. **whack** *noun*

whaikorero *noun* formal speech. [Māori]

whakairo *noun* the art of carving. [Māori]

whakapapa *noun* an account of a person's descent from his or her ancestors; a family tree. [Māori]

whale *noun* a very large sea-animal.
a whale of a (*informal*) very good or great, *We had a whale of a time.*

whaler *noun* a person or ship that hunts whales. **whaling** *noun*

whanau *noun* an extended family. [Māori]

whangai *noun* **1** an adoption. **2** an adopted child within a whanau. [Māori]

whare *noun* **1** a house or hut. **2** a communal building. [Māori]

wharekai *noun* a dining hall. [Māori]

wharenui *noun* a meeting house. [Māori]

whare whakairo *noun* a carved meeting house. [Māori]

wharf (*say* worf) *noun* (*plural* **wharves**) a quay where ships are loaded and unloaded.

wharfie *noun* (*NZ, informal*) a watersider.

what *adjective* used to ask the amount or kind of something (*What kind of bike have you got?*) or to say how strange or great a person or thing is (*What a fool you are!*).

what *pronoun* **1** what thing or things, *What did you say?* **2** the thing that, *This is what you must do.*
what's what (*informal*) which things are important or useful.

whata *noun* a raised storehouse. [Māori]

whatever *pronoun* **1** anything or everything, *Do whatever you like.* **2** no matter what, *Keep calm, whatever happens.*

whatever *adjective* of any kind or amount, *Take whatever books you need. There is no doubt whatever.*

whau *noun* a New Zealand tree with light wood, also called *cork tree.* [Māori]

wheat *noun* a cereal plant from which flour is made. **wheaten** *adjective*

wheedle *verb* (**wheedled**, **wheedling**) coax.

wheel *noun* **1** a round device that turns on a shaft that passes through its centre. **2** a horizontal revolving disc on which clay is made into a pot.

wheel *verb* **1** push a bicycle or trolley etc. along on its wheels. **2** move in a curve or circle; change direction and face another way, *He wheeled round in astonishment.*

wheelbarrow *noun* a small cart with one wheel at the front and legs at the back, pushed by handles.

wheelchair *noun* a chair on wheels for a person who cannot walk.

wheelie *noun* (*slang*) **do a wheelie 1** lift the front wheel of a bicycle or motorcycle from the ground while riding. **2** spin the wheels of a car when moving off.

wheeze *verb* (**wheezed**, **wheezing**) make a hoarse whistling sound as you breathe. **wheeze** *noun*, **wheezy** *adjective*

whelk *noun* a shellfish that looks like a snail.

whelp *noun* a young dog; a pup.

when *adverb* at what time; at which time, *When can you come to tea?*

when *conjunction* **1** at the time that, *The bird flew away when I moved.* **2** although; considering that, *Why do you smoke when you know it's dangerous?*

whence *adverb & conjunction* from where; from which.

whenever *conjunction* at whatever time; every time, *Whenever I see it, I smile.*

whenua *noun* ground or land. [Māori]

where *adverb & conjunction* in or to what place or that place, *Where did you put it? Leave it where it is.*

where *pronoun* what place, *Where does she come from?*

whereabouts *adverb* in or near what place. **whereabouts** *plural noun*

whereas *conjunction* but in contrast, *Some people enjoy sport, whereas others hate it.*

whereby *adverb* by which.

wherefore *adverb* (*old use*) why.

whereupon *conjunction* after which; and then.

wherever *adverb* in or to whatever place.

wherewithal *noun* things (especially money) needed for a purpose.

whet *verb* (**whetted**, **whetting**) **whet your appetite** stimulate it. [from Old English *hwettan* = sharpen]

whether *conjunction* as one possibility; if, *I don't know whether to believe her or not.*

whetstone *noun* a shaped stone for sharpening tools. [from *whet* = sharpen, + *stone*]

whey (*say* **as** way) *noun* the watery liquid left when milk forms curds.

which *adjective* what particular, *Which way did he go?*

which *pronoun* **1** what person or thing, *Which is your desk?* **2** the person or thing referred to, *The movie, which is set in Venice, will be shown on Saturday.*

whichever *pronoun & adjective* no matter which; any which, *Take whichever you like.*

whiff *noun* **1** a puff or slight smell of smoke, gas etc. **2** a hint of an idea or scandal.

while *conjunction* **1** during the time that; as long as, *Whistle while you work.* **2** although; but, *She is dark, while her sister is fair.*

while *noun* a period of time; the time spent on something, *a long while.*

while *verb* (**whiled**, **whiling**) **while away** pass time, *We whiled away the afternoon on the river.*

whilst *conjunction* while.

whim *noun* a sudden wish to do or have something.

whimper *verb* cry or whine softly. **whimper** *noun*

whimsical *adjective* impulsive and playful. **whimsically** *adverb*, **whimsicality** *noun*

whine *verb* (**whined**, **whining**) **1** make a long high miserable cry or a shrill sound. **2** complain in a petty or feeble way. **whine** *noun*

whinge *verb* (*informal*) whine, grumble, complain.

whinny *verb* (**whinnied**, **whinnying**) neigh gently or happily. **whinny** *noun*

whio *noun* a native duck of mountain rivers, also called *blue duck* or *whistling duck.* [Māori]

whip *noun* **1** a cord or strip of leather fixed to a handle and used for hitting people or animals. **2** an official of a political party in Parliament. **3** a pudding made of whipped cream and fruit or flavouring.

whip *verb* (**whipped**, **whipping**) **1** hit with a whip. **2** beat cream until it becomes thick. **3** move or take suddenly, *He whipped out a gun.* **4** (*informal*) steal something. **whip up** arouse people's feelings etc., *She whipped up support for her plans.*

whippet *noun* a small dog rather like a greyhound, used for racing.

whirl *verb* turn or spin very quickly. **whirl** *noun*

whirlpool *noun* a whirling current of water.

whirlwind *noun* a strong wind that whirls round a central point.

whirr *verb* make a continuous buzzing sound. **whirr** *noun*

whisk *verb* **1** move or brush away quickly and lightly. **2** beat eggs etc. until they are frothy.

whisk *noun* **1** a device for whisking things. **2** a whisking movement.

whisker *noun* **1** a hair of those growing on a man's face, forming a beard or moustache if not shaved off. **2** a long bristle growing near the mouth of a cat etc. **whiskery** *adjective*

whisky *noun* (*plural* **whiskies**) a strong alcoholic drink.

whisper *verb* **1** speak very softly. **2** talk secretly. **whisper** *noun*

whist *noun* a card-game usually for four people.

whistle *verb* (**whistled**, **whistling**) make a shrill or musical sound, especially by blowing through your lips. **whistler** *noun*

whistle *noun* **1** a whistling sound. **2** a device that makes a shrill sound when air or steam is blown through it.

whit *noun* the least possible amount, *not a whit better.* [from an old word *wight* = an amount]

White *noun* a person with a light-coloured skin. **White** *adjective*

white *noun* **1** the very lightest colour, like snow or salt. **2** the transparent substance (*albumen*) round the yolk of an egg, turning white when cooked.

white *adjective* **1** of the colour white. **2** very pale from the effects of illness or fear etc. **whiteness** *noun*
white coffee coffee with milk.
white elephant a useless possession.
white heron (*NZ*) kōtuku.
white pine a New Zealand tree used for timber, the kahikatea.

whitebait *noun* (*plural* **whitebait**) (*NZ*) a tiny silvery-white fish, the young of the inanga.
whitebait season the period when one is permitted to catch whitebait (normally August to November).

whitebaiting *noun* the catching of whitebait. **whitebaiter** *noun*

white-eye *noun* (*NZ*) the silvereye.

white-hot *adjective* extremely hot; so hot that heated metal looks white.

whiten *verb* make or become whiter.

whitewash *noun* a white liquid containing lime or powdered chalk, used for painting walls and ceilings etc. **whitewash** *verb*

white water *noun* rapids and fast-flowing areas of a river.

whiteywood *noun* (*NZ*) the māhoe.

whither *adverb & conjunction* (*old use*) to what place.

whiting *noun* (*plural* **whiting**) **1** (in Britain) a small edible sea-fish with white flesh. **2** (in New Zealand) an edible sea-fish similar to this.

Whitsun *noun* Whit Sunday (the seventh Sunday after Easter) and the days close to it.

whittle *verb* (**whittled, whittling**) **1** shape wood by trimming thin slices off the surface. **2** reduce something by removing various things from it, *whittle down the cost.*

whiz *verb* (**whizzed, whizzing**) **1** move very quickly. **2** sound like something rushing through the air.

who *pronoun* which person or people; the particular person or people, *This is the boy who stole the apples.*

WHO *abbreviation* World Health Organisation.

whoa *interjection* a command to a horse to stop or stand still.

whoever *pronoun* **1** any or every person who. **2** no matter who.

whole *adjective* complete; not injured or broken.
whole number a number without fractions.

whole *noun* **1** the full amount. **2** a complete thing.
on the whole considering everything; mainly.

wholemeal *adjective* made from the whole grain of wheat etc.

wholesale *noun* selling goods in large quantities to be resold by others. (Compare *retail.*) **wholesaler** *noun*

wholesale *adjective & adverb* **1** on a large scale; including everybody or everything, *wholesale destruction.* **2** in the wholesale trade.

wholesome *adjective* good for health; healthy, *wholesome food.* **wholesomeness** *noun*

wholly *adverb* completely; entirely.

whom *pronoun* the form of *who* used when it is the object of a verb or comes after a preposition, as in *the boy whom I saw* or *to whom we spoke.*

whoop (*say* woop) *noun* a loud cry of excitement. **whoop** *verb*

whoopee *interjection* a cry of joy.

whooping cough (*say* **hoop**-ing) an infectious disease that causes spasms of coughing and gasping for breath.

whopper *noun* (*slang*) something very large.

whopping *adjective* (*slang*) very large or remarkable, *a whopping lie.*

whore *noun* a prostitute.

whore *verb* **1** work as a prostitute. **2** use the services of a prostitute.

whorl *noun* **1** a coil or curved shape. **2** a ring of leaves or petals.

who's (*mainly spoken*) who is; who has.

> USAGE Do not confuse with *whose.*

whose *pronoun* belonging to what person or persons; of whom; of which, *Whose house is that?*

> USAGE Do not confuse with *who's.*

why *adverb* for what reason or purpose; the particular reason on account of which, *This is why I came.*

wick *noun* **1** the string that goes through the middle of a candle and is lit. **2** the strip of material that you light in a lamp or heater etc. that uses oil.

wicked *adjective* **1** morally bad or cruel. **2** very bad; severe, *a wicked blow.* **3** mischievous, *a wicked smile.* **wickedly** *adverb,* **wickedness** *noun*

wicker *noun* thin canes or osiers woven together to make baskets or furniture etc. **wickerwork** *noun*

wicket *noun* **1** a set of three stumps and two bails used in cricket. **2** the part of a cricket ground between or near the wickets.

wicket-gate *noun* a small gate used to save opening a much larger one.

wicketkeeper *noun* the fielder in cricket who stands behind the batter's wicket.

wide *adjective* **1** measuring a lot from side to side; not narrow. **2** measuring from side to side, *The cloth is one metre wide.* **3** covering a great range, *a wide knowledge of birds.* **4** fully open, *staring with wide eyes.* **5** far from the target, *The shot was wide of the mark.* **widely** *adverb,* **wideness** *noun*

wide *adverb* **1** widely. **2** completely; fully, *wide awake.* **3** far from the target, *The shot went wide.*

widen *verb* make or become wider.

widespread *adjective* existing in many places or over a wide area.

widgeon *noun* a kind of wild duck.

widow *noun* a woman whose husband has died. **widowed** *adjective*

widower *noun* a man whose wife has died.

width *noun* how wide something is; wideness. [from *wide*]

wield *verb* hold something and use it.

wife *noun* (*plural* **wives**) the woman to whom a man is married.

wig *noun* a covering made of real or artificial hair, worn on the head.

wiggle *verb* (**wiggled, wiggling**) move from side to side; wriggle. **wiggle** *noun*

wigwam *noun* a tent formerly used by American Indians, made by fastening skins or mats over poles. [American Indian word, = their house]

wiki *noun* a website or database on which several people can add information.

wild *adjective* **1** living or growing in its natural state, not looked after by people. **2** not cultivated, *a wild landscape.* **3** not civilised, *the Wild West.* **4** not controlled; very violent or excited. **5** very foolish or unreasonable, *these wild ideas.* **wildly** *adverb*, **wildness** *noun*
wild Irishman (*NZ*) the matagouri.

wilderness *noun* (*plural* **wildernesses**) a wild uncultivated area; a desert.

wildlife *noun* wild animals.

wile *noun* a piece of trickery.

wilful *adjective* **1** obstinately determined to do what you want, *a wilful child.* **2** deliberate, *wilful murder.* **wilfully** *adverb*, **wilfulness** *noun* [from *will*[2] + *-ful*]

will[1] *auxiliary verb* used to express the future tense, questions, or promises.

USAGE See the entry for *shall.*

will[2] *noun* **1** the mental power to decide and control what you do. **2** a desire; a chosen decision, *I went to the party against my will.* **3** determination, *They set to work with a will.* **4** a person's attitude towards others, *full of good will.* **5** a written statement of how a person's possessions are to be disposed of after his or her death.
at will as you like, *You can come and go at will.*

will[2] *verb* use your will-power; influence something by doing this, *I was willing you to win!*

willing *adjective* ready and happy to do what is wanted. **willingly** *adverb*, **willingness** *noun*

will-o'-the-wisp *noun* **1** a flickering spot of light seen on marshy ground. **2** an elusive person or hope.

willow *noun* a tree or shrub with flexible branches, usually growing near water.

will-power *noun* strength of mind to control what you do.

willy-nilly *adverb* **1** whether you want to or not. **2** in a disorganised fashion. [from *will I, nill* (= will not) *I*]

wilt *verb* lose freshness or strength; droop.

wily (*say* **wy**-lee) *adjective* cunning; crafty. **wiliness** *noun* [from *wile*]

wimp *noun* (*slang*) a weak or cowardly person. **wimpish, wimpy** *adjectives*

wimple *noun* a piece of cloth folded round the head and neck, worn by women in the Middle Ages.

win *verb* (**won, winning**) **1** be victorious in a battle, game, or contest. **2** get or achieve something by a victory or by using effort or skill etc., *She won the prize.*

win *noun* a victory.

wince *verb* (**winced, wincing**) make a slight movement because of pain or embarrassment etc.

winch *noun* (*plural* **winches**) a device for lifting or pulling things, using a rope or cable etc. that winds on to a revolving drum or wheel.

winch *verb* lift or pull with a winch.

wind[1] (*rhymes with* tinned) *noun* **1** a current of air. **2** gas in the stomach or intestines that makes you feel uncomfortable. **3** breath used for a purpose, e.g. for running or speaking. **4** the wind instruments of an orchestra.
get or **have the wind up** (*slang*) feel frightened.
wind instrument a musical instrument played by blowing, e.g. a trumpet.

wind[1] *verb* cause a person to be out of breath, *The climb had winded us.*

wind[2] (*rhymes with* find) *verb* (**wound, winding**) **1** go or turn something in twists, curves, or circles. **2** wind up a watch or clock etc. **winder** *noun*
wind up make a clock or watch work by tightening its spring; close a business; (*informal*) end up in a place or condition, *He wound up in prison.*

windbag *noun* (*informal*) a person who talks at great length.

windbreak *noun* a row of trees or shrubs that protects something from the wind.

windfall *noun* **1** a fruit blown off a tree by the wind. **2** a piece of unexpected good luck, especially a sum of money.

Windies *plural noun* (*informal*) the West Indian cricket team.

windlass *noun* (*plural* **windlasses**) a device for pulling or lifting things (e.g. a bucket from a well), with a rope or cable that is wound round an axle by turning a handle.

windmill *noun* a mill worked by the wind that turns projecting parts (*sails*).

window *noun* **1** an opening in a wall or roof etc. to let in light and often air, usually filled with glass. **2** the glass in this opening. **3** an opportunity or chance. **4** an access to knowledge.

windpipe *noun* the tube by which air passes from the throat to the lungs.

windscreen *noun* the window at the front of a motor vehicle.

windsurfing *noun* surfing on a board that has a sail fixed to it. **windsurfer** *noun*

windward *adjective* facing the wind, *the windward side of the ship.*

windy *adjective* with much wind.

wine *noun* **1** an alcoholic drink made from grapes or other plants. **2** dark red colour. [from Latin *vinum* = wine (compare *vine*)]

wineberry *noun* (*NZ*) = **makomako**[2].

wing *noun* **1** each of a pair of projecting parts of a bird, bat, or insect, used in flying. **2** each of a pair of long flat projecting parts that support an aircraft while it flies. **3** a projecting part at one end or side of something; **the wings** the sides of a theatre stage out of sight of the audience. **4** the part of a motor vehicle's body above a wheel. **5** the area on a rugby or soccer field etc. close to the touchline; a player positioned in that area. **6** a section of a political party, with more extreme opinions than the others.
on the wing flying.
take wing fly away.

wing *verb* **1** fly; travel by means of wings, *The bird winged its way home.* **2** wound a bird in the wing or a person in the arm.

winged *adjective* having wings.

winger *noun* a player in rugby or soccer etc. positioned on the wing.

wingless *adjective* without wings.

wink *verb* **1** close and open your eye quickly, especially as a signal to someone. **2** (of a light) flicker; twinkle.

wink *noun* **1** the action of winking. **2** a very short period of sleep, *I didn't sleep a wink.*

winkle *noun* a kind of edible shellfish.

winkle *verb* (**winkled**, **winkling**) **winkle out** extract; prise a thing out.

winner *noun* **1** a person or animal etc. that wins. **2** something very successful, *Her latest book is a winner.* **3** a winning goal or shot.

winnings *plural noun* money won.

winnow *verb* toss or fan grain etc. so that the loose dry outer part is blown away.

winsome *adjective* charming.

winter *noun* the coldest season of the year, between autumn and spring. **wintry** *adjective*

winter *verb* spend the winter somewhere.
winter over (*NZ*) remain in Antarctica over winter.

WINZ *abbreviation* Work and Income New Zealand.

wipe *verb* (**wiped**, **wiping**) dry or clean something by rubbing it. **wiper** *noun*
wipe out cancel, *wipe out the debt*; destroy something completely.

wire *noun* **1** a strand or thin flexible rod of metal. **2** a fence etc. made from wire. **3** a piece of wire used to carry electric current.

wire *verb* (**wired**, **wiring**) **1** fasten or strengthen with wire. **2** fit or connect with wires to carry electric current.

wireless *noun* (*plural* **wirelesses**) (*old use*) **1** radio. **2** a radio set.

wiry *adjective* **1** like wire. **2** lean and strong.

wisdom *noun* **1** being wise. **2** wise sayings.
wisdom tooth a molar tooth that may grow at the back of the jaw of a person aged about 20 or more.

wise[1] *adjective* knowing or understanding many things; judging well. **wisely** *adverb*

wise[2] *noun* (*old use* or as a *suffix*) manner or direction, *It is in no wise better*; *otherwise*; *clockwise*; *crosswise.*

wish *verb* **1** feel or say that you would like to have or do something or would like something to happen. **2** say that you hope someone will get something, *Wish me luck!*

wish *noun* (*plural* **wishes**) **1** something you wish for; a desire. **2** the action of wishing, *Make a wish when you blow out the candles.*

wishbone *noun* a forked bone between the neck and breast of a bird (sometimes pulled apart by two people; the person who gets the bigger part can make a wish).

wishful *adjective* desiring something.
wishful thinking believing something because you want it to be true.

wisp *noun* **1** a few strands of hair or bits of straw etc. **2** a small streak of smoke or cloud etc. **wispy** *adjective*

wistaria (*say* wist-**air**-ee-a) *noun* a climbing plant with hanging blue, purple, or white flowers.

wistful *adjective* sadly longing for something. **wistfully** *adverb*, **wistfulness** *noun*

wit *noun* **1** intelligence; cleverness, *Use your wits.* **2** a clever kind of humour. **3** a witty person.
at your wits' end not knowing what to do.

witch *noun* (*plural* **witches**) a person, especially a woman, who uses magic to do things. **witchcraft** noun

witch-doctor *noun* a tribal magician or seer with powers of healing and foresight.

witchetty or **witchetty grub** *noun* the larva of a kind of long-horned beetle, eaten as food in Australia. [Aboriginal]

with *preposition* used to indicate (**1**) being in the company or care etc. of (*Come with me*), (**2**) having (*a man with a beard*), (**3**) using (*Hit it with a hammer*), (**4**) because of (*shaking with laughter*), (**5**) feeling or showing (*We heard it with pleasure*), (**6**) towards, concerning (*I was angry with him*), (**7**) in opposition to; against (*Don't argue with your father*), (**8**) being separated from (*We had to part with it*).

withdraw *verb* (**withdrew, withdrawn, withdrawing**) **1** take back or away; remove, *She withdrew money from the bank.* **2** go away from a place or people, *The troops withdrew from the frontier.* **withdrawal** *noun*

wither *verb* **1** shrivel; wilt. **2** cause to shrivel or wilt. **3** make a person feel subdued or snubbed. [from *weather*]

withers *plural noun* the ridge between a horse's shoulder-blades.

withhold *verb* (**withheld, withholding**) refuse to give or allow something (e.g. information or permission). [from *with-* = away, + *hold*]

within *preposition & adverb* inside; not beyond something.

without *preposition* **1** not having, *without food.* **2** free from, *without fear.* **3** (*old use*) outside, *without the city wall.*

without *adverb* outside, *We looked at the house from within and without.*

withstand *verb* (**withstood, withstanding**) endure something successfully; resist.

withy *noun* (*plural* **withies**) a thin flexible branch for tying bundles etc.

witness *noun* (*plural* **witnesses**) **1** a person who sees or hears something happen, *There were no witnesses to the accident.* **2** a person who gives evidence in a lawcourt.

witness *verb* **1** be a witness of something. **2** sign a document to confirm that it is genuine. [from *wit*]

-witted *adjectival suffix* having wits of a certain kind, *quick-witted.*

witticism *noun* a witty remark.

wittingly *adverb* intentionally. [from *wit*]

witty *adjective* (**wittier, wittiest**) clever and amusing; full of wit. **wittily** *adverb*, **wittiness** *noun*

wizard *noun* **1** a male witch; a magician. **2** a person with amazing abilities. **3** a software tool that demonstrates functions and processes. **wizardry** *noun* [from *wise* (originally = *wise man*)]

wizened (*say* **wiz**-end) *adjective* full of wrinkles, *a wizened face.*

woad *noun* a kind of blue dye formerly made from a plant.

wobble *verb* (**wobbled, wobbling**) stand or move unsteadily; shake slightly. **wobble** *noun*, **wobbly** *adjective*

wobbly *noun* (*plural* **wobblies**) (*NZ, informal*) a tantrum, *throw a wobbly.*

woe *noun* **1** sorrow. **2** misfortune. **woeful** *adjective*, **woefully** *adverb*

woebegone *adjective* looking unhappy.

WOF *abbreviation* (*NZ*) warrant of fitness.

wok *noun* a Chinese cooking-pan shaped like a large bowl.

wolf *noun* (*plural* **wolves**) a fierce wild animal of the dog family.

wolf *verb* eat something greedily.

WOMAD *abbreviation* World of Music and Dance, an international festival, the New Zealand venue being New Plymouth.

woman *noun* (*plural* **women**) a grown-up female human being. **womanhood** *noun*, **womanly** *adjective*

womb (*say* woom) *noun* (also called the *uterus*) the hollow organ in a female's body where babies develop before they are born.

wombat *noun* an Australian marsupial with a thick heavy body and short legs.

wonder *noun* **1** a feeling of surprise and admiration or curiosity. **2** something that causes this feeling; a marvel.
no wonder it is not surprising.

wonder *verb* **1** feel that you want to know; try to form an opinion, *We are still wondering what to do next.* **2** feel wonder.

wonderful *adjective* marvellous; surprisingly good, excellent. **wonderfully** *adverb*

wonderment *noun* a feeling of wonder.

wondrous *adjective* (*old use*) wonderful.

wont (*say* wohnt) *adjective* (*old use*) accustomed, *He was wont to dress in rags.*

wont *noun* a habit or custom, *He was dressed in rags, as was his wont.*

won't (*mainly spoken*) will not.

woo *verb* **1** (*old use*) court a woman. **2** seek someone's favour. **wooer** *noun*

wood *noun* **1** the substance of which trees are made. **2** many trees growing close together. **3** a golf club with a broad face, made of wood or metal.

woodburner *noun* (*NZ*) an enclosed domestic fire designed for burning of wood.

woodcut *noun* an engraving made on wood; a print made from this.

wooded *adjective* covered with growing trees.

wooden *adjective* **1** made of wood. **2** stiff and showing no expression or liveliness. **woodenly** *adverb*

woodland *noun* wooded country.

woodlouse *noun* (*plural* **woodlice**) a small crawling creature with seven pairs of legs, living in rotten wood or damp soil etc.

woodpecker *noun* a bird that taps tree-trunks with its beak to find insects.

woodwind *noun* wind instruments that are usually made of wood, e.g. the clarinet and oboe.

woodwork *noun* **1** making things out of wood. **2** things made out of wood.

woodworm *noun* the larva of a kind of beetle that bores into wooden furniture etc.

woody *adjective* **1** like wood; consisting of wood. **2** full of trees.

wool *noun* **1** the thick soft hair of sheep and goats etc. **2** thread or cloth made from this.

wool-classer *noun* (*NZ*) a person who grades fleeces. **wool-classing** *noun*

wool-clip *noun* the amount of wool produced in a year.

woollen *adjective* made of wool.

woollens *plural noun* woollen clothes.

woolly *adjective* **1** covered with wool or wool-like hair. **2** like wool; woollen. **3** not thinking clearly; vague or confused, *woolly ideas.* **woolliness** *noun*

wool-press *noun* (*NZ*) a machine which compresses wool into bales.

woolshed *noun* (*NZ*) a shed where sheep are shorn and the wool is packed.

woolstore *noun* (*NZ*) a warehouse for storing wool.

wop-wops *plural noun* (*NZ, informal*) remote rural areas, the backblocks.

word *noun* **1** a set of sounds or letters that has a meaning, and when written or printed has no spaces between the letters. **2** a promise, *He kept his word.* **3** a command or spoken signal, *Run when I give the word.* **4** a message; information, *We sent word of our safe arrival.*
word for word in exactly the same words.
word of honour a solemn promise.
word processor a program or computer used for storing, editing, and printing text entered from a keyboard. **word processing** *noun*

word *verb* express something in words, *Word the question carefully.*

wording *noun* the way something is worded.

word-perfect *adjective* having memorised every word perfectly.

wordy *adjective* using too many words; not concise.

work *noun* **1** something you have to do that needs effort or energy, *Digging is hard work.* **2** the use of effort or energy to do something (contrasted with *play* or *recreation*). **3** a job; employment. **4** something produced by work, *The teacher marked our work.*
at work working.
out of work having no work; unable to find paid employment.
the works 1 everything. **2** (*NZ*) a freezing works.
work of art a fine picture, building, etc.

work *verb* **1** do work. **2** have a job; be employed, *She works in a bank.* **3** act or operate correctly or successfully, *Is the lift working?* **4** make something act; operate, *Can you work the lift?* **5** shape or press etc., *Work the mixture into a paste.* **6** make a way; pass, *The grub works its way into timber.*
working class people who work for wages, especially in manual or industrial work.
work out find an answer by thinking or calculating; have a particular result; engage in physical exercise.
work up make people become excited; arouse.

workable *adjective* usable; practicable.

workaholic *noun* a person who is addicted to working.

worker *noun* **1** a person who works. **2** a member of the working class. **3** a bee or ant etc. that does the work in a hive or colony but does not produce eggs.

workhorse *noun* a reliable or diligent person, animal, or machine.

working bee *noun* a group of volunteers doing work for their own or for others' benefit.

workman *noun* (*plural* **workmen**) a man employed to do manual labour; a worker.

workmanship *noun* a person's skill in working; the result of this.

workout *noun* a session of physical exercise.

workshop *noun* **1** a place where things are made or mended. **2** a meeting for people to practise a craft or activity or to share ideas, etc.

work-shy *adjective* avoiding work; lazy.

workstation *noun* a desk with a computer; the computer itself.

world *noun* **1** the earth with all its countries and peoples. **2** the universe. **3** the people or things belonging to a certain activity, *the world of sport.* **4** a very great amount, *It will do him a world of good.*

worldly *adjective* **1** of life on earth, not spiritual. **2** interested only in money, pleasure, etc. **worldliness** *noun*

worldwide *adjective & adverb* (occurring or known) throughout the world.

World Wide Web an information system on the Internet that allows the user to move from document to document when searching for information.

worm *noun* **1** an animal with a long small soft rounded or flat body and no backbone or limbs. **2** an unimportant or unpleasant person. **3** a computer graphic displaying progress in a sports match or contest. **wormy** *adjective*

worm *verb* move by wriggling or crawling.

wormwood *noun* a woody plant with a bitter taste.

worried *adjective* feeling or showing worry.

worry *verb* (**worried**, **worrying**) **1** be troublesome to someone; make a person feel slightly afraid. **2** feel anxious. **3** hold something in the teeth and shake it, *The dog was worrying a rat.* **4** chase or kill sheep. **worrier** *noun*

worry *noun* (*plural* **worries**) **1** the condition of worrying; being uneasy. **2** something that makes a person worry. [the verb originally meant 'to strangle']

worse *adjective & adverb* more bad or more badly; less good or less well.

worsen *adjective* make or become worse.

worship *verb* (**worshipped**, **worshipping**) **1** give praise or respect to God or a god. **2** love or respect a person or thing greatly. **worshipper** *noun*

worship *noun* **1** worshipping; religious ceremonies. **2** a title of respect for a mayor. [from *worth*]

worst *adjective & adverb* most bad or most badly; least good or least well.

worsted *noun* a kind of woollen material.

worth *adjective* **1** having a certain value, *This stamp is worth $100.* **2** deserving something; good or important enough for something, *That book is worth reading.*

worth while worth the time or effort needed, *The job was not worth while.*

> USAGE Use *worthwhile* when it comes before the noun (e.g. *a worthwhile job*).

worth *noun* value; usefulness.

worthless *adjective* having no value; useless. **worthlessness** *noun*

worthwhile *adjective* important or good enough to do; useful, *a worthwhile job.*

> USAGE See *worth* for the use of *worth while.*

worthy *adjective* having great merit; deserving respect or support, *a worthy cause.* **worthiness** *noun*
worthy of deserving, This charity is worthy of your support.

would *auxiliary verb* used (**1**) as the past tense of *will*[1] (*We said we would do it*), in questions (*Would you like to come?*), and polite requests (*Would you come in, please?*), (**2**) with *I* and *we* and the verbs *like, prefer, be glad*, etc. (e.g. *I would like to come*; *we would be glad to help*), where the strictly correct use is *should*, (**3**) of something to be expected (*That's just what he would do!*).

would-be *adjective* wanting or pretending to be, *a would-be comedian.*

wouldn't (*mainly spoken*) would not.

wound[1] (*say* woond) *noun* **1** an injury done by a cut, stab, or hit. **2** a hurt to a person's feelings.

wound[1] *verb* **1** cause a wound to a person or animal. **2** hurt a person's feelings.

wound[2] (*say* wownd) *past tense* of **wind**[2].

wowser *noun* (*NZ*) **1** a spoilsport. **2** a teetotaller.

wraith *noun* a ghost.

wrangle *verb* (**wrangled**, **wrangling**) have a noisy argument or quarrel. **wrangle** *noun*, **wrangler** *noun*

wrap *verb* (**wrapped**, **wrapping**) put paper or cloth etc. round something as a covering.

wrap *noun* **1** a shawl, coat, or cloak worn for warmth. **2** an end of a recording session. **3** a folded filled bread or pancake.

wrapper *noun* a piece of paper etc. wrapped round something.

wrath (*rhymes with* cloth) *noun* anger. **wrathful** *adjective*, **wrathfully** *adverb*

wreak (*say* reek) *verb* inflict, *Fog wreaked havoc with the flow of traffic.* [from Old English *wrecan* = avenge]

wreath (*say* reeth) *noun* **1** flowers or leaves etc. fastened into a circle, *wreaths of holly.* **2** a curving line of mist or smoke. [compare *writhe*]

wreathe (*say* reeth) *verb* (**wreathed, wreathing**) **1** surround or decorate with a wreath. **2** cover, *Their faces were wreathed in smiles.* **3** move in a curve, *Smoke wreathed upwards.*

wreck *verb* damage something, especially a ship, so badly that it cannot be used again.

wreck *noun* **1** a wrecked ship or building or car etc. **2** a person who is left very weak, *a nervous wreck.* **3** the wrecking of something. [same origin as *wreak*]

wreckage *noun* the pieces of a wreck.

wren *noun* a very small brown bird.

wrench *verb* twist or pull something violently.

wrench *noun* (*plural* **wrenches**) **1** a wrenching movement. **2** pain caused by parting, *Leaving home was a great wrench.* **3** an adjustable tool rather like a spanner, used for gripping and turning bolts, nuts, etc.

wrest *verb* force or wrench something away, *We wrested his sword from him.*

wrestle *verb* (**wrestled, wrestling**) **1** fight by grasping your opponent and trying to throw him or her to the ground. **2** struggle with a problem etc. **wrestle** *noun*, **wrestler** *noun*

wretch *noun* (*plural* **wretches**) **1** a person who is very unhappy. **2** a person who is disliked; a rascal.

wretched *adjective* **1** miserable; unhappy. **2** shabby. **3** not satisfactory; causing a nuisance, *This wretched car won't start.* **wretchedly** *adverb*, **wretchedness** *noun*

wriggle *verb* (**wriggled, wriggling**) move with short twisting movements. **wriggle** *noun*, **wriggly** *adjective*
wriggle out of avoid work or blame etc. cunningly.

wring *verb* (**wrung, wringing**) **1** twist and squeeze a wet thing to get water etc. out of it. **2** squeeze firmly or forcibly. **3** get something by a great effort, *We wrung a promise out of him.* **wring** *noun*
wringing wet so wet that water can be squeezed out of it.

wringer *noun* a device with a pair of rollers for squeezing water out of washed clothes etc.

wrinkle *noun* a small crease; a small furrow or ridge in the skin.

wrinkle *verb* (**wrinkled, wrinkling**) make wrinkles in something; form wrinkles.

wrist *noun* the joint that connects the hand and arm.

wrist-watch *noun* a watch for wearing on the wrist.

writ (*say* rit) *noun* a formal written command issued by a lawcourt etc.
Holy Writ the Bible.

write *verb* (**wrote, written, writing**) **1** put letters or words etc. on paper or another surface. **2** be the author or composer of something, *write books* or *music.* **3** send a letter to somebody. **writing** *noun*

writer *noun* **1** an author. **2** a person who writes. **3** a computer device that copies data or text.

writhe *verb* (**writhed, writhing**) **1** twist your body because of pain. **2** wriggle. **3** suffer because of great shame.

wrong *adjective* **1** incorrect; not true, *the wrong answer.* **2** morally bad; unfair; unjust, *It is wrong to cheat.* **3** not working properly, *There's something wrong with the engine.* **wrongly** *adverb*, **wrongness** *noun*

wrong *adverb* wrongly, *You guessed wrong.*

wrong *noun* something morally wrong; a wrong action; an injustice.
in the wrong having done or said something wrong.

wrong *verb* do wrong to someone; treat a person unfairly.

wrongdoer *noun* a person who does wrong. **wrongdoing** *noun*

wrongful *adjective* unfair; unjust; illegal. **wrongfully** *adverb*

wrought *adjective* (of metal) worked by being beaten out or shaped by hammering or rolling etc., *wrought iron.*

wry *adjective* (**wryer, wryest**) **1** twisted or bent out of shape. (Compare *awry.*) **2** showing disgust or disappointment or mockery, *a wry smile.* **wryly** *adverb*, **wryness** *noun*

wrybill *noun* a New Zealand wading bird with a beak bent to one side.

WTO *abbreviation* World Trade Organisation.

WW I, WW II *abbreviations* World War One (1914–1918), World War Two (1939–1945).

www *abbreviation* World Wide Web.

xenophobia (*say* zen-o-**foh**-bee-a) *noun* strong dislike of foreigners. [from Greek *xenos* = foreigner, + phobia]

Xerox (*say* **zeer**-oks) *noun* (*trade mark*) a photocopy made by a special process. **xerox** *verb*

Xmas *noun* Christmas. [the X is short for *Christ*; it represents the Greek letter (= ch) which is the first letter of *Christos* = Christ]

X-ray *noun* a photograph or examination of the inside of something, especially a part of the body, made by a kind of radiation (called *X-rays*) that can penetrate solid things.

X-ray *verb* make an X-ray of something.

xylophone (*say* **zy**-lo-fohn) *noun* a musical instrument made of wooden bars that you hit with small hammers. [from Greek *xylon* = wood, + *phone* = sound]

yacht (*say* yot) *noun* **1** a sailing-boat used for racing or cruising. **2** a private ship. **yachting** *noun*, **yachtsman** *noun*, **yachtswoman** *noun* [from Dutch *jaghtschip* = fast pirate ship]

yachtie *noun* (*informal*) a person who is keen on yachting.

yacker or **yakka** *noun* (*informal*) work, *hard yacker.* [Aboriginal]

yahoo *noun* a wild or coarse person. [from the name of a race of brutish creatures in Jonathan Swift's *Gulliver's Travels*]

yak *noun* an ox with long hair, found in central Asia. [from Tibetan]

yam *noun* **1** the edible tuber of a tropical plant. **2** (*NZ*) a small reddish tuber of the oca plant.

Yank *noun* (*informal*) a Yankee.

yank *verb* (*informal*) pull something strongly and suddenly. **yank** *noun*

Yankee *noun* an American, especially of the northern USA.

yap *verb* (**yapped**, **yapping**) bark shrilly. **yap** *noun*

yard[1] *noun* **1** an imperial unit of length, equivalent to about 0.91 of a metre.

yard[2] *noun* **1** an enclosed area beside a building or used for a certain kind of work, *a timber yard.* **2** (*American* and *Australian*) the garden of a house.

yardstick *noun* a standard by which something is measured.

yarn *noun* **1** thread spun by twisting fibres together, used in knitting etc. **2** (*informal*) a tale or story; a chat.

yarrow *noun* a wild plant with strong-smelling flowers.

yashmak *noun* a veil worn in public by Muslim women in some countries.

yawl *noun* a kind of sailing-boat or fishing-boat.

yawn *verb* **1** open the mouth wide and breathe in deeply when feeling sleepy or bored. **2** form a wide opening, *A pit yawned in front of us.* **yawn** *noun*

ye *pronoun* (*old use*, in speaking to two or more people) you.

yea (*say* yay) *adverb* (*old use*) yes.

year *noun* **1** the time the earth takes to go right round the sun, about 365 ¼ days. **2** the time from 1 January to 31 December. **3** (**Year**) a class in school, *Year 12.* **yearly** *adjective & adverb*

yearling *noun* an animal between one and two years old.

yearn *verb* long for something.

yeast *noun* a substance that causes alcohol and carbon dioxide to form as it develops, used in making beer and wine and in baking bread etc.

yell *verb* give a loud cry; shout. **yell** *noun*

yellow *noun* the colour of buttercups and ripe lemons.

yellow *adjective* **1** of yellow colour. **2** (*informal*) cowardly. **yellowness** *noun* **yellow card** a card shown by a referee to a player who is being warned.

yellowbelly *noun* a New Zealand flatfish with a yellow underside.

yellowhead *noun* a New Zealand bird rather like a canary.

yellowtail *noun* (*NZ*) any of several kinds of yellowish-green fish.

yelp *verb* give a shrill bark or cry. **yelp** *noun*

yen[1] *noun* (*plural* **yen**) the unit of money in Japan. [from Chinese *yuan* = round thing]

yen[2] *noun* a longing. [Chinese dialect word]

yes *adverb* used to agree to something (= the statement is correct) or as an answer (= I am here).

yesterday *noun & adverb* the day before today.

yet *adverb* **1** up to this time; by this time, *The mail hasn't come yet.* **2** eventually, *I'll get even with him yet!* **3** in addition; even, *She became yet more excited.*

yet *conjunction* nevertheless, *It is strange, yet it is true.*

yeti *noun* (*plural* **yetis**) a very large animal thought to live in the Himalayas, sometimes called the 'Abominable Snowman'. [from Tibetan]

yew *noun* an evergreen tree with dark-green needle-like leaves and red berries.

YHANZ *abbreviation* Youth Hostels Association of New Zealand.

yield *verb* **1** surrender; do what is asked or ordered; give way, *He yielded to persuasion.* **2** produce as a crop or as profit etc.

yield *noun* the amount yielded or produced, *What is the yield of wheat per hectare?* [from Old English, = pay]

YMCA *abbreviation* Young Men's Christian Association.

yob *noun* (also **yobbo**) (*informal*) a lout or hooligan.

yodel *verb* (**yodelled**, **yodelling**) sing or shout with the voice continually going from a low note to a high note and back again. **yodeller** *noun*

yoga (*say* **yoh**-ga) *noun* a Hindu system of meditation and self-control.

yoghurt (*say* **yoh**-gert or **yog**-ert) *noun* milk thickened by the action of certain bacteria, giving it a sharp taste. [Turkish]

yoke *noun* **1** a curved piece of wood put across the necks of animals pulling a cart or plough etc. **2** a shaped piece of wood fitted across a person's shoulders, with a bucket or load hung at each end. **3** a close-fitting upper part of a garment, from which the rest hangs.

yoke *verb* (**yoked**, **yoking**) harness or join by means of a yoke.

yokel (*say* **yoh**-kel) *noun* a simple country fellow.

yolk (*rhymes with* coke) *noun* the round yellow part inside an egg.

Yom Kippur (*say* yom kip-**oor**) the Day of Atonement, a solemn Jewish religious festival, a day of fasting and repentance. [Hebrew]

yon *adjective & adverb* (*dialect*) yonder.

yonder *adjective & adverb* over there.

yore *noun* **of yore** of long ago, *in days of yore.*

Yorkshire pudding baked batter, usually eaten with roast beef.

you *pronoun* **1** the person or people being spoken to, *Who are you?* **2** anyone; everyone; one, *You can't tell what will happen next.*

young *adjective* having lived or existed for only a short time; not old.

young *noun* children or young animals or birds, *The robin was feeding its young.*

youngster *noun* a young person; a child.

your *adjective* belonging to you.

you're (*mainly spoken*) you are.

yours *possessive pronoun* belonging to you. **Yours faithfully**, **Yours sincerely**, **Yours truly** ways of ending a letter before you sign it. (*Yours faithfully* and *Yours truly* are more *formal* than *Yours sincerely*.)

> USAGE It is incorrect to write *your's*.

yourself *pronoun* (*plural* **yourselves**) you and nobody else. (Compare *herself*.)

youth *noun* **1** being young; the time when you are young. **2** a young man. **3** young people. **youthful** *adjective*, **youthfulness** *noun* **youth hostel** a place providing cheap accommodation for tourists and travellers, especially young people.

yowl *verb & noun* wail; howl.

yuan *noun* (*plural* **yuan**) the chief unit of money in China.

yucca *noun* a garden plant with white flowers.

yule *noun* (*old use*) the Christmas festival, also called **yule tide**.

yuppie *noun* (usually derogatory) a young professional person with an affluent and trendy life style. [from young *urban* (or *upwardly* mobile) professional]

YWCA *abbreviation* Young Women's Christian Association.

Zz

zambuk *noun* (*NZ*) an ambulance officer or first aid attendant, especially at sporting venues. [from the name of an ointment]

zap *verb* (**zapped**, **zapping**) (*informal*) **1** attack or destroy something forcefully. **2** change quickly from one section of a videotape etc. to another. **3** use a remote control to mute or change a television channel etc. **4** cook something in a microwave oven. **5** delete electronic text, *Let's zap that file.*

zeal *noun* enthusiasm; keenness. **zealous** (*say* **zel**-us) *adjective*, **zealously** *adverb*

zealot (*say* **zel**-ot) *noun* a zealous person; a fanatic.

zebra (*say* **zeb**-ra) *noun* an African animal of the horse family, with black and white stripes all over its body.
zebra crossing (*British*) a place for pedestrians to cross a road safely, marked with broad white stripes.

zebu (*say* **zee**-bew) *noun* an ox with a humped back, found in India, East Asia, and Africa.

zenith *noun* **1** the part of the sky directly above you. **2** the highest point, *His power was at its zenith.* [from Arabic *samt arras* = path over the head]

zephyr (*say* **zef**-er) *noun* a soft gentle wind. [from Greek *Zephyros* = god of the west wind]

zero *noun* (*plural* **zeros**) **1** nought; the figure 0; nothing. **2** the point marked 0 on a thermometer etc.
zero hour the time when something is planned to start. [from Arabic *sifr* = cipher]

Zespri *noun* a trade mark for New Zealand kiwifruit.

zest *noun* **1** great enjoyment or interest. **2** the coloured outer rind of citrus fruits. **zestful** *adjective*, **zestfully** *adverb*

zigzag *noun* a line or route that turns sharply from side to side.

zigzag *verb* (**zigzagged**, **zigzagging**) move in a zigzag.

zinc *noun* a white metal.

zing *noun* (*informal*) energy, enthusiasm, *She added some zing to the team.*

zip *noun* **1** a zip-fastener. **2** a sharp sound like a bullet going through the air. **3** liveliness; vigour. **zippy** *adjective*

zip *verb* (**zipped**, **zipping**) **1** fasten with a zip-fastener. **2** move vigorously or at high speed.

zip-fastener or **zipper** *noun* a fastener consisting of two strips of material, each with rows of small teeth that interlock when a sliding tab brings them together.

zit *noun* (*informal*) a pimple.

zither *noun* a musical instrument with many strings stretched over a shallow box-like body.

zodiac (*say* **zoh**-dee-ak) *noun* a strip of sky where the sun, moon, and main planets are found, divided into twelve equal parts (called **signs of the zodiac**), each named after a constellation. [from Greek *zoidion* = image of an animal]

zombie *noun* **1** a corpse said to have been brought back to life by witchcraft. **2** a dull person, one who seems to have no mind or will.

zone *noun* **1** an area of a special kind or for a particular purpose, *a pedestrian zone.* **2** a catchment area, *a fishing zone or school zone.* [Greek, = girdle]

zoo *noun* (*plural* **zoos**) a place where wild animals are kept so that people can look at them or study them. [short for *zoological gardens*]

zoology (*say* zoh-**ol**-o-jee) *noun* the study of animals. **zoological** *adjective*, **zoologist** *noun* [from Greek *zoion* = animal, + *-logy*]

zoom *verb* **1** move very quickly, especially with a buzzing sound. **2** rise quickly, *Prices had zoomed.* **zoom** noun
zoom lens a camera lens that can be adjusted continuously to focus on things that are close up or far away.

ZPG *abbreviation* zero population growth.

zucchini (*say* zoo-**kee**-nee) *noun* (*plural* **zucchini** or **zucchinis**) a courgette.

Zulu *noun* (*plural* **Zulus**) a member of a Bantu people in South Africa.